FRANZ LISZT

FRANZ LISZT

Selected Letters

Translated and edited by

ADRIAN WILLIAMS

CLARENDON PRESS · OXFORD

1998

Oxford University Press, Great Clarendon Street, Oxford OX2 6DP

Oxford New York

Athens Auckland Bangkok Bogota Bombay Buenos Aires
Calcutta Cape Town Dar es Salaam Delhi Florence Hong Kong Istanbul
Karachi Kuala Lumpur Madras Madrid Melbourne Mexico City
Nairobi Paris Singapore São Paulo Taipei Tokyo Toronto Warsaw

and associated companies in
Berlin Ibadan

Oxford is a registered trade mark of Oxford University Press

Published in the United States
by Oxford University Press Inc., New York

British Library Cataloguing in Publication Data
Data available

Library of Congress Cataloging in Publication Data
Liszt, Franz, 1811–1886.
[Correspondence. English. Selections]
Selected letters / Franz Liszt ; translated and edited
by Adrian Williams.
p. cm.
Includes bibliographical references (p.) and indexes.
1. Liszt, Franz, 1811–1886—Correspondence. 2. Composers—
Correspondence. I. Williams, Adrian, 1940–
ML410.L7A4 1998 780'.92—dc21 [B] 97–50595
ISBN 0–19–816688–5

1 3 5 7 9 10 8 6 4 2

Typeset by Graphicraft Ltd, Hong Kong
Printed in Great Britain
on acid-free paper by
Biddles Ltd
Guildford & King's Lynn

To the memory of my mother

CONSTANCE MARY WILLIAMS

In life one must decide whether to conjugate
the verb *to have* or the verb *to be*.

Franz Liszt

There is
One great society alone on earth:
The noble living and the noble dead.

William Wordsworth

PREFACE

'In Weimar I made the acquaintance of Franz Liszt . . . and each further meeting has increased the high esteem and admiration I feel for him. To be the greatest performer on an instrument, and with one's playing to have thrilled and captivated the whole of Europe, is already no slight glory. To this glory, however, Liszt has added the higher one of disregarding the plaudits bestowed upon him for his virtuosity and, earnestly seeking the sublimest goals of art, of creating works, such as his *Saint Elisabeth*, which will secure him a place of honour among our composers. At the same time, he has for more than half a century ceaselessly, and in the most self-sacrificing way, striven to promote every talent, to seek recognition for what was unrecognized, and to bring neglected musical treasures back into the light.'

Those words by Adolf von Schack, in his memoirs *Ein halbes Jahrhundert*, neatly encapsulate Liszt's outstanding contributions to both the art of music and to humanity at large: the playing which moved and enraptured thousands—he was not only the nonpareil of pianists but, in all probability, the most wonderful performer there has ever been on any musical instrument; his great, inspired, and enduring musical creations; and the support, moral and material, he extended selflessly and unwearyingly to the many major and minor talents who so often—'slow rises worth by poverty depressed'—found themselves in need of that strong helping hand. When we add to all this his numerous appearances for, and donations to, charitable causes, his unstinting giving of alms, and his refusal—other than, perhaps, during his early years in Paris—to accept remuneration from any of the hundreds of pupils who passed through his hands, we have some notion of an outlook wholly lacking in materialism and of a life of unceasing service to others.

It requires no special powers of perception to see that Liszt was one of what have been called the 'dominant 5 per cent of the human race', those with the drive, initiative, and staying power, coupled with sheer talent, who become the leaders and achievers. By no means every member of this élite, however, is as ready as Liszt to help others climb the ladder.... And how often his life interacted with the lives of other persons of prominence whose activities compel the attention of posterity! Among those he knew and associated with were such men and women as Alexander von Humboldt, the Abbé Lamennais, Alphonse de Lamartine, Gioacchino Rossini, Honoré de Balzac, Victor Hugo, Hector Berlioz, George Sand, Felix Mendelssohn, Fryderyk Chopin, Robert and Clara Schumann, Richard Wagner, George Eliot, César Franck, Bedřich Smetana, Camille

Saint-Saëns, Henry Irving, Edvard Grieg, several of the leading Russian composers, countless other personages of distinction in the literature, art, music, theatre, science and politics of the period, two popes, a sizeable clutch of cardinals, and a galaxy of crowned heads, their consorts and offspring.

It is rather remarkable that until now so few of the letters of this magical man and musician have been made available to an Anglophone readership. In 1894, less than a decade after Liszt's death, Constance Bache brought out an English translation of the first two volumes in the series edited by La Mara. A collection of the composer's letters to a variety of correspondents, it contains not a few of interest and importance—the best of which can also be found in the present volume—but almost wholly lacks letters to members of his family, to his closest women friends, and to such associates as Hans von Bülow, Baron Antal Augusz, and the Grand Duke Carl Alexander, all of whom are represented here.

An English translation of the Liszt–Wagner correspondence first appeared in 1888, a few years after the deaths of the two composers, but the only versions available to the translator, Francis Hueffer, were those, published in German (some of Liszt's earlier letters are in French), in which a great amount of material had been suppressed by Liszt's daughter Cosima, the widow of Wagner. The source of a score of Liszt's letters to his son-in-law translated for inclusion in the present selection was the uncensored and almost complete correspondence published early this century.

Liszt's letters to Princess Marie Wittgenstein and Baroness von Meyendorff have already appeared in English (see under Hugo and Waters in *Selective List of Other Works Consulted*), and so, accordingly, none is included in this volume.

In the Biographical Sketches I have provided brief information about each of the hundred or more recipients of letters in this selection, and also about many other contemporaries mentioned therein. The very names of such figures as the Comte de Circourt, Adolf von Schack, and Henrik Ketten, and even those of Aladár Juhász and Cardinal Simor, may be unknown to some readers of these letters; but since these figures were all gifted and interesting individuals in their own right as well as being friends or acquaintances of the composer, I have not hesitated to accord them greater space in the Biographical Sketches than might seem to be warranted by their small importance in his life. Something of Juhász, Liszt's most talented Hungarian pupil, certainly deserves to be known to students of the history of piano-playing; likewise, the name and achievements of Count von Schack cannot be overlooked by those who aspire to carrying in their heads detailed knowledge of nineteenth-century European culture and not merely its main outlines. Circourt and Ketten can be regarded as curiosities—but curiosities worth knowing about.

Many of the letters presented here are only extracts from longer communications. Omissions have been necessitated not only by the exigencies of the space available, but also by the very natural fact that some passages in the letters are of less interest to posterity than others.

Salutations and valedictions are lacking in many of the letters—because Liszt did not write them. The closer his relationship with a correspondent, and the more spontaneous and informal the letter, the less likely it was that he began with a 'Dear So and So' and ended with a 'Yours, F. Liszt'. The reverse also holds good: letters to the Grand Duke Carl Alexander, for example, have both a form of address (usually, in his case, 'Monseigneur') and a formal signing-off. With his nearest and dearest Liszt often plunged straight *in medias res* and, on finishing, dashed off a 'signature' which was just an unreproduceable squiggle that may or may not originally have been an 'F'.

The place where an addressee is known to be—if known for certain—is given for the first letter to that person in any year, but not for later communications in the same year, unless he or she is definitely known to be in a different place.

It would be a shame if these very personal—sometimes impassioned and emotional—writings were to be sunk under the weight of too burdensome and oppressive an *apparatus criticus*; while endeavouring to clarify the occasional obscurity and opacity, therefore, I have preferred to err, if error it be, in furnishing too few annotations rather than too many. I hope, however, that the result is about right, and that many of the footnotes interest as well as illuminate.

Chronological summaries of Liszt's activities provided at the beginning of each year are followed by the titles of works dating from that year. Because of the paramount importance of saving space, no attempt has been made to include every last and least of these. Nevertheless, the great majority, and certainly those of major significance, are given. The 'S' number with which they are identified is the number allotted to them by Humphrey Searle in his book *The Music of Liszt*, an amplified version of the catalogue of which was published in *The New Grove Early Romantic Masters I*. (For details, see *Selective List of Other Works Consulted*.) For this reason, when, in due course, a revised edition of *The New Grove* makes its appearance, with yet another catalogue devoted to works of Liszt, readers should still be able to identify those works without difficulty.

I am happy to be able to acknowledge here the support for this project given by Bruce Phillips and his colleagues at the Oxford University Press; and I am especially grateful to Mary Worthington, not only for the impeccable copy-editing, but also for the probing queries and penetrating comments which induced me to reconsider certain points and to make worthwhile changes to text and annotations alike.

It is also a pleasant duty to record the assistance of one kind or another that I have received from various friends and colleagues. They include two of the world's foremost Liszt specialists: Pauline Pocknell, of McMaster University, Ontario, whose forthcoming edition of Liszt's complete letters to Agnes Street-Klindworth has long been eagerly awaited; and Charles Suttoni, of New York, author of *Liszt Correspondence in Print*, a vade-mecum through the labyrinth of Liszt's published letters which no one engaged in serious work on the great musician can possibly dispense with. To each of these justly admired scholars I am indebted for information that I might not otherwise have encountered, and without which this book would have been the poorer.

Warm thanks are also owed to Mario Becchetti, who, apprised of my intention to write a footnote on a now vanished monument of his native city, almost immediately supplied me with not only a useful and informative article on that monument, but even several photographs of it taken at various times in the decades before its demolition earlier this century. After such invaluable help, I can only hope that my few lines on the *Meta sudans* will not be found wanting by other lovers of Roman antiquity who may read them.

Above all I wish to record my deep gratitude to two remarkable women here in London, fellow members of our little literary and lexicographical coterie in Gough Square. The first to respond to my plea for a fresh pair of eyes to be cast over my labours was the French-educated and acutely intelligent Margaret Eliot, who generously devoted many hours to mulling over my draft translations of Liszt's French, and time and again, when I was floundering, almost instantly coming up with the *mot juste*, or the perfect idiomatic expression, that had eluded me. Margaret's sudden and lamented death, when barely a third of the work had been completed, was an enormous loss. After further progress had been made, however, Mary Bingley most helpfully agreed to look through the letters in a spirit of constructive criticism, a task to which, as a former editress, she brought an admirable mastery of the English language and—my Achilles' heel—its correct punctuation. Reading through almost the entire batch of finished translations, and very nearly the complete Biographical Sketches, she, like Margaret, offered numerous ingenious and imaginative suggestions for improvement, of the majority of which I was only too happy to make use. To both Margaret and Mary I owe a debt that is quite incalculable. *Manibus O date lilia plenis!*

ADRIAN WILLIAMS

CONTENTS

SELECTED LETTERS 1811–1886

Contents

LIST OF PLATES

(between pages 536 and 537)

LIST OF LETTERS AND THEIR RECIPIENTS

NOTE TO THE READER

The Biographical Sketches contain more than 150 entries providing information about approximately 200 people, all of whom are either recipients of letters in the present volume or regarded as interesting and important enough to justify the inclusion of biographical data for them over and above what could be supplied in a footnote or in the Index. The former are identified by an asterisk only if their name appears in the text before the first (or only) letter addressed to them; the latter are identified by an asterisk at the first mention of their name. In a few cases it has been found more convenient to call attention to the Sketches in a footnote.

It can be taken for granted that there are entries in the Sketches for members of Liszt's family and for the two women of the greatest significance in his life, Comtesse Marie d'Agoult and Princess Carolyne von Sayn-Wittgenstein.

The majority of Liszt's letters were written in French, the language which was so very much his preferred medium of communication that he used it even for some of his earlier letters to such ultra-German correspondents as Schumann and Wagner. In the present selection a G has been placed at the end of the heading for those letters originally written in German. When the G is followed by an F in parenthesis, it implies that the letter was written in French but that the only source from which the English translation could be prepared was a version in German. Where—as is generally the case—there is neither a G nor a G (F), the implication is that the letter was written in, and has been translated from, French.

Omissions from the letters are indicated by spaced dots (. . .); Liszt's own dots are unspaced (...).

Footnote references to the Bible and the prayer book use the following abbreviations: AV—Authorized Version, BCP—Book of Common Prayer, Vulg.—Vulgate.

SELECTED LETTERS
1811–1886

1811–1831

When, on 11 January 1811, Adam Liszt, who had studied philosophy, theology, music, and Latin and was now in his thirty-fifth year and an employee of Prince Nicholas Esterházy, married the 22-year-old, barely literate Anna Lager, a former chambermaid, it may have seemed a classic example of a mismatch. In reality, the union could hardly have been more inspired, for it produced, in their son Franz, a man who, as creative and execut-ant musician, as teacher and philanthropist, was a remarkable and outstanding example of *homo superior*—courted as such by, *inter alios*, popes, cardinals, kings, queens, em-perors, and princes—and one of the most charismatic spirits of the nineteenth century.

He was born in Raiding (Doborján), a village in western Hungary,[1] on Tuesday, 22 October 1811, and the following day given the baptismal name of Franciscus. (His godparents were Franciscus Zambothy and Julianna Szalay.) His name-day—he was the child of practising Roman Catholics—was 2 April, feast of St Francis of Paola.[2] Indica-tions of exceptional musical gifts, as well as of natural piety, were already in evidence by the time he was 6, when he heard his father play a concerto. 'Leaning against the piano, Franz listened intently,' recalled Adam. 'In the evening, when he came back into the house after a stroll in the garden, he was singing the main theme of the work. . . . That was the first sign of his genius, and he entreated me to let him begin learning the piano.'

Little Franz was soon performing with rare skill and also trying his hand at com-position. In October 1820, the month of his ninth birthday, he took part in a concert at Sopron (Oedenburg), and was rewarded by an ovation. Appearances followed in Eisenstadt and Pozsony.[3] In the spring of 1822, with unwavering belief in his son's tal-ent, and with his financial problems eased by the generosity of Hungarian magnates who set up a fund for the young prodigy,[4] Adam Liszt moved his little family to Vienna, where Franz began piano studies with Czerny*, composition lessons with Salieri, and made the acquaintance of Rossini. His Vienna début, in December, was with Hummel's* Concerto in A minor and an improvisation. '*Est deus in nobis!*' enthused a critic.

A second Vienna concert, of 13 April 1823, seems to have been marked by the pres-ence of Beethoven,* who bestowed a kiss on the brow of the young artiste. A month

---

[1] Since the boundary change after the First World War, Raiding has been in the Austrian province of Burgenland.

[2] Spending his early life at Paola, his birthplace in Calabria, Liszt's name saint, founder of the Order of Minims, played less conspicuous a role on the national and international stage than did his namesake of Assisi. In middle age, however, he was summoned to France, to succour Louis XI, who was facing death in a state of terror. Remaining in that country for the rest of his life, he died, like the King, at Plessis-lez-Tours.

[3] Known also, at that time, under its German name of Pressburg, Pozsony is now Bratislava, capital of the Slovak Republic.

[4] In 1842, when correcting the biography written of him by J. W. Christern, Liszt noted in the margin that he had received from Counts 'Thadé d'Amadé, Szapáry, and Michael Esterházy a six-year pension of 600 fl.'.

later, accompanied by his father, Franz made a brief return to Hungary, with several well-received appearances at concerts in Pest. Leaving Vienna in September, journeying via Munich, Augsburg, Stuttgart, and Strasbourg, with concerts in each of these cities and, in the first, a kiss for Franz from the King of Bavaria, the Liszt family arrived in Paris, where they took accommodation at the Hôtel d'Angleterre, rue du Mail. As a foreigner, and to his great chagrin, Franz was refused admission to the Conservatoire, but before long was having composition lessons from Ferdinando Paër.

The 12-year-old's first Paris concert, of 7 March 1824, was enormously successful. 'His little arms can scarcely stretch to both ends of the keyboard, his little feet scarcely reach the pedals, and yet this child is beyond compare; he is the first pianist in Europe,' opined a reviewer. As a result of the concert, the young prodigy's portrait was exhibited in the Louvre. Two months later, father and son visited England, where Franz played in London and Manchester and delighted George IV at Windsor. 'This boy surpasses Moscheles, Cramer, Kalkbrenner and all the other great players, not only in the actual playing but in the wealth and development of his ideas too,' declared the music-loving King. During his stay in England the young composer also worked on a one-act opera, *Don Sanche, ou le Château d'Amour* (S1).

Early the following year he encountered the 16-year-old Mendelssohn, later made a second visit to England, and, at the Paris Opéra on 17 October, five days before his fourteenth birthday, attended the première of *Don Sanche*, which achieved a *succès d'estime*. Towards the end of the year Anna Liszt returned to Austria to stay with her sister in Graz.

In 1826 Franz played in the French provinces, reaping further triumphs. 'All the panegyrics in the world would not suffice to give a notion of his splendid talent; to analyse it one would have to define perfection,' wrote a reviewer of his playing in Marseilles. Later in the year he had lessons in counterpoint and fugue from Anton Reicha. By this time, however, he was disillusioned with the life of a performer and a prey to melancholy. 'I would sooner have been anything in the world than a musician in the pay of the aristocracy,' he was to write some years later.

The year 1827 can be said to mark the end of Liszt's childhood. Beginning with a Swiss tour, and continuing with another visit to London (where, on 27 May, he composed the Scherzo in G minor, S153, for piano solo), it culminated in a catastrophe: the death—in Boulogne on 28 August—of Adam Liszt from typhoid fever. Returning to Paris from Austria, Anna Liszt was reunited with her son, and they set up home together, first at 38 rue Coquenard, later at 7 rue Montholon, near the church of St Vincent de Paul.

Nor was 1828 a happy year for the 16-year-old, whose blossoming romance with his pupil Caroline de Saint-Cricq* was brought to an abrupt end by her father the Comte de Saint-Cricq. Shattered by the shock and humiliation, and by the enforced separation from his first real love, the young musician became reclusive and for a long time made no public appearances. In October he was even rumoured to be dead, and an obituary was published.

In the years 1829–31, his general education having been rather neglected—the Bible, the *Lives of the Saints* and *The Imitation of Christ*,[5] the main reading of his childhood, had nevertheless provided substantial spiritual nourishment—Liszt read intensively and extensively, laying the foundations of an exceptionally wide self-acquired education and culture.[6] Going out into society once again he made the acquaintance of numerous other outstandingly gifted individuals: Chateaubriand, Ballanche, Lamartine, Heine, Balzac, Dumas *père*, Hugo,* Mérimée, Quinet, Sainte-Beuve, de Musset and Gautier among men of letters, Berlioz* and Chopin* among musicians, Delacroix and Scheffer* among painters. Attracted by the social and political teachings of the Saint-Simonians, some of whose meetings he attended, he also enjoyed a romance with the Comtesse Adèle de Laprunarède—fifteen years older than he—with whom he spent the winter months of 1831[7] at Marlioz, her *maison de campagne* near Geneva.

Among other compositions of Liszt's early years are the Variation (S147, 1822) on a Waltz by Diabelli, *Etude en douze exercices* (S136, 1826), and Grand Fantasy (S385, 1829) on the Tyrolienne from Auber's opera *La Fiancée*, all for piano solo; a Concerto in A minor (1827), now lost, but probably an early version of the so-called *Malédiction* of 1833 for piano and strings; and sketch of a Revolutionary Symphony (S690) inspired by the July Revolution of 1830.

Of the letters written pre-1832 may be mentioned that of 24 August 1827 to his mother from Boulogne, reporting his father's grave illness and asking her to return to France; two affectionate letters (December 1828 and August 1830) to Czerny; and what has been described as a 'fan letter' (*c.*1829) to the singer Maria Malibran.

[5] *De Imitatione Christi*, the 15th-cent. devotional work attributed to Thomas à Kempis.
[6] August Göllerich, a pupil of Liszt's old age, even described him as 'the most *universally* educated musician who has ever lived'.
[7] A letter to his mother reporting his safe arrival bears the date 9 Jan. 1831.

1832

28 January. Liszt gives a charity concert in Rouen.

26 February. He attends Chopin's first Paris concert, at the Salle Pleyel, and applauds with great enthusiasm.

25 March–1 June. Niccolò Paganini gives a series of concerts in Paris, overwhelming, and inspiring, Liszt with his spell-binding virtuosity.

2 April. At a concert in the Salle Chantereine at which he takes the *secondo* part in a duet with a pupil, Liszt makes his sole public appearance—in Paris—of the year.

16 April. Liszt plays Beethoven *chez* Victor Hugo; in the evening, Weber at the Austrian Embassy.

Late August–1 October. He sojourns in Bourges, where he attends the wedding of a former pupil, the daughter of General Petit.

December. In the salon of the Marquise Le Vayer, Liszt makes the acquaintance of the Comtesse Marie d'Agoult.[1]

30 December. With Rossini, Chopin and others, Liszt takes part in a soirée musicale at the Austrian Embassy.

WORKS. PIANO: *La romanesca* (S252*a*, *c*.1832, published, as a supplement, in the *Gazette musicale de Paris*, 6 April 1833); *Grande fantaisie de bravoure sur la Clochette* (Paganini) (S420, 1831–2).

1. To Pierre Wolff (fils), Rue de la Tertasse, Geneva

Nous disons: 'Il est temps. Exécutons! c'est l'heure.'
Alors nous retournons les yeux—La Mort est là!

Ainsi de mes projets.—Quand vous verrai-je, Espagne,
Et Venise et son golfe, et Rome et sa campagne,
Toi, Sicile, que ronge un volcan souterrain,
Grèce qu'on connaît trop, Sardaigne qu'on ignore,
Cités de l'Aquilon, du Couchant, de l'Aurore,
Pyramides du Nil, Cathédrales du Rhin!

Qui sait?—Jamais peut-être![2]

---

[1] Their first meeting was possibly in Jan. 1833—but in any case not as late as 1 Feb., date of the Marquise Le Vayer's death.

[2] From Victor Hugo's *A Mes Amis L.B. Et S.-B.*—a poem, dated 14 May 1830, which evidently made a deep impression on the young Liszt; and the verse (beginning 'Here's a sigh to those who love me') from Byron's *To Thomas Moore* which Hugo had used as an epigraph for the poem, he took as a motto of his own. The initials refer to Louis Boulanger and Sainte-Beuve.

Earthly life is but a sickness of the soul, an excitement which is kept up by the passions. The natural state of the soul is peace!

Paris, 2 May. For the past fortnight my mind and fingers have been working away like two lost spirits. Homer, the Bible, Plato, Locke, Byron, Hugo, Lamartine, Chateaubriand, Beethoven, Bach, Hummel, Mozart, Weber, are all around me. I study them, meditate on them, devour them with fury; and in addition I spend 4 to 5 hours practising exercises (thirds, sixths, octaves, tremolos, repeated notes, cadenzas, etc. etc.). Ah! provided I don't go mad you will find an artist in me! Yes, an artist such as you desire, such as is required nowadays!

'And I too am a painter!'[3] cried Michelangelo the first time he beheld a masterpiece.... Though poor and unimportant, your friend has not left off repeating those words of the great man ever since Paganini's last performance. René, what a man, what a violin, what an artist! Heavens! what sufferings, what misery, what torments in those four strings! Here are a few of his characteristics:

---

[3] 'Son pittore anch'io', but usually attributed to Correggio.

As for his expression, his manner of phrasing—they are his very soul![4]

8 May. My good friend, it was in a fit of extravagance that I wrote you the above lines; some compulsory work, late nights and those violent desires (for which you know me) had set my poor head on fire. I was going from right to left, then from left to right (like a freezing sentinel in winter), singing, declaiming, gesticulating, crying out; in a word, I was raving. Today both the one and the other, spiritual and animal (to use the witty language of M. de Maistre), are in slightly better equilibrium; for the volcano of my heart is not extinct but is working away silently.—Until when?—

Address your letters to Monsieur Reidet, postmaster-general in the port of Rouen.

A thousand friendly greetings to those Boissier* ladies. Some day I'll let you know the reasons which prevented me leaving for Geneva—on this subject I shall call you in evidence.

Bertini is in London—Madame Malibran is doing her tour of Germany; Messemaecker (how is he getting on there?) is eating his Brussels sprouts, Aguado has the illustrious maestro Rossini in tow.—Ah—Hi—Oh—Hu!!!

2. To Anna Liszt in Paris [Bourges, Friday, 21 September] G (F)

Dear Mother!

With luck, I'll embrace you in Paris on Monday morning; but I can't promise you that today with certainty, for I haven't yet reserved my seat in the mailcoach.

Thank you for the nice letter you took the trouble to write to me. I was waiting for it impatiently. The answer to the details you ask me about I think it will be better for me to save for when we see one another. For the moment I'll content myself with telling you that M. Hatton (the young bridegroom), and also the General and his ladies, are being very good and kind to me. Our domestic life is very simple: at 10 o'clock breakfast, at 6 o'clock dinner; in between, a little work, a little boredom, a walk, some horse-riding; in the evening, tea and écarté. That is how we spend the day in Bourges. As with every time I am away, now too, once again, I can only properly appreciate the whole value and charm of my life with you, with my books, my music, and a few friends.

Visit Mme Garcia[5] and give her news of me. The slippers you intended for the General I advise you to keep for his return to Paris.

---

[4] If Liszt was inspired to become 'the Paganini of the piano', he succeeded most decidedly, in the opinion of some even surpassing his dazzling predecessor. Thus, for example, a reviewer in England eight years later: 'To judge of his greatness, he must be heard; language would fail in the description. He is, indeed, "greater on his instrument than was Paganini on the violin"' (*Leeds Intelligencer*, 12 Dec. 1840).

[5] Probably Joaquina Garcia, widow of the Spanish tenor Manuel Garcia *père* (who had died in June), and mother of the singer and teacher Manuel Garcia *fils*, and the singers Maria Malibran and Pauline Viardot-Garcia.

3. To Anna Liszt [Bourges, Sunday, 23 September] ^{G (F)}

My good mother!

I am really put out: just imagine, there is no seat in the mailcoach until next Saturday—not even on the wretched imperial! I have in vain run from one bureau to the other, made all imaginable enquiries, raved and cursed—all to no avail: no seat, and so physically impossible for me to leave for another week. Good God, how that vexes me!

Should no further letter from Frater[6] arrive, come and meet him at 10 o'clock on Sunday morning at the arrival point of the Lafitte express coach. Let Mlle Moreau and Mlle Kautz[7] know of his return and that he will expect them as usual at 3 and 4 o'clock on Monday. And send Frater himself a couple of words by the next post, so that he can endure his bad luck more patiently. But you must post your letter before 2 o'clock.

Farewell, my good mother, and think of me a little. Cordial regards to my good friends, especially Chopin, Manuel Garcia and Mme Vial. Should there be any letters for me, open them and just let me know what they are about.

4. To Anna Liszt [Bourges, Friday, 28 September]. ^{G (F)} Once again, dear Mother, there is a delay; but this is the last. We owe it to Mme Petit, who has exchanged my seat in the coach for hers. Instead of Saturday, as I wrote to you, I can't depart until Monday morning. So Tuesday, dearest Mother, Tuesday at 10 o'clock you will see me arrive without fail.

No more at present, for the coach is waiting for me.[8] Here there are only parties, outings in the carriage, invitations to lunch, etc. I am, thank Heavens, as healthy as I possibly could be.

I embrace you.

Frater

---

[6] Anna Liszt's nickname for her son.
[7] Two pupils. Clémence Kautz was the dedicatee of the *Réminiscences de La Juive*.
[8] The mailcoach, to take the letter.

1833

This is at once the year in which Liszt resumed his professional career—apart from his brief appearance in April 1832 he had not been heard at a public concert in Paris for nearly three years—and that of his growing intimacy with the Comtesse d'Agoult.

12 March. Liszt and Manuel Garcia give a concert in the Salle du Wauxhall.

23 March. At Ferdinand Hiller's concert in the Salle du Wauxhall, Liszt and Chopin join Hiller in a performance of a triple concerto by Bach.

2 April. Liszt takes part in a concert given at the Théâtre Italien for the benefit of the Irish actress Harriet Smithson.

3 April. Liszt and Chopin play at the Herz brothers' concert.

Spring. Liszt pays his first visit to Croissy, the Comtesse d'Agoult's country château.

3 October. Liszt is a witness at the marriage, in the British Embassy,[1] of Hector Berlioz and Harriet Smithson.

24 November. Liszt participates in a *représentation extraordinaire* mounted for the benefit of Harriet Smithson-Berlioz.

22 December. At Berlioz's concert in the Paris Conservatoire, Liszt plays Weber's *Concertstück* to an audience which includes Paganini.

WORKS. *Malédiction* (S121), for piano and string orchestra. PIANO SOLO: *Harmonies poétiques et religieuses* (S154, published, in a revised version, in the *Gazette musicale de Paris* of 7 June 1835);[2] transcriptions of *L'idée fixe: andante amoroso* (Berlioz) (S395, ?1833), *Symphonie fantastique* (Berlioz) (S470), *Ouverture des Francs-juges* (Berlioz) (S471), *Die Rose* (Schubert) (S556).

5. To the Comtesse Marie d'Agoult [Paris, 4 April]. I believe, Madame, that the other evening you asked me to *take* and introduce to you our celebrated compatriot Heine. He is one of the most distinguished men in Germany, and did I not fear to wrong him by the comparison I should gladly use about him the famous adverb *extremely*, thrice repeated. After this preamble, will you allow me to bring him with me on Tuesday week?....

---

[1] The elegant and costly building at 39 rue du Faubourg Saint Honoré for which in 1814 the Duke of Wellington had paid Pauline Borghese, Napoleon's sister, £36,000 was already well known to Liszt from the time, several years earlier, when he had given lessons to the daughter of the Ambassador, Lord Granville.

[2] A single piece, not to be confused with the great set of pieces of the same title dating from later years.

As for my friend Chopin (haven't you taken offence at this name?), I haven't yet had a chance to pass on to him your very gracious message, but tomorrow (quite certainly) I shall go and wake him gently and affectionately with your invitations and entreaties.

Nor shall I fail to speak to him again of Mme de Rauzan,[3] for whom I am positively pining away with a mad and hopeless passion. On both knees I ask you for the secret. Chopin is the only person to whom I dare speak freely of her, for the Marquis or Chevalier of the rue *Niaise* [*Silly* Street] is a little jealous of me.

Poor Berlioz!... How I *occasionally* discover myself in his soul. He is here beside me. A few minutes ago he was weeping, sobbing in my arms... and I am so impudent as to continue to write to you!... [...]

6. To Marie d'Agoult. 1.00 a.m., Friday [3 May]. Here, first of all, Madame, are the two pieces of music you ask me for. I am very grateful to you for having preferred to give me this commission; I hope you will like them and that you will have no scruples about asking me again, and often. Talking of music, at the literary-Europe soirée yesterday evening I heard Berlioz's *Symphonie fantastique* once again; never had this work made so complete, so true, an impression on me. If I am not killed between now and the end of June I shall probably get down to arranging it for piano, however difficult and troublesome such an undertaking may be. I am convinced that you will be still more astonished reading than hearing it. Ad... will be compelled to hold the warming-pan ready on the day that you go through it. M. de Montcalm who was also there (and who most kindly came to ask after you), was, I am sure, very moved by it. So far as I am concerned, emotion is more or less non-existent now, but admiration remains. I listen without total understanding, but I know that it is very beautiful; I say so, I think so.

Oh! I haven't become wiser yet!

Mme d'Apponyi[4] is to give me a lot of *Mehlspeisen, Dampfnudeln* [puddings and dumplings] next Monday, for she insists on my putting on some weight. That woman really is charmingly kind and cordial to me. I almost had tears in my eyes when leaving her home this evening. . . .

I feel ready to drop with fatigue: I have not had a single night of rest since your departure; yesterday I got home at four o'clock, the day before at two, and

---

[3] Clara, Duchesse de Rauzan, daughter of the Duchesse de Duras, was one of the leading *salonnières* of the Faubourg Saint-Germain and the dedicatee of the first of Liszt's *Apparitions.*

[4] Wife of the Hungarian magnate who was one of the first of Liszt's patrons and Austria's Ambassador in Paris at this time.

so on. Happily, I have to endure all that for only another week. Pardon, a hundred times pardon, Madame, for all this chit-chat; you have accustomed me to so much kindness that I involuntarily (and from my natural propensity for going to excess) often abuse it. . . .

7. To Marie d'Agoult. Wednesday.[5] No, I shall not be leaving for the country. I shall go neither to the Duchess's, nor to granny's, nor to Mme Boissier's nor to Mme Merlin's.[6] I am suffering and need to be alone. You seem not to understand this word *retreat*—this is what I mean by it. First thing tomorrow, I shall make myself at home *chez* my excellent friend Erard,* who is in London. I shall occupy a small room, rue du Mail, where I shall read, work, and study from morning to night. Only my mother and Berlioz have permission to force their way in; all my other friends and acquaintances will believe that I am away. . . . One *passion alone*, one belief alone, remains alive within me: a belief in, a passion for work. What does it matter?... I shall at least be able to fret and torment myself at my ease. If you have some further commission to give me, send to the same address; my mother will take care of the correspondence. Mlle Boscary is marrying Miramon; I am very pleased about it. Adèle in Geneva is overwhelmed by sorrows. That, too, is good. Mme de la Trémoïlle, Mme d'Hérici, de Bellissen, talk to me at length of the châtelaine of Croissy; I let the conversation drop. . . .

Oh! you see, Madame, there are men whom God has marked on the brow, to live and die in vain... eternally deceived and undeceived, hope itself becomes for them an ignoble, unbearable torment... May their destiny be fulfilled. They will find it quiet and refreshing to lie in the grave.

8. To Marie d'Agoult. At last a letter from you!... God be blessed. I was despairing!... Oh! don't be surprised by the dryness, the cold concision of my letters; you know me, you know all the *mockery* that occasionally breaks into my submissiveness, and the bitterness sometimes lurking within this apparent calm (my *second nature*, as you so aptly said). Besides, I write in so commonplace a manner; everything I say and can say I find so insignificant that I am

---

[5] Many of Liszt's letters to Mme d'Agoult at this time bear no date, and the order in which they are presented here must be regarded as to some extent conjectural. Unless there are obvious reasons for differing from it, that followed by Daniel Ollivier in his edition of the Liszt–d'Agoult correspondence has been retained.

[6] The Comtesse Merlin, another of the salon hostesses.

ashamed to add to its length even when I feel like gossiping a bit. Do you remember this line of Petrarch's:

Chi po dir com'egli arde è'n picciol foco.[7] . . .

Talking of letters, I must tell you a short story, or rather something I said in my childhood. An excellent lady who had the incomparable merit of always arriving escorted by big boxes of toys (punchinellos, *saintes chapelles*, little carriages on springs, etc.) and whom, for a thousand other reasons that I imagined at that time, I loved to the point of adoration, asked me when I left for London if I would write to her from time to time. To begin with, I promised to do so, then, thinking about it, added hesitatingly: 'But if I didn't know what to say, would I still have to write?'

V.H. (I should have put Gothic letters for you to understand the initials more easily) told me the other evening that the Abbé de Lamennais, Lamartine, and others had often written to him without his ever having sent them so much as a word in reply, the reason being that he writes no letters at all, a reason springing from time and circumstances. Writing letters has always seemed to me to be rather a good way of expressing oneself; nevertheless, you are free to consider him ill-mannered and I to reply for the hundredth time that Genius is essentially ill-mannered and insolent.

Last Sunday there was a grand *scena patetica* at the rue des Anachorètes: CH... (l'amico) and your very humble servant were the chief and only interlocutors. Entreaties, tears, rages, reproaches, sobs: it lacked nothing; it was magnificent. If that interests you, I shall tell you about it some day, but it would be impossible for me to write it down for you. To excite your curiosity still further, I shall add that the Corinne du Quai Malaquais[8] was mentioned at great length.

Schreiben Sie bald [Write soon].

My way of life is perhaps quite as strange as yours. I am absolutely alone, not six leagues[9] from Paris but in Paris itself, the centre of Paris. Apart from my mother I have seen no one since Friday. Need I tell you that I feel the same aversion, the same suspicions you tell me of... I have written nothing; sometimes towards evening I make my way slowly towards the church of the Petits Pères which is a few paces away from my new retreat. At other times I go through the faubourg Saint-Antoine. I sleep a lot. My health is improving, I assume.— Oh! do you understand? If you have no further need of *Les Pleurs*,[10] send it back to me. Alexandre Dumas is asking me for it. . . .

---

[7] From the sonnet 'Più volte già dal bel sembiante umano': 'He who can express his ardour, burns but a little.'
[8] Marie d'Agoult herself.   [9] The distance from Paris of Croissy.
[10] Lyrical poems by Marceline Desbordes-Valmore.

9. To Marie d'Agoult. Friend Chopin had planned to pay you a brief visit yesterday morning (Sunday); I was intending to entrust him with the enclosed second volume of *Obermann*,[11] which I ask you to be so good as to accept, underline, and annotate. When you get back, I shall myself have the honour of handing you the first volume, which you know already. . . .

I can quite definitely no longer listen to *pretty* music, Madame. To please my good mother, I accompanied her this evening to the Opéra Comique, where they were performing the *Pré-aux-Clercs*,[12] which I didn't know (since 1829—i.e. since Caroline—I hadn't been back to that theatre), but I heard and saw nothing, for I found it impossible to listen to and look at those singing marionettes. It really is pitiful, all that!...

Ballanche whom I ran into the other evening is very busy with the publication of his *France religieuse et poétique* (which will appear under his editorship in about a fortnight, I believe). I *almost* asked him, and he *almost* proposed, to take me to Mme Récamier's,[13] so that we shall probably end up going there one of these evenings. I seemed to remember that you *desired* me to do so.—You doubtless already know that Chateaubriand has accepted the title and diploma of honorary Benedictine; wouldn't it be possible for you to meet for a second time 'the illustrious genius', whom you even outdo with the higher rank of the *Comtesse* over the *Vicomte*, and for you to proclaim yourself Abbess and foundress of a new religious order... and the woman of the renaissance! Oh, forgive me, I was forgetting... all this is only *half* joking, as you know. . . .

There is absolutely no point in sending back to you the letter you are asking for, which is very simple and very suitable. It was my unfortunate imagination (call it what you will) which did everything. As for those places where I have been *unintelligible* and mysterious—laugh at them, have a good laugh at them. Like the good Montaigne: 'I am not melancholy in myself, but a dreamer.' . . .

10. To Ferdinand Hiller in Frankfurt. 20 June.[14] This is at least the twentieth time that we have arranged to meet, sometimes at my place, sometimes here,[15] with the intention of writing to you, and some visit or other unforeseen obstacle has always prevented our doing so. I don't know if Chopin will be up

---

[11] Senancour's pre-Romantic epistolary novel (1804) of gloom, melancholy, and despair was the inspiration for Liszt's *Vallée d'Obermann*, which he dedicated to Senancour and prefaced with a long quotation from the novel.

[12] Three-act comic opera by Hérold, first performed at the Opéra-Comique, 1832.

[13] Chateaubriand's friend and former mistress, renowned for her beauty and her salon at the Abbaye-aux-Bois, rue de Sèvres, of which her devoted admirer Ballanche was an *habitué*.

[14] This letter penned jointly by Liszt and Chopin was also signed by Auguste Franchomme. The parts written by Chopin are here presented in square brackets.

[15] At Chopin's lodgings, of which the address is given further on in the letter.

to offering his apologies; as far as I am concerned, it seems to me that our rudeness and bad manners have gone beyond the point at which excuses are either
permitted or possible.

We very much sympathize with you in your bereavement,[16] and, even more,
would very much wish to be with you, so that we might try to alleviate your
sorrow as much as we possibly could.

[He has said everything so well that I need add no special apologies for my
negligence, idleness, 'flu, or absence of mind, or, or, or——As you know, I explain
myself better in person, and when, this autumn, I take you along the boulevards to your mother's in the late evening, I shall try to obtain your forgiveness.
——I am writing to you without knowing what my pen is scribbling, because Liszt
is at this very moment playing my *études*[17] and transporting me away from any
decent ideas. I should like to rob him of his way of playing my own *études*. As
regards those friends of yours who are in Paris, this last winter and spring I have
often seen the Léo family[18] and their associates. There have been some soirées
in the homes of certain ambassadors' wives—and at not a single one of them has
anyone failed to speak of someone in Frankfurt. Madame Eichthal asks to be
remembered most kindly to you. The whole Plater family were grieved at your
departure and asked me to send their condolences.] Madame Apponyi was very
annoyed with me for not having taken you to see her before you left: she hopes
that when you return you will be so kind as to remember the promise you made
me. I shall say the same of a certain Lady who is not an ambassador's wife.

Do you know Chopin's wonderful Etudes?——[They are admirable!—and
yet they will last only until yours appear] = an author's little bit of modesty!!!
[A little bit of rudeness on the part of the tutor—for, to tell you the truth, he
is correcting my spelling] according to Monsieur Marlet's method.

You will come back to us in [September, won't you? Tr]y to let us know the
day, as we have decided to give you a serenade (or *charivari*). The company of
the most distinguished artistes in the capital = M. Franchomme (present), Madame
Petzold, and the Abbé Bardin, the *coryphées* of the rue d'Amboise (and my neighbours), Maurice Schlesinger, uncles, aunts, nephews, nieces, brothers-in-law,
sisters-in-law, and and = [others still more distant etc.

The editors responsible]

F. Liszt

[F. Chopin]   ([Aug. Franchomme])

[By the bye, I ran into Heine yesterday, and he asked me to send you his warmest
and most heartfelt greetings.—

---

[16] Hiller had lost his father.

[17] It was in 1833 that Chopin's Douze Grandes Etudes, Op. 10, were published, dedicated 'to his friend F. Liszt'.

[18] Auguste Léo was a banker and the dedicatee, ten years later, of Chopin's Polonaise in A flat, Op. 53.

By the bye again, forgive me for all these *vous*[19]—I do beg you to excuse them. If you have a moment to spare, give us your news, which we would very much welcome. Paris, rue de la Chaussée d'Antin, No. 5. I am using [Hermann] Franck's lodgings at present, as he has gone to London and Berlin. I feel very comfortable in the rooms which were so often our meeting-place. Warmest greetings from Berlioz.

As for *père* Baillot, he is in Switzerland, at Geneva, and so you will guess, correctly, that I can't send you the Bach concerto.]

11. To Marie d'Agoult. 30 August. We shall be able to visit la S[20] only on Thursday (the 5th) from 8.30 to 10.00 a.m. M. Mitivié, a medical celebrity who has promised me that he will have us admitted despite the prohibition, is there at that time only; but if you are at all interested in other curiosities, we can arrange to form some big *party* on the very day of your arrival.

M. Henri Herz has had his return reported in several newspapers; the sentence is official because it is reproduced everywhere in the same way; thus, if I am not mistaken: 'M.H.H. is back from his visit to London, where he obtained the greatest success.' I told him the other evening of the admirable way in which you played the *Variations sur Euryanthe*. 'Oh! You don't say!' he replied; 'I didn't think she was equal to giving a good performance of such a difficult piece.' I in my turn politely said that you had started studying the piano again this winter and that you had made immense progress.

J. B. Cramer is still in Paris. I certainly won't be able to escape him. I shall have to dine and spend tomorrow evening with him at Pape's, where several artistes will gather. Need I tell you what makes me go back there? There are bizarre coincidences. Moreover, it seems that the poor man is at his last gasp. At Mme Pleyel's* last Monday he played a *courante*...

The [transcription of the] *Symphonie fantastique* will be finished on Sunday evening; say three 'Our Fathers' and three 'Hail Marys' expressly for it. . . .

Lady Blessington's *Conversations*[21] are rather difficult to find, but you will have them at the end of the week; i.e. tomorrow or the day after at the latest. . . . I am reading, writing and working all day long.—Goodbye—Don't forget me completely.[22]

La Salpêtrière is in the direction of the Jardin des Plantes.

---

[19] Instead of the more familiar *tu*.

[20] The hospital of La Salpêtrière, named from being erected, during the reign of Louis XIV, on the site of an arsenal and saltpetre works. In the early 19th cent. it was best known as an institution for treatment of the insane.

[21] See under Blessington in Biographical Sketches.   [22] The last fourteen words written by Liszt in English.

12. To Marie d'Agoult. I don't know what error (voluntary or involuntary) caused me to carry away the second volume of *La Salamandre*.[23] If you take the trouble to read it you will probably be better pleased with it than you were with the first. The character of Szaffie which, in my opinion, has only the fault of being a bit too hide-bound, is admirably drawn and developed. The chapters entitled 'Une Nuit d'Eté', 'Une Voile', and above all the 'Calenture', the dreadful, frightful Calenture, are magnificent. An astonishing chorus of drunken sailors could be made out of this last orgy in *La Salamandre*. If E. Sue consents to put this episode into verse for me, I shall try my powers. At least, I am very tempted to do so.

My poor good mother has been very worried about me; she had planned to set out yesterday evening in little Musc.'s carriage. I was obliged to tell her that I had been poorly, in bed, and that the doctor had forbidden me to leave my room on Monday and Tuesday... For the rest, we are getting on much better than before. . . .

On Sunday morning I shall lunch at Dr Esquirol's with two old friends of mine who have asked me to go and examine with them a really curious individual: an old woman of sixty, an idiot, a total idiot, but gifted with the strange ability of being able to retain and repeat all the tunes she hears sung, played, or hummed. . . .

I have a thousand things to think of—Berlioz is making an unexpected visit—people are waiting for me, the bell is ringing, and yet never have I *lived* so outside all these sad and ponderous realities. Pity me, Madame, pity me.

Don't forget your old and new promises either; I sometimes have such a need of rest, and can no longer seek it within myself. Adieu, Madame, and a hundred thanks.

13. To Marie d'Agoult. Barring a definite and categorical order, signed by the Comtesse d'Agoult (by Ma.), an order that I shall gladly undertake to have carried out by the royal constabulary, don't in any way count on a visit from the celebrated pianist F. Chopin, for the aforesaid friend and pianist decamped last week and at this moment is probably in Tours, in the company of M. Franchomme (celebrated bass,[24] and not *base celebrity*) and, as you might be so naughty as to think, beside some beautiful, simple, and naïve Tourangère,[25] etc....

Lacking him, and as a kind of consolation, I shall have the honour, Madame, to send you through little Musc.... the pink Mazurkas which it seems to me I promised you a long time before you asked me for them. . . .

---

[23] Novel (1832) by Eugène Sue.   [24] Player of a bass instrument: Franchomme was a cellist.
[25] A female native of Tours, the usual word for which is Tourangelle.

Some sinister recollection of Croissy holds sway over me, strangely bothering me—if you can guess what it is, Madame, and if you feel something similar,
tell me in writing... if the professorial duties leave you enough leisure . . .

You will receive *Atala* and *Le Dernier des Abencérages*[26] by tomorrow's carriage.

14. To Marie d'Agoult [Monday, September]. The Abbé Deguerry* will
not be back until the end of the month; he has to preach at Saint-Roch's on St
Denis's Day [9 October] and every Sunday in October; I shall be able to keep
you well informed of his sermons and to write out summaries for you, for I am
determined not to miss a single one. In the mean time you are subscribed at
Mongie's, Boulevard des Italiens; Lady Blessington's *Conversations* can't be found
for the moment; I have asked for them in three reading-rooms... Mongie (who,
incidentally, didn't want my money, because, he said, my *celebrity* is a good enough
guarantee) has given me a definite promise for them by the end of the week.
Here, anyway, are three volumes of Jacob the Bibliophile[27] which are rather well
known... You would be doing a great kindness if you read them to some extent
for yourself and to some extent for me. Not knowing them at all, I am very
keen to know your opinion. . . .

Dessauer was delighted with your splendid soirée; Marquise[28] in particular
caught his eye. He compares you, Mesdames, to Anna and Agathe in *Der Freischütz*,
Anna ever absorbed in unconscious perseverance and Agathe so loving, so
gently ingenious in consoling and distracting her friend... I found that pretty
accurate. . . .

You were *sublime* on Saturday morning; yes, simply sublime... Never have Goethe
and Schubert been understood like that... never has greater emotion chilled the
depths of my being and burnt my brow... Oh! Could one only die after these
hours of enthusiasm and delirium. What Singing, what Poetry... Yes, it came to
me clearly at that moment that the Universe is merely the garment, the veil...
the *soul* is God.

On Sunday morning (yesterday), on opening my Bible, at mass, I came across
this verse:

'God is our refuge, our strength and our help in distress, and *extremely* easy
to *find*'[29]—'therefore will we not fear...'—that is sublime too! . . . You know,
Madame, that it is only you to whom I can talk of *Art* and Poetry. . . .

---

[26] Respectively Chateaubriand's *Atala, ou les Amours de deux sauvages dans le désert* (1801) and *Les Aventures du dernier
Abencérage* (1826).

[27] The bibliographer, scholar, and novelist Paul Lacroix was known as 'le bibliophile Jacob'.

[28] Marie's friend the Marquise de Gabriac, daughter of the Russian general Count Davidov.

[29] Ps. 46: 1, of which the version in the AV runs: 'God is our refuge and strength, a very present help in trouble.'

15. To Marie d'Agoult. [Monday] 16 September. Thank God and be grateful to me for my clumsiness. 'If Cleopatra's nose... Cromwell was going to lay waste...' It is, however, not a question of either Cleopatra, or Cromwell, or Egypt, or Revolution, but of a simple and modest little bottle of red ink costing *six sols Parisis*.—What, you can't guess?... Well! learn that without that wretched little bottle spilt over a still more wretched letter, you would perhaps have struck your forehead against the ground the whole day long; and then in the evening the coming of tears and sobs would not have failed to ravage your beautiful face... and after that, who knows?... You would perhaps have torn your eyes and teeth out, split your mouth open, burnt your hair—for my letter was frightful, pathetic, sublime [*sic*], enough to make one die of boredom. Wretched red ink, I'll get my own back!

I don't entirely share your fine contempt for the Novel. The Novel is nowadays our epic poem... whatever you do, you won't be able to escape it completely.—You will find it everywhere, in history (the most unlikely story of all), in memoirs (novels of a prosaic and restricted kind), in the *Gazette des Tribunaux*, in religious and philosophical systems, in your memories, in your hopes, in the Lives of the Saints, and under the guillotine during the Terror.—In a word, everywhere. Of course, I shall never send you an anonymous work, but if by chance you now and then receive some orphan, be it even a bastard, receive it hospitably, and remember this Indian (or Chinese or whatever) proverb: 'The wise man is the one who learns from everything.'

I have written so many notes this morning that I can hardly hold my pen... I suffer greatly from the cold, and it seems to me that my circulation is bad. . . . Without farewell, see you soon. . . .

16. To Marie d'Agoult. [Paris, Wednesday] 30 October. It is *once again* a very long time, Madame, since you gave me a sign of life; not one single errand, not one poor little message, nor shopping, nor books, nor parcels, nor music... Are you perhaps poorly, ill?... But no, I flatter myself much too much—you have simply forgotten me—with and after so many others, I am now consigned to oblivion...

The Berlioz performance is definitely announced for Sunday, 10 November (Sunday week), at the Théâtre des Italiens.

I thought you would be interested to see Madame Dorval in *Antony*[30] and (after eleven months) to hear another performance of the *Symphonie fantastique*,

---

[30] Drama (1831) by Dumas *père*.

which will be played by more than a hundred musicians; and then, pardon this little egoism, I too have a slight but ambitious part in this soirée... for I have to play Weber's *Concertstück*. It's only *seven* months since you heard it, and I am practising hard so that I can play it deliriously and with all the disdain of my twenty-two years.—In short, all these considerations (they are rather tangled together) have made me commit an indiscretion, an enormous indiscretion, in your name. This morning I reserved a four-seat box, the ticket for which I shall have the honour of sending to you at Croissy if you wish, or simply to the rue de Beaune, for I think I heard you say that M. de Flavigny[31] would be in Paris from the 10th to the 15th and that you would probably come and join him. Isn't that like pointing a pistol at people's heads and asking for their money or their life?. . . .

Do please send me a couple of words in reply, so that I may know for sure if I am to expect you on Sunday evening at the Italiens. But you'll do so soon, won't you, for I am longing to have your news. . . . If you could manage to send *Werther*[32] back to me on some suitable occasion and, above all, my little *harmonie lamartinienne*[33] without key or bars, I should be extremely grateful. I greatly value those few pages. They remind me vividly of an hour of suffering and delight.

[**Later.**] Berlioz's concert has been metamorphosed into a Grand Benefit Performance. The *Symphonie fantastique* will be replaced by *Antony* (Dorval and Firmin are entrusted with the two principal roles).—Miss Smithson will give us an act from *Hamlet*—all this for 10 or 12 November at the Italiens. What a feast!... You'll try to come, won't you?. . . .

17. To Marie d'Agoult. [Saturday] 2 November. Always delays. Oh! it's unbearable. Mme Dorval won't be back until about the 10th, and so the Berlioz performance is perforce postponed until tomorrow fortnight, Sunday, 17 November.[34] The content of the show remains the same: *Antony*, the last act of *Hamlet*, and the concerto. You will come. For pity's sake, come, Madame. . . .

---

[31] Marie's brother, Maurice de Flavigny.

[32] *Die Leiden des jungen Werthers* (1774), Goethe's celebrated epistolary novel about the torments suffered by young Werther in unrequited love, and his consequent suicide.

[33] The *Harmonies poétiques et religieuses*, inspired, like the later set, by Lamartine's collection of poems published under this title in 1830.

[34] This *représentation extraordinaire* eventually took place on Sunday, 24 Nov.

1834

19 and 26 January. Liszt plays in concerts at Pleyel's and Erard's.

25 February. He plays at a concert in which a fellow performer is Chopin.

April. About this time he is introduced to the Abbé Lamennais.*

May/June. Liszt stays with the d'Haineville family at the Château de Carentonne in Bernay (Normandy).

13 September. He leaves Paris to stay with Lamennais at La Chênaie, the Abbé's home near Dinan (Brittany).

Mid-October. Liszt returns from Dinan to Paris where, not long afterwards, Alfred de Musset introduces him to George Sand.*

5 November. He plays *La Clochette* at a charity concert.

24 November. He and Chrétien Urhan play Beethoven's Kreutzer Sonata at the church of St Vincent de Paul.

Christmas Day. At a matinée in Stoepel's Institution Musicale, Liszt and Chopin—'the two greatest pianoforte virtuosi of the age', according to the *Gazette musicale*—play Moscheles' Grand Duo and Liszt's own *Grosses Konzertstück* for two pianos on themes from Mendelssohn's *Lieder ohne Worte*.

WORKS. *Apparitions* (S155), three pieces for piano. *Grande fantaisie symphonique on themes from Berlioz's Lélio* (S120), for piano and orchestra. *Grosses Konzertstück über Mendelssohns Lieder ohne Worte* (S257), for two pianos.

18. To Marie d'Agoult [Paris, New Year's Day?]. So I couldn't see you yesterday and I can't see you today. Today, when everyone is well and everyone is eating sweets, I am coughing and drinking barley water. What does that portend for 1834? So do write me a word. It is you alone in all the world who are life for me and whom I grieve not to see. Write to me. Tell me about yesterday, about last night. How did you do your hair? Did you cough? Did you waltz? Tell me all that. May my illness be like an absence, like a couple of days spent far away from you. Let me read you. I am better this morning. I should like to be able to go to the [Théâtre des] Italiens tomorrow. In other words, I should like to be able to see you. When will that be? Cursed cold—if only I hadn't lost a brother from a chest complaint.[1] There was a time when I would have been delighted for a chill to put an end to my life. Now, I should be very sorry to

---

[1] Nothing is known of a brother of Liszt.

die. Why? I love you. I want to see your fair hair again, and your blue eyes, and to hear you speak again, and to read more of your letters. I want to live. I love you. And, you see, I shall live because I love you. An illness is to be feared only if one catches it in a moment when one's heart is empty of love. If one loved for a hundred years one would live for a hundred years. If ever you are unwell, therefore, I shall prepare a tribute. You who do not love, or so people say, at least. But if it isn't true, it's a calumny. To prove it to me, write to me. Two or three words, quickly, very quickly. . . . Let me know if your 1834 note-paper is the same as your 1833 paper. Do you still want red wax to be *à la mode*? Do you still want me to be here? But, adieu, a fit of coughing is stopping the man *à la mode*. Adieu, and two words.

19. To Marie d'Agoult [Paris, 1 May]. You feel it, you know it. As far as I am concerned there is no longer anything but mourning, tedium, and bitter, poignant sadness in all things. Nevertheless, I am not wholly extinguished; however arid and monotonous the road I shall walk, I want to travel it to the end.

I shall have to remain in Paris for ten days or so, then I shall leave for Normandy. Happily, I find myself able to perform a few small services for a friend (P. Erard); that keeps me busy and gives me pleasure. It was on one of his pianos that I improvised yesterday before His Citizen Majesty[2] and his august family in the Exhibition Hall. L. PH. found that I had changed a great deal, and I permitted myself to reply that many other things had changed a lot too.[3] An hour later, I went to Janvier's for dinner. Lamartine, Lacordaire, the Abbé Gerbet, and Dubois of the *Globe* were there. Lacordaire, who separated from Lamennais some time ago, talked to me a lot. If I am not mistaken, his Catholicism would edify you greatly and bore you a little. I found him quite perfect. As for the Abbé Gerbet (author of the magnificent book on the generative Dogma of Catholic Piety, which I urge you to read and reread), he is, I believe, a very beautiful soul, a pious soul, most deeply Christian, and even outwardly Christian. That, at least, is the impression he made on me. You know that I make no claim to being able to judge people, either on a first or a hundredth meeting. The *Paroles d'un Croyant*[4] came out yesterday. If you want it, I shall be delighted to send it to you. One little question, Madame: did you carry off Lesage's *Atlas*? If not, will you allow me to take it from *chez vous* and keep it until your return? I shall take great

---

[2] The *roi citoyen*, Louis-Philippe.
[3] This exchange cost Liszt his first nomination to the Legion of Honour, of which he was made a Chevalier eleven years later.
[4] For this, *L'Avenir* and the *Essai sur l'indifférence*, see under Lamennais in Biographical Sketches.

care of it, and my mother will wrap it in grey paper like the album. Talking of grey paper, I have here a splendid volume of white music paper, which I want to fill this summer and which my bookbinder had the sense to bind in grey without my telling him... It gave me childlike joy... I sometimes feel an inexpressible desire for poetry, common sense, life... then it seems to me that all of it is in you, Madame, and I dream and ponder endlessly... *Nicht eines Engels, nicht Gottes, nur Dein* [Not an angel's, not God's, thine alone]. . . . See you soon.

20. To Marie d'Agoult. Wednesday. You are probably in a bad humour today, for I feel deeply troubled and weighed down by sadness. . . .

Your advice on what to read is excellent. I had already made it my duty to try to read seriously Montesquieu, H... (the sceptic[5]), one or two German historians, Niebuhr and Müller, a few Greek and Latin authors, and finally Michelet, Lacretelle, and Sismondi; within the next three years I shall become a little less ignorant. As for La Harpe, Schelling, and the philosophical mediocrities, I am very glad to know them; it amuses me. These last few days I have read Saint-Just's *Les Institutions républicaines.* It contains this fine remark: 'An unhappy man is above governments and worldly authorities. He must speak to them *en maître.*' As regards intellectual debauchery, do you know Diderot's *Le Neveu de Rameau?*[6] Don't read it—although I found it enormously amusing. If you hadn't so often reproached me with explaining too much, I should explain the *proud* and the *absolute* (without admitting them) by the need for dignity and correctness.

I have seen Lamartine quite often; all in all it has been good for me to know several men: my judgement has changed and lost something of its unjust asperity. Here, I always defend the Poet-Deputy with great warmth when he is attacked, which happens often, for this poor L... has had the fate of all moderate men, that of displeasing everyone to begin with. Alfred de V[igny] has said very wittily: 'L... doesn't oppose, just contradicts.' . . . .

21. To Marie d'Agoult [Paris, *c.*12 May]. It is fully understood, fully agreed, that every line, every word from you is dear and precious to me; nevertheless, I cannot accept your advice and reproaches about Lamennais's book. . . .

---

[5] Perhaps Baron d'Holbach, the *encyclopédiste*, whose best-known work, *Système de la Nature* (1770), advances a materialist philosophy.

[6] Written *c.*1762, and first made known through Goethe's German translation, this celebrated novel in dialogue form had in 1823 been printed from a copy of Diderot's manuscript, but was not to be printed from the manuscript itself until 1891.

I understand all the restrictions, all the wise observations that can be made about this magnificent volume. But in all conscience, is it for you, is it for me, is it for us, to cast a stone at the great priest who through his fiery mouth and his brazen pen is sanctifying Liberty and Equality, those two great dogmas of Humanity?

I no longer have a moment to myself, being continually assailed by acts of kindness and friendship. I am writing to you in the company of most excellent people. . . . On Friday I leave for Normandy. This is my address: *chez* Mme d'Haineville, Château de Carentonne, near Bernay, department of the Eure. We talked a lot with the Abbé, who came to see me yesterday evening. Farewell. I had read *Leone*[7] before you did. Here is a splendid remark of Mme Sand's: 'Don't take me for a virtuous woman; I don't know what virtue is. I believe in it as I believe in Providence, without being able either to understand or define it.'

22. To Anna Liszt in Paris [Château de Carentonne, Saturday, 17 May]. [G] [(F)] Arrived safely at 2 o'clock without any mishap, dear Mother. It's a delightful district; my room is spacious and attractively furnished. M., Mme, and Mlle d'Haineville are so obliging and friendly as to drive a dried-up and gloomy fellow like me almost to distraction. Could I become a child, a real child, again I believe I could be happy once more! I am allowed much freedom, and people even want me to use it; I hope to do so, for I shall work. I must go forward and not look back. The *Imitation of Christ* teaches: 'What is undertaken must be brought to a conclusion.'—

Write to me this week, but not too quickly, for I should like to have a long letter. Did you give the *Paroles d'un Croyant* back to Hortense? Mme Vial I shall write to in the next few days. In the mean time, talk to her about the good-for-nothing, who goes to bed every evening at 9 o'clock. How is Fratras? I'd gladly have brought her with me, for she would here have been treated gently and lovingly, poor creature!

Affectionate regards to Mlle Delarue—and *to her alone*; for the others, greetings are enough. Nini should come here with her pupil, if for only a fortnight. Our valley is delightful. Tell her and try to persuade her mother.

Farewell, dear Mother. I have lost nothing, had no accidents when getting in and out of the mailcoach. Tomorrow, Whit Sunday, my hair is to be cut, etc. etc.

---

[7] George Sand's novelette *Leone Leoni*, published that year.

23. To Anna Liszt [Château de Carentonne, 19 May]. ^G ^(F) My wretched piano has still not arrived. Do go to Erard's at once and let him hear my complaints and reproaches so that he will send for the coachman and find out exactly what has happened to the instrument. If you can, send me the three volumes of Chopin Mazurkas[8] and Bertini's Studies through the post. I should be grateful. Adieu. F. Liszt

24. To Marie d'Agoult [Carentonne, May]. I should be *well* and *happy* here: Mme d'Haineville and her daughter are really friendly and attentive to me; her son, an ex-sailor of 30 with whom I argue from morning to night, and sometimes from night to morning, is sincerely fond of me, and I likewise feel affection for him—he is so good, so kind!—All my time is taken up by study and reading. The environs are delightful—my room is very similar to the one I had at Croissy, the fireplace and my bed being positioned in the same way... Oh! why can't I weep, weep on your knees!... My head is on fire... I need your hand, here, on my brow, in my hair... I can no longer hear, sense or see either the trees, or people moving and bustling about, or the sky... The sky!... It is clear and cloudless! Derision! despair! incomprehensibility!... And so we shall never live!... and we don't know what it is to *die*!

> Taisons nous
> et adorons!
> et taisons nous encore!

Tomorrow I shall have a few words from you, I hope. Tell me something of how your days are spent, tell me candidly if you can easily endure all that pack of bothers and anxieties which make up life. As for me, I tell myself that I must work and work! I have an immense need (immense is very ambitious) to know, to learn, to study—and am going through everything again from the beginning. I am reading Bayle, the Bible, the history of philosophical systems, and that good classic La Harpe, whom I have never had the courage to read from beginning to end. The great V. [Hugo] told me one day that it was a colossal heap of ineptitudes—but no matter! I am also practising many cadenzas, octaves, and tremolos—it's head-splitting. I have with me the *études* of Hiller, Chopin, and Kessler. Hiller's I find very good, very remarkable, but I doubt if they will have any *success*; the good Public and the *dilettanti connoisseurs* aren't ready for them yet. . . .

---

[8] Chopin's Mazurkas Op. 6, 7, and 17 had been published by this time.

I can stay here only until 20 June. Erard needs me in Paris about that time. I hope to see you there. Perhaps Sainte-Beuve and I will go to La Chênaie at the end of July. Again it will be for only a month. We shall come back via Croissy.

For the rest, I am quite well, apart from when I feel low. . . .

Why tell me that I shall never feel certain things? That offends me and gives me too bad an opinion of myself. I have not written to Adèle.[9] To Mme Laborie[10] I have said more or less everything that I had to say, that I shall return the letters, not out of duty, nor religion, etc., etc., etc., etc. I said it curtly, bitterly, and scornfully, in a way that deeply distressed that poor Charlotte and brought tears to her eyes. Perhaps I shall write to her when you return, but I'm not sure—and yet *I love that woman*!

Oh! you sometimes understand me very badly indeed! Mme L... is very anxious to know if I am keeping some copy of those letters, and is rather keen for the marriage promise not to have been burnt. I am telling you all this because I now know that you are annoyed when I am reticent... A failing. Don't talk to me much of Adèle, and for goodness' sake *never* mention other names; that hurts me, hurts me deeply. If you wish, I shall speak to you one last time about my life from 1830 to 1833. It is very simple and very sad, very little like that of a Don Juan—but, all your acuteness of mind notwithstanding, it is impossible for you not to form a wrong opinion of it; sharper minds would get it wrong too. That is quite agreed, isn't it?... A few days before leaving I saw Hortense again. That poor beautiful girl made me very ashamed... She has remained so pure, so humbly resigned. Hegel was entitled to say on his death-bed: 'Ein einziger hat mich verstanden und auch dieser... [Only one person has understood me, and even he...].' . . .

In the isolation in which I am living, *love* is tormenting and destroying me—but I shall find some relief in the grave. . . .

25. To Marie d'Agoult [Carentonne, May] . . . Last Sunday they got me to climb up to the Bernay organ, which was an event for the town. M. d'Haineville and others are talking of a soirée on behalf of the poor. It goes without saying that I am making no difficulties and will do my best.

Despite all the friendly attentions people are so good as to pay me, I live very much alone. Armand spends a great part of the day in my room. We are very fond of one another. Sometimes we take a walk together while arguing like madmen. He's a very good sort, very much a believer, very much a legitimist, but

---

[9] The Comtesse Adèle de Laprunarède.
[10] Mother of Charlotte Laborie, who a year or two earlier had been a proposed bride for Liszt.

politely and with what seems to be moderation. As for me, I frighten and ter-
rify him. 'You know, it will be a dreadful sorrow for me to have known you:
you are destined for many misfortunes,' he said the other day. As far as women
or ladies are concerned, I neither see, nor want to see, any. It's a physical aversion; apart from Herminie V and Hortense I find them all unbearable. I take
that to ridiculous lengths.

Someone from Normandy apparently said of his intended: 'Physically she's
an animal, and morally she's destitute.' Nice, isn't it? Do you know Chopin's
Mazurkas dedicated to Mme Freppa?[11] They are delightful. I am practising an
enormous number of cadenzas and tremolos. I hope you will find some
progress. Quite often *my father's idea comes back to me.* Oh! I shall have to work
enormously. Adieu. . . .

26. To Marie d'Agoult [Carentonne, late May or early June]. It is
four o'clock. I have only time to tell you three times, laughable, laughable and
laughable!!... I don't know by what chance all these letters that you do me the
honour of returning to me, and that you would have done better to put I don't
know where, were in that wretched cardboard box. *They all date from* 1831—
the time when, to calm me down, my *mother* and *Madame D...*[12] *were determined to marry me to that dear young lady who...* but I don't want to say anything
smacking of self-conceit. It was also the time of Hor... and to some extent of
Mme G... a time of struggle, anguish, and lonely torments—a time when I was
shattering, destroying, and violently annihilating Adèle's love. It was then that
I wrote 'I *am* and would like not to be. I have to suffer, suffer alone... for your
own sake, *leave me, leave me.*' (You perhaps don't remember, for you have a bad
memory, that we had for a long time been living in the same house, that her
mother was *intimate, more than intimate* with mine, that this poor young lady
had passed through all the gradations, etc. etc.) Nevertheless, as Marquise
would say, *despite the exchange of 'tu'* there was no *sin.* . . . If you had read well,
you would at least have seen at the foot of a torn-up letter: 'From now on there
can no longer be anything in common between you and me.' This letter was
written six weeks after the first one, *in October* 1831. Since then, despite all the
splendid *despair* and even a few *threats,* I haven't once seen that young person
whom I did not love, but *whom I momentarily thought of marrying* in order to
make it up with my mother, wearied by all my follies. My mother!... you know
what this word is for me!... She has never doubted me! But, in the name of

---

[11] Op. 17.   [12] Perhaps Mme Didier.

Heaven, give up once and for all these fine discoveries, they are simply too ludicrous. Neither of us will ever be a Columbus or a La [Pérouse]. I'll tell you once again: *truth is as it can be and has no other merit than that of being what it is.* God is my witness, I have certainly been true with you; will one of us one day have to blush?

Let all that be forgotten; I don't even have to forgive you, although you were in the wrong. Reply soon. . . .

In the evening of 22 June Liszt arrived back in Paris.

27. To Mademoiselle Valérie Boissier in Rome [Paris, late June or July]. I have several times been told that real courage is needed to remain a friend of mine. I don't know if, despite all the reasons with which you could support it, you are of the same opinion; but however that may be, allow me, Mademoiselle, to tell you again how happy and grateful I am for your so kind remembrance of me. Putting aside compliments and fine phrases, it is extremely sweet and flattering for me to learn from you that during the too short hours we had together in Paris I awakened some feeling for art and thought in so elevated a soul as yours.

So you are in Rome, the eternal city, and among the *Italians* of Rome, as Duclos remarked with so much scorn. The disappointments and disenchantments of every kind which have greeted you there do not surprise me at all. Several people, among them Berlioz and M. de Montalembert (one of the contributors to *L'Avenir*), had already told me much the same. The former very amusingly compared Italian orchestras to those bands, made up of musical charlatans, which perform at fairgrounds, and found it difficult to find enough absurd and abusive words to stigmatize the alleged *musicality* of the Italians. As for M. de Montalembert, he regarded himself as favoured by a special grace because, after having spent three months in Rome, he still had the same faith in Christ and in Catholicism, so devoid of intelligence and religion did he find the inhabitants of Rome.—And yet something still tells us Christians that Rome is not dead, but sleepeth; and the day is perhaps not far off in which she will rise again in her archangelic splendour, then to be more than ever all-powerful, dominating men and societies through Charity and Science.

'There are men'—wrote Novalis shortly before his death—'who say that there is somewhere today a kind of union which will grow each day until it has embraced the world in its roots, and soon, when this principle of eternal peace has embraced everything, there will be in this world only one science and one mind just as there are only one prophet and one God.'

The 4 luminous points of your travels (le bazu [Cefalù?], Sorrento, Malibran and St Peter's)[13] have by no means made me laugh. All great things can be brought together; they are as it were *related by blood*. Few people are as worthy as you are, Mademoiselle, of understanding *in breadth* the magnificent genius of Mme Malibran. I thank you for having to some extent associated me with your admirations; you have long known of my exclusive enthusiasm for her... and Paganini. Talking of Mme Malibran, one question, perhaps an indiscreet one: would you by any chance have encountered, in Naples or Rome, Mme G. Sand (Mme Dudevant)?... She is another woman of quite extraordinary genius—very bitter and very painful in its power. No doubt you have read *Indiana*, *Valentine*, and above all *Lélia*; but perhaps you don't yet know *Leone Leoni*, and a magnificent *Letter* on Italy that she has just published in the *Revue des Deux Mondes*.[14] —I strongly urge you to peruse them when you return home... Pending the time when you admit us into the confidence of your own feelings and emotions, she is unquestionably and beyond any comparison the 'strongest' (in the biblical sense) woman, and the most astonishingly gifted.

In a fortnight I shall have the honour of sending you the first copy of the [transcription of the] *Symphonie fantastique*; then, you will successively have a quantity of rather *big* things. I should very much like to be able to promise you a month in Geneva with your so excellent family, but that won't be possible before next spring, if by chance you haven't forgotten me by then. The whole of my summer is given or cast away. In a fortnight I set out from here to La Chênaie, the country seat of the Abbé de Lamennais, where I shall probably stay until August. (Are not the *Paroles d'un Croyant* a prodigious Prophecy? It is quite simply sublime, sublime three times over.) I absolutely have to be back in Paris by the beginning of September, and I have made a score of promises for the beginning of the autumn. . . .

The author of [the transcriptions of] *Die Rose* and *La Fiancée* (a poor author hissed and booed on the one hand, flattered and extolled on the other!) very humbly thanks his illustrious pupil for being so good as to undertake publicity in Italy. He asks her to remember the aforesaid booed author to Mme Boissier and never to doubt his sincere affection and devotion...

[13] Valérie Boissier's impressions of her travels in France and Italy were later published, anonymously, under the title *Voyage d'une ignorante dans le midi de la France et l'Italie* (2 vols.; Paris, 1835).

[14] The very successful *Indiana* (1832), George Sand's first novel (without a collaborator), was written at the time when she had just separated from her husband, Baron Dudevant. *Valentine* appeared, likewise to acclaim, in late 1832. *Lélia* (1833), which enormously impressed Liszt, and shocked many others, concerns the love between Lélia and a young poet, Sténio; the latter's life ends in debauchery and suicide, Lélia's in a convent. The famous *Lettres d'un voyageur* (1834–6), impressions of the authoress's early years in Paris and her trip to Italy with Alfred de Musset, have been said to 'reveal the true and better side of George Sand, the loyal and devoted friend, the mother who under happier conditions might have been reputed a Roman matron'.

28. To Marie d'Agoult. . . . I have seen V.H., Chopin, and Berlioz again
with real, heartfelt satisfaction. When I have spent a few hours with V.H. I feel a
host of hidden ambitions stir within me. Yesterday he said something very nice:
'We have reached that point in civilization when defects are ugly, very ugly.'
Next Sunday an article[15] of his about a workman is to appear in the *Revue de
Paris*. Its conclusions are wholly religious, arch-religious. It is agreeable and consoling to see all superior men nowadays rallying around those few truths outside which there is no salvation for the world. Chopin is very much looking
forward to spending a few days at Croissy when you are so good as to invite
him. As for me, I am making neither plans nor promises. Since my return to
Paris I feel almost in good sorts in my sadness.—Probably and because I shall
soon be at the end of my exile. . . .

[Pierre] Wolff told me a scandalous little story about M. de Ginestous and
Adèle, which ended with Adèle humbly enduring some lashes with a hunting-
crop. It seems that she hasn't gone back into society since then. That amused
me. I await instructions regarding our big scene. Don't you find that very rash?
My good mother said to me the other day: 'Ich weiss nicht, warum du immer
das Apartement Ratzenloch heisst, es sind doch keine Ratzen darin. Du solltest
mehr Respect haben dafür... es kostet 200 Franken [I don't know why you always
call the apartment a rat hole; after all, there are no rats in it. You should have
more respect for it: it costs 200 francs].'. . . .

29. To Marie d'Agoult. [Paris] Friday morning [4 July]. Yesterday evening
I went to *Lucrèce Borgia*;[16] today we are to go on a donkey ride to the Bois de
Vincennes with V.H. and his wife. That's two *rapprochements*. So read his 'Claude
Gueux' in Sunday's *Revue de Paris*. It's tremendously fine. He told me yesterday
that he was going to follow that *vein*... Do you remember our drive through
the faubourgs and the question I put to you about a *popular* novel or short story.
I am very pleased to see one of my dreams realized by a man as outstanding as
V.H.

Sainte-Beuve has written a few words in the ugly album you entrusted me
with. I am going to take it to Obermann.[17] As for M. de Chateaubriand, I dare
not ask him for anything. I know that he doesn't like writing in albums. Yet I
hope to find some Jesuitical way. Erard is going to have the great Gold medal,

---

[15] 'Claude Gueux', a story written as an indictment of the social system, was published in the *Revue de Paris* of
6 July.
[16] Historical drama in prose (1833) by Victor Hugo.   [17] i.e. Senancour.

which gives him appreciable pleasure. I shall go and choose another piano for you this week; it will certainly be better than the previous one.

Loneliness is bad for me. I have told myself every day that I couldn't bear for very long what other people call happiness, for I should find life all but intolerable. . . .

It's good of you to ask how I spend my evenings, but you evidently forget that I know thirty thousand people in Paris and, willy-nilly, have to endure some of them.

On Monday evening Obermann has a small gathering at his place, rue de la Cerisette...

Mme Goussard complains about me quite a lot; we live almost next door to one another and I never go to see her. Herminie S...[18] has many pupils thanks to Mariotte's[19] good recommendations. As for the Labories, there is a whole story there that I don't want to write to you. . . .

30. To Marie d'Agoult. [Monday] 25 August. I didn't get back from Versailles until yesterday evening. Ch[opin] won't be able to come to you before the end of the week, around Saturday or Sunday, and even that isn't very certain. He is now living at 5, rue du Mont Blanc. Perhaps it would be better not to invite him until after my departure, which, since you wish me to, I shall delay for a few days.

The Abbé de Lamennais has just written to tell me that he expects me at the beginning of September, between the 3rd and the 7th. If it is possible for you to give me four or five days at Croissy next week, I shall come. Plan it carefully, for I should like henceforth to spare you any vexation.

Mme Sand arrived a day or two ago. Alfred de Musset talked to me about her a good deal the day before yesterday. He will introduce me to her at her place if he sees her again. Meanwhile he is leaving on a visit to the banks of the Rhine. Our little theological argument about *Obermann* we shall resume orally. Mariotte isn't yet as entirely right as she has convinced herself.

The charge that the ending of *Lélia* is flawed seems admirably founded... in an empty head.

Tomorrow it will be seven years since I lost my father at Boulogne-sur-Mer.[20] Pray for me a little. . . .

---

[18] Herminie Seghers, wife of the violinist François Seghers.   [19] Marie d'Agoult herself.
[20] Either the letter is carelessly dated or Liszt's memory is at fault: his father died not on 26 Aug. but the 28th.

31. To Marie d'Agoult [Friday, 5 September[21]]. There are in your latest letters an extraordinary *gentleness* and *depth* of feeling. Never before had you written to me like that. My own letters are very dry, I feel, but what can I do? With every day that passes I am becoming drier and harder, and am living in a state of extreme discontent. The years of my life that are past seem so shameful, so pitiful! And so many fetters and chains in the present!... Oh! do not try to console me, even you could not do so... Only when you return so that I can see you, and see you again, shall I tell you that I am happy, and I shall be.

The Abbé de Lamennais has just written me a brief note which has made me blaze with joy. 'Please,' he says, 'try to prolong as much as you can the happiness I shall owe to you. Think what I shall suffer when we separate'; and further on: 'Come quickly, dear child, so that I can press you to my heart, which at that moment will throb with a quite new life.' I *love* that man. . . .

You reproach me with not replying to all your questions, but it seems to me that I do nothing else. Henceforth Thoughtful[22] will be careful to write only every three days; probably that will be only twice more, for he leaves here a week tomorrow. If Mariotte had set out clearly and precisely the reasons for this ternary arrangement, Thoughtful would have spared her all those little vexations which he has to endure more than she does. Until Wednesday, therefore, and then Saturday, and then good night. How charming of Mariotte to advise me to read Plutarch's great men.[23] Know, Madame, that I have read them, which is an excellent reason for reading them again. I gladly accept the augury of Guido d'Arezzo and of Saint Augustine, though I am not likely to invent a scale and will certainly not be canonized... which is an injustice. The comparison between E flat and D sharp is lovely. Can you believe that I was impertinent enough to believe that I was D sharp? Incidentally, didn't I already make this same comparison for you (perhaps it was an F sharp or a G flat) last winter? . . . .

Mendelssohn's opinion was known to me, which has not prevented me speaking highly of his works to you (as to everyone). Hiller, Berlioz, and many others (with a few shades of difference) share it. Our *Harmonie* will be dedicated to Lamartine; I shall publish it by itself at first, later I shall write half a dozen. . . .

Taking Ballanche's *Orphée* to read on the journey, Liszt left for La Chênaie in the evening of Saturday, 13 September. Apart from a brush with a gendarme in Alençon because he had no passport, his journey was uneventful.

---

[21] The letter can be dated from its reference to Liszt's departure (for La Chênaie on Sat. the 13th) a week and a day later.

[22] Nickname for Liszt himself.   [23] The celebrated *Bioi parellēloi* or 'Parallel Lives'.

32. To Anna Liszt in Paris [La Chênaie, *c.*21 September] G (F)

Dear Mother,

After a pleasant three-day journey I finally arrived safe and sound, with only 70 francs in my pocket, at La Chênaie. If within a fortnight you could manage to let me have just as much, or a little more, through a banker in Rennes or St Malo, I should be very glad. If not, I shall try to save as much as possible, although it will be difficult.

Now, I have a small errand for you. Will you be so kind as to order from Richard the *Revue de Paris* which contains Victor Hugo's 'Claude Gueux'. Also, get Schoelcher* to give you back my copy of the *Dernier Jour d'un condamné*[24] —a large yellow volume. These, plus the others which M. de Lamennais is already expecting daily, Richard is to send to him without delay. You forgot, it seems, to pack the letters of Sainte-Beuve and Ballanche in my trunk. If you can still find them—and please look—send them to me at once. The Abbé is altogether charming, quite extraordinarily kind—after Longinus[25] he is my greatest passion. I have a very attractive room, good food, very many *agréments spirituels*— in short, I have never felt better.

Farewell, dear Mother; I embrace you as warmly as I love you.

Speak to the good Mme Vial about me now and then, and let me have news of her. Ask her, too, how you can send money to me, for I believe I shall need it.

33. To Marie d'Agoult. Tuesday, 6.00 a.m. . . . You perhaps imagine that

La Chênaie is a small market-town, or at the very least a small village with a priest, mayor, and innkeeper; but not at all. We are obliged to go a good half hour to hear mass (at Saint-Pierre), and if we felt the desire to have a drink, we should have to go the same distance to find a tavern. To be sure, there are a few houses scattered in the fields here and there, but bringing them together under a common name is purely ideal. And so we shall call La Chênaie (not to fail to conform) the home of the good and sublime Abbé, my host.

The house is rather ordinary and by no means new, but fairly comfortably arranged. The dining-room and salon are on the ground floor. The Abbé's room, and Thoughtful's, are on the first; there is also a third room and additional library (for the whole place is congested with books), which is at present inhabited by

---

[24] Novel written (1829) by Hugo as an indictment of the death penalty and the manner in which it was then carried out.

[25] Another nickname Liszt had given to Marie, presumably because he thought her 'sublime'. (The title of the best-known work usually attributed to the Neoplatonic philosopher Longinus is *On the Sublime*.)

an extremely ingenuous and distinguished young man, M. [Eugène] Boré, the Professor of Armenian's deputy at the Bibliothèque. On the second floor are several attic rooms which, like the dining-room and those on the first floor, all overlook a small parterre—a kitchen-garden about thirty paces long, at the end of which is a tiny and very modest little chapel beside some melancholy Scotch firs. M. de Ker,[26] a young man of twenty-three, and two other young fellows (one of fifteen, the other of thirteen) live in them. I have already told you the names of all the people here, and they could not be pleasanter or more agreeable. Outside the fairly narrow enclosure there is a rather spacious pond surrounded by trees and bordered by rocks, where our Newfoundland dog gambols about artistically, to the great amusement of the excellent Abbé and of the whole party. Thoughtful also splashes about in it from time to time, and that does him a power of good. All around are the woods, which our good Father makes us walk through every day *prestissimo*; Thoughtful, with his good legs, sometimes even has considerable difficulty in following him. It is a vigorous, abrupt, nonstop gait—the gait of a man of genius, entirely peculiar to Lamennais. The several avenues of trees he has planted are by no means the least picturesque. His grave he has already chosen under one of the rocks by the pond. We sit there occasionally, talking of God and of mankind's sufferings. The whole region is extremely uneven, varied, full of delightful landscapes; it is almost a little Switzerland, and I think you would enjoy yourself here.

Now, after the topography, the ethnography. And in the first place, the life we lead here is very uniform. Thoughtful, who sleeps well, gets up at roughly the same time as his illustrious neighbour, who does not sleep, or at least very rarely: about 7.00. (Today, to write to Mariotte, he got up earlier.) For an hour or so Mgr. Th... is a sluggard; he reads a bit, puts his tie on, strums the piano for a while. On the stroke of 8.00 his coffee is brought him, and the Abbé usually comes and takes it tête-à-tête with him, which, as you can imagine, gives quite a different intellectuality to this already so intellectual substance. Next, the good father quite often begins to walk rapidly up and down the whole length of the room, while talking and speaking very copiously; that's a habit of his. Scarcely has the conversation become animated, and it takes no more than two minutes for that, than off he charges—frequently for hours at a time, without his even noticing, I believe. He really is a man of perpetual motion! I sometimes think that this mode of conversation would be quite unbearable to Mariotte, who cannot endure people standing, and who has often reproached me for similar idiosyncrasies. It is true that I do not like what necessitates them and makes them characteristic.

---

[26] Elie de Kertanguy, who later married Lamennais's niece Augustine Blaize.

From nine o'clock until midday, Th... works at his exercises in the salon and the Abbé remains in his room. At midday he always has a cup of chocolate, and Thoughtful lunches completely alone. Soon afterwards we meet again and usually take a short walk together, then continue our labours, each for his own part, until dinner is served punctually at five o'clock. It is the only meal we all take together, for the other gentlemen breakfast at 9.30, which suits neither Thoughtful nor the Abbé. Our dinner always takes us three quarters of an hour, and although very abundant in its simplicity (a simplicity which allows, however, partridges and good fowls), it is hardly more than a pretext for a conversation, always a very rapid one, between Th... and the master of the house. M. Boré and M. de Kertanguy are very taciturn, which puts Th... very much at his ease. As soon as the pudding is finished, the Abbé (constantly dressed in an extremely poor, threadbare old grey frock-coat, and always wearing the same blue stockings like a coarse peasant, plus enormous shoes, rarely polished, perfectly in keeping moreover)—the Abbé, our good father, takes his straw hat, which is very shabby and even torn in several places—he has been wearing it for eight years —and says to us in a *voce simpatica*: 'Allons, mes enfants, allons promener', and that sees us out in the open for hours on end. Truly, he is a wonderful, prodigious, and quite extraordinary man. So much genius and so much heart. High-mindedness, piety, passionate ardour, perspicacity of mind, a wide and profound judgement, the simplicity of a child, sublimity of thought, and power of soul—in him can be found everything which makes man in the image of God. Never yet have I heard him say the word *I*. Always the Christ, always the sacrifice for others and the voluntary acceptance of opprobrium, scorn, misery, and death! But I can't write anything to you about him. It's all still too mixed up in my mind. Fortunately, I have made for you a little memorandum of our talks, which we shall soon go over together, for I shan't stay here any longer. I am suffering here, and you know why, you who *stupidly* say to me: 'Ich liebe dich wie du mich [I love you as you love me].'

Before returning to Paris I shall go to Saint Malo and perhaps to Mont-Saint-Michel. The equinoxes are magnificent on the shores of Brittany, and, besides, I need to hear that music. I shall also spend a day in Laval; there is a Trappist monastery I want to visit. In a good fortnight we shall be together again. . . . Pray for me a little. In my room there is a prie-Dieu at which I often kneel.

I am very glad that you reread the *Essai* [*sur l'indifférence en matière de religion*] at the same time as Th..., who is rereading the whole of Lamennais and Ballanche. I should like you to have had the La Chênaie commentaries, which make the book far more interesting. In sum, it is an extremely remarkable and vigorously convincing work. You would do well, I think, to reread it again in parts. The chapter 'Importance de la religion pour l'homme' is admirable. The discussion with J.J.[27] astonishing. . . .

The other day the good father said to us: 'I would give a lot of money to see Louis-Philippe adrift on the Seine in Laffitte's empty coffer; in the middle, as a mast, I would put a police bâton at the end of which, as a sail, I would gladly attach the tie with which they strangled that unfortunate Duc de Bourbon.'

Hiller's number (your engaging him will give me pleasure) is 17, I believe. Moreover, you have only to ask Chopin or my mother. Incidentally, has she sent you a chambermaid? I don't know if you will be able to decipher all this; my pen is execrable. . . .

34. To Marie d'Agoult. [La Chênaie] 9 o'clock. Today it was I who delivered your letter. Imagine my joy if you can!... We (Thoughtful and the Abbé) were right in the middle of a game of écarté. I had just turned up the King of Clubs, when our lame messenger from Dinan arrived. To jump on the packet, untie it, extract from it and hand over a lot of letters which were in it, took but a moment. Finally, still breathless, I saw at the bottom the one from M... 'Oh! this one,' I said hurriedly to L..., 'is not for you, although it is addressed to you.'

Heavens, what a pretty little seal—and then what charming little handwriting!... (not one crossing out, not one scribble) and finally, what a delightful, ravishing, and marvellous epistolary style!.. What prodigies, what miracles of amiability, wit and grace!.. Truly, of the truest truth, without any doubt, without any shadow of doubt (as my illustrious host frequently says), Mariotte is a woman beyond compare.

Yet I have one little reproach. Why say nothing to me of that so laughable and so droll idea mentioned in the first missive?... Is that malice or absent-mindedness?... Well, I am eager, utterly and completely eager, to know about it. And so don't forget, I implore you, to tell me in your next letter, which please address to M. Masson, notary in Alençon (department of the Orne). I shall be there next Thursday at the latest. Believe it or not, I can already no longer endure the admirable life I am leading here. Th... cannot remain so far from Mariotte. Laugh at that, if you will, but it's true. My stupid and hateful existence in Paris, with all its wretched fatigues, its torments and its empty and profound tedium, but where I can find from time to time my poor M..., I still prefer a hundred times to this unceasing celebration of intelligence and soul, to these active, seri-

[27] Jean-Jacques Rousseau.

ous, varied, and singularly fortifying days at La Chênaie, where she has never been, where she will not come, where I am making myself pine away by seeking and asking for her on all sides... Oh! God, how I suffer!!! Tomorrow I leave for Dinan; from there to Saint Malo is not more than two hours. The steamer will take me on Friday morning. For the whole of that day and the next I shall not leave the beach. I feel an inexpressible thirst for the music of the ocean. I shall have, I fear, to abandon my plan to visit Mont-Saint-Michel, for I have no permission and very little money. On Sunday morning I shall return here, and leave again on Tuesday, Wednesday, or Thursday morning. I shall stop in Laval; the Trappist monastery (the haven of refuge) is two leagues from there, and the next evening I shall be handed M...'s letter in Alençon, where I will probably be kept two days. I shall take advantage of it to finish a new fantastic enormity[28] of which I have written $\frac{2}{3}$ at La Chênaie; the remainder is done in my head, but I feel that I really no longer have the courage to remain in this room any more; this life of remoteness is killing me. It seems to me that I shall be a hundred times better off at Alençon. We shall be no more than 50 leagues [from one another]. Oh! if I could only go via Chartres. . . .

So all being well I shall resume possession of the Ratzenloch[29] on Sunday evening, 14 October... Phew!... What a relief!... I shall try to de-sublimify myself in order not to disquieten the noble châtelaine, and I shall quietly wait for her to consent to give me a day and time... But above all write to me once more by way of Alençon. I should be altogether too sad to return home like this!

What you tell me of your dreams gives me extreme pleasure. I solace myself very easily for mine which are (with very few exceptions) horribly vulgar and occasionally atrocious. Just imagine, last week I dreamt that... Mme de G.... (the rest can't be written)... it's abominable, but that makes you laugh, and I now laugh at it too. But when I awoke I felt really distressed about it. . . .

---

[28] The *Grande fantaisie symphonique on themes from Berlioz's Lélio.*
[29] The small apartment, or 'rat hole', rented by Liszt for his own use. See Letter 28.

1835

March. Liszt and Marie d'Agoult's long separation following the death of Marie's elder daughter, Louise, in December ends with an emotional reunion. Some weeks later Marie finds that she is pregnant.

9 April. During his concert at the Hôtel de Ville, his first in Paris—apart from that given jointly with Garcia in March 1833—for seven years, Liszt faints at the keyboard.

26 May. Marie writes to tell her husband (at Croissy) that she is leaving him. 'After eight years of marriage we are going to separate for good. . . . I have nothing to reproach you with; you have always shown me affection and devotion. . . . Adieu, it is my wish that, lacking the happiness which is possible neither for you nor for me, you may at least find rest and peace.'

28 May. Marie leaves for Basel, where Liszt joins her on 4 June.

14 June. The lovers embark on a tour of Switzerland, visiting, among other places, the Rhine Falls at Schaffhausen, Lake Constance, St Gallen, Lake Walenstadt, Einsiedeln, Goldau, Weggis, Brunnen, Gletsch, and Bex.

19 July. They arrive in Geneva, where on the 28th they move into an apartment in the rue Tabazan.[1] Liszt renews acquaintance with Pierre Wolff and the Boissiers, and he and Marie are soon enjoying the company of some of the most distinguished local *savants.*

1 October. Liszt takes part in a charity concert, playing Weber's *Concertstück* and the Fantasy on *La Fiancée.*

9 November. The first lessons are given at Geneva's newly founded Conservatoire de Musique; Liszt undertakes to give instruction, gratis, to ten students.[2]

18 December. Blandine-Rachel Liszt is born in Geneva.

WORKS. VIOLIN AND PIANO: Duo (Sonata) (S127, *c.*1832–5), based on Chopin's Mazurka, Op. 6/2; *Grand duo concertant* (S128), on Lafont's *Le marin.* PIANO: *Réminiscences de La Juive* (Halévy) (S409*a*). PIANO AND ORCHESTRA: *De profundis* (unfinished) (S691).

WRITINGS. 'De la situation des artistes et de leur condition dans la société', published in six instalments, plus epilogue, in the *Gazette musicale.* 'Lettre d'un voyageur', dated 23 November and addressed to George Sand, published in the *Revue et gazette musicale*[3] of 6 December.

---

[1] The house is now 22, rue Etienne-Dumont.

[2] 'It is a great honour for me to hold the same Chair as Liszt,' wrote the great pianist Dinu Lipatti when, 109 years later, he too was appointed Professor of piano at the Conservatoire.

[3] In November the *Gazette musicale* and *Revue musicale* merged, with a new title hereinafter abbreviated to *RGM.*

35. To Anna Liszt in Paris [Basel, 4 June] ^{G (F)}

Dear Mother,

Against all hope we arrived in Basel at 10 o'clock this morning. My boxes, cases, and pockets are full; I gave no alms to the crowds of beggars *en route*, and my purse is still well filled. Longinus is here, as is her mother.[4] I know nothing definite yet, but in four or five days we shall probably leave here with her *femme de chambre*. We are both in rather good spirits and have no thought of being unhappy.

I am healthy, the Swiss air improves my appetite. Chevelus[5] could really be taken for a good German language teacher here. You can't imagine what an abominable German the Swiss speak.

Farewell, many good wishes to Puzzi[6] and Mme Sand. I'll write again soon.

36. To George Sand [27 June]

Dear George,

I was planning to climb the St Gotthard this morning, but since for the past 24 hours it has done nothing but snow (can you imagine what snowy weather is like on 27 June?), I am compelled to remain in my room. And so finding nothing *better* to do, I want to write to you without knowing exactly what to say to you; but no matter!

Puzzi, who has rather surprised me by sending me a letter, tells me that you are leaving for Berry, where you will have '*open house*, a splendid table, and joyous festivities for your *innumerable* friends!' All right!—but what about the *intended* trip to Switzerland? And until when are you postponing our outings in the mountains?... Oh! I very much fear you will find some good but wretched reason to excuse you from coming to join your poor brother the *musician*!...

In three weeks we shall be in Geneva, and if your plans haven't changed I solemnly urge you not to fail to come and see us at once, for I know a certain person[7] with whom you have dined twice who will be able to give you excellent information for your trip—and don't believe that in this case good advice is useless. You can have no idea of the *charlatanism* of these good Swiss, who

---

[4] Marie had been accompanied from Paris by her brother-in-law August Ehrmann (widower of her half-sister Auguste Bussmann), who had departed shortly after the arrival of Marie's mother, the Vicomtesse de Flavigny, travelling from Frankfurt and unaware of the real reason for her daughter's journey. At last apprised of this—by a note the fearful Marie slipped under the door of her room—she too, after the first shock and ensuing nervous attack, left Basel, initially to stay in nearby Arlesheim, where Marie took leave of her on 14 June before rejoining Liszt.

[5] From this nickname for Liszt himself it may be inferred that he already had the famous long hair, a style which he retained for the rest of his life.

[6] Liszt's pupil Hermann Cohen. See Biographical Sketches.   [7] Marie d'Agoult.

make one spend hours travelling miles just to see nasty little landscapes which are 'pretty, pretty, pretty', as the illustrious G. Sand says. Talking of this illustrious individual, I have to tell you that an impertinent fellow called F. Liszt has had the impudence to name her (in a very innocent manner, it is true) in an article in which Berlioz, the *man of genius*, is mentioned.[8] If the said article were by some mischance to fall into your hands, please forgive me this very great liberty.

I am in a very fanciful mood today—and were I not held back by my profound ignorance of physics, would certainly write you a splendid treatise on the snowfalls, the thaw, etc., etc.

And you, dear brother, what are you up to? Do you play the piano? Do you sing romanceros and fandangos, as in the past? And our friend Ste-Beuve, is he definitely becoming a Benedictine? For that, let him come to *Einsiedeln*;[9] there he will find St Meinrad's beautiful *black* virgin. She is more than a thousand years old, but none the less still an immaculate virgin. That is the place to become a hermit—beautiful forests (owned by the monks), a magnificent monastery that looks like a barracks, good people who come in their thousands to prostrate themselves before pictures depicting miracles of the past—excellent white wine, a whole army of joiners, blacksmiths, bakers, dyers, cobblers, braziers, coach-builders, etc. etc. etc., all dependent on and at the disposal of Messeigneurs the Benedictines—splendid!.. but in Paris, in the rue du Montparnasse, among the philosophical friends of the *Revue encyclopédique*[10] and the *Peri* of the Quai Malaquais, seriously to think of finding salvation as a good Catholic—that's going too far!

Once again, and a thousand more times, come, and come soon, at the risk of being bored to death by my superb descriptions of *the Devil's Bridge*, of the *nineteen* lakes that can be seen from the top of the Rigi, of William Tell's Chapel, of the views from Lake Lucerne, of the Furka, of the Grimsell ... and what else besides! ... come, O YOU ... I have forgotten the rest—which is a great pity.

Marie feels in extreme need of reading something of yours. And so give us a new masterpiece soon—pending the time when *we* can realize our plan of a *literary* and *musical* union one solemn night when Planchian criticism[11] will not be admitted. But above all write me a good and very *personal* letter. Give me news of your children. Tell me, too, what Trozzi [a cat] and Puzzi are up to.

Write to Geneva, poste restante. I shall be there about 20 July—and shan't budge again until the spring.

---

[8] Referring to the fourth instalment of 'De la situation des artistes', published on 26 July.

[9] The best-known pilgrim resort in Switzerland, 25 miles south-east of Zurich. Its Benedictine abbey was founded in the 10th cent. on the site of the cell of St Meinrad, murdered in 861.

[10] Popular literary and scientific review which appeared 1819–35.

[11] Referring to Gustave Planche, feared art and literary critic of the *Revue des Deux Mondes*.

Remember me to Michel,[12] whom I have had occasion to defend very warmly—a beautiful aristocratic kiss to the handsome Sos.,[13] patron of arts and letters.

Adieu, I shall write to you from Mont St Bernard.

P.S. Were I less disposed to be cheerful, I would tell you of my Saint-Simonian readings, which made a profound impression on me during my journey from Paris to Basel. In the volume of Sermons, as in the second one setting out the Doctrine, there are things of very great significance, wondrously beautiful in warmth and emotion. I should like you to tell me what you think of Rodrigues' *Letters on Religion and Politics* that Puzzi was to deliver to you. If it doesn't bore you too much, let me know what you have been reading and working on. Adieu.

You know that I am fond of and wholly devoted to you—and so there is no need for me to say these things to you once again in every key and every mode. It is understood once and for all.

37. To Anna Liszt [Geneva, 26 July] ^{G (F)}

Dear Mother,

Your letter made me very sad. You have known for a long time that I am muddle-headed, thoughtless, in a word am *Frater*. The life I have had to lead has perhaps made my innate shortcomings still worse; but Heaven forbid that my heart ever knew of such intentions as you suspect to be in me. Trust me, trust me absolutely. My love for you is deep and immutable, and my memory of your goodness and self-sacrifice will never fade. I should like to be able to find words to convince you how very much I love you, how greatly my heart is filled with reverence and gratitude towards you.

Today is your name-day,[14] dear good Mother. I should have been so glad to send you something; but here there is little opportunity, and I really don't know what might give you pleasure. Mme d'A., too, would like to give you a small present, if she only knew what. Do me the pleasure of taking 100 francs from the money of mine that you are looking after and buying yourself something nice from both of us. Don't say no—I could never forgive you! Just write and let me know what you have chosen, so that I know what it is and can be pleased about it.

---

[12] The lawyer Michel de Bourges, one of Mme Sand's lovers.   [13] Sosthènes de la Rochefoucauld.
[14] The letter can be dated from this reference to St Anne's Day, 26 July.

If you have not already rented accommodation, don't do so before receiving further news from me. We have a splendid residence in Geneva. Couldn't you perhaps come to us? We'll speak about it again.

Mlle [Zoé] Delarue, to whom I am writing at the same time, will, I hope, undertake to buy the books a list of whose titles I enclose. Would you be so good as to give her the necessary amount. I have made two separate notes, one of things to buy, the other of things and books which are with you. Entrust Mlle Delarue with the whole of the book department. They will have to be covered in very thick paper and, in addition, well wrapped in linen, sheets, towels, dressing-gowns, clothes, etc.—otherwise they will be spoilt and damaged like those I brought with me. . . .

Ask *Puzzi* to see to everything relating to my compositions and Mlle Delarue to my Library. . . .

From my *compositions* are to be added:

The *Concerto* (the copy made by Belloni*), with the piano part and the score from which he copied it.

The *Fantaisie symphonique* on themes of Berlioz (which was performed at my concert) in Belloni's copy, bound. The orchestral parts are unnecessary.

A thick blue volume in which there is another *symphonic concerto*, composed last winter in the Ratzenloch.

An *old exercise book* in grey paper, which Puzzi knows and which contains several pieces of mine.

The copy, made by the Pole, of my *sextet*. (Incidentally, has Puzzi asked him if he has copied out the Polish and Tyrolean songs for me?)

All the folk-songs I have collected; a *Duo* for piano and violin on a Chopin Mazurka; the *Schubert Lieder* in a green bound volume; and a *Waltz* in E flat which I wrote for Mme Goussard's album. Puzzi is to borrow this from her. Ask Belloni to copy out both pages for me. I absolutely must have the piece.

Give me news of Mme Sand. She hasn't replied to my letter. The Duchesse de Rauzan passed through Geneva; she sent word to me and I paid her a call.

Farewell, dear Mother; I embrace you with childlike love.

Mlle Delarue is to be so kind as to buy:

Bernardin de St Pierre. 2 vols.

Fénelon. Collected edn.

Bossuet. Ditto.

(Add to them a note of the collected editions which are coming out or have come out.)

Vol. 2 of the *Panthéon littéraire* containing the Confessions of St Augustine, the Meditations, Speeches of St Bernard, etc.—it costs 5 francs, I believe, at Delloye's, place de la Bourse. . . .

Things and books which are *at rue de Provence* and which must be sent to me.
(The *large* trunk won't be too big—perhaps it will even be necessary to use another
as well.). . . .

Books—(Mlle Delarue, Librarian)—

Italian–French (and vice versa) *Dictionary.* 2 vols. in 8vo.

Ballanche. 4 vols. in 8vo.

Shakespeare, in English. 1 vol.

Byron, ditto. 1 vol.

Euler's letters to a German princess.[15] 2 vols.

Mme d'A.'s Bible. 1 vol.

Atlas historique of Lesage, Comte de Las Cases.

Jarry de Mancy's *Atlas des Littératures.*

Duval's *Atlas.* . . .

Works by Reicha relating to composition—

My *collected*—my *splendid collected editions!* Chateaubriand, Massillon, Bour-
daloue, Plutarch, Montesquieu, the French moralists, Montaigne, Rabelais, La
Fontaine, *Théâtre français* (4 vols.), La Harpe. . . .

I shall here point out that, although my books were very well packed, they all
got damaged *en route.* Fortunately they were only paper-bound or badly bound books,
and just a small number. The *Lamartine* and Ramonon's [gift of] the *Imitation*
were saved only thanks to the precaution I had taken to cover them in very strong
paper and to *wrap them in linen.* (I ask and entreat my mother and Mlle Delarue
not to fail to take the same care. They absolutely must be *wrapped* in linen.)

The sheets and towels that Mme d'Agoult has asked for will serve admirably
to this end.

In Heaven's name don't let me receive my dear books soiled and dirtied or
in pieces like several of those I have here, with which nevertheless care was taken.
Put them among my shirts, in my dressing-gown, with my clothes and above
all with the sheets and towels I have just mentioned—otherwise I shall be utterly
inconsolable. . . .

My pipe and my tobacco. . . . André Chénier—V[ictor] H[ugo']s *Les Orientales*
—Lamartine's *Harmonies.* . . . Le Globe, *Atlas classique universel.* . . . Shakespeare
(in French), 2 vols., I believe. . . .

1 copy of each of my publications... *Clochette, Apparition,* etc. . . .

Again I urge that the utmost care be taken with my books!!![16]

---

[15] The *Lettres à une princesse d'Allemagne sur quelques sujets de physique et de philosophie,* by the great Swiss mathematician Leonhard Euler, were first published, in 3 vols., at St Petersburg, 1768–72. Written for the Princess of Anhalt-
Dessau, they expound, amongst much else and with great lucidity, the principal facts of mechanics, optics, acoustics,
and physical astronomy.

[16] The source for this letter has here been corrected, in certain particulars, from passages reproduced by Bellas, 'François
Liszt et le "département des livres" '.

38. To George Sand [Autumn]

Dear Georges [*sic*],

I simply can't express the joy your two letters have given me. You can guess and understand it without my saying anything, can't you? To tell the truth (leaving out of account the *volume* and my flattered *vanity*), I should find it difficult to choose between the one brought by Puzzi and the one in the *Revue des Deux Mondes*,[17] not knowing which of the two touched me more. When I received the first, it had been such a long time since we had seen one another! So many hours had passed! Were they enjoyable or did they hang heavily on you? Was I still to believe in the religious and brotherly affection that I so indiscreetly required of you?—Although not generally inclined to give way to anxieties of a sentimental nature, every time I thought of you (and God knows how often that was!) a thousand bad and sad thoughts came back to me. From the fact that you had not written to me I lost no time in inferring that you had doubtless forgotten that I am a grumpy individual—that after all it was madness to count on the friendship of a woman for whom one has done nothing—and that I could certainly expect to see you laugh in my face the first time we met—and umpteen similar things.

And so, didn't this Puzzikoffian letter do me good! How I pressed that poor child, still out of breath and quite covered in dust from his journey,[18] to give me *there and then* a detailed account of what had become of you during those three months, and how stupid he seemed, never to reply in a way that matched the level of my curiosity!—

So, dear brother, you shut yourself up for a month at Quai Malaquais, from what Madame Puzzi tells me, and not in that deserted house[19] you describe so admirably?—But why didn't you come here? If you knew how happy we are here, how easy it is to work, how comfortable and agreeable life is, how beautiful and delightful the countryside! Oh! I implore you, come, come.—If you can't do so immediately, because of the good Michel's imprisonment, promise me that it will be next spring at the latest. If you like, we'll go on foot as a trio, Puzzi, you, and I, to Chamonix—into the Oberland, and even into all 22 cantons, if you so wish. It will take six weeks at most. Then you will return here to shut yourself up with us for as long as possible, and you will certainly write as you have never written before. The fair peri [Marie] asks you as insistently as I do; in a few days you will be hearing from her.

---

[17] George Sand's 'Lettre d'un voyageur'—its opening sentence addressing Liszt ('mon cher Franz')—published in the *Revue des Deux Mondes* of 1 Sept.

[18] To resume lessons with Liszt, and with mother and brother in tow, Hermann Cohen had arrived in Geneva on 14 Aug.

[19] The home of Michel de Bourges.

Since arriving in Geneva she has been keeping herself very busy. The Bible, Ballanche, Chateaubriand, Bernardin de St-Pierre, Pascal, Montaigne, and Lamennais (of whom I have found here an admirable three-volume edition) are her habitual company. From time to time she shuts herself away the whole day long to write—but Lélia, or rather George, makes her despair. 'If our friend hadn't yet had anything published,' she sometimes remarks, 'perhaps I should venture to face the wind of publicity, but the way that a woman now has to set about soiling paper to *compose Chynodie* or *Thomas Morus*!'[20]—Even so, unless I am very much mistaken (and you know that I am not excessively biased towards her), there are some excellent things in her loose leaves, and I should be glad if you would encourage her a little, for she too easily allows herself to fall into a state of dejection.

Thank you very much for the information about Lavater.[21] I have for a long time been intending to read his book—in the mean time, I am delighted that it interested you enough for you to share a few fragments with us. Although I know phrenology and physiognomy only very superficially and solely from hearsay, I am convinced that when these two systems are completed, the one through the other, magnificent results will be achieved. What you say about the pro-pagation of the former and the slow progress made by the latter, is very fair: let us add that a society of physiognomists working in the flesh would necessarily be very impertinent and almost intolerable. You have been struck by the resemb-lance between Lavater and Erasmus—but have you never happened to compare this Christian doctor's physiognomy with that of the Abbé de Lamennais? ... If you call in at Basel, don't fail to go to the Library: you will enjoy seeing the portrait of Erasmus by Holbein.

Talking of the saint of Brittany, you too must be very distressed by the fact that he is going to keep silent.[22] This silence is a veritable calamity for the great cause of the people.

Why is he waiting for those contemptible persons to be swept away like mud in the gutters on a stormy day?... I don't know—I should have liked him to speak, and yet I bow respectfully before the resolve of this sublime priest whom no one, even the most dedicated and audacious, can rightly accuse of lukewarmness.

Puzzi tells me that you were planning to go to La Chênaie; will you do so? Do you at least write to the good father?...

Now that all that is far off, I can tell you that you really do owe him a little gratitude for the very affectionate way in which he sought you out in your art-istic garret. You can't imagine the quantity of anonymous and other letters (filled

---

[20] Respectively *Cynodie* [*sic*], a novel (1833) by Antoinette Dupin, and a work (1832) by the Princesse de Craon.

[21] Johann Kaspar Lavater, subject of the 'Lettre d'un voyageur' addressed to Liszt.

[22] Lamennais was in fact merely taking a few months of retreat in order to prepare his next book.

with parallels between 'the author of the *Essai sur l'indifférence* and the author of *Lélia*—the sanguinary priest and the debauched woman etc. etc....') which were addressed to him. In order to ignore so many remonstrances and insinuations (that *common* friends would probably not have spared him had an opportunity come along), he needed all his superiority of mind and heart. You can well understand what I mean by this.

And yet I don't want to urge you too strongly to make a journey to Brittany, for I shall no longer be able to do it with you, and La Chênaie and Geneva are too far from one another to *permit me to hope* (a phrase à la Sosthènes?) that you will do us the honour and pleasure of coming to see us.

You know that that is what I desire above all; first and foremost for us, and also a little for you yourself, in the interests of your health and of your work. Here, you will be able to *botanize* with M. de Candolle, *historicize* with Sismondi, and *metaphysicize* with everyone—for Geneva, this cave of honest people, as Byron called it, is essentially a metaphysical city.

I shan't speak to you of Music, and that out of *modesty*. And so, ... 'if you are happy, don't sacrifice to me a single one of the beautiful days of your life; those days are so rare! But if you are alone, if you aren't reluctant to come'—come.

I can't bring myself to finish this enormous letter yet—and so let's chat a bit more—if it bores you, throw it on the fire or light your cigar with it.

On arriving here I set about rereading several St Simonian works, and I admit to my shame that I was even more struck by them, even more moved, than in the past. Beyond all question, Père Enfantin is a great man, notwithstanding all the well- and ill-bred jokes and gibes. Dare I tell you?... What astonished me above all is the so worthy, so wise caution he showed on the notorious question of women. I believe I remember having heard you find great fault with *alleged* St Simonian opinions on women. I have in front of me the pamphlet 'Réunion de la famille', followed by a note on marriage and divorce, and it seems to me that the question posed in these terms is perfectly acceptable to all serious-minded persons, as it is to all *chaste women*. It is important to know this note in order to judge with full knowledge of the case, and I doubt if you have read it attentively.

An article on the Christian mysteries in an old issue of the *Revue encyclopédique* also interested me greatly. You really ought to use your influence with Buloz to induce him to publish in the *Revue des Deux Mondes* (now that the *Revue encyclopédique* has merged with it) the series of articles on the Trinity that Leroux announces at the end of the first one. It is an admirable work and worthy of attracting the serious attention of the depraved animals who have the misfortune to think.

Do you see Ste-Beuve from time to time? Is he working on his history of Port-Royal?[23] Give me news of him, for I no longer write to anyone. Orders from music-sellers and, even more, a rather big task I have imposed on myself, are taking all my time.

Puzzi has asked me to accompany him in a duet that he wishes to dedicate to you. Before long I hope to be in a position to keep an old promise with regard to a dedication. Material difficulties that would here take too long to explain have got in the way up to now.

Tell me, too, something about Lamartine. You were to dine with him at Jules Janin's a week after I left. His speech[24] to the Chamber was good, save the trite exaggerations on the abuse of the freedom of the press—the too numerous comparisons of the drunken Spartan, the blood-stained robe, Caesar, etc. etc. On the whole it was one of the best he has given.—I shall say nothing to you of the Fieschi-Sauzet politics;[25] words can't express what one feels about it. May God deliver us from this *evil* which weighs so heavily on the whole world. Are we to hope that it will be soon?—I think not. Nevertheless, it is not the time for us to fall asleep; let us ceaselessly keep watch, act and pray—the time is at hand, and our lives very short. Indeed, we shall neither of us fail to be at our posts when the hour of combat strikes—brother, it would be beautiful to die there together.

Write to me as and when you wish—if you do so through the post, address to Geneva, poste restante, where I shall spend the whole winter and summer. If through the *Revue*, don't give yourself the trouble of sending it to me, for it is available in all the reading-rooms.

If my friends ask you about me, tell them that I won't be returning for three years—for the least one can do is spend six months in Naples, and the same in Rome.[26]

Adieu, dear George—we never stop talking of you, and we have *hung you in effigy* since the arrival of Puzzi, who every day looks forward to our future

---

[23] Sainte-Beuve's six-volume *Port-Royal* (1840–59), a history of the Cistercian convent near Chevreuse to the south-west of Paris, and very much more besides, was the published form of lectures given in 1837–8 at the Academy of Lausanne.

[24] Lamartine's parliamentary speech of 21 Aug. 1835.

[25] In what has been described as 'one of the most diabolical assassination plots of the nineteenth century', a Corsican conspirator named Giuseppe Fieschi had, by means of an infernal machine of his own devising, attempted to dispatch Louis-Philippe and his sons as they rode in procession in the morning of 28 July. The intended targets survived unscathed, but eighteen others,including Marshal Mortier and a 14-year-old girl, were killed and many more wounded. Upon Fieschi himself, who was also severely injured by the discharge of his machine, were lavished the attentions of the most skilled physicians so that in due course, and in the company of his accomplices Morey and Pépin, he could be tried, condemned, and guillotined.

[26] In the event, Liszt spent much of his life in Rome—but never visited Naples.

campaigns through Switzerland. I have been obliged to promise him that all three of us will climb to the very highest peak of Mont Blanc! Nothing less.

Adieu, adieu, kiss your son for me—and talk a little about frantz [*sic*] with my mother.

Yours for life,

Frantz Liszt

39. To Anna Liszt [Geneva, *c.*mid-November] ᴳ ⁽ᶠ⁾

Dear Mother,

You know what I did with my pupils last winter: I let them wait three, four, sometimes five hours; then at noon I came home to change and apologized by saying very feelingly: 'Oh, how sorry I am; my forgetfulness is really terrible!' etc.—whereupon everything was all right again.

So, dear Mother, today I shall say to you too, how sorry I am to have distressed you with the idle letters in which I asked you to do errands for me, and how unworthy I feel of so devoted and tender a love as yours. After these few words, you will not, I should like to believe, be more unrelenting than my pupils, who have forgiven me not only once but seventy times seven times. Since being here I have written only two letters, the first to Mme Sand, the second to Lamartine. I am enclosing his reply for you, so that you can show it to Hermine and Mlle Delarue. Please let me have it back through the post in about three weeks.

From 9 o'clock in the morning—I get up no earlier than that—until 11 at night, my entire day is filled. The mornings belong to the Conservatoire, to the Method,[27] and to my compositions. The afternoons I devote to reading, piano-playing, visiting, or writing articles. In the evenings I copy or do nothing at all.

Day after day I intend to write to one person or another. In this manner I salve my conscience which, as you know, is very tender. ('My son, you are a hypocrite!!!') But as yet I have required neither pen nor ink. Perhaps, instead, I shall devote the whole of December to letter-writing.

You, dear Mother, I believed I had sufficiently informed about what I had and had not been doing through the letters I sent to my old children Hermine and Mlle Delarue. In any case, little more remains to be said about me other than that I am happy, very happy, extremely happy. Only one timid little ambition remains unsatisfied. Whence it comes and whither it aims, you know. Thank God for everything—and to do me honour eat in all tranquillity of mind an almond cake! Just admit that you have a son who is neither as stupid nor as crazy as people say.

---

[27] A *Méthode de Piano* which Liszt had undertaken to write for the Geneva Conservatoire.

Honny soit qui mal y pense!

Do try to get Schlesinger to have the piece on *La Juive* engraved immedi-ately, for it must be published before January. Of all my pieces it's the most urgent. The others can wait for who knows how long, and have time enough; I'm not bothered about them. So far as terms are concerned, I long ago agreed with Schlesinger that I would likewise bear *the costs*, as with everything I don't give to Bernard [Latte], whose conscientious way of doing business is greatly to my liking, so that I am very much inclined to let him have a lot of my things.

Mme d'A. has written to you about our travels. In one way or another we shall see one another again in 1838.

Look after yourself and ask my friends not to take offence at hearing from me so seldom. I am very busy, and gladly allowing myself to be lulled from my egoistic life and happiness. All my love to my children,[28] many affectionate greet-ings to my brother spirits; for all others, the accustomed phrase and a friendly remembrance are sufficient.

Visit George. I am writing her a long letter about Geneva in the *Gazette musicale.*

---

[28] His pupils.

1836

May. Liszt gives three concerts in Lyons (2nd, 5th, 7th) and then proceeds to Paris, where he stays until early June. At the Salle Erard he plays, *inter alia*, the *Hammerklavier* Sonata of Beethoven, proving, writes Berlioz, that he is 'the pianist of the future'.

Summer. Liszt and Marie d'Agoult holiday at Veyrier and Monnetier; during this time Liszt also gives concerts in Lausanne and Dijon.

7–15 September. With George Sand (plus children), Major Pictet and Hermann Cohen, Liszt and Marie journey by mule through the mountains from Chamonix to Fribourg, where Liszt improvises, unforgettably, on the great organ of the cathedral.

16 October. He and Marie return to Paris, where they take an apartment in the Hôtel de France. The salon is shared with George Sand, to whom Liszt at this time introduces his friend Chopin.

18 December. Liszt plays at Berlioz's Conservatoire concert, deeply impressing the young Charles Hallé, who writes to his parents: 'Such execution, such limitless—truly limitless—execution no one else can possess. He plays sometimes so as to make your hair stand on end! He who has not heard Liszt can have no conception—literally no conception—of what his playing is.'

WORKS. PIANO: *Album d'un voyageur* (S156), Book III (Nov. 1835–1836), *Paraphrases*; *Fantaisie romantique sur deux mélodies suisses* (S157); *Grande valse di bravura* ('Le bal de Berne') (S209); *Rondeau fantastique sur un thème espagnol* ('El contrabandista') (S252); *Réminiscences des Puritains* (Bellini) (S390); *Réminiscences de Lucia di Lammermoor* (Donizetti) (S397, 1835–6); *Marche et cavatine de Lucie de Lammermoor* (Donizetti) (S398, 1835–6); *Grande fantaisie sur des thèmes de l'opéra Les Huguenots* (Meyerbeer) (S412); *Divertissement sur la cavatine 'I tuoi frequenti palpiti'* (from Pacini's *Niobe*) (S419, 1835–6); *La serenata e L'orgia, grande fantaisie sur des motifs des Soirées musicales* (Rossini) (S422, 1835–6); *La pastorella dell'Alpi e Li marinari, 2me fantaisie sur des motifs des Soirées musicales* (Rossini) (S423, 1835–6).

40. To Anna Liszt in Paris [Geneva, 14 January] ^{G (F)}

Dear Mother,

Many thanks for your kind and affectionate letter. Don't worry any more about the *event* that in Paris has given rise to gossip. On 18 December Mme d'A. was safely delivered of a sweet and extraordinarily beautiful baby girl. All necessary precautions had been taken in good time, and up to now I can only congratulate myself on this addition to the family. I should very much like you to come to us in the spring to see the little creature; for otherwise three or four years could go by until we are together again.

You didn't reply to Mme d'A. Why not? Do write to us as often as possible. Your letters always give me such great pleasure.

I need not tell you that I wish you to speak to no one about this matter. Just let people go on talking and prattling, and as hitherto tell them that you know nothing. I recommend complete discretion.

I would have let you have the news earlier, had someone not asked me to say nothing. You understand—and I may say no more. Just keep calm—there is no danger in any respect—and let people prattle! Adieu, adieu!

I'll tell you again that Filliotte—as we call her—is quite unusually beautiful and that everyone admires her. I am really proud.

41. To Anna Liszt [Geneva, March] ^{G (F)}

Dear Mother,

It has been a long time since you heard anything from me; in compensation I write today with an errand. Please be so good as to take my passport to Count Rudolf Apponyi I with a letter which you have to explain to him. The passport, you see, was originally issued for Switzerland, the Tyrol, and Austria. Now, however, I have decided first to spend a year in Naples and then six months in Rome, and finally to go via northern Italy and the Tyrol to Austria. For this, is a new passport necessary or, according to what the rather strict local police say, would it be sufficient for the Austrian minister in Zurich to endorse my old one with a visa? And so ask Count Rudolf I (people call him that to distinguish him from his son Rudolf II), to do me one last service either by providing me with a new passport, or by adding a visa to the old one. I am, after all, complying with all official regulations.

Please take the trouble to look in my trunk or cupboard for four pieces of music by F. Liszt which 13 or 14 years ago were published by the Demoiselles Erard. They are entitled:

Variations on an original theme, dedicated to Sébastien Bach [*sic*],
Variations, dedicated to Mme Panckoucke,
Two pieces dedicated to Count Amadé.[1]

---

[1] Respectively, the *Huit variations* (S148), published 1825 as Op. 1 and dedicated to Sébastien Erard; *Sept variations brillantes sur un thème de Rossini* (S149), published 1824 as Op. 2; *Allegro di bravura* (S151) and *Rondo di bravura* (S152), both published 1825.

Further, look, if possible with Herminie's help, for a copy of my published *Etudes* and, still better, try to find the *manuscript* of the 12 *Etudes* which is lying on the floor in a pile of music. Also, the beginning of a manuscript Sonata in C sharp minor on small-sized Italian paper. . . .

I have nothing new to report. Longinus has already answered the questions you sent me. This last week she has been really unwell. We are expecting you for your birthday in May. If you see Berlioz thank him for his letter, which I shall be replying to as soon as possible. Tell him, too, about your journey in May, and ask him to entrust you for two months with the score of his Harold Symphony. I should like to arrange it for piano, if that suits him. He would have no need to be afraid for his score, it seems to me, if you bring it to me and hand it over to him again on your return.

If you see Chopin, tell him that I am as fond of him as ever, and that I would give much, very much, if he would spend a month or two with us in the most beautiful season of the year. Mme d'A. is very keen to see and hear him again. Do try to persuade him; we would do our utmost to make his stay with us a pleasant one. If George is in Paris, do visit her. For the last three months I have found no time to write to her. Why Hiller hasn't replied to me, I don't know. Ask him if he got my letter. Should his silence be deliberate, tell him I find that infernally stupid.

Thalberg* I should like to know. Those works of his that I have seen I find *so so*. The newspaper eulogies impress me little. Let me know if it is true, as I have been told, that without knowing you he sent you a ticket for his concert.

We hope that in two months we shall see you here, for I shan't be coming to Paris for some time; fate, which sometimes plays bad tricks on us, would then have to take me there.

Farewell, dear Mother; I am very busy, but content to be so, and as happy as I can be without you, whom I love tenderly and with whom I should always like to be united.

Good night. I embrace you with all my heart.

F. Liszt

42. To George Sand. Geneva[2]

Dear George,

I know neither where nor how these few lines will find you; it matters little, provided that for a few minutes they remind you of a friend, a brother, whose devotion and affection you can count on for ever. The three or four letters you have written to M and which she has shown me (contrary to her usual habit),

---

[2] The letter is undated but apparently written on 20 Mar.

have given me real pleasure. Your reiterated promise to come and see us this spring also delights me. Nevertheless, I still hesitate ever so slightly to believe in the reality of your difficult-to-imagine advent in Geneva. Admit that it is a reasonable and almost justifiable scepticism; but God grant that you silence it for good and as soon as possible. These last few days your name has gone the rounds throughout Geneva. It seems that your *sot-système*[3] is in correspondence with Mme Clermont-Tonnerre, and that he has informed her of your imminent arrival. Whereupon, great uproar and alarm in these parts, as you can well imagine. Unhappily, it is like Mr Shakespeare's play *Much to do about nothing* [*sic*], of which, since I am not sure that you know English, this is the relevant French translation: 'Beaucoup de bruit pour rien'.

If you come, you will find me enormously dulled and stupefied! For six months I have done nothing but write, scribble and scrawl notes of every kind and colour. I am convinced that if anyone counted them they would be found to amount to a few thousand million. So, I repeat, I have become shamefully stupid; indeed, as the proverb has it, *stupide comme un musicien*. Perhaps I shall be more to your fancy like this, for I remember the profound aversion you had to my philosophical and ontological knowledge, which was very sensible of you. '*O vous, non pas Lélia, mais,*' etc., etc.

With regard to your former friend Sainte-Beuve, what is your opinion of the episode of a humanitarian poem 8,000 lines long? For my own part, I admit that I shall not very willingly side with those who are devotees of this new incarnation of God, a little mysteriously hidden this time. While admiring certain details, certain days of certain epochs, and above all some lines here and there which are truly sublime, I find it impossible to accept *Jocelyn*[4] as a great work, taken as a whole. Nevertheless I dare not express any further opinion to you, for I am terribly afraid that you may find the whole thing, from first syllable to last, magnificent and unparalleled.

Until the time when we can talk about it at greater length, let me crudely tell you that I would rather have written thirty pages of *Lélia* than the whole of this episode in which mediocrity of thought and feeling so often appears through nebulous clouds of a conventional sentimentalism.

Truly, Sainte-Beuve has committed a *tour de force* in likening *Jocelyn* to *Robinson Crusoe*, and without Lamartine being the least bit aware of it. It is a Jesuitical trait on which he must be complimented.

These last few days I have been told that Didier (of Geneva) is going to stay with you for a while; tell me if there's anything to this new story, which I shall believe in only as much as you want me to. It has been a long time since

---

[3] A jocular allusion to their friend Sosthènes de la Rochefoucauld.

[4] Narrative poem in nine 'epochs' by Lamartine, an episode in an unfinished epic retracing the destiny of humanity.

you contributed anything to the *Revue*; your legal proceedings have doubtless cost you a good deal of time. I hope you are at last completely rid *del marito*,[5] who is *par excellence* a character in a play, one who should never have any other reality. What is delightful in this business is the confident manner in which newspaper articles announce your return to conjugal duties (*vide* the *Chronique de Paris*, amongst others) and Your Ladyship's consummate diplomacy. I am extremely curious (and for one of the first times in my life) to hear you relate the beginnings, the middle and the end of this affair which, I doubt not, must have turned entirely to your advantage.

Were you the man to tell me in advance the day of your arrival (once the hypothetical possibility of the thing is admitted), I would go and await your coach with a sedan-chair, as is the practice here, plus some peripatetic musicians, in order to bring you triumphantly back to the rue Tabazan! Rousseau's street, to Rousseau's house in which we are living.

Since Puzzi has ventured to tell me that it was above all a material obstacle, extremely common at this time, which was detaining you down there, I renew on my own behalf the offer made to you the other day by M. . . .[6]

43. To Baron d'Eckstein in Paris. Geneva, 31 March. You have always been so extremely good to me, my dear Monsieur d'Eckstein, that I feel the greatest need to remind you of me and to ask for a token of your remembrance.

In the time—not far short of a year—since I left France, I have lived the life of the hunters of chamois, indeed, even that of bears, amidst the alpine snows; so that I had almost *decivilized* myself, when one fine day I was caught in a musical trap which is going to keep me in Geneva until next July.

The why and wherefore is that a Conservatoire de musique has been founded here (although there was absolutely nothing to *conserve*, I assure you, for the locals are the devil's own Protestants, protesting even against time and intonation). It was thought that I might be good for something, and so I have had to marshal, discipline, and metronomize fifty young people of both sexes. . . .

I don't know if you know Geneva. It is a serious city, only moderately sociable, although it contains all the elements of a most excellent society. Whatever the void left by the deaths of Mme de Staël and Benjamin Constant, a good number of very distinguished men and women can still be encountered here.

You have doubtless read Mme Necker de Saussure's fine work, *L'Education progressive, étude du cours de la vie*. Despite her sixty [seventy] years, this worthy

---

[5] Literally, 'of the husband', referring to George Sand's divorce suit against Baron Dudevant.
[6] The end of the letter is missing.

kinswoman of three great celebrities[7] is proceeding with her work with a devotion and perseverance all the more admirable in that they are wholly free from vainglory.

M. de Sismondi gives the same example of assiduous and untiring work. Before leaving for Italy (where he is at present) to see his aged parents, he deemed it a matter of honour to offer to the public the 28th volume of his *Histoire des Français*, which will probably be the last. 'I shall stop at Henri IV,' he told me one day in his scholarly but naïve way, '*for I do not know modern history well enough to go any further.*' He is, besides, rather busy with a two- or three-volume work that is part politics, part economics and part philosophy.

Another scholar, M. Adolphe Pictet* (nicknamed here *l'Universel* and, like you, a passionate enthusiast of oriental tongues), is working away at the origins, relationship, and migrations of languages. To the *Journal asiatique*, published in Paris, he has just addressed a rather important work on these subjects. I should be very interested to know your opinion of the value of this research, which is so completely inaccessible to my too ignorant curiosity.

M. de Candolle, the Atlas of the botanical world, has just undergone a wretched iodine cure which brought him to within an inch of death and made him fall for more than two weeks into the strangest delirium. He, the gentlest and most pacific scholar that ever lived, all of a sudden convinced himself that he had robbed, killed, and assassinated, and that he hardly had time left to prepare himself for the scaffold. Poor human reason! Happily, milk and treatment brought him entirely out of danger. And now, admire this psychological phenomenon, or the effect of the iodine: he, who until this time had always *cordially* detested music, is now a passionate music-lover. May the homoeopaths take careful note of this precious miracle!

But that's quite enough of Geneva. What about you, my dear Monsieur d'Eckstein? Will you permit me to call you to account more directly, and to ask you if your great work on India is making progress, and if the *great Brahma* of the forests of St Germain has not changed his retreat? In other words, what are you thinking and writing of? Shan't we soon be having a few fragments? Or shall we have to languish until the last i has been dotted, the last t crossed?

As soon as I saw the prospectus of the *Université Catholique* I hastened to become a subscriber, in the hope that you will take part in editing it. What do you say (candidly and without friendly bias) to this undertaking? In my opinion these gentlemen are wrong to publish their miscellany only once a month; people are influenced less and wearied more by such infrequent publications.

---

[7] Presumably, the Swiss physicist and Alpine traveller Horace-Bénédict de Saussure (her father), Mme de Staël (her cousin by marriage), and the latter's father, the famous Swiss banker Jacques Necker.

M. Ballanche is taking a very long time, it seems to me, to build his *Ville des Expiations* (someone said to me recently, when talking about his works: 'I am waiting to read his "Ville des Explications" '). I am unfortunately neither an Amphion nor an Orpheus; if an excellent grand piano could aspire to replace the three-times-holy Lyre, I should feel a passionate desire to come to his aid so as to hurry on his mystagogical constructions.

What a lot of nonsense; will you pardon me for it, my dear Monsieur d'Eckstein, and will you find a moment to write me a few lines before my departure for Italy? That would make me happy, very happy; I could believe myself with you again, again enjoying all those rich treasures of mind, knowledge and goodness that you possess and which have left such lively memories, and such constant regrets, in me.

Again, farewell. Please remember me affectionately to your Hindu companion, the Upanishah Pollet, and believe in my lasting feelings of profound esteem and affection.   F. Liszt

44. To George Sand [Geneva, April]. I hear that you are in Paris, dear George, and that you are preparing to leave. And where in the world are you off to?—Are you aware that you have given us no sign of life for more than three months? Why is that?—Your court case must have finished long since,[8] and you are now doubtless rich and independent; but you are no longer giving anything to Buloz—and the poor readers of the *Revue* are really *suffering* as a result. On the other hand, *de Musset* (I don't know how far I may go in speaking to you about all that?) is addressing some charming verses[9] to you. Truly, you have to be a very ferocious Lélia to withstand such reproaches. Unfortunately not everything in life is poetry, and de Musset does not always write beautiful verses!

Be that as it may, you can always boast of having written admirable prose. I have recently reread about sixty pages of *Lélia*, which brought me out in goose pimples. My God, it's so beautiful!—

I don't know if you have glanced through Mme Necker de Saussure's work on *progressive education*. It's a very remarkable book, and the woman who wrote it no less so, in spite of her sixty years, her deafness, and her relationship to M. de Broglie.[10] I have for some time been lending her *bad* books, beginning with *La Femme de la démocratie*[11] (which, incidentally, I found rather rambling and heavy going, despite the rare qualities to be found within its pages); and today

---

[8] Far from being over, the divorce proceedings were being conducted more vehemently than ever.
[9] *Nuit de mai* (published 15 June 1835) and *Nuit de décembre* (published 1 Dec. 1835).
[10] Mme de Staël's daughter had married the Duc de Broglie.
[11] Hortense Allart's *La Femme et la démocratie de nos temps* (Paris, 1836).

I have sent her *Lélia,* which she does not know at all. She professes the highest admiration for your talent—but it's a different matter with regard to the Doctrines you represent. You know my response when an argument gets under way on this topic; up to now it has always succeeded marvellously.

Talking of that, J. J. [Jules Janin] has behaved towards you like a thorough rascal. It was only to be expected from the dear Marquise; for it is certainly she who will have insisted on her lover writing the nonsense he has published in the *Débats,* where much more of it is published too.

My mother (who is to come here in a week) has told me of your kindnesses to Mme Jal. Poor woman! By making public proceedings easier for her, you have put new life into her. God knows what awaits her afterwards; but no matter; it is still an enormous service you are doing her. I can assure you of her deepest gratitude.

Remember me kindly to her when you see her.

M[arie] sends you a thousand greetings, and awaits your second missive, promised long ago.

I shan't tell you again to come to Geneva; but please note that I shall be leaving here at the end of June, on 3 July at the latest.

Puzzi, who has changed skin and name (we call him Dottore Ratissimo and risolutissimo) will write to you the first day he can. The poor devil is overwhelmed with business and lessons.[12] He has become quite a somebody; you will find him much changed.

Give me news of Ste-Beuve, of the blond St Simonian and of Everat.[13] Have you finally seen Hiller and Meyerbeer? Tell me about both of them. I have no local news to give you; this is a land of marmots. For the last six months there has been only one event in Geneva—and that event *is me!* That will tell you how lively and animated Genevan society is.

This is now the 3rd letter I have written to you without receiving a single word in reply. If you go on like this I shall send you a packet every week, until you write to me what M. de Lamennais wrote to the *curé* in Geneva: 'I have to tell you, Monsieur, that the postal charges are ruining me.' Very, very, very nice!

Farewell, dear Georges [*sic*]. Yours affectionately,   F. Liszt

45. To Marie d'Agoult in Geneva. Lyons, 23 April. Bonjour, bon Saas! . . . Mme Montgolfier and the Pavy family have given me an excellent welcome. They have gone ahead with regard to the concert, and the *first* will probably take place next Saturday. (Consequently, and parenthetically, send me at the earliest

---

[12] Like Liszt, young Hermann had been engaged as a piano professor at the Geneva Conservatoire.
[13] Respectively, Adolphe Guéroult and Michel de Bourges.

the concert tickets which are at rue Tabazan and ask Puzzi to give you my Duo or at the very least the second piano part which is copied out separately.)

I am living on the sixth floor. There is a little upright piano in a corner. Thus far I have committed no folly, but am tremendously tempted.

In your next, which I am expecting the day after tomorrow, tell me again about the shawl you want, for I very much wish not to do something idiotic.

I played through an extremely mediocre fantasy by Thalberg on *La Straniera*; it has in addition the fault of resembling, poorly, his previous ones. I definitely believe this man has nothing in either his belly or his head. We shall see.

Rudolf Apponyi has written me a charming letter in which he speaks to me of Thalberg (necessarily!), telling me that he is going to visit England, as an *artiste*; i.e. determined to earn as much money there as possible. As you see, M. Sigismond is not so aristocratic! I shall bring you this letter of Apponyi's, which is extremely gracious. I put one in the post yesterday, from my mother. Your shoes are here; tell me if you want them at once.

Mlle Mérienne has again sent to ask if she may do a portrait of me; I shall bring it to you by way of a surprise. She has done a remarkable one of Mme Montgolfier.

You will have a very long letter the day after tomorrow. Forgive me these perpetual trivialities, but I cannot write you just a few words. Do please reply, I love you so much. I am ceaselessly yours and with you. . . .

Send the *Apparitions* with the Duo. Puzzi has them.

Please don't delay in sending to me at the Hôtel de Milan, place des Terreaux, the two or three little things I ask you for.

46. To Marie d'Agoult. Lyons [Monday] 25 April. You don't write to me; that grieves me. You know that I can't live without a few words from you. Dear Marie, each of us is so necessary to the other!

Trying to arrange my concert is keeping me pretty busy. M. Cattin[14] had an immense success at la Montgolfier's yesterday evening. The whole of Lyons is fired up by this time. Everyone is making me wonderful promises. We'll see if things turn out as in Geneva. Meanwhile we are charging five francs a ticket.

Two old whores have just been chasing after me. When I bowed deeply before them I bit my tongue so as not to burst out laughing. One of them, Mlle F, is a singer at the Theatre and, I believe, a pupil of Herz. Perhaps you know her?

---

[14] Cattin, Cretin, Cretino, nicknames for Liszt himself.

Mlle Mérienne, who incidentally is deaf, is to begin my portrait today. That will again mean a lot of wasted time. I am *truly* only doing it for you. It seems to me that it will give you pleasure to have a nice portrait of Cretino. For my part, I know nothing more boring than posing, especially for a deaf lady of 40.

I would like to have finished these wretched *Soirées de Rossini* here, but am being left no peace. I have sometimes told you of the desire I had to do a provincial tour. Well! my expectations were perfectly accurate. Within the next week I shall become a very popular fellow in Lyons. You can understand how that will amuse me.

Happily, to console me for all these boring diversions, I have your Memorandum. Every evening on returning I *religiously* read a few pages. It's my prayer, my poem, my regeneration.

Dear, dear Saas. You are such a sublime.[15]

Send me a letter every day if possible. Write to me of yourself, or of others, it doesn't matter—but write to me!

Adieu.

There is already talk of a second concert; in the mean time we'll have to see how the first turns out.

47. To Marie d'Agoult. Lyons [*c.*Wednesday, 27 April]. Your two letters have reached me, dear Saas. A thousand thanks for all the details you give me.

I am indeed grateful to you for your determination to do some riding. In one way or another Saas needs to gallop; and you can understand that I far prefer the less metaphorical way. Write and tell me what time of day you go riding, and also when you generally take an outing, for I like to know everything.

You don't mention your piano practice. Why are you refusing me this kindness? I am so sad to think that I have been the indirect cause of a deprivation of this kind. Oh! I beseech you, don't be obstinate, start working at it again from this very day; a week or ten days will be quite enough to get your fingers back in practice, and it will give me so much, so very much, joy!

In my life in Lyons there isn't much that could interest you. Still, I know that you are obligingly fond of the most trifling details when they have some connection with Cretin. So here is a summary of my four days.

Saturday: Got up at 9.00. Prelude until 10.00. Breakfast at the Café Grand (cup of coffee). M. Pinondel came to take me to Saint-Jean's and to Saint-Nizier's.

---

[15] This sentence written thus by Liszt in English.

I knew both churches. In the first I admired an enormous stone clock in the style of the one described by Dumas in his *Impressions de voyage* (Berne), with four Evangelists and a procession of the apostles, etc., etc. It stopped in 1786!!! —and Catholicism too!

At Saint-Nizier's there is a magnificent altar (modern) in white marble. That's all. Between 2.00 and 3.00, visits to the engravers, one of each sex, who vied with one another in cursing me. At 3.00, to Mlle Mérienne, who has asked me to go again.

At 5.00, dinner at Mlle Pavy's (tête-à-tête with three or four people), trivial conversation about Lamartine, *Jocelyn*, etc. At 7.00 with Mme Montgolfier to the concert given by M. Cherblanc (violin). People began to notice Vecchio,[16] who scandalized the audience by twice dropping his big walking-stick.

After returning from the concert, which we left after the third piece, Cretin played two or three pieces of his own composition (*La Juive*, *La Fiancée*, and a bit of the *Clochette*) to la Montgolfier, who made clear her admiration for them.

Sunday: In the morning Cretin worked at the *Soirées de Rossini* (a wearisome chore), bathed at 1.00, taking some chocolate while doing so, in honour of la Fina; and between 2.00 and 5.00 was at la Montgolfier's, where Vecchio read through several pieces at the piano and talked about music with M. Montgolfier. At 5.00, dinner tête-à-tête with la M. and her daughter (a young married woman); after dinner, at the Café, and then a soirée at la M's where were gathered the town bigwigs. Vecchio caused one lady (wife of M. Moker, the most notable pianist in Lyons) to faint, and aroused an enthusiasm difficult to describe. . . .

On Monday there was a splendid article in the *Courrier de Lyon*, reporting in high-falutin' language Maestro Cretino's arrival. At 8.30 a.m. M. Cherblanc came to see me. We went to the theatre manager to make the arrangements. He was not in town, and we learnt that we should have to wait until 2.00 on Tuesday. Vecchio posed *chez* Mlle Mérienne who is deaf. Dinner at 5.00 at Mlle Pavy's, with Mlle Mérienne, M. Arlès, a merchant who, knowing that I was to be there, had invited himself, and M. de la Polinière, a doctor. Enormously long conversation about Saint-Simonism. . . .

Cretin felt unwell after dinner because of having eaten radishes. Tea was prepared for him and he was coddled. M. Arlès asked him to come and spend the rest of the evening at his place (*without piano*). Vieux accepted; and we chatted pleasantly until 10.00, Cretino's bedtime. Read Belle's Memorandum!!!

Tuesday: Negotiations with the Manager, who cannot give Vecchio the crush-room, but suggests he play in the Theatre. Vecchio and the Manager both ask for twenty-four hours to think it over. The matter will be decided tomorrow,

---

[16] Vecchio and Vieux, nicknames for Liszt.

doubtless in the affirmative. I shall have half the takings, like Ole Bull and Hauman. . . .

At 6.00, grand dinner at Mlle Pavy's—M. Arlès and his wife, M. Bonnefonds the painter (Director of the Lyons Museum), and several others. Vecchio felt rather poorly and spoke very little. . . .

Adieu, dear Saas. Love me always; I shall try to be worthy of it.

Continuation tomorrow, but please go back to the piano.

48. To Marie d'Agoult. Lyons [*c.* Thursday, 28 April]. To express to you faithfully how I feel in my heart, I could not do better than copy word for word the beginnings of your letters while substituting Cretino for Saas. Indeed, had I not so much to say to you today, I should venture to do so, but my *correspondence*, which will be voluminous, would not, I fear, be finished in time.

I have struck a bargain with M. Provence, the theatre manager, for next Monday. We'll share the takings after the costs (i.e. 350 francs), which I am obliged to give him, have been deducted. The price of seats will be a little higher than usual, the best being five francs. . . . On Tuesday morning I'll give you full details on this topic. Barring accidents, I shall play the Weber Concerto [*Concertstück*] and *La Fiancée* at the first soirée, *La marche d'Alexandre*[17] and my *Divertissement* at the second. If it proves possible to arrange a third concert, we shall see. . . .

A word or two now about my trip to Paris.

First of all, I have *no desire of any kind* to go to Paris at present. The two or three people that, at other times, I should perhaps have been quite glad to see again, have become *profoundly antipathetic* and *foreign* to me (don't think I am exaggerating, and above all take care not to believe that there is the slightest bitterness in my heart against... I can't finish...).

Thalberg hasn't been there for the last ten days. Mme Montgolfier has told me nothing striking about him, and the new works of his that I have seen are decidedly mediocre. We'll talk on this topic at greater length when I see you again.

Oh! since this temptation has now passed, and for ever, I shall admit frankly that for two or three days I have been tormented beyond measure by an unbridled desire to go to Paris and, on the very day of my arrival, to go and sit down in the orchestra at the [Théâtre des] Italiens, at Thalberg's concert. I felt, I knew, that the spectator would draw more of the audience's attention than the principal actor could do. It would have been all but a return from the island of

---

[17] A brilliant piece for piano solo by Moscheles.

Elba. I would have wanted to applaud him and to cry disdainfully 'Bravo', for at present I feel something loftier, stronger, beating in my breast. . . .

But now, I say it again, all that is far away. . . .

49. To Marie d'Agoult. Lyons [Sunday] 1 May. This morning two letters from you at once, both of them nice and deeply loving. Forgive me, forgive me a hundred times, my beautiful Saint, for that dull and ridiculous packet I sent you the day before yesterday. Throw it in the fire at once and forget about it completely. For my part I no longer know what I wrote to you that day, for I find it utterly impossible to reread the letters I send you.

I shall absolutely and definitely not go to Paris. I would never have spoken to you of that wretched trip had you not put the thought in my head. I now defy the Archangel Michael and Satan himself to make me go there. . . .

Marie, Marie, oh! give me back my life, give me back your love, let your beautiful brow once again bend voluptuously over mine, let your adorable tears flow down refreshingly like a celestial dew upon my poor heart, my worn and withered heart.

Listen to me no more, therefore, when I speak to you of anything but love and happiness; tear up and burn all the pages in my letters where there happens to be any name but yours, any thought unworthy of you; fling into the wayside dust and dirt of the gutters all memories, all affections, all the miseries that have come together and collided in my life which, before you came into it, was so bare, so crippled, so calamitous.

Marie, Marie, teach me the mysterious language of your soul, enable us to talk to one another in our sleep, and to respond to one another on some deep, inner level without outward sign. Put your hand in mine and let your fair, noble head and golden locks softly caress my chest, within which beats so heavy a heart. . . .

Don't despair. Our bodies are still young; love can glorify them! And *our* soul (for we have only one between us) is predestined to great and magnificent joys. The day will come when we shall see and clearly understand what in our terrestrial darkness we can only vaguely glimpse and hope for. Love will initiate us into the most sublime, most terrible mysteries! And then, you will remember those blazing words that we could neither of us hold back, for they would have broken our bones and destroyed our mortal lives, those words we uttered one night... there in that room into which you came...

Dear heart, why did I leave you? Why did you let me go? Alas, we are so pitiably rational!

Oh! if you feel some desire to see me, come, you will find me alone, alone! For without you there is nothing for me to gaze upon; there is neither sun, nor nature, nor God, nor temple, nor life.

Nevertheless, I dare not ask it of you as I should like. The journey could tire you. You might perhaps suffer some accident... and, besides, in about ten days I shall see you down there... Yes, in ten or twelve days I shall be in Geneva. . . .

50. To Marie d'Agoult. Paris, 14 May

Dearest one,

You know that my journey was melancholy. We were broken-hearted when parting[18]—how shall we find one another again? Oh! you will still be you, won't you, and I me, but you and me indissolubly united for ever? Leave me this hope, the only one to which I surrender my useless life.

Did you find my letter in Geneva? Have you written to me? So far as I am concerned, I couldn't wait until Monday as I had told you, and, although I have absolutely nothing to say, I imagine that these few lines which give me a little comfort will be agreeable to you too. My mother finds me sad and pensive. It's impossible for me to sit down even to eat; I do nothing but walk about the room. Chopin, whom I saw this morning, loves me tenderly and exclusively. The manner in which he spoke to me today gave me extreme pleasure. He professes a certain measure of criticism for Thalberg, and above all cannot admit that there can be the least comparison between the two of us.

I have just been brought a letter from M. de F...[19] This is what he says:

'My sister writes to tell me, Monsieur, that you wish, and that she herself very much wishes, me to have an interview with you. Calling a truce to any other sentiment than that of my deep concern for her, I shall come to you tomorrow between eight and nine in the evening. If this should be inconvenient, please let me know.'

So the purpose of my journey has been served and I no longer regret it. On Monday, the day after tomorrow, I shall write and let you know the outcome of our interview, which, I hope, will be satisfying for all three. . . .

The five or six persons I have already seen have been very nice to me. Meyerbeer, above all, whom I happened to catch sight of in a shop, seemed very friendly.

---

[18] Marie seems to have joined Liszt in Lyons for a few days, after which he journeyed to Paris and she returned to Geneva.

[19] Maurice de Flavigny, Marie's brother.

He offered me a ticket for *Les Huguenots*,[20] seeing that it is impossible to obtain one and that he is anxious for me not to go other than with a complimentary ticket from the composer.

If I am not mistaken, this brief visit of six or seven days, not very important in itself, will leave a good impression of me in Paris. . . .

Farewell. *Adesso e sempre.*

51. To Marie d'Agoult. Paris, 22 May. Bonjour, Marie. I am in low spirits, but less desperate than yesterday. I tell myself that you probably didn't want to write to me during the two or three remaining days of my stay here, and now you doubtless assume that I am in the coach. And I would indeed be in it were it not for that unfortunate letter I wrote to the Abbé [Lamennais], when Boré told me he would be coming! Oh! if you knew what it costs me to prolong my stay like this! But I don't want to vaunt my sacrifice too much. Although I have had no reply from La Chênaie as yet, I fear I shall have to wait at least a week for it. I don't know what will become of me during this time. Sweltering heat, perpetually troubled days. Not the shadow of a consoling thought, and nobody, nobody to see... If only you would write to me! . . . .

I have seen Principessa [Belgiojoso*]. She is always charming to me; compares me with no one at all and makes fun of the Thalbergois. She has promised me several good letters. Rossini will give me some too, and M. Bertin de Vaux is doing one for me for Ingres.

Yesterday I wrote... guess to whom? To Duchesse... in these terms:

'If Mme la Duchesse de Rauzan would be so kind as to indicate to me a day and a time when I could come to see her, *alone*, I should do so with alacrity, in order to renew to her the expression of my respectful gratitude.'

I thought about it for three days before deciding on this step. I don't know what the outcome will be, but it seems to me that it is far better not to avoid this woman. And, then, we shall have a good conversation. I feel so strong, so proud, *vis-à-vis* all these people!

The Wednesday matinée I have already told you about was splendid. The Rubini [Rossini?] piece, *La Juive* and *L'Orgia* make a prodigious effect. No one, it seems, was expecting such a thing. It is very flattering for me. Berryer is ecstatic, and several of my former antagonists have turned coat and are quite ready to adopt me. No thank you!

I am terribly tired of all that, and a month's rest in Geneva to allow me to recover to some extent will not be too much. . . . Duchesse has just replied: 'I

[20] Opera by Meyerbeer, first performed at the Paris Opéra on 29 Feb. that year.

shall be very happy to see you again, Monsieur; you are very kind to have thought of me during such a short visit. Come on Monday, you will certainly find me at home, etc.'

I'll write and tell you about our interview. Adieu, dearest; don't stop loving me. In ten to twelve days we'll be together again.

52. To Marie d'Agoult [Paris, May]

Dear Marie,

It is 1 o'clock in the morning; I have just taken Horace home. There was a light on in your room. A thousand jumbled memories excite me. I feel almost happy, and I can finally write to you.

Perhaps you were expecting me today! Oh! how I need you, but, you yourself, what are you thinking, what are you doing, how are you living? Does my absence seem as long, and as sad, to you as it does to me? Sincerely, I should not like to have to undertake such a trip again; it has just about killed me! . . .

I lunched with de Musset, who spoke to me with candour and propriety. We have completely made it up. He quoted a charming remark of Saas's: 'Ce qu'on appelle le monde est si peu de chose dans le monde' (taken from a letter of Belle's to Horatio, who shows his letters like Cretino). Alfred, it seems, has been and repeated this remark to several people who found it delightful. He will probably be coming to the baths at Aix this year. I gave him a promise to introduce him to you. You will like one another, I think.

Duchesse and I had a long interview, the outcome of which seems to me to be a good one. I told her that I had been offended by her inquisitiveness last summer and that I had then been able to do nothing but mock her. As I entered her room I pronounced your name very clearly. She asked several questions about you, your pursuits and plans, etc., etc.... I don't know if you will blame me for having assumed this responsibility, but I am convinced that when I have given you a detailed report (which can't be done in writing) of the whole of our conversation you will be pleased with Vieux. I ran into M. de Montalembert there, who was very civil to me. . . . My visit lasted two and a half hours in all. When I left, Duchesse thanked me with *interest* for having come to see her. In short, I am conscious of having done well. Furthermore, I believe I have been clever. I shall tell you everything better down there. . . .

Three people have got me to talk of you—de Musset, Chopin, and Schoelcher; I did so high-mindedly—without any self-satisfaction and making plain my veneration for you.

Tomorrow I have to see Ballanche, Montalembert, and de Vigny, at their places. Principessa (who has definitely made herself my admiring supporter) will have me to dinner with the Abbé Coeur.[21] . . .

I have been to the theatre only once, to see *Robert le Diable*.[22] *Les Huguenots* has been postponed because Mlle Falcon is unwell. . . .

I can't tell you in what a feverishly nervous state this lack of a letter [from you] leaves me. I can neither read, nor write, nor work, nor think, nor not think, of you, nor live, nor die. I hope for the next day, and then again for the next day!! Whatever happens, you have my heart and my life. Have I kept back anything for myself? Am I not wholly devoted to you? Haven't you an absolute right to any and every hour of my life? Where shall I go now if not to you? Haven't I told you a hundred times that God himself would not mean to me what you do?

Adieu, dearest Marie. I shall write to you tomorrow morning. Try to be just a little bit content, a little bit happy, if you can. Walk, go riding, keep busy and don't let solitude depress you. I suffer from it even more bitterly. Farewell again. See you soon, and for ever and always. . . .

53. To the Abbé Deguerry [May]

Monsieur le Curé,

I have just learnt that you have told several people that you reprimanded me during the sermon given by Monsieur l'Abbé Bautain at Saint-Roch.

That is utterly untrue.

Since my return to Paris I have not been to Saint-Roch. It is to be regretted that before *relating* so unlikely a story you did not take the trouble to make more accurate enquiries.

I am, Monsieur le Curé, yours very truly,

F. Liszt

54. To Marie d'Agoult. Midnight, Saturday [28 May]. Your four lines have put life back into me. I feel somewhat relieved. There is air in my lungs. Oh! Marie, how I love you!

This is a table of contents for future *causeries de salon* [salon conversations]:

1. I went to the Abbé Deguerry's this morning. I spoke plainly and unambiguously, and to everything I said he replied with absolute and categorical denials,

---

[21] A supporter of the Gallican party in the Church, this famous preacher was said to be a descendant of Jacques Cœur, the celebrated silversmith of Charles VII. In 1848 General Cavaignac appointed him Bishop of Troyes.

[22] Opera by Meyerbeer, first performed at the Paris Opéra, 21 Nov. 1831.

even repeatedly offering to give me a signed document in which he would declare that he had never made such remarks, etc., etc.... In short, it is impossible to ask for fuller satisfaction.

2. I have at last seen *Les Huguenots*, which had not been put on again since my arrival. It contains some very remarkable things. The work that has gone into the orchestration and *mise-en-œuvre* is prodigious.

3. I gave a big dinner at the Frères Provençaux today, to Ballanche, d'Eckstein, Montalembert, Meyerbeer, Adolphe Nourrit, Ferdinand Denis, Leuret, Théophile, Chopin, Delacroix (the painter), Boulanger, Barrault, *et al.*, *et al.* After dinner we gathered at Erard's, where we chatted a lot. Vecchio played the *Valse mariotique*,[23] part of the first Swiss piece, the *Soirées de Rossini*: greatest success imaginable.

4. Dantan is to do a small bust of Vecchio.

5. I am dropping with fatigue; while not exactly going out into society, I am up late every day. My brain is withering away, and furthermore I am sleeping badly.

From what the Abbé de Lamennais writes to me, I fear I may yet be obliged to stay another week at least, which is dreadful. Nevertheless, since I have already spent this last week waiting, I might as well go on waiting patiently until the end. . . .

It saddens me to ask you for a few more lines. I am so longing to see you again! But write at once, and with a few details if possible; do it out of charity.

Good night, Marie, I am ablaze with love for you.

Having finally seen Lamennais, Liszt left Paris on Friday, 3 June, and three days later was reunited with Mme d'Agoult in Geneva. In October they returned to Paris.

---

[23] Nickname for the waltz, composed for Marie, which was published that year (with a dedication to Pierre Wolff) under the title *Grande valse di bravura*.

1837

28 January; 4, 11 and 18 February. Liszt gives a series of chamber concerts at the Salle Erard with Urhan and Batta. The main item on each occasion is a work by Beethoven; in addition, Liszt plays various solo pieces, by himself, Chopin, and Moscheles.

February. Marie d'Agoult stays with George Sand at Nohant, where they are joined at the end of the month by Liszt.

31 March. Liszt and Thalberg play at a charity matinée in the home of the Princess Belgiojoso.

9 April. At a concert in the Salle Erard, Liszt plays several of the unpublished *Etudes*, Op. 25, of Chopin.

Early May–24 July. Liszt and Marie again stay at Nohant.

August. With Adolphe Nourrit*, Liszt gives a concert (3 August) in Lyons to benefit the city's indigent silk weavers. *En route* to Italy, he and Marie then visit Chambéry, Saint-Point (to see Lamartine), and the Grande Chartreuse.

17 August. They arrive at Baveno (Lake Maggiore). Later in the month they explore Lake Como and journey to Milan.

September/October. Liszt and Marie stay at Bellagio. Here Liszt works on his *Grandes Etudes*, and under the plane trees of the Villa Melzi the lovers read the *Divina Commedia*.

10 December. Liszt takes part in a concert at La Scala, Milan.

24 December. Francesca Gaetana Cosima Liszt is born in Como.

WORKS. PIANO AND ORCHESTRA: *Fantasie über Motive aus Beethovens Ruinen von Athen* (S122, *c.*1837). PIANO SOLO: *Grandes Etudes* (S137);[1] first sketch of *Après une lecture du Dante, fantasia quasi sonata* (S161/7); *Hexameron* (S392).[2] Arrangements of Beethoven's symphonies Nos. 5, 6, and 7 (S464); *Harold en Italie* (Berlioz) (S472), with viola part; *Ouverture du Roi Lear* (Berlioz) (S474); the accompaniment (S476) to Louise Bertin's four-act opera *Esmeralda*; *Soirées musicales* (Rossini) (S424); *Lob der Tränen* (Schubert) (S557); *Lieder* (Schubert) (S558, 1835–7): 1. *Sei mir gegrüsst* 2. *Auf dem Wasser zu singen* 3. *Du bist die Ruh* 4. *Erlkönig* 5. *Meeresstille* 6. *Die junge Nonne* 7. *Frühlingsglaube* 8. *Gretchen am Spinnrade* 9. *Ständchen* ('Horch, horch! die Lerch') 10. *Rastlose Liebe* 11. *Der Wanderer* 12. *Ave Maria*.

WRITINGS. 'Thalberg's "Grande Fantaisie", Op. 22, and "Caprices", Op. 15 and Op. 19', published in the *RGM*, 8 January. 'To Professor Fétis', *RGM*, 14 May. 'On C. V. Alkan's Piano Works (Trois morceaux dans le genre pathétique)', *RGM*, 22 October. 'Robert Schumann's Piano Compositions, Op. 5, 11, 14', *RGM*, 12 November.

---

[1] Based on the juvenile studies of 1826 and dedicated to Carl Czerny.

[2] A set of bravura variations by Liszt himself, Thalberg, Pixis, Herz, Czerny, and Chopin, on the March 'Suoni la tromba' from Bellini's *I Puritani*; it was dedicated to the Princess Belgiojoso.

'Lettres d'un bachelier ès musique', *RGM*, 12 February (to a 'Poet Traveller' [George Sand]) and 16 July (to George Sand).

55. To Marie d'Agoult at Nohant. Midnight, Saturday [4 February]. I have just got home, and here I am with little Zio.[3] The soirée was a tremendous success; you have never seen me understood and applauded quite like that. The public is coming to us quite definitely. Thalberg was stupefied with amazement. In front of several people he said aloud that he had never heard anything like it. He even added that he would be 'incapable of playing four lines of my piece'. If I am not mistaken, he must be feeling sad. Nevertheless, I don't want to give free rein to my suppositions in this respect.

A rather odd incident at the soirée was Herz coming to shake my hand, to tell me that he had never heard me play better. Well, you know what articles I have done on Herz. As for Thalberg, he withdrew into his narrow solemnity. I prefer it to be like that, although he'll pay for it, enormously.

Ronchaud and Mallefille will be writing to you with the details.

I cannot continue; this cough is choking me.

10 o'clock, Sunday morning. I am resuming my letter at the point where I left off yesterday evening. . . .

You must be installed by now. Your camellias are doubtless already on your mantelpiece; I imagine your room to be large and low, with blue curtains and blue furniture throughout...

Mine has been very lonely since you last set foot in it. Poetry has flown from my retreat, as I remarked the other day to Cretin's Universal friend [Pictet], who comes to see me. I am getting him to read [Ballanche's] *Vision d'Hébal,* to mix his ideas up a bit. . . .

Tell me what newspapers you receive down there, so that I can arrange to have you sent what you want. *Le Temps* and *Le Monde* must be reaching you through George; tell me if you want *La Presse.*

My health is good, apart from an abominable cough which seems not to want to go away. I hope to join you at the end of the month; how delightful that will be.

56. To Marie d'Agoult. Monday, 13 February. I'm now more or less recovered, chère Belle. Your letter has done me extreme good. . . .

My soirées are a continuous *crescendo* in effect and artistic importance. This latest one was first-rate. Moscheles' *étude* (in chromatic scales) was encored, as

---

[3] Zio and Zyo, nicknames for Marie.

was the *Valse mariotique*. Generally speaking, people are asking me to put on a further four soirées—in any case, they couldn't take place until my return from Nohant. I am longing to get out of all this hurly-burly. Since you like details, here are two or three:

1. A delightful blunder made by the audience last Saturday, in confusing, with unbelievable self-assurance, Pixis's style and Beethoven's. According to the programme, Beethoven's Trio was the first item and Pixis's the last. But as Pixis had begged me not to sacrifice him, we reversed the order, and there was everyone applauding the alleged Trio by Beethoven... and saying that beside it the other seemed very tame!... Isn't that marvellous?

2, 3, and 4. Thalberg!...

But there are so many things to say that I don't know where to begin. Let's take them in chronological order. Last Thursday Pixis was to bring us together at dinner. Putting aside all my reservations, at 6.00 I was at rue Taitbout! Pixis had just received a brief note of apology from the illustrious pianist, who had *had a relapse*. We contented ourselves with laughing merrily at his absence, and adding a little buffoonery to our hearty dinner; Chopin alone was averse to it. The next day, despite what his friends maintained, we learnt that he had actually been only very mildly indisposed. All things considered, I prefer matters to proceed no further; that is stupid, you will tell me, but how can it be helped? Thalberg is a very weak young man who is very easily influenced. His friends are extremely mediocre; so much the worse for him. Henceforth it will be very difficult for us to meet. Besides, his concert, which is to be on 24 February, will probably be the occasion of a new article. For Fétis is now about to interfere. Yes, Fétis, the worthy professor (paid, or so Chopin believes, by M. Dietrichstein,[4] who is in Brussels at this very moment), is to address a letter to me in the *Gazette musicale* about my (or our) article on Thalberg.[5] Schlesinger showed me a note he had just received from him in which he asks if it would suit the *Gazette* to publish this letter in which, he says, he will observe all the proprieties due to so great an artist as Liszt.

As you can well imagine, I have given Schlesinger the go-ahead to print Fétis's article, which has not yet been received. I shall reply according to what his letter says; it could all become very amusing.

---

[4] Prince Dietrichstein, adoptive father of Thalberg.

[5] The article, describing Thalberg's music as mediocre, monotonous, and pretentious, which had appeared in the *RGM* of 8 Jan. Fétis's defence of the Austrian pianist—which rashly hailed the latter as 'the man of a new school' and charged Liszt with being 'the product of a school which is ending and has nothing further to say'—was published in the issue of 23 Apr. Liszt's response was an open letter to Fétis (*RGM*, 14 May). Rebuking the Belgian musicologist for meddling when his information was inadequate, and writing of the whole debate as 'resembling the title of Shakespeare's *Much Ado About Nothing*', he concluded with the words 'Truth will not fail those who have believed in and suffered defeat for her.'

I don't know if you will be able to read this dreadful scrawl, but would you believe that since Saturday I have had something wrong with my wrist, which is preventing me from playing and writing. Tomorrow I shall go and consult Cloquet the surgeon. It's only a very small sore, I think.

Thalberg's concert is announced for 24 February (fateful date!) at the Gymnase musical. Oh! how I should like to leave immediately afterwards! How I long to clasp you in my arms! How I need to love you. The lion is roaring in my chest! . . .

The 'Lettre d'un bachelier' appeared yesterday. Legouvé came to compliment me on it; he claims that *my style* is improving from day to day. On Thursday, I believe, it will be reprinted by *Le Monde*. If I am not mistaken, it will be very favourably received. When I come to Nohant I shall commission one or two articles from you. Decidedly, little Zyo is a great writer!

My departure depends entirely on Thalberg's concert. If the opportunity seemed good, I would perhaps give a concert during the week. What do you think? . . .

I have just got back from Cloquet's. My sore is quite unimportant; nevertheless, he has forbidden me to play for the next few days. I am sad; I need you. . . .

Tell me what you are reading and what you and George talk about. As for me, I have neither read nor said anything else since being without you. You are the only person in the world with whom I can talk now and again. . . .

Zopin [Chopin] is always very good to me. He will come and see you this spring.

Adieu, dearest. Write to me soon. I need it. Adieu, adieu.

57. To Marie d'Agoult. Paris [*c.*18 February]. I have just heard Thalberg. Really, it's utter humbug. Of all the things called superior, it is assuredly the most mediocre I know. His latest piece (composed recently), on *God save the King*, is much worse even than mediocre. 'He is a *grand seigneur manqué* who makes an artist still more *manqué*,' I remarked to Chopin. . . .

The portrait arrived this morning. . . . The couple of words accompanying it touched me. There is a deep-seated affinity between us. I, too (and perhaps more than you), am tired of my isolation. What makes me stay is the necessity of struggling against a crowd of idiots, the need to overcome one by one all the difficulties standing between me and the development of my personality.

Dearest one, when shall I see you again? I may be wrong, but I believe it would be a mistake for me to leave Paris just now. Jullien returned this morning. I have asked him for 3,000 francs to play at four concerts. He is not far from giving me this sum, which is appropriate, don't you think? Furthermore, it is possible that Schlesinger will put on a concert for me at the Opéra, next Sunday, 25 [26] February; that would be splendid, even though it would bring me only 1,000 francs. Thalberg is rather worried; he still doesn't know where he will give his concert, not regarding the Gymnase musical as aristocratic enough. Besides, he wants at the same time to earn a lot of money. For ten days one word has been weighing on me, and I dare not say it to you: Come!!!

58. To Marie d'Agoult. Paris [*c*.20 February]. Today, chère Belle, I write with a request—which for some time I have been doing quite often. It concerns an article about the four musical soirées, which I ought to do, but dare not, since the enormous success of the 'Lettre d'un bachelier' which everyone has been complimenting me on.

This, roughly, is how the article in question, which will appear above my name, should be set out:

Whatever the public's fondness for things frivolous and its passion for showy mediocrities, etc., etc., Paris nevertheless contains a considerable number of men who are seriously devoted to Art and who work conscientiously at their music education. (It's basically little Zyo's idea, in the first article published in *Le Monde*[6] on Berlioz.)

Had we had any doubts about the existence of this public, the select throng who attended four concerts the programmes of which were not of a nature to lure the dilettanti and the dandies of the Italiens dress-circle, would have converted our doubt into assurance.—Then a couple of sentences on the impotence of the obstacles and on the necessity for progress in the art of music in France.

Then, at last, turn to the four soirées musicales. Say that people listened with religious attention, and passionate interest, to things which at many concerts would probably have caused yawns. Of course, you shouldn't say a word about me, but restrict yourself to giving worthy praise to the talent and individuality of Urhan; emphasize how strict and conscientious he is, artistically speaking; say that if violinists like Lafont and de Bériot have more elegance in their manner, no one could be superior to him in dignity and seriousness. No one understands the great works more profoundly, etc.... Give praise, too, to Batta (who has been a really good fellow this last week); mention his beautiful tone and the charm of his playing. Lastly, praise Erard's splendid, aristocratic, candle-lit salons, and his piano which brings together two qualities which are generally mutually exclusive: power and mellowness of tone. Mention, if you wish, the effect I made at the

---

[6] The issue of 11 Dec. 1836.

Conservatoire and at the Italiens, where with my piano I drowned the orchestra; say, which is true, that with no other instrument would I have found it possible to produce such an effect.

Finish, finally, by saying that these four sessions are, as it were, only preparatory. Although we have already played five Beethoven Trios, there still remains a very considerable number of things which are played nowhere and which it is important to make known to the public.

Announce that these concerts are ending, temporarily, but that we shall resume them in Holy Week, and that we shall devote three days of that Week (if it occurs to you, make something out of Holy Week) to performing exclusively compositions by Beethoven, Schubert, and Weber.

The final sentence you can do as you like; I wouldn't mind if you said that it was time for highly-placed artistes to abandon for good the trade of public entertainers and to undertake to instruct their audiences and initiate them into things great and noble. Let no one be mistaken: the duration of their reputation, and the importance of their position, henceforth comes at this price.

That's roughly the outline of the article, which shouldn't be too long, unless you want to make it long. It will have to be done in my personal name. The thing is important for me, and is a real service I am asking of you. Try to send it to me within five days, so that I can put it in the Sunday, 26 February, issue of the *Gazette*, and also in *Le Monde*.

Four people have been waiting in this room for more than half an hour; impossible to continue.

Love me as I love you.

I shall write you a couple of words tomorrow.

Yours, yours alone.

Spending much of the summer with Mme Sand at Nohant, Liszt and Marie then proceeded to Italy, and by November were living in Como.

59. To Princess Belgiojoso. Como, 15 December. I really don't know, beautiful Princess, how I could have written you a letter foolish enough to suggest a conclusion of the kind you mention. As a general principle, in all honesty, I prefer not to receive letters, so that I am spared the bother of replying to them. But what have general principles to do with it when it concerns you, you who were born as an exception, who live as an exception, and who, whatever you may do, will willy-nilly also die as an exception? And so let's not talk about it any more, and may it be understood and agreed once and for all, that you will write to me as and when you can; in a word, that you will always write to me, were it only to tell me that I am insufferable, detestable, etc. etc.

I shall now tell you that I am quite the little somebody in Milan, which when all is said and done is not displeasing. Thanks to the presence of Rossini, the musical life of these parts is no longer without some interest for me. I don't know why I am using this expression *musical life*, for in reality there is hardly any more of it than there is of political or literary life. There is Rossini, whom I see frequently, and that's all. There are also Hiller and Paër, who are old friends of mine. *The rest do not deserve the honour of being named.* But I am in error, forgetting Pompeo Belgiojoso, who is certainly the finest and most agreeable basso-profondo we know. I should very much like the example of Candia, and a few debts (you see how charitable I am in my desires), to induce him to take up an artistic career. But perhaps he would then deteriorate. Instead of singing *en grand seigneur,* as he does now, he would shine as a professional, his faults, his carelessnesses, would cease to have a certain grace. He would have to become a *vocalizer,* and all the charm would be destroyed.

Rossini receives every Friday. A lot of ensemble music is performed at his place. It is admirable to see what care and trouble he takes to get the choruses to rehearse two or three times a week, and even the Friday soloists. I admit that I entirely fail to understand the great man's condescension, and in his place would beware of this excessive obligingness; would put my feet on the andirons, and the *musicailleurs* and dolts, who abound in his salon as elsewhere, I would send packing.

Last Sunday I gave my concert at La Scala. The evening was a very brilliant one; I pocketed a good number of zwanziger (positive result) and the gathering seemed more than content with my performing-dog tricks. I will certainly not leave Milan without giving another two or three concerts. Next time, I shall play your *Puritains* piece (which several publishers have re-engraved here, without the mistake in the Dedication) and also the *Hexameron,* definitive title of the monster piece...

60. To George Sand. Como, 15 December

My good Piffoël,[7]

As you don't insist on your friends writing interesting things to you, I really don't know why Cretin shouldn't likewise put himself on the footing of being a correspondent of yours, my dear illustrious one. Were it a question of writing

---

[7] Nickname bestowed upon herself by Mme Sand.

to the observer of observation (Balzac), one would at least have to be *witty*; if to Planche, *learned*; if to Nisard, *eloquent*; if to Ste-B., *ingenious*; if to L'anier,[8] *full* of *subtle* allusions; if to Bocage, *aurora borealis* (for a change); if to Michel, *sans culottes*[9] (and it's very cold), etc., etc. But for you, most excellent Piffoël, who have the sense merely to be the most unpretentious and original genius of our time, there is no need for any of that. So the Cretin is writing to you and will go on writing to you just as long as that gives you any pleasure at all.

To say something, therefore, I shall tell you that of all mortal beings I am the most fortunate. *Lac de Côme is very bello. Mi piace more que lago di Ginevra* [Lake Como is very beautiful. I like it more than Lake Geneva]; apart from Mont Blanc, however, with which I had begun to establish intimate relations.—The princess is ever the most adorable of beings. We are living alone and incredibly happy with one another. As an occasional distraction from my happiness I do some work. I believe that, musically speaking, I have made some progress—but what does it matter? Shall I accidentally make myself need the wretched satisfactions of vanity?... No, my friend, whatever may be said by certain people who will never know me other than very superficially, I have no need of vanity. I need only a certain emotion, just as it is, and that's all. You know that too. What don't you know besides? Piffoël is certainly a doctor of Psychology.

Talking of psychology, guess whom I met in Milan? I'll give you a hundred guesses. BARCHOU DE PENHOEN *I tell you and that's enough.* Yes, my friend, I have seen Barchou's card, have seen his feet, his legs, his belly, and even his backside —and he is by no means, I promise you, a metaphysical entity. Holy hell, what the Barchou does that matter to you! It was only on beholding him that I could understand that the absolute was eternally identical with itself, which, translated into intelligible language, means that an idiot is an idiot, witness little *B.*

Princess Mirabelle[10] has doubtless given you all the details of our stay in Como and at Bellagio.

It is impossible to be happier than we are—unless, however, Piffoël comes and sees us, which I shall find quite natural. When, how, and in what way, you can arrange with the princess, to whom you write more often.

Why haven't we yet had any news of Mallefille?... Ask him if he is in the habit of dropping his old friends when he finds it convenient?

If Leroux still remembers me, give him my most affectionate regards; although the *Encyclopédie* has been put on the Index in Milan, the French Consul is sending me each number as it comes out, and you know with what fervent interest I read this splendid book.

---

[8] A play on words: Lasnier was a lawyer at La Châtre; *anier* is the French for a donkey-driver.
[9] The *sansculottes* were the rabid republicans at the time of the French Revolution.
[10] Another nickname for Marie d'Agoult.

And you, my dear Piff, when will you give us a splendid book once again—which means when will you deign to publish one? And won't you be continuing your admirable *Lettres d'un Voyageur?*—Forgive me this indiscreet insistence, but, you see, it has been a long time since I read anything that gave me goose flesh, and I feel a singular *appetite* for your *beautiful words.*

Chopin has just sent a charming dedication to the princess.[11] These twelve new *études* are extremely remarkable. When you go to Paris, see something of him. He is a real friend to me.

Embrace Duteil, and give a good handshake to your other Nohant friends, from me. As for yourself, continue to give me your sincere and discerning friendship, and count ever, and seriously, on mine.   F. Liszt

Avis important: Piffoël né pas obligé d'écrire à *Krétinos, attendu que Piffoël has better thing to far* [*Important note*: Piffoël is not obliged to write to *Cretin,* seeing that *Piffoël has better things to do*].

---

[11] Chopin's first set of piano studies, the Twelve Grand Etudes, Op. 10 (published 1833), had been dedicated to Liszt; this new series, the Twelve Etudes, Op. 25, was dedicated to the Comtesse d'Agoult.

1838

February/March. Liszt gives and takes part in concerts in Milan.

16 March. He and Marie d'Agoult leave for Venice, where he appears in concerts on 28 March and 1 April.

10 April. Liszt arrives in Vienna, where he makes the acquaintance of the 18-year-old Clara Wieck. His first concert—to benefit flood victims in Pest—is given on the 18th. Many others follow; his success is unparalleled. In Venice, however, Marie d'Agoult, who has fallen ill, is deeply disturbed at his long absence.

27 May. Liszt leaves Vienna to rejoin Marie.

Summer. They stay in Genoa and Lugano.

6 September. Liszt attends the coronation of the Emperor Ferdinand I (as King of Lombardy-Venetia) in Milan Cathedral.

Early October. Liszt plays at Cattaio, near Padua, to members of the Imperial family, among whom is the ex-Empress Marie Louise, widow of Napoleon.

Mid-October. Liszt and Marie arrive in Florence, where during their three-month sojourn Liszt plays in public on several occasions and sits—as does Marie—for the sculptor Lorenzo Bartolini.

December. Spending Christmas in Bologna, Liszt plays at the Casino with enormous success and enjoys the company of Rossini.

WORKS. PIANO: *Album d'un voyageur* (S156), Books I (?Sept. 1837–Jan. 1838), *Impressions et poésies*, and II (?Jan.–May), *Fleurs mélodiques des Alpes. Grand galop chromatique* (S219). Arrangements or transcriptions of *Nuits d'été à Pausilippe* (Donizetti) (S399); *Soirées italiennes, six amusements* (Mercadante) (S411); *Ouverture de l'opéra Guillaume Tell* (Rossini) (S552); *Der Gondelfahrer* (Schubert) (S559).

WRITINGS. 'Lettres d'un bachelier ès musique' in the *RGM* of 11 February (to Adolphe Pictet), 25 March (to Louis de Ronchaud), 27 May (to Maurice Schlesinger, on La Scala), 8 July (to Heinrich Heine), 22 July (to Louis de Ronchaud), 2 September (to Lambert Massart).

61. To Marie d'Agoult at Como. Milan, Friday, 2.00 a.m. I don't know why I feel a kind of satisfaction in thinking that you suffered all yesterday. As for myself, I was overwhelmed and discouraged, in a way that I hadn't been for a long time... Oh! how wrong you are, dear good Marie, to torment yourself with things that you suspect to be hidden inside me and of which you never hear me speak. Dear, beautiful child, if you but knew of the profound tenderness, the ineffable affection for you—like those of a brother and friend—which lie buried within the depths of my heart! Oh! fret no more, suffer no more. That would be cruel and unjust. Be aware that all the sincere and loving things I have been able to say to you are only the cold, dull shadow of what you have made me feel and understand. Oh! how I wish you could open up my heart, and with your beautiful hands take hold of, and keep, my soul and my entire life! Sometimes in those hours of enchantment and delight in which through you everything seems so beautiful, so pure, so divine, when I believe I can touch and feel all around me a world more entrancing than the one it is given men to dream of, in those hours which I sometimes rashly seek to recall—when I loved and possessed you entirely—I deluded myself that my life was no longer my own: I had ceased to exist for myself, was wholly merged in you, and we spoke to one another soul to soul... A presentiment of our future destiny? Allow me to believe so.

Farewell. I am dropping with exhaustion. At Rossini's, Nourrit sang the duet from *William Tell* admirably. He was applauded rapturously. As for me, I improvised on themes from the same opera, with prodigious success. I was also introduced to the Governor. But I really can't tell you more about it. It is as though I have been blind and deaf since being here. . . . On Tuesday, at the latest, I shall be in Como. Don't expect me before that. I have done all your errands.

Try not to be sad. For my sake do your utmost to be just a little bit content.

62. To Marie d'Agoult. Milan, Monday morning. I almost sprained my wrist during my improvisation at Rossini's, and became aware of it only the next day. The whole of yesterday it gave me great pain, and for several hours I found it impossible to use my right hand.

I am extremely vexed about it. Francilla[1] makes her début tomorrow in *La Cenerentola*[2] and Pixis has absolutely begged me to stay. My own business is more or less finished, which doesn't mean that I shall bring back either money or a carriage. I would so much have wanted to give you this little joy, but I really dare not choose it without first consulting you again. It would be rather foolish, it seems to me, to hurry too much.

You have hardly written to me this time, which rather hurts me. Nourrit will certainly be coming to Como, but perhaps only towards the end of the

---

[1] The singer Francilla Pixis, adopted daughter of J. P. Pixis.
[2] Opera by Rossini, first performed in Rome, 1817.

week. I may possibly come back to you with him, in Martini's carriage. He is a delightful fellow and very amusing. For three days I have been slightly unwell and am looking a sorry sight once again, which doesn't prevent me being very much *à la mode.* . . .

I shan't begin to breathe a little until Wednesday morning, at the top of that delightful slope in Como. I can no longer live without you. Everything that isn't you makes me suffer. Are you quite aware of that? Will you always believe in my love? Will it be enough for you?

Farewell, dear Marie, let us love one another, and then let us learn, since we have to, how to take the rest patiently and compassionately.

In two days!

63. To Adolphe Pictet in Geneva. Milan, 31 January. No indeed, *Caro Universale*, I have not yet thought of dying, and even if the whim of descending *to the sombre regions of Pluto* (classical style) had taken hold of me, your letter, full of so much that is friendly and heartfelt, would be enough to make me think again. A thousand thanks, *carissimo* and *savantissimo*, for all the kind and affectionate things you wrote. You have known for more than two years that you are one of the very small number of men whose esteem and affection I genuinely value; you know, too (and I hope this conviction will only increase), that we *suit* and complement one another; consequently, that we are formed for everlasting friendship.—I have never, I believe, abused the beautiful word friend; be assured that I shall equally never fail in any of the duties it imposes.

I greatly look forward to publication of the *Conte fantastique*;[3] we shall spend a few pleasant evenings reading and commenting on it. Do not fail to post it to us *subito* [at once]. It is out of the question that Doctor Piffoëls [George Sand] will take offence at it; he has too much good sense for that.

Incidentally, guess whom I have run into here? I'll give you a hundred guesses, but it won't help you: Barchou de Penhoën, who, in Milan, introduced himself only under the name of *Baron de Penhoën*. Imagine how we burst out laughing the first time we caught sight of the end of his nose at La Scala. To begin with, it was like a grotesque vision which Marie simply couldn't believe in; Barchou in Italy, Barchou pursuing us with his objective subjectivity; she considered it quite impossible!... In the end, however, she had to accept the fact, and now

---

[3] *Une Course à Chamounix: Conte fantastique* (Paris, 1838), Pictet's picturesque account of the holiday with Liszt, Marie, and the Sand family in Sept. 1836.

the beautiful Comtesse and the philosopher—Baron—staff Captain—are going to be on the best of terms. I intimated to Marie that I wouldn't find it the least bit offensive to be cuckolded by transcendental Philosophy in person. It will be a precedent...

Since my arrival here I have been working quite hard. The instrumental task that I am especially keen to bring to an end is progressing very smoothly. With the *12 Etudes*—monsters—and a small volume entitled *Impressions et Poésies* which I have just finished, I am not displeased. Since you are so good as to take an interest in these trifles, I should tell you that my publicity arrangements are improving singularly. My agreements with the publishers are far better, and on several other points I have become quite a *grand seigneur.* Within 2 or 3 years, I hope, my artistic position will be altogether settled. I have received several invitations to go to England, Germany, Russia; other very favourable proposals have been made to me too—but I shall not be able to think about all that for another year or 18 months....

Before then we shall probably see one another again in Geneva, whither I shall return in the spring in search of a child I already love deeply. I don't know why I have never spoken to you of her. Forgive this silence. We are both of us terribly *backward,*[4] as you said. . . .

Around 10 to 15 March we set out for Venice. The first days of spring are magnificent there, apparently. For Marie, a moss or a lichen is worth more than all the *carnavals* you can imagine. And so she means at all costs to do Botany again. My own pursuits are perfectly simple: I have nothing else to do but abandon myself to the enjoyment of all the happiness with which she surrounds me. Art itself, which I had made my entire life, is very much taking second place at present—and as an organizational necessity rather than a voluntary result.

You don't mention Mme Pictet? How are the vocal exercises, the *frequenti palpiti,* the harp solos, etc., coming along?—Please remember me affectionately to her and renew the offer of singing, harp, and piano lessons and of anything she might wish or permit. *Honni soit qui mal y pense.* Yet the temptation is great!

Adieu, *Caro Universale,* write to me as and when you can, and never doubt my sincere and cordial friendship.   F. Liszt

[Postscript by Marie d'Agoult, referring to the verse dialogue by Goethe:]
Do me the pleasure, dear Universal, of telling me how you would translate into French: *Künstler's Erdewallen.*

---

[4] This word written by Liszt in English.

64. To Lambert Massart in Paris. Milan, February. . . . I have left my delightful Lake Como to return to Milan for good. After those two months of work and solitude I am now leading a completely worldly life: going to balls and paying umpteen visits to La Scala (quite the fashion, moreover, and one which they should adopt in Paris); further, I go riding, and am even learning a little Italian without giving too much thought to it. In short, I am quite the agreeable little somebody here, and think I am almost *à la mode*. Rossini is still in Milan . . . and is still Rossini; i.e. a man of genius whom success and popularity have made almost a great man. . . . We see one another very often, and very *gladly*. I really can't but be pleased with my relations with him thus far, and am convinced that that is how they will always be. From the beginning of April onwards he will be spending the entire summer in Bologna, where I shall probably pay him a visit. As for me, in mid-March I set out for Venice. From there to Bologna, Florence, Genoa, etc....; if the coronation[5] takes place in Milan in September, as per the official announcement, I shan't fail to return here at that time. In any case, I shall spend next winter in Rome.

Now let's talk business. . . . The Beethoven symphonies are also on sale in Germany, Italy, and England.[6] I am not anxious to sell them in Paris, but attach real importance to their being published there. Kalkbrenner's work is *pitiful*; since becoming acquainted with it, I have been extremely keen for my own to be known to the public. I would gladly consent to give them *for nothing*, but only on condition that they be well *advertised*; in a word, well *published*. I should be glad if the brief preface I sent you could be printed separately, and if a few newspapers would review the work I have done taken as a whole. . . .

Send the proofs of the monster piece (which I want to call *Hexameron*) as soon as possible. Tell me, too, if Schlesinger has published in his paper the 'Lettre d'un bachelier' about my stay at Nohant (at G. Sand's). When you see him, tell him that I have two others that are completely ready, but that I shan't send them to him until this present one has come out. . . .

Farewell, my dear, kind Massart. I don't want to weary you any more with my English handwriting. A thousand friendly greetings to Léon and to good Madame Kreutzer. Remember me kindly to other friends of mine that you see there, especially d'Ortigue,* whom I don't advise to come to Italy talking of Beethoven and Weber. . . .

Adieu, *carissimo*. Ever yours affectionately, F. Liszt

---

[5] Of the Emperor Ferdinand I.

[6] Liszt's transcriptions for piano—by this time, Nos. 5, 6, and 7; the rest later—of the Beethoven symphonies, which had also been arranged by Kalkbrenner.

65. To Adolphe Nourrit in Rome. Milan, 7 February. I feel the need not to remain wholly separated from you, my dear Adolphe. So if you think it a good idea, we can from time to time tell one another what we are doing, thinking or dreaming!—Our last meeting, in Milan, made a deep impression on me. Never had I felt so fully how much this keen and devoted affection that you have always inspired in me held a real place in my heart. Have no doubt, my excellent friend: sooner or later we shall meet on the same paths; we shall toil at a common work. And even if some wretched bad luck put us at a distance of a thousand leagues from one another, we should be no less steadfastly *brothers* and *companions* in thought.

You were much spoken of again in Milan, my friend. The words *engagement at La Scala* have several times been pronounced in front of me, *in high circles*. No doubt when you return here you will have the best luck imaginable. For your friends, the evening in which you appear on this immense stage, to which you alone can give some life at present, will be a beautiful one.

I have hardly seen Hiller since his return. We have not yet resumed our postprandial *disputes*.

I am becoming prodigiously worldly once again. It's a month to cast to the winds. Besides, I have worked enough at Como to allow myself, without too much compunction, to do the rounds of the Milanese salons (but on the express condition that I never make music there, as you know). Between 10 and 15 March I expect to leave for Venice, where I shall remain until the end of April. If in the mean time you revisit Milan, I shall not fail to come and see you for a few days. I am making a holiday of this spring in Venice. It must be something quite marvellous!—And then, it's been my dream for the last five years!

Farewell, dear Adolphe. Consider me wholly at your service, and continue to believe in my friendship.

Yours most affectionately,   F. Liszt

On 7 April Liszt left Venice to travel to Vienna, where he proposed to give a concert in aid of flood victims in Pest.

66. To Marie d'Agoult in Venice. Vienna, Thursday morning, 12 April. Let's look back together over these two or three days, dear Marie.—My journey was much less boring than I feared. Instead of the chambermaid, I had for companion a certain Sig. Bedini, sent to Vienna as secretary to the Papal Nuncio. The first two days we chatted little; but towards the end of our journey he abandoned himself to a kind of friendly and almost affectionate trust which was all but moving. I haven't yet met so simple a priest—I could almost say one so naïf—without attaching our usual bad meaning to this word. In our two or three hours of conversation I provided as usual three quarters of the topics and ideas. In return, he told me two or three stories about travels with a Roman lady; their romantic interest was only very slight, but coming from him that seemed rather droll. The whole thing interspersed with reminiscences of arias by Donizetti, Bellini, and Ricci, which he hummed very agreeably. When we arrived in Vienna, at midnight on Tuesday, we spent the first night together in a room with two beds, but were too worn out by the journey to resume our talks. In a few days from now I shall go and see him; it will be one of the thousand and one friendly relationships that I go through the world tying and untying.

The part of Vienna [Austria?] which we travelled through is not particularly attractive, with the exception of Lake Wörth, which I found melancholy and bewitching. (We no longer define words, do we, dear Marie?—You know what I mean by melancholy; it has nothing in common with the predilections of the Duchesse...)

The main road which runs alongside it is bordered by admirably picturesque pinewoods. As I gazed at those sad but beautiful woods, tears came into my eyes and I thought intensely of you, my fair archangel (that is what I wish always to call you). A thousand confused ideas passed through my mind. I felt that divine anguish which your image always arouses within my breast when we are far apart. Then while staring at those fir-trees, ever green, ever sad, but ever grand and noble, I said to myself: 'She, too, has not known the illusions and childish joys of other women; there has been for her neither flowering nor opening out... only bitterness and desolation.' Oh! how I felt at that moment everything that is noble and sublime in you! . . .

I'll postpone details about Vienna. But my arrival is reported in all the newspapers, and if I am not labouring under delusions as big as Mallefille's fists, I shall create an immense effect. My first concert, for the flood victims, will probably be next Wednesday. In the next forty-eight hours I shall have heard Clara Wieck* (who has stayed expressly for me) and also have seen some of the important people again, Metternich, Dietrichstein, *et al.* . . .

Adieu, my beautiful Myoult. . . .

67. To Marie d'Agoult. Vienna. 6.00 a.m., 13 April. On my route from Venice to Vienna was Klagenfurt. I don't know why that name struck me. . . .

As far as society people are concerned, I have as yet seen no one other than Amadé and the two Dietrichsteins. Amadé is delighted; he does not like Thalberg and is already ablaze with joy when hearing me. Nevertheless, I believe that he does not want to compromise himself too much just yet, and that the measure of his enthusiasm will not be complete until after my concert. Dietrichstein, Thalberg's father, is an old man with white hair and an affectionate and princely manner; he has been extremely charming and attentive to me. . . . He told me that Thalberg had written to him a long time ago to ask him to put his piano at my disposal when I arrived in Vienna. He informed me, too, that Thalberg had been in Bordeaux, and that on his way back he had given concerts in Tours and Angoulême. You can see that we are more *grands Seigneurs*, at least. Venezia, Napoli, and Genova have a better ring to them than do Carpentras and Pondichéry. At 3 o'clock tomorrow I dine at Prince Dietrichstein's. His brother, Count Moritz D., seemed a man of polish. We won't associate very much with one another, I believe; it will probably be limited to a dinner. . . . As for my letters of introduction, I haven't delivered many as yet, and have seen none of the people to whom they are addressed. Tomorrow, Monday,[7] I have to call again on Princess Metternich, who, as a matter of etiquette, did not receive me the first time.

The most important thing is done. My concert for the people of Pest is fixed for next Wednesday and even placarded already. When you receive these lines I shall already be a consecrated man in Vienna. Yesterday and the day before I played to about fifteen artistes: Czerny, Mayseder, Merk, Lachner (from Munich), Clara Wieck,[8] Haslinger, a certain Tischhof, professor at the Conservatoire, etc., etc. There was an enthusiasm of which you can have no idea. Without any doubt I shall have an *overwhelming* success on Wednesday morning. For Weber's *Concertstück*, the Fantasy on the *Puritains*, the Valse and the Etude in G [minor], I have accepted Prince D's offer, and shall play them on a piano of Graf's with which I am very pleased; the delicate, rippling passages in particular go marvellously. I am hoping that Belgiojoso (Tonino) will sing. I shall take care to send you the newspapers.

Best of all, is that I am certain not to exceed the time agreed for my return. I have pushed matters on greatly, and have also found people who have helped me, more than elsewhere. My second concert will follow fairly soon after Wednesday's (a week later, I think). Places are already retained for that second one, and even for a third. I still expect to bring back a little money, which will please me.

A single word about Clara Wieck—*distintissimo* (but not 'uomo', of course!). We are staying in the same hotel, Zur Stadt Frankfurt, and make music as best

---

[7] This letter, begun on Friday the 13th, was evidently continued on the Sunday.

[8] Writing two years later (22 Mar. 1840) to Robert Schumann, Clara Wieck remarked: 'When I heard Liszt for the first time, I was overwhelmed and sobbed aloud, it so shook me. Don't you feel the same, that it is as though he wanted to be absorbed by the piano? And then again, how heavenly it is when he plays tenderly. . . . In comparison with Liszt other virtuosi seem so small, even Thalberg.'

we can after dinner. She is a very simple person, very well brought up, not in the least c...,[9] entirely preoccupied with her art, but nobly and without childishness. She was flabbergasted when she heard me. Her compositions are truly very remarkable, especially for a woman. They have a hundred times more invention and real feeling than all the past and present fantasies of Thalberg. She played the *Frequenti palpiti* here with unbelievable success, at her concert first of all, then at a few soirées, and finally before the Empress, which is an entirely new honour for me.

But, because of my conscientious salon talk, I am forgetting to tell you, my fair Archangel, that I received your letter yesterday, and that it was the first and only hour of joy since we took our leave of one another. . . .

Write soon. It's my sole happiness!

Farewell, farewell, continue to love me. . . .

68. To Princess Belgiojoso. Vienna, 13 April. This time I am not complaining. You have written me the most *excellent* and most charming of letters. I thank you warmly. . . .

Although my stay in Milan was prolonged well beyond my expectations, I shall naïvely[10] confess to you that I have no great fondness for that city.

One can feel too much emptiness in it, and people and things alike sound too hollow. With the exception of the Duomo, squeezed by the wretched huts pressing against it (and similar, in this, to those great souls of our time who are capable of emotional and intellectual understanding of the religious synthesis, and who, even when they arrive at a gigantic unfolding of the power that God has revealed to them, always lack space and air, obstructed and diminished as they are by the little people surrounding them), and Leonardo da Vinci's *Last Supper*, half destroyed by time and even more by the sabre cuts of the regiments who have lived in the refectory (symbol!)—with the exception of these two marvels, I really don't know anything that has made an impression on me.

As regards individuals, I met several agreeable ones, and since people were generally very kind to me I sank gently into what was basically a rather pleasant social life, unobjectionable if rather tedious and silly in its form. . . .

Your errand to Madame Bisi was faithfully carried out.[11] I made her really weep when reading out the part of your letter in which you spoke of her; besides, it is impossible to write lines more deeply felt.

---

[9] Probably, *coquette* (coquettish).   [10] The Princess was a native of Milan.

[11] As Ernesta Bisi had reported to the Princess in a letter from Milan of 22 Feb.: 'Liszt has been here, Liszt has played, Liszt has written with this selfsame pen with which I am writing to you. . . . Over the years I have lost none of my power of feeling, and was moved to my very depths by the enchantment of Liszt's music. The piece from *I*

Talking of writing, how is it that you told me that I write to everybody? To whom, then, if you please? Would your *everybody* be referring to Emilio [Belgiojoso], to whom in fact I wrote three lines of thanks for his kindness in sending me three letters of introduction? I don't know why this kind of reproach, against which I would not dream of justifying myself if reproach it really were, and were it possible that I deserved it, piqued me a little. Yes, please do be aware, dear, beautiful and ideal princess, that I still keep to my claim, which unfortunately matters to you hardly at all, of going only to your home and of writing only to you; and my kind of Don Quixotism is sincere in this respect. If, therefore, you don't want to vex me too much, don't tell me any more that I write to everybody, seeing that it isn't true.

I shall speak to you another day of Venice and Vienna, where by an odd chance I happen to be at the present moment; in a fortnight I shall be returning to Italy. Venice, Bologna, Florence, etc. etc.

Thousands of friendly, affectionate and devoted greetings.   F.L.

Two things which gave me extreme pleasure:
1. Your dress (Venetian bodice, I believe) for the Court Ball, which I insist on seeing when I get back.
2. The kind of small *furore* made in Milan, Venice, and Vienna by the old piece I dedicated to you pending something better or not so bad.

69. To Marie d'Agoult. Vienna, 18 April. End of concert—3 o'clock. The post is leaving. Just two words. Enormous success. Cheering. Recalled fifteen to eighteen times. Packed hall. Universal amazement. Th[alberg] hardly exists at present in the memory of the Viennese. I am truly moved. Never have I had such a success, or one that can be compared with it. It would have pleased you.

Dear Marie, I think only of you. Be happy. Be happy: that is my sole wish.

My thoughts are confused. Wouldn't you like to come here? Is it too late? This part of the world would amuse you for a few days. True, the journey is very tiring.

I shan't advise you to travel in your own carriage. That would be very expensive and the pleasure not in proportion to the cost.

Do what you think fit. I believe in you.

Puritani dedicated to you was played by him—on my supremely bad piano—with that mastery that you know, and despite the inferiority of the instrument the effect was magical. A profound impression was also made on me by Liszt's noble physiognomy. . . .' (A. Malvezzi, *La Principessa Cristina di Belgiojoso*, ii, Milan, 1936, 236–7).

My second concert is arranged for Monday evening. All seats are taken in advance. Once again, you cannot imagine this morning's *furore*. I shall probably give at least two more concerts.

Otherwise nothing interesting. I dine in town almost every day, but haven't yet made a single interesting acquaintance. Princess M[etternich] has all the charm of the Duchesse d'Angoulême. Everyone is giving me a good welcome just now. What's the good of it all? I shall have a little money. That's the best of it.

Farewell, farewell, dear Marie. Love me always.

70. To Marie d'Agoult. Vienna, 10.00 p.m., Monday [23 April]

Dearest,

Forgive me for talking to you once again of my Viennese successes. You know that I am by no means inclined to exaggerate the effect I produce, but here there is a *furore*, a mania of which you can form no idea.[12] Seats for today's concert were already sold out by the day before yesterday, and doubtless tomorrow none will be left for the third, which doesn't take place until Sunday morning. Each of these two concerts will bring in roughly three thousand zwanziger [20 pfennig pieces], all expenses paid. There is no reason why I shouldn't give another two at least, which will make a profit of nine thousand zwanziger in all. Afterwards I have to play *chez* the Empress. Unless you come here, I shall leave on about 6 or 7 May. What joy it will give me to see you, I can't tell you. I am terribly tired. I am having bad nights; in the daytime I haven't a moment's peace. It is much worse than ever. I haven't been able to see anything here, nor hear anything. Every day I am invited out to dinner, twice if anything. Every morning my room is full of people.

The Thalbergites (for these comparisons will never end), who prided themselves on their impartiality to begin with, are beginning to be seriously vexed. In living memory no one has had such a success in Vienna, not even Paganini. I could easily give another half-dozen concerts, but want to restrict myself to

---

[12] Hardly an exaggeration, as is made clear in the writings of contemporaries. Thus Wilhelm Kuhe: 'Liszt had come to Vienna for the purpose of giving a concert in aid of the unfortunate people who were suffering from the disastrous inundations in Pest. Would that I could adequately describe the effect produced by that phenomenal artist! Suffice it that Vienna—artistic, music-loving and enthusiastic Vienna—was in a state of excitement such as I have rarely or never seen. Such playing had never been heard before. It was almost more than human. This was the universal expression of opinion, and everyone appeared electrified. That first and memorable concert was followed by many others, at which the same rapturous enthusiasm and indescribable excitement prevailed' (*My Musical Recollections*, London, 1896, 131).

another two, which will make four in three weeks. If you write to Paris to my mother, ask her from me to have a translation done of Saphir's article, which is creating a great sensation here.

My sole amusement is to buy a few miserable pipes, with which I am delighted. They have cost me two Napoleons [20 franc pieces] in all, but give me immense pleasure.

I am also reading [Lamennais's] *Livre du peuple*. That is not amusing, as Sue says. Incidentally, do continue your correspondence with d'Eckstein; it's something I set great store by.

I have no common sense this evening. My head is hurting terribly... *Ach! könnte ich ihn küssen und fassen ihn* [Oh! If I could only take hold of and kiss it]!

I saw you in a gondola this evening, just for a moment, when I sat down at the piano!

What makes me very happy, is to think that with the bit of money I have just earned here we shall be able to live in tranquillity this summer...

If you came here I believe you would like the town. It must be lovely here in the spring.

But no, it's better for us to be reunited in Venice! But that's so long! Another fortnight.—But not more, of course.—I shall not go to Hungary.—What's the point? You are my homeland, my heaven, and my sole repose.

Yours, for ever yours.

71. To Marie d'Agoult. 8 o'clock, Wednesday, 25 April.[13] I am rather unwell this evening. The Viennese climate is testing me a little, and yesterday and today I have coughed a lot. . . . Your letters are making a great impression on me, and I don't know what would become of me if you didn't write so often. I should like to write to you too, and good, long letters like yours. Why can't I? And why don't I know how to? Forgive me, my fair Archangel, and never doubt my love. Good night, I am going to bed now, being terribly tired. I shall continue this letter tomorrow.

Thursday, 2 o'clock. I am still in bed, but the homoeopathic doctor tells me that it will be over in thirty-six hours. It's a heavy cold accompanied by migraines; in other words, nothing at all. What wouldn't I give to see you? How I need to be with you!

---

[13] Dated 26 Apr. in Ollivier's edition—but Wednesday was the 25th.

My third concert is arranged for Sunday [29 April] and the fourth, for which all seats have been taken, for Wednesday or Thursday. I shall remain here for the whole of next week because of a concert for the Blind at which I am obliged to play. I hope to be able to leave in about twelve days. I shan't go to either Pest or Pozsony, or anywhere else. That would take too much time, and I have too great a need to see you. So in two or two and a half weeks I shall be with you.

The beautiful days will have come back and we shall be happy again.

Adieu, dearest one; love me ever.

72. To Marie d'Agoult. 28 April. I'm now more or less well again, my dear, good Marie. Three powders have restored me to health. *Petites causes et petits effets.* . . . I think I shall have to stay here for at least another fortnight. I am doing absolutely splendid business, and expect to bring back no less than ten thousand zwanziger—all expenses paid. With no exaggeration, never since Paganini has anyone made such an impression. My fourth concert is next Wednesday. The hall is already fully booked; here as elsewhere that is something unprecedented.

Big news: Thalberg arrived yesterday evening. We have to dine together today *chez* Prince Dietrichstein, who sent to say that he would be delighted to bring Castor and Pollux together in his home. I am very glad about the arrival of the Ostrogoth, for I can now be accommodating with no great effort.

Would you believe that there has been such intrigue at court that the Empress's concert has been postponed? By the strangest chance, you played a small part in my lack of favour, the Empress's devoutness being taken advantage of for the benefit of some childish animosities or other. Even so, it is more than probable that the Court will ask for me before my departure. Public opinion is too unanimously for me. I'll give you a detailed account of the petty scheming and shabby intriguing that took place on this occasion.

I have made no friend here, but still have very many courtiers. My room is never empty. I am the man *à la mode*. Fifty copies of my portrait have been sold in a single day. You won't wrong me by thinking that that makes the least impression on me, will you?

One sole desire, one sole passion, possesses me entirely. You know me by heart, don't you?

On the whole I am fairly calm. If you haven't left when these three lines arrive, don't leave. That will be safer. But let me hope that perhaps they won't find you there. In any case, write often. I need you, for you are all I have.

Yours, for ever yours.

73. To Robert Schumann in Leipzig[14]

My dear Herr Schumann,

I shan't attempt to tell you how grateful I am for, and how touched by, your friendly letter. Fräulein Wieck, whose acquaintance I have been so happy as to make here, will express to you better than I could all my fellow-feeling, all my admiring affection, for you. I have latterly been such a nomad that the pieces you were so kind as to send to Milan for me reached me only on the eve of my departure from Venice a couple of weeks ago; and since then we have talked about you so much, from morning till night, that it hardly occurred to me to write to you. But today to my great astonishment I received yet another token of your friendly remembrance of me, and I really don't want to delay in sending my renewed and repeated thanks. And so to write these few lines to you I have just left the company of some extremely pretty ladies. Actually, no need to be grateful to me for this little sacrifice, for it gives me very great pleasure to have a brief chat with you.

Your *Carnaval* and *Fantasiestücke* I find exceptionally interesting. I play them with real delight, and God knows that there are not many things of which I can say as much. Frankly and plainly speaking, it is in general only Chopin's and your works which have a powerful interest for me.

The rest do not deserve the honour of being mentioned... at least, with a few exceptions—to be conciliatory, like *Eusebius*.[15]

In the next 6 to 8 weeks I shall send you my *12 Etudes* and half a dozen fantasy pieces (*Impressions et Poèmes*)—I consider them to be less bad than other things of mine, and shall be happy to think that you do not dislike them.

Shall I confess that I was not greatly impressed by Henselt's* *Etudes*, and that I found them not up to their reputation? I don't know if you share my opinion, but all in all they strike me as very *careless*. They are pleasant to listen to, very attractive to look at, make an excellent effect, and the edition (thanks to our friend Hofmeister) is first rate; but on the whole I doubt whether H. is anything but a distinguished mediocrity. For the rest, he is very young and will doubtless develop. Let us hope so at all events.

I very much regret that I am unable to pay you a brief visit in Leipzig at present. To make your personal acquaintance and to spend a few days with you is one of my keenest desires. But since this cannot be done just now, let us at least try not to remain entirely apart, and to combat as best we can the laziness about writing which is, I believe, equal on both sides.

---

[14] An undated letter from Vienna received by Schumann on 5 May.
[15] The name used by Schumann to designate the dreamy, gentle side of his personality, as opposed to the stormy, passionate Florestan.

In about a fortnight I return to Venice, and shall be back in Milan at the time of the coronation (towards the end of August). I plan to spend next winter in Rome, if the cholera or some other plague doesn't thwart me. I shan't urge you to come to Italy. Your sympathies would be too grievously offended. If it is there known from hearsay that Beethoven and Weber have ever existed, that's about as much as is known.

Won't you have printed what you sent me? Haslinger would have it gladly, I believe, and it would give me great pleasure to see my name associated with yours.

Were I allowed to make you a request, I should ask you to write some trios, or a quintet or septet. I feel that you would do them admirably, and it is a long time since anything remarkable was published in this line. If you ever decide to do something like that, let me know at once; I covet the honour of making it known to the public.

Farewell, my dear Herr Schumann. Do please retain your friendly feelings towards me, and accept once again the expression of my warm sympathy and devotion.   F. Liszt

74. To Marie d'Agoult. Vienna, Tuesday evening, 8 May

Dear Marie,

I couldn't begin to tell you what sadness your letters cause me. To know that you are unwell and not to be with you... to gather hour by hour, minute by minute, those beautiful treasures of goodness and unutterable love. Not to read more than a few lines from your hand... not to see you, not to kiss you gently, religiously on your brow..., no longer to make you smile... no longer to hear the sound of your beloved voice... Oh! I am mortally sad. At every moment I ask myself why I came here, what I have to do here, of what use to me are these plaudits of the multitude and the meaningless noise of puerile celebrity... Yes, Marie, I am mortally sad. Nothing can make me forget for even a quarter of an hour that you are not here, and that I shall never be able to live without you!

All the requests and entreaties being made to me not to leave are unbeliev-able. Without this unfortunate arrangement whereby a carriage leaves for Venice on Saturdays only, I should already have left; or, rather, I should be there beside you, there where I should be. Yesterday I tried to borrow a carriage, but no one will agree to lend me one. I am worn out, exhausted, distressed... The letter I received from you this morning takes away from me all hope of seeing you. Since it is not I who arrange my concerts, I have already entered into public engagements which I could not fail to keep without disadvantage. This morning my fourth concert (which is actually my sixth, though those for the people of Pest and in the Redoute don't count) was even more brilliant than the previous one. Every concert brings in 3,500 zwanziger (minimum). I know this from Haslinger, who does everything for me and keeps my money at his place. . . .

I do nothing but think of Filliot.[16] I have an immense desire to see her again. She will resemble you, I hope. Oh! my lovely Marie, I should so much like to tell you, and to make you feel in the profoundest depths of your soul, how much I love you...

Do you know what is admirable in this city?—the spire of St Stephen's! In whichever direction one goes, in whatever corner of the city one happens to be, one everywhere sees this motionless mass towering above all else. Sometimes it is awesome, at other times heavy and oppressive... It is the only great thing I know here. And it has a prodigious effect on me. This spire pursues me, harasses me, torments me. Comparisons abound... I'll spare you them. . . .

Give me some more errands. I shall be so happy to bring you back something that may give you pleasure. But I haven't yet entirely given up the idea of seeing you here. If you came, this (barring a better opinion, which would be yours) is what we would do. First of all we would go to Hungary for a while. Celebrations are being held in Pest on the 26th of this month.—At the beginning of June, on about the 10th, we would go into the Tyrol for two months, entirely alone. Before or afterwards we would see Munich, and then we would return to our dear Lake Como for the coronation. Florence we would leave for the autumn, and our planned visits to Rome and Naples would still hold good for the winter. But, once again, it is only an idea in the air. Do and arrange everything as you think fit. As you know, I put no trust in my own ideas. . . .

Nothing to tell you that is either interesting or curious. My life is prodigiously monotonous. I am adulated, cajoled, and fêted by everyone, with the exception of half a dozen individuals, rather influential ones for that matter, who are fuming and fretting about my successes. Princess M[etternich] is behaving better to me than she did in the early days. Thalberg is more to the liking of these people. But they don't know what to do about it, because of the great mass of people who have come out unanimously in my favour, thereby consigning the Ostrogoth to the second rank... A Viennese *bon mot*: 'L... ist das Mandl, Th... das Weibl [Liszt is the man, Thalberg the woman].' Have you received my portrait? An enormous number of copies of it have been sold. . . .

A thousand kisses on your archangel's brow. . . .

---

[16] Blandine.

75. To Marie d'Agoult. Vienna, May. And I, too, my poor angel, am mortally sad. The torment of great thoughts, the thirst for the impossible, the wild and passionate aspiration towards what cannot be—are not these the heaviest of all our tribulations? No, never have I so suffered from all my lonely follies as during this past week. To have to endure the din and bustle of Fame (as it is called), constantly to be the cynosure of a thousand eyes—it all makes me feel even more bitterly the absolute isolation of my heart. Why did I not leave during the first few days? Or, rather, what made me decide to come here at all? I swear to you, my good, my only Marie, I do not believe I am in the wrong. I am suffering just as you are; less nobly but just as profoundly. I still feel worthy of your love, of your compassion.

I cannot conceive what there was in my letter to Emilio[17] that could have caused you such deep distress. It was, I believe, kind and sincere towards him. It is true that I should not have written, but should have left immediately. I was prevented. The other evening I heard some of Schubert's *Lieder*, sung by a friend of his. I listened to only three or four, then I came home and dissolved into tears. Surprised by my abrupt departure, a couple of people came in search of me and then spread it about from one end of the city to the other that you were making me extremely unhappy, etc. etc. I do not know why this publicity given to my most sacred emotions so angered me.

I shall certainly come and meet you half-way. But, for goodness' sake, get well, recover, and calm down. In a week, you tell me? Does that really seem possible? And so you would leave shortly after this letter? Heavens, how happy I should be to see you!

You are doubtless saying to yourself what I say to myself with profound bitterness night and day: vanity and self-interest in effect dominate a man's entire life. There is no room for love...

And yet I love you, yes, love you with all my strength. I belong only to you. You alone have a right to my whole being, for you alone possess the secret of my life, of my fortunes and of my misfortunes.

Dearest, I suffer, but it is for you, because of you. I shall write to you again tomorrow. Farewell.

It is to Klagenfurt that I shall go to meet you.

On Thursday, 24 May, the Comtesse d'Agoult penned the following note to her absent lover:

I no longer understand anything at all. After two days had gone by I wrote, on three successive days, three letters which must have reached you last Thursday, Friday,

---

[17] Count Emilio Malazonni, a young Venetian of their acquaintance who was looking after Marie during Liszt's absence.

and Saturday. Those three letters told you that I could not leave Venice; then I received yours informing me that you would be departing on Saturday evening. I waited for you the day before yesterday, yesterday, this morning... and finally your letter arrived... When are we going to see one another again?

I await you, and cannot yet leave my room. In Heaven's name, delay no more.

Leaving Vienna on Sunday, 27 May, Liszt reached Venice a few days later. By early July the couple were in Genoa.

76. To Adolphe Nourrit in Naples. Genoa, 9 July. I am very behind with you, my excellent friend. Your letter arrived only at the end of my stay in Vienna, where I spent one of the best months of my life, spoilt, adulated and, better than that, *seriously understood* and accepted by an outstandingly intelligent public....

But let us rather speak of you, my noble friend, so richly gifted from on high— of you, likeable, profound, and understanding artiste, whom neither ridicule, nor calumny, nor hatred have ever been able to reach.

How I look forward to seeing you again in Naples, and how happy I am in advance for everything that will be able to give you some satisfaction in the legitimate success which, beyond any doubt, you will there enjoy! You know that I have always been of the small number of those who understood and approved your *leaving* the Opéra. Now, more than ever, it seems to me, you must congratulate yourself on having had the strength to take that decision, which spares you a multitude of small but irritating bothers, and easily *increases your stature* in the opinion of even our dress-circle gapers.

Talking about decisions, I have just taken a very small one which will perhaps make you laugh. I am going to Constantinople![18] In late September, at Pest, I shall be embarking on the Danube, and returning via Naples in the spring....

I hope that when we next meet you will find me changed for the better. From day to day I am becoming calmer, more *sedate*, more *practical* (consequently more sociable). A remark of yours often comes back to me: '*Let us strive, my friend, to win over those whose sympathies we have squandered,*' you said to me one day. I don't know why that has remained with me.... I frequently repeat it to myself, while thinking of you, of our *stars*, of the life which is passing, and on which you will leave so beautiful and noble a mark.... And I, nothing!

Keep me acquainted with all that concerns you. Remember me affectionately to Madame Nourrit, and always remain my good friend.

Cordially yours,   F. Liszt

---

[18] Liszt did indeed visit that great city, but not for another nine years.

77. To Anna Liszt in Paris [Genoa or Lugano, late July or early August] ^{G (F)}

Dear Mother,

Send to me poste restante Lugano (Switzerland, Ticino canton), from my library:

Plutarch: *Lives of Celebrated Men*,

Voyage du jeune Anarchasis,

Homer's *Iliad* and *Odyssey*,

Balbi's *Geography*,

the *Mythologie pittoresque*,

and ask Mme Sand to have Edgar Quinet's book on modern Greece obtained for me.[19]

I have just spent a month in Genoa, and my health is improving more and more. When I return to Paris—which admittedly will not be for at least a year, but will then be for good—you will find me physically and morally to your liking. My handwriting alone is not improving, but rather becoming ever more illegible. On the other hand my music is easier to read, having become more song-like and intelligible.

Write me a nice letter. Tell Massart that I have written him an open letter in the *Gazette musicale*, and that he will receive it shortly.

If you want to have a splendid trip, visit me in Lugano, where I shall remain until the end of August. I don't know why it is, but I cannot tear myself away from Switzerland. More than anything I love the mountains; only amidst the mountains does my work prosper.

Mme d'A. is quite restored to health and will write to you before long. Farewell, dear Mother, continue to be fond of me and don't lose courage. 'Ende gut, alles gut und's Ende wird schon gut werden [All's well that ends well, and the end is going to be all right].' Just keep calm.

Wholly yours, even if at a distance.

78. To Adolphe Pictet. Florence, 8 November. You are a wicked man (which is not in the least incompatible with your being the most profound philosopher, the most learned philologist, the most transcendent critic, and inventor of rockets à la Congreve, and Major Federal!).

---

[19] He was at this time hoping to visit Athens, and the books requested were presumably part of his preparatory reading. The second book on the list is Jean-Jacques Barthélemy's very successful *Voyage du jeune Anarchasis en Grèce, vers le milieu du quatrième siècle avant l'ère chrétienne* (4 vols., 1787), in which the author, in relating the imaginary travels in Greece of his young Scythian hero, intended to share with his readers some of his wide-ranging knowledge of the civilization of the ancient Greeks; the 'Geography' is the *Abrégé de Géographie* (Paris, 1833) of the Italian geographer Adriano Balbi; the final item is Quinet's *De la Grèce moderne et de ses rapports avec l'Antiquité* (Paris, 1830).

Yes, dear Universal, you are a wicked man for not coming to see us in Lugano. On the off-chance, and I hoped it would be favourable to us, I had had three rooms prepared for you, plus kitchen and cellar. At the *Caffè bains* there was an ample supply of fugues, canons, gigues, sarabands, etc., on and beneath the piano. Pistol shooting and bathing in the lake were arranged for you.

The sarabands and gigues have taken advantage of this last activity, in the Major's absence. They are still swimming as I write. Perhaps they will arrive at Malagny one of these mornings—by some fanciful link between Lake Lugano and Lake Geneva!

My plans for Turkey are postponed until next spring. Instead of embarking at Trieste, we shall do so at Naples. By then the *Voyage à Chamounix* will be translated into Greek and Turkish, which will naturally oblige you to come to Athens and Constantinople with us.

Talking of the *Voyage à Chamounix*, didn't you ask me to use my wholly minimal influence to have it *puffed* in a few newspapers? Tell me what has been done in this regard since I heard from you, so that it won't be done twice over. I shall give myself the pleasure of writing to Ernest Legouvé, Fortoul, Coste (editor of *Temps*), Viardot, and Guéroult. I can't tell you exactly what news-papers these gentlemen are working for at present, but I am convinced that they will certainly bring some goodwill to it and that you will have nothing to complain of. It would only be necessary for them to be sent a copy of the work so that they can give an account of it. If I were in Paris, that would be done quickly. And so there may be a slight delay, but that really doesn't mat-ter very much. Let me know definitely if you wish me to write to them, or if you prefer to send them a couple of lines direct. In the first case, you have only to have five copies of *Voyage à Chamounix* delivered to my mother, rue de Provence 43.

Now, if you are the least bit curious to know what I have been up to, I shall tell you that I was one of the gapers who attended the coronation in Milan, and that if you have bothered to glance at the official programme you know as much about it as I do. At the end of September, His Highness the Duke of Modena having done me the honour of inviting me to his palace of Cattaio, I spent three or four days there while Their Imperial and Royal Majesties[20] were paying a short visit. From there I was asked to dinner by another, rather less ceremonious, Majesty, Rossini, who is at a loss what to do other than stroll up and down the dreary streets of Bologna.

Before arriving here we rather impertinently went to conjure up the genius of Dante and of Byron (incidentally, I am in the grip of an unbelievable passion

---

[20] Among them the ex-Empress Marie Louise, widow of Napoleon and now ruler of the Duchy of Parma.

for the latter) in the famous pinewood on the beach near Ravenna.[21] I know nothing so desolate, so profoundly melancholy, as that landscape. Now we are in Florence, which you know, I believe. There are such prodigious numbers of visitors here that the hotels can no longer cope. Travellers are sometimes compelled to sleep in their post-chaises, which they doubtless find rather weird.

George has gone to the Balearic Isles, or so I hear from Paris. Have you direct news of her?

Farewell, my most excellent friend. Give us a sign of life as soon as you can; and, above all, continue to be my good, agreeable friend—for your friendship, as you know, means a great deal to me.

Cordially yours,   F. Liszt

Address: Florence, at Ricordi's.—We shall stay for another three weeks.

79. To Adolphe Nourrit. Florence, 28 November. I don't know, my dear Adolphe, if you received the few lines I wrote to you from Genoa around mid-July. Many troubles and anxieties have come your way since then; but finally the time to *rejoice* has arrived—for you and for all of us who love you. Mlle Ungher told me this evening that your début was splendid. It's just what was needed; and you know that I, for my part, never doubted it. Poor friend! I can see you from here, still wholly shaken, wholly overwhelmed by that evening. You have retained so much of your youthfulness, so much freshness of imagination and of heart! Suffering grips you on so many sides! But you are now just a little bit joyous, just a little bit happy, aren't you? Tell me that, my excellent friend, before I come and shake your hand. Write me a few words, if you have the time; I shall really appreciate them. In Milan, Vienna, and Florence I did nothing but talk of you. But I am rather sad not to have news of you more directly.

Has Pixis written to you about *Robert le Diable*?[22] I doubt if that will suit you. Besides, your Naples engagement won't release you for a long time.

I shall be giving myself a really splendid holiday by spending some time with you this spring. I shall arrive about the end of March, and will probably take up my abode in Sorrento or Castellemare for the whole summer, so that I can arduously prepare myself for the vast journeys I shall be undertaking at the beginning of winter (Germany, England, Russia, and even Constantinople). Tell me

---

[21] See Dante, *Purgatorio*, XXVIII. 16–21, and Byron, *Don Juan*, IV. 105.
[22] Apparently Pixis wanted his daughter to appear in *Robert*, with Nourrit, in Milan.

a little about what you plan to do this coming summer, if you will be singing at San Carlo, etc., etc.

I shall be staying in Florence until 10 December. About the 25th I shall be in Rome.

So see you soon, my dear Adolphe. Always remain my good friend, and never doubt that I am yours.   Affectionately,   F. Liszt

1839

New Year's Day. Liszt returns to Florence.

15 January. Brought by her nurse, Blandine Liszt joins her parents.

Late January/early February. Via Pisa, they travel to Rome.

8 March. Giving a *monologue pianistique*—a concert without the participation of other performers—in the Russian Ambassador's rooms at the Palazzo Poli, Liszt inaugurates the modern solo concert.

9 May. Daniel Henricus Franciscus Joseph Liszt is born in Rome.

11 June. Liszt and Marie visit Tivoli with Sainte-Beuve.

26 June. Liszt, Marie and Blandine take up residence in the Villa Massimiliana, near Lucca.

September/early October. They stay at San Rossore, near Pisa.

19 October. Taking Blandine with her, and collecting Cosima *en route*, Marie leaves for Paris. Liszt sets out for Vienna, where the enormously successful concerts he gives between 19 November and 14 December inaugurate his career as a touring virtuoso.

WORKS. *Les Aquilons* (Autran) (S80/2), for male voices and piano/orchestra. The song *Angiolin dal biondo crin* (Bocella) (S269/1). PIANO: *Etudes d'exécution transcendante d'après Paganini* (S140, 1838–9); *Valse mélancolique* (S210); *Fantaisie sur des motifs favoris de l'opéra La sonnambula* (Bellini) (S393). Arrangements of *Mélodies hongroises* (Schubert) (S425, 1838–9);[1] *Adelaïde* (Beethoven) (S466); *Schwanengesang* (Schubert) (S560, 1838–9): 1. *Die Stadt* 2. *Das Fischermädchen* 3. *Aufenthalt* 4. *Am Meer* 5. *Abschied* 6. *In der Ferne* 7. *Ständchen* ('Leise flehen') 8. *Ihr Bild* 9. *Frühlingssehnsucht* 10. *Liebesbotschaft* 11. *Der Atlas* 12. *Der Doppelgänger* 13. *Die Taubenpost* 14. *Kriegers Ahnung*; *Die Winterreise* (Schubert) (S561): 1. *Gute Nacht* 2. *Die Nebensonnen* 3. *Mut* 4. *Die Post* 5. *Erstarrung* 6. *Wasserflut* 7. *Der Lindenbaum* 8. *Der Leiermann* 9. *Täuschung* 10. *Das Wirtshaus* 11. *Der stürmische Morgen* 12. *Im Dorfe*. PIANO AND ORCHESTRA: Concerto No. 2 in A (1st version) (S125).

WRITINGS. 'Lettres d'un bachelier' in the *RGM* of 13 January (on the *Perseus* of Benvenuto Cellini), 28 March (to M. Schlesinger, on the State of Music in Italy), 14 April (to d'Ortigue, on Raphael's *Saint Cecilia*), 24 October (to Hector Berlioz, on San Rossore and Rome). In *L'Artiste*: 'Venice' (in five instalments, 16 June to 11 August); 'Genoa and Florence' (3 November).

---

[1] Based on the *Divertissement à la hongroise*.

80. To Anna Liszt in Paris. Florence, 8 January ^{G (F)}

Dear Mother,

Once again I write with a request. Bartolini, one of the finest sculptors in Europe, whose busts in particular are quite unparalleled, has just finished a magnificent bust of me. Like me, he wants it to be included in this year's Exhibition, and to the same end also wants to send to Paris the busts he has done of Mme Thiers and Marshal Masson. Please be so kind, dear Mother, as to ask either Schoelcher, or Mercier or Massart, but best of all a sculptor, to have my bust taken on arrival to the Exhibition and to attend to all the formalities connected with it. There won't be any difficulties for, if I am not completely mistaken, this bust will be the outstanding one in the Exhibition. And so do see to it that we don't miss being admitted in good time.—

One of these days I shall write to Mortier. The letter he sent me in October reached me only the day before yesterday. The gentleman he asked to bring it to me suffered various mishaps *en route*. Actually, it's better to write to me simply by post, which is safer and quicker. Write to Rome, poste restante, where I arrive in a fortnight.

Did you know that we have sent to Geneva for the little one? We expect her any day now. At the first opportunity I shall be sending you a little brooch, which I hope you will like.

Farewell, dear Mother; continue to be good to me!

P.S. Pay Berlioz the subscription price for his Requiem.

81. To Lambert Massart in Paris. Rome, Via della Purificazione 80, 1 March. I am replying at once, my dear Massart, to your kind and friendly letter. Do keep everlastingly harping on the same string, as you put it, and do be convinced that nothing could give me more genuine pleasure.

I am extremely vexed at all the delays suffered by publication of the Princess Belgiojoso's piece. With the other publishers I stipulated the date of 15 March; there is no doubt that they will publish it very punctually. Do make sure that it will be the same in Paris and that we won't have to make further mention of this unfortunate piece, which in any case won't really be published until I play it in Paris. . . .

An important service I beg you to do me is as follows. Have printed, as well and as soon as possible, the two Beethoven symphonies (Pastoral and C minor), of which you will be receiving the German proofs. I should like them to appear at the end of next July, at the latest. In print they will come to approximately eighty pages. The German proofs (Leipzig, Breitkopf & Härtel) are extremely clear and attractive, so that there will be no difficulty for the Paris engraver. Nevertheless, choose one of the most intelligent, someone like Marguerie, for example, and fix the cost of the plate; and if you need to give him an advance, please do so. I shall reimburse you the whole sum at the earliest.

I leave this matter *totally* in your hands, convinced that you will bring it to a good and speedy conclusion, as a friend and a man of intelligence. My mother will give you the proofs at the end of the month.

Do me also the favour of dropping in on Bernard Latte and telling him about a small parcel he will receive from Ricordi one of these days. It's the *Nuits d'été au Pausilippe*. Three pieces (because I couldn't succeed in finding any more in that wretched album) after Donizetti. Ask him, on my behalf, to publish them in an album format. They are three *baubles* I have been asked for here and which are worth neither praise nor blame. I don't want to write to Bernard about so small a matter, but will send him a long letter when dispatching proofs of the *Album d'un voyageur II*, for I regard this latter work as an important one. The German edition will be ready very shortly, and I want Bernard to publish it next autumn, after my return to Paris has to some extent been prepared.

The twelve *études*, the six after Paganini, the twenty-five (*études mélodiques*) after Schubert, the Beethoven symphonies, the *Soirées italiennes* and the *Album d'un voyageur*—all these things (and a few other trifles) must be brought out this year. Next year, I shall bring you a new harvest.... You will see that I have not entirely wasted my time.

Rome suits me, above all the Rome which is no more, for I have no liking for the new one. The Campo Vaccino,[2] the Forum, the Colosseum, the Baths of Caracalla, the Palatine ruins, these are my favourite walks. Nothing can give one any idea of the feeling that comes over one in the presence of these remains; I am thoroughly imbued with it, but doubt if I shall ever venture to attempt to express it.

As regards St Peter's, I go there very rarely; with those innumerable works of his, Bernini desecrated and defiled it. Apart from the two lions, Canova's tomb[3] is detestably mediocre. His, incidentally, is very much a usurped reputation. I'll gladly say the same of Thorwaldsen, who has also done a papal tomb in St Peter's: the whole thing very cold and stiff.

Michelangelo's *Moses* (at San Pietro in Vincoli), on the other hand, I found sublime. Sculptors reproach him with many things, but the impression he creates is simply prodigious.

---

[2] Wrongly transcribed as 'Vanino' in J. Vier's edition of this letter.
[3] That sculptor's tomb of Clement XIII, completed in 1792.

I see M. Ingres fairly often, and he is very kind to me. We feel compelled to make music together. Did you know that he plays the violin very nicely? We plan to go through the whole of Mozart and Beethoven. . . .

In Rome I have also run into Spontini, Cramer, and Pixis again. The two first-named will be giving you news of me very shortly. Cramer plans to settle in Paris. He's an utter scoundrel who had only a rather mediocre opinion of me until now, and who, at the present moment, is awaiting only a very small opportunity (which he won't lack, I hope) to spit the grossest flatteries into my face. That, moreover, is the attitude of a rather large category of people towards me. We'll see it in Paris, in '40; it will probably be amusing.

I am delighted with d'Ortigue's letter. Now *there* is someone loyal and affectionate. I love and esteem him (and you know that I wouldn't easily say as much of many people). His friendship is precious and valuable to me, and that is also why I want it to be total and unrestricted, for I feel worthy of it. I grieved him quite inadvertently; a glass of champagne less and there would never have been the slightest disagreement between us. He in his turn distressed me a little, but deep down I am convinced that all that is nothing. I rely on him and he can rely on me. Remember me most warmly to him. I am going to attend indirectly to his books. Tell me how many he wants me to send him, for it will be a very big parcel.

Do you see Charles Gay[4] from time to time? Someone else I am very fond of! If you knew what excellent letters he writes me!

Don't take too much trouble over the *Lettre d'un bachelier*.[5] In my opinion it is not the least bit suitable for the *Journal des Débats*, but just the thing for *L'Artiste*. I have a better opinion than you have of the helpfulness of Jules Janin, who for no particular reason has always been very kind to me.

You give me most excellent advice, my good Massart, with regard to my correspondence; but apart from the fact that I should find it more or less impossible to write letters of *friendly self-interest*, I don't believe it would be suitable for me to solicit—directly or indirectly—articles of any kind whatsoever.

I have written to d'Ortigue because I regard him as a friend. That is not the case with several persons to whom you would perhaps like me to make more definite overtures (I shan't name them, but you know whom I mean). These good people have never been more than three-quarters good to me, and it would not be right for me to do for them what I do for my friends. We shall always

---

[4] Wrongly transcribed by Vier as 'Say'. Making Liszt's acquaintance in Milan the previous year, Charles Gay had been impressed by 'the most inexhaustible mind that can be imagined'. 'I find it difficult to understand how, without early studies, and having acquired the most admirable talent in a speciality generally very exclusive, he knows all the things he does and is a stranger to none of the ideas which are current in the world' (Bellaigue, 'Un Evêque Musicien', 398).

[5] On Venice.

get on well together, invite one another to dinner, and to smoke a pipe in one another's homes. If need be, I could also ask them to do me a small service—but that's as far as it would go. I need real, loyal friends who, when the occasion arises, have the courage, as you have had, to look people straight in the face and tell them that I am incapable of behaving shabbily. You are one of them, Gay is another, Berlioz and d'Ortigue a third and a fourth. So I have written to you, and, with God's help and given the opportunity, I shall be able to reveal my devotion and gratitude to you ever more clearly.

Farewell, my good Massart, a thousand affectionate regards to Madame Kreutzer and a good and loyal handshake to Léon.   Ever yours,   F. Liszt

82. To Adolphe Nourrit in Naples. Rome, 5 March

My dear Nourrit,

Your letter of 15 December reached me on 20 February. Assuredly, not the least of the annoyances attached to the nomadic life are these continual postal delays.

Before you wrote me those latest kind lines, for which I thank you heartily, I knew in full and thorough detail of your successes in Naples, either from the newspapers or from the numerous travellers from Naples that I met in the Florentine salons and elsewhere. Since then, a lot of people I had asked to do so must have given you friendly greetings from me. I hope you haven't been too bored by them.

At the home of M. Ingres the other evening I was told that one of the Academy's boarders, whose name escapes me, had heard from you that you would be coming to Rome in Holy Week. Do try to keep your promise. For me it will be a very great pleasure to see you again, and here, and with a *little continuity*!—for to date we have met rather more by chance than really known and associated with one another. For my part, I admit that I rejoice in advance at this opportunity, now so near, for us to see one another, and—forgive me this expression—to *touch* and become more thoroughly *imbued* with one another. And what more beautiful occasion than that of Holy Week in Rome? How sweet and solemn we shall find it, to talk of the *future* amid the so stately ruins of ancient Rome! What religious emotions we shall share at the sight of so much vanished greatness!

Come then, my excellent friend. Quit the din and bustle of the theatre for a few days; leave behind you your argand lamps and your boards, to spend an evening strolling along the Via Sacra by the light of the stars.

Have you read d'Ortigue's pamphlet about Berlioz's opera? It is said to be a vigorous protest against the intrigues of the rue Lepelletier,[6] which you know better than anyone!

Talking of protests, you have doubtless already seen Spontini, who has made one of his own—against the *abomination of desolation*[7] *which has entered the temple*, as the excellent Choron used to say. He has presented the Pope with a splendid memorandum for the reform of church music. As you know, in the majority of churches in Rome and the Papal States, at present, it is cabalettas by Donizetti and Bellini which pay for the solemn ceremonies of Catholicism. Spontini has written some very good things in his dissertation. The Pope has bestowed on him the Order of Saint Gregory—and that is as far as the reforms will get!...

I believe I shan't be coming to Naples before next autumn. Rome charms and chains me.

See you soon, then; I hope so, at least. Please present my most respectful compliments to Madame Nourrit; and if any of your daughters still remembers the *gentleman with the long hair*, kiss her hand from me.

[Henri] Lehmann,* whom I found here, and whom I see every day, asks me to remember him to you. He is a delightful fellow and will, I believe, be a great artist. He works enormously hard, and his latest pictures bear witness to a most remarkable progress. Moreover, I have become very fond of him.

So farewell, dear Nourrit. Affectionately yours,   F. Liszt[8]

83. To Adolphe Pictet in Geneva. [Rome, April]. . . . I am truly vexed by this lack of publicity for your delightful *Conte*. There will be every reason, I think, to return to this topic when we get back. I fear you have made a bad choice of publisher, and I don't know if you are aware of this little detail: for any book which ought to be mentioned in most newspapers (and the main ones), a preliminary formality is required—that of appearing among the *paid advertisements*. If this precaution is not observed, the newspapers accept almost no article relating to new books. You will easily be able to persuade yourself of this by inspecting the newspapers: the *feuilleton* always follows the paid advertisement. I regret that you couldn't tell me earlier of your publishing arrangements; I should probably have been able to be of some use to you. Had I been in Paris when the *Conte* was published, things would not have happened thus.

At present, there is nothing to do but keep silent, perhaps republishing the *Conte* later, 2nd edition (imaginary, of course), and supporting it with some piquant novelty. . . .

George Dudevant *Kamaroupi* has left us without news since the beginning of the Chopin era (about 9 months). She is definitely at Marseilles with Chopin, whose health by no means improved on the Balearic Isles. Doctor Piffoëls's latest productions (*Aldini*, *Spiridion*, and *Les Sept Cordes de la Lyre*[9]) have left a painful impression on me. *Lélia* and the *Lettres d'un voyageur* are assuredly other kettles of fish; evidently weariness, exhaustion, and decline have set in since then. But let's wait further; and since we have been her friends, let us say these things only *quietly* and *between ourselves*.

Mallefille has justified our friendly expectations of Lake Geneva. He is an excellent and decent lad; unfortunately he is not poet enough to be able to dispense with common sense! . . .

Marie told you, I believe, that I had conceived a beautiful and lasting passion for Lord Byron. But now I am experiencing another enthusiasm. Guess for whom? For Johann Sebastian Bach. Do you know his *Passion*[10] at all well? What a masterpiece, my friend! It is truly prodigious. I recommend to you above all the opening Chorus—the exposition; the way the two Choruses and the Chorale are done is admirable. When we see one another again, I shall get you to touch and absorb these marvels. The 6 *Fugues with pedal* are magnificent too. If you don't possess them, I shall send them to you.

Have you made the acquaintance of Mickiewicz*, who is in Lausanne? When you see him, please give him my respectful and affectionate regards.

I shan't tell you anything about Rome. Marie will do it infinitely better than I. In about a fortnight we shall make our excursions to Albano, Frascati, etc., and then on about the 20th of next month (at the latest) we shall settle in the neighbourhood of Lucca for the whole summer. Why the deuce don't you come and spend a month there with us? Your *Cours d'Esthétique* will be finished by then, I think, and Mme Pictet and your children will be very glad to move a little. Lucca will be brilliant this year... but I give up trying to tempt you, seeing that I have so signally failed to do so up to now.

Blandine is becoming a fine girl. She has a great talent for architecture.

As for me, I have worked pretty hard, and above all composed. Willy nilly the public will have to put up with me, despite people's wish to be rid of me.

---

[9] Works dating from a year or two earlier. The full title of the first—which Mme Sand herself described as 'trash'—is *La Dernière Aldini*.

[10] The St Matthew Passion, the famous performance of which under Mendelssohn in Berlin ten years earlier had made a significant contribution to the Bach revival.

At the end of next winter I shall spend 5 or 6 weeks in Paris. From there I shall go to England, to try my luck as a capitalist. Journeys to Russia and Germany will come soon after.

Then, we shall see! . . .

Adieu, my excellent friend. Write to us soon and do believe in my keen and sincere affection.

Yours in all friendship.   F. Liszt

A thousand respectful and affectionate greetings to Mme Pictet.

Send your letters poste restante Florence, unless you have to write to us at once; in this case send to Rome. We won't leave before the 1st of June.

84. To Princess Belgiojoso in Paris. Albano, 4 June. It would be vanity on my part, Princess, to complain of your silence. For me, your letters have always been a favour, a charm. That is not to say that I have the least right to them. However, since you no longer reply to me, I hope you will at least allow me to tell you how much I appreciate the very slightest tokens of your goodwill, and how much I value any indication that you remember me.

Some issues of the *Gazette* or *Revue musicale*, which came into my hands by chance in the home of one of my Russian friends (for in this blessed motherland of the arts, and of music in particular, no one, as you can well imagine, is silly enough to spend 30 francs subscribing to the *Revue musicale*), informed me that you had positively erected altar upon altar and made your charming salon resound with magnificent music. In that, I admit, lies perhaps my one regret of the winter. I should so much have wished to be there, to admire you, to applaud you. Several people who had the good fortune to attend those so select soirées have given me a rapturous account of them.

What a contrast to the tiresome *musical soliloquies* (I know not what other name to give to this invention of mine) which I have devised specially for the Romans, and which I am quite capable of importing to Paris, so boundlessly impudent do I become! Imagine that, failing to concoct a programme which would have any kind of sense, I dared, for the sake of peace and quiet, to give a series of concerts entirely alone, affecting the style of Louis XIV and saying cavalierly to the public, 'Le Concert—c'est moi.' For the curiosity of the thing, here is the programme of one of these soliloquies.

1. Overture to *William Tell*, performed by M. L.
2. *Réminiscences des Puritains*. Fantasy composed and performed by the above-mentioned!

3. Etudes and fragments, by the same to the same!

4. Improvisations on given themes—still by the same.

And that's all; neither more nor less, except for lively conversation during the intervals, and enthusiasm, if appropriate!

A propos of enthusiasm, I ought at least to talk to you of St Peter's. That is *de rigueur* when one writes from Rome. But in the first place I am writing to you from Albano, from where I can make out only the dome; and, secondly, this poor St Peter's has been so dressed up, so embellished by garlands of papier mâché, of wretched curtains for the alcoves, etc., etc., all in honour of the 5 or 6 latest saints His Holiness has just canonized, that I am doing my utmost to dismiss it from my memory. Luckily there have been no miracle workers to glorify at the Colosseum or Campo Vaccino, otherwise living in Rome would have been quite impossible.

All being well, I still expect to spend the end of next winter (March and April) in Paris. Will you permit me to come to the rue d'Anjou at that time to fill up all the gaps in my correspondence? As ever, I count on your friendly and in-dulgent kindness. But will you extend this to the point of giving me a sign of life before the end of my sojourn in Italy? I don't know. In any case, letters addressed poste restante Florence will reach me up to 1 September next.

Please accept, Madame la Princesse, the expression of my sentiments of pro-found respect and devotion.

F. Liszt

Would you be so kind as to remember me affectionately to Madame your sister[11] and to M. d'Aragon.

85. To Robert Schumann in Leipzig. Albano, 5 June

My dear Herr Schumann,

At the risk of seeming very monotonous, I shall tell you once again that the latest pieces you have been so kind as to send to Rome for me I find admirable both in inspiration and craftsmanship. The Fantasy dedicated to me[12] is a work of the highest class, and I am really proud of the honour you do me in linking my name with so imposing a composition. And so I intend to study it and absorb it thoroughly, to draw all possible effect from it.

As to your *Kinderscenen*, I owe them one of the greatest pleasures of my life. You know, or you don't know, that I have a little 3-year-old daughter whom

---

[11] The Princess's half-sister, Teresa Visconti, wife of the Comte d'Aragon, had been a pupil of Liszt's in Paris.

[12] Schumann's Fantasy in C, Op. 17.

everyone agrees in finding *angelic* (what a commonplace!). Her name is Blandine-Rachel, and her nickname *Moucheron* ['gnat' or 'midge']. It goes without saying that she has a peaches-and-cream complexion and that her fair golden hair reaches to her heels just like a savage. She is, moreover, the most silent, most sweetly serious, most philosophically gay child in the world. I have every reason to hope, too, that she will not be a musician, from which may Heaven preserve her!

Well, my dear Herr Schumann, two or three times a week (on fine and good days!) I play your *Kinderscenen* to her during the course of the evening; this enchants her, and me still more, as you can imagine, so that I often play the first repeat 20 times over without going any further. I really think you would be pleased with this success, could you be a witness to it!

I believe that in one of my previous letters I have already expressed my wish to see you write some chamber pieces, trios, quintets, or septets. Will you forgive me for further insisting on this point? It seems to me that you would be more capable of doing so than anyone nowadays. And I am convinced that they would not fail to achieve success, even a *commercial success*.

If between now and next winter you could complete some chamber piece, it would give me real pleasure to make it known in Paris, where such compositions, when well performed, have a greater chance of success than you perhaps think. I should even willingly undertake to find a publisher for your manuscript, if you wished, which, moreover, would by no means prevent you from disposing of it *for Germany*.

In the mean time I plan to play your *Carnaval* in public, plus some of the *Davidsbündlertänze* and *Kinderscenen*. The *Kreisleriana* and the Fantasy dedicated to me are more difficult for the public to digest, and I shall reserve them for later.

Thus far, the only works of yours that I know are the following:

Impromptu on a theme of Clara Wieck;
Pianoforte Sonata, dedicated to Clara;
Concerto without Orchestra;
Etudes symphoniques; *Davidsbündlertänze*; *Kreisleriana*;
Carnaval; *Kinderscenen*; and my Fantasy.

If you would be so kind as to complete your works for me, it would give me great pleasure; I should like to have them bound together in 3 or 4 volumes. Haslinger for his part will send you my Etudes and my other publications as they appear.

What you tell me of your private life has greatly interested and touched me. If I could—I don't know how—be the least bit helpful or useful to you in these circumstances, regard me as wholly at your service. Come what may, count on my total discretion and my sincere devotion. *If it is not asking you too much*, tell me if it is of *Clara* that you speak. But should this question seem *out of place*, ignore it.

Have you encountered in Leipzig Herr Frank [Franck], the current editor of the Leipzig *Allgemeine Zeitung*? From the little I know of him (for he has been on much closer terms with Chopin and Hiller than with me), I believe him to be capable of understanding you. In Rome, people were quite charmed by him. If you see him, give him my most affectionate regards.

My plans are still the same: I intend to be in Vienna at the beginning of December and in Paris at the end of February. I shall be capable of coming to Leipzig to look you up if you allow me to do the journey to Paris with you. Do try!

Farewell, my dear Herr Schumann. Write to me soon (*c/o Ricordi's in Florence*; I shall be in and around Lucca until mid-September), and count at all times and on all occasions on my sincere esteem and lively affection.

Yours with friendly good wishes   F. Liszt

86. To Princess Belgiojoso [San Rossore, September]. I have just been making desperate efforts to describe the forest in which I have been living for nearly a month (see the *Gazette musicale* No. ... which one, I don't yet know[13]), and so shan't tell you about it for fear of involuntarily incurring new reproaches of plagiarism. In the mean time, all you need to know (although you're probably not interested) is that its patron saint is San Rossore, that on one side it touches the Cascine of Pisa, and on the other the sea, and that it is stocked with camels, buffaloes, and deer. It is in this gracious society, which is at least worth many others, that I am living! What will be the moral, intellectual, and *artistic* (pardon this barbarism!) results, I know not. The fact remains that I feel very sad at the thought of leaving Italy in perhaps another fortnight.

Were it not for the need of hearing a little music suited to my mind and my heart, I would certainly have spent next winter in Naples, which I do not know. But I have now been telling myself for at least six years that my musical career will have to begin in the year '40: and here is the year '40 fast approaching! Treat that as childish or however you like, it doesn't make it any less true that in hurling myself recklessly, as I am going to, into public life, I am yielding to a kind of superstitious impulse. Besides, it is more than time for me to think

---

[13] The 'Lettre d'un bachelier' published in the *RGM* of 24 Oct. 1839.

of *real things*—dreaminess, passion, and follies have taken up only too much of my life. Some sort of activity (basically mean and wretched though it be) will always do me some good. And then, my purse is empty. A trip to Germany and England will fill it again. And so, amen!

I don't know how I dared intercede for Puzzi with you, while I myself had such great need of intercession! Pondering over our past relations, I have discovered in myself so many faults and failings (of form, at least) that I am really infinitely grateful to you for not having entirely despaired of me. Do you still remember that unfortunate dinner to which I didn't turn up, when you had had the kindness to invite, in my honour and expressly for me, Meyerbeer, Chopin, Herz, and others?

Do you remember, too, my ridiculous exclusion of Mme J.[14] and that ill-starred box at the Opéra? Truly, the more I think of all these details (which are coming back to me three years later without rhyme or reason), the more they amaze me. What a temperamental and incorrigible boor I was at that time! And how right the illustrious historian of the French Revolution (M. Mignet) was to say of me: *There is a great deal of confusion in the head of that young man!*[15]

Happily, you have consented to forgive and forget (*tout comprendre, c'est tout pardonner*—M. Sue's motto) and to take into consideration only the sincere and delicate devotion you have always inspired in me from the very first days onwards...

If you are good enough to write to me within the next fortnight, do so to Trieste, poste restante. I shall be spending the last ten days or so of October there, and then going to Vienna. I am very curious to hear Mendelssohn's *St Paul*, to be performed there at the beginning of November, and will tell you about it in my next letter.

Farewell, believe in my sincere devotion and keep me a little of your kind friendship.   F.L.

In October, after Marie's departure for Paris, Liszt set out on his journey to Vienna, stopping *en route* in Venice and Trieste.

87. To Marie d'Agoult. Hôtel de l'Europe, Venice, Friday, 25 October.

It is here, Marie, that I bid you a full Farewell. Henceforth I shall find you only in my heart and in my thoughts. But here, too, all things, the sea and the sky, St Mark's and the gondolas, speak to me of you and repeat your beloved name.

---

[14] Probably Cristina's friend Caroline Jaubert.
[15] The words uttered by Mignet apparently in connection with the young Liszt's impetuous demand: 'Teach me, Monsieur, I beg of you, the whole of French literature!'

It was here that we first came together, that we parted from one another and found one another again! It was here that you were dying, and here too that you came back to life!

Oh! Venice, Venice! Into what mood of deep enchanted reverie do I fall at the sight of your lagoons...

You know how childlike I can be, what importance I attach to feast-days... First thing in the morning of 22 October I said to myself: 'Today is not the day that I want to celebrate my twenty-eighth birthday; that will be the day after tomorrow in Venice...'

So at about midday yesterday, joyously and in good heart, I left Padua, alone in my *calessino*. The banks of the Brenta seemed much more charming than I had expected. The very large number of villas and palazzini which continue as far as Fusina, and to which we didn't pay enough attention, makes this whole region singularly pleasing. The architecture of several of them you would certainly like very much.

I read Montesquieu and Lamartine as we went along, but, unusually with me, my own ideas and feelings provided more agreeable company... In my mind I went over the days gone by, and from my eyes flowed tears of benediction.

At 9.30 I reached Fusina. Being alone, instead of coming on that abominable mailboat which you and I took, I hired a very light gondola, from which I had the *felze* removed. The sun was sinking and I fell into a long reverie. Then, all of a sudden, I looked round. Oh! why weren't you there to see that magnificent sunset behind the Paduan hills! It was sublime, sublime. . . .

At the Hôtel de l'Europe, Rodolphe came to meet me. I asked him for the room that you occupied, but unfortunately he couldn't give it me as they are putting down carpets in it. But the room I have been given is directly below, on the mezzanine floor. It has the same air, the same view (two windows) and, I believe, the very carpets and furniture that were in your room.

The servants call me Signor Conte [Count].

I immediately hastened to the Piazza San Marco. . . .

I hurriedly swallowed two cutlets and a cup of excellent coffee (at about 6 o'clock). But the birthday celebrations, the real celebrations, began only in the evening. Think of something superior to so much emotion and so many wonders. You can't. Well, it is nevertheless extremely simple. Going back to my room, I turned my trunk upside down. Right at the bottom I found your diary, which I hadn't wanted to open before then, having reserved it for my birthday celebrations in Venice. I reread the whole of our stay in Venice, then those in Florence and Rome...

I was about to write to you when someone knocked on my door. It was Fana, whose cousin, who had seen me pass by, had told of my arrival. . . . On leaving Fana, who made me have another excellent coffee, I hired a gondolier for a trip along the Grand Canal. Neither of us said anything until we came to the Palazzo Foscari, which he pointed out to me.

'The Emperor came here to see the celebrations—and here (at the Palazzo Mocenigo) lived Lord Byron.' (He pronounced it the English way.)

'What?—Lord Byron?'—'Si Signore.'—'Did you know him?'—'Si Signore. L'ho servito cinque giorni, perché uno dei suoi battellieri era ammalato [I served him for five days, because one of his boatmen was ill].'

Thereupon he gave me several details about Lord Byron, Signora Guiccioli, and la Teresa, who is still in Dolo where she runs a *botteghino dove si prende caffè e liquori* [little wine bar where one can have coffee and liqueurs].

The gondolier told me, too, that he had made a copy of a couple of pieces by Lord Byron while Milord was riding on the Lido. He recited them to me. The first was a hymn of praise to Italy; the second a satire and curse on the same country. I listened without understanding too well what he was saying. Thinking that I had a 'man of letters' before me, I asked him to sing me something from Tasso, which in a raucous and broken voice he did. The melody is very much like the one I wrote down.

At past 10 o'clock I went home to bed. Before going to sleep I reread a few pages of your journal, promising myself to write to you at length the next day. The boat doesn't leave until ten in the evening.

Later. At 8.45 Fana fetched me to go and have breakfast at Florian's. Venice is a perpetual delight to me. It is you, you sorceress, who are doing that. After breakfast we walked along the Riva degli Schiavoni as far as the public garden. . . . When we went our separate ways I went into St Mark's and climbed the Giants' Stairway, then went by gondola to visit Byron's house. Thence, to the Rialto. There I committed a minor extravagance, spending 45 zwanziger on a superb *marinara*.

At midday *chez* Fana, to whom I played my new pieces. He was taken aback by the Dantesque fragment. At 2.00 I returned here to write to you. At 4.00, *table d'hôte*; at 5.00, alone at the Emperor of Austria café. Smoked.

I noticed in the *Allgemeine* an announcement of a work which must be interesting: *Rafael*, a biography by Passavant,[16] two volumes. . . .

Farewell, dear Marie, I shall find your news at Trieste. . . .

Adieu, a long kiss on your beautiful brow.

---

[16] J. D. Passavant's *Rafael von Urbino u. sein Vater G. Santi* (3 vols., 1839–58).

88. To Marie d'Agoult. [Trieste] **Saturday evening, 9 November.** I have not written for five days, having done nothing worth mentioning.

I always see the same people: Alberti, Likl, Nicolai, Jaëll, and a few others. I have made myself a reputation here as mistress of the house. . . . Would you believe that, to the great satisfaction of the assembled company, I made tea—at Nicolai's and twice at Likl's. I tried to the best of my ability to imitate you. . . .

But I must tell you about my concert of last Tuesday. And first of all I want to tell you what the takings came to (all expenses paid, they are still rather considerable): 2,200 zwanziger! That's something unheard of in Trieste. Even Paganini didn't do so well. My success was entirely in keeping, and I was recalled more than twenty times during the evening. You have never been present at such a *trionfo* (as the local journalists put it). . . . I played the *Frequenti palpiti*, the Andante from *Lucia*, the *Galop*, and finally the *Hexameron*. Then, as the audience did not cease to applaud and call me back, I played the Polonaise from *I Puritani* as an encore.

In short, I played really well, rather as I did at the theatre in Venice, with extreme delicacy. Mariani and la Ungher completed the programme with an aria, two canzonette from Rossini's *Soirées* and the quartet from the *Puritani*.

An all but ludicrous incident nearly compromised the success of the evening. Shortly before the entry of the theme from *I Puritani*, a string broke. The tuner immediately came on to extract it, but without managing to do so. As the string was not getting in the way of anything else on the piano, I went on playing; and as the tuner likewise went on fiddling about unsuccessfully with the string, I told him two or three times to go away and leave it. This worthy tuner didn't hear me. In the end, growing impatient, I gave him a violent slap on the hand, while continuing with my piece. It, the slap, could be heard all over the hall. A few malicious people tried to stop the applause which broke out at the end of the theme. The audience were in two minds; the tuner had returned to the wings. Aware of that, I stood up and, facing the audience, told the tuner to remove the piano I was using and to bring on another which was waiting there in reserve; and this was done in less than two minutes. That was time enough to erase the bad impression made by the slap (which the *Osservatore Triestino* called a *gesto poco garbato* [ill-mannered act]); and in the following variation I was greeted by a storm of applause. That determined attitude of mine that you know was perhaps not without some effect on the audience here, which without bothering to learn the facts often boos excessively the artistes most in favour. . . .

As for the tuner, a few people tried to applaud him when he came out later to examine the piano, but a larger number hissed. The poor devil really spent a bad quarter of an hour. I plan to send him a 20 franc piece for his evening. . . .

As Mendelssohn is not coming to Vienna, I am infinitely less eager to hear his *St Paul,* which anyway I shall hear very easily in England. . . .

Will you believe me if I tell you that life weighs on me and is dreadfully tedious without you! I find you so beautiful, so pale, so adorably loving. I kiss your brow with sadness and with love.

For me, Trieste is a lazaretto. I am living here as though in quarantine. The sea is there in front of me, but I find it stupid and lifeless. Oh, our glorious sunsets at San Rossore! Here, nothing like them, just a few merchant vessels, steamers, and some semi-English fog. Also, I often dream of London! For in London I shall be able to see you again. You will come, won't you?

The town is very clean, paved with large flagstones, and many new buildings. In short, it doesn't look unpleasant. . . . Society here is zero, absolutely zero. *Non ragioniam di lor.*[17]

People smoke tremendously in the cafés and casinos. . . . Adieu...

89. To Marie d'Agoult. Vienna, 9.00 p.m., 15 November

Dear Marie,

On arriving in Vienna I found a letter from you; it was the only thing I wanted to find here.

My journey was pretty tiring. I thought back to the time when I made roughly the same trip while you stayed in Venice. Then, all those mountains were bearing down on me, oppressing me. Now... I found it almost a joy to make progress, and still more progress. . . .

No indeed, darling, I shall not shorten this journal. If you find the least pleasure in it that's enough to give me profound joy in going into the most minute details. For physical reasons I couldn't write to you during the journey. The mail-coach stops only for the time needed for lunch and dinner. Moreover, the road offers little of interest. I went through Laibach, Marburg, and Graz. The Mur valley as one leaves Graz is delightful. It has some analogy with certain parts of Switzerland. But the general look of Styria has something indescribably melancholy and painful about it that I didn't encounter in Switzerland. Perhaps that results from the nature of my impressions at that time, but in Switzerland everything seemed strength and plenitude, whereas here I am conscious of a distressing emptiness, a dreary impoverishment...

Alberti is still the same, very sarcastic and full of common sense and discretion. We talked music: Thalberg, Rossini with the variations you know. In

---

[17] 'Let's not talk of them' (Dante, *Inferno*, III. 51).

connection with you (for he knows you through the dedications, and la Samoyloff has also spoken to him about you), I said to him: 'Wissen Sie, dass ich nicht bloss verliebt, aber tief verwundet bin [You know, I am not merely in love, but deeply wounded]!'

Getting here from Trieste took us more than sixty hours (three nights plus two and a half days). Haslinger and Lannoy hastened to me at 8.00 in the morning. My first concert is arranged for next Tuesday. All seats are taken and, what's more, nearly 300 people have put their names down for every one of my Vienna concerts. (If you wish to have this publicity published in the *Gazette musicale*, you are free to do so: the fact is correct.)

This morning I went to see Dessauer, who has some very elegant accommodation. . . . About midday I went to Haslinger's to practise. At three o'clock he, Lannoy, Alberti, and I went by fiacre to Hietzing, where Czerny, Graf, and Saphir joined us for an excellent dinner. . . . On rising from the table Saphir and I went to the Kärntnerthor [Theatre], where a big concert was being given for the benefit of poor women who have the patronage of the Dowager Empress...

I could have wished for you to be a witness of the welcome I received. The entire hall turned towards the place where I was sitting with Saphir. A score of people even tried repeatedly to applaud, but the Empress having not yet arrived, and the purpose of the concert being to honour an institution under her immediate protection, she was accordingly to be applauded on her arrival in the hall and it would have been unseemly for me to be greeted with acclamation before her (or even after).

Nevertheless, the impression made on the audience by my humble self was enormous. I stayed only a quarter of an hour. . . .

So far as satisfied vanity is concerned, I don't believe anyone could aspire much higher in my very modest sphere.

In Pozsony and Pest really extravagant behaviour is expected.

I feel profoundly moved by this welcome, and every day am practising like a madman, so that if possible I may keep myself up to the level of this tide of enthusiasm, of which moreover a good part relates to my personality. . . .

You know already that I totally approve of your conduct with regard to Mme Sand. Continue in the same way and don't doubt that she will end by admitting that she is in the wrong.[18] If not, then—what does it matter?—she can go to Jericho.

---

[18] It was Marie d'Agoult—guilty of making spiteful remarks about George Sand in letters to a common friend—who was really at fault. Having perforce to side with his mistress against the novelist he so admired and wished to remain on friendly terms with, Liszt was nevertheless (already or later) under no illusions about which of the two women was to blame for the estrangement, as he told Mme d'Agoult candidly many years afterwards: 'Although *au fond* I regarded you as being in the wrong, I stood up for you none the less.' (See Letter 480, 29 June 1861, to the Princess Wittgenstein.)

We have explained ourselves sufficiently on this point. However, I still feel convinced that she will come back to you completely. Your personal magnetism is quite irresistible; you are a noble soul and a noble woman.

I am vexed that my mother wasn't more helpful to you. Don't bear her a grudge, and be nice to her, poor woman, for in so many respects she truly deserves it. . . .

Where should I address my letters to you? Write to me often.

Above all, don't yield an inch with George.

Our friends (Chopin, Massart, Berlioz, *et al.*) don't know me at all and can't pass judgement. Success alone can exonerate me, and it is success, too, which condemns me in their eyes. It matters little! Come what may, I shall remain worthy. Goodnight and farewell, dear and unique Marie. I shall soon write to you at greater length. Tomorrow and the day after I have to practise like a drudge. . . .

90. To Marie d'Agoult. Vienna, 7.30 a.m., Tuesday, 19 November.
The Vienna air has put me to the test again this time: the whole of yesterday and the day before I was obliged to spend almost entirely in bed. I swallowed a dozen powders, sweated profusely, and here I am back on my feet for today's concert (12.30 p.m.). I feel a bit weak this morning, but the concert will restore me, I believe.

You can't imagine my ever-growing popularity here. . . . The good Dessauer . . . fancied he would find that I had become very puffed up, quite unbearable, rather ill-mannered, etc., and was astounded to find me so unpretentious, so nice a chap, and above all so much more advanced as both pianist and composer. Frankly, I believe he was very prejudiced against me and that on several occasions he had given (always with that certain restraint that we know) a negative opinion of me. But at the present moment he has been won round completely, saying very nicely that there is something irresistibly fascinating about me, etc...

8.30 p.m. My first concert was a total success. Packed hall, plus the Dowager Empress and the Archduchess Sophie.

The audience was expecting to find its favourite again. It sensed that it was dealing with a man. Of all the pieces, it was the *Hexameron* that was the biggest hit.

As for the *Ave Maria*, I played it for you, while praying. Only the few sensed that; the others applauded. I am displaying boldly my claim to deserving more legitimate successes than the first time, both in composition and performance. I have really got the upper hand with the public, friends and enemies (for a good many would ask nothing better than to see an end to my successes!) alike. With God's help I shall come through safely.

The Pastoral Symphony was understood by only half the audience. But, as always, I maintain and uphold the artist's right to impose on the masses the best and most beautiful. The fashionable society which comes to my concerts in large numbers is wholly Italian. . . .

After the concert I dined at Dessauer's with Bauernfeld (the poet), Kriehuber, Alberti, and a few journalists. . . .

10.00 p.m. Haslinger has just come in with your letter. Profound emotion. To thank him, I embraced him. I'll reply at once to the two or three principal points.

(1) I am entirely of the opinion that the Mouches[19] be brought up at my mother's. You will of necessity control their education in all points, as also their physical and moral regime, their times of going to bed and getting up, their outings, the food they eat, etc. Mlle Delarue seems to me to be the worthiest and most suitable person to take your place during those hours in which you would not be free. When things are more advanced, I shall write her a long letter to ask her personally. In the mean time be indulgent to her; she is very warm-hearted. . . .

Don't delay in putting the Mouches with my mother, for from what you tell me that is the main point for your family; and it is right and proper to yield to them on this point.

As for the rest, no and again no. If your husband wishes to go to extremes, I shall come to Paris immediately and we shall have done with it once and for all. Come what may: I am absolutely resolved, and you yourself would be unable to change anything.

According to law you are, no doubt, his possession, body and soul, but things don't rest at that in this world. People temporize, make shift, come to an agreement, as they can when they hate one another. . . .

(2) Berryer is your legal representative just as Koreff is your doctor. He suits you completely. Don't take any other, and if you have another, change him. I can't understand how we didn't think of him sooner.

(3) Your relations with Mme Sand are moving along as well as possible. Never fail to be generous and friendly to her, and, if you see her again, may it be to some small (?) extent with the avowed intention of bringing her out of her literary tricks and nonsense. . . .

(4) Berlioz will be to me what I make him. My position in Paris must change completely. In the mean time, it matters little. Thank you for the step you got Massart to take. He is a splendid fellow. If you have an opportunity, see

---

[19] Nickname for Blandine and Cosima.

d'Ortigue too. I plan to get him to redo my biography, which will now form a complete volume and immediately be translated into German and probably into English. Give my apologies to Massart if I don't write to him very often. I am overwhelmed with people and things. . . .

(5) I wrote to you from Bologna and from Padua (have the letter claimed, poste restante, at Lyons). In my second letter from Trieste I entered into all the details you ask me for.

(6) I am delighted that you have seen Sainte-Beuve again; he is the friend I would have chosen for you. Continue to give me full details of your social life; they interest me enormously. . . .

91. To Marie d'Agoult. Vienna, 6 December. I have given my third concert, and yesterday, Thursday, my fourth.

Ever-increasing success. My new fantasies, on *Lucia* and *La Sonnambula*, make a hell of an effect. I am regularly made to repeat two pieces a concert. On Sunday, the day after tomorrow, I shall give my fifth, and at the end of the week, probably on Saturday, my sixth concert. After that I shall leave for Hungary where I shall stay for a fortnight.

I am sending you a letter from Count Festetics in response to a few lines I wrote him. You will see from it what a pitch of enthusiasm my compatriots have risen to.

But I am compelled to give myself another six days of rest, for were I not to do so the dinners and banquets in my honour would kill me... That is why I am leaving an interval between the fifth and sixth concerts here.

On my return from Pozsony and Pest I shall probably give another two concerts or else a single one in the hall of the Redoute, which should bring in at least 7 to 8,000 francs. The usual, net amount brought by my concerts thus far is 1,600 to 1,700 florins each time (a little more than 4,000 francs). Yesterday, however, because of several subscribers who didn't collect their tickets—why, isn't known—only 1,500 florins were taken, but it's a small difference.

There was also a concert at Court last week. I played the same duet from *La Sonnambula* with Bériot and then, alone, the Andante from *Lucia* with great effect.

At the end the Empress sent to ask me to play a song by Schubert. I chose the *Ave Maria*, but in the very second bar the Princess of Saxony began to cough —and went on doing so for about twenty bars; I was furious. The Princess Vasa noticed my chagrin and burst out laughing in a manner that was almost scandalous...

Farewell, dear one. At the same time as this you will receive a pile of news-papers in a wrapper, a more economical way of getting them to you. This is almost a business letter, but thus far in Vienna I have done nothing but give concerts, practise my pieces, take medicine, and keep to my room.

Kiss Mouche and Cosima for me.

To complete this letter I still have to tell you that yesterday after my concert I played, at the Concert spirituel, the Beethoven Concerto in C minor which I didn't know and learnt in twenty-four hours (improvising the cadenza) with the most unheard-of success.

So far as satisfying one's vanity is concerned, it is impossible to ask for more, in every kind of respect. The biggest bigwigs, Herr von Kolowrath, Count Sedlistky, the minister of police, Herr von Mett[ernich], *et al*... have not only received me and shown me all possible honour and attention, but it was they who first indicated their wish to see me.

As for the women, it's a universal infatuation. I don't need to tell you that I pay very little attention to it. I know absolutely no woman here whom I like even slightly, physically speaking, and you know that that is the only way I can be caught in times of distraction or excessive boredom. Princess Schwarzenberg isn't back yet. As for Baroness Toti, I go to see her only in the evenings, at a time when her husband is always there. Eskeles and I had it out so categorically that I have had little to say to the Baroness. I merely permitted myself to observe to her that her behaviour to me had been at once impertinent and tactless, and that I asked her not to begin again, seeing that if it happened a second time I should find it impossible to accept any words of reconciliation whatsoever. She seemed rather nettled by my totally correct behaviour. . . .

Eskeles has become more charming to me than ever. Knowing that I like read-ing the *Journal des Débats*, he very kindly sends me a copy every morning. Yesterday he made me a present of a hundred first-rate Spanish cigars. . . .

I reply to one point in your letter for fear of forgetting it. I am very anxious for you not to make me a subscriber to the small newspapers. They're utter tripe deserving of no consideration from me. The *Journal des Débats* and the *Revue des Deux Mondes* are a very different matter. You will do well, I believe, to take out a subscription in my name, beginning from the 1st of January. . . .

La Pleyel arrived here four days ago; she is now staying in the same hotel as I. She gives her concert tomorrow. I have heard her play at length. She has a splendid talent, unquestionably the finest pianistic talent there is.

She asked me if I remembered Chopin's room... 'Certainly, Madame, how could I forget?' etc.... Count Dietrichstein's arrival then cut our conversation short, and I left.

Yesterday and today she asked me several things relating to her concert. I was in a position to oblige her and even to do her a few small services, which of course I did.

Forgive me, dear one, for such short, dry letters. It's a very long time, five days, since I had a word from you. As I was kept in bed for seventeen days and couldn't visit anyone, the multitude of obligations to which I am now to some extent forced to submit is quite frightful. In the evenings, between ten and midnight, I am compelled to practise, for all the pieces I am playing here are new to me, and I simply cannot risk not preparing them.

Next Saturday I give my sixth concert. On Sunday I play for Saphir's benefit, and on Monday I leave for Pozsony, where I shall be done to death by celebrations, banquets, and honours of all kinds. I shall write to you about them in the greatest detail. . . .

92. To Marie d'Agoult. Pozsony, 9.00 a.m., Thursday, 19 December.

Oh! my untamed and far-off homeland! Oh! my friends! Amen!

Arrived in Pozsony at 5.00 yesterday morning. At noon today my first concert. Dinner yesterday at Count Batthyány's (leader of the current opposition in Hungary); saw Széchenyi, who was very kind to me. He has lost almost all his popularity over the matter of the Pest bridge, but is an extremely distinguished man. Grand soirée at the residence of the Governor of Fiume, M. Kiss, to which the whole of society came and where I was lionized. Although Pozsony audiences are reputed to be dreadfully unresponsive, everyone is convinced that they will be positively enthusiastic. A charming detail is that the Palatine has postponed an important sitting that was to have been held today, because a majority of the Magnates would rather attend the concert than the sitting. After the concert I shall add a couple of words to my letter, but I must first tell you about something that rather appeals to me.

It is probable that a month from now, and perhaps sooner, the Hungarian Diet will ennoble me. As it is a national matter, which I have in no wise sought, requested, or coveted, I admit that it will give me pleasure. I didn't want to mention it to you until the thing was done. But there is this little difficulty, which isn't one. If I am given letters patent of nobility, I shall need to be given arms too; and I should like you to devise them for me. Thus far Festetics has found only an owl admissible, for a lyre, harp, and scroll would be absurd; but something with an owl, and something meaningful, is still needed.

Try to think of something, and let me know immediately.

Address your next letter to Pest, c/o Count Leó Festetics. All this may quite possibly be just a nine-day wonder; however, it is very much a topic of conversation at present, and Hungary has, in this respect, special privileges. . . .

Do I need to tell you about Mme Pleyel? Why not? On arriving in Vienna she at once wrote to ask if I could go and see her or else receive her *chez moi*. I found it impossible to go out just then, and in reply sent a couple of words to say that, if it were not being too ill-mannered, I should be delighted to see her at my place at any hour of the day, seeing that the doctor had categorically forbidden me to go out. Five minutes later she was in my room. I couldn't help feeling a kind of surprise at seeing this unfortunate woman still on her feet, fresh and good-looking. She played me several things, including my Fantasy on *Les Huguenots*, admirably. I strongly advised her not to delay in being heard in public; her own opinion is quite the reverse, and she wants to wait.

We talked things over and I ended, as is my commendable habit, by being almost offensive to her, for I was firmly convinced that she had only one means of salvation: that of not worrying about me and my concerts, and of setting up openly as an artiste who neither seeks nor avoids any kind of comparison at all.

(In this connection, at St Petersburg she seems definitely to have bested Thalberg, whose third and fourth concerts were almost total flops—what a good omen for me. La Pleyel has invested 50,000 roubles in St Petersburg alone.)

When she left me her opinion was diametrically opposed to mine, and she said that she wanted to wait until I left for Pest, that the public would be grateful to her for this kind of modesty, etc... When she came back the next day she had completely changed her mind and now entreated me to abuse her as I had done the previous day and to supervise her public behaviour during her stay in Vienna. It's beginning to be embarrassing. She was very insistent. And so her first concert was fixed for Thursday, 12 December.

A few days before the concert she asked me if, when the day came, I would give her my arm to lead her out before the audience. I said no, because it would look as though I was being patronizing, something that I absolutely loathe. More than a score of people told me that I should do it, that it would be helpful to her, etc... I refused, knowing what I was talking about. But when the day arrived, a quarter of an hour before the concert la Pleyel asked to speak to me and again begged me to do her this favour. Amen: I therefore presented her to the audience and the audience began to applaud and to call out in praise of my courtesy and my perfect gentlemanliness. (I was wearing a charming morning coat with gold, dog's-head buttons, polished boots, and an incomparable waistcoat!)

She had a great success, although her choice of pieces was generally considered too severe: Hummel's Concerto, a Fantasy by Döhler, and the *Concertstück*, which was encored. But very sincerely, and with no self-conceit whatsoever, no pianist on earth could play in Vienna at the present moment, and I alone could give la Pleyel her three-quarter success. Last Tuesday she gave her second concert; my name did not at first appear on the programme, and the number of tickets sold by Sunday evening was very small indeed. To spare her a probable embarrassment, I suggested accompanying her in Herz's duet from *William Tell*, the effect of which was prodigious. . . . The public is so infatuated with me and my person that, the moment I showed myself, the audience began to applaud, which was all the more flattering for the fair beneficiary. . . .

2.00 p.m. My concert has just finished. Enthusiasm impossible to describe. I played the *Frequenti Palpiti*, the *Orgia*, the *Ave Maria* (I always play it because of you), the *Ständchen*, and the *Galop*. At the end, when the applause went on and on, I played as an encore a Hungarian melody (the one you like); incidentally, I have just written two new ones, which you will surely like too. From the very first bar it was received with cries of 'Éljen, éljen! [Hail! Long live!]' which moved me to tears. . . .

Farewell, my beloved, a thousand times beloved. Don't worry in the least about my health, which is excellent. I have brought along with me an enormous box of homoeopathic remedies for every possible eventuality, plus the necessary instructions, but, with God's help, I quite expect not to touch them. . . .

93. To Marie d'Agoult. Pest, 25 December. I'll just finish what I was telling you about Pozsony. On Friday, the day after my concert, I played at the theatre in aid of the poor. The hall was packed, something extremely rare in Pozsony. My name was down for only a single item (the first part of the Fantasy on *Lucia* and the *Valse Mariotique*), but as the audience did not leave off calling me back I was obliged to go to the piano again. The applause redoubled, and then, when I began the opening chords of the Rákóczy March (a very popular melody in Hungary which I have just arranged in my own manner), there was only one cry to be heard throughout the hall: 'Éljen! Éljen!' You can't imagine that, but notwithstanding your Stoic indifference so far as success and applause are concerned, I am convinced you would have been moved, for the people here are not a people who yell and shout as they do in Vienna and elsewhere; they are a stout-hearted, generous, proud people...

A few minutes later I paid a visit to the box in which sat Countess Batthyány (flower of the Pozsony aristocracy). As soon as I opened the door the ladies began clapping, and as I entered the box the audience imitated those ladies and applauded me *en masse*.

After the theatre I was presented at the casino (dei Nobili, of course), where I lost about fifty francs at whist, which was only a minor nuisance that evening.

On Sunday came my second concert, in the hall of the Redoute. Same number of people, same success. . . .

In the time between my two concerts I was obliged to pay certain visits, first to the Palatine (brother of the Emperor Franz) and then to two or three persons of high rank. . . . Most of my time I spent in the hotel, busily transcribing the second part of Schubert's *Divertissement à la hongroise* and preparing some orchestral parts to be copied out, a task I am far from having finished.

At Pozsony I received a few lines from you in which you ask if we can meet in Munich. Alas, my darling, that will hardly be possible. You must not move from Paris, even to go six leagues to meet me. I shall take care not to let you know the exact day of my arrival so that you don't do anything rash. Just think what a journey of that kind would be for you, at this time of year. You haven't my strength—far from it (and I haven't brought five or six children into the world and suffered two or three illnesses that might have been fatal). . . .

Perhaps we shall be able to travel together to the Tyrol and Munich next autumn, on my return from England. This is an idea I find very appealing. . . .

I am truly ashamed of my letters, which are about nothing but concerts, applause, money... But bear in mind that such things are my whole life at present. What have I got in this world? What can I think of? Sky and earth alike are hidden from me by thick fogs. All my limbs feel cold and raw. And then, I am so alone, so naked... Sun and warmth will return, I hope. I shall see you again, shall be with you again. You will press me to your bosom once more and I shall not be unworthy of it. But now! . . .

We arrived safely in Pest at about 4 o'clock the day before yesterday. I am staying with Count Leó Festetics. All the hotel proprietors are extremely vexed about it. One of them in particular (at the *Palatine of Hungary*) had made splendid preparations to receive me. . . .

Farewell, dearest, time is passing; I am suffering dreadfully from a back tooth which I am going to have extracted.

I await the owl impatiently. It will be delightful, I feel sure.

Adieu, adieu. Yours, and yours alone.

94. To Marie d'Agoult. Pest, 29 December. How far we are from one another, dear Marie. Your letter of the 12th reached me only yesterday evening, the 28th. This distance is for me a burden of incurable sadness.

I have taken a dislike to my piano. I should like to play only for you, and I don't know why this crowd listens to me and pays me.

I'll reply immediately to two or three points in your letter. What you tell me about my mother distresses me a little, but I very much approve of your telling me. What point would there be in silly restrictions between us? Besides, didn't I in some way take the initiative by speaking to you of your family without mincing my words in the least? So far as the children are concerned, we'll try to find a plan within the next two months which may at one and the same time satisfy the demands of society (to which in my opinion you should yield on several points while maintaining your role of scorning it) and the more imperative demands of your heart and mind. That will perhaps not be impossible. . . .

I shouldn't like you to take Chopin's rudeness too seriously. I imagine that by this time you have punished him enough for it. You know, moreover, what a deplorable influence the chaotic Piffoëls clan can be. You don't need to overdo the resentment against Chopin for his gaucherie. Sharper people than he (although he is very sharp and above all believes himself to be enormously sharp) would lose their way in it.

Berlioz is wonderful to me in his *feuilleton* in the *Débats*. Our permanent relations will be decided in two months. They will be good, I am convinced.

Give my very friendly apologies to Massart for not writing to him any more. I truly don't know which way to turn with all the business, correspondence, and obligations of every kind that I have to attend to.

A few words now on my stay in Hungary. The matter of my letters patent of nobility is making progress. Several magnates have decided that they will go to Vienna to ask for them direct from the Emperor, whose consent is absolutely indispensable. . . . The matter will very probably be decided before I leave Vienna.

For the rest, you must have seen from an article in the Pest newspaper that, were I really bent on an aristocratic origin, I could easily claim one. . . .

Yesterday evening I went to the Hungarian Theatre for the first time. They were doing *Fidelio* (in Hungarian). When I entered the box the entire audience began to clap and shout 'Éljen! Éljen!' I greeted them three times like a king, no more and no less. All this is unparalleled in this country, and elsewhere too, I believe.

At noon today my second concert. Audience and success increasing in size. At 5 o'clock the flower of the Hungarian aristocracy now present in Pest gave me a magnificent banquet (to which had been invited about ten ladies, Szapáry, Zichy, Festetics, Venckheim, *et al.*) in the hall of the casino. There were more than fifty of us at table. Half a dozen toasts were proposed in Hungarian in my honour and to no one else, except to the ladies.

I responded with a toast in French to the well-being, progress, and liberty of 'our common fatherland', which was received as you can imagine.

After dinner, the idea came to someone or other to propose a subscription for a bust of me. In less than ten minutes the figure of 1,500 francs had been reached. These gentlemen would like to have it done by an extremely mediocre Hungarian artist, but I shall try to persuade them simply to ask for a copy of the one by Bartolini. . . .

I don't know if these details amuse you and give you pleasure. As for myself, they strengthen me in the conviction I have held for two or three years, that serious obligations are imposed on me. . . .

Adieu, dear Marie, don't worry about my health any more, and write to me as much as possible.

Would you do me the kindness of letting me have my mother's exact address?

1840

January. At the end of Liszt's concert in Pest of 4 January, Hungarian magnates present him with a jewel-studded sabre of honour; in Pozsony, on the 27th, ladies of the nobility present him with a golden goblet.[1]

February. He gives concerts in Vienna.

19 February. He visits his birthplace in Raiding.

March. After a series of concerts in Prague, Liszt leaves for Dresden and Leipzig, making several appearances in both cities.[2]

4 April. He and Marie d'Agoult meet in Meaux, and a few days later return to Paris, where Liszt remains until early May.

May. On the 8th he makes his first appearance in London since his childhood; on the 11th takes part in a Philharmonic Society concert; on the 25th plays to Queen Victoria.

June. On the 7th Marie d'Agoult arrives in London, taking accommodation at Richmond; on the 8th Liszt again plays at a Philharmonic Society concert; on the 9th and 29th he gives the first ever 'recitals'.

July to mid-August. He gives concerts in or near the Rhineland. At Ems he plays before the Tsaritsa, who invites him to visit Russia.

Late August. Liszt takes part in concerts in Chichester (17th), Portsmouth (17th), Ryde (18th), Newport, Isle of Wight (18th), Southampton (19th), Winchester (19th), Salisbury (20th), Blandford (20th), Weymouth (21st), Lyme Regis (22nd), Sidmouth (22nd), Exmouth (24th), Teignmouth (24th), Plymouth (26th), Exeter (28th and 29th), Taunton (31st), Bridgwater (31st).

September. Concerts in Bath (1st and 2nd), Clifton (3rd), Cheltenham (4th and 5th), Leamington (7th), Coventry (7th), Northampton (8th), Market Harborough (9th), Leicester (9th), Derby (10th), Nottingham (10th), Mansfield (11th), Newark (11th), Lincoln (12th), Horncastle (14th), Boston (14th), Grantham (15th), Stamford (16th), Peterborough (16th), Huntingdon (17th), Cambridge (18th), Bury St Edmunds (19th), Norwich (21st), Ipswich (22nd), Colchester (23rd), Chelmsford (24th), Brighton (25th and 26th).

October and early November. After sojourning with Marie d'Agoult at Fontainebleau, Liszt proceeds to Hamburg, where he gives and takes part in several concerts.

24–30 November. In the first week of a long tour of the British Isles, Liszt plays in Oxford (24th), Leamington (25th), Birmingham (26th), Wolverhampton (27th), Newcastle under Lyme (28th), Chester (30th).

---

[1] Sabre and goblet are now on display in the National Museum, Budapest.
[2] Full details of Liszt's concerts in Germany in the 1840s are given by Saffle, *Liszt in Germany*.

December. Concerts in Liverpool (1st), Preston (2nd), Rochdale (3rd), Manchester (4th and 15th), Huddersfield (5th), Doncaster (7th), Sheffield (8th), Wakefield (9th), Leeds (10th), Hull (11th), York (14th), Dublin (18th, 21st and 23rd), Cork (28th and 30th).

31 December. Liszt and his colleagues visit the Cork Lunatic Asylum.

WORKS. SONGS: *Il m'aimait tant* (Delphine Gay) (S271, *c.*1840); *Am Rhein* (Heine) (S272, *c.*1840). PIANO: *Mazeppa* (S138); *Morceau de salon, étude de perfectionnement* (S142); *Venezia e Napoli* (S159, *c.*1840): 1. *Lento* 2. *Allegro* 3. *Andante placido* 4. *Tarentelles napolitaines*; *Galop de bal* (S220, *c.*1840); *Heroischer Marsch im ungarischen Styl* (S231); *Hussitenlied* (S234); *I Puritani, introduction et polonaise* (Bellini) (S391); *Réminiscences de Lucrezia Borgia* (Donizetti) (S400); transcriptions (S547) of songs by Mendelssohn: 1. *Auf Flügeln des Gesanges* 2. *Sonntagslied* 3. *Reiselied* 4. *Neue Liebe* 5. *Frühlingslied* 6. *Winterlied* 7. *Suleika.*

WRITINGS. 'Sur Paganini, à propos de sa mort', published in the *RGM*, 23 August.

95. To Marie d'Agoult in Paris. Pest, midnight, Tuesday, 7 January.[3]

Four letters on my table from you at once! I am opening them very happily. It is more than a week since I had a single word.

All good, loving, deeply moving. . . .

I mentioned a splendid day. The word is not exaggerated. I shall write about it to no one, and even to yourself I shall write about it extremely badly, because things like that cannot be written. On 4 January I played at the Hungarian Theatre the Andante from *Lucia*, the *Galop*, and, the applause being unending, the Rákóczy March (a kind of aristocratic Hungarian *Marseillaise*). Just as I was about to return to the wings, Count Leó Festetics, Baron Bánffy, Count Teleki (all magnates), Eckstein, Augusz* and a sixth whose name I forget,[4] came on, all in Hungarian gala costume, with Festetics holding a magnificent sabre (worth 80 to 100 louis), decorated with turquoises and rubies etc. Addressing me briefly in Hungarian before the entire audience, which applauded frenziedly, he then girt the sabre on me in the name of the Nation. Through Augusz I asked for permission to address the audience in French, and in a firm and solemn voice pronounced the speech that I shall send you tomorrow, in print. It was several times interrupted by applause. That done, Augusz came forward and read out the same speech in Hungarian.

You can have no idea of the serious, solemn, and profound excitement of this scene, which anywhere else would have been ridiculous. . . . It was magnificent. It was unique. But that wasn't all.

---

[3] Dated 6 Jan. in Ollivier's edition—but Tuesday was the 7th.
[4] Pál Nyáry, Director of the Hungarian National Theatre.

The performance over, we got into the carriage. Lo and behold—an immense crowd was filling the square and 200 young people with lighted torches, a military band at their head, were crying 'Éljen! Éljen! Éljen!'

And note what admirable tact. Hardly had we taken fifty paces when a score of young people rushed forward to unharness our horses. 'No, no,' cried the others, 'that has been done for wretched dancing girls, for la Elssler; *him*, we must fête otherwise!' Wasn't that remarkable!

Festetics' house, in which I am staying, is a very long way from the Hungarian Theatre. When we were roughly a third of the way there, I said to Festetics, 'I'd rather not any more; let's get out and not play the aristocrats in your carriage.' I opened the door, and the cheering which had not ceased for ten minutes increased with a kind of fury. People stood aside at once and we walked, Festetics, Augusz, and I (in the middle), all three of us in Hungarian costume (mine, incidentally, cost me a thousand francs and is only a very simple one —it was a necessary expense).

Impossible to give you any idea of the enthusiasm, love, and respect of the entire population! At 11 o'clock in the evening, every street was full of people. (In Pest, everyone, including society people, even the most elegant, goes to bed at 10.00, with the exception of perhaps five or six people.) The cheering did not cease. It was a triumphal march, such as was experienced by Lafayette and a few men of the Revolution.

As we turned a corner, I asked Augusz, who is very practised in public speaking (he is protonotary of an extremely turbulent committee), to address these young people; and he acquitted himself admirably. The theme I had given him was 'that I could in no wise have deserved, nor at present deserve, the welcome given me in my native land. But that I accepted these more than flattering tokens as imposing new duties on me to fulfil, etc...'

To the first words they responded with a most categorical, unanimous, and resounding denial. 'Yes, yes,' they all cried, 'you deserve it, and much more as well.'

Wasn't that admirable?

At the door of my house the military band stopped, but about thirty young people escorted me with their torches as far as the entrance to my apartment. It was nearly 11.30. The military band played a few more pieces. I was twice called to the balcony. Finally Festetics addressed them from the balcony, to dismiss them. I was exhausted.

It is one thirty in the morning, my head is burning, my heart full of sadness and love.

Wherever you are, whatever you are doing, whatever you are dreaming, I belong to you, to you alone.

P.S. (Wednesday morning.) After such a demonstration (in which, no exaggeration, Society took part as did the entire population), I was bent on doing something for my own part for town and country. And so I extended my stay in Pest by a few days (I shall not leave until Monday) and proposed, for next Saturday, an immense concert at the Hungarian Theatre on behalf of the Pest Conservatoire, funds for which are going to be voted for by the Diet and which will be afoot in a year or eighteen months. I shall conduct the orchestra and the choirs—i.e. the whole thing—and shall in addition play Beethoven's Grand [Choral] Fantasy, with choruses, and Weber's Concerto,[5] and anything they want. There is no way that one can haggle with a public like this. Tomorrow I shall write to you with the programme of this performance, plus the famous speech (which you will perhaps find full of faulty French, but which I delivered superbly). . . .

96. To Marie d'Agoult. Pest, 13 January

Dearest,

The tedium of giving concerts in Pest is now behind me. Yesterday morning (Sunday) my farewell concert put an end to them. I shall stay here tomorrow as well, to rest a little, and on Wednesday leave for Pozsony, stopping for only twenty-four hours in Győr. . . .

I enclose my famous speech with a long article in Hungarian which you will be able to have translated at leisure through my secretary (incidentally, I have engaged him on a permanent basis and hope you will be pleased with him), when I return to Paris. If you like the speech, tell me; if not, let it not be mentioned again. It is something which suited the occasion, and which I wrote and expressed from heart and soul.

The letter addressed to Count Leó Festetics in Pozsony hasn't reached me. I regret it doubly—you can guess why. I'll probably be given it when I get there.

I am going to remain at least ten days without news of you. So don't be annoyed with me if I don't reply to your questions. I am detained here two extra days because of the excessive cold and also because of the illness of a friend (Herr von Schober*) who is to travel with me.

You ask me for permission to be unfaithful! Dear Marie, you name no names, but I assume it is Bulwer.[6] It matters little. You know my way of looking at

[5] The *Concertstück*.

[6] The diplomat Henry Lytton Bulwer, who in 1848 married a niece of the Duke of Wellington, was the elder brother of the novelist Edward Bulwer-Lytton. He had been paying assiduous court to Marie, who found him 'minus the grimace, and also the grace', as like Chopin 'as one fly is like another'. Although she was flattered by his attentions, it is evident from her letters that she was not seriously interested in taking Bulwer as a lover; and her request for

these things. You know that for me deeds, gestures, and acts are nothing; feelings, ideas, nuances (above all nuances), everything. I want and wish you always to have your freedom, for I am convinced that you will always use it nobly and delicately, until the day when you say to me: 'What I am, and what I can be, such and such a man has felt more energetically, understood more intimately, than you have done.' Until that day there will be no infidelity, and nothing, absolutely nothing, will change between us. That day, allow me to say, will not arrive and cannot arrive; such is my profound inner conviction.

If it is a need, or a pleasure, or simply a distraction to talk to me about Bulwer, do so; I shall be pleased and flattered. If not, I shall never say a word about him.

Truth![7]

Farewell, yours and yours alone.

Continue to send your letters to Haslinger's; I shall certainly give three more concerts in Vienna, two for myself and one for the poor.

97. To Marie d'Agoult. Vienna [6] February. You wouldn't believe how bored I am with Vienna. Once again, your letters are my sole joy and I thank you from the bottom of my heart for writing to me so often.

Yesterday I lunched at Pückler Muskau's. He is a reserved man who aims at people of distinction, I believe, but having dealings with him is pretty agreeable to me. He got me to smoke four or five of the most admirable Turkish, Egyptian, and Chinese pipes. Then he took me to see his Arab horses. They filled me with delight! The joy of a child!

I immediately thought of buying the most beautiful one for you! But the price is enormous (15,000 francs, I believe)—and then, how to bring it to Paris? You cannot imagine the impression those creatures made on me, and how vividly they turned my thoughts back to you. I want to go and see them again, and often. Regard it as ridiculous, bizarre, whatever you will, but the sight of those horses brings me nearer to you; I see you galloping to meet me, the air parting before you...

Rudolf Apponyi came to see me. I was kind and affectionate to him, and invited him to supper today. It will be a wholly aristocratic supper, the main

permission to be unfaithful was a rather obvious attempt to arouse Liszt's jealousy. His sage reply effectively called the bluff, and although she later complained that he had not actually answered the question, she also admitted that his response had 'filled her with respect' for him.

[7] This word written by Liszt in English.

guests being Prince Pückler, Prince Fritz Schwarzenberg, Count Apponyi, Count Hartig, Baron Reisach (a nice lad), Count Széchenyi (the illustrious one), Count Waldstein, Count Paul Esterházy, *et al.*, *et al.*...

It will probably be rather cold, but of the best kind. This morning I am just about dead, having played more than six times at the Hofburgtheater; prodigious success, prodigious proceeds too (for the sisters of charity). . . .

The way you mention B[ulwer] makes me extremely curious to know or at least observe him, if, as is likely, we have no reason to meet. If you are not greatly mistaken about him, he seems to me to be almost worthy of your affection... Our future relations will be decided in the first half hour that we talk together. . . .

98. To Marie d'Agoult. Vienna, 22 February.

This week I have made my excursions to Sopron, Eisenstadt, and Pottendorf, written to Miri, M. Ingres, and Bartolini by way of a young painter who is travelling to Italy, plus several other letters (Neipperg, correspondence with Hungary, etc.), attended to a multitude of bills, bought a coupé, engaged a servant, etc., etc.... I am bored to death with all that. I can't tell you how much Vienna depresses me; I hope to make my departure the day after tomorrow. My friends were very insistent on my giving one more concert (for the statue of Beethoven). I refused. The piano is wearing me out. All that I am in a fit state to do is write a page or two of my Hungarian melodies, which I wish to keep on with indefinitely. It is a good seam to work. . . .

Last Wednesday, the day after the concert I gave in Sopron for the poor, I went on a pilgrimage to Raiding. As we went along I recognized all the villages, the bell-towers, the crossroads, and even some of the houses. I fail to understand the persistence of childhood memories, which for me, as you know, have so little attraction. Two leagues from Raiding, a score of mounted peasants, very picturesquely rigged out, came to meet me, and escorted me as far as the judge's house. The entire population (about a thousand people) was assembled. The children, boys and girls alike, bent the knee as I passed them. I had all the trouble in the world to persuade them to get up.

A few peasants came to kiss my hands, the greater number staying at a respectful distance. The priest who had come to meet and welcome me took me to my birthplace, which is in more or less the same condition as when I left it. I saw it all again without emotion—you were not with me. To you alone goes my love, and with you alone can I be completely natural.

The priest said low mass, the crowd filling the church the while. Then we returned (Alberti and Schober, whose verses I sent you from Pest, had accompanied me) to the judge's house, where an omelette and coffee had been prepared for us. I had wine served to the peasants outside, and urged the musicians who had preceded us until then to play waltzes. It was a complete open-air ball in the snow.

The peasants brought me their most attractive daughters, asking me to dance with them. I don't know why I began to think of a note you wrote me from Croissy in which you also told me about a *bal champêtre*. The memory of it cast an indefinable melancholy over this whole scene.

Finally, at about one o'clock, I set out again, escorted by the same peasants, after having left a hundred ducats or so for the parish. At 3.00 we reached Sopron... an immense public dinner for about eighty people in the small hall of the Redoute.

I am vexed that my letter from Gattendorf did not reach you. I am no longer equal to rewriting it.

Your own letters are little masterpieces. Write as you speak... that is to say, as you write. Your portrait is ever here on my table. Tell Lehmann again how grateful I am to him for it. . . .

I want to tell you, too, of a kind of passion to which I abandoned myself for forty-eight hours. Don't be jealous. It concerns the very beautiful [blank in MS] woman at Sopron, the only one for three months for whom I have felt a decided taste. Farewell, dear one.

Strike out these last lines if they vex you. Farewell.

99. To Marie d'Agoult. Prague [Wednesday, 11 March].

I have now been in Prague for a week, and this morning was my fifth concert. . . . The Bohemian aristocracy, the proudest in the Monarchy, have been most charming to me. Here, as elsewhere, the women are on my side. The men give in to this influence, although with a little ill humour. The day before yesterday I had Prince du Rohan (with whom I am almost intimate), Prince Lichtenstein, Count Schlick, the Counts Thun, *et al.* to dinner. We were about a dozen in all. Hermann (you'll have a good laugh at this), who seems to me to have definitely increased in wisdom and stature, as was said of Our Lord Jesus Christ,[8] was one of us. The Grand Burgrave, Count Chotek, who occupies the imperial box at the theatre in the absence of His Majesty, had asked me to go there to rest between

---

[8] Luke, 2: 52.

each piece at the concert for the poor. When, at the end of the concert, after having already played one piece more than was on the programme, I went there to thank him and to say farewell, he and his wife began to applaud openly and to call out my name. The whole audience understood what that meant and thunderous applause obliged me to return to the platform. There were more than 2,000 people in the hall.

The Prague audiences, please note, are extremely musical and have the reputation of being a kind of Supreme Court of Appeal for Viennese reputations. According to what everyone says, my success surpasses even that of Paganini, which here as everywhere is the ultimate yardstick.

Lo and behold, I've inadvertently come back to the concerts which bore me so much! *Basta così!* . . .

It goes without saying that in Paris I shall play only at my concerts. Whatever the musical apathy you have noticed there, I don't despair of rousing those audiences. They and I are old acquaintances and I believe I know exactly what they need. . . .

If you see Erard, let him know that I shall ask for his salon at least twice. My first two concerts must not take place anywhere else. There will be a crush at the second, you'll see. . . .

Shall I be able to stay at my mother's? I should very much like to do so because of the Mouches. Would you undertake to have my room prepared for me at her place, and to have the two or three necessary pieces of furniture put there for me? An hotel would be extremely expensive and would have other disadvantages as well. My secretary, Kiss, an adorable but clumsy individual, would be able to lodge nearby in a small *hôtel garni*. Only a servant's room would be needed for Ferco, who is the perfection of servants and whom I find absolutely indispensable. I am convinced that you will in every respect be pleased with him. . . .

These last two months my thoughts have often gone back to Venice, to a Palazzo Foscari that we would live in, to a comfortable and poetic existence that it would be difficult to have elsewhere.

To be able to write to you, I have had my door shut; more than twenty people have been turned away. Now I have to dress to go to the concert. I am always asked for the *Ave Maria*. A certain passage, which I shall play to you, I never come to without being possessed by you; it is the only thing which makes this impression on me, constantly and invincibly.

Farewell... Yours.

In the second half of March Liszt gave a number of concerts in Dresden and Leipzig and saw much of Schumann and Mendelssohn.

100. To Marie d'Agoult. Leipzig, Friday evening, 20 March. I was to
have given my second concert the day before yesterday, Wednesday, but at about
3 o'clock I began to shiver so violently that I had to go to bed. Today the machine
is in perfect order, although I'm not going out yet because of the frightful weather.
Don't be the least bit worried; you know that around springtime I am always
compelled to spend a day or two in bed. The fever was already gone by yesterday. The tedious part of so untimely an incident is that I am forced to spend
three more days here.

Mendelssohn, Hiller, and Schumann hardly leave my room. Mendelssohn brings
me syrups, conserves, etc. I am very content with him; he is much simpler than
I had imagined.[9] Further, he is a man of remarkable talent and a highly cultivated mind. He draws marvellously, plays the violin and viola, reads Homer fluently
in Greek, and speaks four or five languages with ease. Hiller is having an oratorio performed here next week (*The Destruction of Jerusalem*). He has asked me
to say a thousand flattering things to you. Schumann came to Dresden to seek
me out. Note that it was perhaps only the second time in his life that he had
gone there, although Dresden is a mere four hours from Leipzig. Mendelssohn,
moreover, has never been there.

Schumann is an excessively reserved man, who speaks hardly at all, except
with me now and then. I believe he will be extremely devoted to me. People
here have quoted your remark about Thalberg and me: he being the first and I
the only pianist. This does not please Schumann, who maintains that I am at
once the first *and* the only one.

Incidentally, Thalberg's remark to the King of Saxony is correct; he repeated
it to several other people. The King had invited me for tomorrow, but out of
consideration for the public I was obliged to send to ask him to postpone it until
next Wednesday. It is, moreover, impossible to be kinder than is His Majesty. I
haven't yet had the honour of seeing him (he was still in Vienna when I gave my
Dresden concert), but Lüttichau has given me the most gracious messages from
him. He has told everyone that he no longer desired to hear any pianist but one
—but that one he *did* wish to hear; you can guess who this pianist is? etc. . . .

I plan to leave here on the 29th. I don't know if I shall be strong enough to
travel day and night as far as Meaux, but I shall certainly try. I should so much
like to be there on 2 April![10] I shall write positively and tell you which day you
are to arrive there.

---

[9] Liszt and Mendelssohn had met, in Paris, in early 1825 and again in the winter of 1831/2. It was on this latter
occasion that Mendelssohn, after witnessing his new Piano Concerto in G minor being played at sight ('with the utmost
perfection') by Liszt from the all but illegible manuscript, claimed that he had seen 'a miracle, a real miracle'.

[10] It was Marie who was eager to visit the town of Meaux (about 28 miles east of Paris), perhaps because of a special interest in Bossuet. 2 Apr. was Liszt's name-day.

Two errands:

1. I have entirely decided on the Hôtel de Paris next to the Hôtel des Princes. And so book me from 3 April (and from the 1st if necessary) a fully furnished apartment, consisting of an ante-room, sitting-room, and bedroom, plus a servant's room, for 250 to 300 francs if possible.

2. Give my mother 200 francs for her in her turn to give immediately to Frau Cohen.

Farewell, beloved. I am thinking happily that when you receive this letter there will be no more than a week between us. Before leaving here I shall obtain exact information about distances, and will let you know the day you are to arrive in Meaux.

Adieu.

101. To Marie d'Agoult. Leipzig, Sunday, 22 March. Mendelssohn could definitely not be more charming; he has been kind and attentive to me from the very first day. During the forty-eight hours that I spent in bed he came to see me eight or ten times. Lastly, he yesterday invited more than 250 musicians, as many singers as players, to give me a kind of musical party tomorrow, Monday, in the Grand Concert Hall, to which only about sixty people (to whom he is sending personal letters of invitation) will be admitted.

It's a delightful idea, isn't it? I admit that since the ball given for me by the Ladies of Pest nothing had flattered me so much. Everyone accepted eagerly; not a single clarinettist jibbed. The hall will be splendidly illuminated.

The programme has been drawn up thus:

Symphony by Schubert (unpublished, said to be magnificent).
Psalm (As the hart panteth!) for choir and orchestra by Mendelssohn. It, too, is a very beautiful piece.
Calm Sea and Prosperous Voyage, overture by Mendelssohn.
Two choruses from Hiller's *new oratorio*.
Overture, *Fingal's Cave*, by Mendelssohn.
Concerto by Bach for three pianos, played by Mendelssohn, Hiller, and me.

If you can have a couple of words inserted in the *Débats*, and in the *Revue musicale* ('We are informed from Leipzig, etc....'), I should be glad. I particularly wish them to give praise to Mendelssohn, who is certainly the most eminent composer in Germany at present. . . .

Farewell. I need to practise the whole evening.

24 March. The concert Mendelssohn put on for me yesterday was a magnificent success. I'll give you full details in twelve days. He behaved like a man of superiority and tact. . . .

On Wednesday, 6 May, Liszt arrived in London.

102. To Marie d'Agoult. London, 9 May. I have had an immense success this evening,[11] dear Marie. My London business is nearly done. There is already no parallel possible, unless with Paganini, and *him* I don't mind. I have been given an admirable welcome. Many people still remember Master Liszt. I have seen no one in society; on the other hand I am surrounded by publishers and artistes. On 5 June I shall give my concert alone, a way of doing things that I definitely want to adopt. Forgive me for talking to you so much about concerts, but here that has a kind of importance.

On Monday I play Weber's *Concertstück* at the Philharmonic, an evening which will settle the matter completely.

Aren't you going to write to me? I haven't had a single word from you thus far. I'm not annoyed with you about that, but you must know that the least word from you is beneficial for me in a way that I find difficult to describe. I am very isolated, very alone, when you don't come to me.

Farewell for the time being. . . .

103. To Marie d'Agoult. London, Wednesday, 13 May. What we believe as children, could it be true? Is there a good and bad angel attached to our steps? Could the significance of so many things which seem to me to be doubtful, to say the least, be so simple? I don't know! I don't know! I don't know! But I feel singularly moved and touched by your remembrance. . . .

Tell me about your health. I have received only two letters from you thus far. . . . I have sent you the newspapers and shall continue to send them to you so that you may know to some extent about my public life. Here, that is the only life I have. I don't know anyone yet, except Mr Reeve (a friend of Alfred de Vigny), whom I find charming. He has translated Tocqueville into English.

---

[11] Despite the apparent date (if correct) of the letter, it is to Mrs Toulmin and John Orlando Parry's Hanover Square concert of Friday, 8 May, in which he participated, that Liszt refers.

I have refused to be introduced to Lady Blessington, having no need of any-one at all. My success here is unparalleled; I am sending you the programme of my first concert, an occasion for which a word has been specially invented.[12]

The season is only just beginning. In June I shall probably play nearly every day for 30 guineas a soirée. I have three concerts this week already. Enough on this topic. . . .

104. To Marie d'Agoult. London, Thursday, 14 May. You are very hard on the Princess [Belgiojoso]; to my mind, she has always been truthful and kind rather than false and spiteful. For the rest, I have no fixed opinion on her. It struck me that she might suit you as an acquaintance and perhaps please you as a person. She has had more attraction for me than George (genius apart), and I like her way of being *herself.*

As for the scandal of the concert, as you put it, I haven't for a moment thought of being scandalized. Mesdames M.G.R. *et al.* are at liberty to talk about it as they find fit. The grievances of thin-skinned souls affect me little. If I had listened to them, we should probably not be writing to one another at this moment.

Your tendency towards severity is increasing greatly. What you write to me is admirably said and energetically felt.

Nevertheless, I believe you are mistaken in believing me incapable of under-standing any other language than that of the most absolute flattery. No, Marie, it isn't flattery that I need. It offends me more, is still more out of tune for me than is severity. Isn't the experience of life sad enough, reality harsh and distressing enough, for us not to add artificial afflictions (a hundred times more cruel) to all those that we are condemned to suffer here below? What is the good of aggrav-ating our wounds and overwhelming ourselves with burdens we cannot bear?

I am happy to learn that you have seen your family again; in your relations with them try to be as sweetly obliging as you can. To behave thus won't cause you any serious disadvantage. I have written for Mme d'Obreskoff a waltz that has nothing in common with Mariotte's waltz. . . .

Have you heard Ole Bull?* He is a great artiste; or, at least, has in him all the stuff of a great artiste. And you know that I count barely four such in Europe. He made a profound impression on me in the Beethoven Sonata dedicated to Kreutzer. He is certainly wholly out of the common. If his reputation is not ten times greater than it is, that is perhaps the result of his ignorance of the rules of composition and also of certain clumsinesses which are part and parcel of his

[12] The word 'recital' to describe a musical performance was used for the first time in connection with Liszt's con-cert at the Hanover Square Rooms of 9 June.

being. He is a kind of savage, very ignorant of counterpoint and fugue, but a savage of genius who is brimming over with charming and original ideas.

In short, he moved me, and it is a long time since that happened. And so we see one another constantly; i.e. he spends his days at my place. He is one of the Puzzis on whom you wage war tooth and nail.

Tell me about your health. Do you think you will be able to come here? You will like this country (apart from the Sky!—but Heaven is in our hearts, isn't it, Marie?). . . .

105. To Marie d'Agoult. London, Monday, 18 May.[13] You don't write to me—but you could do. Few things interfere with your inner life. Unfortunately it isn't the same with me. The struggle between the real and the ideal is too strong. Balancing them is perhaps impossible. Yet I often dream. Polez told me the other day that he would rather go 300 leagues than write a letter... That is true for all men of action who think they are being truthful when they express their feelings.

Yesterday morning, Sunday, there was a party at my place: Moscheles, Batta, Lord Burghersh, d'Orsay, Polez, and about ten others. Ole Bull played a Mozart quartet admirably, Batta an *étude* and the *Romanesca*; I, the *Tarentelles*. Everyone delighted.

In the evening went to Lady Blessington's. (Incidentally, she made a nice remark about me to Reeve, who had introduced me to her on Friday evening: 'What a pity to put such a man to the piano!')

That reminds me of Bulwer's 'Why didn't Monsieur L... choose another profession?' Lady Blessington is, it seems, enchanted by my person and my wit (I am repeating what Reeve told me). She introduced me to everyone without my asking her: Louis Bonaparte,[14] Lord Castlereagh, Chesterfield. There were only men in her salon, one of the first being General Alava. . . .

Lady Blessington's salon gave me a lot to think about.

D'Orsay is charming to me, and has invited me to spend a few days in the country with them. I shall accept.

106. To Marie d'Agoult. London, 22 May. What do you expect, dear Marie? Your letters always give me extreme pleasure and often do me great good. That is why I think that you don't write to me enough. Forgive me for being so demanding.

---

[13] Wrongly dated 17 May in Ollivier's edition.
[14] The subsequent Emperor Napoleon III, much admired by Liszt.

I am going to try to find you a country house four miles from here, the kind I should like you to have. I am told that it will cost 25 guineas a month. Do what you can to get here on about 7 June, and stay until 7 July, when, taking the steamer, we shall be able to get to Baden in 48 hours. That would give us six weeks together. Why fear our disagreements? Why always fear and never hope? My heart is filled with joy at the thought of seeing you again. . . .

Next Monday I play *chez* the Queen, which everyone regards as great progress, since she never asks for instrumentalists. It was d'Orsay who arranged it by saying everywhere that the Queen was very foolish always to allow herself to be bored by Italian singers while artistes like Bull and myself were in London. . . .

I dined yesterday at Lady Blessington's, who is definitely one of my supporters here. I like her pretty well (not physically, of course). . . .

Adieu.

107. To Marie d'Agoult. London, Monday morning, 25 May. I went to Hampstead yesterday morning to find a *ratzenloch* for you. The scenery is delightful. I think you will be happy there. The air is very healthy. It's the highest point in the environs of London, recommended to certain patients (not to consumptives, of course, because there is a sharp breeze there). Just let me know and I'll rent you a cottage with which you will be content, I hope. We shall be able to spend nearly all our days together. Bring Annette (and perhaps your valet). The house servants will wait on you. Prices will not be exorbitant.

Once or twice a week we shall be able to go on delightful excursions to Richmond, Greenwich, etc.... You will greatly like this part of the world, I imagine; and I, too, will begin to enjoy it when you are here. . . .

I have come to an agreement with Lavenu for September, October, and November.[15] I shall have 500 guineas a month, plus my personal expenses and Ferco's, in all about 37,000 francs net. It's a wonderful engagement, especially for my first year.

In London itself I don't expect to earn an enormous amount (all this is between the two of us). To begin with, I arrived a little late. Secondly, the season is very bad. Then again, my terms being extremely high, only a certain number of concerts is possible.

It's generally thought that my concert will go splendidly; for my own part, I'm rather apprehensive. Moreover, that will prove nothing. Once again, and for the last time, my business is assured, my position made.

---

[15] For a tour—eventually two tours—of the provinces.

Don't you want to bring Lehmann with you? I could launch him very well here through d'Orsay and Lady Blessington, who are wonderful to me.

You can't imagine the daubs they have here in their Exhibition. It seems to me that a painter could find an excellent position in London. In any case he could spend three or four weeks here, and promote himself a little. . . .

Give me news of the Mouches. What is Daniel doing down there [in Italy]?

I am very glad that you have received Mme de Flavigny:[16] relations with her are necessary. Try (and forgive me for insisting on this point) to maintain them as agreeably as possible.

Do you want me to send you newspapers?

108. To Marie d'Agoult. London, 27 May. I am happy at what you tell me about the improvement in your health, and am still convinced that you won't dislike it here. M. de Flavigny did well to persuade you. I don't know why, but I have no great fear that you will be bored in London. Coming via Rouen seems to me to be an extremely good plan. Don't fail to visit the church of Saint Ouen when coming through Rouen. I took there the first letter you wrote to me, more than six years ago.

I can't get away from reprintings and proofs; I have also arranged melodies by Mendelssohn.

As I don't want to give any lessons except at an enormous price (100 francs), I haven't yet been asked to do so. As for society, I am on the point of going into it a little. D'Orsay got me invited to dinner at the Duke of Beaufort's. I made a pretty good impression there, I believe. On Sunday I am again invited to dinner at Lady Blessington's. Prince Esterházy is due to arrive; he will settle the whole question for me. Thus far no brick has been dropped, either by me or anyone else. . . .

The Queen was more or less alone with Prince Albert the other evening; I believe I amused her. She laughed a lot (which she likes doing) when I told her that 'my vanity was not at all wounded by her not remembering me' (her mother had just asked me if I had not played at her home 14 years ago).

Thank you for writing to me as much as you do. I am profoundly bored here and only staying out of necessity. . . .

It would be impossible for you to accompany me in the provinces: we shall be a troupe of strolling players. You couldn't, without lowering yourself, have the least contact with us during those three months. . . .

---

[16] Marie's sister-in-law Mathilde de Flavigny, née Montesquiou-Fezensac.

Let me know roughly when you expect to leave, and also find out on what boat you will be embarking, so that I can go to the Tower to meet you. . . . Adieu.

109. To Marie d'Agoult. London, Friday, 29 May. I am trying to find a cottage for you. . . .

Talking of publishers, Wessel, who has published Chopin's collected works and is losing more than 200 louis on them, has come to ask me to play some of his pieces, in order to make them known here. As yet, no one has dared risk it. I shall do so at the first good opportunity, perhaps at the Philharmonic Concert or at one of mine (if, as is probable, I give several). You can tell him that when you see him. I am delighted to be able to do him this small service. I shall play his *Etudes*, his *Mazurkas* and his *Nocturnes*, all things virtually unknown in London.[17] That will encourage Wessel to buy other manuscripts from him. The poor publisher is rather tired of publishing without selling. . . .

D'Orsay has done a portrait of me which he is going to publish. It's an aristocratic kindness for which I am grateful to him. Lady Blessington maintains that I resemble Bonaparte and Lord Byron!!!

Farewell, dear one. I have an immense need of rest. I should like to sleep, and dream as well. Let me lean my head against your bosom, and if possible let the bitter tedium, the deadly remorse, which have dug so deep a furrow in my heart be swallowed up in the immensity of your love.

Don't forget to have my two Hungarian frock-coats packed (the one in velvet and the other with the fur lining).

Mme d'Agoult arrived in London shortly before Liszt's concert of 9 June, and took accommodation, not in Hampstead, but at the Star and Garter Hotel, Richmond.

110. To Marie d'Agoult in Richmond [Saturday, 20 June]. 'I can do nothing else at this moment, and probably for ever, than live utterly alone.'

That is what you had to say to me! Six years of the most absolute devotion have brought you only to this....

And that is how it is with so many words of yours! Yesterday (to recall but one day) for the entire journey from Ascot to Richmond you spoke not a

---

[17] Liszt included several of the Polish composer's works in his recital of 29 June at Willis's Rooms, thereby becoming the first pianist to play Chopin, in public, in London.

single word which was not hurtful or offensive. But what is the good of coming back to such sad things, of counting all our inner wounds one by one in this manner? Is it not better to suffer and be silent? You will perhaps add these words to the number of those that you will no longer acknowledge! My language is so changed! At least, that is what you say.

Midnight. Love is not justice. Love is not duty—nor is it pleasure, and yet it mysteriously contains all these things. There are a thousand ways of feeling it, a thousand modes in which to practise it, but for those whose souls thirst for the absolute and the infinite, it is one, eternally one, without beginning and without end. If it reveals itself anywhere on earth, it is above all in this total trust of the one in the other, in this invincible conviction of our angelic nature, inaccessible to any defilement, unfathomable by anything which is not it. And so let us not argue about words (or even about things), not haggle about them or weigh them. If love still remains in the depths of our hearts, everything is said; if love has vanished, there is no longer anything to say. . . .

Farewell. I feel extremely tired. I should like to talk to you a little more, but the memory of your words restrains and freezes me. . . .

Adieu. I don't despair.

In mid-August Liszt returned to England for the first of the two tours organized by Louis Lavenu.

111. To Marie d'Agoult. Chichester, 17 August.[18] My travelling circus life begins today; or, rather, it's only a new fashion, a transformation (and I even have memories which are by no means on the same level as the present realities) of the career I bravely embraced eighteen months ago.

This morning, therefore, concert in Chichester; fifty or sixty people in the hall. This evening, concert in Portsmouth (I shall bring back for you papers with views of each of the towns), with an audience of about thirty.

But Lavenu was prepared for this, and regards these two concerts as mere rehearsals.

The programme always remains the same, of course; for the curiosity of the thing I enclose one with this letter.

Throughout this week we shall be giving two concerts almost every day.

The party consists of Mlle de Varny who has just married the editor of *L'Alliance*, a new French newspaper published in London. . . . *Prima donna assoluta*; i.e. absolutely detestable. Miss Bassano, who has nothing in common with the Duke,

---

[18] Wrongly dated 19 Aug. in Ollivier's edition.

is a nice unpretentious girl. Mori and I plan to buy her a cloak, for her own is too frightful. John Parry, whom you heard in London, is our Grazioso.[19] Lavenu and Frank Mori (the latter asked after you, which made him more interesting to me).

Fortunately, Lavenu, as you will see from the programme, has left two of my pieces *ad libitum*, so that I can play what I think fit. For the rest, we have a good carriage and the postilions go admirably. It's a pleasure that I enjoy all the more keenly seeing that it's the only one. We are looking forward to playing whist the whole day long on Sunday, and have a profound yearning for that day. . . .

Tell me how things are with the Mouches, and kiss them for me.

112. To Franz von Schober in Vienna. Stonehenge, Salisbury, 20 August.[20] It is with an inexpressible feeling of sadness and vexation that I write to you today, my good and excellent friend!—Your letter had done me so much good; I was so happy to think that we should meet again no later than the end of the autumn; I so needed to lean on your arm, experience once more your goodness of heart, your indulgence and fraternal counsel—and now I have to abandon the whole idea, or at least postpone it once again....

An unfortunate engagement that I have just renewed, and which will keep me in England until the end of January, makes it impossible for me to say to you the one word I should like to say: 'Come.'

England is not like other countries: the expenses are enormous. I'd really not dare to invite you to travel around it with me, for we should be almost ruined. Besides, it would be difficult for us to be together, for I have 3 or 4 *compulsory* companions from whom it is impossible for me to separate.

I was hoping to be rid of all that by the beginning of October, but, lo and behold, I have to begin again in mid-November. My trip to Russia, a journey I am as it were obliged to undertake after the gracious invitation extended to me by HM the Tsaritsa at Ems, is the most I shall have time for this year. On 15 May next I return to London once again, probably by the steamer coming direct from St Petersburg.

Where shall I find you in another twelve or fifteen months? Quite possibly I shall come and seek you out in Vienna, but in that case I shall certainly not leave again without taking you with me.

---

[19] It is the diaries kept by the versatile and popular *buffo* singer John Orlando Parry on this and the later tour which remain the best source of information about Liszt's concerts in the English provinces, Ireland, and Scotland.

[20] Wrongly dated 29 Aug. in La Mara's* edition. In my book *Portrait of Liszt* I have explained why, although he was in its general vicinity, Liszt is unlikely actually to have visited Stonehenge.

I have half a mind to spend the following winter in Constantinople. I am tired of the Occident; I should like to breathe in perfumes, bask in the sun, exchange the smoke of coal for the sweet smoke of the narghile. In short, I long for the Orient! O mein Morgenland! O mein Aborniko!—

My uncle wrote to say that you had been very kind and helpful to him. My hearty thanks.—Do you run into Castelli from time to time? When you see him, ask him from me to translate the article that I contributed to the Paris *Revue musicale* (of 23 August) on Paganini,[21] and to have it published in the *Theater-Zeitung*. I should also be very glad if it could be translated into Hungarian, for the *Hírnök* [Herald] (forgive me if I am spelling it wrongly!), but I don't know who could do it.

Talking of Hungarian! I shall always greatly value your work[22] on my visit to Pest. Send it to me as soon as you possibly can, and address it to Madame la Comtesse d'Agoult, 10 rue Neuve des Mathurins, Paris. A thousand friendly greetings to Kriehuber. His two portraits of me have been copied in London, and are unquestionably the best.

Farewell, my good excellent Schober. In my next letter I shall ask you about something I regard as of major importance. It concerns a Cantata for Beethoven, which I should like to set to music and have performed at the great Festival we intend to put on in '42 when the Statue is unveiled in Bonn.

Ever yours most affectionately,   F. Liszt

113. To Marie d'Agoult. Exmouth, 24 August. I have just had three days of severe fever, dear Marie. Fortunately, yesterday was a Sunday, and thanks to British religiosity I was able to spend the whole day in bed. Today I feel appreciably better. I believe I've done something rare in finding a sensible doctor who has promised to allay my fever without using too violent means. He is, besides, the type of man one believes, and I am convinced that I am going to be well. . . .

Our concerts are mediocre, and Lavenu is losing quite a lot of money at present. The expenses are enormous. For two days we have had four horses and two postilions. Everywhere we are putting up at the best hotels. In this respect, nothing could be more convenient—but I am sorry he is not doing better business. To tell the truth, we have so far been in small places only (except for Southampton), and he is counting on Bath, Exeter, Plymouth, etc. to make up.

---

[21] Who had died in May. Liszt's tribute to the great violinist ended: 'May the artist of the future set his goal within, and not without, himself; may virtuosity be a means and not an end for him; and may he never forget that though the saying is *Noblesse oblige*, still more than nobility—*Génie oblige!*'

[22] *Briefe über F. Liszt's Aufenthalt in Ungarn* (Leipzig, 1842, and Berlin, 1843).

The countryside we have just come through is delightful. Sidmouth and Exmouth, from where I am writing to you, I find particularly attractive. Everywhere there are admirable parks. The cathedrals of Chichester, Winchester, and Salisbury are remarkable. At Salisbury I went to warm myself in the sun near the tombs surrounding the church.

For my part, I enjoy solely the pleasure of going quickly, and luckily we have as yet had only the most excellent postilions. . . .

I wrote to you from London on arrival and from Chichester the next day. So this is number 3. Perhaps it would be best if you numbered my letters.

Farewell, dear Marie; write to me soon.

114. To Marie d'Agoult. Exeter, 28 August. I continue to be well and shan't mention my health to you again, since I am now fully recovered. Nor shall I mention the invincible boredom I feel at every hour, every minute; it is not only the foundation on which my life is built, it is the whole of my life. What is remarkable is that among six such variegated individuals, not a single striking incident comes along, not a single remark worth remembering is made. Every day is like the day before and the day after. It's a series of jugs of water which are removed from the table after dinner.

Our caravan has been enlarged by the presence of M. Lemoine (husband of the *assoluta*), a man of about fifty, a former magistrate, bloated, blotchy, and bespectacled. . . . He's a little less insufferable than we were expecting, and, besides, provides a fourth for the Sunday whist!

Yesterday, however, we had rather an amusing adventure. We were at Plymouth, where we had given a very fair concert the previous day. Lavenu had announced a second for one o'clock in the afternoon; but at 1.15 there were not four people in the hall. A crowd of more than 10,000 was making its way to the port, where a huge 120-gun ship was to be launched. Just think what an attraction for all classes of society!

Not losing heart, Lavenu immediately ran in search of seven men, whom he decked out in enormous placards announcing the postponement of the concert until the evening. These seven men spent the whole day walking around the town and the port. At 8 o'clock the hall was lit up, but nobody came; eventually, after we had waited a good half-hour, half a dozen people arrived, whose money—to their great discontent—was returned to them at the door, and the concert was called off for a second time. Actually, as a slight consolation we have been told that at *his* concert Thalberg had fewer than twenty people.

At Plymouth I visited a splendid park belonging to Lord Edgecombe [Edgcumbe]. Imagine the Villa Serbelloni, or rather the entire coast at Bellagio, laid out as a park, with fine groups of trees and numerous lawns such as can be seen only in England, exotic plants and flowerbeds interspersed artistically here and there, the whole thing by the sea with a view of the port and of the city of Plymouth in the background. It really was most beautiful, and I thought sadly of how much I should have enjoyed it had you been there.

I also visited some very beautiful cathedrals at Chichester, Salisbury, and Exeter. They are all surrounded by magnificent widely spaced trees. In France, when we have a beautiful monument, we can hardly wait to suffocate it under a pile of stalls, poky little houses, and filthy buildings. Look at Notre Dame, the cathedrals of Lyons, Metz, etc. Here in England they respect the majesty of the edifice. Its grandeur preserves it from vulgar contact. I have sometimes compared those beautiful monuments in France and Italy, surrounded by the wretched little shops leaning against them, to the great men of all times and all countries, forever bothered, badgered and exploited by the lowest rabble motivated by the vilest self-interest! . . .

I can't tell you what pleasure it gives me to know about your sojourn in Fontainebleau. You will still be there at the end of September, won't you? There, at last, is a goal, a desire, a hope for me.

We shall be able to spend a lovely, soulful week together, forgetting the past and heedless of the future! Try to see that nothing disturbs us at that time, that there are no people there (by people, I don't mean Rey or Mlle Delarue). Order a piano even—but not a square one, as I can't bear them. Have *Obermann* and Lord Byron on your table. I'd like the children and my mother to be there, but not too close, if possible. Come and pick me up in Paris; I'll tell you when. . . .

Please give my news to my mother. Buy Benjamin la Roche's translations of Byron and Shakespeare (one volume Byron, two volumes Shakespeare).

115. To Marie d'Agoult. Bath, 3 [2] September. Oh, our beautiful sunsets! Pisa, Rome, Venice, and soon Fontainebleau! The evening of our youth will be beautiful too; an invincible presentiment tells me so. . . .

Today is almost a holiday for me. I have done half my time. The audiences and the English newspapers are unanimous in their praise of me. Unfortunately we have two sets of rivals: Grisi and Tamburini on the one hand, Persiani and Rubini on the other. They do great wrong to Lavenu, who is in any case not yet known to the public as a concert organizer, something enormously important to the success of the undertaking. I am everywhere having the honours of the encore, and all the people are very much pleased.[23] Takings are still mediocre; there are

---

[23] The last eight words of this sentence Liszt wrote thus in English.

twenty reasons for that, but next year will be superb, everyone says. This is a country apart, as I have often told you. Nothing is proved, nothing done. . . .

Chopin's anxieties amuse me. I have written a very long letter to Neipperg; no one writes to me.

Do give my friendly greetings to Ferdinand Denis; he is one of the finest fellows I know.

Farewell, dear one; I have to dress for the concert.

One of the good things about this artistic tour is the reading. Between each of my pieces I read a dozen pages; the same in the carriage. In less than a fortnight I shall have finished my bulky Villemain volume.

Again, farewell.

116. To Marie d'Agoult. 10 September. It seems to me that I am no longer writing to you, dear Marie, and that saddens me.

We give two concerts almost every day, and the rest of the time travel the highroads. Often we hardly have time left for a meal. So don't be surprised or worried not to hear from me more frequently. I am well; my sole, sweet, fortifying, and unbounded thought is always you, my delightful and angelic Marie.

We shall be in the vicinity of Newstead Abbey[24] tomorrow, and so I have asked them to stop there. My fellow-feeling for—I could almost say affinity with—Lord Byron remains the same. After you (a long way after), it is to him alone that I feel deeply attracted. I know not what burning, whimsical desire comes over me from time to time to meet him in a world in which we shall at last be strong and free, and living a real life—where Cain will no longer ask 'And wherefore should I pray? Wherefore should I offer sacrifices?'

Farewell, dear one; in seventeen days I shall be back in London, and soon afterwards we shall see one another again.

117. To Marie d'Agoult. 16 September. At Newstead Abbey I lay on the grass in the bright sunshine. Swarms of rooks were cawing above my head, and for a long while I listened to their funereal music. Then I entered the rooms. I was shown the cup which Lord Byron had had made for himself from the skull of a monk, and the grave of his dog. As I was leaving, the moaning of the pine trees awakened corresponding harmonies within me, and hollow-voiced I sang and mused out loud. I shall write all that down one day. I don't know if it was the too great excitement, or the sun and the dampness of the lawn on which

---

[24] Ancestral home of the Byron family.

I lay too long—but an hour later I had a temperature again. I was prescribed quinine night and morning. Next day I was appreciably better; but I wanted to wait until I was fully recovered before writing to you.

My companion made me think, too, that I was very imprudent to leave off my flannel vest in London. I began wearing it again this morning.

Oh! indeed the 'meekly melancholy' beauties of Fontainebleau will delight me. Indeed I shall spend long, beautiful evenings there. I shall no longer seek Switzerland, the supernatural and the impossible; I believe I am very close to being happy. Provided you don't fall ill again! . . .

When shall we go to Italy? Florence, Venice, Rome, Naples! I in my turn am feeling that extreme thirst for Italy which you felt four years ago!

Be calm and happy. My exile is going to finish soon.

So far as anecdotes are concerned, I recently met a young man who travelled from Constantinople to Paris with Bulwer. When I asked him what he thought of him, he replied: 'He is a very debauched character I think.'[25] As a matter of fact this young man is still reading law at Cambridge, and had no idea that, according to one's point of view, he could have been praising his travelling companion. . . .

I, for my part, have taken up Roman history again. Incidentally, I should like you to ask Denis if a fairly inexpensive edition of Bayle's Dictionary is available. I very much wish to read it. . . .

I shan't give you any description of the countryside I am travelling through, and so on this point am emulating the classical writers of the century of Louis XIV, and for two very simple reasons: firstly, because I hardly know how to describe; secondly, because all this nature (if nature is what it is) says nothing whatever to me. Yet I find it all very beautiful. We passed Warwick Castle and Kenilworth. The one place which has made an impression on me is Newstead Abbey—and that was because of the man associated with it.

After a short holiday with Marie at Fontainebleau, Liszt left for Hamburg.

118. To Marie d'Agoult at Fontainebleau. 20 October[26]

Dearest,

At 7.30 in the evening I have stopped in a hole called Solre-le-Château, where the postmaster has invited, and to some extent compelled, me to stay the night. The roads are dreadful, and I was made to fear for the carriage. I finally yielded,

---

[25] Quoted by Liszt in English.
[26] Probably the date of the postmark, as by the 20th Liszt seems to have progressed as far as Dinant.

and here I am writing to you surrounded by three old women sitting around the stove, and Ferco smoking a cigar I have given him.

I am reading Alfieri[27] and Fourier. The former I dislike less than I had imagined, and am reading him with fellow feeling. Perhaps he takes his rivalry with the jockey a little too aristocratically. His mistress's taste inspires no such scorn in me. An English jockey is certainly worth many Italian and other *grands seigneurs*. I smiled a little, as you can imagine, when I read these lines, referring to his chance perusal of the English newspaper:

'Reading this almost made me fall dead, and only when I had to some extent come to my senses did I realize and thoroughly take in that this perfidious woman had *spontaneously* confessed everything to me after the journalist had, that very Friday morning, revealed everything to the public.'

I regret that this Petrarch quotation was not given in Italian:

'He who understands is overcome by him who wills.'

It must be a beautiful line.[28] If you know it, write it to me.

I also very much like the farce, *I Poeti*, which follows his *Cleopatra*. As he himself says, they're not the stupidities of a fool. But what delighted me above all was this chapter title: 'A love worthy of me finally binds me for ever.' Were I to read three or four books of this kind, I should probably take it into my head to write my own life. . . .

Farewell, dear one. . . .

119. To Princess Belgiojoso. Dinant, 20 October. You are utterly charming, or if you find this word too insipid, let's say kind, friendly... but that doesn't mean the same thing at all. No matter. There are occasions when I hate the precision of words. Isn't it always better to leave some things only hinted at in relationships which have some charm?

Your gracious letter was handed to me in London a few hours before my departure. All I did [in Paris] was stroll through the Boulevards. Heine accosted me breezily, as is his wont, asked for news of you, and ended up with the most gigantic, most enthusiastic, and the justest encomium of the beautiful princess. He can't get at all used to your absence, and bewails you more with every day that passes. But he will be writing all that infinitely better to you one of these mornings, because he asked for your address, which I didn't give him.

A few paces further on, lo and behold—Balzac! Same questions, same regret, although more restrained. He is engrossed in his *Revue parisienne*, on which,

---

[27] The famous *Vita*, which Liszt was reading in a French translation.

[28] 'E chi discerne è vinto da chi vuole' (from the sonnet 'Come talora al caldo tempo sole').

every 25th of the month, he expends a prodigious amount of intellect; this, how-ever, does not prevent him keeping himself very active with three or four great dramas, of which we shall be seeing at least one before the end of the winter. It will probably be *Mercadet*, the man of genius grappling with financial prob-lems, creditors, usurers, bailiffs, etc., a very topical subject which the author has unfortunately had the good luck to study in depth, and which will doubtless arouse the sympathies and memories of a great number of speculators, who are anything but people of genius for all that.

Still in these same Boulevards, I ran into Chopin (who takes after Prince Porcia[29] a little, I fear), Berlioz (who has just written a funeral symphony[30] for the July heroes, who were at the very most worth the trouble), Koreff (whose wife is unwell), Panofka (who is going to adopt French citizenship, in case of war! How proud one is to be French, etc., etc.); Panofka, I said, and I don't know who else besides. Finally, amazed, enraptured, dazed, charmed, and delighted by so much wit, genius, and transcendence of every kind, I left for Fontainebleau. On the way, I was asked what impression Paris had made on me. 'That of an old cloak which is not yet worn out enough to be thrown away, but which one puts on one's back only with disgust and displeasure.'. . . .

This letter will bear the postmark of Dinant, where I am detained for the whole evening thanks to the rumours of war which are causing the gates of Namur to be closed as early as 8.00. In three days I should be in Hamburg. . . .

One more question. I have mentioned Neipperg, and told you how devoted I am to him. Would it be possible, and not disagreeable, for you to receive him? Wouldn't people be shocked by the presence of an Austrian (I am not joking in the least, believe me) in your Milanese salon? Answer me sincerely on this point. I know he wants to be presented to you. If you see no major drawback to that, I shall give him a few lines of introduction to you.

Bien à vous,
                                                                                    F.L.

120. To Marie d'Agoult. Hamburg, 3.00 a.m., 26 October. I've at last arrived in port, making my (solitary) entry into Hamburg shortly before 9 o'clock. Parish not being at home, I have taken accommodation in the old Stadt London, the hotel used by crowned heads. Schuberth and Puzzi, to whom I sent word with the *valet de place*, came running, and took part in my supper.

---

[29] Prince Porcia, whose acquaintance Liszt had made in Milan, was a friend of Balzac, who dedicated to him the novel *Splendeurs et Misères des courtisanes*.
[30] The *Symphonie Funèbre et Triomphale*.

They are both very sorry that I didn't give them notice of the day of my arrival; it seems that a serenade had been prepared with members of the Liedertafel, and la Baudu was also to have played the *Galop chromatique* to me under my windows. But I arrived like the son of man, stealthily, like a thief.[31]

I think I ought to be tired after these five nights in the carriage, but find it impossible to sleep. I have tried to read, but can't. Not sleeping on the day of my arrival in a town is an old habit of mine. . . .

The four volumes I brought on my journey I have read to the end: Fourier, Reybaud's *Etudes sur les Réformateurs*, [George Sand's] *Spiridion* (Oh! Oh!), and Alfieri's *Vita*. This last gives me little pleasure. I generally feel no great fellow-feeling for these choleric, full-blooded temperaments. I shall certainly not read his works, short of being forced to. As for his life, it's my opinion that it must be especially interesting for editors and compositors, seeing that it goes on incessantly about proofs to correct and recorrect. More than a third of the volume is taken up by these wretched proofs [*épreuves*]. It was a severe trial [*épreuve*] for me to read to the end, and, had it not been for the pelting rain, a good many cigars and the absence of any other reading, I would certainly not have succeeded. I began by making a few notes on it, but didn't have the heart to make a mess of the whole volume. . . . There is in truth nothing of interest in this book other than a few memories of childhood and adolescence, and his passion for horses, which I don't yet share.

Spiridion seemed very long. There are some fine remarks here and there, but I definitely feel no taste for those things, said by a woman. . . . The words she puts into Bonaparte's mouth about the deadly war between the elements, the animal and vegetable kingdoms, are fine, but how far they are from M. de Maistre's pages (*Soirées de St Pétersbourg*[32]) on the same subject. . . . I prefer, too, the Third Act of *Robert le Diable* (the scene of the Branch) to all the Dantesque phantasmagoria of Spiridion's tomb.

Two errands: ask my mother for Duval's *Atlas des Sciences* (given me by Mlle Delarue), which she forgot to pack. . . . Secondly, remind Belloni that he needs to learn German, and if necessary advance him the money he will require to do so.

In Fourier there is a sublime remark: 'This well-being, comparable to that of the Eagle which glides without beating its wings.'

Isn't that what both of us feel when we are alone together?

[31] Rev. 16: 15.

[32] Joseph de Maistre's *Les Soirées de Saint-Pétersbourg, ou Entretiens sur le gouvernement temporel de la Providence* (1821), consists of dialogues, taking place in eleven evenings spent on the banks of the Neva, in which the speakers discuss the fortunes of virtue and vice in the world and the role played by evil in the scheme of Providence. The book contains a celebrated panegyric on *le bourreau*, the executioner, without whose work there would be social chaos.

After his concerts in Hamburg, Liszt crossed the Channel once again for a tour of the Midlands and North of England, Ireland, and Scotland.

121. To Marie d'Agoult. Birmingham, 27 November. I have donned my cope of lead (or of whatever you like) again.[33] The sole happy event in my present life can only be a letter from you. Write to me at length. Talk to me of politics and literature. For two months (Lavenu expects to keep me until 20 January) I shall know nothing of the outside world but what you tell me. Don't send me my letters. It's a physical aversion which is becoming more and more pronounced.

I should very much like to have one or two books. Through Père Brugeaud you could send me Montaigne's *Essais* (if possible Lefèvre's condensed one-column edition, duodecimo, like the Montesquieu you saw, otherwise the one-volume edition I have at my place) and Lord Byron's poems (*Childe Harold* and *Don Juan*), Bibliothèque Charpentier. If you add Leroux's book or the *Revue Parisienne* (should it be interesting), that will be welcome.

I expect to do a lot of reading. I am already a third of the way through Montesquieu (in two days) and hope to continue in the same way.

Our company is more or less the same. Only the *seconda donna* has become *prima assoluta*. That's Miss Bassano, if you still remember her, who replaces Mlle de Varny. Lavenu has fallen out with young Mori, whom I consider a nasty little dog, so we are rid of him. It's a notable improvement. Parry, Miss Bassano, and Miss Steele are all persons of composed, placid demeanour. We no longer play at either écarté or whist. We shall be bored more decently when there is time for it, but thus far that hasn't been the case.

Of all the ways of earning money, this is certainly the one that suits me best. I am completely away from everything. I read, write, and play the piano, returning to everyone, as the occasion arises, indifference for indifference and, if need be, contempt for contempt, while always, as is to be expected, doubling the amount.

Our first concert, in Oxford, went very well; yesterday's, in Leamington, less well. So far as today's is concerned, we are undecided. Perhaps there will be 40 people, perhaps 300 or 400: a very serious and worrying topic of discussion for my travelling companions, and which torments me violently as you can imagine.

---

[33] The wearing of leaden copes is the penalty devised by Dante for hypocrites (*Inferno*, XXIII). Liszt is not accusing himself of hypocrisy, however, but merely indicating that he has resumed the wearisome burden of the life of travel and concert-giving.

Ferco stayed in London. Lavenu has a man who couldn't be a better replacement. Besides, I have no need of anything: provided the parcels are registered and my tie-pin attached, that's all that's necessary. . . .

Do try the mixture of porter with ordinary beer. It will be something like the *half and half.* . . .

We did 50 miles the day before yesterday, 47 yesterday and 25 today. It's a little dizzying. For the rest, our tour will be a lot less tiring this time. We hardly ever have two concerts a day. On 18 December we arrive in Dublin, where we shall spend roughly a week because of Christmas.

Don't forget my books. They will be a great resource for me. If Shakespeare could be obtained in an edition something like the Bibliothèque Charpentier's, I should be absolutely delighted. But as far as I know there isn't one. Remember to send me the Byron volumes, *Childe Harold* and *Don Juan*, with Brugeaud.

I shan't say anything to you, even farewell.

122. To Marie d'Agoult. Liverpool, 1 December. I have never been so horribly nervy as this last week. It reached the point when I was reluctant to write to you. I have thought of you almost constantly with sorrow and bitterness. . . .

I am in the mood for work and reading. I shall even have to take care not to overdo it. I am still finding Montesquieu agreeable. He charms and stimulates my intellect; is at one and the same time piquant and invigorating. I was delighted by his two pages on Alexander. On the other hand, the *Discours sur l'histoire universelle*[34] which I picked up *en route* I find quite sickening. For me there is a certain impotence beneath this priestly pomp. Truth itself would put me off, I believe, dogmatically boomed out like this from the pulpit....

I yearn for Montaigne and Lord Byron. They will be two pillows, one for rest, the other for insomnia. I had an opportunity to buy them and didn't want to. Can you understand that it will give me joy to have them from you?

Your letter, which I was hoping would be longer, has revived me, has made me very happy this evening. . . .

Write to me as much as you can. As for myself, I am doing nothing but travelling the highroads and doing my tricks for the astonished people! For the last week I haven't seen a soul, still less a mind or anything resembling a man or a woman. . . .

Thalberg has only got to flood the public with arpeggios for the flood victims, and indeed to drown himself for the benefit of the drowning; I don't care a button.

---

[34] Presumably the work by Bossuet (1681).

Our concerts last week were (apart from the one in Oxford) pretty bad. True, the towns we went through were rather unimportant ones. At the theatre in Liverpool this evening all the boxes are taken. There will be more than a thousand people.

123. To Therese von Bacheracht in Hamburg. Manchester, 4 December. What a lovely ray of light amidst the thick fogs which were oppressing me! A letter from you, Madame, and so full of kind things so charmingly expressed!

How I thank you for it and how delighted I am with it! I had really dared not flatter myself that you would remember me after all this time, and in so agreeable a way!

Since I left Hamburg it has been my lot to *live* for four or five days. At present I am merely *supporting* myself, after a fashion, amidst things and people that are all but insupportable. I have to get used to it however, if I am not to die on the job like Harlequin's horse, or like poor Malibran, who died in this very room from which I am writing to you. We spoke about her, I believe. *She was an abundant woman* (as Victor Hugo once remarked to me), who perhaps did well to go before her time. Who knows? She might well have finished up by going to St Petersburg and singing out of tune like la Pasta.

Sad awakening of things human.

You have reread the *Lettres d'un voyageur*: in my opinion it is the most original book in contemporary literature and the one which most profoundly reveals George Sand's individuality. The letters to Malgache and Rollinat, in particular, I find quite marvellous. As for the one you mention, I have always borne my illustrious friend a slight grudge for making me utter therein one more nonsensicality than I have done. (*Isn't Enfantin a splendid man?!*) I have never been able to stomach that.[35] For the rest, the bit about the Fribourg organ and the letter to Meyerbeer are entirely worthy of her.

You are right to express no wishes for my happiness. More than six years ago I said to Arabella [Marie d'Agoult]: '*I would rather be richly unhappy than poorly happy.*' Fate has perhaps served me according to my wishes....

I no longer remember very clearly what Heine published about me. I only know that I replied in the *Revue musicale*, in which his article had appeared. If you are curious to know my letter, I shall send it to you.

---

[35] Liszt is here perhaps splitting a hair or two. In Letter 38 of Autumn 1835 to George Sand he certainly wrote: 'Incontestablement, le père Enfantin est un grand homme. . . .'

124. To Marie d'Agoult. 10 December. You write me letters full of charm and interest. In replying, I totally sacrifice all *amour-propre*. Indeed, what can I say about my days and my hours? Yet I am to some extent beginning to get used to them. Besides, in a week there will be a great improvement in my concerts: instead of having to play four or five times an evening, as I do at present, there will be only two piano pieces on the programme. I'm delighted about that. For the rest, our concerts are much better this time, and, if Dublin is a success, Lavenu will at least get his money back.

At Manchester I saw a brother of Lehmann. He looks agreeable and seems very capable. His is more or less the only human face with which I have exchanged a few words during the last eighteen days. . . .

The Madre [mother] topic grieves me all the more seeing that I see no immediate solution to it. That is one of the misfortunes of my life—being compelled to be surrounded and importuned by common people. I have suffered greatly from it and see no end as yet. When I get back to Paris I shall try to determine the possible and relatively acceptable terms between my mother and you. Perhaps you are a little too distressed by these *Gemeinheiten* [dirty tricks]. The audience my mother has at her disposal is extremely restricted and of no importance; I also strongly suspect Puzzi's mother, and I don't know who else besides, of exaggerating things dreadfully and saddling my mother with the blame for things for which they are responsible. There is a language to which you haven't the key, and which unfortunately is that of 99 out of a 100 bipeds. The words they use have an entirely different meaning from the one we are accustomed to give them. They often cause strange misunderstandings and violent clashes. Do you remember my indignant outbursts at innkeepers and *vetturini* [cabmen] in Italy?

Didn't I talk a lot of nonsense with regard to Emile [de Girardin]? I don't know why you tell me about his simplicity, his tranquillity of mind, etc... as though they are a discovery. Once more, I have never doubted them. Strong characters have more than one spring. Monsieur Thiers, from what his friends say, is thoroughly unpretentious too, and more preoccupied with his history of Florence and with paintings than with politics. . . .

Alcibiades was undoubtedly a model of simplicity, which does not mean that I shall do him the honour of comparing him to Emile. . . .

Send me my Byron volume (the Laroche translation), the one you bought for Fontainebleau, and the Montaigne bound in one volume (Panthéon edition), which is in my library, or just one of them if Brugeaud can't manage so many things. . . .

1841

January. The Liszt party performs in Cork (1st), Clonmel (2nd), Dublin (7th, morning and evening, 12th and 13th), Limerick (9th and 11th), Belfast (15th), Edinburgh (19th, 21st and 23rd), Glasgow (20th and 22nd), Newcastle upon Tyne (25th), Sunderland (26th), Durham (26th), Richmond (27th), Darlington (27th), Halifax (29th). Of this last appearance of the tour, the *Halifax Guardian* (30 Jan.) reports: 'We never remember a concert which was marked by so much enthusiasm, or so many rapturous encores, as that of last night.'

3 February. Liszt plays in the Hanover Square Rooms, London.

February–April. He gives concerts in Belgian cities (Brussels, Liège, Ghent, Antwerp) and then returns to Paris. Here, on 27 March and 13 April, he gives matinées musicales at Erard's, and on the 25th, at the Conservatoire, a 'grand concert whose proceeds will be sent to the subscription opened in Germany for the Beethoven monument'.

26 April. Liszt attends a concert given by Chopin, about which he pens a poetic critique for the *RGM* (issue of 2 May).

7 May–2 July. He makes appearances in London.

5 July. Liszt arrives in Hamburg; on the 7th he plays at the North German Music Festival.

15–26 July. He gives concerts in Copenhagen. King Christian VIII bestows upon him the Order of the Dannebrog.

29 July. He again plays in Hamburg.

August to early November. Liszt and Mme d'Agoult holiday on Nonnenwerth, an island in the Rhine. During this time he plays in such towns as Bonn, Ems, and Wiesbaden.

18 September. Liszt becomes a Freemason.

November. He gives concerts in northern Germany.

25 November. Liszt visits Weimar for the first time. On the 26th he plays to the Grand Duchess Maria Pavlovna and her circle; on the 28th takes part in a court concert; on the 29th gives a public concert. On the evening of his arrival he also runs into the Schumanns.[1]

December. He gives performances in Dresden (4th, 9th, 11th) and Leipzig (13th and 16th), and also makes an appearance at a concert given in Leipzig (6 Dec.) by Clara Schumann.

27 December. The first of Liszt's series of concerts in Berlin is enormously successful.

WORKS. FOUR-PART MALE CHORUSES (S72): 1. *Rheinweinlied* (Herwegh), with piano; 2. *Studentenlied aus Goethe's Faust*, unaccompanied; 3. *Reiterlied* (Herwegh), 1st version, with piano; 4. *Reiterlied*, 2nd version, unaccompanied. *Das deutsche Vaterland* (Arndt)

---

[1] Robert Schumann and Clara Wieck had married on 12 Sept. 1840.

(S74), for four male voices. SONGS: *Die Loreley* (Heine) (S273); *Die Zelle in Nonnenwerth* (Lichnowsky) (S274, *c.*1841). PIANO: *Feuilles d'album* (S165), Galop in A minor (S218, *c.*1841); paraphrase of *God Save the Queen* (S235); *Réminiscences de Norma* (Bellini) (S394), *Réminiscences de Robert le Diable: Valse infernale* (Meyerbeer) (S413), *Réminiscences de Don Juan* (Mozart) (S418); transcription of Beethoven's Septet, Op. 20 (S465).

WRITINGS. 'Lettre d'un bachelier ès musique à M. Léon Kreutzer', published in the *RGM* of 19 September.

125. To Marie d'Agoult in Paris. London, 14 May. Your letter puts a little life back into me, dear Marie. So you will come to the Rhine, or somewhere else. We shall, therefore, be able to spend a month or more together! . . .

I still don't know what I shall do between now and July. Business is dreadful in this country, where, however, my personal position is being consolidated in a way that couldn't be better. My first paying concert is on Monday (Benedict's); my own is arranged for 5 June. If some suitable engagement does not come along between now and then I shall return to France, but dare not count on it too much.

In the mean time I am working like a madman at some tremendous fantasies. *Norma*, *La Sonnambula*, *Freischütz*, *Maometto*, *Moïse*, and *Don Juan* will be ready in five or six days. It is a new vein I have found and want to exploit. The effect these latest productions make is vastly superior to my previous things.

When I am with you I shall work at more serious things, so as not to be entirely unworthy of my poor, dear Marie. . . .

I saw Rachel in [Corneille's] *Horace* yesterday; same impression: artificial talent, lacking tenderness, grace, or love, but grand and magnificent in disdain, scorn, irony. In a word, truly and sublimely Jewish. It is the bitter, resounding voice of a people who have been hunted down and degraded. . . .

I shall send you a couple of words for Ricordi, which Mlle Lagrange will take him. As for la Samoyloff and Neipperg, it's better for you to write, for I have just recommended my cousin very warmly and cannot renew the request immediately.

Write to me a lot; I need it. For me, anything which is not you, or doesn't come from you, or doesn't lead to you, is dead.

126. To Marie d'Agoult. London, 31 May. . . . All these last days I have done nothing but fret and fume. To be living in a business country without doing business is awful.

But, lo, a very small star is rising for me. Yesterday the Cambridges asked for me; I played there with enormous success. Next Saturday Rachel recites verses for the Poles at the Duchess of Sutherland's.[2] I have postponed my concert for a week (until 12 June) to be able to play there. People are beginning to talk of me. *Cosa importantissima*, my relations with artistes and with society are getting on to a very good footing. My concert will probably be very brilliant. Esterházy, the Russian and French ambassadors, the Cambridges, the Beauforts, *et al...* will be there. In fact, I am going to hire a gig by the week! Am I not being very simple to bother with these trifles?

Nothing easier than my incognito. We shall at last have an ideal rat-hole! But do try not to be ill! I shall be responsible for the rest.

To spend all my days, all my nights, with you and you alone, to see you, adore you, lose and transform myself in you, what a dream, what happiness! Am I to some small extent worthy of it?

Do send me d'Ortigue's article. Has Kreutzer published the biography in the *Musée des familles*? I should very much like to have it too. Nevertheless, if you forget to reply to these two points, I promise not to grow impatient. . . .

127. To Marie d'Agoult. London, 1 June. No, my dear, I am not la L[oewe]'s lover, nor shall I be. We see one another quite often, but without exchanging either looks, or words, or even loving silences. She is rather a refined lady with an artistic instinct. Her manners, as you know, are those of a lady, which is rare, not to say unheard of, in this category. She is, in addition, rather choosy about the company she keeps, and by no means makes herself commonplace (in London, at least).

For fear of forgetting, I am replying to all your questions.

1. Firstly, I asked Polez for the dresses before you mentioned them.
2. Yes, I believe I sent the money to Abate, but through you.
3. I shall write to la Martellini on the first day.
4. I have received [Meyerbeer's] *Moine* and [Beethoven's] *Adelaïde.*

On rereading your letters I find a kind of question relating to a Hungarian songstress. No, I tell you.

Now that I have replied to more or less everything, I shall tell you that I am writing to you from my bed, seeing that I was nearly killed yesterday evening. A wretched cab overturned and I got a bump on the head and sprained my left wrist a little.[3] I have just had eight leeches attached to the said wrist, and by the time you receive this letter I shall be thriving.

How I envy your doing botany and astronomy!

Talking of astronomy, your friend Greville came to see me. We talked of you a lot, and when I bestowed inordinate praise upon your intellect he said naïvely:

---

[2] Stafford House, now named Lancaster House.

[3] Fellow occupants of the cab were la Loewe, her sister, and the Austrian diplomat Philipp von Neumann.

'That's strange—she must have changed considerably.' I then pounced on one of your letters and read it out to him grandiloquently. The one I chanced upon was the one containing your appraisal of the talent of M. Arago. Poor Greville couldn't get over your superiority! . . .

Farewell, dear one; I kiss you tenderly.

128. To Marie d'Agoult. London, 5 June. These last few days I have been so annoyed, so enraged, by my accident, that I am reproaching myself for not sparing you any anxiety by writing more often, dear Marie. But in the first place my accident is absolutely nothing, although it completely prevents me from playing the piano, which altogether vexes me. Further, I have remained without any letter from you, which hasn't put me in a mood to write. Today a few nice lines have arrived. I reply at once.

1. I haven't the least knowledge of Camilla's[4] trip to Paris, if she has made it. In response to one from me she recently wrote me a letter which is neither curious nor interesting.

2. I can only repeat what I have already written to you about la L[oewe]. I am even so preoccupied with avoiding anything excessive that I sent to ask her not to come and see me during my illness, although five or six women (including Lady Blessington) visited me. So la Loewe did not come, and all these quite unfounded rumours will probably soon be at an end.

Do you know what I am going to do this morning? For the benefit of the Poles, and since my left arm is necessarily in a sling, I shall be playing my duet with Benedict with one hand alone.

Farewell, dear one. I have to rehearse and leave at once for this wretched concert. I shan't be able to write to you until Monday. In the mean time, a thousand loving kisses on your beautiful brow.

There is absolutely no reason at all for you to come here.

129. To Marie d'Agoult. London, 10 June. . . . Your letters are distressing; my life still more so. This confounded sprain exasperates me. Yet I am hoping to play on Saturday.

The Sutherland matinée created a certain sensation. The Duchess was extremely kind and gracious to me. After the concert she invited me to go round her apartments, which was very much noticed. . . .

[4] Marie Pleyel.

Tomorrow I dine at Chiswick with the Duke of Devonshire. Prince Esterházy has asked me to go and dine with him whenever I may have nothing better to do. After my concert he will give a soirée for me. The Queen, they say, is also to invite me to play to her shortly. D'Orsay and Lady Blessington have so graciously renewed their invitation to me to spend a few days with them that I shall probably go next Tuesday and stay for a week.

I have made no new friends. My relations with la L[oewe] are at exactly the same point. The Secretary of the Russian Embassy, Count Cryptowich, is the only person who didn't send me his card when I hurt myself. (Between ourselves) the reason is certainly the matinée for the Poles. In a couple of weeks I shall come and spend a fortnight in that beautiful, agreeable room of bear's-ear velvet, you being the velvet and I the bear.

My lack of money enrages me, but when I am with you I shall forget about it. Parish is to find me an engagement for a festival in Hamburg around mid-July. That would suit me splendidly. It would make a good return to Germany.

At the beginning of August you could come to the Rhine, which would enable us to spend our autumn together. Does that still strike you as a good idea? Haven't you had enough of me? Whatever happens, you know that my life and thoughts belong to you alone.

I have read part of Hugo's *Discours*.[5] It seemed fine, but that lack of consistency in thought which doesn't exclude a wealth of ideas I found perceptible in this piece as elsewhere. I am glad that you see him. He is one of those rare men who attract one strongly to begin with, then stop one and make one retreat with bitter regret.

There are so to speak bronze boundary stones on his mental horizon. But he is often very great and very splendid. His conversation is powerful, rich, luxuriant, and yet a certain artificiality and theatricality is always mingled therein. Tell me what impression he has made on you.

Farewell, dear one; I kiss you tenderly.

130. To Marie d'Agoult. London, 14 June.[6] Your letter, though sad, is doing me good, dear one. My head and my nerves are horribly disturbed too. Like you, and perhaps more than you, I need air. Where to breathe, where to dream, where to live?

Close to you and with you alone!

---

[5] The speech pronounced by Hugo when received into the Académie française, 3 June.
[6] Wrongly dated 16 June in Daniel Ollivier's edition.

This fatal artistic calling is a sore trial to me. My life is as prosaic, harsh, and gloomy as a gambler's, and the game I am playing a long and listless one. You understand me, don't you, dear Marie? And feel some pity for me?

My concert brought me hardly any money. The public at large failed to come. It was a bad day, people are saying generally. But as a social success it would have made you content. The Cambridges, the Duchess of Gloucester, the Duchess of Sutherland, the entire Austrian Embassy (I dined again yesterday at Prince Esterházy's), the Morpeths, Lady Jersey, Lady Carlisle, Ashbourne, Lincoln, *et al*..., the Cryptowiches and even the B's, were there. An audience like that has been seen at none of the season's concerts, and at none has there been such unanimity of praise for the unfortunate beneficiary.[7] My wrist still being swollen, I could play only four pieces; it is impossible for me to do wide stretches with the left hand. That puts me in a fine humour, as you can imagine. I cried my eyes out after my Fantasy on *La Sonnambula*, which nevertheless made a splendid effect despite the weakness of my wrist.

Everyone is urging me to give a second concert. I'll see. I don't want to leave here for another fortnight. It's a matter of money and obstinacy.

This evening I am playing Hummel's Septet at the Philharmonic [Society]. My left hand is not necessary for this piece. The remainder of the week I shall be resting at d'Orsay's, whose hospitality I am definitely accepting. From Wednesday onwards I shall be staying at Gore House, but continue to write to the Erard address. Belloni will bring me your letters.

I have received the Abbé [Lamennais]'s volume and immediately lent it to la Blessington. I have read only a third of it and can't yet give you any opinion of it. By the end of the week I shall have read it all and will speak to you about it at length. . . .

Bohain came to see me yesterday. He has known Girardin for a long time. His conversation is curious and very whimsically substantial. I made him a gift of a remark on the legitimist party: 'There are parties whose tail is bad, but the legitimist party is lacking in its head, and hasn't even got one.' He found that just, and told me that on some suitable occasion he would use it. . . .

You ask me to let you know the threads that make me move in one direction rather than another. This, in a couple of words, is what it boils down to. I need a reputation and I need money, and, as much as possible, both at the same time. The great Festival being prepared in Hamburg for the first ten days or so of July gives me an excellent reason to return to Germany, where, strictly, it is true, I have no need to return. However, as I shall there be able to make

---

[7] Reviewing this matinée of 12 June at Willis's Rooms, King Street, *The Times* (14 June) reported: 'The Duke of Cambridge honoured M. Liszt with his presence, and appeared highly delighted with his performance. Indeed, no laurelled conqueror could desire a more complete triumph than M. Liszt was greeted with on this occasion.'

at a stroke 5 to 6,000 francs net, I think it is sensible to accept the invitation made directly to me and to go there. My present lack of money quite determines me to do so. If I had earned about 10,000 francs here, I would have declined; but as it is, unless you tell me not to, I have to follow the rough and bitter road which cries to me: 'Shift yourself, vagabond!' . . .

The weight of the day is heavy to bear, but the evening will be beautiful, very beautiful, and night's dreams divine.

Yours, dear Marie, yours alone.

131. To Marie d'Agoult. London, 19 June. So you will be coming to Nonnenwerth! After all, I see no great inconvenience in your journey to the Rhine. . . .

You will have, or rather we shall have, our two years [months?], which will be the happiest, most fruitful, the sweetest and most passionate of our lives. I ask for nothing better than to come totally and tyrannically under your Napoleonic influence.

I dined at Prince Esterházy's yesterday with about thirty people. Next Friday there will be a soirée musicale at his place which he has asked me to compose (I had written conduct) for him. I have invited Rubini*, la Loewe, and Staudigl (who, incidentally, has the most splendid basso-profondo voice imaginable). I am rather counting on the effect this soirée will make.

In short, I am beginning to make my way fairly well in London society. Mr Chorley, whom you heard last year, told me: 'A year ago we wanted to hear you because you were the latest; this year we want to listen to you because you are the best!' This shade of difference is pretty accurate.

These last few days I have been suffering from both toothache and stomach ache.

Yesterday I got down to work again. I have paid Moscheles and Beale fully. Nothing is left now but the debts—amounting to 120 louis—in Brussels, which will be paid in a month. I am thrilled to be freed. You wouldn't believe how that was bothering me! Besides, Moscheles finished quite differently from how he began. The Jewish character revealed itself. No matter; I shall tell you the details when we see one another. I am reluctant to write these things.

The journey to the Rhine with Belloni will be productive in a very different way. And if you come to Nonnenwerth my star will shine on me again—at present, instead of a star I have only a candle. That is the best comparison for this indescribable *amour propre* or point of honour which makes me continue the sad and interminable game I am playing with all my might. In the end I shall have to finish by having... What? A kind of reputation and position in Europe. I feel everything, I understand everything, and that's my misfortune. Pity me and love me.

Tell Bovy to send a dozen medallions to Hamburg, addressed to Schuberth, music publisher.

132. To Marie d'Agoult. London [Wednesday] 23 June. I have had no letter from you since Thursday. It's a very long time. I've been suffering dreadful toothache, haven't slept a wink these last three nights, and am still quite done in.

You are probably right as regards Brussels. In any case, do ask Felix [Lichnowsky*] on my behalf (and on yours) to make no approaches whatsoever either for the Cross (which would positively vex me) or for the Professorship that you take to be a serious mistake.

Although I am rather tired of my ideal value and would sometimes gladly exchange it for a mess of pottage, I nevertheless ask for nothing better than to remain such as I am. The fixed sum of 6,000 francs and the possibility of being able to work for three months in the year had rather attracted me to Brussels. I know full well that, in St Petersburg, if I wanted 30,000 francs, I would have them, but Russia is impossible for me. France is distasteful to me. There is no position there but the journalist's. England... not for anything in the world would I like to live here. And so what remains? Venice, Florence, Albano, or anywhere on earth that pleases you.

I take the boat from London to Hamburg next Tuesday, 30 [29] June.[8] The *Musikfest* concerts are fixed for 5, 7, and 8 July. I shall play on the 7th and my own concert will probably take place on the 10th. I reckon on about 10,000 francs from this trip, for I shall probably play in Bremen and in Hanover. I need this money to spend a month quietly with you. Whether it is on Nonnenwerth or in Paris I don't yet know. I shall decide that in Hamburg. . . .

I could have spent 48 hours with you before Hamburg, but am so morose that I haven't the heart to come to you. I need to play my Hamburg game, which will be successful, I imagine. After that we shall have a month and perhaps two. Tell me if you definitely believe the Rhine to be too compromising for you. I don't know why I can't get that properly into my head.

The day after tomorrow there is a grand soirée at Prince Esterházy's, who decidedly couldn't be better to me. The season has been entirely taken up by

---

[8] In the event, Liszt left London at midnight on Friday, 2 July.

politics, yet I am digging my hole in this Great Wall of China. Were it not for my wrist, which is taking so long to get better, I would have given a second concert. . . .

Farewell. Do write more; I am thoroughly depressed. Belloni does all he can to make me laugh—with very little success.

133. To Marie d'Agoult. London, 26 June. . . . Darling, you are adorable, and I am madly, crazily in love with you.

My letter of the day before yesterday answers, I believe, your objection to Hamburg. Such a big Festival as the one for which I am engaged, won't come my way again. I saw a great chance to make, immediately, a certain amount with which to pay my travelling expenses in the Rhineland. Besides, the crossing takes no more than 54 hours at this time of year, and Holland and Belgium are no good just now.

Whatever people may say, as regards business I believe I can manage as well as anyone. About 20 July I can be in Frankfurt. Perhaps the best thing you could do is take the mailcoach from Paris to Frankfurt. It will take you 52 hours at most. That is tiring, true, but less disagreeable than any other way. Tell me if that frightens you, and be of good cheer.

You will have your dresses within a fortnight.

I created a stupendous effect at Prince Esterházy's yesterday. The cream of London (about 60 people) was there. I accompanied la Loewe (of whom I am still not the lover, or even the doting friend), Rubini, and Staudigl. I played three or four pieces (despite my wrist, which is being obstinately slow in making a full recovery). You would have been pleased.

Instead of Tuesday, I shall not leave until midnight on Friday because of a soirée at Lady Ashbourne's to which the Cambridges and the same people as yesterday will be coming. . . .

Do send me a copy of the Kreutzer biography at once. I am rather curious to read it in printed form. Schober has just sent me a long description of fifty to sixty pages,[9] which I shall send you, of my visit to Hungary.

Let me know very quickly if you think you will be free around 15 to 20 July. The environs of Frankfurt, or Mainz or Heidelberg, would perhaps suit you better than Bonn. In any case we shall have the choice. I am somewhat fearful of the Committee[10] and of the prodigious attention you will attract in so small a town with a large student population.

---

[9] See Letter 112 n. 22.   [10] That formed for the Beethoven monument.

Farewell, dear one, I kiss you tenderly.

Belloni left for Hamburg last night.

134. To Marie d'Agoult [London, late June]. Why ask 'what am I good for?' Don't you really know that you are more than good for me, that you are necessary to me! I couldn't live, live with intensity, with energy, with pleasure and with resignation, what is called living, without you. I dream only of you and think only of you. It is truly in you, as Saint Paul said, that I live, and move, and have my being. I shall say all that to you better than I could write it; or, rather, I shall say nothing to you, or something else. But tell me, do tell me, that beating in the depths of your heart you feel my love, my passion, my tenderness! Oh! tell me that, and let me know that you are happy!

For two days I have been living at Gore House, d'Orsay's place. I am still very content with them, d'Orsay in particular.

Since you like my remarks, here is one which Lady Blessington liked: there are two categories of lovers, differentiated by the auxiliary verbs 'to have' and 'to be'; those who wish to *have* their mistresses and those who *are* theirs (I think I said it better, but no matter).

Who the deuce could have told you the story of the duck? Something like that did actually happen, but I would never have imagined that it could have travelled as far as you. Quite simply, I threw myself into a pond for the amusement of two ladies that I haven't seen since. One of them (Miss P...) published a dozen pages about my sojourn in Hungary.[11] The other was completely unknown to me. There is absolutely no *galanterie* in this incident, any more than in my relations with la Loewe.

Don't send your reply to this letter to London but to Hamburg. Put Parish's address. Tell me how you are. Are you putting on weight?

Tell me how you expect to come to the Rhine. Would you believe that I had even thought of the possibility of the Hamburg route? As you don't suffer from sea-sickness, that would perhaps tire you less and we should see one another a fortnight earlier. But you will not be free immediately, and so Frankfurt seems the best itinerary. Next Friday, at midnight, I embark at the Tower of London, and no later than Saturday evening I shall be in Hamburg, either at the Alte Stadt London [Hotel] or at Parish's. . . .

The idea of sending the medallions to Schott, in Mainz, is excellent. If you can, pay the 80 francs back to Bovy.

---

[11] Julia Pardoe in her *The City of the Magyar, or Hungary and Her Institutions in 1839–40* (London, 1840).

135. To Marie d'Agoult. Hamburg, 6 July. No, it is true, you rid my poor life of none of its tedium, you chase none of the clouds from my brow, you bring no smile to my lips... but there is a smile in my heart when I receive a few kind words from you; a ray of heavenly light shines through all my clouds when I think of your beautiful brow; and my lips crease with that irony which is perhaps of genius, perhaps of greatness, when amidst my trite anxieties your name is pronounced, your memory recalled, when there comes to my mind the least word you have uttered, when there meets my gaze the most trifling object you have touched.

I don't know if that is happiness, but perhaps it is love.

I didn't mention Hamburg to you until late. You neither could nor should come here. So prosaic a town is quite impossible for you. I believe I should suffer to see you here. Mainz, Nonnenwerth, fine. I shall certainly be there around 25 to 30 July and hope to arrive with full pockets. Plutus[12] is decidedly obsessing me: I cannot bear to think of not having enough money. By the next post I shall tell you of a plan which will, I believe, put me on a sound financial basis and strike you as thoroughly odd. Don't laugh, and above all don't look sad. I need to go to Copenhagen! I believe I shall find some money there, and to go from Hamburg to Copenhagen takes no more than twenty-four hours. I shall probably leave on Tuesday. Continue to send your letters to Parish's, where I am staying, or else to Schuberth's, which is even better.

I shall spend no more than ten or twelve days in Copenhagen, at most, going from there direct to Frankfurt.

Tomorrow I play at the Festival in a hall which holds 4,000 people. My concert, arranged for Friday, will be a complete success, I feel certain. I shall probably give a second immediately afterwards, for I am in a hurry, a real hurry. . . .

136. To Marie d'Agoult. Copenhagen, 22 July. It's now more than a fortnight since I had a word from you. I don't know what to think, what to believe!

In any case I shall leave here on 26 July (Monday evening). On the 28th I shall be in Hamburg. I don't know how and why I imagine that I shall find you there. I have an immense need to see you, and, thank God, shall be able to do so very comfortably, for I shall have 10 to 12,000 francs available. My Copenhagen concerts have succeeded admirably and the Court has been more

---

[12] Greek god of wealth.

than charming. I am at last beginning to breathe, or, rather, can foresee the day when I shall breathe very freely.

I hope that in Hamburg I shall at least find a letter from you telling me of my destination; if not, I shall leave on the 30th for Amsterdam and wait for a word from you in Rotterdam, poste restante; I shall be there on 3 or 4 August. In ten days we shall finally embrace one another.

Yours, yours.

Don't wait for any more letters from me. I am out of my mind from waiting!

137. To Marie d'Agoult. Hamburg [Tuesday] 27 July. I definitely leave for Amsterdam at midnight on Friday, dear Marie. On Monday morning I shall be in Amsterdam and in the evening at Rotterdam; on Tuesday, if there is a boat, I leave for Düsseldorf, which I shall reach in the evening. I shall continue my journey on Wednesday. I shall first look for you (as Mme Mortier Defontaine) at the Hôtel des Bains, Rotterdam, then in the two or three main hotels in Düsseldorf, and finally at the Rheinischen Hof in Cologne, where I hope to find you on Thursday at the latest.

Were my letter not to reach you in time for you to be in one of those three places, I should not look for you any more until Mainz, Rheinberg, where I expect to arrive on Friday. But I should very much like you to come at least as far as Cologne.

Adieu, adieu, I am writing to you from a bad inn where I am detained by raging toothache. Your three letters reached me simultaneously, but we shall explain all that. Meanwhile, let it be enough for you to know that I attained the object of my trip to Copenhagen.

Present at Liszt's concert in Hamburg two days later was Emma Siegmund (later the wife of Georg Herwegh), who penned about it what was probably the greatest tribute ever paid to Liszt, *qua* pianist, for it could hardly be surpassed: 'It was not Liszt who was playing, but only his mortal frame, being used by God.'

138. To Princess Belgiojoso [*c.*October[13]]. I had come to the Rhineland to have some rest and to recover my breath a little before my journey to Russia. It has been quite impossible. Independently of obligatory trips to Ems, Baden, Wiesbaden, etc., I have had to practise my trade of concert-giver in a lot of

---

[13] The Princess replied to this letter on 9 Nov., from Locate (a village near Milan).

places whose very names would prove too much for your geographical knowledge, so that I am finally getting round to this blessed Russian expedition when already worn out with fatigue and exhaustion. The cold will give me back some strength and colour, I hope.

'Try to convince yourself that it's restful for you to write to me,' you tell me. I would have no great difficulty in convincing myself of many things concerning you about which you would not even care that I am convincing myself. But should I tell you so? My unwavering and idealistic cult for you (and don't take this for twaddle) has not exactly made my relations with you easy for me, as you say. I was always somewhere you were not, and now again am appealing much more to what is undefined and unexpressed between us, than to what we have been able to say or write. My life is full of obstacles, of worries, of wretched little pettinesses. From time to time, and from afar, a ray of light has shone on me, and I have felt heartened and uplifted. You have been full of gentle forbearance and noble kindness towards me during a time in which many others have shown little forbearance, little kindness. I shall never forget that first year in which I had the honour of knowing you. Since that time you have been something, if you will allow me, *more* for me...

Shall we ever be able to talk freely and at length? Let me hope that it will be next autumn in Venice. Oh! don't regard this Venice plan as a mere castle in the air. I have a need to go back there, I want to go back there. The apparent reason for this return will be my *Corsaire* (I tell you this in confidence, and you alone, while asking you to mention it to no one else whatsoever). Although my career as a virtuoso has expanded since we took our leave of one another, and although at the present moment—forgive me once again this arrogant self-conceit—I am on the point of being the only one of my breed, I should nevertheless not like to grow old in this trade. In three years, and no more than that, I shall be closing my piano. It will be in Vienna and Pest, those places where I began my career, that I shall bring it to an end. Before that, as early as the winter of '43, I want to put on an opera of mine (*Le Corsaire*, after Lord Byron), and it is in Venice that I shall do so. Had it not been for financial reasons, this would already have been done. Once more, don't mention this plan to anyone at all; as yet, I have confided it to one person only.

In the mean time I have just written something that I am very glad to have written. It is a male chorus on a philosophically patriotic German text by Dr Arndt, very well known and popular in Germany. The sentiment and conclusion of the text is German unity. I am going to have this piece performed in Leipzig and Dresden by the *Liedertafel*—a word which is untranslatable, because it refers to something which exists nowhere but in Germany. The literal translation would be 'song table'. In every town there are gatherings of from 40 or 50 to as many as 200 people from different social classes who get together every week to eat, drink, and sing. A great many pieces unknown abroad have been composed by German composers, of all ranks, for these gatherings. Next year, when the Beethoven statue is unveiled, I should be in a position to bring together in Bonn the *Liedertafeln* of Frankfurt, Mainz, Cologne, Aachen, Düsseldorf, and other places; and 500 male voices will then sing 'Was ist des Deutschen Vaterland'! (I ask forgiveness of your lovely and melodious Italian ears for these barbarous words.)

I don't know if you were joking when you asked me to tell you about my successes. In any case, I am reluctant to give you a report of my concerts which, thank God, are all succeeding like love-children. However, two things stand out in the vagabond life I have been leading these last 14 months: firstly, a small personal success in Paris (March and April), and then the warm and friendly fellow-feeling I have found in the Rhineland this autumn.

In a fortnight I shall be in Berlin. Be very kind and write me a few lines poste restante. And above all don't ask me any more to retain some 'memory of my friends'. You know that I am devoted to you with heart and soul, and that I want to retain my little *cult*, and not a memory. Wholly at your feet.

F.L.

139. To Marie d'Agoult. Bielefeld, Saturday, 13 November. After I had said goodbye to you, soon after, I felt a profound need of oblivion. Throwing myself on to my knees in that room in Düsseldorf that you had just occupied, I asked God for patience, strength, an upright will! . . .

In the evening of the day when I left you, a concert in Krefeld (an important town because of its silk factories,[14] which are the foremost in Germany); on Sunday, 7 November, a concert in Wesel (for the benefit of two poor people, both of them interesting, which is rare). At Wesel I also made the acquaintance of a music critic, headmaster of the town's *Gymnasium* [grammar school], with whom I got on very well... On Tuesday the 9th, a concert in Münster, very brilliant (like all my concerts thus far). . . .

A *bon mot* of mine. Prince Benthein approached me during the concert, and after a few compliments told me that the Archbishop of Cologne (who is always in Münster) had the previous day asked him if I always appeared, at my performances, with the sabre from Pest: 'For my performances, as for his services, the sabre is not obligatory.'. . . .

---

[14] *fabriques de soies.* In his edition of this letter Daniel Ollivier erroneously transcribed the last word as *scies,* saws.

Thursday the 11th, my second concert in the Münster theatre. An unheard-of crowd, to the point that the entire stage and wings were filled by members of the audience. Several people had come to Münster from Osnabrück and Bielefeld, to invite me to play in those towns. I gave a concert in Osnabrück yesterday, and give one this evening in Bielefeld.

As regards reading, I haven't done any. On the other hand I have transcribed the Funeral March from the *Eroica* Symphony which I shall send to Mechetti for his Beethoven Album. (What a stupid association of ideas, Album of Beethoven!) I expressed myself very sharply about it in a letter to Löwy in which I told him bluntly that if Beethoven were alive he would give us, the contributors, an enormous kick in the backside, and that if Mechetti had any common sense he would have entrusted me with the editorship of this publication: the end is excellent, undoubtedly, since five hundred copies will be sold for the monument, but the means strike me as being fairly ridiculous. The part I have taken, and shall take, in the matter of the monument would, besides, make it all very natural, and, that being the case, I would have found another title than that of Album which I cannot stand for a serious publication.

Mechetti, moreover, wrote me so prodigiously polite and despairing a letter that I couldn't refuse to send him my own contribution to the aforementioned album.

I believe, too, that I have finished the *Loreley*, but it will not be written down until the day after tomorrow. . . .

Don't be worried if I don't reply to your letters immediately. At the distance we are at, with unforeseen circuits and detours, it's hardly possible to be punctual. . . .

Tomorrow I go to Detmold. It was there 'wo Varus seinen Hermann fand';[15] I only hope I don't happen to find mine!

140. To Marie d'Agoult. Leipzig, 7 December. There are many things I should like to say to you, but I must contain myself. My heart speaks to you incessantly. My conversation is no longer to heaven but very much with you, dear Marie. And yet I have to live, work, roam the world far away from you! For how long?

I shall send you shortly a ring from the Grand Duchess of Weimar.[16] It is extremely beautiful. As you know, the Grand Duchess is a sister of Tsar Alexander.

---

[15] Literally, 'where Varus found his Hermann', referring to the battle, in AD 9, in which Quintilius Varus, and the three legions accompanying him, were surrounded in the Teutoburg Forest by Teutonic tribesmen led by Hermann (known to the Romans as Arminius), overwhelmed and annihilated—occasioning Augustus Caesar's grief-stricken cry: 'Varus, Varus, give me back my legions!'

[16] Maria Pavlovna, consort of Carl Friedrich. See under Saxe-Weimar in Biographical Sketches.

She has been the friend and protectress of everything outstanding that Germany has produced in art and literature. No one could have been more gracious to me than she has been; and it is certainly to her that I am indebted for my decoration of the Falcon, which has given so much pleasure to my friends. I don't know if you were even aware of the existence of this order which, moreover, they don't give to anyone and everyone. Its motto, *Vigilando ascendimus*, is a beautiful one and suits me in all respects. I hadn't to make any move to obtain it.

A friend of mine whom you know only by name, Alex de Villers, said what was necessary, everything that was necessary, and nothing but what was necessary. I paid no visit nor uttered a word relating to this decoration. The Grand Duchess and the Grand Duke showed remarkable tact in the matter. At the end of a concert the proceeds of which I had offered to the Frauenverein, an institution to which Her Highness gives her special patronage, the Court Marshal came and handed me two boxes in red morocco, one of which contained the decoration (from the Grand Duke), the other the ring (from the Grand Duchess).

The concert had produced 2,000 francs net.

In all I spent five days in Weimar, during which time the Grand Duchess, who is an excellent pianist and a real connoisseur of music, thrice asked me to play *chez elle*, either to a small, select gathering or to a larger number.

The Grand Duchess has dedicated three rooms in the Weimar Schloss to Goethe, Schiller, and Wieland, and is having them frescoed with subjects from their works. 'In the preceding rooms,' she told me, 'I shall put busts of other men who have contributed to Weimar's renown: Cranach, Bach, and Hummel.'—'It falls to Your Highness to take every noble and charming initiative,' I replied, and she understood.

Before Weimar I spent forty-eight hours in Göttingen, one of the most celebrated university towns in Germany. The concert I gave there brought in 1,700 francs. It was here that Felix joined me, and we went together to Weimar, Jena (where I gave a concert at which my *Rheinweinlied* was performed for the first time, making such a very great effect, and again yesterday at Frau Schumann's concert, that it was encored, from beginning to end), Leipzig, and Dresden. . . . Before leaving here I shall write to you at length, and will give you a complete résumé of my stay.

Meanwhile I reply to your questions:

1. I have not taken the Lord Byron.

2. Schubert's *Schwanengesang* and *Winterreise* must be among my music at my mother's.

3. Your name is on the Ricordi edition of the *Ave Maria*, for it is the only one I have corrected. Ricordi has also published the Pixis *duet* (it is, I believe, a duet) dedicated to you. Write and ask Ricordi to send you both things.

4. Tell Hermann's mother that her son's letter reached me in Dresden and that the music publisher Meser, with whom Hermann kept the accounts of my concerts of two years ago, has undertaken to comment on his letter.

According to the most authentic figures, it has been made clear to me that Hermann stole 1,500 francs from me at the first concert and almost as much at the second. This, added to so many, so very many, other things... You understand, in short, that it is impossible for me to make any response whatsoever to his letter and that I very much hope not to hear from him again. Make that plain to his mother. I am truly reluctant to go into all the details of these nasty tricks of his.

5. Little Cordier[17] has had her autograph for more than a fortnight. Her Nonnenwerth portfolio contains your letters.

During the week I shall write to you at greater length. Today I have a splitting headache and can hardly write any more.

I kiss you lovingly.

141. To Marie d'Agoult. [Berlin] 11.00 p.m., 24 December. I have had no news from you for more than two and a half weeks. I am looking at that view of Nonnenwerth and rereading a few sentences from your old letters. I should like to know that you are calm and occasionally happy. Tell me if that is the case.

Since you take an interest in this nonsense, I'll tell you of a few further remarks which will perhaps appear in the *Lisztiana*!

I don't know if you know that in several music magazines absurdly eulogistic articles have been written about Kalkbrenner's son. At Weimar the Hereditary Grand Duke spoke to me of them and at the same time asked my opinion of papa: 'It is to be hoped, Monseigneur, that he will follow in his son's footsteps!'

The people of Leipzig who idolize Mendelssohn still hope that one of these days he will leave Berlin to throw himself into their arms and say: 'At last! I shall never leave you again!' When he told me of his rather uncertain position here and of the fondness he still had for Leipzig, I replied by saying that the people of Leipzig willingly paraphrase the inscription that the Académie française put beneath the bust of Molière (after his death, it is true): 'He lacks nothing for his glory—we lacked him for ours.'

25 Dec. I am ashamed to mention these things to you, and I don't even know how to mention them, but when all is said and done, you understand me; it seems to me that now and then these matters are on your mind.

---

[17] Daughter of Liszt and Marie's landlady on Nonnenwerth.

In short, since I left you not a single woman has preoccupied me for half a second. . . .

At Dresden I ran into la Sappho[18] again. It was she who wrote to me in the first place (to ask me for good seats at a concert). Her husband, whom I regard as a distinguished man (although totally lacking in polish), came to see me in Leipzig with my old friend Schober. They spent several days with me and we parted on good terms.

Not a word was uttered between la Sappho and me; no *sous-entendu* was possible... In a word, total silence on both sides. On just one occasion was there a kind of intelligent gesture between us. We were at table and Schober was saying that he couldn't understand how it was that so many people got me wrong. La S... interrupted him, saying: 'People who cannot understand L... intuitively will never understand him. He is at one and the same time a very superior man and a woman, by which I mean a marchioness, a very spoilt one.'

How could you have been so uneasy about Hamburg? I shall certainly not go there since you attach this terrible importance to it. But I admit, to my shame, that I don't understand. . . .

26 Dec. This is my Berlin news thus far. On arrival I paid visits to Meyerbeer, Mendelssohn, and Spontini. The first two get on well enough together; the last-named cannot get on with anyone. Meyerbeer introduced me to Count Redern (Intendant of the King's Music), who invited me to have dinner with him today, but by yesterday evening had not returned my visit. I told everyone that I would not dine at his place unless Count Redern returned my card. . . . I already had my letter of excuse prepared. The matter came back to Redern's ears, and yesterday at Meyerbeer's he apologized profusely for having been unable to come and see me, and at 11.00 this morning Count R... was announced. Half an hour later Herr von Humboldt* (who is an intimate of the King's), to whom out of discretion I had not paid a visit, came to me first. I admit that since Count Walmoden's visit in Milan no visit has given me such pleasure. All Berlin is talking just now of this visit of Herr von Humboldt's. Count Trautmansdorff, my Ambassador, likewise did me the honour of paying me a personal visit in return for a card I had left him. For the rest, I have hardly gone out. As you can imagine, after these three visits my room doesn't empty.

Monday evening, 27 Dec. My first concert has just taken place. Unheard-of success.[19] More than 800 people: that is, a packed house. I played entirely alone.

---

[18] The singer Caroline Ungher, now married to Sabatier.

[19] An opinion endorsed in the diary of the writer Varnhagen von Ense: 'In the evening, in the hall of the Sing-akademie, Liszt's concert, without orchestra. He played quite alone, marvellously, matchlessly, magically, earning himself universal and tempestuous applause. Not since Paganini have I heard such a master. . . . Our places were quite near the front, and we had a very good view of this brilliant, clever, handsome man. . . . The King was in his box; present

The King[20] (without my having made any approach or issued any invitation) did me the honour of coming to it, and applauded me greatly. In doing so, he made a real exception for me, as Court mourning is very strict. I assume that it is to Humboldt that I am indebted for it. . . .

too were the Count of Nassau, Prince and Princess Karl, Prince August, and the Crown Prince of Württemberg. As well as Meyerbeer, Felix Mendelssohn, Spontini, Rellstab, and a whole crowd of other acquaintances' (K. A. Varnhagen von Ense, *Tagebücher*, i, Leipzig, 1861, 385–6).

[20] Friedrich Wilhelm IV.

1842

New Year's Day to 3 March. Liszt's remaining concerts in Berlin are received with unparalleled enthusiasm.

3 March. After his final concert (for charity), at the Hôtel de Russie, Liszt is given a memorable farewell by the people of Berlin.

14 March. The philosophical faculty of the Albertus University, Königsberg, awards Liszt the degree of Doctor of Music *honoris causa.*

16 April. He arrives in St Petersburg, where his first concert, four days later, is attended by Mikhail Glinka as well as by the Tsaritsa and the entire Court.

23 April. Present at Liszt's second concert is Tsar Nicholas.

Mid-June. Liszt arrives back in Paris.

20 July. He plays in Liège.

24 July. He gives a concert in Brussels; King Leopold decorates him with the Order of Leopold.

13 September. Liszt plays in Cologne, donating the proceeds towards completion of the city's great cathedral.

2 November. He is appointed Kapellmeister Extraordinary to the Grand Duke of Saxe-Weimar.

15 November. Liszt and Rubini give a concert in Frankfurt.

Late November/December. Liszt gives concerts in The Hague, Rotterdam, Leyden, Utrecht and Amsterdam.

Late December. He arrives in Berlin, where he renews acquaintance with Richard Wagner.*

WORKS. PIANO: *Elégie sur des motifs du Prince Louis Ferdinand de Prusse* (S168); *Petite valse favorite* ('Souvenir de Pétersbourg') (S212); *Deux mélodies russes* ('Arabesques') (S250): 1. *Le Rossignol* 2. *Chanson bohémienne; Valse à capriccio, sur deux motifs de Lucia et Parisina* (Donizetti) (S401). SONGS: *Titan* (Schober) (S79), for baritone, male chorus and piano; *Mignons Lied* (Goethe) (S275/1); *Comment, disaient-ils* (Hugo) (S276/1); *Es war ein König in Thule* (Goethe) (S278/1); *Der du von dem Himmel bist* (Goethe) (S279/1); *Oh! quand je dors* (Hugo) (S282/1); *Vergiftet sind meine Lieder* (Heine) (S289).

142. To Marie d'Agoult in Paris. Berlin, 6 January. Impossible to write, especially to you. You can't possibly imagine my life. I have been ill for two days. At moments I feel as though my head and heart were bursting.

I love you very deeply.

My fourth concert takes place on Sunday, 9 January. Don't be in the least bit worried. I need to be as well as I can be, at the risk of soon being exhausted.

I am ill from concerts and successes. My room is always full, but no longer of Puzzis. Berlin outdoes even Vienna. Meyerbeer doesn't cease telling me that my successes in Paris and Vienna are nothing in comparison with here.

Here are a few newspapers. I am sending you by preference Rellstab's articles, because Rellstab* was to have been my adversary. He is the critic *par excellence* in Berlin. I refused to pay him the first visit. After my first concert he came to see me, and, although of differing opinions on several points, we can understand one another, as you will see from the lines he has written about me.

Write to me, but kindly and gently. Tell me that you suffer from the fact that we live apart like this—but don't tell me that I make you suffer. That fills me with despair. . . .

I need another week or ten days to tell you about Berlin. Yesterday I saw the King for the first time; the Princess of Prussia[1] has asked to see me tomorrow (but without piano).

I also have to send you two or three letters to keep for me, above all one from Herr von Humboldt.

Farewell—the whole of the evening of your birthday, 31 December, I wept.

143. To Marie d'Agoult. 11 January. Your letter is very kind, very gentle. I don't know how I imagined that you would respond ironically to my idea of writing to you every evening, and worrying about that prevented me from writing. I now resume, and happily.

To give you a full report on Berlin, I still need a week. On the 16th the King leaves for London. In the mean time I have given four concerts (the fourth being for Cologne Cathedral—more than 5,000 francs were taken), which brought me 10 to 12,000 francs. On Sunday the 16th I shall give my fifth, and three or four days later my sixth. The hall of the Singakademie is extremely favourable for the piano. The public and society *en masse* are protesting against anyone else taking part in my programmes, even someone of great ability. . . .

People wish to hear me as much as possible, and only me. At my third concert there were two vocal items on the programme. People complained, and many had their tickets reserved for the next concert at which I shall play alone.

As a success, and a satisfaction to one's *amour-propre*, it is splendid, but awfully tiring. My friends say I have become embittered, and I have a fever almost every day. I am longing to finish with this trade.

---

[1] Augusta (the later Empress), daughter of the Grand Duke and Duchess of Saxe-Weimar.

The King has come to three of my concerts, something very rare. I was presented to him at a soirée at Count Redern's, following which he sent me through Count Redern the *Huldigungs* medal in gold, as a token of his personal goodwill. This medal has been awarded only to ministers, to heads of missions, and to generals.

So far as artistes are concerned, the King spoke to me alone that evening. Hauman, who played too, was furious. And that is the case with several of the local artistes, my old friend Felix Mendelssohn not excepted, although our relations are still on a very good footing.[2] What can I do? There are many people who will never understand me and who will spend their lives envying me for what I would gladly make them a present of.

The Prince of Prussia and his wife (daughter of the Grand Duchess of Weimar) are my avowed patrons. She asked for me the other morning to talk to me. She is a charming and gracious princess. Her husband is *ein ganz ritterlicher Herr* [a thoroughly chivalrous gentleman]. Take it for a weakness or, if you wish, for the baseness of a courtier, but yesterday, at a matinée *chez* the King of Holland, when the Prince tapped me on the shoulder as a sign of approbation I realized that one could joyously give one's life for a master.

Manly feeling is not extinguished in me... And love, yes, the deepest, purest, most ideal love, you will rekindle and fecundate within my innermost being.

Here are the newspapers and the continuation of the *Lisztiana*.

The Princess of Prussia: 'You are very fond of the Rhine; you have stayed there a long time, haven't you; is it very picturesque?'—'It is what is most German in Germany.'

After a performance of Mendelssohn's *St Paul*: 'I should like to be able to compose so beautiful a work and not to have composed it.'

144. To Marie d'Agoult. 25 January.
You have guessed correctly, dear, dear Marie: I am horribly nervy, sick, exhausted. Four days ago I fell backwards, was delirious for more than two hours and, at the present moment, have retired to another room in the hotel, leaving my apartment to Belloni and Lefebvre and requesting all my friends not to visit me for at least four days. I feel an overwhelming need for rest.

Eight consecutive concerts, four matinées at the home of the Princess of Prussia, at which I alone, absolutely and exclusively alone, did the honours, playing seven or eight pieces each time.

---

[2] They did not remain so.

Dinners, soirées, balls, smoking-parties, non-stop conversations, proof-correcting, writing, and scoring: it all provides a physical explanation of my physical state. . . .

Look, dear Marie, here on my table is a bracelet that Belloni has had made for me, I believe. My medallion is reproduced in it rather clumsily, it seems to me, but you will be able to conceal that and have it covered (for people mustn't see my forehead on your arm) by a stone or some other adjustment, which can best be done for you in Paris according to your instructions. The bracelet is rather beautiful; tomorrow I'll find a way of sending it to you safely. Write and tell me if you find it wearable. If not, give it to my mother, but, for her, don't have it adjusted and tell her that I want her to wear it.

I am adding to it a small ring whose form seemed original to me here in Berlin—but in Paris that will probably already be known. Do with it what you will. . . .

Thank you for the Hugo volumes. I am going to read them; and in the mean time have lent them to the Princess of Prussia, who is always extremely kind to me.

Send me as soon as possible, when there is an opportunity, the medallion of Lord Byron by David. I still feel the same liking, the same passion for L. B. Hugo called Virgil the moon of Homer; when I flatter myself, I tell myself that I shall perhaps one day be B's. In any case my highly-strung infirmity will some-how unite with his morbid sublimity.

Tell Bovy, too, to send through the Embassy at least twenty of my medallions to St Petersburg for me. Had I had thirty of them in Berlin, they would all be sold. The Princess of Prussia purchased one; Herr von Humboldt showed one to the King, who spoke to me about it. Involve yourself in this sending of the medallions, for Bovy, as you know, is not exactly practical. . . .

Every day I get up at about nine. Between then and one or two o'clock, about fifty people come and go in my room. The other day, Schober told me that when he happened to take a stroll along the Unter den Linden (the central point of Berlin) just after leaving me, it seemed almost deserted in comparison. What do all these people want of me? Most of them—money. A few (especially the young) come merely to see me seated or standing; others to be able to say that they have seen and visited me; yet others (above all the *Lumpen* [scoundrels]) to write about it in the newspapers. While chatting and smoking, I dictate (for writing tires me dreadfully) to Lefebvre, Schober, and Villers the indispensable replies to the hundreds of letters I receive, arrange my programmes, put my papers in order, and, now and then, when an idea comes to me, jot down some music. In this past fortnight I have written two new songs, one for myself and the other for you,[3] dear Marie. . . .

---

[3] Respectively *Titan* and *Oh! quand je dors.*

Continuation of my letter of 25 January. Here are a few of Rellstab's articles, which are by far the best. I want to add a few comments to the one about the concert for the students. The latter had sent to ask, through Rellstab, if I would give a concert in the theatre, seeing that the admission charge at my usual concerts is too high for their pockets. For several reasons I prefer not to play at the theatre just now, and so I replied that I was very flattered by their desire to hear me, and that I was eager to comply fully with their request. Instead of waiting to be begged, I asked them to arrange a concert in the University hall and to fix the cost of tickets at 10 Gros (25 sous), reserving the right to send the entire takings to the parish of Raiding. This proposal, as you can imagine, was received with cheers. The concert took place yesterday. The hall was absolutely packed, and I was as it were obliged to promise a second concert of the same kind, to compensate the students who couldn't obtain tickets this time.

A dozen people who were very keen to take part in this truly curious entertainment induced me to hand out a few visiting cards which served them as entrance tickets, in exchange for which each of them gave me a louis d'or. Meyerbeer two, even.

Without my having informed her of this strange concert, the Princess of Prussia was so delicately thoughtful as to send me 25 louis for my Raiding parish.

In the evening more than 500 students congested the street and the hall of the Hôtel de Russie (the *maître d'hôtel* was almost torn to pieces) and serenaded me. It occurred to me that perhaps that would have given you pleasure.

I see two women here quite often, Bettina von Arnim* and Charlotte [von] Hagn.* The former made herself the sublime servant of genius: *Sie ist ein Kobold magnetischer Intelligenz* [She is a sprite of magnetic intelligence]. The latter has been the favourite odalisque of two kings; in talent she seems to be the Mlle Mars of Germany. I shall send you Bettina's two books, *Briefwechsel mit Goethe* and *Günderode*, which are most remarkable. They will interest you all the more because of the lines, or rather the pages, she has added to them for me.

This packet has become so large that there is no disadvantage in making it still larger. So I am adding to it my letter to Herr von Humboldt and his reply. This is what happened: Herr v H... paid me the first visit. I called to see him the next day, but he was out. The day after that he came to my place again. When taking him home I asked permission to pay him a further visit. 'Let me come to you,' he replied, 'for I am not sure of the time when I can be at home.' After which I sent him my medallion with the enclosed letter. No need for me to tell you how greatly I value his reply.

How the deuce do you manage to write letters so full of interesting and engaging things? Don't go and take this for a joke, but it gives me a childlike joy to reread them during these four days of nervous retreat, and it was largely what induced me to shut myself away and see no one. . . .

145. To Marie d'Agoult. Berlin, 15 February.[4] No, dear Marie, it isn't Belloni who is going to write to you. So long as I have a single finger remaining, it is I who will write and no one else. As far as I am concerned, anything you may know through others (notwithstanding your old complaints about being better informed about me by the most insignificant people than by myself), anything that others can say, invent, comment on, is non-existent. . . .

You ask how long I shall remain in Berlin. Probably another eight or ten days. In any case, reply here. The King returns the day after tomorrow. After the truly unbelievable brouhaha I have caused here, it would have been at the least improper for me to depart four or five days before the arrival of the King.

Whatever Belloni might say, it seems to me that I have done well to remain. Moreover, the eagerness, I could almost say the mania, of the public continues to increase. For tomorrow, my twelfth or thirteenth concert (including those I have given for charity), there have been no tickets left . . . since midday yesterday. On Saturday I shall play again (for the orphans) at the Opera House. The tickets are likewise all taken in advance, and they have been obliged to put policemen in the office. The King will probably ask me to go to him one morning or evening, unless the new mourning for a princess of Mecklenburg-Strelitz, a close relative, prevents it.

I had accepted an invitation from the Duke of Mecklenburg who, through his son, was offering me an apartment in the palace and all possible diversions at Strelitz, when this sad news arrived from Rome.

Summary of my ten days. Last Tuesday, 7 [8] February, I was promoted to the second degree in Freemasonry. The Prince of Prussia took part in this ceremony. . . .

The next day but one the Prince of Prussia got his entire military band, about three hundred men, to assemble, and made them perform five or six pieces. The only guests were the Princes of Bavaria and of Würtemberg, the chamberlains, Meyerbeer, and I. I was evidently, manifestly, as Lichnowsky said, *l'eroe del giorno* [the hero of the day]. In the evening, a concert in the hall of the Theatre. The programme consisted of half a dozen patriotic choruses, three piano pieces, and the *Rheinweinlied, die Ratt' im Kellernest* and *Was ist die Kleine Flavigny* performed by 150 male voices accompanied by about fifty brass instruments. I stood on a chair to conduct my two choruses, which strike me as really fine. The effect they made was very satisfactory. After the *Kleine Flavigny*, choir and orchestra struck up a song, 'Long live Meister Liszt!', which really moved me. I thanked the audience and musicians with a few emphatic words. Tears were choking me.

---

[4] Published under the date 15 Feb. 1843 in Daniel Ollivier's edition. However, there are indications that the letter belongs to Feb. 1842.

A detail I haven't told you of: at the last of my concerts in the Singakademie, on going to the piano I found a laurel wreath. As it happened, on the music rack there was a volume of Beethoven sonatas. Taking the wreath, I placed it around the volume, but nicely and unostentatiously, and so that it was noticed by only half the audience. . . .

After the concert for the students, there was a concert for the players. On Wednesday, 9 February, at ten o'clock, more than 500 dramatic artistes, singers, dancers and actors of both sexes, gathered in the hall of the Hôtel de Russie. I played them four or five pieces, and afterwards invited la Hagn, the Russian chargé d'affaires, and Brockhaus the bookseller, for a meal.

Yesterday I was nominated a member of the Berlin Academy. Next Friday the University and the Academy are giving me a banquet; there will be 150 guests, I believe. Everyone of distinction in Berlin will be there.

On Saturday after my concert the dramatic artistes are giving a supper for me.

It has been decided that, on the day of my departure from Berlin, all the students who can afford a horse will accompany me as far as the first post. There will probably be more than 500 of them.

I anxiously await your portrait. I have chosen for you a bracelet mounted with turquoises and a beautiful opal. You will receive it through the Embassy together with Felix's second volume. . . .

The Princess of Prussia has sent me the works of Prince Louis Ferdinand of Prussia and the autograph score of a flute concerto by Frederick the Great, the whole thing magnificently bound and enclosed in a very beautiful box in velvet with his arms.

The Prince of Prussia also sent me a beautiful walking-stick studded with diamonds. I shall send you the first of these presents through the Embassy.

Forgive me all these details. You know that they interest me only as much (and all the more) as they can interest you.

I am so happy that you finally believe in my profound love.

146. To Marie d'Agoult. Marienburg,[5] 8 March. I wanted to write to you when leaving Berlin. In that very room I had been living in for more than two months, that room which had seen such a succession of faces and things, I very much wanted to tell you that one thing alone, one face alone, was constantly with me, constantly needed by me.

Just when I was about to write to you, the postman brought your last letter, and, two minutes later, the hotel was besieged, the streets congested, more than

[5] In Prussia, now Malbork in Poland.

50,000 people having gathered to say to or shout to me a final farewell. Felix, who accompanied me as far as the second post-station, will have sent you details of that extraordinary day. I asked him, too, to tell you how a beastly little ring was sent to me from His Majesty, for I was loth to tell you about it. He is to send you all the newspapers as well.

One remark I cannot pass over in silence. You tell me, you of all people, that my heart has succumbed to a more serious feeling than it has ever done before. And where have you got that from? And who told you? Can you seriously believe in another serious feeling in my life? I understand nothing of these inexhaustible riches of the human heart. As far as I am concerned, I have nothing to give, therefore nothing to accept. The gamble I very openly took with my life was once and for all, and I have neither the strength, nor the inclination, nor the will to do it a second time.

If I have been unable to instil a little more peace and gentleness into you, it's cruelly and bitterly disappointing...

But let's leave it at that. I don't doubt the practical excellence of M. de Girardin's advice. Even so, can I not without self-conceit believe that there are things that I alone have the right to say and do for you? I don't know why I foresee that the publicity will turn out unpleasantly for you. I should be so happy, so proud, of an opportunity which would allow me to leave off this stupid incognito in your regard. Do believe that I should do so with all possible restraint.

I continue to wait for your portrait. Is it like the sketch he did at Lucca that Lehmann has drawn you?

It was in Marienburg that the Order of the Teutonic Knights was founded. I have just gone over the castle. A windowpane bears this inscription:

> Wer kein Krieger ist,
> Soll auch kein Hirt sein![6]

Do you understand why I am writing to you from Marienburg?
Yours and no one else's. . . .

147. To Marie d'Agoult [St Petersburg, 25 April, NS]. I don't in the least wish to recriminate, but how can it be that you saw irony and anger in my silence! *To die, to sleep*[7]... Silence is a sleep too, a heavy sleep, full of oppressions from which some women, perhaps, are not to awake other than in the tomb.

My views seem to displease you more and more; so let's not speak of them any further. . . .

---

[6] 'He who is not a warrior, should not be a shepherd either!'   [7] *Hamlet*, III. i. 60.

This is how my first week in Saint Petersburg went. Arriving on Saturday evening (ten days ago), I was summoned to the Tsaritsa the next day, Sunday. Grand Court soirée. The Tsar accosts me thus: 'We are almost compatriots, Monsieur Liszt.'—'Sire?'—'You are Hungarian, are you not?'—'Yes, Your Majesty.'—'I have a regiment in Hungary.'

During the course of the soirée I naturally asked HM for permission to play him a *Marche hongroise* (which, be it said in passing, I played remarkably), telling Wielhorsky, who is wonderful to me, that until HM came to experience the rhythm of Hungarian sabres, it would perhaps be a distraction for him to listen to their musical rhythm.

Two days later, at 2.00 on Wednesday, my first concert, in the great Hall of the Nobility. I played eight to ten pieces.[8] A concert unique in St Petersburg, with which none of the concerts given by other artistes can be compared—not only in the present season, but for twenty or thirty years. The hall being immense, I set moderate prices. The concert turned on myself alone: six pieces for piano. *Basta.* The Tsaritsa and the entire Court, save the Tsar, were present. The next day, Thursday, the Tsaritsa and the Grand Duchess [Elena Pavlovna] invited themselves to Count Wielhorsky's to hear me. I played the Weber piece with orchestra. I don't know why, but I can never play that work without thinking of that opposite box at Berlioz's concert in the [Théâtre des] Italiens! At the end of the evening, the Tsaritsa asked me for another three or four pieces.

Saturday, the day before yesterday, my second concert in the same hall (in which, incidentally, neither Thalberg nor any of the artistes who show off abroad dared give a concert, apart from Mme Pasta, who had only 700 people). . . . This time HM the Tsar came, an extremely rare honour. At his entry I said to Wielhorsky and some others: 'The hall is fuller than last time seeing that HM has deigned to come.'

Financial result of the past week, more than 40,000 francs net. From yesterday until Easter Tuesday, neither plays nor concerts are possible because of the ceremonies of Holy Week. On Easter Wednesday I shall give my third concert in the hall in which Thalberg gave his. On that evening, or rather on that week, will depend how long I stay in St Petersburg. As far as I can see, I don't reckon on stopping here beyond a month. As for my subsequent plans, it is you who will decide them. Do you sincerely wish me to join you? Do you want to spend two months in Fontainebleau or on Nonnenwerth? If you decide in favour of Nonnenwerth, it will only be necessary to take care to shut ourselves up and make it known that we will see no one whatsoever, otherwise it will

[8] At this concert of 20 Apr. (NS), Liszt actually played seven pieces, not counting any encores: Overture to *William Tell*, the Andante finale from *Lucia di Lammermoor*, Fantasy on *Don Giovanni*, transcriptions of Schubert's *Serenade* and *Erlkönig*, and of Beethoven's *Adelaïde*, and the *Grand galop chromatique*.

be unbearable. I feel a great weariness in living and a ridiculous need of rest and ... repose.

If you don't reply to this last page of my letter, I shall know what that means and I shall probably go to Stockholm and Copenhagen, or to Warsaw and Breslau, or anywhere. My table is littered with letters addressed to me from all over the place. I really don't know how I shall manage to rid myself of this virtuoso career.

Write to me as and when you find fit; and give me political and literary news, for I am living in the most absolute vacuum. . . .

After spending the summer together, Liszt and Marie briefly went their separate ways, he to Cologne, she to Paris.

148. To Marie d'Agoult. 40, Cäcilien-Strasse, Cologne, Saturday, 10 September. Got to Cologne at midday yesterday, and am staying with Lefebvre, who made ready a charming set of rooms for me. I have paid no visits. At 7.00 p.m. I received the King's command to go to Schloss Brühl (you remember our drive there with Lefebvre and Diezmann).

I could not get there until the end of the evening, as the messenger who had been sent and I passed one another, for I had taken Lefebvre to Brühl, from where I had to return to dress and go back there again. It was 10.30 when I arrived at the Schloss. The King, Queen, the King of Würtemberg, and the royal princes were there.

All were extremely gracious to me. The Prince of Prussia again readily gave me the chivalrous handshake which so pleased me in Berlin. The Queen stood up to compliment me. In the most affectionate and refined way, Herr von Humboldt chose his seat at dinner next to me—to do so even moving, very politely, a gentleman who had already sat in that place.

Petit Fichtre[9] can definitely say the very opposite of what Pelican[10] said: 'Never was anyone more appreciated and less humiliated.'

The concert for the Cathedral will probably take place on Tuesday the 13th. As Herr von Metternich is at Johannisberg,[11] I plan to ask him for an audience, which I hope he will not refuse me.

After that I shall be completely free, and awaiting your orders. Belloni is to stay in Paris until we decide differently.

Kiss the Mouches twice.

---

[9] Liszt himself.   [10] Nickname of Eugène Pelletan, former tutor of Maurice Sand at Nohant.
[11] Crowning a hill overlooking the Rhine valley near Rüdesheim, the castle of Johannisberg, with its famous vineyards, had been given to Metternich by the Emperor Francis II of Austria.

In the third week of October, after several weeks in Paris with Marie, Liszt resumed his concert tours.

149. To Marie d'Agoult. Weimar, 22 October. Today is the 22nd of October. On getting up I found your letter; it's a complete celebration, and the celebration will be all mine. I kiss and embrace you with all my heart, with all my thought, dear, unique Marie. . . .

The pain in my arm has gone. Tomorrow, the 23rd, a concert at Court. The audience will consist of the Weimar Court, the two Princesses of Prussia, Wilhelm and Carl, and the new bride,[12] daughter of the King of Holland.

Rubini has limitless confidence in me, and thus far our plan to give concerts together has suffered not the least set-back. I am very much preoccupied with the idea of obtaining for him honourably an honourable decoration. I hope to succeed. . . .

During the journey I read *Consuelo*.[13] The first volume, apart from a few details, I found boring. The second, absurd. The third will probably unite both qualities. In my opinion it is a complete falling-off of her talent. . . .

When we were passing Nonnenwerth two dry leaves fell into the carriage; I at once told myself that I would send them to you, but, before I could pick them up, Belloni had thrown them out.

With regard to H[14]—if it is the Czettritzes[15] who are keeping you informed of my words and deeds, I pity them for having nothing better to do and no longer hold it against them. Being spied on by my *valet de place* is a matter of no importance to me. . . .

Incidentally, the Czettritzes haven't received your letter, and have gone three weeks without news of you. If you want to give them pleasure, write to them. . . .

150. To Marie d'Agoult. Gotha, 8 November. Let me tell you straightaway something which gives me great pleasure. Rubini has received the decoration of Saxe-Coburg, the Order of Ernst, which is at present the *Hausorden* [family order] in England, Belgium, Portugal, and even France, through Prince

---

[12] Sophie. See under Saxe-Weimar in Biographical Sketches.

[13] Novel (1842–3) by George Sand containing many of her ideas on music. (One of the characters is the young Joseph Haydn.) Its sequel was *La Comtesse de Rudolstadt* (1843–5).

[14] Charlotte von Hagn.

[15] Robert and Marie von Czettritz, a Prussian general and his wife who had made the acquaintance of Liszt and Marie d'Agoult on Nonnenwerth in 1841.

Albert, King Leopold, the King of Portugal, and the Duchesse de Nemours. For him it was as difficult as it was important. I have at last succeeded, plainly and simply, without his having said a word or taken any step whatsoever, thanks to the tact and kindness of the Duke.[16]

There had at first been talk of giving me the decoration, and Rubini a ring. I said quite flatly that I gladly renounced all my own claims, and that I very much wished him to have the decoration; after many *pourparlers*, two concerts, two Court dinners (an entirely new honour for me), the Duke finally made up his mind. . . .

Between Tuesday, 1 November, and Monday the 7th, I stayed in Coburg, whither your letter was forwarded to me from Weimar.

Since you are harking back to the rendezvous in Koblenz, I must tell you the truth on this subject. During the whole of my stay in Paris I received no letter at all from la H[agn]. When I got to Cologne, I found on my table two letters telling me that she would be arriving in Bonn that very day. She was to stay at Schlegel's. Joseph Maria [Lefebvre] had also received a letter in which she asked him to send me those addressed to me and, I believe, even to reply giving precise information about my arrival in Cologne.

In her second letter to me she wrote: 'I hope to see you in Bonn; but in any case, after having spent two or three days there I shall be coming to Cologne.'

I sent no reply, telling Lefebvre that I would not be going to Bonn; as for Cologne, we would see when she arrived. (A singular rendezvous, as you can see!)

Those letters were already four or five days old. The next day, or the day after that, she wrote: 'I am forced to return straight to Berlin because of an engagement there; I shall stay in Koblenz until Monday morning—I don't know the day of the month—do try, etc....' This letter reached me on the Thursday or Friday. I neither set out nor replied, reserving the right to apologize humbly some other time.

While this was going on, it came into my mind to ask for an audience with Herr von Metternich, and I sent Jacob to Johannisberg. M... replied in the note that I have shown you, giving me an appointment in Koblenz, where I arrived not on the Monday indicated [by la Hagn], but on the Tuesday evening [13 September].

The interest provided for me by this visit to Herr von M. was, as you know, that of curiosity to begin with, but which might perhaps promise something for the future. It had no connection whatsoever with a rendezvous in Koblenz. . . .

---

[16] Ernst I, father of Ernst II (see Biographical Sketches) and of Albert, consort of Queen Victoria.

Ecco la storia del dolce amore [That's the story of the sweet love].

Felix spent this week in Coburg; he was extremely helpful to me in the matter. It must be admitted that there is no one like him for carrying things off, sometimes by being unrelenting. Apart from Meyerbeer (who had composed a marriage cantata), no artist has been decorated by the Duke up to now. He doesn't hand them out lavishly even to his chamberlains.

Tomorrow evening I shall be in Frankfurt. Hiller is there. Thalberg has just spent a fortnight in Pest without playing. Incidentally, Felix knows the story of Thalberg's decoration: the 6,000 francs etc. It's really pitiful. Döhler gave a concert there four or five days ago. . . .

La Sheppard threw herself at Felix with many passionate outpourings. He kept her in Frankfurt for a week or so, but is very disillusioned and claims that she no longer smells good, but without having bad breath.

I don't know how to say farewell to you after such stuff, and, to continue, will wait until Frankfurt.

151. To Marie d'Agoult. Frankfurt, 11 November

On arrival in Frankfurt.

This time our correspondence is beginning very sadly. Perhaps I don't really understand the letter I have just received. I am rereading it, and forgive me if I am mistaken, but I have the impression that a quarrel, or rather a complete and immediate break, would give you pleasure. Let neither that, nor any other things, be an obstacle. I shan't claim any credit for it. But if you wish it to be a violent break, try to put me on the positive track of some treachery (there must be several instances; I have always believed, even, that parts of my letters, which moreover will have told you nothing interesting, had been sent on to you); try, if possible, to send me a letter or anything at all which will authorize me to quarrel. Otherwise, which is more reasonable (although I am utterly tired of this role of reasonableness amidst so much folly and stupidity!), I shall flatly and naturally break things off before the end of the year, and it will be very simple. . . .

Tell me plainly what you want me to do and I certainly shan't argue. To return to Paris at the present moment would be difficult for me; however, if you wish me to I shall leave the very next day.

Kiss my children and, if possible, don't give way to emotion.

Reply at once and to Frankfurt.

152. To Marie d'Agoult. (On the steamer from Mainz to Rotterdam) 16 November

Here I am in front of Nonnenwerth once again, dear Marie.

> Nicht die Burgen, nicht die Reben
> Haben ihr den Reiz gegeben.[17]

I am going to sing those lines and set them to music, although I am in a mood neither to sing nor to write, but quite simply to weep.

Your reply didn't reach me in Frankfurt; I shan't have your news until the Hague. . . .

Yesterday, Tuesday, a most magnificent concert in the Weidenbusch Hall. The entire diplomatic corps, all the Rothschilds (seats reserved at 3 florins 30, a great innovation in the free city[18]), and a packed hall. In the days prior to the concert there was something for the whole town to gossip about. This is what it was. Frau [Charlotte] Rothschild sent a pianist to ask me to go and play at her place and to engage Rubini. I replied evasively. I was asked my terms; none suited me in the least. As for Rubini, since he knew Frau R... in London, I urged him pressingly to accept. He didn't want to part company from me (and, incidentally, I have every reason to be extremely happy with him; it would be impossible for anyone to behave more agreeably than he has done). Frau Rothschild went to the Roman Emperor [hotel] and asked for Belloni. He, Lichnowsky, and others tried to persuade me to accept at a charge of a hundred louis. I refused quite emphatically, stating my reason thus: the Roths. have never thought of doing me the slightest courtesy, and no one in the world, crowned heads excepted, has a right to send for me as one sends for a *valet de place*.

Frau R... remarked to Belloni that these [illegible] gave concerts, however. I responded by saying that Prince Esterházy sold his sheep, but that people did not for that reason take it into their heads to ask him for cutlets, and the same with Prince Metternich and his Johannisberg, etc... Frau R... persisted; and *I* persisted in my refusal. Finally, after a great many *pourparlers*, I got Rubini to call on Frau R... and to accept, which he did solely for my sake. So on Sunday there was a grand soirée, with Rubini and Döhler.[19] The former received 50

---

[17] 'It is neither the castles, nor the vines, which have given it its charm.' From *Nonnenwerth*, Lichnowsky's poem on Marie d'Agoult.

[18] Frankfurt was a Free Imperial City until 1886.

[19] In a letter of the 17th, Frau Rothschild's brother, Anthony, reported on both the soirée—'Döhler, though not so wonderful [as Liszt], plays beautifully'—and Liszt's concert: 'I had an excellent opportunity of hearing and seeing the most extraordinary player in the world. I say *seeing* because he is as curious to look at as to hear, with his long hair at times streaming over his face, at others completely thrown back by a violent toss of the head, his wild eyes, which he now and then turns on every side as if to see what kind of impression he is producing. . . . He is an agreeable, talkative man in society. . . .' (Derek Wilson, *Rothschild: A Story of Wealth and Power*, London, 1994, 121).

ducats, the latter 15, which he immediately sent back with a very polite note. What would have been still better would have been to invest them at 3% with the Baron.

As for me, instead of going to the R.s... I preferred to be conspicuous by my absence, and consoled myself for my loss of 50 ducats by winning a few florins at whist at the Prussian military envoy's. . . .

The next day [Anselm] Rothschild paid me a visit, without finding me at home, and through Lichnowsky invited me for today. All things considered, I preferred to depart. . . . You do think I'm in the right, don't you?

Have I told you the motto of my new decoration: *Constanter et Fideliter*.

153. To Marie d'Agoult. [The Hague] 30 November. . . . It is certainly your letters and not mine which are delightful and full of interest. It is to them that I owe the only enviable quarter-hours (for I spend a long time reading them) of my so monotonous life. . . .

The theatre arrangements have forced me to spend a week in The Hague before my first concert, and I hate waiting. In the mean time there have been two or three grand soirées at Court. The King [Willem II] is assuredly a distinguished man; I'll tell you about him at greater length in another letter before long, when I shall be less under the influence of the humid weather prevailing here. Belloni certainly exaggerated Holland's resources; even so, I shall very probably do acceptable business here. Our first concert went off very well, with two encores, something unheard of for this country. The King and Royal Family gave the signal for the 'bravos'. After yesterday's soirée, which took place in the magnificent Gothic gallery that the King has just had built and in which I rediscovered the paintings we admired together in the Prince of Orange's palace in Brussels just over two years ago, the chamberlain on duty gave Rubini and me a snuff-box each. Possibly they won't confine themselves to that. In the mean time I have given mine to Belloni (with whom I am very pleased at present), for the very simple reason that I don't know what to do with it since I don't take snuff, and also and above all because, by some mistake or other, my snuff-box is inferior in value and effect to Rubini's, and it doesn't suit me not to be (in things like this, at least) on an equal footing with him.

That may cause a bit of fuss in town, but it's a fate to which I must resign myself. I've already reprimanded the Prince of Orange's chamberlain rather sharply, for lack of due form; in the present case it's not a question of a reprimand, for I have neither the right nor the desire to give one, but of a very short *avis aux lecteurs*. . . .

I shall write to Blandine.

Write to The Hague. I leave for Amsterdam tomorrow, but return here in three days. . . .

154. To Marie d'Agoult. Utrecht, Friday morning, 9 December.[20] The day is dark and cold. The only ray of light which comes to me, the sole source of life and warmth, is my remembrance of you, dear Marie. I am thinking of our awakenings in Como and Florence (you had flowers which you made beautiful). It is the month in which our two daughters were born. I feel as though I have forgotten how to live. My dreams are becoming confused and the years are digging an abyss of misery for me. Yet we should need but few things, if it were what you wanted.

I haven't been able to attach myself to anything; I shall leave off all these so artificial and pointless tasks, just as one leaves off a threadbare coat, on the day I believe you will again be happy to live with me. But, whether this is a temperamental failing, hardness of heart, or blindness of mind and heart at one and the same time, I haven't believed that I was sufficient in your life, and, as an alternative, I have preferred this wandering life to a sickly stagnation which would have killed me without giving you life.

I do not conceal from myself the fact that for three years my life has been only a series of feverish and often wilful excitements, ending in disgust and remorse. I have to spend, and go on spending, life, strength, money, and time without enjoyment in the present or hope in the future. I have compared myself to a gambler. Minus the ceaseless excitement, the unfailing thirst, I could also compare myself to a man wandering through the fields, uprooting and throwing to the winds flowers, fruit, trees and seeds, without sowing, ploughing, or grafting.

My health has remained of iron. My moral strength has not diminished, my character has perhaps grown more vigorously firm. Are these the conditions of happiness? Is the ideal still possible? I cannot answer. It is for you to decide.

155. To Marie d'Agoult. Münster, 20 December.[21] I live in expectation of a letter from you, dear Marie, and have only one thought, only one desire, to rest in and gain new strength from your love.

---

[20] Dated 8 Dec. in Ollivier's edition, but Friday was the 9th.
[21] Wrongly dated 26 Dec. in Ollivier's edition.

I have written to Blandine; today is her birthday[22] and I want to kiss you on the brow.

I am rather poorly and trying to work. External distractions are too violent and beginning to weary me greatly. In three days I shall be in Berlin. You haven't replied to the suspicion I voiced concerning letters sent to you. I shan't mention it again, but will keep my conviction in this regard. The whole thing is a chapter over and done with, one which it would have been better never to have begun.

Give me news of everything and everyone, for you do it most charmingly, and I am no longer reading anything. I am in a hurry to cast these four months behind me.

I don't want to forget Cosima; it's her birthday too. I love those children, and think of them constantly. Take care of them.

Write to the Hôtel Saint-Pétersburg, or simply Berlin.

[22] Blandine's birthday was the 18th, Cosima's the 24th.

January/February. Liszt plays in Berlin, Frankfurt an der Oder, Breslau (now Wrocław in Poland), Liegnitz (now Legnica), Potsdam, Fürstenwalde, and Posen (now Poznań). At Breslau on 1 February he conducts a performance of Mozart's *Die Zauberflöte.*

March. After playing in Glogau (now Głogów), and again in Liegnitz and Breslau, Liszt arrives at Krzyzanowitz, near Ratibor (now Racibórz, Poland), where he is the guest of Felix Lichnowsky.

28–30 March. He gives three concerts in Cracow.

April. After four concerts in Warsaw, Liszt proceeds to St Petersburg. Here he makes the acquaintance of Countess Eveline (Eva) de Hanska, the mistress—and later the wife—of Honoré de Balzac. 'Liszt', she notes in her diary, 'is in performance what Beethoven is in composition, alone and unique.'

May. After a series of concerts in Moscow, where he is very well received, Liszt returns to St Petersburg.

Summer. Liszt, Marie d'Agoult and their children have a last holiday together on Nonnenwerth.

October. Liszt plays in Frankfurt, Würzburg, Nuremberg, Augsburg, and Munich.

November. Concerts in Augsburg, Stuttgart, Tübingen, Heilbronn, Ludwigsburg, Hechingen, Donaueschingen, Karlsruhe, and Heidelberg.

December. Liszt makes appearances in Karlsruhe and Mannheim, and spends Christmas in Weimar.

WORKS. PIANO: *Ländler* (A flat) (S211); *Seconde marche hongroise—Ungarischer Sturmmarsch* (S232); concert paraphrase of *Gaudeamus igitur* (S240); transcriptions of the Circassian March from *Ruslan and Lyudmila* (Glinka) (S406), *Russischer Galopp* (Bulhakov) (S478), Overture to *Oberon* (Weber) (S574), Wielhorsky's song *Ljubila ja* (I loved him) (S577).

SONGS: *Bist du* (Metschersky) (S277); *Du bist wie eine Blume* (Heine) (S287, *c.*1843); *Was Liebe sei* (C. von Hagn) (S288/1, *c.*1843); *Morgens steh' ich auf und frage* (Heine) (S290/1, *c.*1843); *Die tote Nachtigall* (Kaufmann) (S291/1, *c.*1843); *Oh pourquoi donc* (Mme Pavlova) (S301*a*); *Ihr Auge* ('*Nimm einen Strahl der Sonne*') (Rellstab) (S310).

156. To Marie d'Agoult in Paris. Berlin, 11 January (write to Berlin).
So far as my plans are concerned, dear Marie, none is possible (I mean of those I want to speak to you about) before my return from Moscow. Towards the end of June I shall return to Paris, or you will come to the Rhine, or somewhere or other, and then we'll talk and decide.

In the mean time I have recaptured my Berlin public. I'll not conceal from you that it was a difficult game. Well! I believe I have won it completely. Two days before my first concert (which I gave alone, without Rubini, following several little disagreements relating to his stage career which, in my opinion, he resumed so clumsily here, and only as a result of his wife's foolish advice), a caricature was published in which on the one hand I was shown playing to empty seats, and on the other a lot of women were throwing me baskets (*Korb geben*[1]) etc... Instead of that, there was a tremendous crush at my first concert [8 January]. The King, Queen, and entire royal family were present, and I had a genuinely enthusiastic success.

Talking of women, I nevertheless believe that I am on the point of receiving a big basket; you will be able to judge from the letter I enclose. Read it and throw it on the fire at once, for I shouldn't like it to be seen by other people. You will see that the beautiful person in question also explains many things through pride and ambition... why not? And since we are on this topic, I have to tell you at once that I disliked a sentence in your letter, as follows: 'If you put as much publicity into breaking as you have into, etc...' Is there, then, any such thing as publicity between us? I find it difficult to understand that. . . .

Let's turn to *Hervé*.[2] It's absolutely splendid. Perhaps the woman's corruption is not drawn quite adequately. I can't identify very well with this character who to some extent takes after George and to some extent after Camilla. The comparison with the tower of Pisa is extremely beautiful. All in all, it's a really charming story. . . .

Daniel's mistakes in versification delight me. Blandine has written me a nice letter, a little too wise. The next time she has to write to me, let her do it *chez vous*; don't let anyone dictate anything to her; let her write nonsense to me, so long as it is her own. I love that child, and should like her to be herself with me. I fear she is being brought up too well. What would be the good of that...

What is the use of making her so learned, so well informed? If she has any taste for music, let her be put to it a little. I should be glad if she played the piano tolerably well. . . .

The opera-glasses have been ordered; the watch will come afterwards.

Tell me if the Princess Belgiojoso is in Paris. Also, send 500 cigarettes to the Russian Embassy, addressed to Count Nesselrode in Berlin.

I am up to my ears in tasks to be attended to. I have to learn new pieces, rehearse with singers and orchestra, conduct choirs, correct proofs, etc. etc....

I shan't be writing to you a lot, but you can be sure of me.

Adieu.

---

[1] *Einen Korb geben* (to give a basket), meaning 'to refuse someone', 'turn down an invitation'.
[2] A short story by Marie d'Agoult, published in *La Presse*, Dec. 1842.

157. To Marie d'Agoult. Breslau, 22 January. I'm now sixty leagues further away from you, dear Marie. Rubini having foolishly and imbecilically re-entangled himself in the strings of the Berlin theatre, I found it fitting to push on to Breslau, a move which will give my purse as well as my little bit of dignity something to be pleased about. Arriving yesterday, I am already all but on the same footing here as three years ago in Vienna, and last year in Berlin. But perhaps I am mistaken; be that as it may, these are my plans, geographically speaking.

From Breslau I shall go and spend forty-eight hours with Teleki, at Felix's. Whether I return through Sweden and Denmark, or take the boat to Le Havre, around the end of June I shall be back in Paris. There we shall talk.

Weimar is to be for the autumn in general and this year in particular; but *au fond* I am under no obligation and shall always come to a satisfactory arrangement with the Grand Duke.

I am greatly tempted to go to Hungary next year, and should be very glad if you could join me in Vienna. Will you? Don't reply on this point; for I don't want you to say no. And so long in advance you can't say yes.

I am entirely of the opinion that I shall soon have to bring my virtuoso career to an end. Hungary is the natural and necessary conclusion. I fancy you will love that country, and I cherish the idea of spending some time there with you: 'O ma sauvage et lointaine patrie'. Perhaps we shall finally realize our old plan of Constantinople. Perhaps! Perhaps!

'Hope, child, tomorrow and then again tomorrow!'

Incidentally, I don't know how to arrange your *Valse*, but it seems fine, just as it is. . . .

I have recently become quite a close friend of one of your cousins, young Bethmann Hollweg, whom I find a charming lad, entirely *comme il faut*. Teleki, whom I mentioned to you, did the journey from Berlin to Breslau with me; we shall stay together for the whole of this fortnight at least. In July he will be coming to Paris. I am very fond of him.

It's about ten days since I last had a word from you. It's almost impossible for me to write much to you. My time is eaten up by every imaginable vexation, and I cannot change my life just now.

Believe in me and love me. . . .

About 8 February I have to be back in Berlin. The Princess of Prussia is being so kind as to await my return for one or two big concerts. The King has plans of the same kind, and I for my part will certainly give another two or three concerts. . . .

Around the end of February I shall take the same road as last year, probably again accompanied by Rubini as far as Saint Petersburg. There he and I will separate once and for all (if not before!). I shall spend only a short time in Petersburg, so as not to miss Moscow this time...

158. To Fryderyk Chopin in Paris. Posen, 26 February. There is no need for an intermediary between Rellstab and yourself, dear old friend. Rellstab is too eminent a man, and you, for your part, are too well bred, for the two of you not to hit it off quite marvellously and at once (however badly artistes generally get on with critics); but since Rellstab does me the pleasure of accepting a few lines from me, I am taking good care to remind you more especially of myself, and wish to take advantage of this opportunity to tell you once again, even at the risk of seeming monotonous, that my affection and admiration for you will ever remain the same, and that on any and every occasion you can make use of me as a friend.   F. Liszt

159. To Marie d'Agoult. Monday, 6 March. When writing to you yesterday, I had a temperature; my letter must give that away by being markedly curt in tone. I don't want to reread it; but don't go and examine my words in detail, and be kind.

It is rather remarkable that I am standing up to this life of travel, of fatigues, of vexations, of incessant dinners and suppers, in the way that I am. You must think that I could easily change it if I wanted to. If it were possible for you to be my companion for a fortnight, you would see that that's more difficult than you believe. I shan't weary you any further with an account of my concerts and of the details of my present life, but for the last fortnight I have been making a very careful collection of letters and other items which may have some sort of interest for you. If you ever have the patience to go through them in Paris, you will, I am convinced, be more indulgent to me.

In three days I go to Felix's, which suits me as little as it seems to suit him a lot; but I have to. From there I shall write and let you know where you should address your letters to me.

I have so many things to say to you that I have forgotten, I believe, to thank you for the biography.[3] Frankly, I wasn't hoping for you to put so much zeal into it and am truly grateful. It's not very important, it seems to me, under whose name it appears, but I don't want to make any decision about it. Belloni would be delighted, but that is no reason for putting his name to it. As regards selling

---

[3] That of Liszt in the *Pascallet* collection.

it in Germany, I have a perfect publisher at hand: Schlesinger in Berlin. He won't give me much money for it, but will publish and launch it to perfection. You can send the proofs to him direct (but without any markings in your own hand). . . .

160. To Marie d'Agoult. Krzyżanowitz, 18 March. We are here leading such a life of plenty that, this last week, it would have been really difficult for me to marshal my thoughts enough to write to you. Feasting and revelry don't leave off at Krzyżanowitz, and every day outdoes the one before. One certainly needs a great stomach capacity and a very well-developed bump of amusability to take it. This is roughly the programme of the week's festivities:

On Monday, a great vulture and gerfalcon hunt; the prince's entire hunting staff in full uniform. Symphonies and bugle fanfares, etc... Felix will be sending you a stuffed vulture from our hunt.

Tuesday, excursion to Grätz (a magnificent castle six leagues from here), and, on the way, visit to sheepfolds and half a dozen splendid farms. Belshazzar's feast prepared at Grätz, ascent in a balloon, fireworks, etc...

Wednesday, federal shooting-contest (reception of deputations from Ratibor and Troppau).

Thursday, eagle hunt (we lay in wait for several eagles, but didn't kill any), then a hunt on the lake (with about twenty boats); the lake is two leagues round. Geese and wild duck came crashing down in thousands.

And every day a Grand Lunch, Extremely Grand Dinner, Rout, Whist, Ball—and a Concert into the bargain, of course.

Finally, the day after tomorrow, I shall have to tear myself away from all these delights. Buying a new carriage, which obliged me to send my manservant to Vienna, is causing me a compulsory delay of four or five days. Write to Warsaw, for I shall probably spend only three or four days in Cracow. But allow me to urge you to be very discreet in your letters and, when there are certain things to say, resort to our usual hieroglyphics during these two months. . . .

161. To Marie d'Agoult. Warsaw, 5 April. I am having to contend with all manner of vexations, minutiae, and carriage accidents (I have just ordered a four-seater from my old manufacturer in Vienna, who has sent me a hut —I have to send it back to him). Meanwhile, complications with cases and trunks, etc.

The authorities have intervened in the fixing of ticket prices; there has been a lot of wrangling and pettiness, and into the bargain I have just been unwell and spent three days in bed. It was a bad cold accompanied by a temperature, so nothing serious or worrying.

I arrived here four days ago, and will leave a week today at the latest, being driven away by Holy Week. It will be impossible for me to give more than three concerts, and of these three I am forced to drop one at the Theatre. Such is the local practice. I shall need at least six days to get from here to Petersburg, where I shall probably spend even less time than in Warsaw. It is Moscow that I am aiming at first and foremost.

When writing, put Count Wielhorsky's address, Petersburg. Write a little more than you did to Ratibor, but more or less in the same agreed style.

I am very distressed at what you tell me about my mother. Your advice to make her return to Germany is good, but it will be difficult to persuade her to do so. The only way will be to make her come with me when I return to Vienna and Hungary. Once she is there, we'll try to pamper her (as Mme Laborie used to say), and she isn't someone who can resist being pampered.

It will be difficult to get her back to her family, because she hasn't really got a family. To be sure, she has a sister, who is excellent but lives an extremely retired life in Graz, and I can't see my mother deciding to live in Graz now that she is used to the comforts of Paris. As for her brother, he is in a state of irremediable poverty because of the mass of children he has sired so inopportunely.

Nevertheless, however difficult it may be to make my mother swallow this pill, I shall certainly succeed. . . .

Now for Koettlitz, who is an abominable scoundrel.

Send to the Hôtel des Princes for Beker, who served me as a *valet de place* when I lived in the Hôtel d'Antin. Promise him 100 francs, and get him to beat Koettlitz black and blue with a big stick, as thoroughly, positively, and simply as possible.

Tell my mother that if she doesn't want to lay herself open to abuse from me, she must dismiss Koettlitz at once; and, if he were to be dying of hunger at the door in the rue Pigalle, I forbid her to send him so much as a crust of bread. . . .

Lichnowsky got me to read *Julien*,[4] the publication of which I don't much approve of after *Hervé*. Buloz is right; you need to extend your range. And so, do a romance. Do it soon and make it long, involved, rich, and great. There are a hundred times too many ideas and shades of feeling in the two things you have just published. . . .

---

[4] Another of Mme d'Agoult's short stories, published in *La Presse*, Feb. 1843.

I shan't respond to your advice. I regard it as excellent, and above all expressed very persuasively. Your judgement is correct, fair, and noble, but I still maintain that you can't justly appreciate certain circumstances.

They say la Sappho is in Paris. La Hagn is to go there. La Camilla will be arriving there at the same time, I think. They have only to enjoy themselves as they find fit.

Adieu.

162. To Marie d'Agoult. Saint Petersburg [27 April, NS]. Between now and my return from Moscow I shall do no more than reply to your questions. In the first place, I am by no means free to write to you as I should like, and then I probably couldn't write to you spontaneously at the moment, being so pestered and harassed on all sides and having umpteen thousand bothers and vexations to grapple with.

Perhaps it would be as well for you to have another hundred copies of the *Pascallet* [biography] run off; 300 seems to me to be a suitable number, but of course I am entirely of your opinion (and believe I have already told you so) regarding publicity in France. My opinion would even be not to put it on sale at all. I shall have a good number of copies bound which I shall give to anyone I regard as a fitting recipient. . . .

I am delighted at your *Lucrèce* reading.[5] . . . Your contribution to the *Allgemeine* is a very good thing; so far as publicity is concerned, it is the equivalent of your relationship with Lamartine. You are right to say that there is a favourable wind, and I in my turn can say: Columbus must pity La Pérouse (!), for I am far from forging ahead.

In three or four days I leave for Moscow, and at the end of May or beginning of June I shall be able to embark here, either for Hamburg, or for Le Havre or Rotterdam. . . . My plans at that time will depend totally on your wishes. Heligoland tempts me quite considerably; but why won't you take Blandine to the seaside? She gives so little trouble, poor child, and will perhaps be glad to see me again. Besides, the pension in Berne attracts me very little. But we'll speak again about all this.

When shall I begin my travels again? I can't be too precise by myself alone. I shall have to speak to you, and you will have to let me more into the secret

[5] A tragedy by Marie's protégé François Ponsard which had been read in her salon on 12 Apr. before Lamartine, Sainte-Beuve, and other invited guests.

of your situation in Paris. The only thing I am obliged to do is to be in Weimar in February. In March I shall probably return to Vienna, and at the beginning of May should like to be in Hungary. . . .

Petersburg makes me horribly nervy and sickly. I am learning many new pieces, which forces me to practise the piano more than I have done for two years. The instrument I have had made has turned out pretty well; I should like you to be able to hear it. Yesterday I gave my only Petersburg concert. I believe you would have been pleased with me. On Sunday there is Count Benckendorff's concert for the hospitals, at which Rubini and I are doing the honours...

I kiss your beautiful brow; a thousand greetings to Lehmann.

'The Moscow public have been extremely kind to me,' Liszt reported to Marie from that city on 22 May (NS). 'I shan't succeed in leaving before the end of the week, and shall need to spend at least ten days in Petersburg.'[6] By the last week of June he was in Hamburg, where he gave a concert on the 26th.

163. To Marie d'Agoult. Hamburg, 25 June. I have given up the idea of going to Stockholm. My chances with public and Court were uncertain. Besides, the King of Denmark is not in Copenhagen; it will be a separate trip that I shall perhaps have to make in the autumn.

So I shall come to Aachen to meet you. Reply, as you reply, in a precise and positive manner to Joseph Maria Lefebvre's address, 40 Cäcilien-Strasse, Cologne. In any case, in the evening of 12 July I shall take accommodation in Aachen, at Dremel's, Hôtel de l'Empereur, I believe—but it will be enough to name Dremel, who is the Liszt of Germany's hoteliers—phew!—and will be looking out for you. Your quarters on Nonnenwerth will be prepared, and by me, if you please.

Nothing else today.

Bring Charles de Saint-Laurent's *Dictionnaire encyclopédique universel*, which I need. Further, send to my mother's to ask for the *Encyclopédie musicale* (Gathy's German dictionary), which I also need. And don't forget at least a dozen copies of the *Pascallet*, with which I am delighted, more than delighted. I shall kiss your incomparable little feet in gratitude.

Yours, and yours alone.

By early October, after the summer holiday on Nonnenwerth, Liszt had returned to his life as an itinerant virtuoso.

---

[6] To which city Liszt returned from Moscow accompanied by two bear cubs which had been presented to him.

164. To Marie d'Agoult in Cologne. Würzburg, 5 [6] October. I am
detained in Würzburg for another couple of days. Of course I don't see a living
soul here apart from Schad, who doesn't leave me from midday until six o'clock.

Just imagine, this splendid fellow lives right next to the Reichsgraf, who is
a Würzburger *par excellence.* The magnificent Palace of the Bishops, which
Napoleon added to crown property, was built by a Schönborn, Prince Bishop
of Würzburg, Bamberg, and Mainz in 1700 and something. It contains a hall
of mirrors with chinoiserie, unique in the world. Without being of great artistic
interest, the architecture is none the less excellent and impressive. . . .

In Frankfurt I dined with Aloys Schmitt and Vollweiler. The latter still remembers the harmony lessons he gave to 'Little Flavigny'![7] But Aloys' memory is less
good. I courted the good-natured fellow by playing several of his early studies
to him from memory.

Neither Bettina nor my cousin was in Frankfurt, nor anyone else. I saw only
Mme G... whom I have always regarded as a pleasant woman. The Cambridges
asked after me, but I found it impossible to pay them a visit.

Belloni has arrived—married to Zelia Belloni. He claims to have had no honeymoon, seeing that my letter reached him the day after his marriage and that
he respected his wife on the wedding day. O Blagoxi!

Tomorrow a concert in Würzburg; on Monday probably one in Nuremberg,
etc., etc.

Write to Munich; I shall be there, I hope, at the end of next week.

165. To Marie d'Agoult. Nuremberg, 12 October. Here, at last, are a
few rays of sunshine, and I am writing to you, dear Marie. Nuremberg is a marvel, and I couldn't tear myself away from it so quickly. Belloni and Lefebvre left
for Munich two days ago, but I shan't be there until the day after tomorrow.
Heideloff, whom I see every day, all day long, is a man of my stamp. 'Ich möchte
die Welt bauen [I should like to build the world]', he said when I first expressed
my admiration for the gigantic profusion of drawings that he showed me! He
is nearly 60, but still radiates the youthfulness given by contemplation of things
eternal. He's something between Orbis Pictus[8] and Bartolini, and also resembles
the Abbé [Lamennais] a little. I shall send you his book *Ornaments of the Middle
Ages,*[9] which seems to me to be a magnificent work.

---

[7] Marie d'Agoult herself.

[8] This shortened title of an illustrated encyclopaedic reader first published by Comenius in 1654 was one of the
nicknames of young Henri Lehmann.

[9] *Les Ornements du Moyen Age: Die Ornamentik des Mittelalters* (Nuremberg, 1843).

It is agreed between us that he will begin my Album, and with the design of a Sänger-Burg that he wants to build for me at Grafenwerth. Would you believe that the cost will be only from 50,000 to 60,000 francs! I have given him a promise to return to Nuremberg and to introduce to him a young architect whose artistic education he will have to finish. The idea of bringing you here next summer greatly appeals to me, for I am convinced that you will be very happy here.

Two months out of twelve, is horribly sad. If you could know how bored I am, in what a shrinking and suffering state I spend my days, you would love me for it a little, I am sure.

But there is nothing to be said on this topic at the moment, since there is nothing to be done about it. . . .

I have purchased a dozen delightful statuettes of the Apostles for you. I am sending them via Cologne. . . .

Farewell; I kiss you and with great difficulty refrain from coming out with any kind of ridiculous sentimentality.

A thousand greetings to Orbis Pictus.

166. To Marie d'Agoult. Munich, 22 October. I can't in the least understand how it can be that you are not here. Will this restless desire of mine to see you, will this need I have to live and breathe in you, really never be assuaged!?

I am thoroughly depressed, quite sickened, at the thought of having to go on living like this.

You asked me to give you my impressions of Munich. I found here what I was expecting, and even more. What the King's[10] ardent enthusiasm has achieved with this intractable bit of land, which seemed so unlikely to become historic through art, is quite prodigious.

You absolutely must come here next year. What will strike you above all is the intelligent grouping, the wise, poetical distribution of so many masterpieces. Not only is everything beautiful, but everything is in its right place, thus doubling its worth. That feeling of confusion with which we were so often wearied by churches in Italy is impossible here, where the set square and the luminous compass preside over all artistic endeavours. To give just one example, in the Ludwigskirche, painted solely by Cornelius, the painter set himself the ingenious programme of somehow making a picturesque *Credo*, and of grouping all his compositions around verses from the Nicene Creed. . . .

---

[10] The art-loving Ludwig I, King of Bavaria 1825–48.

However, Cornelius's frescoes are not in my opinion the finest. Schnorr and Hess seem to me to be superior so far as technique is concerned, and by no means behind him in composition.

A new process (I say new, for it has been used here for only about fifteen years, and I don't know that use of it has been made elsewhere), caustic painting, I like very much indeed. Through this caustic preparation, colours become infinitely more brilliant, and tones and tints more harmonious, with an enormous gain in effect. The Charlemagne frescoes in the rooms of the new palace are painted in this manner; as are forty magnificent Greek landscapes by Rottmann, which are the finest things of this type that I have seen.

The Throne Room with twelve statues of the Bavarian Dukes, each one thirteen feet high, is admirable. It was Schwanthaler (who unfortunately is no longer here) who carried out this immense work. It will be impossible for other sovereigns, when they see what the King has created here with such slender resources, not to feel a kind of shame at their own deficiency of imagination, and their lack of taste and grandeur. Willy-nilly, therefore, they will have to follow his example.

The Grand Duke of Weimar is already having Schiller and Goethe Rooms painted; and in honour and to the glory of visitors to the spa the Grand Duke of Baden has asked Herr Götzenberger to undertake a score of works inspired by legends and chronicles of the Black Forest. The others won't be able to get out of at least looking as if they are doing something too.

As a matter of fact, employees are terribly badly paid (they say), the military are complaining and the roads are awful. But roads will always be made and the employees have only to drink beer.

The country is poor, without doubt, but it would be equally poor without painting or statuary, and in this way it has at least gained a lasting importance. Raphael and Michelangelo have survived in Rome itself. It will probably be the same with Schnorr and Schwanthaler.

Tomorrow I shall send you a more personal letter. . . .

Write to Stuttgart, which I shall probably reach not later than 3 November.

Farewell; I kiss you lovingly. Kiss Blandine for me, and also the two others. Her letter delighted me.

167. To Marie d'Agoult. Donau-Eschingen, Saturday, 25 November.[11]

I've ascended to the source of my native river, the Danube. Two paces from the Schloss, near the entrance to the residence of Prince Fürstenberg, with whom I am staying, there is a small spring, arranged like sulphur water springs, with

---

[11] Liszt's editor Daniel Ollivier has the date 26 Nov.—but Saturday was the 25th.

a stone framework and a short flight of steps. A few small and rare grey fish are swimming in it, doubtless content with their lot. That is the source of the Danube.

Ten paces further on, two small rivers, the Brigach and the Breg, slip unnoticed into the redoubtable river... Symbol and omen.

Another symbol and omen. On arrival here, Edward said: 'Sir, I did find your golden [*sic*] ring.'[12] My sphinx had been lost since Rolandseck. It was found here. Putting it on my finger, I kissed it rapturously. . . .

It's now ten days since I had news of you; I hope to find a few lines in Karlsruhe tomorrow. . . .

Kiss Mouche. . . .

[12] The quoted words written by Liszt in English, reporting the speech of his English manservant.

1844

7 January. Liszt conducts a concert in Weimar and is also the soloist in Hummel's Piano Concerto in B minor.

Mid-January to late March. He gives further concerts in Weimar and also appears in other German towns, among them Gotha, Rudolstadt, Jena, Dessau, Stettin (now Szczecin in Poland), Magdeburg, Brunswick, and Hanover.

9 February. In Dresden, Liszt attends a performance of Richard Wagner's *Rienzi* and enthusiastically compliments the composer. Here, too, he encounters the Irish adventuress Lola Montez.*

April/May. He gives several enormously successful concerts in Paris. This is also the time of the final break with Marie d'Agoult.

June. He stays with Princess Belgiojoso at her home near Versailles.

23 June. In a concert at the Conservatoire, Liszt makes his last ever public appearance, in Paris, as a pianist.

29 June. He arrives in Lyons, where he gives six concerts and is received with rapture. 'More than a great pianist,' declares *La Revue du Lyonnais*, 'he is a great artist, a great soul.'

17 July. Leaving Lyons, Liszt visits Lamartine at Saint-Point (18 July), then spends a few days in Avignon and, lured by its Petrarch associations, makes a brief digression to the village of Vaucluse.

23 July. He arrives in Marseilles, where between 25 July and 6 August he gives several concerts, and from where he also journeys to, and plays in, nearby Toulon.

10 August to early October. Liszt gives concerts in towns and cities in south-western France: Nîmes, Montpellier, Sète, Béziers, Toulouse, Montauban, Bordeaux, Agen, Angoulême, and Libourne.

7 October. He arrives in Pau, in the Pyrenees, where he makes several public appearances and has a moving reunion with his early love, Caroline de Saint-Cricq, now Madame d'Artigaux.

14 and 18 October. Concerts in Bayonne.

21 October. Leaving Pau, Liszt takes the road for Madrid, where his performances are received with an enthusiasm bordering on delirium. Of his first concert, the newspaper *Iberia musical* reports: 'It is impossible to describe his manner of playing, because his Heaven-sent genius constantly inspires him to change it. . . . Never have we witnessed so great a frenzy.' 'No one could believe that it was a mere mortal who sat at the piano,' declares *El Globo*.

7 November. He plays before the Queen of Spain, Isabella II, who presents him with a diamond brooch worth 20,000 reales and makes him a Knight of the Order of Charles III.

December. Liszt plays in Córdoba and on the 17th arrives in Seville, where he spends Christmas.

WORKS. SONGS: *Freudvoll und leidvoll* (Goethe) (S280/1); *Die Vätergruft* (Uhland) (S281); *Enfant, si j'étais roi* (Hugo) (S283/1, *c*.1844); *S'il est un charmant gazon* (Hugo) (S284/1, *c*.1844); *La Tombe et la rose* (Hugo) (S285, *c*.1844); *Gastibelza, bolero* (Hugo) (S286, *c*.1844); *Wo weilt er?* (Rellstab) (S295). PIANO: *Faribolo Pastour* and *Chanson du Béarn* (S236); transcription (S402) of *Marche funèbre de Dom Sébastien* (Donizetti).

168. To Marie d'Agoult in Paris. Weimar, 23 January. Your latest letter made me awfully sad. 'Do you sometimes think of death?' made my flesh creep. My mind went back to the crows which came and pecked at the windows by my father's bed. Last night, in a fit of fever, I dreamt of Louise[1]... and of others. Now and then I feel a bit troubled in mind, but it's nothing.

Happily, when awaking still in the grip of this nocturnal fever, I was brought your letter. . . .

Schober will tell you better than I can what Seydlitz is like. Lich[nowsky] says, I believe, that hanging is too good for him, but I don't take him literally. As you know, he exaggerates a bit. In any case, I didn't want to introduce him to you directly, and just entrusted him with a letter for Mme Apponyi and a copy of my *Lieder*.

I found it more piquant not to address it to you in order to puzzle him all the more—but I bet you will be far more pleased than you imagine with Schober, whom, besides, you will find a mine of information on German literature, which he knows thoroughly. All in all he has, beyond any question, a remarkable mind and a heart of gold.

Your view that Frau von Arnim possesses musical genius, I find most ingenious, even true. I have had copied out for you the replies to your questions.[2] Haven't you received them then?. . . .

You don't weary of humorous anecdotes, it seems. Thank heavens—it appeared to me that I had sent you quite enough of them, if you had already received my packet of letters. I have no very high opinion of Bettina as a practising musician, but her magical insight into the art is certainly deep and almost cabalistic. Those *Lieder* she has just published and dedicated to Spontini are of no great value, but there is an expressive anguish, a *kind of pregnancy* of feeling which does not fail to have a certain interest. As regards a circle of friends, I

---

[1] Marie's deceased elder daughter.

[2] Her disparaging article on Bettina appeared, above the name Daniel Stern, in the *Revue des Deux Mondes* of 15 Apr.

believe that Bettina has greatly lived in herself and through herself. She is on friendly terms, willy-nilly, with a number of people who are eminent in the arts and sciences, and upon whom—it has always seemed to me—she has more or less forced herself when seeking them out. Memories of her brother are of use to her too. Clemens Brentano was very well liked by his circle; indeed, even by the salons and the public. . . .

Bruno Bauer and Feuerbach are intimates of hers now, I believe. She also receives many students. In former days she saw a lot of the Grimms and of her brother-in-law Herr von Savigny.[3] Well, what else do you want to know? I really don't know anything more than what I have told and sent you thus far, and I doubt if your article is so detailed.

So what news do you want of Germany? I myself am living entirely confined to Weimar and know no more than what the *Allgemeine Zeitung* knows five days earlier than I do. Petit Fi... is nevertheless making his very small personal way, but thus far it isn't perceptible. But I have put life back into the orchestra, and mounted some concerts which, without too much self-conceit, would have been more or less impossible without me. . . .

This, therefore, is my programme that I repeat partially or fragmentarily at any opportunity, like that good fellow Marius: 'Delenda Carthago', or General Bertrand: 'I vote for the unrestricted freedom of the Press.' Not *Delenda Carthago*, but *Aedificanda Vimaria*.[4]

Weimar under the Grand Duke Carl August[5] was a new Athens. Let us now think of building the new Weimar. Let us openly and boldly renew the traditions of Carl August. Let us allow talents to act freely in their sphere. Let us colonize as much as possible and try to arrive gradually at that triple result which must be all the politics, all the government, in fact the Alpha and Omega of the whole of Weimar: a Court as charming, as brilliant, as attractive as possible; a theatre and a literature which are not rotting in the timbers of the garret and not drowning in the recesses of the cellars; and lastly a University (Jena). Court, Theatre, University—that is the great trilogy for a state like Weimar, which can derive importance neither from its trade, nor its industry, nor its army, nor its navy, etc., etc....

That, therefore, is my main theme, which I shall sing here in every key, in the faint hope of perhaps doing a little good... but who can flatter himself that he will do any!

I am poorly today and can't write any more. Adieu.

---

[3] The jurist Friedrich Karl von Savigny had married Bettina's sister Kunigunde.

[4] Not 'Carthage is to be destroyed' but 'Weimar is to be built'. The former expression should, however, be attributed not to Marius but to Cato the elder.

[5] For Carl August and his mother Anna Amalia see under Saxe-Weimar in Biographical Sketches.

169. To Marie d'Agoult. Weimar, 4 February. Chancellor Müller[6] has told me about the charming letter you wrote to him; he has probably already replied. The visiting card to Weimar in the Bettina article I accept with eagerness and gratitude. It goes without saying that it is extremely necessary to deal tactfully with the Court, more especially as the Hereditary Prince[7] (to whom Luden has dedicated a history book, *Dem Fürsten der Jugend*) gives evidence of being very much attracted to all that is noble, great, and intelligent, to the point that hopes may legitimately be based on the increase of his influence in the fields of art and literature. Personally, I am wholly devoted to him and, with God's help, we shall find a way of bringing about some good things. His sister, the Princess of Prussia, has just paid a 36-hour visit to her mother, who is still unwell. I had the honour of seeing her, and the dedication of the *Lieder* I intend to hand to her myself, in Berlin, where I shall spend three or four days at most, at the end of the month.

You ask me how it is that with so profound a feeling for nature, and so intelligent a sense of form, Bettina has created nothing. Perhaps I can reply with more authority than others could, that too great a depth of feeling is not favourable to creativity, that impressions which are too intense, too multifarious, destroy the tranquillity of mind needed to bring characters into being, and do not admit the pursuit of a logically consistent and simply observed dramatic development.

Madame Samoyloff has no children; hysteria is barren, and an ordinary English nanny is better gifted by nature. Bettina has done what I have done: used up her creative power (which was perhaps not disproportionate) in understanding, feeling, living, and imbibing all that. . . .

Besides, women are in a deplorable position. Their lives are necessarily artificial and conventional. They haven't the right simply to make mistakes. Talking of which, I believe you are absolutely right about the dedication[8] to Madame Pleyel, but relatively I believe I am less wrong than you make me feel. Be that as it may, the blunder has been committed and, like several others, cannot be uncommitted... unless in another form. . . .

Schober leaves tomorrow and will bring you the opera-glasses. I shall ask him also to acquaint you with my Weimar programme, to which I attach a certain importance. Be nice to him. He has a mind and heart capable of understanding you.

The pens I am writing with are quite impossible.

---

[6] The jurist Friedrich von Müller, who became Weimar Chancellor in 1815, is remembered above all for his association with Goethe. Mme d'Agoult's letter to him, of 23 Jan., is preserved in Weimar's Goethe und Schiller Archiv.

[7] Carl Alexander. See under Saxe-Weimar in Biographical Sketches.

[8] Of the *Réminiscences de Norma*. (See under Pleyel in Biographical Sketches.)

170. To Marie d'Agoult. Weimar, 16 February. In the last lines of your letter there is a Byronism that is terrible in a very different way from mine. You can no longer hope for anything; you can no longer laugh, or weep, can no longer feel either joy or sorrow. What, then, can *I* have? You no longer believe what I tell you, you no longer wish either to understand or to excuse the sad exigencies of my life, such as it has become. What, then, can I say to you? And why write to you!

I don't intend to discuss the dedication any further. Justifying myself has always filled me with invincible disgust, unless anger is mingled with it; and how could I be angry at this moment?

There is no parity, no possible parallel, in our two lives, you tell me. All right, I shan't argue about it. But at least, if my conscience is bad, I shall not undertake an even worse role: that of being your bad conscience. According to you, I have made it utterly impossible for myself to be any good to you, socially speaking, in any way whatsoever. The small quantity of intelligence that nature has allotted to me not being enough to understand this assertion in any way at all, you will permit me simply to take your word for it and, *faute de mieux*, to continue to be devoted to you with heart and soul.

You can be completely reassured about Léon.[9]

'Vulgar publicity' is already not lacking, in your opinion; it is difficult for the orgies in Germany and Warsaw to be surpassed... Still more difficult to add a drop of bitterness to this flood... which I wish to contain.

You bring up Puzzi once again; in that, it seems to me, there is something indefinably cruel and tactless. But I am wrong and always wrong. In any case, I shall be making very short work of that wretch. . . .

The Hereditary Grand Duke is to make me a present of an immeasurably precious album containing autographs of Goethe, Schiller, *et al*... (Isn't that charming? But the young prince is most charming to me, and with every day that passes I am growing fonder of him.) That won't get in the way of the album that you have chosen for me so well, but I believe it would be better to keep it for my return to Paris, on 20 March, than to send it to me. Three hundred francs seem very little for something so beautiful, and I find the idea quite delightful. If possible, don't put off for too long carrying it out. Were Lehmann to draw your portrait on the first page, he would give me very great pleasure.

A sorrow that I shall not deny myself, when we see one another, will be that of quoting to you the six or seven sentences from your last two letters.

I have not heard of the founding of a Conservatoire in Berlin. If people were thinking of me, I should refuse.

---

[9] Léon Ehrmann, a son of Marie's deceased half-sister.

Lichnowsky's visit will probably spare me a journey to Portugal. On the other hand, I shall spend a fortnight at the Wartburg[10] with the Hereditary Grand Duke during the summer. . . .

If you see Schober, be so kind as to tell him that I have done his errands and that I still have the same ideas with regard to Weimar.

The Court here couldn't possibly behave more appropriately towards me. Yesterday, Professor Wolff recited *Faust* at the H. Grand Duke's. I had a few moments of real inspiration while accompanying him. There was an empty seat in the salon for me. You should have been there. . . .

171. To Marie d'Agoult. Weimar, 18 February. Belloni arrived yesterday morning. I at once got him to give me full details of the Puzzi affair. It has neither frightened nor troubled me. At 10 o'clock I left for Erfurt, where I had to play in the evening. Sobs were choking me, but I played without anyone being able to suspect the emotion I was feeling; afterwards, however, I broke down, wept for a long time, quite alone, and am now writing you my thoughts on this deplorable business.

1. I shall in no way try to be diplomatic with this wretch. If he sends me two seconds (as Belloni says), the matter will be settled in twenty-four hours, probably without it coming to a fight. I shall flatly refuse any certificate, but will consent to see him.

2. The letters he may have are not as compromising as you seem to fear. They can only be from 1840. Besides, publishing them is impossible: no newspaper will ever undertake to do so, either in France or Belgium or anywhere else. And so it's mere braggadocio on his part. Belloni argues that he can have them lithographed and distributed: but that would be a matter for the courts, and he will take care not to do so. . . .

I have almost no doubt that I shall force him to capitulate and to beat a shameful retreat.

This isn't the place to respond to your reproaches regarding my carelessness with your letters. Were I to heed only the sorrow caused to me by your reproaches, I very much believe I would decide once and for all to ask you to throw them in the fire *en masse* and never to write to me again. . . .

I only wanted to tell you the details of this Puzzi business, so let's say no more about the rest. The *Norma* dedication must remain as it is. Mme Pleyel's name is only at the head of this too celebrated epistle and nowhere else. . . . I have received a few extremely respectful and grateful lines from her in which

---

[10] The famous medieval castle near Eisenach in Thuringia.

she tells me that she feels mortally ill and that she will probably not drag out her cheerless existence much longer. . . .

Write to Berlin. I leave tomorrow.

172. To Marie d'Agoult. Berlin, 11 March. It was only on my return from Stettin that I was handed a huge packet of letters among which I found one from you, addressed to Weimar. You ask me for the title of Bettina's *Lieder*. They literally haven't got one. The publication of this work was meant to be a deed rather than anything else. It was shortly after the unpleasant quarrel forced on Spontini that Bettina, who did not know him, declared herself his champion, defended him in the press, paid him a visit, and dedicated her songs to him. So this little collection, which harsher judges condemn for having neither head nor tail, has no title either. On the first page are simply these words (taking the place of a title): 'Dedicated to Spontini (followed by some of Spontini's titles) by Bettina von Arnim.' There are about a dozen songs altogether, I believe.

That is the latest information you asked me for. It is possible that from now on providing information will become my exclusive speciality with you. As far as anything else is concerned, it is obvious that our two points of view are diametrical opposites. I haven't saved the Capitol and there can be no question of giving thanks to the gods. However, after having reflected profoundly and painfully, I felt that it was impossible to justify myself and to reply, in any manner, to your letter sealed five times over. I simply enclose with these lines the broken sphinx you gave me in Rome.

It was in Paris, in April, that the final break took place. Some lines from Mme d'Agoult to Liszt at this time run as follows: 'Were it not my conviction, my dear Franz, that I am not and cannot be in your life anything but an affliction and a tiresome irritant, please believe that I should not take the decision that, with the utmost sorrow, I am taking. You have much strength, youth, and genius. Many things will yet spring up for you on the grave in which our love and our friendship are laid to rest. If you wish to spare me a little in this last crisis, which with a little pride and clear sight I should not have postponed so long, you will not respond with anger and irritation to the few requests I have to make. These will be through the intermediary of a third party. Choose whom you would like; M. de Lamennais, if you agree to him, who loves you and has never considered me as anything but a calamity in your life. I consent to accept any wise words which will condemn my desire after a ten-minute interview. My wish is that it may be straight after your concert.[11] It is not good to prolong this state of uncertainty. Besides,

---

[11] Liszt gave a concert at the Théâtre des Italiens on 16 Apr. and another on the 25th.

I shall have material arrangements to make which need to be made sooner rather than later. . . .'

173. To Marie d'Agoult. 11 April. I am very sad and deeply grieved. I am counting one by one all the sorrows I have caused you, and neither anything nor anyone will ever be able to save me from myself.

I no longer want either to speak to you, or see you, still less write to you. Didn't you tell me that I was a play-actor? Yes, like those who would play the dying athlete after drinking hemlock.

No matter. Silence must seal all the torments of my heart.   FRANZ

174. To Marie d'Agoult [April]. I don't understand your indecision. You wished not to see me. I obeyed you.

The question of the children is not something to be decided from one day to the next, especially since it contains within it several other questions about which in the past we have agreed only rarely. You have a simple way of putting questions which doesn't seem to me to be always the right one, but it has its advantages with regard to other people, advantages that you could disdain.

As for my closest friends, I haven't lied to them. I have told them plainly that you disapproved of and condemned my orgiastic life, and that you had there-fore intimated to me that it was better for us not to see one another, and that we would therefore be seeing one another no more. I erroneously said my friends: I have given this explanation to M. Villers alone. The others had no need of it, and I haven't gone into details about you with anyone at all.

If you insist on your idea of a third party, my own preference is for M. de Ronchaud, but it seems to me that we could just as well conclude these mat-ters in writing. Before leaving I shall write to you at length my ideas about the children's upbringing. You will do what you think fit . . .

175. To Marie d'Agoult [April]. Why are you sending me threats? I find it impossible to understand them. If you prefer M. de Flavigny[12] to M. de Ronchaud, so be it.

I have refused you nothing, but since it is a matter of life or death, I find it reasonable to know the exact why and wherefore.

---

[12] Marie's brother Maurice.

It seems to me that the children's upbringing is bound to cause you insurmountable difficulties. And, further, if you set yourself up as an enemy, I shall find it impossible to agree to hand them over to you again.

Once more, I believe you are being very unfair and very touchy towards me. I have given you everything I had: heart, head, and arms. I shan't bring you to book for anything. If you want more, it will be less for me. Take and don't hesitate.

176. To Marie d'Agoult. 25 April. Here are the two seats for Herwegh. I have no other lines from you. There remain only the two notes for Belloni which will be returned to you tomorrow.

If you don't want to cause me real distress, don't return anything at all. I give you my word that if Edward were to bring anything back I would break it or throw it out of the window.

If you have no visitors this evening, I shall come and see you when I leave the [Théâtre des] Italiens.

177. To Marie d'Agoult. Paris, 7 May. Deeply convinced that you will be able to supervise the upbringing of my two daughters better than anyone, I can only be wholly grateful to you for your explicit wish to concern yourself with it more fully than in the past.

I can't see my mother making any difficulties. Thus far, in my opinion, she has carried out quite splendidly the hard task she accepted. Let me hope that you will have fewer worries; let me also ask you to be so good as to give me now and then, or to arrange to be sent to me, news of these children, their health, their studies, etc.

It could never enter my mind to oppose the educational plan you adopt.

You are free to decide if it suits you better to bring them up in your own home, or to have them brought up in a boarding-school. This latter course seems to me to be preferable, but I don't want to insist at this moment, and make only one reservation: I shall intervene once again in this matter that you have made so painful between us when, as a result of the solution you have found, you bring down upon your head difficulties with and interference from your family, which, as much as it is in my power to do so, I am anxious to spare you.

You can be perfectly reassured with regard to the financial arrangements I shall make. The income from the sum I must invest will almost be enough to support the two girls. As soon as the matter is settled, I shall let you know direct and also through your chosen intermediary, M. Massart.

178. To Marie d'Agoult. 12 May. I no more desire to correspond about Blandine's upbringing than you do. You are a great stickler for your principles, which I don't contest in the least, but, in my humble opinion, it made little difference whether it was M. Hall or Mlle Bernard, and, since there is no reason to be dissatisfied with the former, I confess that I would have preferred to spare him this chagrin. You have decided otherwise—so be it.

When a difference between us doesn't seem absolutely essential, I would prefer to let you act without saying and say without acting.

I don't know if it will be possible for me to leave the malachite vase at my mother's. Motives are easy to guess, and, if you are anxious to avoid any scandal, you will do well to leave it in the place it used to occupy.

179. To Anna Liszt in Paris. Nîmes, 5 August ^{G (F)}

Dear Mother,

My journey is proceeding safely, and it may well last longer than I at first thought.

Spain tempts me very much, but I shall decide only in Bordeaux, where I arrive at the end of the month.

The news of the children which you sent to Lyons for me was extremely pleasing. Further news for me, send to Toulouse. From Marseilles I sent you two newspapers. Did they reach you? Rosario's wish cannot be fulfilled. I cannot beg Erard for a grand piano.

How do things stand with your housing plans? What are the Vial-Seghers doing? You must have received news of me from Mlle Pavy in Lyons. Give her my friendliest regards. Give M. Rey about 20 francs and ask him to buy a few flowers for Mme Lamennais [Lamartine?].

As far as Blandine is concerned, I must recommend the greatest restraint. Just let me know everything that goes on; as soon as I return to Paris I shall be able to reach the most suitable decision. Without any further differences of opinion, you have so well and naturally complied with all my wishes that I don't need to give you any explanations at the moment. Just continue to retain the same dignity, moderation, and goodness.

Should Mme d'A. want to have Blandine during her holidays, then let her. If not, consult Mme Bernard[13] about the best way for the holidays to be used,

---

[13] Blandine (from 1844) and Cosima (from 1846) were educated, until 1850, at the boarding-school run by Mme Louise Bernard and her daughter Laure in the rue Montparnasse.

and let me know. Sooner or later we shall have to agree on exact arrangements—for the moment one can only be patient.

Farewell, dear Mother. Health and patience are wished for you by your devoted son   F. Liszt

180. To Anna Liszt. Toulouse, 26 August. G (F) On arrival in Toulouse I found your letter, dear Mother, and by return of post am sending you the desired 1,000 francs.

Thank you for so obligingly attending to the matter of your will, which was the only essential thing at the moment, and something I was concerned about.

I am simultaneously writing to Massart and sending him 2,000 francs for Blandine's board and lodging. Her letter pleased me, but I want her to write to me only when she herself wishes to, and not for people to make it a *duty* for her. Let me know in Bordeaux, which I shall reach in 10 to 12 days, what plans Mme d'A. has with regard to the children.

From several quarters it has come to my knowledge that Mme d'A. is returning to her husband.[14] That seems to me to be the best and most sensible thing to do. Sooner or later it must come to that; the question of the children, too, would be considerably simplified thereby. In the mean time I rely on you to see that my views and wishes concerning them are not disregarded.

My Spanish tour is more or less decided on. I intend to ask Edward to come to Bordeaux and shall tell him direct what he is to bring me. This tour will take at most two months. At the beginning of the winter I shall come and admire your new residence, and at the same time choose the furniture which you absolutely *must* purchase. Three or four cupboards from the rue Pigalle you will have to throw out; for I seriously insist on your furniture being elegant and decent, although it's likely to be a good two years before I can put it to use.

My grandfather has died. Have a requiem mass said for him on the anniversary of my father's death, 28 August. Should this letter not arrive in time, it can be during the week. The children should attend the mass.

Your devoted son   F. Liszt

181. To George Sand. Pau, 8 October. Instead of passing through Paris again to go to Stockholm, I am leaving for Madrid; but before I cross the Pyrenees let me tell you plainly and simply, dear George, how truly grieved I feel not to see you at Nohant as I was hoping. It's all one to you, I know, but not to me.

---

[14] This was not the case.

The art of turning feelings into flowery language is not one with which I have ever been familiar; in any case, how could one venture to use flowery language of any kind to you? But do believe that the memory of your friendship remains deep in my heart, and that the days we spent together have left their noble and genuine mark therein.

At present, I am more alone and more exhausted than ever. I no longer feel up to anything, but, thank Heaven, my artistic ambitions have remained complete. —Others will probably have told you that Mme d'A. and I will henceforth be seeing and writing to one another only on *business*! In Paris I lacked an opportunity to tell you this whole sad and complex story; and even if there had been an opportunity I would have preferred to say nothing. Isn't silence the only mourning which suits great sorrows? Even at the risk of some misunderstanding, I shall continue to keep it.

In a week to ten days I shall be in Madrid, and around the end of December shall have to return to Germany (Weimar). If it wouldn't bore you to hear from me now and then, it would be a great kindness if you would send a couple of lines to let me know; I for my part need hardly say that to see your handwriting again would give me more than pleasure...

Lecourt, who remembers very vividly how kind you were to him in Marseilles, has told me that Algerian chiffons are to your taste; will you allow me to send you one, chosen expressly for you and which I was hoping to bring to you? If you don't like it, give it to Tempête.

Farewell, dear Georges [*sic*]; always and everywhere count on my grateful friendship and respectful devotion.   F. Liszt

182. To Anna Liszt [Late 1844 or early 1845] G (F)

Dear Mother,

You would have every reason to complain of me; instead, you leave it to others, who do it all the more eagerly the less their right to do so.

I enclose a letter from Herr Kirchmayer; on receipt of it, Rothschild will pay you 2,000 francs. A further 3,000 francs you will receive through Mme Belloni, and the remaining half of the promised 10,000 francs will reach you in the same way in the first half of February.

After business matters have been settled, I must admit that I find it rather entertaining when, sitting comfortably at their firesides, certain people complain about my concert plans and calculate the sums I am earning and spending. What have *they* achieved, and where has their infallible wisdom brought *them*? What have *they* earned by their talent and their labours so that in the precise workings of their double-entry bookkeeping they can compare their profits with mine?

Were one to compare small things with great, I should say that they were playing the role of the Committee of Public Safety in Paris, which used to draw up
the plan of campaign of its military commanders and issue orders stipulating
that a general was 'within three days to bombard and take a specified city and
to put to the sword those of its occupying forces which did not surrender'. All
such prattle, sad and serious though it is, sounds ridiculous and reminds me
of the Italian proverb: 'Protect me, O Lord, only from my friends—from my
enemies I can protect myself!'

But if only you, at least, do not lose heart or your trust in me amidst all this
jeering, I shall not complain. Here on earth, those who are conscious of their
worth are pursuing a goal. I feel that I am drawing near to mine, and that suffices
me. Amen!

My Spanish tour is a success, thank God. And so for your letters to reach
me it is quite unnecessary for you to write 'distinguished pianist' or bungler or
similar stupidities on the envelope. My name is enough, here as elsewhere. Also,
pension off your horrible seal, which, notwithstanding all my respect for your
habits of thrift, I should not like to see staying in the family for ever. Order a
small seal with the letters A.L. in reasonable size. Or, if you prefer emblems to
letters, choose a *Mater dolorosa*; or just a dog, symbol of fidelity.

In another fortnight I shall be in Lisbon. Anything urgent you can write to
me there; otherwise, as always, Mme Belloni will convey your letters.

With fondest love,   F. Liszt

1845

January. Liszt plays in Cádiz and then travels into Portugal.

15 January–25 February. He stays in Lisbon, where he gives several enormously successful concerts and also plays to Queen Maria II 'da Gloria', who makes him a Knight of the Order of Christ.

March/April. He proceeds up the east coast of Spain, giving concerts in Málaga, Granada (a second visit), Valencia, and Barcelona.

21 April. At Barcelona he embarks for Marseilles.

27 April. Liszt is made a Chevalier of the Legion of Honour.

May. He gives concerts in cities in Southern France, including Avignon, Lyons, and Grenoble.[1]

Late May. Visiting Lamartine at the Château de Monceau, near Mâcon, Liszt makes a proposal of marriage to the poet-statesman's niece, Valentine de Cessiat,* and is rejected.

Summer. Further concerts in eastern France and in Switzerland.

10–13 August. Liszt is the moving spirit of the Beethoven Festival in Bonn. On the 12th is unveiled the statue of Beethoven, made possible largely by Liszt's own donation of 10,000 francs.[2] He conducts Beethoven's Fifth Symphony and plays the *Emperor* Piano Concerto. At the closing concert he conducts his Beethoven Cantata before King Friedrich Wilhelm IV and Queen Victoria; in the evening plays at Brühl to the same monarchs.

22 August. He gives a concert in Spa.

Late August. He goes down with jaundice and 'utter exhaustion'.

24 October. Liszt arrives in Paris for a holiday with his family. During this time he makes the acquaintance of the celebrated courtesan Marie Duplessis.

24 November. He plays in Luxembourg.

WORKS. *Festkantate zur Enthüllung des Beethoven-Denkmals in Bonn* (Beethoven Cantata) (O. L. B. Wolff) (S67), for soloists, chorus and orchestra. *Les Quatre Elémens* (Autran) (S80), for male voices and piano/orchestra: 1. *La Terre*, 3. *Les Flots*, 4. *Les Astres*.[3] *Le Forgeron* (Lamennais) (S81), for male chorus and piano/orchestra.

PIANO: Ballade No. 1 in D flat (S170); *Grosse Konzertfantasie über spanische Weisen* (S253).

SONGS: *Tre sonetti di Petrarca* (S270/1, 1844–5): 1. *Pace non trovo* 2. *Benedetto sia 'l giorno* 3. *I' vidi in terra angelici costumi*; Songs from *Wilhelm Tell* (Schiller) (S292/1):

---

[1] In Liszt's audience at Grenoble, and 'bowled over' by his playing, was Nanci Pal, elder of the two surviving sisters of Hector Berlioz.

[2] Long afterwards La Mara wrote, simply but justly: 'The German nation has in large measure to thank Franz Liszt for the monument erected in Bonn to its greatest composer.'

[3] For No. 2, *Les Aquilons*, see under 1839.

1. *Der Fischerknabe* 2. *Der Hirt* 3. *Der Alpenjäger*; *Jeanne d'Arc au bûcher* (Dumas) (S293/1); *Es rauschen die Winde* (Rellstab) (S294/1, *c.*1845); *Ich möchte hingehn* (Herwegh) (S296); *Wer nie sein Brot mit Tränen ass* (Goethe) (S297/1, *c.*1845); *O lieb, so lang du lieben kannst* (Freiligrath) (S298, *c.*1845); *Schwebe, schwebe, blaues Auge* (Dingelstedt) (S305/1); *Gestorben war ich* (Uhland) (S308, *c.*1845); *Ein Fichtenbaum steht einsam* (Heine) (S309/1, *c.*1845).

183. To Princess Belgiojoso in Paris. Cádiz, 6 January. Although you have not replied to my last letter, I am again writing to Paris on the off chance, assuming that you will have been detained there. For my part, I am making scant progress in my peninsular peregrination and tending to linger in every town. As a matter of fact, notwithstanding Madame Bedwar's predictions, which were in perfect agreement with those of most of my friends, I have every reason to be satisfied with this tour; and even had I done no better than mediocre business, I should still find it a sufficient pleasure to look at the droves of oxen grazing on the aloe hedges, and the black mantillas playing at chiaroscuro with the most beautiful sunbeams, a sight of which I have not yet wearied and on which my bump of dissatisfaction has taken no hold. Not that that entertains me greatly, nor is my mood brightening appreciably, but at the distance where I am it almost does me good to feel that I am out of reach of a mass of bothers and vexations. . . .

So far as music is concerned, Spanish folk-songs and the guitar are giving me enormous enjoyment, especially when the songs are sung by some blind man— a very frequent occurrence in Spain where, in general, blind people are made use of more than elsewhere. At the Escorial it is a blind man who acts as your guide—and what a guide! There is no cattle-shed, no painting, no historic spot which he does not point out to you with the most scrupulous accuracy! In Madrid, in the theatre and at balls, you find parties of blind men who perform for you fandangos, boleros, and jotas, whose modulations make your hair stand on end! In Seville it is a blind man who tunes the instruments, and the same at Jerez. I have no doubt that somewhere or other there is a blind professor of painting or teacher of ballet.

As regards painting, the museums of Madrid and Seville contain some dazzling marvels; and with such a painter as Velasquez, Philip IV was well able to console himself for his lack of success in war. Talking of the Seville museum, I found myself the hero of a party which deserved a more brilliant one. All the rooms were illuminated, the great gallery had been chosen as the gathering place, and dinner was given in the room reserved exclusively for works by Murillo. Here can be seen, among others, the celebrated *Piété à la serviette*, painted after dinner with the Franciscans, who outdid the graciousness of our present-day *maîtres de maison*—since the latter are generally satisfied with an album sketch or some little flight of fancy of no special importance—by demanding of him as a digestion piece nothing less than a great painting.

Poor great Murillo! M. de Vigny forgot him in his *Stello*![4] In Paris, have you come across Federigo Madrazo? His paintings contain great feeling and beautiful lines. His latest picture, of the Duke of Ossuna, seemed to me to be quite remarkable. People are surprised to find such beautiful paintings in Spain nowadays. Villamil is also a great talent. The only things of his I know are genre paintings and landscapes. His great work on the historical monuments of Spain (lithographed in Paris) is engrossing him.

So our friend Lehmann has produced some masterpieces? Have you seen his magnificent paintings in the Cloître St-Méry?[5] Tell me what you think of them.

As I have already told you, I no longer receive news from Paris, unless it is from time to time through the *Journal des Débats*, for which I still have my old partiality. Berlioz tells us of a great composer, Félicien David. Have you heard his *Désert*? The poetical programme does not seem very varied! In Madrid we had two operas by Verdi, *Nabucco* and *Ernani*, and after my departure they put on *I Lombardi*. It is splendid, ever splendid and never better. The orchestration is pretty carefully done, the accessories nicely maintained, etc.

But I always come back to the fact that, even to make jugged hare, one first needs a hare. 'Ideas,' remarked Hugo to me one day, 'rare game in the forest of words.'. . . .

184. To Blandine Liszt in Paris. Gibraltar, 5 March

Dear child,

I shall not be seeing you as soon as I should so dearly like to, for my travels will of necessity have to drag on. The best consolation for the sorrow this causes me is the one you are giving me by applying yourself to your schoolwork and your progress, as I have been very pleased to learn from my mother, Madame Bernard and M. Massart. Nor am I for my part, you can be certain, sparing myself either work or pains to ensure that your name will one day give you a right to the respect and goodwill of those who will know you. Continue in this

---

[4] A volume of tales inspired by the tragic destinies of the young poets Thomas Chatterton, Laurent Gilbert, and André Chénier.

[5] Frescoes in which Lehmann had depicted the recipient of this letter as well as Mme d'Agoult and Liszt himself. See Pauline Pocknell, 'Clandestine Portraits: Liszt in the Art of His Age', *Analecta Lisztiana II* (ed. Saffle and Deaville), Pendragon Press, 1997.

way, dear child; grow and fortify yourself through your heart and your intelligence. Later, you will reap the fruits of a good education and will bring into
my life the greater part of its happiness.

Write to me soon; tell me where you have got to with your different studies.
Is it still Mlle Kautz who gives you piano lessons? Remember me kindly to her,
and thank her from me, and also on your own behalf, for the pains she is taking with a poor little child like you.

I should also like to know which of your studies you like best and most enjoy
working at.[6]

Are you still cultivating the little bit of garden I knew? I should very much
like to send you some beautiful flowers from Spain, but they would spoil on
the journey, and the most beautiful of them would freeze in your flowerbed. As
I want you to remember my name-day, however, I shall ask *Grandmama* to send
you some rose-bushes on 2 April.

Farewell, dear child; pray for me, and may Heaven's blessings always be with
you.

185. To Lambert Massart in Paris. Gibraltar, 6 March

Dear Massart,

My journey is nearing its end; Málaga, Granada, and Barcelona will take me
no more than six weeks, and about 15 April I shall surely be in Marseilles. I
don't yet know what *detour* I shall then make not to return to Paris; for—shall
I admit it?—Paris has become odious to me. As my friend, you will forgive me
this very sincere confession, for you know better than others to what sad and
unique cause to attribute this aversion to a country to which, moreover, I am
bound by so many ties; but, hand on heart, I feel that I shan't be able to live
there for a long time, that I would there be shattered at every step; and even
your friendship, loyal and tactful as it is, couldn't help me to exorcise sorrows
which would burst out despite everything.

Last spring I had, on the one hand, a kind of personal struggle to sustain,
face to face with the public; on the other hand, the final word which was to tear
the veil from my youthful dreams and do away with ten years of my life had
not yet been definitively pronounced.

There was, therefore, still *struggle* and *doubt* for me; you know me well enough
to know that intermediate proposals don't suit me. So I am well rid of them! But,
as success came to me from without, *unhappiness* took hold of me within. Without

---

[6] Blandine replied: 'I am learning grammar, French history, geography, ancient history, the catechism and Bible
stories, English and sol-fa. What I enjoy most is English and ancient history. It is still Mlle Kautz who gives me piano
lessons. I am now playing Cramer's studies.'

writing poetry, as is said by those people who speak bad prose without knowing it, I shall tell you that the bitter feeling of knowing that the life of my heart
was shattered for ever, as was fully revealed to me during my last visit to Paris,
was what made me travel to Spain. I certainly have no reason to regret it, even
if I have remained '*Gros ou maigre Jean*'[7] as before. I have seen some beautiful
regions and met some distinguished people. Sometimes, too, I find that my thoughts
are ripening and my sorrows ageing under this profound and scorching sun.

Be that as it may, I am determined not to return to Paris for several years;
but as I very much wish to see my mother and at least one of my children, *try
to arrange* for them to come and see me in Marseilles, or at the latest in Heidelberg
(on the Rhine), during the summer. I shall spend a month in the environs, and
hope not to waste it. At the beginning of autumn I shall probably go to Sweden
and Denmark. Next, I shall have to resume my duties in Weimar, duties I am
coming more and more to regard as of serious value. I shall spend the remainder of the winter in Vienna, and the following spring in Hungary. There, I shall
make new plans. I am very much tempted to go to Constantinople, Athens,
and Naples[8] before finally crossing, and in Italy, my dramatic Rubicon—i.e. before
risking my operatic fiasco on any stage whatsoever. All things well considered,
I haven't the courage to risk it in Paris, as I was expecting; the neighbourhood
of the rue des Mathurins[9] would too directly poison for me any success I might
have. Regard that as puerile if you like, it won't make it less true.

In the mean time [Louis] Boisselot,* the charming, loyal and worthy fellow who
has just done the whole of this journey with me, and whom I shall ask to give
you my news when he goes through Paris, is to build me my piano-orchestra
with two pedal-keyboards. I have no doubt that he will succeed, and grandly.
It will be not only an improvement, but a *complete* transformation, of the piano.
'For new wines new bottles are needed,' as the Gospel says,[10] and my ideas will
then be realized more freely! He expects to have it finished in October. I shall
then be thirty-four; by the age of thirty-six or thirty-seven I hope to have shut
up shop as a pianist celebrity!

I don't know exactly what money you need for Blandine. Would you be so
kind as to let me know through M. Belloni and ask him for the necessary sum?

To come to a decision about Cosima, I am waiting for a few lines from you.
Be so kind as to talk to Madame d'A. about it, and let me know her wishes and
her figures on this topic, unless she prefers to write to me direct.

Belloni will in any case journey to Paris while I make my way to the Rhine.
Since for the moment it's only a matter of money, he will be able to settle
everything.

<hr/>

[7] To 'Gros Jean', implying a lout or rustic, Liszt has added its opposite.
[8] Liszt eventually reached Constantinople, in the summer of 1847, but never visited Athens or Naples.
[9] Mme d'Agoult's home, at this time, was at 10, rue Neuve-des-Mathurins.   [10] See Matt. 9: 17.

Josy will join me in Weimar at the beginning of winter.[11] Try to get him to learn something between now and then.

As you see, my dear Massart, one doesn't have with impunity a friend such as myself, and it is a terribly [indecipherable word] business, that of being my Pylades.[12] But don't weary of it yet and stay with me to the end.

Affectionately yours,   F. Liszt

186. To Marie d'Agoult in Paris. Marseilles, 2 May. I have always thought, Madame, that there was no need of a third party between you and me, and, in accepting those you had chosen, my intention was simply to do you a courtesy. Whatever your irritation in my regard nowadays, I am addressing you directly, to bring to a rational end a dispute which is as painful as it is pointless. Massart and my mother write that you wish to have Blandine with you until the holidays; this arrangement, which, it seems to me, will be of no use to Blandine, is not of a kind to give me much satisfaction either.

About a year ago, Madame, I was able to think that the unbelievable opinion of me which you had invented for yourself, and had expressed to me in several letters, remained a secret between us alone. From your past, so full of ardent devotion for me, I had even concluded that to everyone else you would be as discreet about me as I had elected to be about you. But I have now had to abandon this illusion, for it is impossible for me to remain unaware any longer that you are telling all and sundry the silliest and most foolish things about me. If you would only reflect for a moment, you would realize without difficulty that it is quite impossible for anyone to find the least substance to any of the accusations that you are hurling at me. But it no longer behoves me to get into this argument again, and that is not my intention in writing you these lines. Their sole purpose is to ask if you seriously believe that it suits me to have Blandine brought up in your home so long as you are keeping up hostilities towards me at any price. . . .

187. To Anna Liszt in Paris. Avignon, 6 May. G (F) Enclosed, dear Mother, is a letter for Berlioz, which please let him have at once. I also ask you to subscribe as soon as possible to the *Journal des Débats*, from 1 May onwards. That will cost you 80 francs annually; but it is fitting for Mme Liszt to subscribe to this magazine.

---

[11] A violin-playing gypsy boy who had been entrusted to Liszt's care in 1844, the strenuous—but futile—efforts to educate whom he later described amusingly in his book on the Hungarian gypsies and their music.
[12] Figure of Greek mythology whose friendship with Orestes has become proverbial.

I shall shortly send you a copy of an excellent memorandum on the subject of the children; it was written by a lawyer and puts an end to all my hesitations. Show it to Massart and keep it *chez vous*. I await your and Massart's replies in Lyons and hope that both will be satisfactory so that I can save myself a trip to Paris at a time when there is no point in my being there.

I hear through Edward that you have often changed the children's governesses. That is not to my way of thinking. Wouldn't it be possible to find a decent and dependable person who can be kept for several years, if her services are rewarded accordingly? Do try to aim at this; I don't like such frequent changes.

I daresay you heard that I have been awarded the decoration of the Legion of Honour. The way it happened was very flattering to me. I am sending Massart a copy of the two ministerial letters. If you are curious, ask him to show them to you.

Farewell, dear Mother; maintain your good composure towards everyone. Don't encourage the hangers-on who press upon you, to cheat you, and don't hand out too many alms. But if you give, give generously and try to help substantially. Stinginess is always a bad thing.

For the rest, rely on me. Time and patience are in the habit of bringing many a thing to a good end.   Your loving son   F. Liszt

188. To Marie d'Agoult. Lyons, 15 May. You tell me, Madame, that you do not know what to reply to my letter; and I, in my turn, find myself in a similar difficulty.

Arguments have never brought happy solutions between us. In our best days, I remember, you told me repeatedly and incessantly that I had indeed the power of inducing you but not that of persuading you. With how much greater reason, nowadays, have I to mistrust even the most sensible things I could say to you?

Allow me, therefore, to restrict myself to expressing to you purely and simply my desire and my wishes with regard to my two daughters: it is that nothing be changed in their present situation, which, moreover, you yourself decided upon last year.

I ask you therefore to leave Blandine at Madame Bernard's and Cosima at my mother's.

You have long known that I shall never find it fitting for you to contribute a centime towards the cost of my children's upbringing. Well, to avoid henceforth all the additional annoyances one might have to put up with following this irritating question of the settlement of accounts, I shall write and let Madame

Bernard know that in future all expenses incurred on Blandine's behalf will be paid direct by M. Massart, or by my mother, if you find that more suitable.

This measure, which seems to me to simplify and reconcile everything, cannot in any way diminish your influence on Blandine's upbringing; and so I like to think that you will approve of it.

As for what regards me personally in your letter, however much I may appreciate the abatement of your anger towards me, I cannot, even so, in any way reproach myself for the past. Each and every day of that past, Madame, was full of true and passionate devotion for you; the faults and aberrations that could be found in it were never, in any way whatsoever, either serious or lasting. The hand you promise to hold out to me, one day of forgetfulness, I shall be happy to take and keep hold of everlastingly, but I cannot, no, never shall be able to, tell myself that that hand had to leave me for a single moment.

189. To the Abbé Félicité de Lamennais. Grenoble, 18 May. You could not doubt the great value I attach to the genuine and kindly interest that for several years you have been so good as to take in me. If it has not yet been given to me to deserve it as publicly as I would have wished, do please believe that the fault is not entirely mine, and that certain pressing circumstances in my life, in imposing a greater reserve on me towards you, have also played a large part in the delays in my career and my standing.

From the lines you honour me by writing to me, I believe I am justified in assuming that the reserve and the silence I have maintained—and which come naturally to me from my profound respect for your character and a rather long habit of discretion—have not been maintained *elsewhere*.

Be that as it may, since you are so good as to inform me of your concern for my children, allow me to respond today by stating the exact conditions pertaining to this matter (an extremely simple one basically, although complicated just now by all sorts of extraneous circumstances which could not in any way alter it) and by briefly expressing my views.

They are restricted to two main points: the *education* it is fitting to give my children at the present time, and the steps to take to ensure, as far as it depends on me, the future of their position, especially with regard to *legality*.

As far as their education is concerned, it seems to me that it would be difficult to find a better *middle course* than the one I adopted last year at Mme d'A.'s suggestion. The way in which my elder daughter is being brought up at Mme Bernard's could not be better. Judging by all the letters which come to me on this subject, her physical, moral, and intellectual development proceeds most satisfactorily, in parallel. 3,000 francs a year, which I send regularly every 4 months to M. Massart (again at Mme d'A.'s request), suffice at present for all the expenses of her education.

Cosima, younger and more delicate in health, could not be better looked after than she is by my mother, who adores her, and who has for 5 years constantly kept my three children in her home, lavishing on them all her love and solicitude.

My desire and my decision, as I have just written to Mme d'A., are therefore that nothing be changed in the present situation of these children, which, moreover, ten months ago Mme d'A. herself not only approved but decided.

In my opinion, and with the unanimous agreement of the persons from whom I could accept advice, it is the wisest and worthiest course to keep to, if not the most desirable. . . .

Were you in this connection to feel the slightest doubt and to deem it apposite to address some questions to me, I would reply with complete sincerity about everything which concerns me personally; but for the moment allow me to pass to the second point in the matter occupying us: knowing what steps need to be taken to assure the children's position in the future.

It is obvious that they can in no way be regarded as *French*. My elder daughter was born in Geneva, Cosima in Como, and Daniel in Rome. All three bear my name and I have over them an absolute right, which of course imposes an equivalent duty on me. Now, being my children, they necessarily take the nationality of the father: they are therefore, willy-nilly, *Hungarian*; and, as such, subject to the law of the country. The best and most decisive thing I can do in their interest, therefore, is to ask the Emperor, through the Palatine of Hungary, for a *complete legitimization* (which, according to the civil code, corresponding in that with Roman Law, is a prerogative of the prince).

The same concession, enabling him to make his son his legatee, was obtained by Paganini in Piedmont; and this precedent, which I shall cite in due time and place, will probably give me a similar right. In any case, it is the important step that should be taken before any other; and, when I arrive in Vienna early next winter, I shall try to take it without delay. If, as I have some ground for hoping, the outcome is favourable, my children will then be in the best possible position, and I shall have made good my youthful follies as honourably as the situation allowed.

It is therefore from Vienna, and absolutely not from Paris, that I await the definitive solution of the difficulties about which you have necessarily been informed rather inaccurately; for this reason it is to Vienna, not Paris, that I have to return.

Do please forgive me these long and wordy details—which your few lines seem to call for—and allow me to hope that, before you withdraw from me a particle of the esteem that I shall always do my best to deserve, you will not on any occasion refuse to admit the vindication of my actions, for this can be the only result of a simple statement of the facts.

I have the honour to be, my illustrious and venerable friend,

Your wholly grateful and devoted   F. Liszt

190. To Therese von Bacheracht. Strasbourg, 17 July.

Alas! No, I shall see neither your mountains nor your lakes. Instead of listening to the marvellous symphonies of your waterfalls, I shall have to go and conduct the Symphonies of Beethoven at the celebrations in Bonn. I shall be passing Nonnenwerth again! . . .

Madame de Staël says somewhere: 'Glory is only the glittering mourning of good fortune' (an essentially feminine maxim!). Have I had good fortune? I know not. Will glory touch me on the nose one of these days? I know still less. Be that as it may, I shall go to Bonn in the mean time, and very much in the mean time! The *Beethoven festival*[13] promises to be magnificent; what's more, and to crown it all, HM the King of Prussia, who doesn't weary of being extremely kind and gracious to me, has just sent me, through Meyerbeer, an invitation to take part in the concerts which will take place on the occasion of Queen Victoria's visit to the castle of Stolzenfels.[14]

This will certainly lead me back to my *Swiss tours*, but not into the Oberland. So farewell the chalets and *tables d'hôtes*, the *ranz des vaches* and the waterfalls, the sunsets (which I always prefer to the sunrises, and for good reason!) and the indefinable donkey rides!

A plague on the brouhaha of my celebrity, which ever compels me to go right when the fancy takes me to go left! Look, if you really felt like being charitable, you would from time to time send me some of the lines you perfume so charmingly with wit and grace, to console me a little for all the vexations and annoyances I have to endure! I promise to reply more punctually than in the past. Overcrowded though my days may be, I nevertheless succeed better than formerly in *making time for myself*; it is an alchemy like any other and the only one within my reach. So don't let too many months go by without letting me have your news, and please be so kind as always to count on my sincere affection (of which, for that matter, you have no need) and my respectful devotion (which I would be glad for you to put to some test or otherwise make use of).

Wholly at your feet,   F. Liszt

---

[13] Of 10–13 Aug. 1845. Full details of this memorable event, and Liszt's outstanding part in it, are provided in Alan Walker's *Franz Liszt: The Virtuoso Years*, 417–26, and my *Portrait of Liszt*, 214–21.

[14] Liszt played before Queen Victoria at Brühl on 13 Aug. and again at Stolzenfels on the 16th.

191. To Anna Liszt. Freiburg [im Breisgau] 18 October. ^G I shall most probably arrive in Paris in the morning of 22 October, and stay with you in the rue Louis le Grand. In the mean time invite M. and Mme Seghers, plus Mme Vial, Massart, Kreutzer, and his mother to our family dinner, and ask them to tell no one else of my so speedy return. I intend to remain in Paris a week at most.

Your loving son   F. Liszt

Don't forget Blandine, so that we shall meet *au grand complet.*

192. To Ary Scheffer in Paris. Nancy, 12 November

My dear friend,

The honour of handing you these lines belongs to M. César-Auguste Franck,* who has the disadvantage (1) of being called Caesar Augustus, (2) of being a serious composer of beautiful music. You have had confirmation from Meyerbeer of the opinion I gave you of his oratorio *Ruth,* and the great master's *sincere* approbation seems to me to make the matter conclusive.[15]

It is now essential for this young man to make a way for himself. If there could be annual or decennial exhibitions for works of music as there are for paintings, I have no doubt that he would distinguish himself most honourably, for among the young people who sweat blood and water to set down some ideas on cheap music paper, I know not three who are his equal. But having talent is not enough; in addition, and above all, one has to push oneself forward.

For such a result to be achieved, many obstacles have to be surmounted and many steps climbed. This man will probably have more difficulty than others, for, as I have said, he has the handicap of being called Caesar Augustus and, besides, seems not to possess that blessed *worldly wisdom* which enables one to thrust oneself in everywhere. This is perhaps a reason for people of heart and mind to come to his assistance; and the noble affection you have shown me for several years makes me hope that you will pardon anything indiscreet in my approach to you today.

The object of these lines is therefore quite simply: to ask you to be so kind as to send a couple of words to M. de Montalivet about M. Franck's special merit, and to persuade His Excellency to allow him to have his oratorio performed in the Salle du Conservatoire this winter.[16]

---

[15] During his visit to Paris (late Oct./early Nov.), Liszt, along with Meyerbeer, Spontini, Adolphe Adam, Moscheles, Alkan, and others, had attended a private performance of *Ruth* specially mounted by the composer's father.

[16] The Comte de Montalivet, Minister in charge of the Civil List. The work was indeed performed at the Conservatoire (4 Jan. 1846)—but with a disappointing critical response.

Whatever the outcome, I shall be grateful to you for the part you have been so good as to play, and before long will come and thank you.

Yours in admiration and fellow feeling,   F. Liszt

193. To Pierre Erard in Paris. Angers, Friday, 26 December

My dear Erard,

I owe you a report on your victory in Nantes; it was most brilliant and most complete, I assure you! But also what an instrument, or rather what a mass of instruments, in this grand piano! There is really only one word to be said, to be repeated, to be written on every key, as Monsieur de Voltaire wrote on every page of [Racine's] *Athalie*: Admirable! Admirable! Admirable!

Bewler, who behaved with much tact and good grace during my visit to Nantes, cannot understand how qualities which seem to be so incompatible can be brought together: extreme lightness of touch with so powerful a volume of sound. As for myself, I never seek to understand anything and for good reason; but I am adjusting to it quite marvellously. After three consecutive concerts each containing 7 pieces, my fingers have not felt the least bit tired, and if I am not mistaken I didn't fail in a single passage. It is the first time I have had an experience like that with instruments as magnificent as the Erards; or even with other instruments, cheaper and less magnificent, Parisian or English. Hitherto, in Vienna alone, as I told you, have they managed to make pianos which my fingers liked, and the pianos that Boisselot sent to Spain for me came near them in the touch; hence my predilection. . . .

Tomorrow I give a concert in Angers; and on Monday a concert in the salons of the Conservatoire Brewler, where all the nuances and perfections inherent in your codal product[17] will be appreciated even better than in the theatre. Next weekend I shall spend in Rennes, and between 5 and 8 January shall be back in Paris (for 4 to 5 days), without it being as apparent as usual. You will give me a bottle of your excellent Burgundy, and I shall try to tell a few merry stories to your wife, whose hands in the mean time please kiss for me. As for Lise, embrace her effusively and vigorously: you know that these have been my faithful loves for 20 years!

Yours in long and sincere friendship,   F. Liszt

Don't take the trouble to reply: you won't have time.

I am writing with vile lodging-house pens which make my writing even more illegible than usual. . . .

---

[17] i.e. grand piano—the Italian for which is *pianoforte a coda*.

1846

13 January. Liszt provides the piano accompaniment in a private performance of his Beethoven Cantata at a soirée in the home, in Paris, of Jules Janin. The élite audience call for an encore.

17–24 January. Concerts in Lille, Douai, and Valenciennes.

22 February. Liszt plays and conducts at a charity concert in Weimar.

1 March–17 May. Vienna: Liszt gives ten concerts and makes several charity appearances, travelling and playing elsewhere between whiles.

12, 14, 24 March. Concerts in Brünn.

13, 16, 19 April. Concerts in Prague.

26 April. Concert in Olmütz (Olomouc).

3–13 May. Five concerts in Pest; Liszt sits for the painter Miklós Barabás.

20 May–12 June. Liszt stays with Prince Lichnowsky at Grätz and gives recitals in Troppau (Opava), Ratibor, and Teschen.

Mid-June to early October. He spends the summer in Vienna (charity concert with Johann Strauss the elder in the Brühl on 20 July), with excursions to and concerts in Graz, Marburg (Maribor), Rohitsch-Sauerbrunn (Rogaška Slatina), Agram (Zagreb), and Sopron (from where he makes a brief visit to Raiding). The last of these appearances is at Kőszeg (Güns) in north-western Hungary, where he is elected a freeman of the town.

Early October. He takes the steamer to Pest, and gives a charity concert here on the 11th.

Mid-October. Liszt stays with Baron Augusz in Szekszárd, gives a concert on the 18th and on the 22nd celebrates his thirty-fifth birthday.

Late October. He is the guest of János Scitovszky, the Bishop of Pécs, where he gives a recital and also plays the cathedral organ.

2 and 4 November. Concerts in Temesvár (Timişoara).

8 and 10 November. Concerts in Arad, of which Liszt is made a freeman.

Mid-November. Concerts in Lugos (Lugoj), Temesvár again, and Nagyszeben (Sibiu).

24 November–8 December. Liszt stays, and gives four recitals in, the Transylvanian city of Kolozsvár (Cluj).

8 December. Charity recital in Nagyenyed (Aiud).

16 December. Liszt arrives in Bucharest, where he gives recitals on the 21st, 23rd, and 31st.

WORKS. *Ave Maria* (S20/1), for chorus and organ; *Pater noster* (S21/1), for unaccompanied male chorus. *A patakhoz* (To the brook) (S81*a*), for male-voice quartet. PIANO: Hungarian Rhapsody No. 1 (S244/1); bravura paraphrase (S386) of the Tarentella from *La Muette de Portici* (Auber); *Capriccio alla turca sur des motifs de Beethoven* [*The Ruins* *of Athens*] (S388); transcriptions of Weber's *Der Freischütz* overture (S575) and *Jubel-Ouvertüre* (S576); of *Sechs Melodien* (Schubert) (S563) and *Müllerlieder* (Schubert) (S565).

In 1846 Liszt also began to plan an opera, *Sardanapale* (Sardanapalus), the libretto of which was prepared, through the intermediary of the Princess Belgiojoso, by an Italian writer named Rotondi. In the event, however, although more than a hundred pages of piano score were completed, the opera remained unfinished.

194. To Marie d'Agoult in Paris. Valenciennes, 23 January.[1] A singu-lar correspondence, ours! But since we no longer have anything but words for one another, why not say them? They will not close our wounds, it is true, but they will not reopen them either. To what are we condemned? Do we know? We used both of us to be noble natures, and you have cursed me, and I have banished myself from your heart because you misunderstood mine. Is it a test we are undergoing—or an affliction of fate? The future will tell us. . . .

195. To Marie d'Agoult. Weimar, February. Our letters crossed. Yours is most excellent in content and charming in form. Thanks doubly, therefore. Whatever made you take up your pen, I accept the result with gratitude, with-out seeking the cause. . . .

Having nothing to say to you today, allow me to give a little time to dis-cussing two or three points in your latest letter, the only ones which betray some kind of strange preconceived ideas or, rather, some wilful malice against my doings and activities. . . .

And so I copy out pedantically the whole of this paragraph of yours:

'I have had news of your Cantata. My instinct hadn't deceived me: it wasn't in little, low, suffocating, congested salons, under the ridiculous patronage of Janin, that you were to recover from the momentary failure of Bonn.'

At these words I stop you...

Failure? What failure?

Was it a failure to have brought to a good end so enormous an undertaking, especially one so enormously mismanaged, of which not only my friends but the great majority of the musicians and public of Bonn and Cologne were utterly despairing at the time of my arrival?

Was it a failure to have formed a majority, indeed a unanimous majority, leav-ing a minority of only one to seven, and among other things to have brought

---

[1] Incorrectly dated 27 Jan. in Ollivier's edition.

about in ten days, and to the great astonishment of residents and visitors alike, the construction of a hall large enough to hold 3,000 people?

Was it a failure to have understood that at my début as a conductor it was in good taste to share the conducting honours with Spohr, veteran of the German classicists, and to have shown him, contrary to his expectation, all possible deference and respect?

Was it a failure so to have arranged matters that, instead of a deficit of several thousand thalers, which they were all dreading, there was eventually a surplus of a thousand thalers?

Was it a failure modestly to have postponed the torchlight procession that the students and people of Bonn were wanting to give me, and for which everything was prepared, and to have accepted no other honour than that of allowing my name to be given to a new street close to the Beethovenstrasse?

Was it, finally, a failure to be addressed in this manner by the King at Brühl: 'I am aware, Monsieur Liszt, of everything that the city of Bonn owes you; allow me to compliment and thank you, etc....'?

And so envy (of which I have indeed been, and am, the object—I really don't know why, for nothing and no one will ever take away from me the only thing I care about), envy was not mistaken, and in the most fulminating article published against me—in the *Morning Post* (because I had declared that no pianist other than Mme Pleyel would play at the Bonn celebrations, and that Moscheles, Mme Dulken, and other English pianists who were there were waiting in vain, having put their trust in the hollow promises and invitations from the President and the Directors)—in this article, therefore, in which my Cantata is described as a wretched rag-bag and my influence on the Beethoven celebrations as disastrous, stupid and inconceivable, you will be able to read, in conclusion: 'The Beethoven celebrations should have been entitled thus: "Beethoven Festival, in honour of Liszt!"' (They even took the trouble to print it in capital letters!)

I could add many other details, but this is too long already. And so I resume my transcription of your paragraph: 'Not many of these things (such as the Janin soirée) would be needed for you to be left behind by younger rivals.'

At these last words I stop you again. Who are my younger rivals? Who can they be? Do you really believe that young rivals with as much to stake as I, and joyously eager to stake it, can easily be found? I very much doubt it.

Your remark would look very fine if published in *La France* or the *Gazette musicale*, even in the *Courrier* or *La Presse*, but truly has no admissible meaning whatsoever.

As I told you, the Janin soirée was only an affectionate courtesy on my part, in recognition of his past and present kindnesses. I am not in the least seeking to get myself talked of as a composer (as people say); for the time being it is enough for me to earn 50 to 60 thousand francs from concert tickets, and I don't care a rap for the aesthetes, or the critics for that matter.

Consequently, I wanted neither the Opéra nor the Théâtre des Italiens nor the Conservatoire, either for my Cantata, my *Quatre élémens*, or my other musical lucubrations. I simply asked for my turn at the Opéra and nothing else, for it truly doesn't suit me after five years of a European career to offer myself as a candidate with 'younger rivals'... . . .

If M. de Girardin really said 'He's making a lot of headway and getting nowhere', he uttered a fine witticism and a fine bit of nonsense.

Do you remember that six years ago your instinct (and it wasn't wrong at that time) told you that I shouldn't give a concert in Paris? Well! Compare that situation to my concerts of two years ago, when, alone, without assistance, without preparation, without protection, either in the press or in society, barely a week after my arrival in Paris... isn't that getting somewhere?

Recently, again, Vatel offered me 15,000 francs for two concerts at the Italiens, in memory of those three soirées.

You may remember, too, with what difficulty I found publishers six years ago; nowadays things are somewhat changed. Isn't that getting somewhere?

I shan't mention here the ribbons that have been bestowed upon me or what you call (wrongly) the charlatanism of my career. But which of my colleagues, of my rivals, of my confrères, has established a position like that of your very humble servant *vis-à-vis* the Courts, Society, the Press, and the Public? Isn't that getting somewhere? . . .

Certainly I shall not get, and cannot get, where M. Delarue has got. The Grands Cordons of the Legion of Honour and marshals' batons are not reserved for small fry like us; but if on the one hand you take account of the fact that it was necessary for me to earn a minimum of 60 to 80,000 francs a year, proudly and without it being apparent, and on the other you take the trouble to run through merely the lists of my concerts and of my works, such as they are, not to mention my travels and my frightful correspondence, you will see that I have hardly had time to amuse myself very much, and to lead this alleged life of debauchery and immorality which makes it every decent woman's duty to shun and repudiate me!!

Let us, as and when necessary, candidly and unhesitatingly separate what *is* from what *is said*. . . .

And since I am in the process of calling facts in evidence, let me again, to make an end of it for today, quarrel with you about one last remark: 'None of your lies takes me in', you tell me. With a clear conscience I can say that I have always been conscious of never having lied to you—but let's turn to details.

Die I lie when I said to you in '33: 'Marie, I have neither experience, nor education, nor fortune, nor name, but perhaps I have a head and a heart...'?

Did I lie when I said: 'At every hour, at every minute, in all countries, in all circumstances, I shall belong to you'? (Remember what Lichnowsky said!)

Turning to bigger details, did I, lastly, lie to you with regard to Mme S[amoyloff], the Princess [Belgiojoso], la Pl[eyel], etc.... and if I sometimes happened to be timid, embarrassed, confused, unhappy, and broken before you, were those things lies?

No, Marie, boldly expunge this word from the dictionary of your memories. It cannot stay there long.

But I am trespassing on your time and, being unable to be anything other than appallingly personal, I am necessarily being quite insufferable and very boring. Besides, I am writing with such dreadful rapidity that you will have still more difficulty than usual in reading me. . . .

As far as local news is concerned, I shall be going to Gotha tomorrow to attend the first performance of *Zaire*, an opera for which the reigning Duke (Ernst, brother of Prince Albert) has composed the music.

196. To Princess Belgiojoso. Vienna, 2 April. My name-day, feast of St Francis of Paola. For a month I have been leading a life, following a trade, which would kill several horses, but it is impossible for me to unharness myself at present. Vienna has kept and more than kept to what it promised. I cannot but take that very much into account, and, happy though I should be to spend a week or two at Locate, I am compelled to practise usury with my time and, dividing them as convenient between Vienna, Prague, and Pest, to give some fifteen concerts in the space of six weeks. The summer is advancing in leaps and bounds; the fable of the cicada comes to mind and I feel very little in the mood for Terpsichore. The little house on Montparnasse tempts me enormously, but to make this delightful dream come true one shouldn't sing too much during the summer lest one be forced to dance when winter comes. Oh! money! money! What a frightful corrosive!...

Belloni tells me that at the end of May he will be in a position to make final arrangements with Mercier. For my part, I admit that I feel a little less hopeful. It is true that a foolish characteristic of mine has always been to doubt good fortune in those few moments in which it was coming to me from all quarters. On the other hand, I have always quite vigorously rowed against the winds and tide, convinced that the candle-end which served me as star was not going out just yet.

To return to our building project, I could have 20,000 francs available within the next two months, and before the end of next year another 20,000. So if costs do not rise beyond that, accounts will easily be settled, but if it were a matter of a larger sum than 50,000 francs I might well be in difficulties. The idea of marriage that you very delicately slip into your letter is far removed from my way of thinking. In any case, if there ever were such a possibility, it would assuredly simplify the settling of my accounts, for I should certainly never marry a woman who had only a cottage and her heart to offer me in exchange for my long, greying hair and extracted teeth.

I am told of the imminent arrival of *Sardanapalus*, which I shall have the honour of sending to you at once. Within the next 6 weeks I shall probably also know something definite about the date it is to be staged and the principal singers. Barring unforeseen and adverse events, I think people in Vienna will have a chance to boo me in May '47. Between now and then I am not too sure what will become of me; a trip to Constantinople tempts me greatly as an autumn 'villeggiatura'; I hope to be sufficiently in funds to undertake it. For the time being, far-off countries suit me best... Spain was splendid, and I fancy that in Constantinople and Athens I shall work like a madman; and, as you know, the best ingredient of rest, or even of a kind of happiness, is music paper in a smoky atmosphere. . . .

When you have a free quarter of an hour and a fit of philanthropy, write me one of those so adorably sensible letters, those so seriously good and persuasive letters, which you write so well and which always make me very happy...

Wholly and admiringly at your feet and with a *shake-hand* [*sic*] of respectful friendship.

197. To Marie d'Agoult. Prague, 14 April. 'Publicity conditions', as we used to say in our good days, have engrossed me terribly these last six weeks: nine concerts of my own (with no other pieces on the programme but mine, and constantly changing pieces, making a total of about fifty, a good third of which I had to practise again, which was a great nuisance), plus three concerts in Brünn, two Court concerts, five concerts given out of kindness or for charity, making altogether about twenty acts of public drudgery... In a few hours I begin again in Prague, and at the end of the month in Pest. On 18 May I shall have to go to Ratibor, or rather to Grätz, on the occasion of the first mass said by Lichnowsky's brother, and then return to Vienna before paying a few quick visits to Pozsony, Sopron, and Graz in Styria, all of which will take me to mid-June; after which I shall ask for a month or two's reprieve. Besides, I am behind with my paperwork and absolutely itching to compose. Unfortunately the things I should like to write bring in hardly any money (look at poor Berlioz, who in the very midst of his successes has real difficulty in making ends meet), and no recipe has yet been found for earning 40 or 50,000 francs a year by busying oneself with works of art!

There remains the theatre, it is true, *e vedremo il nostro Sardanapalo*! . . . My patience and my courage are being fully tested; and, thanks to God and my mother, my health is of iron.

I shall probably put this autumn to use to realize my old dream of Constantinople and Athens. . . .

Were Donizetti's illness unfortunately to be incurable,[2] it is very probable that a ray of high favour would fall on me; I should at least be a unanimously nominated candidate for this position, or any similar one. A salary of 10,000 francs for six months' duties, or non-duties, is not exactly to be disdained, and the Vienna post is unquestionably one of the best possible. . . .

Felix Lich[nowsky]'s brief visit to Vienna (he stayed only three days) provided me with a good excuse for inviting Prince Fritz Schwarzenberg and getting to know him better. His is a splendid name, nobly and intelligently borne. In Vienna, Prince Fritz's word is law in matters of honour. When committing his follies he always remained serious and honourable, and to him could be applied Shakespeare's words 'every inch a king'. . . .

Despite all my efforts I have not thus far been able to obtain *Nélida*,[3] the success of which sincerely delights me.

Try not to allow too much time to elapse between subsequent works, and write bad things (if that were possible) rather than none at all. If by chance you need information on German literature, before my departure from Weimar I came to an agreement with Professor O. L. B. Wolff (referred to by Prutz in his *Politische Wochenstube*[4] as 'Der finger stumpf-abschreibende O. L. B. Wolff'[5]) that he would provide you with anything you needed, and more. But please write direct to him, signing Daniel Stern, and make use of him as of a friend of mine who will be very happy to become yours. . . .

Wolff is a treasure-house of information, quotations, and knowledge. God knows anything he doesn't know! (Between ourselves, it was he who gave me the reviews you made use of to do such an abominable article on Frau von Arnim, an article whose aptness I don't dispute and for which I have had to pocket a

---

[2] For the last few years of his life Gaetano Donizetti suffered from general paralysis of the insane. The position in Vienna to which Liszt refers was that of Court Composer and Master of the Imperial Chapel.

[3] See under d'Agoult in Biographical Sketches.

[4] Prutz's satirical comedy in verse *Die politische Wochenstube* (1843).

[5] 'O. L. B. Wolff, whose fingers have been worn down by writing.'

few eulogies from right and left, but which, had I still the right, I would well and truly disown.) . . .

Independently of German literature and bibliography, Wolff has a remarkable knowledge of foreign literatures, notably Italian and Spanish, not to mention French, from which he quoted me a few remarks of Daniel Stern's. In a word, he is a veritable milch-cow, as we used to say rather picturesquely.

And can it be that we no longer speak the same language? That our joys and sorrows are no longer through one another? I, for my part, have bravely torn my heart from my chest, thrown it to earth and broken it into a thousand pieces, but if you were by chance to discover some few fragments of it through my life or the works of my mind, you would find in them the still blazing reflection of your radiance and of our youthful love. . . .

198. To the Hereditary Grand Duke Carl Alexander. Aboard the 'Galatea', between Pozsony and Pest, 6 October

Monseigneur. . . .

Now that I have left, for a few days at least, those human ants' nests that are called great cities, and find myself once again on the waters of my native river, the Danube, letting each and every current carry me along as it pleases, I enjoy thinking first of all of Weimar, my fixed star, whose beneficent rays shine down on the long journey of my life ... of Weimar, homeland of the Ideal, where I should aspire to gaining freedom of the city one day—of Weimar where, five years ago, the understanding indulgence of an august Princess first gave me a kind of serene and serious awareness of my future!

Indeed, I shall never forget the flattering encouragement that HIH the Grand Duchess deigned to give, then and since, to my feeble endeavours, and the kindness with which she welcomed—I could almost venture to say divined—my desire humbly to link my own efforts to Weimar's glorious tradition. In entrusting me with a post which ought henceforth to bind me ever more securely to your royal and illustrious House, she gratified one of the dearest wishes of my pride as an artist, thus rewarding well beyond their deserts some good intentions, some laboured sketches. . . .

As I had the honour of telling YRH when I left Weimar, my *programme* is fully drawn up; it only remains to have it accepted and approved by the public, which is not the easiest part of the matter. The moment is coming (*Nel mezzo del cammin di nostra vita*[6]—35 years!) for me to break out of my chrysalis

---

[6] 'In the middle of our life's course'—the opening line (*Inferno*, i. 1) of Dante's *Commedia*.

of virtuosity and to allow my thoughts to take free flight. . . . Were it not for the wretched money matters which so often keep me in a stranglehold, and also the various more or less alluring whims of my youth, I could be 4 or 5 years more advanced. Such as I am, thank God, I have not lost too much, and honour, too, is saved. My life has not been sullied in any way, and, chance having come to my assistance, it has even been given to me to do here and there a certain number of trifling good things which now and then console me for having delayed.

My last thirty concerts in Vienna, Prague, and Pest, the subscription of 3,000 florins (for a splendid present that the *Kunstfreunde* [art lovers] of Vienna intend to make me) on which appear the finest names of the aristocracy, of literature and of the bourgeoisie, my triple nomination as *honorary citizen* (*Ehrenbürger*) in Hungary, and my double nomination as *assessor* (*Gerichtstafel-Besitzer*) of the counties of Sopron and Bars, mark *einen Zeitabschnitt* [a period of time] for me, after which I can without too much philosophical resignation remain indifferent to all kinds of petty barkings, dull-witted recriminations, and shrill jealousies. *Die Hauptsache ist bloss ein ordentlicher Kerl zu sein und den innern Kern und Samen durch Werk und That herauszubilden* [The most important thing is simply to be an honest fellow and to form one's inner core and essence by one's work and achievements].

If I am to do that, my travels, instead of being at once the means and the main object of my life, as they have been until now, will soon become only an accessory matter, a kind of hors d'œuvre. What, moreover, is left for me to see? At most a bit of the Orient and of Italy, Sweden, and, at the very end, perhaps America. None of that is by any means urgent, and I am thoroughly determined to take and leave it only at complete leisure.

The goal which matters to me before and above all else at this time is that of *conquering the theatre with the products of my mind*, just as during the last six years I have conquered it with my personality as an artist; and I trust that before the coming year has passed I shall have arrived at a more or less decisive result in this new career. . . .

I don't know if Herr Genast will have deemed it necessary to speak to YRH of the rumours circulating in Vienna, which have been echoed by several German papers, about my impending appointment *als k.k. Kammer-Kapellmeister*[7] (what a lot of K's!), in succession to M. Donizetti. No decision can be taken on this topic before next spring. For if on the one hand, and I very much hope this will be the case, M. Donizetti, although gravely ill, eventually recovers, on the other, I shall have various conditions to stipulate before coming to a final decision. . . .

---

[7] The ubiquitous 'k.k.' stood for *kaiserlich-königlich* (imperial-royal).

When passing through Prague I had the honour of paying my respects to HIH the Archduke Stephen. This young Prince enjoys great popularity in Bohemia. The day he consented to receive me, I took the liberty of speaking to him of YRH. Then, when I congratulated him on the warm applause which had greeted him the previous day as he entered the theatre, where the birthday of HM the Emperor was being celebrated, he replied more or less as follows: 'Aren't you aware of what can become of popularity? High tide and roaring waves in the morning—low tide and muddy sand in the evening!'—I no longer remember who it was who told me that at the Duke of Wellington's he had seen adorning the mantelpiece a huge pebble which one day during a riot had been thrown at the windowpanes of his study ... And those windows look straight out on to the colossal statue of the Duke in Hyde Park! An eloquent proximity, don't you think? . . .

By mid-March I hope to be back, with bag and baggage, from my travels through all kinds of far-flung regions. Will you allow me, Monseigneur, to send you my news from Odessa or Constantinople? Were YRH to find a few moments of leisure in which to write to me, you would need only to address it to Mechetti, Court Music Publisher, Vienna. . . .

Before the end of the winter I shall come in person to renew to Monseigneur the expression of the profound and respectful attachment with which I have the honour to be Your Royal Highness's very humble and grateful servant

F. Liszt

199. To Marie d'Agoult. At Leó Festetics's, Dáka, 8 October. You complimented me on my last letter; that embarrassed me. From sheer self-esteem I was wanting to remain at my own level, and to write you a letter equally good and still longer... but to do that I needed to find time. Well, I really believe it would have been easier to obtain money than time during this latest sojourn of three or four months in Vienna, so overwhelmed was I with visits, dinners, publishing chores, theatre and libretto discussions, etc., etc., etc. Forgive me, therefore . . . and above all don't be sulky with me, for I should truly be too punished if you took as long to reply as you would have a right to! . . .

Among my forthcoming publications, if you have time to pay any attention to them, you will be able (after dinner) to look at three Petrarch Sonnets (*Benedetto*, etc... *Pace non trovo*... and *I' vidi in terra*) for voice, and also very free transcriptions of them for piano, in the style of nocturnes! I regard them as having turned out singularly well, and more finished in form than any of the things I have published.

During my visit to Hungary I collected a good many bits and pieces with the help of which one could fairly well recompose the musical *epos* of this strange country, whose Rhapsode I am appointing myself. The six new volumes (about a hundred pages in all) that I have just published in Vienna under the collective title of *Mélodies hongroises*—there were already enough for four volumes six years ago—form an almost complete cycle of this extraordinary, half-Ossianic (for these songs give one the feeling of a vanished race of heroes) and half-gypsy *epopoeia*. As I proceed, I shall write another two or three volumes to round off the whole thing.

No need to tell you of the smaller stuff (Schubert, *Müllerlieder*, Marches, Tarantellas, *Capriccio alla turca*, piano arrangements of Weber overtures, Berlioz's *Idée fixe*, etc.). Chores such as this are going to cease completely, and, as regards piano pieces, I shall attend only to my three concertos and my volume (about two hundred pages) of *Harmonies poétiques*, of which two-thirds are done.

Phew! That's quite enough of me, isn't it! . . . What is the correct name of the American philosopher[8] you have discovered? . . .

200. To Anna Liszt in Paris. Szekszárd, 22 October. ^G Thirty-five years! In the middle of my life, amidst my plans and strivings, it is to you, dear Mother, to you who have always been so kind and good to me, that I turn with profound emotion and the most heartfelt yearning. Thus far I have not succeeded in building the cabin which is to shelter my renown and my ambition, although I am not short of material or even of the land to build it on. Doing the work and erecting the walls will cause me much hard labour and painful anxiety, until I can lay the different floors according to my fancy—but don't for that reason become impatient and lose confidence in me! You can be sure that serious and unshakeable determination, plus an original talent strengthened and developed by study and experience, can achieve much. Very soon the completed work will have to make itself known.

Through Messrs Löwy and Belloni you have learnt of my current plans and travels. So nothing remains for me to tell you. During the next three or four months continue to write to Vienna, to Haslinger, who always carries out very promptly his task of forwarding my letters to me. My itinerary includes Klausenburg [Kolozsvár], Bucharest, Jassy, Odessa, perhaps Kiev and Constantinople. At the end of March I intend to be back in Vienna. Perhaps I shall stay there for some time. You have probably heard that I have it in mind to have my first opera

---

[8] Ralph Waldo Emerson.

performed in Vienna. There, too, I have a good chance of a very decent position as k.k. Court Chamber-Kapellmeister with a salary of 4,000 gulden for a mere six months' service a year. If these assumptions and probabilities come to nothing, I would go from Vienna to Weimar for a couple of months and then put new plans into effect.

Your decision to find other accommodation for Daniel and Cosima I can in all respects only approve. Apart from the nights, when he is asleep, it is impossible for you to keep Daniel any longer, and I believe Cosima will feel very comfortable at Mme Bernard's. . . .

Please give to Mlle Chazarin the thanks which next year I hope to express in person. Tell her that I am convinced she is directing Cosima's musical studies in the right way. I merely want Cosima to practise reading music and gradually to learn to play by heart. Incidentally, no method need be prescribed to so intelligent and talented a teacher as Mlle Chazarin.

In a few days you will receive a visit from Baron and Baroness Lannoy, who are among the best of my Viennese friends. I commend them particularly to you, and want you to be most gracious and kind to them.

By the next post I shall send you 2 or 3 letters which I ask you to forward. Today you will receive a whole packet for the children, Kroll, and Mme Seghers. I would have written to Massart too, had I not wanted to wait for his letter. Since, however, I assume that it requires an answer, I am postponing my own epistle. In the mean time tell both him and Mme Kreutzer that I shall never forget their steadfast and proven friendship.

Farewell, dear Mother; spare me henceforth advice about my health and my career. Certainly, were I to listen to anyone on this topic, it would be *you*. But, as things are at present, any anxiety or admonishment I find quite superfluous. I can adopt no other course, cannot change my habits and convictions. The mistakes I make are not serious ones; they are more easily made good than those into which suggestions from another person would cast me. Up to now, no one can seriously accuse me of having steered my life's ship badly. Among my colleagues I see none who has managed it better. To be sure, I realize that if I want to avoid becoming a half-wit or an idiot, I must exchange this ship for a better, roomier, and more comfortable one. Well, a lot of ballast will then have to be thrown overboard—but I shall land where and when it pleases me.

Write to me in detail about everything that happens and about what interests you. Do you see Erard occasionally? I have owed him a letter for ages; but I have so little time, and then it isn't easy to write to one's friends from a distance of 300 miles. What is Berlioz doing? How is Chopin?

I for my part am achieving everything I can, and often think I must be crazy!

I embrace you most lovingly.

F. Liszt

201. To Baron Augusz in Szekszárd. Temesvár, 10 November

Dear Augusz,

I am beginning to miss you very often since we took our leave of one another—and in all manner of ways. To begin with, I am all but vexed with myself for not having lumbered you with me for a few more days in those charming rooms at Szekszárd in which you provided me with such elegant and comfortable accommodation; on the other hand I miss you in Temesvár too, and in Arad and Lugos, which, were it possible, outdid even Szekszárd and Pécs as regards goodwill and patriotic fellow-feeling towards me. . . . Guido Karácsonyi (whom you met in Pest, I believe) is with princely munificence doing me not only the honours of Bánlak, but even of all the relays and the most splendid carriage-horses, not to mention the amazing illuminations and fireworks at Bánlak, Temesvár, and Arad. In a word, it is the most fantastically glorious journey that ever an artist could have dreamt of, and without my having had the least inkling of it beforehand—rather like the 'Bourgeois Gentilhomme', who did not realize that he was speaking *prose without knowing it!*

'Of all living artists' (I have just written to a friend in Vienna), 'I am the only one of which a proud fatherland can proudly boast... Whereas the others laboriously struggle in the shallow waters of the ever thriftier public, I sail freely forwards on the full tide of a great nation. . . .'

The golden laurel wreath that a score of the most notable persons of Temesvár presented to me after my second concert turned out admirably, and it will make a splendid appearance among the half-dozen things which mark the principal dates of my career.

I enclose with these lines some verses by Sárossy which seem to me to be stamped with deep and exquisite feeling. But talking of verses, do please try to find an opportunity to give my very humble thanks to Mme Salamon (if I am murdering the name, forgive me, but you know to whom my thanks are rightly due), who was so kind as to address me some charming verses in Szekszárd which unfortunately did not reach me until the moment of departure. Do tell her that I am infinitely grateful, and that I should be glad to renew personally the expression of all my regard for her... Haslinger will send you the Hungarian Rhapsodies; the dedication to Mme Augusz[9] will not long delay. . . .

Farewell, my dear, excellent friend; retain your affection for me, and count on all of mine.

F. Liszt

---

[9] When, in 1853, the majority of the Hungarian Rhapsodies were published, No. 8 was dedicated to Baron Augusz himself.

1847

13 January. Liszt arrives in Jassy (Iaşi), the capital of Moldavia, where he gives concerts on the 17th, 20th, and 23rd.

2 February (OS). Present at Liszt's soirée musicale in the hall of the University of St Vladimir, Kiev, is a new acquaintance, the 28-year-old Princess Carolyne von Sayn-Wittgenstein.[1]

Later in February. Liszt is the Princess's guest at Woronince, her estate in Podolia.

13 April. He arrives in Lemberg (Austria, later Lvov, now Lviv in the Ukraine), where he gives and takes part in several concerts.

24 and 25 May. Concerts in Černovcy (Austria, now in the Ukraine).

8 June–13 July. Liszt sojourns and gives concerts in Constantinople, where he is warmly received by Sultan Abdul-Medjid.

Early August. He arrives at the Black Sea port of Odessa, where he gives ten concerts and spends several weeks with Princess Carolyne. Here, too, he meets her estranged husband and her mother.

Late September. At Elisavetgrad (now Kirovograd), Liszt gives the last concert of his career as a professional pianist.[2]

October–January. He again stays at Woronince with the Princess.

WORKS. SONGS: *Isten veled* (Farewell) (Horváth) (S299) and *Le Juif errant* (Béranger) (S300). PIANO: *Magyar Dallok* (S242*a*, 1839–47) and *Magyar Rapszódiák* (S242*b*, 1839–47); Hungarian Rhapsody No. 2 (S244/2); *Grande paraphrase de la marche de Donizetti composée pour Sa Majesté le sultan Abdul Medjid-Khan* (S403);[3] transcriptions (S553) of Rossini's 'Cujus animam' (from the *Stabat mater*) and *La Charité*.

202. To Marie d'Agoult in Paris. Bucharest, 3 January.

You protest at my transcribing[4] and at my naïve arrogance. In this, as in a thousand other things, you are perfectly right, but I confess to feeling an almost invincible dislike of repeating the same things, and, since I possess neither a stylistic talent nor the

---

[1] According to La Mara, the Princess 'for the rest of her life preserved the programme of that memorable evening like a holy relic'. Liszt played the *Hexameron*, a concerto (probably the *Concertstück*) by Weber, his own transcription of Schubert's song *Die Forelle*, an Etude by Chopin, Weber's *Invitation to the Dance*, and an improvisation on themes submitted by the audience.

[2] In the years and decades to come Liszt occasionally played the piano in public—generally for charitable causes—but never again to earn money for himself.

[3] The composer of the march was not Gaetano Donizetti but his brother Giuseppe, who had come to Constantinople in 1828 and later been appointed Chief of Music to the Ottoman Armies.

[4] To spare himself the bother of having to reword the same information, Liszt in his letter to Marie of 8 Oct. had copied out (with minor changes here and there) a long passage from his letter of 6 Oct. to Carl Alexander.

rare ability to vary indefinitely the same content in different forms, I find it more convenient simply to quote myself, as the Abbé Deguerry used to do! It even seemed to me that, having arrived at a certain degree of intimacy, one could, without arrogance or *naïveté*, practise a mutual exchange of letters of the official type, and I saw no mischief in transcribing—or, rather, copying out—for you my letter-programme to the Prince of W.

For the rest, you know that I am not even so lucky as to possess in my own person all possible faults at one and the same time, and, while charging myself with being hard-headed, I believe I am thin-skinned enough not to want voluntarily to expose myself to incurring the same reproaches too often. And so I shall transcribe no more, and, to enter into original matter, I reply first and foremost to your questions about *Nélida*.

No, a hundred times no, reading this book did not offend me for a single moment. This is what I have said and repeated a score of times to a hundred people, who maintain, just the same, that it has filled me with bitterness. In general, in Paris as in Vienna, in Berlin as in Milan, this novel has been taken as an attack on my poor self. Madame de Sagan, the Princess of Prussia, my mother, and the Princess Belgiojoso have judged it from the same viewpoint as M. de Girardin. Why!? I really don't know, unless it is that in our works we all carry a little of our destiny; and yours and mine alike, although in different degrees, is to be somewhat tossed about. In Germany, the stupid, pedantic critics hostile to me have seized upon *Nélida* to draw all sorts of conclusions against the sincerity of my feelings and the relative morality of my life. . . . In fine, *Nélida* has had several successes at once: *succès de curiosité*, *succès de scandale*, sales success, stylistic success... Will these various successes eventually come together in a serious and lasting success which will maintain the book in the higher region of élite novels such as *Adolphe*, *Delphine*,[5] and *Leone Leoni*, or will you have made only a pendant to Lady Bulwer's novel, a kind of devil's advocate speaking against an artist's passion, like Milady against the conjugal habits of the celebrated novelist?[6] That seems to be the real question. So far as I am concerned, I do not hesitate to hope for the most enviable fate for *Nélida*, for I have never for one moment doubted both the superiority of your heart and the superiority of your intelligence; and it seems to me to be impossible for the combined power of these two forces not to carry within itself the conditions of life and durability. . . .

---

[5] Respectively, the celebrated novel (London, 1816) by Benjamin Constant and Mme de Staël's epistolary novel of 1802.

[6] Rosina, wife of Edward Bulwer-Lytton, devoted much of her life, after their legal separation in 1836, to persecuting him for the wrongs, real or imagined, that she had suffered at his hands. Her novel *Cheveley, or the Man of Honour* (1839), in which he was portrayed as a villain, was the first in a long series of similar attacks upon his character and behaviour.

Look at what happened to *Lélia*. What book ever had more stupid abuse heaped upon it in the Salons and in the Press? Well! Has all that prevented *Lélia* from establishing Mme Sand's reputation on a wider and more definite basis? While selling only moderately well, *Lélia* nevertheless remains to this day the only poem in the French language, as was remarked to you by Mickiewicz.

To conclude this topic, I shall only add that in response to the hail of questions, insinuations, condolences, and malignities of every kind which have fallen upon me *en masse* in regard to *Nélida*, I have always imperturbably replied that I have never in my life had any intention of doing any painting, still less of dining in the servants' hall of any Highness, and, finally, that so long as my full baptismal name be not spelled out, nor my present address given . . . I shall always flatly and absolutely refuse to recognize myself in the articles and books in which people are so kind as to concern themselves indirectly with my humble self.

If you have a good memory you will recall that I already established this principle at the time of the publication of *Béatrix*[7] and of the short story by Théophile de Ferrière.[8] You know that I don't change my ideas much, once I have got one fixed in my head, and that one has served me perfectly well, once again, to rid me very thoroughly of all the sympathy and sentimentality I have no need of...

Brava, therefore, one last time and quite unequivocally for the form and content of *Nélida*. Everything I have written to you about it is the whole truth, considered and unconsidered; and, before writing to you, I had said it at greater length even to the two persons to whom I had made a present of the first two copies I could obtain: my friend [Simon] Löwy in Vienna, and Mme Revicsky[9] whom you perhaps remember from Florence, and for whom people in Vienna were fairly generally attributing me with more tender feelings.

Someone writes to you from the Rhine to tell you that there is talk of my getting married in Hungary. Thus far that does not even begin to be the case... but you know that several times already the newspapers have taken it into their heads to marry me... among others to Mlle Montez.

Talking of this too celebrated Anglo-Hispanic, have you heard that HM King Ludwig of Bavaria has asked her to sacrifice her theatrical successes and is keeping her in Munich (where he has bought her a house) with the rank of favourite sultana?

---

[7] Novel by Balzac which had been inspired by the story of Liszt and Mme d'Agoult. As the model for the eponymous anti-heroine, the latter was treated with particular severity. The first two parts were published in 1839; the third and final part in 1845.

[8] *Brand Sachs*, which appeared in the *RGM* of 24 Apr. and 1 May 1836 above the name Samuel Bach.

[9] Countess Sidonie Revicsky, to whom Liszt later dedicated his Fifth Hungarian Rhapsody.

My two opera subjects, of which thus far almost nothing has been done, are *Sardanapalus* and *Richard in Palestine* (after Walter Scott). Have you heard [Berlioz's] *La Damnation de Faust*? Tell me about it. . . .

In four or five days I leave Bucharest for Jassy. If you reply quickly, write to Kiev, Russia; I am curious to see the famous contracts[10] which take place there about 20 January Russian style (2 February). . . .

203. To Anna Liszt in Paris. Woronince, 10 [22] February.[11] G (F) I can give you good tidings of myself, dear Mother. In a fortnight from now you will be receiving 15,000 francs that I don't know what to do with. On my name-day you will have another 10,000. Then there will be a break until the end of autumn; for in the summer I shall probably need all my money myself.

If people ask you about my itinerary, say that via Bucharest and Jassy I have reached Kiev. In a couple of weeks I go to Jassy again, and from there to Odessa. Thither please send my letters up to 20 March or later; for they get to me within a fortnight. In mid-April I arrive in Constantinople, where I plan to spend three weeks, and finally in June I return via Lemberg to Vienna.

It occurs to me: if you want to do me a pleasure, throw both your old sofas out, and at once. Spend 600 to 700 francs on furnishing your salon decently. If I find that horrible junk, bought fifteen years ago, still there when I come to Paris in the summer, I shall be really cross. Celebrate my name-day on 2 April by renewing your furniture. Mme Seghers, who possesses taste and understanding, can give you good advice about it. But avoid green and light-yellow, colours I loathe, and buy a couple of things on which one can sit comfortably.

Together with your old sofas kick out the tedious hangers-on whom for years, on one pretext or another, you have tolerated far too indulgently. Mark what I have so often told you: one can only effectively help those who help themselves. Too many experiences have taught me to be inexorable.

My Uncle Eduard conducts himself splendidly and will, I hope, make a good way for himself in Austria. I do all I can to help him, because he deserves it.

Continue to do kindnesses to the Berliozes (who now have a household of four!). It is my wish. How is Guiselin? Give my most cordial regards to Mlle Chazarin. They are fine people.

I enclose a note for Mme Sonzoff, to whom I wrote from Bucharest. Isn't she a pretty woman; indeed, a charming one? Send her my note at once.

---

[10] Contracts made by local and provincial landowners for the supply of sugar, beet, grain, and other produce, and for the sale of property. Princess Wittgenstein was one of the landowners in the city for this purpose.
[11] Wrongly dated 2 Feb. by La Mara.

Give me news of the children; and also ask Mlle Laure Bernard to write to me at Odessa (Russia), poste restante. (I believe it must be stamped as far as the frontier.)

Farewell, dear Mother. Continue to be to me what you have always been, and be certain that I am always striving for what is highest and best.

With all my heart,   F. Liszt

204. To Marie d'Agoult. Woronince, 10 [22] February. . . . Above all, thank you for the good and singular news you give me about your new volume.[12] Bless my soul! That's what can be called making headway! Mme de Staël and George Sand outstripped at a stroke! Nothing less! The approbation of [D. F.] Strauss's translator seems to me to be tremendously flattering, and the newspapers' determination to treat you as an authority an extremely rare phenomenon in this time of silly jokes about anything and everything. I really couldn't be more impatient to devour your new masterpiece, but unfortunately it still can't be found in this corner of the world, where perhaps the title alone will be enough to delay its admission. Meanwhile, be so kind as to go on telling me about it, for this splendid indifference that you display (with, in my opinion, so much grace) towards what we call publicity, I don't possess in the least.

Lucrezia Floriani[13] hasn't got here either, with the exception of one single copy which I was so stupid as not to appropriate on the spot. What do you think of it? Is it a success?

Is Mme Sand's break with Chopin permanent? And for what reasons? If you know any details, share them with me. For my own part, I am living outside a society which itself lives outside all these things; and so I know nothing at all, which for that matter provides me with a certain peace of mind which could be favourable to the development of my reason... if reason and development there could be. . . .

Do you know the latest? It is that I have just met at Kiev, by chance, a most extraordinary woman, a truly extraordinary and outstanding woman... so much so, that I decided, with great joy, to make a detour of twenty leagues to spend a few hours chatting with her. Her husband's name is Prince Nicholas Sayn-Wittgenstein and her maiden name Ivanovska. It is from their home that I am writing to you.

---

[12] Mme d'Agoult's *Essai sur la liberté*.

[13] Novel by George Sand inspired by her relationship with Chopin, whose character is analysed, not flatteringly, in her portrait of Prince Karol.

In about a month I shall be in Odessa, where I shall await the first fine days to embark for Constantinople. Don't forget, I beg you, to address Lamartine's letter to Odessa, for I desire to know Reshid[14] through other intermediaries than those who would be at my disposal in the Embassies.

About mid-July I shall be back in Weimar, where I shall finish my three acts... Paris doesn't tempt me in the least, but perhaps I shall arrange for the children to come somewhere. . . .

You ask me for details of my intimate life. This question embarrasses me singularly. To make jugged hare, a hare is needed, they say. To have an intimate life, some, or at least one, intimate relationship is needed. I readily admit that since our altercations I haven't given a moment's thought to such a thing.

I try to observe, to understand, and to feel in order to arrive at a certain number of true and valid opinions. This seems to me to be a duty. The rest of the time I play the piano, scribble, lunch and dine, etc.... with the most perfect lack of concern about the opinions of other people that you could imagine. . . .

Until the end of May write to Odessa, and, if it's a matter of indifference to you, sign Nélida rather than Daniel. This latter name, as you know, has never been to my taste. . . .

It was on Good Friday (2 April) that Liszt penned the first (apart from some brief notes) of the many hundreds of letters he was to send to the Princess Wittgenstein during a period of nearly forty years.

205. To Princess Carolyne. Czarny-Ostrov, Good Friday. Do you remember B's *vague* musical fantasies? Well, Mme la Princesse, taking up my pen to write to you I am experiencing a feeling very similar to B's when at W[oronince] he sat down at the piano with such excellent intentions of delighting and surprising me! And yet in this comparison the advantage remains entirely on the side of our charming blond Jesuit. For what have I to say to you that you do not know infinitely better than I could tell you? And what event or incident in my life would be worth your taking an interest in for 5 minutes? Be that as it may, I shall gladly put aside all vanity and all modesty to continue to be simply *Filzyg-Midas*[15] as before!

---

[14] Mustafa Reshid Pasha, the Ottoman statesman who was Grand Vizier (chief minister) at the outbreak of the Crimean War and whose reforms included abolition of the slave trade.

[15] Nickname for Liszt, from Filzyg, the piano teacher at Woronince of the young Princess Marie von Sayn-Wittgenstein (see Biographical Sketches), and Midas, the semi-legendary Phrygian king whose fingers transformed into gold everything they touched.

Wasn't it on a Good Friday that Dante first set eyes upon Beatrice? Or was it Petrarch who came upon Laura?[16] Although I am writing to you from a room splendidly stocked with several hundred of the choicest volumes, I don't want to clear up this uncertainty of my crass ignorance, relying on your omniscience for the solution. A remarkable coincidence of this year which touches my superstitious chord is that the 1st of January was a Friday, the 2nd of April, feast of my patron saint, is Good Friday, and the 22nd of October, my birthday, will again be a Friday!

'What about us?' said Bossuet, of daily memory at Woronince! Talking of Bossuet, our Tacitus is wonderfully to my liking. To certain Bossuetic propositions which we discussed together could fairly justly be applied what he says of the Cimbri (they have more been got the better of than conquered) . . .

I have rather cleverly found an abode here at Czarny-Ostrov in the home of Count Przezdziecki, stepfather of our attractive young woman of Niemirov, and government Marshal for 27 years. I am lodged in a charming apartment (his stepdaughter's) with a splendid fireplace and a singularly well-chosen library. Since, fortunately, there is no woman in the house, I am enjoying very great freedom— the whole morning until 2 o'clock I don't budge from my room. . . .

The evening after dinner is divided between whist and the Count's orchestra, the best in the region, I believe, and well enough made up to perform quite tolerably a few overtures by Rossini and Donizetti, and even *Freischütz* and *Oberon*. . . .

On Easter Tuesday I shall be leaving Czarny-Ostrov, giving a concert on Thursday at Kremenets, and on the Sunday or Monday after that will be in Lemberg, to which I beg you to address your letter, if indeed you have leisure to write to me at all. . . .   Filzyg-Midas

206. To Marie d'Agoult. Lemberg, 1 May. Thank you for being so charmingly prompt in attending to my concerns. Your letter of 1 February (enclosing Lamartine's letter of introduction[17]) wasn't able to reach me until 20 April in Lemberg... all pinned and labelled as it was . . . for it had done the return journey from Odessa to Jassy. . . .

This tour is getting longer and, like all my tours, is being prolonged for me, and, not now having a central point where some magnet or other attracts me, I allow my mind to be made up only by the course of events and by certain proprieties. So Belloni is perfectly delighted to see me doing business so

---

[16] Of these two fateful occurrences, it was the latter (6 Apr. 1327), as related in certain of the *Rime*.
[17] To Reshid.

sensibly; indeed, even saving money. My poor capital will be increased by a hundred thousand francs after Odessa, and it is not impossible that I shall add a few more thousand to it by spending the summer and autumn in Russia, not returning to Weimar, via Kharkov, Vilnius, and Königsberg, until about the end of next January. But I shan't decide on my route until I am in Odessa.

The sum I have mentioned shows you pretty well that I am continuing to forge ahead very successfully. The details would be of no particular interest to you. . . . My relations with Weimar are the best and most flattering possible. When arriving here I again found a long letter from the H.P.[18] which really moved me, and in no circumstances will I abandon this position, of which in three years I shall make something. . . .

I have found it impossible to obtain the *Essai sur la liberté*. The title is a frightful bogy for all the censors in the smaller towns. It has been read by only one of my correspondents, who praises it to me. Lichnowsky, who has made a very intelligent début at the Diet of Berlin, has also written me a couple of words about it. . . .

I thought *Lucrezia Floriani* delightful, and when I was reading it all my old affection for George returned. Tell me how things stand between her and Chopin, and if, with his malady, Chopin can go on living. His *Polonaises, Etudes,* and *Mazurkas* I have played a great deal in Podolia, Volhymnia, and Galicia, where I am constantly in Polish society, which even spoils me a little, it is claimed; if, indeed, there is anything still spoilable in me.

What do you think of the extraordinary performances in politics and diplomacy of L.M., Countess Starhemberg, in Munich?[19] I, personally, am delighted with them and fully approve what the King has done. The impetus she has given to the old ministerial hovel in Bavaria can only be favourable to the country. Admit that I am singularly skilful at unearthing people who undergo sudden changes of fortune!

And that poor Mariette Duplessis[20] who has died... She is the first woman I have been enamoured of who is now in some cemetery or other, delivered up to sepulchral worms! Indeed, she told me so fifteen months ago: 'I shall not live; I am an odd girl and I shan't be able to hold on to this life which I don't know how not to lead and that I can equally no longer endure. Take me, take me anywhere you like; I shan't bother you. I sleep all day; in the evening you can let me go to the theatre; and at night you can do with me what you will!'

[18] The Hereditary Prince (or Hereditary Grand Duke) Carl Alexander.

[19] Referring, of course, to Lola Montez.

[20] The 21-year-old Marie Duplessis, one of the most celebrated of French courtesans, immortalized in literature and the theatre as *La Dame aux Camélias* and in the opera house as *La Traviata*, had made Liszt's acquaintance in Paris in late 1845 and quickly lost her heart to him.

I have never told you how strangely attached to this delightful creature I became during my last visit to Paris. I had told her that I would take her to Constantinople, for that was the only reasonably possible journey I could get her to undertake. Now she is dead... And I know not what chord of antique elegy vibrates in my heart at memory of her!

Forgive me for talking to you of her at such length, but I don't know how not to speak to you heart to heart, whatever the interpretation you have sometimes given to my words!

Would you do me a kindness? The answer is yes, isn't it? Do be so kind as to buy something pretty, beautiful, and charming as a gift for Mme Belloni, either a bracelet, a shawl, or a piece of furniture, etc... something costing between two and three hundred francs, and have it delivered to her from me. As far as making purchases is concerned, and other things too, it is only your taste that I rely on completely.

If you reply to me at once, write to Jassy, Moldavia, and tell me the cost of Mme Belloni's present, so that I can discharge this little debt immediately.

Let me know what you are doing, what you are writing, publishing, etc... At Odessa I shall be able to obtain the *Essai*, about which I am very curious. Who is the closest to you of the men you see? I shall write to Lamartine from Constantinople, where I don't expect to arrive for another two or three months.

From May onwards write to Odessa.

P.S. I have given three enormous concerts here, plus a concert for the poor; also conducted the Musikverein concert and played for Lipinski and la Bohrer, both of whom you have heard in Paris.

207. To Princess Carolyne. Černovcy, 23 May. In three days I shall be in Jassy. . . . I have read *Lucrezia Floriani*, which is worth reading, even by the people who make only a light meal of products of this kind. The ideas and style are of a rare concision and clarity. The main character is in some way the authoress's *portrait* in prose and dressing-gown—just as *Lélia* was her statue and, if you feel like taking the comparison further, the *portrait* in poetry and the loose-flying draperies of her lyrical garment. The second character, Prince Karol, is drawn with a subtlety and mournful spite that can be completely felt only by the small number of those who might wish to be *beside themselves* with love, raving and ecstasizing in a delirium of expansiveness and unending devotion, but very quickly coming down to earth and repenting when, one fine day, making the sad discovery that the game isn't worth the candle. *A revoir donc bientôt*, Mme la Princesse; do, please, always regard me as your wholly devoted and grateful

Filzyg-Midas

208. To Princess Carolyne. Jassy, May. . . . How happy I am at what you tell me about Berlioz,[21] and that you really do seem to understand and empathize with him both intellectually and emotionally. In Odessa, if we think of it, we can discuss your thesis 'that it is easier to have genius than perfect taste'; a thesis which contains much emptiness, like all those which at first impress one with their soundness and their depth. In the mean time I do not know if Dr Pico della Mirandola[22] himself would not be a little nonplussed if he were asked to cite his *heroes of taste*... with or without genius. It's neither Shakespeare nor Dante nor Byron nor Goethe nor Voltaire nor Mme Sand nor Molière nor Béranger nor *et al., et al.* Taste is a negative thing, and genius ever affirms and affirms.

But let's keep these quibblings for Odessa, where, as I wrote to you, I shall arrive at the beginning of July. In three days I shall be embarking at Galatz for Constantinople, since I far prefer to go there straightaway so that we can have our full month of July in Odessa, seeing that you will not be getting there until the end of June. I have just had a beastly cold which I have not yet shaken off, despite four days of bed and perspiration. Perhaps even my journey to Constantinople will be delayed by a week or so, since I am hardly back on my feet; and if I can manage to write without my head swimming, it's the very most I can do.

During this week of compulsory retirement I have gone through one of the volumes of Lamartine's [*Histoire des*] *Girondins*. It is very noble, very congenial, very humane, and in fact very beautiful, despite all the mean, petty or systematic criticisms of Lamartine's person that people have managed to come out with.

As regards *Lucrezia Floriani*, about which I spoke to you in my last letter, someone[23] has written to me from Paris: 'L.F. is generally disliked. Talent has not adequately cloaked the vulgarity of this confession. It still seems that she wants to leave Chopin from sheer boredom, and that he is hanging on. However, there has already been a removal, and she will shortly be leaving for Nohant

[21] Whose acquaintance Carolyne had just made in St Petersburg.
[22] Celebrated 15th-cent. Italian polymath who at the age of 23 published a list of 900 theses, announcing that he was prepared to defend them against all comers.
[23] Marie d'Agoult.

alone. In short, the public is in on the secret of a struggle between pity and distaste, in which, for those who know Mme Sand, it is certain that she will not be swayed by pity.'. . . .

These are the first lines I have written since my six days in bed. Let me soon have news of you; write to the Austrian Embassy in Constantinople. Wholly at your feet.   F.L.

209. To Marie d'Agoult. Jassy, May. I returned here with a feverish cold which for five days has confined me to bed... where the doctor intends to keep me for another week, but I doubt if I shall be able to endure it.

To console me for this annoyance, two old letters of yours (of 13 and 28 March) were awaiting me in the post, forwarded from Odessa, and both have given me extreme pleasure. I was especially delighted with the couple of paragraphs on Lola and that poor Mariette, for, to be perfectly frank, I was beginning to reproach myself for having mentioned them to you in my last letter from Černovcy, fearing that you might find those two subject-objects ever so slightly licentious. If I had happened to be in Paris when la Duplessis was ill, I would have had my quarter of an hour as Des Grieux[24] and tried to save her at any price, for hers was a truly delightful nature in which practices commonly held to be corrupting (and rightly so, perhaps) never touched her soul. . . .

Having everywhere sought and asked for the *Essai sur la liberté*, I have been promised that it will be sent to Constantinople for me by the second boat, for it seems that it is in the customs here. So far as I am concerned, despite my malady (I am writing to you from my bed), I intend to leave . . . next Sunday (barring a relapse, which the doctor is threatening me with); fifty-four hours after my departure from Galatz I shall arrive in Constantinople, where I shall spend the whole of June. . . .

Berlioz has sent me a long . . . letter from Petersburg through the Princess Wittgenstein (who is my new discovery in princesses, as Mme Allart said, with this difference, that we have not the least intention of falling in love with one another). He has given four concerts and tells me he has every reason to be delighted with his success and the money he has earned there. The King of Prussia has invited him to put on *La Damnation de Faust* at the Berlin theatre, and he will accept; but the tone of his letter is as despairing as a funeral knell. Poor great genius grappling with what is three quarters impossible!

[24] In the Abbé Prévost's *Histoire du chevalier des Grieux et de Manon Lescaut* (1731), des Grieux tends and watches over his lover Manon during her last moments.

Blandine writes to tell me that she is to take her first communion. Wouldn't you like to see her on that occasion? To be sure, I should never dream of asking you either a grace or a favour on this topic, but it seems to me that it would be right for you to see her. If you think differently, let nothing further be said. . . .

210. To the Hereditary Grand Duke Carl Alexander in Weimar. Galatz, 4 June

Monseigneur,

The two letters that YRH did me the honour of writing to me during the winter finally reached me at almost the same time, on my return to Jassy, after suffering endless delays and several times being redirected. The constant change of my itinerary during these three or four months of travel through the provinces of Kiev, Podolia, Volhynia, and Galicia made regular postal communications impossible for me.

Although still detained in bed by a very heavy cold, following an intermittent fever which had already kept me company for ten days or so, I nevertheless could not delay, Monseigneur, in expressing my sincerest thanks for your constant and repeated kindnesses. . . .

Herr von Ziegesar's appointment, in succession to Baron von Spiegel, as Intendant of the Court Theatre, gives me great pleasure and will lead, I am convinced, to happy and desirable results for Weimar. Since becoming more closely acquainted with Herr von Ziegesar—and that already goes back several years— I have had this unvarying opinion of him: that he belongs to that rare category of men who are so *comme il faut* that they are always *ce qu'il faut* and *tels qu'il faut*, trusted and accepted in every position to which they are appointed.

As regards the theatre, one can't labour under any great delusion. It seems that we have entered fully into the years of the seven lean kine of Pharaoh's dream[25] (which, however, does not prevent singers of both sexes from growing commendably stout!). The dazzling light cast by very exceptional and almost extravagant individualities warps the public's ideas by over-exciting its appetites. People now want Linds, Rachels, and Rubinis, at every turn and in every shape. But where to get hold of them, and where the banknotes to use as bait? . . .

As far as the opera in Weimar is concerned, the most urgent reforms and improvements to be carried out, as soon as possible, will have to turn:

1. On the choice of *new jeunes premières*!
2. On organization of the choruses, these being at present less than 0.

[25] Gen. 41: 1–36.

For the honour of your theatre, Monseigneur, new people need to be taken on and new, effective measures adopted to ensure the most thorough rehearsals and most carefully prepared staging of all works to be performed. With regard to tragedy and comedy, it will also be necessary to practise a little more the so reasonable system, so eminently in keeping with the legitimate trends of our century, of *admitting* and of *permitting new ideas* (especially in *dramatic economy*), and not mutilating, by brutal and absurd censorship cuts, the new talents and great conceptions called for by our present, 'pregnant with the future', as was remarked so profoundly by Leibniz.

As corollary of this wise toleration of ideas, it will be necessary to assure advantageous *royalties* to German authors and composers, who are beginning, with good reason, to grow tired of having to pay the piper on behalf of others. Perhaps this measure has already been taken by the Weimar theatre, and in that case I like to believe that it will have been taken with the best and most honourable of intentions, with no economic reserve springing from caution; but in any case, since YRH allows me to give him my frank opinion, I consider the 'royalty' system to be not only the most honest and progressive, but one which will of necessity soon be adopted generally.

The enlightened benevolence and superior taste of Your Royal Highness being valued by the men of letters who have had the honour of conversing and of establishing an understanding with you, and this having become widely known in Germany, it will be easy for you, I am convinced, to induce some of our celebrities either to have one of their new works premièred in Weimar, or to secure from them a promise to come and conduct the rehearsals of those of their works that success has already consecrated. But for it to be convenient for Monseigneur to take such a step, the company must be put on a respectable war footing and the artistes must have *breathed into them* a certain life-giving fluid and spirit of honourable rivalry.

On my return to Weimar I will gladly talk at great length about all these things, and about the most appropriate means of accomplishing them, with Herr von Ziegesar, who, one can be certain in advance, will respond worthily to the trust with which you honour him, and who through his intelligent activity and ceaseless zeal will succeed in having *good* works *well* performed, and in gradually raising the standard of the Weimar theatre to that of the four or five theatres in Germany with the highest reputation. . . .

I venture to ask you again, Monseigneur, to be so good as to lay at the feet of HIH the Grand Duchess the expression of my most profound respect, and to deign to accept that of my unfailing gratitude and of the total devotion with which I have the honour to be, Monseigneur, Your Royal Highness's very humble and grateful servant   F. Liszt

211. To Marie d'Agoult. Galatz (in quarantine), 17 July. Before I entered quarantine an indulgent friend arranged for me to be handed on the steamer some letters and the *Essai sur la liberté*. Yesterday I read the first four books in a single session, and I hold out my hand to you—a hand which is proud and happy for having perhaps, through its past embraces, caused to vibrate within you such valiant harmonies of thought and feeling. . . .

You ask me if I send anyone fuller details of the lands I am travelling through. Absolutely not, I assure you. . . . I don't breathe a word to anyone at all in Paris. It is more than eight months since I wrote to Princess Belgiojoso, the only person with whom I have to some extent kept in contact through correspondence, a contact which is limited to a brief exchange of messages and of whatever news there may be. Now and then I write to my mother and to the children... From Constantinople I sent a fairly long letter to Mme Bernard in response to a few very sensible and well-written pages she had sent me.

You will have learnt through the newspapers that His Majesty the Sultan was extremely gracious to me, and that after having recompensed me both in money . . . and with a gift (a charming enamel box with brilliants), he conferred on me the Order of Nichan-Iftihar[26] in diamonds. I admit that I was greatly surprised to find His Highness so well informed about my bit of celebrity that long before my arrival he had told both the Austrian Ambassador and his Master of Music, [Giuseppe] Donizetti, that as soon as I had disembarked they were to take me to his Palace of Cheragan.[27] I shall write, through you, to thank Lamartine for his letter to Reshid Pasha.

I am delighted by the huge success of the *Girondins*; I have only been able to read one volume, when I was unwell in Jassy. At Constantinople no one but [the French Ambassador] M. de Bourqueney had received a copy, but I didn't see him until the end of my visit, because of his wife's illness. Two people I was very glad to see there were E. Boré and Count Zamoyski (Ladislas); with the latter I went on quite a long excursion into Asia. As you know, he is the leader of the Polish *émigrés* in Paris. His sister is the celebrated Princess Sophie whom I saw quite often in Lemberg. . . .

You haven't let me know the cost of Mme Belloni's bracelet, which delighted her. Don't forget to tell me. I might well have another commission for you, but a much more delicate one, which could well cost you three or four mornings; and I confess that I hardly dare ask you unless you encourage me a little. It concerns a Preface or Postface to my *Rhapsodies hongroises*, for which I would of course give you a good many notes and instructions. I greatly value this work,

---

[26] Meaning, roughly, Order of Glory.

[27] The royal palace of Cheragan stood some three miles north of Constantinople proper, on the west bank of the Bosphorus.

and it is absolutely necessary for the deep and inner significance of this series of compositions to be made eloquently clear to the public. . . .

A fortnight from now I shall be in Odessa. Perhaps, when passing through Constantinople again in October, I shall go to Athens. In December I shall be back in Weimar. . . .

Yours in admiration and fellow-feeling (not to mention all the rest).

212. To Pierre Erard in Paris.[28] I owe you abounding thanks, my dear Erard, for the charming zeal you showed in sending one of your magnificent instruments to Constantinople for me. Even before I embarked at Galatz, the Constantinople newspaper had informed me of this kindness in such good taste on your part; but I was none the less agreeably surprised when, at the Palace of Cheragan, I let my fingers wander over an instrument 'of such power and perfection', as you put it so felicitously in your letter to M. Donizetti, which the Constantinople paper published in its entirety. After having twice made a dazzling appearance at His Imperial Majesty the Sultan's and twice at my concerts (the last of which was held in the splendid salons of the Russian Embassy, where the view extends from the Bosphorus to the Sea of Marmara, from Pera to Constantinople, from the Seraglio promontory to Mount Olympus, from Europe to Asia!), the piano was sold for 16,000 piastres to a young man, M. Baldigi, who has offered it to his beautiful bride-to-be....

This instrument's fate is quite a romantic one; and it must be conceded that, for the classic qualities it possesses, it well deserves it.

During the course of last winter I often had an opportunity to make the most of (or, rather, to make the most of myself on) your *Erards*; amongst others in Jassy and Kiev, whither M. Branicky arranged for the piano his sister had just received to be transported 25 leagues. The sole observation I would have to make would again bear on the *touch*, which is a little heavy and above all too *yielding* for me; but this is truly a quarrel about nothing, for I have singularly spoilt myself with these comfortable and agreeable Viennese slippers, as you would gladly call them.

When will it be given to me to make instruments 'of such power and perfection' once again resound and sparkle in Paris? I don't know. My return is extremely uncertain and in any case very much postponed. In September I shall probably visit Athens, and in December I have to return to Weimar, to resume the duties which have been too long interrupted.

---

[28] An undated letter received by Erard on 5 Aug.

Let me have news of you from time to time through my mother, who is full of praise for your kindnesses, for which I am most sincerely grateful to you.

A thousand compliments to Madame Erard, and please remember me most kindly to Lise.

Yours affectionately,   F. Liszt

P.S. Mme Raymond of Jassy will bring you a few lines from me. She is an outstandingly distinguished woman to whom a most excellent instrument is justly due.

213. To Anna Liszt. Nikolayev, 5 September $^{G\ (F)}$

Dear Mother,

During the next three months send me your letters through Messrs Halpérin, bankers in Berdiczev, government of Kiev, Russia.

Thither, too, send me something I should like you to buy, and to which I ask you to devote the greatest attention. Be so kind as to obtain for me a bonnet for a lady, a very distinguished lady. Ask Mme Seghers to give you advice and order the head-dress at Mme Camille's or some other milliner's of artistic taste. It should be extremely elegant, fashionable, and becoming. The lady for whom it is intended is approaching thirty and wears only white or black. Don't let yourself be talked into buying some gaudy piece of frippery, better suited to a grisette, which would go badly with the lady's habits and dress. The price is irrelevant; the dearer the better. If necessary, I'll place 300 francs at your disposal. If you find nothing specially attractive you can send several bonnets. This little present means a lot to me. So do start searching for one at once and see that it is sent off as speedily as possible.

In the same parcel you can put, without damaging the bonnet, the daguerreotype of the house at Raiding in which you brought me into the world. If I am not mistaken, you have two copies of it, or else two different views of Raiding. In any case, send me your copies and have others made by the best daguerreotypist that Herr Roth can recommend.

My affairs are as satisfactory as my health. Continue to devote yourself to the children and, when associating with friends and acquaintances, to be moderately reserved. In this respect do be ever more cautious.

The solution to the problems in my life is drawing near. An event as unexpected as it is crucial seems to be tilting the scales of destiny on to the side of happiness and to be presenting me with a life's task which I feel equal to—for it would take very unfortunate and unforeseeable events to prevent the realization of my hopes. The year '47 is bringing me luck. Celebrate my birthday and pray with the children for me!

In January I shall be back in Weimar, and in April will come to Paris, to embrace you—and will then, too, if necessary, make new arrangements for the young scamps.

Various people will bring you news of me. Receive them with your usual politeness. Should, however, someone as my 'friend' try to 'touch' you, then equally politely show him the door.

Should you need money, let me know. However, I suspect that the capital you have at your disposal, and always will have, will suffice. A position with very substantial advantages is being offered to me. It is not wholly out of the question that I end up doing very good business with it, but I dare not speak of it, for fear of being laughed at.

Farewell, dear Mother. We'll see one another when the leaves are turning green. In three days from now I shall be in Elisavetgrad, where HM the Tsar of Russia will be reviewing more than 100,000 men. From there I shall be returning via Berdiczev to the Princess Wittgenstein's estate of Woronince, from where I wrote to you last winter. There I want to spend two or three months without concerts, without bothers, without fatigues. That will be something quite new for me.

Kiss the children and bless me!   F. Liszt

Should Mme d'A. send a reply to my letter, forward it to me at the said address.

214. To the Hereditary Grand Duke Carl Alexander. Woronince, 15 (27) October

Monseigneur,

I am taking advantage of the departure of my secretary, M. Belloni, whom I have instructed to make ready my winter quarters in Weimar, to send YRH this reminder of me.

The birthdays of Their Imperial and Royal Highnesses being at the beginning of February,[29] and winter being in general the most favourable season for amusements of all kinds, including those of music, I thought I would be doing right and responding as best I can to the kindness with which the Weimar court is so good as to honour me, by arranging my affairs so that I can devote the months of January, February, and March to the duties entrusted to me, which

---

[29] The Grand Duke Carl Friedrich (birthday 2 Feb.) was a Royal Highness; as daughter of an emperor, the Grand Duchess Maria Pavlovna (birthday 16 Feb.) was an Imperial Highness.

I shall always be eager to perform in accordance with the Spanish motto of mine that you have been pleased to notice: *Pundonoroso!*[30]

The beginning of 1848 I shall therefore be putting to very good use, and if, as I have every reason to believe, Herr von Ziegesar's ideas and mine are in agreement, I shall try to see that this time is equally not wasted for Weimar, whose glorious tradition you are so nobly bent on maintaining. In any case, Monseigneur, I venture to count on your sympathy and support, which, I know in advance, is given to men of *goodwill*, even if they ought not to limit themselves to *good intentions*, which, I hope, will nowhere be used as paving.[31] . . .

I was promising myself the great pleasure of writing to YRH from Constantinople; but at the sight of that world metropolis I felt something akin to what your great Goethe experienced when he for the first time beheld Rome and the masterpieces of antiquity. By virtue of that fatality which causes the infinitely small to feel the inferiorities of the infinitely great, I said to myself as he did, that 'great things are seen properly only on the second occasion, for at first sight of them our astonishment mingles with the thing itself, whose life one seems to share, losing oneself in the pure feeling of its value.'[32] Now, since in August I was expecting to see Constantinople a second time, and to take the sea route by going via the ancient Athens to return to the new one,[33] I made no haste to acquaint YRH with my first impressions. Later, my plans changed, and of necessity had to change. Instead of by sea, I shall be travelling overland, leaving here in early January.

And so I am postponing to the earliest interviews that you will do me the honour of granting me, an account of what in my travels might be of some interest to YRH. I shall mention only one detail, a big one in fact, that of the 80,000 men whom HM the Tsar of Russia inspected, three weeks ago, at Elisavetgrad. I attended those manœuvres, to look with all my eyes and to admire with all my admiration. For me, Elisavetgrad also marks the last stage of the concert life I have been practising throughout the year. Henceforth I expect to be able to make better use of my time, and I am meanwhile holding myself in repose so that I may advance more rapidly.

I venture to call upon you to be so kind once again, Monseigneur, as to consent to lay my very humble respects at the feet of HIH the Grand Duchess; and I also ask you to believe in the unvarying and grateful devotion with which I have the honour to be Your Royal Highness's

very humble and obedient servant   F. Liszt

---

[30] 'Punctilious', 'honourable', 'scrupulous'.

[31] Referring to the proverb *L'enfer est pavé de bonnes intentions*, (the road to) hell is paved with good intentions.

[32] From Goethe's *Italienische Reise* (Italian Journey) (1816–17).

[33] Because of its former literary glories Weimar was often called 'the Athens on the Ilm' (the stream flowing through the park and outskirts of the town).

215. To Marie d'Agoult. Woronince, 10/22 December. Instead of writing to you from Athens, as would have been the case if I had kept to my previous travel arrangements, I am doing so once again from the same room that I occupied last February. If I remember correctly, I wrote to you then (for I can't lose my longstanding habit, whether it be good or bad, of telling you what I feel to be the real truth, even though I know that you regard it as the product of my imagination) of the profound attraction I felt, *a prima vista* [at first sight], for a great character joined to a great intellect. This attraction has since increased so much, that Mme Allart's former prediction, which we have always kept as a tradition between us, looks like becoming a true prophecy. . . . And, come what may, I no longer feel that I shouldn't do all I can to bring about the fulfilment of this prophecy. . . .

Where have you got to with your works and your celebrity? I found it impossible to obtain *Valentia*.[34] If you have a copy left, send it with your other new things to my Weimar address, and don't doubt that I shall ever remain *ein sehr dankbares Publicum* [a very grateful public]. As for myself, I have been leading a very quiet life these last two months. Belloni, who will be spending part of the winter in Paris and whom I take the liberty of recommending to you in my turn, will be able to give you topographical details about the province of Podolia I am living in.

Publication of the *Rhapsodies hongroises* I told you about will be finished in the course of the winter, and before long I shall have brought to an end the complete volume of my *Harmonies*.

After writing to you from Galatz I spent six weeks in Odessa and a fortnight in Elisavetgrad, where HM the Tsar mounted a large-scale review of troops. At the beginning of January I shall leave for Weimar (without stopping *en route*) and in early April spend a fortnight in Paris to see my mother and make a few pilgrimages to your Tabor of the rue Plumet, assuming that you don't consider me far too Russified. . . .

---

[34] Short story by Mme d'Agoult, published in *La Presse*, July 1847.

1848

Mid-January. Liszt leaves Woronince and, via Radziwilow, Lemberg, Cracow, Ratibor, Krzyżanowitz, Löbau, and Dresden, returns to Weimar, which he reaches in early February.

16 February. He conducts Flotow's opera *Martha*.

28 February. He conducts Gustav Schmidt's opera *Prinz Eugen*.

18 April. Liszt and Princess Carolyne are reunited at Schloss Grätz.

Late April/early May. They journey, via Prague, to Vienna; and from here visit Eisenstadt and Raiding.

9 June. In Dresden, *en route* to Weimar, Liszt spends the evening with Wagner and Schumann, but falls out with the latter.

In Weimar, the Princess—who hopes the Grand Duchess Maria Pavlovna will prevail upon her brother, Tsar Nicholas, to grant her a divorce—moves into the Altenburg, a thirty-room mansion in the outskirts of the town. Liszt's official residence is for some time the Erbprinz Hotel (centrally situated in the market-place), until in due course he moves into a side wing of the Altenburg. For appearances' sake, the Court continue to address communications to him at the hotel.

18 September. In Frankfurt, Liszt's friend Prince Felix Lichnowsky is killed by a mob.

12 November. At a Court concert Liszt for the first time conducts music by Wagner: the overture to *Tannhäuser*. He also plays the Andante from Henselt's Piano Concerto and a piano solo, and conducts Act IV of *Les Huguenots*.

WORKS. Mass (S8/1) for 4 male voices and organ. *Hungaria-Kantate* (Schober) (S83), for soloists, male chorus, and piano/orchestra. The symphonic poem *Les Préludes* (S97). SONGS: *Kling leise, mein Lied* (Nordmann) (S301/1); *Weimars Toten* (Schober) (S303); *Le Vieux Vagabond* (Béranger) (S304, *c.*1848); *Ueber allen Gipfeln ist Ruh* (Goethe) (S306/1, *c.*1848). PIANO: *Romance* (S169); *Trois études de concert* (*Il lamento, La leggierezza, Un sospiro*) (S144, *c.*1848); *Consolations* (S172, 1844/1848); *Glanes de Woronince* (S249, 1847–8); arrangements of Verdi's 'Salve Maria de Jérusalem' (*I Lombardi*) (S431), Wagner's *Tannhäuser* overture (S442), Weber's *Einsam bin ich, nicht alleine* (*La Preciosa*) (S453) and *Schlummerlied* (S454), Schumann's *Widmung* (S566).

216. To Princess Carolyne at Woronince. Löbau, 29 January.[1] . . . I have just finished *Paradise Lost*, which I thank you for having lent to me. It is very much the sort of thing I like reading, and Milton will make me take up Dante and Homer again. I have marked a mass of passages while thinking of

---

[1] Although not important in itself, this excerpt has some interest in that it shows Liszt, so much of whose reading life was devoted to Dante and Goethe, giving time and thought to the third of the four great 'Prophets of Heaven and Hell', as the authors of the *Aeneid*, the *Divina Commedia, Paradise Lost*, and *Faust* have been called.

you. I planned at first to write them out for you, but that would take half a volume, and I prefer to wait and speak to you about them. One thing, among many others, pleased me: the full and frank affirmation of love between man and woman, not of mystical and figurative love only, but real and substantial love, contrary to the pedantic theologians to whom Milton allows not the least say in the matter. As for *Satan*, I would willingly say of him what you said about the *necessity* of Hegel. It isn't great—for Satan gets excited, does things, discourses, battles, reasons, becomes a diplomatic negotiator, etc. Now in my opinion Satan has nothing to do with all that. Satan magnified into infinite proportions can only be Doubt, mute Sorrow, total Silence. He stands out well—as Sun—*Spirit* of Darkness, rays of *Negation* and of Death—but is himself in his essence not affected by them. He does not deny, does not die—he suffers and doubts. As a matter of fact, a Satan made of this stuff does not easily let himself be put into an epic poem—but, rightly or wrongly, it seems to me that this conception of him would be more in accord with our poetic feeling of today. . . .

217. To Princess Carolyne. [Weimar] 28 February. My heart is swelling, my brain burning and desiccating ... Is this living, is it loving, to be feeling and thinking with such pangs as I experience? Let me be swallowed up in and repose in you; that is my sole destiny, and with God's blessing it will be a glorious one! In the mean time I am making an effort to keep to the practice of the motto I had engraved on a signet-ring I gave to Caroline d'A[rtigaux]: *expectans expectavi* [I have waited in hope]. Although this is a quietist[2] motto, I assure you that I feel eaten up with disquietude. . . .

The letter to my mother moved me deeply. When reading it, she will surely have shared my emotion. Since you forbid me to show gratitude, at least allow her to keep in the depths of her heart the keenest feeling of gratitude that it is given to a mother's heart to feel. . . .

I have conducted the rehearsals and two performances of Flotow's *Martha*, which has been a complete success. This evening a new work by a young composer called Schmidt is being performed: *Prinz Eugen*.[3] At Schmidt's request this, too, is being conducted by me. . . .

Henselt's Concerto has been played twice, at Court concerts, by your very humble Filzyg-Midas. Her Imperial Highness has had a note about it sent straight to Petersburg, so that the very high praise I gave it might be repeated in high

---

[2] Pertaining to Quietism, the doctrine of asceticism and contemplative devotion which is embodied above all in the works of the 17th-cent. Spanish mystic Miguel de Molinos.

[3] Gustav Schmidt's opera *Prinz Eugen der edle Ritter*, first performed in Frankfurt, July 1847.

places, to Henselt. The conducting baton[4] had the stupefying effect which was to be expected, but the name of the giver I revealed only with extreme discretion!

Tomorrow a French play will be performed by amateurs belonging to Weimar's *haute volée*. In a week's time a charade with *tableaux vivants* will be acted at Court, plus, as an operatic interlude, *Erwin und Elmire*, a text by Goethe set to music by the late Duchess Amalia. Shortly afterwards we shall have *Fidelio*, with which I shall take great pains, and perhaps there will still be time to stage an unpublished opera by Schubert, *Alfonso und Estrella*, to a text by my friend Schober. When not busy with my duties in the theatre, I have the Court concerts to prepare, 4 or 5 singing lessons a week to give to Her Royal Highness the Hereditary Grand Duchess [Sophie], a very intelligent young princess, the timbre of whose voice is quite delightful; plus a male-voice choir to train, and, which is unbearable, endless correspondence to attend to. From this enumeration you can see that here in Weimar my days of leisure are very few indeed. . . .

Prince Pückler and Mme de Sagan have been here, the former for a fortnight, the latter for three days. Mutual gratitude was the order of the day between Pückler and me, and I hope not to be out of favour with Mme de Sagan, whom, in response to her most friendly and pressing invitation, I shall visit *chez elle*. Conradi and my Hungarian sculptor are here also. The Princess [Augusta] of Prussia dropped in for only one day, her father's birthday [2 February], and I could have no more than a few quick words with her.

I am getting my friend Professor Wolff to dedicate to you his *family Shakespeare*,[5] which you will like, I hope; it comes out at the end of June.

The cipher F.L. appears on about twenty very well-bound volumes which are filling me with childlike delight. What extravagance these opals from Brazil, and how shall I dare thank you for them?

Lieutenant or Captain Heygendorff in the service of Saxony is reputed to be the most brilliant horseman in the Saxon army. His mother[6] is a great celebrity, as a singer and actress of the time of Carl August. After the death of the Grand Duke, who had given her letters patent of nobility and a *Rittergut* [estate] which did not prevent her playing all her roles to the great plaudits of Germany, sometimes in plays by Shakespeare, Schiller, *et al.*, sometimes in operas by Mozart, Gluck, *et al.*—after the death of Carl August, as I say, she left the theatre and from that time forward has had nothing to do with it. The publication of her memoirs is announced, containing many justificatory passages which will very naturally have little difficulty in also being accusatory. From time to time I have

[4] A solid gold baton adorned with precious stones, a gift to Liszt from Carolyne.
[5] Written thus by Liszt in English, referring to Wolff's book of selections from Shakespeare, *Familien-Shakespeare*.
[6] Caroline Jagemann (who died later in 1848) had borne children to Carl August and in 1809 been elevated by him to the name and title of von Heygendorff.

the pleasure of waiting upon her. Her conversation, in the rare free time I can manage to find, and when I am ever so slightly in the mood for chatting, charms and interests me. Moreover, she goes out very seldom and is never seen at court and in semi-official circles. . . .

Ary Scheffer has just sent me a note recommending a young composer. As soon as I have sent a reply I shall send it to you for your autograph collection. . . .

At this very moment the most incredible news, about the latest events[7] in Paris, is arriving by telegram from Strasbourg. The implications of these events will be immense, but as yet they haven't been confirmed. . . . According to this telegram, it's a matter of nothing less than the taking of the Tuileries, the abdication of Louis-Philippe, the Regency of the Duchesse d'Orléans, and a Molé-Thiers ministry. . . .

218. To Princess Carolyne. 12 March. Events are proceeding at such a pace that it is impossible to abandon oneself to plans. For myself, I can only proceed towards you and with you—in you, all my faith, all my hope and all my love are concentrated and summarized, *et nunc et semper.* Have you received my last rather short letter, in which I informed you of events in Paris? The implication of these events is incalculable. Nevertheless, there is a possible hope that peace in Europe will not be disturbed immediately. . . . Whatever happens, here are the fixed points I propound and which I shall carry out to the letter. I shall in any case leave Weimar at the end of your March. Barring unexpected obstacles—which will have to be foreseen and forestalled—I shall come as far as Lemberg to meet you. But should there be drawbacks or hindrances to this journey, I shall take up my abode at Lichnowsky's, in Ratibor, which is only four hours away from the Austro-Prussian frontier and eight hours from Cracow. Perhaps you will prefer to settle on our meeting there, since I can guarantee its total security, notwithstanding the objections found to it 4 months ago. If, which is very unlikely, there were *obstacles* even to my waiting for you in Ratibor, I should quietly return to Weimar, where I should remain, arms crossed, until I received further information from you. Today, I am so shaken by these events—we have even had a big scare in Weimar—that I shan't write any more. The day before yesterday I was in Leipzig again. My affairs are in quite good order, despite the terrible holes being made in my pocket, and my health is bearing up. I hope you will find me *well.* In everything I do and can do, the magnetic needle,

---

[7] The year was marked by revolutionary events throughout Europe. In France they led to the short-lived Second Republic.

unerringly turned towards the same pole, is sensitive. Be both my *grace* and my salvation.

219. To Princess Carolyne. 24 March. Even at Woronince you were complaining that, if one wished to follow the newspapers fairly conscientiously, one had no time for anything else. What, therefore, would you say now, when it is no longer a question of merely the *Helvetians* and of a few incomplete movements in Italy, but of *anything* and everything at any hour of the day? The newspapers are full of what goes on and what people say and think. What play could compete in interest and emotion with present events? What sermon better persuade us of the vicissitudes of human destiny? What professor in his chair or what salon wit enthral us enough to compensate us for the interrupted reading of the most modest newspaper!?

I, who have always hated politics, admit that I can no longer justify such an attitude. My compatriots have just taken so decisive, so Hungarian and so unanimous a step that it is impossible to refuse them a tribute of legitimate sympathy. As I write these words my eyes fall on the statuette of Goethe which is on my table, and this plaster smile cuts me short.

What is certain is that business is in a deplorable state at present. Bankruptcies follow bankruptcies. Two of my best friends are going to be very severely tested, and probably reduced to destitution. I wanted to try to save them, but in vain. Belloni writes from Paris to tell me that Rothschild is temporarily suspending payments and will perhaps be obliged to go into liquidation.

I shall bear with very simple resignation the great disasters which could befall my very modest fortune. You know that I have never invested money other than for conscience' sake, so as to be able to prove, if need be, that I had never so constantly lacked common sense as people have tried to claim. I understand only two things: work, and Chapter V of *The Imitation of Christ.* Oh! What sublime and beautiful things there are in your letter to me! They have seared my very soul. Yes! I shall wait for you, for I have nothing else to think of or do, if it be not to wait for you. It is only necessary for this *waiting* to be worthy of you. I shall try!

This last month I have often had the honour of seeing the Grand Duchess, who through all these events is retaining the most admirable steadfastness of character and goodness. The cult I had devoted to her for several years has grown still stronger during these two months. Monseigneur the Hereditary Prince, with whom I have always been on the very best terms, has just been so charmingly kind as to give me the plan and design of a house he has sketched for me, and for which the Grand Duke is so good as to offer me a very fine plot of land in the middle of the park. Let us trust in God, who, as St Augustine says, 'could very well create us without us, but can only save us with us'.

Before 12 April I shall be at the frontier; in a week I leave Weimar!

On 26 March Liszt set out for the home of his friend Felix Lichnowsky at Krzyżanowitz, near Ratibor, where he spent a fortnight or more before proceeding to Castle Grätz (another Lichnowsky residence) for the reunion with Princess Carolyne.[8]

Before leaving Weimar he had received a letter from the 24-year-old Bedřich Smetana in which the young and unknown Czech composer had related something of his past life and present financial troubles, asked for a loan of 400 florins to open a music school, and enclosed a copy of his *Six morceaux caractéristiques* for piano solo. 'I stand before you and ask you', he had written, 'to be *so kind, so very kind, as to accept this work and have it published!* Your name will enable it to find acceptance with the public, your name will be the basis of my future happiness, of my everlasting gratitude!'

220. To Bedřich Smetana in Prague. Krzyżanowitz, 30 March ^G

Dear Sir!

The *Morceaux caractéristiques* and the letter enclosed with them were delivered to me barely a quarter of an hour before my departure from Weimar. I want above all to express my most cordial thanks for the dedication, which I accept with all the more pleasure seeing that the pieces are among the most excellent, finely felt, and subtly worked out which have latterly come my way. The sole criticism I would perhaps allow myself would be in reference to the title of the very first piece, 'Gretchen im Walde'. The canon form seems to me to be rather too academic for 'Gretchen', and in my opinion the simple title 'Im Walde' would be preferable.[9]

Difficult though it is, nowadays, to find a decent publisher for a decent work, if it is not signed by a name which is already celebrated and saleable, I nevertheless hope to be able to send you word very soon of the *publication* of your *Morceaux caractéristiques*, and will in any case do my best to make active contact with the publisher to ensure that you are sent a fair and encouraging payment. If, as is likely, my way brings me through Prague this summer, I shall give myself the pleasure of calling on you and offering you my thanks in person. In the

---

[8] It is also possible that the reunion took place at Krzyżanowitz, and that almost immediately afterwards they journeyed to Grätz, where Liszt was certainly installed by 22 Apr., the date of Letter 222 to Schober.

[9] Smetana took this advice: in the published edition of the work (Op. 1) the piece in question bears the title *Im Walde* (In the Forest).

mean time, dear Sir, please accept the assurance of my sincere esteem and cordial good wishes.

F. Liszt

221. To Princess Carolyne. Krzyżanowitz, Sunday, 2 April. I have just come from the Krzyżanowitz church. Shall I soon be taking you there? That is my sole thought, from evening to morning! During mass, people sang hymns in *your* language [Polish], and the priest spoke to them in the same tongue.

How can I tell you of the inexpressible heartbreak I felt when those accents that I understand only in you, and which I love so much through you, came to my ears and my soul like waves of light!

Oh! May I see you again soon, for all that I possess in heart and soul, in faith and hope, is only in you, through you and for you. May God's angel guide you, O my radiant morning star!

The house is absolutely deserted and I see not a living soul, apart from the servants looking after me. Far from there being any disadvantage in your coming here, it is perfectly opportune, and you will surely be of my opinion. Here, far more easily than elsewhere, you will be able to make your travel plans, which will doubtless have to be adapted to events.

222. To Franz von Schober in Weimar. Castle Grätz, 22 April ᴳ

Dear friend,

Your kind letter has brought me still closer to you in the frenzy of the *estro poetico* [poetic afflatus] inspired in me by your 'Hungaria'[10]; and it is my hope that, thanks to this good influence, you will not be dissatisfied with the composition.

Since my Beethoven Cantata I have written nothing of so distinctive and uniform a character. Any day now the orchestration should be finished, and on some suitable occasion we can have it performed at Weimar in your honour, together with *Weimars Toten*.[11]

Despite the closing of the Russian frontier, the P.W.,[12] accompanied by a special official outrider, passed safely through Radziwilow and Brody, and for the last four days she and her charming and interesting daughter have been in residence

---

[10] The *Hungaria-Kantate*.   [11] 'Weimar's Dead', a setting of a dithyramb by Schober.

[12] Before setting out, the Princess, who was accompanied by certain members of her household as well as by her daughter, had left letters for her husband and mother-in-law informing them of her decision to join Liszt; and to the relevant church authorities had sent a petition for divorce.

at Castle Grätz. As it is still rather early in the year to take the waters, I should like to persuade her to spend a couple of weeks in Weimar before her 'cure' in Carlsbad (which unfortunately has become very necessary!). If I succeed in doing so, I shall arrive in Weimar between 10 and 15 May to prepare a suitable apartment or house for the Princess.

I should be so pleased if you had an opportunity of getting to know the P.W. She is beyond any question a quite extraordinary and *utterly* splendid example of soul, mind, and intellect (plus, of course, immense *esprit*).

It won't take you long to understand that from now on I can dream of very little personal ambition or of any future involving myself alone. *Serfdom* of the political kind may come to an end, but the *bondage of the soul* in the realm of the spirit, is not that said to be indestructible?....

You, my dear, esteemed friend, will certainly not answer this question in the negative.

And so I hope that in three weeks we shall see one another again. Be so kind as to remember me to our young lord.[13] What you wrote to me about him pleases me. As soon as possible you will hear further from me, with more details. Don't write to me until then, for my address will in the mean time be very uncertain; but continue to be fond of me, just as I love and honour you.   F. Liszt

---

[13] The Hereditary Grand Duke Carl Alexander.

1849

16 February. Liszt conducts a performance of Wagner's *Tannhäuser*, the first production since the Dresden première of 1845.

Mid-May. He shelters Wagner, on the run after the Dresden uprising.

28 August. The 100th anniversary of the birth of Goethe. Liszt conducts the première of his *Tasso, Lamento e Trionfo*, a work composed as a prelude to Goethe's *Tasso*, which is also performed.

September. Liszt and the two princesses holiday on Heligoland.

Late September–December. *En route* to Weimar they visit the spa of Bad Eilsen (near Bückeburg) and, when Princess Marie falls ill with typhoid fever, are detained here for several months. On 15 October Liszt takes part in a concert given in Bremen by Carl Reinecke.

WORKS. The symphonic poems *Ce qu'on entend sur la montagne* (1st version) (S95, 1848–9) and *Tasso, Lamento e Trionfo* (1st version) (S96). *Festmarsch zur Goethejubiläumsfeier* (Goethe March) (S115), for orchestra. SONGS: *Die Macht der Musik* (Helene, Duchesse d'Orléans[1]) (S302); *Hohe Liebe* (Uhland) (S307, c.1849); *Anfangs wollt' ich fast verzagen* (Heine) (S311, c.1849). PIANO AND ORCHESTRA: Concerto No. 1 in E flat (1st version) (S124); *Totentanz* (1st version) (S126);[2] arrangement of Weber's *Polonaise brillante*, Op. 72 (S367).

PIANO SOLO: *Grosses Konzertsolo* (S176, ?1849). Paraphrases or transcriptions of 'Halloh! Jagdchor und Steyrer' from *Tony* (Duke Ernst of Saxe-Coburg-Gotha) (S404); *Ernani* (Verdi) (S432, c.1849); 'O du mein holder Abendstern' (*Tannhäuser*) (S444). *Années de pèlerinage, deuxième année, Italie* (S161, 1837–49): 1. *Sposalizio* 2. *Il penseroso* 3. *Canzonetta del Salvator Rosa* 4. *Sonetto 47 del Petrarca* 5. *Sonetto 104 del Petrarca* 6. *Sonetto 123 del Petrarca* 7. *Après une lecture du Dante, fantasia quasi sonata* (Dante Sonata).

WRITINGS. The essay *Tannhäuser and the Song Contest at the Wartburg.*[3]

223. To Richard Wagner in Dresden. Weimar, 26 February

Very dear friend,

So much do I owe to your valiant and superb genius, to the blazing and magnificent pages of your *Tannhäuser*, that I feel wholly at a loss in accepting the thanks you are so kind as to address to me with regard to the two performances I have had the honour and good fortune to conduct. Nevertheless, your letter

---

[1] Born a Princess of Mecklenburg-Schwerin, hence the language.
[2] The Concerto was first sketched in 1832, the *Totentanz* planned in 1839.
[3] Published in the *Journal des Débats* in May, and two years later in German.

has given me one of the keenest pleasures of friendship, and I thank you with all my heart for your words of thanks. Once and for all, number me from now on among your most zealous and devoted admirers; near or far, count on me and make use of me.

Messrs Ziegesar, Genast, and Biedenfeld have sent you details of the impression made on our public by your masterpiece. In the *Deutsche allgemeine Zeitung* you will find a few lines that I sent to Brockhaus* at his request; it was Biedenfeld who drafted this brief article. I shall send you by post the article published in our *Gemeindeblatt*, in which there appears, too, the prologue by Schober, who had the sense to turn *Tannhäuser* to very good account.

Talking of people of good sense, do you know what I have taken it into my head to do:

Neither more nor less than to adapt for the piano, in my own way, the overture to *Tannhäuser* and the whole of the 'O du mein holder Abendstern' scene from the Third Act. The former will, I believe, find few performers capable of overcoming its technical difficulties, but the 'Abendstern' should easily be within reach of pianists of the 2nd class.

And so if you felt like asking Meser to publish it, or allowing me to offer it to Härtel or Schlesinger, I should be glad if it came out soon. Perhaps, if you had no objection, I could even use it for an album on behalf of which I have been pressed into service these last two months—the album published by a 'women's society' for the benefit of the *German fleet*!! In vain have I told them that I am myself on the rocks as far as manuscripts or ideas are concerned; they won't take no for an answer, and now once again a letter has come from a beautiful lady badgering me more than ever!

Drop me a line on the destination you prefer for your 'Abendstern'; and when we see one another again I shall be so impertinent as to play your overture to you with my own two hands, as I have rewritten it for my special use.

Do please remember me very affectionately to Tichatschek; he has been an admirable artiste and a charming and excellent comrade and friend. So it will give me real pleasure to see him here again in May as he has promised us; and if, this time, you had a few free days, how happy we should be to see you spend them here.

In the mean time, very dear friend, believe me with heart and soul your devoted admirer and friend   Fr. Liszt

P.S. A very beautiful and accomplished hand[4] wishes to add a few lines to this letter; if you are tired of reading me, you can have no better compensation.

---

[4] That of Princess Carolyne, who wrote of her own appreciation of *Tannhäuser*, thanked Wagner for his kindness to her during her visit to Dresden the previous year, and intimated her desire to express her admiration in person.

224. To Anna Liszt in Paris [Weimar, late February or early March[5]]. G (F) Your letter, dear Mother, moved me to my very depths. Your words are words of wisdom, of truth and of love. Be sure that my life will justify your trust and that your old age will be spared the distressing worries inflicted upon you by my early years!

Your admiring affection for the Princess makes me happy. Your maternal instinct does not deceive you. The better you get to know her, the more you will admire her glorious intellectual gifts and be overcome by her noble-minded greatness of heart and by her love.

I do not know in what connection Princess G[agarina] told you that the Princess Wittgenstein is not beautiful. When the opportunity presents itself, tell your friends and acquaintances from me that I believe myself to be as good a connoisseur of beauty as anyone, and that Princess W. *is* beautiful, very beautiful even, for she possesses that rare and imperishable beauty which can be imparted to the countenance only by a radiant soul. If, as I hope, it is granted to me to bring her to Paris as my wife this year, she will certainly create a sensation, and the cream of Parisian society will rectify the absurd opinions of common clodhoppers. Disgraceful machinations against the Princess jeopardize so many vital interests that I have little desire to re-establish contact with my Parisian friends. I have neglected them only too much; yet they who know me will neither lose patience nor their trust in me.

Kiss the children from me. I shall certainly see them this summer, whether at a seaside resort or elsewhere. I am even thinking of having Blandine and Cosima with me for some time. Everything hinges on the main question, which takes priority over everything else—my marriage.

Farewell, dear Mother; pray for me and love me! F. Liszt

The opening of a letter in French of 14 May from Liszt to Gaetano Belloni in Paris runs:

Dear Bell,
Richard Wagner (Kapellmeister at Dresden) has been here since yesterday. That's a man of admirable genius; indeed, a very experienced genius which is evidently destined to beat out for itself a new and glorious path in art. The latest events in Dresden have impelled him to make a great resolution, in the accomplishment of which I have decided to do everything I can to help him.[6]

---

[5] This undated letter (written before 8 Mar.) is a reply to Anna's of 13 Feb.
[6] Translated from the facsimile of the holograph (of the opening of the letter only) given in Weilguny and Handrick's *Franz Liszt: Biographie in Bildern* (Leipzig, 1967), 23.

Unfortunately the remainder of the letter is available only in an incomplete German version;[7] and since that version perpetrates two gross blunders[8] in its rendering of even the foregoing few lines, it has not been regarded as trustworthy enough to use as the basis of an English translation here. The purpose of the letter, however, seems to be to ask Belloni to give what help he can to Wagner when the latter arrives in Paris; above all in regard to obtaining a success—perhaps in London—for his latest opera, *Lohengrin*.[9]

225. To the Hereditary Grand Duke Carl Alexander.
Weimar, 23 May

Monseigneur,

The times are so rich in events that there no longer seems to be any room for letters and conversations, that exchange of a number of ideas and rather unnecessary intermediate sentiments, when parliaments and even constitutions depart and have given themselves formal notice to be gone, neither more nor less than did the gods of old!

Nevertheless, having been so good as not to forget me entirely, YRH will forgive me for taking up your spare time in camp[10] by these lines of mine, with which I enclose by way of escort some extremely peaceful columns that have just appeared in the *Journal des Débats*.

As you will realize very quickly, this poetical analysis of Wagner's [*Tannhäuser*] libretto was for me only an opportunity to express something that I feel very deeply, and I could wish it were given to me to be able to prove in some still better way my respectful admiration for the august Princess [Maria Pavlovna] whose touching kindnesses and flattering patronage keep me here in Weimar!

Wagner spent a few days here and attended two rehearsals of his opera [*Tannhäuser*]. The excellent result we obtained gave him a satisfaction that was almost a surprise. Unfortunately, by a singular coincidence, on the very day of the performance the Leipzig newspaper published the *Steckbrief* [arrest warrant]

---

[7] Published by Wilhelm Tappert in the *Neue Musik-Zeitung* (Cologne) of 1 Oct. 1881 and reproduced in La Mara (ed.), *Franz Liszt's Briefe* (8 vols., Leipzig, 1893–1905), i. 75–6.

[8] Liszt's 'un génie très pratique', for example, was misread as 'un génie trépantique' and accordingly rendered in German as 'ein schädelspaltendes Genie'. This was in its turn translated in all innocence by Constance Bache (in her English version of the first volume in the series edited by La Mara) as 'a brain-splitting genius'—which, whether or not an apt description of Wagner, is hardly what Liszt meant.

[9] In the event, the première of *Lohengrin* took place not in London but at Weimar (28 Aug. 1850), and the conductor was Liszt himself.

[10] Carl Alexander was away on military duties at Horsens, East Jutland.

which compelled him to leave at once.[11] I don't know if it is the road to Dresden or the one to Paris that he will have taken. Come what may, I did everything possible to dissuade him absolutely and completely from any participation in political *discord*. Art has nowadays no need to join in the raucous cries from the barricades; its territory is purer and more exalted, and its influence at once more salutary and more lasting. Without the distressing touchiness that so many years of painful struggles have left in him—struggles brought about by the difficult-ies arising from his position, his renown, his ambition, and his legitimate pride (leaving out of account his rare make-up as poet and artist, already necessarily made sensitive by the grace of God)—it can be assumed that he would in no way have ventured into this regrettable situation, and I am even convinced that he is more compromised in appearance than in fact. Moreover, as a woman of heart and intellect yesterday said so rightly: *Ausserordentliche Menschen muss man nicht mit dem gewöhnlichen Massstabe messen* [Exceptional people are not to be measured by the usual standards].

If, as I hope, he arrives safe and sound in Paris, he will there find as much of that tranquillity he so greatly needs, by bringing out a new work which won't lack success ... and then his political cure will be achieved. 'Que diable allait-il faire dans cette galère!'[12]

In a few days we shall be putting on once again the Duke of Coburg's opera [*Tony*], on the subject of which I have had published in ten or a dozen French newspapers, including Frankfurt's, the brief account which Monseigneur will find enclosed with this letter. If YRH deemed it opportune to show it to the com-poser of the score of *Tony*, and at the same time to remember me to his good-will, I should be greatly obliged.

Has news of the death of Madame Récamier[13] reached you, Monseigneur? One would wish to speak with grace of that reign of grace which would like-wise seem to be disappearing. What, then, shall we have left? What always remains: to strive and to merit. It will be difficult to fill the gap that this death will leave in your correspondence!

HRH the Hereditary Grand Duchess has just given me very appreciable pleas-ure by resuming her [singing] lessons, in which the teacher will naturally have more to learn than the pupil. When YRH returns, I think the runs and roulades

[11] Following his part in the ill-fated rising in Dresden, Wagner had sought refuge in Weimar. An undated note from Liszt to Princess Carolyne of *c*.20 May runs: 'Can you give the bearer 60 thalers. Wagner is obliged to flee, and I can-not come to his assistance at the moment.' Crossing safely into Switzerland, Wagner then made his way to Paris and later to Zurich. Ahead of him lay eleven years of exile.

[12] The famous repeated exclamation of Géronte in Molière's *Les Fourberies de Scapin* (II. vii): 'What the deuce was he doing in that galley?'

[13] The celebrated *salonnière* and beauty had died on 11 May.

of *Le Prophète*[14] will have their most accomplished performance, thanks to the brilliant vocalization of a royal *assoluta*.

In the hope that these long Schleswig war trials will soon give place to a glorious and lasting peace, I impatiently await the return of YRH, so that I may be able to repeat *viva voce* the tribute of respectful devotion with which I have the honour to be, Monseigneur,

Your very humble and faithful servant   F. Liszt

226. To Carl Reinecke in Bremen. Weimar, 30 May. Many thanks, dear Herr Reinecke, for your kind lines; I am pleased to hope that you arrived safely in Bremen, which must be quite delighted to possess you. The musical taste of that town I have always heard spoken of very highly, and I feel sure that its inhabitants will have the good taste to appreciate you at your full worth, and that with little difficulty you will there create for yourself a really splendid position.

Wagner, who will probably have to lose his own position in Dresden as a result of recent events, came and spent a few days here with me. Unfortunately, news of the *Steckbrief* arrived on the very day of the performance of *Tannhäuser*, which prevented him being present. He must by now have arrived in Paris, where he will surely find a more favourable ground on which to make full use of his dramatic genius.

With the aid of success, as I have often said, he will even end up being recognized as a great *German* composer in Germany, provided that his works are first performed in Paris or London, following the example of Meyerbeer, not to mention Gluck, Weber, and Handel!

Wagner told me of his regret at being unable to respond better to the note of introduction I had given you for him. If you should ever find yourself in his vicinity, don't fail to go and see him on my behalf; you can be sure of a good welcome.

I am very much obliged to you for having spoken of me to Schumann in such a manner as he at least ought to think of me. I should be very interested to know his setting of the Epilogue to *Faust*.[15] If he publishes it, I shall try to see that it is given a suitable performance here, either at Court or in the Theatre. When passing through Frankfurt recently I had a glance at the score of *Genoveva*,[16] having been told that it would be performed in Leipzig by mid-May at the

---

[14] Five-act opera by Meyerbeer, first performed at the Paris Opéra, 16 Apr. 1849.

[15] Liszt conducted Part III of Schumann's *Scenes from Faust* at Weimar in August as part of the Goethe centenary celebrations.

[16] Schumann's four-act opera (based on Hebbel's tragedy of the same title) about St Geneviève. The first performance, conducted by the composer and attended by Liszt, was in Leipzig on 25 June 1850.

latest. I very much fear that Schumann may find himself grappling with the difficulties and dilatoriness which usually accompany the performance of any elevated work. One could say that, to counterbalance for a time the glorious creations of genius, a wicked fairy presents the most vulgar works with a magnificent success and sees that they become widely known, favouring those whom inspiration has passed by in order to relegate its elect to the shadows. This is no reason to lose heart, for what matters the *sooner* or *later*?

A thousand thanks for the cigars you sent me so punctually and helpfully. If you have an opportunity to send me some samples of a kind neither *too thin* nor *too light*, within the price range of 20 to 25 thalers a thousand, I shall gladly place an order which might be followed by a larger one.

Schuberth of Hamburg has just sent me your Schumann *Lieder* transcriptions, which have given me real pleasure. If you publish other things, kindly keep me informed; for you know the sincere interest I take in both yourself and your works. I hope to have an opportunity of proving this to you more and more.

In the mean time, believe me yours affectionately,   F. Liszt

P.S. I have not forgotten the little commission you entrusted me with relating to the *Fantasie-Stücke*, and in a few weeks I shall send you a copy of the new edition.

227. To Robert Schumann. Weimar, 5 June ^G

Dear friend,

Allow me, above all, to repeat to you what, next after myself, you ought to have known best for a long time—namely, that no one honours and admires you more sincerely than my humble self.

When the occasion arises we can by all means have a friendly discussion about the importance of a work, of a man, even of a town.[17] For the present I especially rejoice in the fact that your opera [*Genoveva*] is to be performed soon, and I entreat you to notify me about it a few days in advance; for I shall most certainly come to Leipzig on that occasion, when we can also talk about staging the same opera as soon as possible thereafter in Weimar. Perhaps, too, you can there find time to acquaint me with your *Faust*. I am very eager to know

---

[17] In his letter to Liszt of 31 May from Bad Kreischa, following Reinecke's visit and enquiry on Liszt's behalf about the *Scenes from Faust*, Schumann, quoting words uttered by Liszt at the time of their quarrel the previous year, had asked if the work would not be '*too Leipzigerish*' for him.

how you have set about it; and your plan to give this work greater length and breadth seems to me to be wholly appropriate. A grandiose subject generally also requires grandiose treatment. Although in its small *dimensions* Raphael's *Vision of Ezekiel*[18] attains the culminating point of greatness, it was in fresco that he painted the *School of Athens* and all the *Stanze* at the Vatican.

Manfred is glorious, passionately attractive![19] Don't let anything hinder you; it will refresh you for your *Faust*—and German Art will point with pride to these *twins.*

Schuberth has sent me your *Album für die Jugend* [Album for the Young], which, to say the least, I like very much. Your splendid Trio[20] we have played here several times, and rather satisfactorily.

Wagner spent a few days here and in Eisenach. Any day now I expect news of him from Paris, where he will surely enhance his reputation and his career quite dazzlingly.

Would your dear wife (to whom please give my friendliest regards) not for once like to make a rural and romantic excursion into the Thuringian Forest? The environs are quite delightful, and I should be very glad to see her again in Weimar. You will find here a very good grand piano and a couple of intelligent people who are attached to you with true fellow-feeling and admiration.

In any case, there will appear in Leipzig as a *claqueur*

Your invariably devoted friend   F. Liszt

228. To the Hereditary Grand Duke Carl Alexander.
Sunday [24 June]

Monseigneur,

If I find no special reason to come to you today,[21] please ascribe this to nothing more than legitimate discretion; may it be allowed me, however, to associate myself in mind and heart with the good wishes expressed to you, which it is my confident hope that you will realize.

Next Thursday, at Ettersburg,[22] I shall take the liberty of offering YRH the volume of Dante that you reminded me about the day before yesterday. These last few years he has become for my mind and spirit what the column of clouds

---

[18] In the Pitti Palace, Florence. The *School of Athens* fills a wall of the Stanza della Segnatura in the Vatican.

[19] Schumann's overture and incidental music to Byron's dramatic poem of the same title was completed that year.

[20] Probably the Piano Trio in D minor; possibly the one in F.   [21] Carl Alexander's thirty-first birthday.

[22] Hunting-lodge, belonging to the Grand Dukes of Saxe-Weimar and dating from the early 18th cent., situated on the Ettersberg hill near Weimar.

was for the children of Israel when it guided them through the desert. At this very moment I am leaving the poet just as he left Virgil,[23] and YRH will not find fault with me, I hope, for inscribing the date of 24 June 1849.

On all dates, in all circumstances, be pleased to make use, Monseigneur, of the unchanging and serious devotion of

Your very humble and faithful servant　　　F. Liszt

229. To Blandine Liszt in Paris. [Bückeburg] 22 October.

You want a letter, you tell me, dearest child, and you want it very promptly and without delay; but yours (which, like Mlle Laure's, should be dated 12 July, I assume) did not reach me until after mid-September; and, without wishing to make excuses on this point, these last weeks I really haven't found a favourable hour for our correspondence, and kept this pleasure for my first free day.

Finally, today, 22 October, my 38th birthday, I want to give myself something of a celebration too—and since I imagine that you have not forgotten me, I should not forgive myself if I put you off any longer. Here, then, is your letter, dear Blandine; and my heart has so much fatherly love and so many fond dreams to murmur to you, that could my pen write it all down speedily and faithfully you would be receiving a whole volume.

Let me kiss you, therefore, my poor child, and in response to my prayer may God's blessing descend into your heart; and may you, and your sister, be a lasting consolation for me; may you both be fully aware that being gentle and good to those who love you will make you happier than anything else in this world. And who could love you as deeply as I do?

Your progress in education and intelligence gives me keen satisfaction. I see with pleasure that your handwriting is improving. Try to write more and more legibly and elegantly, if possible—and take care not to imitate me on this point. The lessons in literature and history with abstracts of Homer and of the Greek tragic poets that you tell me about must have had a beneficial influence on the development of your mind, for which we must not in future neglect to provide healthy and substantial nourishment. And so I find the choice of Homer and the Greek tragic poets wholly suitable. I should be glad if you would do me the pleasure of sending me by Grandmama, who will be visiting me in Weimar at the end of December, some of your analyses (that of the *Iliad*, for example, and of *Antigone*[24]), copied out neatly and put between covers.

---

[23] It was Virgil who departed, leaving Dante overwhelmed with sorrow (*Purgatorio*, xxx. 49–54).
[24] The tragedy by Sophocles.

Add to them, also, two or three of your drawings, which I shall honour with frames and hang above my desk. On that occasion, don't forget to tell me the names of your drawing master and your teacher of literature and history.

Please don't fail to thank Mlle Kautz, as nicely as you can, for the care she is taking with your musical studies. I am most grateful to her, and very much wish you to prove ever worthier of her excellent lessons. When Grandmama returns to Paris, I shall give her a large album chosen from among new works of mine published in Germany, which I shall ask her to offer on my behalf to Mlle Kautz, to whom in the mean time please convey my most sincere greetings.

Farewell, dear child; write to me soon and often. Keep me informed of your studies, and do not fail to send me samples (as commendable as possible) of your knowledge and ability, which could find no one more sympathetic and appreciative than your father, who will be so happy to become ever so slightly proud of and for you.

230. To the Hereditary Grand Duke Carl Alexander. Bückeburg, 24 October

Monseigneur,

Detained in Bückeburg for a month and more because Princess M.W. has been seriously ill, and even now has not reached the convalescent stage, I cannot foresee that I shall be back in Weimar before early December. Permit me, therefore, to entrust to the post the enclosed letter from Herr [Gustav] Schmidt, who has the honour to thank Your Royal Highness for so graciously intervening in a way that has had the practical result of obtaining for him the post of Kapellmeister at the Wiesbaden theatre. Allow me to join with it the renewed expression of my keen gratitude for this further kindness of Your Royal Highness's to me, one which follows so many others.

Would my very long letter about the Goethe Foundation,[25] sent from Hamburg more than a month ago, have had the unlucky fate of not reaching Monseigneur?

---

[25] Liszt was at this time giving thought to his remarkable essay *De la fondation-Goethe à Weimar*, in which he proposed that a foundation, named after Goethe, should be set up which would promote the arts through annual competitions, whereat in one year poets, in the next painters, in the third sculptors, and in the fourth musicians would compete for prizes, the judges to be invited from all over Germany. Every year the winning work would be 'crowned' and performed, printed, or exhibited under the aegis of the foundation; and every fourth year there would be a music festival at the Wartburg, the medieval castle near Eisenach associated with the Minnesingers (as well as with St Elisabeth and Luther). Unfortunately nothing came of this imaginative proposal, which, with goodwill and support from others, might have led to the creation of one of Europe's outstanding arts festivals. As was remarked eighty years later by the Liszt scholar Peter Raabe: 'To put such a plan into action, and to maintain the foundation permanently, would have been possible only if men such as Liszt himself—in whom selflessness and humanity were combined with a noble mind—were the rule and not rare exceptions.'

If so, I shall easily console myself by asking YRH for permission to send him a copy of it.

The misprints which crept into my article about the Goethe celebrations (published in the *Journal des Débats* of 25 September) greatly vexed me. 'Père' instead of 'Prince' Anton Radziwill is quite ludicrous; and finding the word *impassible* [impassive] distorted into that of *impossible* did not fail to disturb my more or less impossible *impassibilité* [impassiveness]. I take pleasure in hoping that YRH will have greeted this *feuilleton*, such as it is, with some indulgence, in favour of my good intentions which cannot be doubted.

I have the honour to be, Monseigneur,

Your very humble and grateful servant   F. Liszt

1850

5 January. Liszt and the princesses return to Weimar.

Mid-January to mid-March. Anna Liszt stays at the Altenburg.

25 June. Liszt is present at the première, in Leipzig, of Schumann's *Genoveva*.

24 August. Liszt conducts the première of his *Prometheus* overture and choruses.

25 August. The statue of Herder is unveiled before Weimar's town church; Liszt's *Festchor* is performed.

28 August. Liszt conducts the première of Wagner's *Lohengrin*.

Mid-October. Joseph Joachim[1] begins his duties as leader of Liszt's orchestra.

Late October. Illness obliges Princess Carolyne to return to Bad Eilsen, whither she is accompanied by her daughter and by Liszt.

WORKS. *Festchor zur Enthüllung des Herder-Denkmals in Weimar* (S86), for male chorus and piano/orchestra. The symphonic poems *Ce qu'on entend sur la montagne* (2nd version) and *Héroïde funèbre* (S102, 1849–50). Overture (S99)[2] and choruses (S69) to Herder's *Prometheus Unbound*. ORGAN: Fantasy and Fugue (S259) on the chorale 'Ad nos, ad salutarem undam' from *Le Prophète* (Meyerbeer).

PIANO: *Valse impromptu* (S213, *c.*1850); *Mazurka brillante* (S221); arrangements of Wedding March and Dance of the Elves from *A Midsummer Night's Dream* (Mendelssohn) (S410, 1849–50) and *Illustrations du Prophète* (Meyerbeer) (S414, 1849–50): 1. *Prière, Hymne triomphale, Marche du sacre* 2. *Les Patineurs* 3. *Chœur pastoral, Appel aux armes.*

PUBLISHED. *Liebesträume* (S541), arrangements for piano of the songs *Hohe Liebe, Gestorben war ich,* and *O lieb, so lang du lieben kannst.*

A major preoccupation remained the upbringing and education of Blandine, Cosima, and Daniel.

---

[1] This young violinist (see Biographical Sketches) had made Liszt's acquaintance at Vienna in 1846, and, in a private performance at Liszt's hotel, played the Mendelssohn Concerto to him, with Liszt accompanying at the piano. 'To this day,' wrote Joachim's biographer half a century later, 'Joachim cherishes the memory of Liszt's wonderful playing, particularly of the manner in which he accompanied the finale of the concerto, all the time holding a lighted cigar between the first and middle fingers of his right hand' (A. Moser, *Joseph Joachim*, London, 1901, 70).

[2] Which in 1855, after revision, became the symphonic poem *Prometheus.*

231. To Anna Liszt in Paris. Weimar, 25 March

Dear Mother,

I was delighted to learn direct from you that your journey passed without incident and that you got back to Paris in perfect health. Let me hope that you will not make yourself needlessly ill with regard to the change which must *of necessity* take place in the children's domestic arrangements, a change that I should like to see brought about without your working yourself into too anxious and agitated a state. If you will consider the matter, and take the trouble to remember some conversations we have had on this topic, you will find it entirely natural and perfectly appropriate for me to stick to my determination to take the children from Mme Bernard's, just as it was natural and appropriate for me to leave them there when, five years ago, I decided to, despite the abuse and recriminations that their mother was at that time pleased to heap upon me on this subject. . . .

Let there therefore be no further question of getting me to abandon a decision taken after much thought and which you have merely to see is carried out *à la lettre*; for you know that, as far as serious things are concerned, I never think of changing anything I have resolved to do. You have the best proof of it in the way I behaved towards the children five years ago, when I brought all Madame d'Agoult's fury down on my head by firmly refusing her any more direct interference in their upbringing; and, had she left me no alternative, would, to that end, have had recourse to the law. You later approved of what I did at that time; and since my present approach is its inevitable outcome, I am convinced you will approve of it likewise when you have seen its good results. In the mean time don't allow yourself to be too softened by Blandine's tears. . . . It is quite natural that she and Cosima bewail the loss of Mlle Laure, and it would even be a pity were they not to do so; but it is still more natural for these children to comply lovingly and trustingly with what I want for them, which has always been their best counsel and firmest support, and for their education to be continued and completed by moving on to the higher level I seek for it.

For the moment you need do nothing else but purely and simply keep the children in your own home; and as soon as possible give them a change of air by taking them into the country and staying there with them in order to keep them for the time being from any *idle* relations. It matters little that their piano studies have been temporarily broken off; but, to make up for it, I want them to read a lot and to remain actively occupied. So give them about ten of M. de Chateaubriand's volumes: the *Génie du Christianisme*, the *Martyrs*, and the *Itinéraire de Paris à Jérusalem.*[3] They are also to have M. de Ségur's universal history, which is in my library, and to go on with their historical studies as best they can. In addition, I shall get Belloni to bring them a few volumes which will interest them and provide them with some good spiritual nourishment.

By about mid-July I expect to have found someone who will be able to assume full responsibility for their education and to justify all the confidence I shall place in her. . . .

And so, dear Mother, do please help me carry out my duty as a father such as I understand it; and don't amuse yourself by listening to the foolish advice of some people and the tittle-tattle of others. As behoves sensible and serious-minded people, let us simply do what we know to be right.

As regards the four thousand francs, my express wish is that they be paid to you annually; do therefore make with Belloni the arrangements necessary for all the papers to be perfectly in order and for there to be nothing to come back to on this point.

Farewell, dear Mother; may God keep you and bless you through your children.

F. Liszt

232. To Joseph d'Ortigue in Paris. Weimar, 24 April. I am truly very grateful to you, my dear friend, for the trouble you have so kindly taken in devoting a few hours to a perusal of my *Chopin* manuscript[4] despite your own urgent affairs. The kind judgement you pass on three-quarters of my work gives me most flattering encouragement, and I thank you very cordially for your observations on the fourth quarter, of which I shall not fail to take advantage when the special considerations which make me defer publication of this little volume are put aside. As regards my *Chopin soirée*, I admit that I am rather keen on it. It is by no means an invention, but really did take place, and on two occasions, in the rue du Mont-Blanc, with the persons whom I have tried to characterize in my own way. I imagine that these details will be more or less to the taste of the public to whom a work of this kind is more especially addressed,

---

[3] In *Le Génie du Christianisme, ou les Beautés poétiques et morales de la religion chrétienne* (1802), Chateaubriand's intention was to demonstrate that of all religions the Christian is the most poetical and the most humane; *Les Martyrs, ou le Triomphe de la religion chrétienne* (1809) deals with the triumph of Christianity over paganism in the Roman Empire in the early 4th cent.; and the journey Chateaubriand made (1806–7) to collect material for that work is described in *L'Itinéraire de Paris à Jérusalem et de Jérusalem à Paris* (1811).

[4] Six months earlier, during his sojourn at Bad Eilsen, Liszt had been deeply shocked—apparently bursting into tears when coming unexpectedly upon the announcement in a newspaper he was reading—to learn of the death of Chopin (17 Oct. 1849). He had asked d'Ortigue (and also Sainte-Beuve) to look through and comment upon the memoir and appreciation, co-authored by Princess Carolyne, that he had later drafted in tribute to the Polish composer.

and which is neither that of the usual newspaper readership nor that of those who reflect upon their reading, but a public between the two, consisting mainly of women who are understood or misunderstood, plus a certain number of people who like to dream when reading. . . .

Your affectionate and devoted   F. Liszt

233. To Franz Dingelstedt in Stuttgart [Weimar, 13 May]

Dear friend,

Herr von Ziegesar's letter has already informed you of the affectionate and courteous reception that naturally awaits you here—notwithstanding people's memory of the stinging darts you are accused of having formerly hurled at the *bornes et borgnes* [boundary stones and one-eyed people] of Weimar; but let this be said in parenthesis and entirely between ourselves, reserving the right to come back to it orally when you get here. . . .

While waiting for the official arrangements (which should soon be made) of the festival programme, this is what I propose:

For the Herder anniversary, 25 August,[5] at 11 o'clock: unveiling of the Statue. —At midday: *Der entfesselte Prometheus* [Prometheus Unbound], dramatic scenes by Herder, with Choruses composed by yours sincerely.

Evening: Handel's *Messiah*, grand performance in the town church.[6]

For the Goethe anniversary, 28 August. In the morning: gathering of members of the Committee of the Goethe Foundation and definitive fixing of the programme of the competition for next year, which will have to be made known at once through the newspapers.

Luncheon at Court.

Evening: Prologue by Dingelstedt and *Lohengrin*, grand opera, not yet performed, by Richard Wagner.

About this work I have had a letter sent (with Wagner's authorization) to the Intendancy at Dresden, which possesses the manuscript score. As soon as we have received it I shall send you the libretto, which you may possibly be able to make use of for your Prologue. In my opinion, this Prologue will have to refer even more to Weimar, its past and its future, than to Herder, for whose anniversary it seemed to me preferable not to propose a theatrical celebration. The performance of an oratorio in church is obviously a more appropriate way

---

[5] Date of Herder's birth in 1744.
[6] An appropriate venue, for it was to take up the post of Moderator at the Stadtkirche that Herder had come (1776) to Weimar in the first place.

of commemorating a Court Preacher, Moderator, and Senior Councillor of the Consistory!—especially since Herder never wrote anything for the theatre. . . .

A thousand sincere and friendly greetings from   Yours, F. Liszt

234. To Feodor von Milde in London.[7] **Weimar, 2 August.** Thank you for your excellent letter, my dear friend, which although rather belated gave me great pleasure. For five days we have been hard at work on *Lohengrin*, and however enormous the task for the forces at our disposal, I am convinced that we shall acquit ourselves with honour, for gradually and by degrees all our artistes will grow passionately fond of this masterpiece, will thoroughly absorb its content and live its life, which is the *sine qua non* for a performance such as I intend ours to be. To achieve it, we have already had 4 hours of rehearsals every day this week, and next week we shall have two every morning and two every afternoon, seeing that it will be necessary to divide the orchestra into stringed and wind instruments, for separate rehearsals.

Do try, my dear friend, to get here no later than the 12th, if you can manage it; you will find us already in the midst of dress rehearsals in the theatre. I shall ask you into the bargain to be so good as to undertake a few score bars in *Prometheus*, which will be performed on 24 August, eve of the unveiling of the statue of Herder, and for which I have composed eight choruses and a long overture.

On the 25th I plan to have Handel's *Messiah* performed in church, and on this occasion I am of a mind to have choirs and orchestra placed in the apse, from the front seats to the altar.

If you could induce Ernst (to whom please give my most cordial regards) to come here from 20 to 30 August, I should be delighted; nevertheless, if, as is to be assumed, he has *more profitable* engagements for that time, he should not put himself out, for Weimar has unfortunately no material advantage to offer him. But be so kind as to tell him that HIH the Grand Duchess has several times deigned to ask me 'when Herr Ernst will return here, as he promised....'

I enclose, dear friend, a bill of exchange for *15 francs*—and take pleasure in hoping that you will not have to make use of it.

Fräulein Agthe[8] (who is adorable in her role of Elsa) asks me to give you her most affectionate compliments—to which I add without more ado the sincere good wishes of your affectionate and devoted   F. Liszt

---

[7] Where he was studying with Manual Garcia.   [8] See Biographical Sketches under Milde.

At Weimar's Court Theatre on Wednesday, 28 August (101st anniversary of the birth of Goethe), was given the première of *Lohengrin*. Liszt conducted; and the parts of Lohengrin, Elsa, Telramund, and Ortrud were sung, respectively, by Karl Beck, Rosa Agthe, Feodor von Milde, and Josephine Fastlinger. As part of the Goethe celebrations, a reading of Dingelstedt's Prologue preceded the performance.

Among the musical and literary notabilities present were Giacomo Meyerbeer, Gérard de Nerval, Jules Janin, and Bettina von Arnim.

235. To Richard Wagner in Zurich. Weimar, 2 September

Dearest friend,

Your *Lohengrin* is a sublime work from beginning to end; in many places my very heart poured forth tears. The whole opera being a single and indivisible wonder, it would be impossible for me to lay stress on any particular passage, combination, or effect.

Just as a pious ecclesiastic once underlined word for word the whole of the *Imitation of Christ*, I could underline note for note the whole of your *Lohengrin*. In that case, however, I would begin at the end; that is, with the duet in the Third Act between Elsa and Lohengrin, which is in my opinion the acme of what is beautiful and true in Art.

Our first performance was relatively satisfactory. Herr von Bülow,* who will be seeing you shortly, will give you very exact details. The second can't take place for another ten or twelve days. The Court, as well as the few intelligent people in Weimar, have great feeling and admiration for your work. As for the public at large, they will certainly make it a point of honour to find beauty in, and applaud, what they cannot understand. As soon as I can find some leisure I shall give attention to the *feuilleton* which will probably appear in the [*Journal des*] *Débats*. In the mean time Raff* (whom Bülow will tell you about) will do a couple of articles for Brockhaus's paper and the Leipzig *Illustrirte Zeitung*. Uhlig will attend to Brendel's* music journal etc.

If you can find a moment, don't forget to write to Genast, who took a very warm interest in the success of *Lohengrin*; you can be entirely reassured about the fate of this masterpiece in Weimar, which is doubtless a little surprised to have such works to perform. But before the end of the winter *Lohengrin* will necessarily become a 'hit'!!!

When shall we have *Siegfried*? Write to me soon, and always count on your devoted friend and servant   F. Liszt

236. To Anna Liszt. 5 October ^{G (F)}

Dear Mother,

I would have preferred these lines to be delivered to you by Mme Patersi,[9] into whose hands I ask you to put both my daughters, since it is to her that, from now, I wish to entrust their upbringing. Thank you from my heart for all the love with which you have accepted the children these last few months; and for all the care and trouble which you took with them in their early childhood, they will remain as grateful to you as I am.

Unfortunately Mme Patersi fell ill immediately on arriving here, and cannot come to Paris for another fortnight. But, since you are moving house, her sister Mme Saint-Mars, who will live with my daughters and her at rue Casimir Périer No. 6, Fbg. St Germain, is being kind enough to collect the children and keep them with her until the arrival of Mme Patersi.

After receiving this letter, therefore, will you hand Blandine and Cosima into her charge. Please also be so kind, dear Mother, as to have the furniture you told me of, and all the other household items you have assured me you can dispense with, taken to Mme Patersi's aforementioned residence. I hope you will often give my daughters the pleasure of dining with them, and I want Daniel, too, to present himself at Mme Patersi's quite often. Six silver cutlery sets, glass and china, table linen, sheets and pillow-cases, will therefore be necessary. Since I would have to buy everything new, I should be very much obliged if you would let them have any things of this nature that you yourself no longer need.

I have asked Mme Patersi to bring my daughters to see you frequently, and to accompany them everywhere. I am convinced that on closer acquaintance you will think highly of her, and also like her, when you see that she is having a good influence on the children. She alone has to decide what is or is not allowed them. She knows the views I hold on their education and their future, which fully accord with her own. It is my hope that under her influence the bad and worrying results of the education given them by Mme Bernard will soon disappear.

Farewell, dear Mother; remain healthy and cheerful and give your full trust to your loving son   F. Liszt

237. To Blandine Liszt in Paris. Weimar, 5 October. Your latest
letter, dear Blandine, has satisfied me no more than did the preceding ones. I have for long had to be content with their banality, attributing to your great youth the absence of any individual thoughts which might inform me of the

---

[9] Mme Patersi de Fossombroni, a lady in her early seventies who had been the governess of the young Princess Carolyne.

real state of your soul and of the reach of your mind. For some time they have been less banal, it is true, but they express opinions and depict a mood that I find rather unreasonable; and I should like to hope that they spring from your present ignorance of the value of certain feelings and of certain facts. From now on this ignorance will no longer be an excuse, for I have had the good fortune to meet someone who, in the course of a life of sorrow and frustration, has given proof of a character so rare, and of a mind so sound, that she will know how to show you the better path you will have to follow to become a respectable and distinguished woman. She will teach you what solid piety (that essential foundation of honour and dignity), discernment, prudence, and common sense consist of, all more necessary in your position than in others. Obey her, I order you; give her your trust, and you will be happy to have done so. . . .

I shall not say to you 'love Madame Patersi', for I wish to believe that you have too good a heart not to be sincerely attached to her rare qualities and grateful for the intelligent care she will devote to you. Her tender heart will make her sympathize with your errors of thought, which can easily degenerate into errors of sentiment and of conduct. She will show you more explicitly than I can do, through letters, why I call errors those outbursts which prevent you from understanding that my wishes for you are dictated by reason and a serious concern for your welfare. Listen to her with attention and respect, for I have told her truthfully and with emotion of the difficulties you have caused me in more ways than one. She knows what I want and desire for you, and also how determined I am to neglect nothing that might induce you, in the difficult position in which destiny has placed you, to live as a pious Christian, an honest woman, and a rational human being, worthy of the wishes that I, and others close to me, have for your future.

You will be going to live with Mme Patersi, and I presume that in her company you will soon forget those sorrows which you try to alleviate, you say, by strumming on your piano. Study it seriously; take the trouble to acquire some talents and you will soon see that work and study don't go with idle musings. Apply yourself in particular to acquiring a good knowledge of geography and history, which Mme Patersi promises me to make you give serious attention to, and of the languages in which she will supervise your progress. Your letters in English and German are not bad at all, assuming that your teachers have not corrected them. In those which in future you will write to me regularly on the first of each month (without expecting equally regular replies, for I have other tasks to attend to), while your chief concern must be to satisfy me, you will tell me what you have been reading, of the impressions you have gained from it, and of the persons you meet and of the things you see, so that I may better than hitherto be able to judge the development of your moral and intellectual understanding. . . .

I embrace you, dear Blandine, and bless you.

238. To Anna Liszt. 21 October ^{G (F)}

Dear Mother,

Mme Patersi brings you my best wishes for a happy celebration of 22 October. I hope you have got over your removal difficulties quite splendidly and are enjoying radiant health. Where, then, are you actually living at present? Are you near to or far from the children? Let me have more details in your next letter, so that I know where and how you have made a nest for yourself.

Since Mme Patersi naturally needs many books, will you please put the whole of my little library at her disposal. I should even be glad for the majority of my books to go to her residence, to adorn the children's study.

It gives me great satisfaction to know that my daughters are now growing up in normal and in every respect satisfactory circumstances. Mme de Patersi's high-mindedness and proven experience give me ground for hoping that my earnest endeavour to ensure them an appropriate future will meet with success. I have no doubt that you too will establish pleasant relations with her and come to like the new state of affairs, which with God's help could continue indefinitely until the girls get married.

The day after tomorrow I travel to Eilsen, where I shall spend the months of November and December. In a fortnight from now Belloni will be visiting me there and, I trust, bringing me good news of you and the children and of everything that interests me in Paris.

A thousand good wishes for the happiness and peace of mind which he prays to God to grant you, are sent to you by your faithfully loving son   F. Liszt

239. To Blandine Liszt. Bad Eilsen, 5 November. . . . Thanks to the

considerable change which has just come about in your circumstances, I take pleasure in hoping, with total confidence, for a profitable completion of your education, and for good and happy years for both of you. Madame Patersi, by giving you, and you alone, her time and attention, will give your studies a coherence and solidity which even the best boarding-school could not achieve. Your minds and characters will develop normally. Further, you will have an excellent opportunity to learn and practise the household arts, an indispensable condition for the well-being and dignity of women. You will soon know how to keep your little accounts properly, will apply yourselves to good needlework and, later, to making your dresses and embroidering your collars, gradually reaching the point of finally being able to run, perfectly properly, your own little homes.

I haven't yet made up my mind about your piano lessons. However obliged I am to Mlle Kautz for the progress you have made with her, and glad though I should be to accede to your wish to keep her as your teacher, it could nevertheless be that, in consequence of more cogent reasons than I can explain to you, I should find it advisable for you to change tutors; in this case it will probably be Mme Seghers and her husband whom I shall ask to keep an eye on your wrong notes.

You tell me you have played Weber's Sonata in D minor, which you regard as one of the most beautiful pieces you know. Not knowing what works of this kind you have studied hitherto, I am not aware of the comparisons you are making, and of what in particular you like and find more striking about this sonata. I should be glad if you would enter into more detail on this subject, as on others, in your next letters, for to utter generalities is to say almost nothing; and as I am anxious for your taste to become more refined and for your judgement to spring more and more from genuine understanding, I shall give myself the pleasure of talking over with you the causes and reasons which must necessarily have a part in it. I, too, have a great fondness for this sonata, notwithstanding its rather obvious defects, such as the abrupt and shortened ending of the first and second part of the opening movement, and a certain lack of proportion between the Allegro, the Andante, and the Finale—a proportion which, it seems to me, is handled much more successfully in the same composer's Sonata in A flat, and even in the one in C (dedicated to the Grand Duchess of Weimar), which both form a more harmonious and complete ensemble.

What Etudes are you working at? Have you learnt the 24 Preludes and Fugues in Bach's *Well-Tempered Clavier*, of which you will find at Grandmama's an old edition that I once used? What do you know by Beethoven? Have you a good memory and do you play easily and correctly by heart? Give full replies to these questions so that I may be able to give both of you some profitable advice.

This letter being already fairly long, I shall keep for another time a discussion of your Roman enthusiasms and your appreciation of what you refer to as 'a little book' by Montesquieu, on *La grandeur et la décadence de Rome*.[10] This little book is full of grand things, great ideas, and firm judgement. No cultivated mind can afford not to read and reread it, and to ponder its contents carefully; but

---

[10] Montesquieu's historico-philosophical work *Considérations sur les causes de la grandeur des Romains et de leur décadence* (1734).

you are still a little young to devote yourself to such an occupation, for which in any case you lack the intermediate steps and those leading up to it.

Since you are fond of the Romans, you will do well to acquaint yourself successively with their principal historians: Livy, Sallust, and lastly Tacitus. In the excellent Rollin you will find substantial extracts, well within your grasp, of these authors. When you have sufficiently read and digested them, you will better be able to understand and enjoy Montesquieu, and you will no longer base your preference for the first part of this work over the second on impressions which, very valuable in other matters, are irrelevant for the philosophy of history, an expression used almost to excess since Montesquieu, which does not prevent his book remaining one of the most accomplished models of its kind.

Your observation about the absence of great female characters in Greek history does not lack a certain justness. Tell me sincerely if that comes from your own thinking, or if you have heard it argued by someone else, and by whom.

Give Cosima a loving kiss. She is a sweet and excellent creature, not for her love of the Greeks and Romans but for love of you and of your father, who blesses you and will keep you in his heart. . . .

240. To Anna Liszt. Eilsen, 11 December. [G] The impression your letter made on me, dear Mother, was a very disturbing one! Although you made no specific mention of it, I can nevertheless tell, from your anxieties and the whole train of your thought, that you have fallen into a state of depression, which I find most regrettable. The various reasons for it I can understand, without perhaps being able to approve of them.

Don't let your straightforward and admirable common sense, or your maternal feelings, do anything to influence you—just have more trust in me. Despite everything, it will become more and more apparent that my ideas, my plan, and the steps I have taken are the most appropriate ones and best lead to the high goal I am aiming at and with God's help will reach.

In the mean time do be entirely reassured about my health, my tobacco-smoking, and my present sojourn 'at the seaside', as you put it. Unfortunately in the state of Bückeburg there is not a drop of sea water to be seen; indeed, there is not even a small stream like the Ilm. The Princess is simply making use of the Eilsen sulphur springs for her liver complaint. In winter, cures of this kind are very frequently taken in Carlsbad and elsewhere. Incidentally, this winter is truly a very mild one, and I remember having frozen more in Florence and Madrid than here. Thus far, we haven't seen a trace of frost and snow.

I regret very much that Mme Patersi does not live in the Faubourg Saint-Honoré too, and that my daughters are not in your neighbourhood. But this drawback can probably soon be remedied.

Both now and later I most earnestly desire you, dear Mother, to have the best and most sincere understanding with the two ladies. Mme Patersi is a woman of excellent character. By her antecedents and her outstanding culture she is superbly suited to the task she has to accomplish: that of imparting solid knowledge to my daughters and at the same time training them to be refined and practical. I regard it truly as a definite piece of good fortune to have found in this most estimable woman a satisfactory guarantee of the fulfilment of my wishes concerning the supervision of my daughters. Thanks to her experience and the pains she will take, the period of transition—always difficult—in which girls grow into women will for Blandine and Cosima prove to be beneficial and productive.

Once again, put aside unnecessarily melancholy thoughts and unhealthy brooding; abide by your splendid common sense, while continuing to trust firmly in your most affectionately loving son   F. Liszt

1851

Much of the first eight months of the year Liszt spends in Bad Eilsen with the two princesses, several times returning alone to Weimar for brief resumption of his duties.

WORKS. The symphonic poem *Mazeppa* (S100). PIANO: Scherzo and March (S177); Two Polonaises (C minor and E major) (S223); *Grandes Etudes de Paganini* (S141, based on the earlier *Etudes d'exécution transcendante d'après Paganini*); *Etudes d'exécution transcendante* (S139, based on the earlier *Grandes Etudes*): 1. *Preludio* (C) 2. (A minor) 3. *Paysage* (F) 4. *Mazeppa* (D minor) 5. *Feux follets* (B flat) 6. *Vision* (G minor) 7. *Eroica* (E flat) 8. *Wilde Jagd* (C minor) 9. *Ricordanza* (A flat) 10. (F minor) 11. *Harmonies du soir* (D flat) 12. *Chasse-neige* (B flat minor). Arrangement (S366, *c*.1851) for piano and orchestra of Schubert's Wanderer Fantasy; arrangement (S657, *c*.1851) for two pianos of Beethoven's Ninth Symphony.

PUBLISHED. Hungarian Rhapsodies Nos. 1, 2, and 15 (Rákóczy March). The memoir of Chopin (in instalments in *La France musicale*, and a year later in book form). The essays *Tannhäuser and the Song Contest at the Wartburg*;[1] '*Lohengrin', grand romantic Opera by R. Wagner and its first performance in Weimar on the occasion of the Herder- and Goethe-Festival in 1850*; *De la fondation-Goethe à Weimar.*

241. To Blandine Liszt in Paris. Bad Eilsen, 17 January. Madame Patersi must have told you, dear child, that I was satisfied with your last letter, being better written, having no repetitions and no trite, flabby turns of phrase. There is only one sentence that needs to be looked at: 'Mme P.', you say, 'who detests usury in general' (I assume that the same applies when it is in particular) 'understood no better than I' (your measure of understanding, dear child, is not yet a term of comparison) 'that modifications exist which can fittingly extenuate what honest people like us' (oh, oh) 'regard in their ignorance as an abominable theft.'

It is out of irony, I think, that you use the word ignorance, for you are not unaware that usury is considered by religion to be a great evil. As for the economists, they look on it as a scourge. This irony is therefore neither subtle enough, nor marked enough, nor sharp-edged enough to have the wit and piquancy without which irony becomes platitude. The debate in the Chamber turned on a motion aiming to rank usury among criminal offences, while until now it has

---

[1] In German; as already noted, it had been published in French two years earlier.

counted only as a civil offence. A criminal offence is pursued by the law from the moment it is suspected, and he who has committed it is punished as guilty towards society. A civil offence is a matter for a lawsuit; that is to say, for disputes between private individuals, when one of them complains of having been wronged or deprived by the other. The law, when one of the parties seeks redress from it, decides against the one and for the other, without punishing personally the one not found in the right. Indeed, my child, you cannot have an opinion on so difficult a question, which can divide the opinions of the most competent authorities; but you can without difficulty understand that it is very much beyond your irony, all the less appropriate seeing that no one has tried to sing the praises of usury. In saying 'honest people like us', you were doubtless repeating an expression used by Mme P., without reflecting that it was inappropriate for your little fifteen-year-old mouth. Mme P. can very well say 'honest people like us', for as you know, or will one day, she has her whole life long given proof of an heroic and truly rare integrity; but you, dear children, have not yet had any opportunity to prove in any way to honest people that you would practise or refuse usury. And so in your remarks retain the modesty which befits your age; avoid the absurdity which clings to little persons using expressions ill befitting their extreme youthfulness. This might cause you to lose youth's special charm and in no way credit you with an impossible maturity, but rather serve to deny it. In the children of kings and noblemen, an impertinent manner of speaking often inspires hatred in those who, because of their subordinate position *vis-à-vis* the parents, have to listen to them patiently; in those who are so fortunate as not to have sycophants compelled to listen to them with feigned respect, such a manner of speaking arouses only a mocking smile, and gives a poor idea of the natural good sense of the young persons using it.

Since this letter I have learnt of the sorry scene of 3 January. Mme P. having also told me that you finished by sincerely asking her forgiveness, and with real repentance, I shall not scold you further, since you already feel how unreasonable you were that day. But think, Blandine, to what point ill-considered outbursts can have troublesome and unforeseen consequences for the unreflective minds which surrender themselves to them. Mme P. did you a favour by teaching you what you had the bad taste to forget: politeness towards an old friend of your father, who gives you lessons so zealously and conscientiously, and who practises with honour and distinction a profession that your father long practised and might well wish to continue. And you could even complain of this alleged severity to your Grandmama, with whose affection for you is naturally joined some weakness! Nature does not generally give the strength necessary to look after more than one generation. Maternal tenderness almost always takes on a softer character with regard to the children's children. You should consider this weakness with gratitude and respect, since grandmothers, not being destined to bring up their grandchildren, lose with age the energy which they perhaps possessed formerly.

Almost all grandmothers are inordinately indulgent. Also, in the present case, what resulted from your complaining? Grandmama was more touched by your tears than was necessary, and instead of giving you a good talking-to there and then, as you deserved, was annoyed with Mme P. for not spoiling you as, from her excessive fondness for you, she would have done. What you have to do now, Blandine, is speak to your Grandmama. And so do it as soon as you can; tell her that you realize that you were wrong, and ask her not to aggravate your fault by bearing a grudge against Mme P. for what was the more her duty to tell you the less you were prepared to understand it. It is enough to call attention to a mistake committed inadvertently, but a wilful lack of consideration must be reprimanded severely, for it springs either from bad feelings or from foolish pride. Speak to Grandmama in a way that will convince her that you are capable of understanding all you owe to the advice and instruction given to you, even when at first it imposes on you temporary restraints and constraints to which you have unfortunately not been sufficiently accustomed.

On this occasion I shall tell you again that I see in you, with sorrow, a tendency to tears and scenes, an extremely trying tendency with women in general, and you in particular, for I have a sovereign aversion to all that.

Nobility of soul, real unselfishness, great feelings, sublime resolutions are expressed with simplicity. Tears are beautiful only on those solemn occasions which—thank God!—are rare. Snivellings are a parody of those beautiful tears, and as such, I detest them. Instead of touching me, sobs for trifles put me out of all patience; far from moving me they are repugnant to me as evidence of a feebleness of heart and spirit injurious to women's dignity. Understand this, my daughter; try in future to lose your taste for these daily dramas which inspire me with neither interest, nor esteem, nor sympathy. Live simply; carry out your duties with humble gratitude for the Providence which has permitted them to be well taught to you; be of serene and equable humour; reflect seriously but without becoming sullen—and the less you make these untimely outbursts, the less you are tearful and lachrymose, the less you seek problems where there is none, the more I shall love you, the more you will please me and become what I wish you to be.

Correct, now, the trouble you have caused us all, and henceforth take things calmly.

Kiss Cosimette from me; tell her that I was pleased with her last letter, and learn both of you to make life easy and agreeable for those who surround you, for that is women's destiny.

242. To Princess Carolyne. [Halle] 21 January. Good evening, dearest! As the train has not taken me further than Halle, I am writing you these few lines between which I should like you to be able to read all my love, all my tenderness, all my exclusive and ardent passion.

When you return from Eilsen—I am already thinking of it, but not sooner than you, am I?—try to leave by the same 7.00 a.m. train. The compartments are much better and there are almost no stops at intermediate stations. At Brunswick, which you will get to before midday, you will be able to lunch on a light beefsteak, very comfortably, since you will have a good three-quarters of an hour for this purpose; and at Magdeburg you will have a rather bad coffee, in a narrow, smoky, and badly lit room. At 8.15 you will finally reach Halle, where I shall be waiting for you and where I shall prepare your quarters in this same Thuringian railway hotel in which we have already eaten, and even dined, several times! The rooms are freshly decorated and tolerably well furnished, and in any case we shall here be able to indulge in all our customary rustic pleasures. . . .

No mishaps *en route*. Until Brunswick I was alone in the compartment, and from Brunswick to Magdeburg not twenty words were exchanged among the passengers. Further on, I had willy-nilly to surrender myself to the charms of a few conversations, all the more so since I found myself with some old acquaintances who kept me agreeable company.

I have finished the *Phaedo*[2] and the first volume of [the *Meditations*[3] of] Marcus Aurelius. When we see one another again I shall tell you in what way, in times past, I found the 'beautiful danger' of Socrates more enticing than the '*morisque*' of Pascal, although there is, *au fond*, much similarity in the thought.

As for Marcus Aurelius, I shall willingly put his bust—without forgetting yours!—among my household gods. . . .

At Brunswick station I ran into Herr von Radowitz, but without recognizing him, supposing him to be in England. He was going to Erfurt, probably via Halberstadt, and from there *en poste*—where his wife still is. I envy him neither his diplomatic post nor his intimacy with the King—but utterly and completely the happiness of going to join his wife! Marcus Aurelius quotes among other things this line by an ancient poet: 'Our lives must be harvested, just like ears of corn.' All right—so long as you and I are not uprooted from one another! . . .

---

[2] Plato's *Phaedo* relates the discussion, about the nature of death and the probable immortality of the soul, which took place between Socrates and his disciples during the last hour of his life, and the manner and circumstances of his dying.

[3] The reflections and memoranda—written in Greek—of this 1st-cent. Roman emperor and Stoic philosopher.

243. To Princess Carolyne. [Weimar] 8.00 p.m., Wednesday, 22 January. Here I am, in this room, at this table, near these windows where I have so many times seen you—suffering so much, weeping so much, loving so much! All the objects which surround me are known to, and full of, you, and they speak to me in a language of ineffable sorrow and eloquence! But when you come back you will find in this room an object which was not here when you left, and which, at the thought that it would give you some small pleasure, has given me a very great one. I don't want to make a mystery or surprise out of it, and will simply say that Bartolini's bust of me has arrived, and that I find it quite splendid.

Alighting from the train at 10.00 this morning, I found no one at the station, where Hermann[4] and my friends had been misinformed about arrival times. The servants Jetty and Therese were naturally delighted to see me—and the dog 'Black Mux' came to show me all his tricks, rather commonplace and very demonstrative ones, in my little room. Don't fail to give this important detail to our little one, who loves to call herself 'White Mux'. Hermann told me that Black Mux sometimes played very bad tricks on ladies by his affectionate assaults—especially on those who wear long sleeves, which he doesn't like. Now and then he takes it into his head to knock little girls over.

At about 11.30 I went to the rehearsal of [Raff's opera] *King Alfred*, quartet and choruses, about which I shall later have occasion to talk to you at greater length. When leaving, I could no longer put off, as you can well imagine, my visit to Ziegesar, whom I found still the same excellent and most excellent fellow that you know. He suggested that I accompany him tomorrow to Gotha, where *Le Prophète* is being performed—but it suits me best not to budge from here before your return. . . . With what emotion I once again saw my little books in their green bindings—your gift—and my Histories, which I shall probably never read but which are likewise one of your beautiful presents; and the Bible in 18 volumes, and Proudhon, and so many other gifts of yours! Truly, when I ponder and reflect now and then, I wonder if it wasn't you who once made me a present of my eyes and my hands—and if each evening it isn't you who *wind up* the movements of my heart—so much have you done, and are still constantly doing, for me! In any case, this poor heart hasn't a single beat which isn't yours or for you! . . .

---

[4] Liszt's manservant.

244. To Princess Carolyne. Sunday, 26 January. . . . My conversations of yesterday and the day before have made me so extremely hoarse, and given me such a heavy cold, that I shall be obliged to spend today, and perhaps tomorrow, in my room. . . .

As I didn't want to face the bad air outside, Joachim, Stör, Walbrül, and Cossmann came here and played two beautiful quartets by Mozart and Beethoven, for I am anxious to spare myself, and because of my bad cold refused an invitation to dine at the Schloss. Your letter was handed to me at the moment of a sublime melody in the second quartet which was not unworthy of harmonizing with your tears. And when you get back I shall ask them to repeat it, especially for you. Ziegesar is going to atone splendidly for the blunder of *Zar und Zimmermann* by assigning the proceeds of the first performance, on 1 February, towards bringing relief to the family of the composer,[5] who has just died in very straitened circumstances leaving a wife and half a dozen children destitute. . . .

An opportunity having come along, I very frankly and explicitly gave Raff my opinion of his volcanic eruptions—and in all probability his cure will not even present disquieting or dangerous symptoms. If I felt that I possessed to a somewhat greater degree a talent for writing letters of narrative interest, I should be able to relate several details which do not lack a certain piquant *naïveté*.

While we wait for our hero quickly to get over his infatuation, he has with great passion set to work on his *Alfred*, whose Fourth Act will at last be finished in three days. After which I shall ask him to betake himself to Leipzig, assuming that by that time you have sent me the proofs. As for the overture, he plans to write it, like Mozart, only at the very last moment, and in hopes of the total success of his work he is at present very comfortably smoking his cigar. . . .

245. To Princess Carolyne. Monday, 27 January. My poor adorable one! You talk dazzling nonsense in your latest letter, and 'the serpent which writhes in your heart' has seductions still more powerful than the serpent which seduced our mother Eve. I am truly grieved that you have put your nose into that correspondence, of which I authorize you to burn everything you wish, since for me it has long been only a past of ashes. Alas! Long before Odessa even, I was hardly justified in playing seriously the role of juvenile lead—*Helden- und Liebhaberfach*, as they say in German. Yet it is all that would have been required ... for you to show me well and truly to the door. In the human heart, love is

---

[5] Lortzing, who had died of a stroke on 21 Jan.

tinged and shaded into infinity. Its main gradations and graduations can be arranged in groups—but the peculiar essence of certain love is *mystery*. It reveals itself more than it can be explained. In a few years I shall probably be in a better position to talk of certain things. The bruises I have acquired through others or through myself will then be healed—and I shall have regained my true youthfulness, and vindicated myself from the reproach made to me[6] of 'living as though I were immortal!' Then, too, will have disappeared, I hope, your bruises, your perturbations, and your feverish emotions, against which the best arguments for the use of juvenile leads would unerringly fail. . . .

Unfortunately I have to reprimand Raff severely for not having completed the Fourth Act of his *Alfred*, which has prevented copies being made and the whole of this Act being rehearsed. . . . When, this morning, I asked the Intendant to give Raff a major dressing-down, he told me that he had already done so a couple of times; but that in response to his *serious* admonitions, Raff had done nothing but laugh heartily. . . .

This morning the Grand Duchess sent for me, to show me a *great* number of new compositions. . . . Towards the end of our musical session, Monseigneur [the Grand Duke] came in and said that when hunting this morning he had wounded a hare—but that it had died rather a long way away, or so he had been told. The Grand Duchess took care to inform him at once of the improvement in Magne's[7] health. She had earlier done something very gracious. After having shown me her portfolio of manuscripts, *very much filled* with new pieces and sketches for compositions, and having as usual got me to sit at the piano to show them to me, she asked: 'Have you news of Princess Marie's health? *We should have begun with that.*' Monseigneur seemed delighted with your Magne's recovery, and then, resuming his account of the morning's events: 'When passing by the Belvedere, I heard a nightingale sing... There are already nightingales at Belvedere... If Princess Marie could hear those nightingales sing, it would surely contribute to speeding up her convalescence.' And at that moment the excellent and worthy old man was assuredly more of a poet for me than he imagined! . . .

Herr von Plötz has just been decorated by the Duke of Dessau with the cross of Commander of the Order of the *Bear*. That isn't a joke, for the Order of the Bear is the *Hausorden* [family order] of the family of princes of the house of Bernburg, whose origin goes back directly to the first created bear and is consequently of an antediluvian antiquity and renown, as is shown by the etymology of their name *Bärenburg*, which has become *Bernburg*. Had I been given this cross, I would not fail to adorn myself with it 'on great occasions!'

---

[6] By Princess Belgiojoso.
[7] Magne, Magnet, Magnette, Magnolet, Magnolette, nicknames for the young Princess Marie Wittgenstein.

Voltaire's maxim 'petites causes, grands effets' is unhappily going to find an application which will be distressing to me, for all sorts of disagreeable little causes will probably prevent my writing to you for two or three days. I am encumbered with tasks: continuing the proofs of *Chopin* with the *żal*,[8] which I like immensely in print; adding the phrasing and expression marks to the piece Raff will have to take to Leipzig; tomorrow's rehearsal and Court concert; one or two theatre rehearsals for *Alfred* this week—indefinite negotiations with the musical tribe ... and over and above everything about ten long letters to write. . . .

Oh, our beautiful hours in Eilsen! When shall we resume them? These 18 days of waiting are going to be so gloomy and so long! . . .

246. To Princess Carolyne [31 January]. Dear one, you have written me an adorably admirable and sublime letter today—and I am truly ashamed not to know what to write back to you other than stylistic frigidities and twaddle. But since you do not weary of giving and casting out, in an immense profusion that knows no bounds, the inexhaustible pearls of your imagination, the unheard sobs of your soul—how can I do other than keep my own soul *wide open*, so that I may incessantly breathe in these marvellous perfumes, before which exaltation and poetry itself would remain silent?—What have I to say to you, and what words would be given to me to express my rapture? Were I obliged to respond to your letter, I would truly need the Archangel Michael for my secretary!—But although I despair of ever writing to you as I *mean* to, I cannot do otherwise than write to you unceasingly, while having nothing to say to you. Like your comparison of the automaton 'which begins by taking a few steps to the most general satisfaction, and which all of a sudden, without apparent cause, stops short and makes no further movement—and even if he were given a push would do nothing more than fall on his nose'—how just and charming a comparison! My God! what a mind you have, what grace and lofty originality beside *this genius* of your heart!—Don't contest this word; it is no more than strictly accurate. . . . Alas! my good and beautiful one, you also see Herschel's *six moons*[9] and yet others that even the Herschels of the future will not discover. . . .

8 The Polish word, implying regret, grief, sorrow, to which Liszt in his memoir of Chopin (co-authored by his Polish princess) devoted several paragraphs, mentioning *inter alia* that Chopin would repeat the word over and over again, as though his ear thirsted for its very sound. The Polish-born pianist Artur Rubinstein described *żal* as 'a beautiful word, impossible to translate'. 'It means sadness, nostalgia, regret, being hurt, and yet it is something else. It feels like a howling inside you, so unbearable that it breaks your heart.'

9 Victor Hugo's *Mazeppa*, which this year inspired Liszt's symphonic poem of the same title, contains the line: 'Les six lunes d'Herschel, l'anneau du vieux Saturne'.

When shall I be given 'barszcz'—tell me how to spell this word, which I should like to know—and 'zrazy'?[10] When shall we be resuming our open-air breakfasts? . . .

Raff leaves for Leipzig tomorrow. The 'Correcturprobe [corrective rehearsal]' with orchestra, of his *Alfred*, acquainted me very favourably with his score, and I must say in all sincerity and justice that it is a really remarkable work which promises to be a splendid success. The day after tomorrow, for Monseigneur's birthday, I have to inaugurate the new chairs and music-stands that Ziegesar has had made for the orchestra—at a cost of nearly 300 thalers!—by conducting, before the play, Weber's *Jubel-Ouvertüre* [Jubilee Overture]. When I go to Halle to meet you, inside myself I shall be performing a very different one. . . .

Lohengrin

247. To Princess Carolyne. 7 February. Happy birthday! . . . I didn't write to you yesterday, and that greatly saddened me when I was going to bed. But my day was spent in the theatre having Raff's opera rehearsed for $3\frac{1}{2}$ hours in the morning and for just as long after lunch. Fräulein Rosalie Spohr,* niece of my colleague in Cassel, arrived with her father, who is an architect in Brunswick and strongly resembles his brother. Although the Grand Duchess has declared very firmly that artistes from elsewhere are not to be admitted to Court concerts, she was so gracious as to take into consideration my recommendation, through Ziegesar, of Fräulein Spohr, and instructed me to invite her to yesterday evening's concert, the programme of which I am sending you. She is a young artiste of 18, rather intelligent and interesting. Her hair style is like my own. Exceptionally, I told Ziegesar to ask Their Highnesses to excuse me, making a pretext of the fatigue caused by my rehearsals—and giving as a reason my lack of taste for performing frequently at such crowded soirées, necessarily consisting of rather unmusical audiences. At the same time I laid claim to the honour of showing, one of these mornings, several of my recent compositions to the Grand Duchess and the Princess [Augusta] of Prussia—and I assume that within a few days I shall be summoned for this purpose. My two *Lieder* were sung delightfully and most soulfully by Götze—and the first of them, *Du bist wie eine Blume*, the Grand Duchess immediately asked to hear again. The second, *Schlummerlied*, which is much longer, seemed to make a generally very good impression. I wrote this *Schlummerlied* at the same time as I was transcribing Weber's, at Krzyżanowitz, when waiting for you in April '48. Götze will sing it

---

[10] Polish dishes: 'beetroot soup' and 'meat cut in slices and stewed'.

for you. The Pcss of Prussia seems to retain some kindly feelings towards me—
that, at least, is what she told me, with all the charm that you know. . . .

248. To Princess Carolyne [Weimar, 8 February]. My poor, poor darling! And so you are now at grips with an abscess! I don't really know what that
is, never having had to suffer one, but I have always heard that it is extremely
painful.... Dear Lord, be kind to my dearest one, who is so kind, so kind to
me! . . .

Yesterday evening, feeling very tired, I went to bed at 10.00 and fell asleep
while rereading your letter. I had spent the morning at the theatre—*Alfred*—
and the period after lunch at Winterberger's with Sacha and Jadassohn. Talking
of Jadassohn, he is coming back from Leipzig where those gentlemen of the
Gewandhaus committee, Moscheles in particular, treated him as a *turncoat*, shutting him out of their concert and deploring the bad direction he is following
at Weimar. This visit to Leipzig will be pretty salutary to Jadassohn, and if he
goes on as he is he will within two years be able to have a good revenge! Between
6.30 and 9.00 I was at the Russischer Hof Hotel with la Spohr, who played me
half a dozen pieces by Parish-Alvars quite splendidly. I could have wished for
you to hear her, for I imagine that you would like the sonority of the instrument and its *Aeolian undulations.* Poor darling, if I could only send you all the
harps of the angels, and all the choirs of the Thrones, Dominions and Powers
to sing to you of our love, and to sweeten your sorrows with all the splendour
of their harmonies! . . .

To give myself a *compulsory* occupation, I am this morning going to get down
to preparing the new edition of my *Etudes*—which will certainly take me the
whole of this month. The Grand Duchess will not be resuming her lessons on
a regular basis before the end of February, I imagine—thus far she has sent for
me only twice. At the end of the concert the day before yesterday, Monseigneur
very particularly charged me with remembering him to you and conveying his
respects. The Pce of Prussia is expected shortly. Thank Magnette for her dear
little letter, which I liked very much—I shall write to her this evening or tomorrow. For the first time since my return I have some idea of spending two or
three hours at the piano—as Magne claims that under my fingers nightingales
sing. Alas! I very much fear that owls, and cranes in particular, screech and croak
there still more! Farewell, my beautiful eagle eyes and talons—'*occhi griffanti!*'[11]
Don't flood them with tears—and try to *live*, in order to love!

---

[11] Liszt here seems to be quoting (or misquoting) from Dante's description (*Inferno*, IV. 123) of the shade of Julius
Caesar, the usual reading of which is 'Cesare armato con li occhi grifagni'—'hawk-eyed Caesar'.

249. To Princess Carolyne. Tuesday evening, 11 February. This morning I was obliged to take an oath in court, 'that I did not order and receive some bottles of champagne from the firm of Katz in Strasbourg!' What frightful abuses, what dreadful immorality in these legal proceedings! I have never had any experience of them in France, but in Germany in the last few years I have four or five times been compelled to take an oath in cases where the oath was an odious absurdity. When the law interferes in this way to the detriment of honest people and to the advantage of rogues, how to respect it other than as a lesser evil? All this red tape and these formalities, are they not a barbarism worse than that of savages? And yet as long as we belong, in whatever class, to any state whatsoever, it will be very difficult to follow literally the Gospel teaching which tells us to go two miles with him who would compel us to go one mile, and to surrender one's cloke to him who is taking away our coat![12] Over what abyss of confusions, errors, lies, injustices, contradictions, cruel tyrannies, and deadly necessities, are we not sometimes obliged to walk? Oh! Compassion for the weak! Compassion even for the guilty! . . .

I dined alone at the Altenburg today after the rehearsal of *Alfred*, which is already going marvellously and will certainly be one of the best performed works to have been heard here. . . .

I have got down to correcting my *Etudes*, which is a job for me. Tomorrow I shall have some letters to write and will perhaps neglect you. Try to remain fairly calm and peaceful. In a week we shall resume our '*bon café*'. Bonsoir to Magne, and endlessly and unceasingly to you.

250. To Princess Carolyne. 7.00 p.m., Thursday, 13 February. . . . Fräulein Agthe is confined to bed by a sudden attack of 'flu, and so Raff's opera can't be performed on the 16th.[13] We have had to put together a concert programme very rapidly, to make up as much as possible for this disaster, for which there has been no precedent in Weimar, in February, for the last 20 years—and which I take pleasure in attributing to Messire Raff's ill luck. The day after tomorrow I'll send you the programme. You will be surprised to find my name at the end, but from what Ziegesar told me of the Grand Duchess's particular wish to hear me that day, I thought I couldn't refuse. That very morning, when the *Alfred* rehearsal was interrupted by the frightening and dismaying message about the Agthe 'flu, I stated most emphatically that long years, at the very least, would pass before I would consent to practise the profession of *acorn*, to be devoured

[12] See Matt. 5: 40–1 (AV).   [13] Birthday of the Grand Duchess Maria Pavlovna.

by swine. The comparison is not very elegant, but appropriate enough in the circumstances. When Ziegesar went to the Schloss at about 1.00, to report the calamity, apologizing as best he could and expressing the chagrin it caused him, he at once spoke to the Grand Duchess about a concert. She immediately asked if there were any way of inducing me to play. Ziegesar tells me that he replied thus: 'Madame, the Weimar public is truly not worthy to hear such an artist'— and eventually she said: 'I don't want to ask it of him, but if he wished to, it would give me great pleasure and I should be grateful to him.' This notwith-standing, I showed no great eagerness—not, it goes without saying, because of the Grand Duchess, who can of course dispose of my humble self in all circum-stances. I am making that only too clear, perhaps, by my present sojourn in Weimar. I balk at the sight of the imbecile Weimarians, who in no time at all would regard me as meat for their pies! Ziegesar for his part (I must do him this justice) did not insist—and at the end of the conversation I had the pleasure of politely offering my co-operation at Sunday's concert. I shall end it with the Fantasy on the Skaters' Waltz from *Le Prophète*, after which Ziegesar will make the Peterhof fountains play, with a decoration *ad hoc. . . .*

I kiss your dear little feet, and ask the Good Lord to make you suffer no longer!

251. To Anna Liszt in Paris. Eilsen, 21 February ^{G (F)}

Dear Mother,

Hardly had Princess Marie's long illness come to an end, when her mother, probably as a result of weariness after 9 weeks of incessant nursing duties, had herself to take to her bed. From what the doctor says, she won't be able to get up for another fortnight. Of course, as soon as I could, by which I mean a day after the birthday of HIH the Grand Duchess, I hastened to Eilsen from Weimar, and shall stay here until both patients are recovered, and then accom-pany them home.

I was very glad to learn from Mme Patersi (whom in your letter you did not mention) that you often visit them and that on Sundays she brings the chil-dren to see you. At my daughters' present stage of development, I want them, for valid reasons, to remain exclusively under Mme Patersi's supervision. I fully concur with her choice of company for the children. During our long conversa-tions in Weimar, before her departure for Paris, we agreed on all essential points. And so I should be very grateful if you would stop seeing difficulties where none exists. The easiest, safest, and most agreeable thing you could do, would be to trust, wholeheartedly and with conviction, in my views, in the way I am guiding my Parisian family; indeed, no one can judge the situation with more serious interest than I.

I also ask you, dear Mother, to spare me correspondence as much as possible. I really lack the time for it, and pointless letters make me still more impatient than pointless conversations, which, as you know, often provoke me to undisguised impatience. Your sister Therese in Graz isn't one of the obtrusive ones, and I shall write to her on the first free day. I am really fond of her, although we haven't much to say to one another, and I gladly avoid the hackneyed expressions between nephews and aunts. My sonorous phrases would soon be transformed into sonorous coins for the benefit of my thirty or forty uncles, aunts, nephews, and nieces.

As far as my family is concerned, I made my position clear in Weimar. My true family consists of the small number of those who understand, help, and support me. I haven't time to waste, nor can I squander my money. I implore you too, dear Mother, to be more careful in your dealings with others; don't allow your kindness to degenerate into weakness and be tempted into handing out money to unworthy people who will never pay it back. I say this to you not only from economic misgivings, although these alone would justify my warning; I place still more weight on the social disadvantage which such ill-chosen and equivocal relations result in.

Farewell, dear Mother; God keep you healthy in body and soul. Have no worries about your loving son   F. Liszt

P.S. As I am very pleased about the influence that Mme Patersi has on Daniel, I want him to spend all his free time with her. She alone is to decide whom he and his sisters should meet or associate with.

As you do not like my letters in German, I shall in future write to you in clear and precise French. So far as my handwriting is concerned, you will have to put up with it. For your part, don't take delivery of too many letters to me from other people. They give me only the trouble of replying, without saying anything and usually without being able to do anything. But write to me yourself oftener than hitherto, and be convinced in advance of the joy with which each and every one of your letters is received.

Throughout the 1850s Liszt continued to exchange letters with the exiled and often deeply dejected Wagner, to whom he never failed to give what moral, practical and —when possible—financial help he could. The German translation of his essay on *Lohengrin* had been done by Hans von Bülow and Carl Ritter, and revised by Wagner himself.

252. To Richard Wagner in Zurich. Eilsen, 1 March ^G

Dear Wagner,

When and where I am writing these lines will tell you sufficiently well in what sorrow and distress I have been living for months. I did, it is true, spend about 3 weeks in Weimar; but immediately after the Grand Duchess's birthday (16 February) I returned here, where, alas, I found the Princess still very unwell and confined to bed.—On the 7th I have to go back to Weimar to conduct Raff's opera: the work is too important for Raff's career for me to neglect it. But the thought of that journey, while here at the sickbed I have to leave my whole soul, my whole faith, and all my love, fills me with dread.—Let's talk about you.

I could never think of forgetting you, and still less, if that's possible, of being cross with you. Forgive me for not having expressed to you before now my sincere and heartfelt thanks for Bülow and Ritter's German version of my *Lohengrin* article. Your letter in particular gave me great delight—and very much flattered me. That you are content with my conception of so glorious and magnificent a work of mind and soul as your *Lohengrin*, is my exceedingly rich reward. As soon as I am back in Weimar I shall arrange for it to be printed (perhaps the *Illustrirte* will publish it in *one* number) and then send you the proofs, which I ask you to attend to *as quickly as possible* and return straight to [J. J.] Weber.

Ritter can go through the article quite carefully in one day and send it back to Leipzig by return of post.

As regards the French original, I shall probably publish it as a separate pamphlet with my article on the Herder Festival (without the cuts and alterations made by Janin in the *Journal des Débats* of 22 October) under the title *Fêtes de Herder et Goethe à Weimar, 25 et 28 Août 1850.* . . .

Wieland is still under lock and key in Weimar, together with my scores and manuscripts.[14] As soon as my manservant returns I shall send you *Wieland* at once—but don't want to call in any everyday, prosaic locksmith to give him his liberty.

I am very much looking forward to your book;[15] perhaps on this occasion I shall try to grasp your ideas a little better, not having managed to do so too well with your *Kunst und Revolution*—and make a French sauce with it.

My pamphlet on the Goethe Foundation (*De la fondation Goethe à Weimar*) was published the other day by Brockhaus, and when there is an opportunity I

[14] Wagner had sent Liszt his poem *Wieland der Schmied* (Wieland the Smith)—an operatic project which he himself had abandoned—inviting him to use it as the libretto for an opera of his own. Liszt had declined with thanks: 'Great as is the temptation to forge your *Wieland*, I must abide by my decision *never* to compose a German opera. I have no vocation for it, and entirely lack the *patience* to bother with German theatrical affairs. . . .'

[15] Wagner's *Oper und Drama* (Opera and Drama) had been finished several weeks earlier; his long essay *Die Kunst und die Revolution* (Art and Revolution) had been written in 1849.

shall send it to you. My essay on Chopin, which is appearing in *La France mus-icale*, and likely to be spun out to around 15 numbers, you probably haven't heard about in Zurich? Bülow read the original in Weimar.

Farewell, be happier than I—and write soon to

Your faithfully devoted friend   F. Liszt

253. To Eduard Liszt in Vienna[16]

Dear, excellent Eduard,

Sharing in your joy will give me real joy of my own, and I thank you most cordially for having thought first and foremost of me as your child's godfather. I accept this office very willingly, and sincerely wish that this son may be worthy of his father and contribute to adding to the honour of our name. Alas! It has been only too much neglected and even compromised by the vast majority of our relatives, who have been wanting either in elevation of feeling (like my uncle A.[17]), or in the intelligence and talent (some of them even in education and the basic rudiments), necessary to give a higher impulse to their career and to deserve serious esteem and consideration. Thanks be to Heaven, it is quite otherwise with you, and I cannot tell you what sweet and noble satisfaction that gives me. The intelligent perseverance you have shown in overcoming the numerous difficulties that were impeding you; the solid learning you have acquired; the distinguished talents you have developed; the sound and judicious honesty you have unceasingly kept to in word and deed; your sincere filial devotion to your mother; your attachment, resulting from reflection and conviction, to the precepts of the Catholic religion—these twenty years, *in fine*, that you have spent and employed so honourably; it all deserves the highest praise and gives you every right to the respect and esteem of decent and sensible people. So I am glad to see that you are beginning to reap the fruits of your endeavours, and the distinguished position to which you have just been appointed[18] seems to justify the hopes you once confided to me and which I treated, probably wrongly, as so much *naïve ambition*. At the point you have reached, for me to hurl advice or untimely counsel at you would be totally uncalled for. Permit me merely, because of my deep affection for you and the bonds of kinship which draw us together, to make just this one recommendation:

'To thine own self be true.' Be true to what you feel to be the highest, best, noblest, and purest that is within you. Give no thought at all (barring those

---

[16] The letter is undated but evidently written shortly after 2 Mar., date of birth of Eduard's son, Franz Maria Liszt.

[17] Anton Liszt, a son of the second marriage of Liszt's grandfather.

[18] Eduard Liszt had in 1850 been appointed Assistant Public Prosecutor.

occasions when it may be expedient and necessary) to being or becoming *something*; but work perseveringly and laboriously to be and to become more and more *someone*.—Since the difficult and formidable task of judging men, and of pronouncing on their innocence or their guilt, has fallen to you, *look long and deeply into your own heart*, so that you may not yourself be found wanting at the tribunal of the Supreme Judge;—and in grave and determinative circumstances pay heed only to your conscience and to God! . . .

Before the end of the winter I shall send you a parcel of music (of my publications) which will give you some distraction in your leisure hours. I am trying to work as much and as well as I can, although I sometimes feel a kind of despondent terror at the thought of the task I should like to fulfil, and for which I still need at least ten years of health and strength in mind and body alike.

Do please give my fond respects to Frau Liszt; from now on the two of you form the whole of my family on my father's side; and do believe in the deep and unchanging affection of

Your devoted   F. Liszt

254. To Blandine Liszt. Eilsen, 8 March

Dear Blandine,

Your letter gave me pleasure, by making me hope that your handwriting will soon be formed. I am tolerably satisfied with it, and think that from now on, being able to do so well, you will do still better. And so I really expect no longer to receive letters written less well. In your progress take good care not to advance like that pilgrim of the Middle Ages who went to Jerusalem by taking three steps forwards and two steps backwards! In your next letter tell me about your lessons and your reading. Inform me how your hours are divided through the week, so that I know how your time is used. Have you already begun to study with Mme Patersi? At what point are you resuming your studies? Are you reading some work, outside the lessons, with Mme Patersi? Have you also some special reading? Is it the same for you and Cosimette? Let me have your impressions, and also a summary, of it.

On Saturdays you have visitors, and you have also both been out from time to time to soirées. Tell me how the two of you spend those evenings when you remain alone at home. I assume that in your school you had to learn pieces of poetry by heart. I should be glad if, every month, each of you would undertake to learn a number of well-chosen poems. You are too big for this exercise to be part of lessons; take the necessary time out of your leisure hours. Also ask your teachers of English and German occasionally to show you some pieces to get by heart from the great poets of their language. The winter is drawing to its close; we are entering Lent and the springtime; you will have fewer distractions and be going out less, and consequently more free moments in which to cultivate your memory.

You say that you are jealous of Daniel because of Mme P.'s fondness for him. I shall answer your joke seriously by saying that jealousy is absurd in the sense that if we wish to be more loved, we have only to make ourselves more lovable. In noble hearts which are for ever unaware of the vile torments of envy, objects of jealousy are transformed into objects of emulation.

Be the most grateful to Madame P. for the pains she is taking with you, be the most affectionate, the most loving, the quickest to understand her, the keenest to obey her, the most responsive to her, the most eager to spare her occasions for reprimand and to receive her reprimands submissively, as tokens of her affection for you and of her conscientious zeal in taking my place—and I tell you that it will be you of whom she will be fondest. But can you reasonably hope that that will be the case so long as she encounters in you the bitterness, inflexibility, and recalcitrance shown in the incident following M. Seghers' lesson?... Are you still possessed by the same feelings? Examine your conscience, examine your conduct, and you will have the answer. Are you already such that Mme P. must love you with all the devotion that you certainly have it in you to deserve and to aspire to from her? Are you so docile, so cured of your faults and so determined to cure yourself of them?... The more we value someone's affection, the greater the pains we must take to deserve it, when we are no longer little children and urchins. . . .

You tell me you were under the weather, which was the cause of your letter being delayed for a couple of days. Were you unwell, or just engrossed in the carnival? If the latter, all you needed to do was tell me so; I would certainly not have been annoyed with you. I love you to be gay, but still more wish you to be truthful. Get into the habit of being scrupulously sincere with me.

I again met with some repetitions in your letter, which spoil its style. It would not be a waste of time for you and Cosima to make drafts of your letters. They would thus become rather a profitable kind of exercise for you; and so that you can judge your progress I shall give you exercise books intended for these drafts.

How is your needlework coming on? By Easter you should already be a good seamstress.

In all my good advice, dear child, be aware of your father's deep and devoted affection for you.

In early April Liszt again returned to Weimar.

255. To Princess Carolyne in Eilsen. Saturday, 12 April. I gave myself a treat by dining alone, in our study—and immediately afterwards began to read your 'satires', which I hadn't yet been able to go through for want of an hour or two to be able to devote to them. Your pages on the Monasterżyska library and the three books which made so vivid an impression upon you in your child-hood: the *Bible de Royaumont*,[19] the Roman history, and Shakespeare with *Romeo and Juliet*—moved me deeply. You really do have the most adorable, most prodigious, most loving and unbelievable womanly nature that could ever be dreamt of or hoped for! I have long known it, but the deep-seated awareness I have of the height of your flight—for you are soaring, soaring right up to the angel Gabriel whom you see in a ray of light, intercepted by the Venetian blinds of the Monasterżyska library, above the Virgin—at times causes me ecstasies that I couldn't describe. But you, on the other hand, *you* know how to talk, and my good Sansonnet[20] is truly sublimely eloquent when reminiscing about her childhood. . . . Have you Gervinus's *Shakespeare?*[21] If you haven't yet bought it, don't—for you will find it here.

My poor *Hingehn!*[22] Have I shown you a copy with the expression marks added by me in red pencil—the one I had sent to Haslinger for printing? At the top of the first page I wrote, in some town or other (not Lemberg) in Galicia, these words: 'This *Lied* is my youthful testament.' I hardly suspected, at that time, that there would be found *someone* to listen to it in that way—for how could I have imagined that I would meet such a woman—and that this woman would want to become mine! . . .

256. To Princess Carolyne. 7.30 a.m., Easter Tuesday [22 April]. . . . The music of our Catholic church, and more especially the organist, jangled my nerves so much on Palm Sunday that I wondered whether to go to church at Easter—feeling quite incapable of turning my thoughts to God during an hour of such discordant sounds. When you are there, it is quite different. My eyes turn to you, and that serves me for prayer; but without you this music

---

[19] The *Histoire du Vieux et du Nouveau Testament représentée avec des figures et des explications édifiantes tirées des Saints Pères*, published in 1670 under the pseudonym of Sieur de Royaumont, Prieur de Sombreval, is often referred to as the *Bible de Royaumont*. Its principal author is believed to have been the hagiographer and theologian Nicolas Fontaine, who was attached to the schools of Port-Royal and, as a Jansenist, imprisoned for several years in the Bastille.

[20] Starling, nickname for the Princess.

[21] G. G. Gervinus's four-volume *Shakespeare* came out between 1849 and 1852. A decade later appeared his ill-received *Händel und Shakespeare*, in which he contrived to show that the intellectual affinity between his favourite poet and his favourite composer sprang from the Teutonic origin common to both.

[22] Liszt's song *Ich möchte hingehn wie das Abendroth*, composed in 1845 and inspired by the emotions aroused in him by his reunion the previous autumn with his youthful love Caroline de Saint-Cricq.

assails my ears so severely that I can no longer pray. Yesterday I enquired at what time our parish priest celebrates low mass, and tomorrow I shall go at six thirty in the morning. In general, as you know, my piety goes no further than low mass. Perhaps there is even a musical reason for that—but I don't want to examine the reasons for my half-heartedness, and shall tell you quite simply that on Easter Day, after having written to you, I preferred to go to my piano. At about 10.00 Hermann brought me a visiting-card from Prokesch,* formerly Austrian Minister in Athens and now Ambassador in Berlin. I knew him slightly in Vienna and he always showed me great goodwill. He is a remarkably distinguished man, considered one of our best diplomats. In his youth he also published several books on the Orient, etc. I am still wondering in what connection and for whom he came to Weimar, where he stayed only a few hours, having come from Berlin and leaving again in the afternoon for Leipzig. He didn't want to present himself at Court, and saw no one here. So the Grand Duchess did not fail to accost me at once, after the Easter Day lunch to which I had been invited, with these words: 'You have had a visit from a great diplomatist.' I still fail to understand how the Russian Easter managed to coincide this year with our Easter?—In short, Prokesch spent rather more than half an hour at the Altenburg, and I offered to serve him as *cicerone* for the Goethe, Schiller, Wieland, and Herder rooms at the Schloss—which he accepted. His conversation interested me greatly. Among other things I remember a striking remark about Herr von Radowitz, whom like everyone else he considers a man of distinction: 'Alle seine Berechnungen sind richtig, aber die Zahlen sind falsch [All his calculations are correct, but the figures are wrong].'

So I stayed with Prokesch until midday, and took good care to show him Preller's three paintings in Tsar Nicholas's room. In one of them he detected an analogy with a Titian group in Rome, and he was struck by Preller's talent to the point of saying that so far as he knew there was nowhere else in Germany a painter of so vigorous a talent, capable of executing three such landscapes.

On leaving Prokesch I went to Joachim's. By chance they played one of Beethoven's last quartets, the one in A whose Adagio is headed: *Canzone di ringraziamento offerta alla Divinità da un guarito*. That was my real Easter....

257. To Princess Carolyne. Midnight, Wednesday, 30 April. I have just got back from my *Favorita*,[23] where, so far as the public is concerned, there was no one—but in the ducal box were Her Imperial Highness plus Pce and Pcss Carl of Prussia. The performance having truly been pretty good, as much

---

[23] Opera in four acts by Donizetti, first performed at the Paris Opéra, 2 Dec. 1840.

on the part of the orchestra as of the singers, Their Highnesses sent me their special compliments by Ziegesar. Stahr,* who arrived at 6.00 this evening, sent his card to the orchestra for me during one of the intervals, and as soon as the performance was over I of course went to thank him. Don't be annoyed about that, dear one; Stahr is a remarkably distinguished man who knows a multitude of things, and who has soul. During the two hours I have just spent with him, he quoted to me without muddle or pedantry—Horace, Heine, and Vischer— who are wonderfully of *our* opinion. Tomorrow I shall probably suggest that he stay at the Altenburg—and shall mention him to Monseigneur as a possible secretary of the Goethe Foundation. He is perfectly qualified for this position, and in a couple of years that plan may well come to fruition. La Lewald today went to one of Weimar's literary and learned dinners—at Frau Pogwisch's [24]—where were uttered the most amusing *absurdities* about our essay, which I shall keep to relate to you orally. . . .

My time being terribly taken up by local matters . . . I have done no more than skim through the letter received from you today. I immediately sent you the *History of Spain* and, for want of a history of Russia, not to be found in this collection, 2 vols. of the *History of Germany*. I am going to read your letter. Although I am sleeping less than usual, it is impossible for me to find time to read anything but your letters, which are manna in the desert of my heart.

258. To Princess Carolyne. Saturday, 3 May. Dear one, I have a job to give you: that of formulating biographical questions relating to *our Schubert*,[25] for which [Simon] Löwy will have to gather the necessary material. Do me, therefore, the kindness of sending me a sheet of searching questions, such as you know how to do—so that we shall be able to get down to the task this summer. I enclose Löwy's letter, which you will have difficulty in deciphering; Magne will help you. The Schubert article is on the last three pages.

Talking of Schubert, I'll give you some good news: the *Siegfried* affair is in order. Ziegesar is writing to Wagner this evening—but as it has to remain a secret, *don't tell anyone*. Wagner will be given 300 thalers (100 on 1 July, 100 on 1 November, 100 on 1 March 1852), plus another 200 if the score is delivered by 1 July next year, making 500 in all. . . .[26]

---

[24] Ulrike von Pogwisch, sister of Ottilie von Goethe, Goethe's daughter-in-law. The essay in question was presumably *De la fondation-Goethe*.

[25] Liszt's planned biography of Franz Schubert was unfortunately never realized.

[26] Nor, needless to say, did this attempt by the Weimar Court Theatre (influenced of course by Liszt) to help itself and Wagner by commissioning from the latter his opera or music drama *Siegfrieds Tod* (Siegfried's Death) ever come to fruition. Re-entitled *Götterdämmerung* (Twilight of the Gods), and forming the final part of Wagner's *Ring* cycle, it was ultimately not completed until Nov. 1874—when it was certainly not delivered to Weimar.

You ask me what I am doing. I read your letters and reread them, and then I feel you suffer, within yourself and within me. That is a powerful and sombre echo of the soul; in the same way, the gaping passengers on the Rhine steamers, when listening to those tremendous thunderclaps reverberating through the heart of the rocks, can hardly imagine that they can resound. I wake up at 7.30 or later, and often stay in bed until 11.00, writing and receiving people who come to see me on business. Generally I lunch alone, at the Altenburg. Apart from in rehearsal hours, I write a mass of letters.

259. To Princess Carolyne [Weimar, 4/5 May]. . . . If you could know how my hours are employed, and could observe the people I see, you would have no reason, it seems to me, to express your dissatisfaction with the way my days are divided up. Your absence cuts me in two, and even were I living somewhere totally uninhabited, from the moment that the post got to it I should find it difficult to *sing* while you were not there. You know that without being breathlessly active I cannot be accused of idleness. But to set about the work I have to do I really must have a rather better base than I have had for a month.

Here is a short summary of the *things* that have taken up my time. Wagner's *Siegfried*, a matter which is now concluded in the way that I have written to you. Conversations and letters relating to the Goethe Foundation: I am going to write some more today, in reply to a proposal made to me by an extremely intelligent man, whose three-volume novel *Nach der Natur*, which has made a very great sensation, I urge you to read—the author is a very good Silesian gentleman of the name of Hauenschild, who uses the literary pseudonym Max Waldau. Determining the arrangements to be made so that we can set up our orchestra on a permanent basis within the next month or two: attending to pensions, new appointments, and the purchase of instruments. The Monday Institute, which will be functioning well and truly at the end of this month, and will be really important for Weimar. Rehearsals and performances of *Lohengrin* and *Favorita*; and, for this week, of *Fidelio* and *Robert le Diable*. Two court concerts, and a third on Tuesday week. Plus three or four lessons to give to the Grand Duchess, and about five or six to Jadassohn and Sacha Winterberger. The dispatch of two manuscripts to Härtel, which I first had to revise. Sending Brockhaus the *Lohengrin* with the indications you gave me. Copying out the *Harmonies poétiques*, plus Schubert's Fantasy which I should like to send off shortly. Correction of the proofs of the First Hungarian Rhapsody, and dispatch of the Second, and also my *Etudes*, to Senff, etc.

I can assure you, dear one, that I try to waste as little time as possible and that I can bear your absence only with great despondency, which does not allow me to indulge in my faults of sociability. Don't think I enjoy taking people to and fetching them from the station! . . .

If you will be so good as to take into consideration on the one hand the heavy burden of my duties in Weimar, and on the other my little aptitude for the epistolary style, I believe you will judge with more indulgent patience the life I am obliged to lead, and which it seems to me will later be deemed honourable. My wishes, my partialities, my ambitions—you know them. For me, it can all be summed up in what is for the world a laughable banality, but which is the expression of the ardent yearning of my soul: 'a thatched cottage and her heart'.—

But why has your poor Woronince been taken from you? Why am I obliged to put Weimar back on its feet, and to suffer one by one the inevitable consequences, even at this very moment, of my personal position? Why am I compelled to be an *apparently serious* man, something antipathetic to my loving, dreamy, even forgetful nature? When shall I be able to dream, write, compose, and love you in tranquillity?

Dear God, be blessed, since You have given her to me, and do not abandon us!

260. To Princess Carolyne. 10.00 p.m., Tuesday, 6 May. Brava, Magnet, bravissima! She has guessed correctly and won her bet with you—so that there are two winners, and even three, if you consent to admit me into your illustrious company. La Lewald has not set foot in the Altenburg, and I have carefully explained to her how impossible it is for me to invite her before your return, without compromising her. I have twice dined with her in the past week—and I find Stahr of real interest, for his wit, knowledge, intelligence ... and character. It seems to me that when you see him again you will form a better opinion of him than you did on Heligoland—and I should be very glad if later on he could contrive to settle in Weimar. He would make a perfect secretary of the Goethe Foundation, and first thing tomorrow I shall drop a hint about it to Monseigneur [Carl Alexander], who got back from the Meiningen baptism only yesterday.

Stahr has lent me two volumes which I should like you to read. Frau Kinkel's *Memoirs*, written during her husband's imprisonment and worthy of the wife of a Brutus artist and philosopher—and Jung's *Geschichte der Frauen*.[27] Ask Gerhard for this volume; it's worth the trouble. As for Frau Kinkel's *Memoirs*, they are

---

[27] Referring, presumably, to Alexander Jung's *Frauen und Männer oder über Vergangenheit, Gegenwart und Zukunft der beiden Geschlechter* (Women and Men, or concerning Past, Present and Future of both sexes) (Königsberg, 1847).

in a Stuttgart magazine, the one which published those verses by Heine on my alleged apathy as a renegade Magyar, and are strictly banned, or else I would have sent them to you. . . .

Have I told you a little story related to me by Plötz, with whom I have re-habilitated myself by very simply approaching him at a Court soirée, and, after a hint from his wife, paying him a visit? You perhaps remember that we wrote to a Pcss Czetwertynska to turn down the Cracovian concert in Dresden last summer. Well, this same Pcss Czetwertynska remarked at a soirée, in front of Mme Maltitz, that she was at least very pleased to have one more autograph. She added that in the whole of Podolia there was not a single honest person who did not pay total tribute to your great qualities of mind and to the com-plete purity of your life. This big truth, related to me by the big Plötz, never-theless did not fail to give me palpable pleasure.

You have noticed a certain irritation in my letters. Alas, my epistolary style is frightfully mannered, and a terrible parody of the Napoleonic manner. I gen-erally know *what* to say, but not *how* to say it.... It's my way of thinking—and it is much worse when you are far away. You are a chatterbox, but an admirable, ravishing, inspiring, thrilling, bewitching one—in short, you know how to speak. While I, my poor self, suffer from a mental *crick in the neck*, which is, I feel, one of the most stupid weaknesses imaginable. But you forgive me and resign yourself to loving me, despite everything, don't you? For myself, I love you with all the abandon, all the excess, and everything positive that is in me. . . .

261. To Princess Carolyne. Midnight, Wednesday [7 May]. Utter idiot that I am, to imagine that I was doing well in doing other than what you want. You have this advantage over Homer himself, whom Horace sometimes allowed to nod[28]—that you never nod off over a single iota of the least of your instruc-tions. In my stupidity I had simply believed that it was better not to jumble Magne's brain with Spain and Sweden at one and the same time. Since the his-tory of Russia that you were asking for is missing from my collection, I thought it was better to send you 2 vols. on Germany. But nay! It is Sweden that you are calling for, and here is Sweden coming to you. . . .

I have just conducted *Fidelio*—and had a long tête-à-tête chat with Stahr, whom I most certainly consider an *eminent* man. . . . You tell me that Heine and Horace are the ABC, and I am really quite astonished at this discovery! But what is less ABC is to have published at the age of about 20, as he did, 8 or 10

---

[28] An allusion, of course, to the Horatian line which has given us 'Homer nods': 'Indignor quandoque bonus dorm-itat Homerus' (*Ars poetica*, 359).

vols. of Aristotle, with commentaries quoted eulogistically by Cousin, Ravaisson, Jourdain, *et al.* I assure you, dear one, that his conversation is a mine of totally extraordinary ideas and *aperçus*, and when you summon up the patience to listen to him, I am sure you will be of my opinion.

The Grand Duchess has asked me to go to her at 11.30 tomorrow. I can assure you that she is in the best of humours in your regard. In the evening I hope to be able to do a little work, which will be soothing for me. Writing this pile of letters has really worn me out. For goodness' sake, come back as soon as you can, so that I may be a little less unbearable to myself. . . .

262. To Princess Carolyne. 8.00 p.m., Thursday [8 May]. . . . Your last letter but one was very short, and I have just received another of only three small pages! And so you have taken a turn for the worse once again! My God, what can I say to you? If you're not better in another five or six days, I shan't be able to stand it any longer and will return to Eilsen. . . .

You were wanting to write to ask Szerdahély[29] what I am doing at different hours of the day. But I have told you, and you can guess without my telling you. I read your letters and drag myself like a ghost through these rooms to which my Sansonnet no longer brings enchantment, where my sweet Harpagon no longer hoards her treasures, where my Chrysostom no longer waxes eloquent![30] Oh, absence means only gloom! . . .

263. To Princess Carolyne. 7.00 p.m., Saturday [10 May]. Dear and beloved! How the hours and days get sadly longer—and, as a crowning sadness, how your letters get shorter! Here are three, of barely two pages. My poor darling, if by the end of the week you are not better I shall once again journey to Eilsen, for I cannot get used to this distance, as long as I know that you are ill. What nonsense I am talking! If you were not ill, would there be a distance?

I have started working again, to some extent, and began yesterday by finishing my Polonaise. During the week I hope to finish revising copies of the *Harmonies*

[29] A Hungarian living in Weimar at this time, apparently for the sake of Liszt, by whom, in a letter of 1 Feb. to the Princess, he was described as 'a charming boy and very discreet'. 'He generally comes at about 9.00 to enquire if I need his services in any way—for going on errands, taking messages, copying letters, etc.'

[30] A teasing allusion, using the name of Molière's miser, to the Princess's tight-fistedness, followed by a tribute to the persuasive fluency of her speech, Chrysostom—an epithet applied most famously to the great 4th-cent. preacher St John (of Antioch)—being Greek for 'golden mouth'.

and of the Schubert Fantasy, done by that poor devil Reissmann. He's a boy who has remained a burden to me, but whom it would have been *inhuman* to send away. Perhaps he will be up to doing something later, but he isn't good for much at present. His copying is very defective, and obliges me to be very impatiently patient! I have also almost finished the two *Harmonies* Nos. 7 and 8, 'Tombez, larmes silencieuses!' and the *Miserere*; I shall try to write them down at once. The Court, the theatre, and the flood of correspondence have taken me all this month, as you know—and, then, when you are not here, I truly can't do anything worthwhile. Don't take that for a foolish and convenient excuse. Even to think and breathe, I need you totally!

Raff is preparing a little pleasure for you. It is the *facsimile*, of which I shall have 100 copies run off, of *Ce qu'on entend sur la montagne*. I have very carefully revised this score which he is copying out yet again, and from this copy he will have a second one run off with chemical ink, which will be multiplied a hundredfold by the autographic process. As there is now a very good lithographer here, the appearance of the thing will be splendid, and according to our calculations the hundred copies will cost us no more than 45 thalers. If, as I am assured, this trial attempt succeeds, I shall do the same with the *Tasso* overture and the Goethe March. That will make in all an expense of about a hundred thalers, which seems reasonable. It will be our luxury, and I hope you will not disapprove of me for having embarked upon it. . . .

At what cup of injustices, brimming over with gall and bitterness, you have been forced to drink, my poor and unique Carolyne! What other woman would not have sunk in the very first days! And this glorious martyrdom of love and of your unshakeable greatness of soul you will soon have been enduring for three years! Alas! How small and feeble I feel beside you, and above all how wretched I am when I am far away from you! I dare not even speak to you of my love— but you will understand me. You feel the beating of my heart in yours—don't you? And God will take pity on us! . . .

264. To Princess Carolyne. 9.00 a.m., Tuesday, 13 May.

The whole of yesterday was wasted. The *Lohengrin*, as I wrote to you, attracted 8 or 10 persons to whom I had to show some attention. Mme Schlick's protégé arrived on Sunday likewise. Between 11.00 and 1.00 that day there was a quartet session at the Altenburg, in which was repeated Beethoven's Quartet with the Adagio *Canzone di ringraziamento alla Divinità da un guarito*. Between 2 and 5 we lunched and chatted at the Erbprinz. Herr and Frau Moscheles, Robert Franz and his brother-in-law Hinrichs, Kühmstedt—whom the Grand Duchess had had invited for *Lohengrin*—and Stahr did most of the talking. I invited no one to lunch or supper, and restricted myself to having served, on Sunday and yesterday, two bottles of champagne, of which I drank not half a glass! After the performance, which really went very well, Their Highnesses sent for me, to compliment me in their box, while, below, a dozen people persisted in calling me back to the stage—a good and very praiseworthy intention to which I naturally did not respond. . . .

Even though we shortened the intervals, the opera did not finish until about 10 o'clock. Afterwards we all met at the Erbprinz, and I didn't get tipsy. Among the visitors was Prof. Hensel, Court painter in Berlin and widower of Mendelssohn's sister, of whom he has had a delightful portrait engraved, which I shall show you as he has just given me a copy. His wife was an extremely distinguished musician, and Mendelssohn owes her the ideas for several of his most successsful works, amongst others the *Lieder ohne Worte*, of which a number are entirely Frau Fanny Hensel's invention. Härtel is engaged in bringing out quite a considerable number of his posthumous works, and this afternoon we shall be playing a trio of *hers*, which seems most interesting. Among other things Hensel told me that the King,[31] asking him to give his *Grüsse an Liszt* [greetings to Liszt], had added that he was truly curious to learn whether Liszt was *seriously* enough in love with the Pcss W. *um sie nicht sitzen zu lassen* [not to walk out on her]. I am quoting the exact words, expressed with His Majesty's usual lack of ceremony. Naturally I replied *mit dem schönsten Klangwort der deutschen Sprache* [with the finest-sounding words in the German language], as His Majesty put it at his enthronement: *Ja—und abermals Ja!* [Yes—and again Yes!]—for I can declare before both God and man that I love you with all my soul and with all my strength, with all my past and with all my future! The oath of fidelity which I hope soon to take is at once the sweetness and supreme ambition of my existence! Do you remember these words from the Bible—'This is now bone of my bones, and flesh of my flesh!'[32]

Yesterday morning, Monday, was spent chatting with Kühmstedt, whose lot in life I shall try to ameliorate—for he is evidently out of place in Eisenach. Then came Kral, who will play the viola d'amore at the court concert on Thursday. After that I went to David's, and from there we went to Winterberger's —where Dresel, a former quasi-pupil of mine from New York, joined David and Cossmann in a trio by Mendelssohn. Since Frau Moscheles was extremely insistent that I should go to the piano, I declined peremptorily, for I found it

---

[31] Friedrich Wilhelm IV.   [32] Gen. 2: 23.

inappropriate to be thus called to give an account of myself, in something from *Lohengrin* into the bargain. But in order to moderate the impression of my lack of obedience to her wishes, I suggested that Moscheles and I play together his latest Sonata for piano duet—and chose the bass part. At 1.30 the Grand Duchess sent for me, and I stayed with her until 3.00. Moscheles and his wife departed at 4.00, and at Winterberger's in the evening we made music until midnight with David, Franz, *et al.* Raff came out with some astounding theories with an unbelievable display of intelligence. It left us all open-mouthed. . . .

I am writing to you in bed. Ziegesar has just spent an hour with me, and shown me Wagner's reply, which, with a gratitude that could not be better expressed, accepts the *Siegfried* proposal. But he is first composing a *Young Siegfried*[33]—which will be performed in February '53 at the latest, in order to prepare the public for the *death* of Siegfried, of which you know the poem. That will be, I think, Wagner's outstanding work. One really must bow very deeply before a man of this genius. . . .

265. To Princess Carolyne. Friday, 16 May. The Altenburg has been bought by the Grand Duchess, who wished to put an end to Stock's *vandalisms.* Just imagine, he was planning to have all the small woodwork on the stairs cut away so that he could have a beer cabinet installed there. Yesterday, Vitzthum[34] *particularly* assured me that the Altenburg's present tenants would not be shown the door.

Yesterday evening's concert went perfectly. Frau Schlick's protégé made a very good impression. . . .

You will be receiving Stahr's two latest volumes. He was presented today to Carl Friedrich, and to the Grand Duchess. La Lewald is behaving very sensibly and in no way pushing herself forward. She has had the good judgement to imitate your example, in not going to Frau Plötz's on *Friday* mornings, although, to be agreeable to Monseigneur [Carl Alexander], Frau Plötz urged her with some insistence. Later on, I believe, you will not be discontent with Stahr, who will be infinitely more valuable to us than Dingelstedt and Gutzkow. I do not despair of seeing him settled here, as Monseigneur's secretary for the *Fondation Goethe* and editor of a magazine. . . .

On 20 May Liszt returned to Bad Eilsen for the last time.

---

[33] Wagner's *Der junge Siegfried*, re-entitled *Siegfried*, was to become the third part of his *Ring* cycle; its first performance was at Bayreuth, 16 Aug. 1876.

[34] Baron F. A. J. Vitzthum von Egersberg, Grand Cup-Bearer at the Weimar Court.

266. To Adolf Stahr. Eilsen, 26 May. I leave you in order to reply to you, dear friend. Your *Two Months in Paris*[35] have been a delightful intellectual recreation for us during the first days of the melancholy retreat away from which I could not for long go on living. On many a page of this book facts and ideas become of particular interest through the happy lucidity of the way in which they are set out and the artistically economical light with which you illuminate them!

The Princess, who is still very unwell, asks me to thank you very affectionately both for your kind thought in sending her this work and for the pleasure it has given her. I hope that in a fortnight or so she will be convalescent enough to think about returning home. Between now and then I shall live as though half dead!

Your journey to Jena will, I hope, bear fruit for Weimar, for I like to think, from what you have told me about him, that in Hettner you will find a man of *enlightenment*. His book on Goethe, that is being sent to me from Leipzig, I shall read at the same time as your study of *Faust*.

When you do me the kindness of writing to me, please tell me if the question of the *magazine* has been raised *officially*, and in what manner?[36]—In Weimar, unfortunately, there would in certain respects be every reason to repeat this parody of Racine's line: 'I fear *everything*, dear Abner, and have no other fear!' . . .

Do you know if Mgr. the Hered. Gr. Duke has already invited Hauenschild? Was it through you or did he do so direct? It will be very agreeable to me to meet, *en personne naturelle*, the author of *Nach der Natur*, and I fancy we shall have no difficulty in understanding one another. Perhaps he will manage to come while you are in Weimar, and we should then make a *Goethe Foundation quartet* which would be worthy to harmonize with the *Canzone di ringraziamento da un guarito* (which Joachim made so comprehensible to us one Sunday morning), even though we are still very ill!

Wagner has sent me his pamphlet on the Zurich theatre.[37] It is well intentioned and well written—but his puppets' strings are too openly visible for us to be taken in. Most of the time he quite fails to chew on anything at all, through excess of appetite. Even so, Wagner will remain what he is, the most admirable *Zwillings-Genius* [twin genius] of musical composition and dramatic poetry. Add to that the fact that he is at the same time the dramatist, decorator, machinist, copyist, Kapellmeister, and schoolmaster *par excellence* when it concerns his own works, and tell me if he hasn't in him the stuff of some Indian god with any number of heads and hands? . . .

Ever yours, F. Liszt

---

[35] *Zwei Monate in Paris* (2 vols., Oldenburg, 1851).   [36] The planned magazine never came into being.
[37] *Ein Theater in Zurich.*

267. To Anna Liszt in Paris. Eilsen, 29 August ^{G (F)}

Dearest Mother,

I leave Eilsen tomorrow morning to travel to Weimar, and don't intend to budge an inch until next summer. The Princess, thank Heaven, has almost recovered, and I hope we shall have a mild winter.

I should be very glad indeed to take possession of my books once again, so please will you send me my entire Paris library, books and music. Have them packed up at once and ask Belloni to send them here by freight.

To my great joy I read that at the London Exhibition Erard was awarded a medal. In the next few days I shall reply to the friendly letter in which he tells me this. Should you see him, give him my heartiest greetings and assure him of my constant devotion.

Unlike Erard, M. Daniel has unfortunately no such results to show, and also seems not to have deserved them. I hope he will distinguish himself better at next year's prize-giving, and I ask you not to spoil him by being too indulgent to him. It would be painful to me if the boy became only a silly jackanapes! I forgive him his levity only on condition that he work hard from now on and make a point of bearing my name with propriety.

How are the Seghers? Remember me to them. Mme Patersi is delighted with the hours that M. Seghers is giving to the girls, and under his supervision they seem to be making good progress.

My own aspirations are likewise directed towards progress, and indeed towards tremendous progress, please note! My Parisian friends won't have to reproach me with laziness when we see one another again.

Mme Patersi will give you a couple of German newspapers to read which report on my essay on the *Fondation Goethe*. May that give you reason to remember Weimar, where in a few years I hope to greet you once again.

With a child's love,   F. Liszt

In late August Liszt and the two princesses left Eilsen and returned to Weimar, *en route* lingering in the Rhineland and visiting the Schumanns in Düsseldorf.

268. To Richard Wagner. Weimar, 1 December. ^G Your letter,[38] my

glorious friend, has given me great joy. In your extraordinary way you have reached an extraordinarily great goal. The task of forming a dramatic trilogy out of the *Nibelung* epic, and composing the music for it, is worthy of you, and

---

[38] Of 20 Nov., accompanying the poem of *Der junge Siegfried*.

I have not the slightest doubt about the monumentally successful outcome of your work. Of my sincerest interest and most heartfelt fellow-feeling you are already so assured, that no further words are needed. In the 3 years you are giving yourself for it, many things can change to your advantage in your outer circumstances. Perhaps, as many newspapers are already reporting, you will soon return to Germany; perhaps, too, by the time your *Siegfried* is finished the means of a performance will be available to me. Just get down to it and, *regardless* of anything else, apply yourself to your work, for which the same programme could be set out as the one that, when Seville Cathedral was being built, the cathedral chapter gave to the architect: 'Build us such a temple that future generations will be obliged to say the chapter were mad to undertake something so extraordinary.' And yet the Cathedral stands there still!

I enclose a letter from Herr von Ziegesar, the contents of which are indeed known to, but not suggested by, me. Ziegesar is a man of dependable, excellent, and worthy character, one on whom you can always count as a friend.

I hope that, as soon as his painful eye trouble allows him, he will once again (next spring, I think) take over the Intendancy.

Your extremely well-founded and justified apprehensions about my activity in Weimar, I shall not reply to; they will actually be proved or disproved during this couple of years in which you will be living with your Nibelungs. In any case, I am prepared for better and worse, and hope to be allowed quietly to proceed along my modest path!

Bülow, to whom I showed your letter, is working on an Overture to *Julius Caesar*, which in a fortnight's time we shall perform with the tragedy. As a piano virtuoso (if you still want to know anything about such people), he is making significant progress, and if, as I am advising him to, he makes a real career out of it in the next few years, it will unquestionably turn out very much to his advantage. . . .

Hearty thanks, dear friend, for sending *Der junge Siegfried*. Last week, unfortunately, everything was so chaotic here that I couldn't find a quiet hour in which to read it—but I expect you can let me keep it until Christmas?[39]

When are your three dramas *Fliegender Holländer*, *Tannhäuser*, and *Lohengrin* coming out? Have you revised the preface? Härtel has promised it me, but thus far I have received nothing. Perhaps you have another publisher for it? When the occasion arises, let me know through Bülow, who is writing to you simultaneously.

Farewell, and, if you can, live in harmony with the upper world as well as with your lower abdomen, to which in your letter you even attribute things for

---

[39] As Wagner explained in his next letter, it was a gift.

which it is not quite responsible. People may think as they like, but I for my part cannot get away from this definition: 'L'homme est une intelligence servie par des organes;' and that your own organs do you splendid service is demonstrated by the fact that you are writing your *Nibelung* trilogy, with Prologue.

May the living God bless and preserve you!

Your affectionately devoted friend   F. Liszt

1852

Most of 1852 Liszt spent in Weimar, composing, teaching and carrying out his demanding duties as Kapellmeister. In June he directed a music festival at Ballenstedt; in July attended a music festival in Brunswick; and in November mounted in Weimar a Berlioz Week during which he conducted two performances of his friend's *Benvenuto Cellini* and Berlioz himself conducted his *Roméo et Juliette* and Parts One and Two of *La Damnation de Faust.*

Among other visitors this year were the versatile young composer Peter Cornelius,* who became a keen supporter and good friend of both Liszt and Wagner; and Hans Christian Andersen, who in the spring spent three weeks (19 May–10 June) in Weimar and was on several occasions the guest of Liszt and the Princess, appreciative listeners to the tales Andersen read out to gatherings at the Altenburg and elsewhere.

WORKS. Fantasia on Hungarian Folk Themes (S123, ?1852), for piano and orchestra. The song *Es muss ein Wunderbares sein* (Redwitz) (S314). PIANO: *Ab Irato* (S143), a revised version of the *Morceau de salon, étude de perfectionnement* of 1840; transcription of *Bénédiction et serment, deux motifs de Benvenuto Cellini* (Berlioz) (S396); *Soirées de Vienne* (S427) ([9] *Valses caprices d'après Schubert*); *Harmonies poétiques et religieuses* (S173, 1840 [No. 2], 1845–52): 1. *Invocation* 2. *Ave Maria* 3. *Bénédiction de Dieu dans la solitude* 4. *Pensée des morts* 5. *Pater noster* 6. *Hymne de l'enfant à son reveil* 7. *Funérailles* 8. *Miserere, d'après Palestrina* 9. *Andante lagrimoso* 10. *Cantique d' amour.*

269. To Richard Wagner in Venice. Weimar, 15 January ^G

Dearest Friend!

I am probably the last to write and tell you how we have all once again been most profoundly delighted and stirred by your glorious work! How can we thank you for it? How am I more especially to express my thanks?.... Bülow and Brendel have written to tell you that the 6th performance of your *Lohengrin* can be called a relatively satisfactory one. What I wrote to you after the very feeble and defective 1st performance has proved correct. At every performance the artistes' understanding and comprehension has increased simultaneously with the public's—and I am convinced that on Saturday (24 January) the 7th performance will be even more successful. Next season we shall at once attack your *fliegender Holländer*, which for local reasons that I have explained to Bülow I didn't want to propose for this winter. Then, too, we shall probably be in a position to improve things in regard to the scenery etc. in *Lohengrin*. You can certainly rely on me to bring performances of your works in Weimar more and more up to scratch, just as our theatre will gradually eradicate various economic considerations and make the necessary improvements and replenishments not only to the scenery but also to the chorus and orchestra! Excuse my bad German style; I am better at *doing* a thing than writing about it.

Hearty thanks for your splendid present of *Siegfried*, of which I ventured to arrange a reading at Ziegesar's for the Hereditary Grand Duke and Duchess. Ziegesar, who had already read your poem, is very enthusiastic about it, and the small circle (about 15 people) he brought together that evening was picked quite exclusively from among the most ardent *Wagnerites*; and was, therefore, the *crème de la crème*!—I am extremely curious to know how you will set about the work, musically speaking, what proportions the different movements will have, etc.

So do get down to it soon; perhaps the whole work will take you even less than 3 years. As regards the performance, we shall manage to arrange it somewhere by carefully complying with your orders and instructions. With all the genius of your imagination, you are so eminently experienced and practical that you will certainly write nothing that cannot be achieved. Difficulties are necessary—so that they can be overcome. In the unlikely event of your not being back in Germany by then, put the whole thing in my hands; I only ask you to give me a detailed programme, which I shall follow totally, of everything that you desire and require in the performance of this gigantic work. People and things shall be found for it somehow. I hope, however, that I shall have the pleasure of enjoying your Nibelung trilogy quietly from the stalls or a seat in the balcony, and then of inviting you for 4 consecutive evenings after the performance to supper in the Hôtel de Saxe (Dresden) or Hôtel de Russie (Berlin), if you are still able to eat and drink after all your exertions.

About the conclusion of your preface to the 3 operatic poems I shall say nothing. It struck me in my heart of hearts, and I wept a manly tear over it.

My portrait I am sending you through Härtel. The medallion I shall have to order for you from Paris, as in Germany only galvanoplastic copies are available.

After the performance of *Lohengrin* the Princess wrote a few words for you which I enclose.

Farewell, and live as tranquilly as possible, my glorious friend—and let me soon hear something of you.   Your   F. Liszt

270. To Richard Wagner [early to mid-May [1]**].** ^G That I was unable to fly to your *fliegender Holländer* [2] was not my fault; how delighted I should have been to see you again, and what a wonderful treat your glorious work would have been for me, I need not tell you, most excellent friend. The news that has reached me from several sides about the performances of *Der fliegende Holländer* is naturally very agreeable to me. Next winter you shall also have news of our performance in Weimar, for we can't delay it any longer, and it is to be hoped that the artistes will have a great success (for of the work itself there can be no doubt at all). Be so good as to let me know as soon as possible of the exact changes, omissions, and alterations you have made to the score, for I want to have the copies made at once. Recently I again laid down the principle that our first and chief duty in Weimar is to mount Wagner's operas entirely *selon le bon plaisir de l'auteur*. With this, you will doubtless agree—and so we must do *Lohengrin* without cuts, as we have already done, and study afresh the *whole* of the finale of the Second Act of *Tannhäuser* (apart from the small cut in the Adagio that was made in Dresden). This will be done by the next performance. Send me, therefore, necessary *instructions* for mounting *Der fliegende Holländer*, and be assured that I shan't deviate from them by one iota.

Thank you very much for your kind offer of the designs, which I jump at. Send them to me as soon as you can—we now have here a very clever young scene painter and machinery man, Herr Händel (formerly of the Hamburg Theatre), who will make a point of meeting your demands to the very best of his ability. I have notified the Intendant, Herr von Beaulieu-Marconnay,* that you will be sending the designs, and the honorarium (5 louis d'or) will be sent to you at the end of August; if you would prefer to receive this small sum earlier than that, I'll send it you by return.

I have asked Bülow to tell you of the *crime* I committed when His Majesty the Tsar of Russia was here. *Tannhäuser* had been announced for the evening when it was hoped that HM would visit the theatre—but Knopp and Milde couldn't sing a note, and Frau von Milde was likewise very hoarse. Since it was impossible to put on a complete opera, I coolly took the First Act of *Tannhäuser* as far as the end of the Pilgrims' Chorus (closing in G major)— and then after a short interval resumed in that key with the prelude to the Third Act of *Lohengrin*, and continued with the whole Act to the end of the duet—bringing the performance to a close with the *Carnaval romain* overture and the Second Act of *Benvenuto Cellini* (omitting the baritone aria).

---

[1] The letter is undated, but probably written in the first half of May, and certainly not later than a few days before the 24th, date of Wagner's reply.

[2] Referring to three performances in Zurich between 21 Apr. and 1 May.

Fräulein Frommann[3] was present and has probably written to you about it.

The Tsaritsa is expected at the end of this month, and *Tannhäuser* is again announced for the 31st. Beck is undertaking the part of Tannhäuser, and the finale of the Second Act will be done complete. But the new ending will unfortunately have to wait until next season, for a new scene is being painted for it and can't be finished in time; otherwise, everything is ready and copied out.

Spohr's *Faust*, with new recitatives, is down for next season, and at the beginning of June we are doing Schumann's *Manfred*. About the music festival at Ballenstedt with the Overture to *Tannhäuser* and the *Liebesmahl der Apostel* you have probably heard.

Your Faust Overture went well and created a sensation.

Farewell, and get down to your *Siegfried*.

Your   F.L.

271. To Robert Schumann in Düsseldorf. Weimar, 8 June ^G

Very dear friend,

I am glad to be able to tell you that the first performance of *Manfred* is to be next Sunday, 13 June, and to give you a friendly invitation to be present. At this time of year your commitments in Düsseldorf will allow you, I trust, to come here for a couple of days—probably with Clara, to whom please remember me most kindly. Should you come alone, however, I beg you to stay with me at the Altenburg, where you can make yourself perfectly comfortable and at home. The final rehearsal is to be held on Friday afternoon: perhaps you will be able to attend it, which would of course be very agreeable to me. Your friends in Leipzig will see the announcement of this performance in the papers, and I imagine you will consider yourself duty-bound not to fail to be here with us.

While cordially wishing you ever the best of spirits for your work, plus good health and 'every other good that appertains thereto', I remain unalterably

Yours most sincerely   F. Liszt

272. To Robert Schumann. Weimar, 26 June ^G

Dear friend,

I very much regret that you were unable to come to the 1st[4] presentation of your *Manfred*, and believe that you would not have been discontent with the way in which, musically speaking, we prepared and performed this work, which

---

³ Alwine Frommann, a devoted supporter of Wagner, was reader to Princess Augusta of Prussia.

⁴ Transcribing this word as '2ten' (2nd), Liszt's editress La Mara conceded that it could equally well have been '1ten' (1st).

I regard as one of your most genuinely successful. The whole impression was, as I had expected, a thoroughly noble, profound, and elevating one. The part of Manfred was undertaken by Herr Pötsch, and rendered with an understanding that did him honour. As far as the staging is concerned, one or two things could be said; but it would be unjust for our debt to the producer, Herr Genast, not to be acknowledged. It seems to me, therefore, that it would be appropriate for you to write Herr Genast a couple of friendly lines of thanks and ask him to pass on your compliments etc. to Herr Pötsch and the other artistes.

Perhaps I may make just one observation. The music introducing the Arimanes chorus (D minor) is too short. About 60 to 100 bars of orchestral music, of the kind you can write so well, would be of decidedly good effect. Do think about it and then go afresh to your writing desk. Arimanes can stand a few lines of polyphony, and on this occasion can be allowed to rage and roar quite comfortably.

Am I to send your manuscript score back to you, or will you make me a nice present of it? I am by no means an autograph collector, but the score, if you have no further need of it, would give me pleasure.

A thousand friendly greetings to Clara, and do ask her soon to let me hear something of you once again.

In sincerest admiration and friendship,

Yours   F. Liszt

273. To Princess Carolyne in Weimar [Brunswick, 3 July]. The post is an *Institution* which functions even worse than Ziegesar's, don't you think? It's now 6 o'clock on Saturday morning and I still haven't had a word from you. To be sure, it isn't your fault—you who always write, and who are always adorable.

The festival here has put me in mind of M. de Talleyrand's remark: 'When I look into myself, I find that I am pretty worthless; but when I compare myself with others, I think less badly of myself.' That is entirely the case as regards Ballenstedt and this place. With all the external advantages which I lacked in Ballenstedt, the people here wholly fail to reach a result equal to the one I achieved. For the rest, the locals are generally rather charming, and each and every one of them possesses a certain gift of affability and good grace—to which we are rather unaccustomed in Weimar. I spent yesterday evening at a Major Holland's, whom I didn't know before. It was one of those gatherings which do honour to the master of the house by being agreeable to the guests, and having, therefore, very little in common with those *conducted* by Maltitz *et al.* . . .

As far as distinguished non-local artistes are concerned, there is only Moscheles to mention. He came to see me even before yesterday's concert, in the company of Litolff, with whose name my own has three letters in common—but he lacks the *conclusive letter*, the *z*—and his paraph is worth very little. Yesterday evening, after the Holland soirée, he played me a Ballade and an Elegy which are more impressive than what I knew of his work until now. . . .

7⁵ o'clock is striking, and I have just been brought your letter. Loving thanks for your kind words—God is giving me courage and hope. . . .

I shall continue my letter later. A piano is just arriving for me from a manufacturer who was foreman at Erard's in London, in 1825. He is doing me this courtesy in memory of the hours we spent together at that time, playing all sorts of boys' games in the little garden in [Great] Marlborough Street. . . .

274. To Princess Carolyne. Saturday, 8.00 a.m. [Brunswick, 3 July].

Yesterday's concert with Beethoven's Ninth Symphony was decidedly inferior to ours in Ballenstedt—notwithstanding the 700 singers and 300 players, of whom nearly half are imaginary. Some half a dozen people, who had attended the Ballenstedt festival and were among the audience here, expressed themselves about it very plainly. That gives me a slight satisfaction. . . .

This morning I shall be hearing a Trio at the recital given by Müller, whose fraternal quartet enjoys great fame in Germany. The four brothers are currently forming a new quartet, with their sons! Moscheles will likewise be appearing, in a Duo for two pianos—some *Homage to Handel* or to Beethoven of his composition! At the theatre this evening there is *La Fille du Régiment*⁶ with Mme Marra, a singer of good reputation with whom I renewed acquaintance yesterday. I went neither to the *Festessen* [festival banquet] nor to the ball, and managed to dine alone in my room on a beefsteak, and to go to bed at about 11.00 after spending an hour at the Spohrs',⁷ who had the good taste to invite no one else. They are the excellent people that you know, and with whom there are no snags to fear. I shall presently be going to see Rietschel's statue of Lessing, which is to be unveiled this autumn. You know that this statue has established Rietschel's reputation, and since he is to come to Weimar I shall be glad to be able to speak to him about it. . . .

---

⁵ Wrongly transcribed by La Mara as '9'.
⁶ Two-act opera by Donizetti, first performed at the Opéra-Comique, Paris, 11 Feb. 1840.
⁷ The home, not of the composer (who lived in Kassel), but of his brother Wilhelm and niece Rosalie.

275. To Princess Carolyne. Halle, Thursday, 8 July.[8] . . . Getting here after 7.00, I went into town to see [Robert] Franz, whom they haven't been able to unearth anywhere. In compensation, I looked at a lively flock of swallows flying around the church of St Ulrich. They told me a thousand things *in the air* that I should like to be able to bring you as the swallow flies. On the train I read the first number of Lamartine's *Civilisateur*, of which this is the conclusion: 'To be admired, one has to ascend; to be useful, one has to descend.' This assertion is one of those which seem to me to overstate what it is unnecessary to say. . . .

Here is Franz coming to me in this same room in which we dined with Magnolet. . . .

276. To Princess Carolyne [Ettersburg, 14 July]. I didn't write to you yesterday evening, dear unique one, and am reproaching myself bitterly for it this morning. The Princess [Augusta of Prussia] had given me a love poem to set to music, between dinner and the soirée. Wanting to do it without delay, I wasn't able to go back to the tea until about 9.00—and later, by dint of thinking about you I forgot you.

The verses the Princess gave me to set are from *Amaranth*,[9] as follows:

> Es muss was Wunderbares sein
> Um's Lieben zweier Seelen!
> Sich schliessen ganz einander ein,
> Sich nie ein Wort verhehlen,
>
> Und Freud und Leid und Glück und Noth
> So mit einander tragen—
> Vom ersten Kuss bis in den Tod
> Sich nur von Liebe sagen!

We know something about that, don't we?

During Liszt's visit to Ballenstedt in June, his mother, who had been staying at the Altenburg, had set out on her journey back to Paris, but in Erfurt suffered an accident.

---

[8] La Mara has the date 6 July—but Thursday was the 8th.

[9] Narrative poem (1849) by Oskar von Redwitz. The song (with 'ein' not 'was' in the opening line) inspired by these two verses is one of Liszt's best and most popular. C. F. Manney's translation (*Franz Liszt: Thirty Songs*, ed. Carl Armbruster, Boston, 1911) runs: 'A wondrous rapture must it be, | The love of two souls plighted, | Whose faith, from all concealment free, | No word or thought has blighted. | Come joy or pain, come weal or woe, | Each shares the same emotion, | From that first kiss e'en unto death | With love's unchanged devotion.'

277. To J. B. Streicher in Vienna. Weimar, 6 August

My dear Herr Streicher,

I was expecting to ask my mother to hand you these lines, but an unfortunate accident as a result of which she has for more than six weeks been confined to bed in Erfurt, does not allow me to hope that she will be in a state to undertake the journey to Vienna that she was planning for this year. The fracture of the bone in her left foot has been healed for some days, but the sprain, which is the worst part of the accident, will not allow her freedom of movement for several months, according to the skilled doctors who are tending her. Next week we shall try to bring her here, where the crutches awaiting her will enable her, *poco a poco*, to give herself up to the distractions of a journey around her room!

Since the house I live in is in process of being completely rearranged and refurnished, I should be glad to take possession of the Beethoven Piano[10] that I owe to the friendly generosity of Herr Spina, and which I left in store with you. Allow me, my dear Herr Streicher, to ask you to be so good as to send it to me without delay so that it can be placed in the salon intended for it. My cousin Dr Eduard Liszt, who will bring you this letter, will pay the dispatch and carriage costs. But do please see that all necessary care is taken with the packing, so that it is protected from any accidents *en route*, and order a *special packing-case*, the price of which will be included in the costs of transport.

Perhaps you will one day have the good idea of paying me a little visit with Frau Streicher, which would give me great pleasure. In the mean time, be so kind as to give her my most affectionate regards; and receive, I beg of you, the best and most cordial good wishes of

Yours sincerely,   F. Liszt

278. To Daniel Liszt in Paris. Weimar, 22 August. The news of your *first prize in history* has given me the most agreeable satisfaction, and I am grateful to you, my dear Daniel, for having responded in such a manner to the trouble I am taking, and to the expectation I have of you. Once seriously entered upon a life of application and study, it is to be presumed that you will not feebly stop half-way, and that you will have the ambition to aspire to successes and satisfactions ever more difficult to obtain. You would not be my son, and I should have to disown you as such, if you were not animated by a sincere love of work, by a passionate zeal for the task it is given you to accomplish. Realize once and

---

[10] The famous Broadwood piano given to Liszt by Spina in 1846 and bequeathed by Liszt to the Hungarian National Museum in Budapest.

for all, and remind yourself unceasingly, that it is only by dint of constant work and sustained efforts that, by the gradual ennoblement of his faculties and his character, man is permitted to acquire his freedom, his morality, his value, and his greatness. And so the best aspect of any success we achieve is that it spurs on in us the need we have to extend the limits of our intellectual *power* and enlarge our horizons. . . . 'Idleness is the mother of all vices' is the simple proverb which can serve you as a text. It will lead you straight to the corollary maxim, which I recommend you alike to ponder and to practise: 'Work is the father of all virtues.' By virtue we mean strength, superiority, nobility, greatness....

Yes, dear child, since God has ordained that man must work, it is through work that he fulfils the twofold law of his expiation and his rehabilitation. To work on oneself and on others, to work to make one's own the knowledge acquired, to work to increase it, extend it, make it bear fruit—such is the purpose of our life on earth. Let us glorify God therein, for it is on this condition that we gain our glory and our salvation!

I should be interested to have further details about how you won your first prize—what task you had to carry out, what topic had to be discussed, etc. Tell me in your next letter—and prepare yourself in a way that next year will enable you to win *two* first prizes. It will double your pleasure, and in this way you will be making ready to distinguish yourself in your chosen career.

I embrace you very lovingly, dear child, and bless you for the joy you have given me. F. Liszt

279. To Richard Wagner. Weimar, 23 August ᴳ

Most glorious friend!

You have once again given me real, *God-sent* joy with your dedication of *Lohengrin.* Accept my sincerest and most heartfelt thanks, and be convinced that to be worthy of your friendship will be my life's task. The little that I have thus far been able to do for *you*, and thereby for the honour of Art, has chiefly this merit, that it encourages me to do even better and more decisive things for your works in the future. Just let me proceed simply and quietly along my path, and, when the goal is reached, you will surely be content with me.—But why are you concerning yourself with the bad jokes going the rounds in a couple of newspapers, and accusing me of having been the cause of them? The latter is quite unthinkable, and Hans has probably already told you that the manuscript of *Siegfried* has not been out of his hands for months. Earlier on I lent it, as you wished, to Fräulein Frommann alone, and the reading of it which took place at

Ziegesar's at the beginning of last year[11] for the Hereditary Grand Duke could surely not have given rise to the bad jokes in the *Kreuzzeitung*. In any case, the joke is quite innocuous and insignificant, and I earnestly ask you totally to ignore such tittle-tattle once and for all.

What does it matter to you if other people come out with absurdities about you and your works? As the French proverb has it, you have *d'autres chats à fouetter* [other fish to fry]! And so, for your own sake and for mine, don't let yourself be diverted from publishing the *Nibelungen* tetralogy[12] as soon as it is finished. . . .

As you know already, *Der fliegende Holländer* is down for HIH the Grand Duchess's next birthday, 16 February. We shall make it our business to mount and stage this opera appropriately. Ziegesar is a passionate admirer of your genius, and will set to work with great love and enthusiasm. The corrected score was taken to the copyists immediately, and in 6 weeks the work will be rehearsed *comme il faut*.

The theatre season will begin with Verdi's *Ernani*, soon to be followed by Spohr's *Faust* with the new recitatives. In mid-November I expect Berlioz, whose *Cellini* (with a fairly considerable cut) is not to be shelved—for despite all the nonsense talked about it, *Cellini* is and remains a very significant and highly estimable work. I am sure you would like many things in it.

Raff has undertaken some big changes in the orchestration and arrangement of his *Alfred*—and in its new form this opera will probably be even more effective than before, although it was much applauded at the first 3 or 4 performances. All in all I regard the score of this opera as the best that has been written by a German composer for the last 10 years. Naturally I don't include you in that—you stand alone; and so you can be compared only with yourself.

I am very glad that you have allowed yourself this trip. They are splendid fellows, those glaciers, and in my youth I too struck up friendship with them! For next year I recommend you a tour around Mont Blanc, which is what I did to some extent in '35. But my travelling companion soon became tired—and made me even more tired....

Farewell, live in peace with yourself, and bring out your Nibelung poem before long, to prepare the public and put it in the right mood for it. Disregard all manner of *Grenzboten*, *Wohlbekannten*, *Kreuzzeitungen*, and *Gazettes musicales*, and don't let such rubbishy scribblings bother you. Rather drink a good bottle of wine—and aim at and work towards eternal, immortal life.

Your affectionately grateful and truly devoted   F. Liszt

[11] Actually the beginning of the present year. See Letter 269 of 15 Jan.

[12] Liszt sometimes refers to the *Ring des Nibelungen* as a trilogy, sometimes as a tetralogy. Strictly speaking it is the former, preceded by what the Germans call the *Vorabend* or preliminary evening (*Das Rheingold*).

280. To Clara Schumann in Düsseldorf. Weimar, 11 September. It is not without regret that I give in to your wish, Madame, by returning to you the autograph score of *Manfred*—for I confess that *in petto* I had rather flattered myself that Robert would leave it with me by virtue of friendly ownership. As our theatre possesses a very accurate copy which will serve us for subsequent performances of *Manfred*, I was tempted to send you that copy, which would suffice for correcting the proofs; but some kind of scrupulous integrity kept me from doing so. Perhaps you will find in that a ground for giving generous encouragement to my rather shaky virtue; in which case you will have no difficulty in guessing what would be to me a precious reward....

How is Robert's health? Have the sea baths done him good? I hope he will soon be fully restored to his domestic happiness—and to his composing desk.

I should have been very glad to repeat our last year's visit to Düsseldorf, and was very touched by the way you so graciously remembered it in your letter!—but alas! an unfortunate accident suffered by my mother, who nearly broke her leg when going downstairs, has obliged her to stay in bed for more than nine weeks, and even now she can walk only with the help of crutches, and will need several months to recover completely.

As she was forced to remain in Weimar, I didn't want to leave her throughout the summer, and had to deny myself the pleasure of a holiday excursion.

Princess Wittgenstein and her daughter, who has become a very tall and charming young woman, ask to be remembered most affectionately to you and Robert, to which I add my own most sincere wishes for our friend's speedy recovery, together with cordial assurances of my unceasing friendship.   F. Liszt

281. To Rudolf Lehmann. Weimar, 22 September. .... As regards news of Weimar, I have little or nothing to tell you. You have probably heard that this little town is to be enriched, within the next two years, by a grand monument which will consist of a [double] statue of Goethe and Schiller. The work has finally been entrusted to Herr Rietschel of Dresden, who has promised to send his sketch by the end of October. The Court here is undertaking to pay the sum asked for the model (about 6,000 thalers), and HM King Ludwig of Bavaria has taken it upon himself to have the statues cast at his own expense in Munich—so that, for the pedestal and the accessory cost of the unveiling, only a few thousand thalers are still needed, and can easily be obtained by a subscription.

Further, Herr Gasser of Vienna is busy modelling a statue of Wieland, which he has likewise promised to finish in two years, and which, judging by the things he has already done, promises to be a splendid work of art. As you can see, the Court of Weimar is making it its duty not to neglect its fine traditions, and it may be that after having, through these four statues to Herder, Goethe, Schiller, and Wieland, thus nobly perpetuated the memory of Germany's great poetical period, it will be given to it to do yet more. . . .

282. To Carl Czerny in Vienna [September or October]

My honoured master and friend,

Permit me to make a particular recommendation to you of Professor Jahn, with a number of whose interesting works of musical literature and criticism (amongst others his Introduction to the original score of Beethoven's *Leonora*, published by Härtel of Leipzig), you are doubtless familiar.

The object of Herr Jahn's visit to Vienna is to collect documents for a biography of Beethoven, which will, I am convinced, meet the serious requirements (thus far, so ill-satisfied) of musicians and public alike. In honour of the great man whom, to your credit, you understood and admired long before *hoi polloi* began to *chorus* their approval of him—do, please, open to Herr Jahn the treasures of your reminiscences and of your knowledge, and accept in advance my sincere thanks for the good service you will thereby be doing to Art.[13]

It is with unchanging devotion that I remain, dear master, your very grateful and devoted

F. Liszt

P.S. When will the *Gradus ad Parnassum*[14] come out?—The copy of my *Etudes*, that are dedicated to you, will be handed to you in a few days by Herr Löwy.

283. To Wilhelm von Lenz in St Petersburg. Weimar, 2 December.

I am doubly indebted to you, my dear Lenz (you will allow me to reciprocate by dropping the *Monsieur*,[15] won't you?), firstly for your book, so deeply imbued with that sincere and earnest passion for the Beautiful without which no one

---

[13] Otto Jahn never completed a biography of Beethoven, but became the outstanding 19th-cent. biographer of Mozart.

[14] Czerny's *Nouveau Gradus ad Parnassum*, Op. 822, written in admiration of Clementi's *Gradus ad Parnassum, or the Art of Playing on the Piano Forte*.

[15] In his book *Beethoven et ses trois styles* (St Petersburg, 1852), as well as recalling his studies with Liszt at the latter's home in the rue Montholon, Paris, in the late 1820s (and again in 1842), Lenz had written: 'Although very much alive, Liszt is already one of the great names in the history of the piano; to call him *Monsieur* Liszt would be an anachronism.'

will ever penetrate to the heart of works of genius; secondly for your friendly letter which reached me shortly after I had obtained your book, the announcement of which had singularly aroused my curiosity. . . .

Your friendly recollection of our talks, in the form of lessons, in the rue *Montholon,* means a very great deal to me, and the flattering testimony that your book gives to those long-past hours encourages me to invite you to continue them in Weimar, where I should find it equally agreeable and interesting to see you for a few weeks or months, *ad libitum,* so that we could enlighten one another on Beethoven. . . .

For us musicians, the works of Beethoven are like the pillars of cloud and of fire which led the children of Israel through the wilderness—a pillar of cloud to guide us by day, a pillar of fire to give us light at night, '*so that we can proceed both by day and by night*'. Their obscurity and their light equally mark out for us the path we are to follow; they are each of them a perpetual commandment, an infallible revelation. If it fell to me to categorize the different periods of the great master's thought, as revealed in his Sonatas, Symphonies, and Quartets, I should not, in all honesty, come to a halt with the now fairly generally adopted division into *three styles,* which you have followed—but, simply taking note of the questions raised thus far, I should frankly ponder the big question which is the axis of criticism and musical aestheticism at the point to which Beethoven has led us: namely, how far does the traditional or accepted form necessarily determine the manner in which the thought is organized?

The solution to this question, as it emerges from the works of Beethoven himself, would lead me to divide those works not into three styles or periods —the words *style* and *period* here being corollary and subordinate terms, of vague and equivocal meaning—but, quite logically, into two categories: the first, that in which the traditional and agreed form contains and governs the master's thought; the second, that in which the thought stretches, breaks, recreates, and shapes form and style in accordance with its needs and inspirations. Proceeding thus, we doubtless come straight to those unceasing problems of *authority* and *liberty.* But why should they frighten us? In the realm of the liberal arts they happily involve none of the dangers and disasters that their oscillations give rise to in the political and social world, for, in the domain of the Beautiful, genius alone has authority; thus, with the removal of this dichotomy, notions of authority and liberty are brought back to their original identity. Manzoni, in defining genius as 'a stronger imprint of Divinity', has eloquently expressed this very truth. . . .

Please accept, my dear Lenz, the sincerest expressions of feeling, and the warmest thanks, of

Your very affectionate and obliged   F. Liszt

284. To Richard Wagner. Weimar, 27 December. ^G Forgive me, dearest friend, for my long silence. That I can do so little for you, to help you, is deeply distressing to me! Your last letter (of about 6 weeks ago) brought home to me very clearly all your sorrow and misery! Over your wounds and afflictions I wept bitter tears. For the time being, alas, the only remedy open to you is to endure and persevere. How sad for a friend to be able to say no more than this! Of all the tiresome and disagreeable things I am having to put up with, I shan't speak to you—don't think of them either—and today I want before all else to tell you something agreeable: that some time next summer I shall pay you a visit (probably in June). I shan't be able to spend a long time in Zurich, where you alone are of interest to me. It is possible—*but must not yet be spoken of*—that on the way back I may direct some kind of festival in Karlsruhe. Can you by that time prepare me an orchestral work for it? Perhaps your Faust Overture, for I should be glad to have a new work of yours performed along with the Overture to *Tannhäuser.* . . .

Reports in several newspapers, that I am leaving Weimar and settling in Paris, are quite unfounded. I am remaining here, and can do nothing but remain here. What brought me to this carefully considered decision, you can guess without difficulty. Before all else I must faithfully fulfil a serious duty. In this feeling of the most profound and most steadfast love, belief in which fills my whole soul, my exterior life must either be lifted up or go under. May God protect my honest intentions!

How far have you got with your *Nibelungen?* What joy it will give me to be able to grasp your creation directly through you! For Heaven's sake don't let yourself be distracted from it, and go on confidently *forging your wings*!

All is transitory; God's word alone remains eternal—and God's word is revealed in the creations of genius.

Yesterday we had a performance (on a non-subscription night and to a *packed* house) of your *Tannhäuser.* New scenery had been painted for the revised conclusion, and for the first time I had the whole of the Second Act finale (a glorious, masterly finale!) and the whole of Elisabeth's prayer in the Third Act done without a cut. The effect was quite extraordinary, and I think you would not have been dissatisfied with the whole performance. . . .

On 1 January Joachim goes to Hanover as orchestral leader. A very able violin virtuoso, Ferdinand Laub, has been engaged for our orchestra. . . .

I am very glad that my comments on your Faust Overture have not displeased you. In my opinion the work would gain from a couple of passages being *extended.* . . .

Au revoir then in a few months. I think of that moment with joy. . . .   F.L.

1853

June. The 20-year-old Johannes Brahms visits the Altenburg, and is amazed and delighted by Liszt's rendering, at sight, of his Scherzo in E flat minor and part of his Sonata in C.

Early July. Liszt visits the exiled Wagner in Zurich.

8 July. The Grand Duke Carl Friedrich dies; his son Carl Alexander becomes the new ruler of the Grand Duchy.

Late July to mid-September. Liszt holidays in Carlsbad and Teplitz (Teplice).

October. He directs the music festival in Karlsruhe at which his *An die Künstler* is performed. With Bülow, Cornelius, Joachim, and others, he then proceeds to Basel for a rendezvous with Wagner, who accompanies him and the two princesses to Paris.

December. Liszt visits Leipzig for performances (on the 1st and 11th) of works by Berlioz, who is also present. Here, too, he renews acquaintance with Brahms.

WORKS. *Domine salvum fac regem* (S23), for tenor solo, male chorus, and organ/orchestra; *Te Deum II* (S24, ?1853), for male chorus and organ. *An die Künstler* (Schiller) (S70), for soloists, chorus, and orchestra. The symphonic poem *Festklänge* (S101). PIANO: Ballade No. 2 in B minor (S171), Sonata in B minor (S178, 1852–3), *Huldigungsmarsch* (S228), and transcription (S421) of the *Andante finale* and March from Raff's opera *King Alfred*.

PUBLISHED. Hungarian Rhapsodies Nos. 3–14 (S244/3–14).[1]

WRITINGS. *A Letter on Conducting; a Defence. Sobolewski's 'Vinvela'* (published in 1855).

285. To Richard Wagner in Zurich. Weimar, 23 January [G]

Dearest Friend!

I cannot thank you for your more than royal present other than by accepting it with the deepest and most heartfelt joy. You yourself can best feel the overwhelming impression made on me by receipt of your glorious gifts, and how I greeted the 3 scores with eyes full of tears! Long ago the Florentines carried Cimabue's *Madonna* in triumphal procession through the city amidst the ringing of bells;[2] were it only granted to me to prepare a similar celebration for your

---

[1] Including a new version of No. 9, first published in 1848.

[2] Cimabue's *Madonna with Child and Angels*, now attributed to Duccio, so delighted the people of Florence, that it was taken to the church of Santa Maria Novella (for which it had been painted) in a solemn procession, 'to the sound of trumpets and amid scenes of great rejoicing' (Vasari, *Vita di Cimabue*).

works and for you! In the mean time the 3 scores will repose in their own special *niche* here with me; and when I come and see you I shall give you more details.

To begin with, the 3 works must be given a decent performance here. . . . *Der fliegende Holländer* presents no great difficulties to our now well-drilled artistes, and I am promising myself a better performance of it, relatively speaking, than of either *Tannhäuser* or *Lohengrin*. The latter work, however, goes far better than it did at the first 4 performances—and all in all there's no reason to be dissatisfied. . . .

Until the end of May I have to stay in Weimar, much though I long to see you again. The wedding festivities for the marriage of Princess Amalia (daughter of Duke Bernhard, brother of our Grand Duke) with Prince Hendryk of the Netherlands (brother of the reigning King of Holland and of our Hereditary Grand Duchess) are to take place in May, when *Lohengrin* or *Tannhäuser* will probably be put on again, as well as a grand orchestral concert in the hall of the Schloss. . . .

Once more I thank you with all my heart—and remain unwaveringly

Your truly devoted   F. Liszt

286. To Adolf Stahr in Berlin. Weimar, 4 March

Very dear friend,

A few days ago Wagner sent me his great work *Der Ring des Nibelungen, ein Bühnen-Festspiel für drei Tage und einen Vorabend*. It consists of four dramas ('Das Rheingold'—'Die Walküre'—'Der junge Siegfried'—and 'Siegfried's Tod') of which he has had a few copies run off *for his friends*. Asking me to send you a copy, he writes: 'Stahr ist die erste deutsche literarische Notabilität, die mich als Dichter beachtet hat, wofür ich ihm stets zu Danke verpflichtet bin [Stahr is the first German literary notability to pay attention to me as a poet, for which I shall always be obliged to him].'—And so you will shortly be receiving this gigantic work, your opinion of which would be of great interest to Wagner—an opinion which, I like to hope, will be favourable to him. If after having read it at your leisure you wish to do him the pleasure of writing to him, please be so kind as to send your letter through me, so that I can make use of it for my own instruction.[3]

---

[3] Writing to Wagner on 8 Apr., Liszt remarked: 'Stahr wrote me a longish letter in which he declares quite plainly that your poem is a total mistake etc. I have not sent you this letter, because I regard it as pointless, and can in no way share his opinion.'

I don't apologize for not having replied sooner to the kind letter of yours that Joachim brought me. Unhappily, I am reduced to keeping silent more often than not about the things we most care about!...

The late Duke of Oldenburg usually spent his evenings playing *patience*; the one that fate obliges us to submit to, much more than to play, is less entertaining!... More than once I regarded HRH with an envious eye as he indulged in this harmless amusement at the Belvedere,[4] while in a corner of the salon quite good music was being performed. He has gone to his rest now, and I have to continue *my* patience. May God help men of goodwill!

Frau Stahr, accompanied by her elder daughter, has twice called to see me, and as a way of thanking her for the charming present which came to me from Jena for Christmas Day, I am going to send her some pieces of mine that have just been published. . . .

The plaster model for the Goethe and Schiller monument that Rietschel has sent here, I like enormously; it has met with almost universal approval. In a couple of years the statue will be finished and unveiled. That would be a fine moment for the Goethe Foundation; but probably, like others, it will be allowed to pass, for want of money they say. However, the Hereditary Grand Duke is persevering in his plans for it; and has even got Schober to make a German translation of my essay on the *Fondation Goethe*. Let us, therefore, resign ourselves to further waiting, while looking at 'l'herbe verdoyer et le soleil foudroyer!'

Weimar was crowded even more than usual with Royal and Most Serene Highnesses on the Grand Duchess's birthday (16 February), and a score of them could be counted in the grand-ducal box at the performance of Wagner's *fliegender Holländer* that evening. The King of Saxony[5] is expected in a few weeks —and in May celebrations, similar to those you witnessed two years ago, will be held for the marriage of Princess Amalia (Duke Bernhard's daughter and, incidentally, a woman of very fine mind) to Prince Hendryk of the Netherlands. . . . Shortly afterwards I shall take wing to Zurich, where I want to spend a few days with Wagner and in his company breathe some mountain air for a while. We are putting on his three works (*Der fliegende Holländer, Tannhäuser, Lohengrin*) *this very week*. Perhaps it will one day be decided to do them in Berlin —and, if so, it is very probable that I shall go there, for Wagner has made my participation in the preparation of his operas a *sine qua non* for their performance in that city. . . .

Do please, dear friend, remember me affectionately to Fräulein Lewald, and believe me, invariably, yours very cordially   F. Liszt

---

[4] Grand-ducal Schloss in the outskirts of Weimar.
[5] Who was at this time, and until his death in a carriage accident a year and a half later, Friedrich August II.

287. To Heinrich Brockhaus in Leipzig. Weimar, 22 March

My dear Herr Brockhaus,

In thanking you for so kindly sending me the entry under my name in the *Conversations-Lexikon* [Encyclopedia], I particularly wish not to go beyond the limits of the most scrupulous delicacy, which in matters of this kind should, it seems to me, be kept to all the more properly seeing that they are far more often exceeded. Consequently, all I shall do is draw your attention to three factual errors in the article concerning me: firstly, my alleged capacity as an ex-St Simonian; secondly, my imagined journey to America; thirdly, my diploma from the University of Königsberg, which my biographer has arbitrarily changed into a diploma of *Doctor of Music*, which was not the one awarded to me.

I have never had the honour of being a member of the association, or to be more exact, the religious and political family of St Simonism. Despite my personal liking for this member or that, my zeal did not go further than that shown at the same period by Heine, Börne, and a score of others whose names are in the *Conversations-Lexikon*, who restricted themselves to going fairly frequently to hear the eloquent sermons given in the Salle Taitbout. I can affirm that among my numerous tailors' bills there is none for any *burbot-blue* coat; and, since I have mentioned Heine, I should add that my fervour has remained far short of his, for I have never had the least desire to '*commune through space with Père Enfantin*' by correspondence or dedication, as he has done!

Furthermore, I can also assure you that my practical course in European geography has not extended beyond it, and that the other 4 or 5 parts of the globe are totally unknown to me. And when you come to see me in Weimar, I shall be able to show you among other awards the one from the University of Königsberg, by virtue of which I have the honour to belong, exceptionally, to the class of Doctors of *Philosophy*, an honour for which I have always been particularly grateful to this illustrious University.[6]

As for the summary judgement this article passes on myself and my works, you will easily understand that I can accept it only as *transitory* and with the necessary reservations, however obliged I am to the author for his kind intentions. After having attained, or so my biographer avers, a primary objective of my youth—that of being called the Paganini of the Piano—it is quite natural, it seems to me, that I should seriously aspire to being called by my *own name*, and that I rely enough on the results of persevering determination and work to

---

[6] One hesitates to contradict Liszt about the degree conferred upon him (Mar. 1842) by the university in question, but K. G. J. Jacobi's presentation speech, as reproduced in Lina Ramann's *Franz Liszt als Künstler und Mensch*, clearly states that the honorary doctorate was of Music, albeit awarded by the Philosophical *Faculty*.

hope that in one of the next editions of the *Conversations-Lexikon* a place will be made for me that is more in accordance with my aims.

Accept, dear Herr Brockhaus, the sincere and affectionate regards of

Yours truly   F. Liszt

288. To Princess Carolyne in Weimar. [Karlsruhe] Thursday, 30 June.

This morning I was awakened with your letter—a splendid sun of love: it wasn't yet 7 o'clock when I received it. At about 8.30 Eugène[7] came to take coffee with me; later I had to go and see two riding-schools, to justify my choice, already made, of theatre for the proposed concerts. At midday I was to wait upon the Grand Duchess [of Baden]—but before that we went with Eugène to the picture gallery, where I admired a very beautiful Berchem and had pleasant thoughts of you. Eugène made several discerning observations about German painters—for example, that their cartoons were generally composed and carried out extremely well, whereas their paintings rarely rose above a more or less admitted mediocrity. As for Overbeck's style, he characterized it as 'the affectation of clumsiness'. The fresco at the top of the staircase, depicting the inauguration of Freiburg Cathedral, was painted by Schwind. It is nobly felt and thought, but has rather a dull effect—and can also be reproached with not causing eyes and mind to concentrate on any one point. . . . As we were coming out, Leiningen apostrophized a head of the dead Luther—admirably painted by Cranach, who was called *Müller* and born in Cranach!—with the energetic monosyllable S.....! In his opinion, people would have done better to smoke him like a Mainz ham than extol him for the Reformation. 'Opinions are free'—according to what Her Imperial Highness thinks. The Grand Duchess is extremely gracious and kind. She and I gossiped a good deal about Weimar and Gotha, and I am pleased to imagine that she will on the whole have retained a good impression of the three-quarters of an hour I spent with her. . . .

I received two letters this morning: one from Joachim, who is forced to stay in Göttingen, the other from Wagner, who is expecting me the day after tomorrow. I am touched by the pleasure my visit seems to give him. If only you had been able to come with me.

So Magne will be confirmed tomorrow. Bless her in the name of the Father, the Son, and the Holy Ghost—Power, Wisdom, and Love. . . .   F.L.

---

[7] Prince Eugène Wittgenstein, Carolyne's nephew by marriage.

289. To Princess Carolyne. [Zurich] 8.00 a.m., Sunday, 3 July. May the peace and blessing of God be with you, and with your child! I had no more time to write to you from Karlsruhe, on Friday the 1st—and after lunching with Leiningen, and chatting with him at great length, I left at about 1 o'clock for Basel, and from there with the post, at 10.00 p.m., for Zurich. The journey takes nine hours. . . .

Wagner was waiting for me at the arrival point, and we almost smothered one another with our embraces. In his voice there is now and then the cry of a young eagle. On seeing me again he wept, laughed, and stormed with joy—for at least a quarter of an hour. We went to his place straightaway and spent the whole day together. He is capitally lodged, has acquired some splendid furniture—among other things a sofa, or rather a *chaise longue*, and a small armchair in green velvet—and has had the piano scores of *Rienzi*, *Tannhäuser*, and *Lohengrin* superbly bound in red. He is keen to keep up a show of luxury, but a very moderate one—more or less as you are keen not to deprive the Erholung balls etc. of the ornament of your person. He looks well, while having got rather thinner in the last 4 years. His features, particularly his nose and mouth, have taken on a remarkably clear-cut and energetic character. He dresses rather elegantly, and wears a hat of a faintly pinkish white. His demeanour is by no means democratic—and he has assured me twenty times over that since he has been living here he has completely broken with the refugee party—and even got well in with the bigwigs of the local bourgeoisie and aristocracy. His relations with the musicians are those of a great general who has only a dozen candle-makers to discipline. His logic regarding artistes is merciless in its acerbity. As for me, he loves me with heart and soul, and doesn't cease to say: 'Sieh, was du aus mir gemacht hast [Look what you have made of me]!'—when it is a question of matters pertaining to his reputation and his popularity. Twenty times a day he has thrown himself on my neck—then rolled on the ground, caressing his dog Peps and talking nonsense to him turn and turn about—and abusing the *Jews*, which is for him a generic term with a very extended meaning. In a word, a grand and magnificent nature, something like a Vesuvius spitting out fireworks, emitting sheafs of flame and bouquets of roses and lilacs. 'Die Kunst ist nur Elegie [Art is only elegy]', he said to me among other things—and when developing for me this theme of the infinite sufferings an artist has to endure at every hour of his life, he led me to say to him: 'Ja, und der gekreuzigte Gott ist eine Wahrheit [Yes, and the crucified God is a Truth].'

His wife[8] is no longer beautiful, and has grown rather stout—but she is a good manager, and does her own housework—even the cooking. For today, he

---

[8] Minna, née Planer, whom Wagner married in 1836.

wanted to kill the fatted calf and throw a big party. We had difficulty in moderating him on this score, and in reducing the dinner invitations to 10 or 12. Hermann will wait at table, for he has no male servant.

290. To Princess Carolyne in Carlsbad. [Zurich] Monday morning, 4 July.

. . . I didn't go to see *Lohengrin* at Wiesbaden—but yesterday we did better, Wagner and I, by setting ourselves to sing the whole of the duet between Elsa and Lohengrin. 'Ma foi, c'était superbe,' as our poor friend Chopin used to say, and we understand one another like twin brothers. In the evening we went to see Herwegh, who is living with his wife in a house beside the lake, and has accumulated a mass of scientific books, chemical and optical appliances, etc., etc., just like the late Dr Faust. . . . I found him changed to his advantage, his head almost bald—the lower part of his face framed by a big beard, and rather robust in body. For several years he has been devoting himself uninterruptedly to natural history studies, and latterly has also given much attention to Sanscrit and Hebrew. He is planning a long epic work, something like the *Divina Commedia*. Aiming just a little high, don't you think?

Around Zurich the lake much resembles Lake Como—minus the wealth and variety of vegetation. It would seem that one could live here happily—and were I to see you here that is what I should doubtless be. I have always been very fond of lakes, and can easily become intimate with their waves and their physiognomy. They are more in harmony with the tone of reverie which is habitual to me, than the great rivers or the ocean. . . .

Wagner made it known that during my stay here he would keep open house from morning to night. I feel some misgivings about the expense I am putting him to, because there are always a dozen people at table for lunch at 1.00 and supper at 9.30. I have asked him to come and dine with me at my Hôtel du Lac today—and tomorrow or the day after I think we shall go on a 24- or 48-hour trip into the mountains, with just Herwegh. This evening he wishes to begin the reading of his *Nibelungen*—I am told that his manner of reading is quite fascinating and simply can't be imagined. The four evenings of readings that he gave to a select, non-paying audience created a great sensation in the city and environs of Zurich—as did his concerts at the theatre, which won him 'all the votes', even those of the *citoyens-Philistins* who were strongly prejudiced against him. A common friend of ours told me in confidence yesterday that during the first years of his residence here, when he was alienating everyone by his ways, Wagner nevertheless did not fail gradually to gain ground in the esteem and consideration of the local people—but that since the concert rehearsals and performances he had become so agreeable that he could no longer be resisted. So great things, my interlocutor says, await him. This week again he will be appointed an honorary member of several music societies—which will have to be no more than a prelude to his diploma of *Ehrenbürger* [honorary citizen] of Zurich—which will take him straight to the dignity of Kapellmeister-in-Chief of the Helvetic Confederation. It seems that he has no kind of relations with the other *émigrés*, whether German or foreign—and he has sworn to me on his *Nibelungen* that he will never again meddle in politics. Several of his friends and patrons belong to the ultra-conservative group. However, he suspects that one of the spies charged with reporting to Dresden or Berlin is personally hostile to him—and bears him a grudge for having in former days looked down on him. Which, be it said in passing, is his usual practice, even with people who put much effort into being obsequious to him. His manner is decidedly domineering, and he keeps anyone and everyone at a distance rather obviously. For me, however, there is complete and absolute exception. Yesterday he remarked once again: 'For me, thou art the whole of Germany'—and he lets slip no opportunity to make this clear to his friends and acquaintances. His whole demeanour, and his overflowing mind, would please you greatly, it seems to me. He has decided that he is plainly an extraordinary man, whose minor preoccupations alone can be appreciated by the public. He protests energetically against the alleged system that boobies have wished to extract from his writings—and we make great game of interpretations and commentaries accorded to the words *Sonderkunst* [special art] and *Gesamtkunst* [total art]. It was not he but Uhlig who invented the word *Sonderkunst*—and Brendel strikes him as a manufacturer of cat food. As for Raff, he is naturally antipathetic to him—and he assumes that his articles have done him, if anything, a bad turn. Among his disciples and fanatics it is Ritter to whom, while taking into account his absurdity, he shows particular affection. The Ritter family give him a regular subsidy of more than 1,000 écus a year—and his standard of living seems to me to require at least double that, if not triple. His cellar is very well stocked, from what Hermann tells me —and he has a pronounced taste for luxury and elegant habits. He is not abandoning his theatre plans in Zurich, and there is a question of building a new hall, for which a number of shareholders would guarantee funds. In any case, he will give himself the pleasure of mounting something *unparalleled*, when he has finished composing his *Nibelungen*, and I gladly support him in this idea. If, as I believe, his importance continues to increase, and to become wholly predominant in Germany and Switzerland, there is no doubt that the 100,000 francs needed to enable him to realize his idea of a *Bühnenfestspiel* [stage festival drama] will be found. I assume that in the summer of '56 he will assemble here the artistes he needs to mount his four dramas—and probably even speculation will turn out well, in a financial respect, since, for a festival such as this, he will easily be able to bring several thousand visitors here. If Monseigneur takes my advice, he will offer him Weimar or Eisenach to carry out this colossal project—but it is to be feared that our customary parsimony and niggardliness may be an obstacle. We shall see where we have got to after the festivities for the Schiller and Goethe monument.

291. To Princess Carolyne. 7.00 a.m., Wednesday, 6 July. . . . It is today that we begin our trip, from which we shall not get back until the day after tomorrow. Herwegh, with whom I am in sympathy (he has extremely good manners), will be coming with us. Our goal is Lake Lucerne. Wagner will be taking his *Siegfried*. Yesterday and the day before he read to us with unbelievable energy and intelligence of expression his *Rheingold* and *Die Walküre*—and this evening we shall have *Der junge Siegfried.*

In response to Magne's delightful little letter, I shall be writing to her. I have purposely delayed our departure in order to wait for the post, which will probably bring me another letter from you. My departure from here is still fixed for Saturday. With Herwegh I have touched on the topic of *Christus*, such as I should like to compose it—and it is not out of the question that he will undertake this work, and do so successfully. Frau Herwegh makes a very good impression on me—and for several years she has been giving her husband exceptional proofs of devotion and self-sacrifice. On some suitable occasion I shall tell you about them. From time to time 'Nélida'[9] writes to him, to tell him of the praise bestowed upon her books by the newspapers. She used formerly to define friends as 'messengers raised to the power of two'. Among other things, Frau Herwegh told me yesterday that when, running an errand for someone, she went to see Proudhon in Sainte-Pélagie,[10] he received her with these words: 'Another one!' Yet he finished by kissing her on the brow, in a way that made her feel she had been given a slap in the face. It seems that so far as women are concerned Proudhon *understands* only the *female*—and that he has habits of a repellent vulgarity. . . .

Yours and at your feet.   F.L.

292. To Princess Carolyne. Friday morning, 8 July. The day before yesterday, at 3.00 in the afternoon and in the brightest sunshine, Wagner, Herwegh, and I embarked on the Lake Zurich steamer to go to Brunnen, one of the loveliest places on Lake Lucerne. It was I who suggested this threesome trip, firstly

[9] The Comtesse d'Agoult.
[10] Paris prison in the rue du Puits-de-l'Ermite, demolished 1899. It was for his violent journalistic utterances that the French socialist Pierre-Joseph Proudhon—remembered, *inter alia*, for the famous paradox 'La propriété, c'est le vol'—had (1849–52) been incarcerated therein.

to get away from the visitors who threaten to hamper us here, and, if the opportunity arose, to be able to talk without restraint to Wagner. I also had a secret need to give myself up to one of those powerful impressions that the great beauty spots make on me, and to this end resigned myself to spending a hundred francs or so. After 2 hours on the boat, followed by 4 or 5 in the carriage, we reached Brunnen, by way of Richterswyl and Schwyz, at about 11.00 in the evening. *You* were everywhere and uninterruptedly present, by those mysterious emanations of the heart which bind us together. . . .

Yesterday morning, Thursday, at 7.00, we hired two boatmen to take us to the Rütli—one has to say Grütli—and the Chapel of William Tell. At the Grütli we stopped at the three springs, and the idea came to me to propose *Brüderschaft* [fellowship] with Herwegh by taking the water in the hollow of my hand at each of the three springs. Wagner did likewise with him. Later we spoke again, and in some detail, about our planned *Christus*—you know what I mean—and I believe he will carry it out soon and splendidly. It will be the work by which I shall speak to *you* of my faith and my love, and if my powers do not fail me there will be *greatness* and *beauty* in it. At William Tell's Chapel we stopped for several minutes. The boatman told us that during Ascension Week 16 masses are celebrated there every day. When we are together once again, remind me of the letters M and N, so that I can acquaint you with a fragment of conversation we had in this chapel. By 10.30 we were back in Brunnen, whence via Lake Zug we returned here at 6.00 in the evening. . . .

At this very moment a telegram has reached me from Talleyrand, informing me of the death of the Grand Duke.

293. To Princess Carolyne. Frankfurt, 8.00 p.m., 13 July. . . . There was a short concert in the theatre yesterday. I heard la Wagner[11] sing three Schubert *Lieder*. She is more a conventional talent than someone outstandingly gifted. She has, to be sure, some bell-like sounds in her throat, but all in all she made on me the impression of those German landscapes which I love no more than you do—something like Königstein, if you accept this simile. As she was to leave again this morning, I went to see her in her 'camerino' at the theatre, where she very kindly invited me to go and see her at her place after the concert, to speak to me more comfortably. She justified herself after a fashion for not having sung *Tannhäuser* here—which I find a real scandal, and which I had no scruples about saying. I tried to be at once polite and plainly explicit with her—and she finished

---

[11] The singer Johanna Wagner, adopted daughter of Richard Wagner's brother Albert.

by offering to come and sing Elisabeth and *Ortrud*! in Weimar during the winter—which I accepted, subject to Ziegesar's approval. I shall certainly have no better luck with celebrated female singers. This category of artistes has lagged completely behind my preoccupations and aspirations during the five years that you have made me understand true glory. The tawdry finery of the theatre, some publicity and applause suffice them—and there is no longer anything in common between us, apart from perhaps a few external details. Wagner defines art: *Ein ohnmächtiges Surrogat des Lebens* [A faint substitute for life]. Most artistes are unfortunately only a poor 'substitute' for art. For the rest, la Wagner and I parted amicably enough, although I told her pretty frankly what was my own way of understanding the works of her uncle, etc. etc. . . .

At midday today I presented myself at Prokesch's. He invited me to lunch, which I accepted. He and his wife were truly charming to me, and I shall neglect no opportunity to cultivate this relationship. It was a small family and head-of-the-mission lunch. At table there was also an abbé, who is, I believe, entrusted with the education of the younger son. I believe I told you that Frau von Prokesch had had the idea of the 'Orpheus' medallion—which you have in your cupboards in the green closet. Consequently, they didn't have to beg me to play a few trifles after the meal; and I invited myself back to their place the next time I am passing through. Tomorrow I shall take a little trip to Mainz and Wiesbaden—and the day after I shall happily return to Weimar. I am longing to see our blue room again, your writing-table, all the wallpaper and carpets you chose, and your daguerreotype, and even those wretched little busts Dosnay did of you and Magnolet! . . .

294. To Princess Carolyne. Blue room, midday, Saturday, 16 July. . . .

About 3 o'clock this morning I entered our room again. Here, everything speaks and sings to me of you. Our memories—are the lakes and well-loved mountains of my soul! You are my unique portion, my glory, my treasure, and the sweetness and peace of my life. I cannot understand how I can be anywhere you are not—but here, at least, resentment at your absence is mitigated by your steps, your words, your tears; and your image is present everywhere.

I went to bed for a few hours, and at about 9.00 found three letters from you in Kostenecka's[12] room. I needed a few hours to read them. . . . This evening I shall go to the Belvedere to see Ziegesar; and Vitzthum has sent to ask me to call on him tomorrow morning. I think I shall simply write my condolences

---

[12] Carolyne's housekeeper, who had come with her to Weimar from Woronince.

to Vitzthum, for him to present them to the Grand Duchess. . . . I shall see if there is any way of coming to join you before the end of this month, and will let you know. The 'white lion' is a charming symbol,[13] and I, too, am of the opinion that I don't need to stay anywhere else. Magne has made a charming invention of the 'owl's insignia'. We shall be able to combine the white lion with Minerva's owl—and put the Golden Fleece to shame. . . .

Tomorrow and the day after I shall put my correspondence in order, and on Tuesday I hope to begin to find a few hours for the compositions I am planning. I found it absolutely impossible to write anything during the fortnight's travelling—and I really need to write music to keep my equilibrium. When I spend several days without music paper, I feel as though I were dried up. My brain becomes congested and I feel incapable of taking pleasure in external things. This is something I have often noticed; it is a kind of sickness which has increased with the years. Music is the breathing of my soul; it becomes at once my work and my prayer. . . .

Please give the Duchesse de Sagan my most appreciative thanks for her remembrance of me. You know that I am not ungrateful, and that I can appreciate certain kindnesses at their full value. I hope she will still be in Carlsbad when I get there—if not, I shall go to Teplitz to see her. In the mean time I am very happy to learn that your relations with her are developing well, just as I hoped and desired. She can learn a lot from you, I am convinced—but many people can also learn a lot from her, for she stands out as one of the most accomplished types of worldly skill and intelligence, and several acts in her life prove that she has not lacked heart. In sum, she is a worthy model for Balzac's subtlest brush —much superior, in my opinion, to women of the type people are in the habit of calling attention to as a 'femme supérieure'. . . .   F.L.

295. To Princess Carolyne. Midday, Monday, 18 July. The gifts of the Holy Ghost are diverse and harmonic—roughly like the 7 notes of the scale. Invoke your guardian angel—an act of piety to which you brought me, and which I enjoy practising—to prompt one according to what is needed at that moment: *strength*, or *prudence, purpose, faith, knowledge, wisdom*, and *awe*. You possess all these gifts. And so walk straight along your path with humility before God, and without anxiety or worry about mankind. Remember that verse of the Gospel in which Christ recommends his disciples not to prepare their sermons to the world's great and mighty, 'for it is the Father who will speak through your mouths'.

---

[13] The princesses' hotel in Carlsbad was named the White Lion.

You are a *living testimony* to faith in love, to conviction in duty. Be therefore calm and steady, so that you can persevere to the end!

What is this Archduke Ferdinand—young or old? In any case you needn't worry about complimenting the *savants*—for with the exception of the Archduke John and Duke John of Saxony, I know hardly any Imperial or Royal Highness who particularly prides himself on his learning. Further, there is no reason to abuse any category of individuals whatsoever, and jokes about scholars are no newer than those about tailors, etc. Since as a Pole you have strong national dislikes, you willingly add to them other additional dislikes—and the *scholar* being always more or less 'Niemiec',[14] you make him the embodiment of a 'profound feeling of tedium'. There is nothing but innocence in that, provided it isn't repeated too often, and doesn't become habitual—for it would then be unjust. And no one more than you makes rather greedy use of the scholars you encounter— when they are of good enough stuff to let themselves be questioned perpetually on Brahma and Vishnu, the stars of medium magnitude, superimposed strata, etc. etc. . . .

At 6.00 yesterday evening, Sunday, Talleyrand, Riencourt, Reményi,* and I went to Ettersburg. Monseigneur had gone for a walk. The footman having shown me the path he had taken, I ventured to follow his track and caught up with him fairly quickly. One of the first things he said was: 'The Word must now be made action.' I drew his attention to the date 28 August,[15] and then handed him Wagner's letter, which seems to me to be very fine and made quite an impression on him. Later, when we sat down on a bench in the shade of an oak, to divert him I read him Berlioz's letter—and he asked me to write to Berlioz on his behalf and tell him that he had every reason to take the Covent Garden hisses in very good part and the failure of *Cellini* for a serious success. When I made to take my leave, Monseigneur asked me if I felt like staying for tea and supper. Talleyrand and Riencourt had come only for the ride, and did not present themselves. I did not reflect long before accepting, at the risk of returning home on foot. At 8.30 I went to the usual salon. There were the *reigning* Grand Duchess, Watzdorf, an aide-de-camp of the King of Prussia, and an envoy from the King of Saxony, Herr von Gersdorf, former Ambassador in London. These two gentlemen on an official mission naturally kept the conversation going— which I for my part was very glad about, for I was by no means in a mood for talking. London, the Caucasus, and the exotic races of men formed the burden of the conversation, to which I had almost nothing to contribute. They retired

---

[14] Polish for 'German'.

[15] Carl Alexander was to be installed as Grand Duke of Saxe-Weimar-Eisenach in a ceremony on 28 Aug., a date which had several associations for Liszt. It was the day of his father's death (1827), of Goethe's birth (1749), and of the première of *Lohengrin* (1850).

at 10.00, and when wishing me goodnight Monseigneur asked me to compose a March for his installation—*Huldigung*—of 28 August. I shall make a start on it tomorrow—and when returning in the calèche with the Prussian Lieutenant-Colonel, Herr Hiller from Gärtringen, I believe I found a pretty good theme which I need only develop. The Grand Duchess is very simply and thoroughly in her place. Her manner has remained the same, for me at least—charming and sensible. Her rank and her personality, which she displays to wonderful advantage, at one and the same time or turn and turn about, require one to speak to her with respectful sincerity and veracity. The King of Prussia will be coming here tomorrow, Tuesday, to pay his visit of condolence to the Dowager Grand Duchess—who has henceforth to be called in German *Grossherzogin-Grossfürstin*—and will be spending a few hours at the Belvedere. The Princess of Prussia will be staying with her mother until 4 or 5 August. . . .

Today I've been able to do virtually nothing. At 5.00 I went to the Belvedere to see Ziegesar and take him the Czerny volume.[16] A heavy rainstorm took me by surprise, and I was forced to spend a couple of hours there waiting for the arrival of a carriage from Weimar—for I had gone on foot, to have some exercise, which turned out very badly for me. So you won't catch me at that again. I have told my mother that I shan't take her back to Paris until the end of August—and even that seems very uncertain. . . .

296. To Princess Carolyne. 10.00 a.m., Friday, 22 July. . . . Yesterday I finished my March for 28 August.[17] It has more than 200 bars in 4 time, and seems to me to have turned out pretty well. The military bandmaster will arrange it for his band, and Raff will score it for the theatre orchestra. I have written it only for piano, giving just a few instrumental indications. It is more than twice as long as the March from Mendelssohn's *Midsummer Night's Dream*—and I believe it will make rather a fine effect. I spent the whole day in our room, and propose to do the same until Tuesday, barring summonses from the Belvedere and Ettersburg. God knows, and so do you, that I am not at all ungrateful, and that it comes naturally to me sometimes to magnify immeasurably the least word, the most trifling gift. But when I see you suffering from and crushed by the multiple blows of the most odious harassment—my heart bleeds, and it is only with an effort that I can keep silent. We'll talk of my hopes for the new reign. The date of 28 August is auspicious—and I am confident that the Prince will

---

[16] The *Gradus ad Parnassum*, dedicated to the Grand Duchess Maria Pavlovna.
[17] In the event, the March was not performed at the ceremony, as Carl Alexander explained to Liszt: 'Fearing that having music in the castle itself would offend my grieving mother, I decided to omit your March.'

hold fast to his excellent intentions. No one in the world has the power to extinguish[18] this sacred flame in our hearts, which is our dignity, our liberty, our *raison d'être*. We hold it inviolable from our God, and we shall render it up to Him pure and intact on the day of eternity—when we shall be *one*, in the life of truth and love. The appearances of this world change and pass. What care we about its grimaces and the warts on its nose!

I can't understand why M. Wieniawski did not wait upon you. I fully approve your not having been to his concert, and going to Laub's. Give my regards to the latter, who will probably still be in Carlsbad when I get there. Expect me on the 27th, in the evening. I take it that the visa in my passport will not oblige me to spend more than a few hours in Dresden.

Farewell, dear Carolyne. May the dews of Heaven refresh your soul!

297. To Princess Carolyne. [Karlsruhe] 26 September. . . . I assume you will manage to see Ulm on Saturday; as for Stuttgart, there is absolutely no need for you to stop there. We shall be able to go there together another day. If, however, between one train departure and another you have an hour to spare —go and see the statue of Schiller, since it was claimed, a few years ago, that I resembled it. . . .

I am very pleased that you are seeing King Ludwig[19]—and, if he consented to it, that you are seeking to keep up some contact with him. I have always sincerely admired him, and his name will remain great, despite the pettinesses which are attached to his reign. He is the art patron of the century, and he well performed an extraordinary and truly royal task. He can hold out his hand to the Medici and to Pericles and say to them: 'I am your equal!' Things beautiful and great have been for him not merely ways of filling his leisure hours—he has lived with them on familiar terms. . . .   F.L.

---

[18] In her transcription of this letter La Mara here has *attendre* (wait for), which is meaningless; and it can be assumed that what Liszt wrote was *éteindre* (put out, extinguish).

[19] Ludwig I restored Munich's reputation as a centre of the arts, but his infatuation with the adventuress Lola Montez had made him deeply unpopular, and in 1848, the year of revolutions, he had abdicated in favour of his son Maximilian II, father of Wagner's patron Ludwig II.

1854

7 January. Liszt attends the first Leipzig performance of *Lohengrin.*

16 February. He conducts the first Weimar performance of Gluck's *Orfeo* and, as an introduction to that opera, the première of his own symphonic poem *Orpheus.*

Late March. To prepare and conduct the première of Duke Ernst's opera *Santa Chiara,* Liszt spends a fortnight in Gotha.

Mid-May. He makes a brief visit to Leipzig, on the journey reading the recently published *Memoirs* of Berlioz.

Late May. He visits Joachim in Hanover and Litolff in Brunswick.

July. Liszt attends a music festival in Rotterdam; also visits The Hague, Scheveningen, Brussels, Antwerp, Cologne, and Bonn.

August to November. George Henry Lewes and Mary Ann Evans (George Eliot),* in Weimar to do research for Lewes's *Life and Works of Goethe,* are frequent visitors to the Altenburg.

19 October. Liszt completes his Faust Symphony.

20 November. First meeting of the New Weimar Club, founded to enable Liszt and his circle to obtain a 'centralization of common endeavours'. Liszt is elected president and Hoffmann von Fallersleben vice-president.

Among other premières conducted by Liszt this year: the symphonic poems *Les Préludes* (23 February), *Mazeppa* (16 April), *Tasso, Lamento e Trionfo* (final version) (19 April), *Festklänge* (9 November),[1] and the first concert performance of *Orpheus* (10 November); Schubert's opera *Alfonso und Estrella* (24 June); Anton Rubinstein's opera *The Siberian Hunters* (11 November).

WORKS. The symphonic poems *Orpheus* (S98, 1853–4), *Hungaria* (S103) and *Ce qu'on entend sur la montagne* (final version). *Eine Faust-Symphonie in drei Charakterbildern* (Faust Symphony) (S108). SONGS: *Ich scheide* (Hoffmann von Fallersleben) (S319); *Blume und Duft* (Hebbel) (S324). PIANO: *Berceuse* (1st version) (S174). *Années de pèlerinage, première année, Suisse* (S160, 1848–54): 1. *La Chapelle de Guillaume Tell* 2. *Au lac de Wallenstadt* 3. *Pastorale* 4. *Au bord d'une source* 5. *Orage* 6. *Vallée d'Obermann* 7. *Eglogue* 8. *Le Mal du pays* 9. *Les Cloches de Genève.*

ESSAYS. *Gluck's Orpheus; Beethoven's Fidelio; Weber's Euryanthe; On Beethoven's music to Egmont; On Mendelssohn's music to A Midsummer Night's Dream; Scribe and Meyerbeer's Robert le Diable; Schubert's Alfonso und Estrella; Auber's La Muette de Portici; Bellini's I Capuleti e i Montecchi; Boïeldieu's La Dame blanche; Donizetti's La Favorita; Richard Wagner's Der fliegende Holländer;* Clara Schumann.

---

[1] At a gala concert celebrating the 50th anniversary of the arrival in Weimar of Maria Pavlovna.

298. To Princess Carolyne in Weimar. [Gotha] Tuesday, 21 March

Very dear and unique one,

Just a note to wish you goodnight, for it is nearly 10 o'clock. I shall say my prayers to God for a while, and must then chat with you for a while, mustn't I? It's true that when you're not here I have a terrible lack of things to chat about. For today I have nothing to tell you unless it is that on the journey I was accompanied by Herr Gross the younger, who told me that he would be marrying Fräulein Staff, which I didn't know or had forgotten. At Erfurt, 'Soestchen',[2] as Preller says, and Fräulein Schreck were so kind as to come to the station to present me with a bouquet—which caused Herr Gross to say that I was a fortunate mortal. When I finally arrived in Gotha, a superb *negro* met me, on behalf of Monseigneur, and drove me in a pretty little brougham to the Schloss, where I have the same room as a year ago. The negro is my personal servant and permanently installed at my door. His name is Philippe, and he is an old acquaintance of Hermann's—seeing that he was part of the 'show' put on by Hermann's uncle, Becker the conjuror, a professor of magic. At 10 o'clock Wangenheim took me to the rehearsal, from which I returned here at about 1.30. At 5.00 I dined at the Duchess's, who is as ever a most charming and gracious lady. As far as visitors are concerned, there was only a young Pce von Leiningen, in Austrian uniform. The Duke will not get back from Berlin until the evening of the day after tomorrow, and the performance of his opera is to be on Sunday week [2 April[3]]. Between now and this coming Sunday I shall stay here and hardly leave my room, except at rehearsal times.

Today I revised my *Années de pèlerinage*, in which there are only a great many minor corrections to make. Tomorrow evening I shall resume work on my *Montagne*, which I expect to finish by Sunday. . . .

May the guardian angels keep and sustain you! Love to Magnolet—and don't forget   Lazybones

299. To Princess Carolyne [Gotha, n.d.] . . . As Monseigneur is dining at 3 o'clock today, I am taking advantage of the two hours of freedom remaining to me to write to you first of all. Here are a few words for Caroline.[4] I have neither the leisure nor the talent to write a long letter on this topic. Her father

---

[2] Marie Soest, a pupil of Liszt's.

[3] This being Liszt's name-day, to greet the Princess he went briefly to Weimar in the early morning and then returned to Gotha for the performance.

[4] Carolyne was initiating a correspondence with Caroline d'Artigaux, née Saint-Cricq, Liszt's first love, whose acquaintance she made in Paris in 1855.

did both of us much harm, with the most reasonable intentions in the world. I have never borne him a grudge, and for 6 years have done more and better than forgive him. I hope that one day or other fate will bring us closer to Caroline. She is the only person whom I wish you to know. You will do her good and she will be charming to you. Write to her at some length. You know how to speak and write—which I succeed in only rarely, unless you help me. . . .

What an admirable pantomime, the story of your handkerchief! The whole of the *Ring des Nibelungen* couldn't touch it! Be for ever blest!

300. To Eduard Liszt in Vienna. Gotha, 29 March

Very dear friend and beloved cousin,

For quite a time I have been wanting to write to you unhurriedly and at some length, for you are one of the very small number of persons whom it gives me pleasure to tell of my thoughts and feelings. And so I am taking advantage of the first moment of leisure granted to me here to come and chat to you. To begin with I'll explain how it is that these lines come from Gotha. For about a week I have been living here *chez* Monseigneur the Duke, who has asked me to conduct the rehearsals and first performance of his new opera, *Santa Chiara*. This 3-act work, with a text by Frau Birch-Pfeiffer (who, it must be said in paren-thesis, is one of my literary antipathies), will be performed here next Sunday, 2 April, and you will find a mention of it in the newspapers.

The Duke of Gotha . . . is a remarkably intelligent and active prince with the knack of doing something notable. These last twenty-five years his house has been under what can fairly be called a *star*—and he in particular will not fail to behave like a *sagacious* astronomer who doesn't nod off when there is some-thing better to do. The invitation to be his guest for a fortnight was as flatter-ing as it was agreeable, and his acquaintance, on a closer personal footing, offers much of interest. His new work (as also the earlier ones) contains several things that are striking and distinguished—but perhaps lacks certain qualities which can be found only in the creations of the great artists and which alone ensure that a work will last: consistency and originality of style, wealth and relation-ship of ideas, and lastly that indefinable something which counts for more than anything.

In your latest letter you ask me to tell you about Wagner. A lot could be said. By himself alone, through his books (*Oper und Drama*, *Das Kunstwerk der Zukunft*,[5]

---

[5] 'The Art-Work of the Future', a pamphlet dating from late 1849.

Die Kunst und die Revolution) and his three dramas, *Der fliegende Holländer*, *Tannhäuser*, and *Lohengrin*, Wagner has performed the labours of an entire corps of engineers and sappers. At least a dozen years will be needed for his ideas to be digested and for the seeds he has sown to bring forth their harvests. In the mean time, there is already a 'Wagner literature'—I have contributed to it myself, and am waiting to broach the subject more deeply when he has *finished* and mounted a performance of his great *Nibelungen* trilogy, of which he has thus far *finished* only the poem and of which a complete presentation will take *four* evenings. It was not without reflection that I hoisted his banner, and the partial failures that this or that work or idea of his may suffer here and there mean very little so far as I am concerned. The extraordinary impulse he has given to opera, or rather to *drama*, is noble; his genius is powerful, imposing and by its very nature turned towards the sublime; the goal he is pursuing, notwithstanding some contradictions in thought and detail, deeply *Christian*—consequently, true and necessary. To do him full justice, this appreciation would need long pages—you will supply their want. When there is an opportunity I shall send you the volume that Brendel has just published, *Die Musik der Gegenwart und die Gesamtkunst der Zukunft* [Music of the Present and the Total Art of the Future]. Raff, whom you met in Weimar, will also be bringing out quite soon his book *Die Wagner Frage* [The Wagner Question], which you will read with interest.

For a work on harmony and counterpoint etc. I recommend you Marx's *Compositions Lehre.*[6] For a teacher of composition I don't know whom I could direct you to in Vienna. . . .

You ask about the relation between Schumann and Wagner. It's difficult to express in a few words. For my own part I have a *very high opinion* of the talent of Schumann, who is an outstanding master of *musical* style and frequents the higher regions of art. However, I can best convey my impression by saying that I regard him as a kind of *Arius* in the little Church we are trying to build.

The news given by some newspapers about my Faust Symphony is correct—and I hope to have finished this work by the end of the autumn. Revising and making some slight alterations to the nine *symphonic poems* before they are published is taking a lot of my time—but I hope to have brought this task to an end in another six weeks, and soon thereafter shall be devoting myself exclusively to the Faust [Symphony], for which I have already jotted down several themes and combinations. . . .

A thousand best greetings to your wife, dear uncle-cousin—write soon to Weimar, and don't fail to count on the warm, unchanging affection of your

F. Liszt

---

[6] A. B. Marx's *Die Lehre von der musikalischen Komposition* (2nd edn., Leipzig, 1841).

301. To Daniel Liszt in Paris. Weimar, 20 April

My dear Daniel,

That's a beautiful Easter egg you have cooked for yourself with your diligence, and I congratulate you on it with all my heart. Try to add to your library of *prizes*, of which the Sallust you have won in this competition makes such a splendid adornment.[7] I always remember with pleasure a library of this kind which was at my disposal about twenty years ago; it had been given as a college and examination prize to M. de Ferrières, the present French Minister in Weimar. Until now I have always envied its owner; but if you acquire a similar one for yourself I shall be consoled for not having been able to put my own youthful years to greater profit. However much one applies oneself later on, those who have not gone through the progressive steps of a college education always lack a certain fund of knowledge that can easily be called upon and put to good use; and to this day I regret having neglected the lecture courses I should rigorously have attended after the death of my father. But on the one hand I knew no one who possessed the higher outlook which would have enabled them to give me more judicious advice; and on the other, from the age of twelve I was obliged to earn my living and support my parents. This necessitated specifically musical studies, which absorbed all my time up to the age of sixteen, when I began to teach the piano (and even harmony and counterpoint), and, as well as I could, to make my way as a virtuoso both in the salons and in public. In fact, I managed to acquire a fairly lucrative position quite quickly, and to make a reputation as a kind of artistic personality. Nevertheless, I should have done better to apply myself more, and regularly, to cultivating my mind and thus to putting myself more on a level in real learning with the outstanding men with whom I had the advantage of associating when I was still very young. A number of them honoured me with their friendship, and this led me to reflect on different subjects and to compensate as much as possible, by attentive reading, for my lack of regular studies; and to distinguish myself in this too, perhaps, from other members of my *profession* who aspire to nothing very much beyond their semiquavers and the humdrum round of ordinary—*too ordinary*—bourgeois life.

As your own circumstances are more favourable, my dear Daniel, it is right that you are learning more than your father could at your age, and it gives me real joy and sweet satisfaction to see that you are responding so well to what I took pleasure in expecting of you. Continue in the same way, dear child, and vigorously make ready to go out into the world with an adequate ballast of solid

---

[7] Daniel's prize was presumably a copy of this Roman historian's *The Catiline Conspiracy* or *The War against Jugurtha*, the only works of his to have survived.

knowledge. It will not only stand you in good stead in your career but also add pleasure and delight to your life. Make, therefore, a thorough study of *your human-ities*,[8] so that, later, you will be a complete *man* from head to foot.

I embrace and bless you.   F. Liszt

302. To Anna Liszt in Paris. 20 April ^G

Dearest Mother,

Daniel has done well once again. The lad truly is better than his Papa—isn't he, Mama? You prefer him too, and I really ought to be jealous. Well, later, I too want to learn something proper, and he can lend me his Sallust for that purpose. Then perhaps I'll no longer need to 'torment myself with a lot of scrib-bling', as Salomon Heine wrote to his nephew Heinrich. Do you remember, dear Mother, that nice little story that I have probably told you several times? Heine once wrote to his rich uncle in Hamburg to touch him for money. The uncle sent not a farthing, but instead the good moral that it was truly a pity that his nephew had not learnt something *proper*—for then he would 'not need to write books and ask for money'. By the words 'learn something *proper*' the good man meant possessing safe capital in shares and properties. In time, per-haps Daniel too will learn something equally proper; for the present I am con-tent with his achievements and have written to him today.

How is your foot? Can you walk and stand? Fortunately you have Daniel nearby, and with the boy's nimble legs he can be beside you with a single bound. But do spur him on so that he won't fail to win his expected prize in the next competition. After the success he has achieved I am thinking of giving him a present.

Here at the *Alten*burg everything remains as of old [beim *alten*]. At the same time I too am getting old and not much cleverer. But for domestic use my clever-ness is still adequate. A pity that you have become such a dyed-in-the-wool Parisienne and can no longer bear to be anywhere else if some extraordinary mishap doesn't force you to be! If your foot is quite better, come to Weimar and have a good laugh at Wedel[9] for his too scientific, unrefined gallantry!

As you see, dearest Mama, I still have a sense of humour. Write to me soon, kiss the children and me too, for when all is said and done I am your good-hearted child   F. Liszt

---

[8] The expression *faire ses humanités* means above all study of the language and literature of Ancient Greece and Rome.
[9] The surgeon who had tended Anna Liszt after her accident two years earlier.

303. To Blandine Liszt in Paris. May.[10] You are a sensible girl with the right way of viewing things, my dear Blandine. Your letter gives me wholly conclusive and pleasing proof of it. On this long and serious topic of marriage, I have up to now spoken hardly a word to you. On the one hand, I have lacked opportunities to communicate to you in any detail my ideas on this subject, and on the other I was waiting for your own to be expressed with some significance. This is what has just happened in connection with M.L., and you are perfectly right to believe that I love you too much ever to force you into a marriage against your will. Further, you are entirely of my opinion in finding that you are still young enough to wait with impunity.

Marrying in haste is the most foolish and immoral of occupations. And so I have never been able to find any taste for certain ways of doing things which cannot later be undone, and under the burden of which one can one's whole life long be bowed and broken.

If you believe me, therefore, my dear daughter, you will make no haste to enter the married state. All things considered, and barring some fluke of Providence, I by no means desire you to change your name before you find the perfect match for you. Better one 'here it is' than two... 'you'll have nothing's!'[11] Continue to learn and to study. Follow the dictates of your heart. The rest will be found. I hope that it will not be long before we see one another again. In the mean time I embrace and bless you.[12]

304. To Princess Carolyne in Weimar. [Hanover] on getting up at 7.30, Monday, 29 May. . . . Even with a wait of 2 hours at Halle and a meal stop of 40 minutes at Magdeburg, it doesn't take more than 11 hours from Weimar to Hanover; and at 2.15 I found Joachim and Cossmann on the platform. From Magdeburg onwards I had the very agreeable company of Frau von Bonin and her daughter. Herr von Bonin was for many years the aide-de-camp of the Pce of Prussia, and since '48 has been devoting himself to landscape

---

[10] In reply to a letter from Blandine of 13 May in which she had given her father her impressions of a prospective suitor: 'I have twice seen M.L.D. His outward appearance I neither liked nor disliked. A week later we had another meeting, in the Winter Gardens, where a general conversation got going and gave rise to nothing very special. . . . He hasn't that distinction I should like my husband to have, so that I can find him worthy of being your son-in-law. In short, it can't be said that he is common, but it can't be said that he is distinguished. . . .'

[11] A twisted ending to the proverb *Un 'tiens' vaut mieux que deux 'tu l'auras'* (roughly equivalent to 'A bird in the hand is worth two in the bush').

[12] Blandine's next letter, of 26 May, began: 'Your letter has made me so happy that I don't want to lose a moment before expressing all my gratitude, for decidedly M.L. did not please me, and, while recommending him to me for his excellent moral qualities, M. Buquet told Mme Patersi that that indefinable something he lacks, and which strikes one straightaway, I was inevitably bound to notice, as you would undoubtedly have done at a single glance. . . .'

gardening, in the environs of Magdeburg. His daughter has taken a liking to the Turks, and on catching sight of my red fez, which she assumed must be covering a 'true believer', induced her mother to climb into the compartment in which I was sitting in solitary state—thanks to the protection provided for me by the railway staff as a result of Hermann's procedures. Great was the surprise to find so little of native *Turkery* in me—but I flatter myself that after the three hours in the train I did not remain very far below her opinion of the real Turks.

I arrived in Hanover at the height of the festivities for HM the King.[13] There was a gala celebration at the theatre yesterday evening, lasting from 7.00 until gone 11.00. They did Spontini's *La Vestale*, with Fräulein Ney of Dresden as Julia, and Bötticher of Berlin as high priest. I stayed to the end, and the performance interested me. It is certainly the splendid high-flown style of Gluck, but already made a little conventional—something like David in painting. It has talent, passion, subtle and profound intentions, genius even—but the whole thing is slightly stilted and as though *made uniform*.

A favourite promenade of the residents of Hanover is called *die List*—we are to go there today. The rest of the day I shall spend making music tête-à-tête with Joachim, who is very pleasantly housed in the most attractive district in the city. Above his piano hang Beethoven and Shakespeare, between two views of Egypt: Karnak, Thebes, sphinx with a human head and a ram's head—and Medinet Abou, Thebes, later constructions. The Arnims have put verses beneath these lithographed photographs, which I shall try to acquire too, to offer them to you, you who have *penetrated* all the wisdom and learning of Egypt.

I am expecting a letter from you for this evening, and until lunch am going to the piano. Love to dear Magnolet, and don't forget   Lazybones

In early July Liszt attended a music festival in Rotterdam, journeying thither via Mainz, where he wished to visit the Schott publishing-house.

305. To Princess Carolyne in Weimar. Hôtel du Rhin, Mainz, 8.00 p.m., Saturday, 8 July. . . . At supper I skimmed through the *Journal des Débats* of 8 July, in which there is a short article by Saint-Marc Girardin on the King of Prussia's visit to the Wartburg. 'This castle', it says, 'is beloved of all German patriots on several grounds, and we are not surprised that the Grand Duke of Saxe-Weimar, who studies the history of Germany *no less zealously than*

---

[13] In celebration of the thirty-fifth birthday, on 27 May, of the blind George V, last King of Hanover (which in 1866 he lost to Prussia).

successfully, has had the splendid idea of restoring the Wartburg and even of housing therein a museum of old arms and armour. The Wartburg will be for the
Germany of the Middle Ages what Versailles is for 17th-century France!' There
follow the Wartburg's four phases: (1) its foundation by Ludwig, Landgrave of
Thuringia, mingled with the origins of the house of Saxony; (2) St Elisabeth,
'for in his enlightened cult of history, the Grand Duke has not forgotten that
Catholicism has had its times of greatness and holiness in Germany, and he wants
the Wartburg to represent the memory of those times too; (3) the Minnesingers,
with their great poetic tournament; (4) Luther. The Wartburg will thus represent four great moments in the history of Germany: the feudal system and the
origins of the house of Saxony, Catholic holiness with Elisabeth of Hungary,
the poetry of the Middle Ages with the Minnesingers, and finally Protestantism
with Luther.' To crown it all, Saint-Marc Girardin makes the King of Prussia
say when leaving the Wartburg, where he had shown full approval of the archi-
tects and the plan of restoration devised by the Grand Duke: 'I have just learnt
a good deal more about our Middle Ages, which I thought I knew pretty well
already'—praise for the Grand Duke of Saxe-Weimar's restoration scheme which
couldn't be more appropriate!!

The Dutch boat departs from Mainz at 9.00 tomorrow morning, and gets to
Rotterdam at 3.00 the day after. Lazybones has already booked his cabin, and
when passing the Loreley will think of 'Juliet'! Good night, and may God bless
you, you and Magnolet. . . .

306. To Princess Carolyne. 9.30 a.m., Sunday, 9 July, in sight of Mainz.

The Dutch steamer, the *Agrippine*, is setting out. Gazing upon them, I am still
greeting the towers and domes that you submitted to your architectural investigations—and in thought am kneeling on the steps of the altar at which you
prayed. Mainz has always made a special impression on me, something like a
question mark between the real and the fanciful. Frauenlob, Gutenberg—that
liberator of the liberators of the human conscience—; the Rhine, whose width
is considerable here, but which nevertheless seems to seek to inspire awe by its
just proportions alone, rather like an oratorio by Handel or a poem by Pope;
the fortress of the German Diet—in 1814 the fortress was surrendered by France
to General Hünerbein, who in 1815 restored it to the Grand Duke of Hesse;
memories of my adventures with Lichnowsky, whose acquaintance I made at
Mainz; and Schott, publisher of Beethoven's *Missa solemnis* and Ninth Symphony,
as well as of the *Muette de Portici* and the Sonata by Schulhoff ... and of my
Années de pèlerinage. All these things and these names are reflected in my mind
at the sight of Mainz—roughly as the clouds, crags, and hillsides are reflected

in the waters of the river. The first time I crossed the Rhine was on the bridge at Mainz, at the end of March 1840. It was about one o'clock in the morning. Hermann [Cohen], nowadays Brother Augustin, was accompanying me—for he had come to Prague to see me, to get out of a scrape he was in as a result of some stupidities on his part. I was returning to Paris for the first time after 3 or 4 years of absence—during which I had become a kind of phantom of celebrity in Vienna and Pest, and to some extent elsewhere too. I remember that in a hushed silence I long listened to the noise of the river, which that night was rather majestic. My own destiny has never filled me with either fear or anxiety. With some kind of presentiment of the unknown, which secretly urged me on in all moments of solitary reflection, I was on my way to meet things which I already knew only too well. This resilience did not break in me until a day rather close to us, that in which I felt that I was loved even more than I was forgiven and understood—that in which you revealed to me the limitless love which is my soul's thirst. May you be everlastingly blessed for it!

The Dutch steamers are charming. Believe it or not, I am writing to you in a kind of small 'Crystal Palace', built on to the bridge, from which one has a perfect view of the landscape, while being sheltered from the wind and rain. Happily, we today need fear neither the one nor the other, it being a mild Sunday morning. At 6.00 I was awakened in bed by a few brightish rays of sunshine, which I sent in thought to you and Magnolet, while thanking God for thus uniting our hearts. Before getting up, I skimmed through part of the piano score of Halévy's *Juif errant*.[14] It is a work done carefully, calculatedly, and with talent —but, decidedly, the old concept of opera, with its divisions into arias, trios, duos, etc. ceasing and unceasing at every turn, with the symmetry and artifice of garden ornamentations in pebble, like those frequently seen in the villa-palazzi of northern Italy—such a concept has become inadequate, and is not to the taste of present-day ideas and feelings. New wine shouldn't be put into old bottles! *L'Etoile du Nord*[15] and the *Juif errant* are here to bear testimony to Wagner, who is truly something very different from a mere dreamer. . . .

A boat is just passing us on which I can read in golden letters: *Schiller*—3 shots are then fired so that the echo isn't left idle. That reminds me of the rules of a conservatoire in Rome, which used to oblige its singers to do their exercises in places known for their echo—so that they might better get to know their faults! Worthy *naïveté* of an age which displayed its vanities less than does our own. . . .

The Rhine country gives me, poetically speaking, the impression of attractive stoves in green faience. It is very historic and tolerably beautiful—but it is

---

[14] Fromental Halévy's opera *Le Juif errant* (The Wandering Jew), dating from 1852.
[15] Three-act opera by Meyerbeer, first performed in Paris, Feb. 1854.

not here that I would find you a residence. Talk to me of the countryside at Pisa, of the Roman Campagna, of Constantinople—and even of Venice, Lake Lucerne, Lisbon, or the forest of Fontainebleau! Later on we must go to Italy. However vulgarized and abused it may be, that land still retains primordial energies and qualities which speak to the profoundest depths of the soul. Italy is to nature what the Vénus de Milo is to art: however far from her one may be, one never leaves her! . . .

307. To Princess Carolyne. Rotterdam, 7.00 a.m., Tuesday, 11 July. A very good day to you, dearest one—here is news of Lazybones. At Cologne the evening before last, [Anton] Rubinstein* came on board the *Agrippine*. He was coming back from Berlin, where he had spent a few hours in honour of the beautiful eyes of Fräulein Emilie Genast. . . .

My night from Sunday to Monday was pretty bad. The boat's engine made a terrible row, and the reverberation in my cabin was quite diabolical—so much so that I was even seized by fear, and somersaulted out of bed to see if there had been some accident.

Yesterday offered me nothing of interest except, perhaps, meeting four or five musicians who are attending the music festival. Ritter, from Magdeburg, whom you saw in Weimar and at Merseburg, was one of them. At 3.30 we reached Rotterdam. My host M. van der Hoop was waiting for me on the quay, the time of arrival having been telegraphed to him by one of the Dutch steamboat agents who had done part of the journey with me. This M. van der Hoop is not the banker, nor even a relative of the latter. His status is that of a notary. His house seems very well run, and Mme van der Hoop most agreeable. Nevertheless, I assume that I shall not be staying here long, seeing that there is no room for Hermann, who has accommodation in the Hôtel des Pays Bas rather far from here, which is extremely inconvenient for me. Rubinstein is also staying at that hotel.

An hour after my arrival I went to the rehearsal of *Israel*.[16] It lasted until 10.00. I shall tell you later about the work and the performance. . . .

308. To Princess Carolyne. [Rotterdam] Monday, 17 July. This is how my day went yesterday, Sunday. At 10.00, left by train for The Hague with Hiller plus a gentleman and a lady whose portrait Scheffer has painted. In less than an hour we were in The Hague, where we went by carriage to Scheveningen,

---

[16] Handel's oratorio *Israel in Egypt*, first performed in London, 1739.

a journey which takes no more than 25 minutes. The road is charming—a splendid avenue of trees, which the Baedeker Guide informs me was planted by Charles V, takes one almost to the beach. The first people I saw when getting out of the carriage were the little Hereditary Prince of Weimar and Kämpfer. Little Carl August looks absolutely splendid, and runs the whole day long. Then we went up to Scheffer's, with whom I had a long chat. His wife went to Paris a few days ago, because of her mother's illness. Scheffer is staying there in Scheveningen with his daughter Mme Marjolin, a daughter of his brother Henri, and two or three children of his late brother. He looks pretty well, his face ever so slightly bloated and his hair very definitely grey. Cutlets were served for lunch, and then we took a stroll on the beach, which is very pleasant for walkers. I hardly looked at the sea, which seemed to me much like a lithograph. Scheffer gave me some all but unbelievable details about M. de Lamennais,[17] which I shall tell you when I get back. The Introduction and the entire translation of Dante are finished, and will soon be published. . . .

It seems that four years ago Monseigneur had the notion of getting Martersteig to paint the Wartburg, which Scheffer strongly advised him against. For my part, I didn't press him to come to Weimar—but simply told him that Rietschel, of whom he thinks very highly, had just finished a delightful bust of Magnolet. Incidentally, I ought to give you a severe scolding for the negotiation on the sly over the portrait of Chopin. I am most decidedly opposed to it—and in any case Scheffer cannot deliver it before finishing it as he intends. We'll talk about it further.

At 6.00 I dined at Pce Hendryk's, there being just a few of us. I turned the conversation to all manner of topics. Before taking leave of me, the Princess asked after you. . . . The Prince was so kind as to show me several fine paintings— among others a Rembrandt self-portrait and a *St Sebastian* by Luini, both from his father's collection. I also saw Nieuwerkerke's equestrian statue of William the Silent; it creates a splendid effect and is nicely positioned—under the arch in the centre of the entrance to the castle built by the late King, and opposite the palace which is presumably the King's residence. In a square there is also an execrable statue of the late King Willem II in uniform. In it he greatly resembles M. Hutschenruyter, military bandmaster, whom we saw in action at the Yacht Club. At 11.00 p.m. I was back here. Mme van der Hoop had arranged a grand soirée musicale. Before my arrival Pischek had sung, several amateurs had played the piano—and to round off I obliged with two pieces: my Etude and the *Patineurs*—Amen! . . .

---

[17] Who had died in Feb. that year.

309. To Princess Carolyne. Brussels, 7.00 a.m. [Thursday] 20 July.

You are so constantly amongst us, through all our thoughts, all our affection, and all our love—that I find it strange and bizarre to have to write to you. Escorted by Belloni, Mme Patersi and the girls arrived punctually at the Hôtel Bellevue at 8.00 p.m. on Tuesday. I, for my part, went from Rotterdam to Antwerp on Tuesday night—a 9-hour journey, from 1.00 in the morning until 10.00. From Antwerp to Brussels takes no more than an hour, so that instead of finding myself late at the rendezvous, I was there several hours early. . . . Yesterday we dined at 6.00, and at 10.00 this morning I shall be taking the whole party to Antwerp—to see the beautiful Rubens in the Cathedral and in the Museum. We have yet to see how we shall spend tomorrow—and the day after that, Saturday, we shall go our separate ways. It is possible that I shall stay for a further day between Bonn and Düsseldorf, and that I shall not get to Leipzig until Wednesday. I called to see Fétis and Mme Pleyel. There will be no excess in our relations, 'for the moment'. Fétis was very ill a few months ago, but I found him fully recovered, sprightly and vigorous. 'That', said Mme Pleyel, 'is the advantage of ugly people—they don't change!' . . .

Friday. I went to sleep over your dear letters, and at 7.00 Blandine came to awaken me. The children are fine—looking well and cheerful. We'll talk about them at greater length in a few days. Just now I am entirely at their service. I chat with them, or rather I speak *in front of* them and *for* them. Mme Patersi is as excellent and perfect as ever, just as you know and love her—keeping always a perfect *order*, even through a certain number of confused ideas. I flatter myself that I am totally in agreement with her on all the main points.

Yesterday we went to Antwerp where we spent the day, which was very fine, strolling in the zoological garden, the most renowned in Belgium, and giving ourselves the pleasure of inspecting lions, tigers, vultures, and ostriches. From there, we went to the Museum to see some superb Rubens: the spear thrust, the Adoration of the Magi, the Trinity—marvellously foreshortened! At 6.30 we dined at M. Kufferath's, with the Schotts. I went to the piano after the meal . . . and played the *Konzertsolo*, my invariable Etude, and the *Patineurs*. I shall be recommencing the session this evening, playing the Ninth Symphony with Rubinstein. . . .

Au fond, I have only one thing to say, but it is one which contains more than a sentence, more than a book, and even more than an entire library—that I need to see you again. Wednesday evening or Thursday afternoon you will see me arrive. Love to Magnolet.

310. To Princess Carolyne. Cologne, 7.00 a.m., Sunday [23 July]. . . .

I had to chat to the children until the last moment. Only at about 11.00 did I make two or three visits [in Brussels], among others to Jósika, the Hungarian novelist, 2 of whose volumes you have read. He and his wife are very well bred. I learnt from them that the 'learned Diotima' had been to Brussels fairly recently, to consult General Bedeau and obtain documents from him, for her history of the '48 revolution.[18]

Have I told you that the 'Marquis de la Tigrière' [Reményi] arrived in Brussels on Wednesday morning? He is always the same, very stylish and altogether magnificent. Belloni, too, for his part is absolutely unchanged. Just fancy, he fancies that he will be appointed *editor* of *L'Art Journal*, which will appear during the Universal Exhibition in Paris! He is seriously convinced of his chances —talks of the falling-off of Meyerbeer, of the *Etoile du Nord* being a mere shooting star (!), of the advent of Verdi, who is to have his *Vespri siciliani* performed at the beginning of spring, etc.

The journey from Brussels to Cologne offered no interest to the passengers, whom an excessive heat made unfit for anything. On arriving at the Hôtel Royal, Rubinstein and I first of all went and had supper. Then Hiller, Franck, and Gouvy arrived, and a little later Marschner, Inkermann, and Diezmann. We chatted until 1.00 in the morning. . . .

I have already told you, I believe, that Fétis and Mme Pleyel *können mir gestohlen werden* [can be stolen from me], as Raff says. I saw them together the day before yesterday for an hour, and have had enough of them for a long time. . . . Au revoir!

311. To Peter Cornelius. [Weimar] Sunday, 3 September ᴳ

Dear Friend,

Rubinstein got here at midday today and longs to see you![19] Don't keep us waiting, and come back on Wednesday at the latest.

At the Altenburg you will meet my son, who is already outgrowing me *au physique*—may he soon do so *au moral* too.

Wasielewski from Bonn also arrived here today, and for Wednesday Genast is planning a *soirée d'artistes*, to which I am to invite you especially.

I for my part have nothing newer to tell you than that I am very fond of you, and that you no longer need to be conspicuous by your absence—for

---

[18] Referring to the Comtesse d'Agoult and her *Histoire de la Révolution de 1848.*
[19] The text of Rubinstein's opera *The Siberian Hunters* had been translated into German by Cornelius.

you will certainly be much more conspicuous by your presence!—(Editorial annotation!—)

A revoir donc, cher ami, et

Bien tout à vous   F. Liszt

Friendly regards from the residents of the Altenburg—and cordial greetings to your mother.

312. To Blandine and Cosima Liszt in Paris. Weimar, 25 September. Greetings, dear girls. Daniel is returning to you with a supply of descriptions and narrations, pictures, parallel definitions, etc., just as in literary courses. I hope that as Weimar's historiographer he acquits himself well, and that what he tells you will give you a few hours of pleasure. He is also to inform you of two things I want you to do—and which I hope you will carry out faithfully.

How goes it with your piano strumming? Do you practise? Is M. Seghers giving you regular lessons? Try to make good use of the coming winter, in which you will not be bothered by other teachers since you are already accomplished and model examples of an excellent education and have finished learning how to express in several languages the ideas which will come to you later.

Music being the universal language, and even to a certain extent able to dispense with ideas, it is by no means my intention to end your studies with M. Seghers. But try to learn by yourselves what even the best teachers cannot convey through lessons; and, until the day when I try to shape your talents to my liking, I kiss you most tenderly.

February. Another Berlioz Week is held in Weimar. On the 17th, Liszt is the soloist in the première of his Piano Concerto No. 1 and Berlioz the conductor; on the 21st, Berlioz conducts his *Symphonie fantastique* and *Lélio* (in which Liszt undertakes both the piano part and that of the Chinese gong).

17 May. At a concert in Leipzig's Catholic church, Liszt conducts his *Ave Maria* (S20/2) for four voices and organ.

26–30 May. He attends the Lower Rhine Music Festival in Düsseldorf.

10–11 June. He visits Eisenach and Gotha.

21 July. Carl Tausig* becomes a pupil.

21 August. Blandine, Cosima, and Daniel Liszt arrive at the Altenburg for a fortnight's holiday with their father. In September the girls take up residence with Frau von Bülow in Berlin.

October. Liszt spends several days in Brunswick where, at a concert on the 18th, *Orpheus* and *Prometheus* are performed.

6 December. He conducts several of his works, including *Les Préludes* and the première of Psalm 13, at a concert in the Singakademie, Berlin.

WORKS. *Missa solennis zur Einweihung der Basilika in Gran* (Gran Mass) (S9), for soloists, chorus, and orchestra. Psalm 13 (S13), for tenor solo, chorus, and orchestra. The symphonic poem *Prometheus* (rev. version). ORGAN: Prelude and Fugue on the name BACH (S260).

ESSAYS. *Berlioz and his 'Harold' Symphony*; *Robert Schumann*; *Robert Franz*; *Marx and his Book 'Nineteenth-Century Music'*; *No Entr'acte Music!*; *'Das Rheingold'.*

313. To Adolf Stahr in Berlin. Weimar, 5 February. ^G These lines, dear friend, bring you my heartiest good wishes for tomorrow[1] and my sincere participation in your joy. I thank you for having thought of me, and ask both of you always to consider me a loyal and devoted friend at your service.

The loss of your friend Hauenschild grieves me too. Shortly before his death he had written to our Grand Duke, and it was quite possible that he might have come to Weimar for a long time. I knew him only through you and a couple of quite charming letters which he was so kind as to write to me after publication

---

[1] Stahr's long-desired marriage with Fanny Lewald was finally taking place.

of the *Fondation Goethe*. This, however, was sufficient for me to admire him as a truly distinguished man of the rarest gifts; and so I again recently expressed to the Grand Duke my wish that He would induce him to come to Weimar. Now he has gone to see the great dead, and certainly feels more at home with them than with the so many half-dead people ambling around whom in this life one cannot avoid! . . .

Our only literary event here this winter was a 5-act play *Duke Bernhard of Weimar*. It was performed 3 times and received with great applause. The author is the young Genast (public prosecutor here), and several pieces of music were composed for it by Raff.[2]

I am expecting Berlioz in a few days; he will be conducting the Court concert for the Dowager Grand Duchess's birthday (on 16 February), and afterwards putting on in the theatre his new oratorio *L'Enfance du Christ*. I for my part am working hard at my *symphonic poems*. Nine of them are already finished, and the scores will be published later this year (by Breitkopf & Härtel of Leipzig). . . . I have also completed a Faust Symphony (in 3 character pieces: 'Faust', 'Gretchen', and 'Mephistopheles') ... *en attendant mieux et davantage*!—

What plans has your wife for the summer? Isn't anything bringing her back to Weimar? I should be delighted to see both of you again. Your daughters are coming here after Easter, and I shall make it my business to make their stay a pleasant one. My mother, too, will probably spend some time in Weimar this summer.

A thousand friendly greetings from the Princess, to which I join the sincerest regards of your very affectionate   F. Liszt

Do you see Hans von Bülow in Berlin? I recommend him to you once again as a personality and a quite remarkable artiste, one whom I count among the small number of those to whom I am truly devoted.

314. To Anton Rubinstein. Weimar, 21 February. Your *fugue*[3] of this morning, my dear Rubinstein, is very little to my taste; I far prefer the 'Preludes' you wrote earlier in that same room which, to my great surprise, I found empty when I came to fetch you for the Berlioz rehearsal. Does this music really jar on you? And after the sample you had at Court on that other occasion, did a resolution to hear more of it seem too hard to take? Or did you take amiss a few remarks I made to you which, I give you my word, were meant in all friend-

---

[2] Wilhelm Genast and Raff became brothers-in-law not long afterwards when Raff married Wilhelm's sister Doris.
[3] The word comes, of course, from the Latin *fuga*, flight.

liness? Whatever the reason, I don't want any explanations in writing, and I send these lines only to let you know that the surprise caused me by your nocturnal flight was by no means an agreeable one, and that you would in every way have done better to hear the *Fuite en Egypte* and the Fantasia on Shakespeare's *Tempest*.[4]

Let me have your news from Vienna (if not sooner) and, whatever *rinforzando* of 'murrendo' may take possession of you, please do not do wrong to the sentiments of sincere esteem and cordial friendship invariably harboured for you by

F. Liszt

315. To Baron Carl Olivier von Beaulieu-Marconnay. Monday, 21 May

Dear Baron,

It is not exactly with absent-mindedness, still less with forgetfulness, that I could be reproached regarding the Programme of this evening's Concert. The indications that HRH the Grand Duchess is so good as to give me are too precious to me for me not to be most eager to carry out all my duties, at the very least. If, therefore, one of Beethoven's Symphonies does not appear on today's Programme, it is because I believed that in this way I would be complying better with HRH's wishes; and I ventured to guess what she did not find occasion to convey to me this time. His Majesty the King of Saxony's[5] predilection for the Symphonies of Beethoven certainly does honour to his taste for the beautiful in Music, and no one could subscribe to that more sincerely than I do. I shall merely observe that on the one hand the Beethoven Symphonies are extremely well known, and that on the other these admirable works are performed in Dresden by an orchestra having at its disposal far greater resources than we have here; and that consequently our performance would run the risk of seeming rather *provincial* to His Majesty. Besides, if, after the example of Paris, London, Leipzig, Berlin, and a hundred other towns, Dresden now stops at Beethoven (to whom in his lifetime people far preferred Haydn and Mozart), that is no reason for Weimar—I mean the musical Weimar that I can modestly claim to represent— to come to a complete stop there too. Nothing better, doubtless, than to respect,

---

[4] Respectively the second part of Berlioz's *L'Enfance du Christ* and a work of his dating from 1830.

[5] Who was now Johann I, a man of remarkable powers and unusual culture compared with most other princes of the time, according to his obituary in *The Times*: 'He was a well-read and acute jurist, an accomplished archaeologist, a profound student of Dante. Personally very few of the sovereigns of Europe could pretend to be superior in intellectual capacity and attainments to King John of Saxony. But political wisdom did not seem to accompany these literary gifts. . . .'

admire, and study the illustrious dead; but why not also occasionally live with the living? This is the method we have tried with Wagner, Berlioz, Schumann, and a few others, and it would seem that it hasn't thus far turned out so badly that we have any reason to change our minds without urgent cause and put ourselves at the tail-end—of many other tails!

The significance of the musical movement of which Weimar is at present the very centre, lies precisely in this initiative of which our public doesn't generally understand very much, but which is none the less acquiring its share of importance in the development of contemporary Art.

For the rest, dear Baron, I shall hasten to put everything right for this evening by following your advice, and for the 3rd item on the programme will ask Messrs Singer and Cossmann to join me in a performance of the magnificent Trio (in B flat, dedicated to the Archduke Rudolf) by Beethoven.

Affectionate regards,

Yours,   F. Liszt

In late May Liszt attended the music festival in Düsseldorf, journeying thither via Halle and Brunswick.

316. To Princess Carolyne in Weimar. At Litolff's, Brunswick, 25 May.

I bless and cherish you, dear unique one! . . . At Halle I went to see Franz, who remarked to me very wittily about [Haydn's] *Creation*: 'Also führt man noch diese Thierbude dem erbauten Publikum vor [So they're still presenting this menagerie to an enthusiastic public]!' To understand this witticism, you need to know that in the *Creation* there are numerous portrayals of animals: a lion, a stag, birds, etc. It is like a small musical Buffon. Franz has promised me that he will return to Weimar during the course of the summer, and that he will give me notes for some articles about his works and his lyrical genius that I have long been intending to write.

Litolff arranged accommodation for me at his place, and it was simpler to accept without too much standing on ceremony. His wife is well bred, reserved, and ladylike. He and I made a little music together this morning, and will be continuing shortly. At 4.00 he got together the regimental band, which is really excellent here and exceptionally well provided with string instruments. It first of all played an overture by Fétis, the programme of which could be summarized thus: 'Will she love me? Yes, she loves me.' The question not being vital for me, I took only a rather objective pleasure in it. Then came two overtures by Litolff: *Les Girondins* and an *Ouverture triomphale* on the Belgian national anthem. These two works by no means lack talent—but they belong somewhat to the *flamboyant* style, which in my opinion is close to being *flambé* [done for], in music. And so I advised Litolff to cultivate this field no more, since he has, in my opinion, better things to do. . . .

317. To Princess Carolyne. [Düsseldorf] Saturday evening, 26 May. About 9.30 I passed Bückeburg. The Eilsen valley has remained *holy* in my heart; and so, immersing myself in it with all my soul, I gazed upon it as long as I could. The railway also runs alongside an avenue of poplars where, during Magne's illness, we on several occasions went for walks. We talked about Chopin; and it was there, too, that you gave me the sensible advice to break completely free from servitude to the public, and even to give up that half-way stage I had rather clumsily stopped at, of playing in public from time to time without either pecuniary or artistic profit—not yet understanding that I should adopt a definite position. In this, as in a thousand other things, you were more than right—and I would gladly box my own ears for not having understood you more quickly. We so loved one another at Eilsen! The whole firmament was in our hearts! And what adorable disputes about *Chopin, Lohengrin,* etc., which were written there!—All these memories made my heart swell with happiness, and as they came back to me the tears gushed from my eyes—and the distant landscape seemed to me like a crater still smoking with our love! The *Harmonies poétiques, Cantique d'amour,* and the Polonaises date from that time!—Oh, if I could ever find in music the *Geistes-Körperlichkeit* [spiritual embodiment] of what you made me feel! . . .

318. To Princess Carolyne. [Düsseldorf] Tuesday morning [29 May]. I was interrupted by visitors yesterday, and after the concert, at 10.30, we went for supper to the Breidenbacher Hof. In sum, this *Musikfest* teaches me nothing and satisfies me little. I can hardly profit from the *Creation*—and the rather pale moonbeams of the *Peri*[6] are no more to my taste than need be. It was with a rather reserved tolerance that the audience received this work which does, however, contain some fine moments. Schumann's great merit definitely lies in the distinction of his style. He has certain ways of saying certain things

---

[6] With a German text translated and adapted from the second of the four Oriental tales in Thomas Moore's *Lalla Rookh*, Schumann's cantata *Paradise and the Peri* was composed and first performed in 1843.

which no one else has known how to. About a beautiful pedal effect, Joachim remarked to me: 'He's a *man!*'—'Or at least a *musician*,' I replied. As for Chorley, he doesn't mince his words, finding *Paradise and the Peri* a 'paradise lost'.

Hiller's conducting is like his whole personality: easy-going, all right, very seemly, even distinguished—but without energy and elasticity, and so without authority or communicative electricity. He could be reproached with lacking faults, and with not paying sufficient heed to criticism. . . . In general, this *Musikfest* lacks that contagious something which must be in the air to rouse and excite the public willy-nilly. Everything is more or less all right, but nothing strikes one or makes its mark with vigour. In Holland, there was a more pronounced meaning to all this bustle. One could see that the Dutch were making an effort to put themselves on a level with Germany's musical culture, and making laudable progress. Here, it is done from sheer habit, to the requisite and established extent. In one way or another the different groups of the performers and of the public understand this situation, and this comprehension always makes itself felt more or less directly. La Lind, because of her popularity, effectively conceals the irremediable emptiness of the festival—but even that isn't an advantage, for after virtuosi have been so much railed against, it is to say the least rather illogical to put them in the foreground like this, when that place should above all be given to Art. As a matter of fact, the committee is sure to have good receipts, thanks to the contribution, gratis, of la Lind. Nevertheless, in Hiller's place I would not congratulate myself on it any more than Rubinstein had reason to for his pianistic successes in Vienna. Further, Hiller's conducting and what some call his lack of character, *Charakterlosigkeit*—a term more than severe in this case—do not fail to meet with rather unfortunate criticisms. Joachim among others told me yesterday that he approved of almost none of the tempi taken by Hiller—still less his transitions from one tempo to the next. People find him *pomadig* [sluggish], lacking *élan*, applying himself to no more than is strictly necessary to the work in hand, and not mastering it even to the degree necessary to communicate its sense and meaning. In a word, the opposition formed by Schumann's supporters accuses him of turning this festival to account to enable him to continue his 'Etudes rythmiques' as conductor.

Mme Kalergis* bewails her depression and melancholy, etc. Did you know that the London *Press*,[7] Disraeli's newspaper, has flatly accused her of having, in company with Chreptowich, had Tsar Nicholas assassinated![8] Applying it to herself, she told me a well-known story of a famous Italian Punchinello, who, in the grip of chronic depression, consulted a doctor. The latter asked him

[7] A weekly journal to which Disraeli had contributed the first leading article in the first issue, in 1853, and of which he was for several years the inspiring spirit.
[8] The formidable Iron Tsar had died in his Winter Palace on 2 Mar.

if he had liver trouble, stomach pains, or a headache. 'No, but I feel mortally sad.'—'Well, to amuse yourself, go and see the celebrated Punchinello; that will cure you.'—'The remedy may be excellent, but unfortunately I cannot avail myself of it—I *am* the celebrated Punchinello!' She has come from The Hague, and goes back there tomorrow. Thence she will return to Brussels, and if the [Crimean] war continues, will go back to Petersburg, to reside once again for some time with her uncle, the Chancellor [Nesselrode]. She tells me that he cannot manage without her—any more than Mme de Lieven can adapt to her absence. . . .

If Liszt was not enamoured of the music he heard in Düsseldorf, the same could not be said of his feelings towards a visitor to the festival who left before he did, and to whom, before he took his own departure, he penned the lines that follow.

319. To Agnes Street-Klindworth in Brussels. [Düsseldorf] 6.00 a.m., Thursday [31 May]. It is in this same room that I am writing you these further final words. Taking possession of your apartment when I got back here at about 5 o'clock yesterday, I didn't budge from it until 9.00. During the morning we had music at Frau Schumann's. She played Schumann's Sonata (D minor) with Joachim, the Overture to *Genoveva* with me, and the *Etudes symphoniques* (one of Schumann's early, good works); I, too, had to oblige, despite my lack of inclination. Not wishing to offend her, after Frau Schumann had made repeated entreaties I gave in and played them Bach's Chromatic Fantasy. Then I went to lunch with Joachim, Brahms, Wasielewski, and Lührss at a confectionary-cum-restaurant, and it was not until about 5.00 that Hermann handed me your letter, which did me a great deal of good, for I was able to shed many tears.

This morning the birds nesting in the trees of the Museum opposite awakened me with a kind of 'funeral song'. In an hour I leave for Kassel with [Ferdinand] David . . . who told me yesterday evening that Weber had the habit of almost always writing the same maxim in albums: *Beharrlichkeit führt an's Ziel* [Perseverance leads to the goal], and that he, too, possessed this autograph by the composer of *Der Freischütz*. Rossini's method is similar but more complicated, for he has certainly composed about a hundred different musical versions, scattered in numerous albums all over Europe, of these lines by Metastasio:

> Mi lagnerò tacendo
> della mia sorte amara,

> ma ch'io non t'ami, o cara,
> non lo sperar di me![9]

The first line has always seemed to me to be an ironic allusion to the album mania ('Mi lagnerò tacendo'), which I for my part have opposed for a number of years by imperturbably refusing my signature to what Berlioz calls lovers of *albuminations*.

Kassel, Friday morning, 1 June. Before leaving I reopened Dante and reread the final canto (the 33rd of *Paradiso*), which ends with these 3 lines:

> Ma già volgeva il mio disio e 'l velle,
> Sì come rota ch'igualmente è mossa,
> L'amor che move il sole e l'altre stelle.[10]

I passed the journey chatting with my two travelling companions, David and Lührss. In the evening we went to Wilhelmshöhe, and, when we got back to the King of Prussia Hotel, had 3 rubbers of whist. Spohr, whom we saw again during our dinner, wasn't free in the evening, and doesn't seem very eager to do us the honours of Kassel, as we deserve; consequently, we shall depart this morning at 11.30, and at 6.00 I shall be in the Altenburg. Spohr is an excellent and worthy man, *bieder und tüchtig* [upright and capable]; he is now about 75— and of all the musicians of his period I regard him as by far the best and most valuable. His double career as virtuoso and composer is equally honourable; but both the one and the other have lacked that element of the extraordinary which, quite simply, is what we mean by genius. . . . He is a patriarch of art—but no longer a prophet nor an apostle. Among other merits he has that of taking an interest in the works of Wagner, and he has had *Der fliegende Holländer* performed here several times, before anyone thought of doing it elsewhere. David told me that he has also written a kind of Violin Concerto entitled *Sonst und Jetzt* [Formerly and Now], adding that the *Jetzt* is particularly distinguished from the *Sonst* by a triangle and cymbals accompaniment, which is neither more mischievous nor more characteristic than necessary!

At Düsseldorf on Wednesday evening I received a letter from Mme d'Agoult in rather a gentler tone, with her old seal 'in alta solitudine' around a rhododendron she has had made in Geneva. She strongly urges me to come to Paris for 48 hours, so that she and I can discuss the arrangements to be made with regard to the children should they find themselves without Mme Patersi. I shall

---

[9] An adaptation of lines from *Siroe, re di Persia*, II. i. 'I shall complain in silence | of my hard lot, | but that I do not love thee, O my darling, | don't hope that of me!'

[10] Although Liszt seems to have written these lines as though they formed a *terzina* (tercet) in themselves, they actually consist of the second and third lines of the final *terzina* followed by the single line that, famously and sublimely, brings the entire *Commedia* to a close: 'The Love that moves the sun and the other stars.'

deny myself this trip, although at the end of her letter she assures me that I shall 'not regret having devoted this short space of time to deep and lively affections', and shall reply to her from Weimar. . . .   A.A.

320. To Richard Wagner in London.[11] Weimar, 2 June ^G

Dearest Richard!

Wearied and dulled, I got back here yesterday from the Düsseldorf music festival. Hiller, who directed the whole thing, had invited me, and it interested me to take part in something like that for the nonce, to hear *Paradise and the Peri*, and to applaud la Lind. I need not tell *you* anything about it, and am not much the wiser myself. Although the festival as a whole can be considered a great success, it nevertheless lacked something which was indeed not to be expected from it. In the world of art there are many and various laurels and thistles, but you need bother very little about such things: 'The eagle flies to the sun.'

So you are reading Dante. He's good company for you, and I for my part want to provide you with a kind of commentary on that reading. I have long been carrying a Dante Symphony around in my head—this year I intend to get it down on paper. There are to be 3 movements, *Hell*, *Purgatory* and *Paradise*— the first two for orchestra alone, the last with chorus. When I visit you in the autumn I shall probably be able to bring it with me; and if you don't dislike it you can let me inscribe your name on it. . . .

When will you be returning to Zurich? In Düsseldorf people were saying that you had already left London! The ordinary and humdrum in their envy were rejoicing at this news, which I was not loth to spoil for them. *Whatever* may come to pass, and *however*, I most earnestly ask you to

hold out and *persevere.*

As *poeta sovrano*, you must, as Dante says of Homer, proceed on your way quietly and peacefully, *sì come sire.*[12] All that other rubbish is no concern of yours. Just work away at your *Nibelungen* and be content to live on as an immortal!

Later on I shall ask Klindworth to send me the piano arrangement of the First Act of *Die Walküre*. How do things stand with that of the *Rheingold*? Has Hans kept it? Tell me, so that I may know how I can get my hands on it.

I have strongly advised Hans to settle in Berlin, where his position at the Music Academy suits him very well. There is little to be gained from travelling

---

[11] Having been invited to conduct the concerts of the Old Philharmonic Society, Wagner lived in London (22 Portland Terrace, Regent's Park) from early Mar. to late June 1855.

[12] Alluding to *Inferno*, IV. 86–8, when, following Virgil through Limbo, Dante beholds Homer, the 'sovereign poet', coming forward 'as sire', ahead of Horace, Ovid, and Lucan.

around, nowadays. Later he should go to Paris and London; but to begin with Berlin will be a favourable terrain for him for a couple of years.

I shall stay here during the summer, until I go to Esztergom at the end of August. The musical work keeping me busy is a new and rather altered score of my *Prometheus choruses*, which I want to publish next winter. As soon as it is finished I shall return to my Dante Symphony, which is already partly sketched.

Farewell, dearest, most unique friend, and write soon to your serf in body and soul,   F.L.

The Kapellmeisterin[13] and the Child send you cordial greetings.

321. To Agnes Street-Klindworth. Weimar, Tuesday, 5 June.[14] For the last three days I have in vain been trying to find a moment to write to you. . . . Yesterday evening the Grand Duke thought I was looking so unwell that he invited me to spend some time in the country, offering me *inter alia* Goethe's apartment at the castle of Dornburg—but I shall not leave Weimar until the end of the month. To round off the theatre season, which ends on the 24th, I have to conduct two or three operas. Yesterday we had a five-hour rehearsal of *Tannhäuser*, which will be performed this evening in honour of the Princess of Prussia, whom it gave me great pleasure to see again. For the last dozen years she has consistently been extremely kind to me, and seems disposed to go on being so. . . .

I have a pile of letters to write before I resume work on my *Prometheus*. From Paris I have been sent some issues of the *Revue contemporaine* with M. Guizot's article 'Nos mécomptes et nos espérances', and another by Pontmartin on Madame Sand's memoirs.[15] In this latter article, which treats the author of *Lélia* very harshly, there is rather a droll passage: 'After the endless bragging of the author of the "Musketeers", after the comical self-conceit of the *Bourgeois de Paris*,[16] it was thought that nothing more was possible; well, we were mistaken, there was one more step to take, and, to the general amazement, Mme Sand has just taken it. There was the writer, the artist, the celebrated woman, with much ado announcing her memoirs, and believing that she had the right and the power to interest her readers by telling them the story of her life .... before her birth.'

---

[13] 'Kapellmeister's wife', referring jocularly to the Princess; 'the Child' (das Kind) was Wagner's nickname for young Princess Marie.

[14] The letter is dated Tuesday, 4 June in La Mara's edition—but Tuesday was the 5th.

[15] *Histoire de ma vie* (1848–54).

[16] *Mémoires d'un bourgeois de Paris* (6 vols., 1853–5) by Louis-Désiré Véron, author, publisher and, 1831–5, director of the Paris Opéra.

Further on, he sets these memoirs of '*before the cradle*' beside [Chateaubriand's] of *beyond the grave*. The fact is, that to publish *nine volumes on the story of her life*, and by the ninth to have got no further than the *age of seven*, can seem somewhat singular; but the explanation given by M. de Pontmartin (developing the thesis of the *inheritance of organism* put forward by Mme Sand) is that Mme Sand belongs neither to the aristocracy nor to the people, bastardy[17] no more giving her rights to the one, than the lax morals of 'Marie Rainteau, a lady of the opera, calling herself by her *nom de guerre* Mademoiselle Verrières— one of the innumerable victims of the Maréchal de Saxe and great-grandmother of Mme Sand—and of Antoinette-Victoire-Sophie Delaborde, abandoned in her youth to *terrible risks*', justify her in claiming an origin among the people.

How are your own concerns? My thoughts follow you constantly through these labyrinths of negotiations and expectations, so that I am perhaps more agitated by them than you are yourself. After all, 'but one thing is needful'—and so let us follow Mary rather than Martha[18]—

Cœur nobyle cœur immobyle. A.A.

322. To Agnes Street-Klindworth. Stadt Altenburg [Hotel], Gotha, Midnight, Sunday, 10 June

'Even thine altars, O Lord of hosts!'[19]....

It was in these same rooms that I read to you, 3 months ago, the magnificent passage from the *Soirées de Saint-Pétersbourg* on the Psalms. My whole soul was breathing at that moment; and your letter, arriving this evening, has brought me as it were the perfume of that thrilling hour. I implore you, be from time to time the 'unreasonable child', or whatever you want to call it, just as you were. Write and tell me what goes through your heart and make me your 'confessional', as you so well put it. Your tears are beautiful, pure, and holy! I can't say more of them than that; but hear what I do say, and let the rays of my affection spread out and penetrate like balm into the deepest recesses of your soul.

I'll tell you how I happen to be in Gotha. Rietschel has just spent two days in Weimar finishing the marble bust of Princess Marie, which is a masterpiece. As he wanted to see Schwind's paintings at the Wartburg, this morning we set out for Eisenach with Preller, of whom I have a very high opinion, as much for

---

[17] Of Mme Sand's ancestor the Maréchal de Saxe, natural son of Augustus II, Elector of Saxony and King of Poland, and Countess Aurora von Königsmark. By his adventure with Marie-Geneviève Rainteau he sired Aurore Dupin de Francueil, whose son Maurice Dupin and daughter-in-law Sophie, née Delaborde, were George Sand's parents.

[18] The classic New Testament contrast between two sisters, referred to several times in Liszt's letters. Mary's priority is the quest for spiritual enlightenment, Martha's the efficient running of the household (Luke 10: 39–42).

[19] Ps. 84: 3.

his rare artistic gifts as for his noble personal qualities. On our return journey we are spending the night in Gotha, and I took advantage of the first half-hour of freedom to unseal your letter. Tomorrow morning we leave for Weimar, where *Tannhäuser* is being performed again in the evening. . . .

Bussenius has finished the biography [of Liszt], of which you have the first 2 instalments. He would like to send you the whole thing; but I should need your exact address, for he will probably ask Baron Jósika, who lives in Brussels, to deliver it to you. Jósika is a novelist with a distinguished reputation; his political conduct during the events in Hungary was most honourable; he stood fast to the end, even though, having moderated his earlier opinions, he could easily have adopted a more prudent line. For some years he has been living a retired life in Brussels with his wife, who is likewise of good birth and wholly devoted to her husband. If you have an opportunity to make his acquaintance, speak to him the language familiar to minds and characters of this stamp. Several of his novels have acquired great popularity in Hungary, and been translated into German and French. . . .

I received this morning a long letter from Wagner on Dante. The *canard* reproduced by several newspapers about his abrupt departure from London is of roughly the same magnitude as the one reporting my departure for America. Wagner will remain quietly in London until the end of the Philharmonic Society concerts (the 26th of the present month); and it goes without saying that I, for my part, am not leaving Weimar. . . .

In Munich did you hear any mention of E. Förster? He is a very deserving man who married Jean Paul's daughter and usually resides in Munich. His *Handbuch* for Germany and Italy is very widely known. He will soon be bringing out a large folio on the Blessed Fra Angelico of Fiesole, with a good many engravings after drawings he did in Italy, where he also translated into 8 volumes the Vasari published by Cotta. The Princess saw a lot of him in Munich, and he has been spending a few days at the Altenburg, where he plans to remain for a couple of weeks. I often go and keep him company while he sketches a group of angels after Fra Angelico.

'Hope, child' and be blessed! Don't complain too much about the uncertainty of your lot; distressing it may be, but a place where you can rest your head you will always find in my heart.

323. To Agnes Street-Klindworth. Halle railway station, 6.00, Saturday, 7 July. 'All that doesn't prevent me being horribly sad', you wrote to me recently, Agnes. These words continue to resound in my heart ... but you know that my maxim is that one has to *stifle* and suppress certain emotions, and take no account of that inexpressible feeling which is the foundation of our life itself!

You can't imagine how much I grieve at my inability to be *of any use* to you whatsoever! However graciously you scold me for the few words I let slip on this topic in my last letter, I don't want you to be mistaken about my feelings by supposing that I fail to appreciate yours. This need to be *something* to *someone* is a youthful wound of mine which has never healed. There is a beautiful letter on this theme in *Werther*, which, if I am not mistaken, begins thus: 'I would willingly break my skull' ... etc.; and I remember that the first time I read it, 25 years ago, I dissolved into tears and flooded the whole book with them. But let's not speak of emotions or tears—and at least know how to keep silent about what we suffer and endure!

I left for Dresden in the evening of the day before yesterday, and in a few hours I shall be back in Weimar. You know the reason for this trip—and probably Frau Ritter will agree to have my daughters in her home for a year or two —after which it can be assumed that they will get married. The Paris *atmosphere* is becoming more and more unhealthy for them. (Incidentally, I believe that it was in last month's issue of the *Revue contemporaine* that their mother published rather a long extract, entitled 'Power and Liberty', from an *Histoire de Hollande*[20] which is announced. If by chance you go to the reading-room, ask for that issue of the *Revue contemporaine*. As you know, Mme d'Agoult's penname is Daniel Stern.) On the other hand, I neither can nor wish to keep my daughters under my roof at the Altenburg. But I believe it would be to their advantage to spend some time in Germany—and, to this end, Dresden or Berlin seem to me to be the most suitable towns. I have told them nothing of this plan as yet, and shall inform them of it only when I *see* them again. . . .

324. To Princess Carolyne (visiting Berlin). [Weimar] 8.30 p.m., Saturday, 14 July. . . .

After accompanying you to the train—on which may God, as well as Magnolet, keep you company—I went to the Ritters' with Bronsart. There we found Frau Röckel, wife of Wagner's old friend—who will have to spend I don't know how many years in the *Zuchthaus* [convict prison]. The Röckels are close relatives of Frau Hummel[21] and Frau Moritz, and this Frau Röckel I rather like, although I know her only slightly. At Ritter's request I played one of my Rhapsodies—No. 2, the one which delighted Panin at Teplitz, and which Ritter wants to arrange for violin and orchestra. After chatting for at least an hour, I paid a quick visit to Götze in the Frorieps' garden. Alma, Bertha, and

---

[20] Mme d'Agoult's *Histoire du commencement de la République aux Pays-Bas.*   [21] Widow of J. N. Hummel.

their mother were present. Shortly before 6.00 I got back to our blue roost.
. . . Throwing myself on to my knees, I asked God to take care of you, and to
accept all three of us into His eternal dwelling-place. Then I went in search of
Bach's *Passion*, of which I went through the whole of the first part, 100 pages
of score, in these $2\frac{1}{2}$ hours. This work is still one of my own passions, unhack-
neyed for me, and every time I immerse myself in it its attractions redouble. If
we were not so badly off in Weimar, it would give me great pleasure to mount
a performance, such as I know how, of this colossal marvel. The one you heard
in Leipzig can give you no more than a very feeble idea of it, despite the considerable number of players and singers assembled for the occasion.

I envy you your tomorrow morning at the *Domchor* [cathedral choir in Berlin],
and will do my utmost to get the Grand Duke to arrange for those singers to
come here next winter. . . .

I am being summoned to have supper tête-à-tête with Miss Anderson.[22] So
good night, *très chère, seule et unique*! Tomorrow morning I shall continue my
Passion, and will probably not be writing to you until after I have received your
first letter. . . .

325. To Princess Carolyne. [Weimar] 9.00 a.m., Saturday [21 July].

Your letter of Thursday, dearest one, didn't reach me until rather late yesterday
afternoon—but in compensation I have just received Friday's, which was delivered rather earlier than usual. I am delighted with your *systematic* and practical
course in the plastic arts, and certainly expect you on your return to allow me
to profit from it by telling me about the *statues*, just as Magnolet often tells me
about the plays she has seen. The methodical and intelligent way in which works
of art are displayed and grouped together in the Berlin museum is renowned
among connoisseurs, and the credit for it probably belongs to Olfers, and perhaps to the King himself. . . . I urge you to take notes and to write them down
in the handbook containing the catalogue of the statues and pictures. Your connoisseur's success with regard to the placing of the *Vénus de Milo*, of the *Medusa*,
of the *Jupiter*, and of the *Antinous*, earns for you an esteem which you can put to
excellent use, to add to the splendid fund of knowledge and intelligence that you
possess already. So look carefully and don't fail to ask questions of and, when necessary, to *confess* people who have taken the trouble to look carefully before you!

I have never had a very high opinion of the painting of Begas. The whole
of that school, with the exception of Cornelius and Kaulbach,* gives me the

---

[22] Princess Marie's governess Janet Anderson (see Biographical Sketches), whose nickname at the Altenburg was 'Scotland',
'Scotch', or 'Scotchy'.

impression of being roughly on a level with the one represented in music by Marschner, Lindpaintner, *et al.* As for Kaulbach, he is another kettle of fish, and I do indeed believe that he is really someone. Do tell him that I have always had this feeling about him, and that I set very great store by his friendship. When I am finished with my *Dante* [Symphony], I shall see if I can set one of his paintings to music—*Hunnenschlacht*, for example, or some newer work, which would suit me still better; for I imagine that during these last years his talent has greatly increased! I shall speak to him about it when next we see one another, and when you have given me some information about his Berlin paintings. . . .

As for Humboldt, I surrender him to you completely. But don't forget that while having established his dwelling place in the immensities and infinities, his regular promenades through the Milky Way and the nebulae have never caused him to lose his balance on the slippery floors of the Courts. He is a kind of pope of science: infallible on 'dogma', and marvellously subtle and supple— having in him something of both cat and monkey—in the ordinary circumstances of life. If you succeed in *getting on* well with him, I shall be very happy. If he deigned to give me his patronage with the King, who could one day or other order something from me for the *Domchor*—perhaps a rather large-scale work: if need be, a Greek tragedy would suit me quite well under those conditions—he would be doing something kind, for which I should remain truly grateful. . . .

Wholly at your feet and in your heart. F.L.

326. To Princess Carolyne. Monday morning, 23 July. Very dear, adored and adorable one, how good of you to take so much bother and trouble with my girls, and how shall I ever be able to thank you enough for everything you do for me! It goes without saying that I fully subscribe to whatever you may deem advisable and fitting for their stay in Berlin—and that the flat in Bärenstrasse has my complete approval. And so please tell Frau von Bülow to take it. That the doctor lives nearby strikes me as very convenient, and I have no objection to M. Hans, whom I love like a son, living under the same roof as my girls. He will be able to be very useful to them, as much by his music lessons as by his really outstanding culture and intellect. . . . Before you leave, see if there is any reason to tell Varnhagen and his niece about my girls. Since they will be inseparable from Frau von Bülow, they will be seeing them as a matter of course.

I protest about the *witticism* that has been made up on my behalf about compositions by the Princess of Prussia. In general people don't succeed in attributing wit to me, and more than once I have been almost vexed by the stupidities that people have taken the trouble to invent on my account—even when they seem to have been found amusing enough to be often repeated. . . .

327. To Princess Carolyne. Tuesday, 24 July

Infinitely dear one,

This visit from Lewy, who arrived yesterday at 5 o'clock, has given me great pleasure, first and foremost because he brought me news of you. For the rest, I should have preferred to have a certain amount of solitude this week, for, as I wrote to you yesterday, I have begun work on my Psalm[23]—and if I am not disturbed too much I shall have made great headway, almost finished it, by your return. Disturbances of all kinds have always been so much part and parcel of my life—that I have ended up by accommodating myself to them and persuading myself that it must be thus. . . .

As for my Mass,[24] it calls for a certain *piety* and a certain *faith*, things quite unknown to our usual musical practice. I fear that without my own participation it may go a little awry—and consequently may not produce the impression I have wished for and felt. In everything I do I believe I have something quite new to say; and so it is essential that *my* thoughts and *my* feelings are assimilated, so that they are not betrayed by a ruinous performance. Karlsruhe was a very useful lesson for me in this respect, and I shall try to turn it to good account. Albeit to a lesser degree than Wagner, I need *men* and artists—and cannot be satisfied with manœuvres and a mechanically regular performance. The Spirit must breathe on these sonorous waves as on the great waters of the Creation. . . .

I have also accepted a new pupil, that little Tausig from Warsaw whom I mentioned to Magne. He has an *astonishing* talent, and will get himself talked about later. He is $13\frac{1}{2}$, and although of the tribe of Jacob will not displease you, I believe. He will probably spend 18 months or 2 years here, after which he will be perfectly ready to embark on a fine career as pianist and composer, for he is already very advanced on both counts.

Greet our Magnolet tenderly from me. I am delighted that Kaulbach wants to do a portrait of her, and will do him a *Hunnenschlacht* in exchange, which won't be worm-eaten either![25] Use will naturally have to be made of a long *pianissimo* effect, with which it will be necessary to end—to leave the hearer gazing

---

[23] Liszt's setting of Psalm 13 ('How long wilt thou forget me, O Lord?').
[24] The Gran Mass or *Missa Solennis*, composed for the consecration, in 1856, of the great basilica at Esztergom (Gran).
[25] The symphonic poem *Hunnenschlacht* (Battle of the Huns) was completed in 1857.

on the battle in the sky, as though terrified and dazzled by these *shades* unsated by combat! And I, too, sometimes feel that I am a Hun, to the very marrow of my bones. When my bones are broken, and reduced to dust or decay, my spirit will breathe in the combat, the valour and—your love!

Dearest one, this evening or tomorrow morning Hans will give you my news, not very new for you. As soon as he has gone I shall set to work, and will try to keep my doors closed. During these 4 days I have been unable to write anything—which makes me rather ill-humoured. My congratulations to you on having so satisfactorily finished with your Berlin museum, and I again strongly advise you to devote yourself equally conscientiously to your subsequent studies. Your idea of going to Tegel[26] on the pretext of admiring sculptures, I find excellent, and I am curious about the news you will shortly be giving me of the principal personage. . . .

Here, nothing new is happening—and consequently I have nothing to tell you. Sometimes the melancholy swaying of the trees in the garden, the promenading of the splendid peacock bought very recently by Henri, or the musical twitterings of the birds, cause all kinds of ideas and dreams to steal upon me. Since I possess no descriptive talent I shall not weary you with them by letter, and restrict myself to keeping you silently present in this dear blue room—and to loving and cherishing you in my own way, which is perhaps not a good way, but is at least *a* way, as Mme Sand used to say. Incidentally, in this morning's *La Presse* there is a rather curious chapter of hers on marriage, which will amuse you on your return. . . .

At your feet,   F.L.

328. To Princess Carolyne. [Weimar, late July]

Infinitely dear one,

Yesterday, my day was still more wasted than the others have been, for I didn't write to you. However, I got down to work to some extent and shall try to finish soon the Psalm I have begun. . . .

I am accepting Tilke's manuscript, and will probably manage to have it engraved by Körner of Erfurt, who is a very good publisher for organ music. The Fantasy which precedes the Fugue on the chorale from the *Prophète* seems to me not to be disproportionately long, whatever the opinion of Haupt, whom it would greatly

---

[26] Schloss Tegel (which the princesses visited on Sunday, 29 July), the Humboldt lakeside estate a few miles to the north of Berlin. It was here that, four years later, the remains of the great Alexander were interred in the family cemetery amidst the pine trees.

interest me to know, and to whom I ask you in the mean time to present my best compliments.

There is nothing very enigmatic about Humboldt's remark. It means merely that a literary programme could have been made for *Hungaria* without too much fear of offending the conservative susceptibilities of the German public. But as there are yet other susceptibilities I have to spare, I believe it has been better to dispense with one—besides the fact that, for my own part, I prefer to refrain from *barking* when the possibility of *biting* is taken from me. For me as for Humboldt, patriotism is only a *very* relative and mutilated form of *feeling*. In so far as I am an artist, I have little taste for *cockades*, which very easily lend themselves to the *comic*, and in the regions that we frequent are simply out of place. For the rest, when you see Humboldt I urge you not to hark back to his remark, which has no other intention than that of ingeniously lengthening his very ingenious note. The words 'artificially liberal' are a little dig at the displays of democracy currently being put on in the North of Germany, and in no way related to our 'muttons' of prefaces. . . .

Thank you for your researches into Holbein's *Todtentanz* [Dance of Death], which we shall be able to turn to good account when the occasion arises. . . .

Thank Frau von Bülow for her excellent letter. I shan't write to her again until after I've seen you. Love to the 'Infanta'[27]—and love from afar this poor Lazybones, who loves you with all his poor heart.

329. To Princess Carolyne. [Weimar] Sunday, 29 July. Look inside some bush or other at Tegel, and there you will find your poor Lazybones, present in mind and heart. You are his entire *Cosmos*, and much more besides! I am sending your letter for Schwind to be posted, and am absolutely delighted that this matter is finished according to your wishes. And so you will possess *The Seven Works of Mercy*![28] May God guide you and heap upon you all the blessings which my wishes, my prayers, and my tears can call down. Is Kaulbach to begin Magne's portrait in Berlin? I supposed that he would do it here, from beginning to end. My idea of doing a *Hunnenschlacht* is not a mere whim. I definitely intend to set about it as soon as I have finished the Psalm; i.e. at the end of August. I only need to have another look at the engraving of this battle, which you possess, I believe, in your cabinet of masterpieces. Visitors are announced, and I am again obliged to break off. And so, until tomorrow!

---

[27] Humboldt's nickname for Princess Marie.
[28] Moritz von Schwind's cartoons for the frescoes painted in the Wartburg. The Princess was purchasing them as a gift for her daughter.

330. To Princess Carolyne. Monday, 30 July. I am writing a pile of letters today, to Berlioz, Augusz, Mme de Gasparin,[29] *et al.* Here are a few words that I ask you to get Marx to hand straightaway to the father of little Ketten*— the young prodigy from Poznań whom you saw here. . . . I am very curious about your visit to Tegel, and rejoice in advance at the account of it that you will be sending me tomorrow. Look after your chill, *très uniquement chère.* Everything you have said and done thus far seems to me to be quite marvellous—continue in the same way and all will end well! With people who are at a high level of talent and intelligence it will always be easy enough for you to get on well. And so have your further week or more in Berlin with a clear conscience. Seeing you again will be a delight for me—but I wouldn't like to hasten it. Resign yourself, therefore, to being blessed through letters for a few more days yet!

331. To Princess Carolyne. [Wednesday, 1 August]

Infinitely dear and gracious one,

Leaving by the 4.30 train I got to Wilhelmsthal[30] a little before 9.00. . . . Having conscientiously read Proudhon's booklet *Philosophie du Progrès*, I admit that for a long time no book has given me so intense a feeling of the truth of my belief in the 'Man-God', of which Proudhon's confidence in the divinity of the 'collective man' is only the shadow and the reverse. If it were established that all the metaphysical arguments in support of the existence of God were annihilated by the arguments of philosophy, there would still remain an altogether invincible one: the affirmation of God through our lamentations, the need we have of Him, the aspiration of our souls towards His love. For me, that is enough, and I need nothing further to make me remain a believer to my very last breath. Proudhon's writing is summed up by this conclusion: 'Affirmation of progress, denial of the absolute.' But he inadvertently makes of the word progress an *absolute* and a most incomprehensible and inadmissible fetish. For him, change is everything. It is a perpetual bustle without goal or end—for the deification of man becomes meaningless from the word go when one has got rid of the idea of God. The pages on art struck me. 'Art is humanity,' he says. I shall have the impertinence to modify his formula thus: Art is humanity's heart, science its brain, industry its arms and hands, commerce its feet—and politics and government its stomach.

---

[29] Liszt's former pupil Valérie Boissier, now the Comtesse de Gasparin.
[30] Grand-ducal hunting-lodge, to the south of Eisenach.

I have learnt nothing new at Wilhelmsthal, unless it is that the Grand Duchess Marie will be unable to get back from her cure in Franzensbad until mid-September. . . .

332. To Anna Liszt in Paris. [Weimar] 13 August ^{G (F)}

Dearest Mother,

Since you cannot bring yourself to leave Paris, and I cannot manage to come there, I should at least like to see my children again and spend a week with them. Frau von Bülow is being so kind as to collect them in Paris and accompany them to Weimar, where I shall give them a welcome which will leave them with a pleasant memory. Perhaps it is not particularly agreeable for you to put Frau von Bülow up; nevertheless, I ask you, dearest Mother, to accommodate her as comfortably as possible during the three or four days of her stay in Paris, until all the travel arrangements are made. You know what a high opinion I have of Frau von Bülow and how fond I am of her son, whom I regard as the most qualified of my pupils to carry on my work in the world of art and to take the brilliant position he has fairly earned. So do give Frau von Bülow a friendly welcome and don't let her notice if her presence should be to some extent a nuisance in your little household. That is the simplest way of practising hospitality.

I hope that at today's prize-giving Daniel will have the desired success, and am very much looking forward to seeing him and his sisters again. If you have time, write to me before their departure and give them your letter to bring with them. I am thinking of remaining in Weimar for the whole summer; on the other hand, for next winter I am planning some trips to Leipzig, Berlin, Hanover, Brunswick, where some of my newest orchestral works are to be performed under my direction. If the things the newspapers may publish about me are not too bad, I shall send you a couple of their reports so that you too will have a little pleasure from them. Until then I am devoting myself to work and striving to improve, as is fitting for your affectionately devoted son   F. Liszt

333. To Princess Carolyne (visiting Paris). Wednesday, 22 August, Feast of St Symphorian, according to our Weimar almanac. Good day,

therefore, in Paris! I take it that you arrived there safely yesterday morning, and that at this moment you are getting ready to go to the exhibition. Accompanied by Frau von Bülow, the family trio also made its arrival yesterday, at 3.30 p.m. The game of whist I had started with Henselt was broken off by it. This morning Henselt starts back to his Schloss, the *Rittergut* [manor] of Gersdorf, 4 hours from Dresden. Daniel, as I had assumed, took about ten prizes again this year, first and second in his school, independently of his two *proxime accessits* in the general competitive examination, which does him great honour. The trio are in splendid humour, and have invented a new form of government, which they call 'dinocracy' and which is in full voice at the present moment in the Altenburg. I had a meal with them, for they had not eaten *en route*—but from today we shall be keeping to our Weimar hours of dinner at 1.00 and supper at 9.00. Then, when it had already gone 10.00, and after having taken them to their rooms and wished them goodnight, I went to rejoin Henselt at the Russischer Hof Hotel. On returning, about half an hour past midnight, I saw a light in the drawing-room and found a a very wide-awake Blandine and Cosima who, without giving me prior warning, had been waiting for me while reading M. de Maistre's *Pape*. We chatted until 1.30 a.m., but I shall not weary you with details of my conversations with the 'dinocracy', and am keeping a recital of the stories and narratives for your return. . . .

On Saturday and Sunday I stayed at Wilhelmsthal, dining, boating, and driving, and chatting about this and that with the Grand Duchess, who is always very kind and *spirituelle* with me. . . .

At 7.30 Blandine came to give me the surprise of waking me. I have decided that I shall not breakfast with 'the gang', but for the whole of their stay will, somehow or other, keep the morning to myself till lunchtime. . . .

Rellstab is expected today or tomorrow. My poor Psalm—and my poor *Beatitudes*! However, I shall have to try to find a few hours to *finish* them, before your return.

For her part, Mme Sand has finished the stories she is telling us in her *Histoire de ma vie*. In the issue of *La Presse* for 17 August, which contains the last chapter of this work, I was agreeably surprised to come across this passage: 'People have claimed that in one of my novels I had portrayed the character of Chopin with great analytical accuracy. They have made a mistake, because they believed that they had come upon some of his traits of character. In adopting this system, which is too convenient to be safe, Liszt himself, in a life of Chopin which is rather exuberant in style but filled nevertheless with very good things and very beautiful pages, has gone astray in good faith.'

Brendel dropped in on me this morning from the moon, or rather from Gotha, where a 'Mozart Foundation' is being set up, which I shall be obliged to set aside half a day for, tomorrow or the day after. . . .

5.00 p.m. Your letter of Thursday has just reached me, and I renew my congratulations to you on Magnolette's success with Scheffer. Don't worry about paying for it until the portrait is in Weimar. . . .

I am curious about the news you will be giving me of Lamartine and Girardin. Don't expect too many letters from me. I shall be able to write to you only 2 or 3 times a week—for the children and the cousin, not counting Brendel and *tutti quanti*, are eating up my time quite dreadfully. I bless you—and can live and come to life only through you.

334. To Princess Carolyne. Saturday, 25 August. The question of the *agreement* between reason and faith was considered, admirably, by Pascal. What he says about it, as well as his manner of saying it, I have always found as convincing as conclusive. 'Faith declares what the senses do not declare, but never the contrary. It is above but not contrary to them. If we submit everything to reason, our religion will lose everything mysterious and supernatural; if we offend against the principles of reason, our religion will be absurd and ridiculous.'[31]

'Reason', says St Augustine, 'would never surrender if it did not consider that there are occasions when it must surrender. It is therefore right for it to surrender when it judges that it ought to surrender, and for it not to surrender when it judges, rightly, that it ought not to. But one must be careful not to deceive oneself.'

After Pascal and St Augustine it is *your faith* that came to seal my convictions. I say to you upon my oath that there is no room in my heart for the empty dreams of unbelief. . . .

Eduard [Liszt] arrived yesterday morning, and we spent the evening, *tutti quanti*, at Tiefurt. Frau von Bülow yesterday morning received a letter from Hans which has made her wish to return to Berlin at once. There is nothing inconvenient in the girls' staying here alone with me. When you get back I shall tell you in detail of how things have gone, domestically speaking. In the mean time, try to manage in Paris more or less as you did in Berlin—and to bring back with you a good harvest of drawings and keepsakes.

335. To Princess Carolyne. Monday, 27 August. Your *entente cordiale et artistique* with the Scheffers gives me the greatest pleasure, very dear, sole, and unique one. I urge you only not to speak too highly of me to them! It is a pity that you won't be seeing Lamartine in Paris—but I still fancy that some lucky chance will help you make his acquaintance. . . .

[31] From the *Pensées*, which also quote the words of St Augustine reproduced by Liszt in his next paragraph.

I didn't want to have this letter posted without having received my daily *manna*—but today, unhappily, I have had to do without it, for the postman brought me nothing from Paris. My letters to you I shall from now on address to the Hôtel des Princes. Tomorrow and the day after I shall try to get rid of my appalling correspondence, and then get down to writing my Fantasy on BACH for the inauguration of the organ at Merseburg, which will take place on 21 September. Hoffmann told me that I enjoyed particular esteem in Merseburg. Did I tell you that Rellstab came to see me? We parted as good friends, despite our differing opinions. In a few days I shall write to Frau von Bülow, and will probably dispatch the girls to her at the beginning of next week. She has promised me that she will come as far as Halle to meet them. Nothing new happening in Weimar. Consequently I have nothing to tell you about it—unless it be that you are loved throughout time and eternity, *in saecula saeculorum.*   F.L.

You know what deep feelings I have retained for Mme d'Artigaux—and so speak to her about me as you find fit. Love to Magnolette. Tell her that at twilight yesterday evening I absent-mindedly called Cosima Magnolette.

336. To Princess Carolyne. Tuesday, 4 September. . . . At 1.30 I am taking the girls to Merseburg, where we shall find Frau von Bülow, who will take them back to Berlin tomorrow. I shall probably not get back until tomorrow evening, for the girls are in no hurry to leave me. On Saturday and Sunday I wasted my time at Reinhardsbrunn, at Mgr. de Gotha's, with Litolff who seems, moreover, to be grateful to me for the small sacrifice of time I made for him in this matter. I hope a ribbon will not be lacking, which will be a link between Litolff and me. Eduard leaves for Vienna on the same train which is setting us down at Merseburg.

Bravo for the Scheffer visit at nine o'clock in the morning! I'll accommodate myself very gladly and willingly to those denials! Here are a few lines for Delacroix.[32] Invite him to come and see us in Weimar. It is not altogether out of the question that he would enjoy himself here. . . . Perhaps a little studio of sorts could be arranged for him. In the mean time send him 300 very good and fine cigars, while assuring him that he will probably find better ones here. . . .

Have you seen Zénéïde Lubomirska? Don't forget to pay her a visit. Is David the sculptor in Paris? Has he exhibited? Etex did a big medallion of me in times past. If you went to his studio you would be able to add it to your vast

---

[32] As his *Journal* shows, Delacroix had been visited by the 'très aimable' Princess and her daughter on 26 Aug., and dined with them on the 28th.

collection, which also lacks, if I am not mistaken, a little bust by Mercier. I am very glad that you are going to Fontainebleau. It is Obermann's forest. I remember it fondly, although I did no more than stroll in it for a couple of hours. . . .

F.L.

337. To Princess Carolyne. Friday, 7 September. Ask Delacroix for the booklet that George [Sand] quotes, and if George returns, make her acquaintance. If necessary, I shall send you a few words for her. Write to me only if she comes back in time.[33]

The youngsters are still at the Altenburg, and won't be leaving for Berlin until tomorrow, Saturday. They will be accompanied by Frau von Bülow, who came very punctually to our rendezvous in Merseburg last Tuesday, expecting to take them to Berlin by the night train. When we left the church, Blandine was so insistent that they should spend a few more days at the Altenburg, that I hadn't the heart to refuse her, and they came back to Weimar that same evening with Frau von Bülow. Latour d'Auvergne, who is always extremely kind to me, will give these young ladies a passport—and tomorrow evening they will be going to bed in Berlin. . . .

If you see Verdi again, tell him that his *Due Foscari* will be performed here for the Grand Duchess's birthday, 8 April. It is one of Her Royal Highness's favourite works; she greatly enjoyed it in Rome—and Beaulieu and I agreed that it would be done here this season. . . .

Why don't *you* want to pose for Scheffer for a few hours? If he has had the idea of painting this portrait, I strongly urge and even beg you to take him at his word. Scheffer would be able to do this portrait either for me or for Magne, to whom I am writing the couple of words enclosed; and who, it seems to me, would have to undertake to resume this little artistico-diplomatic negotiation. Don't brush this idea aside and don't reject my request, I implore you. Just imagine, M. Ingres, from what I am told by Blandine, charged 18,000 francs for his portrait of the Duchesse de Broglie. At that rate, M. Scheffer paints gratis!

You are doing well to see Chasles. Is Mickiewicz still in Paris? Find out and, if he is, write him a few lines in Polish. I await your response about Mme Sand, to send you a few words addressed to her. Sainte-Beuve could perhaps be got

---

[33] The two women dined together on 20 Sept. Liszt's note of 9 Sept. to Mme Sand had asked her to 'give a cordial and friendly reception to Madame la Princesse Wittgenstein, about whom I have nothing else to tell you than that for eight years I have been wholly devoted to her, and, were it otherwise, would be unable to live'.

hold of somewhere. See if you have leisure for him. [Blaze de] Bury did a long article on la Ristori in the 15 August issue of the *Revue des Deux Mondes*. The moment has perhaps come to let him know that you are in Paris. For the rest, if you don't do so, I shall have nothing against that. . . .   Yours,   F.L.

338. To Agnes Street-Klindworth. [Weimar] Tuesday, 11 September. . . . You tell me of your plan to give lessons. Would that be in Brussels?— If so, I urge you to go and see Mme Pleyel from me and tell her unreservedly of your position. She could be useful to you, recommend you to Fétis—and, if you wish, I'll send you a few lines for the latter as also for Mme Pleyel. . . .

My daughters are now settled in Berlin with Frau von Bülow. Hans will make sure they don't neglect their piano practice, and to all appearances they will fairly rapidly reach a very good standard, for they are already pretty advanced and have heard a lot of good music. The elder has quite adamantly declined to accept any of the three suitors (very suitable and which suited me perfectly) suggested to her. We'll see if new candidates have better luck. They are both highly intelligent—and, notwithstanding a certain unsettled imagination and sensitivity, good and upright characters. As for my son, he is wonderfully promising; is guileless without being unsteady, and will, it can be assumed, maintain a rather harmonious balance in the development of his faculties—out of the ordinary ones, for that matter. . . .

Having in October spent a few days in Brunswick, where his *Orpheus* and *Prometheus* were performed in a concert on the 18th, Liszt went in late November to Berlin, where he stayed at the Brandenburg Hotel with Agnes Street-Klindworth and on 6 December conducted the première of his Psalm 13.

339. To Princess Carolyne in Weimar. [Berlin] 8.00 a.m., Tuesday, 27 November. I barely managed to make half a dozen visits yesterday, from 10.30 in the morning to 8.00 in the evening. On going out I first went to see Schlesinger, who kept me for more than an hour, and then to 'those girls', who are very decently lodged and both in perfect health. How delighted they were to see me again, how they kissed and cajoled me! As I was delayed, they and Frau von Bülow had already set out for my hotel. . . . At about 2.30 Tausig and I had an *à la carte* snack together in *your salon*, with which I am very content— as I am with the hotel carriage and *valet de place*, Ulrich.

After lunch I called at Bock's, and paid two long visits to Dorn and Marx. By 8.00 I had returned to the Wilhelmstrasse, where I found Stern, Conradi, Kroll, Laub, Prosch, and Hahn. An unexpected arrival towards the end of the evening was young Grimm,[34] whom you know from the Arnim period in Weimar. He seems rather taken with those girls, who, moreover, are tolerably pretty and Parisian. Among other amusements Blandine undertook that of mimicking Philarète Chasles. She really made me hoot with laughter when imitating the gestures and manner of speaking, and even the fluent erudition and eloquence, of the Professor lecturing. Quite remarkable is the flow of words and professorial turns of phrase which come to her. Hans tells me that she made this kind of entertainment last more than an hour, not long before my arrival. Chasles's lectures are very widely attended—M. Philarète is in vogue here. I shall attend his next discourse.

Wednesday, 7.30 a.m. . . . At about 11.00 [yesterday morning] I saw face to face the Chimborazo of science and amiability,[35] of whom Mme Gaggiotti has just finished a very pleasing and thoughtful portrait which I was shown.

When I arrived I was carrying a bouquet which I placed on his table—and which, incidentally, cost me 4 écus without being particularly splendid. He did me the honours of a few cutting slanders on the slanders of Berlin. He deplores the mania for criticism and disparagement which is the ever-prevailing sickness of this capital of Germanic intelligence, citing Meyerbeer as an example—as a victim, of course. As a token of her esteem, Mme Gaggiotti has given him a fine portrait of herself, curiously lit on the right cheek. Lichnowsky's portrait being near the window, I made a point of commenting on it. That led him to speak of Mme de Sagan, in whom he has known 'many attachments'—I believe he even used the expression 'aberrations of the heart'—but who was 'utterly broken' by her passion for Felix. This topic having taken rather a pathetic, sentimental turn, I permitted myself to observe that in love as in religion one could always be happy to come to 'a beautiful end'!

When taking my leave I made friends with his footman,[36] who had welcomed me most cordially, recognizing me at once and assuring me that His Excellency would be delighted to see me again. To crown this splendid welcome he showed me some of his master's books and portraits, while warmly urging me to present my regards and respects to Mme Gaggiotti—who paints like Raphael, plays the harp like Parish-Alvars, sings like Malibran, and lives in Dorotheenstrasse, whither I shall not fail to go to pay my court. . . .

---

[34] Hermann Grimm, who in 1859 married Gisela von Arnim.   [35] Obviously, Alexander von Humboldt.
[36] Probably Johann Seifert, Humboldt's servant-master during his last years.

340. To Princess Carolyne. Wednesday morning, 5 December. . . . On
Monday morning I called on la Frommann, who the previous day had written
to ask me to make Rellstab and Kossak favourably disposed towards Wagner, or
at least to tone down their critical swipes at *Tannhäuser*. Naturally I told her
that I took no part in boiling up porridge for cats[37] and that she was much too
much *Jenenserin, Kleinstädterin* [the Jena provincial] in her anxieties about the
fate of Wagner's works. Our topics for discussion not offering me much in the
way of current interest, I several times changed the subject. After a good half-
hour of conversation, and with a wish coming over me to see a beautiful face,
I betook myself to Mme Gaggiotti. She was out, but the servant told me that
she would be there the next day at noon, so I returned yesterday. Both mother
and daughter won my heart by singing your praises in all the keys—and I shall
not fail to return there several times, if possible. It seems that you wrote them
a delightful letter, which did not surprise me, but the manner in which they
spoke of you quite charmed me. I am very susceptible to a certain *melody* in
praises, which comes naturally to Italian women. At their place I ran into the
Pce of Baden, brother of the Regent, who is on military service here.

After the vocal and orchestral rehearsals, I spent an hour with the girls. From
there I went to Schlesinger, who had prepared a Sardanapalian supper—to
which were invited the bigwigs of the opposition critics, Kossak, Lindner,
and about twenty other persons belonging more or less to the party hostile to
the *Zukunftsmusik*. We didn't go to table until about 11.30 and we stayed until
past 3 in the morning—but without *excessive* cognac on my part, as I asked
Frau von Bülow to write to you yesterday. I talked a lot. In reply to a toast proposed to me by a Herr von Löwenstein, poet and critic, I said roughly: *Über
dem Künstler steht die Kunst. Als herrschender Künstler bin ich aus Berlin aus-
gezogen; als Diener der Kunst kehre ich wieder zürück* [Above the artist stands
Art. As a ruler in the realm of Art I left Berlin; as a servant of Art I return
again]. I made myself as clear as I could—and we'll have to see in what way I
am *treated*. In any case, I shall abstain from lamentations, apart from the *Lamento*
of my *Tasso*.

Yesterday morning I wrote to Humboldt and Olfers. Tomorrow, Thursday,
Olfers has given me a rendezvous at the Museum at 11.00. . . . Yesterday evening
was spent with the Bülows, the Sterns, and Mundt, at the Marxes. Since none
of us seemed in much of a mood for conversation, I went to the piano and
played *Funérailles* and several pieces from the *Années de pèlerinage*. . . . This evening
at 6.00 I shall be going to another of Marx's lectures—he will be talking on

---

[37] That is, doing something pointless (cats don't eat porridge).

Aeschylus. . . . Going to the museum tomorrow morning, and the dinner at Humboldt's, will serve me as *preludes* to other *Préludes*. . . .

Dated Monday the 3rd, the invitation to dinner with Humboldt on the 6th, the day of Liszt's concert, had run thus: 'Monsieur and illustrious colleague! Please don't refuse me! I beg you to be so good as to take dinner at my place at 3.00 next Thursday with Messrs Rauch, Eduard Hildebrandt, Mariette—Director of the Egyptian Museum in Paris who made the immense discovery of the temple of Apis with 63 granite sarcophagi; Herr Brugsch, a Prussian, very young but the possessor of a fine talent and Mariette's companion in the ruins of Memphis; Herr Ehrenberg, traveller in Syria and Abyssinia and my companion on the Siberian expedition; Herr Alexander Mendelssohn, cousin of Felix—people worthy of You. Don't refuse, for You will be free at 5.00, later to receive all of us, sceptre[38] in hand. . . . The soup will not be Crocodile nor young Rhinoceros tongue.'[39]

Liszt went to the dinner, and to the young Princess Marie Wittgenstein reported, 'There was a marked tone of goodwill on the part of the Greatest of the Great towards your poor little Lazybones.'

[38] Conducting baton.   [39] La Mara, *Briefe hervorragender Zeitgenossen*, ii. 60–1.

1856

7 January. Liszt attends the first Berlin performance of *Tannhäuser.*

27/8 January. He conducts the Mozart Centenary concerts in Vienna.

16 February. In Weimar, he conducts Berlioz's *Benvenuto Cellini.*

13 May. Liszt plays the organ at a concert in Merseburg Cathedral; his pupil Alexander Winterberger gives the first performance of the Prelude and Fugue on the name BACH.

12–15 June. Liszt attends a music festival in Magdeburg.

July. Blandine and Cosima Liszt spend a fortnight at the Altenburg.

Early August. Liszt travels to Hungary.

31 August. At the consecration of Esztergom (Gran) Cathedral, he conducts the first performance of his Gran Mass.

4 September. The Gran Mass is performed in Pest.

8 September. Liszt conducts the première of *Hungaria.*

15 September. In Vienna he attends a concert given by Johann Strauss.

21–9 September. He stays in Prague, and on the 28th conducts another performance of the Gran Mass.

October/November. Liszt, Carolyne, and Marie visit Wagner in Zurich.

23 November. At a concert in St Gallen, Liszt conducts *Orpheus* and *Les Préludes,* Wagner the *Eroica* Symphony of Beethoven.

Late November/December. Leaving Switzerland, Liszt and the princesses spend a fortnight in Munich before returning to Weimar.

WORKS. *Eine Symphonie zu Dantes Divina Commedia* (Dante Symphony) (S109, 1855–6). The song *Wie singt die Lerche schön* (Hoffmann von Fallersleben) (S312, *c.*1856). *Concerto pathétique* (S258, *c.*1856) for two pianos, based on S176. PIANO: *Festvorspiel-Prélude* (S226); *Vom Fels zum Meer, deutscher Siegesmarsch* (S229, 1853–6).

ESSAYS. *Mozart: On the Occasion of his Centenary Festival in Vienna. Dornröschen: Genast's Poem and Raff's Music of the same Title.*

341. To Princess Carolyne in Weimar. [Vienna] 9.00 p.m., Wednesday, 16 January. . . . I've been wanting to write to you for the last 12 hours, and have found it impossible to find a single moment to myself since 9.00 this morning! Getting to Prague yesterday evening at 7.00, I immediately took the night train which was leaving 10 minutes later, and which in 13 hours brought me here. On arrival I took a fiacre, to give Eduard a surprise. After we had had a coffee at his place and quite a long chat, he accompanied me to the *Kaiserin von Oesterreich* [Hotel], where I am very comfortably lodged. Marchesi, Haslinger, Löwy, Spina, Riedel von Riedenau, Streicher, Willmers, Glöggl, Hellmesberger, *et al.* have called to see me. At 4.00 I had a meal in my room with Eduard, who is thinking and acting wonderfully. At 7.00 we went together to a choral rehearsal, about 4 or 500 persons—all of that will go off perfectly, like clockwork. Some *excellent friends* will probably turn up, among whom Eckert in particular has been mentioned to me. But in this instance they will be neither warm nor cold. If they have any tactics at all, they will end by rallying, even if it is only to protest *doubly* against my works next time. Tomorrow I shall begin my round of visits, less extensive than in Berlin—and between now and Sunday I hope to have put my little affairs in order.

My journey went very pleasantly, apart from the fact that in Dresden I had time to swallow only half a beefsteak, and in Prague only a quarter of an excellent piece of roastbeef—so much did the guard hurry us, on the pretext that the train was late. In compensation I nourished my mind by reading Lenz's volume, which I finished conscientiously, and nearly 200 pages of Ulibishev,[1] for, from Bodenbach to Prague and as far as Brünn, there was an excellent lamp in the compartment. I feel perfectly fit and well—and 'whatever happens, I shall remain worthy', as friend Bocage used to say. . . .

342. To Agnes Street-Klindworth. [Kaiserin von Oesterreich Hotel]

Vienna, 18 January. . . . I believe I told you in my lines from Berlin that I had to prolong my stay there by 48 hours in response to the gracious invitation from the King, who in this matter was again extremely kind to me. Two days after the 1st performance of *Tannhäuser* there was a grand concert at the palace (*im weissen Saal,* with more than 2,000 candles and from 1,200 to 1,500 guests), which I attended as a spectator, without taking part in the programme.

Among other pieces, an Overture by Count Redern and the finale of Mendelssohn's *Loreley* were performed, and Taubert gave an extremely mediocre rendering of the 1st movement of Beethoven's Concerto in E flat. Between the two parts of the concert HM did me the honour of talking with me for a few minutes; and, complimenting me in the most wittily affable manner on my *Tasso,* he laid particular stress on the *Court scene.* Taking the opportunity, I told the King that I planned to return to Berlin quite soon; 'for after working fairly hard

---

[1] Presumably referring to the *Nouvelle biographie de Mozart, suivie d'un aperçu sur l'histoire générale de la musique et de l'analyse des principes œuvres de Mozart* (3 vols., Moscow, 1843; later published in German and Russian), in which, by way of praising Mozart, Ulibishev had penned sharp criticisms of Beethoven's later style—animadversions which he maintained and reiterated in *Beethoven, ses critiques et ses glossateurs* (Leipzig and Paris, 1857).

these last 3 years it now behoves me to *volatilize* my products a little'.—'I understand', he replied with a strikingly apt remark, 'you now need *chimneys*'—and this conversation assures me that the King will deign to continue the kindnesses he has always shown me and for which I have remained, as you know, most sincerely grateful.

On the eve of my departure my two daughters unexpectedly came to see me at the Brandenburg Hotel to ask me, most insistently, to take them back to Weimar for a couple of days. Giving in to their entreaties I escorted them to Weimar, where they were to stay until the end of this week so that they could return to Berlin with Frau von Bülow, who came for them the day before yesterday after paying a visit to her sister Frau Frege in Leipzig. The Princess was very surprised by this quite unexpected appearance, and welcomed them with all the truly *maternal* affection that she has not ceased to feel for them. . . .

On my return to Weimar I found Dawison there. He is a *great artist*, and there is an affinity between his virtuosity and mine: in reproducing, he creates. His conception of the role of Hamlet is entirely new. He does not take him as a dreamer, sinking under the burden of his mission, as people have agreed to regard him since Goethe's theory (in *Wilhelm Meister*[2]), but as an intelligent and enterprising prince with lofty political aims, who *waits for* the favourable moment to take his revenge and at the same time achieve the goal of his ambition by having himself crowned in place of his uncle. This latter result could obviously not be reached in the 24 hours—and the expectation Shakespeare contrives to bring to the role of Hamlet, his dealings and negotiations with England, clearly reported at the end of the play, in my opinion fully justify Dawison's conception, with all due deference to Herr von Goethe and the general run of aesthetes. At the same time, Dawison also very positively solves the question of knowing whether Hamlet loves Ophelia or not. Yes, Ophelia is loved; but Hamlet, like any exceptional character, imperiously demands the *wine* of love from her, not contenting himself with the *milk*. *He wishes to be understood by her, without submitting to the obligation of explaining himself.* It is thus Ophelia who corresponds to the generally received notion of the character of Hamlet; it is she who is overwhelmed by her inability to love Hamlet as he *needs* to be loved, and her madness is only the *decrescendo* of a feeling whose fragility does not allow her to sustain herself in Hamlet's sphere. . . .

People here (contrary to the opinion in Berlin) consider me to be looking very well, but I feel full of worries and fatigue—though you won't have to complain of me! A.A.

---

[2] Goethe's celebrated novel about theatrical life contains a long discussion of *Hamlet*, a performance of which is given by a troupe of actors in whose company Wilhelm finds himself.

343. To Agnes Street-Klindworth. Prague, 3 February. Your lines from
Cologne reached me a few hours before I left Vienna. Forgive me for not writing to you sooner; it was certainly not for want of thinking of you! From morning to evening, and until fairly late at night, all my hours were taken and divided
up by a crowd of visitors to be received, music to be heard, courtesies to be performed, and tedia to be endured, not counting the obligatory series of lunches
and dinners. All in all, this sojourn in Vienna, while tiring me greatly, has, I
believe, turned out fairly well. Notwithstanding the '*good*' services that some
of my very honoured colleagues sought to do me, the two concerts of 27 and
28 January which comprised the *Mozart-Feier* had the *most complete* success, and
the official eulogies made to me about them perfectly well express the general
impression. The Burgomaster, the Council, and the Festival Committee could
not have treated me better—and I am taking home (to enrich the cupboard in
the green closet at the Altenburg) a conducting baton with this inscription: *Die
Stadt Wien dem Dirigenten der Mozart-Feier* [The City of Vienna to the Director
of the Mozart Festival] etc., plus the laurel wreath which adorned the colossal
bust of Mozart during the two concerts, presented to me by the Burgomaster
and the President of the Committee. The large hall of the Redoute, freshly decorated and splendidly illuminated, looked very beautiful. Several days beforehand it was impossible to obtain tickets. Their Majesties the Emperor and Empress[3]
were present, and the general effect of the performances given by more than
500 artistes was very satisfying. From Weimar (where I shall be back in the evening
of the day after tomorrow) I shall send you some reviews, plus the article that,
on my arrival in Vienna, I published about this festival, which serves me as a
preparation for the solemn ceremony in Esztergom, and as a general *transition*
to my present position. Although very much a partisan of what people are pleased
to call *Zukunftsmusik*,[4] I don't entirely intend us to be postponed to the Greek
calends! . . .

    I saw Prince M[etternich] again; but to my regret couldn't accept his invita-
tion to dinner, for that same day a dinner was given by the Burgomaster to the
Festival Committee (and, if I am not mistaken, to me in particular), which I
was necessarily obliged to go to. The Prince is perfectly well preserved and is
maintaining his status quo, even after all the disturbances experienced by that of
Europe, continuing to concern himself with sovereign lucidity with all things,

---

   [3] The young Emperor Franz Joseph had in Apr. 1854 married Elisabeth, a daughter of Duke Max in Bavaria. The
beautiful and tragic Empress had come into the world on the same day as Cosima Liszt, and, many years later, the two
women—each, in her way, among the most remarkable of the century—made one another's acquaintance in a box at
the Bayreuth Festspielhaus.

   [4] 'Music of the Future', the name bestowed upon the music of Wagner, Liszt, and their associates by Professor Bischoff
of Cologne in mocking allusion to Wagner's *Art-Work of the Future* (1849) and its advocacy of a powerful new alliance
between music and the drama.

not excepting those 'which others don't concern themselves with', as he remarked to me about Mme Sand's memoirs, which he assured me he had read from first line to last. . . .

I made the acquaintance of a delightful young woman, Countess Nákó, who plays gypsy airs (*Zigeunerweisen*) entrancingly, with the spirit and passion peculiar to them. She also maintains at her own expense a small band of gypsy musicians (in the Banat) whom she recently got to play to Meyerbeer; when I arrived they had already departed again, but I had no reason to miss them for Mme Nákó is by herself alone worth a host of *Zigeuner*. In addition she occupies herself fairly seriously and not unsuccessfully with painting, and I saw several of her studies of heads and portraits (in oils), which seemed to me to have turned out very well. In a word, she is an outstanding person who has decidedly more understanding of art than had her predecessors. . . .

344. To Agnes Street-Klindworth. Dresden, 4 February. . . . After hearing one act of *Don Giovanni* I got back on the train and arrived here at 4 o'clock this morning. It was my second night on the railway—and to my extreme weariness of heart and mind is added a tiredness in all my limbs which isn't exactly making me livelier. Obliged to break my journey here (where I have to arrange a concert for next month) and for a few hours in Leipzig, I shall not be back in Weimar until tomorrow evening—at roughly the time that you will be returning to Brussels. . . .

The day after tomorrow, Wednesday, I shall go to Gotha to attend Berlioz's concert. *L'Enfance du Christ* is to be performed—and I shall write you a few words when returning to the Stadt Altenburg Hotel.

Since I left Weimar the only news I have had of the children has been through the Princess and you. Your opinion of my daughters corresponds perfectly with hers. . . .

345. To Hans von Bülow in Berlin. Weimar, 14 March

Very dear friend,

So many things and so many tasks have been burdening me since my return from Vienna that I have found it impossible to reply earlier than this to your splendid letter of last month. A few days after receiving it I had occasion to talk at some length about you, your person and your talents, with HRH the Regent of Baden, the Princess of Prussia, and her daughter Princess Luise. The Regent

referred very tactfully to the remark accompanying your *bow* after the performance of the Faust Overture, and pointed out how it helped turn the audience's
rather hesitant show of enthusiasm in the right direction. The Princess of P. and
her daughter spoke most charmingly of your amiability and your talent; and
I was delighted to learn from Their Highnesses of your successes as virtuoso
and teacher. Regarding your idea of becoming a *Hof-Pianist* [Court Pianist], I
should very much like to know if you have told anyone else (and whom) of this
idea before I venture to say anything more definite. So do please write and let
me know where things have got to with this impulse of yours to be a courtier;
and if you think it would be useful for me to be your mouthpiece, I should be
so with great pleasure, convinced as I am that I should encounter not a single
voice that would not be wholly favourable to such a wish on your part. If need
be, I could even write direct to the Princess of Prussia. . . .

Since my trip to Berlin I have found it impossible to get down to work, at
most finding enough time to correct the proofs of six of my symphonic poems,
which will at long last be out in another fortnight and which I shall send to
you at once. You will see that I have taken great pains with them, and on the
final proofs I have again made some quite notable changes. Two-piano arrangements of these same pieces will appear successively, and I hope you will find
them reasonably to your liking.

Berlioz spent three weeks here. The performance of his *Cellini* was very satisfying this time, and Caspari sang the principal role perfectly. A week later, at
the Princess of Prussia's request, we did *Lohengrin*, which Berlioz found little to
his taste. We didn't speak to one another about it, but to others he expressed
himself in no uncertain terms, which vexed me. For the rest, this performance
of *Lohengrin* created an enormous sensation here, and I fancy you would not
have been dissatisfied with it. There were some admirable moments from the
two Mildes and Caspari, and Fräulein Marx (of Darmstadt) declaimed and acted
her part most valiantly. As for myself, I confess that my admiration continues
to grow for this marvellous work, which is in my opinion the highest manifestation of dramatic genius. . . .

Litolff created a *furore* in Gotha with his *Robespierre* and *Girondins* overtures
etc., and was between Gotha and Weimar when *Cellini* and *Lohengrin* were performed, but didn't want to hear *either of them!*—which doesn't prevent his 4th
Concerto being an excellent work.

Griepenkerl has just given here two 'Vorlesungen über den kunsthistorischen
Fortschritt in der Musik und der Poesie [Lectures on art-historical progress in
music and poetry]' in which he mentioned neither Wagner nor Berlioz, doing no
more than compare Haydn with Wieland, Mozart with Goethe, and Beethoven
with Schiller, and beating the air with his fat paws on the subject of 'programme

music' which, to please his new friends in Weimar and elsewhere, he pronounced an absurdity. It was too ridiculous for words! Among other comicalities he thought he ought to remonstrate in a friendly way with me about the wrong path I had strayed on to, one which could lead only to disappointments, advising me to reflect on it and to take into consideration all the historical, critical, and aesthetic importance of the *principles* of a man as weighty as Griepenkerl! I thanked him politely for his good advice, and left off seeing him, for I haven't the patience to endure, even over a hot toddy, all that mish-mash of twaddle and self-importance. . . .

Send me some good news of yourself before long. Imitate the King of Sardinia, whom Louis Napoléon praised so highly when he said that 'he wasn't looking behind him'—and that you will keep in good health of mind and body is what is wished for you by

Your affectionate and devoted friend   F. Liszt

346. To Dionys Pruckner in Vienna. Weimar, 17 March ^G

Dearest Dionysius. . . .

Your intention of spending several months in Vienna and its charming environs, I entirely approve of; as, too, of the fact that you will be coming into closer contact with Czerny, a master whose manifold musical experiences can be of great benefit to you, both practically and theoretically. Of all the composers now living who have especially concerned themselves with playing and writing for the piano, I know none whose views and opinions measure up so exactly to what has actually been achieved. In the '20s, when for most musicians the greater number of Beethoven's creations were a kind of sphinx, Czerny played Beethoven *exclusively*, with an understanding that was as excellent as his technique was adequate and efficient. Nor, later on, did he close his mind to the progress that had been made in technique, but by his teaching and his works made a substantial contribution thereto. One can only regret that by excessive productivity he necessarily weakened himself and proceeded no further along the path of his first Sonata (Op. 6 in A flat) and some other works of that period —works of which I think very highly and regard as important and beautifully constructed compositions of the highest quality. But, unfortunately, Viennese social and publishing influences at that time were of a detrimental kind, and Czerny did not possess the requisite dose of toughness to evade them and uphold his *better self*. This is generally a difficult task, the solving of which brings with it many an inconvenience even for the ablest and highest-minded.

When you see Czerny, remember me to him as his grateful pupil and devoted, sincerely admiring friend. If I come to Vienna this summer I shall be very glad to spend a couple of hours with him once again. . . .

Yours in all friendship,   F. Liszt

347. To Richard Wagner in Zurich. Weimar, 25 March ᴳ

Dearest Richard!

At last I can inform you that at the *beginning* of May you will receive 1,000 francs. When you wrote to Vienna to me about this matter it was impossible for me to tell you anything definite, and even now I am not in a position to take on an *annual* commitment.

It always grieves me to send you disagreeable news, and so I waited for the moment when I could let you know that the sum in question would be sent to you. I have several times spoken to you of my difficult financial circumstances, which simply amount to this: that my mother and my three children are decently provided for by my earlier savings, and that I have to manage on my salary as Kapellmeister: 1,000 thalers a year plus a further 300 thalers as a present for the Court concerts.

Since, several years ago, I took the serious decision to devote myself to my artistic career, I have no longer been able to count on additional money from the music publishers. My symphonic poems (of which in a fortnight's time I shall send you a few in full score) bring me in not a ha'penny—in fact, even cost me the considerable sum I have to spend on copies to distribute to friends. My Mass and my Faust Symphony are likewise quite *unprofitable* works—and I have no prospect of earning money for several years yet. Fortunately I can just about keep going; but I have to pinch a good deal and avoid getting into difficulties, which might affect my whole position very badly. So don't take it amiss, dearest Richard, if I don't agree to your suggestion, because at present I really cannot undertake regular obligations. If, later on, my circumstances improve, which is not quite impossible, it will be a pleasure for me to make your situation easier for you.[5]

About my trip to Zurich I can tell you nothing before I know when the Cathedral at Esztergom is to be consecrated. Several newspapers announce that this ceremony is to take place in September. Should that be the case I would come to you earlier (at the beginning of August)—as soon as I have official news

---

[5] Wagner's next letter began: 'Your letter made me very distressed. Because you can't respond as you would wish to my request for new financial assistance, do you really think it necessary to apologize by giving me an exact description of your situation? If you only knew how deeply ashamed and humiliated I feel!'

about it I'll write to you. In the mean time I must remain here. On 8 April (birthday of the Grand Duchess) I have to conduct Verdi's *Due Foscari*, and at the end of April your niece Johanna's performances.

Carl Ritter's visit I unfortunately missed. I had gone to Gotha that day to hear the Duke's opera *Tony*; Carl Formes sang the title role. But I hope to see Carl in Zurich. Give him my friendly regards. Through his sister Emilie you have doubtless had news of our latest performance of *Lohengrin*, which went off very well. Caspari sang Lohengrin far better than it had been heard here before. The Princess of Prussia had asked for this performance, and for want of an *örtliche* [local] Ortrud (Frau Knopp, who used to sing the part here, has terminated her contract and is going to Königsberg) we sent in great haste for Frau Marx of Darmstadt. That we had a packed house and a keenly attentive audience goes without saying. Berlioz was present.

Do you correspond with Councillor Müller? He is very sincerely devoted to you and well intentioned.

Dingelstedt, who was here recently, intends to put on *Lohengrin* next winter and *not before*. Of the very *decided* success of the Prague performance you have probably had detailed news. Fräulein Stöger, daughter of the manager, sang Ortrud and wrote me a very enthusiastic letter about the enthusiasm of the audience and of the musicians. Until last season she was one of our artistes here in Weimar.

Farewell, be as patient as you can, dearest friend, and write soon to

Your   F.L.

348. To Anna Liszt in Paris. 2 April. ^{G (F)} As you are not with us today, dearest Mother, allow me at least to spend a few moments with you by letter and to celebrate my name-day by a heart-to-heart talk with you. Daniel, too, abandoned you in Easter Week and will probably—since his holidays were lengthened in honour of the birth of the Prince Imperial[6]—arrive in Paris only this evening. He will bring you, I hope, the best of news from Berlin, where the girls are getting on splendidly. They have quite enjoyed themselves this winter and seem to have gained more poise. Were their mother miraculously to come to her senses, we could hope the best for their future. In any case, I shall do everything possible for them.

Between ourselves there is much talk of a marriage between Hans von Bülow and Cosima. She seems very attracted to him. I have nothing against it; but I remain true to my resolve not to influence my daughters' free choice. That is

---

[6] Born on 16 Mar., the son of Napoleon III and Eugénie escaped to England during the Franco-Prussian War, entered the Woolwich Academy and was killed in the Zulu campaign of 1879.

the most convenient and at the same time the wisest position for me to take in this situation which I did not create but which was forced upon me, and the disadvantages of which I should like to avoid as much as possible, for myself as well as for my daughters.

Daniel will certainly have been the diplomatic intermediary between his mother and the girls. I am not letting him stay in Weimar, so as not to disturb him in this role which he will—I fear—set about rather clumsily. It would have been disagreeable to me to see him just now; for with the best intentions the good boy is naïve enough to burden his heart with all manner of nonsense, which exhausts my patience.

I am fairly well and hope in a few days to get back to work, which has become my *raison d'être*.

Farewell, dear Mother; bless your respectfully and lovingly devoted son

F. Liszt

349. To Agnes Street-Klindworth. Merseburg, 23 June

'Manibus O date lilia plenis!'[7]

It has been impossible for me to write to you this last week. At Magdeburg I had to involve myself actively in the *Musikfest*, Litolff having suddenly fallen ill. Things were none the worse for that, I fancy, and I even believe I was sufficiently praised for conducting the Ninth Symphony, which went marvellously with a women's chorus (made up of absolutely first-rate vocal societies from Brunswick and Magdeburg, and a very large orchestra, etc.), about a dozen members of which count among the notable talents of our time. A few hours later (on Sunday [15 June]) I was called back to Weimar in honour of HM the Dowager Tsaritsa of Russia,[8] who has always been very kind to me, and this time too seemed to put up with hearing me. And so, to get to the Belvedere in time, I spent the night on the train. The next day there was *Tannhäuser*—and since then I have done nothing but work at the second part of my Dante [Symphony], which is now completed in my head, and which I shall have finished writing down by the end of the week.

This afternoon I have come to Merseburg to go through a few organ pieces with Winterberger, about whom I have already spoken to you. He is a first-rate organist who will not take long to acquire the reputation he deserves. Before

---

[7] 'Oh with full hands give lilies!'—a graceful compliment from Liszt to his lady friend, for these are the words which Dante (*Purgatorio*, xxx. 21), borrowing from (and slightly adapting) Virgil (*Aeneid*, vi. 883), gives to 'cento ministri e messaggier di vita etterna' to announce the imminent—and prodigious—appearance of Beatrice in the Earthly Paradise.

[8] Alexandra Feodorovna, widow of Tsar Nicholas.

returning to Weimar I wanted to wish you good night—and now, stupidly, I have nothing to say to you.

Do you know what that means?[9] Yes, undoubtedly; but *I* no longer know what it signifies *to me*, so much have I succumbed, body and soul, to my malady.

Forgive me for being so silly and so monotonous in my silliness—yet I sometimes fancy that, one day, some sense will be discovered in all that.

I shall probably not go to Hungary but to Switzerland, around mid-August. If you're not too far away, I'll try to pay you a quick visit at that time.

If you can, write to me at somewhat greater length.

350. To Richard Wagner. Weimar [9 July]. [G] My trip to Hungary has these last few weeks quite unexpectedly become less certain, so I hesitated to write to you, dearest Richard, until I knew something more definite; for the date of my visit to you will be arranged according to whether that trip takes place or not. The consecration of the cathedral at Esztergom is fixed for 31 August, and if I do still go there to conduct my Mass I should be with you in Zurich around the 15th or 20th of September; but if I am exempted from going to Hungary I shall be in Zurich no later than the end of August. I hope to know by the end of next week what I am to do, and shall then ask the Kapellmeisterin to give you more precise details. But, accustomed though I am to *waiting*, I didn't want to wait any longer before telling you how much I hunger and thirst to be with you again and to go through our programme of *nonsense*. As *hors d'œuvre* (which, as is well known, possesses the quality of exciting appetite and thirst) to your banquet of the *Rheingold* and *Walküre*, I shall bring you my symphony to Dante's *Divina Commedia*, which I finished yesterday and which belongs to you. It lasts a little less than an hour, and may give you some pleasure. . . .

So far as your pardon is concerned, the status quo will remain for the time being, but I hope you will be able to come to me next winter, and in the mean time am preparing your quarters at the Altenburg. *Tell no one of this.* What I have heard I shall inform you of *in person*. Above all, take care of your health

---

[9] From Chopin's Etude in A flat, Op. 10/10.

and try to ensure that prospects open up before you which are rosier than the roses that erysipelas has painted upon your face. Unfortunately, as far as external matters are concerned, I can offer you little that is rosy, even though to all appearances I must be counted among the fortunate ones. And indeed I am fortunate, as fortunate as any mortal can be; I can confide this to *you*, because you know by what a boundless, selfless, and inexhaustible love my whole existence has been sustained these past eight years! Why need I be disturbed by other troubles? All else is only a way of expiating my sublime good fortune!

And now don't reproach me with not telling you anything of myself, since I have confided to you the secret of my usual silence. . . .

During my visit to Berlin I found Alwine Frommann in a touching state of anxiety about the articles which might be appearing in the Berlin press about the performance of *Tannhäuser*. Though I very much appreciate her friendship for you (which also maintains friendly feelings between the two of us), I could not help offending her through my indifference. In the same way, when she was last here, about three weeks ago, I could not refrain from making a couple of bad jokes about the *enthusiastic* interest with which she attended a performance of Auber's *Le Maçon*[10] in our local theatre—and she very nearly took offence at my bad jokes about the *many-sidedness* of her taste, or, rather, the want of taste revealed in her admiration of this wretched *musique de grisettes*. When the occasion arises I shall try to make amends to her.

Of the truth of what you write about the trouble and inconvenience we experience in associating with heterogeneous people, I have only too often had an opportunity to learn—although I might boast of possessing a much thicker and more *impermeable* skin than you, as well as a far larger portion of tolerance.

But for today, with all this prattle, I have tested your tolerance quite enough. In a few weeks we shall communicate without the need of ink and paper, which is the right and wholesome thing for us.

This time, the Kapellmeisterin may come to Zurich too.   Your   F.L.

351. To Richard Wagner in Mornex, near Geneva. Weimar, 1 August. [G] How I thank you, dearest, most unique of men, for having sent me the scores of your *Rheingold* and *Walküre*! For me the work has the fabulous power of attraction of the magnetic mountain, which takes irresistible hold of ships and mariners. Hans has been with me for a few days, and I could not deny him the joy of gazing upon your *Valhalla*; and so he strums away on the

---

[10] Opera first performed at the Opéra-Comique, Paris, May 1825.

piano, hammering out the orchestra, while I howl, groan, and bellow the vocal parts. This by way of prelude to *our* great rendering in your Zurich palace, to which I look forward most longingly.

A week from now I travel to Hungary, and on the 31st my Mass will be performed at the ceremony in Esztergom for which it was composed. For a number of secondary reasons I have afterwards to spend a couple of weeks in Pest and Vienna, so I shan't get to Zurich until about 20 September. The Kapellmeisterin will probably come too, with her daughter.

Franz Müller will be visiting you in Mornex about the middle of this month, bringing you his work on the *Nibelungen*.

The two scores I shall leave here to be looked after by the Kapellmeisterin, until you write to tell *her* that they are to be sent to the Härtels.

Your idea of becoming a house owner in Zurich is quite a singular one, and I congratulate you most heartily on all the building delights which await you. Dawison told me recently that his guest appearance in Berlin had enabled him to buy a villa near Dresden. You, with your scores, should proportionally be able to acquire at least the whole of Zurich plus the Seven Churfürsten and the Lake!

Whether Madame Erard will place a grand piano at your disposal on the favourable terms you suggest, is a questionable question, which on some suitable occasion I shall question her about!

But first and foremost see that you are well; the other *arrangements* will come about in due course.   God be with you.   F.L.

Hans (who sends you heartiest greetings) and I are just about to tackle the end of the *Walküre*.

At the end of the first week of August, Liszt set out for Hungary, and more especially for Esztergom (Gran), where on Sunday the 31st his specially commissioned *Missa solennis*—now generally known as the Gran Mass—was to be performed at the consecration of the town's great new cathedral.[11] 'I may say that I have *prayed* it rather than *composed* it,' he had written to Wagner the previous year after completing the Mass.

352. To Princess Carolyne in Weimar. Queen of England Hotel, Pest, 6.00 a.m., Monday, 11 August. I had this paper purchased in Esztergom yesterday and wanted to write to you after I had seen His Eminence. . . . I believe things will go pretty well in Esztergom, whither I shall return in about ten days.

---

[11] One of the oldest towns in Hungary, and the residence of the Cardinal Prince Primate, Esztergom, situated some 36 miles north-west of Budapest, is famous above all as the birthplace of St Stephen, the country's first 'apostolic king'. The imposing basilica, modelled on St Peter's in Rome and standing in a commanding and picturesque position 215 feet above the Danube, its huge dome visible from afar, was built between 1821 and 1870.

. . . Bishop Fekete is still very lively and fit, although close to 70. I didn't stay with him yesterday, which very much surprised him, but I intend to make use of his hospitality when I return. During the festival several generals from the Emperor's suite will be in neighbouring rooms—for Fekete has taken over the provision of accommodation for the military, and has told me that there will be neither canon nor bishop in his home at that time. It is he who has undertaken to direct the *batteries*. His tall figure and strong build qualify him perfectly for those duties. There will be an 101-gun salute when the Emperor arrives, on Saturday evening, 30 August. The next day there will be several salvoes during the consecration ceremony, which will last from 7.30 in the morning until at least 1.00 p.m. The basilica's acoustics seem excellent and the organ perfect. . . .

My friends in Pest did something rather nice. On receiving news of my arrival they mounted a big dinner in my honour, and several people told me that they were preparing to welcome me with *pompa di festa*. For this reason I arrived here on the sly, at 5 o'clock in the morning. Having got off the train, I set off on a good quarter of an hour's walk along the Danube, conjuring up some memories and thinking of you and Magnolet. Grosse, who is thoroughly enjoying his trip and serving me marvellously, took a carriage to the hotel—and installed me in the very same room which was my bedroom 10 years ago. He has a small adjoining room, and for both together I am paying 3 fl. 30 kr. a day, slightly more than 2 écus, which is not exorbitant. My two very large windows, one of which has a small balustrade, face the mountains, the Palatine's Palace, the old ruined fortress, and the Buda observatory. It is a splendid view, and from morning onwards there is a great but fairly quiet traffic of boats, rafts, and steamers on the Danube. This population, which has none of the characteristics which give coarseness and greed for gain to trading peoples, I have always found more likeable than any other: their *gatya* drawers, cut roughly with wide flaps, rounded and let out below, white and completely dirt-proof—the *guba*, a kind of peasant's greatcoat, likewise white—their waistcoats of coarse blue cloth with white metal buttons—their carts and teams of oxen, the way they walk and smoke: everything has a special character. Nothing anywhere else can take the place of these things and these racial features when they are connected with childhood memories, and when this music of the heart, which is one's feeling for one's native country—for the Hungarian as for the Pole—has been kept unsullied. So I felt very emotional even at the frontier, when I glimpsed one of those so simple tableaux of a shepherd squatting nonchalantly 'in the custody of' his sheep and his oxen—for it was he who looked as though he were being guarded by his animals. Like an injured dove my thoughts flew lovingly towards you, my good angel—towards your peasants, your fields, your Podolia, your sunrises, and those long-past days which burn your soul with so ardent a flame!! Dear, adored, unique one, you left everything for me, to give more than everything to me—to me who am only a vacillating shadow, unable to give anything to you, do anything for you! Say nothing to me of that!—Leave me my incurable sadness and suffering! Just fill me now and then with your strength and your celestial sweetness, and let us hope in God who made us one for the other! . . .

353. To Princess Carolyne. [Pest] Wednesday, 13 August. Augusz lives in a villa an hour away from here. I dined there yesterday and the day before, which took me nearly 5 hours each time. Augusz is more and better than a somebody—he is a brain. He has behaved wonderfully to me, and I believe I can count on very marked goodwill on his part. This morning I shall pay some formal calls with him. When I entered the box of the Intendant, Count Ráday, yesterday evening, the audience began spontaneously to applaud me, and I made several bows of acknowledgement. Unanimous opinion is very much in my favour, and Festetics[12] will have only the role of Fieramosca in the final scene of *Cellini*. Nevertheless, I am beginning to doubt whether he will stand fast until the day my Mass is performed—and think he will leave Pest and Esztergom on some family pretext. You can have no idea of the harassment and insults he has been subjected to, and which despite all my conciliatory goodwill haven't yet ceased. The fact is, he has displayed astounding maladroitness and all the stupidity of enormous vanity—not to mention a strong dose of lies and duplicity. It would take too long to write all these things in detail; but we shall soon have an opportunity to chat about them in our blue room. I should like to be able to put at your window the magnificent view I have before me. You would give an even more magnificent description of it, by absorbing the warm hues of this splendid sun, which would remind you of your Podolian summers. I don't know what the temperature has risen to—but the fact is, we are roasting.

The day after tomorrow, the 15th, a Mass by Weber is being performed at the parish church, between 10.00 and 11.00. I shall be there, and will take advantage of my stay here to hear some other masses as well, perhaps one of the 4 by Cherubini, for vocal and instrumental music is performed regularly during services at the main churches here. On the 18th the Emperor's birthday is being celebrated, and on the 20th, St Stephen's Day, I shall return to Esztergom. . . .

---

[12] Count Leó Festetics, magnate, composer and Intendant of the Hungarian National Theatre, in earlier years so great a friend and admirer of Liszt the virtuoso, had been intriguing against Liszt the composer, apparently in the hope that a work of his own might be performed at the consecration ceremony.

This evening I am going to the German Theatre, to see Fräulein Seebach play Adrienne Lecouvreur.[13] Afterwards I shall hasten to the gypsies, as I did yesterday evening. You know what a special attraction this music has for me—so I plan to steep myself in it. I could be defined pretty well in German: 'Zu einer Hälfte Zigeuner, zur andern Franziskaner [Half gypsy, half Franciscan friar]!' There is, however, still something else which holds sway over these two contrary elements, isn't there, my adorable darling? It is this something else which is writing to you, thinking of you, and blessing you unceasingly!

You can send me by the next post the packet containing my orchestral parts, deposited in your cellar oratory. But have it very well wrapped in oilcloth. Now that you are more or less *au courant*, I shall perhaps let 3 or 4 days go by without writing to you. My rehearsals begin tomorrow. I have all but committed an extravagance—by buying, or rather ordering, a piano for roughly 500 florins from Beregszászy, who won a first medal at the last Paris Exhibition. I was seduced to some extent, I believe, by the portrait of Louis Napoléon next to the maker's name—and also by the wood which is very essentially Hungarian, *Eschenholz* [ash]. When all is said and done, I find these instruments excellent and admirably constructed. The manufacturer was delighted with my order, as you can imagine, and will give me credit for as long as I like. This new piano will very advantageously replace my Tomaschek, and it seems to me to be in good taste to buy a piano in Pest. . . .

354. To Agnes Street-Klindworth. Queen of England Hotel, [Pest] 13 August. Here is a small picture of Esztergom,[14] which for centuries has been the see of Catholicism in Hungary. The solemn ceremony in which this basilica will be consecrated is to take place on the 31st of this month. The Emperor and four Archdukes will arrive the previous evening with a retinue of 60 dignitaries and high-ranking officials; assembled here, too, will be four cardinals, seven or eight archbishops and about forty bishops. If you are interested, I'll send you a detailed description of this great ceremony, which according to the programme will last more than six hours (from 7.30 a.m. until 2.00).

As a result of the foolish wounded vanity of an old friend of mine, who claimed for his own work the honours of performance on this day, that of my Mass was put in jeopardy. But at this news there arose a really energetic and unanimous protest in *all* Pest and Buda's German and Hungarian newspapers; and the musicians, and everyone who has some idea of a piano, a violin, or a note of music,

---

[13] The title role (later much associated with Sarah Bernhardt) in the play by Scribe and Legouvé.
[14] An illustration on the notepaper he was using.

and even many of those who have only heard tell of these things, showed their fellow-feeling with me quite resoundingly. The result of this was that the opposition (by now reduced to one individual plus his shadow), which 3 weeks earlier had managed to persuade His Eminence the Cardinal Archbishop-Prince Primate[15] of Hungary that my Mass would last *three hours* and be exorbitantly expensive, in consideration of which it had been decided that a work other than mine would be chosen—the opposition, I say, was every day and almost every hour for a fortnight so disgraced and decried in the newspapers, the salons, the cafés, at the theatre and in church, that it gained me in advance an almost unheard-of triumph. It is now established and undisputed that I form an integral part of the national pride, and when I entered the Intendant's box at the Hungarian Theatre yesterday evening the audience applauded me warmly. I should need to be a dreadful imbecile not to do honour to so exceptionally favourable a position, and despite a few difficulties which will not fail to arise I shall try to get a firm foothold and take root. . . .

Your letter reached me punctually an hour before I left Weimar. I stopped for only a few hours in Prague and half a day in Vienna. In Prague, Dreyschock had arranged for me to dine with several distinguished persons who are of interest to me. It is not out of the question that I may return to Prague for a few days; they are planning to follow Weimar's example and celebrate a Wagner Week there, by performing Wagner's 3 operas during the same week around mid-September. . . .

Prague occupies rather a remarkable place in the annals of music. After the rebuffs Mozart had in Vienna with his *Nozze di Figaro*, to which the Viennese preferred some work or other that has since been totally forgotten, he found in Prague a warm welcome and lively appreciation. 'It was for Prague that I wrote my *Don Giovanni*!' he said; and it was there, too, for the Emperor's[16] coronation that he had his *Clemenza di Tito* performed for the first time. On this topic I'll tell you an anecdote which has not been recorded by any biographer, but which has been guaranteed to me as authentic. After the First Act of the *Clemenza di Tito*, HM left the theatre: the manager arrived in a fright to give this disastrous news to Mozart, who fully conscious of his own genius replied point-blank: 'Um so besser, da haben wir einen Esel weniger im Theater [All the better—now we have one donkey fewer in the theatre]!' I am far from approving such

---

[15] János Scitovszky, who had been Liszt's host ten years earlier when Bishop of Pécs. The great musician, who had enchanted Scitovszky with his 'wonderful playing, extensive culture and outstanding human qualities' (the words of the Liszt scholar Margit Prahács), had at that time promised to compose a mass for a ceremony to be held after completion of restoration work on Pécs Cathedral. Since, however, the work of restoration had been long drawn out, and Scitovszky had in the mean time (1849) become Cardinal Prince Primate with a residence in Esztergom, he had asked Liszt to compose, instead, a mass for the ceremony at which the great new basilica in that town was to be consecrated.

[16] Leopold II.

remarks; but sometimes they come to mind when I hear uncrowned donkeys pontificating about things of which they haven't the least idea.

During his travels in Germany in the '40s it was in Prague, as well, that Berlioz met with most enthusiasm; and now a sizeable part of the public is showing rather elevated taste in preferring *Lohengrin* even to *Tannhäuser*. And so for someone like me it is rather a curious phenomenon to observe at closer quarters. . . .

Until 1 September write to me at the Queen of England Hotel, Pest (Hungary), where from my window I enjoy a very grandiose view over the Danube, the town, and the mountains of Buda. I rise early to have just a little bit of leisure to dream empty dreams!   A.A.

355. To Princess Carolyne. [Pest] Monday, 18 August. I have only good news to give you, my beloved. Everything is proceeding in the way I hoped, and it would be all but impossible to find elsewhere so full and superabundant a measure of sympathy, consideration, even respect, as I am given here. The little incident I told you about of my reception at the theatre made a sensation in high circles. Every evening when I enter or leave one of the public places, the Hoppegarten, Lloyd Casino, etc., where after the theatre I regularly go for supper—people greet me warmly with prolonged *éljens*. My deportment is, I believe, what it should be: simple and serious. I hear a good deal of music, at the theatre and in church. Yesterday the Haydn Mass known as the Nelson was performed; and today, for the Emperor's birthday, I shall hear Cherubini's 4th Mass. Tomorrow I go to Esztergom, and return here in the evening of the next day. My rehearsals are going well—and the performers are beginning to understand my work and to find it very much to their taste! Next week we shall decide what remains to be done after Esztergom. At all events, between the 24th and 29th we shall have two big final public rehearsals of my Mass. Around the 4th or 6th of September, a grand concert. I have also just been sent a very appropriate letter from Prague asking for my Mass, which could be performed on 28 September, feast of Wenceslas, patron saint of Bohemia. I haven't yet decided to accept, although the proposal is a very agreeable one and extremely opportune. For his part, Haslinger has written to me from Vienna to offer to have the Mass engraved—but I shall try to make other arrangements about that. You will have a good laugh when I tell you the details of the censorship this poor Mass was forced to undergo before my arrival. All these antecedents, moreover, have been extremely favourable to me, and I should have to be a frightful idiot not to achieve a complete and extraordinary success. . . . My preliminary correspondence having become almost public, and the Viennese salons having taken notice of it, I am told that, about a quotation made from one of my letters, 'Ich habe die Messe mehr gebetet als componirt [I have more prayed the Mass than composed it]', Mgr. Viale Prela, the Apostolic Nuncio, exclaimed with that touch of malice familiar to *Monsignori*: 'Gott sei Dank, dass Liszt doch betet [Thank God that Liszt *does* pray]!' . . .

356. To Princess Carolyne. Friday, 22 August. Since yesterday I have been staying at Karácsonyi's, in Buda. Immediately on my arrival in Pest he had got his steward to offer me this very spacious and elegant set of rooms, in which a new piano had already been placed expressly for me. As Karácsonyi was not here, and had not written to me, I had some scruples about accepting. When his steward made repeated visits, those scruples disappeared, and I am now making use of his carriages, his horses, and his servants quite shamelessly—until Karácsonyi and his wife, née Countess Marzipani, get back tomorrow from Bad Ischl. According to the custom of the country, it is practising hospitality to accept without standing on ceremony that which is offered one. In short, I am rather more tranquil here, and since there is no lack of horses in the stable I shall not be hindered in my movements. Karácsonyi is returning for a few days only, in honour of the invitation extended to him by the Cardinal for the ceremony in Esztergom, without which he would probably have gone to Switzerland and Italy. He is having built the most beautiful house in Buda, a kind of *palazzo*, next to the temporary accommodation I am now living in. This taste for architecture will cost him several hundred thousand florins; but since his fortune is one of the best administered in the country he will hardly notice this expense, which, moreover, squares with his habits of display. The whole town is taking an interest in this building, and when it is finished it will be one of the city sights, and honoured with a coloured lithograph. . . .

Your letter of the 19th and Magnolette's reached me yesterday evening. I kissed it fervently and fell asleep while reading it. Remember me kindly to Tausig, whom I am very fond of; his reflections on *Marino Faliero* and *Hamlet* delighted me. I believe in a great future for this sharp fellow. Pruckner arrives on the 24th; Winterberger,[17] whom I took to Esztergom, is looking cheerful. This evening he and I will play *Tasso* to a very small number of artistes *chez* Brauer, director of church music in Pest, who is behaving marvellously to me. My rehearsals are going extremely well, and although I am already very tired of my Mass—for I have hardly any patience for the study of my works—it is nevertheless giving me all sorts of personal gratification to which I cannot be wholly indifferent.

---

[17] Who played the organ part at the performance of the Mass.

But my hunger and thirst for work and production is becoming still more intense. I should so like to be back in our blue room, for here it is absolutely impossible for me to work! . . .

357. To Princess Carolyne. 7.00 a.m., Wednesday, 27 August. . . . Singer will have sent you the poster of the first rehearsal of the Mass, which took place at 3.30 yesterday in the charming hall of the National Museum, unfortunately too small for this event. Although the cost of tickets had been slightly increased —3 fl. for the best seats, 2 fl. for second best, and 1 fl. for third—there were many people who had been unable to obtain any, and from what I am told the hall has never been filled like this at any of the Philharmonic and other concerts which have been given here for years. The heat, too, was literally unbearable, and I left bathed in perspiration—which prevented me from writing to you immediately, since I had to change clothes in Pest, my Buda lodging-place being half an hour away. The vocal and instrumental performers had already grown passionately fond of my Mass at the earlier partial rehearsals—and in town it is quite generally being said: 'Das ist wohl ganz neue Musik, aber zum Niederknien [This is entirely new music, but for kneeling to].' Each section was much applauded, and at the end I was recalled 3 times. The performance was good, while still lacking several half-tints which will increase the impression very considerably. My thoughts and feelings are not, I believe, altogether understood by the public here—but people are keenly aware that the work is something out of the ordinary. . . .

I saw Countess Batthyány again yesterday, Lajos Batthyány's widow, who has been back here for some time, to take her daughter into society a little, and also, I believe, to regain possession of some property. She is a very noble woman, and her elder daughter, aged 17 or 18, is charming. She had come to my rehearsal, and in the evening I spent an hour in her box at the Hungarian Theatre. The *Nordstern*[18] was being performed, and again affected me disagreeably. I really can't be reconciled to its vulgarity, however artistically disguised. . . .

358. To Princess Carolyne. [Esztergom] 31 August. It is a quarter to 3. The last Amen of the Mass has just been pronounced. HM the Emperor, who is staying opposite, is returning to the sounds of the melody of Haydn's *Gott erhalte*—and I am coming to kiss your hands, and those of Magnolette, while

---

[18] Presumably *L'Etoile du Nord.*

telling you that everything went according to your wishes, and that God blessed me. My Mass began at 1.30. As I had estimated, the whole work lasts only 45 to 50 minutes at most, watch in hand. The performance was perfect, even admirable in several places—without the least little hitch, without the shadow of a Karlsruhe *bassoon*.[19] In all, we were more than 130 singers and players. Unless I am greatly mistaken, the general impression produced by the work is beyond what I could have flattered myself I would obtain. I shall be sending you newspapers and letters, which will give you a detailed account of today's 'date'. For the moment, I want only to thank and bless you for having inspired me with good thoughts and helped me to work for God! Be blessed 1,000 and 1,000 times! I shall sing of you on harps and organs later! More details tomorrow.

359. To Princess Carolyne. Tuesday, 2 September. I have been back in Buda since 11.30 yesterday evening. It was impossible for me to write to you again from Esztergom. I shall add only a few things to my brief report of the day before yesterday, keeping back several details for our conversations in the blue room. On the day of the consecration I was not invited to the Primate's table—and declined an invitation to the other table, to which Leó Festetics, Count Ráday, Karácsonyi, *et al.* had also been invited, and who likewise made their excuses. I dined on the boat with all the artistes, Festetics and Ráday. . . . As a résumé of the impression made by my Mass, I can tell you that throughout almost the entire performance all heads were turned towards the choir.[20] At a rough count there must have been 4,000 people in the church.

Yesterday morning, Monday, I had a visit from the Bishop of Transylvania, Haynald,* who is one of the heads of the Hungarian Church. . . . He is a man of about 40, rather tall and slim, with noble, delicate features. He speaks French and Italian marvellously, is intimately acquainted with [Baron] Bach and already strongly tipped as a future Primate of Hungary. I am grateful to him for coming to see me, as a particular courtesy, and we later did the short journey from Esztergom to Pest together. There was another banquet at the Primate's at 1.00 yesterday, attended by the Cardinal Archbishop of Agram, the Graeco-Catholic

---

[19] At the Karlsruhe Music Festival in Oct. 1853 a bassoonist had made a wrong entry during a performance, conducted by Liszt, of Beethoven's Ninth Symphony. 'In a passage where the [bassoon] enters on an off beat, the player made a mistake and came in on the even beat', recalled Liszt's pupil William Mason. 'This error, not the conductor's fault, occasioned such confusion that Liszt had to stop the orchestra and begin again, and the little fellows [the critics] made the most of this opportunity to pitch into him.'

[20] That is, towards Liszt himself. Perhaps, however, he was leaving out of account the consuming interest of his compatriots in his own person, as reported by Vilmos von Csapó when writing of this return of Liszt's to Hungary: 'He was a phenomenon whom, despite themselves, people simply could not take their eyes off.'

Archbishop of Grosswardein,[21] the Archbishop of Udine, who did me the honour of hailing me in Italian as '*la gloria dell' Ungheria*', the Bishop of Brünn, Augusz—in all, about sixty people. I was seated between Count István Károlyi and Bishop Haynald, who seemed almost to be having something of an advance look at 'his dwelling-place'. The Primate proposed a toast to me in Latin towards the end of the dinner, to some extent taking the hint given him by Haynald. You know Count Károlyi by reputation. Already the previous day he had expressed himself very warmly in favour of my Mass, and tomorrow I shall pay him a visit in Fót, where he has had built the most successful church, architecturally speaking, in Hungary. It contains paintings—remarkable ones, apparently —by Blaas of Vienna, and an organ by Moser, costing 12,000 florins. It is Fót which is the active centre of Catholic propaganda in Hungary.

Here, now, is what I have still to do: last performance of my Mass at the parish church in the course of this week; concert at the Hungarian Theatre with *Les Préludes* and *Hungaria*; rehearsals and performance of my first Mass, for men's voices only—it will probably be sung on the day of the consecration of the *Herminie Chapel* in memory of the daughter of the deceased Palatine, sister of the Archduke Stephen, on 8 September. That will take me until about 12 September. On the 15th, Strauss (!) is performing my *Mazeppa* in Vienna, and proposes to give me a grand serenade. . . .

I hope that Magnolette and you, my good angel, are in good health of mind and body—and bless you with all my heart.   F.L.

360. To Princess Carolyne. [Buda] Friday, 5 September. Thank you for your dear heather! It blooms on the smoking altar of my heart. Cassel's verses I handed to Augusz, who yesterday did me the honour of coming to dinner here with his wife. Karácsonyi and his wife having left for Ostend, there were only five of us at dinner: the Auguszes, Winterberger, and a M. Bakits, Karácsonyi's lawyer and businessman. . . .

Yesterday my Mass was performed admirably in the Pest parish church, which barely contained the enormous crowd of the curious that this performance had attracted. The sonority was far better than in Esztergom, and the musicians in even better form and even more imbued with an understanding of my work. And so it created prodigious emotion. From what I have been told, many persons wept, and Augusz tells me that he was obliged to support Count Károlyi, who had been so kind as to come from Fót—2 hours away—to hear my Mass

---

[21] Now Oradea in Romania.

again. Singer will have sent you the *Lloyd* and an article published separately by Engesser. Several Viennese newspapers, the *Fremdenblatt* and the *Oesterreichische Zeitung*, which have taken a position of spiteful prejudice against me, accuse me of transplanting the *Zukunftsmusik*, and even the Venusberg, into the Church, which is a fairly well calculated *coup de Jarnac*.[22] But the clergy will not be taken in, and, in the person of several of its leaders, is making a show of adopting me openly. On this topic I enclose a copy in Latin of the opinion expressed by the Bishop of Temesvár. . . . I have two or three small changes to make to my score, and will try to shut myself up for 24 hours to attend to them before returning to Vienna. . . .

After a preliminary 2-hour rehearsal, I spent the rest of Wednesday at Count Károlyi's in Fót, where I met two bishops and several ecclesiastical personages. Augusz accompanied me, and I can only greatly praise the splendid welcome given me by the Count. Among his other courtesies was that of placing me on his left at dinner. I shall subscribe about 100 florins to his work of Catholic propaganda, which moreover is greatly prospering. In Vienna I expect also to make the acquaintance of the Revd Father Klinkowström, the most celebrated of the preachers of the Company of Jesus. I shall give you orally my impressions of the church in Fót, for which Count Károlyi has already spent nearly a million francs. . . .   F.L.

361. To Princess Carolyne. Friday, 12 September. I have arrived at the end of my stay here, and it only remains to ask God to bless the little that I have done. . . . I have nothing of particular interest to tell you of these last three days, unless it is that I am going to be admitted as 'confrater' by the Franciscans, who will send my diploma to me in Weimar. I dined with them yesterday, at the same table at which I sat in 1823, '40 and '46. My old affection for this monastery has not diminished with the years, and the Franciscans welcomed me as one of their own. A talented painter, Giergl, is doing an oil portrait of me, and Singer is bringing you a photograph which, notwithstanding my reservations about photography in general, I find not too disagreeable. I shall try to be ready to leave tomorrow evening, Saturday, and despite His Eminence's invitation will probably not be stopping in Esztergom. By Sunday evening at the latest I shall be in Vienna, and will write to you with a little more leisure— for here I find it all but impossible to gain half an hour's rest during the day,

[22] An unforeseen blow or 'stab in the back', from the duel fought before Henri II in 1547 by Gui Chabot, Lord of Jarnac, and the seemingly invincible duellist and swordsman La Châtaigneraie, when, by a trick learnt for the occasion, Jarnac passed his opponent's guard, wounding and vanquishing him.

and since suppers go on until 1 or 2 o'clock in the morning, I am worn out when I get back. Despite everything, I look well, and your dream gave you a false impression of my face, which is in rather good condition. Endless *tendresses* to you, dear, unique and adored one. I yearn for the moment when we shall see one another again, in the first days of October. . . .

362. To Princess Carolyne. Kaiserin von Oesterreich Hotel, Vienna, Monday morning, 15 September. On my arrival here yesterday evening I was at once handed your dear letter—and fell asleep over your dear advice about sleep. . . .

My last days in Pest brought nothing new. At 7.00 a.m. on Saturday I took Augusz to the boat for Szekszárd, settled a few bills, lunched in the house, with Erkel,* having earlier made a little music, took leave of Ráday at the Hungarian Theatre—and then left, as I had arrived, without drums or trumpets, at 9.00 in the evening, conscious of having done more or less what I had to do, and as I was to do it. I shall give you an oral summary of the facts of my present stay, and presume that you will approve of my restricting myself to only one concert in Pest. Singer will bring you a few more newspapers, plus two photographs which will convince you, I hope, that I am not looking too bad. . . .

This evening, at the Volksgarten, Strauss is performing several excerpts from *Lohengrin*, and the March finale of *Mazeppa*. . . .

363. To Princess Carolyne. Vienna, 16 September. . . . I have just received, a few moments ago, a definitive letter from Prague. I shall be there on Sunday morning, and in reply to these lines write to me until 28 September at the *Gasthof zum schwarzen Ross* [Black Horse Inn], where we spent a day in '48. There is a *Naturforscher* [naturalists] congress here at present. People were expecting Humboldt, who of course isn't coming; but Carus,* whose brother is here, and Schleiden are still expected. Tomorrow I shall see Bach and Klinkowström. The Strauss evening went off very well, and the concluding part of *Mazeppa* was encored, as were the two pieces from *Lohengrin*. The programme bore the words *Zu Ehren der Anwesenheit des Herrn Doctor Liszt* [In honour of the presence of Dr Liszt]. There is a very strong possibility of my Mass being performed.

Your advice to Wagner was perfect. One would like to hammer him as flat as possible. That isn't nice, but it's how it is. Happily, he has it in *him* to do something good—and after his death a statue will be put up to him, as to poor

Schiller. Such is the law of destiny that it is good to understand, so as to submit to it only to the degree necessary! . . . F.L.

While in Prague Liszt twice wrote to a certain Hungarian actress.

364. To Lilla Bulyovszky in Pest. Prague, 22 September

Madame,

Fräulein Seebach whom I had the pleasure of seeing yesterday morning told me that you have been so good as to devote further time to looking for my spectacles. Alas! It is field-glasses for looking a few hundred leagues into the distance that I need rather than spectacles which would help me only to see more distinctly what I have not the least desire to look at! But be that as it may, I am no less grateful to you, Madame, for having ... remembered me after my departure, and for thus agreeably lending me an *excuse* for thanking you. For the rest, as regards excuses I was keeping another in reserve and proposing to write to tell you that I feared I hadn't told you how much ... I attach to the visit to Weimar that you have promised me; and I ask you not to forget that this little town which Mme de Staël defined as 'a Schloss surrounded by a village' will necessarily be on your route when you go to Paris. Allow me, therefore, Madame, to count on the favour of your memory, and please be very much assured of the great pleasure it will give me to see you again and to do you the honours of the memorials of Schiller and Goethe which are the glory of Weimar.

During the few days I have just spent in Vienna I found it impossible to go either to the opera or to the Burgtheater, and I did not even set eyes on the smallest part of the procession of the illustrious company of 'Naturforscher' (which formed the most interesting spectacle of the moment)—with the exception of Dr Tormay, whom I caught a glimpse of on the railway platform. The day before yesterday I sought him out again, but with no more success than you had with my spectacles, which compels me to ask you further to give him my most affectionate compliments plus all my thanks for the pamphlet and the newspapers he sent me on the day of my departure from Pest.

I cannot tell you, Madame, with what profound and inalienable emotion I recall the welcome given to me during this latest sojourn of mine in Pest; and I am eager to find a little peace and solitude so that I can sing to myself some of the music which, in fitting response to that emotion, throbs in my heart. The 'long-eared ones' will doubtless get nothing out of it—but why worry about them?

If you are in a kind mood send a few lines to me at the 'Black Horse', Prague, where I am staying until next Sunday (28 Sept.), after which I shall go to Zurich to see Richard Wagner.

A thousand respectfully admiring and sincerely affectionate compliments,

F. Liszt

365. To Lilla Bulyovszky. Prague, 28 September

Madame,

I am replying at once to your *second* letter. Your dream is the dream of a child: I am too old to love a young girl—and I do not remember experiencing, even in my youth, a similar infatuation. How to define what I *understand* by this word love? If in your capacity as a novelist you have some psychological interest in this topic, read the chapter in the *third* book of *The Imitation of Christ* (on 'the effects of divine love'). You will find therein the familiar nourishment of my thought, the heavenly manna on which my soul has subsisted during long years in the desert of this earthly existence—and when you come to Weimar I shall be able to continue this chapter for you in person; if, that is, your curiosity and your novelist's patience are not at an end!

In any case, I promise you a *compatriot's* welcome, without nonsense or pedantry of any kind. You have accused me of coquetry of the spirit, and I have permitted myself to remark that you are mistaken. If you retain for me a little of the goodwill that I dare lay claim to, you will, I am convinced, perceive your error and understand me better. 'You live as though you were immortal!' a very intelligent woman once said to me.[23] 'Why not?' I replied. My task in this world is an arduous and resigned one. I am like one of those age-old mountain peaks where the roses do not grow but from which the gaze of my thought embraces a vast horizon and is brightened by the appearance of some friendly star.

But what's the point of all this chatter which doesn't concern you? Thank you for your letter—and we'll meet again, won't we? I leave Prague tomorrow morning and in about a week shall be in Zurich, where I shall be seeing Wagner, who is busy completing the most prodigious dramatic work yet attempted. It is called 'Der Ring des Nibelungen, ein Bühnenfestspiel in 4 Abenden', and he is writing words and music alike. Two of the works in this tetralogy (*Das Rheingold* and *Die Walküre*) are finished—and the two others (*Der junge Siegfried* and *Siegfrieds Tod*) will be ready in a year or two at most. When their author is dead

[23] See Letter 245 n. 6.

there will be subscriptions to put up a statue to him; but in the mean time he lives in exile overwhelmed by sufferings and anxieties!

A revoir again, Madame, and a thousand respectful and admiring compliments.

F. Liszt

Don't write to me *until after* I have told you *where* to address it.

On 13 October Liszt arrived in Zurich, where he stayed at the Hôtel Baur (as did Carolyne and Marie who came soon afterwards) and, despite being confined to bed for more than a fortnight with a skin complaint, was for several weeks able to enjoy the company of his friend Wagner.

The following letter to his royal patron in Weimar went largely unheeded, and Wagner's theatre was eventually built not in Weimar but at Bayreuth, which was also the venue for the first complete performance, twenty years later, of *Der Ring des Nibelungen*.

366. To the Grand Duke Carl Alexander. Zurich, 10 November

Monseigneur,

It is my duty to call your attention once again to something great, and I shall broach the subject without further preamble. For the honour and interest of the patronage that Your Royal Highness accords to the fine arts, and also for the honour of the initiative and of the priority that I venture to ask you to claim and maintain for Weimar in these matters, as far as is possible, it seems to me not only appropriate but necessary and, as it were *essential*, for Wagner's *Nibelungen* to be performed *first of all* in Weimar. This performance will unquestionably be no very easy matter; exceptional measures will have to be taken, such as the construction of a theatre and the appointment of an *ad hoc* personnel in accordance with Wagner's wishes; difficulties and obstacles will be met, but in my opinion, and all things well considered, it will be enough for Your Royal Highness to apply himself to wanting it seriously for matters to go as though by themselves. As for the material and moral outcome, I do not fear to answer for its being in all points such that Monseigneur will have reason to be satisfied.

Wagner's work, of which half is already finished and the whole of which will be completed in two years (summer '58), will tower above this age as the most monumental achievement of contemporary art; it is unparalleled, marvellous, and sublime. Would it not therefore be deplorable were petty considerations of *medio*cracy—which in certain circumstances rules and governs—to succeed in preventing it from shining and radiating over the world? Allow me firmly to believe that this will not be the case and that Your Royal Highness will not hesitate in the accomplishment of the noble task which has fallen to him.

For the last week a malady which is not very serious but extremely tiresome has kept me in bed, where I am writing these lines[24] so as not to delay further in giving expression to a sentiment which prevails over any other consideration. I still need another ten days or so to be more or less back on my feet, and expect to return to Weimar by about the end of the month. I shall do so full of confidence in Your Royal Highness's kindness to me, more disposed than ever to work and well deserve it, if possible, by serving you according to your wishes, Monseigneur, and remaining very sincerely

Your devoted and grateful servant   F. Liszt

367. To Baron Augusz. Zurich, 20 November [G]

My dear friend,

Even if absence does not prevent a continuation of the empathy of mind and feelings that is characteristic of true friendship, the fluent and substantial expression of that empathy, achieved without difficulty when friends are together, is nevertheless much reduced; and so there often comes over me a yearning desire not to be separated too long from the few who take me as I am. To write to you I was merely waiting for the quiet kind of day that can be used comfortably to set down a number of things that have occurred. Unfortunately for a couple of weeks I have had to keep only too quiet, my doctor having ordered me to bed. My indisposition by no means gives cause for concern; but, to be fully restored to health, I shall have to take things easily for a time and look after myself. . . .

I had some very agreeable news the other day from my cousin Dr Eduard Liszt. HE the Minister v. Bach was expecting my request and has given orders for the full score and piano edition of the Gran Mass to be published at government expense by the Imp. and Roy. Printing Press in Vienna. A final copy of the manuscript, containing a number of facilitations, improvements, and not insignificant additions, which occurred to me at the Pest and Prague performances, when the general impression became still more powerful and spiritual (for example, the closing fugue in the Gloria and 4 entries instead of 2 in the words 'Et unam sanctam catholicam et apostolicam Ecclesiam', plus a Heaven-soaring climax in this movement!), I am now having prepared after spending about a fortnight writing down these additions and revising the entire work. For the musically knowledgeable to ascertain what the score contains, it is essential for them to examine and inspect it, both before and after performance. . . .

---

[24] With which was enclosed a letter of 31 Oct. to Carl Alexander from Wagner.

The glorious paprika you sent to Prague for me, and for which I thank you most warmly, is a guarantee that you forget nothing and *tempore opportuno* will obtain whatever is appropriate.

As soon as I can depart I shall go to Munich for a few days, and about the middle of December I intend to be back in Weimar, to spend the winter there and make progress with my work. If you can from time to time find a free quarter of an hour, a letter from you will give me great pleasure. Later on, let me know two or three months in advance *if* the Kalocsa ceremony takes place. This, it is to be hoped, will not clash with the Grand Duke Carl August centenary celebrations, which would unfortunately prevent me (as I told you earlier) from going to Hungary. From 25 August to 8 September I shall have to remain in Weimar. The Goethe-Schiller monument (the work of Rietschel in Dresden) is to be unveiled then, as is the statue of Wieland (done by Gasser, in Vienna). On this occasion there also has to be some music, with a contribution from my humble self.

About Wagner, whom I came here to visit because he may not cross the Swiss border into Germany, I'll tell you a few things when we meet, if they are of interest to you. We see one another every day of course, from morning till night. His new and colossal work (*Der Ring des Nibelungen*, a tetralogy), which he has almost half completed (i.e. the first two dramas, *Das Rheingold* and *Die Walküre*), won't fail to create an enormous stir if it comes to a performance, which it will do, one hopes, in '59. Such a text and such music are quite unparalleled, and a great part of the audience will certainly sit there totally flabbergasted. . . . May there only be as many well-meaning people as the Hungarian schoolmaster of whom you told me, who had 'wanted to do that!' For my own part, at least, I don't want to neglect most modestly doing mine. Amen!

A thousand affectionately grateful and devoted regards and respects to Mme Augusz, and many friendly greetings to the children, with whom I hope next summer to continue my ballet exercises.

Bien tout à vous,   F. Liszt

As soon as I am in Weimar I'll send you the medallion which Rietschel has done of me. It appeared in the Paris Exhibition and is unanimously regarded as a masterpiece. At the weekend I shall also write to Karácsonyi.

I still feel a scruple, or even two, which I venture to ask you to allay. It's possible that in Pest I still owe about 10 florins, which haven't been claimed from me moreover; and since it concerns two people you recommended to me I should be most obliged if you would pay them on my behalf. The first is the French artiste who shortened my locks for me; the second, Skriván the hatter, who didn't deliver my hat until the very moment of my departure. As you will have occasion to see both of them, I implore you to set my conscience at rest for 10 florins *without drawing at sight* on L.F.[25] as part of the musical expenses of Gran.

After a week in St Gallen, and the concert of 23 November, Liszt and the two princesses spent a fortnight in Munich before returning to Weimar.

368. To Blandine Liszt in Paris. Munich, 30 November. You are acquiring strange manners, my daughter, and your lessons in Paris are profiting you quite perceptibly! My habit of giving a reason for my decisions and of not changing them lightly being known to you, I shall await the end of the period of time I stipulated for your removal from my mother's home to see if you intend to go on failing to keep the promise you made me before your departure from Weimar,[26] and to go on deliberately opposing my express wishes, which are so entirely in agreement, I say it again, with outer proprieties and my own conscience.[27] If that is how it is to be, I shall naturally have to see later about a way of intimating those wishes to you still more expressly.

For today I note two further points in your letter. The first is merely meaningless nonsense; the second, something worse. You assume to begin with that I shall hasten to Paris to chatter with you about the greater or lesser degree of attention that you will deign (or disdain) to pay to what I advise and ask you, and then you casually, and with a wholly piquant laconism, drop the remark that you have received proposals from 'two honourable suitors', without taking the trouble to be more confiding than if it were a matter of telling a schoolfriend about some new fashion in dressing-gowns that you had seen in a shop.

Reflect a little, my daughter; look into your heart and ask yourself if this is the way to behave and to write to me.

369. To Baron Augusz. Weimar, 30 December G

Dear Friend!

From the newspaper report according to which I appeared in St Gallen as a *pianist*, you can once again see how intent people are on doing me a good turn in the press and reporting my activities in accordance with the truth. I for my

[25] Leó Festetics.

[26] Blandine and Cosima had spent a fortnight at the Altenburg in July, *en route* to Paris, whence in September Cosima had returned alone to Berlin.

[27] In a letter to Blandine of 11 Nov. Liszt had written: 'I find it essential that in Paris you do not live at Grandmama's; and I am stipulating the 1st of January as the date by which I wish this temporary arrangement to be ended.'

part am so used to all the crudest distortions and misrepresentations which for several years the leading newspapers have published about me, that I no longer take any notice of them and can only advise my friends to treat them with similar indifference. Better people than I are no better off in this respect; indeed, there is even something rather flattering about being attacked by all kinds of nonentities for stupid and contemptible reasons, and this has thus far hindered me little. I enclose (from the St Gallen newspaper) the programme of the concert, in which I conducted the first part and Wagner the second (*Sinfonia eroica*). The excellent performance of 2 of my symphonic poems—*Orpheus* and *Les Préludes*—must surely have been disagreeable to some ill-wishers (whose breed has spread everywhere); consequently they had nothing more urgent to do than hold forth on my *imaginary* piano-playing. From the dogged bigotry of people like this, incidentally, still more mischievous behaviour can be expected, and they have already several times tried to do me far worse. Nevertheless, I remain confident that decent people will eventually be found who will do justice to the upright man and artist I feel myself to be. It is to be hoped that the bad comedy which antagonists of the so-called 'Music of the Future' have been playing for some years, will soon be at an end; but of course I shall have to serve them as a point of attack still longer, which does me honour. One of their leaders recently said, rather naïvely: 'If we don't bestir ourselves and resist very energetically, the public might easily get to like Liszt's works. Onward, therefore, Handel, Bach, Haydn, Mozart, Beethoven, Mendelssohn, and all the classics, and thus at our leisure use the dead to kill the living.'

Fortunately we are not so easy to kill, and we even toughen ourselves still further by a more zealous study of the classics than is the practice of the gentlemen who are usually content to show off with a few uncontroversial works and names (which, however, in their time were also much contested!), without gaining any further insight into the matter. And so if it is agreeable to you, tell Count Ráday that my piano-playing in St Gallen is as true as my trip to America (which has appeared in all the newspapers several times), or my intention of smuggling the 'Venusberg' into church music. . . .

From several places I have received invitations to conduct my works, but intend not to leave here this winter, firstly because I am still rather unwell (and having to write to you from my bed, so as not to delay the answer to your enquiry), but mainly because what matters to me most is being able to continue working on, and finishing, several symphonic works, for which I need total peace and seclusion. My Pest malady has been increased by another: for 2 months I have been in the grip of several dozen boils, an illness as healthy as it is unpleasant. However, the doctor promises me that by the beginning of next year I shall be jumping around like a *stag*!

Mille respectueuses hommages à Mme d'Augusz (the lullaby shall be composed); et bien tout à vous de sincère et reconnaissante amitié.   F. Liszt

P.S. HE the Cardinal Primate most graciously deigned to send me a small prayer book, and to write a few words therein, for which last week I wrote him my thanks.

1857

7 January. At Weimar's Court Theatre Liszt conducts the premières of the Piano Concerto No. 2 (played by Bronsart) and the final version of *Ce qu'on entend sur la montagne.*

26 February. At a concert in the Leipzig Gewandhaus Liszt conducts *Les Préludes, Mazeppa,* and the Piano Concerto No. 1 (played by Bülow).

31 May–2 June. His direction of the 35th Lower Rhine Music Festival (Aachen) is very successful despite a determined opposition.

Late July to mid-August. Several boils having remained on his legs after illness earlier in the year, Liszt returns to Aachen to take the waters. Here he has a clandestine reunion with Agnes Street-Klindworth.

18 August. He attends the wedding, in Berlin, of Cosima and Hans.

3–5 September. A festival is held in Weimar to commemorate the centenary of the birth of Carl August, the foundation stone of whose monument is laid. On the 3rd, the double statue of Goethe and Schiller is unveiled and Liszt conducts the première of *Weimars Volkslied*; on the 4th, the statue of Wieland is unveiled and Liszt conducts the première of *Festvorspiel*; on the 5th, he conducts the premières of two works inspired by Goethe and Schiller: the Faust Symphony and *Die Ideale*. A visitor to the festival, and to the Altenburg, is Liszt's friend Bedřich Smetana.

22 October. In Florence, Blandine Liszt marries Emile Ollivier.

7 November. At the Theatre Royal, Dresden, Liszt conducts his *Prometheus* and the première of the Dante Symphony.

10 November. Moritz Schön conducts the première, in Breslau, of *Héroïde funèbre.*

29 December. At a concert in Weimar's Court Theatre, Liszt conducts the première of *Hunnenschlacht.*

WORKS. *Weimars Volkslied* (Cornelius) (S87). The symphonic poems *Hunnenschlacht* (S105) and *Die Ideale* (S106). SONGS: *Ich liebe dich* (Rückert) (S315); *Muttergottes Sträusslein zum Mai-Monate* (Müller) (S316). Arrangement (S356) for orchestra of the *Festvorspiel.* Work is begun on the oratorio *The Legend of Saint Elisabeth* (S2), completed in 1862.

ESSAY. *Weimar's September Festival in Celebration of the Centenary of the Birth of Carl August.*

370. To Princess Carolyne in Weimar. Leipzig, Wednesday, 25 February.
Two days since I saw Minette[1] and Magnolette—bad days! . . . The two preliminary rehearsals, quartet and wind instruments separately, on Monday and Tuesday were excellent. This morning's full rehearsal went marvellously.

---

[1] Nickname for the Princess.

Nevertheless, it will be safer to have an extra rehearsal tomorrow, which will be for *Les Préludes*, *Mazeppa*, and the Concerto. A good many of the musicians seem to be taking a liking to my things, but will probably not dare to express it. Rietz[2] left the hall at the entry of the triangle in the Concerto, although he had listened without shuddering to the much more frequently used triangle in the Vieuxtemps Concerto, rehearsed shortly before. [Ferdinand] David is behaving perfectly to me, while showing that he has reservations about the main thing. He was waiting for me at the station on Monday, and I had coffee at his place before going to my accommodation at the Hôtel de Bavière, the rehearsal having to be held half an hour after my arrival. On Monday I dined entirely alone in my room, at 3.00. Senff came to see me, as next course after the soup. Then I slept for a good hour, and at 6.30 called on Lobe and Brendel. To end the evening I had invited myself to a whist party at David's, with R. Dreyschock, *Conzertmeister*, and one of the Gewandhaus conductors, Dr Petschke. On Tuesday I lunched tête-à-tête at the home of our friend [Clara] Riese, but with her mother and cousin. There I found your short letter in German, which I read right through with emotion. In compliance with your instructions, I went back to have a '6-minute' sleep, after which I paid a visit to the Mildes, to Hauptmann, Freytag, and Pohl. At 8.30 there was whist again at Dreyschock's, with David, followed by supper for 5 or 6 people, as on the previous day. . . . Hans got here at 4.30 this morning, and made a great effect at the rehearsal. He plays this Concerto admirably. . . .

La Riese is absolutely radiant. I applied to her Napoleon's remark about Polish women, telling Bülow that she was the only man 'man enough' in Leipzig.

371. To Richard Wagner in Zurich. Weimar, 19 April. [G] By your letter, dearest and most unique of men, you have made my Easter Day very beautiful; and by the loving *azymes* you offer me therein, with such real kindness and affection, you have strengthened me, reinvigorated me, and made me wholly oblivious of all other leaven! My sincerest thanks for it; and may the giving to me of so much and such heartfelt joy be a joy to you too. This joy shall not be spoilt for us by a couple of misprints and omissions. The important thing is that you hold me dear and consider my honest aspirations as a musician to be worthy of your sympathy.

This you have said in a manner that no one else could say it! I candidly admit that when I brought my things to you in Zurich, I did not know how you would

[2] Julius Rietz, the Leipzig Kapellmeister at this time, was inexorably opposed to the music of Liszt, Wagner, and their followers.

receive them, what you would think of them. Having already had to hear and read so much about them, I no longer have any real opinion on the subject, and go on working only from inextinguishable inner conviction, without laying claim to recognition or approval. Several close friends of mine—Joachim, for example, and formerly Schumann and others—have displayed a strange, doubtful, and unfavourable attitude towards my musical creations. I by no means hold this against them, and cannot retaliate, because I continue to take a sincere and comprehensive interest in their works.

Imagine, then, dearest Richard, my ineffable joy during our hours together in Zurich and St Gallen, when your radiant glance penetrated my soul so life-enhancingly, so winningly, embraced it so lovingly! . . .

Things are in a sorry state at the Altenburg. The Princess has been quite seriously ill for the past three weeks and cannot leave her bed. Princess Marie has had to take medicine too, and is not allowed to leave her room; and I, after being kept in bed for a full six weeks, have only this last couple of days progressed to the point of being able to hobble around the theatre and the Schloss. Nevertheless, I should like to hope that better and the best things will soon come to my dear ones, as to you, who have so high a place in my heart, and to whom I feel and confess that I wholly *belong*.[3]   F. Liszt

At the beginning of next season Dingelstedt takes over the Intendancy from Herr von Beaulieu. He has been here for the past fortnight, and his position, although not yet officially announced, has been guaranteed by the necessary signatures.

At your recommendation, Frau Rauch makes a guest appearance as Ortrud next Sunday. Herr Althaus too, whom you introduced to me, has been staying in Weimar for a month. But I doubt whether I can be especially useful to him. His vocal talent is said to be very slight as yet. Otherwise he has made a good impression on me, and I shall hear him shortly.

Again, all, all my thanks for today, when I didn't want to write to you about anything else.

372. To Anna Liszt in Paris. [Weimar] 27 April G (F)

Dearest Mother,

As you can no longer read German fluently, I want to say to you in French, and from the bottom of my heart, that I love you with a childlike love and that your letters always give me great joy. Try to retain your good health for many

[3] Words that put one in mind of those of the Hungarian statesman Count Albert Apponyi, who in his memoirs wrote of his 'innermost conviction that those three great men [Beethoven, Liszt, Wagner] belonged to one another'.

a long year yet, as well as that beautiful equanimity of soul which you possess to so great a degree that you are even able to transmit it to others whose frame of mind is less harmonious.

I am glad that Rubinstein's success[4] has so pleasantly reminded you of the applause bestowed upon me before my journey to Italy. My own memory of that time, and even of the period following it, which surrounded me with still more pomp and hullabaloo, is somewhat dim and nebulous. Whatever people may say, I feel conclusively that the foundations of my true fame and of the real purpose of my life as an artist have been laid only by my works of the last four to five years. Through them alone will my name go honourably down to posterity, which will base its judgement on what I achieve and not on the hostility shown to me and the attacks perpetrated upon me, to which, thanks to the envy and jealousy clinging to me, I shall probably be subjected lifelong. Instead of regretting that I turned my back on an activity now over and done with, I am more inclined to reproach myself for not having finished with it ten years earlier. And indeed I should have done so, had I not, because of obligations undertaken, had to be preoccupied with earning money.

If, dearest Mother, we are not of the same opinion in this matter, I know all the same that you are not angry with me because I am incapable of subordinating my higher convictions to the vacillating goodwill of the public. I believe I can promise you with certainty that my works will have greater justice done to them when they are better understood and judged more impartially than at present, when I have a very hard battle to fight—which nevertheless neither worries nor disheartens me.

Your news that Blandine is now living at her mother's is very welcome to me. I think that when the occasion arises she will take the trouble to inform me of this herself, and I shall wait for her to do so before I write to her. As you know, I was against her staying with you permanently. Everything is now arranged in the best possible way. Cosima's wedding will take place during the course of the summer, and towards the end of June I shall let you know the exact date. Naturally, I have to make the necessary arrangements in Berlin beforehand, so that I can be there again for the wedding.

The time between 20 May and 5 June I shall spend in your neighbourhood in Aachen, where on the three days of Whitsun I am to direct the music festival. At the third concert Bülow will play one of my concertos. After that, and until September, I intend to remain in Weimar, to finish some large-scale compositions—work which requires several months of undisturbed peace and quiet.

[4] Anton Rubinstein had made a sensational appearance in Paris earlier in the month.

With a thousand heartfelt wishes for your health and happiness I remain, dearest Mother, your faithful son F. Liszt

373. To Princess Carolyne. [Aachen] 22 May. Thanks be to Heaven for your dear, sweet lines. . . . My introduction to the committee at the town hall, yesterday morning, made rather a good impression on those gentlemen, among whom are distinguished by kindly feelings in my favour: the president, van Houten, possessor of several *quartets* of stringed instruments, two violins, viola, and cello —by Stradivarius, Guarneri, Amati, and Magini—making a collection that is probably unique in Europe; the town architect, named Ark; and a poet by the name of Joseph Müller, celebrated for poems in the local dialect. This last-named has just sent me several of his little volumes, with very flattering inscriptions, and also a small miscellany of Catholic poetry: *Muttergottes-Sträusslein zum Maimonate.* After some explanations which had been asked of me, Dahmen the burgomaster took me into the town hall's large hall to show me the venue. Unhappily it hardly lends itself to a big musical festival because of the large pillars which go right through the hall, on the one hand preventing the conductor being seen by all the performers, and on the other dividing the audience in two, which is bound to be to the disadvantage of the general impression.

In this hall are some large frescoes by Rethel, the composition of which I found imposing and bearing the stamp of genius. Rethel is sharing Schumann's melancholy fate, in a lunatic asylum in Berlin, and the vulgar herd say that it is the result of wounded vanity. He was able to finish only half the job, and it was his pupil Kehren who was asked to paint the remainder, from Rethel's cartoons. I have been told that many unpleasant tricks were played on him here, and that he had to endure the most scathing criticisms from 'experts', who understand painting no more than they understand music—the secrets and the mystery of art don't reveal themselves when they are at the mercy of arrogance and mediocrity. I shall go back to those frescoes with Kehren, and will try to tell you about them in greater detail. . . .

Before going out this morning I wrote a few lines to Hiller and to Bronsart, whom I am urging to come and see me before the rush of the full rehearsals. I also saw the theatre hall, which has very favourable acoustics, and am very satisfied with the excellent arrangement of the music-desks and the general layout. We shall have 52 violins, 16 violas, 19 cellos, and 13 double-basses. That's enough to delight Berlioz himself.

Please send word to Frau Milde that I await her anxiously. She will be staying in the same house as myself at the Suermondts', as will Frau Pohl. Also remind

Cornelius to send me by Frau Milde the score and piano score of [Berlioz's] *L'Enfance du Christ*, plus a packet of my visiting-cards, which were forgotten. Poor darling, it was you, unwell though you are, who wanted the job of putting paper in my writing-pad, of putting the envelopes, sealing-wax, and pens in order. Thinking about it this morning, I could not hold back tears of emotion! Send Cornelius to the Mildes at once, so that they will be here on Wednesday morning at the latest. . . . I am really clamouring for Frau Milde. Having seen the hall this morning, I am convinced she will make a great impression. . . .

Greet Magnolet from me, and give, too, all my regards to Scotland, as well as to the nightingale which sings in the little clump of trees in the Altenburg garden. Wholly at your feet and in your heart.   F.L.

374. To Princess Carolyne. 5.00 p.m., Saturday, 23 May. . . . Nothing new to tell you, unless it is that my room has been enriched by three beautifully painted heads, which Suermondt himself came to hang this morning.[5] He is busy putting the whole house in order, and is in difficulties because of the sheer quantity of his pictures. The first is a very fine portrait of Gluck, painted by Kupetzky—at a time when the original could have been about my age. The second a *St Jerome* by Ribera, of which Suermondt wishes to make me a present—and the third a Dutch lady with the huge collar fashionable in the 17th century. The *St Jerome* is of an admirable vigour, and has in it at one and the same time something of an anchorite, of a Titan and of Faust. As for the Dutch patrician lady, she seems to me to be well painted, well burnished, and of a charm which is both pleasing and dignified. While not standing too much on ceremony, she seems to compel one to do so with her! . . .

At 6.00 I shall be going to the rehearsal of *L'Enfance du Christ*, and tomorrow morning at 7.30 I shall be attending a low mass, which a choir of school-children is accompanying with hymns. . . .

375. To Princess Carolyne. Monday morning, 25 May. Yesterday morning Turányi and I went together to the 7.30 mass in the cathedral. . . . Afterwards we spent a couple of hours tête-à-tête and I played him my Mass, which he finds admirable and an advance on Beethoven's. He has for his own part done half a dozen Masses, and in the afternoon acquainted me with three of them,

---

[5] Liszt's host was an art patron and collector.

as well as some other compositions—amongst others a setting of Schiller's *Die Macht des Gesanges* for choirs, soloists, and orchestra—overtures, quartets, *Lieder*, symphonies, all unpublished. In my humble opinion these works are more to their advantage in this manuscript obscurity, despite the qualities of experience, learning, and scholarship that they reveal. He lacks, as many writers do, a certain something which seems to me to be absolutely indispensable—and he knows too well beforehand what he wants to do, to succeed in doing it well. . . . I had lunch with Suermondt's stepbrother and sister-in-law. The two brothers married two Coqueril sisters, and at table there was also an unmarried third sister aged about 24. It seemed to me that after the coffee was a good occasion to display my little talents as a pianist, and I played them a couple of pieces by way of thanking them for being so obliging and for the consideration they continue to show me.

Milde has just written to tell me that he has been refused permission to come to Aachen, and that his wife will not be able to get here until Thursday morning, because of a performance of the *Merry Wives*,[6] which he finds pretty *unmerry*. Please send word to Frau Milde once again that the *Musikfest* awaits her just as the dry earth awaits the dew. I beg her to come straight to me on arrival. Her room is prepared, on the same floor as mine, and she can be assured that she will be petted and pampered. Urge her too to bring with her the parts of the couple of pieces she will have to sing at the third concert: perhaps the prayer from *Genoveva* which she sang in Leipzig, or the one in *Tannhäuser*, the parts of which could be copied with all possible speed; plus some volumes of *Lieder* by Schubert and Schumann. I am expecting, too, a little packet of visiting-cards, and 3 copies of the *Künstlerchor*. . . .

May God's angels bring their *Musikfest* into your great and gentle heart, infinitely dear one! Love to Furet-Schahatte,[7] and don't either of you forget your

Lazybones

376. To Princess Carolyne. Tuesday morning [26 May].

The full rehearsals with the Aachen musicians, who in the choirs and orchestra number about 300 and form the nucleus of the festival performers, began yesterday afternoon, Monday. I was anxious to make the acquaintance of my players and singers, with whom I hope that I shall very soon establish the best relations. I have always noticed that at the moment of the performance, and despite all the offensive remarks that are uttered or printed about me, the musical personnel

---

[6] Otto Nicolai's opera *The Merry Wives of Windsor*, first performed in Berlin, 9 Mar. 1849.

[7] Nickname for Princess Marie.

have willy-nilly felt drawn towards me and followed me with fire and docility. Here, unquestionably, it will be the same. When I entered I was greeted with the usual fanfares, and I expect that after the last chords of the *Musikfest* the applause of the great majority will be joined to them. The Suermondts tell me that my ways do not displease, so that my *persönliche Liebenswürdigkeit* is in rather fine fettle. It would even appear that the members of the opposition are beginning to join and merge with us, when they see how the silly things said about me have such little foundation in fact.

This morning I shall do a second rehearsal with the orchestra alone, and at 7.00 this evening with choirs and orchestra. *L'Enfance du Christ* has been learnt only reluctantly, just as I foresaw. For all that, it will go well and create a good effect. For my own part, I admire it only to a certain extent. As soon as my *Elisabeth* is finished, we shall have to compose the *Christus*, in the way that we understand this work. . . .

To bring you completely into my modest way of life in Aachen, I must tell you that the dining-room is on the ground floor and adorned with two pictures placed opposite one another. I sit at the 'head' of the table, with Frau Suermondt on my left, and he on his wife's left. The painting on my left depicts an enormous pelican surrounded by Chinese ducks and other such fowl which are enjoying paddling about, while the pelican contemplates them in the manner of Prince Metternich—'der auf solche Einzelheiten nicht eingehen kann [who cannot go into such details]'. In the opposite painting, whose subject is the disciples at Emmaus, Our Lord Jesus Christ is shown with SS Peter and John and a cornfield. I don't know if Suermondt, placing them there, thought of the analogy there is between the pelican and Jesus Christ.[8] This latter painting is the work of Otto Rethel, brother of Alfred, who began the frescoes in the Town Hall. The two brothers belong to the Düsseldorf school—and the pelican is by Hondekoeter, 1660. The drawing-room with the Erard piano and the Velasquez is wholly at my disposal for receiving visitors. All the furniture is covered with dark green velvet, as is that in the adjoining room, in which among other choice paintings is an admirable study of a head, by Rubens. In my last letter I told you that Suermondt had put three paintings in my room. Having to go out, I'll add only—to prove to you how much my travels contribute to my education— that among the preciously preserved treasures in the Cathedral is Charlemagne's hunting horn with this inscription, one which according to the archaeologists

---

[8] The parallel becomes clear when it is remembered that in the Middle Ages the pelican was believed to feed, and even resuscitate, its young with its own blood from a self-inflicted wound in the breast—a fable of which, whatever the limits of his ornithological knowledge, Liszt would certainly have known from his readings in Dante's *Paradiso* of the lines (xxv. 112–13) in which Beatrice identifies St John as 'colui che giacque sopra 'l petto del nostro pellicano'.

has remained mysterious and incomprehensible, and which I for my part understand so well: *Dein Ein.*

Bronsart has written to say that he will probably be arriving this evening. Berlioz's not very kindly attitude towards my activities and inclinations has become known here, and is not helping to show him in a better light, for most people explain it simply as envy, and are perhaps not entirely mistaken. Tomorrow I shall write to Daniel, whose letter reached me a moment ago with Bronsart's.

377. To Princess Carolyne. 7.00 a.m., Tuesday [2 June]. You have brought me luck, and since yesterday evening my victory here, as the Suermondts say, is complete. At the rehearsals, *Festklänge* had a success with the orchestra; so the performance had a good deal of fire and zest—and the salvoes of applause and bouquets which burst out in the final bars make modesty easy for me. As for Berlioz, it was impossible to save him, notwithstanding all my efforts. Without the illness of Dalle Aste, who couldn't sing two notes yesterday evening and had already been forced to leave the hall after the first recitative in *Messiah*— without this fortunate illness which made it possible for me to withdraw without cowardice the first and last parts of the Berlioz trilogy, it was evident that the work would have been a disastrous failure. Schneider sang very well the narration of the *Fuite en Egypte*, and Frau Suermondt behaved heroically in organizing the invisible choir. . . . Every piece in the concert went marvellously, and although we lacked Dalle Aste I changed nothing in the order of the programme. Reinthaler, composer of the oratorio *Jephthah*, successfully performed in Cologne, London, Berlin, Erfurt, etc., undertook the bass part in [Schumann's] *Sängers Fluch.* But I had to omit the first and last parts of the *Enfance du Christ* and end the concert with an admirable chorus and colossal Fugue with three trumpets by Bach. The great success of the evening was the Schubert Symphony and my *liebenswürdige Persönlichkeit*, in honour of which *Festklänge* was given a reception which completely surprised me and with which you can be content. Bronsart and Bülow are writing to you by the same post. Just as I hoped and told you before leaving, my reputation as a 'conductor' is brilliantly established, and my adversaries will be forced to beat a retreat on this point. Out of 550 singers and players, there are certainly more than 500 who like me and who follow me with a kind of affection, which is the result of the musical authority I exert and shall maintain more and more. . . .

La Milde's success is prodigious. She is the *star* of the *Musikfest*, and even the party opposed to me praises her to the skies. Hiller and the people from Cologne and Düsseldorf are delighted with her. I am reserving the whole of this little bundle of stories for our 'Causeries' of Monday, Tuesday, Wednesday,[9] etc. . . .

378. To Princess Carolyne. 8.00 a.m., Wednesday [3 June]. In everything good that happens to me, as in everything good that I do, it is to you that my heart and my thoughts go back—because it is you whom I have to thank for being the little that I am! This feeling, which fills my whole soul, is my peace of mind, my blessing, my glory, and will follow me beyond the grave; or, rather, precedes me thither, for it is through you and in you that my soul aspires to Heaven!

The situation in Aachen has been favourable to me. Everything went off very well—my friends are much cheered and the opposing party all but put out of countenance. Yesterday's concert went perfectly from beginning to end. There was talk of repeating *Festklänge*, which made a sensation here. But since the concert had, in accordance with tradition, to be brought to an end by a chorus —Handel's *Hallelujah*—and since the ovation which had been prepared, as is also customary in such a situation, was most suitable to end with, it was better to make no change to the programme. Müller, whom I have told you about and who is on the committee, caused to rain down after the *Hallelujah* a thousand copies, in all colours, of the piece of verse I am enclosing, which perfectly expresses the opinion of the great majority. Fräulein Dahmen, the burgomaster's young and pretty daughter, simultaneously presented me with a laurel wreath, to the accompaniment of a fanfare, a shower of bouquets, and cheering from the entire audience. La Milde's success has something prodigious about it. Singer was much applauded, as was Bülow, who played like a lion. Hiller complimented him through a third party on his talent as a performer, regretting only that he had not chosen another piece.

After the concert I had invited myself to the van der Hopes', at the Hotel Nuellens. Part of the *Liedertafel* went there to serenade me. In the neighbouring salon Hiller was dining with some of the people from Cologne, all of them less than delighted with the success of the Aachen *Musikfest*. Although I had to go through this first room, to reach Mme van der Hope's, Hiller and I didn't even exchange greetings. After the meal, when escorting Mme van der Hope to the door, I drew a little to the left, to avoid passing too close to the stout person of my former friend!

---

[9] A jocular parallel with Sainte-Beuve's famous weekly essays *Les Causeries du lundi*, so called because they appeared on Mondays.

At 11.00 this morning a session of the Weimar quartet takes place: Singer, Stör, Walbrül, and a local substitute for Cossmann. Bülow and Singer will play the Beethoven Sonata dedicated to Kreutzer, and Frau von Milde will sing *Lieder* by Franz and Schubert. . . . On Sunday I shall be back in Weimar. . . .

379. To Richard Wagner. Weimar, 10 July ^G

Dearest Richard!

At your recommendation I am reading the correspondence between Schiller and Goethe. Your last letter found me at this passage:

'It counts as one of the greatest happinesses of my existence that I am experiencing the completion of these works, that this comes at a time when I am still striving and aspiring, and that I am able to drink at this pure spring; and the beautiful relationship that exists between us makes it a kind of religious duty for me to make your cause mine, and out of every reality that is in me to form the purest mirror of the spirit inhabiting this mortal frame, and thus, in a higher sense of the word, to deserve the name of your friend.' (Page 163, Vol. One)

When I think of the breaking off of your work on the *Nibelungen*, I can only weep! Should the great *Ring* really not free you from all the little chains shackling you? You certainly have many reasons to be bitter—and even if I keep more quiet about it, I am no less distressed. It is impossible for me to get any further with the Grand Duke at present; yet it would be foolish to abandon all hope. A more favourable hour will come—but it must be waited for, and in the mean time I can only ask you not to do your friend an injustice and not to spurn the 'virtue of the mule', as Byron calls patience.

Tristan seems to me an extremely happy idea. You will undoubtedly create a glorious work—and can then return refreshed to your *Nibelungen*. We'll all come to Strasbourg and form for you a *garde d'honneur*.[10] I hope to see you at the beginning of the autumn, although I can't draw up any definite plan just now. The Princess is still confined to bed and will not be fully recovered for a long time yet.

As for me, and despite all my resistance to the idea, I shall have after all to make use of the baths at Aachen, which is more than disagreeable to me. Next week I go to Berlin for a couple of days, to make various arrangements for the Bülow wedding, which is to take place next month. From there I travel to Aachen,

---

[10] Wagner was at this time intending to make his *Tristan und Isolde* a work of rather modest dimensions, and to finish it in time to have it produced in Strasbourg a year later. In the event, the première did not take place until 10 June 1865, in Munich.

and intend to stay there, taking the waters, from 22 July until 10 August. By 14 August I shall be back here again, awaiting the Grand Duke's orders with regard to the September festival. The excavations already undertaken for the Schiller-Goethe monument will, it is feared, cause a dangerous subsidence of the soil near the theatre, and it is quite possible that the two 'fellows' may find no secure position in Weimar. A telegram was immediately sent to Rietschel in order to decide how matters can be remedied. Perhaps I shall be told not to engage in any more *Zukunftsmusik*, lest the town be ruined completely. In which case I should have to seek refuge with you in Zurich, so that in your home I could play you my Faust Symphony (which has been lengthened by the addition of a closing chorus of male voices singing the last eight lines—'the eternal feminine'—of Part Two) and my latest symphonic poem, inspired by Schiller's *Ideale*.

Please give Frau Wesendonck my most affectionately devoted and humble greetings. When one visits you, one runs no risk of becoming a rustic [sich zu verbauern], even in Baur's *Hôtel du lac*, and I have qualms about being a burden to your so charming friend if I am her house guest.

Whether the Princess will be fit to travel this year remains very doubtful; but Princess Marie will in any case not leave her mother. If they are both able to undertake this year the Swiss tour they missed last year, then of course I shall stay with them at the Hôtel Baur, where your wife will not deny me the boon of providing me with excellent coffee and a practicable coffee machine, for the slops served in the hotel under the name of coffee I can endure no more than a *pièce de salon* by Kücken etc.; it spoils my morning hours.

How did you manage to get at HM the Emperor of Brazil? Tell me this. It would be appropriate for him to send you the Order of Roses set in brilliants, even though you care nothing for flowers or orders.

Rosa Milde is to make some guest appearances in Dresden shortly, and has asked for Elisabeth as her first part. If la Meyer's voice does not improve, I advise you to choose la Milde as Isolde. I believe you will be content with her, notwithstanding the fact that she was so highly praised by our *friend Hiller*.

Your faithful   F.L.

380. To Princess Carolyne. [Aachen] 9.00 a.m., Wednesday, 22 July.
. . . Neither accident nor incident interrupted my journey, which was favoured by weather made a little cooler by the storm. I arrived here at 7.00 p.m., having changed trains only once, at Düsseldorf, where the Rhine has to be crossed.

8 of the 16 hours of travel I used to read Chateaubriand's *Mémoires*,[11] which interested me to the point of making me want to read the remaining volumes. The elaborate style attracts me, and I like, too, the detailed political and philosophical ideas, reserving the right to extract from them what suits me best. There are in it a great number of admirably coined expressions, such as 'turn lies into putting up statues', 'old people enjoy being secretive, having nothing to display which is worth having'. . . . Even if the narrative were not as accurate as it might be, and the portraits not perfect likenesses—they retain no less value as composition and art, more or less like landscapes of the idealistic school. This book is a fitting conclusion to the career of the author of the *Génie du Christianisme*, and could be entitled the *Génie du Chateaubriandisme*.

I am temporarily staying at the Hotel Nuellens, which is packed with people, and where I have found only a small room on the ground floor, looking out on to a garden courtyard. At 9.00 yesterday evening Rodenburg[12] came to see me. He expects very good results from the cure I began this morning by swallowing two glasses of sulphurated water. At 11.00 he will accompany me to the bath, and I shall write to you in more detail of the prescriptions he will give me. I shall probably be allowed coffee in small doses, for most of the patients are taking it—and even a *Schoppen* [glass] of Moselle at lunch, which as a precaution I shall do without. On the visitors' list I noticed the names of Branicki —the forename is not indicated—and Counts Alexander and Vladimir Komar, with a Countess Alexandrine Komar *mit Gesellschaftsdame* [with lady companion], listed separately and staying in the same hotel. If Meyerbeer stays in Spa for another fortnight or so, I shall pay him a visit there.

From what Rodenburg tells me, a regular cure generally takes 6 weeks, but I reckon on getting off with half that expense at most. What is certain is that I shall decamp as soon as I reasonably can. . . .

381. To Princess Carolyne. Thursday, 23 July. From Saturday my quarters will be at the Bains de la Rose, where I shall be occupying a small room leading into the garden and adjoining a closet which will house Grosse. The total bill will be 6 francs a day. The baths being in the house, I shall have to go out only in the mornings, to go to the arcade where the waters are drunk. Among the drawings I brought back for you from Aachen, you will find a view

---

[11] The monumental *Mémoires d'outre-tombe*, published after Chateaubriand's death, hence the title.
[12] Doctor in Aachen.

of this arcade, in which, at 6.30 this morning, I took my second walk. Half an hour later I immerse myself in the bath, heated to a temperature of 26 degrees, for 25 to 30 minutes. Then I have breakfast with coffee or tea, smoke and work. I shall manage to lunch *à la carte* with a beefsteak in the Kurhaus restaurant, which is opposite the Bains de la Rose, and on rainy days I shall have the meal brought to my room. Between 3 and 5 o'clock there is music in the garden or the Kurhaus hall; I shall go and listen to it quite regularly. I also mean to attend the theatre performances. There is opera 4 times a week during the bathing season, and no *Schauspiel* [play]. . . .

Rodenburg firmly believes that by the simple means of the water and the baths I shall be completely cured. I am keeping to my Weimar diet and voluntarily going without wine. In 3 or 4 days we shall see if my little sores will make up their minds to close for good. For the moment they have of course reopened, the bathing having removed the crusts. I take care not to let my mind dwell on them, and am happy to think that they will soon be leaving me in peace. By today's post I am sending to you, or rather to Magnolet, the score of *Die Ideale*, to which I finished adding the expression marks this morning. . . .

Apart from Rodenburg I have not yet seen any of my acquaintances here. Suermondt was in Liège yesterday, and I shall let 2 or 3 days go by before going to see van Houten, Turányi, *et al.* I have written a couple of notes to Suermondt and Müller. I am spending my time quietly thinking of you and Magnolet. Goethe and Schiller's correspondence is pleasant reading for me, and I am coming across a good many passages perfectly suited to the present-day musical situation. The views and opinions are perfectly just but in too restricted a sphere to interest us deeply, and if the names of Schiller and Goethe were to be removed from these 2 large volumes, people would pay little attention to them. The ceaseless repetition of a crowd of incidents which are utterly trivial and commonplace wearies the reader needlessly. The rind and shell are too greatly disproportionate to the fruit, and mar the flavour one would find in the latter—had some literary errand-boy done us the service of releasing it from the trappings overloading it. . . .

On Sunday I shall be going to Father Roh's sermon, and shall try to see him again later. The local newspaper, *Echo der Gegenwart*, which I shall send you, reported my arrival in a very appropriate manner. In the same issue is mentioned as 'curiosissimum' that the Grand Duchy of Weimar contributed only 1 fl. 30 kr. to the subscription for the statue of Luther which they are planning to erect at Worms. In such a case one can say with Lamartine: 'There is not a single idea which outweighs an écu!' I have had no letter from you, either yesterday or today—the evening post will probably bring me your news. I love and bless you.   F.L.

382. To Princess Carolyne. Bains de la Rose [Aachen] Saturday, 25 July. I can in all veracity give you good news of my cure, which is going very well. Not only are no more pustules coming, but even the old ones are looking better, and as far as I can see are closing up without further encrusting. I hope to be almost rid of them in about a week—although Rodenburg is trying to persuade me that to go *sano* one has to go *lontano.*[13] Tomorrow he will send you his book of medical spells, plus Liebig's short article on the substances contained in the Aachen waters.

At about 1 o'clock I took possession of my accommodation at the Bains de la Rose, consisting of one room with two windows and another with only one. This latter room is being used by Grosse, which suits me very well, and the splendid fellow is taking all imaginable care of me. The furniture is very decent, of birch, if I am not mistaken, looking slightly yellow. I have hired a small piano made by Pape of Paris, peculiarly slender and unusual in its shape, which I shan't attempt to describe to you. My room looks out on a neat and tidy little garden, and I enjoy total peace and quiet outside. The whole of this afternoon I devoted to revising my Marches, which are making a din [*tintamarre*] inside my head. Alas! my dear, unique and adored 'Tintamarro' is far away! I am progressing more slowly than I should like with these Marches, but shall persevere. Perhaps they will turn out all the better. I have begun to reread Chateaubriand's *Essai sur la littérature anglaise*—which I bought for 10 gr. (a cretin's illustrated edition) and am finding to my liking. . . .

It is 10.00 p.m. . . . Good night, most infinitely dear one, you who alone are necessary to me, in both this world and the next—for I don't know what to do with myself when you are not beside me. God be with you and Magnolet!

F.L.

383. To Anna Liszt. Aachen, 28 July. ᴳ ⁽ᶠ⁾ I want to embrace you, dearest Mother, on your name-day,[14] when I remember with special tenderness the countless tokens of your kindness to me, your loving care and devotion. If during my life I have uselessly squandered much time, I nevertheless hope I have not entirely wasted it, and as I inherited your good health and your good heart I also live in the confidence that I have turned to the better and unwaveringly carried out that commandment of God's which corresponds with the impulse of my own heart: 'Honour thy father and thy mother!'

---

[13] Inverting the Italian proverb *Chi va sano, va lontano* (Good health will take you far).
[14] As already noted, St Anne's Day is actually 26 July.

The ailment that laid me low for part of last winter seemed to want to settle in my legs permanently. So on doctor's orders I decided to take the cure in Aachen. I am drinking sulphur water and taking daily sulphur baths, which after only a week has brought considerable improvement. By the end of next week I hope to be rid of my malady and shall proceed to Berlin for Cosima's wedding with Hans von Bülow. Both have already had their banns published. The ebullient youth each of them possesses will merge, I believe, in a happy marriage. Their characters suit one another quite splendidly, and for Hans I foresee a distinguished artistic career. I love and esteem him for his rare talent, his acute intelligence, and the great uprightness and distinction of his character. With Cosima too I am very content. Always my favourite, she has made great strides in poise and intellectual superiority. She seems to me to have a better and sounder understanding of things than does her sister, who is too inclined to allow herself to be guided by airy and sentimental fantasizing. I do not know how Blandine will view the marriage. Her ideas are very different from mine, being too similar to those of her mother, who entirely abandoned herself 'au vague des passions'. So I fear I shall be unable to help her as I would wish.

Daniel seems to be liking it in Vienna. He has doubtless given you his news, which on the whole is satisfactory. Things will continue to boil and ferment in him for two or three years until he reaches maturity. His school-leaving certificate has been found. I hope he will give me the joy of continuing his legal studies in Vienna as dazzlingly as he began them in Paris. There is almost only good in the boy; but he must become firmer and manlier. The change of air was therefore not only useful for him but necessary.

Do you remember, dearest Mother, a practical proverb that you used to reproach me with when, as a youth, I showed little appetite: 'Lazy in eating, lazy in everything.' Gradually, according to the rules of moderation and even of good taste, I have learnt to eat—and, what's more, to digest many things as well. I hope that my children will likewise manage to do so. To satisfy me completely, they should not content themselves with being idle in the world and dozing the day away. They must be reborn in the spirit and sense of the best that is in me—only then will they be wholly *mine*.

That brings me back to God's commandment, which I should like to carry out fully and completely by honouring, loving and blessing you as your loyally affectionate and devoted son   F. Liszt

384. To Princess Carolyne. [Aachen] Friday, 31 July. What an inexhaustible treasure trove of goodness, strength, advice, gentleness, and wisdom, most infinitely dear one, your heart incessantly pours out over me! How to praise you, bless you, sing of you, and glorify you as I need to? My soul's every wish invokes you, my heart's every fibre throbs at thought of you; and, not knowing how to speak the language of angels, I say to you with Shakespeare:

> Hang there like fruit, my soul,
> Till the tree die![15]

My recovery is making excellent progress, and I hope you will not disapprove of my haste to return to you. At the latest I shall leave here at the end of next week, but even hope to set out as early as Thursday. My work on the Marches is drawing to an end, and on Sunday I shall begin to orchestrate the *Festvorspiel*. Bronsart and Winterberger will be arriving here with Hahn on Sunday or Monday. We shall make music from morning to night. Your letters are being brought to me very punctually by the postman, without going via the Hotel Nuellens. There is need of no other address than my name—but, as I wrote to you, for this last week I have been staying at the Bains de la Rose. They are in the centre of town, and known to every child, because it is an ancient establishment which, like mahogany, improves with age.

So far as things ancient are concerned, I have been to see the relics kept in the cathedral sacristy: Charlemagne's skull and arm (his body is in a splendid shrine which is never opened, given by Frederick Barbarossa), the Virgin's knitted girdle, Jesus Christ's leather belt, the cord by which Jesus Christ was bound during the scourging, the sponge soaked in vinegar with which his thirst was quenched on the Cross, a robe belonging to the Virgin, and a piece of cloth from the beheading of St John. Victor Hugo describes Jesus Christ's belt thus: 'a small thong twisted and rolled around itself like a schoolboy's whip'. Opposite it is the Emperor Constantine's *sigillum* [seal]. It fell in later times into the hands of Haroun Al-Raschid, who made a present of it to Charlemagne. Since I entirely lack any descriptive talent, I am sending you V. Hugo's 9th Rhine letter[16] to give you precise information about these miraculous objects. Magne will be able to read you these 15 or 20 pages without tiring. Among others is this sentence which appealed to me: 'Charlemagne, whose tomb shines down to us through

---

[15] *Cymbeline*, V. v. 264 (the words of Posthumus when he is embraced by Imogen in the reunion scene). Readers conversant with events in the life of Tennyson—inspirer of Liszt's only English song—will recall that when, on his death-bed, that poet asked for a volume of Shakespeare to be put into his hands, it was to these same lines that he turned.

[16] *Le Rhin: Lettres à un ami*, a two-volume work, first published in 1842, based on letters written by Hugo to his wife in 1838 and 1839 during visits to Germany and Switzerland. The ninth letter is entitled *Aix-la-Chapelle—Le tombeau de Charlemagne*.

10 centuries, left this world only after he had enshrouded his name in these two words, to earn himself a double immortality: *sanctus, magnus*, holy and great, the two most majestic epithets with which Heaven and earth can crown a human head!'

Thank you, too, for having sent me Lamartine's *Entretiens*, which will be a treat for me in the evenings. . . .

385. To Princess Carolyne. [Aachen] 8.00 a.m., Sunday, 2 August.
The arrival of Sacha Winterberger and Hahn prevented me from writing to you, for my afternoon was taken up by a stroll with Müller, and the evening by a kind of celestial concert given by the *Liedertafel*, of which Rodenburg is temporarily acting president. Winterberger brought me a new *Sonata quasi fantasia*, which I found an advance on its predecessors, and Hahn will read me today and tomorrow the main chapters of his work on Chopin, in which he has treated questions of form *ex professo* and *à fond*. Bronsart will come by this morning's train, which will make permanent music for us. These young people having become my 'nearest', it is my duty to busy myself with them and their work for a few hours every day, all the more since they have taken the trouble to come and find me here. Not to remain idle for my own part, I shall set two of the *Lieder* of Müller's *Muttergottes-Sträusslein*, which will be of the simplicity of a rosary. My Marches are completely finished and it only remains for me to add the expression marks, which will be done by tomorrow. This morning Beethoven's first Mass in C is being performed in the Cathedral, to some extent especially for me. To attend it I shall be forced to miss Father Roh's sermon, which I regret, for I am not altogether one of those people whom Pascal writes of as 'going to a sermon as one goes to vespers'. At 1 o'clock I shall lunch in town with the Suermondts, and perhaps later go to their country house. *La Juive* is announced for tomorrow with Steger, the bawling tenor from Vienna. The day after tomorrow there is the grand concert of the Concordia, to benefit those who suffered in the Moselle fire; it will also receive a few écus from the exhibition of the portrait of Pcss Luise, Grand Duchess of Baden, painted by Winterhalter. . . . This portrait has already been exhibited in Karlsruhe for a similar end, which is a wholly modern way of making princely effigies popular. . . .   F.L.

386. To Princess Carolyne. 10.00 a.m., Saturday, 8 August

Infinitely dear one,

Cornelius's verses[17] were a veritable obsession with me throughout yesterday. Neither at dinner nor in the theatre was it possible for me to free myself from the spell. Magnolet and Miss Anderson, to whom I beg you to give my very sincere regards, would have had a good laugh, seeing me light my cigar-case instead of my cigar and put red wine in my coffee instead of sugar. I am finally clear about what I want to do, and I fancy it will be magnificent! The whole of today and tomorrow will be spent on it, for while retaining the popular character in the melody, which I shall have sung in unison without any alteration to the 5 stanzas, I shall very perceptibly vary the orchestral accompaniment, which will oblige me to write 8 to 9 pages of full score. But the thought of seeing you again in a few days puts me in a good mood, and I hope to have finished by tomorrow evening or the morning of the day after. . . .

I had some slight thought of going to Spa to visit Meyerbeer, but have learnt from the newspapers that for at least a week he has been back in Paris. It goes without saying that I am writing to no one and seeing only unavoidable visitors: Rodenburg, Bronsart, Suermondt, Formes, Steger, Father Roh, and a M. Cavallins, Intendant of the Stockholm Theatre. Suermondt has three seriously ill sons in the house, of whom two are down with typhus. Father Roh has just sent me a little book of prayers, *Marienandacht*, for which I shall go and thank him this afternoon. Aachen's musical tribe have almost disappeared from my horizon. I haven't the bother of ridding myself of them, and will leave those people to paddle about in the pool of their *amours-propres* and their narrow interests, as before.

So far as reading is concerned, *Fabiola ou l'Eglise des catacombes*[18] by Cardinal Wiseman, and a piquant little volume of Chamfort's *Maximes, pensées et anecdotes*,[19] which I bought in Cologne, with Lamartine's *César* and *Cromwell*, provide me with some distraction during the half-hour of the daily bath and the one preceding my sleep. Thank you for your Lamartine quotation, which is indeed the best definition of 'character' that could be given. Here are a few of Chamfort's thoughts to which you will subscribe:

---

[17] Those that Liszt was setting in his *Weimars Volkslied*.

[18] *Fabiola or The Church of the Catacombs* (London, 1854). Distinguished as scholar and polyglot as well as for ecclesiastical eminence, Cardinal Wiseman wrote this historical romance (among whose cast of characters are SS Agnes, Pancras, Tarsicius, and Sebastian) as he slowly journeyed towards Rome during illness. It became very popular, was translated into most European and several Asiatic languages, and—*pace* Liszt, who faulted its 'starchy goodness' (letter of 11 Aug.)—can be read with interest and enjoyment even today.

[19] Of which Liszt particularly liked to quote, and apply wryly to himself, the epigram: 'Celebrity is the punishment of talent and the chastisement of merit.'

'The public does not in the least believe in the purity of certain feelings and certain virtues—and, in general, the public can hardly *raise* itself other than to *low* ideas.'—'There is a deep indifference to the virtues, which surprises and scandalizes much more than the vices.'—'Courtiers are paupers enriched by begging.'—'No one in the world has more enemies than an upright, proud, and sensitive man who is disposed to leave people and things for what they are, rather than take them for what they are not.'

How much more does this last thought apply to a woman who, like you, blessing of my life, adds to these qualities a superior intelligence, the shrewdest sagacity, and all the courage of a steadfast character! . . .   F.L.

387. To Agnes Street-Klindworth. Aachen, Tuesday, 11 August.[20] As I write these words to you I am still in Aachen.[21] The doctor has insisted on my taking at least 21 baths, and I have submitted to this course of treatment, albeit reluctantly. While gliding by, the hours have often weighed upon me here, and I hardly needed further confirmation to know what to believe about the incurability of my ailment. On Sunday, Winterberger and Hahn (from Rotterdam) and Bronsart came to spend a few days with me. Since their departure I have hardly gone out, so that I can bring to an end the task I have set myself for the September celebrations in Weimar, and which has been made bigger by a poem of Cornelius (the original of which I am sending you). My setting of it has turned out well, I fancy, and the *choral* theme of the March written for the Grand Duke served me splendidly as a starting point for this *Volkslied*. So that it can be used more, I have been compelled to write it twice: a first version for male chorus (accompanied by a dozen brass instruments) which can be sung in the open air, when the statues are unveiled or during the procession, and a second version for chorus and soloists, male and female, accompanied by full orchestra, varied in each verse and commenting on the meaning of the text, which will probably be performed in the theatre on two evenings in succession. The whole thing comes to about twenty pages of full score, on which I have worked uninterruptedly.

As regards books, I have been reading Cardinal Wiseman's *Fabiola*, which has the fault of a certain *starchy goodness* not really in keeping with the character and freedom that are the life and charm of novels. And so I shall not urge you to read it, although the second heroine is your patron saint (Agnes), and a part

---

[20] La Mara has the date 12 August—but Tuesday was the 11th.
[21] As already noted, Liszt and his lover had contrived a clandestine reunion in Aachen, from which Agnes had by this time taken her departure.

of the Saint's office can be found in it. But if there falls into your hands a small volume in the Hetzel collection, entitled *Esprit de Chamfort*, do glance through it. . . .

For my reading *en route* I am taking Lamartine's *Jules César*, which I shall read turn and turn about with the end of *Fabiola*.

I shall be in Weimar in the morning of the day after tomorrow, and two or three days later in Berlin, whence I shall write to you. Don't reply to me until after my return from Berlin at about the end of this month. . . .   A.A.

388. To Blandine Liszt in Florence. Weimar, 24 September

Dear Blandine,

You have made me so little accustomed to being taken into your confidence, to having you open your heart to me, that at first your latest letter rather took me by surprise. I am heartily grateful to you and should be glad if we could continue to walk this path, which is at once the best, the simplest, and the most natural.

M. Emile Ollivier* is known to me through the renown which clung to him at the time of the last elections. I remember in particular some very laudatory articles with which *La Presse*, the only Parisian newspaper that I occasionally read in Weimar, supported his candidature. You tell me that the two of you are as one in heart and intelligence and that you are 'twin souls'. That certainly suffices for love; but, so far as your marriage is concerned, let me put to you some questions of a more specific nature. What has been agreed between you, your mother,[22] and him on this topic? When do you intend to get married? Is M. Ollivier continuing to practise as a lawyer in Paris? Does his family approve of this union? What are your financial arrangements?

For my part, without having the least intention of opposing your choice, and fully prepared as I am to have an excellent and high opinion of M. Ollivier, I should nevertheless very much like to know my son-in-law personally, and believe I should not be demanding too much by asking him to come to Weimar, if only for a day or two.

In your next letter please give me more details about M. Ollivier. Tell me where he comes from, how his name happened to come into prominence, and if he has published anything; and if, as I hope, your feelings for one another are growing ever stronger, I assume that he will write to me for his own part.

---

[22] It was in Mme d'Agoult's salon in Paris that Blandine and Ollivier had first met. They had then drawn closer together when members of a group—which included Mme d'Agoult—visiting Italy; and it was from Florence, where the wedding eventually took place, that Blandine had written to tell her father of her engagement.

I am expecting Cosette and Bülow in a few days. They will spend a week here before settling permanently in Berlin.

I embrace you, dear Blandine, with most fervent wishes for your happiness and with all my true love and affection.

389. To Lyudmila Shestakova, née Glinka, in St Petersburg. Weimar, 7 October

Madame,

I wish I could tell you how deeply moved I was by the letter you have done me the honour of addressing to me. Thank you for having remembered me as one of the sincerest and most zealous admirers of the splendid genius of your brother, who was above vulgar successes and for that very reason so worthy of a noble glory. Thank you, too, for being so graciously kind as to inscribe my name[23] on one of his orchestral works—works which will always be esteemed and favoured by people of taste.

The Dedication with which you honour me I accept with real gratitude, and shall find it at once a pleasure and a duty to contribute as best I can to propagating the works of Glinka, works for which I have always professed the most genuine and admiring appreciation. Of this I beg you, Madame, to allow me to assure you once more, and also to accept the most respectful compliments of

Yours very sincerely,   F. Liszt

By the same post I am writing to Herr Engelhardt in Berlin to thank him for his letter and to tell him how very flattered I am to see my name attached to a score of Glinka's.

390. To Blandine Liszt in Florence. Weimar, 9 October

My dear Blandine,

As this letter is probably the last you will receive from me before your marriage,[24] I send to you in it not only my consent but also my most loving blessing.

I ask God from the bottom of my heart to protect your future so that, above all, whether in prosperity or in adversity, you always retain that immaculate purity

---

[23] By dedicating to Liszt her deceased brother's *Capriccio brillante* (on the 'Jota aragonesa'), also known as First Spanish Overture, the score of which was published in 1858.

[24] Which took place before the high altar of Florence Cathedral, under the great dome of Brunelleschi, on 22 Oct., Liszt's forty-sixth birthday. Among those present, in addition to the bride's mother, the groom's father, and others, was the painter Edouard Manet, a friend of Ollivier.

of the heart, that integrity and equity of desires, judgement, and hopes which alone are capable of inspiring in a husband the respect, trust, and protective love that a woman has the right to expect from him when she knows that she deserves them.

May you in your new state be free of all the pettinesses which only too often creep into the minds of women, whose advice and actions alike can have so fatal an influence on the career of a man dedicated to public affairs.

I enclose five thousand francs which will be helpful to you, I imagine, for your immediate expenses, and I particularly ask you to acknowledge receipt of the bill of exchange on this occasion.

In my letter to M. Ollivier you will see my reply to all the points which are of interest to you at the present time, and, so far as your dowry is concerned, you have known for several years what I want to, and can, do for you.

May Heaven inspire and guide you as much as I beseech it to do.

Your affectionate father.

391. To Richard Wagner. Hôtel de Saxe No. 17, Dresden, 3 November ^{G}

Dearest Richard!

How could I not think of you ever lovingly and with sincere devotion—above all in *this* city, in this room, where we first came closer to one another, when your genius shone before me!

Rienzi still rings out to me from every wall, and when I enter the theatre I cannot help greeting you before everyone, as you stand at your desk. With Tichatschek, Fischer, Heine, and other of your friends in the orchestra here I speak of you every day. These gentlemen seem to be well inclined towards me, and show a keen interest in the rehearsals of *Prometheus* and the Dante Symphony, which will be performed next Saturday at a concert for the benefit of the Court Theatre chorus's pension fund. Bülow and his wife arrive here that day and will give you news of the performance. The Kapellmeisterin and her daughter arrive this evening. The Child is crazy about your *Tristan*;[25] but, by all the gods, how can you think of making it an opera for *Italian singers* (or so Bülow tells me)? Well, the incredible and impossible have become your elements, and perhaps you will bring this off too. The subject-matter is glorious, and your treatment of it quite wonderful. However, I have some slight misgivings about the way in which the part of Brangäne is rather spun out, because

---

[25] That is, the poem or libretto, the music for which was not yet written.

I simply cannot bear *confidantes* in a drama. Forgive me this silly comment and pay no further attention to it. When the work is completed my misgivings will undoubtedly vanish.

For 16 February, birthday of the Dowager Grand Duchess, I have proposed *Rienzi*, and hope Tichatschek will sing in our first two performances. Dingelstedt will be writing to you shortly. The Third Act will necessarily have to be very much shortened; Fischer and some others even said we ought to omit it completely. The Weimar stage, like the Weimar state, is little adapted to military insurrections. Let me know sometime what attitude I should take with regard to it. Rehearsals begin in January.

Let me give you my heartiest thanks once again for your friendly reception of my daughter. She is a dear, good child and devoted to you with all the enthusiasm of her young soul.

In Florence on 22 October her sister Blandine married Emile Ollivier (*avocat au barreau de Paris* and a *democratic* deputy of the city of Paris). From all sides I hear the greatest praise of the character and abilities of my new son-in-law, whom I shall meet for the first time this winter.

I long to be back at my work soon; but unfortunately the inevitable interruptions caused by my thousandfold relations and obligations leave me little chance of it this winter. Oh, could I only live with you on Lake Zurich and go on writing quietly!

God be with you!   Your   F. Liszt

392. To Blandine Ollivier in Paris. Weimar, 24 December. To give you the simplest pleasure, dear Blandine, is always a very appreciable one for me.

And so I thank you for your thanks while most sincerely wishing to give you a reason for them as often as possible. Having heard the *Tannhäuser* overture in Berlin, you will easily realize what is inadequate in a duet arrangement of such an overture.

For example, the luminous sparks of the violin passages which accompany the Chorale at the end cannot be reproduced on any other instrument than that collective one called the orchestra. In the arrangement I made for Hans and which you doubtless know, I tried to compensate for the inadequacy of the piano by varying and gradually increasing in intensity the patterns and figures in the accompaniment; but in the duet arrangement one is limited to copying closely the violin figuration whose effect on the piano is rather paltry, not to mention the fact that it is diminished on it by being continuous, whereas in the orchestra it grows ever greater and greater.

As for *Les Préludes,* I sent this work to you so as not to refuse you—but do take care not to make publicity for it in any way, for on the one hand I feel no need to persuade people for whom I have no regard, and on the other I should be very sorry to expose you to filial disappointments!—For the rest, notwithstanding all the nonsense uttered and printed about my *symphonic poems,* these works are making their way astonishingly on this side of the Rhine, and one day people will have the surprise of hearing them in Paris and—who knows?—perhaps even that of applauding them. For my part, I have only one thing to do: to continue my work without troubling myself about all the rest—which in any case is never a great difficulty for people who know what they are doing.

But let's talk of something which interests me more: your forthcoming visit here, which will give me true joy. Both of you will be welcomed wholeheartedly and with open arms—and so don't keep us waiting too long. Bring me in person (and in book) *Les XV joies du mariage,*[26] and know that I am fully prepared to increase their number, in the best sense, of course!

---

[26] Blandine had enjoyed, and brought to her father's attention, this anonymous 15th-cent. satire on marriage, which has been attributed—probably erroneously—to Antoine de La Sale.

1858

Early January. Blandine and Emile Ollivier spend several days at the Altenburg, Liszt's first meeting with his new son-in-law.

11 and 14 March. At the first of two successful concerts in Prague, Liszt conducts performances of the Dante Symphony, *Die Ideale* and the Piano Concerto No. 2 (with Tausig); at the second, *Tasso* and the Piano Concerto No. 1 (with Pflughaupt).

22 and 23 March. Performances in Vienna of the Gran Mass. On the 22nd, Liszt has an audience with the Emperor Franz Joseph.

10 and 11 April. Performances in Pest of the Gran Mass. On the 11th, in a ceremony at the Franciscan Church, Liszt is made a *confrater*.

14 April. In Vienna, Liszt is presented with a silver music-rack adorned with busts of Beethoven, Weber, and Schubert.

Late April. Liszt, Bülow, and Tausig are the guests at Löwenberg (Silesia) of Prince Constantin von Hohenzollern-Hechingen.*

Summer. Among visitors to the Altenburg are the dramatist Friedrich Hebbel, the poet Otto Roquette (author of the text of Liszt's *The Legend of St Elisabeth*), Kaulbach, Varnhagen von Ense, and Serov.

Late August to October. Liszt holidays in the Austrian Tyrol and also stays in Munich and Salzburg.

December. Liszt tenders his resignation to the Grand Duke after the première, on the 15th, of Cornelius's opera *The Barber of Bagdad* is received with a hostile demonstration covertly organized by the General Intendant, Dingelstedt.

WORKS. The symphonic poem *Hamlet* (S104).[1] SONGS: *Lasst mich ruhen* (Hoffmann von Fallersleben) (S317, *c*.1858); *In Liebeslust* (Hoffmann von Fallersleben) (S318, *c*.1858). The dramatic monologue *Lenore* (Bürger) (S346).

ESSAY. *Criticism of Criticism: Ulibishev and Serov.*

393. To Felix Draeseke in Dresden. [Weimar] Sunday, 10 January. G

. . . A couple of virtuosi we have heard here several times recently are Sivori and Bazzini. . . . A well-known piece by Bazzini, 'la ronde des lutins [Dance of the Elves]', was, by a printer's error, called 'ronde des crétins [Dance of the Cretins]'! What an immeasurably large public for such a 'dance'! . . .

---

[1] The short central section depicting Ophelia was added later.

394. To Richard Wagner in Paris. Weimar, 30 January. ^G In Calderón
you have once again found a friend in Paris, dearest Richard; *à la bonne heure*
—he is certainly a fellow with whom one can forget all the rogues and their
rogueries. I know him only very superficially, I regret to say, and have not yet
succeeded in taking him into myself. Grillparzer used to tell me wonderful
things about him, and if you remain much longer in this element I'll look at
some of his works again. When convenient, let me know what I should begin
with. The two main elements, *Catholicism* and *Honour*, are both very dear to
me. Something musical might be made out of them, don't you think? I have
read Cardinal Diepenbrock's translation of a quite wonderful sacred drama in
which heaven, air, earth, and all their powers are set in motion. I forget the title
at this moment, but will look it up.² Perhaps you can tell me how this material could be formed and fashioned for musical purposes.

Rienzi has to be postponed until May. We want to invite Tichatschek for it.
Whatever *can* be done, we shall do; but it vexes me that this will always be on
so petty a scale. Fischer (Dresden) has written in some distress to tell me of the
temporary frustration of his hopes to put on *Rienzi* there this winter. Like
Tichatschek and many others he is sincerely devoted to you, and we shall certainly all joyously do our duty as best we can.

Lohengrin will be performed here very shortly. I have already held a couple
of rehearsals because Ortrud, the Herald, and the King have to be recast. I can't
tell you how deeply the work moves me every time. When we last did it I felt
proud for my century—for possessing such a man as, in this work, you show
yourself to be! With *Lohengrin* the old opera world comes to an end; the spirit
moves upon the face of the waters, and there is light!

About your chances in Paris I have little to say to you. Certainly, of all your
works *Rienzi* seems to me to be the most suitable for the Parisians; but whether
they will take you up in earnest, and, in that case, whether you can count on
favourable relations with the management, the artistes, and the press, I regard
as very questionable. Nevertheless, you have done well to go to Paris yourself.
But read Calderón assiduously so that you can patiently endure the Parisian way
of doing things, one which stands in such complete contrast to your genius and
your temperament.

Keep me *au courant* of your adventures there, and if I can be of service to
you in anything it goes without saying that you can make use of

Your faithful Franciscus

---

² Probably *El mágico prodigioso*.

395. To Princess Carolyne in Weimar. Prague [Saturday] 6 March.

Leaving Leipzig at 6.00 a.m., I got here at 7.00 p.m., having stopped for just three hours, 9.00 to 12.00, in Dresden. The journey took place without any incidents or accidents, and thanks to the corrupt measures taken by Grosse I remained quite alone between Dresden and here. Our friend Meissner was waiting for me on the platform, as were two very young people, Musil and one of his colleagues from the medical school, and the two theatre directors: Stöger, our ex-Irma's papa, and Thomé. Wagner is in rather active correspondence with the last-named, who is counting on being the first to do *Tristan*—in Prague and conducted by Wagner! I offered him my congratulations, promising him in advance that I would not be entering into rivalry with him, natural though it would seem for Wagner to give me the priority. Poor Tristan! Here he is already wandering from Strasbourg to Karlsruhe, and from Karlsruhe to Prague—perhaps ultimately to come back to me in Weimar, just like [Doppler's] *Judith* and [Raff's] *Samson*! These intemperate gaucheries of Wagner's would be enough to vex one—but let us never accuse those who are suffering misfortune!

In Dresden I went straight to Draeseke's. He showed me two pieces from his opera [*König Sigurd*], both of which I found superb and entirely equal to what is needed. At Whitsun he will bring his finished score to Weimar, and I'll try to have the work put on next winter. While at Draeseke's I sent Grosse to get hold of Reubke. This gallant and charming young man has not long to live, I fear, despite the care being lavished upon him by 3 or 4 doctors, including Carus. Chest diseases which have gone this far are rarely cured; but the patients generally delude themselves up to the very last moment and have a gentle death. The Ritter sisters are alleviating his unfortunate condition with multiple proofs of the friendliest and most tender interest. They have undertaken to serve him as nurses, and send him whatever he needs. He has just given a concert at the Hôtel de Saxe with some success, and if he manages to live will continue to succeed likewise.[3] . . .

At 2.30 this afternoon *Tasso* is being performed at the Conservatoire, and we shall then rehearse the Dante and *Die Ideale*, which are the subject of every musical conversation in Prague at the moment. The 7/4 and 5/4 and the unresolved dissonances still have their interest in this city, where I assume that I shall find the majority of musicians fairly well disposed towards them. Meissner will be lunching with me at 1 o'clock, and I am going out to pay some necessary visits. I love you.   F.L.

---

[3] Liszt's pupil Julius Reubke died on 3 June.

396. To Princess Carolyne. [Prague] Monday evening, 8 March. Your programme for the Dante is a masterpiece, and despite my taste for bagatelles I found barely three or four words to change. Thank you for having sent it to me so quickly; and although a police regulation requires printed matter to be deposited with the police three days before publication, I hope it can be issued on Thursday. The proofs are carefully read and corrected and you will be receiving the two copies for Pohl. . . .

My rehearsals here are going marvellously, and, if I am not mistaken, there is enough goodwill for me in the Prague air at the moment. . . . This morning I paid a few visits, among others to Mme Cibbini and HE Cardinal Schwarzenberg. I noticed in his study a large rubber ball quite close to a crucifix on a console-table. Škroup told me that His Eminence does many physical exercises, walks round his room on stilts, plays ball, etc. For the rest, there are neither curtains nor carpets in this large study—but quite a number of mediocre paintings which he probably bought to encourage the pious sentiments of their creators.

My dinner yesterday, which will cost me roughly 70 florins, went off pretty well. Ambros* was sparkling in wit and prodigiously erudite. Ricard and Meissner were of the company. The last-named often quotes to me Mozart's relevant remark, 'Meine Prager verstehen mich', and flatters himself that his fellow citizens will be entirely of his opinion when it's my turn.

The post brought me nothing from you today; probably you had your letter posted too late. Tausig has just arrived; tomorrow and the next morning we shall have our two last rehearsals. . . . Your injunction to me to make my health my penultimate concern is too witty for me to do other than follow it. And so I shall try to sleep, and will not abuse spirituous liquor, although passion plays a part therein, to some extent! Tell Magnolet that I think of her a great deal and that I love her most tenderly. Patience—if we lack roses, we can clasp hands! . . .

397. To Princess Carolyne. [Prague] 7.00 a.m., Thursday, 11 March. Thank you, my sweet love, for your dear letters. Since the Vienna playbill gave you a moment of joy, I am very happy that the thing was settled amicably. May the God of the weak and the oppressed be with us!

Corinne must be in my bedroom, under the dummy piano, or right beside it. . . .

Here's a phenomenon for you! Yesterday, at the rehearsal, somewhere in the middle of Francesca's melody, about a hundred people began to applaud enthusiastically, in such a manner as almost to bring the rehearsal to a halt. My arms

fell to my sides. In this respect, as you know, I am not accustomed to being
spoilt, unless by my very dear domestic critic, to whom I owe all that is agreeable and good in my poor life. . . .[4]

398. To Princess Carolyne. Prague, 13 March. You are doing very
well to spend a few weeks in Berlin. But take care, my very dear ones, not to
catch a chill in some minor gallery, and don't get up as early as you did during
your first stay in Berlin, at 6 o'clock in the morning, even if it were to write to
Lazybones! . . .

I shall get Meissner to send you the local newspapers, which this time will
be more restrained than when the Mass was performed. Ambros yesterday plunged
into a series of articles which look like continuing throughout the week. He is
beginning by quoting Sesostris,[5] which will please you. . . .

Yesterday my day was spent visiting the Vice-Chancellor of the University
and a few other people of lesser calibre. I lunched at Count Salm's and spent
the evening at Ambros's, giving him great pleasure by playing him some charming little pieces of his own composition, somewhat in the style of Schumann;
he has just published them under the title *Auf der Wanderschaft*. . . .

399. To Princess Carolyne. [Vienna] Thursday, 18 March. 'Bene-
dicimus te, gratias agimus tibi', I sang in my Mass—and the better part of my
heart comes back to you!

For today, I haven't as yet anything new to tell you of Vienna, unless it is
that preparations for and rehearsals of the Mass are going well. On Friday and
Saturday the last full rehearsals will take place. . . .

Daniel has moved in with Tausig on the 3rd floor of the Empress of Austria,
where there are two beds, of which Daniel has taken one for himself. I breakfast with them at 7.00 a.m. The Easter holidays having come, on Tuesday evening
Daniel will leave for Dresden; for the term just ended he has obtained two very
good certificates at the university. This hotel arrangement is no invention of
mine. Hidalgo [Tausig] concocted it before my arrival, and I was notified only
yesterday evening when first going into the room, where I found them lodged

---

[4] In a note to the Princess that evening, after the concert, Liszt reported that 'the performance was excellent, full of
life; I believe I was recalled half a dozen times after the final chords of the Dante. . . . Tausig played admirably.'

[5] Our sole source of information about this mythical Egyptian king is Herodotus, who attributes to him just one
utterance (inscribed on his stone image): 'By the strength of my shoulders I won this land.'

together. There is no objection to be made to it, and I am even very glad that in this way I shall have more opportunity of seeing Daniel. . . .

Before my departure I warmly recommended Stör to have Mendelssohn's *St Paul* performed on Palm Sunday, for the benefit of the pension fund. All these Weimar trifles, both great and small, affect me little, and I shall always manage to have other fish to fry. Remember me most politely to the Old Man of the Mountain,[6] and also most affectionately to Varnhagen. Perhaps you'll be seeing the Arnims? Ask and take Magnolette's advice about this. . . .

The success of sorts of my Concerto for two pianos played by Kroll and Hans gave me a pleasant surprise. Oh, when shall I be able to work, and work yet more!! My head is full and more than full, and I feel that I shall now really do something good. . . . I am interrupted by visitors—farewell, may God be with you!

400. To Agnes Street-Klindworth. Aboard the steamer *Junon*, from Vienna to Pest, 31 March. No indeed, you are not mistaken, I cannot recover from my sickness. At certain moments it floods my every fibre, my every vein; I suffer from an unquenchable thirst, and prayer even increases its ardour. This feeling for the impossible becomes apparent, it seems, in my works, and on hearing my Mass one of my compatriots said: 'This music is religious to the point of converting Satan himself!' What people call success went far beyond my expectations at the two performances of 22 and 23 March—and even the critics, who cannot do other than show hostility to my endeavours, considered themselves obliged to hold a few reservations in my favour. The brief note you saw in the Augsburg *Gazette* comes from an individual I have on several occasions had shown the door, and who deemed it fitting to take revenge thus. For the rest, a good part of the Viennese press, notwithstanding the adverse precedents, praised me, and my few friends are very confident of victory. . . .

I can't tell you how much the kind of life I am obliged to lead, when I am away from Weimar, is becoming more and more unbearable. Ever to have to be talking to a lot of people to whom most of the time I have nothing to say, putting up with the customary stupidities and duplicities, incessantly paying and receiving visits, spending a mass of money for the pleasure of being bored to death—what a laughable torment! And so I said yesterday that I envied my driver, who at least has over me the incontestable advantage of remaining on his box-seat like a veritable philosopher, while I am delivered up to the obligations of worldly life, to which I no longer feel the least bit suited.

---

[6] Humboldt's nickname for himself.

I shall spend only a very few days in Pest, whither I am going solely to visit my four singers (who have consented to go out of their way for a week by coming to Vienna to sing my Mass); without their co-operation the performance was becoming impossible, seeing that Count Lanckoronsky had refused the theatre singers *permission* to take part in it. This unkind behaviour is ascribed to a touchiness unworthy of the high-ranking personages to whom it is attributed —in connection with the following.

During my last stay in Vienna, about 2 years ago, a person rather unqualified for this purpose asked me if I wished to be heard at a *Court concert*. I naturally replied that I had given no concerts for ten years, and consequently no longer belonged in the category of artistes who are invited to Court concerts. This was taken in bad part and very wrongly—for if Their Majesties had sent to ask to hear me in a small gathering, and without other colleagues (who are no longer my colleagues), then as a very humble subject of the monarchy I would certainly have given proof of obedience, and thus after a fashion satisfied their curiosity; but to insist on my continuing to practise a profession which I gave up without any exception many years ago, I could only find doubly uncalled for, both with regard to the Court and with regard to myself. As it generally happens that the one towards whom one has behaved badly is further punished into the bargain, Count Lanckoronsky made the most of the first opportunity which came along to make me feel the effects of this distributive justice, of which in high circles very frequent use is made.

This time I paid no visit to Herr von Metternich, finding it simpler not to bother His Highness with my humble person. His son Richard having ignored me during my last visit to Dresden, I thought it prudent not to seem too eager.

On the other hand I presented myself at His Majesty's, to thank him for the edition of my Mass which is being prepared at the Imperial and Royal Printing Press, and to assure him viva voce 'dass ich es mir in meinem künstlerischen Streben angelegen sein lasse, dem Lande, dem ich angehörig verbleibe, Ehre zu bringen [that in my artistic endeavours I am making it my business to bring honour to the country to which I belong]'.

To go to Egypt and not see the pyramids would be nonsensical; in the same way it would not be permitted to spend a few days in Prague without visiting the K's.[7] I spent a thoroughly original and delightful evening there, details of which I shall give you when we next meet. One of the two sisters is arthritic, but the other still full of vitality and vivacity. For this soirée their salon was thronged by the most attractive young people of Prague high society (the Lobkowitzes,

---

[7] Probably the Kittls.

Auerspergs, *et al.*), and I finished by declaring to Mlle K that she was herself so extraordinary that willy-nilly something extraordinary had to be done in her honour—whereupon, *without taking off* my gloves, I played the 'Sehnsuchts-Walzer', to the general satisfaction. . . .

Let me tell you again that I am delighted to learn that you have resumed your piano-playing, and even that you are giving some lessons. You know that I have always appreciated your talent as a pianist and I should not like you to give it up entirely. Music is indeed not a kind of *amusement* for me—but it fills a gap which, without it, would remain yawningly open in my soul.

When you come to Weimar I shall ask you to play me several things that I no longer want to hear played by others. . . .   A.A.

401. To Princess Carolyne. At Karácsonyi's, Herrengasse 10, Pest, 9.00 a.m., 1 April. This is the first quiet and pleasant awakening I have had since I left you. I attribute it to a small thatched cottage in bronze, exactly like the one in your room, which without my noticing it was close to my bed last night. Karácsonyi is still obliged to look after himself a lot and to keep to his room, following a rather serious illness he has just had. His wife is confined to bed, and at present the whole household has an air of peace and melancholy which suits me perfectly. Perhaps I shall spend a week here. . . .

If the Mass is performed in Brussels, I shall have to go there about a week earlier. I am terribly vexed by the inevitable expense which journeys of this kind bring, and don't find the moral gain to be in proportion. Oh, why do I not know how to paint, were it only water-colours for Magne's portfolios, and why cannot I stay peacefully at home to work, without having to take part in all the discordant hullabaloo of the world! The necessity of dragging my person about in public, and of needing the co-operation of so many other individuals before my work can be produced, I am finding more and more unbearable. Truly, after the dancer the musician is the most badly placed of all artists when, as I do, he finds the hubbub of the human anthill a distressing spectacle. The advantage possessed by painters, sculptors, and writers, of being able to put forth their ideas with no intermediary other than colour, marble, and typography, and to lead quiet, withdrawn lives independently of other human beings, strikes me as a boon beyond compare. And so I should greatly envy them, did I not finally know that each of us must bear his cross in this world and trust only in the Good Lord! Be blessed for having attached yourself to mine; and, through your love, making it light and agreeable for me! . . .

402. To Princess Carolyne. [Pest] 8.00 p.m., Saturday, 10 April, after the performance of the Mass in the museum hall, put back a day because of a change in the theatre performances

'Celebrations, verses, flowers, infinite love'—what a telegram, and signed Carolyne, Marie! All I could do was weep with joy and gratitude. But how to reply? Nevertheless, my soul flew towards you, even more quickly than the telegraph. . . .

I have only a few moments to write to you today. The Mass was perfectly performed, and equally well listened to, this afternoon. The whole aristocratic and fashionable world and a large audience were gathered in this charming museum hall, whose sonority is unfortunately a little too strong; but there was no reason to be disagreeably affected by it this time. Hearts throbbed—and in the auditorium there was that indefinable feeling brought about exclusively by works bearing the stamp of genius. Tomorrow the Mass will be performed in the parish church once again, during divine service. Immediately afterwards, the Superior of the monastery will say a low mass for me—for my solemn reception as *confrater*. By order of the Franciscans, Augusz will be admitted to this title tomorrow at the same time. I have just been shown the draft of the Latin address to be made to me by the Superior. It is a masterpiece of wording and I shall send it to you. I do not know if the newspapers will interfere in this matter, but that is totally indifferent to me—and the ceremony will be held with a solemnity of a kind ultimately to reduce even the greatest ill-wishers to silence. At 1 o'clock there will be a banquet in the refectory to which several of the most respected townspeople have been invited. You will have news of it in my next letter from Vienna. . . .

403. To Princess Carolyne. Vienna, Tuesday, 13 April. When I got here yesterday evening your dear letter was waiting to welcome me. . . . At 10.00 on Sunday, 11 April, my Mass was performed in Pest's parish church. It was packed, and close to the altar there were about a dozen reserved seats, occupied by people whom M. Santóffy, the parish priest, had invited specially, by sending them texts printed in Latin, German, and Hungarian which I shall forward to you. . . . Immediately afterwards I had to return to receive a deputation from the Conservatoire, headed by its president, Baron Prónay, which was coming to thank me for having destined for the Conservatoire the takings from the previous day's concert at the Museum.

At midday I went to the Franciscan Monastery. The Superior said a low mass for me, during which a male-voice choir sang, very well, several pieces from an

extremely simple mass, with organ accompaniment. The Franciscan church is one
of the most attractive and spacious in Pest. There is a small memorial there to
Albach,[8] with an example of the medallion which is in my ground-floor room.
I took a seat on a bench near the high altar and prayed for you and Magnolette.
At 12.30 we gathered in the refectory. On my right was Augusz and on my left
Karácsonyi. Beside Augusz was Danielik, the canon who has just published
what is said to be a very scholarly biography of Christopher Columbus, and is
regarded as one of the best minds in the Hungarian clergy. A very sedate and
dignified man, he communicates with the *Univers catholique* and will shortly be
going to Constantinople and Rome, there to carry out research for a work on
Hunyady. The illustrated book on St Elisabeth which you know, is also by him.
Several copies of this work (which was presented to the Emperor and Empress)
went for 1,000 florins each. For my part, I limited myself to 50, which is already
a very reasonable price. Beside Danielik was Santöffy, priest of the parish church,
and among the guests were several *Honorationen* [notabilities]. With the 12 or
so Franciscans who were present, we were about forty people at table. My bust
and portrait had been put in the refectory. Before we ate, one of the friars addressed
me with the allocution in Latin which I have spoken of to you as a little masterpiece of its kind. Haas, a canon and a school principal, was the author, for
the Franciscans are not equal to this standard of writing. It will be published
in Latin and German in a religious newspaper, *Der katholische Christ*, which you
will receive. During the meal the Superior proposed a toast to me in Latin,
and others to Augusz, Karácsonyi, *et al.*, who replied to them in Hungarian. At
about 4 o'clock we went our separate ways, and as I had to depart during the
evening the diploma of *confrater* and the allocution, which has yet to be translated, will be sent to me here. The diploma is dated 20 June '57. Count György
Károlyi, who, incidentally, when two estates were entailed had to have his fortune ascertained formally and proved that he had an *income* of 900,000 florins,
was likewise named a *confrater*, some years ago. Augusz and Karácsonyi will be
receiving their diplomas in due course. As you see, I am in very good and reliable company. Preoccupied with economizing as I have been for a month, I was
content to give the Superior, through Augusz, 200 florins, which moreover is
quite sufficient. . . .

Daniel is not back here yet. When I got here at 7.00 yesterday evening I at
once went to Hellmesberger's quartet session, where there was a crowd which
would have made Singer and Stör envious. Ole Bull, who had just arrived, was
there. . . .

[8] Pater Albach, whom Liszt had known in his boyhood and to whom he had dedicated several of his sacred choral
works.

This morning Mosenthal brought me almost the whole of the First Act of *Janko*.[9] I fancy you will like it pretty well. . . .

404. To Princess Carolyne. Friday, 16 April. At last I am very nearly finished with Vienna, and tomorrow I shall be able to set out in full tranquillity of conscience. The famous music-rack was presented to me the day before yesterday, at 5 o'clock, and it was again Assmayer in his capacity as Hofkapell-meister who undertook the speech, to which I responded with just a simple thank you. However, I added to it the vow of soon bringing out some works which would be worthy of being placed on such a rack, and also worthy of being offered in homage to the three patron saints of music, Beethoven, Weber, and Schubert, whose busts seem to command me to walk my path and to carry out my task. . . . With the exception of Weber's bust, which is rather a failure, the whole rack seems to me to have turned out very well. It is a beautiful *objet d'art et de luxe* whose natural place is in the salon—where we shall put it on Beethoven's piano.[10] . . .

The day before yesterday there was also a grand soirée at Countess Bánffy's. Tausig and Laub played. As Count Lanckoronsky had refused the Italian singers permission to sing there, I took it upon myself to compensate Mme Bánffy for this disappointment. She had written a most crushing letter to the Count, who had irritated her extremely, but I begged her not to send it. In return, at the end of the soirée I played a couple of pieces which obtained much more success than they deserved. It was a most elegant party. Among the guests were Pce Wolkonsky, Pcss Zenaïde Wolkonsky's son, appointed Minister at Dresden in succession to Schröder, and his wife; Pcss Khevenhüller, Felix [Lichnowsky]'s sister, and her daughter Pcss Brezenheim; the Duchesse d'Acerenza, sister of the Duchesse de Sagan; a charming young woman, Countess Zamoyska; the Batthyánys; Brunswicks; *et al.* As far as the bourgeoisie are concerned, I noticed only Laube, manager of the Burgtheater, and his wife. The Countess has already several times asked me to remember her most kindly to you, and I shall be bringing you two small Viennese objects, one for you and one for Magnolette, from her. She and her acquaintances were all fire and flame at the two perform-ances of my Mass, and say aloud that journalists who take it into their heads to criticize me are 'infamous!' Notwithstanding all my dislike of salon music, I believed that it was better to give her pleasure just this once—all the more since

---

[9] A Hungarian opera (libretto by Mosenthal after a novel in verse by Karl Beck) that Liszt was planning at this time but ultimately never composed.
[10] See Letter 277 n. 10.

she committed not the least indiscretion in this respect, and sincerely wishes *us* well. . . .

I bless you and remain eternally your F.L.

405. To Princess Carolyne. [Löwenberg] 7.00 a.m., Tuesday, 27 April.

. . . Tausig, who left at the same time as Hans, will be back in Weimar at the same time as this letter. Put him up at the Altenburg until he finds something else, and give him a good welcome. Since Vienna he has been very melancholy and leaves his room only reluctantly. During the last month he has made the piano arrangements of the Dante [Symphony], of the Faust [Symphony], and of *Die Ideale*, and dwells in this sphere alone. I shall speak to you in more detail about him, for I am making it my duty to be useful to him, something in which I hope to succeed. . . . He has it in mind to change his name, and through his fingertips to gain a big reputation.

I hope you will not refuse me some crumbs from the table of your erudition on the subject of Buddhism, so well prepared for you by Koeppen,[11] if I have read the name right. Although my 'siege is done'[12] in this respect, I shall take great pleasure in hearing you speak on this infinitely fertile topic. In my opinion you are perfectly right to protest against the reconciliation[13] which a few similarities in form in no way authorize. The resemblance in rites hardly matters, when there is such a difference in dogma and feeling. Schopenhauer has very lucidly brought out the differences between Greek philosophy and Christ's religion in his Dialogue on Religion, which is in the second volume of the *Parerga*[14] and contains two of the finest and most powerful pages known to me in defence of Christianity. None of the doctors of the Church has better shown the infinite distance between Aristotle and Plato on the one hand and the Gospels on the other—for nothing can be compared with Love, just as nothing can replace it. As far as you are concerned, most infinitely dear one, whose whole life is but the fulfilment of this supreme law, I can well understand your indignation at false semblances and lying analogies. If ever you take the time to write down your thoughts on Koeppen's book, I am certain that you will with complete spontaneity say the most beautiful things. . . .

Do give my regards to Scotch, whom I shall be so happy to see again!

[11] C. F. Koeppen's work *Die Religion des Buddha.* Vol. i, *Die Religion des Buddha und Ihre Entstehung* (The Buddha's Religion and its Origin) had been published in 1857; vol. ii, *Die Lamaische Hierarchie und Kirche* (The Lamaistic Hierarchy and Church), appeared in 1859.

[12] Receiving for his history of the Knights of Malta some notes on the siege of Rhodes, the Abbé Vertot is said to have rejected them with the words 'mon siège est fait'—a remark which has become proverbial to indicate a stubborn adherence to ideas or opinions despite information that might correct them.

[13] Between Christianity and Buddhism. [14] Schopenhauer's *Parerga und Paralipomena* (Berlin, 1851).

406. To Blandine Ollivier in Paris. Weimar, 4 May. Like you, my dearest Blandine, I have wound up my travels—i.e. by the two days I have just spent in Berlin with Cosette, which will remain one of my most agreeable memories. I wanted to write to you from her home, but our conversations went on from morning to night, and she seemed so content with my presence that I had no scruples about letting those two days go by without thinking of anything other than her.

The wholly public life (less and less to my taste) that I had been obliged to lead these last two months made me feel all the more, by contrast, the charm and intimacy of her affection. At bottom, I am no longer good for anything other than steadily continuing to make progress with my work, my only goal being that of giving expression, as clearly as possible, to a very firm Ideal in my mind—and, in so doing, of loving the few souls who love me, while totally forgetting the people who busily do the opposite. . . .

The great admiration I profess for the political and civilizing genius of Louis Napoléon, whom I believe a worthy heir to his uncle—for if the latter could with good reason call himself the man of destiny, Napoleon III seems to me to be very much the man of the force of circumstances—does not make me in the least unjust towards other convictions, and in any case I hardly pride myself that I can pose as an expert in matters political ever to think of wrangling with Ollivier about anything he may or may not resolve upon doing. But despite my deliberate impartiality, I admit that I found it very agreeable to learn from Cosette that he had refused to undertake the defence of Pieri;[15] such calamitous individuals no longer belong, in my opinion, to civilized society, and their only recourse is to the infinite mercy of God, who pardoned the good thief. In this sense, M. de la Bourdonnaye's remark, which has been treated as barbarous—'Send them back to their natural judge'—is only just; but it is distressing to think that the intermediary between the delinquent and the natural judge still exists in our societies: the Executioner—and I for my part pray that before long the death penalty will be abolished.

I don't know how to effect a transition from that to something else. As a contrast to Louis Napoléon and Pieri let's turn to... Choka![16]—This fine and charming boy has been given a good scolding by Cosette who, like you, understood nothing of the holiday trip he made so opportunely during my visit to Vienna. I alone understood, and consequently urged him not to impose any filial constraints on himself. Moreover, they have a very high opinion of him in

---

[15] Accomplice of Orsini in the attempted assassination of the Emperor (Jan. 1858), for which, like Orsini, he went to the guillotine.

[16] Nickname—from '*cho*colat' and '*café*'—for Daniel Liszt.

Vienna, and I take it that he will accomplish his legal studies there with distinction, which is the main thing for the moment. Later we'll see what will have to be done for him and what he will be able to make of himself.

Someone who is a friend of ours (and who is indeed someone), occasionally, like Daniel, puts me in difficulties over what I have to do for him, seeing that he possesses a special talent for handling his affairs very badly. You can't guess whom I mean, but won't be surprised when I say that it is Wagner. With his immense genius which becomes more and more indisputable through all the foolish disputes he has to embark on, he unfortunately can't manage to rid himself of the most trying domestic vexations, not to mention all the disappointments of his fantastic expectations. In this way he resembles those lofty mountains, radiant at their peaks, but shrouded in fog up to their shoulders—the difference being that the figurative fogs contain many more real drawbacks than do the others.

Tell me something of him in your next letter, for I love him with all my heart and admire him as Germany's finest *génie-artiste*.

I have had 300 francs sent to the Lamartine subscription. Does Ollivier encounter him sometimes? Do Michelet and d'Eckstein visit you? Let me have news of them, and give them my affectionate regards.   Yours.

407. To Anna Liszt in Paris. 8 May ^{G (F)}

Dearest Mother,

The apple, pear, and plum trees in the Altenburg garden are in fullest bloom and ripening against the time when someone will go and 'rütteler' them. This word of your invention has not yet found a place in the Dictionary of the Académie française.[17] It reminds me, however, to 'rütteler' at my laziness in letter-writing and to chat with you to my heart's content.

Fortunately I can give you excellent tidings of all those who are dear to you, myself included. Daniel is in good health and moving as nimbly as a mountain goat along the Vienna pavements. Cosima looks very well and is filling out a bit; I have just spent a couple of days with her in Berlin, without setting foot outside her very attractively furnished home. On returning to the Altenburg I found everyone well and cheerful, thank goodness, although both in and outside myself there are all sorts of unbearable things to bear.

Your dear letter I received in Pest punctually and with great joy on my name-day. The honour done to me there by the Franciscans will have delighted you

---

[17] Anna had been thinking of the German 'rütteln', to shake.

too. I am sending you the speech made when I was admitted into the Order as a *confrater*. It will explain the whole proceedings to you, and you will be moved by the way in which my father was remembered therein. I remember how in my childhood—which seems still to be lasting—you often called me 'clumsy Frater!' Was that a presentiment of my present dignity? It will, I fear, only further increase my clumsiness in many of life's circumstances—such as my inability to amass money by being prudently economical, or to prevent all sorts of nonsense about me going round the world.

Please give Belloni the enclosed note, which requires a reply. I should be delighted to stay with you when I come to Paris, if Blandine, who is putting accommodation at my disposal in her home, were not contesting me with you. Perhaps I could visit you in the autumn. The whole summer I must do good; by which I mean keep quietly to myself so that I can finish a big work I have just begun.

Loving good wishes, dearest Mother, from your sincerely devoted son

F. Liszt

408. To Ernst Pasqué in Weimar. Salzburg, 8 October ^G

Dear Friend!

Even if *der deutsche Michel* [the typical German] has concocted a Mozart resembling himself and thereby often practised a dubious idolatry, it behoves us none the less wholeheartedly to venerate the real, great, and beloved Mozart and to pay homage to his genius. Filled with this feeling I came to Salzburg, where I take delight in gazing upon the statue of our glorious, cheerful, and superabundantly gifted master. You won't blame me for delaying my return to Weimar for a few more days: I can certainly *rely on* Lassen,* and without *disturbing* Stör [18] may surely stay a little longer with Mozart!

Your friendly letter reached me an hour before I left Munich, and the business part of it I have already dealt with in my letter to Lassen. I shall be back with you in about a week. *Comala* [19] should then be launched at once—but please don't forget the *beautiful clouds* I asked for earlier on. Nor do I want to keep Cornelius's *Barber of Bagdad* waiting. We can probably get the barber's set-up prepared quite nicely by the beginning of November.—Rietz's new comic opera will be very acceptable to me, and I shall be pleased if my zealous Leipzig adversary achieves a success with us, to contribute to which I'll gladly do all I can. [20]

---

[18] Puns on Lassen and *verlassen*, Stör and *stören*.
[19] Opera by Sobolewski, the première of which Liszt conducted on 30 Oct.
[20] Rietz's one-act opera *Georg Neumark und die Gambe* was performed in Weimar the following May.

Rietz will certainly come up with a clever, subtle, and decent score. That is something that always gives me pleasure, and I am happy if it is shared by the audience. Fortunately this is mostly the case in Weimar, where, without flattering ourselves, we are juster and more impartial than elsewhere when it comes to understanding and appreciating new works. . . .

Sincerely and affectionately yours,   F. Liszt

P.S. At the local theatre yesterday I saw Bauernfeld's comedy *Die Virtuosen*, and was amused by the inevitable apparition of the 'Music of the Future'. . . .

409. To Richard Wagner in Venice. Salzburg, 9 October ^G

Dearest Richard,

The news about you in the papers this last month was so varied and contradictory that I did not know where to write to you. First, it was reported that you had arrived in Vienna; then, when this premature announcement was retracted, someone wrote to tell me that you had gone to Florence or Paris. From your last letter, which reached me on the day I left Munich, I finally learn that for the time being you intend to remain in Venice, and that the government will make no objection to your staying there. With all my heart I wish that you will find peace in Venice, that you will be comfortably settled there, and that you will resume and complete the works interrupted by such distressing events. *Fiat pax in virtute tua* is a prayer in the Mass which I cry to you from the very bottom of my heart!

The enquiries I had made about your safety if you stayed in Venice were certainly not answered satisfactorily enough for me to be able to recommend it as the most suitable place for you to stay in, even temporarily. I still have a few doubts, which, however, I hope will prove to be groundless. It is a great pity that we cannot live together, and I have an unutterable longing for the day when this will be possible! I recently spoke again to the Grand Duke about your situation, and implored him to do everything he could to bring about your return to Germany—which he promised me he would do! . . .

Another point in your letter, dearest Richard, almost hurt me. I can quite understand if, amidst the vexations and excitements which made your latest stay in Zurich so miserable, you regard as '*trivial*' the official engagements which prevented my coming there, and if you take as little account of Jena University's anniversary celebrations as you do of the consideration I have to show to the Grand Duke (if only so that I can now and then be of use to you in various small ways). When you are in a calmer mood, however, you will easily understand that I cannot and may not leave Weimar at any moment—and will surely feel that the delay in my journey to Zurich was caused by no kind of *triviality*. When I wrote to say that I would be with you again on 20 August, I certainly assumed that even in the event of your earlier departure from Zurich you would indicate another place—Lucerne or Geneva—where I could meet you. Since you did not do so I came to a conclusion that on your word I am happy to abandon, although, as I remarked to you recently, I have for years had to be prepared for many unbelievable and deeply offensive things from the Comtesse d'A.[21]

But enough of this, dearest Richard! We shall remain what we are—inseparable, true friends, and such another pair will not soon be found!

During the first half of September the Princess, her daughter, and I roamed around the Tyrolean mountains and spent a few days quite solitarily in the Oetz valley. Driven away by bad weather we returned to Munich, quietly witnessed the festivities, and saw our friend Kaulbach every day. . . .

So as not to abandon our original travel plans, and to assert our rights even against the bad weather, we have come to Salzburg and in about a week shall be back in Weimar. There I shall probably find the proofs of the Dante Symphony, which I shall soon be sending you as the truest child of my sufferings.

When will the joy of reading *Tristan* be mine?—The Härtels tell me that the piano score is already in print.[22] Have you decided where the first performance is to take place? From what I hear, they are very much counting on it in Karlsruhe. May God grant that *Tristan* will, as I hope, bring your exile to an end!

At Weimar this winter we shall have *Rienzi*, with Tichatschek. Before that I go to Dresden, where I have promised Rietschel to pay my old debt to Weber, and to make just *one* exception by playing several of Weber's piano pieces at a concert for the benefit of the Weber monument (the model of which Rietschel has completed with incomparable mastery). . . .

Write to me at Weimar soon, to let me know how you like the city of the lagoons. Presumably Carl Ritter is with you. If, as I should like to think, his ill humour towards me is now over,[23] give him my friendly greetings and tell him

---

[21] Writing to Liszt on 27 Sept., Wagner had reassured him: 'As regards the Comtesse d'A., I made her acquaintance when Cosima stayed with me. On several occasions mother and daughter came to my place in the evening, for music. She seemed to take great interest in my *Nibelungen*. Unfortunately I was not in the mood to become better acquainted with her mind: to argue about art is something I like less and less; and she showed no inclination to induce me to do so. In the little contact I had with her otherwise, she was very reserved towards me, in a critical, superior kind of way. Nor did she ever speak of you to me—your avowed and intimate friend. I alone touched, inadvertently, on the artistic value of your new creations: an opinion to which she listened in silence. Thus my relations with the Comtesse d'A.'

[22] In a letter to Wagner of 26 Dec., after receipt of the First Act, Liszt enthused: 'What a heavenly Christmas present Härtel has sent me. All the children in the world put together cannot be so delighted with their trees hung with golden fruit and glittering presents as I, in my one person, am with your unique *Tristan*!'

[23] Ritter seems to have been unfortunate in the features with which nature had endowed him; and at Zurich in 1856 had taken as a personal insult Liszt's use of the word 'baboons'. See Wagner's *My Life*.

that I sincerely approve of the sonatas of his which Härtel has published. But he should not wait too long to bring out several things, and not become engrossed in this stupid musing.

Most sincerely and affectionately I remain

Your steadfastly loyal   F. Liszt

410. To Blandine Ollivier. Weimar, 21 November. And so these last few days, dearest Blandine, you have been back in your nest in the rue Saint-Guillaume, where I enjoy visiting you in thought. During the months of your stay in Florence I travelled through the mountains and valleys of the Tyrol, which contains scenes of great beauty: Lake Achen and the Oetz valley in particular made a profound impression on me. We also spent a few days in Innsbruck and Salzburg. In this latter town, birthplace of Mozart, whose statue adorns the main square, at every hour of the day the Town Hall's chiming-clock very stupidly played not one of the melodies of the 'divine Wolfgang', as Blaze de Bury used to say, but a rather insipid theme from Donizetti's *Linda di Chamounix*. I was assured that September was the wrong time to be there, and that usually, for at least seven months of the year, the carillon didn't permit itself such pranks, not taking it into its head to ring out with anything but themes of Mozart.

On the way back from our excursions in the Tyrolean Alps we spent three weeks in Munich, so that we could at our leisure visit the great art exhibition and take part in the extremely brilliant celebrations marking the 700th anniversary of the city's foundation. Kaulbach, with whom I have been on friendly terms for many years, did a full-length portrait of me. It is a masterpiece and a page of history in the manner of the finest portraits of Van Dyck.

In Munich I also ran into Mme Ungher-Sabatier, who sang Emile's praises while expressing regret at not being in Florence (where by chance I renewed acquaintance with her about twenty years ago) to do you the honours of her villa. She told me she would be spending a few weeks in Paris, and so perhaps you will see her there.

Since 20 October we have been peacefully reinstalled in the Altenburg, where Emile's letter for 22 October reached me and gave me very great pleasure. Please tell him, dear Blandine, how anxious I am to continue to deserve his good opinion and to work for the fulfilment of his good wishes, for which I am most sincerely grateful. An enormous arrears in correspondence, plus other matters to which I have had to give priority, has prevented serious resumption of my work, interrupted for several months. However, I have corrected the proofs of the Dante Symphony (which I played to you here), in score and also for 2 pianos, as well as those of my symphonic poem *Die Ideale*, after a poem of Schiller's. These two works will be out by Christmas, and when Cosette goes to Paris she will bring them to you with the Gran Mass, which will be published at the same time. If you have an opportunity, show them to our common friend Lecourt (of Marseilles), who wrote me an altogether delightful letter telling me of the friendly interest he now has in both of you, and of the superlatively favourable impression that your own person and intelligence made on him. My paternal vanity was noticeably flattered, and I am delighted to share his opinion, something you have no reason to be uneasy about! . . .

Baron Alexis Des Michels (of the Foreign Office in Paris), who tells me he has occasionally met Emile in Marseilles, has just spent about ten days here. I very much enjoyed making his acquaintance, and if you run into him in Paris I presume you will share my impression. He is a close friend of Gounod, and his musical opinions are more sensible than those of the general run of people. Talking of Gounod, try to hear his *Médecin malgré lui* at the Opéra-Comique, and also his *Faust*, which is currently being performed at the Opéra, and tell me very sincerely what you think of them. I should be delighted if these two works were on a level with the high opinion I have formed of Gounod's talent. And so to begin with, as I said to Des Michels, I am quite prepared to have his *Médecin malgré lui* put on in our theatre.

A thousand hearty greetings to Emile. I remain faithfully at one with you, in heart and soul.

411. To Agnes Street-Klindworth. Meiningen, 7 December. I have just spent a couple of days in Coburg (at Monseigneur's). The first performance of a new opera (in 5 acts, this time), entitled *Diana von Solange* and composed by HRH, took place on Sunday and, as one might expect, enjoyed a complete success. The Duke had brought together on this occasion several intendants and a few literary celebrities (Putlitz, Tempeltey, *et al.*); Dingelstedt appeared in *both capacities*. Herr Kücken, author of the very celebrated *Larme*,[24] was there too, and he told me (which, however, I knew already) that *Tannhäuser* would shortly be performed in Stuttgart, for all that a highly placed personage is supposed to have said, some time ago: 'Von einem solchen Lumpen braucht man keine Musik zu hören [One doesn't need to hear the music of such a scoundrel]!' —I don't imagine that this opinion has changed since then—but Wagner's works are not only making a noise everywhere, but well and truly making *money*.

---

[24] F. W. Kücken's once popular song *Die Träne* (The Tear), Op. 52/3.

Consequently, all managements are obliged to put them on, whatever people say. . . . For my own part I need attend to them no more, especially *Tannhäuser*, which I no longer even conduct and which has now become a *pons asinorum* in every theatre in Germany, without exception.

Meiningen has become a railway station between Eisenach and Coburg. I broke my journey here yesterday to call and see the Hereditary Prince (who has just got married again to a very charming young person: the Princess of Hohenlohe-Langenburg[25]), with whom I have established friendly relations. My day passed between lunch with his father and a small private soirée in his own residence.

In 5 hours I shall be back in Weimar. On Sunday, Mme Viardot-Garcia will sing Norma. Cornelius's opera, of the music of which I have a very high opinion, will be performed during the course of next week. Lassen has all but finished his *Frauenlob*; but I doubt if it can be put on this winter, for we have a very full programme. However, I shall try to find some good opportunity, which one must do one's best to bring about while never counting on it; and I should like in this matter to give Lassen a further proof of the very friendly interest I take in him. . . .

The great event in our little town this winter is the stir being caused by Dingelstedt, as much by his manner of running the theatre (thus far, extremely profitably for the Grand Duke's coffers) as by his *Vorlesungen* [lectures] for the benefit of the Schiller Foundation. We have already had several storms in our tea-cup, and it looks as if the tempests will continue—but on the whole Dingelstedt, who has not yet fallen out with me, despite the longing people had for him to do so, is getting on with things very well. . . .

Today I just wanted to tell you that I am still in the land of the living, without really knowing why; for my mind and heart frequent regions which are little known to others, and were I asked *what was the matter with me*, I should find it very difficult to reply.   A.A.

The 'falling out' came only too quickly. On 15 December a hostile faction, covertly organized by Dingelstedt, opposed the première of Peter Cornelius's sparkling comic opera *The Barber of Bagdad* with determined booing and hissing. Liszt, Dingelstedt's real target, then submitted his resignation to the Grand Duke, but conducted a Beethoven concert already planned for the 17th.

In a letter on the 19th, Cornelius explained matters thus: 'Liszt wants—Art; Dingelstedt—himself. Hence the conflict.'

---

[25] Feodora, daughter of Queen Victoria's half-sister.

1859

Early January. An exchange of letters brings a brief—but serious—misunderstanding between Liszt and Wagner.

27 February. Liszt conducts a concert of his works in Berlin.

10 April. The Emperor of Austria awards Liszt the decoration of the Iron Crown, in consequence of which an hereditary knighthood is later bestowed upon him.[1]

1–7 May. Liszt stays at Löwenberg.

9 May. He attends a concert in Breslau.

Early June. Liszt is present, and works of his are performed, at the music festival in Leipzig at which the Allgemeine Deutsche Musikverein is founded. His acquaintance is made by the young Arthur Sullivan.

23 June. Liszt's patroness, the Dowager Grand Duchess Maria Pavlovna, dies in Weimar.

Summer. Bedřich Smetana stays at the Altenburg.

15 October. Princess Marie Wittgenstein marries Prince Constantin von Hohenlohe-Schillingsfürst and leaves Weimar to live in Vienna.

15 November. Liszt conducts his *Prometheus choruses* in Zwickau.

13 December. The 20-year-old Daniel Liszt dies in Berlin.

WORKS. *Die Seligkeiten* (The Beatitudes) (S25, later incorporated into the oratorio *Christus*), for mixed chorus and organ; Psalm 23 (S15) and Psalm 137 (S17); *Festlied zu Schillers Jubelfeier* (Dingelstedt) (S90/11), with baritone solo; the recitation *Vor hundert Jahren* (Halm) (S347); *Totentanz* (rev. version) (S126), for piano and orchestra.

PIANO: *Venezia e Napoli* (rev. version) (S162):[2] 1. *Gondoliera* 2. *Canzone* 3. *Tarantella*; *Ernani: paraphrase de concert* (rev. version) (Verdi) (S432); *Miserere du Trovatore* (Verdi) (S433); *Rigoletto: paraphrase de concert* (Verdi) (S434).

PUBLISHED. The book *Des Bohémiens et de leur musique en Hongrie* (the German and Hungarian translations, by Peter Cornelius and József Székely respectively, came out in 1860 and 1861) and the essays *John Field and His Nocturnes* and *Pauline Viardot-Garcia.*

---

412. To Richard Wagner in Venice. Weimar, 4 January. ᴳ So that I shall no longer be exposed to the danger of boring you with an '*earnest and pathetic*' way of speaking, I am sending back to Härtel the First Act of *Tristan*, and asking not to make the acquaintance of the remainder until it is published.

---

[1] A higher degree of nobility than a mere 'von', it would have enabled him, had he chosen, to call himself Franz Ritter von Liszt. However, in 1867, having by then no male heir of his own, he was granted permission to transfer the knighthood to Eduard Liszt.

[2] Published in 1861 as a supplement to the *Années de pèlerinage, deuxième année, Italie.*

Since the *Dante* Symphony and the *Mass* are not valid as bank shares, it would be superfluous for me to send them to Venice. And in future the receipt, from there, of offensive letters and telegrams of distress I shall regard as no less superfluous.[3]

I remain, *most seriously and loyally,*   Yours,   F. Liszt

413. To Princess Carolyne in Weimar. [Berlin] 7.00 p.m., 25 February. This, most infinitely dear one, is how my day has gone. At 9.00 this morning, preliminary rehearsal at the Singakademie. Hans [von Bülow] did me the honours of *Die Ideale*, which he conducts admirably, with a perfect understanding of the work. The orchestra is consequently very well prepared, and it will be easy for me to add to it in several places the 'indefinable something'— *una certa idea*, as Raphael says, which I imagine will make an impression upon the audience. From there, at 11.00, Cosima and I went to see Fräulein von Jasky, after which I called on Cosmos. He gave me a most gracious welcome, saying among other things that he very much hoped I would be staying *longer* in Berlin. By that he was referring to a rumour going around for some years that HRH the Pcss of Prussia would choose me as Meyerbeer's successor—something of which there is absolutely no reason to think. As that was the last thing in my mind when Humboldt mentioned it, he repeated it more distinctly, at which I could only bow. He spoke of Weimar's school of art, and in particular of Kaulbach, his symbolism and his awaited *Christopher Columbus*, talking very graciously about our friend. As I handed him your letter only on my arrival, he did not read it until after my departure—but in the kindliest way asked after you, etc. Mention was made, too, of Meyerbeer's new opera [*Dinorah*] and of my *Elisabeth*, and he told me that this latter work would be particularly well received in Darmstadt—as the ruling family prides itself on its descent from St Elisabeth. For my part, I remarked that Thuringia and Hungary likewise laid claim to this saint.

Although his conversation is still lively and alert, Humboldt is ailing and shrunken. Stilke, whom I saw just now, told me of having dined with him

---

[3] In a letter, marked by bitter and awkward humour, of 31 Dec., Wagner had bidden Liszt send 'your Dante and Mass. But first—money!' 'Don't write to me again earnestly and pathetically!' he had added. 'God! I have already told you recently how tiresome you all are. . . .' Having given Wagner unfailingly generous moral and material support for many years, bowed down at this time with numerous problems and worries of his own, and regarding such a missive as a more than peculiar reply to his letter (26 Dec.) of glowing admiration for *Tristan*, Liszt had responded with the irate communication reproduced here. Before receiving it Wagner had already written (2 Jan.) with what was tantamount to an explanation and apology (followed by further long elucidations on the 7th and 8th)—but, unhappily, the two letters had crossed in the post. Cordial relations were soon resumed, but the misunderstanding—which has been called a 'fateful' one—seems to have caused these two great but fundamentally very different men to tread rather more warily with one another from this time forward until, two and a half years later, their correspondence came virtually to an end.

yesterday—and that he was pleased to tell of having dined in days of old with Voltaire.[4] As for Frederick the Great, that doesn't count and goes without saying! From Humboldt's I went to Mitzi Genast's, then returned to the Hotel Brandenburg, which you so wittily styled an hotel for ruined noblemen, or so Cosette tells me. I dined there tête-à-tête, not with Voltaire or Frederick the Great, but quite simply with Cosette, who is thoroughly good and kind. . . .

414. To Princess Carolyne. [Berlin] Midnight, Sunday, 27 February.

One single thing is needful! It is you, beloved Carolyne, my faith and my love, my earth and my Heaven!

Although you told me not to telegraph this evening, I got Cosette to do so. I take it that her telegram reached you before you went to bed, and gave you some pleasure, as well as to dear Magnolette. By his little bit of success today, Lazybones is becoming almost a gentleman. Brendel, Kroll, and all our party are delighted. Hans played admirably, and his symphonic prologue for Byron's *Cain* is the work of a master. Mitzi's success was not below what I expected —on the contrary. After the Schubert *Lieder* she was recalled twice, and once after *Mignon*. She will sing the *Loreley* at the Strauss concert, next Wednesday, in which Bülow will also play several pieces. I beg you to pass on Mitzi's splendid and complete success to her father and family, through Pohl or some other intermediary.

At the Pce Regent's concert the Duke of Ratibor came up to me very affably. I shall pay him a visit tomorrow, Monday, at 11.00, as well as to Hugo Hohenlohe, a cousin of his whose acquaintance I made in Stuttgart, and whom I ran into that same evening. The Pce of Prussia received me with perfect amiability, and the Princess was so very flatteringly gracious as to spend half an hour at Hans's concert, for which I am most grateful. She arrived towards the end of the Faust Overture, heard the Schubert *Lieder* and the *Caprice turc*,[5] after which she had to leave. Early that afternoon, at 1 o'clock, she had talked to me for a quarter of an hour about Weimar, giving me, as she put it, a 3-point sermon on this topic. Much of it concerned Weimar as a place of refuge, and I was strongly given to understand that I could only find myself much worse off anywhere else. I shall give you further details of the sinuosities of this conversation.

---

[4] One wonders if this was an old man's memory playing him tricks—for the aged Voltaire had died when Alexander von Humboldt was only 9.

[5] The Fantasia on themes from Beethoven's *Ruins of Athens*, for piano and orchestra, with Bülow as soloist.

415. To Agnes Street-Klindworth in Brussels. [Weimar] 18 April. This is to ask you a favour: that of giving me your news and of telling me how you are keeping in health, mood, and humour.

Until the 29th of this month I shall remain here, the Grand Duchess[6] having asked me to attend to a programme for the celebration of the birthday of her nephew, the Tsar of Russia (29 April). The next day I shall leave for Löwenberg (in Silesia), to pay a very cordial visit to Prince Hohenzollern, and from there I shall return to Leipzig, where there will be some musical tasks to see to in early June (music festival, concert, and performance of my Mass, etc.).

The Princess and her daughter left for Munich the day before yesterday. Kaulbach is painting a portrait of Princess Marie, which is an exceptional mark of friendship, for my illustrious friend has still less to do with portraits than I with piano-playing (which is hardly anything at all), and has refused several *august* commissions in this genre.

What are your plans for the summer? Either in September or December, Wagner's new work, *Tristan und Isolde*, will be performed at Karlsruhe, and it is likely that he will obtain permission to enter, and temporarily to stay in, the Duchy of Baden, to conduct the first performances. I shall go there without fail at that time, and expect even to go and see Wagner beforehand in Lucerne (whither he has returned—the government of Saxony having, from what people say, protested about his sojourn in Venice).

I shan't mention several other rumours of the 'what is being said' and 'what is being printed' kind, for I take it that you have given no more credence to the newspaper reports according to which I am going to Paris (where I have nothing to do), than to the one maintaining that I have fallen out with the town and court of Weimar.

Nothing has changed in my position, which in its outer aspects is getting rather better than worse; and so I like to consider my trip to Paris, by order of the newspapers, as a progress—for in times past I was just as unceremoniously made to travel to America.

Do believe that I remain unvaryingly just as I am, just as you know me by heart.   F.L.

416. To Princess Carolyne in Munich. Wednesday morning, 20 April. Your sweet letter from Nuremberg has just reached me, and I assume you didn't miss the one I sent you there. I took it that you would stay there on Monday and not get to Munich until yesterday.

---

[6] The reference is evidently to the Dowager Grand Duchess, Maria Pavlovna, aunt of the reigning Tsar Alexander II, for the Grand Duchess Sophie was his cousin.

On Monday evening Herr Dingelstedt quoted to us the inscription placed on the sign-board of the Globe Theatre in Shakespeare's time. It was in bad Latin and meant 'The whole world plays the comedy'. In early years the theatres were set up in the inns, and nowadays the profession of intendant does not differ greatly from that of the innkeepers, in my opinion at least. Dingelstedt gave us rather a detailed picture of the exterior arrangements of the theatre under Shakespeare. Just as in France under Molière, there were two companies or troupes of rival players, those of Blackfriars and the Globe—the former taking their name from a priory. Fashionable society sat on the stage around the actors, roughly as the *beau monde* sat near the violin and double-bass stands, and even the timpani, at my concerts in Vienna. The ladies were masked. The show began at 3.00 in the afternoon. Tragedy, the performance of which did not exceed $2\frac{1}{2}$ hours in length, was always followed by a farce. The parts of Juliet, Ophelia, and Cordelia were played by young boys. A blackboard showed the name of the place where the scene was set—and the loss of such a method is certainly deplored by more than one patron of the arts and sciences. There was no scenery, but a scenic arrangement favourable to episodes, such as the play in *Hamlet*, the battle in *Macbeth* and the balcony scene in *Romeo*. And there was quite a large band, which, however, did not participate to the point of meaning something by and for itself, being limited, fortunately, to announcing the entrance of princes and kings through fanfares of trumpets, of lovers through flutes and hautboys, and so on.

All of this was perfectly expressed and delivered, and formed a genre picture which was altogether pleasing. Later, when it was a matter of dealing with the nature of Shakespeare's genius, Dingelstedt came out with nothing but platitudes, made extremely complicated by his alleged claim to be saying something almost new; but not so new that it could not be felt and applauded right from the start. Lessing, naturally, was made use of. *Der muss immer herhalten, um auf das deutsche National-Gefühl zu pochen* [*He* is always the one to suffer, to give German patriotism something to boast of]![7] The *coda* ended elegiacally with a lamentation about the lack of ground for development of the German theatre. The theatre, he said, is and remains essentially demagogic—not, however, in the sense in which the police understand this word. When it is directed by the Courts, it becomes trifling and conventional, as in France under Louis XIV; when by the clergy, it petrifies, as with Calderón in Spain. Shakespeare and England have given us an example of what its vitality and greatness can be when it takes

---

[7] In the famous 17th letter of the *Literaturbriefe*, and later in his *Hamburgische Dramaturgie* (1767–8), Lessing had extolled Shakespeare (not, at that time, highly regarded in Germany), arguing that his plays came closer to the essence of Greek classical tragedy, and were therefore worthier models for German dramatists, than the French classics with their restrictive and devitalizing adherence to the unities.

root in the soil of a free people. 'The rest is silence'—*Hamlet*, last scene. Then he got up and added a few remarks on the *Schillerfeste*[8] having been cancelled—in the circumlocutory manner of the Weimar correspondence in the Augsburg *Gazette*, 16 April, No. 106. It is there stated that HRH the Grand Duke has had to subordinate his love of art to his love for the fatherland.[9] . . . Not to contradict himself, Dingelstedt talked about the *Pfingstwein* [Pentecostal wine] of the poets, which in the Weimar Theatre he was hoping to have sprinkled from beneath the traps and through all the wings. He was probably confusing the descent of the Holy Ghost at Pentecost with the Last Supper! Marshall was delighted with all this eloquence, which was applauded by the Grand Duke and Duchess, the Archduke Stephen, and a large audience.

Wholly at your feet,   F.L.

417. To Princess Carolyne. Leipzig, 8.00 a.m., Good Friday [22 April]

Infinitely dear one,

I did not write to you yesterday, while doing nothing but think of you and even preparing for you a little surprise—which I shall tell you about at once. Between 9.00 and 1.00 the *Beatitudes* were composed almost in their entirety—nothing remains but to find an ending, which won't be difficult. The piece is of a total simplicity—poor in spirit and humble of heart. The baritone solo intones each of the first 3 verses, which the chorus repeats, but once only. To avoid monotony and gain movement—in the 4th, 5th, 6th, and 7th verses, 'they which do hunger and thirst after righteousness, the merciful, the pure in heart and the peacemakers'—the baritone solo sings only half the verse: 'Blessed are they which do hunger and thirst after righteousness!' 'Blessed are the merciful' etc., and the chorus finishes them: 'for they shall be filled', 'for they shall obtain mercy'. Finally, in the 8th verse, 'Blessed are they which are persecuted', I first of all repeat between the chorus and solo voice the words 'Beati, beati', and several times the whole of the verse which ends 'regnum coelorum'. The whole contains about 80 bars, without accompaniment. I shall perhaps add to it around the middle a few chords on the organ, to support the voices. The whole thing will last only 5 to 8 minutes. On Monday morning it will be finished, and perhaps I shall have it engraved for you. . . .

---

[8] The festivals planned in celebration of the Schiller centenary.
[9] The Austro-Italian War, which was about to break out, was arousing strong feelings in Germany too.

418. To Princess Carolyne. Löwenberg, 6.00 a.m., 2 May. An arrears of correspondence . . . that I should like to put in order, will shorten my letters from Löwenberg, which I reached with Brendel and Bronsart at 6.00 yesterday morning. The Prince is, as ever, most charmingly kind and affectionate to me. Unfortunately, he is compelled to spend two-thirds of the day in bed, in the company of a ferocious gout which has been tormenting him for 4 months, in all sorts of ways and quite unceremoniously. He does not dine at table, and, by having himself carried into his box, has attended only 3 concerts out of about 20 which have taken place here this winter. For the rest, he is exceedingly good-humoured in conversation, and takes the keenest interest in the progress of *Zukunftsmusik*, which in these parts, thanks to his strongly avowed liking for it, is going well. Although the series of concerts given by the Prince's orchestra is over, and a third of the musicians scattered far and wide—I can very well manage to spend my time without violins or flutes, reserving the right to lay them under contribution another time. For the moment, we are restricted to small-scale music: Bronsart's Trio, his *Frühlingsfantasie*, *Die Ideale* on 2 pianos, etc., all of it with no audience other than the Prince in his dressing-gown, listening in the room adjoining the salon, plus his sister-in-law and his wife, and the 8 or 10 people who form part of the Prince's household. . . . Monseigneur told me yesterday, in a very sprightly way, of the visit that Louis Napoléon, his cousin through his first wife, Pcss von Leuchtenberg, made to Hechingen, up until two days before the assassination attempt in Strasbourg. Later, Pce Hohenzollern met Louis Napoléon again at Arenenberg, where the latter took pleasure in singing the duet from [Rossini's] *Semiramide*: 'Va, va, superbo, al trionfo, alla gloria!' When some serious topic was being discussed, Louis Napoléon generally remained silent, or else responded with 'I'll think about it'—and then returned to the same topic the next day, armed with his arguments from top to toe. His outstanding genius in action is thus in perfect balance with his guarded impassivity in words. Among other anecdotes, I note in addition this one about Spontini, who said one day to Pce Hohenzollern: 'I do not know *forte* and *piano*—I need *fortissimo* or *pianissimo*.' That can be applied perfectly to music as to other things, and corresponds with my maxim: Either well or not at all!—which you practise at its best. My soul sends you, *il più fortissimo* possible, all its *tendresses*.

F.L.

419. To Princess Carolyne. [Breslau] 8.00 a.m., Tuesday, 10 May. Damrosch's concert is one more stage along the road I have to travel, and all in all there is every reason to be satisfied with the result, so far as the audience's opinion and the impression made on it is concerned. Bronsart will give you more detailed news, and I shall send you the newspapers, which will probably be two-thirds favourable. I regret only that various circumstances had a detrimental effect on the takings, for I should have been glad to leave Damrosch well in pocket. First of all the bad weather—the hall which had been chosen being a good half-hour from the centre of town, the rain prevented many people from coming. Then a performance by Mme Bulyovszky, who is creating a *furore* just now. The theatre management obliged her to appear yesterday evening, despite her wish to postpone the performance until today—proof of which she provided for me by two letters from the manager. Lastly the financial crisis and the unsettled general situation, not counting the unsettled musical one—Damrosch having succeeded in occupying the ground, but not yet in establishing himself firmly thereon. For all these reasons, of which the bad weather was the main one, the hall was barely half-full, but that's already quite something; for, as I told you, it is immensely large and holds more than 3,000 people. Frau von Bülow would have noticed in it the predominance of the *dritte Gesellschaft* [third estate]. Taking into account the rain, the war, the bankruptcies, and the difficulties of our position, I am perfectly content with the rest. The performance was extremely commendable, and the audience gave the best reception to my 2 works. For a wonder, the *Künstlerchor* was warmly applauded. From what I have been told by Hesse, Gottwald, Brosig, Kapellmeister at the Cathedral, Seifriz, and Damrosch, it created a sensation. The principal tenor part was sung by the synagogue cantor, with a manly vigour which delighted me. As for *Tasso*, it was already accepted here as in Prague, for the *thematische Bearbeitung* which the connoisseurs concur in recognizing in it. Damrosch conducted the Ninth Symphony very well at the end of the concert, after playing the Beethoven [Violin] Concerto in masterly fashion.

At Damrosch's this evening we shall have the pendant to the Bülow soirée in Berlin. About twenty right-thinking people have been invited, and I shall probably play Bronsart's Trio and some solo piece or other. For tomorrow evening a big public dinner is being prepared for me, and on Thursday morning I shall be returning to our blue room, which I long to see again. Perhaps I shall find in it the photograph of Magne's portrait, at which I rejoice in advance. . . .

                                                                    F.L.

420. To Princess Carolyne [The Altenburg, Weimar, 13 May]. Your blessing welcomed me on the threshold of this house which your love and devotion have transformed into a heaven on earth for my heart. Every one of its stones and atoms speaks to me of you. . . .

Rehearsals of the Mass are going well. St Thomas's Church [Leipzig] has been granted us after some rather lively discussions, and everything seems to be in fairly good order. Brendel handed me your letter dated Monday the 9th, which has given me great joy. At Breslau I had received that dated the 7th, and so I lack but one, which will be sent back here to me. The one which Augusta, *Prinzess-Regentin*,[10] gave me on the staircase, on my return to the Altenburg, bore the postmark 10 May, and the one received this morning, the 11th. . . . Our grand and beautiful life as a threesome, who are but one in God, will recommence only after 4 June. We shall see what we have to do during the rest of the summer to enable Lazybones to keep his promise to Magnette and you, to finish the *Elisabeth*. To this end, it is all but indispensable for me to have four months of peace, from 1 July to 22 October, with my mornings devoted to work and my evenings made happy by your presence. Incidentally, don't spoil your stay in Munich with 'blue' anxieties concerning me.[11] That will come in its time. New appointments are made only on the King's birthday in November, and I do not know if there will shortly be a vacancy for a musician. There will perhaps be a chance for me after the death of Spohr—but may God yet long preserve this venerable Nestor of the chromatic scale!

Have you read the *Allgemeine Zeitung's* obituary of Humboldt?[12] The words with which it finishes are rather well found: *Ehrenbürger der ganzen Erde* [Honorary Citizen of the whole Earth]. It could even have gone so far as to say *Ehrenbürger des ganzen Weltalls* [Honorary Citizen of the entire Universe]—the stars and comets would not protest! During your stay in Berlin you wrote me a charming remark about Humboldt's kindness, which you compared to the refreshing shade of a beautiful palm-tree: it neither gives nourishment nor quenches thirst, but inspires an inward-looking mood which allays life's memories and fears, and mysteriously fills us with the feeling that the best of life is to await what will be taken care of by God! The whole of last night the birds in the garden sang me a lovely serenade, which I send to you, to you and Magnette, with all the love in my soul.

F.L.

421. To Agnes Street-Klindworth. Weimar, 20 August.

An event of major importance in our Altenburg life as a threesome is about to occur. It is still a half-secret which I tell you in confidence. Pcss Marie is to be married to Pce Constantin Hohenlohe-Schillingsfürst (younger brother of the Duke of

---

[10] A jocular reference to Augusta Pickel, Carolyne's lady's maid at the Altenburg, on the analogy of Princess Augusta of Prussia (the later German Empress), consort of the Prince Regent (the subsequent Emperor Wilhelm I).

[11] Carolyne was hoping that Liszt would be admitted to the Order of Maximilian—a decoration eventually bestowed upon him in 1866 by King Maximilian's son, Ludwig II.

[12] Who had died on 6 May, a few months short of his ninetieth birthday.

Ratibor), a major and aide-de-camp to the Emperor of Austria. He is a man of nearly thirty, of perfectly gentlemanly sentiments, and very well born in all respects. He went through his first campaign in Italy in '48, and this last time performed his duties very well beside the Emperor at Magenta and Solferino. His devotion to Pcss Marie is wholly sincere, and I am convinced that in this union she will find every desirable chance and guarantee of happiness. The wedding will take place here, shortly after the indispensable assent of the two Emperors[13] has been obtained, probably at the beginning of October. Until then I shall not be able to leave Weimar, and to my great regret I have had to call off the visit I had planned to make to Lucerne at the end of this month to see Wagner. He will probably already be on his way to Paris, where he expects to stay for some time. It is the simplest and least costly thing he can do in the circumstances now obtaining, and I had already urged him to do it last year when he was going to Venice. He has just finished his *Tristan und Isolde* (3 acts), and there is a strong possibility of the première being at Karlsruhe in December. I shall be there without doubt, but if this performance were delayed I would try to join Wagner in Paris for a few days, and in that case I would travel via Brussels.

Berlioz and Mme Viardot* have just sent me a very friendly invitation to attend the Baden Festival, on the 29th of this month, at which Mme Viardot will sing the grand Duo from Berlioz's new opera *Les Troyens*.[14] (This work is likewise now completely finished, but has little chance of an early performance in Paris because of Berlioz's singular position *vis-à-vis*, or rather *opposite*, as they say in English [!], the grand Opéra.) I am told wonders of this duet, which I should very much like to hear, but that will not be enough to make me budge.

In the mean time my life goes by in working, dreaming, and praying. I have just finished two Psalms, 'The Lord is my Shepherd' (Herder's German translation) and the well-known 'By the waters of Babylon'. I have also tolerably well enlarged and better proportioned Psalm 13, 'How long wilt thou forget me, O Lord?', which I shall publish this winter, at the same time as *The Legend of St Elisabeth*, which I shall have finished by Christmas.

I shall shortly be sending to Brussels for you my volume on the *Bohémiens* which has just come out in Paris, plus the arrangement for 4 hands of three of my symphonic poems. You will easily find a partner to play them with. . . .

F.L.

---

[13] Franz Joseph of Austria and Alexander II of Russia.

[14] The opera which Berlioz dedicated, appropriately, to the Princess Wittgenstein, who, during a visit of his to Weimar, had spurred him on with the words: 'If you shrink from the difficulties this work may and must bring you, if you are so feeble as to be afraid to face everything for Dido and Cassandra, then never come back here—I refuse to see you again.'

422. To Kálmán von Simonffy. Weimar, 27 August

Sir,

I would have found your letter rather surprising, had I not known from experience how, when some sensitive spot has been touched, the best intentioned men easily allow themselves to be deceived by the most evident untruths.

You tell me that you have not read my book on the Gypsies (which, for that matter, has not yet been published), but, giving credence to a malicious rumour—disseminated by some newspapers—which has no basis in fact, you tell me that you will treat me 'with all the severity I deserve', and that you will do so because people say (without having read me) that I have done injury to Hungarian music and consequently to my patriotism.[15]

Set your mind at rest, Sir, such is not the case, and indeed it is to me in this whole matter that people are doing injury. So far as patriotism is concerned, there is no one who could reasonably pride himself on remonstrating with me, and when you read my book you will realize without difficulty that it has been inspired by the feelings of fervent devotion I have for my country.

It was the pleasure I felt in hearing several of your charming Hungarian compositions that induced me to reply to your letter, but I do not for this reason consider myself obliged to follow the same procedure with all persons who might take it into their heads to talk to me of the so-called 'storm' raised by my book. I beg you, Sir, not to see these lines as any kind of *captatio benevolentiae*—for I in no way desire to escape being judged with all the severity I deserve, convinced as I am that in this matter, as in others, I shall have only to gain therefrom, provided that those who set themselves up as my judges (or, if you prefer it in German, 'die sich zu meinen Richtern aufwerfen') are capable of justifying themselves in all conscience.

I am, Sir, yours very truly,

F. Liszt

423. To Princess Carolyne in Paris.[16] [Weimar] 20 October. Your very dear letter from Frankfurt arrived this morning, and I had already learnt through Gieseke of your meeting with Magnet in Gotha. . . .

Hans has sent me Wagner's letter,[17] and its sense corresponds well enough with what you foresaw. Although he does not explain himself clearly, and even

---

[15] Liszt's book on the Hungarian gypsies and their music aroused displeasure in his native land, owing to his belief that Hungary possessed no music but that of the gypsies—which was not the case, for much of what he had heard played by the gypsies, albeit in their own manner, was genuine Magyar folk music, which was not to be studied scientifically until the advent, several decades later, of Béla Bartók and Zoltán Kodály. As well as their own music, the gypsies also performed pieces—of the salon type—composed by Hungarians of the middle classes.

[16] After her daughter's wedding, Carolyne was spending a fortnight in Paris.   [17] A letter to Bülow of 7 Oct.

retains a certain delicacy of language which he has not used in other circumstances, it is apparent from this letter that he wishes to put asunder those whom God hath joined: that is, you and me. He complains about my reserve, about the unbound copy of my Dante [Symphony] that I sent him (6 weeks after publication!), about the unreceived copies of my Mass and the *Bohémiens*, and about Pohl's few lines on the subject of the introduction [*Prelude*] to *Tristan*, in which it is said that the harmonic texture of this piece is indebted to a study of my symphonic poems, etc. etc.[18] In sum, he seems to wish to insinuate to Hans that you exert a regrettable influence over me, one which goes against my real character. If Wagner hasn't the merit of having invented this foolish idea, I for my part am far from sharing its absurdity. Every time people have tried to lampoon me in such a manner, I have put a quick end to it—regarding such a falsehood as a triple injury done to me. Wagner is now living at 16, rue Newton, avenue des Champs Elysées. Perhaps you will see him. I almost urge you to. But treat him very gently—for he is sick, and incurable. That is why we must simply love him and try to serve him as best we can.

Yours in eternity,   F.L.

424. To Princess Carolyne. [Weimar] Monday morning, 24 October.

Endless love and affection, my unique one. . . . Your sweet letter of the 21st reached me yesterday evening, and I envy you for having heard the duet from *Les Troyens*, while thinking it charming of Berlioz to give you this lovely surprise. Poor great friend, he is making a sad departure from this world of woe, 'bleeding from every pore', as you tell me! If one could at least alleviate his troubles a little—but it is difficult to imagine how. Tell me again how deeply devoted to him I have remained, and how happy I should be if I could be of use to him in anything.

Wagner wrote me a nice letter for the 22nd—and our friendship will continue without too much stumbling, if *he* continues in this way. Perhaps you will bring me back some news of him? Have you received 4 letters from me, addressed to the Hôtel des Princes? Magnette's letter was in one, and in the last but one, if I am not mistaken, was the draft of my letter to Hans about Wagner.

I am not expecting you until about the end of the week, and strongly urge you to see M. de Lamartine this time, even if it were to cost you 1 or 2 extra days. He won't be here much longer—and is certainly one of the finest and noblest natures God has created. So do see him! . . .

---

[18] Wagner had written, *inter alia*: 'There are many matters which we are quite frank about among ourselves (for instance, that since my acquaintance with Liszt's works my treatment of harmony has become very different from what it was formerly), but it is indiscreet, to say the least, of friend Pohl to babble this secret to the whole world.'

Cosette is still with me and does not go back to Berlin until tomorrow. I kiss your dear hands, and breathe only in your soul.   F.L.

425. To Princess Carolyne. [Weimar] 27 October. God be praised, after I have spent 2 long days of waiting 2 good letters of yours have just arrived at the same time. . . .

I thank you, dearest one, for your kindness to my old friend Ferdinand Denis. He deserves it because of the most excellent feelings he has cherished towards me for nearly 30 years. I hope you will see Lamartine, and also Villemain and Sainte-Beuve. If Mme Sand is in Paris, it seems to me that you should go and see her. The *Les Troyens* soirée at Pauline [Viardot-Garcia]'s is in very good taste, and I take delight in advance at the splendid account of it that you will give me. Perhaps it will give you an appetite for *Tristan*? But it is understood that you will do solely as you deem fit, and in this matter I can advise you neither for nor against. Wagner is living at 16, rue Newton, as I have already written to you. I don't think you can leave Paris before next Tuesday, and so try to fill your time as best you can. Incidentally, are you not thinking of seeing Eugène Delacroix again? I feel that he has a right to special attention.

My *Festlied* being finished, I am going to get down to my correspondence, which has been considerably encumbered by 22 October. My Mass for male voices, the Napoleon III one, was successfully performed in St Augustine's Church [Vienna]—where the Canova statue is erected—on 23 October, anniversary of the founding of the *Männergesangverein* [Male Choral Society], of which Herbeck is conductor. Cornelius and Herbeck have given me most satisfying news about both the performance of this work and its reception. In March, the *Prometheus choruses* will probably be done, and, to give Herbeck a small pleasure, I am going to orchestrate for him a couple of Marches by Schubert which he very much desires. You know that I am always led into temptation by these little accessory tasks, which, moreover, are not too pointless for me at present. The Polish melodies[19] will soon be out, and Schlesinger has just written me an appropriate letter in which he finally agrees to publish my *Lieder*; i.e. to undertake the publishing expenses, etc. As the piano score of Gounod's *Faust* has now come out, you will do me a kindness by bringing me a copy—but don't ask Gounod for it, simply buy it.

Nothing has arrived for you these last few days, nor has anything worth mentioning happened either in the house, which I hardly leave, or in town. I saw

---

[19] The *6 Chants polonais*, Liszt's transcriptions (S480) for piano solo of songs by Chopin, published in 1860 with a dedication to Princess Marie Hohenlohe.

Dingelstedt again at my supper of the 22nd, and also at the Altenburg. Our relations have got back on to a good footing.

So I expect you on Thursday, a week today, and in the mean time I praise you, bless you, and glorify you at every hour of the day, with all my soul, which is wholly in you.

426. To the Grand Duke Carl Alexander. Weimar, 4 December

Monseigneur. . . .

The time has perhaps arrived for me to narrow more and more the range of subjects on which, in obedience to your wishes, I have taken the liberty of speaking to you up to now with the conscientious candour that expresses what I feel and also springs from my sincere devotion to your self. However distressing my last years in Weimar have been, the tokens of affection and esteem that you have so kindly granted me have always cemented my dedication to your service —but this very dedication now compels me not to enter Your Royal Highness's confidence even further, not knowing if I have long left to enjoy it. The news I am receiving from Petersburg in the matter of the Princess Wittgenstein's divorce makes it very clear that covert ill will continues to have the upper hand. For this reason, I cannot go on in Weimar any longer. While it was a question of a daughter during her minority being threatened by circumstances beyond one's control, the unbearable had to be borne; but at the present moment I foresee that despite the sorrow it would cause me to leave you, Monseigneur, I shall soon have to seek far from Weimar a way of life which will be less burdensome to me than here—less systematically thwarted on the outside and repressed within. My unshakeable determination to withdraw during my years of maturity from all *personal* contact with the public, of which nearly forty years have given me a surfeit, obliges me to give thought to new considerations, in view of the career that still lies ahead of me. Whatever the circumstances I remain, Monseigneur, invariably

Your very humble and devoted servant   F. Liszt

P.S. As regards the oratorio *Judas Iscariot*, the score being as unknown to me as the sentiments of this individual I am unable to recommend it to you.

In early December, while the guest in Berlin of his sister and brother-in-law, the 20-year-old Daniel Liszt fell gravely ill. His father arrived in the city during the evening of 11 December.

427. To Princess Carolyne. [Berlin] Thursday, 15 December.[20] This, most infinitely dear one, is how these 4 days have been spent. Just as we agreed, I did not stop at the Anhaltstrasse when I got here at 10 o'clock on Sunday evening. When I went there the next day at 8.30, the only person up was the housemaid, who told me that Cosima had been sitting up with Daniel until 6.00 in the morning. A few minutes later he arrived in the dining-room, pushed along on his couch; he seemed very happy to see me again. My first impression was that he was near to death, his weakness extreme; but he was hardly aware of it. Neither Hans nor Cosima who came into the same room shortly afterwards, where the coffee was already prepared, had the least inkling of what was to occur so soon! We breakfasted quietly, Daniel remaining as usual and gently complaining that for several days he had quite lost his appetite. He was given some milk. His breathing was extremely laboured, and his words painfully broken, although there was no sign of his reason being affected; and indeed his intelligence remained unclouded to the very last moment, save that he already lacked the strength to exercise it. Although he appeared to take a certain interest in the conversation which developed quite animatedly between Hans, Cosette, and me, I felt that he was not in a condition to follow it, and urged him to be patient. He spoke to me about resuming his legal studies soon, and Cosima told me that the previous day he had wanted to read a book of his, Puchta on jurisprudence. Hearing this helped him concentrate his mind a little, and he explained to us slowly but precisely the 5 categories of obligation according to the law.

At 10.00, Bücking[21] arrived. Cosima told him that the night had been a very bad one and that Daniel had not managed to get to sleep until past 5.00 in the morning. To sustain and revive him a little, he was prescribed a few sips of Tokay. After the medical consultation I took Bücking aside and told him that I was prepared for the worst. Despite his caution and his wish not to fear too much, he was unable to reassure me. He dwelt only on the fact that the illness was not in the nature of an ordinary pulmonary or consumptive malady, that there was absolutely nothing contagious about it, that in fact no organ was seriously threatened, and that if he should succumb it would simply be from depletion of his vitality. 'Should it come to the worst, he will simply pass away, very quietly, without a struggle and probably without pain.' This prediction came to pass with well-nigh unbelievable accuracy, as you will see later. But Bücking at once added that his condition had not reached the point at which a possibility of a change for the better could be ruled out—still less the moment pin-pointed when he would make, in the words of the French peasants, 'une fin de vie', with no malady other than that of no longer being able to live!

---

[20] The letter was begun on the 15th and finished on the 16th.   [21] A Berlin doctor.

So as not to tire Daniel, who was dozing off, Hans and I went into the drawing-room to talk music a little and to look over the proofs of a Bach concerto. This incident, which I mentioned in the lines I wrote to you the same day, you seem to have taken amiss, dearest one. It is probable that on this occasion, as usual, you are entirely right in thinking that I should have put those moments to use in preparing Daniel for the mystery of death, and in inducing him to desire to receive the sacraments of the Church. But please bear in mind that he was no longer in a condition to gather his thoughts, and that after listening a few days earlier to the suggestion made to him several times by his sister about taking communion together at Christmas, he had decided that it was better to wait until Easter. Where feelings of this kind are concerned, it would have been dangerous to force it on a nature as sensitive as Daniel's. A half-consent would have been deeply distressing to me, and arousing the emotion which any intimation of mine might have created would have been so extremely risky—that I lacked the courage for it. Bücking, in whom I felt full confidence, did not anticipate that the end was so near, and was of opinion that his condition would fluctuate somewhat before the end; and I knew no priest in Berlin on whom my thought could fasten with some reliance in this matter. Even so, on receiving your latest letters I felt that I had been wrong. Some way of inducing Daniel to receive the sacraments might still have been found had my faith been more active.

The rest of Monday was spent around his couch, which after breakfast we pushed into the dark drawing-room. Two letters arrived for him, one being from Mlle Szerafina of Pozsony.[22] Cosima read it to him, and I tried to engage him a little in conversation about this young person in whom I assumed he was taking some interest. But he was no longer aware of things external to himself, and his strength was so reduced that it scarcely sufficed to keep him alive. We gave him a few more drops of Tokay, and at 2.00, while we were lunching, he took a cup of broth. His sister's nursing had become indispensable to him. When she moved the least distance away from his couch he asked for her again. He dozed off repeatedly, but whether he was awake or asleep the only outward sign of suffering was his laboured breathing. To stay alive was not within his power! Towards evening Fräulein Franz and Dohm arrived; and at 9 o'clock we took Daniel into his little room, which he would leave no more—other than to go to the last resting-place of his mortal remains!

About 11.00 in the evening I returned to the hotel with Cosette. She at once went back to her brother, read some psalms from the prayer book you gave her, and after a few hours managed to get him to sleep. The next morning, Tuesday,

---

[22] Szerafina Vrábely, who in 1864 married Carl Tausig.

at 9.00, Hans came in tears to tell me that there was no more hope, and I went to Daniel. His face was not drawn, just extremely pale. Up to the very moment in which the coffin was closed his features retained their expression of gentle composure. His beard and hair had a slight reddish tinge, causing Cosima to remark that he resembled a Christ by Correggio. In one of his drowsy states he pronounced, quite clearly, these words: 'Je vais préparer vos places!!' Bücking, however, thought that he would still survive the night. Cosima and I knelt by the bed and asked God that His holy will be done—and, especially, that He might associate us with that Holy will by granting us the grace steadfastly to do it.

This dear and noble child and I opened our hearts to one another—and I shall tell you orally of the beautiful thought which came to her, and that she will carry out. Daniel reminisced to me once more about his legal studies, which he was expecting to resume in the spring! Hans, Cosette, and I stayed by his bed in turn—but His name was pronounced only between my daughter and me. Daniel was nearer to Him and to the Kingdom of Heaven which the Lord has promised to those who have become as little children! At 10.00 in the evening I lay down on the bed which had been put in the room with the piano. Without anyone having alerted me, at 11.15 I got up and went into Daniel's room. Cosette was kneeling. There was only silence—silence and mystery. A few minutes went by, grains of sand on the shore of eternity. 'I can't hear his breathing any more,' I said. She placed her hand on his heart—it was no longer beating. A moment before we had heard the merest sigh. He had gone to his rest in the Lord. 'Let us die thus unto ourselves, to live in God from this moment onwards. Let us cast from us our foolish passions, our vain attachments, all our futile triflings, so as to aspire only to Heaven. God will not reject us if we go towards Him single-mindedly!' That is more or less what I said to my daughter, as well as many other things of a like nature that I no longer recall. '*He* is happy', she replied, 'and we are happier than he, since our merit can be the greater!' Then we prayed with all our souls. May God grant our prayers! Amen.

I felt that it was better not to inform Hans, who was rather badly affected by it all, until the next day. I urged Cosette to lie down on the sofa in the piano room, and I slept for a few hours on the bed. The next day, Wednesday, Hans and I undertook the necessary visits to the church, the police, Bücking, etc. While we were out, Cosima washed Daniel's body herself. No one helped her, even her maidservants being overcome by horror of death. The sacristan, who showed me every kindness, sent a fine garment for Daniel's body. My daughter dressed him in it—and placed a portrait of Pascal at his feet. They had recently spoken constantly together about Pascal. This portrait remained in the coffin, which we had to put in the dark drawing-room since it was too large to go in the little room in which he died. With that piety which comes from the heart, and which counts for more than any regard for the conventions, she made a kind of *chapelle ardente* and grouped around the body her paintings and other pictures on religious subjects: a madonna, a St Cecilia, a second madonna, the beatitudes ornamented by Schulze that Magnette gave her some time ago, and Rubens's *Christ with the Four Sinners* that you gave her as a present. They are the four great penitents: Mary Magdalene, the good thief, St Peter, and David. On a table she then put a crucifix and candles. Your prayer book was there too; and it is the only one we used, she and I.

At 9 o'clock I took Hans and Cosima to the Brandenburg Hotel, to take tea. I had urged Cosima to spend the night there, but she insisted on going back to Daniel, and so I yielded. She went at 10.30. I wanted to accompany her, but Otto had just arrived with your letters and, all things considered, I decided not to watch over Daniel—and strongly urged Cosima not to wear herself out.

We didn't send for a priest; but you won't disapprove of me for that. The *Propst* [provost] who blessed the union of Hans and Cosima has become a *Feldpropst*, almost an army bishop. His successor asked me if I wanted a priest to accompany the coffin to the cemetery, telling me that it was not customary in Berlin and that a specific request for it would have to be made. This, of course, I did make. As for the mass, I preferred it not to be sung, the music practised in most Catholic churches leaving much to be desired. The sacristan undertook all the arrangements, which were made for the best and as speedily as possible.

We at first thought that the funeral would have to wait until Friday or Saturday; but Bücking having made a statement to the effect that the deceased's illness was quite uncontagious, we obtained a dispensation from the police; so the *Beerdigungs-Comptoir* [undertaker's] was able to go into action yesterday morning, Thursday, at 11.00. That is what it is called in Berlin, the Church not having the benefit of what in France they call the 'Factory'! The *Propst's* successor, not yet designated *Propst* but only curate, observed to me that it was not the custom to take the body to church as in France and, I believe, most Catholic countries. He himself said mass, at 10 o'clock. Only Hans, Cosima, and I were present—the regular masses finishing here at 9.00. Frau von Bülow and Isa[23] would willingly have come, but Cosima and I had a kind of tacit agreement to allow no one to share our grief. At 11.00 the chaplain arrived at the mortuary. He recited the service for the dead, and at 11.30 the procession set off, the hearse in front, 12 men accompanying it, and 3 carriages following. In the first were the chaplain and Hans; in the second, Cosima and I. The third, the hotel's, was empty. The first two were hired from the *Beerdigungs-Comptoir*; the hotel's I had ordered for the return journey from the cemetery with Hans and Cosette.

---

[23] Bülow's sister Isidora, later Frau von Bojanowsky.

The Catholic cemetery is outside the Oranienburg gate, a long way from the Anhaltstrasse. We went through the Oranienburgerstrasse, where Humboldt lived. A magnificent sun shone down on us, and we felt a little of its warmth even at the cemetery.

At the graveside the coffin was lifted up, three sacristans in white surplices shook their censers, while for several minutes a flock of pigeons circled high up in the air, almost vertically above the grave. The chaplain said some prayers aloud, and the coffin, a beautiful oaken one, was finally lowered into the ground. We threw the last spadefuls of earth on to the mortal remains of him who is, as he said, to prepare our places! May God have mercy upon him—upon him and upon us!

We got back here at about 1.30 and stayed until 11.00, just we three. I wrote the first pages of this letter; Cosette, who has something of your facility for letter-writing, wrote 3 or 4 notes about the arrangements to be made, and also 2 letters, to her mother and to Blandine. I added a few lines to Blandine, and I shall entrust her, in accordance with your good advice, with delivery of the letter I shall write to my mother. Tonight my children are staying at the hotel again; I have promised them that tomorrow I shall take them back to their home. We shall probably spend the evening in the same dark drawing-room, with Frau von Bülow and Isa whom I have asked Cosima to invite.

I shall let you know tomorrow by what train I shall be returning on Sunday. In her letter to her mother Cosima said: 'He settled into the arms of death as into those of a guardian angel—one he had long been expecting. He made no struggle: with no aversion to life he was ardently aspiring to eternity.'

My thanks and blessings for everything you tell me. Do not over-exert yourself, my dearest one. The Requiems in Vienna and Weimar are a kind thought from your heart. Cosima is also writing to the Abbé Bucquet, to ask him to say a mass for her brother's soul. All the things that cannot be put in writing I shall tell you when I arrive on Sunday. May God fill you with all the treasures of His tenderness!

F.L.

428. To Blandine Ollivier in Paris. Weimar, 26 December. Your letter, dearest Blandine, has moved me deeply, and those noble, heartfelt words have penetrated my very being!

In your love, dear child, God leaves me a great consolation; and before the coffin which has just closed, our tears, prayers, and hopes come together in even greater intimacy!

Be thanked and blessed for your thoughtful and loving attentions to my dear mother. Continue to help her to bear this great sorrow as painlessly as possible!

May the memory of all her maternal kindnesses to Daniel bring her some solace! She loved him so dearly, spoilt him with such touching devotion!

Please also thank Emile for his affectionate kindness to my mother. Through her upright character and the invariable rectitude of her life she is naturally at one with lofty feelings and noble actions—and I am proud to know that such feelings and such actions are habitual to your husband.

Let us earnestly ask God to grant us the grace of leading good lives, while strengthening us in the practice of the truths and virtues which will allow us to participate in everlasting Truth and Beatitude!

1860

17 *May.* Princess Carolyne leaves Weimar for Rome.

Early June. Liszt is present at the Schumann celebrations in Zwickau; and, in Magdeburg on the 9th, at a concert in which Bülow conducts the Goethe March and *Les Préludes.*

3 July. He attends the funeral in Leipzig of his pupil Clara Riese.

August. Already a Chevalier of the Legion of Honour, Liszt is elevated to the rank of Officier.

14 September. Liszt writes his will.

Mid-October. He goes to Vienna to see the Papal Nuncio.

22 October. Liszt's forty-ninth birthday. At Weimar there is a torchlight procession in his honour and he is made a freeman of the town.

24 November. He is present at the christening in Berlin of his granddaughter Daniela von Bülow.

WORKS. Psalm 18 ('Coeli enarrant')[1] (S14), for male chorus and orchestra. Two Episodes from Lenau's *Faust* (S110, *c*.1860), for orchestra: 1. *Der nächtliche Zug* 2. *Der Tanz in der Dorfschenke.* SONGS: *Die drei Zigeuner* (Lenau) (S320); *Die stille Wasserrose* (Geibel) (S321, ?1860); *Wieder möcht'ich dir begegnen* (Cornelius) (S322); *Jugendglück* (Pohl) (S323, *c*.1860). The recitation *Der traurige Mönch* (Lenau) (S348). ARRANGEMENTS FOR PIANO: Spinning Chorus from *Der fliegende Holländer* (Wagner) (S440); *Danse des Sylphes de La Damnation de Faust* (Berlioz) (S475, *c*.1860); *6 Chants polonais* (Chopin) (S480, 1847–60); *Der Tanz in der Dorfschenke,* known as the First Mephisto Waltz (S514, *c*.1860).

429. To Baron Augusz. Weimar, 14 January

My dear and honoured friend,

Among the numerous expressions of sympathy which have come to me from far and near following the death of my son, you cannot doubt that your letter is one of the dearest to me, because of the feelings of loyal friendship which bind us.

I have spoken little to you about my son. He had a dreamy, gentle, deep nature. His soul's yearnings elevated him above the earth, as it were, and he had inher-

---

[1] The Bible known to Liszt was St Jerome's Vulgate; in the AV and the BCP this Psalm is No. 19 ('The heavens declare').

ited from me a powerful propensity towards that region of ideas and aspirations which brings us ever closer to the divine mercy. And so the thought of entering the priesthood had been taking firmer and firmer root in his mind. My sole desire was that before carrying out this holy resolve he should undertake solid and serious studies, in order to fit himself for the task of giving good service to the cause of religion. You know how much he applied himself to responding fully to my expectations of him, and to what he rightly considered an obligation imposed by his name. After he had carried off the *prix d'honneur* at the *concours général* in Paris, he was preparing to sit his law examination in Vienna, and would, I doubt not, have acquitted himself with honour. On the eve of his death he spoke to me about it again and strove to explain to me the chapter from the *Code* dealing with the different kinds of obligations. A little earlier he had taken pleasure in reciting to me by heart a few lines of Hungarian, to prove that he was keeping the promise he had given me to acquire a good knowledge of this language even before the completion of his legal studies!

May the God of goodness and mercy keep his soul in the everlasting peace of our heavenly homeland!

Our earthly homeland, alas, is in a state of much agitation, and what you tell me, confirming the newspaper reports, is hardly of a kind to make one hope for an imminent and favourable solution to the difficulties of the situation. Patriotism is a great and admirable sentiment, to be sure; but when in its exaltation it reaches the point of disregarding necessary limits, and takes for counsel solely the inspirations of hotheads, it too will end by 'sowing the wind to reap the whirlwind'. It is not for me to get involved in judging these events, for I don't feel called to take an active part in them. Nevertheless, I firmly hope not to fail in my task, and shall apply myself ceaselessly to bringing honour to *my country* (as I told HM the Emperor) by my work and by my character as an artist: even if not precisely in the way understood by certain patriots, for whom the Rákóczy March is more or less what the Koran was for Omar and who would gladly burn—as did the latter the Library of Alexandria—the whole of Germanic music with this fine argument: 'Either it can be found in the Rákóczy or it is worthless.' . . . The fuss made about my volume on the gypsies has made me feel much more truly Hungarian than my antagonists, the Magyaromanes, for loyalty is one of the distinctive features of our national character. Now is it loyal, I ask, to steal from those we have *patronized*? Haven't Bihary, Lavotta, Csermák, Boka, and a score of other gypsies left us a mass of compositions signed with their names and which have taken root in the very heart of our memories? And so why not render unto the gypsies the things that are the gypsies', while retaining for the Hungarians their own rights and possessions?—and have I done anything other than this? . . .

The German newspapers continue to busy themselves with my humble self. I am made to go hither and thither—to Munich, to Dresden, to Berlin (as Kapellmeister). No, thank you! There is no more justification for such news than there is for the obloquy—on the part of the critics—of which I have the honour to remain the object. For the whole of this winter I shall stay here to finish my *Elisabeth* (which still requires several months' work), and in the spring I shall turn my mind to what I have to do and to what is to become of me.

The political situation permitting, I shall probably spend a couple of months in Rome during the course of the year, to do some research necessary to enable me to make progress with and complete a large-scale religious composition. . . .

F. Liszt

430. To the Grand Duke Carl Alexander. 6 February

Monseigneur,

You have on several occasions quoted to me a letter I had the honour of writing to you against my desire and at your most express command.[2] Knowing that it would lead to nothing, I summed up therein what *should* have been rather than what thenceforth might be. The persistence with which you remind me of it makes one believe that you attach more importance to what is written than to what is said, although my conduct for twelve years should have proved to you that for me, even in the face of real catastrophes, *saying* and *doing* were one. I write, therefore, Monseigneur, to reiterate to you at greater length and in a more justified manner what I have already had the honour of saying and writing to you succinctly. I shall not begin by repeating that I cannot remain in Weimar unless I am *married*: you would not wish to impose on me the distressing task of detailing the reasons. If you will be so good as to consider my position more from the point of view of a friend than a Sovereign, you will understand those reasons; and if you find them inadequate, it will be sadly impossible for me to make for you the sacrifice you ask of me in wishing to retain me otherwise. The devotion to you of one of your servants has some value only in so far as you esteem him who gives it—and it is up to him to know and determine the conditions which will assure him this esteem (still more precious than your favour) both in the present and in the future.

The purpose of today's letter is to explain why I cannot resume public duties in the theatre, and it is not in the least at variance with the one you quote; for

---

[2] A long letter of 14 Feb. 1859 in which, as bidden by the Grand Duke, Liszt had drawn up 'the conditions on which depend the efficacity of my co-operation in his theatre'.

you, Monseigneur, well know that declarations of love and declarations of diplo-macy, once they have been considered as null, are no longer valid a year later, for time alters loving feelings, affairs, and situations. A year ago, if you had taken me at my word, which I was naturally not expecting in the least, I should have submitted courteously and continued my optional service at the theatre for another season or two. My absence at the podium would have been brief, and my return sufficiently justified by the use I should have made of it, because it would have been bad grace on my part to sulk.

My determination to divorce from the public does not date from yesterday. Chance was to decide if I should leave it on the occasion of a success or of a failure. Chance has decided: my divorce is a fact, an *accomplished fact.*

After the time which has passed, it would be nonsense for me to return where I have no wish to remain. I have been on the go for nearly forty years and con-sider my task in this respect as largely accomplished, by no means caring to wait for the slumber of old age to take hold of me amidst the orchestra, as it did with Spohr, any more than I have thought of playing the piano, like Moscheles, until the extinction of natural warmth. It would show poor understanding on your part, Monseigneur, to insist on my resuming my public duties when the moment has come for me to quit them. In requiring it, you would be performing a kind of bad action, which it behoves me not to allow you to do. Do not imit-ate the Sovereigns who misuse the abilities of their servants by employing them wrongly; which is not in the interest of the artist, and never in the interest of his patron. If I am wanted, let the *spirit* not the *letter* of my talent be employed. What does it matter if it be I who wield the baton at a performance, provided that it be I who breathe life into it, for this is not dependent on the movement of my arm but on the effect of my mind. What was the fine result of this sys-tem of *status quo* for Hummel, certainly an artist of great talent. That of mech-anizing him, blunting him, and withdrawing him from the world of art, in which his influence as Kapellmeister is equivalent to zero. Weimar morally castrated him—and what advantage did Weimar derive from it? I don't envy his fate, and shall not model my career on his, however proud I might be to put my name to works like his, especially those produced before he vegetated here.

What do you need, Monseigneur? A theatre which does not risk being con-fused with the bad *Stadttheater* [city theatres]: a *Hoftheater* [Court theatre]; that is, an institution for art, not an undertaking whose leader declares that for him the money of the 'gods' smells as sweet as that of the dress circle. Consequently, it matters to you that in your town and at your Court there is a movement which corresponds to a comprehensive view, and a leader whose good name is a guarantee for you that he can assume responsibility for what in music is done and what is not done, at your home and in your theatre. This leader, I can be.

The question poses itself thus: does Your Royal Highness value me? Let us assume that the answer is yes. Why does he? Probably because he believes that I have an intellectual value. Any man of intellectual value can only have his own ideas. If it is desired to make use of these advantages, the result can be obtained only by allowing him to act in accordance with his ideas. Generally speaking, that is. In my particular case, you must take me only on these conditions, in the sense that gratitude can always bind me to the person of Your Royal Highness, and keep me available at your side, but could not impose on me the duty of annihilating myself and doing you a disservice thereby. The Weimar theatre has had significance only under Goethe, and Goethe never needed to appear in it in public. If you desire my services in the musical category, exempt me from the *letter* which kills and thus leave free play to the *spirit* I represent, a spirit of initiative and encouragement in the domain of art. In ten years and without any support I have founded *eine Weimar'sche Schule* [a Weimar school]. It has only been possible for me to have certain works performed; that is something, but that has been all. I defy anyone else to do, with so little means, what I have done. If you help me in good faith, if you give your protection to those I recommend to you, if, through your goodwill, you take an interest in the works I call to your attention, I promise you that Weimar will be in reality what it is only in imagination and very temporarily: the seat of the *neudeutsche Schule* [New-German school]. My sojourn alone—and it alone—in Weimar has identified the name of this town with that of this school. Were I to spend ten years in Lübeck people would talk of *die Lübecksche Schule*! And for more than ten years, I assure you, for victory and the future are ours.

If you want me, Monseigneur, then give me, with a title and position at Court, the possibility of influencing the theatre and music of your city. The *five* points of my aforesaid letter contain roughly the foundations. They would need to be broadened in certain ways, and I should need to have some money at my disposal; for *point d'argent, point de Suisse*[3]—and no music. Put me in a position to spend for the cultivation of my art at your Court three thousand, one thousand —or even five hundred écus a year, according to whether you wish to give it more or less lustre. Once my position is defined, and fairly demarcated according to the requirements of art and the conventions of your Court, I shall devote myself with the zeal that you know to the success of what I believe ought to be agreeable and advantageous to you.

While not reappearing in public, I shall always be at your disposal for any kind of musical duties in your salons, and shall be flattered to act the Kapellmeister therein, although I *completely resign* the *name* from this very moment. When it

---

[3] i.e. nothing for nothing.

is a matter of performing works which interest me, I shall conduct the rehearsals
and the negotiations necessary to bring to a good end the successes it will be a
question of maintaining. So that you may not fear that I shall exploit too exclusively the scope which would thus be given me, I need only remind you that in
the programmes of the Court concerts I have never neglected to take account
of Your Highnesses' personal tastes—that the theatre repertoire will be able to
provide an ample selection of operas to everyone's taste—and that no artist, I
can say, has understood on so extensive a scale as I the hospitality and courtesy
due to talents of every description. Remember, Monseigneur, that to conduct
Le Prophète in '50 I asked for only the *appropriate* costs for the *mise-en-scène*,
being unable to lend my name to performances inferior to those in the neighbourhood; the same with symphonies by Beethoven, the same with operas by
Mozart.—'Célébrité oblige.' Regarding works conceived in a style which is in
decline, I shall recall that it was I who supported Dorn's *Nibelungen*, the subsequent success of which in Berlin compensated for the unfair attacks to which
it was subjected here. And as far as my avowed adversaries are concerned, I have
ignored neither Herr Hiller, nor Herr Taubert, nor Herr Rietz—and it was on
my recommendation that we mounted in Weimar the *Tempest* and the *Neumark*
of the two last-named—the most stubbornly envious of the dazzling renown we
are acquiring.

Yet I do not conceal from myself, Monseigneur, that the greatest difficulty
does not lie in the detail of these arrangements—a talk with HE Count Beust
would certainly be enough to put that right. No one takes seriously the financial
fears formerly expressed on the subject of my influence on the theatre. Not desir-
ing any administrative book-keeping, I run no risk of dragging it to its ruin. Besides,
meine sogenannten Experimente [my so-called experiments] have done no harm
that I am aware of to Herr Sernau, the Intendancy generalissimo of all General
Intendants!

Why should I not speak to you frankly?

It is doubtless not to the taste of your retinue and probably not to yours,
Monseigneur, to see at your Court an artist who, as Prince Talleyrand wittily
said, would be *arrivé* and *non parvenu*, who would not atone through the absurdities of an upstart for the advantage of having married a Princess, and whom
one would thus be more or less obliged to honour and compelled to respect.
Here, it's a question of preventing me at all costs from making a marriage that
my birth has not allotted to me but which, I say without false modesty, I believe
I merit.

This difficulty is such, I realize very well, that I could succumb to it, in Weimar.
Rather than retain me here in the only way in which I can remain, people will
persuade you that you cannot be *good* to me. I am entirely prepared for it, and

if, despite that, I talk to you of the manner in which I could serve you, it is only so as not to respond by a bitter silence to the friendship your words express and for which I am never less than grateful, something I shall remain whatever the circumstances—as, too, Your Royal Highness's very faithful servant

F. Liszt

431. To Princess Carolyne. Whitsun, 8.00 a.m., 27 May.[4] The Whitsun bells are ringing. . . . At this hour you will be *en route* to Rome.[5] May your valiant and holy expectations there receive their crown—and may the end of your tribulations be at hand!

I went several days without news of you, and in my uncertainty about your itinerary didn't write to you. Yesterday morning I received your letter from Nîmes, and on returning home in the evening found the one from Marseilles. You were very wise to stop for a while in Nîmes. The *Maison carrée* and the amphitheatre are splendid architectural 'preludes' to what you will see in Rome. As someone quite uninformed in these matters, I shall even say that certain of these 'preludes', the *Maison carrée* for example, struck me as being more harmonious than the most grandiose edifices of pagan Rome. As for the temples of the goddess 'Reason', with or without the 'modified' programme, I don't venture into them. My heart understands only the 'madness' of the Cross, and breathes only in Jesus crucified and resurrected!

There have been some violent storms hereabouts in the last few days. Great damage has been caused in Gotha, and in several neighbouring villages poor people have lost their little bit of property. I hope you didn't suffer during the crossing from Marseilles to Civitavecchia. Take into consideration, too, the dietary recommendations Hebbel makes to you at the end of his letter. I enclose it with the present lines, plus a letter from Blandine, who warm-heartedly shared our emotion when reading your pages on Daniel.[6]

A very effusive letter I have received from Wagner I am sending to Magnette in the first place, asking her to pass it on to you. It is a reply to the *Herzensgruss* [cordial greeting] I sent him by telegram on his birthday, 22 May. I am going to write to him again, and also steep myself in his *Tristan*. I have done little this last week, while tormenting myself for 6 or 7 hours a day over my work.

---

[4] La Mara's edition of this letter bears the date 28 May (Whit Monday), but it seems clear that Liszt was writing on Whit Sunday, the 27th.

[5] To seek the Pope's permission to marry Liszt.

[6] The obituary notice (anonymous but actually penned by Carolyne) of Daniel Liszt which had been printed in a limited edition for private circulation.

Hoffmann's[7] song, *Scheiden*, got on my nerves quite singularly. I made 3 or 4 different versions of it, tore them up one after the other—and, for the sake of some respite, finished it yesterday evening. It's nothing very special—and I have sworn not to let myself in for another such labour. Like M. Roqueplan, I fancy I succeed better in 'doing large-scale things'. Be that as it may, Cornelius is satisfied—and approves it. In addition, the whim suddenly took me, without rhyme or reason, to set Lenau's *Zigeuner*—and at the piano I quickly found the whole outline. If that can in a way be done by itself, without, right in the middle, running into one of those ferocious and stubborn resistances which are the hardest test the artist has to face—I shall get down to writing it. Otherwise, no, for the time being, for I too foolishly allowed myself to be plagued for several days in seeking the right emphasis, which I found 20 times—and which nevertheless remained unfindable—for Hoffmann's *Scheiden*. . . .

11.30. I have just got back from church. My little Sunday morning world has been taken leave of for today. . . . At the door of our dear dwelling-place, and at the foot of the stairs, I found some shrubs that the servants had put there to celebrate Whitsun. I enclose a leaf for you, with all the blessings of my soul!

F.L.

432. To Agnes Street-Klindworth in Brussels. 28 May. Thank you for your letter and for sending the photograph of Wagner. The little bust of our friend is permanently on my desk. I shall now put with it the picture for which I am indebted above all to you, since, as he wrote to me, it was thanks to you that he had a second copy at his disposal.

The Princess left for Rome about ten days ago. The great concern of her life and heart has at last found a favourable and legitimate solution which but for despicable intrigues could have been obtained *ten years* earlier. Two months ago the *invalidity* of her marriage with Pce N. W. was formally pronounced by the Catholic consistories of Russia, which have responsibility for this matter, and countersigned by the Metropolitan Archbishop of Petersburg. In this respect, therefore, everything is in the most perfect order, just as she desired. What follows will depend on certain proprieties, which there is now no reason to offend or neglect.

I was intending to come to Brussels for a day or two this spring, but various obligations have prevented my budging from here. I shall probably remain here

---

[7] The poet A. H. Hoffmann von Fallersleben, who lived in Weimar from 1854 to 1860 and was on numerous occasions a welcome and convivial guest at the Altenburg.

for the whole summer, for I doubt if the Pcss can be back before mid-July[8] —and in her absence I am on guard at the Altenburg. What are your plans after Kreuznach? It would be very kind of you to tell me of them. Perhaps you will stop in some spot not too distant from Weimar, where I should be able to join you and tell you how truly affectionate, grateful and devoted to you I continue to be.   F. Liszt

433. To Richard Wagner in Paris. Weimar, 31 May. ^G Your letter, dearest, unique one, means more to me than the most beautiful, blossoming May day. May you, too, rejoice in the heartfelt joy it has given me!

How gladly would I telegraph *myself* to Paris! Where could things go so well for me as with you—in the magic circle of *Rheingold, Walküre, Siegfried, Tristan und Isolde*, all of which I yearn for! I mustn't think of this for the time being, however; but I shall certainly come, and as soon as I can.

Your photograph has been announced to me by a very engaging hand, but has not yet made its appearance. I have already told you that the little bust of you always remains on my writing-desk as *unicum*. The photograph shall have a place in the same room, which otherwise contains nothing *artistic*.

Beethoven, Weber, Schubert, and others of the same stamp keep your portrait (the one with the motto 'Du weisst wie das wird') company in the anteroom; *here*, I want to have you alone, together with my *Saint Franciscus*,[9] whom Steinle has drawn for me quite splendidly. On his outspread cloak he strides firmly, steadfastly over the tumultuous waves—his left hand calmly holding burning coals, his right hand giving the sign of blessing. His gaze is directed upwards, where the word 'Charitas', surrounded by an aureole, lights his way!

On the great question which for the Princess is one of life and death, a *definitively* favourable decision has finally been obtained. All the vile and subtle intrigues which for long years were woven against it, have been overcome. After the Princess's return from Rome (where she arrived last Sunday and will probably remain until the end of July) all will be arranged. If I could then also soon have the joy of seeing you *with us*!

Through Fräulein Hundt (to whom, together with her friend Ingeborg Stark, you gave so friendly a welcome) I heard a good many things about your way of life in Paris. And so there will soon be a *Tannhäuser* with ballet and a *contest*

---

⁸ In the event, the Princess never returned to Weimar: Rome was to remain her home until her death twenty-seven years later.

⁹ Liszt's name saint, Francis of Paola, depicted walking on the waters—a legend which Liszt later vividly illustrated in his *Légende de St François de Paule marchant sur les flots*.

of translators as well as of *singers*! It will be quite a tough piece of work for you, and I advise as many walks and cooling baths as possible. During the rehearsals Fips[10] should give you a lecture on philosophic patience. . . .

You know the reasons why I did not beg you to let me have *Tristan* for Weimar—and so you cannot disapprove of my passive attitude. If (as I hope will not be the case) there should be no favourable chances of an early performance of this wonder-work, and you will in the mean time be satisfied with a performance here, I firmly believe that I can arrange it for next season ('61). In your next letter, let me know what you think about it.

Meanwhile, I remain, with all my heart,   Your own   F. Liszt

434. To Princess Carolyne. [Weimar] Sunday, 3 June. . . . Bülow's
concert at Magdeburg is fixed for next Saturday. I have decided to go to it, and even, as a preliminary, to attend during the course of the week the Zwickau *Schumannfeier*.[11] . . . This kind of thing is completely devoid of reality for both you and me at the moment—but in view of the fact that I have had to remain here, I manage or, rather, inconvenience myself in consequence. At Dresden and in Weimar, and so probably elsewhere too, a rumour is going around that I shall soon be joining you in Rome. As you can see, *vox populi* is very flatteringly favourable to us.

Cornelius returns to Vienna tomorrow. He read to me again yesterday the opening chapters of the *Bohémiens*, on which I had only very minuscule observations to make to him. His translation seems to me to have turned out very well—and I am convinced that this book will gradually find its place, and keep it. Augusz made a just remark: if the *Bohémiens* had appeared a couple of years ago, it would have met with an enthusiastic reception in Hungary. We shouldn't hide from ourselves that the Iron Crown changed my public position quite considerably. I am far from regretting it—it is just a matter of continuing in the same way. . . .   F.L.

435. To Princess Carolyne. Monday, 11 June. . . . Through your letters
I can follow you in your peregrinations in Genoa and Pisa; and I have the most vivid idea of your arrival in Rome, as of your first impressions at the mouth of the little Tiber, at the Capitol, at the church of Sant'Andrea dei Frati, and

---

[10] A spaniel given to Wagner by his friends the Wesendoncks.
[11] Commemorating the fiftieth anniversary of Schumann's birth, in that city, on 8 June 1810.

in the underground church of St Peter. You could certainly have taken no wiser decision than that of moving at the earliest into the apartment so courteously offered to you. I am really surprised at the cheapness of your ten-room residence, and of the other arrangements, such as carriage, *valet de place*, footman to serve dinner, etc. . . .

Without ranking in the category of high dignitaries of the Church, the three Dominican Fathers will none the less be personages of importance. One can only gain in instruction and edification in such company, and I strongly urge you not to neglect the opportunity.

The brief trip that I have just made in honour of the *Schumannfeier* and the concert in Magdeburg . . . offers nothing which deserves special mention at the moment. I enclose only the short programme of the Magdeburg concert, which Hans conducted admirably, and which was a total success from beginning to end. . . .

You will doubtless have letters direct from Vienna; despite that, I am sending you the one dated Corpus Christi.[12] It is on this day, if I am not mistaken, that His Holiness gives his 'urbi et orbi' blessing from the balcony of St Peter's. May his blessing fill your heart, too, with joy and consolation!   F.L.

436. To Princess Carolyne. Sunday, 17 June. My whole soul burst into tears of ecstasy at your letter of the 3rd! How good is God to have given me the grace of knowing you, following you, owing you *everything* in my life which is not futility—or bitterness! Be blessed, unceasingly blessed!

Our parish priest[13] paid me a visit yesterday. He has just received numerous marks of affection and respect from his parishioners, it being the 25th anniversary of the beginning of his duties in the Grand Duchy of Weimar. You remember that he was for long years a parish priest in Eisenach. A diploma of doctor in theology, issued in Rome, would be a distinction which he would greatly value.

The whole of this week has passed fairly quietly. . . . The Grand Duke is in Baden, where it could well be that he will attend the 'coucher', of a few little German sovereigns, held by HM Louis Napoléon. After Baden he will join the Grand Duchess in Switzerland—and at the end of the month Their Highnesses will be back in Wilhelmsthal. So far as non-local visitors are concerned, I shall mention only Lenz, who has just completed his 6-volume work on Beethoven. I spent an entire day with him and he will return in the autumn. As a distinguished jurist, he has been appointed assistant public prosecutor to the Petersburg

---

[12] That year, 7 June.   [13] Father Anton Hohmann.

Senate. From what he tells me, he has been very much involved in your business during the lamentable number of years it has had to continue. Given this opportunity, I naturally didn't mince my words on the petty meannesses, extortions, and disgraceful machinations of which you have been the victim!

Yesterday I finished Lenau's *Die drei Zigeuner*, and flatter myself that they will not displease you. . . .

I congratulate you on having met Father Theiner,* and very much urge you to cultivate his acquaintance, if you have a chance. He is considered one of the best and steadiest brains among the Catholic doctors of our time. Signor Visconti,[14] for his part, will not take long to realize that there is no reason to entertain you with twaddle after the manner of the 'Russian princesses'. As for Overbeck and Cornelius, I am totally reassured about the good relationship you will establish with them. They are two princes of art—far rarer than the others —with whom you will naturally be very much at your ease, for you breathe freely in the atmosphere of masterpieces. I strongly approve your enlarging, without further delay, Mgr. Gustav's[15] library with Curmer's *Imitation*[16] . . .

Your letters make Rome more palpably present for me than if I were seeing things with my own eyes. I anxiously await what you will tell me by the next post. . . .   F.L.

437. To Agnes Street-Klindworth. Weimar, 19 June. . . . Wagner's portrait has given me very great pleasure. It is certainly the best there is, and I am waiting to have other copies engraved from it, when a good opportunity comes along. In the mean time, the newspapers announce that the first Paris performance of *Tannhäuser* will be at the end of this year.[17] It shows good taste on the Emperor's part to have commanded this performance—but I very much fear it will bring Wagner many worries and vexations which he will have no little difficulty in bearing. In my opinion, *Rienzi* (with a few changes and cuts) was better suited than *Tannhäuser* to the habits of the Paris Opéra personnel and public, who will not willingly allow the *singers' contest* at the Wartburg to take place without *songs*. This point has already been difficult for a few German aestheticians to accept! Come what may, however, I am very glad that Wagner will *hear his work again*; because, for him, being deprived of this resonance of his genius was like a Trappist's fast which he could no longer endure.

---

[14] Either of two distinguished archaeologists working in Rome at this time: (Baron) P. E. Visconti or his nephew C. L. Visconti.

[15] For this German prelate and his brothers, see under Hohenlohe-Schillingsfürst in Biographical Sketches.

[16] H. L. Curmer's French edn. (1856 etc.) of *De Imitatione Christi*.

[17] In the event, the Paris première took place on 13 Mar. 1861.

Did he show you a few fragments of *Tristan* and the *Nibelungen*? He sings them in his own way, which is gripping and captivating. As for the works themselves, I admire them as the sublimest manifestation of art.

If you are so kind as to write, put simply Weimar.   Yours   F.L.

438. To Princess Carolyne. [Weimar] 24 June. Your pious and adorable letter covering 8 to 14 June reached me punctually a week after the previous one. I thank you on my knees for all your goodness, your patience, your unshakeable devotion. . . .

I have already congratulated you on your acquaintance with Father Theiner, and am delighted to learn that your contact with him continues. Tell me sometime on what work he is now engaged—and, if there is some good portrait of him, bring it to me. If I am not mistaken he is of Silesian origin, and Lichnowsky, among others, often spoke to me of him with that high and admiring esteem which he took good care not to squander. The fortunate chance you have had of participating in the commissioning of Overbeck's frescoes of the Seven Sacraments in Vienna can count as a noble and delightful satisfaction worthy of you. *Für eine Dame*, as Cornelius says, *leisten Sie wirklich Unglaubliches* [For a lady, you achieve what is truly unbelievable]! . . .

At midday yesterday we had a Protestant ceremony in the Schloss chapel, in commemoration of the death of Maria Pavlovna. Dittenberger gave an 'unctuous' address, 'barren' and conventional, in which there was mention—but without defining them—of the *unaussprechliche* [inexpressible] virtues of the deceased, and the 'unutterable' blessings which would be attached to her for evermore. One of my neighbours remarked that in view of this whole array of things which were 'unsayable', the orator would have done well to 'say' less about them. The Pcss Regent and Pcss Carl attended the ceremony. By way of official-style pendant to Dittenberger's address, I am sending you the eulogium in today's *Gazette*. There is a way of burying the living under flattery too! . . .   F.L.

439. To Princess Carolyne. Weimar, Wednesday morning, 4 July. The sending of these lines suffered a 24-hour delay. Our poor Riese has died—and I left by the night train to attend her funeral. It took place at 6.30 yesterday morning, Tuesday, in St John's cemetery in Leipzig, which is at the present moment entirely adorned with the sprays of a thousand rose-bushes in flower. During the address given by the Protestant priest beside the open grave, near the coffin on which was laid a wreath of white roses—the birds were softly singing, the rose-bushes giving off a gentle perfume, and a young birch-tree was plaintively shaking its branches. It seemed to me that it was trying to remember some melody that my son had sung[18]—and some heart-broken strains were added to it by my tears! May God, in His mercy, be the eternal blessing of those we have loved!

Have I told you that I am busy on an instrumental composition which I have long been pondering, and which will be entitled *Les Morts*?[19] Each stanza will fall back on chords which correspond to the verse 'Blessed are the dead which die in the Lord!'[20]

The newspapers report the death of Cardinal Wiseman. You saw him again barely a fortnight ago. I am beholden to him for a quiet and pleasant day in Lisbon. I almost hesitate to send you this little page. Without being, as is vulgarly said, afraid of death—you yet do not wholly share the feeling of radiant serenity with which I shall greet the mysterious messenger, the august patron of our deliverance. Now, believe me: it will be a supreme delight to you—to you who have so greatly suffered, so greatly prayed, groaned, striven, deserved, and loved! Love is victorious over death, even on this earth—and there above, there will be no more death! . . . F.L.

440. To Blandine Ollivier in Paris. Weimar, 10 July. Most affectionate thanks, dearest Blandine, for having written to me at once about the unfortunate accident which has occurred.[21] My confidence in your veracity reassures me about the probable consequences. Please let me have specific news about my dear mother's present condition, however, and if necessary send me a telegram. Tell me, too, if it is on the same foot that was already injured earlier that the operation will have to be performed.

Here are a few lines for you to give to my mother. Don't forget to tell Emile how touched by, and how grateful I am for, his devotion to her. And I know that you, for your part, will neglect and omit nothing that can contribute to easing her painful situation, and that will help her endure it as best she can.

Had I had the choice, I would certainly have far preferred this accident to have happened to me!

The news I receive from Rome is excellent. The Princess is in contact with the most important people there, and being shown quite exceptional consideration

---

[18] The tree reminded Liszt of his son because 'Birch-tree' (*Bouleau*) had been the Princess's nickname for Daniel, whose slim, youthful frame had put her in mind of the birch-trees at the Altenburg.

[19] A setting of a text by Lamennais, *Les Morts* (the first of Liszt's *Trois Odes funèbres*) was composed in memory of Daniel and dedicated to Cosima.

[20] Rev. 14: 13.   [21] Anna Liszt had fractured her femur.

and respect. His Holiness has several times received her with kindness and gentleness.

She will probably be away for a few more weeks yet. I have sent her your letter, which she very much appreciated; and it is a sweet satisfaction for me, dear Blandine, that we have the same feeling about those pages on Daniel which throb with so profound an emotion and so maternal an affection. At the same time as your letter I received one from Mme d'Artigaux, vibrant with a like sympathy. Oh! through the active and permanent communion of beautiful souls, how beautiful could life yet be!

Let us remain one in heart, dearest Blandine, and ask God to grant us His peace here below, and in the hereafter all His light.

I am very happy to learn that my mother will soon be living in your home. Try to arrange for the move to be effected as soon as possible. . . .

441. To Princess Carolyne. [Weimar] 11 July. There has been no post from Rome this week, and I have now gone ten days without a letter from you. . . .

Here is some distressing news that the enclosed letter from Blandine has just brought us. I of course at once wrote to Blandine and to my mother. Let's hope that this unfortunate accident will have no serious consequences. Should that not be the case, I have asked to be telegraphed—for I should probably decide to go to Paris.

In the same envelope I am enclosing a page from Cosima's latest letter, because of the drollery of the manikin and the automaton. Have I told you that Cosima will be lying in in September? . . . The mention of Mme Kalergis in Cosima's letter refers to the service she has just done Wagner, in generously making good the deficit of his Paris concerts by advancing him several thousand francs. This gracious act, which gave me a very pleasant surprise, I was directly informed of by a short letter from Wagner that I have passed on to Cosima.

On Sunday I went to Leipzig to hear Allegri's *Miserere* and Lotti's magnificent *Crucifixus* at a concert given by the Riedel Society. . . . Hearing these works has in a way brought me nearer to you in Rome and put me back, if I may express it thus, on to the 'ascending' slope of my fervent desire to compose religious music. I must soon write the *Stabat mater dolorosa* and the *Stabat mater speciosa*,[22] the text for which has been supplied to me by Emile [Ollivier]. All this music is moaning, singing, and praying within my soul. For the moment

---

[22] Both eventually included in the oratorio *Christus*.

I am entirely absorbed by the work mentioned in my last letter. Do not scold me for not having yet finished the *Elisabeth*—for tasks awaiting me, I haven't always as much free time as I should like. However, I shall keep my word. The *Elisabeth* will be ready in time and as she must be.

The Grand Duke has been back for 4 days—he hasn't yet sent for me. Scotchy is still suffering quite a lot from her rheumatism. For the rest, nothing new. In the last issue of the *Courrier du Dimanche* there is a brilliant article by Montalembert on the monasteries. I have sent Magne her translation of Halm's *Iphigénie*, which has finally appeared in the June issue of the *Revue Germanique*. . . .

442. To Princess Carolyne. 15 July

Infinitely dear one,

At the risk of seeming very monotonous, I must once again heap all kinds of praise upon you. No one in the world is constituted like you, with this twofold understanding that can penetrate ideas and things alike. Your parallel between Raphael and Michelangelo touches on the most hidden secrets of art with a luminous profundity of intelligence—and right beside it, a few moments later, you explain with a finesse of reasoning as practical as it is astonishing, that it suits you best at the moment not to invite people to dinner. If I cannot entirely subscribe to the comparison you are pleased to make between my humble self and the great figure of Michelangelo—feeling rather a dwarf compared to this giant—I am entirely of your opinion with regard to the invitations. . . .

I am very glad that you have had an opportunity to make amends for a slight negligence towards Manning. The news of the death of Cardinal Wiseman has been denied—but he is said to be seriously ill. I should like to flatter myself that you will not find my letter to [Cardinal] Antonelli too badly worded. If another one should be necessary, telegraph me at once. Perhaps you will find a way to send me one of your five photographs via the Viennese Embassy messenger.

Here are 2 rather heartening letters from the Olliviers. With them I enclose two others by Mulinen and Laroche, as well as Montalembert's article on the laxity of religious orders. In it, the 'lay cardinal', as Montalembert has been nicknamed, severely and vigorously criticizes the corrupt practices which have infested the regular clergy—while maintaining intact the original honour of these great institutions. He deploys for them that dominating, moving, lively eloquence of his, laying about him with might and main, consumed with zeal for the house of God.

I shall see Monseigneur tomorrow, at Ettersburg. He had already invited me last week, but the message reached me too late. We haven't anything of great importance to say to one another for the moment. Bronsart, Inga, and the Ritters with their mother, for whom I cherish particular respect, spent several days here once again. . . . Bronsart and Inga left yesterday for Danzig, where they will stay with Bronsart's parents for a couple of months. Our friend Hans II[23] is still as madly in love.

Once again all praise and blessings for you, who are my good angel, my joy, my glory, and my salvation.   F.L.

443. To Princess Carolyne. 16 July. On thinking it over again, it seemed to me that the wording of the opening sentence of my letter to Antonelli, which I did at one go, was a bit too 'local'. I thought it a good one to begin with—but now I almost dislike it. Consider if the one I am sending you herewith is not a little better. Choose the one you find the less unsuitable to be delivered. In today's, I have left the date blank. The earlier one bore the date 11 July, feast of St Pius according to the calendar we have here. Delighted by that discovery, I had forgotten to consult the *Almanach de Gotha*, which contains the three calendars Gregorian, Reformed, and Russian. Only a moment ago did I notice that the Gregorian calendar differed on this day of 11 July from the Reformed calendar, so that my intention of opportunely 'offering a humble present[24] to His Holiness for his name-day' will be incomprehensible in Rome. In all things, I always do better to confine myself strictly to what you tell me. There will probably still be time to rectify my semi-stupidity—and I also assume that my second draft will suit you better. If you find them both equally bad, telegraph me at once, and I shall send you a third, and a fourth if necessary. . . .   F.L.

444. To Princess Carolyne. 24 July. . . . Eloquence has been defined as the art of saying what is necessary, all that is necessary, and only what is necessary. Well, behaviour and practice have an eloquence of their own which yields nothing to eloquence of speech and follows the same rules. You possess it, and give daily proof of it, in a way that is nothing short of prodigious. The title of 'ecumenical' that Cardinal Andrea has bestowed upon you is most felicitous and in perfect keeping with the one given you by Humboldt: *die vielbegeistigte Fürstin* [the many-minded Princess]. . . .

---

[23] Liszt's nickname for Bronsart, Bülow being Hans I.
[24] Apparently a contribution to Peter's pence.

I congratulate you on your acquaintance with the Revd Father Beckx.[25] He must undoubtedly be 'a man', as Napoleon said of Goethe at Erfurt.[26] Order from Paris a second copy of the *Imitation* for Mgr. Gustav. Were His Holiness later to put into effect his idea of establishing, as it were, the 'canon' of church singing on the exclusive foundation of Gregorian chant, it is a work to which I should devote myself body and soul, and one which by God's grace I hope to be in a fit state to carry out very well. Perhaps through Mgr. Gustav you can find a way to get a copy made for me of the memorandum on the reform of church music presented by Spontini to HH Gregory XVI at the beginning of 1839. Spontini showed it to me at that time, but I should like to reread it. For the work I have in mind, I should above all have to use the materials already very well set out in Regensburg by the publications of Canon Proske and the late Mettenleiter. I shall also have to do some research in Brussels, Paris, and above all Rome. In a year's time I could be in a position to submit this work to His Holiness, and if he deigned to grant it his approval it would be adopted by the entire Catholic world. When there is an opportunity I shall probably outline its plan, very simple in itself, for it is above all a matter of holding fast to what is immutable in the Catholic liturgy while adapting it for the requirements of the notation in use at the present time, without which it is impossible to obtain a precise and satisfactory performance. The instruments of the orchestra would all be put aside—and, to support and reinforce the voices, I shall keep only an *ad libitum* organ accompaniment. It is the only instrument with a right to a permanent place in church music—its varied registers will also enable a little more colour to be added. Nevertheless, I shall use it with extreme reserve. . . .

I enclose three letters, from Eduard, Blandine, and also Brendel, since even in Rome these little things retain a kind of interest for you! Of which Cardinal was it said that nothing was either too great or too small for his vast intelligence? . . .   F.L.

445. To Princess Carolyne. 5 August. . . . Take care of your health as best you can, most infinitely dear one! It isn't an essential asset, I dare say—the exaggerated and affected care that certain people take of it would make me inclined to set less value on it than it is worth. But it is necessary to look after it—despite the distrust that St Bernard had of it for a monk—'knowing to what it leads us', adds Bossuet! As for myself, I don't know how I am, but I am going on all

---

[25] Father-General of the Jesuits 1853–87.   [26] 'Quel homme!'

right—and people even consider me to be looking well. This last week I have read several scores by Handel and Bach, and scribbled some tolerable music of my own. The lugubrious composition I told you about is finished—and I have begun the orchestration. The day before yesterday your Psalm, 'The heavens declare the glory of God', came spontaneously back into my mind, and the main phrases gushed from my heart. I need about a week to get it down on paper. If it pleases you a little, I shall be very happy.

Have I spoken to you of your photograph? Your features have an expression of haughty melancholy, and reveal completely the concealed heartbreak. The pose and the clothing have turned out well, and the motion of your hands seems an unanswerable entreaty. I have put this photograph on your desk, alas now quite empty—near your letters which are in the drawer—and often talk with your picture. . . .

M. Desméloizes has lent me the 1 July issue of the *Revue des Deux Mondes*— in which Saint-René Taillandier lets fly rather sharply at Herr von Humboldt in connection with the publication of the Varnhagen–Humboldt correspondence.[27] His article is for the rest very well done and likely to satisfy those in high places. It contains a stroke of originality which borders on the baroque: a vindication of [D. F.] Strauss's 'religiosity' in contrast to the godlessness of Humboldt! In this connection, an ingenious remark quoted from Sainte-Beuve: 'Take the greatest of the modern anti-Christians, Frederick [the Great], Laplace, Goethe; have a good look at anyone who has completely misunderstood Jesus Christ; he has lacked something in mind or heart!' . . .   F.L.

446. To Princess Carolyne. 16 August. There was no post this time, and it's 11 days since I heard from you. I am still hoping that the letter from you that I have been expecting for 5 days will arrive this afternoon or tomorrow. At his invitation, I have just spent a couple of days at Wilhelmsthal with Monseigneur. He told me that he would be seeing HM the Tsar[28] of Russia in mid-September, and very kindly insisted on offering his services. In addition, he mentioned the Duke of Sermoneta[29] as the most intelligent and charming person he met in Rome. He even wrote down for me his forenames, D. Michelangelo, D. of S., and his address: Palazzo di Caserta, on a piece of paper, telling me to urge you to make the Duke's acquaintance. . . .

[27] In his correspondence with Varnhagen, Humboldt had been unsparing in his criticisms of the Court and society of Berlin, and this caused a scandal when, soon after his death, the correspondence was published.

[28] Alexander II, the Grand Duke's cousin.

[29] See under Caetani in Biographical Sketches.

On Monday morning I received a letter from Wagner, to whom the King of Saxony has intimated through Seebach that his government would make no objection if he returned to Germany, anywhere other than to Saxony itself—and so, with the exception of Leipzig and Dresden, Wagner can stroll about in total safety in the 'cara patria', whole and undivided! He at once took advantage of it to take his wife to the baths at Soden, and to pay his court to HRH the Pcss of Prussia in Baden. I am sending you his two notes. At the earnest insistence of Bülow, who told me that Wagner was in extreme need of seeing me again— I had sent a telegram in answer to the first note to say that I could not go to Frankfurt until Thursday—whereupon Wagner wrote me the second note. On thinking it over, I sent him a few lines to Baden, poste restante, fully approving his devotion to Mme of Prussia but adding my apologies and regrets at being unable to accept this new rendezvous. . . .

Yesterday, 15 August,[30] *Te Deum* at the Catholic church for the Emperor Napoleon. At my request they performed the one I wrote when Magne was married, shortly after the Gregorian Mass. It is only a version of the Catholic liturgy; it made a good impression, it seems. M. Desméloizes, with whom I dined, paid me some very kind compliments about it. . . .

I end as I began—sadly. May God protect you—all my prayers are with you!   F.L.

447. To Princess Carolyne. 22 August. The end of your latest letter, 'I am treated so harshly by everything and everyone', breaks my heart! Yet there is no question of weakening just now. Let us remain steadfast, strengthening ourselves through God! We must, by our faith and our love. I shall write to you more often, since you ask me to—although I don't know how to speak to you as I should like. While you were listening to the Psalm 'Coeli enarrant' at Santa Maria Maggiore, I was working at mine for male-voice chorus. I finished it yesterday, and it seems to me that it hasn't turned out too badly. It has just over 300 bars, 30 pages of full score of a very pronounced hieratic character. I have made two versions of it, one in Latin, one in German. I still have to adapt the orchestration in various ways, so that it can be performed with small forces, with organ only, if necessary, or with the whole orchestra, or, again, in the open air, when there is some male-choir festival—very frequent in Germany, Holland, and Belgium. In this last case, it needs only brass instruments, horns, trumpets, and trombones, and at the very most a few clarinets. I shall produce

---

[30] Date of birth of Napoleon I (1769).

the 'Coeli enarrant' for you in these three ways, I hope—and I fancy that you will like the verse 'Et ipse tamquam sponsus procedes'.[31] . . .   F.L.

448. To Princess Carolyne. 28 August. I have just spent five days in Berlin, almost without budging from my room. Your two telegrams reached me punctually. How many tribulations and set-backs for you! May God sustain and guide you!—I saw no one in Berlin of whom I need to tell you. I was proposing to pay a courtesy call on both Pce Latour d'Auvergne and Count Redern; but the former is in Paris and the latter away. On Sunday the Bülows and I went to Herr Seifert's, Humboldt's servant. The 'Old Man of the mountain' bequeathed him everything he possessed, library, collections, and objects belonging to him. For the purchase of the library, the Emperor Napoleon saw to it that an offer worthy of France was made: 70,000 francs for all the books in bulk, and without prior examination to see if the works are complete. Patriotic scruples prevented Seifert from accepting, which in a financial respect will cause him considerable loss. The Prussian Government decided not to buy, and all the books are now in Berlin with a bookseller named Ascher, who is selling them separately! Apparently it was publication of the Humboldt–Varnhagen correspondence that influenced the Government's negative decision—a very unfortunate one for Seifert's interests, and little in keeping with the consideration due to the name, position, and glory of Humboldt. In about a fortnight, on 17 September, the public sale of collections of pictures, prints, photographs, and other items will be held. I have empowered Cosette to obtain for you the Ingres painting which she tells me you liked, the death of Leonardo da Vinci, if the price is accessible. She assumes that in the present situation there will be no great alacrity in Berlin. If a few foreigners, whether private individuals or delegates of their governments, don't suddenly turn up, it is probable that most of the items will be sold below their value. For the rest, and between ourselves, I was surprised at the paltry nature of most of the presents given to Humboldt—especially those from Tsar Nicholas and M. Demidoff; a few pieces of malachite much inferior to the one you possess. The two most splendid gifts in the collection are by French artists: the Ingres painting and the colossal marble bust of Humboldt by David d'Angers. The latter is valued in the catalogue at approximately 2,000 thalers—but it is doubtful whether half that will be obtained for it. Cosette bought back privately from Seifert the specimen of my medallion which I gave

---

[31] Ps. 19 (Vulg. 18): 5: 'Which is as a bridegroom coming out of his chamber.'

to Humboldt in '42, with box in blue velvet—for 5 thalers. This medallion, which is no longer available commercially, sold in Paris for 48 francs.

Yesterday, Monday, there was a play and concert, in honour of Goethe's birthday, at Berlin's Wallner Theatre—a summer theatre with garden. Dawison had come specially from Dresden to play the role of Carlos in *Clavigo*[32]—and today will play this same role again in Dresden. The concert which preceded the performance was conducted by Wieprecht. Among other things my Goethe March was performed quite successfully. During the winter a cycle of *Vorlesungen* [lectures] will be given in Berlin on Goethe as poet, prose-writer, statesman, *savant*, artist, etc. I was asked to undertake the musical part in the great man's *Bestrebungen* [endeavours], which I politely evaded. Schöll will deal with the topic of the statesman, and Prof. Necker, President of the Goethe Committee in Berlin, will talk about Goethe's influence on *Culturgeschichte* [cultural history] . . . .

Friday, 31 August. In my telegram I told you that on my return here I found my appointment as Officier of the Legion of Honour. A letter from Mulinen, chargé d'affaires of the French Legation in the absence of M. Desméloizes, tells me, according to a telegram from M. Thouvenel, that the Emp. Napoleon, in a decree of 22 August issued on the proposal of M. Thouvenel, has been pleased to bestow on Doctor Liszt the rank of Officier of the Legion of Honour. Mulinen, who is always charming to me, has written to you direct on this topic. At the Erholung he was asked why His Majesty had accorded me now this evidence of his goodwill—to which he replied: 'Because M. le Docteur Liszt—is *Liszt*!' That reminded me, all self-conceit apart, of the remark made by M. de Meulnare, Belgian Minister in '43, when he was asked why such and such a Belgian artist had not been decorated in preference to me: 'The reason is very simple—in honouring M. Liszt, the King's government honours itself.' . . .

My Psalm is completely finished. . . . I have promised Schlesinger, with whom I am pretty content, to arrange Meyerbeer's *Schillermarsch* for him, a labour to which I shall add another similar one, by revising and correcting the scoring of my Rhapsodies, of which the half-dozen for orchestra are ready and which I should like to publish during the year. People who can't see further than the obvious can have no idea of the trouble and care required for the revision of scores. It's enough to make one throw in the towel—especially when, like me, one is tormented by the two contrary poles of the simple and the luxurious. . . .

May the peace and the mercy of God be with you!   F.L.

---

[32] Tragedy (1774) by Goethe.

449. To Princess Carolyne. Weimar, 4 September. . . . I thank you and bless you for everything you say, do and suffer. Unfortunately I can lend you only the support of a broken reed. God grant that it suffice—with all the best reasons in the world you have for being and remaining right! It seems to me that I had a clear view of the situation right from the beginning. . . . The details in your letters are only, so to speak, the developments in the scenario I had made for myself shortly after your arrival in Rome. You act as you think, admirably— and your letters are of a divine quality. They have all the backbone of reason and nerve of conduct of those of Mme de Maintenon, with the poetry of Byron— plus your great and holy heart! The impression I feel when reading your letters corresponds to the one which emerges from your marvellous picture of one of those Roman sunsets: 'when the translucent atmosphere is only a golden haze in which swims with voluptuous ecstasy a sun of moonlike whiteness, a dizzy-ing whiteness such as must have been that of Christ on Tabor.'[33] Indeed, my infinitely and ineffably loved one, you have nothing to be modest about, what-ever you say. It is for others, and for me first of all, to practise modesty to the point of embarrassment—in relation to you. . . .

Thank you for the interesting information about music in Rome. It tallies perfectly with my impressions and memories of 20 years ago. If I return to Rome, it will probably be the canons' choir at San Pietro in Vincoli that I shall most frequent. Please find out if the liturgical service as performed by these canons can be obtained. If the expense isn't too great, bring me the score. Meluzzi's and Aldega's compositions interest me too—but a couple of pieces will be enough. When there is an opportunity, tell Meluzzi that it will be very agreeable to me to have his work on the diapason published in our friend Brendel's newspaper. I am rereading Chamfort's little volume with great enthusiasm, and quote a few passages for you on a separate page. . . .

Mulinen is still very friendly—and I have become fond of him because of his discerning recognition of your superiority. Yesterday evening we spent a couple of hours with his wife, plus M. and Mme de Laporte, at the *Schiesshaus* [shoot-ing gallery]—strolling in the menagerie, the cyclorama, *chez* the acrobats, and in the punch shop! . . .

Forgive me these insignificant details—but here I have neither monuments, nor masterpieces, nor Eminences to tell you of. Talking of Eminences, thanks to your latest portraits I know all about their intellectual, moral, and physical features. May Father Ferraris, whom I bless with all my heart, soon be part of the Sacred College![34] Although Mme de Maintenon's remark is not inaccurate:

[33] Mount Tabor, traditionally the scene of the transfiguration of Jesus.
[34] That is, be appointed a cardinal. Ferraris was the Princess's, and later Liszt's, confessor in Rome.

'I know no one unhappier after those who desire the foremost positions—than those who obtain them.' . . .

Scotchy has written to you—she is a little better and spends a lot of time with the Sabinins. Probably Monseigneur will invite me to Wilhelmsthal one of these days; I shall go in any case before he leaves for Warsaw. Through you and for you. Be patient!   F.L.

450. To Agnes Street-Klindworth. Weimar, 7 September. Many days have now gone by without my writing to you. I shall say nothing to you of the worries and sorrows which have filled them for me. You have enough of this baggage of your own!—For the rest, I am still just as uncertain about what will become of me next winter as when I saw you. The Princess will not return until about the end of this month, and I shall decide only then. . . .

Like you, I very much fear that our glorious friend is labouring under something of an illusion about the nature of his chances of success at the Paris Opéra. There is in him something incompatible with the very tyrannical ways and customs of the French theatre, and I doubt whether he will succeed in imposing the tyranny of his genius on them straightaway. As for finding a Germanic *cradle* for *Tristan*, I believe he will have to resign himself to waiting until the Paris performance of *Tannhäuser* is over. In Germany, the Karlsruhe incident has spread general panic among singers of both sexes, and people don't leave off saying that the two principal roles in this work are absolutely unsingable. That is by no means my opinion, and if Wagner had not held, and was not still holding, to financial conditions which cannot be met in Weimar, I would undertake to prepare rehearsals of *Tristan* for him here, in a way that would not dissatisfy him. We shall see later what will have to be done—and if other more eminent theatres dare not risk it, I shall continue to keep ours for him, as a last resort.

During the 5 days (23 to 28 August) I spent in Berlin at my daughter's, Hans and I again went through the score of *Tristan*. It is marvellously beautiful from start to finish, and I know nothing which can be compared with it for intensity of tone and sublimity of emotion.

Talking of things extraordinary, have you heard of the poem *Merlin l'enchanteur* which Edgar Quinet has just published?—The very laudatory analysis of it that I read in the *Courrier du Dimanche* made me desire to know this work, and I have ordered it.

A little volume that I have reread with delight is Chamfort's (*Maximes, Pensées*, etc., published by Stahl, Collection Hetzel). If you don't already know it, have a look at it. Wit of a better kind than is contained therein, in abundance, can't be found. Among a hundred others, here is a very persuasive thought: 'Any man who at the age of 40 is not a misanthrope has never loved mankind.'

When you see my daughter Cosima (to whom I spoke a lot about you recently) again, you will like her. Hers is a rare and beautiful temperament, which in its spontaneity possesses great charm. . . .   F.L.

451. To Princess Carolyne. 17 September. This time, I am 36 hours behind-hand. Your letter up to 6 September reached me very quickly, like the one before it. Monseigneur has gone to Bamberg, where he will be seeing Duke Bernhard [of Saxe-Weimar]. During the week he will be coming here to view an exhibition of paintings in which appear the oil-painting by Schwind that you know, showing the Emperor Rudolf riding to Speyer, where he was to die, and Menzel's picture of the meeting between Joseph II and Frederick the Great. . . .

A fortnight from now, Queen Victoria, accompanied by Lord John Russell, will be arriving at her brother-in-law's in Coburg, there to enjoy, they say, family joys and pleasures. In passing, she will do a tourist's *shakehand* [*sic*] with the Pce Regent of Prussia at Coblenz. When I have seen Monseigneur again, I shall perhaps be able to tell you more about it. As for the French cabinet, it is imperturbably putting into practice, with a virtuosity which far surpasses Paganini's, the proverb 'que ta chemise ne sache ta guise [let not thy left hand know what thy right hand doeth]'. It is virtually impossible that France will give way. But the expected initiative could temporarily be changed and remain stuck until the complications reach the point when the Sphinx reigning at the Tuileries feels that he is in a position to put all his advantages to good use. What you tell me so aptly about another great personage[35] applies perfectly to the Sphinx. The devil himself would not guess what he's up to—what he does without saying, and what he says without doing. . . .

Shall I tell you what I have been applying my thoughts to these last few days? To you, doubtless—and always to you, most infinitely dear one—but this time in an unwonted way. On 14 September, Feast of the Exaltation of the Holy Cross, I wrote my will. To write those 12 large pages, plus a 4-page supplement containing dispositions relating to the publication of my manuscript works, I needed a whole day. Although I felt inspired to do it, the writing became so illegible that I had to make another copy—which again took me a whole day. When you return I shall show it to you—and you will tell me what I should add or change. In the mean time, I am leaving it in one of the drawers of your desk, in our blue room. . . .   F.L.

---

[35] Probably Antonelli.

452. To Anna Liszt in Paris. Weimar, 18 September. ^G Your kind and
affectionate little letter, dearest Mother, brings me heartfelt joy. Thank Heavens
that you have again made such good progress! May you soon be your active,
busy self, once more!

A thousand apologies from scatterbrained Frater for having thus far failed to
send his thanks for the equally agreeable and useful present of the green rug,
duly delivered by Fräulein Hundt. For several months it has been rendering me
excellent service and delighting my eye with its beautiful green colour—the colour
both of hope and of the Holy Ghost. Although silent and mute, it tells me many
nice things about you. It lies in my study under my desk, and while I write to
you warms my feet, which for years have had a silly habit of freezing. That probably comes from the fact that in many things I am rather a hothead. Schiller,
your darling, suffered from the same inconvenience; and, to protect his feet,
had to have some special equipment installed (under his desk), which can still
be seen at his house here in Weimar.

Through Herr Lassen, the Kapellmeister, the gun likewise arrived in excellent condition. True, I shan't make much use of it, for I gave up the pleasures
of the hunt years ago; but if some quite exceptional opportunity comes along,
in your honour I shall try to shoot a hare (not a goat, *s'il vous plaît*) with it.
The animal bagged by me I shall then either have stuffed or made into a pie,
to send to you.

Again a thousand thanks for your letter. Your loving son,   F. Liszt

453. To Princess Carolyne. 20 September. . . . I saw Monseigneur at
the Roman House[36] yesterday, and took my leave of him repeating what I had
said to him earlier: 'I am as resigned as resolved.' In about a week I shall see
him again in Eisenach. He has just got back from Oberammergau, where he
attended the performance of the Passion of Our Lord, which amazed him. He
was accompanied by only Herr von Goethe[37] and Thompson. From what he told
me, he found no one he knew among the 100,000 spectators. The *Schultheiss*
[village mayor], who apparently played the part of Christ admirably, had the
honour of being congratulated by Monseigneur. . . .

To relate a detail from the private life of the Emperor [Napoleon III], it is
said that His Majesty's greatest amusement consists in crossing over a small pond

---

[36] House in the classical style standing in the Grand-ducal park, built—under Goethe's supervision—in the 1790s
as a summer residence for Carl August.
[37] Walther von Goethe, elder of J. W. von Goethe's two grandsons.

near the palace of St Cloud while wearing cork shoes, a feat which he performs
superbly. The people who have the honour of accompanying him are required
to cross over too—and when they are so clumsy as to fall into the water, he is
graciously amused. The beautiful Marquise de Gallifet, second daughter of M.
Charles Laffitte, is named as being recently very much in favour. She has been
married for only a few months, and M. de Gallifet accompanied the Emperor
to Baden, as aide-de-camp. . . .

Cosette has telegraphed me to say that she purchased the Ingres painting—
François I at the death-bed of Leonardo da Vinci—at the Humboldt sale, for 520
thalers. In my opinion it's worth the price. If you have a moment of leisure,
send Eduard a couple of lines from Rome, accompanying them with your photograph. It seems to me that because of his loyal devotion to you he deserves this
distinction. . . .   F.L.

454. To the Grand Duke Carl Alexander in Eisenach [Weimar, 3 October]

Monseigneur,

I shall try to satisfy as well as I can Your Royal Highness's mild curiosity
regarding the Comte de Saint-Germain, necromancer, alchemist, and first-rate
virtuoso violinist. Unfortunately I haven't at my disposal here the biographical
works which would help me to provide further interesting details about this
individual, whose true name and origin seem to be still unknown.

He is assumed to have been Portuguese, because he is sometimes called Aymar
Marquis de Bedmar. The Maréchal de Belle-Isle brought him to France (from
where, is not stated by the German and French encyclopaedias I have consulted).
The Duc de Choiseul presented him to Mme de Pompadour (of the same kind
as the Countess of Landsfeld—Lola Montez—*mit monarchischem Hintergrund*?)
and also to His Majesty the King [Louis XV], who took a liking to him—so
the encyclopaedia says—and gave him an apartment at *Chambord*![38]

An extreme ease of manner with the most highly placed personages gained
him the privilege of saying anything with impunity. (Kings' fools had this privilege in days of yore, and I take pleasure in thinking that it is not their fault if
it didn't make the Kings wiser.) While affecting a profound contempt for riches,

[38] The magnificent château built by François I.

Saint-Germain enjoyed displaying a prodigious quantity of precious stones and diamonds (after the manner of the Duke of Brunswick, who has been living in Paris since '48) and boasted that he had learnt the art of cutting diamonds well on *one* of his first voyages to the Indies.

From the marvellous descriptions he gave of his many travels, he could pass for the prototype of my friend M. Alexandre Dumas, Marquis de la Pailleterie, present director of the Museum of Naples. The arms of the Marquisate de la Pailleterie have been decided upon thus by M. Dumas the younger (from what I have been told): '*Pas* d'argent *sur* fonds de gueule.' Chateaubriand's motto is 'Je sème d'or'.

Apart from his chemical knowledge and alchemical illuminism, Saint-Germain played the violin admirably—so well that people thought they could hear an entire orchestra under his bow—and possessed in addition the talent of writing *equally well* with right and left hand, which I envy him doubly, for my handwriting being horrible and almost illegible, it greatly displeases me.

By means of his elixir of long life, he claimed, he had already lived for 350 years. The same liquor also had the property of turning a woman of 70 into a perfect resemblance of a girl of 17—and, further, made anyone quite simply *immortal*. This idea was carried on, moreover, *without elixir*, in Condorcet's remarkable book *Des Progrès de l'Esprit humain*.[39]

Frederick the Great asked M. de Voltaire for a few details about the Comte de Saint-Germain. 'He is a man who doesn't die and knows everything,' replied Voltaire. He did die, however, in 1784—or 1795—as a *close friend* of the Prince of Hesse-Cassel. This intimacy would explain in rather a singular manner why the present Elector of Hesse governs in the manner of 350 years ago; a method which has succeeded extremely well for him thus far, as it has with others who haven't even the merit of his obstinacy. But the pitcher goes so often to the well that in the end ... it fills itself,[40] says Figaro.

Be so kind, Monseigneur, as to excuse my want of greater erudition, which I shall endeavour to replace as advantageously as possible by the sincerest and most respectful devotion of

Your very grateful servant   F. Liszt[41]

---

[39] In his *Esquisse d'un tableau historique des progrès de l'esprit humain* (written in enforced seclusion and published posthumously in 1795), in which he sketched the history of mankind from the earliest times until the Revolution and expressed his hopes for the future, Condorcet strove to show his belief in the indefinite perfectibility of the human race, above all in the moral and intellectual sphere.

[40] A twisted ending to the proverb 'Tant va la cruche à l'eau qu'à la fin elle se casse [is broken]'.

[41] In his note of thanks (Eisenach, 4 Oct.) Carl Alexander wrote: 'To be fittingly thanked for your delightful letter, my very agreeable correspondent and caustic biographer of M. de Saint-Germain, you should have heard my bursts of laughter. . . . Your letter is worthy of Chamfort. . . .'

455. To Princess Carolyne. Weimar, 8 October. . . . I spent 6 to 7 hours with Monseigneur in Eisenach, last Tuesday—after I had informed him by letter of the favourable result of the Council.[42] His first words were: 'Nothing remains but to go to the altar; please don't postpone it any more!'—However, I was very openly on guard against excessive confidence—and did not conceal some remaining fear which was still troubling my hopes. He suggested taking me to the Wartburg, and on the way offered of his own accord to write a further letter to Antonelli in which he would ask him to hasten the definitive conclusion. I accepted with joy. At the Wartburg he immediately set about writing it—while I waited a good half-hour in the St Elisabeth portico. He then showed me his draft, which because of its intelligent and lucid precision I found perfect. This missive was sent by post with 3 seals, via Marseilles—just as I had recommended. Although at this time there is no more need of it, it still confirms Monseigneur's present good intentions towards us, and can only make a good impression on Antonelli. Ask him if he has received it. If by chance it has gone astray, you can in good conscience assure Antonelli of Monseigneur's persistent support—still more marked this time than previously. In addition, I talked a lot with him about the theatre, the academy, building plans, the music festival, etc. At 5.00 I dined for the first time at the Eisenach Schloss, whither he had taken me on foot. At table there were only his two daughters,[43] Thompson, Frau von Könneritz, and Fräulein Froriep. After dinner we read tête-à-tête a few of Chamfort's maxims and several sonnets by Platen. The Grand Duchess was not due to return until the next day but one. . . . At Coburg the day before yesterday they together paid a visit lasting a few hours to the Queen of England, and this week Monseigneur leaves alone for Vilnius and Warsaw.

Okraszewski[44] has sent me this telegram from Milan, which I received yesterday evening and which took only an hour and 55 minutes to get here: 'The Princess has completely won her case. I am going to Vienna, then to Fulda and Weimar. Set your mind at rest; she is well.' To that I responded with a telegram to Magne: 'I venture to ask you to urge Okraszewski to stop in Weimar first of all, for I wish to accompany him to Fulda.' I simultaneously telegraphed to Eduard in the same terms. At Fulda I shall follow your instructions word for word, and provide myself with all the necessary papers.

---

[42] As Liszt had notified the Grand Duke in a letter of 30 Sept.: 'The Council of Cardinals of the Sacred College, convoked on 22 September for the purpose of judging on the *form* and *substance* of the matter concerning the Princess Wittgenstein, *unanimously* decided in her favour *on both points*.'

[43] 11-year-old Princess Marie Alexandrine and 6-year-old Princess Elisabeth. Fräulein Froriep was their governess.

[44] Wladislaw Okraszewski, the Ukrainian lawyer whom the Princess had employed to bring her marriage annulment petition to a successful conclusion.

Here is a note from Cosette. Do not scold me about the Ingres painting—I hope it will give you pleasure. For 22 Oct. a *Fackelzug* [torchlight procession] is being prepared in town in my honour; several hundred people are to participate. Perhaps I shall be obliged to ask for it to be postponed to another year. In extreme haste!   F.L.

After a brief visit to Vienna, to talk—fruitlessly—to the Papal Nuncio and to Mons. Gustav Hohenlohe about his hoped-for marriage with the Princess, Liszt returned to Weimar on 22 October.

456. To Princess Carolyne. 26 October.

. . . . I hope you won't disapprove of me for that trip to Vienna. Although I could do nothing there, it still had to be made, it seems to me. Why, you will understand without my saying. The Grand Duchess, who is very much in the know, as I was able to see in the talk I had with her a few hours before I left for Vienna, immediately perceived its significance. She is not yet abandoning her former erroneous ideas about the form of our marriage—and while no longer insisting on the necessity of a change of religion, she admits that the marriage tie performed by a Protestant priest would suffice—if we would indeed prefer not to restrict ourselves simply to the registry office!! To hypotheses of this kind, only the most categorical denials can be opposed. I did not fail to do so, as you can well imagine. Without labouring under any delusions about our relative weakness, I am yet very hopeful, and beg you to share the sentiment expressed by the great apostle [St Paul]: 'Si Deus nobiscum, quis contra nos.'[45] For the rest, the Grand Duchess was full of tact, I shall even say of goodwill, towards me in this latest visit. And so I shall not despair of converting her more completely to our cause ... but, for that, a little more time is still needed. I shall return to the Wartburg one of these days. I was only waiting for some news from you, having remained nearly 3 weeks without knowing what was happening. . . .

I am thoroughly abashed and all but heart-broken by your praise of my acumen and of my very slight ability. Alas, I succeed in very few things, and don't know how to do anything at all for you, in the lowly region in which I am constrained to remain—while you show yourself in all things admirable to all and adorable to me! Your new relations with Father Theiner are of real importance, and everything you tell me of Mgrs. de Falloux, Talbot, and Spaccapietro

---

[45] 'If God be for us, who can be against us?' (Rom. 8: 31).

proves what a past-mistress you are in the art of assessing and understanding people. . . .   F.L.

457. To Princess Carolyne. 4 November. All praise and blessings for you, dearly beloved Carolyne, on this day[46] in which the Church celebrates the glory of your patron saint! 'Enter thou into the joy of thy lord, good and faithful servant!'[47] When reading this verse from the Gospel in church today, I choked with tears and could feel your beautiful eyes filling my whole soul with their splendour. You have fought enough, entreated enough and pressed on in season and out of season, in all patience and wisdom, as the great apostle recommends to Timothy, for the crown of justice and joy at last to be your portion. Amen! . . .

I am waiting for your news in order to announce myself to Monseigneur at the Wartburg, where he will remain for at least another fortnight. The last letter I received from you is that of 15 October. Please thank Linange very affectionately for the portrait he has sent me. . . . My 2 or 3 dozen visits in town being more or less completed, I have resumed my work, which is my sole repose, as you know. Time is very short for what I should do—but what long days without you! When shall I see you again? Have I told you that Cornelius's translation of the *Bohémiens* has come out? The volume looks very fine, and I believe that Cornelius has accomplished his task very well. Let us finish our own with full confidence in God, who will not forsake us.

My mother has successfully effected her change of residence. She was of necessity carried in a litter, but is still in very good spirits, and seems content with her accommodation at Blandine's, rue St Guillaume. The latest news from Cosima is very satisfying. I believe she intends to give her daughter the name of Daniela-Senta.

458. To Agnes Street-Klindworth. 16 November. . . . You speak to me of Weimar, where on 22 October there was a torchlight procession in my honour which set the whole town in commotion, following which the *Gemeinde-Rath* [parish council] unanimously named me an *Ehrenbürger* [honorary citizen]. (Incidentally, it is twenty years or so since such an honour was bestowed upon me by the *Gemeinderäthe* of Pest, Sopron, and Jena.) That doesn't prevent me from saying that you are perfectly right to find me as it were out of my element here, where of course I lack the necessary base of operations. Nevertheless, if I

---

[46] Feast of St Charles (San Carlo) Borromeo.   [47] Matt. 25: 23.

have remained a dozen years in Weimar, I have been sustained here on the one hand by a sentiment not lacking in nobility, and on the other by a great idea. By the first, I mean protecting a woman's honour, dignity, and lofty character against foul persecution. By the second, renewing Music through its most intimate alliance with Poetry. . . . Despite the opposition it has encountered and the obstacles raised up against it on all sides, this idea has not failed to make a little progress. Let people do what they may, it will triumph invincibly, because it forms an integral part of the sum of the just and true ideas of our age; and I am consoled by the knowledge that I have served it conscientiously, loyally, and disinterestedly. If, when I settled here in '48, I had wished to attach myself to the *posthumous* party in music, associate myself with its hypocrisy, cherish its prejudices, etc., then because of my previous contacts with the principal bigwigs in that same party, nothing would have been easier. I would certainly have gained outwardly in consideration and acceptance; and those very newspapers which now find fit to heap insults and abuse upon me would have vied with one another in singing my praises, without my making any effort. They would readily have declared me *not guilty* of a few youthful peccadilloes, in order to extol and call attention in every way to the *enthusiastic upholder* of the fine, wholesome traditions from Palestrina to Mendelssohn. But such was not to be my lot; my conviction was too sincere, my belief in the present and future of art at once too ardent and too positive to allow me to put up with the empty objurgatory formulae of our pseudo-classicists who do their utmost to cry out that art is going astray, that art is lost.

The waves of the spirit are not like those of the sea. They have not been told 'thus far and no further'. On the contrary: the spirit 'bloweth where it listeth', and the art of the present century has something to say just as had that of previous centuries—and it *will* say it, without fail.

All the same, I have never hidden from myself that my position has been extremely difficult, and my task a most thankless one, for many years at least. Wagner having so valiantly innovated and completed such admirable masterpieces, my first concern had to be to win for those masterpieces a permanent place which could take root in German soil, at a time when he was exiled from his own country and when any and every theatre in Germany was afraid to risk his name on a poster. Four or five years of *obstinacy*, if you like, on my part were enough to bring this about, despite the slender resources available to me here. Indeed, Vienna, Berlin, Munich, etc. have for 5 years done nothing but what little Weimar (which to begin with they had mocked) dictated to them ten years ago. . . .

I don't know why I have begun to talk to you of things you know at least as well as I do. Being unable to indulge in the 'mania for travelling' (by which M.

de Talleyrand explained Napoleon I's Russian campaign to M. Lazareff), it seems that I am taken by that of chattering with you. It was your remark about my entourage of 'cretins' in Weimar which put me back on the track of my little local exploits. . . .   F. Liszt

459. To Princess Carolyne. 22 November. I saw Monseigneur at dinner, tête-à-tête—and he was extremely kind to me, telling me repeatedly that he valued me singularly and did not admit the possibility of my living anywhere but in Weimar. Actually, having had no news from you for about ten days, I found myself short of a specific request or petition for him; and told him only that the next stage of the affair was to be a second missive from Rome to Fulda. I also explained the reason for my trip to Vienna, telling him of my interviews with Mgrs. Gustav and Luca.[48] For his part, he offered me two things outright. Firstly, to spend a few days at one of his country houses in the environs of Fulda, there to receive the nuptial blessing from the local Catholic priest, with whom Monseigneur is on very friendly terms. Secondly, to apply to the Tsar of Russia for permission to return to Russia for a few days with the object of receiving the same sacrament there. Monseigneur has already raised this point in Warsaw with his cousin of Russia. Both of these proposals are more serious, it seems to me, than several things said earlier on. I await what comes from Rome—and you can then tell me how I should proceed. With regard to the related matter of my Chamberlainship, this, too, Monseigneur is well disposed to settle positively. From what he has told me, I cannot have any doubts about this. You will understand, however, that for the present it would be indecorous of me to insist on it—and so of course I must put off this pleasure *post festum*. As you have so rightly said, the *Ehrenbürgerthum* [honorary citizenship] would not have come to me if in high places there were not a little good wind blowing for me just now. . . .   F.L.

460. To Agnes Street-Klindworth [Weimar, 2 December]. Your letter reached me an hour before I left for Berlin, where I have just spent three days in honour of my *grand*daughter, who was christened . . . in my daughter's home (Anhalter Strasse 11) at 4 o'clock on Saturday. It was in those same rooms that I saw my son Daniel die, a year ago. In affectionate memory of him, Cosima

---

[48] Monsignor A. X. De Luca, the Papal Nuncio.

has named her daughter *Daniela*, joining to it the name of *Senta*,[49] who, for her, represents an ideal type of woman. The association of these two names Daniela-Senta, harmoniously strange, seemed still more singular through the Latin prayers of the baptismal rite. It was Hans's sister, Isa, and I who served as godparents.

I hardly left my daughter during those three days, and put myself out to visit only Redern, Prince Latour, and Meyerbeer. (These three personages live just beside one another in the Pariser Platz. As you know, at a cost of 400,000 thalers the Emperor has acquired a mansion for the French Embassy, in the Pariser Platz. The British Embassy is close by.) Meyerbeer told me that he had two completely finished operas in his portfolio, and a third well advanced. Newspaper reports that the famous *Africaine* will be put on immediately after *Tannhäuser* at the Paris Opéra were not confirmed to me by the *illustrissimo maestro*—on the contrary, he seems 'to prefer to wait'.[50] (You remember that delightful axiom in the *Cuisinier parfait*: 'The rabbit *demands* skinning alive—the hare *prefers* to wait!') . . .

In Berlin, Fräulein Jenny Meyer (a fine mezzo-soprano voice) has just sung *Mignon* and been obliged to *encore* it (!), which will also cause a few copies to be sold! . . .

461. To Princess Carolyne. 28 December. Your telegram of good wishes for the festivities reached me on Christmas Eve, on my return from Frau von Schorn's,* where I had promised to participate in the splendours of the Christmas tree. Arriving late, I found the little candles extinguished, the presents distributed, and Frau von Schorn all alone. However, she had me served an excellent supper, prepared especially for me. Someone went to look for her two daughters and for tall Otto Schorn, now acting as secretary of the Art College; they were at the Frorieps'. The five of us stayed together until 10.30. Your telegram had been delivered a few minutes before I got back, after a journey of 9 hours, which shows that the telegraph line between Rome and Marseilles has been restored. . . .

Twenty years ago, Fräulein von Schultz was a maid of honour in Hanover, where, if I am not mistaken, her father had a junior minister's portfolio. During my very brief stay there [1844] the whole family took a liking to me, especially Fräulein von Schultz, who, a few years later, married Herr von Skupitzin. From what I have heard, it seems that this individual was not conspicuous for the qualities which make a good husband. When we went to Eilsen I exchanged a few words with Fräulein Schultz at Hanover railway station, and I spoke to you

---

[49] The name of the heroine in Wagner's *Der fliegende Holländer*.
[50] The première of Meyerbeer's five-act opera *L'Africaine* took place at the Paris Opéra on 28 Apr. 1865.

of her on that occasion. Ernst the violinist was much loved in that house, and perhaps had had a notion of creating for me a position similar to the one he was occupying, *Conzertmeister* with a large salary. The little differences I had with the late King—who is said to have preferred to put up with certain vulgarities, corresponding to his own, than with a way of life in which he scented some kind of independent opinion, intolerable to sovereigns of his kidney—made things impossible for me in Hanover. Besides, it had never entered my head to seek anything there whatsoever. It was in early '44, before the Belloni concerts in Paris, that those little differences took place. I recall that the Schultzes continued to think well of me and be kind to me. My advice would be for you to see them from time to time, should the occasion arise, since you happen to be living in the same house.

To return to Weimar, I can tell you that the Grand Duke and Duchess are being most gracious and considerate. A week ago I had to speak to them about a little incident at a concert—too trivial to tell you about in detail—and they seemed content with my way of looking at and dealing with things, rather different from that of other persons around here. Monseigneur invited me to lunch, and after chatting about this and that asked me what I was doing in the afternoon. 'I am going home to resume writing.'—'I'll accompany you, and as you have excellent cigars you can give me one.' And thus it happened! Monseigneur came and spent an hour with me—to the great surprise of Heine,[51] who did not recognize him. I had recently had a chat with the Grand Duchess on the topic of presents given to artistes. On Christmas Day she sent me a large and splendid box full of cigars, adding on it in her own gracious hand: 'For M. Liszt.' I shan't show it to anyone, and shall not smoke the cigars—but am telling you this detail, as being something of a sign of good intentions. . . . At this very moment I have received an invitation to a soirée, a non-musical one, at the Grand Duchess's today, and am accepting. . . . A week ago, on Friday, there was a little music in the salon containing the statue of Lucifer. The first two performances of *Rienzi* took place yesterday and the day before. I had busied myself to such an extent with the piano and orchestral rehearsals that people imagined I could not get out of conducting the performance. But I have no intention of getting involved in all that again. . . .

I shall probably spend New Year's Eve with Dingelstedt, who has invited about a dozen people. . . .

The 57th 'Entretien' in Lamartine's *Cours de littérature* mentions a visit I made 15 years ago to Saint Point. I'll copy out for you the whole passage, which most definitely flatters me, although even then we felt something else 'in partibus'!

---

[51] A servant at the Altenburg.

The next issue, No. 58, contains a splendid apostrophe against one of the great ineptitudes of our time—specialization. . . . F.L.

Thank you 1,000 times for all your ingenious and profound remarks about certain new books, especially Krasiński's unfinished poem. How I long to 'intrude' again in some of your readings, as I used to! At least tell me about them when you have the leisure, or when the fancy takes you—and grant in advance your indulgence to my cretinism, which permits me to follow only from afar and at a low level the lofty flight of certain metaphysical ideas that people have more accustomed me to admire than explained to me. However, so that you may not think I am becoming ever more stupid—I'll tell you that I have just read with great interest Leibniz's correspondence (edited by M. Foucher de Careil) with Pélisson, Bossuet, Spinola, the Duke and Duchess of Brunswick, *et al.*, concerning the reconciliation of Catholics and Protestants. It consists of 2 volumes, dedicated to the King of Hanover, which will be followed by at least a dozen others, containing the complete works of Leibniz plus related documents and fragments. It was a letter from Foucher de Careil to Monseigneur which provided me with an opportunity to peruse this work and has put me very much in the mood for similar reading matter. . . .

1861

Mid-February. Liszt visits Prince Constantin von Hohenzollern-Hechingen at Löwenberg where, on the 15th, *Die Ideale* and *Mazeppa* are performed. On the 19th he is in Leipzig, where the *Prometheus choruses*, conducted by Bronsart, are very well received.

30 April. Liszt sets out for Paris, where he wishes to see his mother and the Olliviers. Among the friends and colleagues with whom he associates during his six-week sojourn in the city are Rossini, Lamartine, Berlioz, Wagner, Pauline Viardot, and Gounod. He also makes the acquaintance of Bizet and Baudelaire, has several meetings with the Comtesse d'Agoult, and dines at the Tuileries with Napoleon III and Eugénie. 'I have come to feel a most warm and genuine affection for him,' writes Emile Ollivier; 'and how transported, moved and filled with wonder I have been by his truly supernatural playing, it is impossible to describe.'

8 June. Liszt leaves Paris to return, via Brussels (where he has a reunion with Agnes Street-Klindworth), to Weimar.

5–7 August. The Allgemeine Deutsche Musikverein is inaugurated by a music festival in Weimar which is attended by, *inter alios*, Wagner, Cornelius, Tausig, and the Olliviers. Among the works performed is Liszt's Faust Symphony, superbly conducted by Bülow.

17 August. Liszt leaves Weimar and travels to Löwenberg, where until 19 September he is the guest of Prince von Hohenzollern-Hechingen.

19 September–6 October. He stays in Berlin.

17 October. At Marseilles, Liszt embarks for Civitavecchia.

20 October. He arrives in Rome and is reunited with Princess Carolyne, whom he is to marry on the 22nd. In the evening of the 21st a Vatican emissary brings news that the ceremony is to be postponed, and the marriage plans are subsequently abandoned.

WORKS. *The Legend of St Elisabeth* (further progress on different sections). TRANSCRIPTIONS FOR PIANO: *Valse de l'opéra Faust* (Gounod) (S407), the song *Löse, Himmel, meine Seele* (Lassen) (S494), Pastorale (Reapers' Chorus) (S508) from the *Prometheus choruses*.

462. To Princess Carolyne in Rome. [Weimar] 10 January. May every blessing be with you, most infinitely dear one! . . .

Scotchy got back on New Year's Eve, and the day before yesterday wrote you a long letter about her trip. Her upright and honourable character is most estimable, and it will always prevent her from lacking anything whatever in grateful devotion to you. Nevertheless, from the way in which she told me of her conversations with Magne, I realized that she is not by nature equal to grasping the present situation. Like Magne, she regards it as out of the question that the Hohenlohes are creating difficulties for you, Pce Constantin having assured her that they were doing nothing of the kind—all the difficulty lying in the laws of the Church that the Vienna Nuncio, the Munich Nuncio, the Bishop of Fulda, *et al.*, have declared are totally opposed to you. You can guess the rest of the argument. . . .

The best of what Scotchy told me concerned the harmonious relationship between Magne and her husband, and their splendid status and standing in the Viennese Court circle, the formality and exclusiveness of which have quite surprised Scotchy. She is touched by the reciprocal charm that husband and wife exert on one another. '*She is charming, and he is very tender and loves her. It is beautiful to see her in her dresses*'—runs the description—'*in her nice carriage with 2 splendid english horses,—to see them together at dinner in the evening.*'[1] That's fine, and I am far from taking exception to it! So I sang in chorus with Scotchy: '*She is an angel, and we will hope the best.*' At my request, Scotchy sent toys (costing about twenty fl.) to Eduard's children for their Christmas tree—through Cornelius, who several times visited her in her hotel, the Roman Emperor. Despite Scotchy's lack of insight, she will, by her sincerity, and even her goodwill, at least have contributed to causing Magne to see things in a way which comes nearer the truth, something she couldn't get into the habit of doing in Rauden. I have no doubt at all that the moment I pray for will come, when Magne will be wholly and completely your daughter! For the present, she must be left in her passivity. Like you, I think that an exchange of opinions or explanations by letter between Magne and you would serve no purpose.

Cosette has been here for 3 days, and the day before yesterday we spent a very pleasant evening *chez* Frau von Helldorf, who invited us there when I told her of Cosette's imminent arrival. There were about a dozen of us, the Helldorfs, the Gerstenbergs, Zedlitz, *et al.* Yesterday evening we went to the Mulinens', who are always very affectionate to me. Tomorrow or the day after I shall invite myself to tea with Frau von Schorn, to whom I have introduced Cosette. . . .

Monseigneur went to Potsdam for the King's funeral.[2] Mourning will not be strict here, for no later than tomorrow there will be a grand ball at Countess Wedel's, and others will follow. Two days after the King's death, Monseigneur was in his little box at the theatre. The New Year's Day concert went off very well, and I continue to be on good terms with the masters of the house. Hebbel's *Nibelungen* will be performed on 26 January, or so I am told by Dingelstedt

---

[1] The italicized words written thus in English by Liszt.
[2] Friedrich Wilhelm IV had died at Potsdam (Sanssouci) on 2 Jan.

—who has just spent an hour with me. At the moment when your letter arrived I was revising my Second Concerto (to which, incidentally, I have made a few improvements), which took me 4 or 5 days. 'Respirons l'éternité'! Schott, who is going to publish it with *Venezia e Napoli*, will pay me modestly but appropriately for it. Schuberth is offering to publish the Faust Symphony, and I am rather inclined to give it to him—for he is also publishing the Faust-Parerga, *two episodes from* Lenau's *Faust*: *Nächtlicher Zug* and *Mephisto-Walzer*. All in all, he is not a bad publisher. I shall still need at least ten days to revise the manuscripts thoroughly before sending them to be printed. . . .   F.L.

463. To Agnes Street-Klindworth in Brussels. 24 January. You are truly and admirably kind to write to me thus *in extenso* amidst your family trials and tribulations. If my wishes are useless and my thanks insignificant, you know that at least they proceed from keen and sincere affection.

I don't know how I got hold of the notion that you see the M's frequently; but since that is not the case, I shall take good care not to poke my nose into things. The anxiety many people have, about knowing where *to spend* the evening, has always been unknown to me, and it is not in Brussels that I shall experience it!—I shall need to work steadily to get through all my paperwork between now and 15 February, and, as already mentioned, on the 16th I shall go to Prince Hohenzollern's (in Löwenberg) and on the 19th have to be in Leipzig. And so it is only in the last week of February that I shall make the acquaintance of your Erard.

My daughter Cosima departed 4 days ago, after having spent a fortnight here. She would be very pleased to see you again, and I take pleasure in thinking that you would find her rather clear-cut *personality* agreeable. Her little daughter (whom we jocularly call *Cosma* because of the singularly prominent bumps on her cranium, which give her in the cradle a certain comic resemblance to Herr von Humboldt) continues to be fed from the bottle. Cosima had begun by suckling her, but fell ill after a few days, and the doctor, Frau von Bülow, and Hans were totally opposed to her going on zealously with maternal duties which she was not strong enough to endure. Forgive me these details, which I would certainly not have dreamt of mentioning had you not expressly asked for them.

Hans will be going to Paris for the 1st performance of *Tannhäuser*, rehearsals of which seem to need to be prolonged beyond the time initially prescribed for them. Here, all sorts of things rather disagreeable to Wagner are being related about the confusion into which this new music is plunging the singers and members of the orchestra; but I assume that there is a certain amount of exaggeration, at least, in this *hearsay*. For the rest, it is never without difficulties and lively disputes that new works of major importance manage to take their rightful place. Gluck and Spontini in Paris, Mozart and Beethoven in Germany, encountered difficulties similar to those of Wagner, and Handel very nearly threw a prima donna through the window, the Diva having declared his music unsingable. One can but recall Solomon's saying: 'No new thing under the sun.' . . .   F.L.

464. To Princess Carolyne. 3 February. I am smitten with remorse at sending this letter so late. Various small external circumstances made me fall into this fault of omission, which this morning fills me with bitter sorrow. On awaking I was overcome by a fit of unspeakable sadness. . . .

The first days of the week I was busy with proofs and revisions of music, which I find strangely tiring at present. On Thursday we had the first performance of the *Nibelungen* of our friend Hebbel, who had arrived here in the morning. As he had found only a rather bad room at the *Eagle*, I thought it was my duty to invite him to stay at the Altenburg, and take it that you will not disapprove of this hospitality. His play created a great impression, and the Court seems very well disposed towards him. He has been invited to dine at Monseigneur's, on Friday, with me. At the Grand Duchess's yesterday evening, he read the First and Fifth Acts of the 3rd part of his *Nibelungen*, to about twenty people. Their Highnesses were struck and, as it were, startled by the work's emotional power and loftiness of style. At dinner, where Hebbel and I were seated at the Grand Duchess's table, mention was also made of Geibel's *Siegfried*,[3] which was recently performed in Munich, apparently without great success, for all its poetic merits. To my great surprise, Their Highnesses would admit no possible comparison between that play and Hebbel's. The first two parts of the *Nibelungen* will be put on again next Wednesday, and Hebbel will stay until then. I have asked him to write you a few lines, which he will do with genuine alacrity. Here, too, as during my last stay in Vienna, Hebbel is behaving towards me with the utmost tact and sympathetic regard. I don't know if I told you that at the end of last year he made a brief trip to Paris, on which occasion I sent him at his request a few words for my mother and Wagner. After his return to Vienna he wrote me the letter I am enclosing. It will give you the measure of our good relations.

[3] Meant is Geibel's tragedy *Brunhild* (1858).

I am also adding Blandine's latest letter and a note from Pce Polignac to Wagner, which I ask you to return to me. So far as my participation as player or conductor is concerned, I shall reply in the negative—but will perhaps ask Wagner to conduct *Les Préludes*.

The day before yesterday the New Weimar Club mounted a celebration in honour of Schubert, born on 31 January. There were to have been about fifty of us; but the Court having very graciously invited itself, the whole town wanted to come. Here is the brief preliminary report from the Weimar paper about this *Schubertfeier*, consisting of a concert and dinner and ending with a ball. I managed to get through Schubert's Rondo with Singer and one of the *Soirées de Vienne*, to the audience's satisfaction, it seems. Since it was not a public soirée, and the free invitations had been issued by my colleagues, I decided that I ought not to abstain. May I see you again soon, and resume my true, my only life— beside you, at your feet!   F.L.

465. To Princess Carolyne. Löwenberg, 16 February. Just as I was getting into the carriage in Weimar I received from our dear excellent priest the lines I am enclosing for you. However on guard I may be against surprises, in things of this kind—I gave full vent to my joy. When I get back, in four days, I take it that I shall find confirmation of the news given me by the priest. Meanwhile, the rumour has spread everywhere that you have won your case in Rome. Yesterday evening on my arrival here, Pce Hohenzollern at once said: 'Well, my dear fellow, everything is in order—the Pope has settled the matter!' —As I wrote to you in my last letter, I shall wait in Weimar until all your instructions reach me. Perhaps I shall manage to be in Rome by Holy Week! Before my journey to Paris I shall probably go to Fulda with our parish priest. Monseigneur has shown me the cartoon of Preller's sirens. The rocky landscape seems admirable, and the wings added to the sirens look splendid. Monseigneur did not understand why these ladies, if they desired those gentlemen so much, did not hurl themselves on to the vessel by means of their wings. I allowed myself to explain to him that, with women, the role of passion was not to take or to give—but to *attract*, which he found plausible enough. Preller also sent him the architectonic sketch of the Propylaea, where he would like to paint his *Odyssey*. This project, approved by Cornelius, is very beautiful—but it will not be carried out. The most they will do is build a museum for which Monseigneur has a design—which I find hideous—by Streichhan. But you know that I understand nothing of such matters. . . . May God heap upon you all His blessings!

466. To Princess Carolyne. [Weimar] 6 March. As usual at the approach of spring, I went down last week with an illness which kept me in bed for a couple of days. It has been completely gone since yesterday, and I am resuming my accustomed routine, which for the moment consists in going out very little, and in getting on as well as I can with my musical work. . . .

I have had no letter which might be of any interest to you. The performance of *Tannhäuser* in Paris has been postponed, in the first place because of rather a serious difference of opinion between Wagner and M. Dietsch, conductor at the Opéra. . . .

In Weimar people have given attention to nothing but the great fancy dress and masked ball that the Academy of Art, headed by Kalckreuth, put on in the Town Hall for mid-Lent. Monseigneur went in a costume à la Rubens, his wife as Marie de Médicis; Kalckreuth, Beaulieu, Henckel, Fräulein von Watzdorf, Frau von Helldorf, *et al.*, in Louis XIII costume. Dingelstedt had prepared a dramatic prologue for these festivities, but it was not approved—and it was Herr von Beaulieu who undertook to write it, which was anything but flattering for Dingelstedt, and he did not go to the ball. I, too, refrained from going—and shall not even conduct the small Court concert, announced for Friday. Talking of concerts, have you heard mention of the *Liszt-Conzerte* Tausig is giving in Vienna? The programme contains my works only. Tausig is conducting the orchestra himself, and taking care to repeat at each concert one of the *symphonische Dichtungen* performed at the previous one. It seems that he is pulling things off marvellously, and that this undertaking does not fail to create something of a sensation.

My mind is hardly on all these matters, and I sometimes need to make an effort to attend to even the bare minimum of my musical obligations. I told you that the Faust [Symphony] and the Two Episodes from Lenau's *Faust* were going to be printed. It is Schuberth who is publishing them, and Kahnt is undertaking the *Prometheus choruses*, which will also be coming out in the summer. These last few days I have found it necessary to make a couple of arrangements of the *Schnitterchor* [Reapers' Chorus] for 4 and 2 hands, as well as of the *Nächtlichen Zug*. At the end of this week the whole bundle will be sent off to Leipzig. I shall add to it the *Beatitudes*, which will shortly be published— after having been performed by the Riedel Society in Leipzig. Heaven grant that I may soon get to work again according to the dictates of my heart, beside you, who are for my thought the 'Turris eburnea', ivory tower. When reciting the litanies of the Blessed Virgin, I stopped at this appellation, the full profundity of which I had not hitherto felt. May God guide you and fill you with His grace!

F.L.

467. To Princess Carolyne. 14 March. I have just sent you a telegram to say that I have completely given up the idea of going to Paris. All things considered, I find that I have nothing to do there at the moment, not to mention that I am not in the least inclined to take any pleasure in salon talk, nor to interest myself in any kind of exterior things. . . . Without you I have no desire to see anyone or anything; so let us put off 'our' trip to Paris until later. Wagner will be rather annoyed with me for missing his *Tannhäuser*—but, indeed, I should be of no use to him, whether he has a success or not. If luck is against him, I shall try to arrange a return for him here with his *Tristan*; and to this end I have already obtained Monseigneur's provisional consent. If the truth be told, I should not know what part to play in Paris just now, with regard to *you*. This uncertainty induces me not to show myself. . . . I hope you will be of my opinion—and unless you have some errand to give me for Paris, I shall no longer think of going there. . . .

Your 2 letters covering the period from 16 February to 1 March reached me the day before yesterday. I hope the next post will bring me a beginning of the new one I am expecting.... May your heart tell you all that mine feels in ardent adoration for you!   F.L.

Tomorrow there is a concert at Monseigneur's which I shall conduct. It's now about ten days since I saw him. You have had news of the Leipzig *Prometheus* from Cosette, who came here for a few days after that concert. Her state of health is rather disquieting; more especially as she won't let anyone mention it. The Berlin climate doesn't suit her at all, and the doctors prescribe Nice. She has promised me that she will follow the directions given by Traube, a doctor very celebrated in Berlin for treating chest complaints—and I hope that by doing so in good time she will pull through.

468. To Princess Carolyne. 20 March. How many times, when returning home in the evening, do I catch myself looking for the soft light at the windows of your room.... but alas! it shines only in my heart! The house remains forsaken, gloomy, and in mourning. I feel this all the more when people come here, as they did yesterday—when I had invited someone introduced by Emile Wittgenstein, and also Herr von Ramberg, whom you met in Munich. Talking about you with the latter, I couldn't help a certain enthusiasm creeping into my voice—and among other things I told him that your intelligence was for me a whole starry firmament. That is hardly new, but very true. Besides, I am not in the least getting used to living far away from you! I lack a *raison d'être*—and I sometimes seem to myself a mere shadow. May God grant my soul's wish—by reuniting us soon!

Exceptionally, I have been out several times this week. Four days ago I dined tête-à-tête with Monseigneur, and again asked him for the decoration for Wagner—although, and even because, *Tannhäuser* has met in Paris with a fate similar to the *Barber of Bagdad* in Weimar. I believe I told you that at the first performance of *Rienzi* in December, I proposed to Monseigneur that he send the decoration to Wagner. The idea did not displease him at all to begin with— but he put off carrying it out. Recently, he finally told me outright that stubborn objections to it were being made by Herr von Watzdorf! That vexes me, for I feel that this mark of attention would have done honour to the Grand Duke's good taste, and that at the present moment Wagner would be particularly appreciative of it. I am trying to prepare Wagner a return to Weimar in the autumn with the first performance of *Tristan und Isolde*, which he should be invited to put on and conduct. Monseigneur seems fairly well disposed to the idea—provided that this plan isn't thwarted by some Herr von Watzdorf or other! I am sending you a copy of my note to the Grand Duke about Wagner's decoration. As Cosette is taking an interest in the matter, I have sent her one too. . . .

I spent yesterday evening at Parry's, and the previous day at Herr von Heydebrand's, Prussian Minister and a very celebrated chess player. He has published a volume on the theory of this noble game. The Grand Duke and Duchess were at these two soirées, and today they leave for Berlin, where they will congratulate the new King on his birthday, 22 March.[4] Dingelstedt has preceded them there, to attend the final rehearsals of his arrangement of [Shakespeare's] *The Winter's Tale*, which is likewise to be performed on 22 March—but at the Victoriatheater. . . .

Have I already thanked you for sending the article on the deadly effects of absinth? I read it with Mulinen, who continues to come and see me often— and he confirmed, from several examples known to him, the dreadful ravages caused by this drink. He himself had formerly consumed quite a lot of it, until Rayer ordered him to refrain, on pain of being taken to Père Lachaise in a few months. I promise to follow your advice and recommendations, most infinitely dear one, you who are my Law and my Blessing. Pray for me and cure me of my bad habits, which often cause me to suffer bitterly. Oh, until when, O Lord, will you leave me to pine, far away from her!   F.L.

---

[4] Wilhelm I, who had succeeded his brother Friedrich Wilhelm IV as King of Prussia, was, of course, the Grand Duke's brother-in-law.

469. To Agnes Street-Klindworth. 21 March. I am sad unto death—and can neither say anything nor hear anything. Prayer alone brings me relief at times, but alas! I can no longer pray with much continuity, however imperative the need I feel to do so. May God grant me the grace of coming through this moral crisis, and may the light of His Mercy shine in my darkness....

This morning Lassen came to see me. We spoke only of things which have become rather irrelevant to me—yet I was suddenly overcome by such sorrow that I could not hold back tears. Forgive me for wearying you with such futilities! You have so often been kind and gentle, and I am allowing myself to speak to you as if you were present here with me—which, I can assure you, I do very little indeed with other people.

The opinion of the doctors in Berlin was less unfavourable than I had feared. Cosima has to begin with been prescribed a milk cure; to this end she will go around mid-May to Reichenhall.

If there were some pretext—someone to recommend, a newspaper or book to send—I should be very glad if you would write to Cosima. We often spoke of you during her last stay here, and if she had known how to set about it you would already have received a letter from her. Her address is 11, Anhalter Strasse, Berlin. I enclose a specimen of her style, which I find rather remarkable, to put it modestly. Her intellectual faculties have developed greatly these last few years, and I believe she has in her the makings of a woman very much out of the ordinary. She writes with a rare facility and fluency of pen and mind. Let me have the enclosed letter back under cover, for I want to keep it. . . .

Have I told you of the Book of Job *by Isaiah, rediscovered,* restored to its full length and translated literally by Pierre Leroux? I have been sent only the preface, which has made me singularly keen to know the whole work. Besides, I feel more than ever in a mood to reread this wonderful book. . . .

When you have a spare moment, write me a few lines.   F.L.

470. To Blandine Ollivier in Paris. Weimar, 25 March. I shan't conceal from you any longer, dear Blandine, that I have been very worried about Cosima. Six weeks ago I was notified from Berlin that she was showing symptoms of a serious chest complaint. Her mother-in-law and sister-in-law were doing their utmost to prevail upon her to take care of herself and look after her health —but in vain, for she claimed that she understood the situation better than anyone. Neither her very perceptible loss of weight, nor a dry cough which was tormenting her for hours on end and depriving her of the sleep she so needs, could induce her to take the doctor's advice and undergo treatment. By chance

1. Liszt's birthplace in Raiding (Doborján)

2. Liszt in 1842. Portrait by Franz Krüger

3. The Comtesse Marie d'Agoult. Oil painting by Henri Lehmann, 1843

4. Princess Cristina Belgiojoso. Painted by Henri Lehmann, 1843

5. Liszt in 1845 (daguerreotype)

6. Valentine de Cessiat

7. (*top left*) Fryderyk Chopin.
Portrayed by Winterhalter, 2 May
1847

8. (*top right*) George Sand. From a
lithograph by Thierry *frères*

9. (*right*) Alexander von Humboldt.
Daguerreotype by Hermann Biow,
1847

10. Daniel, Cosima (*rear*), and Blandine Liszt, with Liszt's mother (*left*) and Mme Patersi de Fossombroni. Photograph, *c.*1852

11. Liszt in middle life

12. Hans von Bülow

13. Carl Tausig

14. Liszt's bedroom, dining room, and music room at the Hofgärtnerei
(Goethe und Schiller-Archiv, Weimar)

15. Princess Carolyne von Sayn-Wittgenstein at her home in Rome

16. Cosima and Richard Wagner. Photograph, Vienna, May 1872

17. Liszt Jubilee Committee, Budapest, 1873. From the left (*front*): Archbishop Haynald (Chairman of the Committee), Liszt, Count Albert Apponyi, Count Guido Karácsonyi; (*rear*): Imre von Huszár, Count Imre Széchényi, Ödön von Mihalovich, Baron Antal Augusz, Hans Richter, J. N. Dunkl

18. Queen Elisabeth of Romania (Carmen Sylva)

19. Anton Rubinstein in later life

20. Liszt with Carl and
Caroline Lachmund.
Photograph by Louis Held,
Weimar, 1884

21. The Grand Duchess Sophie.
Photograph by Louis Held,
Weimar, 1892

22. Alexander Siloti, *c.*1904

23. Soirée in St Petersburg. At the piano (*left*), the aged Mily Balakirev

I had arranged to meet her in Leipzig to attend the performance of my *Prometheus choruses*. She did indeed come there on 17 February – and, alas, I could see only too easily how well justified were the fears which had been expressed to me about her condition. To gain the time to see what needed to be done, I suggested that she return to Weimar with me, which she willingly consented to do, and I also gradually managed to get her to agree to being examined by a doctor in whom I have full confidence. He did not hide from me his opinion that it was high time she underwent a proper course of treatment, and temporarily prescribed some medicines for her which have done her some good.

I initially thought of taking her to Paris, there to consult a doctor with a high reputation, and of urging Hans to take her to some place with a mild climate, in accordance with what the doctor would probably advise. She utterly refused to go, putting forward several very sensible reasons against a journey undertaken there and then. Above all she was bent on not troubling, or even disturbing, her husband—and asked me to allow her to wait for Hans in Berlin. I'll spare you details of our discussions, the outcome of which was that on 10 March she returned to Berlin, where, as she had promised me, she consulted her usual doctor, Bücking, and also Herr Traube, a doctor who is celebrated for treating chest complaints and whom Frau von Bülow had urged me to summon to Weimar.

This consultation was, thank God, quite favourable for Cosima, who was prescribed a milk cure ('Molkenkur') at Reichenhall in Bavaria; and, as her constitution has remained quite resilient, I hope she will there be fully restored to health.

Naturally, dear Blandine, to my good mother you won't say more than that Cosima is mildly indisposed, at most. Poor, dear Mother, how I was looking forward to seeing her again!... The few preparations necessary for my journey had been made, and I was expecting to set out on 22 February. It was at that moment that Cosima's condition was at its worst.... lasting for ten or twelve days. According to the latest news I have received from Frau von Bülow, she was looking much better when she returned to Berlin than she had done before her departure, and her cough was not quite so bad.

So, as you see, I could not think of leaving, and in order not to worry you needlessly I could not even let you know why I was not leaving.

Now I have to wait for news which will probably come between 10 and 15 April. I won't be able to tell you until then when I shall be able to see you again—but it will be soon.

In the mean time let me thank you, dearest Blandine, for offering to accompany Cosima to the south; I hope such a trip will not be necessary and that the Reichenhall cure will be enough. Besides, Hans would not agree to his wife being away for several months unless he was with her.... but I am none the less moved by the affection you show your sister. Do, however, take care not to write and tell her too insistently to look after her health, for that is a topic which angers her very easily, as you know. . . .

Kiss my good mother and give Emile a cordial handshake from your loving and affectionate father.

So that you don't have to wait for my reply, I shall send you tomorrow, under separate cover, a bill of exchange for 500 francs which you can put to the same use as the previous one.

Cosima has promised me the *Book of Job by Isaiah*, translated and provided with a fully restored text by Leroux. Tell me if this work, which excites my curiosity in the highest degree, has been published yet. I know only its astonishing preface.

471. To Princess Carolyne. Easter Day, 31 March. Let me begin this day with you, most infinitely dear one. This week has favoured me, for, unusually, your weekly letter from 16 to 22 March has reached me. . . .

Yesterday Monseigneur, with whom I dined, as usual asked me for your news. I likewise replied as usual, saying that your health was, thank God, fairly good, and that Rome's climate suited you. Then he came back for the twentieth time to this question of whether it would be possible to find a priest who could put an end to this weird situation, seeing that everything has been put in order, weighed, and decided. 'That would be very dangerous,' said I.—'But how is it all going to end?' he went on.—'We have to wait.'—'What, wait just now, when Rome itself is so threatened!'—'We shall wait!'—This fragment of conversation was word for word as I have written it down for you.

I come back to Rome where you have to remain—and say in confidence that the prospect of pitching my tent there, for the few years of life that perhaps still remain to me, in this time of 'profound degradation and arrant perfidy', attracts me singularly. The time to make a definite plan has not yet come; and I remark solely that my opinion will be fully in harmony with yours, if you decide to settle in Rome. In any event, I shall not continue my mode of life, such as it has been these last ten years or so. I absolutely must have more peace, solitude, self-communion, and independence. My expenses must also be more restricted and better regulated, my work more continuous, less in fits and starts— it must hollow out its bed like a broad river. God grant that I give you a little satisfaction! . . .

During that same conversation I also told Monseigneur bluntly that I thought the museum blueprint he had shown me was ugly, very ugly, in fact hideous

—quite as hideous as that horrible effusion of Greek architecture which stands in the Karlsplatz opposite the Russischer Hof Hotel and which has been given the designation of reading museum. Although I ostensibly profess to understand nothing of either painting or architecture, I do not know why Monseigneur ascribes to me a certain soundness of impression in these matters, and talks to me of them more often now than formerly.

Seeing that I am giving you these local details, I shall further mention that Dingelstedt has just spent a fortnight in Berlin—you can guess for what purpose! His arrangement of Shakespeare's *Winter's Tale*, with Flotow's music, was performed in the city's Victoriatheater, without any subsidy from the Court. It obtained a complete success. The twelfth performance has been reached already —and the newspapers are unanimous in their praise of Dingelstedt, who in this respect at least has schemed very cleverly. The play having been put on for the first time on the King's birthday, 22 March, Dingelstedt had it preceded by a prologue in which attention was suitably called to, and emphasis laid on, the exalted virtues of His Majesty. This notwithstanding, neither the King nor the Queen granted Dingelstedt the honour of seeing them—but quite simply ignored his presence in Berlin. That rather surprised Dingelstedt, who only last summer at the seaside resort of Ostend had several times been favoured by invitations from the King—and was naturally flattering himself that he would receive a warm welcome in Berlin. . . .

Oh, how I long to read with you the beautiful verses of Tasso and Petrarch! Thank you for the adorable sonnet you wrote out for me. I shall put these two lines under one of your portraits:

> Le degne lodi, il gran pregio, il valore,
> Ch'è da stancar ogni divin poeta.[5]

Thank you above all for the moving account of your solitary evening on Tuesday, 19 March—with the little drama of the fire-log. I feel that I have some resemblance to that log, and shall try to make myself still more like it—so that in your hearth I can maintain a mild temperature and a gentle light!   F.L.

472. To Princess Carolyne. 20 April. . . . The music festival was decided on last December. I thought I had sent you the preliminary announcement published in the 1 January issue of Brendel's newspaper. You will understand why I thought, *at that time*, that August was the most suitable month for this

---

[5] From Petrarch's sonnet 'In nobil sangue vita umile e queta': 'The deserved praises, the great excellence, her worth, | enough to tire any divine poet.'

meeting. I am now no longer free to change the date, 5, 6, and 7 August—but if need be I shall get out of taking part, or else the festival will be postponed to next year. I enclose the initial announcement of 1 January; and in Brendel's next issue, which I shall send you, you will find the programme. First day: Beethoven's *Missa solemnis*, sung by the entire Riedel Society, about 200 people, who will come here for this purpose. Second day: my *Prometheus choruses* and the Faust Symphony—both scores will be published in mid-July. Third day, not yet decided: either a concert programme with Hans, Draeseke, Cornelius, and Damrosch—the New German School—or the Second Act of *Tristan*, with Schnorr and his wife, from Dresden, who have already studied the two principal roles in Karlsruhe and in Dresden recently promised me that they would sing them here. I have written about this to Wagner, who naturally has the right to conduct his own work. But, between ourselves, I doubt that this plan will be realized. As soon as I have a definitive reply from Wagner, I'll tell you about it. As for me, it has been agreed that I shall not conduct. Riedel will take the baton for Beethoven's Mass, Stör for *Prometheus*, and Hans or Lassen will conduct the Faust Symphony. I shall undertake only the preliminary rehearsals. . . .

Deign to allow me a request! Never justify to me what you intend doing or want to do—for I feel slightly humiliated at the thought that you consider yourself obliged to explain your reasons. In any case, August marks the extreme limit of the unsettled life I have been leading for several years. Probably I shall then, as you tell me to, lock up the Altenburg, dismiss the servants, etc. If by some ill chance it had not yet been granted to me to come and join you, I would go and settle in the first corner that could be found. Miss Anderson, to whom I have given your message, will remain here as long as you wish—although the poor woman must be bored to death, for my company is only a very mediocre resource for her; and she often lacks even that. I have agreed with her that the status quo will last until the beginning of August—without giving further explanations, except that by not leaving before then she would be doing you a service. That suits her because of Magne's confinement, during which, she tells me, she would not like to be too far away. Provided she can go back to England at the end of August, that is all she needs. When you write to her, keep her to this resolve which she, as it were, made of her own accord.

My relations with Mulinen have become very friendly, and I am taking real interest in him. We see one another 3 or 4 times a week, and he still keeps up his old habit of taking part in our lunch. His abrupt manner, which is so greatly disliked here, where he treats *tutti quanti* as idiots or worse, doesn't bother me in the least, because I for my own part have nothing to complain of. . . .

Be so kind as to present my sincere respects to Father Ferraris. The kind opinion he has formed of me, from what you have told him, does me an honour which I value highly. I often take part, in thought, in your Italian lessons with him, and thank you for having sent me the radiant sonnet for which you were his inspiration. I at once memorized the last three lines, which I now repeat with delight:

> L'italo accento sul tuo labbro or suona—
> Romano è il tuo pensier, romano il cuore,
> E sarà Roma a tuo desir corona!

Amen! F.L.

473. To Princess Carolyne. [Paris] 16 May.[6] . . . My task from now on will consist of writing things which have some value—and not in personally pushing them forward in the markets of Germany or France. The bit of celebrity attached to my name will effectively prevent their passing entirely unnoticed. To cite only one small detail in support of this opinion, I know that Verdi had several of my scores on his table in Genoa. I am even told that he speaks of them with particular consideration. So Rome suits me much better than any other town, seeing that you are happy there. I hope we shall find it possible to manage fairly economically—for I am more than tired of the enormous expense of our mode of life in Weimar, which I foolishly did not put a stop to immediately after your departure. Had I foreseen so long a separation, I would certainly have seen about another establishment, which would have cost me half the money and in addition enabled me to work uninterruptedly. Be that as it may, I hate lamentations and recriminations, so let's not speak of it any further —and let me just thank you for your sweet indulgence.

Here, I am trying not to spend too much money. My accommodation doesn't cost me more than 7 francs a day—but I need from 15 to 20 francs a day for the carriage. I definitely can't lunch or dine in 40-sou restaurants or at *tables d'hôtes*. I invite no one to dinner, and, contrary to my former habits, I take carriages by the hour, which costs me less. I have also been more or less compelled to spend 500 francs on clothes, it being a year since I had anything made in Weimar. My tailor is the celebrated Chevreuil, and I have ordered two complete outfits from him—one for the morning, the other for the evening. I also need to replenish my stock of underclothing to some extent, and have asked Blandine for advice. Forgive me these domestic details. God grant that I will soon no longer have to bother with all these things, which I know nothing about and which are obsessing me! . . .

---

[6] This letter, begun on Thursday the 16th, seems to have been finished on Friday the 17th.

All that you say about Wagner shows admirable acumen. Mère Elodie was quite right to compare you to Antonelli. I fancy that you could even go one better than he—in what touches on keen insight into certain circumstances of which both great and small are so often the playthings! From the letter Wagner wrote me before leaving Paris, and which I sent you, you have seen that he will not be returning here until next week. However his affairs turn out, I shall play only a rather limited part in them. . . . Forgive me if I contradict you—but Rome will be for us a very different thing from what Zurich was for Wagner. There will be all the difference between Frau Wagner and you, most infinitely dear one! . . . I can tell you that Ollivier has written an extremely severe letter to Frau Wagner who, it seems, made up some very unpleasant tittle-tattle about Blandine. After that, it will be difficult for relations to be renewed. I for my part shan't interfere, experience having taught me only too well the futility of trying to patch things up!

Our poor friend Berlioz is thoroughly dejected and filled with bitterness. His domestic life weighs on him like a nightmare, and outside he encounters only vexations and disappointments! I dined at his place with d'Ortigue, plus Mme Berlioz and her mother. It was dismal, sad, desolate! Berlioz's voice has become feebler. He generally speaks very quietly—and his whole being seems to incline towards the grave! I don't know how he has managed to isolate himself here in this way. In fact, he has neither friends nor supporters—neither the great sun of the public, nor the gentle shade of people close to him. The editorial staff of the *Journal des Débats* still backs and protects him. It is to this that he owes the commission for a little one-act opera[7] which will be performed in Baden-Baden next year. Bénazet, a contributor to the *Débats*, is giving him 4,000 francs for it. As for *Les Troyens*, it has little chance of being performed at the Opéra. In the autumn Gounod's *Reine de Saba* will be put on, followed by Meyerbeer's *L'Africaine*, and then a new work by Félicien David, and another by Gevaërt. The last-named is a protégé of the director of the Opéra, M. Royer, with whom Berlioz has all but fallen out on the subject of some alterations that Royer was insisting on in the libretto of *Les Troyens*. 'That', Berlioz told me, 'is the grain of sand on which I must run aground. The whole of the press is on my side, numerous friends support and urge me on, Count Walewski invites me to dinner, I have the honour of dining at HM the Emperor's—but all to no purpose! M. Royer doesn't want it—and there's nothing to be done!' His article on the Wagner concerts has harmed Berlioz at least as much as Wagner. . . .

---

[7] Actually a two-act opera, *Béatrice et Bénédict*, with words by the composer after Shakespeare's *Much Ado About Nothing*, was first performed at Baden-Baden in Aug. 1862.

Since I am talking to you of matters musical, I'll add that I have established good relations with Gounod—a likely candidate for membership of the Institut at the next vacancy, and much cleverer in his conduct than Berlioz. I also paid a call on Halévy, to thank him for his goodwill towards me—from what Belloni and Ollivier maintain—at the time of my negotiations with the Institut. He will be inviting me to dinner with Sainte-Beuve and a few other colleagues of his next week. As for Rossini, I am hoping for his goodwill too. He welcomed me very paternally, at once asked for news of you and made several very flattering remarks to me. My long hair gave him a desire to touch it and ask if it was really mine. I replied that I considered it entirely mine, to use or abuse as I wished. 'You are very fortunate, my dear friend,' he went on. Then, putting his hand on his own head, 'Look, nothing there any more—and I have hardly any teeth or legs left either.' His musical recreation consists in writing piano sonatas to which he attaches alimentary titles such as 'fresh butter', 'chick peas', or 'green peas', and 'cherries' or 'apricots', and I don't know what else besides. I shall decipher them [play them at sight] tomorrow evening, after dinner at his place.

My relations with the Metternichs* seem to be shaping fairly well. The Princess has invited me to be one of a small gathering at Count Walewski's tomorrow, Saturday. I shall go. M. le Duc Tascher de la Pagerie, to whom I took some charming lines from Hebbel, received me very well. The Sphinx [Napoleon III] will probably do me the honour of seeing me soon. I had to write to him to this end, and Pce Metternich undertook to have my note delivered. . . .

These are my dinner invitations for the week. Tomorrow, Rossini; Sunday, Mère Elodie, which will be a joy for me. Monday, Autran with Lamartine, whom thus far it has been impossible for me to see—he receives only at 8.00 in the evening, and goes to bed at 10.00, but people dine so late that I haven't been able to slip away. Tuesday, *chez* Mme Erard, with the Olliviers and Janin, at La Muette; Wednesday, Ollivier with Leroux, who will read us his translation and recasting of the Book of Job; Thursday, Lacombe—probably with Dollfus, the Kreutzers, Ollivier, *et al.* Incidentally, don't be too reserved in your relations with Ampère.[8] He is perfectly agreeable and *comme il faut*. I met him in times past with Sainte-Beuve, and, as you know, he was one of the intimates of the Abbaye-aux-Bois, with Mme Récamier.

Herr von Reumont is credited with being as witty as he is ugly, which is saying not a little. We had a sight of one another at Wilhelmsthal, *chez* Monseigneur, and the latter corresponds fairly frequently with him. It seems to me

---

[8] Not the mathematician and physicist, but his son Jean-Jacques Ampère, historian and philologist.

that when an opportunity comes along you could also make the acquaintance of Gregorovius.* . . .

May God grant me the grace of seeing you soon!   F.L.

474. To Agnes Street-Klindworth [Paris, 17 May]. Your kind lines of 8 to 15 May reached me punctually, as did the letter from an autograph collector, M. Powell (to whom I shall reply shortly), who had the sense to write to the rue Belliard address. . . .

My mother is enduring her unfortunate condition with exemplary patience and perfect equanimity. She can hardly manage to get up, or rather to have herself lifted out of bed so that she can sit in an armchair, and she will probably be condemned to crutches for the rest of her days. My daughter and her husband are admirable in the solicitude and affectionate regard they show her. It's really moving, and I see in it, as it were, the blessing of Providence for my good intentions, in which I have never been entirely wanting, despite my many follies. Thanks to my mother being given a home at the Olliviers', I am completely reassured about an eventuality which must inevitably arrive in the long run. Alas! (as said M. de Vigny), what sort of world is it in which one arrives with the *hope* of seeing one's father and mother die!

The photographs for which I am indebted to you will be welcome. If you say you are satisfied with them, they have of necessity turned out very well; for I flatter myself that you are harder to please in what concerns my sorry person than I have the right to be myself. Tomorrow morning I have to sit for M. Salomon, a well-known sculptor and photographer here—and will bring you this new example of my likeness, if it turns out well. I shall add to it a photograph of a relief of Chopin which Salomon has promised me.

My relations with my son-in-law Ollivier, whom I barely knew, have got on to the best and warmest footing. He is by nature at once upright, intelligent, and ardent—further, he has a rare and delightful feeling for music.... which is a way of saying that he enjoys mine. Among other things he has taken a particular liking to the phrase in the Dante [Symphony] that you know.

Wagner will be back in 4 or 5 days. He left a few lines for me before leaving —on the very day of my arrival.

M. de Mulinen, with whom I had taken accommodation in a furnished and very neat little house, rue Castellane 5, returned to Frankfurt in the evening of the day before yesterday. . . . I dined with him in a small gathering at the Metternichs' last Monday. Gounod had brought the score of his *Faust*, and for pudding I did him the honours of his Waltz, to the great satisfaction of those present.

There is talk of scraping together a nice little sum for Wagner by mounting performances, *for his benefit*, of *Tannhäuser* or *Lohengrin* on every stage in Germany. Berlin will set the ball rolling, and the others will follow. This practical idea has been dreamt up by Pourtalès, or Hatzfeld—or Pcss Metternich—or even the Queen of Prussia and I don't know who else besides. For my own part, I am all for it—and it is solely a matter of passing on the proceeds to Wagner.

As for our friend Berlioz, he is utterly dejected and embittered. His *Troyens* have been postponed indefinitely, and he is hardly managing to *recover* from his wife. What a yoke!

This evening I shall dine at Gounod's, and tomorrow with Rossini, who welcomed me very paternally . . .

If I am presented to His Majesty it will be through Metternich. . . .

Affectionately yours,   F.L.

475. To Princess Carolyne. 28 May. This last fortnight I have had a kind of St Martin's summer of *fashion*. . . . My official explanation of it is this. Pcss Metternich has deigned to take pleasure in making me *à la mode* again. She has convinced Court and town that I have talent—and that I am a well-behaved fellow whom one can pet. In this she has been surprisingly successful, just as it becomes her to succeed in all things!—The truly gracious kindness shown to me by Their Majesties the Emperor and Empress has been quite exceptional, and I have every reason to be personally grateful to them for it. There is also talk of promoting me at once to the rank of Commandeur of the Legion of Honour. I have already been congratulated on this topic—although I have thus far received no official notification of it. Mme d'Agoult—whom I saw yesterday, after the note I am sending you—did not fail to confirm what I had heard already: people were talking of me a good deal and repeating 'witticisms' uttered by me, or so it is claimed! It was probably an allusion to the loyal response I gave to the Emperor, after dinner at the Tuileries last Wednesday. His Majesty asked me about feelings in Germany with regard to the present policy. 'Of great hostility towards France—quite natural, for that matter.' He remarked that he did not agree that it was *natural*—without for that reason objecting to my reply. During the course of the evening the Emperor showed a certain lack of restraint towards me, saying rather emotionally: 'I sometimes feel as though I were 100 years old.'—You can guess my response![9]

So far as retorts, witty or otherwise, are concerned, here is one that I made in the cutting tone that you have more than once rightly reproached me for.

---

[9] 'Sire, you are the century!'

Mme Delphine Potocka[10] was dining at the Rothschilds'—and over coffee she interrogated me about you, which led to quite a sharp little exchange between us. Continuing, she asked rather abruptly: 'And her daughter, where is she?' —This question, put in a decidedly casual manner, reminded me of the interest taken in you in 'your regions', and I replied: 'I am not obliged, Madame, to serve as your information bureau—but if you are curious about it, you can find out from the *Almanach de Gotha.*' I thus avoided, as she did, pronouncing the name of the Pcss Hohenlohe, which seems to scorch the tongues of certain people! . . .

                                                                               F.L.

476. To Princess Carolyne. 9.00 a.m., Wednesday, 5 June. Franco[11]

has just left me. I had already seen him last Sunday, at his place. Talking to me of you, of your apartment, of your diet, of your progress in Italian, etc., he has made the best possible impression on me. . . . My departure from here remains fixed for Saturday. Although I feel tolerably tired with my *vie de salon* here, I can only be flattered by the welcome being given to me everywhere. To give you the pitch of the vogue which has attached itself to me, I enclose three little newspaper cuttings. The brief note about Lamartine's soirée appeared in *Le Siècle* of 3 June. It's an improvement, it seems to me, on Pcss Belgiojoso's celebrated invitation cards, on which she had added in her own hand: 'M. Liszt will play.' The fact is, people have been singularly curious about me! They have such charming manners in Paris that it would almost be in bad taste for me not to be fairly agreeable too. This does not prevent me from remarking occasionally that I am here practising a trade which I am no longer equal to, and for which I have no taste!

On Monday I dined and spent the evening at the Duchâtels'. M. Duchâtel, a former minister of Louis-Philippe, had signed the document recording my elevation to the rank of Chevalier of the Legion of Honour, and I thought it appropriate not to forget him at this moment. Furthermore, they have been extremely kind to Bülow. They are generally held to be people sitting very comfortably on a fortune of several million, which they put to splendid use—they also possess refined taste in matters of art. Among other things M. Duchâtel possesses Ingres's famous painting *La Source*, an extremely beautiful Ruysdael, and a unique Memling. Yesterday I had another dinner with the Rothschilds

[10] A talented singer, this Polish countess had been on friendly terms with Chopin and was the dedicatee of his Second Piano Concerto and Waltz Op. 64/1.
[11] The Princess's doctor in Rome.

in Boulogne,[12] where they have found a way of making a kind of Versailles. Changarnier, Vitet, the Pce and Pcsse de Ligne, Delphine Potocka, *et al.*, were there. It was agreed that there would be no music—however, it was not possible to refrain from it entirely. This evening I shall be at Lamartine's—and tomorrow *chez* Wagner, who is of course fuming at hardly seeing me. On Friday, Poniatowski is giving me a dinner with Auber, Halévy, Gounod, Théophile Gautier, Berlioz without Wagner, *et al.* This will be for me a kind of prelude to my candidature for the Institut.[13]

'Voilà pour le moment', to quote Belloni—who is naturally in a kind of fever of delight at the fuss people are making of me. Mère Elodie leaves this evening. I am giving her the picture of St Monica. The photograph is not sold separately, but is published in Scheffer's complete works, with a text by Vitet. . . . I am looking forward to finding your letters in Weimar. You know that I can only live through you and for you.   F.L.

477. To Princess Carolyne. [Weimar] Wednesday, 12 June. As I entered this house once again, my whole soul dissolved into blessings for you! No human words could express the intensity, the radiance, the depth of what I feel for you in my heart! This afternoon I shall go to Desméloizes to claim my treasures—but I couldn't sit down at this table without my thoughts winging their way first and foremost to you! I must also apologize for the abbreviated, inadequate letters I sent you from Paris. In the present one I shall try to fill a few gaps. . . . Although I did nothing but play the piano in one place or another during those three weeks, it seems to me that people weren't mistaken in regarding me as having some slight significance. It would be futile now to lay stress on things that can only be surmised. Come what may, I was agreeably moved when, a moment ago, I read the diploma recording my elevation to Commandeur, worded as follows: 'HM the Emperor, by decree of 29 May 1861, has promoted to the rank of Commandeur of the Legion of Honour M. Liszt, Franz, composer. To take effect from that same day. Signed: the Grand Chancellor, etc. Paris, 31 May 61.' The omission of any other little titles of mine, and the perfect simplicity and accuracy of the designation 'composer', add still more to the unexpected satisfaction given me by this diploma—through which the Emperor will certainly not have made an ingrate! If, as is said, opportunity makes the

---

[12] Boulogne-sur-Seine (now Boulogne-Billancourt), south-west of Paris.

[13] The Institut de France, a learned society made up of the five academies: *française, des inscriptions et belles-lettres, des sciences, des beaux-arts, des sciences morales et politiques*. Liszt's candidature was unsuccessful.

thief, it can also, as an exception, make anything else. I have always had a secret instinct that one day it would help me. Hence this strange unconstraint which for long years became as it were my second nature—earning me from Pcss Belgiojoso the reproach that I lived as though I were immortal!

That epithet brings me back to the Institut. At Poniatowski's dinner, last Friday, I found myself in the company of Auber, Halévy, Berlioz, Gounod, and Théophile Gautier, among others. After the coffee I brought up directly the question of my candidature at the next vacancy. Halévy, without being unfavourable to me, laid before me a few observations on the rather unacademic character of my musical leanings, and above all those of my school in Germany—which is taking it into its head to do nothing less than anathematize and burn everything that had until now been adored. My reply was as frank as it was explicit. I declared unreservedly my great admiration for the genius of Wagner, which I have made it a point of honour to profess for the last 12 years, in all circumstances—while distinguishing in Wagner the three elements of theorist, poet, and musician. Nowhere have I written or said that I subscribed to any iconoclastic theory whatsoever; on the contrary, I have everywhere expressed the enthusiasm inspired in me by Beauty—Beauty of any kind, even. As far as art is concerned, theories hardly matter to me. Without denying them a certain critical and relative value, I should find it impossible to ascribe to them the generative power which matters above all else and which belongs to inspiration alone. Wagner is the poet and dramatic musician of present-day Germany—and that is enough for me to pay him full homage. . . .

I don't know if Halévy was entirely satisfied with my explanations. Nevertheless, he asked me if I wished to make them public, when I became a candidate for the Institut, by writing, either to Sainte-Beuve or to some other person, a letter which would reassure my numerous friends in regard to the suspicions which have been raised against me. There would be nothing inconvenient in that, when the moment comes—that is to say, if and when I believe that my chances are more or less certain. Otherwise, no. From what he told me, it is in early autumn that they will set about replacing Rietschel and Chélard as corresponding members. I asked him to inform me about the steps I should have to take at that time, and in the mean time to regard me as a candidate *in spe*. Actually, it's the title of foreign associate member that I aspire to, and which in a given time would come to me—but only Rossini and Meyerbeer occupy this rank. Now, Rossini's natural successor is Verdi—and Meyerbeer's, Wagner. In view of my unusual position as a composer who has written nothing for the theatre, I can compete with neither the one nor the other. Moreover, you know, dearest one, that I am by no means keen to pursue honours, and that the failures I would experience in this field wouldn't trouble me. From a certain point of view, it would be entirely just for the various prominent individuals in art to be part of the academy—and from that point of view I have a right to be one of them. May this be said without any lack of modesty—for true modesty does not lie in ignorance or concealment of one's ability; it is simply one's own moral decency. By virtue of this sentiment, therefore, I can at one and the same time claim my place in the Institut—and remain in perfect equanimity, whether it is granted, or denied, me.

Thursday. My first visit yesterday was of course to Desméloizes, for I was hoping to find your letters there. They haven't arrived yet, and the next post won't be for another ten days or so. As luck would have it, this morning I was brought a short letter, sent to Paris, in which you tell me of the arrival of the photographs. . . .

478. To Princess Carolyne. 18 June. . . . Scotland will leave here in mid-August—and I shall then dismiss the household servants. I should like to make an exception of Otto, however, whom it seems to me more prudent to keep a little longer—either by leaving him here, or by bringing him with me. A few days after the festival I shall do my packing—and will see how I can manage. At worst, I shall go and spend some time at Pce Hohenzollern's or at St Tropez in the Olliviers' cottage. In any case, I shall leave Weimar for quite a long time. Need I tell you that Our Lady of Loreto or Florence would be Paradise for me?[14] . . .

Monseigneur invited me to dinner at Ettersburg on Monday—and gave me a splendid welcome, as did the Grand Duchess. In response to his question about the news I had received from Rome, I said, 'I haven't been expecting any for several months'—thus avoiding entering into details, which would at the very least have been absolutely useless. He also said to me among other things: 'The Emperor didn't ask you to give me his compliments?'—'That's because he didn't consider me worthy.'—To other people who ask me how you are, I reply imperturbably, 'Well, very well, perfect'—or else, 'In perfect health of body and mind.' When, despite the conclusive tone I adopt on these occasions, someone ventures to question me about your return, I cut them short with: 'But the Princess has absolutely no reason or desire to return. I, for my part, very much wish her to remain in Rome, where everything suits her wonderfully.' . . .

Yours with all the anguish and aspiration of my soul. F.L.

---

[14] The Princess was at this time thinking of Loreto and Florence, as well as Rome, as possible places for the wedding.

479. To Princess Carolyne. Saturday morning [29 June]. The whole of yesterday from 2 o'clock onwards I spent at Ettersburg. To begin with, the Grand Duchess kept me alone for a couple of hours. After dinner, the discussion began again, this time with her husband too. Neither of them admits the possibility of my leaving Weimar for good—and told me earnestly how fond they are of me and how greatly they value me. For my own part, I merely paraphrased the letter I wrote to Monseigneur last autumn, I believe, in which I indicated to him that a new phase of my life had now begun. The German newspapers having just spread the rumour that the Emperor Napoleon had appointed me *Ober-Intendant* of the music of his household—they assumed, or pretended to assume, that this circumstance had induced me to leave Weimar. I reassured them on this point, by affirming that I would no more take up musical duties in Paris than in Vienna or Berlin, where there had likewise, and on several occasions, been talk of finding a post for me. As the Grand Duchess did not find my explanations clear enough, I summarized matters for her roughly thus: 'From 1848 until the time of Pcss Marie's marriage, in '59, it was she who remained the centre of gravity, *Schwerpunkt,* of our entire position. Anything that could suit her present or her future necessarily became imperative for us. Since then, my centre of gravity, although it hasn't for that reason exactly changed, can only be Pcss Carolyne. So I have only to concern myself before all, and above all, with her—and her alone! I know that she follows me blindly, and with an affection and devotion that quite preclude any question of sacrifice between her and me. It is my wishes that have kept her in Rome until now—and she will probably remain there for some time yet. However, the moment might come in which I should have to ask her to leave Rome. It is for such an eventuality that I have to keep myself ready to make her existence tolerable. Now, rightly or wrongly, I am so vain as to believe that if all my time is given up to her, her sufferings will be alleviated. The obstacles which have got in the way of our marriage may continue indefinitely. I am no longer taking it into my head to count on a solution favourable to us. On the contrary, I am expecting only bad luck, so that I can as well as possible protect us from its blows. Such as we are made, both of us, we fundamentally need only one another. Several people could undoubtedly, and in good conscience, have done us good turns. But since, instead of that, we have been done only a good many bad turns, it really is necessary to look facts in the face and, without surrendering anything of our right, readily to accept the fate which has been prepared for us.'

As an additional factor, I laid great stress on the enormous expense involved in running the Altenburg—an expense it was impossible for us to be equal to after Pcss Marie's departure. This *de luxe* existence was not only not leading me to anything but, further, was personally disagreeable to me—the emptiness of my artistic position offering me no compensation for the financial burden. Without laying stress on my career or my position, I laid it down as a principle that, you apart, I had become more than indifferent to everything that concerned me—and had long attended to it as only a tiresome second best. Incidentally, I made them realize to some extent how your [our?] ideas on almost all questions of art in Weimar were little suited to the ways and customs of the place—from the project of the *Fondation Goethe* to Dingelstedt's Intendancy and the painting academy. To this they of course responded that I was mistaken, that I was wrong, that I should be aware of the affection surrounding me and of the regard which showed me that I was appreciated, esteemed, coddled, spoilt—in a word, that they neither wanted to, nor could, do without me. I replied gently and without any ill humour that I had hardly noticed it, and that in any case I would not leave Weimar as an ingrate! I even asked Their Highnesses' pardon for talking to them at such length on so slight a topic as myself, assuring them that I had intended not to weary them with it any more. I was thinking of writing to them, plainly and matter-of-factly, after my departure, which will be effected without fuss, and with no sentimentalities or farewell suppers whatsoever, the circumstances in which I am placed not allowing me to derive any pleasure from saying, or in hearing said to me, things which I know better than others do!

You understand, infinitely dear one, the turn this conversation took—the provisional outcome of which I shall tell you further on. All my decisions are based on a negative eventuality, one which so far as our marriage is concerned I regard as probable. When Monseigneur asked me repeatedly if he couldn't do me some service, either by letter or by taking some direct step—I replied explicitly, 'No, and again no!' . . . In thanking him for his goodwill, I asked him totally to refrain from taking any step. I was merely biding my time to tell him at the requisite moment what would have to be done—if he can indeed do anything, which I do not assume. 'For the moment all I need do is leave here quietly.'—'Where will you go?'—'Perhaps I shall stay in the little house my son-in-law Emile Ollivier possesses at St Tropez—perhaps ask Pce Hohenzollern to put me up for a while—or perhaps make a trip to Greece. The Princess cannot endure northern climes very well. She has had some serious illnesses in Weimar. Moreover, she is capable of spending days admiring the shaft or the capital of a Corinthian column. I cannot pride myself on an equal capability, but will certainly share in the pleasure that will give her. Let me assure you, Monseigneur, that I have no other objective than what will suit the Princess. I should be a scoundrel were I to do other than concentrate all my efforts on obtaining for her at least a little peace.' The proposal for us to get married clandestinely at one of Monseigneur's country seats—Zella, in the Oberland I believe, where there is a Catholic priest—was brought up again. Since Monseigneur said, 'That is not unfeasible', I cut him short by retorting, 'Unfeasible thrice over!'—At the very end, the Grand Duchess said: 'One little house is as good as another—accept one of those that the Grand Duke has several times offered you. If you do indeed have such need to live in solitude, go and stay in Dornburg, or at Zella, where rooms suitable for you and your manservant will be prepared. But don't leave those in Weimar until you believe the time has come to join the Princess in Rome. Even then, promise us that you will not consider your absence as other than a journey, from which Weimar will always mark the return.'

All this was said at greater length, with the precision and the grace of mind which characterize the Grand Duchess—so that I could only agree. We thus exchanged thanks and parted good friends—until the time when matters take a more definite turn. . . .

Your 6 letters of May and June reached me simultaneously yesterday, through Desméloizes. As yet I have been able to read only the 3 latest. . . . By the way, Froriep and Preller, the librarian, have died. Thank you for the magnificent description of the feast of St Philip Neri. The carriage bearing Antonelli—whose letter gave me profound satisfaction, and which I'll return to when writing to you tomorrow—I can see from here. . . .

May God soon bring me to you at Our Lady of Loreto!   F.L.

The box for your letters I have ordered at Bauer's.

480. To Princess Carolyne. 29 June.[15] His Eminence's letter has given me one of those rare and delicate satisfactions which, as you know, I appreciate to excess. Notwithstanding the simplicity of its content, which is just a polite note of thanks,[16] it has in form and appearance that character of striking distinction exclusively peculiar to the 'supremacy' born to command, not to insinuate. When you find an opportunity, please, I beg you, tell His Eminence how flattered I am that he took the trouble to pen me these autograph lines. Although I have more or less forgotten the very little Italian I knew 20 years ago, I believe I have perfectly well understood what the Cardinal tells me, as well as the gracious manner in which he does so. There is only one point on which I am not entirely clear—knowing if the words he uses to sign off, 'servitore vero', are a formula very generally used in Italy, or if, as I think, it shows a special nuance of consideration. Be so good as to let me know. As for the phrase 'sensi della mia più distinta e sentita stima', I find it charming and much subtler than the French

---

[15] Evidently written later the same day rather than the next day referred to at the end of the previous letter.
[16] For Liszt's generous contribution to Peter's pence.

'expression' or 'assurance'. Once again, this letter has delighted me—and I doubt whether the Cardinal possesses in his magnificent collection of stones a specimen as pleasing to him as his lines are precious to me.

I promised to tell you about my visit to the Hôtel Montaigne. Alas! The memories which led me there are extremely sad, and the one which has been added to them is not of a kind to make them more serene. Nélida did not see me again to tell me of anything that could have interested us—but only because many people were speaking to her of me, of my little successes and even of my *bons mots*. My daughters' names were pronounced only casually, at the end of my last visit, the day I left Paris. She then asked me why I had prevented Cosima from following her real vocation—that of an artistic career!! According to Nélida, that was what was most suitable! On this point, as on so many others, I am unable to share her opinion. This radical disagreement in our temperaments showed itself right at the start of our first interview, when we chatted about very general things only, such as the principle of nationalities, Hungary and Poland, the politics of the Tuileries and of Cavour, etc. As you know, on the sea of nationalities she proceeds at full steam ahead! Without stopping her fine flow of words I quoted Lamartine's article on Italy, which she found more than stupid. When I observed that this article had created something of a sensation at the Foreign Ministry, she replied with her doctoral aplomb, 'Certainly not; anyone who has spent only a week in Italy will never share M. de Lamartine's opinion!' . . .

When I was taking my leave of her, Nélida asked if I would have dinner with her one day. 'With great pleasure—but I shall find it difficult to find a free day.'—'In that case perhaps you will come for lunch?'—'Thank you, I accept.'—'Whom do you wish me to invite?'—'Whomever you like—anyone who will think me good enough to merit the honour of being in your home.'—She suggested Mme de Pierreclos, Lamartine's niece, whom I ruled out—giving as a pretext my disinclination for female company. I suggested Ronchaud, whom she alleged to be invariably boring. She then mentioned Guéroult of the *Opinion nationale*, Nefzer, and a few others. Eventually I said, 'Arrange it how you like. As far as I am concerned, anything will suit me—either the two of us alone, or *tutti quanti*. Incidentally, I should let you know that I have lost my former habits of sobriety. I eat a lot—having acquired an appetite when eating in the homes of a great many people.'—'You will be served as much as you like, for there is an excellent cook in the house.'—We agreed on a Friday, I believe, for this lunch. . . . It was excellent and served to perfection. All the guests did justice to it, and the conversation flowed along very nicely. Nélida maintained, of course, that in France there was no longer either good taste or good form—that there was no longer either talk or conversation—that all interest in matters of the intellect had disappeared—that plenty of building work was going on, but that it certainly didn't amount to architecture, etc., etc. You can imagine how all this nonsense was to my taste. And so I did not fail to cast a good many stones into the fine flower-beds of her blossoming rhetoric—by maintaining, stoutly, that our own age was at least as good as any other, that there was always a prodigious amount of intelligence in France, and that the Seven Wonders of the ancient world put together did not equal the reconstruction of Paris being carried out by the Emp. Napoleon. Thereupon I took my leave, the first to do so, a few minutes after the coffee, and returned, without having announced myself beforehand, on the day of my departure, about a week later.

I found her alone. We spoke of Mme Sand, whom I had intended to visit at Nohant—but she was still in the south, near Toulon. Her two latest novels have had a very decided success, and in France her name is more popular than ever. The whole mounting tide of newspapers proclaims her the greatest writer of her time. The incident of the prize of 20,000 francs from the Académie established this fact with new *éclat*—so much so that M. Thiers himself was put in the shade. Nélida told me that M. de Girardin had taken it into his head to arrange a meeting between her and Mme Sand—but that this reunion hadn't come any-where near patching things up. I remarked that they had parted too badly—ever to meet again gladly! 'What about you,' she went on, 'have you remained a good friend of hers?'—'Your estrangement rather cooled my relations with her—for although *au fond* I regarded you as being in the wrong, I stood up for you none the less.'—'I believed the contrary.'—'Groundlessly, as of old.'—In connection with Goethe and his biographer, Lewes, I mentioned Miss Evans, George Eliot. It seems that she has written two novels—whose titles I forget—which are very highly spoken of, so much so that several well-known critics in England regard Miss Evans as Mme Sand's only rival. This was a sore point for Nélida. Fortunately her superiority as a historian and publicist remains intact. From time to time she writes articles for *Le Siècle* and also for *Le Temps*—a new paper, founded by Nefzer. After we had chatted about various literary and polit-ical matters, I gave the conversation a more personal turn. Wagner, the Music of the Future, the part I was taking in the present-day musical movement, etc., had been touched upon several times in my very first visit; I returned to these topics in more detail—and showed her very plainly that to continue along my path I needed neither friends nor party nor newspapers. 'Guermann's walls are already painted', I told her, 'and he will paint others too—without bothering in the least about rubbish spoken or printed by others.' She was struck by my voluntary isolation, and perhaps, too, by the strange significance of my artistic life. Not that she has ever much noticed it, but at that moment it seemed to flash upon her. Hearing me talk of myself like that, of my egoism and my ambi-tion, of the part I play for the public and of the one which remains reserved for the artist, of the total identification of my endeavours of former days with my ideas of today, of the permanence of this self that she had found so 'hateful'—she felt some kind of emotion, and her whole face filled with tears. I kissed her on the forehead, for the first time for many long years, and said, 'Look, Marie, let me speak to you in the language of the peasants. May God bless you! Don't wish me ill!'—She could make no response at that moment—but her tears flowed still more abundantly. Ollivier had told me that when he was in Italy with her, he had several times seen her weeping bitterly in various places which reminded her more particularly of our youth. I told her that I had been touched by this remembrance. All but stammeringly, she said, 'I shall always remain faithful to *Italy*—and to *Hungary*!' Thereupon I quietly left her. On my way downstairs I thought of my poor Daniel! His name had not once been mentioned during the 3 or 4 hours I had spent talking with his mother!!! . . .

May God be with you—and bring me to Our Lady of Loreto!!   F.L.

481. To Princess Carolyne. 6 July. By this post I am sending you a letter of Rossini's. When returning to Weimar I had asked him for the titles of his 4 albums—and sent him my Dante [Symphony] and some of my other symphonic poems. The copy of the Dante I skimmed through with him in Paris had been lent to me by Wagner. The 'pure-blooded Italian melodist', as Rossini signs his letter, didn't find himself in his natural element when *reading* my Francesca da Rimini episode, which perhaps borders on a more elevated region of the soul. Yet I fancy that if he heard it, then with that marvellous intuition so suited to his genius he would quickly grasp what I wanted to express. Be that as it may, his letter is charming, and delicately flattering. I am going to write a few lines of thanks to Mme Rossini, for the truly 'superlicocantious' naming of those titles —a word invented by Rabelais which will make you laugh. Please let me have the titles back sometime. Here, further, are 31 photographs of the royal houses of Prussia and Saxony, and the photographs of the Grand Duke and Duchess of Baden. . . .

What becomes of me after 15 August depends entirely on what news I receive from you. In any event, I shall leave Weimar. I have spoken of St Tropez so as to suggest a place in keeping with my financial circumstances—very openly acknowledged in high places—and also to indicate that I shall not be going to Paris. Through my last letter you will have seen the new turn I am giving to the situation. It is not fitting for me to be mysterious *vis-à-vis* Their Highnesses, to whom nevertheless I cannot speak too exclusively of you. Seeing that you think it a good idea for me to take the road to Vienna, it goes without saying that

St Tropez falls into the Mediterranean. I shall continue to speak of it only so as not to go back on what I said. For the rest, you know that I have also mentioned Löwenberg—which, in the case of a longer delay, suits me much better. . . .

Brendel has just spent three days at the Altenburg, to come to an agreement with me on various matters relating to the music festival, the provisional programme of which I enclose. Through you and for you. F.L.

482. To Princess Carolyne. 14 July. . . . . Their Highnesses are spending a few days at Altstedt, a newly furnished hunting lodge 6 leagues from Ettersburg. I had the honour of seeing the Grand Duchess 4 or 5 days ago. She spoke of nothing but violins, asking me to find her one with a bow soft and velvety enough not to grate upon her. I shall try to do as she wishes. For the rest, the Grand Duchess is still, within limits, the same witty, tactful, precise woman—with the utterly charming and noble manner that you know. Have I told you that Monseigneur is working on a history of Saxony that he intends to have printed?— And the Grand Duchess, I am told, is writing her memoirs. The Duke of Gotha is no slowcoach either. He has just mounted a *Turn- und Schützenfest* [festival of gymnastics and rifle shooting] at Gotha which went off with the greatest éclat, enormously enhancing his popularity. People are beginning to call him the Victor Emmanuel, and even the crowned Garibaldi, of Germany. Others, it is true, are reminded of Philippe-Egalité! Time will show!

As regards princely literature, you know that the Duc d'Aumale is writing a life of the great Condé;[17] and the French Empress is said to be writing an epistolary novel, in collaboration with Pce and Pcss Metternich and Pce Reuss, secretary of the Prussian Legation.

Here, nothing worth mentioning has happened all this week. I have been busy with various preparations for the music festival, in honour of which I have to write a good many letters and also undertake some preliminary rehearsals. . . . Oh! How I long to be quit of all this, and to breathe another air! Last night I again woke up saying an Ave Maria and thinking of Our Lady of Loreto! . . .

F.L.

483. To Princess Carolyne. Friday morning [19 July]. After my lunch [yesterday] with Pissareff, who has left again for Prague, I went to Ettersburg, whither Monseigneur had had me invited for dinner. There I found Watzdorf, Werthern, Prussian Minister in Athens, Beust, and Reumont. The last-named

---

[17] *Histoire des Princes de Condé pendant les XVIe et XVIIe siècles* (Paris, 1863–96).

was placed on the left of the Grand Duchess, and I between him and Walther
Goethe. I spoke to him of Ferrières in Florence and Ampère in Rome. From
what I have heard, Reumont's position at present is not one of the most brilliant. He complains among other things of having been obliged to leave his
entire library packed in chests at Florence—which is extremely inconvenient
for him for his work. He tells me that, as a minister dismissed from office, he
no longer has any residence at all! For the rest, I could extract nothing from
him of any interest. Not having read his book about the Countess of Albany,[18]
I deemed it more prudent not to speak to him of it. Over coffee, the Grand
Duke remarked to me, 'Have you ever seen anyone as ugly as Reumont?'—
'On that score,' I replied, 'it is a letter of permanent recommendation, for it
seems impossible for Providence not to have compensated the mind for the flaws
of the face.' . . .

When I got home yesterday evening I found the enclosed letter from Eduard,
to whom I shall reply to say that I expect him and his wife on 2 August. . . . I
shall put off sorting our books, music, and papers until after his departure. . . .

May God grant us a beautiful and noble life—united in faith and love!

F.L.

484. To Princess Carolyne. Erbprinz Hotel [Weimar] 12 August. I
find it impossible to assemble and bring together in concentrated form the emotions of my final hours at the Altenburg. Every room, every piece of furniture,
to the very steps of the staircase and the garden lawn—everything was illumined
by your love, without which I felt annihilated! Just as I telegraphed to you, I
left this house—where for 12 years you so ardently practised the Good and sought
the Beautiful—at 2 o'clock in the afternoon, in full sunlight, arm in arm with
Eduard who, I believe, has faithfully carried out all your instructions. He left
for Vienna at 4 o'clock. When I went through the rooms in the morning I could
not restrain my tears. But after making a final stop at your prie-dieu—where
you used to kneel with me before I went on a journey—a comfortable feeling
of release came over me. . . . Among the numerous objects to which I had become
attached, and which ceaselessly spoke to me of you, there is one which, I know
not why, I now think of as the veil of a sanctuary. Forgive me this rather whimsical comparison. It is the cloth with the flowers and the talisman that you embroidered for me. I saw them in my mind's eye when falling asleep last night—and

---

[18] *Die Gräfin von Albany* (2 vols., Berlin, 1860). Louise, Countess of Albany, was first the wife of Prince Charles
Eduard Stuart ('Bonnie Prince Charlie'), then the mistress of the great Alfieri and, after the latter's death, of a French
painter, François Xavier Fabre.

I sense that I shall never be separated from them again. I carried away with me under my arm your daguerreotype portrait from Petersburg, and the box for your letters, delivered to me by Bauer three days ago, in which I have had your Rome photograph framed. These are my lares and penates—or, to put it more like a Christian, my sweet guardian angels!

Eduard will send you full details of all the formalities carried out, the inventory, correct form of procedure, seals, which he increased rather than reduced, complying for that matter very fully with both the spirit and the letter of your instructions. Our double seal has been put on all the doors—and the seal of the *Hofmarschallamt* [Court Marshal's Office] on the four main doors. The blue room, my bedroom and yours, as well as some other windows, have been barred with wooden planks in accordance with your orders. All measures have been taken so that, in all human probability, no unfortunate accident can happen. I have yet to buy a bracelet costing 150 thalers for Miss Anderson. She is spending a few more days here at the Sabinins', with whom she is on very friendly terms. Before returning to England she will probably go to Vienna.[19] . . .

The music festival went off perfectly. I'll tell you about it at another time. For the moment, here is a brief provisional article which will acquaint you with what was done. Wagner was very nice to me—and last Friday, at the pre-departure lunch, proposed a toast to you, which moved us very deeply. . . .

                                                                        F.L.

485. To Princess Carolyne. Löwenberg, 23 August. I telegraphed you the day before yesterday from Leipzig—and arrived here, as I planned, yesterday evening, Thursday, at 6.00. From 5.00 on Saturday the 17th until midday on Sunday, I stayed with the Duke of Coburg at Reinhardsbrunn. He got back in good health and excellent form from his sea baths at Ostend. His popularity in Germany is increasing. . . .

At Wilhelmsthal, where I have just spent more than two days—from 5.00 on Sunday until midnight on Tuesday—I met the Pces of Orléans, the Comte de Paris, and the Duc de Chartres. They were accompanied by Comte Montguyon and General Trollenveau; and in their honour the Comte de Bouillé and the Marquis de Passy, *fils*, had also come to Wilhelmsthal. M. de Bouillé gave me the impression of being a man of wit and talent. He busies himself with chemistry, possesses a fine fortune, and keeps abreast of the more exalted kind of

---

[19] In his next letter (15 Aug.) to Carolyne, Liszt wrote: 'Miss Anderson has just left for England. She is going back to her brother's, a vicar in Somerset—and will write to you on arrival. We had a very nice leave-taking, with emotion on both sides.'

literature. I dined thrice with the Princes, without for that reason becoming much better acquainted with them. They are reserved, but with pleasant manners. The one and the other struck me as being very young! . . .

I shall tell you one day about my conversation on Sunday evening with Monseigneur; it lasted more than two hours. At a certain moment I said to him, 'If you call democrats those who do not consent to beg—my friends and I are arch-democrats!' On Tuesday afternoon he offered me with extreme good grace a chamberlain's key. He will send the official document here to Löwenberg for me—for I was determined not to prolong my stay at Wilhelmsthal. The Grand Duchess is openly favourable to me—and particularly asked me to tell you about her. I said not a word about the contents of your two latest letters, and limited myself to maintaining my previously mentioned plan of a winter sojourn either at St Tropez or in Athens—in any case, far from Germany, in view of my wish to spend a winter without an overcoat. My conversations with the Grand Duchess were not much shorter than those I had with her husband. She treated me nobly, *en grand artiste*—and as someone of whom she has a pretty high opinion. The opinion I have had of her for several years has been fully confirmed. I flatter myself that I shall remain fairly well in favour with her—which is not very easy. My new rank of Chamberlain changes nothing in the position I have now adopted *vis-à-vis* the Court. Later on, we'll see. . . .

Before leaving Weimar I took leave of no one at all, and paid no visits during the last 3 days. I only took care to ensure that the Altenburg peacocks are well fed until New Year's Day. The caretaker received 4 or 5 thalers for this purpose. I remembered that you loved these creatures—whose very cry pleased you! They need not suffer from our absence. At noon on Saturday I went up to the Altenburg again. . . . After having gone round the garden, given one last look at the windows of your room and of the blue room, I walked to the station. The train for Gotha was leaving at 1.30. . . .

Starting yesterday, 22 August, I have begun to economize. That's something new, isn't it? Well, I shall, I promise you! May Harpagon help me!

Wagner is in Vienna, where he is busy with rehearsals of *Tristan*. Blandine is still with Cosette in Reichenhall, from where she will return to St Tropez. Cosette will be back in Berlin by the end of this month. Perhaps I shall arrange to meet her here, in about ten days. May God watch over you and reunite us soon!

F.L.

486. To the Grand Duke Carl Alexander in Weimar. Löwenberg, 7 September

Monseigneur,

Returning here from a two-day excursion to Primkenau (visiting the Duke of Augustenburg), I was handed the envelope in which Your Royal Highness was so good as to send me my new diploma.[20] I return thanks to you for this kind attention, as also for the Atticism of the expression 'zu Bezeigung unsrer besonderen Zuneigung [as a token of our special affection]', while assuring you that I shall endeavour not to respond to it like a Boeotian![21] . . .

At Löwenberg, where we lead a most agreeable and peaceful *vie de château*, I shall be detained for a few more days yet by the very gracious hospitality being shown to me by Prince Hohenzollern. So far as outside amusements are concerned, during this fortnight there has been only a popular celebration in honour of the victory gained at Katzbach (26 August 1813) by the Prusso-Russian army under Blücher, following which the French army had to withdraw from Silesia. This campaign earned Blücher the title of Prince of Wahlstadt; and it was around his colossal bust, sculpted by Rauch and placed in the centre of a charmingly rural promenade a quarter of an hour away from the town of Löwenberg, that were held the celebrations commemorating one of the glorious feats of arms of the year '13. We went there in a procession to listen to some patriotic speeches and to indulge in all the rejoicings customary in such cases. The previous day, Prince Hohenzollern had given a banquet at which General Count Nostitz, Blücher's aide-de-camp and now an octogenarian, but still very steady on his legs and able to keep a good seat on a horse, was the chief bigwig.

Among other books, I have these last few days gone through the 4th volume of M. Guizot's *Mémoires*. . . .

A volume of 300 pages bearing the title *Reisebriefe von Felix Mendelssohn-Bartholdy* has just been published. The first two letters (21–5 May 1832[22]) are from Weimar; Goethe does all the honours of them, every day inviting Mendelssohn to dine with him. 'In the mornings I have to play the piano to him for the best part of an hour, works by all the different composers, in chronological order, and tell him how they contributed to musical progress; while I do so He sits in a dark corner, like a *Jupiter tonans*. He wanted nothing to do with Beethoven—but I told him there was no escape, and then played him the first movement of the Symphony in C minor. It had a curious effect on him. To

---

[20] The document confirming that Liszt had been made a chamberlain.

[21] Boeotia, the country adjoining Attica on the north-west, was proverbial for the stupidity of its inhabitants (despite being the birthplace of Pindar, Corinna, and Plutarch).

[22] The letters actually date from May 1830. (Goethe died in Mar. 1832.)

begin with he said, "That isn't at all moving; it's only astonishing; it's over-whelming," and he grumbled away like that for a while, and after a long time began again, "It is very great, quite wild, one could fear the house was falling down. *What must it be like when all those men are playing together!*" '

That is the limit of what people were able to listen to in 1832 [1830]—five [three] years after Beethoven's death.

As for Hummel, he is mentioned in only a single line (at the end of the first letter), but with two exclamation marks: 'In *Iphigénie en Aulide*[23] Hummel has struck out octaves and the like!!'

Of Walther and Wolf Goethe, Mendelssohn says: 'They are lively, hard-working, friendly lads; and to hear them talking about "Grandpapa's *Faust*" is simply too sweet for words.'

Permit me to ask you, Monseigneur, to be so kind as to remember me de-votedly to the very gracious memory of HRH the Grand Duchess and to con-sider me

Your ceaselessly loyal and grateful servant   F. Liszt

P.S. If anything notable was said or done at the meeting of the Goethe Com-mittee in Weimar, on 28 August, I trust you will be so good as to let me know.

487. To Princess Carolyne. Löwenberg, 12 September. . . . As I wrote to you in an earlier letter, the sacrament of confirmation was given me in Paris at the church of St Vincent de Paul, more than 30 years ago—so I don't need to receive it again. I shall ask you just to tell me to which confessor I shall have to apply in Rome. If you choose Father Ferraris for me, as I should like, please inform him that I do not know Italian well enough to confess in that language. More definite news, which in all likelihood will not be long in coming, I shall therefore await here. If, however, some other difficulty arises and a postpone-ment becomes necessary, then to begin with I shall spend some time in Berlin, where at the present moment I shall feel easier in my mind than elsewhere. Although Pce Hohenzollern is extremely kind and gracious to me, I don't con-sider it proper to prolong my stay here beyond another 4 or 5 days. I have been enjoying his hospitality for three weeks already—and I am not accustomed to wearying even my best friends with my presence.

Cosette has just spent five days at Löwenberg, where she made an excellent impression on the Prince, getting on so well with him that she has been press-ingly invited to come here again this winter, with her husband. . . .

---

[23] Opera by Gluck, first performed in Paris, Apr. 1774.

Your weekly letters have reached me regularly. The latest post brought me the one from 24 to 30 August. You did well not to start a debate about whether life was or was not—an insoluble enigma! Obviously for those who have faith the key to the enigma has been found. The fundamental task of any and every religion is to reveal this key—more especially the Christian religion, whose divine solution is so astonishingly in harmony with the presentiments, aspirations, failings, and exultations of our souls! The Christ who is the Way, the Truth, and the Life shines in the darkness of life and death—and 'nothing can escape this light!' . . .

A nice remark of Chamfort's to a very rich man: 'I beg you to believe that I have no need of what I lack.'

Cosette, who has returned to Berlin, will write out for you an account of her stay at Löwenberg, which will acquaint you to some extent with the ways of this household. She will also tell you of a trip we made together to Gersdorf—a *Rittergut* which now belongs to Henselt, three leagues away from here—in the company of Henselt, who had come here to see me. The 'malaria' which depresses any genuine artist in Petersburg he feels very badly, to the point that these last 2 or 3 years he has composed nothing. In a few days he will be going back to Petersburg, where his position as inspector general of the piano classes of *all* the private schools for young noblewomen in all the Russias assures him a good salary and much respect. He has been decorated with the Order of Vladimir—a distinction which has as yet been bestowed upon no other artist. . . . F.L.

488. To Princess Carolyne. Hôtel de Pologne, Berlin, 22 September.

I wait and hope. All your letters are reaching me—and each one brings me nearer to the day of my deliverance! May God be blessed in you and through you! . . .

For various little reasons I deemed it opportune to leave Löwenberg, after having spent a month there, 22 August to 19 September. The Prince is still most warmly and sincerely fond of me—and I believe, too, that I got on very well with his entire entourage. . . .

Not to inconvenience the Bülows, I have taken accommodation in a small hotel, very modest but decent, 100 yards away from their home. I spend the mornings here, and lunch at their place at 2.00. Then I go out, and return to have dinner with them, at 8.00. Yesterday, I spent the evening with Rubinstein, Weitzmann, and a Dr Schelle, who spent three years in Rome devoting himself to serious studies of Gregorian chant, Palestrina, etc. In April he will bring out the first volume of his history of the Sistine Chapel—and become Brendel's active collaborator on the Leipzig *Neue Zeitschrift*. Rubinstein has suffered in his own way from the Petersburg 'malaria'. It is very unlikely that he will return there, and I assume he will settle in Vienna for a time, until he finds some post as a conductor, which is what he is aiming at. As usual, he is spending his time composing a mass of works. To my regret, the two latest he played me show no progress over their predecessors—but he is young and robust. If only he succeeds in controlling his productive incontinence—he will reach loftier regions. His Petersburg position, which isn't one, is filling him with a kind of bitterness, and that's in his favour. His character is a nobly proud one. I fear only that the strings of love and sorrow do not vibrate energetically enough in his soul!

I have just read M. de Montalembert's pamphlet on Poland: *A Nation in Mourning*. Its sentiment is beautiful, and the style ardent. . . . His quotation of two passages from Krasiński's *Psalms of the Future*[24] makes me want to know this work which, if no French or German translation has appeared, I shall ask you to translate for me. . . .

If possible, I should like to set out for Marseilles on the 30th of this month, and there await subsequent news. It is for you to decide on the date of my journey. If I don't hurry you any more, it is certainly not for want of aspiring with all the power of my soul to see once again 'my country, city of the soul'!![25] . . . Be blessed without end!

489. To Princess Carolyne. Berlin, 29 September. . . . The day before yesterday, 27 Sept., was the feast of SS Cosmas and Damian, Cosette's name-day. She received your dear and charming letter in the morning, and showed it to me. I am counting on you to translate for me the 3rd chapter of P. Faber's book. The summary you are making for me of the ideas in the *Soirées de Pétersbourg* I find striking—but am surprised at the little value you grant the book's scientific evidence. I was happy to have a higher opinion of it, but without being in a position to produce supporting evidence. Antonelli's remark is charming: 'With the Princes one should always be 24 hours ahead!'—It was to comply with this maxim that I left Weimar, and even Löwenberg, earlier than people expected. . . .

Our Highnesses of Weimar will be very big guns at the coronation in Königsberg, where the Weimar colours will appear beside those of Prussia, in honour of the Queen. The 100 ladies who will congratulate Their Majesties at their entry into Königsberg have to wear sashes in the Weimar colours. There

---

[24] *Psalmy przyszłości* (1845).
[25] Byron, *Childe Harold*, iv. lxxviii. The full line, correctly punctuated, is 'Oh Rome! my country! city of the soul!'

will also be a grand concert conducted by Meyerbeer, who has composed a march and a cantata for this solemn ceremony. I called on the most illustrious maestro, who at once told me that my new title of chamberlain was considered to be the indication of my impending marriage. He, I assume, will receive his letters patent of nobility at Königsberg. Several newspapers, including the *Kreuzzeitung*, have announced my journey to Rome—a piece of news that they dreamt up entirely by themselves, for I have never spoken of this journey as probable. My St Tropez and Athens plan I have maintained stoutly up to the present moment, and shall continue to do so until the end of October!

I have promised, or rather proposed to, Cornelius to make a little music at his place this evening. He gave me a very good welcome, and bestows upon you the title of his *Geheimenrath*—saying that you have corrected and improved his cartoons. His wife made a good impression on me. A German woman would never be able to occupy this position with such simplicity, good grace, and charm. You know that it has been discovered that she descends in a direct line from the family of Raphael! . . .

Cornelius is very annoyed with Kaulbach, who has never sent him the drawing he had promised him in exchange for a small painting. In general, relations between artists are not conspicuous for excessive cordiality or goodwill —something of which I for my part have had more than one experience. It is certain that the practice of the fine arts divides much more than it brings together the persons who devote themselves to it. One has only the sad conviction of noticing that mutual civilities in other fields are no greater! . . . .

490. To Princess Carolyne. [Berlin] 4 October. Blessed be your dear letter of 28 September which settles everything. I telegraphed you immediately after reading it, indicating to you the Hôtel d'Orient at Marseilles. If by chance this hotel no longer exists, like the Hôtel des Princes in Paris, I shall go to the Hôtel des Empereurs.[26] . . .

How to respond to the sentiment which made you choose the 22nd of October, and to the words that this sentiment inspires in you? However long I still have to live will not suffice, in my opinion! I am also happy about the coincidence of your parish church being under the invocation of your patron, St Charles. After him, it is certainly Antonelli who is our great patron in Rome. So I shall try to light a beautiful candle for him on the very Sunday evening in which he wishes to do me the signal honour of receiving me! Please tell me how I can

[26] It didn't and he did.

manage not to displease him, and to be fairly agreeable to him. We shall follow custom with regard to the presents, and I shall try finally to heal your 'too persistent bruises'. Meanwhile, here is a present which delights me—the photograph of your commensal, Mister Puss! Thank you for having sent it to me.

Cosette will be thanking you for your letter for Cornelius, and giving you a description of the evening we spent last Sunday in the home of the modern Raphael. Tomorrow we shall take tea at the Marxes', and in the *prima sera* [early evening] I shall pay another call on Cornelius, in your honour. His *Ezekiel* I find admirable—but when you are not there I no longer dare speak either of painting or of literature, or of the drama, for all my impressions are dull and unreliable. Without your light, I live only gropingly—literally!

Yesterday evening I saw Goethe's *Iphigenie*[27] again. Johanna Wagner made her second début in it and was very much applauded—although she seemed to me to be fairly mediocre, with the exception of some fine poses and of some beautifully spoken lines in the monologue in the Fourth Act. As for the tragedy, I am ashamed to say that for all its sublimity I like it no more than I do Goethe's *Tasso*. But once again—I declare that, without you, I'm at a complete loss! . . .

I shall telegraph you as soon as I arrive in Marseilles, where I shall spend my hours waiting for the dawn of 17 October. If my calculations are correct, these lines will reach you on Wednesday the 9th. That will be the eve of my arrival in Marseilles—however, it's possible that I might linger for a day *en route*. And so don't telegraph me before Saturday the 12th—even if it were still necessary for you to send me a telegram. May God heap His blessings upon you!

Through you and for you.   F.L.

491. To Princess Carolyne. [Marseilles] Monday, 14 [October]. These are the last lines I am writing to you. My long exile is about to end. In 5 days I shall again find in you my country, hearth and altar! May the clemency and mercy of God, who 'raiseth up the poor out of the dust, and lifteth the needy out of the dunghill',[28] be blessed without end! May I give you days of peace and tranquillity, as we approach the evening of our lives!—

I have given up the idea of a trip to St Tropez,[29] and shan't leave Marseilles until Thursday, the 17th. Because of a mistake made by the forwarding agent

---

[27] The Schauspiel *Iphigenie auf Tauris*.   [28] Ps. 113: 7.

[29] Deeply disappointing Blandine, as she wrote on the 25th: 'The shock was so great that I needed some time to get over it. Your room was ready; I had put in it Wagner's table, his inkwell, your music paper and some booklets, and was deploring the absence of dictionaries. . . . While preparing your room I was saying a thousand things to you; I saw myself in your arms, had for a moment left this cold planet, and now have to return to it.'

in Frankfurt, my belongings haven't arrived yet; it could be that I shall embark before receiving them—leaving Otto here to bring them to me later. In 24 hours in Rome it will be easy for me to obtain something to wear. By the boat which arrives this evening from Civitavecchia I shall probably have a few further words from you. I shall go to meet them, by climbing up to Notre Dame de bon Secours, patron saint of sailors. 'Sursum corda!' Thursday's steamer is called the *Quirinal.*

Liszt reached Rome on Sunday, 20 October. In the early evening of the following day he and the Princess took communion together at San Carlo al Corso, the church, dedicated to Carolyne's name saint, in which on the 22nd—Liszt's 50th birthday—they were to be joined in holy matrimony. Later that evening, however, a Vatican emissary arrived at the Princess's rooms to say that the ceremony was to be postponed so that documents relating to her marriage with Prince Wittgenstein could be examined further. The consequence of this eleventh-hour intervention, and her belief that during their long separation Liszt had grown indifferent to her, was that Carolyne now abandoned the marriage plans for good. 'The world with its thousand resources is stronger than I,' she wrote to Liszt's cousin Eduard. 'But God is making resignation easier for me by the joy I have had, not only in seeing Liszt again, and seeing him in good and magnificent health, but still more, and above all, by finding in him again in every circumstance, however unforeseen, that same noble-mindedness, tact, and loftiness of view which make me admire, cherish, and esteem him more than ever.'

492. To Blandine Ollivier. Rome, 25 December

My dear daughter,

Here first of all are my best wishes and felicitations for New Year's Day, and I ask you to perform whole-heartedly your duty as my very dear daughter by giving my mother all my love and respect and Emile my very real and affectionate regards.

I was delighted to learn from one of your latest letters that my good mother was again peripatetic (you will be able to explain to her the Greek etymology, from the school of Aristotle), and I certainly expect you not to fail to tell me of her travels around your rooms. The *Moniteur*, to which the Princess W. subscribes, will give me *in extenso* Emile's speeches to the Corps législatif. Don't for that reason forget to send me the *Droit* or the *Gazette des Tribuneaux* as soon as there is some speech for the defence by your husband, about whom, incidentally, I had in Marseilles the great satisfaction of hearing eulogies in every key

of the political and social scale, from Boisselot, Lecourt, the Pastrés, and a score
of others. There are many reasons why I should like to remain informed about
his oratorical activity, and, since what he says is always excellently said, I fancy
you will enjoy keeping me in the know. . . .

My life in Rome is more peaceful, more harmonious, and better ordered than
in Germany. I am hoping, therefore, that it will be to the advantage of my work,
and that this will turn out well. I am living at 113 Via Felice, close to the Pincio,
in a very attractive first-floor flat in which Léopold Robert lived for seven or
eight years. Tenerani's and Overbeck's studios, the Quirinal, Santa Maria degli
Angeli, and Santa Maria Maggiore are nearby, and I intend to go to them often,
to take possession of them, for beautiful things belong to those who know how
to feel and become imbued with them. On Sundays I go regularly to the Sistine
Chapel to bathe and reinvigorate my spirit in the sonorous waves of Palestrina's
Jordan; and every morning I am awakened by a concert from the bell-towers of
the surrounding churches . . . which charm me far more than all the concerts
of the Paris Conservatoire could do. Our friend d'Ortigue is also keeping me
very agreeable company through his recently published volume *La Musique à
l'Eglise*, and his *Dictionnaire du Plain-Chant*, which is providing me with much
help and instruction, and to which I have done the honours of a binding in
beautiful white vellum in the Roman style, a perfect match for the contents of
this excellent work.

Talking of dictionaries (and, as you know, they are a craze of mine), has the
one announced by Hachette and entitled *Pensées et Maximes* come out yet? Please
enquire, and I shall order a copy. But above all, keep me informed about things
more closely related to me—your new play, and the portrait of you that we saw
begun. Your muse and the painter's palette have not remained idle, I hope? Let
me know, too, what Wagner is up to this winter. He replied so sourly to my
last lines from Berlin that I don't quite know how to set about resuming correspondence with him.

This afternoon I paid a visit to the Cerasari ladies of whom you spoke so
highly. They had the sense to talk a lot about you and Emile, telling me that
you and he made a household of two angels, which I naturally found even more
agreeable to hear than the *scena patetica* from [Verdi's] *Ballo in maschera* which
the elder of the two sisters sang to me. When an opportunity comes along I
shall try to thank them for the 'two angels' by doing them some kindness or
giving them some fruitful introduction.

I embrace you, my very dear daughter, with all my heart.

What is the position with regard to Leroux's *Job*? Have you seen Lamartine
again?

493. To the Grand Duke Carl Alexander. Rome, 25 December (Via Felice 113)

Monseigneur,

In Rome, everything that is good takes on a character of perpetuity. The sentiments which attach me to your person and bind me to the service of your family cannot therefore be obliterated here. And so it is with 'the unleavened bread of sincerity and veracity' that I write to renew to Your Royal Highness, on the occasion of the New Year, all my wishes for his happiness and his renown. May all your good thoughts and noble desires be fulfilled and give you, Monseigneur, that satisfaction full of serenity and of fortitude which is the attribute of great hearts!—

The Rome temperature suits me perfectly; up to now no cold has been felt, and these fine days I am employing effortlessly and without boredom through my work as a composer, through reading, and, as recreation, by paying visits to churches, monuments, galleries, and studios. I hope by Easter to have finished my oratorio *Saint Elisabeth*, and perhaps an opportunity to produce it for you will later come my way, either in Weimar or at the Wartburg.

Among the small number of people whose company I frequent with interest and pleasure, I shall mention in the forefront the Duke of Sermoneta—knowing, besides, that I owe the greater part of his goodwill to me to the recommendation that Monseigneur was so good as to make to him. Among the most distinguished personalities that can be met with in the European aristocracy he has his own distinct individuality, and one finds really great delight in following the sallies and meanderings of his exceptional and lively mind. While 'not believing in geography', as he said to silence someone who was persisting in charging him very dearly for an atlas he didn't need, the Duke doesn't for that reason surrender to 'le vague des passions'; and in practising with as much assiduity as success Benvenuto Cellini's art, so that he has, as it were, created a kind of archaeological jewellery in excellent, exquisite, and erudite taste, he is by no means out of his depth. Furthermore, he cultivates equally successfully another branch of art—that of Bernard Palissy—by maintaining the pottery of Urbino, with, as fellow workers, his wife and his daughter, the most gracious Donna Ersilia Caetani, Contessa Lovatelli, about whom a woman that I should feel almost ashamed to praise for her mind, but whom Herr von Humboldt named with good reason *die vielbegeistigte Fürstin*,[30] has said: 'The noble and expressive type of her beautiful features is at once part Juno and part Titania.'

---

[30] See Letter 444.

I do not know if Monseigneur has seen samples of this artistic pottery that the Duke sometimes further ennobles by Greek inscriptions; but, convinced that you would take great pleasure in them, I urge you to call for a dessert service from this most illustrious workshop, which would certainly make a splendid show on your table.

Your library probably already contains the Duke of Sermoneta's work on Dante and his *Atlas transmondain de la Divine Comédie*, which, as it seems to me, only too well exempted him from 'believing in geography'. It is regrettable that only a small number of copies of this work has been printed and is not available commercially. Very competent judges give it sincere praise and state that the author deservedly has the reputation of being Rome's outstanding authority on the works of Dante—indeed, that he has mastered the *Divina Commedia* to the point of being able to recite every canto from memory.[31] How humbling for a poor ignorant musician like me who has ventured to publish a cacophonous mish-mash adorned by the title of '*Dante*' Symphony!

Were I a little better qualified to speak to you of books, and especially of folios, I would tell you, Monseigneur, of the enormous publications of the Most Revd Father Theiner (of the Oratory, Prefect of the Secret Vatican Archives), the *Vetera Monumenta Hungaricum*, *Vetera Monumenta Poloniae et Lithuaniae*, and the *Codex diplomaticus Dominii Temporalis* (preceded by two remarkable introductions in French). These pyramids of learning are rising in the shadow of the Vatican, by means of a small printing-press that the Holy Father has made available there to the Revd Father Theiner. The last time I visited him in his turret, formerly inhabited by Galileo, he remarked with an eloquent and touching simplicity: 'All my work has not led me to, and will never lead me to, material riches. Here, I am without a penny to bless myself with, and the voluminous results of my researches are published thanks to the munificence of the Holy Father, of the bishops and of a few other people who provide me with the requisite resources. Do you find that shaming?'—'Not in the least,' I replied, 'it is true glory.'—'Well!' he went on, 'since you speak of glory, there is one to which I am not indifferent. It is that given to me by the happy awareness of having done by myself alone, in a dozen years, more work than about fifty of my colleagues in Germany (under the direction of Pertz, I believe[32]) have done in more than thirty years, and thus of having lit for Poland and Hungary two torches which will shine in perpetuity for those two nations.'

---

[31] In the 'Ricordo Biografico' with which he prefaced his edition of the *Carteggio Dantesco del Duca di Sermoneta*, Angelo de Gubernatis confirmed that the Duke did indeed know the *Commedia* by heart—'with the exception of about twenty lines that he complained he had never learnt properly'.

[32] The parenthesis is presumably Liszt's, not Theiner's.

Blessed be the small number of the elect that such awareness sustains through the aridities of life, 'mentre che la vergogna dura'![33] Being unable to aspire so high, I shall at least strive to keep enough oil in my lamp to light my way until the real day comes—when there will be no more tomorrow.

Allow me, Monseigneur, to ask you to be so good as to lay at the feet of Her Royal Highness, the Grand Duchess, the most respectful homage of gratitude and devotion with which I have the honour to be

Your very faithful servant   F. Liszt

P.S. As a small proof of the great value I attach to your kindnesses, Monseigneur, I enclose one of my Rome visiting-cards. It is the first time since I have been using visiting-cards that any title whatsoever has been added to the two mono-syllables of my name.

---

[33] Literally, 'while the shame lasts', referring to the evils that taint the world and discredit humanity. Not a 'quotation from Dante', as stated by La Mara, but from a celebrated quatrain by another great Florentine who revered Dante to the point of wishing he had been 'such as he' ('pur fuss' io tal!')—Michelangelo Buonarroti (in the person of *La Notte*). The full quatrain runs: 'Grato [*or* caro] m'è il sonno, e più l'esser di sasso, | mentre che il danno e la vergogna dura. | Non veder, non sentir m'è gran ventura; | però non mi destar, deh! parla basso!' Liszt prefixed these words to both the piano piece *Il penseroso* and the orchestral work *La Notte* (based in part on *Il penseroso*), second of the *Trois Odes funèbres*.

1862

Among Liszt's new pupils this year, the whole of which he spends in or near Rome, are the gifted young Italian pianist and composer Giovanni Sgambati,* and a 20-year-old Englishman, Walter Bache,* later the foremost champion of Liszt's music in England.

Another new acquaintance is Ferdinand Gregorovius, hard at work on his *History of the City of Rome in the Middle Ages.*

In September Liszt receives news of the death of his daughter Blandine.

WORKS. *The Legend of St Elisabeth. Cantico del sol di San Francesco d'Assisi* (S4), for baritone solo, male chorus, orchestra, and organ. PIANO: two concert studies (S145), *Waldesrauschen* and *Gnomenreigen; Berceuse* (2nd version); Variations (S180)[1] on the bass line from the first movement of Bach's cantata *Weinen, Klagen, Sorgen, Zagen; Ave Maria (The Bells of Rome)* (S182); *Alleluja et Ave Maria* (Arcadelt[2]) (S183); *A la Chapelle Sixtine* (S461), based on Allegri's *Miserere* and Mozart's *Ave verum corpus.*

494. To Xavier Boisselot in Marseilles. Rome (Via Felice 113), 3 January.

I want to thank you first and foremost, dear friend, for one of the most tangible pleasures of my sojourn in Rome: that given me daily by a delightful Boisselot upright piano which is the principal adornment of my sitting-room.

As you know, for 13 years I have kept in my study in Weimar the grand piano that in 1846 [1847] your excellent brother Louis sent to Odessa for me. Although the keys are almost hollowed out, as a result of all the frolics which music of the past, the present, and the future has indulged in upon them, I shall never consent to change this piano, being quite determined to keep it, as a favourite partner in my work, until the end of my days. The upright piano that Mengarini has very helpfully placed at my disposal is distinguished by a most agreeable touch, and also by a splendid sonority, whose volume is as satisfactory as an instrument of this smaller size allows.

---

[1] Inspired by Liszt's grief at the death of Blandine.
[2] The *Ave Maria* was actually an arrangement by P. L. P. Dietsch of Arcadelt's three-voice song *Nous voyons que les hommes.*

The other evening I found at the Duke of Sermoneta's (Caetani) an excellent grand piano from your manufactory, and if, as is probable, I remain here for some time, I shall arrange with Mengarini for him to dispose of several in the same way, to the greater advantage of the few people to whom I shall give the entire benefit of them.

As regards music in Rome, I am wholly enthralled by that of the Sistine Chapel, where everything is grand, majestic, permanent, equally sublime in its general effect and in its radiance. Every Sunday I listen to that singing in the way that one must say one's breviary.

Despite, or rather because of, this, I don't in any way share the opinion of those who claim that everything has been said in church music, that its vein is exhausted. On the contrary, I believe it should be excavated still further, and, at the risk of seeming presumptuous, I shall admit that this task tempts me singularly and that I shall endeavour to accomplish it by writing several works in the style and of the order of inspiration of my Gran Mass and of some Psalms which have been performed in Germany.

For the moment I am wholly absorbed in *Saint Elisabeth*, and before this oratorio is finished (which will certainly take me another three or four months at least), I cannot think of undertaking anything else. Let me know sometime, dear friend, if, in addition to the scores I left with you when departing from Marseilles, you still feel like going through some similar ones of mine, and in that case remind me what address I should give to the Leipzig publisher (Herr Kahnt) for him to get them to you without needless expense or delay.

The French Academy's prize-winners are MM Guiraud and Paladilhe. I haven't run across them very much as yet, nor have I yet tried the Academy's piano (a rather ancient one, I am told), not generally being in a hurry to display my talent, such as it is, which time and again becomes a very disagreeable burden to me, seeing that many people fancy, tacitly or openly, that they are entitled to require me to *entertain* them at any and every turn, opportune or otherwise. At my age and in my frame of mind, that isn't always agreeable, and, besides, I can't see what advantage there can be in making music a too obliging *nice girl*. Whatever one has from it, art is an aristocracy whose company one does not frequent comfortably.

Do please, dear friend, remember me very affectionately to Madame Boisselot; and also tell my godson Franz, who is coming along so promisingly, that he will always find in me the sentiments that his father so well knew were mine. And do be assured, you and yours, of my very true and cordial devotion.   F. Liszt

Don't forget to give my best regards to Lecourt, whom I remember with particular affection. I was delighted to find him to be just the same person I knew; just as vivacious, as forthright, and as unceasingly sprightly and youthful.

495. To Prince Constantin von Hohenzollern-Hechingen in Löwenberg. Rome, 26 January

Monseigneur,

Anything favourable that happens to my *nearest and dearest* mattering to me at least as much as what happens to myself, Your Highness will allow me to thank him first and foremost with the sincerest gratitude for having been so kind as to decorate Herr von *Bülow* with your family order. He will do honour to this honour, I have no doubt, as much by his thoroughly noble sentiments as by his rare talents. . . . His wife has just written me a letter which is quite filled with your kindnesses, and the exquisite liberality with which you dispense alike the spiritual and the material *agrémens* which add savour and flavour to life.

In the description she gives me of her stay at Löwenberg, I was particularly touched by Your Highness's remembrance of me; I shall not cease to respond to it by the most respectfully devoted and affectionate attachment. It was still more flattering for me to learn that you derived some pleasure from following the windings and meanderings of my Faust Symphony without wearying of them. If, during the course of the season, Herr Seifriz is not afraid to add to his 'experiments and ventures!' I shall almost urge him to acquaint you with my 'Valse de Méphistophélès'. It was an episode from Lenau's *Faust*, 'the dance in the village inn', which served me as a programme for this whimsical work, which is stuffed full of seasoning of various kinds and sprinkled with *belladonna!* The manuscript has remained in Leipzig, and to obtain it Herr Seifriz would have only to write either to Brendel or to the publisher Schuberth.

For the time being I am wholly engrossed in my *Legend of St Elisabeth*—which I hope to finish in three or four months. It has been said, without being unjust to Michelangelo, Raphael, or Palestrina, that the Rome climate is the greatest of artists. May it have a favourable effect on my work in a way that will remove from it anything which would run the risk of seeming heterodox to sensitive ears. Are mine among these? They have had to endure such maltreatment that I know not what to think. In any case, I wish to remain a man of *good faith* in my works as in my conduct.

The musical diet known to me here is nowhere near as plentiful and substantial as the one I was used to. Thus far I have heard nothing which has given me the desire to listen to it more attentively—with the exception, however, of masses by Palestrina and his school, whose character of sublime permanence is fully revealed in the Vatican chapel. The number of choristers is rather restricted; but the acoustic proportions of the chapel are so excellent, and the choir so well placed (towards the middle of the nave, but a little nearer the altar), that those 24—or 30 voices at most—produce a very impressive effect. It is a sonorous incense which carries prayer aloft on its clouds of gold and azure!

In other churches a kind of music is cultivated whose attractions and advantages I am far from disputing ... but to enjoy it without restraint a degree of *naïveté* of impression is needed that I despair of attaining. The overtures to the *Gazza ladra* and the *Barbiere di Siviglia*, the cavatinas from *Norma* and *Ernani*, that are sometimes heard on occasions when they have at least the merit of surprise, hold no more interest for me than do theatres in which are performed only works that do not gain from being too well known. As for what in Germany are called Concerts—such as those of Löwenberg, to mention one of the best examples—the kind has not yet been imported into Italy; and if it ever did make its way here, I doubt that it would succeed in becoming acclimatized. This notwithstanding, one here and there comes across artistes who declare their high regard for the *classical* music of Haydn, Mozart, and Beethoven—but it is a little like the way in which in other capitals society ladies can occasionally be heard extolling the profundities of German philosophy, with which they will take good care not to become more closely acquainted. After all, it would be ridiculous to pick a quarrel with the Italians who have indeed the best reasons in the world for doing what they like *chez eux*, and even for becoming ever so slightly infatuated with their environment of feelings and habits.

It is with the sincerest sentiments of gratitude and affection that I remain, Monseigneur, Your Royal Highness's faithful and devoted servant   F. Liszt

496. To Princess Carolyne. [Rome] 27 January.[3] St John Chrysostom[4] sends you this little bouquet. You have more than one characteristic in common with your patron saint—like him you possess learning, eloquence, the sacred flame, and are suffering exile! May the robe of glory likewise be your raiment in the heavenly homeland!   Minimissime Besson.[5]

497. To Princess Carolyne. [Rome] Thursday, 30 January. I doubt that I shall manage to reach the Piazza d'Espagna before 3 o'clock. Tell me then if you are still of a mind to take a drive to the Via Appia.

The columns of St Paul's[6] are magnificent, and, taken as a whole, of a serene and majestic harmony. They sing the glory of God, just as does the whole firma-

---

[3] During the years in which Liszt lived in Rome and saw the Princess almost daily, his written communications to her were naturally no more than mere notes.

[4] Whose feast-day it was. The Princess's forenames, it should be remembered, were Jeanne Elisabeth Carolyne (or, in her native tongue, Joanna Elżbieta Karolina).

[5] From this time forward, when writing to the Princess, Liszt often signed with the word Besson (a French dialect expression for 'twin')—sometimes with Bon Besson or B.B.—as a sign of his affinity with her in mind and spirit.

[6] The great 4th-cent. basilica of San Paolo fuori le Mura (St Paul without the Walls), almost wholly destroyed by fire in 1823 but rebuilt on the original plan. The columns to which Liszt refers are eighty in number.

ment on a beautiful summer morning, when, sensing a divine and loving awareness, everything seems impelled towards auspicious events in this world.

I kiss your dear little hands, and am wholly at your feet!

498. To Princess Carolyne [Rome, February]. Good day dearest, very dearest, one! Yesterday evening I usurped the privileges of Kicy, who nobly refused to take part in my culinary spoliations! That is an example of how, when it comes to dignity, cats have something to teach humans! . . .

The excursion to the Vatican with Visconti and the Lovatelli[7] is arranged for noon today. The Rzewuskis,[8] whom I ran into yesterday evening at Mme Malatesta's, will be taking part—as they will, too, at 3 o'clock, in an archaeological outing, conducted by Mme Malatesta and illustrated by di Rossi, to the Christian Museum in the Lateran. I shall in any case be dropping in on you—not at twilight [*entre chien et loup*] but between Vatican and Lateran! However, I strongly urge you not to expect me for lunch. The *Antinous*[9] might detain us for rather a long time—and between the wonders of pagan antiquity and those of Christianity I might not have enough leisure left to take refreshment! If by chance Visconti were to get carried away by his own eloquence, I should even be obliged to postpone my visit to you until this evening, for it would be impolite to miss the rendezvous with Rossi in the Lateran. See you soon!

499. To Princess Carolyne [Rome, 2 April]. How can I tell you, my good angel, of the sweet joy caused me, when I awoke, by your note and the beautiful gifts you have sent me![10] I had given no further thought to the desk, on which I am writing to you, so that it has been to me at one and the same time a surprise and a memento. If indeed, despite my protests against presents in general, you are maintaining your generosity and munificence to the point of immoderation—you could find me nothing more to my taste than the Schnorr Bible.[11] And so I thank you, most sincerely and unreservedly, for these dear pictures which are more within my understanding than other masterpieces. I shall look at them often, as I am doing this morning, linking thoughts of you to all the beautiful miracles, as our good Ferraris says, of the Old and New Testaments. Moreover, I can see that you have resolved to transform my dwelling

---

[7] Wrongly transcribed by La Mara as 'Savatelli'.
[8] Probably in-laws of the Duke of Sermoneta, whose first wife was a Rzewuska.
[9] An antique statue of Hadrian's favourite.   [10] For his name-day.
[11] Julius Schnorr von Carolsfeld's *Bibel in Bildern* (Bible in Pictures) of 1860, containing 240 woodcuts.

place into a second Vatican. The panther rug represented the *Arazzi*[12]—and so Schnorr is now giving me the *Loggie* and the *Stanze*[13] in the *Via Felice*! May your good and gentle will be done! I resist it no more—and can only praise and bless you with all my soul!   F.L.

500. To Blandine Ollivier in Paris. Rome, 26 April

My dear daughter,

About a week ago an excellent German priest (Herr Landmesser) wrote me a few lines to inform me charitably that there were several letters addressed to me in the poste restante parcels. Not suspecting that among them was one from you, I made no haste to claim them, so that your very nice letter of 2 April did not reach me until after a fortnight's delay. It gave me no less pleasure for that— but, to avoid similar delays (and it is probable that without the intervention of my priest your letter would not have got to me at all), do please from now on write on the envelope: 'Via Felice No. 113.'

Your remembrance of the old Saint-Vincent-de-Paul (rue Montholon!) with regard to the 2nd of April moved me deeply, and I thank you from my heart. Give all my love to Grandmama, and to Emile my best regards. I gladly agree to becoming your child's godfather; and while waiting for the event to take place I pray to God (Who is the true one!) to pour out His blessings upon you, before as well as after, and everlastingly! I can also imagine, while sharing in it, the joy with which Grandmama is already making all sorts of plans and projects for the newcomer. This little creature will make her forget her crutches and the whole world, so happy will she be.

You are known, dear Blandine, to be very skilful and ingenious at charming people into providing you with what you want, and I suspect that you made double use of your skill with regard to my Mass. Firstly, by persuading the *curé* of Saint-Eugène that this work rather deserved his goodwill because of the Catholic feeling with which it is permeated, and then by telling me the most flattering things about his liking for it. If the performance corresponds with my wishes and with the pains people are so good as to be taking to this end, I hope it will make rather a good impression, so that you will not have to regret having vouched for it. Nevertheless, were it to turn out otherwise, there would be no reason to be distressed to the point of grief or discouragement, for religious music above all, which must seek truth, piety, profundity, purity, and intensity of emotion

---

[12] The Galleria degli Arazzi (Tapestry Gallery) in the Vatican.

[13] The latter being the rooms in the Vatican with the renowned frescoes by Raphael; the former being the loggias, or gallery, leading from them, containing biblical scenes designed by Raphael and executed by his assistants.

while refraining from empty effect, also needs sensitive performers and singers who are, as it were, imbued with these feelings. Now, that is not often met with, even apart from the fact that the bitter and occasionally childish disputes about church music disconcert even the better disposed, and in their appraisal of compositions of this kind, people generally bring with them more prejudices and vague or theoretical preoccupations than elevated minds that are prepared for contemplation and self-communion.

M. Cochin has just been announced with a letter from Emile. I shall continue my letter by the next post, for the mail leaves in half an hour.

I embrace you lovingly.

501. To Blandine Ollivier. Rome, 27 April. This is a continuation of the letter interrupted yesterday by the arrival of M. Cochin, which moreover was extremely agreeable to me since he brought good news of you, dear Blandine. . . .

Since he has to go to Porto d'Anzio today, to pay his respects to His Holiness (who is having a holiday of several weeks there, and to whom he has as yet been able to be presented only in a general audience here—on Easter Saturday—at which there were about a hundred people), I asked him to introduce me to Mme Cochin straightaway, and there and then took them to Overbeck's.

The 7 large cartoons depicting the 7 Sacraments are, I believe, Overbeck's outstanding work, and will best determine his place in the history of art.

As Emile had told me that Mme Cochin was interested in painting and that her mentor was Flandrin, I saw to it that she became more fully acquainted with Overbeck, who also has pleasant memories of his relations with Montalembert, for whom in former days he drew the picture of Saint Elisabeth, the engraving of which forms the frontispiece of Montalembert's work.[14] . . .

Mme Cochin was very pleased with our outing, and, on her return from Porto d'Anzio, I shall take her to two or three other studios. As she had the sense to say some nice things about you and Emile, I am delighted to be helpful to her, which I wasn't induced to be to the d'Haussonvilles you mention. This is why: I did the crossing from Marseilles to Livorno with Mme and Mlle d'Haussonville, and had several conversations with them on the boat. Like mother, like daughter, so far as intelligence is concerned, and I gladly pay them tribute and do them full justice in this respect. At Livorno, M. d'Haussonville met his wife and daughter and took them to Florence to see the galleries and the

---

[14] *Histoire de sainte Elisabeth de Hongrie, Duchesse de Thuringe (1207–1231)* (Paris, 1836).

exhibition. Saying 'au revoir à Rome', which I reached about a fortnight before they did, we went our separate ways. At the beginning of November I ran into M. d'Haussonville in the Sistine Chapel. We exchanged a few polite words, as we also did in the reading room which I was going to quite often just then; he told me vaguely that we would see one another again, probably expecting me to visit him. There's the *rub*; for in the exceptional position in which I am placed I have had to make certain rules for myself and to keep to them strictly. Among these rules the simplest is not to forestall people who have arrived in Rome since I did, but quietly to wait for them to intimate to me that it would be agreeable to them to see me. This is in all countries the practice among well-bred people neither of whom is subordinate to the other. In Paris it would be for me to pay the d'Haussonvilles the first visit, if I wished to cultivate their acquaintance; but in Rome it is for d'H. to visit me first. He refrained from doing so, and consequently I did no more than run into Mme d'H. and her daughter two or three times at the French Academy and at performances of classical music, where we resumed our conversations of the boat, she from her position of *supériorité tranchante*, and I from mine of *infériorité... dubitative*. When talking with society people, either because of a taste for paradox, or because of the mood I am in, or because of anything else at all, I generally find myself varying in twenty different ways the theme given by this celebrated response of Cardinal Antonelli's: 'It is perhaps like that, but it isn't thus.'

The fact is that, if I have little to offer society, I feel that I have still less to seek from it; we are therefore more or less quits, and you replied very subtly to Mme d'Haussonville by giving her to understand that one can grow surfeited with 'one's calling of making people happy'—especially when this can be practised only to the detriment of one's own dignity.

Write soon to let me know that you are well, and kiss my good mother for me.   Yours.

Please give my regards and greetings to Lamartine and Delacroix. . . .

502. To Princess Carolyne.[15] I was deprived of the joy of seeing you yesterday evening, my good angel—and I still feel grieved about it this morning! It was gone 10.00 when we got back from our archaeological outing. Visconti was most agreeable and interesting—and we all enjoyed ourselves. After exploring

---

[15] This and other notes to the Princess interspersed here and there in the following pages cannot be dated exactly and might have been written at almost any time in 1862. The present one was obviously not written until after the publication, this year, of Hugo's celebrated novel *Les Misérables*.

the Villa Negroni, where the Quirinal, the Viminal, and the Esquiline[16] meet, we had supper at the Baths of Titus, at the local Véfour. Over the Paris one it has the undeniable superiority of being less expensive—since the cost for the six of us was only 3 scudi. Visconti came too, bringing a first-class appetite and a thirst to match! Don't hurry your visits—I shall come at about 2 o'clock, and will wait for you while going on with *Les Misérables*. 'The tempest in a skull', which I read a moment ago, is awe-inspiring!

May the Good Lord fill your soul with all His blessings! F.L.

503. To Blandine Ollivier. Rome, 9 June. My thoughts often fly to you in your retreat, dear Blandine, and there has been no reduction in the part of my prayers devoted to you. That God will grant you the grace called for by your present condition, and pour out His blessings upon your motherhood, is what I ask ceaselessly. May the accomplishment of the duties it involves ever be accompanied for you by all the joys, delights, and satisfactions of a devout and clear conscience! May the doleful spectacle of the sorrows which follow forgetfulness or neglect of God's law serve to keep you well on your guard; believe me, there is no sophism in the world specious enough to atone for our faults. Let us therefore not flatter ourselves through the deceptive illusions of a wisdom of our own invention, as opposed to the true wisdom, the one which existed before us and will remain when we are gone, but strive simply to be good, upright, and sincere with ourselves and with others, without ever seeking happiness which does not go hand in hand with practice of the Good and the cult of the Beautiful, which alone lift us up to that region where our souls breathe freely.

Your latest letters, dear Blandine, are quite permeated with the sentiments that I love in you. And so to read your small handwriting, with its characters formed so firmly and prettily, gives me great joy and delight.

Have you already decided on your baby's names, for I assume you will bestow several patrons[17] upon him? Tell me what they are. After your confinement you will probably go to Saint-Tropez, where I should certainly come and join you did not compelling reasons detain me in Rome. Poor Grandmama! How I feel for her at not being with you when the great event takes place—but she will make up for it later, and the baby's totterings will lend wings to her crutches! Emile must soon be at the end of his legislative duties for this session. He has just sent me his photograph by Desmaisons, plus the one of me. Although they have turned out well, it seems to me that Emile's expression is a little too solemn.

---

[16] Three of the Seven Hills of Rome, the others being the Palatine, Capitoline, Caelius, and Aventine.
[17] Name saints.

Have you received the buttons with Minerva's owl that I gave to Herr Heilbuth (a very talented painter—a native of Hamburg but very Parisian in his manner and occasionally even in the informality of his conversation—and recipient of a medal at the '61 Exposition)? These buttons are a product of the Roman goldsmiths' craft. Before sending them I wore them expressly for you, and hope you will find them to your taste.

Tomorrow, the Cochins set out on their journey back to Paris. Our relations became mutually affectionate without effort on either side. When you return home, do go and see Mme Cochin from time to time, something that would be made all the easier by the pleasant way she spoke to me of you.

They are thoroughly respectable people and interesting to talk to. They made a very good impression here, and Roman high society, which is not suspected of being excessively effusive towards outsiders, received them most graciously. I learnt that they quite often saw the Borghesi, who lord it over the conservative salons, and also frequented Princess Rospigliosi* (née Cadore), who is said to feel towards the Borghesi as the Capuleti [Capulets] did towards the Montecchi [Montagues]. For my part, I ran into the Cochins in the homes of neither the former nor the latter (for I have not been introduced to the Borghesi and go only very rarely to the Princess's), but simply in the Sistine Chapel and at Saint Peter's. We also visited a few *ateliers* together, and the day before yesterday I was their guest for dinner. That is enough to leave me with a very agreeable memory of them.

If you are still reading the newspapers, you know that Catholic Rome is quite radiant just now because of the presence of 370 bishops, archbishops, patriarchs, and cardinals, come from all quarters of the globe to attend the canonization of twenty-six Christians, almost unknown during their lifetimes, who were martyred in Japan in the seventeenth century.[18] It is a majestic spectacle for the faith, an imposing affirmation for thought, this ecumenical assembly, more numerous and united in feeling than at the most memorable councils, forming an indestructible bundle to the principle of divine authority personified in the Pope. In an infinitely more exalted sense than was imagined by the good La Fontaine, couldn't one say with him:

'All wasted their time, the bundle resisted.'?[19]

And France, that hotbed of revolutions, is resisting with more fire and fervour, so to speak, than the others. Its 68 bishops present here leave no doubt of it; and of whatever opinion one may be on this or that question of politics or

---

[18] At Nagasaki in 1597. Six of the martyrs were Franciscan missionaries from Europe, most of the remainder Japanese laymen. They were put to death simultaneously by a kind of crucifixion.
[19] From the fable *Le Vieillard et les Enfants*.

philosophy, a prevailing fact that has to be recognized, under pain of blindness, is the immense vitality and unrivalled power of Catholicism.

I pray for you and embrace you from the depths of my heart.

Write soon: Via Felice 113.

504. To Princess Carolyne. The storms in *William Tell* and the Pastoral Symphony are but trifles in comparison with the one that the Good Lord is this evening performing by Himself! However, I flatter myself that the one in *Elisabeth* is not very much inferior—I should like to play it to you, to lull you to sleep this evening! There was literally not a cat in the street—even the Pincio sentinel had become invisible! Good night, my good angel—you who are my peace, my tranquillity, and my light!

505. To Princess Carolyne. However pleasant this day may have been, it is no less a day lost for me—since I haven't seen you! Let me at least tell you for the thousandth time that you are the best and sweetest part of my life—and that I have neither desire, nor fantasy, nor ambition outside this feeling! I shall come again at about 9 o'clock to give you an account of our trip to Ostia.[20]

506. To Blandine Ollivier in Gémenos (a village near Marseilles). Rome, 8 July. Grandmama has written me a wholly charming little letter in her most beautiful handwriting. Among other things she tells me about the Geneva portrait of me which belongs to that city's Conservatoire, and of your fondness for that picture. I can't tell you how moved I was to know this, and what inner happiness it gives me to talk with you, dearest child, in the chapel of my heart into which enter only those special thoughts which are an earnest of immortality! On the other hand, the memories which are connected with your birth in Geneva have been vividly illuminated recently by the presence of someone who had no reason to notice it, and to whom I did not even mention you very much. Guess who? The Revd Father Hermann[21] in person. He has just spent a month here and I saw him quite frequently. His entry into religion has benefited his intelligence as much as his heart and his manner; moreover, he

---

[20] The ancient port of Rome, near the mouth of the Tiber. Excavations here were being supervised by the elder Visconti, and it was probably he who gave Liszt and his companions a conducted tour, just as he did at sites in Rome itself. (As something of a student of hagiology, Liszt was doubtless also aware that St Monica, mother of St Augustine, died in a house in Ostia.)

[21] Liszt's former pupil Hermann Cohen.

practises in an exemplary way the rule of the discalced Carmelites which, as you know, is one of the strictest of the monastic orders, for it obliges one to sleep usually on a plank and to abstain from meat throughout the year; and it imposes many penitences and mortifications.

Hermann preached here once, at S. Luigi dei Francesi; his sermon made a considerable impression. His kind of eloquence could be characterized by the term 'ejaculatory', which is used only for certain prayers. It moves and persuades those who are not too arrogant and pretentious to receive it. The Holy Father received Hermann very kindly, and Cardinal Wiseman invited him to go at once to England and there devote himself to founding a Carmelite monastery. This order has glorious antecedents there through the Blessed Simon Stock (in the XIIIth century), to whom the Virgin Mary transmitted the scapular. Hermann, who has already been a prior in Lyons, will probably be one again in London, unless he is appointed General of the Britannic province. He departed yesterday morning, and since he will be going via Paris I have asked him to give my news to Grandmama. On reflection, however, I remembered that she had no liking for monks in general, or for Hermann in particular, and I consequently found it advisable to forewarn her of his visit, and to appeal to her philosophic tolerance so that she won't treat him as a *Jesuit* (!) and won't take fright at the cowl and the scapular!

For the rest, Carmelite dress has some grace in its austerity, and Hermann told me that Lacordaire remarked to him one day that it was easy to see that it was a woman (St Teresa) who ordered and perhaps devised it.

From the Carmelites to L. Veuillot the transition is easy. I have seen him two or three times, and since I have a high opinion of his talent we got on quite well, if I am not mistaken. Before his departure he handed me a copy of his latest work, *Le Parfum de Rome*, with this autograph inscription: 'To M. Liszt, memento of an admirer who hopes to become a friend.' . . .

All blessings on you and our dearest Daniel-Emile.[22]

May the joy and the peace of God be ever with you.

507. To Blandine Ollivier. Rome, 19 July. I am very happy, dearest Blandine, that the happy event took place so safely, and that you not only accomplished your task well but, further, that you had no excessive suffering to endure. The requisite amount must still have been quite enough, and so I attribute to the

---

[22] In a letter to Liszt of 22 June, Blandine had written: 'Do you approve of the names we have chosen? If it is a boy, *Daniel*-Emile; if a girl, *Geneviève*-Rachel. Geneviève is the name of Emile's mother, and Rachel one of mine.' Her son Daniel was born at Gémenos on 3 July.

fine quality of your character the total acceptance you showed in enduring and thus overcoming the painful agitation of this travail, which though natural is none the less violent and terrible.

While taking pleasure in hoping that 'mother and child are doing well', and that the loud cries of the little creature continue without your having to add to them any moans or groans of your own, I'll resume chatting with you, as previously, and counting as ever on your intuition to supply what I don't say, and what you know better than I could say.

During the hot season, which thus far hasn't inconvenienced me in the least, visitors and native members of society alike are away from Rome. That suits me very well, and I am turning it to account to complete my *Legend of St Elisabeth*, which will be ready in a month.

Before I get down to something new (probably the Choruses of Byron's *Manfred*), I shall lounge about a little in Albano, Frascati, and Rocca di Papa, where several people of my acquaintance—the Duke of Sermoneta, Visconti, and Overbeck—are holidaying. I foresee that my visits will be short, for someone with my outlook cannot develop a taste for habits and diversions which last several hours. So I have carefully avoided various picnics that people have been so kind as to suggest to me, and I haven't failed to admit candidly that milk, meadows, and even honey don't suit me either literally or figuratively.

The fact is, I am comfortable only in my own company and in that of the very small number of those I love and with whom I feel at one in thought and feeling. So far as other relationships are concerned, a good deal of reserve is advisable, seeing that people generally communicate only to be mistaken about one another. This maxim is borne out by a small recent experience, one to which I would once have been more sensitive.

You know what sincere esteem and liking I have always had for the talent of Gounod, and how affectionate our personal relations were. Well! Can you believe that he spent more than six weeks in Rome without taking the trouble to come and see me, and that we didn't once see one another? He took about and sang his *Reine de Saba*, his *Faust*, and his *Vieil Habit* of Béranger at the French Academy and elsewhere. A score of people asked after him, knowing that we were closely acquainted; I for my part could only say that I should steadfastly and in good conscience continue to praise his works, which it would always be interesting and agreeable for me to know and admire, despite the regret I felt at his decision not to find time for me. . . .

I pray for the three of you, Blandine, Emile, and Emile-Daniel, while blessing God for what he grants me through you, and persevering in the most absolute monotony of my devoted and loving feelings for you.

Let me know how M. Emile-Daniel is getting on. Have you taken a wet-nurse?

508. To Franz Brendel in Leipzig. Rome, Via Felice 113, 10 August. ^G

What an agreeable bouquet of surprises your letter brings me, dear friend! So
Pohl really has got down to the Faust article—and even Schuberth is not letting the piano arrangement of the Faust Symphony moulder in a drawer. How
odd all this sounds, precisely because it is so exactly what is needed and what
I desire! If you are back in Leipzig, please send me soon a couple of copies of
the Faust article (the issues of the *Zeitschrift* containing Pohl's essays have not
reached me), and enclose with them the 2-piano arrangement of the Faust
Symphony (when convenient, several copies). The parcel Kahnt told me of, containing some of my things arranged for duet, hasn't yet come, and as I have
got hold of a very capable young pianist here—Sgambati by name—who is
proving a first-rate partner in duets, and who plays, for example, the Dante
Symphony boldly and correctly, I should be glad to go through the whole cycle
of symphonic poems with him. . . .

The *Legend of Saint Elisabeth* is finished to the very last note of the score; I
have now to do only a part of the piano arrangement, plus the duet arrangement of the Introduction, the Crusaders' March, and the final procession—which
should be done by the end of this month at the latest. I shall then send the
whole thing to Weimar to be copied, together with a couple of other smaller
manuscripts. What happens to it later on will depend on... In the mean time I
want to attempt a couple of little trips into the country (to Albano, Frascati,
Rocca di Papa—and to the rather more distant 'Macchia serena' near Corneto,
where in centuries gone by much robbery and violence took place!), and before
the end of September I hope to be able to set steadily to work again, and to
continue with my musical 'robbery and murder'! If, when doing so, I could only,
like you, hear the Sondershausen orchestra, and could conjure up friend Stein
and his valiant phalanx in the *Colosseum*! . . .

What '*amazing* things' are you planning, dear friend? This word arouses my
curiosity; on the other hand I share your superstition about speaking only of
what has actually been accomplished ('faits accomplis'). In Schelle you are gaining a really competent fellow worker. Has his history of the Sistine Chapel already
been published?[23] If so, do please send me the book with the other musical things.

My daughter, Frau von Bülow, tells me great things about Wagner's new work,
Die Meistersinger, writing *inter alia*:

'The *Meistersinger* is to Wagner's other conceptions roughly what *The Winter's
Tale* is to the works of Shakespeare. His imagination, turning to gaiety and drollery,
has evoked the Nuremberg of the Middle Ages with its guilds, its poet-artisans,
its pedants, and its knights, making the heartiest laughter ring out amidst the

---

[23] Eduard Schelle's *Die päpstliche Sängerschule in Rom, genannt die Sixtinische Capelle* (Vienna, 1872).

loftiest and most ideal poetry. Leaving aside the meaning and purpose of the work, the artistic labour could be compared with that of the *Sacraments-Häuschen* [tabernacle] at St Lawrence's (in Nuremberg). Like the sculptor, the composer has lighted upon the purest, most graceful and most fanciful form—boldness in perfection; and just as we see Adam Kraft beneath the ciborium, holding it up with a grave and meditative air, so in the *Meistersinger* we find the calm, profound, serene Hans Sachs sustaining and directing the action.'[24]

And so on. I liked this description so much that, once I had started on it, I could not spare you the long quotation. As you know, the Bülows are in Biebrich with Wagner—who at the end of this month is to conduct a performance of *Lohengrin* in Frankfurt. A detailed report of this event should not fail to appear in the *Neue Zeitschrift*, and, to write it, I could recommend no one better than my daughter. The letters in which she from time to time tells me something of musical events in Berlin and elsewhere are really charming, and full of striking wit and the shrewdest understanding.

Berlioz was so kind as to send me the printed piano score of his opera *Les Troyens*. Although piano editions really do a disservice to the works of Berlioz, a cursory reading of *Les Troyens* nevertheless made an uncommonly powerful impression on me. Its tremendous energy can't be denied; and it certainly doesn't lack delicacy—I could almost say *subtlety*—of feeling.

Pohl will report to you on the performance in Baden of Berlioz's comic opera *Béatrice et Bénédict*. I venture to say that this opera, which requires little outside assistance and is based on a well-known work[25] of Shakespeare's, will meet with a favourable reception. Berlin or any other of the larger German theatres would truly be doing itself no bad turn if it admitted one of Berlioz's operas into its repertoire. In vain do people try to excuse themselves, or rather to justify themselves, by saying that Paris has committed a similar sin of omission—for we should not imitate the faults of others. Paris, moreover, has for a good number of years been developing a dramatic activity and initiative which Germany is far from attaining—and if particular deplorable and personal circumstances prevent Berlioz from putting on his works in Paris, that's nothing to do with the Germans.

Hoping to hear from you soon (even if not yet about the '*amazing* things' hinted at), I remain, dear friend, your cordially devoted   F. Liszt

Who attended to the final proofs of the Faust Symphony? Impress upon Schuberth not to send unworthy editions of my things out into the world. Bülow

---

[24] This passage from Cosima's letter was quoted by Liszt in its original French.
[25] *Much Ado About Nothing.*

will be so kind as to undertake the final revision, if Schuberth will only take the trouble to ask him.

509. To Princess Carolyne. Vincenzo[26] arrived at the very moment when I got to the *storm*, more than half-way through the task of revising and adding the expression marks to the piano arrangement of the *Elisabeth*. Without changing ink I hasten to tell you that I feel perfectly well.

[Cardinal Lucien] Bonaparte came at 4 o'clock, alone, telling me that he had assumed that without company he would have a better chance of seeing me—and that he had consequently got out of his rendezvous with his walking companions. He stayed for nearly an hour, and we had a pleasant chat about a protégé of his called Jacques Trouvé, now aged nearly 18 and a remarkable pianist. I shall tell you about the ups and downs of the Trouvé drama, in which Bonaparte naturally played a very fine role. He really is quite charming, very kind and something more—which gives value to his qualities. His brother Napoleon came to see me at about midday—but, having given instructions, I didn't see him. Besides, Mgr. Lucien and I drew up beforehand a little plan which will be put into effect when his Gabrielli sister arrives. It seems more than likely that I shall get to know very well the different routes leading to the Palazzo Gabrielli! . . .   F.L.

510. To Anna Liszt in Paris. Rome, 12 September

Dearest Mother,

If my letters give you even a hundredth part of the joy that yours cause me, that is enough to make me well content, for it would already be a good deal. Your handwriting, it seems to me, is becoming from year to year ever more beautiful; so much so, that I should like to take lessons in calligraphy from you. Something else which increases for me from year to year is the sweetness of the evidence of your love and devotion. I was moved to tears by your pious remembrance of my father, and thank you with all my heart for having on 28 August thought simultaneously of him and of me. My father's presentiment, that his son was to leave the track beaten by others of his social class and face the hazards of an uncommon destiny, quickly became a real conviction, I could almost say an *article of faith*, with him; that presentiment, I say, conceived in the cir-

---

[26] Servant of the Princess.

cumstances of Raiding, the village, far removed from all civilization, whose social amenities were limited to games of tarot with a few country priests and colleagues in the service of Prince Esterházy, all of them inferior to him in intelligence and understanding nothing more of music than, perhaps, the strumming of his little prodigy of a son, aged eight or nine! How not to be struck by it? He did not hesitate for a moment, nor did he yield to all the rational arguments of rational people. He had to sacrifice his secure position, give up comfortable habits, leave his own country, ask his wife to share a doubtful future, meet the costs of our modest existence by giving Latin, geography, history, and music lessons; had, in a word, to quit the service of Prince Esterházy, leave Raiding and settle in Vienna, so that I could take lessons from our good, excellent Czerny and thereafter face the risks of a very problematical career. And all this with savings of no more than a few hundred francs! Certainly, dearest Mother, you are entirely right when you say that not one father in thousands would have been capable of such devotion, or of such persistence in that kind of *intuitive stubbornness* possessed only by persons of exceptional character. But since, as both a dutiful wife and a most devoted mother, you shared daily and hourly everything that my father [did and sacrificed?[27]] for me, allow me to bring to you, with the most faithful respect and all the emotion of my gratitude, what is due to you. . . .

Your most affectionate son,   F. Liszt

Have you noticed that 28 August, St Augustine's Day, is also the date of Goethe's birth? This Weimar is playing a singular role through the years of my little life. Before placing me under Czerny's guidance, my father wanted to take me to Weimar, to Hummel, who, if you recall, asked for one or several ducats per lesson, which angered my father, who considered it an uncalled-for demand on the part of an old friend. Later, in 1836 or 37, I had the idea of writing from Milan to the Grand Duke of Weimar, whom I did not know at that time, for I came to Germany only in 1839 [1840], to offer myself as successor to Hummel (who had just died) as Kapellmeister. Later still (in 1841), it was in Weimar that, without having thought of it beforehand, I received my first decoration. . . .

On Thursday, 11 September,[28] just over two months after the birth of her son, Liszt's daughter Blandine died at St Tropez.

---

[27] The published source for this letter here has a gap indicating an indecipherable word or words.

[28] A letter from Emile Ollivier to Liszt dated 9 Sept. contains the words 'Blandine died this morning'—but it seems clear that in his distraught state he wrote the wrong date.

511. To Anna Liszt. 27 September. My first, my constant thought in this cruel calamity which has struck us,[29] is you, dearest Mother: you, who played so great a part in this dear, gentle life which, alas, is no more—through the care, love, and devotion which you lavished daily, hourly, on her childhood; you whom she loved so devotedly and whom she felt happy, in her turn, to care for, soothe, cheer, and charm! What melancholy, what a void her disappearance has just caused us in this sad world! I weep and grieve more than I can say. But you, dearest Mother, truly show admirable resignation in such sorrow; and the letter you wrote to Ollivier, and which he has just shown me, gives me the sole consolation to which I am open at this moment: that of knowing that you are bearing your grief like a Christian.

Ollivier arrived yesterday morning, and is staying with me. This morning, feast of SS Cosmas and Damian, I took him to an ancient temple of Romulus and Remus in the Forum, since turned into a church and dedicated to the patron saints of our unique Cosima. I have been very worried about her, and am only slightly reassured. It is with a great many tears that I fête her today,[30] my thoughts going to Blandine and Daniel, who join me in praying for her. These three were just one in spirit, and now we have only Cosima left. May Heaven dwell within her! . . .

Michelangelo said that it was wrong to rejoice at the birth of a child; that, on the contrary, we ought to weep to see one more being about to participate in mankind's sufferings, and to reserve our cries of joy exclusively for those who, after a noble life, die in the Lord.[31] If it is an error, it is only in this sense that, here below, we can rejoice other than 'tremblingly'.

May God be merciful and grant us His blessings and His peace.   F. Liszt

512. To Princess Carolyne [Late October or early November]. I spent a bad night, and this morning I feel totally shattered—it's my nervous condition which takes hold of me for a day or two. I shall probably not resume my seat at your table today—unless I feel a little more presentable by about noon. At present I am doing nothing but yawn and stretch my arms! I am sending my apologies to Bonaparte—if I can manage a little work I shall add the expression marks to the *Clavierauszug* [piano score] of the *Elisabeth*, which I beg you

---

[29] The published version of the original French here has 'vous' (you), surely a misreading of 'nous' (us).

[30] The feast of St Cosmas was, of course, Cosima's name-day.

[31] Writing to Vasari in Apr. 1554 Michelangelo had put it more simply: 'It seems to me that Lionardo [his nephew] hasn't much judgement, and particularly not in making such a feast for the new-born with the rejoicing that should be reserved for the death of someone who has lived a good life . . .' Blandine herself (letter of 23 Jan. 1862) had drawn this remark to Liszt's attention.

to send me. Don't be in the least bit 'inquiètte' [worried]—by writing this word with two t's, like Bon Ecclésiaste,[32] I am just being mischievous! There is no illness at all in my condition—merely a great deal of *Abspannung* [exhaustion]. A day of seclusion in my room will restore me completely. The weather is frightful, and I shall do better not to go out—but I am not making that absolutely definite. At all events, don't wait for me, and don't irritate Kicy's stomach, which needs to be satisfied at set hours! I shall nurse myself so that I am completely cheerful on St Charles' Day,[33] which is my great festival-day! Yours, throughout time and eternity.   F.L.

513. To the Grand Duke Carl Alexander. Rome, 1 November

Monseigneur,

The affectionate kindness of your lines[34] has touched me all the more seeing that I have been remiss towards Your Royal Highness. Your family has suffered a bereavement.[35] I ought to have written to tell you how much I associate myself with all those sentiments which honour the memory of the deceased Prince; forgive me for having failed to do so at a time when so much grief was weighing upon me. There are certain states of the soul in which one hardly knows how one lives; someone else would seem to take this trouble for us! . . .

The Legend of St Elisabeth is finished. May this work contribute to the glorification of the 'dear Saint', and may it disseminate the celestial perfume of her piety, of her grace, of her sufferings, of her resignation to life, and of her gentle submission towards death!

I have in addition written some other works connected with the same order of emotion. One of them is called *Vision at the Sistine Chapel*.[36] Its great figures are Allegri and Mozart. I have not only brought them together, but as it were *bound* them to one another. Man's anguish and wretchedness cry out in distress in the *Miserere*, to which God's infinite mercy and forgiveness respond and sing in the *Ave verum corpus*. This comes close to the sublimest of mysteries; to Him who shows us Love triumphant over Evil and Death.

If this outline were to seem too mystical, then, to explain the musical idea I have indicated, I could fall back on an incident in Mozart's biography. It is known that when he visited Rome he wrote down Allegri's *Miserere* during its performance in the Sistine Chapel, both to retain it better in his memory and,

---

[32] Literally, 'Good Ecclesiastes', one of Liszt's nicknames for the Princess.
[33] The Princess's name-day, 4 Nov.   [34] Of condolence, in a letter to Liszt of 11 Oct.
[35] On 31 July the Grand Duke's uncle, Duke Bernhard of Weimar, had died.
[36] The work ultimately entitled *A la Chapelle Sixtine*.

perhaps, to breach the prohibitive system which, in the good old days, extended even to music manuscripts. How not to remember this fact, in that same enclosed space where it occurred? So I have often sought the place where Mozart must have been. I even imagined that I saw him, and that he looked on me with gentle condescension. Allegri was close by, and seemed almost to be committing an act of penitence for the celebrity that pilgrims, generally little given to musical impressions, have taken care to bestow exclusively upon his *Miserere*.

Then, slowly, there appeared in the background, beside Michelangelo's *Last Judgement*, another shade, of unutterable greatness. I recognized him instantly and with joy, for while still an exile here upon earth He had consecrated my brow with a kiss. Once, He too sang his *Miserere*, and until that time no sobs and lamentations of so profound and sublime an intensity had ever been heard. Strange encounter! It was on Allegri's mode, and on the same interval—a stubborn dominant—that Beethoven's genius thrice alighted, to leave thereon, and everlastingly, its immortal imprint. Listen to the Funeral March on the Death of a Hero, the Adagio of the *Sonata quasi Fantasia*, and the mysterious *Convito* [banquet] of phantoms and angels in the Andante of the Seventh Symphony. Is there not a striking analogy between these three motifs and Allegri's *Miserere*?

Have you retained a memory, Monseigneur, of the *Cantico di San Francesco*?[37] I have also taken it into my head to set it to music, after rereading Ozanam's[38] work on the Franciscan poets in 13th-century Italy—a book of excellent and delightful judgement in which I have found some interesting details relating to this *Cantico*. Probably Herr Hase, with his so justly appreciated talent, will have recorded them in his life of St Francis.[39] And so, at the risk of telling you only things that you in any case already know much better, I cannot resist the temptation of naïvely sharing with you my freshly acquired erudition, as follows:

In the 18th year of his penitence, the servant of God, having kept vigil for forty nights, had an ecstasy, following which he told Brother Leonardo to take a pen and write. He then sang the first seven stanzas of the *Cantico del Sole*, glorifying God for Brother Sun, Sister Moon, Brother Fire, Sister Water, Brothers Wind, Air, and Cloud. (The title of the old Cologne edition is: *Cantico delle Creature, comunemente detto de lo Frate Sol.*)

---

[37] St Francis of Assisi's well-known *Laudes creaturarum* or *Cantico del Sole* (Canticle of the Sun).

[38] Had Liszt in the latter period of his life been asked which three great men of the past he most revered, he might well have named St Francis of Assisi, Dante, and Beethoven. Such a choice would surely have been echoed—so far as the first two names are concerned—by the admirable Frédéric Ozanam (a founder of the Society of St Vincent de Paul), whose writings show him to have been devoted in equal measure to Saint and Poet. It was Ozanam, the cause for whose canonization has been initiated, who 'rediscovered' for the 19th cent. the 13th-cent. Franciscan poet Jacopone da Todi, whose *Stabat mater speciosa* Liszt—like Jacopone and (perhaps) Dante, a member of the tertiary order of St Francis—set to music in his oratorio *Christus*. The book here referred to is Ozanam's *Les Poëtes Franciscains en Italie au treizième siècle* (Paris, 1852).

[39] Karl August von Hase's *Franz von Assisi: Ein Heiligenbild* (Leipzig, 1856).

A few days later a great dispute arose between the Bishop of Assisi and the town's magistrates. The Bishop fulminated and laid them under an interdict; the magistrates placed the prelate beyond the pale of the law and forbade all dealings with him and his followers. Grieved at such strife, the Saint lamented that there was no one who would intervene and restore peace. To his *Cantico* he then added the following eighth stanza:

> Laudato sia, mio Signore,
> Per quelli che perdonano per lo tuo amore,
> E sostengono infirmitate e tribulazione!
> Beati quelli che sostegneranno in pace,
> Che da Te, Altissimo, saranno incoronati![40]

Then he told his followers to go boldly to the leading citizens, to ask them to make their way to the Bishop and, on arriving, to *form two different choirs to sing the new verse.* The disciples obeyed, and, hearing those words, to which God seemed to lend a secret virtue, the adversaries embraced penitently and asked one another's forgiveness.

It is with this verse that I am ending my setting of the *Cantico di San Francesco.* I am therefore omitting the verses and commentaries subsequently added to it, and shall recall only that on 4 October 1226 St Francis breathed his last, after having his *Cantico del Sole* sung to him once more. Could one not say that it was the 'mehr Licht!' that in his last moments was asked for by Goethe? . . .

F. Liszt

514. To Baron Augusz. Rome (Via Felice 113), 10 November

My very honoured friend,

I have long been reproaching myself for not writing to you; but to *you* I would have wanted to write only completely openly. But my situation forces me to be very reserved and even to remain silent about the things affecting me most closely.

Recently, and quite unexpectedly, a great sorrow came to me. Let me keep silence also on this grief and simply resume our old and friendly relations, with which are linked so many fond memories of mine, by telling you plainly and frankly that my friends can be quite reassured about me, that I am in good health, working persistently, and striving to make conscientious use of the time remaining to me here below.

---

[40] 'Praised be Thou, my Lord, | for them that for Thy love forgive, | And suffer tribulation and infirmity! | Blessed are they that shall persevere in peace, | For by Thee, Most High, shall they be crowned!' The Italian stanza, as copied by Liszt, uses more or less modern spelling.

Monseigneur Haynald, who showed me much kindness during his visit to Rome last June, will have given you my news, for I made a special point of asking him to. About the imaginary grievance raised against me in Hungary, he talked to me with a solicitude that I could not but find touching. I cannot admit to any guilt in the matter wrongly ascribed to me, for it does not follow that because I praised the gypsies I depreciated the merit of the Hungarians. Quite the contrary, I spoke very favourably of them, as was only fitting. So I really hope that the time will come when people will perceive their error and see that they have not been fair in this matter.

A letter I have just received from Baron Prónay,[41] written in the name of the Committee of the Pest-Buda Conservatoire, invites me to return to Hungary. I am replying to it at some length, and assume that he will acquaint you with this reply. At my age, and in my exceptional position, to accept Baron Prónay's invitation and 'exchange my residence in Rome for one in Pest' is not as easy as he seems to assume. Five or six years ago matters could have been arranged more simply and it would have been easier to specify what could properly affect my choice of residence. Now, various considerations prevent me, among them being the impossibility of losing sight of my obligations towards HRH the Grand Duke of Weimar, who long ago released me from all my former musical duties (so as not to hinder my work as a composer, which remains the *sine qua non* of my entire life) and associated me with his personal service by appointing me his Chamberlain.

Nevertheless I keenly desire *to do something* for Hungary; perhaps it will come about as the Gran Mass came about, and perhaps, too, it will be you again, very dear friend, who will do me the great service of finding it for me. Were that to be the case, I should be doubly happy! . . .

My *Legend of St Elisabeth* was completed two months ago, and I believe I did not make bad use of the materials you kindly provided me with. . . .

Please, my very honoured friend, do not punish me for my silence, and when you have the leisure for it send your news to your most sincerely affectionate, devoted and grateful friend   F. Liszt

515. To Anna Liszt. Rome, Via Felice 113, 2 December ^{G (F)}

Dearest Mother,

Forgive me for delaying so long before answering your question about my *St Elisabeth*, a work at which I have toiled for more than a year. Today I shall at last do so. I am calling it *Legend of Saint Elisabeth of Hungary*; nevertheless,

---

[41] President of the Conservatoire in Pest.

it can be considered an *oratorio*, a form to which it is linked. In it, music is exalted into prayer. It is sung and accompanied by the orchestra, but not *performed on the stage*. It is addressed to *listeners*, not to *spectators*; the drama is not to find expression through the performers' costumes and gestures. The performance lasts two and a half hours and requires four or five soloists for the parts of Elisabeth, the Landgrave Ludwig, the Hungarian magnate—who takes the child Elisabeth to the Wartburg and puts her under the protection of her father-in-law Hermann—, the Landgravine Sophie and the Emperor Frederick II von Hohenstaufen; plus a large chorus and full orchestra. The main events in the life of the dear saint form the framework of the poetic text, which Otto Roquette, a distinguished and graceful German poet, composed and which I have set to music. It breathes the whole spirit and fragrance of Montalembert's work on St Elisabeth, without the exaggerations in his book which sometimes offended you. This requires readers who are familiar with the legends of the saints and from the outset disposed to understand the supernatural inspiration of a glowing piety which is intensified to the point of heroism, as also the complete renunciation which can be gratified only at the mystical fountains of everlasting life. To be sure, the mores and habits of our time have far departed from such exaggerations of abstinence. We are not saints, and at all times the saints have been exceptional beings, the elect. But why could we not—without raising ourselves to their heights, indeed simply contenting ourselves with the *practice of good*— at least seek in thought to become absorbed in the depths of their souls? If we so often tolerate what stands *below* the level of good, indeed if our tolerance is often subtly transformed into sympathy even, why do people so very much resist what rises *above* the good?

You know, dearest Mother, how for several years on end during my youth I ceaselessly dreamt myself, so to speak, into the realm of the saints. Nothing seemed to me so self-evident as Heaven, nothing so true or so great a source of happiness as the goodness and mercy of God. Despite all the errors and aberrations of my life, nothing and no one have been able to shake the belief in immortality and the salvation of the soul which came to me during my prayers in the churches of Raiding and Frauendorf, at the Mariahilf church in Vienna, and at Notre Dame de Lorette and St Vincent de Paul in Paris. All the storms notwithstanding, the good seed in me has germinated and is more deeply filled than ever before with all the truths of religion. When I now read the *Lives of the Saints* I feel as though after a long journey I am meeting old and venerable friends from whom I shall part no more.

An extraordinary coincidence led me lovingly to St Elisabeth. Born, like her, in Hungary, I spent twelve years—of decisive importance for my destiny—in Thuringia, not far from the Wartburg in which she dwelt. How eagerly I followed the restoration of the Wartburg Castle, which *my* Grand Duke of Weimar undertook; and the Elisabeth passage-way leading to the chapel of the newly-risen castle was painted under my eyes by Schwind. His scenes from the legend of St Elisabeth I adopted for my work, in the following sequence:

1. Arrival of St Elisabeth at the Wartburg in a silver cradle. Children's chorus of welcome.
2. Elisabeth's meeting with her husband, the Landgrave Ludwig, who is returning from the hunt. Miracle of the roses.
3. Crusaders' Chorus. Ludwig's departure from the saint. His journey to the Holy Land.
4. Ludwig dies. The saint is driven from the Wartburg by her mother-in-law Sophie.
5. Works of charity. Chorus of the Poor. Elisabeth's prayer. Last memory of the land of her birth. She dies, entrusting her soul to God.
6. Elisabeth's solemn obsequies at Marburg in the presence of the Emperor Frederick II von Hohenstaufen.

You see, dearest Mother, that there is here no trace of exaggeration and that even the unsympathetic figure of Master Konrad, who in Montalembert's history of Elisabeth could not be avoided, makes no appearance. The music need not illustrate every incident in the story.

But I fear that today, dearest Mother, I have chatted to you for far too long.

May God keep you healthy in body and mind and give you His peace and richest blessing, as is implored of Him by your faithfully loving and devoted son   F. Liszt

Have you news of Ollivier? Is he in Algiers?

516. To Princess Carolyne. I thank you for the good dinner—and above all for your dear words. Had it been given to me to live according to my taste, I should have imitated the example of the Blessed Labre—and hidden myself in a slum of more or less historic ruins. There I should have kept only a beautiful casket to hold all your letters, which, in the periods between prayer, I should have read and reread incessantly like a Divine Service! . . .

1863

20 March. Cosima von Bülow gives birth to a second daughter. Liszt's third grandchild, she is named Blandine after her deceased aunt.
20 June. Liszt moves from the Via Felice to the monastery of the Madonna del Rosario on Monte Mario.
11 July. He is visited there by Pope Pius IX.
16 July. He has a private audience with the Pope at the Vatican.

WORKS. *Slavimo slavno slaveni!* (U. Pucić) (S33), for male chorus and organ.[1] *Salve Polonia* (S113) for orchestra. PIANO: Legends (S175): 1. *St François d'Assise: la prédication aux oiseaux.* 2. *St François de Paule marchant sur les flots*; *Rhapsodie espagnole* ('Folies d'Espagne et jota aragonesa') (S254, *c.*1863).
Liszt also devotes much time to work on his oratorio *Christus* (S3).

517. To Princess Carolyne [27 January].

Today is the feast of St John Chrysostom, one of your patron saints. For my foolish remarks of yesterday my leaden mouth makes due apology to his golden one. I shall come and celebrate your name-day with you—don't change your usual routine in the slightest, but simply order lunch for two at 1 o'clock. Forgive me for having been for several days in rather a distracted mood—it results from my having been unable to continue the work I had begun. As soon as I get down to it again I shall be my usual self—so, this very morning, I shall try to write half a page of music. Till 1.00, therefore, and with no tiff at all.   Yours!

518. To Anna Liszt in Paris. 7 March

Dearest Mother,

For once in a while I have to reproach you slightly, but do so very gently of course, while asking you not to scold me for it. You hadn't told me that your doctor was recommending you the waters of Bourbonne-les-Bains,[2] and it was through our good and excellent Hermann that I learnt of it. The sleeping-cars installed in French trains will make this journey easier for you, and I earnestly

---

[1] The first performance was in Rome on 3 July.   [2] Spa in north-east France, not far from Langres.

ask you to do as the doctor advises. If it will help you make up your mind more quickly, will you allow me to add that I shall come to visit you at Bourbonne-les-Bains, to stroll around your room with you, give you your fill of talk and anecdotes, embrace you and weep with you?...

So it is agreed, dear Mother. You will go and take your cure, and I shall be there while you are doing so. Nevertheless, don't count on my being of any use to you, for, as you know, I am extremely clumsy at anything connected with nursing duties. You will therefore need to take someone from Paris on whom you can rely to look after you. But please let me know a little in advance the sum you will need for your journey and your stay in the spa, and I shall hasten to send it to you. . . .

I embrace you, dear Mother, with all my heart, and am very faithfully yours,

F. Liszt

519. To Anna Liszt. Rome, 8 May

Dearest Mother,

I am happy about the good news you give me of your health and leave it entirely to you to decide what you find advisable to do this summer. As you had told me about a trip to the spa of Bourbonne, I naturally urged you to come to an understanding with your doctor and to take his advice. If he thinks that such a course of treatment would be of no use to you, it would be better to abandon the idea, reserving the right to follow some other, more suitable advice. The most important thing in all this will be to retain that fortunate mental equilibrium which allows you to endure physical sufferings and discomfort so patiently. It is a gift given to you by God, one for which I thank Him from the bottom of my heart, while asking Him to heap upon you all His blessings!

To amuse you a little, dearest Mother, I shall pay you a little compliment. Without being aware of it, you write like Herr von Humboldt. He too, his upright-ness of mind notwithstanding, didn't bother to keep to a *straight line* when pen-ning words on paper, following the direction of telescopes rather than that laid down by teachers of handwriting. And so don't complain about a fault which is a point of resemblance with that great man whom I remember with deep gratitude.

I believe I have already thanked you for sending the moving poem by Ratisbonne.[3] There are noble tears in those verses so melodiously inspired by our dear Blandine. A few months after Daniel's death I reread the stanzas entitled 'Les Morts' that Lamennais published in his volume of *Mélanges*. Each one of

---

[3] Louis Ratisbonne's *Il le fallait*, inspired by the death of Blandine and published in the *Revue Germanique et Française* of 1 Feb. 1863.

them falls back on, or rather reascends to, this simple but sublime exclamation: 'Blessed are the dead which die in the Lord.'[4] This is the reverberation of God's mercy in the human soul and the revelation of the mystery of life and death through the infinite blessing of His love.

When reading Lamennais's verses I involuntarily translated them into music, jotting down these chords, feeble and ineffective though they may be. Later on I shall compose similar music for Blandine. Let us not be too sad about the sorrows of life, dear Mother, since this life is only a beginning and it is given to us to die 'in the Lord', Who loves us and calls us to Him!

Let us believe and our faith will be justified.   F. Liszt

You will shortly receive news of me (in tolerable condition, both physically and mentally) from someone you have certainly heard spoken of, and highly: Princess Marcelina Czartoryska.[5] I have seen a good deal of her here and am flattered by the kindness she has shown me. She has promised me that she will pay you a visit to give you some of those details which interest you as a mother and which, generally, I forget or neglect to write. As you know, Princess Cz. possesses real talent as a pianist, a talent I have made particular use of to compensate myself for the rather unstimulating music I am sometimes obliged to hear. Further, as well as many other merits she has a charm and steadiness of mind which make her stand out even among very distinguished women. For the last dozen years she has been living almost constantly in Paris, but her estates and those of her husband are in Galicia and other parts of old Poland. The present political situation draws her back to Vienna, where she had settled earlier. Our excellent Czerny gave her piano lessons and, during the last years of his life, Chopin as it were breathed into her the ecstasies of his Muse. So you will have a number of things in common to talk about: Chopin, Czerny, Vienna, Poland, Paris, and myself into the bargain. . . .

520. To Eduard Liszt in Vienna. Rome, 22 May [G]

Dearest Eduard,

Weariness or something of the sort put me in mind of my *Berceuse*. Into my day-dreams there then came various other *Berceuses*. Would you care to join my dreams? It wouldn't be difficult; without so much as touching the keys you have only to allow yourself to be lulled into the feelings hovering over them. A really charming lady, endowed with manifold intellectual as well as musical gifts, will

---

[4] Rev. 14: 13.

[5] A compatriot (née Radziwill), pupil and friend of Chopin, the Princess had been among those with the great Polish composer at the moment of his death in the early morning of 17 Oct. 1849.

see to this. She plays the little piece delightfully and has promised me to let it *work its spell* upon you. And so I shall shortly be sending you a copy of the new version of the *Berceuse*, addressed 'to Princess Marcelina Czartoryska, Klostergasse 4'. Wend your way thither—and should you find the Princess not at home, leave the manuscript there with your card. I have told her that you will be calling, and spoken of you as my close relative and friend. In the Princess Cz. you will find a rare intelligence and understanding, a most charming and gracious social manner, a delightfully enthusiastic worshipper at the shrines of *Mozart, Beethoven, and Chopin*, and, over and above all this, the shining faith of the Catholic Church reflected in her feeling for the blood of Poland.

Patria in Religione et Religio in patria might be the motto of Poland. God protect the oppressed!

I should be glad if you would undertake one further errand for the Princess Cz. During her stay here she several times expressed the wish to know some of my compositions (of which, intentionally or not, she had hitherto taken little notice); and the 2-piano arrangements of the symphonic poems *Héroïde funèbre, Tasso,* and *Les Préludes* which I played with her, she received with friendly, courteous tolerance. Without laying claim to more than that—ample experience having taught me that my things more easily gain themselves enemies than friends —I should nevertheless like the musical threads of our pleasant relations not to be entirely broken, and, to make amends, wish to present her first of all with various pages of music. In Rome's sparsely stocked music shops could not be found the works which best suit her talent, and I promised to seek your help in the matter. Please, therefore, my dearest Eduard, have the following works simply and neatly bound together in one volume (in the order given here) and deliver them soon to the Princess Cz.

1. *Glanes de Woronince* (Leipzig, Kistner).
2. *Mélodies de Chopin*, transcribed by Liszt (Berlin, Schlesinger).[6]
3. Mazurka (Senff, Leipzig).
4. 2 Polonaises (*idem*).
5. 2 Ballades (1 and 2 Kistner, Leipzig).
6. *Consolations* (Härtel, Leipzig).

Should the volume not already be too thick, the *Valse mélancolique* and *Romanesca* (2nd edn. by Haslinger) could be added. Naturally the whole thing, contents and binding, is to be charged to me, as a present to the noble artiste. If the things are not available in Vienna, order them speedily from Leipzig through Haslinger or Spina.

---

[6] The *Chants polonais.*

Talking of Spina: hasn't the 2-piano arrangement of my orchestral adaptation of the magnificent C major Fantasy of Schubert been published yet? This delay, or rather negligence, is by no means to my liking.

Most affectionately yours, F. Liszt

521. To Franz Brendel in Leipzig. Rome, 18 June. ^G . . . The day after tomorrow I shall be quitting my rooms in Via Felice and moving to *Monte Mario* (an hour's distance from the city). Father Theiner is so kind as to let me use his apartment there in the almost uninhabited house of the oratorians. The view is magnificent beyond words. I wish now at last to be able to live more *naturally*, and hope that I shall manage to approach more closely to my monastico-artistic ideal. . . .

522. To Franz Brendel. Rome, 18 July. ^G . . . This letter is so packed with royal personages, majesties, and highnesses, that it offers me a natural transition to tell you of an extraordinary, nay, incomparable honour which came my way last Saturday, 11 July. His Holiness Pope Pius IX came to the church of the Madonna del Rosario and hallowed my dwelling-place with his presence. After I had given the Pope a small proof of my skill[7] on a harmonium and on my workaday upright piano, he most graciously addressed some very significant words to me, urging me to strive after heavenly things in things earthly, and through my ephemeral harmonies to prepare myself for those that will be everlasting. His Holiness stayed for about half an hour; Monsign. de Mérode[8] and Hohenlohe were in his retinue—and the day before yesterday I was granted an audience in the Vatican (the first since I have been here), at which the Pope presented me with a beautiful cameo of the Madonna. . . .

523. To Anna Liszt. Rome, 25 July. ^{G (F)} Here I am on your name-day [26 July] once again, dearest Mother, embracing you, fêting you, thanking you from a full heart. To all my wishes for your happiness and well-being I add an apparently selfish one: may my works bear good fruit and my growing fame

---

[7] Apart from some Beethoven, the pieces Liszt played on this memorable occasion—the visit is said to be the only one ever paid by a pope to a musician—were the recently composed *St François d'Assise: la prédication aux oiseaux* and *St François de Paule marchant sur les flots*.

[8] The Belgian prelate Xavier de Mérode was the brother-in-law of Montalembert.

give you some contentment! Bless me, dear Mother, and pray for me to Him who grants fulfilment to blessing!

My health is good and my new residence has awakened within me the greatest desire to work. You know what an exceptional honour the Holy Father paid me, and will understand that after such a visit, to which no worldly honour can be compared, the decision I had already made anyway, to settle permanently in Rome, was only strengthened. I am sending you a small photograph of the parish church of the Madonna del Rosario on Monte Mario. The first window on the left on the first floor is that of my study, and the last one, rather blurred in the photograph, admits light to my dining-room. Apart from me, in the whole building dwell only the priest, a friar who attends to the cooking most excellently, and my servant, whose name, Fortunato,[9] is of good omen. Ollivier will explain to you where Monte Mario is situated; before my windows lies the most glorious panorama of the whole of Rome.

Since my comparison of your handwriting with that of Alexander von Humboldt pleased you, I'll amuse you with a new comparison. Your name-day follows one that is greatly celebrated here—guess which!—Cardinal Antonelli's.[10] You perhaps admire him less than Humboldt; yet with the latter he has in common the fact that the majority of those who talk about him understand no more of his politics than they do of *Cosmos*, if they were even to *read* this in the first place. But I admit that the uncomprehended Humboldt enjoys more trust.

Be that as it may, I have just congratulated His Eminence, who honours me with his goodwill,[11] and so, now that I am in the process of comparing, I want to pass from our good and holy Mother Church to my own gentle and beloved Mother, who is deeply revered by

Her respectful son   F. Liszt

524. To Agnes Street-Klindworth. Madonna del Rosario, Monte Mario, 30 August

Your *Music* is heard; it resounds frequently within my soul.

No need to tell you that there is no great change in me, still less that I have become forgetful. But my life is ordered more simply—and the Catholic piety of my childhood has become a regular and regulating feeling. For a good many people piety consists in burning what one has worshipped. I am far from blaming them—but for my own part I incline, and shall rather seek, to sanctify what

---

[9] See under Salvagni in Biographical Sketches.

[10] Antonelli's Christian name was Giacomo (James), 25 July being the feast of St James the Greater.

[11] Antonelli generally referred to Liszt as 'lo stregone ungherese' (the Hungarian wizard).

I have loved; and, if you will forgive me this comparison between the very great and the very small, I shall say that in doing so I am following the method constantly used in Rome for Christian monuments. The magnificent columns of Santa Maria degli Angeli, don't they come from the Baths of Diocletian? And the bronze from the Pantheon, hasn't it been put to use in the baldachin of the altar at St Peter's?—An endless list of such transformations could be made; for at every step one takes here one is struck by how the divine plan agrees between what has been and what is and will be. And so I am becoming singularly fond of Rome, where I hope to leave my bones, and I repeat with St Bernard: 'Ibi aër *purior,* coelum *apertius, familiarior* Deus [There the air is *purer,* the sky *clearer,* God *closer*]!'

Since the Augsburg *Gazette* has informed you of my dwelling place, I am sending you a small photograph of the Madonna del Rosario, where I live on the first floor—working and praying.

You, too, have changed residence. Write without music and let me know how your concerns and preoccupations are going. . . . I should be interested, moreover, to know your views on the political events in the North. My circle being very restricted, I know only what is said by the *Moniteur,* to which I subscribe from lasting conviction, and two or three newspapers that I read from time to time. And so if you would be so kind as to continue, even to a small extent, your illustrious customary offices for my benefit, I should be most obliged to you. For total security, I ask you to take the trouble of having your letters *registered* at the post office, so that I may be warned of their arrival by a preliminary advice note, just as you have already done for your splendid *music.*

More soon.   F.L.

525. To Franz Brendel. Madonna del Rosario, 7 September ^G

Dear friend. . . .

The summer has gone by quietly, and I have been out and about very little, but rather remained constantly sitting at my work. My abode continues to suit me more and more, so I intend to spend the winter here. With my last letter you doubtless received the photograph of the Madonna del Rosario? Unfortunately the absolutely magnificent, truly sublime view that can be enjoyed from all the windows is something I cannot send. So you'll just have to imagine it taking in the whole of Rome, the wondrous *Campagna,* and all past and present glories. . . .

Weitzmann's 'The Carnival in Rome around the Middle of the Seventeenth Century', I read with great pleasure in the *Neue Zeitschrift.* It is a vivid and

charming sketch, spiced with learning but without leaden pedantry. Has a review of the same author's very remarkable 'History of the Piano' etc.[12] already
appeared in your newspaper? In a recent letter to me, Frau von Bülow wrote
that Hans was busy preparing some essays for the *N.Z.* It is probably he who
is seeing to the review of Weitzmann's 'Piano History', which would be most
appropriate; if this is not the case, I would advise you to entrust it to one of
your staff, and to include several quotations from the work. The confounded
piano has its unquestionable importance, if only because of the way in which
it is generally abused!—In honour of Härtel's edition of Beethoven I have again
been busying myself with studies and experiments in writing for the piano. The
arrangements of the 8 Beethoven symphonies, which I have just sent off to Leipzig,
are not, I trust, unsuccessful. They cost me more trouble—attempting now one
way, now another, correcting, deleting, adding—than I had initially expected. As
we grow old we deliberate more and are less readily satisfied. . . .

Most affectionate greetings from your devoted   F. Liszt

**526. To Agnes Street-Klindworth in Ostend. Madonna del Rosario,
19 September.** . . . I accept with gratitude your promise to continue your dispatches of former days; however, I should not like to take indiscretion too far,
nor to tire you out by adding to your usual occupations. And so let's agree that
you will write to me approximately once a month about what is going on; and
so that the letters reach me safely, do please always provide them with the seals
required for *registered letters.* (Incidentally, write of certain matters, should they
crop up, only sketchily—merely hinting at them, because of the censorship.) As
for now, my servant being obliged to collect letters at the post office, it is also
advisable for them not to attract attention because of their size .... forgive me
for these unnecessary details!

In exchange for the riches of your part of our correspondence, I have unfortunately nothing of interest to offer you; it will therefore be an act of pure generosity on your part, and I shall receive it as such. My *raison d'être* in Rome
consisting in one person alone, and that one person having very little to do with
society, I concentrate on a few fixed points of feeling, study, and work. I finished
my *Elisabeth* oratorio last *summer,* and have made pretty good progress recently
with the one entitled *Christus,* which I hope to complete before Easter. . . .

Among the few people I associate with, I'll name Monseigneur [Lucien]
Bonaparte, Mgr. Nardi, and Baron Felix Meyendorff, since I see them less rarely

---

[12] C. F. Weitzmann's *Geschichte des Clavierspiels und der Clavierliteratur* (Stuttgart, 1863).

than others. Mgr. Bonaparte lives an extremely retired life, never going into society, and even declining invitations to his brothers' homes when people other than members of his family are there. A prelate whose devoutness is very sincere, he is also the possessor of wide-ranging erudition and a most astute and judicious intellect. The kindness and goodwill he shows me, as well as the admiration we share for his *cousin*, make me very attached to him. People will in vain act and speak against the Emperor: he will remain the great man of a great age.—Nardi, who is not entirely of this opinion, has taken the opposite course to Mgr. Bonaparte and is often to be seen in diplomatic and other salons. He appeared recently at the Congress of Malines; did you hear mention of him?—Meyendorff (nephew of the Ambassador to Berlin and Vienna) passed from Stuttgart to Rome as first secretary of the Embassy. He has, it seems to me, everything that is needed to make a splendid career. His wife (one of the daughters of Prince Gorchakov of Warsaw)[13] combines with many other charms that of an extremely original talent on the piano.

Thank you once again for your letter. Be *entirely* reassured about the good use of your time when you want to write to me, and never suspect me of being other than what I am and shall always be—that is to say,

Your wholly affectionate and devoted servant   F. Liszt

527. To Jessie Laussot in Florence. Madonna del Rosario, 15 October.

Here, chère Madame, are a few lines that, not knowing where to send them, I beg you to forward to Frau Ritter (*mère*).[14]

The melancholy familiarity with death that I have had to acquire these last few years, by no means lessens the grief we feel when our loved ones leave this earth. If at the sight of the newly-dug graves I thrust back despair and blasphemy, it is so that I may weep more freely and not separate myself, either in life or in death, from the communion of love.

She whom we mourn was especially dear to me. Her physical weakness had greatly increased her intuitive faculties, and, finding compensation therein, she lived in the beyond... At our first meeting I felt as though I already knew her. It was in Zurich, *chez* Wagner, whose powerful and splendid genius she felt so profoundly. For several weeks at lunch and dinner time she regularly took my arm to go into the dining-room—and exuded an uncommon charm and grace,

[13] Baroness Olga von Meyendorff. See Biographical Sketches.
[14] Julie Ritter had lost her daughter Emilie, sister of Carl and Alexander Ritter.

of sweet and conciliatory affection, in that home in which a certain exquisite part of intimacy was wanting. The secret of making her presence agreeable and harmonious she possessed in a rare degree. Everything about her, even her very silence, showed understanding, for she seemed to *hear*, or rather to discern, the thoughts that words only half communicate, and, in her noble heart, to complete them.

May her soul live everlastingly in the fullness of the light and peace of God!

Very cordially yours,   F. Liszt

Please forgive me the delay in these lines. It was only yesterday that I obtained your address from Sig. Sgambati.

528. To Franz Brendel. Rome, 11 November ^G

Dear friend. . . .

Despite my seclusion and isolation I am forever being badly disturbed by visits, duties of politeness, and musical protégés, as well as by various obligations and a voluminous—but for the most part pointless—correspondence. Among other things the St Petersburg Philharmonic Society has invited me to conduct performances of works of mine at two of their concerts during the next Lent season. The letter is, to be sure, written more reasonably than the one (of which I told you recently) from the committee in charge of work on Cologne Cathedral; but, even so, the good people cannot desist from twaddle about my 'former triumphal processions, unparalleled mastery on the piano' etc., which has come to be thoroughly nauseating to me—like stale, lukewarm champagne. Committee gentlemen and others should really be rather ashamed of uttering such trite superficialities to me, unbecomingly denigrating me by alluding to a standpoint I occupied years ago and which is now quite outdated. Since my departure from Germany only one musical association can boast of forming an honourable exception to this: namely, the 'Zelus pro Domo Dei' society in Amsterdam, which, as a result of their acquaintance with and performance of the Gran Mass, last week sent me a document conferring honorary membership upon me, together with a very kind letter which struck just the right note. . . .

For your wife's amusement, and as a piece of French reading, I enclose a copy of my reply to the letters from Petersburg and Amsterdam. When you have read them perhaps you would send both copies to my daughter in Berlin, as additions to her small collection of my miscellaneous correspondence.

Most cordial greetings from your affectionate   F. Liszt

529. To Agnes Street-Klindworth. 6 December. How to *reciprocate?*

What can I do or say in order to respond to so much grace, kindness, patience, charm, and wit? You inevitably condemn me to a kind of ingratitude, despite the aversion I feel to the very word! May you at least derive some pleasure from dispensing your bounties to me like this, and be quite certain that I am more adept at *receiving* than at giving or repaying. A splendid talent, isn't it? But it is your fault if no other is left for me to lay claim to. However, you would be doing me an injustice if you assumed that I had forgotten our childish little cabbalism of the *Carlsplatz.*[15] It is not an apparition that has vanished—I see and hear you always in just the same way. . . . Two obligations of different kinds will probably induce me to absent myself from Rome this coming spring. I am not making much mention of it as yet, and ask you to imitate me on this point; but when the time comes I shall let you know. For the rest, as I have already told you, a chronic idiosyncrasy of mine is a dislike of travel. What's the good of dragging oneself about? Madame de Sévigné was quite right to say that 'unless one is an ambassadress there is no need to shift one's bones'. I am determined to leave mine *here*, without imposing further pointless fatigues on them.

Father Theiner has fulfilled your wish by obtaining the Holy Father's Blessing for your rosary. I shall send it to you at the first opportunity, and will add to it a rather good engraving of Pius IX (with autographed inscription) for which you will find a good place in your salon. Rosary and portrait will reach you through M. Franchomme (the friend of Chopin), who has come to Rome to visit Princess Marcelina Czartoryska and will return to Paris by New Year's Day. When you have received them (or even before), write a few words to the Revd Father Theiner which I'll pass on to him. He is very busy at present with the new edition of *Baronius* and his continuators, including Theiner himself, which will be published in Paris and will fill 40 to 50 volumes in quarto!—In addition he is continuing his folios of the 'Vetera Monumenta historica' and preparing a 5th volume of very curious documents on Poland, so as not to leave idle the Vatican printing-works which he has set up beneath his turret, formerly inhabited by Galileo. To make still more certain that he is not bothered by visitors and untimely interruptions, around Christmas he will come and spend 6 weeks in the little house of the Oratory Fathers, which adjoins the Madonna del Rosario and is completely deserted in winter. We shall contrive to dine tête-à-tête every day, and, if you are so kind as to continue your *mailings* to me, they will provide our most beautiful intellectual dessert. . . . F.L.

[15] The Weimar square in which Agnes had lived at the time of her affair with Liszt nearly a decade earlier.

1864

21 March. Liszt plays at a concert for Peter's pence.
Mid-July. He is the guest of Cardinal Hohenlohe at the Villa d'Este.
30/1 July. He plays to the Pope at Castel Gandolfo.
August–October. Liszt travels to Germany to attend the Allgemeine Deutsche Musik-verein festival in Karlsruhe. He also visits Munich, Lake Starnberg, Weimar, Löwenberg, and Berlin. After a week in Paris he returns, via Saint Tropez, to Rome.

WORKS. *La Notte*[1] (S112/2, 1863–4), second of the *Trois Odes funèbres* for orchestra. ORGAN: *Ora pro nobis. Litanei* (S262). PIANO: *Urbi et orbi, bénédiction papale* (S184); *Vexilla regis prodeunt* (S185); transcriptions (S464, 1863–4) of the remaining Beethoven symphonies and revision of those completed in earlier years.

530. To Charlotte von Oven[2] in Munich. Rome, 16 February. When the winter frosts were threatening the *symbolic Pine*, you protected and adorned it, enveloping it in flowers of poetry and perfumes of memory. And so its sap will not grow cold, and its evergreen foliage will again be able to smile, dream, and gently murmur.

A great poet has spoken of the aerial moaning of the sea breeze among the leaves of the pines of Italy.[3] In days gone by I often listened to this wonderful concert in the pinewoods at Pisa, and my soul drank deep draughts of ineffable anguish and delight; but here one is more inclined to meditate than to dream. The pine which overlooks the hills of Rome, like a hermit sunk in some mysterious meditation which holds him back on the very threshold of the Holy City, doesn't allow its thoughts to wander into vagueness. It stretches its branches towards the heights where the sign of the redemption of the world appeared in radiant triumph to Constantine;[4] it is to that tree, noble beyond all others, whose leaves, fruits and buds bring forth every grace and every blessing, that it bears testimony; and it is the hymn of the *Crux fidelis* that it urges me to sing.

---

[1] Inspired, as already noted, by Michelangelo. The middle section of the work Liszt prefixed with words of Virgil's: 'Dulcis moriens reminiscitur Argos' (Dying, he remembers fair Argos), *Aeneid*, x. 782.

[2] The former Charlotte von Hagn had visited Rome in the autumn, and, on returning home, written and sent to Liszt a poem inspired by the solitary pine on Monte Mario and by the 'eternally unforgettable hours' spent with Liszt himself.

[3] See Letter 78 n. 21.

[4] In 312, according to the legend, Constantine the Great was converted to Christianity after seeing a vision of the Cross of Christ superimposed upon the sun, accompanied by the words *In hoc signo vinces* (In this sign conquer).

As you know, the chapel commemorating the appearance of the Cross to Constantine on Monte Mario stands very close to the symbolic pine and to my dwelling-place at the Madonna del Rosario. Two Dominican friars have had the idea of celebrating once again, through eloquence and music, the manifestation of the divine sign which on this very site converted the Caesar to Christianity. Eminent prelates have associated themselves with this idea, which the Holy Father has graciously approved. It was at first thought to realize it in the little church of the Madonna del Rosario; but the great gathering of people attracted by so solemn a ceremony will necessitate a change of locality. I shall shortly be sending you the programme, on which a modest place is reserved for me.

Today, let me just thank you for your charming poem; I should like to be able to respond to it more suitably. Nevertheless, since you continue to show me so much goodwill, I hope that you will supplement abundantly everything lacking in

Your very affectionate servant   F. Liszt

531. To Princess Carolyne [Madonna del Rosario, May]. Long live the King of Bavaria![5] That's a truly royal flash of inspiration—and if some imprudence were to be discerned therein, fie on prudence! Hasn't Bon Ecclésiaste done more and better for Lazybones? I am going to make a copy of this miracle of a letter, and will bring it to you this evening. . . .

532. To Princess Carolyne [Villa d'Este[6]] 14 July. . . . One thing alone is necessary and beneficial for me: to be able to work steadily and consistently at my little notes, so that in their entirety they will later do a little honour to Bon Ecclésiaste. I neither want, nor seek, nor desire anything else! After having

---

[5] This enthusiasm for the 18-year-old Ludwig II, King of Bavaria since 10 Mar., is explained and elaborated on in the diary (1 June 1864) of Kurd von Schlözer, Secretary of the Prussian Legation in Rome. Referring to a recent dinner at which he had seen Liszt, Schlözer comments: 'Liszt seemed in a strikingly cheerful and excited frame of mind. As is well known, he is a close friend of Richard Wagner, and he was now overjoyed at the flattering invitation Wagner has received from the young King Ludwig to go to Munich, where he is guaranteed a life free from cares. Liszt read out the King's letter (in transcript) to us. In it the King tells the composer how enthusiastic about his music he has been from early youth onwards, and of the joy it has given him; and so if he now offers him Munich as a place of residence, it is merely an expression of the sincere gratitude he owes him' (K. von Schlözer, *Römische Briefe*, 71). To Franz Brendel, Liszt wrote: 'What a royal and marvellous act is Ludwig of Bavaria's letter to Wagner. It ought verily to be engraved in the Valhalla in letters of gold. Oh that some other Princes would adopt a similar style!' (La Mara (ed.), *Franz Liszt's Briefe*, 8 vols., Leipzig, 1893–1905, ii. 66).

[6] Famed for its magnificent gardens with their numerous terraces and immense fountains, the 16th-cent. Villa d'Este at Tivoli, a town and episcopal see some 18 miles north-east of Rome, had been built for Cardinal Ippolito d'Este by the famous and infamous Pirro Ligorio, architect, antiquary and forger; and it was now the property (as the tenant of its owner, the Duke of Modena) of Liszt's friend Gustav Hohenlohe, the Papal Grand Almoner, who gave the composer an open invitation to stay there whenever he wished.

appreciated many audiences, in general and in particular, I have reached the exact point when one can not only do without an audience—but can even find a real satisfaction in doing without it! Those who don't understand that, don't understand music! *Ergo*, I shall work for Bon Ecclésiaste, and a little for myself. Even if I do not succeed in doing anything worthwhile, it will still be the best use I can make of my time. Since the phrenologists have been telling me for forty years that I possess large musical bumps—I have no alternative but to set them in motion and show them off! . . .   F.L.

In late July and early August Liszt spent a few days in the Castelli Romani region of Italy to the south-east of Rome, staying at Castel Gandolfo, the Pope's summer residence overlooking Lake Albano, and also visiting Albano, Nemi, and Frascati.

533. To Princess Carolyne. Hôtel de Rome [Castel Gandolfo] Sunday, 31 July. I hope my stay at Castel Gandolfo will give you some satisfaction. The Holy Father is most graciously kind to me. Yesterday, Saturday, at about noon, he deigned to receive me and to remark that it gave him pleasure to see me, speak with me and listen to me here. Shortly afterwards, between one and two o'clock, before his lunch, I played him various pieces on an upright piano that Mgr. Hohenlohe had managed to find. Today, at the same hour, I continued to display to him my little repertoire. Yesterday, as today, I had the honour of eating at the Court table, presided over by Mgr. Borromeo. In the evening I accompanied Mgr. Hohenlohe to M. de Sartiges in Albano; and this morning went to Galora, where the Holy Father said low mass in the church of the Jesuit Fathers, in honour of St Ignatius.[7] On Tuesday, day of the *gran perdono*[8] of our dear and adorable San Francesco, I shall attend the papal mass in the Franciscan Monastery at Nemi. For tomorrow, Monday, M. de Meyendorff has invited Mgr. Hohenlohe and me to dinner. Meyendorff is living in one of the numerous palazzi belonging to Cardinal di Pietro, which in Albano they call the Palazzo dei *Cinque*. Baron Bach, who is said to be coming here tomorrow, has taken his *villeggiatura* [country holiday] there for several summers. . . . Before this morning's musical session, to which he came, HE the Cardinal [Antonelli] favoured me with quite a long conversation. I shall probably be unable to return [to Rome] before Wednesday evening; for in addition to luncheon at the

[7] Ignatius Loyola, whose feast-day it was.

[8] In 1216, following a vision of Christ which had appeared to St Francis in the Porziuncola chapel at Assisi, and at Francis's request, Pope Honorius III granted a plenary indulgence (the 'great pardon' to which Liszt refers)—full remission of temporal punishment to a repentant sinner—on one day in the year for visiting the chapel (now *toties quoties* on 2 Aug.).

Saxony minister's in Frascati, on Tuesday, I am promised to Mgr. Borromeo on Tuesday evening. Besides, Mgr. Hohenlohe is so affable and kind when insisting on keeping me longer, that I dare not refuse. . . .   F.L.

The Hôtel de Rome is owned by Nainer; and, thanks to the most obliging good offices of Hohenlohe, my accommodation in it, just ten paces away from His Holiness's Palazzo, is quite perfect.

Nardi lunched at the Palazzo yesterday, and afterwards set off again, to make a two-day retreat with the Camaldolites[9] in Frascati. I am not expecting to hear from you here, where in any case your lines would arrive after my departure.

On 9 August Liszt departed for Germany, the initial part of his journey being by boat from Civitavecchia to Marseilles.

534. To Princess Carolyne in Rome. Grand Hôtel, Marseilles, Friday morning, 12 August.
When I leave you, my soul no longer follows my body. It remains entirely with you, for eternity! I did the little journey from Rome to Civitavecchia, and from there until here, always turned, or, to use the biblical word, 'converted' to you—praying for the day when, instead of looking behind, my eyes will seek you *in front*, on this same road. . . .

Our crossing was only 'variously' good, as the Marseillais says. During the night of Wednesday to Thursday *Frate Vento* [Brother Wind] blew just a little too much in praise of God. Having reached the Cape of Corsica, we enjoyed a horrible pitching and, until we entered the port of Marseilles, were compelled to listen to the strenuous music of the mistral. A vessel so tossed about in beautiful sunny weather offered, for the rest, rather an odd sight, but we were hardly able to analyse it in its details, seeing that we were all sick. . . .

The fair sex was represented on the *Moncibello* only by Mme Marie. That was what the boat's housekeeper called herself; she flattered me singularly by seeking my conversation, and assuring me that she knew me well by reputation! She is of Corsican origin, daughter of an old soldier—and approaching fifty. She admires and appreciates the Emperor and Empress.

Instead of arriving at Marseilles at 4.00, as we were told by the captain when setting out, it was 10 in the evening when we entered the port. It was the over-zealous *Frate Vento* which caused us this delay. On the recommendation of Mme Marie and the captain, I took accommodation at the Grand Hôtel de Marseille, which goes one better than the Hôtel des Empereurs. At 10.30 I was brought

[9] Members of the religious order founded by St Romuald at Camaldoli (Tuscany) early in the 11th cent.

your telegram—and I kissed your sweet name, my good angel. The first lines of the newspaper I was reading as I disembarked told me of the death of Mgr. Gerbet. His sketches of Rome[10] had kept me company for the entire voyage, and I shall finish them before reaching Strasbourg. It is decidedly a masterpiece, and I know no work on Rome which can be compared with it. If in regard to Rome you were not in the position of Mme Néal relative to the *Kreuzzeitung*, I would recommend you Gerbet's book still more warmly. Perhaps for my own pleasure I shall quote some passages from it when writing to you from Strasbourg.

This morning I saw my Boisselot godson and his mother. The young man is doing, and will do, honour to his godfather—I'll introduce him to you some day. . . .

At 5.30 this morning I went to Notre Dame de la Garde. The church is in a noble style which could be called, I believe, Tuscan Renaissance—like the churches of Pisa and Florence. I attended mass, next to about ten sisters of charity, and shall not fail to go there again on my return.

535. To Princess Carolyne. Strasbourg, 4.00 p.m., 15 August, Assumption of the Blessed Virgin. Magne's name-day, and also Napoleon's birthday. At 9.00, high mass in the Cathedral, plainchant suited to the surroundings. Rudimentary, but not offensive, harmony and organ. Large gathering of the faithful. Edifying emotion, the Bishop officiating. At 11.00, military and official mass in the Cathedral. . . . At high mass, as in the military mass, I sang with all the power of my lungs: 'Domine salvum fac Imperatorem nostrum Napoleonem [Make safe, O Lord, our Emperor Napoleon]!' After Rome, however, my ears take no pleasure at all in the pronunciation of Frenchified Latin: *Ing*peratorem and *nong*, instead of *nunc*, I find quite cacophonous. See what an ideal thing is uniformity! Speaking the same language, people pronounce it varyingly, each in his own manner; saying the same things, people understand them differently! Love and charity, which is the perfection of love, alone understand! My ears suffered greatly, too, from the absence of Pio Nono's voice, to which I have grown so accustomed. To Fortunato, who was beside me in the Cathedral, I remarked that if all the bishops on earth sang together, their united voices would not equal the dogmatically resonant and energetic quality of tone of Pio Nono.

As I was praying for Magne, all the beautiful drawings we used to take to her in the mornings of 15 August came back into my mind!

[10] *Esquisse de Rome chrétienne* (2 vols., Paris 1844, 1850).

The slow train that I was congratulating myself on having taken, from Marseilles to Strasbourg, surprised us with several delays. Dijon, which we didn't get to until two or three hours later than indicated by the timetable, we had to stay in for nearly four hours. Then we twiddled our thumbs for three hours in Belfort, and for almost as long in Mulhouse—so that we didn't arrive in Strasbourg until 11.00 yesterday evening. The other passengers were fuming— but I congratulated myself, taking advantage of the slowness of the journey to finish Gerbet's second volume, begin Thiers's *Le congrès de Vienne*, which I bought in Belfort for 2 francs, and reread between Belfort and Strasbourg—guess what?—*Manon Lescaut*! One of those illustrated editions, which in Weimar we used to call the 'cretin editions', had tempted me. I couldn't resist spending 50 centimes on it while having a stroll in Belfort station. There are certainly 'people' and 'feelings' in this masterpiece; and I willingly agree with the author that 'the world doesn't always awaken feelings'—and that 'it often causes them to be lost'! 'Frailty perpetuating itself under remorse', as Sainte-Beuve says, is a rather unattractive frippery! That smacks too much of his 'Transylvanian hotel'! Yet some fine flashes, such as 'I was born for brief joys and long sufferings!' Lastly, the end is adorable. From the archers' attack at the gates of Paris, until New Orleans, one can only weep. How not to be Des Grieux at that last moment— 'I did not find it difficult to open the ground in the place where I was, the soil there being sandy. So that I could dig with it, I broke my sword—but found it less useful than my own hands. I dug a wide grave. There I laid the idol of my heart, after having taken care to wrap all my clothes about her, to keep the sand from touching her.'

I had at first planned to set out again this afternoon. Everything considered, I am remaining here until tomorrow—and will fête Magnette very pleasantly with Bon Ecclésiaste, without concerning myself with either Härtel or Brendel. Besides, from my window in the Hôtel de la Maison Rouge I have a superb view: the back of Kléber, whose statue adorns the square. It was he who said to Bonaparte: 'General, you are as great as the world!' This evening there will be fireworks and the Cathedral spire will be illuminated. I shall do the honours to Fortunato, whom I am serving as *cicerone*. After the military mass, as midday was striking, we admired together the marvels of the famous clock of the Three Kings, with the procession of the apostles, the crowing of the cock, etc.

Have you received my letter from Marseilles? I handed it to the captain of the *Moncibello*, so that it would get to you as quickly as possible. I hope that on Wednesday or Thursday your first lines will reach me in Karlsruhe. Alas, alas! why is it necessary to write to one another? Why am I not still in that Rome 'furrowed in all directions by the glory of men and the splendours of God'

—and, above all, inhabited by my good angel who prays for me, and will see me again soon, very soon! . . .

536. To Princess Carolyne. Erbprinz Hotel, Karlsruhe, Sunday morning, 21 August. My first impressions on returning to Germanic soil have been by no means agreeable. Leaving Strasbourg on Tuesday morning, I got here at 1 o'clock. I at once learnt from Brendel that Bülow was detained in Starnberg with a fever—and would not be directing the festival. Further, Pohl is feverishly editing the Baden *Gazette* and taking no part at all in what will have to be done at Karlsruhe. It is thus that he has understood his duties as 'secretary general' of the Musikverein! Herr von Bronsart and Frau Ingeborg will be conspicuous by their absence. On hearing all this surprising news, I began to wonder what the deuce I was doing here! Nevertheless, Brendel seemed to have no misgivings and, *faute de mieux*, I have begun to share his satisfaction! Seifriz of Löwenberg will be the festival's principal conductor, *Hauptfestdirigent*, which I am pleased about. A replacement for Frau Ingeborg has been found in Fräulein Topp from Stralsund, who is quite simply a marvel. Yesterday she played to me, from memory, my Sonata and the Mephisto Waltz, in a way that delighted me. The laurels of this festival will be divided between Reményi and Fräulein Topp.

On Friday Cosima got here. Not wanting to influence her in any way, and not being very well apprised of Hans's situation in Munich, with regard to Wagner etc., I had refrained from writing to her. She learnt from a third party that I was here, and assumed that I had stopped in Saint Tropez and in Paris, whither she telegraphed and wrote to me, to let me know about Hans's serious illness. For more than a fortnight he has been utterly exhausted—in one of those attacks of 'depression' which make his life absolutely unbearable. Fortunately he was able to see the King again, on his arrival in Starnberg. I hope the move from Berlin to Munich can take place fairly smoothly, despite susceptibilities, scenes, subtleties, and retorts on Hans's part. Cosima is showing a great deal of common sense in this matter, and will manage things very well. It is possible that she will return to her husband tomorrow, to nurse him. I am rather worried about Hans, who wishes to return to Berlin. In the mean time, the King of Bavaria has in the most gracious way offered him a fixed salary of 2,000 florins a year.

Yesterday and this morning Cosette and I went to mass together. The Catholic church is very near the Erbprinz. Its exterior looks rather heavy, but the inside is well maintained, and cannot be compared with Weimar's grubby lean-to. There is not only a bell, but also some splendid pillars. Light comes from above, as in the Pantheon. . . .

537. To Princess Carolyne. At Wagner's, Lake Starnberg, Wednesday, 31 August.[11] I found Hans in so wretched a condition, both physically and morally, that these last two days I have barely left him, and limited myself to sending you a telegram. His illness is mainly a nervous one, according to what I am told by Wolfsteiner, the *Medicinalrath*[12] who accompanied King Max to Rome. For a week or so he had paralysis in his legs; it has now settled in his left arm, causing him acute pain. He has seen the King four times, and dined once with him, without Wagner, tête-à-tête. His relations with His Majesty are of a character as exceptional as they are flattering for him. Indeed, he finds himself more advanced in favour, in a few days, than I was in Weimar at the end of 10 years. As for Wagner's position, it is nothing less than prodigious! Solomon was wrong: there *is* something new under the sun![13] I am fully convinced of it since yesterday evening, after Wagner had shown me several of the King's letters. . . .

Cosette has written to tell you that my works were completely successful at Karlsruhe. It's almost the first time I have had such an experience! I hope my manner, which shouldn't have been anything but simple and reserved, was not prejudicial to it. Neither the Grand Duke nor the Grand Duchess [of Baden] came to Karlsruhe during the music festival. Nevertheless, the Grand Duke did things very appropriately, and without any niggardliness, so far as theatre expenses and arrangements, lighting, etc. are concerned. The Court was at first on Mainau,[14] then in Baden, from what I have been told. I refrained from presenting myself—although the Queen [Augusta] of Prussia, who sent 200 thalers to the Musikverein, had sent word that she would be glad to see me again. Hans's serious illness was sufficient reason for my speedy departure from Karlsruhe. All in all, the festival concerts went off very well indeed. After the Psalm [13], the last item at the first concert, the audience called for me—but I had left the theatre a few minutes before the end. At the final concert I had to show myself twice—after the Mephisto Waltz and *Festklänge*. Hearing this latter work once again, I remembered Carlsbad, where it was written, and your exclamation: 'There I am!'

[11] Dated 30 Aug. in La Mara's edition, but Wednesday was the 31st.
[12] Roughly equivalent to 'senior medical officer'.
[13] Eccles. 1: 8. (Once ascribed to Solomon, the book of Ecclesiastes is now regarded as of much later authorship.)
[14] An island in Lake Constance containing the Grand Duke of Baden's holiday villa, celebrated for its gardens and flora.

For the Psalm, Mme Viardot had come from Baden with Chorley, Turgenev —the Russian novelist—and a brother of Lehmann, a merchant well established in London. Mgr. Haynald did not arrive until the next day but one, and attended the final concert in my ground-floor box, to which for that evening I had invited no one but Cosette. He set off again for Ems, on Saturday morning, and will probably be spending next winter in Rome. . . .

Among those present at rehearsals and concerts, I can further mention Serov, who is most displeased with me because of my sincerity about his opera *Judith* —to which I advised him to do what Judith did to Holofernes! Just imagine, Serov fancies himself to be the Russian Wagner!! Plus Gille,* Lassen, Fräulein Hundt, Brahms, Pruckner, Singer, Riedel from Leipzig, Gottwald from Breslau —and the others whose names you saw on the list at the end of the programme I sent you. . . .

On Sunday morning at 11.00, Cosette and I took our departure, reaching Munich at 9.00 p.m. As you know, Munich wasn't on my itinerary; I decided to go there only after careful deliberation, and earlier on had suggested to Hans that we meet in Augsburg. Since he was quite unable to leave his bed, I no longer hesitated to go and see him. The King is at Hohenschwangau, 6 or 8 hours away from here. There he celebrated his birthday, 25 August, *en famille*. Wagner went to congratulate him—and took him a new March he had composed. According to Cosette, Wagner was invited to spend a couple of weeks with the King at Hohenschwangau. I expected, accordingly, that I wouldn't be seeing him this time—and came solely for Hans's sake. Wagner, who did no more than put in an appearance at Hohenschwangau, got here in the evening of the 25th. I proposed to him to return his visit, as early as Tuesday evening. And so we two left together[15] by the 5 o'clock train yesterday, leaving Hans and his wife in the Bayerischer Hof Hotel. Cosette and I agreed that I should leave Munich on Saturday. Hans will probably also be in a more or less fit state to return to Berlin with Cosette on Saturday—for he is totally against going to Gastein or Wildbad, recommended to him by the doctor. He claims that the Berlin air is the only one which will help cure him! . . .

But let's come back to Wagner, whom I have entitled the Glorious One, *der Glorreiche*. At bottom, nothing can have changed between us. The great good fortune that has at last come his way will sweeten as much as possible certain asperities in his character. For the moment, I have to say that he is very much at his best, in all respects. Naturally we chatted at great length, for 5 hours on end. . . . Wagner acquainted me with his *Meistersinger*, and in return I showed him my *Beatitudes*, with which he seemed more than content! His *Meistersinger*

---

[15] For the Villa Pellet, the house beside Lake Starnberg that had been provided for Wagner by King Ludwig.

is a masterpiece of *humour*, spirit, and lively grace. It is animated and beautiful, like Shakespeare!

Before I left for Starnberg I was brought your sweet and lovely letter of 20
August, addressed to Karlsruhe. The sight of your handwriting warms my heart
with a light whose beauty is very different from that of the dome of St Peter's
or of Strasbourg Cathedral! Do tell our dearest Ferraris, and also Rignano,
Marcellino, and the priest at the Madonna del Rosario, how much I look forward to seeing them again!

I am continuing to go to mass, on rising. Today, as on a couple of other days,
I was prevented from going, which grieved me. Let me kiss your hands for the
communion for Hans, on St Bernard's Day [20 August] . . .   F.L.

In the early hours of Monday, 5 September, Liszt arrived in Weimar. To the Princess
he wrote later that morning: 'At the station there was no room in the only fiacre. When
I was about to get in, I found three gentlemen inside already. I preferred to put Fortunato
with them, and to profit by the dark night to make *my midnight walk*—from the railway to the Altenburg. How many ghosts did I not meet! Schubert's *Doppelgänger* would
be the nearest cousin to this spectral family!'

**538. To Princess Carolyne. [Weimar] Monday morning, 12 Septem-
ber.** The sound of your weeping and of your prayers inside these rooms
resounds within my soul! Court society is away, with the exception of Beust,
who left for Wilhelmsthal yesterday morning. The Grand Duchess is to arrive
there today, and Monseigneur tomorrow. Yesterday, 11 Sept., Monseigneur was
at the family party in Friedrichshaufen—Lake Constance—where Tsar Alexander's name-day and Queen Olga's[16] birthday on the same date were being
celebrated simultaneously. The Tsar and Tsaritsa and the King and Queen of
Würtemberg were all there together. The Empress Eugénie is at Schwalbach,
where the King of Prussia is to visit her. The Count of Paris has sent word that
he will be going to Wilhelmsthal on 14 Sept. Nothing definite is yet known
about Tsar Alexander's visit to Wilhelmsthal, which seems to be expected shortly.
I am going to write to Monseigneur to tell him that I shall be returning to
Weimar on about 20 Sept., and to ask him to let me know where he wishes to
see me. . . .

Herr von Beaulieu—Minister of the Duchies of Saxony to the Diet of Frankfurt, where he now resides—has founded here a *Kunst- und Wissenschaftsverein*
[Society for the Arts and Sciences]. It is popularly called the *Eulen-Verein* [Society

---

[16] Queen Olga of Würtemberg was sister of the Tsar and cousin of Carl Alexander.

of Owls]—because of the seal adopted by this society, on which appears the owl of Minerva. As is to be expected, Kalckreuth, the noble artistes, the *Hofräthe* [Privy Councillors], *et al.*, are members. These gentlemen meet in the most elegant premises in Weimar, at the Erholung. There was talk of inviting me there, but in view of my speedy departure I shall be deprived of the pleasure they were kindly intending to give me. The turn of the wheel is virtually driving Dingelstedt back into my old state of opposition. I was thinking to myself yesterday that there are towns which fulfil their functions in a manner that is the direct opposite of what orthopaedic institutions aim at. What is straight, they make crooked! To the regrets expressed to me about my giving up control of the Weimar theatre, I replied: 'Die Glanzperiode der Weimarer Oper bleibt die, in welcher man am meisten über mich schimpfte [The Weimar opera's most glorious days remain those in which people most complained about me].' . . .

Be blessed with every heavenly blessing!   F.L.

539. To Princess Carolyne. Löwenberg, Friday, 16 September. Having got here on Tuesday evening, I shall be leaving again tomorrow morning for Berlin, where I shall be staying at the Bülows' until Tuesday. Hans is on the road to recovery. He is having to take daily baths with some salts or other, followed by rubbings and sleep. His doctor is also prescribing him an extremely tonic diet of meat and Bordeaux wine to give him his strength back. Cosette is here. Her splendid good humour delights our excellent Prince, who is very kind to her. Generally speaking, palace life offers little variety—and that of Löwenberg is no exception to the rule. However, I am always glad to return to this house, for I am convinced that people here sincerely wish me well. As the Prince's orchestra is still on holiday, the onus of providing the music has now fallen on me, an obligation I carry out very readily, without in the least waiting to be begged. Yesterday I played the Prince our Shepherds and Three Kings,[17] as also the two *St François*. Oh, when will the moment come when I shall belong to myself again—and can continue and complete our *Christus*! I swear to you that there is no other happiness for me than the one you have been giving me for nearly three years by your gentleness, your devotion, and your adorable concern for my true welfare, my sweet guardian angel! . . .

The newspapers are again talking of the Holy Father's grave illness, and of the imminence of the next conclave. I don't believe it in the least, but I should be glad if you would send me some authentic news. For ten days or so I have

---

[17] Respectively the Shepherds' Song at the Manger and March of the Three Holy Kings from *Christus*.

heard not a single remark that could interest you even minimally. Forgive me, therefore, the emptiness of my letters! Next week I shall perhaps manage to glean a few things in Monseigneur's vicinity. In the mean time I am asking Cosette to send you a report of daily chit-chat, in which she will succeed much better than I! Damrosch came to see me this morning, bringing me the score of his opera *Romeo and Juliet*, which I read through from start to finish. Into it he has put his passion as a lover and his passion as an artist! It is a glowing brazier, this work, but I fear the public will be only moderately fired by it, and that the difficulty of performance will be prejudicial to its success. Nevertheless, it contains a good number of vigorous passages, and others of a magnetic dreaminess —which I like very much. Did I tell you that in Weimar I skimmed through the First Act of Cornelius's *Cid*. The première is to be on 18 December.

Saturday morning. The Prince has been so affectionately insistent on keeping me here a little longer, that I have postponed my departure until Monday morning, and so shan't get to Weimar until Thursday. . . . F.L.

540. To Princess Carolyne. Berlin, Wednesday, 21 September. Your two dear letters, my sweet angel, have been sent to me here from Weimar, and give me your news up to 10 Sept. I am happy that you are fairly satisfied with my very precise report on the Karlsruhe concerts. For me they had only one shortcoming, but a very serious one—that of not taking place in Civitavecchia, or Velletri! You cannot imagine the extent to which journeys have become painful and disgusting to me! Arriving somewhere is just as unbearable as departing —and I feel that I can no longer stay anywhere other than at the Madonna del Rosario! Tomorrow evening I shall be back in the Altenburg, where I shall spend the whole of Friday. On Saturday I shall probably make my visit to Wilhelmsthal. Mgr. of Coburg [Duke Ernst of Saxe-Coburg-Gotha] is in England. He is said to have gone off his head, only temporarily, I hope. His popularity is now greatly jeopardized—but I still think he will end by regaining the lost ground, and that he will take a good slice of the cake when they get round to carving it up! If he happens to be back from his trip before I leave Wilhelmsthal, I might decide to go and see him.

Through my mother, Ollivier has offered me his flat, rue St Guillaume, for the week I shall be spending in Paris. I am accepting, and hope to arrive there on 2 Oct. Here, I am staying with Hans, who, happily, is fully convalescent. . . . He plans to go to Munich for 2 Oct., the date on which the King will be making his first visit to the theatre since the death of his father. Wagner will be directing *Der fliegende Holländer*, of which he is now adjusting the *mise-en-scène* and conducting the rehearsals. It can be assumed that within the next 2 years Hans will be appointed Director of the Conservatorium, a position for which the newspapers are already nominating him. I shall see no one here, apart from Weitzmann, who lives on the ground floor. He remains as extremely affectionate and devoted to me as ever.

At noon yesterday Cosima and I went to kneel at Daniel's grave! If I decide to go out today, it will be to see the exhibition of Cornelius's complete cartoons. Having decided to spend only a couple of days here, the best thing I can do with them is make as much music as possible with Hans. . . .

Alas, could I only imitate, belatedly and from afar, the new St Margaret of the Visitation—of whom you tell me that she worked while remaining ever on her knees, being unable to bring herself to adopt any other position in the presence of God. My whole soul is very much on its knees!   F.L.

541. To Princess Carolyne. Weimar, Saturday morning, 24 September. A telegram from Beust informs me that as the Tsar has to remain at Wilhelmsthal until Tuesday, a room is no longer available. Consequently, the Grand Duke will not be receiving me until next Wednesday, the 28th. It's a hitch which sets me back 4 days—but it has to be endured, vexing though it be. The Germanic atmosphere I find extremely oppressive—and yearn only to escape from it and to embark at Marseilles as soon as possible. I expect to be in Paris on 2 or 3 Oct., and in Marseilles on the 12th. Oh, how long and melancholy it is to live like this, far away! Your last letter, up to the 16th and still addressed to Weimar, reached me yesterday. And so I shall have to go for about ten days without having your news!

After reading the newspapers, I cry out: 'Gracious Heavens, what have we come to—so far as nourishment of minds is concerned! Material famine, horrible though it can be, I would find far preferable. In comparison with flaws and failings of the intelligence, death of the body is nothing!'

I spent yesterday revising the duet arrangement that Brand[18] has made of the Gran Mass. . . .

Fortunato's accounts cause me real irritation. Despite all my efforts at economy, recorded by Fortunato's book, my expenses are increasing. Well, I can assure you that I don't indulge in dissipation, invite no one to dinner, and refrain from going about by carriage. But the railway journeys, although I always travel

---

[18] Mihály Mosonyi (see Biographical Sketches).

second class in Germany, are extremely expensive. While systematically restricting my expenses, I cannot avoid spending well beyond what I should like. Forgive
me this foolish admission, which I mention in confidence and of which I am
almost ashamed! If I could at least be of some service to you—all my worries
would fly away still more quickly than my poor écus! . . . Thank you again, my
good angel, for your letter, your thoughts and your prayers! I shall write to you
immediately after seeing Monseigneur, on Wednesday.

**542. To Princess Carolyne. Wilhelmsthal, 7.00 a.m. [Thursday] 29
September.** I wrote to you, my good angel, last Saturday, the 24th, from Weimar.
Beust's telegram had left me uncertain about what to do during the 3 or 4 days
that I had to wait for the Tsar to leave Wilhelmsthal. Having nothing else to
do in Weimar, I decided to spend the feast of SS Cosmas and Damien, 27 Sept.,
with the Bülows in Berlin and return here yesterday, Wednesday the 28th. I did
so—but first have to tell you of something else. On the eve of my departure
for Berlin, the Grand Duke came as far as the Weimar station to meet the Tsar,
first stopping at the Roman House for a few hours. He sent for me at once,
and granted me an interview of an hour and a half, in which the main things
I had to tell him were touched upon. He reminded me that he had several times
written to Antonelli in my favour, for which I thanked him very sincerely, and
equally as much for his assurance that he would always do whatever he could
to show his affection for me. By virtue of this affection and of the numerous
proofs of it that he has given me, he did not hesitate to refer again to the simplicity of the solution that is now possible—being unable to conceive that
people could have pursued a goal for 15 years, only to turn aside from it at the
very moment when nothing any longer stood between them and its accomplishment.[19] I remarked that I had not thus far spoken of this matter to anyone at all, and that I was not planning to break this silence in the future. As
regards questions of position and domicile, there is no reason to give any further thought to them, since my entire desirable position is enclosed within my
inkwell, and this inkwell, being in the care of the Madonna del Rosario in Rome,
could not be better situated. . . .

    1.00 p.m. These lines were interrupted by a visit from Monseigneur, who
stayed in my room for a couple of hours. Our conversation added nothing

---

[19] Carl Alexander could not understand why Liszt had still not led the Princess to the altar, since, with the death
(10 Mar. 1864) of Prince Nicholas Wittgenstein, no spiritual or temporal power on earth could now legitimately prevent their union, were this still their desire.

essential to what I have written above. I indicated only my determination not to leave Rome next year. Since the Tsar's departure the Grand Duchess has been kept in her apartments by a cold. Yesterday, the Grand Duke did not get back from hunting until 2 hours after my arrival here. We dined in the billiard room. One of Tsar Alexander's sons was announced for today—but was put off. I shall stay here tomorrow too; the next day, Saturday, I'll probably leave for Strasbourg, where I shall spend the night, for these railway journeys tire me extremely. Forgive me for writing to you in so abbreviated a fashion. Putting all excuses aside, even that of idleness—how could there be any?—I believe it is better to tell you of certain personal details *viva voce*. In the mean time, I am only anxious for you to be informed of the main things, which boil down to very little. In sum, I hope you will have no reason to object to anything I have done.

This remark of Bismarck's is reported: 'I know I shall not always keep my place—perhaps shan't even last long in it—but I will make sure that Prussia sells me dear!' Another remark by the same personage, when speaking of the liberals and the progressive democrats: 'Sie hassen mich, weil sie wissen, dass ich sie besiegen werde [They hate me, because they know that I shall overcome them].'

Friday morning. I had to go to Eisenach at 2.00 yesterday, so that at the church I could hear the choir formed and conducted by Müller-Hartung, in whom Monseigneur is taking an interest. At about 5.00 I returned here with M. Maltitz, who spoke in a very agreeable way of M. de Sartiges, a memory of Brazil, and of the nuncio Mgr. Ostini, now a Cardinal. He also discoursed on the *elegies* of Propertius, of which he is enamoured. He places them well above the Roman Elegies[20] of Goethe—who did no more than gather two or three drops of nectar fallen from the cup of Propertius. In comparing him to Tibullus, Maltitz claimed that if Tibullus deserved the nickname of nightingale of love—that of peacock of love belongs to Propertius. Enough of this poetic ornithology!

The Grand Duchess did not appear at lunch, nor in the evening. On the Grand Duke's right sat his elder daughter, and on his left his son. The young Princess is very charming—and her brother converses, asks questions, laughs and behaves like a lad of some intelligence. He put his holidays to good use last March by touring in Italy, and got as far as Florence and Siena. He will soon be going to Leipzig, where he will spend his final year at the University, after which he will have to do his military service. As far as visitors are concerned,

---

[20] Goethe's *Römische Elegien* (originally entitled *Erotica romana*), written after his return from Italy to Weimar in the summer of 1788.

the only guest yesterday was an Englishman—whose name I am not sure of—who spent several years in India, Tibet, and China and gave us some very interesting descriptions of them. Among other things he told us that a subsidiary chief, on the borders of British and Tibetan territory, one fine day brought his ministerial council meeting to an end by murdering the 14 persons who formed this council! Maltitz quoted an aphorism which had greatly struck Goethe: 'Für den Verstand ist Alles lächerlich, für die Vernunft nichts [For the intellect, everything is ridiculous; for reason, nothing is].' I retorted that it was only a pity that ridiculous people were usually at grips with *Verstand* and not with *Vernunft*. For my own part, I have no very high opinion of maxims of this kind. . . .

543. To Princess Carolyne. Paris, 29 rue St Guillaume, 4.00 p.m., Tuesday, 4 October, feast of St Francis. I got here at 5.00 in the morning, and am occupying Blandine's rooms on the second floor—my mother is still on the third. Cosima had joined me in Eisenach on Saturday, and came here with me. I breakfasted with the two of them, plus Jules Senart of Dijon—he who in days gone by aspired to be *alone* with me! My mother is in perfect health and retains on many things a thoroughly healthy judgement which she seasons with a charming good humour, not devoid of a certain sweet and honest mischief.

Loving thanks, my dearest good angel, for your three letters from 17 to 26 Sept., and for your beautiful prayer to St Peter on 18 Sept., day of the canonization of St Margaret Alacoque.[21] I repeat it with all my soul. May God grant a holy death to my mother, and a holy life to my daughter! . . .

The weather having cleared up on Saturday morning, I took Cosima to the Wartburg with Lassen, who had come from Weimar to wish me farewell. We spent the evening at the Schwendlers', to whom I conveyed your greetings. . . . Pohl got into the compartment with me at Baden, to accompany me as far as Strasbourg. Mme Mouchanoff-Kalergis was so kind as to shake hands very graciously with me at the station, while assuring me of all the goodwill of HM the Queen of Prussia, who is still in Baden. The Empress Eugénie is expected there today. . . . At Strasbourg I had to stop for half a day longer than planned, because of 2 trunks going astray—which didn't turn up until yesterday evening.

I feel very tired today, and will be going out only to address a prayer to our adorable St Francis, at [the church of] St Thomas Aquinas. Cosima immediately went to see Mme Saint-Mars, on whom I shall pay a call tomorrow, as

[21] Margaret-Mary Alacoque was beatified that year, and canonized in 1920.

well as on Mgr. Bucquet. Hardly had we arrived when I said to Fortunato: 'Soon
we shall be back in Rome, and not budging from it again for a long time.' ...
    Peace and blessings in God!   F.L.

Leaving Paris in the evening of Wednesday, 12 October, Liszt and Cosima travelled together
to Saint Tropez, where they wished to pray at the grave of Blandine. Spending the night
of the 14th here with Emile and little Daniel, they went the next morning their separate ways, she to Germany, he to Rome.

1865

23 March. Liszt's *Beatitudes* are performed at a charity concert in the Palazzo del Senato on the Capitol; he joins two other pianists in a performance of Bach's Concerto in D minor for three keyboards, and also plays a solo.

20 April. In a concert at the Palazzo Barberini he plays the *Invitation to the Dance* and *Erlkönig.*

25 April. Liszt receives the tonsure and moves into the Vatican.

15 August. At the Vigadó concert hall in Pest he conducts the first performance of *The Legend of Saint Elisabeth.*

17 August. At a second concert Liszt conducts the first movement of the Dante Symphony, creating a sensation, and his orchestral arrangement of the Rákóczy March.

22 August. St Elisabeth is repeated.

26–7 August. Liszt is the guest in Esztergom of the Prince Primate of Hungary, Cardinal Scitovszky.

29 August. At a concert in Pest Liszt plays his two Legends (their first public performance), *Ave Maria* and *Cantique d'amour.*

2–9 September. With the Bülows and Reményi he is the guest in Szekszárd of Baron Augusz. He then returns to Rome.

WORKS. Several sections of *Christus. Missa choralis* (S10) and *Ave maris stella* (S34/1), both for mixed chorus and organ. Arrangement (S117) of the Rákóczy March for orchestra. PIANO: *Les Sabéennes. Berceuse de l'opéra La Reine de Saba* (Gounod) (S408, *c.*1865); *Illustrations de l'Africaine* (Meyerbeer) (S415): 1. *Prière des matelots.* 2. *Marche indienne*; *Fantaisie sur l'opéra hongrois Szép Ilonka* (Mosonyi) (S417).

544. To Anna Liszt in Paris. [Rome] 24 January

Dearest Mother,

I shall never be able to thank you enough for your affection and for your dear little letters which make it so lovingly evident! Let me first of all reassure you about the *comfort* of my dwelling place on Monte Mario. It now has two fireplaces which heat the room perfectly and maintain a very agreeable temperature. This improvement was carried out by order of the Princess last summer when I was away. And so nothing is lacking here for my material well-being. I need do no more than take care of the rest by working and behaving sensibly. With God's grace I am trying to succeed in both.

That I did not see our old and most excellent friend [Ferdinand] Denis during my short stay in Paris, is one of my regrets. To tell the truth, I went there this time just to spend a few days with you... and the week went by very quickly! And so do please give my apologies to Denis together with my friendliest greetings.

Princess Marcelina Czartoryska has given me good news of you. She is spending the winter in Rome with her husband (Prince Alexander) and son (Marcel). I very much appreciate the kind affection she shows me and am really delighted at the way she and I keep up our relations. You told me about the visit from Countess Brokmann and her sister Mlle Lannos. They are really charming, aren't they? Do tell them so from me. Princess Czartoryska is now living in their apartment (Via Gregoriana, 5) and it frequently gives me pleasure to recall how pleasant they were. If, as I assume, Count Brokmann prolongs his stay in Paris, I shall be very glad to see him again this spring.

Once again, dearest Mother, be fully reassured about my health, my well-being, and my perfect contentment with my lot, for which I desire no other satisfaction than to prove to you ever more how much I love you with the sincerest and most devoted filial affection.

F. Liszt

P.S. Please don't take the trouble to have your letters stamped in Paris, but simply have them posted.

545. To Agnes Street-Klindworth. 26 January.

St Agnes wasn't forgotten this 21 January.[1] I spent the whole day alone in my room, without any visit or diversion whatsoever. Your nice letter reached me the next day. The *enharmonic* chord by Chopin[2] that you quote still vibrates in my heart, and it is occasionally joined by the angelic voices of Fra Beato....

The compositions I am working on at present are:

A. A Mass (a cappella—without accompaniment) that I intend to dedicate to the Holy Father. It will be finished in about a fortnight.

B. The revision of a big liturgical work, containing the church services for the whole year in Gregorian Chant, in 4-part harmony. It was a Roman prelate who composed this work, and in my opinion it couldn't be done more successfully; for there is nothing stilted or nonsensical or stylistically inappropriate in it to jar with the simple and devotional gravity of the text. The author spent several years perfecting his work and asked me to oversee its publication—which necessitates a certain amount of preliminary work having it copied, and having to

---

[1] That saint's feast-day.   [2] In the Etude in A flat, Op. 10/10.

attend to corrections and arrangements, with which I shall have to busy myself for the rest of the year and beyond. . . .

Let's pass on to Munich. The King's enthusiasm for Wagner is still at the same level—i.e. phenomenal, almost miraculous. Semper the architect has been instructed to design a new theatre which will be built expressly (and in accordance with Wagner's indications) to mount the *Nibelungen*. The King is having a *Nibelung Passage* painted in one of the galleries leading to his apartments; further, he has ordered a *Wagner Gallery*, which will consist of a dozen paintings depicting the main scenes from *Tannhäuser, Lohengrin, Der fliegende Holländer*, etc., and is having published *by order* Wagner's complete literary works, including his newspaper articles and other lucubrations of days gone by.

Tristan und Isolde will probably be performed next May (with Schnorr and his wife, Mitterwurzer and Beck), in the form of a rehearsal at the Residenztheater before an invited audience. This idea of Wagner's has suited the King, who, they say, showed himself to be sensitive to the virtual coldness with which *Der fliegende Holländer* (performed only a couple of times) was received. . . .

Among my new acquaintances here I shall mention Pce and Pcss Caraman Chimay. I take pleasure in *making music* with them, something of which they don't weary. The Prince's diplomatic concerns (Secretary of the Belgian Legation in Rome) don't prevent him from cultivating his talent as a violinist; and so he is eminently successful at doing honour to his teachers, Bériot and Vieuxtemps. As for his wife (née Montesquiou), she plays the piano more or less in the manner of your musical 'Glanzperiode' in Weimar.

The Montessuis have just arrived. I shall run across them at Pcss Czartoryska's. . . .   Yours very affectionately   F.L.

The Revd Father Theiner is restored to tolerably good health, and occasionally takes a stroll in the garden adjoining the one belonging to my *curé* at the Madonna del Rosario.

On Tuesday, 25 April, feast of St Mark the Evangelist, Liszt received the tonsure in the private chapel at the Vatican of his friend Prince Gustav von Hohenlohe, the Papal Grand Almoner. As necessary preparation for so solemn a step, he first spent a few days at the Lazarist Mission.

546. To Princess Carolyne. Saturday, 22 April. *Et ego semper tecum!* I feel very comfortable here, and these 3 or 4 days of transition are very soothing! No austerity is imposed upon me. Apart from extra spiritual reading, which I do very gladly, it is almost my life on Monte Mario. These are the principal points of my *orario*: 6.30: rise, meditation alone, coffee in my room. 8.30: mass

—tomorrow, Sunday, sung mass at 9.30—spiritual reading alone, visit to the Blessed Sacrament. Midday: lunch in the refectory, the meal being far better than my parish priest's. There are about 35 of us; I am seated at a separate table, alone. There is no talking, which suits me extremely well. I don't very well understand the reading aloud done by one of the friars, up in a pulpit, from the beginning of the meal to the end. Yesterday, coffee and water were brought to my room, a courtesy of which I was most appreciative. 1.30: rest. 3.30: spiritual readings, visit to the Blessed Sacrament, stroll in the garden *ad libitum*. 6.45: meditation alone, *per un'ora*. 8.00: supper, silence and reading, as at lunchtime. I returned to my room at 8.30, where the superior, Padre Guarini, kept me very agreeable company until 9.30. All lights must be out by 10.00. . . .

[**Later.**] If it were possible for you to go round to see Hohenlohe this evening, I should be grateful. He has just spent the better part of an hour with me, and I carried out in front of him a preliminary rehearsal of my dress, with which he was most content. Because of an interview with the Cardinal Vicar, he will not be able to come to you today—but you will find him at the Vatican this evening or tomorrow evening, or so he told me. He will probably be taking me to the Cardinal Vicar tomorrow, at about 5.00 or 6.00. I forgot to ask him the time of Tuesday's ceremony, for which, in heart, mind, and will, I feel thoroughly prepared.

The piano will be transported from Nardi's to the Vatican in about ten days, Hohenlohe having assured me that it wouldn't in the least disturb the arrangement of his furniture. The Holy Father has spoken to him about the Latin studies I have to undertake—it will be Solfanelli who will take formal charge of them, which will not prevent me having recourse, exceptionally, to Fabi's good offices, if he wishes to grant me them. Peace and joy in the Holy Spirit!

547. To Princess Carolyne. 3.00 p.m., Monday [24 April]. . . . My three days at the Mission have been very agreeable—I shall retain a profounder and more serene memory of them than of my alleged successes of former days! Man is really only what he is in the eyes of God! This morning I had a visit from the Abbé Bauer; we embraced and chatted to our hearts' content. He will come and see me again at about 9.00 tomorrow morning, after having coffee at D. Achille's; he suggested bringing Père Hyacinthe to me during the course of the week, which I accepted with great eagerness. We read together a chapter of Father Togni's *Instructio*, which has fully informed me of the meaning and significance of the ceremony of the tonsure. When I have received mine, I shall pass on to you my little bit of knowledge on this topic. . . .

548. To Princess Carolyne. 7.00 p.m., 25 April, Feast of St Mark.

Your lines of this morning have shone out over the whole of this happy day. Mgr. Hohenlohe will give you an account of it before you receive this. It gives me pleasure to go over it again with you. I rose before 6.00. After praying and hearing mass, I continued reading an excellent work, *Traité des Sts Ordres*, by M. Olier, parish priest and founder of the Seminary of St Sulpice. The Abbé Bauer was so kind as to borrow it from the head of the French seminary, and to send it to me yesterday evening. At about 7.00, Mgr. Hohenlohe came for me in *frullone*.[3] The two of us went together from the Mission to the Vatican. The constitutive words of the ceremony, which preceded mass, are taken from Ps. 15.[4] I uttered them with heart and tongue at the same time as the Bishop, as he gave me the tonsure: 'The Lord himself is the portion of mine inheritance, and of my cup: thou shalt maintain my lot.' Some prayers and Ps. 83 [84]— 'O how amiable are thy dwellings, thou Lord of hosts!'—concluded the ceremony. At the end, Hohenlohe addressed some very touching words to me. Mgr. Corazzo and Don Marcello served mass, which was attended by Salua and our excellent Ferraris, who had heard my last confession as a layman; and also by Fortunato and Antonio.

As you know, the tonsure must be in the form of a crown—but perhaps you have forgotten what this signifies. It is so that on the head of the cleric, and of the whole clergy, may be imprinted the image of the crown of thorns of Our Lord Jesus Christ. It also denotes the 'royal dignity' of him who is admitted into the ranks of the clergy. The word 'cleric' comes from the Greek *kleros*, heritage, lot.

At 9.30 we breakfasted in the salon—with coffee and chocolate. Shortly afterwards the Abbé Bauer came, and he and I spent an hour chatting pleasantly. Fortunato is in a hurry to return. I shall continue my *diario* tomorrow morning.

May our dear good Lord heap upon you all His blessings! I enclose the *Manuel du chrétien*, in which I beg you to read for my sake Ps. 15 and 83. It is a very poor French translation—but your soul will sing them in their real language! I did not fail, this evening, to speak to the Holy Father of my gratitude and devotion to Hohenlohe, who once again has done everything for the best.

At about 10.00 I took possession of my rooms, which are very comfortable, well arranged and furnished, and suit me extremely well. The view is *ad libitum*. If I go to the window, which I shall do only rarely, I can enjoy the whole of the façade of St Peter's. Otherwise I can glimpse only a *buon pezzo* of the dome, which looks down on my writing table. Apart from the bells, I can hear almost no noise. Do you remember the remark made by Felix Lichnowsky's

---

[3] Open four-wheeled carriage with two seats.   [4] In the Vulg.; Ps. 16 in the AV and BCP.

father, which Felix inserted in an article in the Augsburg *Gazette*, in '41, I believe: 'If Liszt had been an architect, he would have built the dome of St Peter's'?

The Abbé Bauer spent a good hour with me, from 11.00 until noon. During this time the Prior of the Minerva came too, with Father Romito. In the course of the week Bauer will return with Père Hyacinthe, who at Pau saw a good deal of Mme d'Artigaux. I have advised Hohenlohe of their visit. Some reading, and making a copy of a letter to the Bishop of Raab [Győr], in whose diocese I was born, kept me busy until lunchtime. Hohenlohe had brought me the draft of this letter in German. I found it very dignified and confident. Included in it were these words: 'Seit heute Morgen trage ich das geistliche Kleid—und wohne hier unter demselben Dache mit dem Statthalter Christi [Since this morning I have been wearing clerical dress—and residing here under the same roof as the Vicar of Christ].' I copied it word for word, without changing a thing. There were four of us at lunch, the two others being Pce Niky[5] and Don Marcello. The death of the Tsarevitch and of the Grand Duchess of Mecklenburg-Schwerin provided topics of conversation, which otherwise turned on rather indifferent things. . . . After the meal I proposed that, to smoke, we should adjourn to my sitting-room, a suggestion which suited Hohenlohe particularly well as he was expecting a visit from the Arenbergs. For my part, too, I preferred not to seem otiose—as I wish to avoid being even the slightest bit obtrusive as far as Hohenlohe is concerned. 'Rien de trop'—especially never to be *de trop*—is the first rule in my relations with him. I am convinced that they will be sound and lasting. When the Arenbergs arrived, Niky and Marcello went to pay their court to them—leaving Hohenlohe at my place finishing his cigar. It seems to me, confidentially speaking, that there must be some serious agreement between Niky and Pcss Eleonore. In the evening Hohenlohe told me that the elder Pcss had spoken of me to Niky—and asked him how I looked in my new state. 'Sehr würdevoll [very dignified],' replied the young man.

I slept for a good hour and, shortly before the Ave Maria, accompanied Hohenlohe to the Holy Father, in the antechamber coming across Mérode and Ricci. At my audience with His Holiness, no one else was present. I had in no way prepared to say anything whatsoever. Perhaps my emotion did not do me too much of a disservice—but I shan't venture to state that as a fact, since I am hardly aware of the impression I make, unless it be a very sorry one. Pius IX received me with great kindness and gentleness. At my second genuflexion, your recent prayer for the workman and his work came into my mind, and I said more or less this: 'The gospel for this day teaches us that the harvest is great. I, alas, am only a very small and feeble workman—but I feel very happy now to

---

[5] Prince Nikolaus von Hohenlohe-Waldenburg-Schillingsfürst.

belong to you a little more, and implore Your Holiness to make use of me.' The Pope then said: 'You will now have to undertake some theological studies.'—'I have not remained entirely a stranger to them, and shall resume them with all the more joy and zeal. It is also indispensable for me to work at my Latin.' Pius IX: 'The Germans have great facility.'—Ego: 'In particular my compatriots, the Hungarians—my father was an excellent Latinist.' Pius IX: 'A Hungarian recently spoke to me in Latin with a fullness and precision which surprised me, and that I should not be capable of equalling. I shall not say as much of Cardinal Scitovszky's Latin, which is *di modo grosso*, as we say.' The name of Scitovszky, pronounced by the Holy Father, I turned to account by recalling very briefly that I had had the honour of meeting the Cardinal when he was Bishop of Pécs, in 1846. It was because of a promise I made to him then that he commissioned the Gran Mass, performed ten years later. Finally, not to abandon Hungarian territory, I added that I would probably be required to keep another promise I had given, by going to Hungary this year, where during the week of the feast of St Stephen, 20 August,[6] a musical jubilee is to be celebrated in Pest. Since the opportunity did not naturally present itself to touch on Roman topics, I was very glad to pass over them in silence. It matters to me that people are well assured that I neither aspire to nor covet any position whatsoever that might fall to me. But to this end *bisogna dar tempo al tempo* [one should take one's time]. . . . My audience lasted about 10 minutes. At the end the Holy Father gave me his blessing *in extenso*. I shall fill in a few gaps in this *diario* orally.

Wednesday, 26 April. Attended Hohenlohe's mass at 6.30—and after my coffee read some newspapers. Hohenlohe came and asked me to accompany him to the Cardinal Vicar's, in *frullone*. I at once got dressed—Chimay turned up. I chatted with him for a quarter of an hour while waiting for Hohenlohe. . . . We went to the Cardinal Vicar's, who was out. To Hohenlohe's dictation I wrote in the book, with a pen drawn from the catacombs: 'The Abbé Liszt,[7] to pay his respects to His Eminence.' From there I accompanied Hohenlohe to Piazza Colonna, where he had to purchase some paper, and we returned here chatting pleasantly. Remind me to speak to you of Canisius when I see you—probably on Saturday, or Sunday at the latest. At about 1.00 I went up to Father Ferraris's. Salua told me that Hohenlohe went to see you yesterday evening; he sang me your praises. At 2.00 we lunched together, again *à quatre*, with Niky and a clergyman from the banks of the Rhine. . . . At 4.00, Bauer and Père Hyacinthe came. Hohenlohe had unfortunately already gone for a walk in the

---

[6] The feast of St Stephen, King of Hungary, is now 16 Aug.; but in Hungary his chief feast is kept on 20 Aug., the day of the translation of his remains from Stuhlweissenburg (Székesfehérvár) to Buda.

[7] How Liszt—who never became a full-blown priest—was known from this time forward, *abbé* being a courtesy title for a 'secular priest' or an ecclesiastic in minor orders.

famous Vatican gardens—but I asked them to return on Friday at 3.00. To do them courtesy, I accompanied them to Father Ferraris's—where we vied with one another, Ferraris, Bauer, and I, in singing the praises of your theological knowledge. . . .

549. To Princess Carolyne. 9.00 a.m., Monday [1 May]. Sunday, 30 April, was well spent—apart from the lack of work on my music, which always leaves a certain emptiness in me. After leaving you I went to Père Hyacinthe's, and told him that his comparison between Hagar [8] and the nineteenth century was one of the finest pages of *L'Eloquence chrétienne*. . . .

At 12.30, lunch at the French Seminary, where I was given a most cordial and flattering welcome. I certainly expect to go there again from time to time, the Superior having invited me once and for all with an emphasis that persuades me to go there for lunch whenever, in Rome, I have no idea where to go at 12.30. I played with great pleasure, a rare occurrence with me, 2 little pieces on Bauer's piano, before the 3 or 4 people who form the administration of the French Seminary. On leaving the excellent company of the Seminary, Bauer and I went back to Père Hyacinthe's, where we found Mgr. Place. As he seemed to assume that I would soon become a priest, I admitted to him that I felt barred from such a step, because of unworthiness to begin with—and also because of 2 or 3 works that I was extremely keen to finish and which claimed the greater part of my time. I further intimated to him that during my next visit to Paris I intended having the Gran Mass performed there. Anyway, Mgr. Place impressed me with his great goodwill towards me—and tomorrow I shall take him my card. I accepted Bauer's invitation to join an archaeological outing he is going on with Père Hyacinthe—led by the Abbé Michelot, chaplain at the French Embassy. The last-named has been living in Rome for 12 years and, I am told, has appropriated the learning of Visconti and of Rossi simultaneously. The rendezvous is arranged for tomorrow, Tuesday, at the French Seminary. Let me know if I shall find you in after the expedition, at about 7.00, because at the Ave Maria I have to go to Cardinal Antonelli's.

To complete yesterday, in honour of the feast of the Blessed Labre [9] I again visited the church of Santa Maria ai Monti, where his remains lie, and St Catherine of Siena's room, facing the French Seminary. St Catherine knew that the duties of Martha did not in the least militate against the activities of Mary.

---

[8] See Gen. 16: 1–16 and 21: 1–21.

[9] Benedict Joseph Labre was canonized in 1881. The church in which he is buried is usually called Santa Maria dei Monti.

She applied herself to works of charity, and took care of the poor as though she had been their mother. . . .

550. To the Grand Duke Carl Alexander in Weimar.
The Vatican, 3 May

Monseigneur,

I have just accomplished in all simplicity of intention an act for which my inner conviction had long prepared me. On 25 April I entered the Church by receiving the minor orders,[10] and since that day have been staying with Monsignor Hohenlohe, who attaches me to him by true kindness.

This modification or—as a highly-placed person has put it—this *transformation* of my life is by no means leading to sudden changes. Before very long I shall resume my work of musical composition, and shall try to finish by Christmas the oratorio entitled *Jesus Christ*. Other works, sketched or pondered, agreeing with the same sentiments, will be produced in the course of time. Since my new status imposes no hardship on me, I am sure that I can live in it quite naturally while wholly observing the rule, without my state of mind being more bothered by it than I am outwardly bothered by my cassock, on the subject of which people are so good as to pay me the compliment of saying that I wear it as though I had worn it all my life.

Your Royal Highness will not imagine that I am neglecting duties and obligations undertaken previously—and in particular those which sincere gratitude commands. Enclosed with this letter He will find a feeble proof of the *importance* I attach to what touches his service. To the questions that Monseigneur has jotted down on the document he sent me, I have added the replies. But how shall I manage to give you satisfaction by suggesting a Kapellmeister for you? The two personalities on whom I tried to fix Your Royal Highness's choice are no longer available, and it is His Majesty the King of Bavaria who resolutely takes the initiative I aspired to for Weimar.[11] There is no longer any point, therefore, in pondering over what can no longer be achieved—and the best thing to do, I say it again, is to rely on Herr von Dingelstedt. If, however, Monseigneur absolutely insists on my naming some musical celebrities capable of carrying out efficiently the duties in question, I shall obey by citing Messrs Rubinstein, David (in Leipzig), and my ex-friend Hiller (in Cologne), who has excellent antecedents in Weimar, where he studied with Hummel, in Goethe's lifetime.

---

[10] Which he actually received on 30 July that year.
[11] Referring to Liszt's repeated efforts in the 1850s to induce the Grand Duke to do for Wagner what was now being done for him by the King.

As for Herr von Bronsart, I could not recommend him enough, and finding him a suitable position will certainly be advantageous.

Allow me, Monseigneur, to ask you to express to Her Royal Highness the Grand Duchess my profound and unchanging devotion; and deign to believe me unceasingly Your Royal Highness's very humble and grateful servant

F. Liszt

551. To Princess Carolyne. [The Vatican] 4 May, evening. Little to say today. Hohenlohe is in bed with a slight temperature. . . . Tessière came for a chat this morning *alla buona* [without ceremony]—and is very kindly offering to contribute to my Latin and Italian studies. Solfanelli made me recite declensions for nearly three hours yesterday evening—we shall continue on Saturday. Tomorrow, dinner *chez* our incomparable Ferraris—and the day after tomorrow your very small and humble abbé will come to you before one o'clock.

The Nardi piano has been put in Hohenlohe's salon, and I have got rid of the Monte Mario one, which I have had sent back to Mengarini. I long to have the Alexandre, and above all to get back to writing music. But if I continue at this rate with my correspondence, it won't be for another week or so. This epistolary slowness shames and enrages me! See you on Saturday! I have had a charming present from Mme Betsy Meyendorff in Paris: a copy of Raphael's portrait from the gallery in Florence.[12]

552. To Prince Constantin von Hohenzollern-Hechingen in Löwenberg. The Vatican, 11 May

Monseigneur,

Your Royal Highness will understand that I have an inner need to tell you of a very happy circumstance which assures me from now on, in full measure, the stability of sentiment and conduct to which I aspired. Were I not to tell you of the decision I have taken, I should feel that I was committing an act of ingratitude and falling short of the gracious friendship with which you have been so good as to honour me.

On Tuesday, 25 April, feast of St Mark the Evangelist, I entered the ecclesiastical state on receiving the minor orders in the chapel of HSH Monseigneur Hohenlohe at the Vatican. Convinced that by this act I should be confirming to myself that I was on the right path, I accomplished it without effort, in total

---

[12] Presumably the well-known self-portrait in the Uffizi.

simplicity and uprightness of intention. Moreover, it accords with the anteced-ents of my youth, just as it does with the development undergone by my work of musical composition during these last four years—work which I intend to pursue with renewed vigour, since I consider it to be the least defective part of my nature.

To speak familiarly, if 'the habit does not make the monk', neither does it prevent him being one; and in certain cases, when the monk is fully formed within, why not assume the outer garb as well?

But I am forgetting that I do not in the least intend to become a monk in the strict sense of the word. I lack the necessary vocation, and it is enough for me to belong to the hierarchy of the Church to the degree that the minor orders allow me. And so it is not the frock but the cassock that I have donned. And on this subject, Your Highness will forgive me the slight vanity of mentioning that people pay me the compliment of saying that I wear my cassock as though I had worn it all my life.

I am now living in the Vatican, with Mgr. Hohenlohe, whose apartment is on the same floor as Raphael's *Stanze.* My abode is not in the least like a prison cell, and the kind hospitality shown to me by Mgr. H. frees me from any unpleas-ant constraints. And so I shall leave it only rarely and briefly, removals and, above all, journeys having for various reasons become very burdensome to me... Better to work peacefully in one's own home than do a lot of running around elsewhere —except in such cases as are absolutely necessary. One of these awaits me in August, when I shall keep my promise to go to Pest for the musical festivities being arranged in celebration of the 25th anniversary of the founding of the Conservatoire. My *St Elisabeth* oratorio and Dante Symphony form part of the programme.

Next year, if Your Highness were still thinking of carrying out his noble pro-ject of a musical congress at Löwenberg, I should be very happy to take part in it, and place myself entirely at your orders and service.

Allow me, Monseigneur, to express to you once again my most grateful thanks for the tokens of goodwill that you have so generously accorded both to myself and to my works; and be so good as to accept the homage of the invariable feel-ings of most respectful devotion with which I have the honour to be,

Your Royal Highness's very humble and affectionate servant   F. Liszt

553. To Agnes Street-Klindworth. [The Vatican] 19 May. Nothing could be sweeter, more lovingly affectionate, than your letter. I thank you for it with the most religious emotions of my heart. Let me hope that the idea which came to you when reading my last lines will some day be realized. I shall speak further to you about it when I see you—but without *preaching* to you, for it would ill become me to do this to anyone, and with you it would be uncalled for to the point of being ridiculous. . . .

Let's come straightaway to M. George.[13] If he is indeed showing taste and a decided flair for music, he shouldn't be thwarted. Despite my few illusions about the attractions of an artistic career, I should hesitate to turn someone aside from it when there is a probability of his distinguishing himself therein. So far as George is concerned, I urge you only not to interrupt his other studies too soon, so that he can learn, and learn well, by his education and upbringing, to do honour to his mother in all points. It is nowadays more than ever necessary for an artiste to be a man of intelligence, and one who knows not only his own field but a good many things outside it. To be a good everyday musician is no longer enough; and even that will be beyond the reach of those who neglect to acquire suitably well-stocked minds.

As regards a teacher, you cannot make a better choice than M. Léonard. I was speaking of him yesterday to Prince Chimay (who plays the violin with taste and distinction); he repeated what I had already heard from someone else about the thorough instruction given by Léonard and the excellent results of his lessons. You will therefore do well to entrust George to him at the earliest, while instilling into the pupil that we do not come into the world to amuse ourselves, and that to do well, as to live well, we must put all our energy and zeal into the performance of our duty.

When George is more advanced, lend him to me for a while. I shall try to add to his knowledge of certain masters (Beethoven, Bach, *et al.*), and shall busy myself with him fondly. . . .

Thank you for your generous promise to continue the favours of your *mailings* to me from time to time; I accept them with full gratitude.

Yours,   F. Liszt

554. To Kálmán von Simonffy in Pest. The Vatican, 21 May

Sir,

I should be sorry to cause you to lose a bet, but since you are asking me to inform you 'if Beethoven's Ninth Symphony was performed at Pest in 1840', I have to answer that it was *not*.

Nor is there any reason to be greatly astonished at the long delay before this stupendous work was performed in Pest. In Europe in 1840 the Ninth Symphony

---

[13] The eldest of Agnes's children.

was regarded as a most frightful *bugbear* by the majority of musicians and self-styled 'connoisseurs' of music. In two or three German cities, on some exceptional occasion, it had been performed at best mediocrely and fragmentarily, and the rest not bothered with; the Paris Conservatoire did not risk it until later and with no great enthusiasm—and even after the 1848 Revolution it seemed foolhardy to put it on the programmes of the most respectable concert societies, in view of the ill fate attached to the Ninth Symphony because of the foolish and pitiable judgements which had been passed on it.

I am, Sir,

Yours truly,   F. Liszt

555. To Princess Carolyne [Villa d'Este, May]. I had just fallen asleep when I was brought your kind lines at about midnight. Thank you for this sweet awakening—my heart was keeping watch with you! Everything here is perfect, beginning with my 'Patron'. He has arranged 3 rooms very comfortably for me—with piano, harmonium, and various items of furniture which couldn't be better chosen. And so I am very pleasantly installed—as you guess so well, my good Tyrolean humour does not fail me. I spent my day yesterday reading about fifty pages of the *catéchisme de Persévérance* in Italian—and in seeking out a few passages on the piano for the Indian jugglery of *L'Africaine*, of which I shall be the turkey-cock, otherwise known as the dupe![14] . . .

I began my sacristan studies this morning, by serving mass to Hohenlohe. I hope to be able to perform this office properly before long—but since good things mustn't be abused, I am promising myself to devote my small ability as a sacristan exclusively to Hohenlohe, as I have already formally notified Salua.

B.B.

In early August, shortly after passing the minor orders examination for which he had been studying, Liszt left for Pest, there to attend the first Hungarian Music Festival and to conduct the première of his *Legend of Saint Elisabeth*. From Civitavecchia he went by sea, via Livorno (Leghorn), to Genoa and then overland.

556. To Princess Carolyne. Pragerhof, almost on the Hungarian border, 7.00 p.m., Monday, 7 August. The uncommon quality of this paper will tell you that I am writing to you from a country inn. As the Pest train does not connect with the Mestre-Venice one, on which I have just arrived, I shall

---

[14] A play on *coq d'Inde* and *dindon* (*de la farce*).

have to spend the night here, and shan't be setting out again until 9.30 tomorrow morning. From here to Pest takes less than 11 hours. So I shall get there between 8 and 9 tomorrow evening, 8 August—and initially put up at the Queen of England Hotel, as in the past. . . .

Pest, 5.00 p.m., 9 August. It was impossible to continue with the pen and ink at my disposal in Pragerhof. . . . My journey overland could not have gone better. The greater part of the time I was alone. No incident to tell you of other than that between Milan and Pragerhof I read the 2 vols. of Hugo's *Légende des siècles*[15] in their entirety. At Milan, on Sunday morning, I sent you a telegram after having prayed for and with you, in the church of San Carlo and in the Cathedral. The church dedicated to your Saint[16] was on my route as I went to the Cathedral. It is an imposing building, in the form of a rotunda and with a pillared façade, in the Corso Vittorio Emanuele, Milan's principal street. I did not examine its beauties in detail, and confined myself to praying with all my soul. On entering and leaving, I was agreeably impressed by the church's rather modern look of cleanliness and its good state of repair. A few groups of contemporary sculpture seemed to me to deserve appreciation—but I was in too much of a hurry.

As for the Cathedral, it delighted me—and seemed to be much more beautiful this time than 25 years ago. I not only heard mass being celebrated there, but saw it—through the pane of glass covering the underground chapel where lies the body of St Charles. In Rome, the corresponding site at St Peter's, St John Lateran, etc., is called the *confessio*, but there they haven't introduced the use of glass panes, and the chapels are arranged differently.

If this description contains some inaccuracy, please forgive me. To observe more carefully I should have needed some leisure, and I was too full of St Ambrose[17] and St Charles to look attentively. So I did not take advantage of the verger's obliging offer to show me the treasures in the sacristy.

Yesterday evening, at 8.00, the train set me down in Buda. I walked through the new tunnel leading to the bridge joining Buda and Pest, and came back to my old quarters in the Queen of England Hotel, from which can be enjoyed a magnificent view over the Danube, the mountains, the fortress, and the castle of Buda. . . . It is on 15 August, Feast of the Assumption, that the first concert, with the *Elisabeth*, is to be held. The second is announced for the 17th. The Dante Symphony will be performed—and, to conclude, my orchestral paraphrase of the Rákóczy March. I'll send you programmes and newspapers. Reményi is

---

[15] The epic poems in three series (1859, 1877, and 1883) through which, by way of numerous scenes and episodes, Victor Hugo depicts humanity's long, slow march, in different civilizations, towards progress.

[16] St Charles (San Carlo) Borromeo, feast-day 4 Nov.   [17] Sant' Ambrogio, patron saint of Milan.

just arriving—and I shall have to go out with him at once, to see Orczy *et al.* My thoughts and my heart are with you—at the Villa d'Este, where I assume you have been installed since yesterday evening.

557. To Princess Carolyne. [Pest] 7.00 a.m., 16 August. This time I cannot boast of any blow—unless it be those to my obligatory modesty! The *Elisabeth* was greeted with cheers yesterday evening—the newspapers are filled with my name—I have become a kind of public event! Eduard, who has been here since the day before yesterday, will write to you about it, as will Cosima. I enclose the programme of the first 2 concerts; the third will probably take place next Wednesday. To get things to go properly, I had to resign myself to doing the actual conducting—i.e. to conducting the rehearsals and performances of my works. I was very little disposed to do so, as you know—but putting aside all false modesty or foolish vanity, it was impossible to do otherwise. I am convinced that when I have acquainted you with the situation, you will not disapprove. To the 500 performers of the *Elisabeth* were united, so to speak, 2,000 listeners, who by their attention and sustained appreciation 'took part' in the work to a quite astonishing extent. For several days, tickets for tomorrow's concert have been unobtainable. The Vigadó hall, magnificently and sumptuously decorated, is much larger than the one on the Capitol in Rome. It must hold between 2 and 3,000 people.

The *Elisabeth* will be performed again at the third concert, on Wednesday; a fourth will probably follow. Thus far I don't think I have made any blunder. I truly have to take no pains *um mir hier ein Publikum zu schaffen* [to create a public for myself here]! Only I haven't 10 minutes to call my own. These are the first lines I have written for 6 days. My poor jerky style is therefore even jerkier. Visitors arrive from 8.00 in the morning. At 7.00 I go and hear mass in Pest's main church, the Stadtpfarrkirche, beside the Palace of the Stadtpfarrei, where I have a lordly apartment in the parish priest's house. Yesterday, for the Feast of the Assumption, a dinner for 60 was given by my excellent and most cordial host, who is much loved here. Among the guests were Augusz and his wife, Baron Orczy, whose sister has married Steffy Károlyi, Danielik, Mátray, every parish priest in Pest—where, as you know, there are no bishops—Eduard and his wife, plus Hans and Cosette. Tomorrow there is a big banquet for the Emperor's birthday [18 August]. I am trying to do honour to my *vestito* [dress]!

558. To Princess Carolyne. Wednesday, 23 August. You can be content with Pest. . . . Yesterday evening, Tuesday the 22nd, third and last concert at the Vigadó: *Elisabeth*, which lasts nearly 3 hours, largely took up the whole evening—nothing else had been admitted on to the programme this time. After the unimaginable success of the Dante, at the second concert, there was no longer any possible doubt about the continuing, and even the increasing, success of *Elisabeth* at this second hearing. The performance was remarkable. The 500 singers and players forming the choruses and orchestra carried out their task with a kind of passionate piety—and at certain moments with transports of enthusiasm. Furthermore, the part of Elisabeth, sung by a young woman of exquisite feeling, Mme Pauli-Markovics, was given its full halo. I shall continue to send you the *Lloyd*, the German newspaper whose music critic was not favourable to me in former days. He is a man of talent who belongs to the Mendelssohn school. Consequently, he has to make some effort to catch the public mood—which, it is true, far exceeds the normal pitch. . . . Cosette and Hans are charming, and make the best impression on everyone. Eduard, who will be writing to you, and his wife returned to Vienna this morning. It seems that several of the Viennese newspapers are praising the *Elisabeth*. More details on the situation when I see you at the Babuino![18] . . .

559. To Princess Carolyne. Szekszárd, at Augusz's, Wednesday, 6 September. At 6.00 a.m. on Saturday we left Pest with the Bülows and Reményi. To avoid disturbing our hosts by getting up too early, we spent Friday night aboard the steamer. In less than 6 hours it took us to Paks, where 2 carriages awaited us in which we arrived here at 3.30. I have been given the same rooms as in '46, and the Bülows have comfortable accommodation in the other wing of the house, which is extremely spacious and very well kept. There is an ample garden, a billiard room, and 2 pianos, of which we make good and frequent use. Since Augusz's position obliges him to be very reserved, we keep ourselves to ourselves, without making any visits, which suits me perfectly. On Sunday evening I was given a vocal and instrumental serenade, which caused about 7 or 8,000 people—as I am told—to gather in the square. Instead of haranguing them, I had the piano placed near the open windows; Reményi and I played a Hungarian Rhapsody, and Hans and I the Rákóczy March as a duet. Several persons who were among the crowd, and whom I saw next day, assured me that people had been able to hear perfectly. I had intended to depart today, but

---

[18] The Princess's Rome residence was in the Via del Babuino.

couldn't resist the friendly entreaties of Augusz, his wife and children, who are keen to keep us until at least Saturday. Friday being the feast of the Nativity of the Virgin, I shouldn't like to spend it on the train. So we are staying here, where we are leading a splendid *vie de château*. I hope to receive a letter from you on Saturday evening, when I get to Buda—and by Monday evening I shall probably already be in Venice.

Hennig, a first cousin of mine whom I saw frequently at Esztergom in '56, when he was curate in one of the parish churches, has entered the illustrious Company of Jesus, and is now part of the teaching staff at the Jesuit College in Kalocsa, a very well known and flourishing establishment. Vetzko, another of my cousins, is *curé* of a village in the environs of Szekszárd. He came to see me in Pest, and again here yesterday morning. He is an educated man with a good reputation. I confessed to him today, and took communion at his 7 o'clock mass—in communion of heart and soul with you.

Cosette has undertaken to write you a brief account of our trip to Esztergom; I shall enclose it with these lines.

From the 20th to the 21st we shall continue our chats in the Babuino! In reply to this note, write immediately to Venice, poste restante. It is not certain that Cosette will accompany me as far as Venice; but as I am obliged to go through Mestre—which is only an hour from Venice—I shall give myself the pleasure of a stroll around St Mark's Square, and of collecting your lines at the post office.

560. To Baron Augusz in Szekszárd. The Vatican, 20 September

Dear Friend,

Having come home, I at once discovered, on opening my portfolio, the *corpus delicti* of an evident theft committed more or less deliberately at Szekszárd. It is this notepaper, bearing the arms of Hungary, on which I am losing no time in writing to you, and of which I cannot make better use than by telling you how the few days I have just spent *en famille* in your home provide me with an agreeable and happy memory. As early as my first visit to Szekszárd, in 1846, I had felt the cordial charm of your hospitality, which getting some twenty years older has not weakened in the least, not to mention that in growing older myself I have become still better qualified to appreciate the value of so steadfastly devoted a friendship as yours. And so when I return to your home, which I hope will be before long, expect me not to leave for some time. One really feels too comfortable there to desire a change.

As our most excellent friend Schwendtner was so good as to have the Bülows and me at the Stadtpfarrei for another couple of days, it was only last Tuesday

(12 Sept.) that we set out. The Bülows returned via Vienna straight to Munich, and I took the train to Venice. From Wednesday evening to 3 o'clock on Thursday, what marvels! What an imposing and irresistible architectural symphony, the Grand Canal from the Doge's Palace to the Rialto, St Mark and his lion! And thank Heavens one can listen to it, experience it and absorb it in silence, the lagoons ever preventing the prosaic din of other cities from approaching. In Florence, where I was obliged to stop from midnight until 4.00 a.m., I prowled around the statue of Dante[19] in the Piazza Santa Croce, and at the Loggie, where I found an old friend, the *Perseus* of Benvenuto Cellini, of glorious and swaggering memory. The tribulations that Cellini endured at the time of the casting of his *Perseus* reminded me of other, rather similar, artistic quarrels, and in particular of the one caused by my Gran Mass, in '56, when you intervened, dear friend, equally nobly and effectively to bring everything to a good end. Let me thank you for it once again, for it is to your persistence of 9 years ago that I am indebted for the position made for me in Pest this present year, one which without the precedent of Esztergom would have lacked the necessary foundations. Please also give my thanks to my *little prophetesses* of that time (who have since so happily grown up), Ilona and Anna, for having energetically maintained that 'Liszt's Mass was to be performed', and ask them to continue their prediction for the Coronation and Szekszárd Masses. That will bring luck. It was while thinking of you, of your family, of Hungary, of what I still have to do to justify to some extent the good opinion of my friends, that I returned to Rome, where I shall resume my work as soon as possible. In 6 or 8 months I hope to have finished my oratorio on Jesus Christ.

The Holy Father has returned to the Vatican in the very best of health. There is talk of holding a solemn celebration next year to commemorate the eighteen centuries since the establishment of the See of St Peter in Rome. Doubtless the Cardinal Primate and other Hungarian Bishops will be summoned.

Please, dear friend, present my most affectionate respects to Baroness Augusz, and thank her for her gracious kindnesses to Cosima and me. To the children I send the very same best wishes that they and you send me—and to Mlle Huber a thousand affectionate greetings.

With renewed thanks I am most cordially yours,   F. Liszt

---

[19] Enrico Pazzi's work, representing the poet as the *alma sdegnosa*, had been inaugurated four months earlier at the time of the Dante sexcentenary celebrations.

1866

3 January. Liszt conducts his *Stabat mater speciosa* at the church of Ara Coeli, Rome.

6 February. His mother, Anna Liszt, dies in Paris.

26 February. Sgambati conducts Liszt's Dante Symphony at the inauguration of the Sala Dante.

4 March. Liszt arrives in Paris where, on the 15th, his Gran Mass is performed at the church of St Eustache.

21 April. He has an audience at the Tuileries with Napoleon III.

25 and 27 April. Liszt attends concerts in Amsterdam at which works of his are performed by Bülow.

29 April. After a performance of the Gran Mass in Amsterdam, Liszt goes to The Hague to see Queen Sophia, and two days later returns to Paris.

10 May. He plays to the Empress Eugénie at the Tuileries, and in mid-May returns to Rome.

June. Prince Gustav Hohenlohe is appointed a cardinal and vacates his rooms at the Vatican; Liszt accordingly returns to his former abode at the Madonna del Rosario.

22 November. He takes up residence at the monastery of Santa Francesca Romana in the Forum.

WORKS. The oratorio *Christus* (S3, 1862–6[1]), consisting of:
1. Christmas Oratorio (Introduction, Pastorale and Annunciation, *Stabat mater speciosa*, Shepherds' Song at the Manger, March of the Three Holy Kings);
2. After Epiphany (*Beatitudes, Pater noster,* The Foundation of the Church,[2] The Miracle, The Entry into Jerusalem);
3. Passion and Resurrection (*Tristis est anima mea, Stabat mater dolorosa, O filii et filiae,*[3] *Resurrexit*).
Ave maris stella (S34/1, ?1865–6), for mixed chorus and organ. *Les Morts* (Lamennais) (S112/1, 1860–6) and *Le Triomphe funèbre du Tasse* (S112/3), first and third of the *Trois Odes funèbres* for orchestra.[4] Piano piece in A flat (S189); transcription (S491) for piano of *Hymne à Sainte Cécile* (Gounod).

561. To Baron Augusz in Szekszárd. Rome, 1 January. . . . The *Szekszárd nectar* arrived safely on 27 December. It was the feast of St John and the Pope's name-day. I took advantage of this timely coincidence to get Mgr. Hohenlohe at once to offer two crates (50 bottles) to His Holiness as a present, which he

---

[1] Some parts had, however, been composed at Weimar in the 1850s.   [2] Added later.   [3] Added later.
[4] *Les Morts* has a male chorus ad lib. *Le Triomphe funèbre du Tasse* was composed as an epilogue to the symphonic poem *Tasso, Lamento e Trionfo.*

most graciously accepted. That same day Mgr. Hohenlohe had invited about
ten people to dinner, among them some discerning connoisseurs in aromas and
bouquets, of whom I shall mention just Mgr. Lichnowsky (canon of Olmütz)
and Commendatore Visconti (celebrated archaeologist). On the appearance of
the Szekszárd there was, as for certain parliamentary orators, a quickening of general attention; and after we had duly examined and commented on the beautiful labels on the bottles, specified the eminently salubrious qualities of the wine,
recalled the poetry of its vineyard (including your splendid and cordial hospitality in Szekszárd), we refreshed ourselves by drinking it, while unanimously
giving warm praise to your products and gifts.

Through Mgr. Haynald I have learnt that my Dante Symphony has again
been performed in Pest. This continuing sympathy shown by the Hungarian
public, even in my absence, gives me extreme pleasure. What a composer cares
about most of all is to last. Now, you know that, at the risk of displeasing certain
of my so-called friends, I take the title of composer seriously, and fancy that my
works perhaps have it in them to last a while. If I err, at least I do so in perfect tranquillity of conscience and without claiming to be right when I am not.

It seems that in Vienna people have been surprised at my lack of eagerness
to have my *Elisabeth* performed there. Yet that can be explained very naturally,
whatever people choose to say, and I shall exchange my opinion only for a better one. As for the dedication of this work, allow me, dear friend, to defer it to
the moment of publication, which will not be for another year.[5] In Rome, an
unexpected opportunity has occurred for my Dante Symphony. It will be heard
at the end of this month, at the time of the inauguration of a picture gallery,
consisting of 27 immense canvases—painted by contemporary Italian artists—
depicting the principal scenes of the *Divina Commedia*. His Majesty the King
of Saxony has deigned to accept the title of patron[6] of the limited partnership
which has been formed for the purpose of mounting a permanent exhibition of
these paintings; and at the Palazzo Poli (Fontana di Trevi) we have already been
able to see for several weeks the glittering inscription, in large golden letters:
'Galleria Dante'! I enclose an article from the *Osservatore Romano* containing more
details of this exceptional undertaking. I am adding, too, a brief account of the
Stabat mater speciosa, which I composed recently (at the request of an excellent
friend of mine, Father Marcellino da Civezza—a Franciscan), and which will be
performed the day after tomorrow in Ara Coeli, the Franciscan church. . . .

                                                                    F. Liszt

---

[5] The vocal score was published in 1867, the full score in 1869, with a dedication to King Ludwig II of Bavaria.

[6] Appropriately, for under the name of *Philalethes* (Lover of Truth) King Johann I of Saxony, a lifelong Dantist
and collector of a complete library of works on the great Florentine, had given the world a very successful German
translation of, and commentary on, the *Commedia* as early as 1833.

562. To Anna Liszt in Paris. The Vatican, 14 January G (F)

Dearest Mother,

The best thing I have to tell you today is that I shall soon have the joy of seeing you again. A very friendly letter from M. Dufour, mayor of Paris's 2nd arrondissement, informs me that on 15 March my Mass will be performed at St Eustache. The collection which will be taken in the church on that occasion is to go to the Schools Society, of which M. Dufour is president. If, as I hope, my Mass is favoured with a good performance, it won't fail to make a good impression, and it will give me a truly childlike satisfaction to allow you to share the modest success which I shall endeavour to deserve. I shall be coming to Paris on 5 March.

Would you please thank Ollivier for the pamphlet by Z. Marcus which he sent me. In it I read with pleasure some accounts of Ollivier in his youth. His distinguished character, talent, and eloquence are justly appreciated. In Paris this time I hope to go to the Chamber to attend one of his splendid oratorical successes, which are becoming more and more the habit with him.

In about a fortnight a couple of large parcels, addressed to Ollivier, will arrive from Leipzig. They contain the scores and orchestral parts of my Mass and of several of my symphonic poems which are indispensable for the Paris performance of these works. Ask Ollivier to keep them until they are collected by Belloni. I am reluctant to deposit them with some music dealer or other.

Princess Marcelina Czartoryska writes from Vienna to tell me that she will shortly be going to Paris and staying there for several months.

Until we meet again soon, dearest Mother. Thank you for your good, kind letters.   Yours with heart and soul,   F. Liszt

The distressing events in Munich have fortunately had no further effect on Bülow's position; he is surviving there. At the end of February, at the King's request, he will be conducting a grand performance of my *Elisabeth* oratorio.[7]

563. To Baron Augusz. Rome, 14 January. . . . In my last letter, of New Year's Day, I told you of the august and *altissime* approbation accorded to the 'Szekszárd'; and also of the praise bestowed upon it at Mgr. Hohenlohe's dinner. His Holiness, from what I was told yesterday, has it served at table daily, and I hope that the generous juice of your grapes will contribute to his longevity. I have with equal success begun to make a little publicity for the 'Szekszárd'

---

⁷ On 24 Feb. Invited by King Ludwig to attend this performance, Liszt was obliged to decline with regret. Two months later the King, to whom the work was subsequently dedicated, bestowed upon him the Order of St Michael.

on the other side of the Tiber, by presenting a couple of bottles to one of the most discerning connoisseurs in these subtle matters, Count Leo Bobrinsky. The result of his careful, judicious, and comparative examination is that he very much desires to obtain about fifty bottles to begin with, and will instruct his Vienna banker to have them sent to him. . . .   F. Liszt

Madame la Princesse Wittgenstein tells me that she has had recourse to your good offices to obtain a supply of the photographs taken of me in Pest, which I am being asked for on all sides, for they are considered to have turned out much better than many others. If it is more convenient for you to reply to her in German, I can inform you that Princess W. reads and understands this language better than the majority of Germans, although for want of practice she has never got into the habit of writing it correctly.

In early February Liszt received from Emile Ollivier a letter of the 1st which ran: 'Since yesterday your mother has been very seriously ill. I am weighing my words: it is *serious*, but not *dangerous*. When you receive this letter, it will all be over in one way or the other. If her condition worsens, I shall let you know by telegram. . . . The illness is capillary bronchitis. I need not say that we are doing everything we can.'

On 7 February, Ollivier wrote again: 'The improvement I notified you of did not last: yesterday evening, at 11.00, she breathed her last. My brothers and I closed her eyes, had her laid out, and then I deposited a kiss upon her brow—from you, from Blandine, and from myself. She received extreme unction. Tomorrow we shall take her to her resting place.'

Further lines followed on the 8th: 'I have just returned from the melancholy ceremony,[8] and enclose a copy of the address I gave. I have acquired a plot of ground and shall have a stone placed there with her name and this inscription from Ecclesiastes: *Qui inveniet feminam bonam, hauriet jucunditatem a domino*[9] . . .'

564. To Emile Ollivier in Paris [The Vatican, February]. I am profoundly grateful to you for your feelings towards my mother. God will reward you through His blessings, for which your soul, more exalted than the favours or reverses of destiny, is so well prepared. Blandine and Daniel are with their grandmama!— and I shall not tarry. During the time remaining to me it is to you that I shall owe the most effective consolation for my grief: the sanctifying union of my mother's soul and mine through the grace of the sacraments she received when dying.

---

[8] After the funeral service at the church of St Thomas Aquinas, Anna Liszt was buried in the cemetery of Montparnasse.
[9] Actually Prov. 18: 22: 'Whoso findeth a wife findeth a good thing, and obtaineth favour of the Lord.' However, Ollivier probably had in mind a more literal meaning of the Latin: 'Whoso findeth a *good woman* . . .'

Do please give my respects to Mgr. Bucquet, whom I shall go and see at once. I shall be in Paris around the end of this month, and will take your advice on what is the most suitable thing to do about my mother's burial place.

In one of her last letters she urged me to come and stay in your home. Is that still possible, without in any way inconveniencing you?

Yours very truly,   F. Liszt

565. To Princess Carolyne in Rome. [Paris] Monday evening, 5 March.

A good crossing and incident-free journey. In Marseilles on Friday evening saw Belloni and Franz Boisselot, in my room at the Grand Hôtel. Saturday morning, 7.00, departed—Sunday, 11.40, arrived in Paris. I had sent a telegram to Ollivier, who came to fetch me at the station. I am living in my mother's rooms, on the third floor; Adolphe Ollivier[10] is on the second, and Emile on the first. Emile's career is taking great shape—and his next speech at the end of this week, on domestic matters, is awaited as an event. He recently had an interview of an hour and a half with the Empress. He is being strongly urged to become political editor to the newspaper *La Presse*, in succession to Girardin, with whom he is very close. The latter is once again, but certainly not for the last time, making a lot of noise. . . . He came to see me yesterday at about 5.00, and tomorrow I shall be one of a foursome at his place for lunch, with Ollivier and Mme de Girardin. . . .

My arrival is reported in a kindly way by most of the papers. A second performance of the Mass is already being mooted—seeing the enormous demand for tickets. *Vedremo!*

I didn't go out yesterday. At 7.00 this morning I was at [the church of] St Thomas Aquinas. It was in the holy Angelic Doctor's mansion that I attended mass. At 9.00, visit to the *curé* of St Eustache—at 10.00, visited the Mayor of the 2nd arrondissement—later, took the dispatches to Chigi,[11] who received me affably. Chigi told me that through the newspapers he had denied the news of his return to Rome. I have called on Pcss [Pauline] Metternich, Pcss Marcelina [Czartoryska], Mme de Blocqueville, whom I didn't find—and Mme de Chimay, who had sent me a note inviting me to lunch. Tomorrow morning I shall go to see Berlioz, Rossini, d'Ortigue, *et al.*—in the afternoon, Luciano and Bucquet. Permit me for a fortnight or so to write to you in telegrammatic style. Thank you for your telegram. Cosette is sending me some very favourable newspapers. Takings of 40,000 francs at St Eustache for the benefit of schools are being

---

[10] Brother of Emile.   [11] Papal Nuncio in Paris.

spoken of. Tickets are already at 10 francs and will go still higher. In his *feuilleton* in the *Moniteur* today, Théophile Gautier announces the Mass very simply but suitably. I shall pay him a call on Friday or Saturday.

Among those who attended my mother's cortège to the cemetery were, Emile tells me, Mme Spontini, Ferdinand Denis, and Louis de Ronchaud. In the morning of the day after tomorrow I shall go to the Montparnasse cemetery with Adolphe Ollivier. . . .

566. To Princess Carolyne. [Paris] 4.00 p.m., Saturday, 10 March.

I got back here at about 2.00. On my table were your 3 letters, which had all arrived at once. . . .

The partial rehearsals of the Mass finished today. Because of a recent scandal, the Archbishopric is maintaining in all its severity the regulation prohibiting women singers from performing in church. And so we shall be deprived of the co-operation of Mme la Baronne de Cateu and of Mlle Bloch, which I regret more than anyone. Three of the choirboys who have charming voices, and whom I have had rehearsing every morning since Monday, will replace them. Very probably the Mass will be performed a second time, later this month, but I shan't make up my mind on this subject until the day after the performance at St Eustache. As I remarked very plainly yesterday to the person who was trying to come to an agreement with me about the second hearing: 'If my work makes merely a good impression, there will be no point in a repetition. It would need to make a sensation quite out of the ordinary—and after that, we'll see!' Nothing will be decided during these 5 days. I shan't ask to see the Emperor until after the 15th. . . .

On Thursday evening I accepted, as an exception, an invitation from Pcss Metternich. About fifteen people were there. I played the St Francis Legends, the 'fried chicken',[12] as a reminiscence; and, as ordered, the Sanctus and Credo from the Mass, four hands with Saint-Saëns,* a musician of the highest class. This is my week: Sunday and Monday, dined with Ollivier; Tuesday, at Girardin's, with Mme Keller,[13] who sang your praises to me and whom I invited to Mme de Blocqueville's for the day after tomorrow, Monday. On Wednesday, a big Pasdeloup concert at the Cirque Napoléon—a Weimarian programme: Wagner, Berlioz, the Septet from *Les Troyens* encored, Saint-Saëns, etc. On Thursday, dined with Ollivier, John Lemoine, and Saint-René Taillandier at Mme Singer's, sister

---

[12] Liszt's nickname for one or more of his *Soirées de Vienne* after Schubert.

[13] Carolyne's cousin Denise Keller, whose acquaintance Liszt had made at Kiev in 1847 at the same time as that of the Princess.

and niece of the Ratisbonnes. Today, dinner at the Montesquious' with Pcss Caraman-Chimay. Tomorrow, *chez* Mme Erard at La Muette—on Monday, Mme de Blocqueville—on Tuesday, Kreutzer—on Thursday, Pcss Marcelina. Have seen Berlioz, Rossini, d'Ortigue. Not yet seen Mgr. Bucquet, Lucien Bonaparte, Pcss Julie,[14] Lamartine, Sainte-Beuve, Denis, Veuillot, Hyacinthe. I am postponing my visit to Nélida, and would not like to return to any communion of minds with her. I also intend to do without the moral support of the Rothschilds, which I have no need of now. Every morning before 7.00 I go to mass at St Thomas Aquinas's. Tomorrow, or the day after, Adolphe Ollivier will take me to the Montparnasse cemetery. . . .

The news from Rome has given me extreme pleasure. Cesare Cantù at the second performance of the Dante Symphony—advantageously replaces various absent persons! Do you remember that 10 years ago I got you to buy Cantù's *Universal History* for your library?

Impossible to continue today! I receive about twenty letters a day—and just as many visits.

At St Eustache on Thursday, 15 March, the Gran Mass received a barely tolerable performance in what, as Walter Bache noted, were lamentably inadequate conditions: 'Unfortunately there were no women's voices in the chorus, so that the accents, etc. were not given with much vigour: the orchestra and chorus were unfortunately not raised, which of course lessened the effect in so vast a church. . . . There was a detachment of soldiers in the church, and occasionally during the music the officer gave the word of command at the top of his voice! During the Sanctus the drummer performed an obbligato! . . . During the music, lady patronesses came round rattling money boxes, and upsetting chairs with their crinolines! The audience was just like the one at the Palazzo Barberini.'

567. To Princess Carolyne. Sunday evening, 18 March. I am trying to find the right word. Success, yes—sensation even—but a difficult situation. St Gregory will help us! One gains an idea of certain things only by doing them! I was hoping to be able to give you notice, this very evening, of the second performance of the Mass. Three or 4 proposals have been made to me on this subject—no conclusion yet. I shall probably confine myself to the Credo alone, at the Cirque with Pasdeloup on Good Friday. It is a *mezzo termine*, but one which has a certain attraction, seeing that the unbelievers have decided to say and print that the Credo is the weakest and most inharmonious piece in my

---

[14] Sister of Lucien Bonaparte and wife of the Marchese di Roccagiovine.

Mass. Nélida is of this opinion. I haven't been to see her—and through sundry persons she has let it be known to me that she can't understand my absence from her *salon*! At the Théâtre Italien it has been a question not only of performing my Mass, but of exploiting it! No point in telling you in writing of these mercenary details. For the moment I have been made a *lion*! We shall see how this key can be changed without disadvantage, and will try to show ourselves as we are—very seriously serious!

Tomorrow M. Bucquet will present me to the Archbishop. The day before yesterday I asked Pce Metternich to express to the Emperor my wish to be permitted to thank His Majesty for his kindnesses to me. Pcss Julie, whom I saw yesterday for the first time, called me the most sought-after man in Paris! That is much too much, for the little that I am! I am told that the newspapers concern themselves with me daily. Their tune, too, will gradually change. The Nuncio and the Prussian Amb. have left me their cards. Leverrier[15] has invited me to lunch at the Observatory. Pcss Marcelina is very kind to me—but I shall hardly succeed in fitting into her very Orleanist circle. Mme Blocqueville, perfect and charming; after St Eustache she wrote to me with a full heart, telling me that she would tell you of her impression. Ollivier wrote to you on Thursday, in the Chamber. He will be speaking tomorrow. Nearly 50,000 francs takings for the Schools Fund is a fact somewhat overlooked! Up to now, at masses in previous years, the figure of 8 to 10,000 francs had barely been reached. Berlioz, d'Ortigue, Kreutzer, and other friends (??) of mine—Rossini, very kind. At yesterday's dinner he graciously proposed a toast to me. During the evening, more than 100 people turned up, among them the young Rothschilds. Rossini had the tact not to ask me to play, although everyone was expecting to hear me. I deliberately refrained—for newspapers large and small would have torn to pieces this poor pianist, the Abbé Liszt! . . .

Fancy, I have the use of a carriage. My Indian from Rouen, M. Courzon, who lives a very retired life here, has put one of his at my disposal. You remember the incident of his wife's confession. It is a real service he is doing me, for the English horse he has lent me runs like a tiger—and saves me a great deal of time. . . .

Girardin had entrusted Charnacé* with doing the article on the Mass in *La Liberté*! It was Nélida who dictated it, having come to the rehearsal with Charnacé. I have hardly reached the viewpoint of Père Hyacinthe—whom during the week I shall visit at Passy. But life isn't becoming more agreeable for me, nor any easier! Nevertheless, I have no reason to complain. St Gregory and you will not abandon me—of that, I am quite certain!

---

[15] The co-discoverer of Neptune had been Director of the Paris Observatory since 1854.

Tomorrow I shall go to the Chamber for the first time, in honour of Ollivier's speech. Thus far I have committed no blunder, I fancy. In about a fortnight I hope to have more elbow room. May God be with you and us! The best of my time in Paris is between 7.00 and 8.00 a.m., at St Thomas Aquinas's. . . .

568. To Princess Carolyne. Maundy Thursday, 29 March. Be blessed for your dear letters! They have reached me punctually up to 22 March, and I owe them my sweetest moments. . . .

After the *éclat* of the Mass at St Eustache, it could be presumed that my situation would be easier—but patience is still needed. According to the reception given to the Credo tomorrow evening at the Cirque Napoléon, I shall proceed further or continue to delay. Yesterday morning's rehearsal was satisfactory—but I am taking great care not to conclude from it that success is assured for tomorrow. Ollivier and Belloni will give me news of it; for it suits me better not to attend this concert. As there are no boxes at the Cirque, and as I would be, inevitably, the cynosure of all eyes, I far prefer to spend the evening of Good Friday in my room! The breviary is also the greatest of music! To Rossini is attributed this witticism: 'Liszt is composing masses, to get used to saying them!' The truth is that I more prayed my Gran Mass than composed it, and for rather a long time I have been used to singing my breviary! You, who know me by heart, will not find that I abuse the metaphor by saying that, and our good Father Ferraris will not accuse me of heresy either! . . .

Personally, I can only be well satisfied with the genuine courtesy I am generally shown. The Minister for Foreign Affairs has sent me his card, after having, of his own accord and without my seeking him out, renewed acquaintance with me at Nieuwerkerke's. Various other personages, including the Nuncio and the Prussian Ambassador—but Pce [Richard] Metternich excepted—have done the same.

After Easter, Ollivier, his brother and I will sort my mother's papers and a small number of objects she left. . . .

Continue to put up patiently with some stupid and unpleasant articles. The one in *Liberté* was not written by a democrat but by Nélida's son-in-law, Guy de Charnacé. *Poco a poco* my fingers will do my brains less injustice—and my celebrity will no longer stand in the way of my reputation! It's just that the transition is a little too slow! Nothing, however, prevents our putting this time to good use, by loving God and His Church—and by modestly practising the virtues taught us! It is that to which is applying himself your very humbly devoted

F.L.

Has Girardin sent you his plays? He readily promised me to, the day before yesterday *chez* Pce Napoleon,[16] who yesterday was due to leave for Florence and Naples. The Prince had the perfect good taste not to invite me to play the piano in his home—but Pcss Clotilde showed her wish to hear me, in so discreet a manner that I could not refuse. There were in any case no more than 9 or 10 people in her salon. . . . If possible, I shall dine at Girardin's in about a week. Until then I am fully booked. Sainte-Beuve received me very cordially, and likewise wants to invite me. He is still living in his little apartment of days gone by, rue Montparnasse. I went back to Berlioz's, but without finding him. . . .

569. To Princess Carolyne. 2 April. At 6.30 this morning, before I went to St Thomas Aquinas's, I received your telegram *S. Francesco e Gregorio.* Fortunato brought it to me with a beautiful bouquet, and while he was dressing me we talked about Peppina, Liberati, and other people in Rome—even about Lupi and Kicy,[17] whom I envy! The article by Ferraris on the Tenerani statue, [Alexei] Tolstoy's* poems and your annotated card reached me yesterday through Sachs. . . .

The performance of the Credo on Good Friday was flabby and confused— the soloists had colds, the choruses were uncertain, etc. As you know, I did not attend this concert. When he got back, Ollivier gave me a report in more or less these terms: 'It was not a failure, despite a few hisses which were heard. A third of the audience applauded, and a good many people even applauded warmly. A group of about fifteen formed a cabal—some persons rashly called for an encore. Here and there people were saying: "But it's a great work, it should be heard again!" In sum, it's a kind of success—especially in comparison with what happened to Wagner and Berlioz.'—Pasdeloup confirmed the accuracy of this report in a way that is still more favourable, telling me that on that evening a notable advance in public opinion had taken place. He has full confidence in my cause and its ultimate triumph. Nevertheless, one can progress only slowly. My new public will gradually be formed—at the same time that the prejudices and hostilities of determined opponents are lessened or reduced to impotence. . . .

On 15 April, at the last concert of the season, at the Cirque, Pasdeloup will have *Les Préludes* performed. He has very decently offered to withdraw this work from the programme if, at the final rehearsal, I am not satisfied with the zeal and care he and his orchestra bring to it.

---

[16] Prince Napoleon Bonaparte, nicknamed Plon-plon. Son of Jérôme Bonaparte, one-time King of Westphalia, he had in 1859 married Princess Clotilde, daughter of Vittorio Emanuele II, first King of Italy.

[17] Carolyne's parrot and cat respectively.

570. To Princess Carolyne. Friday, 13 April. Your letter of 4 to 8 April has just reached me. Four days ago I sent you my photograph. I have just been given a present which will please you. Gustave Doré this morning sent me a superb drawing of St Francis of Paola. In return, I shall arrange a little soirée, with the Dante Symphony, at his place. Saint-Saëns will undertake the second piano. Only about a dozen people will be allowed to listen—for I am protecting myself tooth and claw against soirées musicales. You say very rightly that an audience for my piano is possible only in Rome or Pest—and yet. . . .

I am still being lionized—but haven't time to pay attention to it. No news yet of the Emperor. No getting away from the Metternichs. I saw the Pcss again yesterday, and fancy we shall remain on good terms. She has had framed the large photograph of me by Munier—which she had bought with her own money—and has put it in her boudoir, in very lofty company. All's well that ends well—and I hope you will be content with me. *Les Préludes* will not be performed at the Pasdeloup concert on Sunday. On Tuesday I shall probably dine with Lagueronnière, at Marie Escudier's—who has married Mlle Kastner, runs a carriage, and lives in a charming mansion in the Champs Elysées. . . .

I have put off speaking to you about Nélida until now—although I have seen her twice, tête-à-tête. Ollivier and others induced me to make this visit, a few days after the Mass at St Eustache. She told me that it was her intention to publish her memoirs. I retorted that I did not believe it possible for her to write them, for what she would entitle memoirs would consist of lies and postures. In saying that, I put plainly to her for the first time the distinction between the True and the False! Those are big words—but it was necessary to use them, to do my duty. Since the continuation of a communion of minds between the two of us is now becoming an immorality, nothing was left to me when seeing her again but to lean on duty. Besides, the role of Guermann is a very silly invention; it is time to finish once and for all with such a doctrinal sentimentalism. Mme d'Agoult does not have to be indulgent towards me. Hand on heart, I believe Right is on my side—and shall have to reproach myself only with having used a little violence in the form. Unfortunately it is impossible to say certain things in a way that is agreeable to those they hurt! Surgical operations are not carried out with wafts of a fan! . . .

571. To Princess Carolyne. Midday, Sunday, 15 April. Emile and Adolphe Ollivier and I have just opened my mother's desk and cupboards. She left very few objects of value—a bracelet, two watches, some rings, a shawl, some lace—that is virtually everything! . . .

The Abbé Latouche, an 84-year-old priest, author of a Hebrew dictionary and various scientific works, proposes to teach me Hebrew grammar in 2 hours. Tomorrow morning I shall be going to Notre Dame, where Baron Taylor is having Labarre's Mass performed, with Offertory by Gounod, violin solo by Alard, and twelve harps. That makes little noise in advance, but will perhaps be the more beautiful afterwards! Forgive me this observation, which is all but a fatuity! Alas, only too much noise is being made about my humble self! My explanatory session with d'Ortigue takes place this [tomorrow] morning. . . .

572. To Princess Carolyne. Saturday, 21 April. My session at Léon Kreutzer's with d'Ortigue, Damcke, and Berlioz has had one good result: that I am completely at ease with two of my old friends, d'Ortigue and Léon. . . . Using the duet arrangement of the Gran Mass, in less than an hour I explained to them how I proceeded in my work, and made a special point of vindicating myself against the unjust charge that I am overturning accepted notions of harmony, rhythm, and melody. Far from overturning, I believe I have developed and enriched them. Damcke agreed that in my Mass there is not a single bar which infringes the rules of harmony. He is a teacher of harmony with a great reputation—but has been opposed to the new school until now, Berlioz excepted. Well, he assured me that he could undertake to teach at any conservatoire with the examples contained in my work. He was not present at the St Eustache performance, of which only false reports had reached him. As for Berlioz, I treated him with all the respectful consideration I owe him. I imagine that this hour of friendly chat has not lessened the good opinion he may have of my bit of musical *savoir-faire*. Naturally we spoke of you—and on this topic we shall always be in agreement! The same evening, Monday, I saw him again at dinner at Mme de Blocqueville's, with Mme Mnischek, Montégut, Léon Masson, and Laprade, who has been a member of the Académie française, if you please, for a good many years. Berlioz brightened up towards the end of the meal, in connection with Shakespeare. Conversation was maintained in a very pleasantly interesting and animated tone. The next day, dinner at the Escudiers', with Lagueronnière, Langrand Dumonceau's partner, and two other financiers. They were extremely disappointed not to hear me play the piano, after the coffee. On the conditions on which I am still in Paris, I must refrain from certain kindnesses—because they would be interpreted very foolishly, to my disadvantage. Better to displease people *en passant*, than continually to be falling out and squabbling with them! On Wednesday, a big dinner at Mme Bénoît Fould's, Ary Scheffer's Maecenas and a close friend of Ollivier and Blandine. Ollivier having undertaken to forewarn the mistress of the house, no piano appeared. . . . The book most talked about in the salons of the cognoscenti is Mrs Craven's *Récit d'une sœur*.[18] It is the story of M. and Mme de la Ferronnays. Mgr. Gerbet in his dialogue between Fénelon and Plato drew an admirable picture of the death of M. de la Ferronnays.

Sunday morning. . . . The day before yesterday I received the following letter, addressed to the Abbé 'Laity': 'M. l'Abbé, The Emperor has been informed of the desire you have expressed to be received by His Majesty. He instructs me to inform you that he will receive you with pleasure, on Saturday, 21 April, at 2.00. Yours etc. Marquis d'Havrincourt, chamb. de service.'—After having ascertained that it was not to the Abbé Laity that the invitation was addressed, I went to the Tuileries at the specified time. The Emperor received me with a Napoleonic grace—and I stayed with him for about half an hour. We talked of Rome, of Lucien [Bonaparte], Ollivier, Bülow, etc. In 3 weeks, I hope, I shall tell you almost word for word what was said to me. Pcss Metternich had also summoned me for 2.00 yesterday. I wrote to her in the morning to ask her for a one-hour delay. Entering her home, I said: 'The Emperor seemed to have forgotten that Pce Metternich had forgotten to ask for me the honour of an audience with His Majesty.'

This morning I went to Lucien's, and took him Tizzani's short article on magic, which came to me very opportunely. Thank you, and again thank you. Tomorrow, Monday, I leave at 7.00 a.m. and reach Amsterdam in the evening. On 3 or 4 May I shall be back here.

573. To Princess Carolyne. The Hague, 7.00 a.m., Monday, 30 April.

As my good and dearest one used to say, 'Holland finished'—and very well finished, with the Gran Mass yesterday morning at the church of Moses and Aaron, run by good Franciscan fathers. This is how my week has gone. Arriving in Amsterdam, at noon last Tuesday, found the Bülows at the station, and stayed with them at the Hôtel Docleu. Wednesday, 25 April, anniversary of my entry into the Vatican, a grand concert in the park hall: Psalm 13 and several piano pieces, among them *St François sur les flots* and the Schubert Fantasy with my orchestration, played by Bülow. The hall was crowded. The Psalm went marvellously, and as the applause went on for some minutes I climbed on to the platform to show my thanks. Whereupon I was presented with a large and very beautiful silver bay wreath, with this inscription in Dutch: 'Art, by those who honour it, to its hero, *Held* F. Liszt. Amsterdam.'

---

[18] This book by Mrs Augustus Craven (née Pauline de la Ferronnays) had been published in January.

On Friday, another concert, a subscription one this time, in the park hall. A decided success for *Les Préludes*, and pieces by Hans. Yesterday morning, at 10.30, a very good performance of the Mass, conducted by Van Brée. At 2.00, left with Cosima and Herr and Frau Heckmann, excellent and charming people, who showed me the most cordial hospitality in Amsterdam, and are keenly supportive of the Music of the Future. The Queen[19] had asked me by telegram if I could go to The Hague at 4.00. I accepted with the most grateful alacrity. She gave me a wonderful, charming, and gracious welcome. My visit lasted about half an hour. On leaving her, I went to Pcss Hendryk's, at the Queen's request. The Princess urged me to stay here today too, but I made my apologies. Cosima has to return promptly to Munich, and she is keen to accompany me at least as far as Rotterdam. This evening I shall be in Brussels, and tomorrow in Paris. Hans got to Munich yesterday evening, from where he will write to you.

Your letter to Amsterdam hasn't reached me—but I told Van Brée to send it on to Paris for me. May S. Gregorio protect us!

574. To Princess Carolyne. Hôtel Bellevue, Brussels, 1 May.

Yesterday I wrote for you, very hastily, a brief summary of my week in Amsterdam. It will bear some fruit, I hope, and I have gained a couple of excellent friends there. Cosima left me at Rotterdam, to return to Munich, where Hans and she are truly doing all that is possible at present, and to the best of their ability. The *Elisabeth* will be performed a third time, before the King goes to his summer residence. Hans's position will soon be regularized by the foundation of the new Conservatorium—if, as is probable, he is successful in his conducting of the *Mustervorstellungen* [model performances] of *Tannhäuser* and *Lohengrin*, for which the leading artistes from various German theatres have been engaged. Wagner has rented a country house[20] near Lucerne for a year. Cosette, Hans, and the children will spend July and August there. What I find desirable above all else— is for Wagner not to return to Munich for a long time.

The Queen of Holland spoke to me about the Emperor Napoleon, in whom she is pleased to recognize an extraordinary fund of goodness and gentleness. With the Queen and Pcss Hendryk I spoke a good deal about Mgr. Hohenlohe and the Villa d'Este. Pcss Hendryk very graciously reminded me that she is related to the Hohenlohes.[21]

---

[19] Queen Sophia of Holland, consort of Willem III and daughter of King Wilhelm I of Würtemberg, was, of course, the sister-in-law of Liszt's royal patrons in Weimar.

[20] Tribschen.   [21] Her maternal grandmother was a Princess of Hohenlohe-Langenburg.

Without yet being anxious, I feel grieved at having had no news from Rome for a week. This evening I shall be back in Paris, and will be departing therefrom as soon as possible. I still have to go to a matinée at Rossini's, with *Tasso* on two pianos, and a Dantesque session at Doré's, plus 3 or 4 explanatory visits and dinners. Ten days or so will suffice for that—and at last, at long last, I shall be able to return to Rome! May God heap upon you all His blessings!

575. To Baron Augusz. [Paris, early May?]

Very dear friend. . . .

If, as you tell me, Hungarian newspapers have declined to reproduce the *Fremdenblatt*[22] articles about me, then they are behaving very decently, in a way that touches me deeply. You recall the *Fremdenblatt's* shrill and vulgar hostility in '56, at the time of the first performance of my Gran Mass. Since then, the zealous ill will of this rag has not abated; moreover, when it is a matter of lies, disparagement, stupidities, and platitudes, it is always in numerous, and occasionally even in good, company. I for my part am not thinking of complaining; people being made as they are, I find it very simple that they should become infatuated with me, should envy me, and should seek all possible means of giving me a hard life. Far better, loftier, and worthier souls than I have been subjected to worse treatment, both now and in days gone by. This, it must be said, is no consolation; but these examples can help to bolster one's courage. A man endowed with some superiority will accomplish his task only at the cost of many sufferings. But so long as we have clear consciences, there is nothing to fear. 'If God be for us, who can be against us?'[23]

Once again, very dear friend, please do not be distressed by attacks upon me, whether spoken or in print. *I* am not going to complain, for I have been nobly loved, far beyond what I could ever deserve. So it is from the depths of my soul that I say and often sing this psalm: 'Convertere anima mea in requiem tuam, quia Dominus beneficit tibi, quia eripuit animam meam de morte, oculos meos a lacrymis, pedes meos a lapsu. Placebo Domino in regione vivorum!!!'[24]

I shall ask Bertha to translate for me word for word the poem of *Szász Károly* [Charles the Saxon], which I shall probably set to music as soon as I have returned to Rome. Your next letter to me, address to the Vatican, where I shall be in a dozen days at the latest.

[22] A Viennese newspaper hostile to Liszt.   [23] Rom. 8: 32.

[24] 'Return unto thy rest, O my soul; for the Lord hath dealt bountifully with thee. For thou hast delivered my soul from death, mine eyes from tears, and my feet from falling. I will walk before the Lord in the land of the living' (Ps. 114, Vulg.; Ps. 116 in the AV and BCP).

In short, I have not the least reason to be dissatisfied with my stay in Paris, but it is not of such newspapers as the *Fremdenblatt* that one should enquire to know what to believe on this point. . . .

A thousand cordial greetings—and very truly yours.   F. Liszt

576. To Princess Carolyne. [Paris] Ascension Day, Thursday, 10 May.
I am very touched by what the Holy Father called me—*il nostro caro maestro* —and aspire to nothing beyond returning to Rome as soon as possible.

The Bavarian Minister in Paris, Baron Wendland, has written to inform me of the [Order of] St Michael. I paid him a visit the day before yesterday and had a fairly long chat with him. Oh, how rightly you say 'the lion's life often equals a dog's life'! However, I have little to complain of, and will try to last while enduring![25] Rossini's matinée, with *Les Préludes* and *Tasso* on 2 pianos— Planté* was at the second piano—succeeded beyond my expectations. People seem gradually to be forming a certain opinion of my talent as a composer— but we are still only at the preliminaries. Yesterday evening, Planté and I again went through *Les Préludes* and *Tasso*, at Pcss Marcelina's, where she had assembled about a dozen well-chosen people to hear them. Tomorrow evening, Saint-Saëns and I will do the Dante, at Gustave Doré's. Planté and Saint-Saëns have grown passionately fond of my symphonic poems, which are beginning to make their little way, on the sly. I also spent 3 hours tête-à-tête with Gounod. He showed me the larks' duet from his *Roméo*[26]—and various other works of his, which I like very much. After the performance of *Roméo* he will be spending some time in Rome, and on this occasion will not forget to come and see me. . . .

Veuillot and I chatted about your letter[27] on Raphael and Michelangelo. He was greatly surprised by it. Since, in this connection, I was speaking highly of the qualities of intelligence of your cousin Denise Poniatowska, he told me very plainly that she would not be capable of writing such a letter. I knew it better than he—but enjoyed hearing him say it. . . .

577. To Princess Carolyne. [Paris] Saturday, 12 May.
I shall be leaving here on Tuesday evening, the 15th, and from Marseilles on Thursday morning. . . .

I believe I have already told you that the Doré soirée went off very well. At my request, *Les Préludes* was played by Saint-Saëns and Planté, and Saint-Saëns

---

[25] An allusion to the saying *Qui dure, endure.*

[26] Gounod's opera *Roméo et Juliette*, first performed in Paris, 1867.

[27] Perhaps a reference to the Princess's essay *La Chapelle Sixtine*, published in the *Revue du Monde Catholique* of 10 Feb. that year.

further played the first movement of the Dante, the Fantasia on themes from the *Ruins of Athens*, and the *St François*. There is indeed not too much to boast of; but one could also find oneself in a less favourable situation than I am in. At the dinner given by Mme Drouyn de Lhuys, I finally ran into the Papal Nuncio and his Auditor. Having had the honour of being placed beside His Excellency, I chatted with him a little about several acquaintances in Rome. After dinner five or six people arrived: the Pce of Denmark, Countess Primoli, Mme Moulton, Mme Catters—and a little music was performed, tastefully. The next day I received cards from the Minister for Foreign Affairs, from Comte Chaudordy, and from Baron d'André.

The day before yesterday, Thursday morning, I received from HM the Empress a summons to go at 3.00 to the Tuileries, where she graciously conversed with me for half an hour. I had not requested this brief audience, of which I retain a most pleasant memory. Nor did Her Majesty ask me to play anything to her, but, the conversation having taken a musical turn, I suggested making my Saint walk on the waters before her, and we went into the salon. The Empress had received me alone at first; but she summoned her two ladies-in-waiting and her chamberlain to the salon—so as not to mortify them! One of them, Mme de Sanley, had the wit to mention the Dante—which gave me an opportunity to give a rough indication of my approach to composing. The *Elisabeth* and the *Christus* oratorio have also come to Her Majesty's knowledge. . . .

May the Good Lord heap upon you all His blessings! F.L.

On 22 June, a month after Liszt's return to Rome, his friend and host Gustav Hohenlohe was elevated to the College of Cardinals, a consequence of which was that he was obliged to vacate his rooms in the Vatican. Liszt then returned to his former quarters at the Madonna del Rosario on Monte Mario.

578. To Princess Carolyne. [Madonna del Rosario] Forgive me for reminding you about the framing of my favourite picture: the 4 great sinners who loved much! If I did not feel so unfit for philosophical theories and aesthetic speculation, I would almost risk a little interpretation, probably a very foolish one, of this sublime painting by Rubens. In saying that the 4 sinners loved much, I yet distinguish in St Peter, love through faith—in the penitent thief, love through hope—in David, love through contrition, humiliation and a broken heart! For Mary Magdalene, it is love quite simply and despite everything! Further, it was to her that Jesus first appeared, at His resurrection! She did not recognize Him instantly, something which we find utterly dismaying and heart-rending—and took Him for the gardener of the place where the tomb was. But Jesus called

her by her name—and she replied 'Master!' I am keen to have this painting in
my study, and shall place it on the right of the piano—where formerly hung
the magnificent Luca della Robbia which you also gave me, and which now adorns
the parlour. I hope the *curé* will not consider Mary Magdalene to be an infringe-
ment of the *clausura*!—

579. To Emile Ollivier in Paris. [Rome, 10 August]

Dear Ollivier,

Your lines about the musical session with Planté have given me extreme pleasure. Of eloquence, it has been said that it is as much in him who listens as in
him who speaks. That is even more true of music, and you have got so used to
listening to mine that you make up for anything it may lack. I shall thank Planté
for his liking for my works and for his zeal in studying them. They necessarily
require a little more goodwill and serious intelligence than are generally met with,
even among artistes who for the most part are perfectly willing to shine cheaply.
I for my part have not sought this kind of economical satisfaction, and spare
neither time nor trouble to find the adequate way of expressing what I feel. Could
I only to some extent confirm what you tell me, and knead some of that 'strong
man's bread' to which I aspire. Its failure to obtain the success of brioches and
pasties bothers me very little indeed! On this score I have long practised, and
without effort, a rule of total renunciation, the consciousness of purer and profounder aims freeing me from vulgar vanities. Besides, what should I complain
of, when my work receives its reward, and beyond its deserts, by such noble
sympathies as yours, dear Ollivier? Do believe that I am very keen to do honour to it with my best *verbo et opere.*

When composing *Die Ideale* I followed stanza by stanza Schiller's poem, of
which the Emperor has done an excellent prose translation,[28] since published
among his *Œuvres.* Bülow will be able to make you well acquainted with my
Ideale, which he knows by heart and keeps at his fingertips.

These last weeks I have resumed work on my *Christus* oratorio, and just finished the *Tristis est anima mea.* I hope that by Christmas I shall have finished
the whole work, where right at the beginning your *Stabat mater speciosa* has found
its natural place between the adoration of the shepherds and that of the Magi.

With whole-hearted thanks,   Yours F. Liszt

---

[28] Napoleon III—who as a boy spent several years at the *Gymnasium* in Augsburg—had translated the poem in
Sept. 1840 when, as Louis-Napoléon, imprisoned in the Conciergerie in Paris.

580. To Baron Augusz. Rome, 2 October. Our thoughts met, dear excellent friend; I was going to write to tell you of my fond memories of my stay with you last September. Those pleasant days will come again, I like to hope, when there is a further opportunity for me to return to Hungary; perhaps, just as I did then, I shall use and abuse your *model* hospitality still longer, if Madame Augusz is so good as to grant me permission. I am very keen to hear the Cardinal's most eminent Bells in E flat ring out frequently; and I thank you heartily for your beautiful idea of putting up my medallion in your church chancel.

Talking of bells and of church, could you give me some information about the Chapel, dedicated to St Louis, King of France, at Balkány (in the county of Szabolcs?)? The Comtesse de Thury in Paris is greatly interested in it and is asking me for a relic that I shall try to obtain for her, for this chapel.

Since Prince Gustav von Hohenlohe, now His Eminence, left the Vatican, following his promotion to the cardinalate (for apart from Cardinal Antonelli no cardinals live in the Vatican), I have returned to my former abode at the Madonna del Rosario, which you know from Reményi's brilliant description. Here, I have more free time than elsewhere, which suits me best, and I have put it to use in the first place to work consistently at my oratorio *Christus*, begun two and more years ago. Yesterday evening I at last reached the final bars of the score, and, to say the *amen* to this work, which will last about three hours, I have now only to turn to the accessory tasks of revision, making the piano arrangement, etc., which will be done in a month. . . .

Thank you for your friendly offer of a new supply of Szekszárd nectar, which, however, you will permit me not to accept until *after the '68 vintage is gathered.* Let us hope that it will be more profitable than that of the present year, during which I must also restrict my expenses to what is strictly necessary and practise a little abstinence. . . .

Princess Constantin Hohenlohe has been in Rome for ten days or so, staying with her mother, Princess Carolyne Wittgenstein. I have told her that my friends in Hungary had spoken highly to me of her husband, and I am convinced that when she comes to Pest she will be especially appreciated there, for she possesses in a high degree the charm and tact of noble feelings.

My affectionate greetings *en famille.*

Yours most cordially   F. Liszt

For address, put simply *Rome*, the Commandeur Abbé L.

Have I told you that the Emperor Maximilian[29] was so good as to appoint me Grand-Officier of the Ordre de la Guadeloupe, and that a little earlier the King of Bavaria bestowed on me the same rank in the Order of St Michael?

---

[29] The ill-fated Emperor of Mexico, younger brother of Franz Joseph of Austria.

581. To Agnes Street-Klindworth in Brussels. [Rome] 24 November.

For more than two months I hadn't received a line from you. This is said without any reproach but simply to explain that I am not late, as you think. The news given by some newspapers about my oratorio *Christus* is only half correct. I have indeed finally finished this work, after having worked on it for a couple of years;—but as for a performance, I know neither *when* nor *where* it will take place. Paris isn't the place for oratorio; this musical form is virtually uncultivated in that city and would perhaps not be accepted there as it is in England and Germany. Besides, my personal circumstances are in several respects at once exceptional and very unfavourable. I can push myself neither to the *fore* nor to the *rear*. What is perfectly becoming and profitable for other composers is no longer suited to my position. To organize concerts, for example, to search for ways to have my works performed, to accept the half-kindnesses of certain proposals, are things entirely forbidden me. And so, standing aside from the beaten track, I am unlikely to make my way. No matter; my mind is made up—and has been for a long time. So long as I had a public position in Weimar, I took an interest in having several of my works performed—for I needed to hear them to form an idea of them; and it was indeed more to this end than to putting them on for an audience that I applied my thoughts. For the rest, as you know, it was never without a very special and *explicit* invitation that I consented to have them heard either in Weimar itself or in a score of other German towns, the different orchestras of which I was keen to know and try out. My experience has now been gained, and I regard it as adequate in order to write with total security. It therefore pleases me to profess complete disinterest in the fate of my works. If they are worth anything, it will be noticed in time, without my needing to bother about anything other than writing them as best I can. . . .

Despite the bad weather looming up on Rome's political horizon, I shall remain here. So as not to vex a few people who are fond of me, I have quit for the winter my favourite dwelling place at the Madonna del Rosario, and since 22 November, St Cecilia's Day, have been living in a splendid apartment still more splendidly situated: right in the middle of the Forum, opposite the palace of the Caesars and facing the full light of the sun, at *Santa Francesca Romana* with its tower. This church is served by some Olivetan monks (in white), who live on the other side of the house.[30] My new apartment was formerly occupied by Cardinal Piccolomini. I have left one of my two pianos and some furniture at the Madonna del Rosario, whither I shall return in the spring.

---

[30] Originally called Santa Maria Nuova, this latest of Liszt's abodes was renamed after the saint, Frances of Rome, whose remains it houses—as it does those of Gregory XI, the pope who in 1377 brought the papacy back to Rome from Avignon.

At the Dante Gallery Beethoven's Eroica Symphony is being rehearsed; it will be a novelty for Rome. Sgambati, who will conduct the performance, is a rare and true artist with something of both Bronsart and Tausig in him: an odd mixture, isn't it, for a pure-blooded Italian who, in addition, has eyes as beautiful as those of the King of Bavaria? After the Eroica, my Dante Symphony will be performed once again (for the third or fourth time). It actually enjoys a kind of popularity here! I would have been the last to believe in the possibility of so bizarre a thing—but it's a fact! . . .

News of *Vienna* would interest me; but, please, do not tire your dear brain when writing to me; and above all be convinced, in the *superlative*, of the unchanging devotion of your sincere friend and servant   F. Liszt

1867

New Year's Day. Among those who hear Liszt play in a spontaneous performance at Nardi's are Mr and Mrs W. E. Gladstone.[1]

8 June. Liszt is present at the performance, in the church of St Matthias, Buda, of his Hungarian Coronation Mass at the coronation of the Emperor and Empress of Austria as King and Queen of Hungary. Leaving the ceremony, he is given a unique ovation by the crowds lining the processional route. 'The crowd gathered on the other side of the river naturally thought it must be the king who was approaching and being acclaimed with the spontaneous emotion of a reconciled people,' recalled an eye witness. 'It was not *the* king, but it was *a* king, to whom were addressed the sympathies of a grateful nation proud of the possession of such a son.'

6 July. Part of *Christus* is conducted by Sgambati in Rome's Sala Dante.

Late July. Liszt travels to Germany, initially to Weimar, where he stays at the Altenburg for the last time.

23–5 August. He attends the music festival in Meiningen.[2]

28 August. He conducts his *Legend of St Elisabeth* at the Wartburg as part of the celebrations marking the castle's 800th anniversary.

31 August–18 September. Liszt is a guest at Wilhelmsthal.

20 September. He arrives in Munich.

9/10 October. Liszt visits Wagner at Tribschen, near Lucerne, and then returns to Munich.

Early November. He arrives in Rome.

WORKS. Hungarian Coronation Mass (S11, 1866–7). The Foundation of the Church (*Christus*). PIANO: *Marche funèbre* (S163/6, eventually included in the *Années de pèlerinage, troisième année*);[3] transcription (S447) of 'Isoldens Liebestod' from *Tristan und Isolde.*

582. To the Grand Duke Carl Alexander in Weimar.
Rome, 4 January

Monseigneur,

My sincerest wish is to satisfy Your Royal Highness, and I hope to succeed this time. The opportunity that He deigns to offer me corresponds to the vow I made when composing *The Legend of Saint Elisabeth*. The honour you intend

---

[1] Catherine Gladstone, née Glynne, had been a pupil of Liszt's in Paris, in 1829. Gladstone (who became British Prime Minister for the first time in 1868) recorded in his diary for 1 Jan. 1867, about this visit to Nardi's: 'Liszt came at 5 for love of C. his old pupil, and played. It was marvellous.'

[2] As does the 23-year-old Friedrich Nietzsche, who is impressed by Liszt's *Beatitudes*.

[3] For the Emperor Maximilian, executed by firing squad on 19 June.

for my work, in designating it for the programme of the Wartburg anniversary celebrations, I accept with gratitude. The exceptional nature of the event will be my justification if, to obey you, Monseigneur, I make an exception to my rule and undertake to conduct the *Elisabeth*. I count on Herr von Dingelstedt being ready to write to me in good time so that we can agree on the arrangements to make, the jobs to assign, the 'gaps to fill', etc. If I had to indicate someone whose participation would be more than agreeable to me, I should name Herr von Bülow. He better than any other would contribute to the significance of the musical programme of the Wartburg celebrations. Your goodwill, Monseigneur, will decide how best to find a way to have Herr von Bülow invited, whether by proposing some choral work to him, or otherwise.

I shall invite Sig. Sgambati to accompany me, and I ask permission to present him to you personally. In him you will appreciate an artist of the noblest quality. As regards his settling in Weimar, his financial requirements would be very modest; all that would matter to him would be to find an employment for his talents in keeping with the future of his reputation.

Next 29 June, feast of SS Peter and Paul, the Catholic Church celebrates the eighteenth centenary of the martyrdom of the first Vicar of Jesus Christ. All Bishops of the Roman Catholic Church, more than 900 in number, are convoked to Rome by the successor of the Apostles who, in St Peter's Basilica, will solemnly proclaim the canonization of several Martyrs and Saints, Christ's servants!

In the opinion of the best-informed persons no political trouble will occur here before that time, and assurances of the most perfect tranquillity are being spread in abundance even by those who generally show themselves to be very much opposed to it.

Judgement and the future belong to God. On earth, it is reserved to men of goodwill to possess peace; it comforts them in even the severest struggles. *Romanus sedendo vincit.*

Deign to do me the kindness, Monseigneur, of remembering very humbly to Madame la Grande Duchesse

Your very grateful and faithful servant   F. Liszt

583. To Agnes Street-Klindworth in Brussels. [Rome] 14 February.

Were appearances not deceptive, I should this time accuse myself of the worst of vices: ingratitude. Your last letter not only greatly interested me, but even did me a service. Thanks to you I have a clear understanding of this most complicated situation in Austria, and if need be I could even adopt a certain knowing look when people mention it. I cannot understand how I so long put off thanking you for your kind generosity in sharing with me some fragments of your consummate knowledge. The blame lies above all with winter, which still condemns me to the sterile coming and going of a mass of necessary obligations. Without frequenting society—for I never go to balls, nor to theatres or grand soirées—I nevertheless find myself associating with so many people that I don't know how to cope. Perhaps I shall end up settling in Subiaco[4] or Assisi, which would be very much to my taste.

This summer, in August, I shall be returning to Thuringia. The Grand Duke of Weimar has invited me to the jubilee celebrations in honour of the 800th anniversary of the founding of the Wartburg. My *Legend of St Elisabeth* will be performed there. Thus far, in Pest, Munich, and Prague, it has been very favourably received—so that friends, full of impartiality, pay me the relatively flattering compliment of telling me that it resembles none of my earlier works and by no means offends their ears.

Here is the programme of an historic concert which is making rather a sensation here. On it you can see, in erudite and illustrious company, my Psalm [137] *Super flumina Babylonis.*[5] Further, the valiant conductor of this programme has been keen to add to it a short commentary in which I am treated as neither a 'young composer' nor as someone launching an attack on the rules of art. On the other hand, people can give themselves this double pleasure in Brussels in respect of the Mephisto Waltz, which you say is shortly to be performed there. The prospect doesn't worry me, and I should not be bothered about it even if, with regard to the propagation of my *things*, I did not resolutely practise that singular virtue that the Jesuit Fathers call 'holy indifference'. It has long been clear to me that I should be even more wrong to aspire to simple and easy successes than I am done wrong in having them denied me. At the risk of appearing insufferably arrogant, I believe that the *understanding* of certain music requires a more elevated, educated, and refined intelligence and moral sense among artistes and their audiences than is generally found. The prevalence of coarse habits, of prejudices, of spite and ineptitude of every kind and in the most varied forms (pedantic or trivial, turgid or scatter-brained) is still excessive in the world of music. Perhaps it will gradually diminish, and perhaps, too, I shall then find *my* public. I am not seeking it and have little enough time left to wait for it. . . .

F. Liszt

To attend the coronation in Buda at which his specially commissioned Hungarian Coronation Mass was to be performed, Liszt left Rome on Saturday, 1 June, arriving

---

[4] Small medieval town in Latium associated with St Benedict who there, *inter alia*, drew up his Rule.
[5] 'By the waters of Babylon' (BCP); Vulg., Ps. 136.

in Pest on the 4th. At the ceremony on the 8th, the conductor was Gottfried von Preyer, Kapellmeister at St Stephen's Cathedral, Vienna.

584. To Princess Carolyne in Rome. [Pest] midday, Saturday, 8 June.

I believe you can be satisfied. The musical success of my Mass is complete. It surprised everyone by its brevity, its simplicity—and, dare I say it, by its character. A well-known critic, Herr Schelle of Vienna, who had come expressly to hear it, said to me yesterday (I quote him verbatim): 'I really believed we had finished with church music, and that in this field hardly anything new could be done which was good, or anything good be done which was new. But your work, or rather your masterwork, for it is one, contradicts me dazzlingly—and in my article I shall take care to say so to the public, for people ought to know what it's about.'

The decision whereby the performance of the Mass was awarded exclusively to the Imperial Chapel in Vienna, was favourable rather than detrimental to the effect of the work. It seems that even during the preliminary rehearsals in Vienna the majority of the Chapel musicians formed a favourable opinion of it. This early good impression increased still more at the final rehearsal and in the performance—as I am told by Hellmesberger, Doppler, and Kapellmeister Preyer, who conducted in place of Herbeck, detained in Vienna by a serious illness. I don't yet know if some approval is granted me in high places. I hope that at least there will be no reason to reproach me with having composed music that is too long or unintelligible; for the contrary opinion is generally held. As you know, Their Majesties are cruelly afflicted by the Archduchess Mathilde's fatal accident,[6] and by the news from Mexico, which I shall believe only when it is impossible to doubt it. The Archduchess Mathilde's funeral will take place tomorrow. According to the newspapers, the horses which were harnessed to the coronation coach in Buda will be used to draw the Princess's hearse! The King and Queen are said to have shed many tears during the coronation ceremony. I had taken a seat in the choir, beside the organ. After the Primate, it was Mgr. Haynald who played the principal part in the various offices and ceremonies. Here is the programme, from which must be deleted the theatrical performance and the evening-dress ball, which Their Majesties cancelled because of the family mourning.

Prince Constantin, who greeted me warmly, I have seen once. He is overburdened with things to do at the moment, but I shall try to see him again

---

[6] In attempting to hide a cigarette which she was smoking in disobedience to her father's wishes, the 18-year-old daughter of the Archduke Albrecht had set her thin cambric dress on fire and been burnt to death.

tomorrow evening. The day before yesterday he was appointed a Knight of the Golden Fleece. The Coronation Mass will be performed at the end of the week, on Friday or Saturday, in the large hall of the Vigadó. I hope to set out on Monday or Tuesday, 18 June—and to be back in Rome on the 22nd or 23rd.

God bless   Bons Bessons

A few weeks after his return to Rome, Liszt travelled north again, this time to Germany.

585. To Princess Carolyne. The blue room, [Weimar] 4.00 p.m., [Monday] 29 July. In this place, thirteen years of joys and sorrows, of *Wahrheit und Dichtung*,[7] press upon me, sing, weep, cry, moan, and shine! Every object—what am I saying?—every atom of air and of light contains a fragment of your soul! It is a glorious, ineffable, immense hymn of all the energy and all the tenderness of Martha and Mary at one and the same time!—You know with what all but childlike devotion I follow the Saints' feast-days. Today's is St Martha's—and Friday's was St Anne's. When I read the epistle of the office of the day, 'Who will find a strong woman? She is more precious than treasures brought from the ends of the earth', these admirable words were illumined for me by remembrance of you in Woronince, in Weimar, and of every single day! . . .

Mgr. the Archbishop of Calcutta, about whom you spoke to me, said mass in Livorno on Thursday. I attended it—and even stayed for a second mass, in commemoration of my mother.

Reaching Marseilles at 4.00 p.m. on Friday, I went up to Notre Dame de la Garde, *Ave Maris Stella*, and left again at ten in the evening on the fast train to Lyons. Before getting on board I purchased a charming volume which I shall bring you: *Le trésor épistolaire de la France*. Being unable to chat with you for a long time, I have to resign myself to seeking distraction by reading letters of Mmes Roland and de Staël, of Chateaubriand and de Maistre. Glancing through this volume, I at once came across Chateaubriand's Roman letter to M. de Fontanes, which I have long had a liking for, despite my little taste for *received* enthusiasm regarding Rome. . . .

Tuesday morning. In this same *Trésor épistolaire* . . . two letters from M. de Maistre to his daughter Constance will please you. They establish, with penet-

---

[7] Truth and Poetry—reversing the title by which Goethe's autobiography (*Aus meinem Leben. Dichtung und Wahrheit*) is usually known.

rating lucidity, that women must not rival men, that they are not by any means condemned to mediocrity—that they can even aspire to sublimity, but feminine sublimity! This same thought will be crystallized by the *Petits Entretiens*![8]

Leaving Marseilles at 10.00 p.m. on Friday, I got here yesterday, Monday, at 11.30 a.m. On Saturday evening I had to stop in Mulhouse, and sleep for a few hours at the Lion Rouge. On Sunday at 6.00 I went to mass; then I continued my journey via Strasbourg, Wissembourg, Landau, and Mainz. It is the first time I have taken this line, which seems a couple of hours shorter than the Kehl, Karlsruhe, Heidelberg one.

Augusta[9] had received my telegram from Strasbourg, but not yet your letter from Rome. I found her at the railway station, where she arrived from Wacha at the same time as I did—and here I am reinstalled most comfortably in the blue room. The Grand Duke is in Ostend and the Grand Duchess at Ilmenau. Their Highnesses will return to Wilhelmsthal on about 12 August. An eyewitness tells me that at the Paris review in honour of the Sultan, His Highness was on horseback on the right of the Emperor, and the Grand Duke of Weimar on his left. You have read that the Emperor paid a visit to the Duke of Gotha at the Hôtel Mirabeau. It is said that *Tannhäuser* will be performed at the Paris Opéra for HM the King of Bavaria. That is a courtesy in the best taste, perfectly Napoleonic! Mme Metternich rightly guessed what would be suitable. . . .

586. To Princess Carolyne. 5 August, Our Lady of the Snows. The week has passed tranquilly—but not without bringing me a disagreeable intimation relating to the Altenburg, of which I am informing you at once. In view of the arrival of the Prussian Colonel in Weimar, and the expected arrival of a Prussian General, Herr von Watzdorf told Count Beust that it was becoming essential to have the use of the 3 or 4 large rooms at the Altenburg which contain your furniture. The whole of the rest of the house is already let. Only your white room, the blue room, and the 3 small adjoining rooms have been spared. Count Beust, whom I saw the day before yesterday, tells me that this apartment, with the small staircase, which it has been necessary to repair, was reserved for me in perpetuity by the Grand Duke. I told His Excellency that your intention had been to come here at the end of this July, and meet your daughter; but that since Pcss Marie's health had prevented her from making this

---

[8] See under Sayn-Wittgenstein in Biographical Sketches. [9] Augusta Pickel.

journey at present, you were postponing your own as well. I asked him to grant you in the mean time the longest respite possible and not to force you into a removal as onerous as it would be distressing, except in case of absolute necessity. The Grand Duchess will be returning in 5 or 6 days. I hope to see her immediately, and shall urge her to be merciful in the matter. Count Beust will inform you at an early date of the decision taken, which I fear won't be favourable. We mustn't resent it, but resign ourselves—and practise the Gospel precept: 'Do unto others what you *would like* them to do unto you.' That does not resemble, generally, what other people do to us! When you receive Beust's letter you can determine the arrangements to be made.

Every morning I go to the mass of our excellent parish priest, Hohmann, who slightly infringes the Roman rule by taking at least 40 minutes to say mass. I leave the house at 7.00 and do not get back here until after 8.30. I avoid going through the town, and up to now have not seen the Market Place. When walking through the park, I think of the rosary you used to say there in days gone by! At 12.30 my meal is brought from the Erholung. Vincenzo (with whom I am extremely content) and Augusta go and have lunch together at the Erholung, at about 1.00. In the evenings, Vincenzo always prepares me some tit-bits very much to my taste, to accompany tea. In the mornings my door remains closed, and I write or read until 12.30; between 2.00 and 6.00 I have visitors. . . .

Soon there will no longer be a green uniform in Weimar—the military will have a new outfit, in the Prussian manner. The Grand Duke still had a green uniform at the Paris review—it's a good ending! . . .

Yesterday evening I went to Frau von Schorn's. She passes her time in bed, in very great pain. Her state of mind is tranquil, although she seemed to have got a little thinner; her eyes and tone of voice retain the sympathetic, agreeable quality showing noble blood. We spoke of you, and of the Emp. Maximilian; and you will soon be receiving a letter from her. Perhaps you will send her your *Chapelle Sixtine* and *monument Tenerani*. I also told her about the *Petits Entretiens*, very great in their content!

Tomorrow I shall go to Jena to hear Schubert's Mass, at a church concert, plus a *Lacrymosa* by Draeseke and a Hymn by Mendelssohn. The *Elisabeth* rehearsals are going well. Müller-Hartung conducts them with remarkable zeal and intelligence. I shall become friends with this young artiste of good stock, the only one here with whom I can get along, for he has what is necessary to be perfectly *comme il faut*. Fräulein Adelheid von Schorn is a member of Müller-Hartung's *Singverein*, and will also be singing in the *Elisabeth* choruses at the Wartburg, exclusively devolving on the Weimar and Eisenach *Singvereine*, consisting of *dilettanti*. The chorus from the Weimar theatre will not be participating, just the orchestra. The whole thing will seem rather like a Court celebration, and will, I hope, be a great success. As far as Meiningen is concerned, I am less sure. *Ce qu'on entend sur la montagne* worries me a little, not that I have to disown this work—but because I feel that the moment to *hear* what I had in my inner ear when writing it has not yet arrived. Nevertheless, I have great confidence in Damrosch, who is conducting. . . .

587. To Princess Carolyne. Monday morning, 12 August. . . . I have made the friendly acquaintance of Comte de Rayneval, French minister in Weimar. His manner is perfectly agreeable, and he also shares his brother's opinions and Roman sentiments. He lived in Rome for several years, as Secretary of the Embassy. Last Wednesday, I dined in a threesome at his place, with the Chancellor of the Legation, M. Henriot. On Thursday, tea and supper at our friend Preller's, whose mood is as beautifully verdant as the trees he paints! The Schölls, Frau Hardmuth, and Fräulein Adelheid von Schorn were at Preller's. He repeated to me what Cornelius had said to him shortly before his death:[10] 'I have from time to time met distinguished women, even superior ones, in my long career—but for depth of feeling and keen understanding of art, none of them can be compared to the Princess Wittgenstein.'

On Saturday evening I visited Steinacker in Buttelstedt, and yesterday [Ferdinand] David of Leipzig, on holiday in Berka. Steinacker is as ever very kind, gentle, active, ingenuously uncomplaining and charitable—*ein Angehöriger der guten Altenburger Zeit* [someone from the good Altenburg time]! His wife's mental illness seems incurable. She is in a nursing home in the outskirts of Weimar. . . . Frau David has for some years been in a state similar to Frau Steinacker's—but apparently with some chance of being cured. He, David, remains vigorous, lively, and unceasingly active. He is indispensable in all matters musical in Leipzig—at the Gewandhaus, in the theatre and the Conservatorium—and everywhere gives excellent service. He is one of the best and most expert musicians in Europe—and more, a man of breeding and a very pleasant companion. Shortly after my arrival here he paid me a call, and I am again very grateful to him for having most kindly offered me his assistance at the violin desks in the Wartburg, which I am accepting most eagerly. To thank him for it, I went to see him yesterday evening in Berka—where I had a good look at the trees! . . .

The Bülows will not be back in Munich until mid-Sept., and the King not until the beginning of October. I'll decide what to do after the Wartburg.

[10] The painter Peter von Cornelius had died on 6 Mar. that year.

588. To Princess Carolyne. Liebenstein, Tuesday morning, 27 August.
The whole of this Meiningen music festival could not have gone better. The Duke's strong personal interest has played a major part in this general and very genuine success. *Ce qu'on entend sur la montagne* was perfectly performed and much applauded. Brendel told me yesterday that he rejoiced at having chosen this symphony for the Meiningen programme. I'll send you some newspaper articles and have asked Mme Laussot to write you a brief account of the 4 concerts, which you will receive at the same time as these lines. Before the last concert, the day before yesterday, the Duke sent to Gille, Reményi, and Damrosch the cross of Chevalier of his order—and to your very humble servant the insignia of Commandeur. These tokens of favour have naturally still further increased the good and charming impressions that my friends and I will take away of this week of music, which passed in perfect harmony. Some of the Duke's acts of kindness to me I shall tell you about *viva voce*.

In an hour from now I shall be going to Eisenach. The Grand Duke, who came first to Meiningen and then here yesterday evening, urges me to stay at the Eisenach Schloss. Ollivier will be arriving there this morning. Half a dozen correspondents of major newspapers will be there too: Gasperini for *La Liberté*, Cornelius for the *Allgemeine*, and so on; probably M. Blaze de Bury will undertake to represent the *Revue des Deux Mondes*. Barring some unexpected occurrence, the *Elisabeth* will have the same success here as in Pest. In great haste the motto of my new decoration: *Constanter et fideliter*.   F.L.

589. To Princess Carolyne. Wilhelmsthal, Saturday, 31 August.
Eduard [von Liszt] came to Eisenach on Tuesday. I arranged an interview for him at the Wartburg with Count Beust, whom I eventually asked to keep the blue room at the Altenburg for me until next year. . . .

Ollivier wrote to you yesterday of the impression made by the *Elisabeth*. The Grand Duchess enjoys this work, about which she said to me after the rehearsal: 'It is at once very beautiful and very charming.'—The Queen of Prussia did not come to the Wartburg. So far as august listeners are concerned, there were only TRH the Grand Duke, the Grand Duchess, and their children. This epithet 'august' reminds me of Herr von Maltitz, whom I haven't yet set eyes on. The Comte de Rayneval and his secretary, the Marquis de Clermont-Tonnerre, were the sole representatives of the diplomatic world at the Wartburg festival. Among the literary and artistic celebrities were noticed Bodenstedt, Roquette, Gottschall, Genelli, Kalckreuth, *et al.* Dingelstedt was conspicuous by his absence—but the Grand Duke told me that he will be coming here in 3 or 4 days. Emile Ollivier was at the Wartburg dinner on 28 August. Yesterday he went from Eisenach to Meiningen, where he wishes to have a serious talk with Bodenstedt on the Slav question. From there he will go via Munich to Prangins, *chez* Pce Napoleon. On my return, I shall speak to you of his ministerial career; he evidently has the finest opportunities. The Emperor and Empress are most markedly kind and civil to him. . . .   F.L.

I observe further that the Catholic parish priests of Weimar and Eisenach, as well as several priests from the environs, were very pleased with the *Elisabeth*. The 2 former heard it in the Wartburg first of all, and came back to hear it again in Eisenach's Protestant church, where the performance, conducted by Müller-Hartung, was remarkably satisfying.

590. To Princess Carolyne. Wilhelmsthal, 18 September.

Your letter of 5 to 8 Sept. got to me here safely yesterday. I am extremely pleased about it, for it means that there will be virtually no interruption in our correspondence. The day after tomorrow I shall be in Munich. This last week I spent from the evening of Wednesday the 11th until Saturday morning in Leipzig, and Saturday in Altenburg—getting back here at 4.00 on Sunday. . . . Everyone here, including the Grand Duchess, shows me the greatest kindness. . . .

So the Brahmins and the Buddhists will appear in your *Petits Entretiens*. 'Das interessirt mich sehr zu wissen [I am very interested to know that]'—as used to be said by our good Pohl, whose sister I saw again in Leipzig. She has married a distinguished philologist, Prof. Lipsius,[11] and I spent a pleasant evening in her home. . . .

In Munich I hope to reacquaint myself to some extent with what's going on. These last weeks I have been able to read neither newspapers nor books—such leisure tires me much more than any work whatsoever. Vincenzo has at least the resource of long walks—but they are no habit of mine, and I wouldn't know how to find time for them. The Grand Duchess said to me just now: 'The atmosphere in Weimar is like a brush!'

Dingelstedt comes today to pay his farewell visit, and I have stayed to some extent expressly for him. The Grand Duke greatly regrets his going, and would like his successor to be some literary celebrity. Nothing doing! The new Intendant will be Herr von Loën, Chamberlain to the Duke of Dessau. I do not know him personally, but some articles of his that I have read make me think that Monseigneur has made a good choice. . . .

[11] Hermann Lipsius, brother of La Mara, and from 1869 Professor of Classical Philology at the University of Leipzig.

Everything concerning Their Highnesses I'll reserve until my return to Rome. On 30 Sept. they will return to Weimar, there to celebrate their silver wedding on 8 October. On your table in the Altenburg I left a large piece of gilt bronze with this inscription: 'Carl Alexander to Franz Liszt'. The Grand Duchess has given me a superb drawing by Fra Bartolommeo, which I shall bring. It shows a monk praying.

You greatly exaggerate the success of *Elisabeth*. What is best about this work is its suitability to the Wartburg programme. I am happy also to have been able to contribute a little to the glorification of the patron saint of the tertiary order of St Francis—and your patroness too! . . .

Meiningen, Thursday, 19 Sept. As Monseigneur has gone hunting this morning, I accompanied him for 2 or 3 stages, and then returned here for Bodenstedt. Tomorrow, or the day after at the latest, I shall be in Munich. Your letter of 9 to 12 Sept. was handed to me yesterday evening—Dingelstedt was in my room. Thank Schlözer kindly on my behalf. I can't blame him for feeling affection for me, and whenever there is an opportunity I speak of him in a way that he wouldn't find disagreeable. His little volumes *Frederick* and *Choiseul*[12] I was praising at table with Monseigneur only yesterday, before I received your letter. . . . [Alexei] Tolstoy will arrive at Wilhelmsthal in a few days. Mme Pavlova, who was there last week, read some scenes from [Tolstoy's play] *Ivan the Terrible*, which will be performed in Weimar this winter.

Please let me know if all my letters have reached you punctually. Do go on as beautifully as you can with the *Petits Entretiens*, from which I hope soon to derive literary and other benefits. May your 3 patrons, St John Chrysostom, St Elisabeth, and St Charles, collaborate on these *Entretiens*—by their inspiration and their grace!   F.L.

591. To Princess Carolyne. Hotel Marienbad, Munich, 26 September. Got here on Friday evening; I hadn't forewarned Cosette, whom I went to see next morning. Finding no room at the Hotel Marienbad, I spent the night in the dependent building of the Hôtel de Bavière. We were there with Magne, 10 years ago, to see the historic procession pass. On Saturday morning, at 6.30, I went to St Boniface's, at 8.00 to Cosima's, and at 5.00 p.m. moved into the Hotel Marienbad. I have a small, quiet apartment looking on to the garden and costing 2 thalers a day. St Boniface's is a hundred yards away, and the Arcostrasse, where the Bülows live, even nearer. I go to mass every morning

---

[12] *Chasot. Zur Geschichte Friedrichs des Grossen und seiner Zeit* (Berlin, 1856) and *Choiseul und seine Zeit* (Berlin, 1848).

at 6.30, and lunch at 1.30 alone with the Bülows. From his cure at St Moritz Hans has brought back a frightful cold and loss of voice. He is obliged to spend half the day in bed. Despite that, he is enormously busy with preparations for the *Musikschule*, which will open on 14 Oct., and rehearsals in the theatre. Last Sunday he conducted *Tannhäuser*. The King, who is on holiday in Berg, near Lake Starnberg, had come for the Friday rehearsal; he left again immediately afterwards, and returned on Sunday evening for the performance, which he attended in the large central box, entirely alone, without any aide-de-camp or chamberlain whatsoever. After the second act, he paid a 5-minute visit to his fiancée, Duchess Sophie, seated in the large box on the left side. The wedding has apparently been postponed to the end of November. His Majesty's matrimonial ardours seem very restrained. Some people even assume that the marriage will be put off again—and perhaps for good.[13] On Saturday, rehearsal of *Lohengrin*, and on Sunday the performance. The King will attend both—and I shall follow his example, Cosette having obtained for me the favour of a back seat in the box of the *Hofmusik-Intendant*, Baron Perfall. It was in this seat that I listened to, but did not see, *Tannhäuser* on Sunday. Perhaps I shall go to the theatre a third time—if they perform Calderón's *Mágico prodigioso*[14] . . .

I shall probably find an opportunity to see the King during the week, before going to Stuttgart; if not, this will be from 10 to 15 October. When one lives at Santa Francesca Romana one doesn't have to run anywhere else. . . .

592. To Princess Carolyne. Stuttgart, 3 October.

Not much news to send you from Munich. Hans is still unwell, but not confined to bed. He has a swelling in his throat—*Halsgeschwür*—and must submit to painful treatment which will last 5 or 6 weeks. The doctor has forbidden him to speak. Nevertheless, he conducted the rehearsal of *Lohengrin*, which lasted more than 6 hours, and the performance. Packed hall, emotion, general enthusiasm! The King was present, alone in his central box as usual. After the first act, His Majesty took a magnificent bouquet to his fiancée, who attended the performance with Countess Trani. The marriage is announced for the end of November. I have not yet seen the King; he will probably receive me on my return to Munich in a week. Pce Chlodwig Hohenlohe told me last Sunday that for several months he had not had the honour of approaching His Majesty. In the winter season

---

[13] It was, for the unfortunate King Ludwig II was not attracted to women. Sophie, a younger sister of the Empress Elisabeth of Austria, a year later married the Duc d'Alençon, and in 1897 perished in a fire at a Parisian charity bazaar.

[14] Calderón's 'Faust' play, set in the reign of Diocletian and written for the Corpus Christi festival at Yepes in 1637. The 'wonder-working magician' of the title is God.

the ministers work turn and turn about with His Majesty on fixed days—but in the summer the King lives apart, and talks only to his secretary and some of the people in his entourage.—'A constitutional minister is little enjoyed by sovereigns,' Pce Chlodwig remarked to me.—'Perhaps more appreciated than enjoyed,' I replied.—I can only be pleased with the good reception given me by Pce Chlodwig. Last Sunday I saw him in his home—for I was anxious not to present myself at the Ministry, unless absolutely necessary. The same evening I paid him a short visit in his box, during the interval of *Lohengrin*, to thank him for his invitation to attend the performance in that same box. . . .

On Cosima's name-day, Friday, 27 Sept., we arranged a small matinée musicale, with Frau Kaulbach, in Kaulbach's studio. Reményi gave an astonishing performance of several pieces, and I entertained the company with H. von Bülow's *Sängers Fluch*. Hans, who goes out hardly at all, was not there. It goes without saying that Kaulbach and his wife asked me to give you their respectful greetings. Zumbusch is doing my bust. Under the large photograph of me by Albert, which costs 100 florins, Kaulbach has written 'unübertrefflich [unsurpassable]' . . .

593. To Princess Carolyne. Munich, Friday, 11 October. Here I am, thank God, nearing the end of my absence from Rome! In a week I shall be on my way back. After spending 3 days in Stuttgart . . . I made a trip into Switzerland. From Sunday evening until Wednesday morning I stayed in Basel —and at 3.00 on Wednesday afternoon I was at Tribschen, Wagner's home near Lucerne. Pohl accompanied me from Stuttgart to Lucerne, whence I returned here yesterday evening. I spent only half a day with Wagner. He has changed quite a lot in appearance—has grown thin and wrinkled. But there is no weakening of his genius. *Die Meistersinger* amazed me with its incomparable vigour, boldness, vitality, richness, verve, and *maestria*. No one but Wagner could have succeeded in creating such a masterpiece.

The first news I learnt on getting here was that of the breaking off of the King's marriage plans. This event is naturally creating a great sensation in town. The proposed marriage with a Russian princess has already fallen through—and no one can forecast where His Majesty will make his final choice. In the mean time, his ideal friendship with Wagner is holding firm with all the signs of real passion. . . .

This evening I shall be going to see the *wunderthätige Magus* [*El mágico prodigioso*], Calderón's Spanish and Catholic *Faust*. My sessions at Zumbusch's are going to recommence. Vincenzo assures me that I am looking very well. You will soon be able to judge—and even if you do not care for my appearance, I hope you will not be discontent with the rest of my poor self! . . .

Liszt's purpose in visiting Wagner had been to discuss the relationship, which had already produced two children (Isolde and Eva), between Wagner and Cosima. 'Liszt's visit', wrote Wagner afterwards, 'dreaded, yet agreeable.' However, in the long run Liszt was unable to save the Bülows' marriage, for a year later Cosima left her husband and joined Wagner permanently. Obliged to stand by the wronged Bülow, whom he loved like a son, Liszt sorrowfully broke off relations with his daughter and her lover. Several years were to pass before a meeting and reconciliation—years of great sadness for Liszt. As Princess Carolyne remarked to Lina Ramann:* 'I went through the death of his son with him, as well as those of his daughter Blandine and his mother—but nothing that can be compared with this despair.'

594. To Princess Carolyne. Munich, 16 October. I have decided to spend another week or so here. Hans is gradually getting better, and very actively busying himself with his Conservatorium. In fact, it is for him, and in response to his pressing request, that I am spending this further week in Munich. . . .

On my return here, news came of the breaking off of the King's engagement. Just fancy, King Ludwig I asked for the performance of a play, translated by him from the Spanish, entitled *Recept gegen Schwiegermütter* [Remedy against Mothers-in-Law]! It was put on on Monday. I am sending you the poster, as well as the portrait of the fiancés. His Majesty [Ludwig II] is at Hohenschwangau, leads a very retired life, and goes riding a lot. I haven't seen him other than in his box from a distance, at the performances of *Tannhäuser* and *Lohengrin*.

On Saturday evening I paid my second visit to Pce Hohenlohe at the Ministry. His manner is always very affable. I believe he is fairly satisfied with the effect produced by his last speech, 'full of nuances'—as was said by a French newspaper which he quoted to me. . . . As for Kaulbach, we took up again just where we left off. For several years he has shut his door, made hardly any visits, and accepted no dinner invitations in town. His coming to the Wertherns' was an exception, made to some extent for me. He has also been to see me twice—and the day before yesterday I dined at his place with Döllinger, whom I shall call on today. The Kaulbachs apologized to me for not having replied to your very kind letter—and I can assure you that they remember you warmly. . . . When you see Gregorovius, tell him that Kaulbach is one of his ardent admirers. He is reading with passionate enthusiasm the *History of Rome in the Middle Ages* and also Gregorovius's work on Corsica—and asks me to give him his very best compliments. For all the bustle, and notwithstanding the honours and glorifications heaped upon Liebig in Paris this summer, the illustrious *savant* still regards the French as very ignorant in matters of science. The only superiority he allows them over Germany is in industry and manufacture. Apart from that, he saw only frivolities, follies, and absurdities in agronomy, chemistry, medicine, etc. He expressed himself very frankly with the Emperor, 'who doesn't understand things very well either!' I took care not to upset Liebig—and confined myself to pleading some extenuating circumstances relating to the mathematical sciences! Then we talked about you—and Liebig took interest and pleasure in having news of you. 'Welch merkwürdige Frau!' he said; 'es ist mir keine solche vorgekommen! In einer Stunde quetscht sie den gescheitesten, geistreichsten Gelehrten vollständig aus [What a remarkable woman! I have never known one like her! In an hour she can pump the cleverest and most brilliant scholar completely dry]!'

Every day I spend a couple of hours posing at Zumbusch's. Yesterday Kaulbach collaborated on my bust, which seems to be turning out well. In Zumbusch's studio I ran into Redwitz. His rather unclerical opinions on the education act, against which the Bavarian episcopate has raised so strong a protest, surprised me a little. His person pleases me more than I would have expected. One generally imagines him wholly steeped in piety—with lowered eyes and a timid manner of speaking, intermingled with sighs! Not he!!

The *Lloyd* has published a few extracts from a biographical notice inserted in the October issue of *Westermann's Monthly Review*; I shall bring it to you. In it you will recognize a female hand[15]—I add immediately that I know the authoress only slightly. The style does not lack elegance—and if anything she praises me too much rather than not enough!

Returning to Rome at the beginning of November, Liszt did not leave Italy again for more than a year.

---

[15] That of La Mara.

1868

20 April. George Grove visits Liszt at Santa Francesca Romana. Of his host, and his host's playing, he writes: 'His hair is grey, his face very refined and *luminous*, and his hands the perfection of delicacy. It was quite different from Rubinstein or any of the great players, and I could have listened for ever.'

21 June. Liszt plays to the Pope, in the Vatican library.

2 July. Liszt and his friend Don Antonio Solfanelli set out on a pilgrimage to Spoleto, Cascia, Assisi, Fabriano, and Loreto.

11 July. They arrive at Grotta Mare on the Adriatic coast, and here enjoy a seven-week *villeggiatura*.

September to December. Liszt divides his time between Rome and the Villa d'Este at Tivoli, giving much attention to preparing new editions of piano works by Weber and Schubert.

New Year's Eve. Two distinguished Americans, the poet H. W. Longfellow and the portrait painter G. P. A. Healy, visit Liszt at Santa Francesca Romana. The painter later recalled: 'The Abbé himself came forward to greet us, holding a Roman lamp high up, so as to see his way. The characteristic head, with the long iron-grey hair, the sharp-cut features and piercing dark eyes, the tall, lank body draped in the priestly garb, formed so striking a picture that Longfellow exclaimed under his breath: "Mr Healy, you must paint that for me!" Our visit was most agreeable, for, when he chose, no man was more fascinating than Liszt. . . . He willingly consented to sit, and I made a small picture, as exact a reproduction as possible of what we had seen, and which gave great pleasure to Longfellow.'[1]

WORKS. Requiem (S12, 1867–8) for male soloists, male chorus, organ, and brass ad lib. *Ave maris stella* (S34/2, from S34/1), for male chorus and organ/harmonium; plus a version (S680) for voice and piano/harmonium. *Mihi autem adhaerere* (S37), for male chorus and organ. PIANO: Technical Exercises (S146) begun; *La Marquise de Blocqueville, portrait en musique* (S190); *Ave maris stella* (S506, *c*.1868), an arrangement of S34/2.

595. To Agnes Street-Klindworth in Paris. [Rome] 13 June. I congratulate you on your new abode. From the *Carl August Platz* to the rue de la Loi [Brussels] was an appreciable advance; but the Boulevard Haussmann is even better, for on the whole Paris suits you more than any other city. *Prospere procede*.

---

[1] The painting hangs in Craigie House, the Longfellow home at Cambridge, Massachusetts.

I for my part remain hidden away at *Santa Francesca Romana*, in the ruins of the Forum. It is the very opposite of the Boulevard Haussmann and of the *Venusberg*, even though from my windows can be seen a row of trees planted as though along a boulevard, and the ancient remains of the Temple of Venus and Rome frame my dwelling-place. Visitors to the city are amazed at the panorama which from the Capitol to the Colosseum takes in a prodigious mass of monuments and ruins, the Palace of the Caesars, the Arch of Titus, the Basilica of Constantine, etc., etc.—of which the daily usufruct costs me a rent of only 1,500 francs a year. M. de Girardin says that 'Rome smells of death', and I am becoming a little paralytic from it. Despite the hot weather, I should not like to budge in the summer, which is the good season for me because of the smaller number of visitors. Father Theiner has cordially invited me to accompany him to Ischia, after St Peter's Day [29 June], and Cardinal Hohenlohe has invited me to stay at his Villa d'Este (in Tivoli). I don't know if my sluggishness won't prevail.

Bravo M. Langrand! His Guarnerius couldn't be better disposed of, and I look forward to hearing M. George on such a beautiful instrument. It will probably be in Weimar (or in Munich, if you prefer), Paris being quite outside my programme. As I told you, longstanding gratitude towards the Grand Duke and Grand Duchess of Weimar commits me to acceding to their wishes and spending some time in their vicinity next year. That seems to be my duty; consequently, I do not hesitate. It goes without saying that in Weimar I shall not resume the Kapellmeister's duties that you saw me perform. I shall live in *retreat* there, abstaining from all obligatory visits and pointless formal calls. My sole ambition consists in quietly dispensing with most people and things, which is far less difficult than putting up with them.

I learn from Munich that the 1st performance of *Die Meistersinger* will take place on the 21st of this month.[2] You ask me my opinion of this work; don't you know it already? Be assured that the *Meistersinger* is a masterpiece, 'un gran capo d'opera', as the Italians say. If I had to write a book on Wagner, I should gladly take for an epigraph this remark of Victor Hugo's about Shakespeare: 'I admire *everything*—I admire like a brute.' My sole reservations have nothing to do with the completeness of Wagner's genius, but very much to do with the intellectual faculties of the public. . . .

I recall that you used to be on very friendly terms with Disraeli. Do you think he will manage to keep his position?   Yours, F. Liszt

---

[2] At the Royal Court Theatre, conducted by Bülow.

596. To E. Repos in Paris. Rome, 1 July

Dear Sir,

Since you are so good as still to remember my *Ave maris stella*, it would be inexcusable of me to forget it. My first manuscript having gone astray, I spent the whole of yesterday rewriting this very simple song, of which on the first possible occasion you will receive two versions at once: one for *mezzo soprano* with piano or harmonium accompaniment; the other for 4 *male voices*, with a simple organ accompaniment. In this latter, please excuse my very bad handwriting over and above whatever defect there may be in the work itself. Here, unlike in Germany, I haven't several intelligent copyists available. The only one I can make use of is ill—and I haven't time to await his recovery, for tomorrow I set out on my pilgrimage to Assisi and Loreto—after which I shall have a *villeggiatura* of at least six weeks at Grotta Mare (near Ancona, on the shores of the Adriatic).

I count on your being so obliging as to send me the final proofs of the *Ave maris stella* at the address I shall give you shortly.

How can I manage to get you the biographical article about me that was published in 1843 in the multi-volume collection of the *Biographie Pascallet*? I really don't know. This article is at once the most accurate, the best written, and the kindest of all those that have appeared about me *in French*. M. Fétis quotes it in the entry under my name in the *Biographie univ. des Musiciens*, and I have advised M. le Chanoine Barbier de Montault to enquire about it at the Angot publishing house. M. Emile de Girardin's library must contain, among other things, the complete *Biographie Pascallet*: but the illustrious publicist has so many important matters to attend to that I should be reluctant to bother him for such a trifle.

In any case, it will be easy to unearth the unfortunate little opus in question at the *Bibliothèque Impériale* where, if necessary, a copy of it could be made for the use of M. le Ch. de Montault.

Please count, dear Sir, on my feelings of sincere affection and esteem.

F. Liszt

A thousand thanks for so helpfully sending me the *Répertoire* of St Sulpice, which reached me punctually.

On Thursday, 2 July, Liszt, his manservant Fortunato, and Don Antonio Solfanelli set out on their pilgrimage, details of which were sent in long letters to the Princess.

597. To Princess Carolyne in Rome. Fabriano, Tuesday, 7 July.[3] Our journey is proceeding smoothly and expeditiously. Tomorrow evening we shall be at Loreto, 3 hours away from Fabriano—and on Thursday evening, or Friday morning, we shall arrive at the goal of our pilgrimage, Grotta Mare. Thus far, no tiresome mishap—for a few fleeting showers of rain cannot be counted as such—and the relatively bearable expense of about 250 francs. The main part of the day is devoted to the duties of ecclesiastical life: mass, the service of Matins and the Hours. The rest of the time passes quickly in reading, meals, and walks, obligatory when travelling. Reaching Spoleto at night, I slept for a couple of hours, and at about 6.00 in the morning, Friday, went for a stroll through the town while waiting for Solfanelli—who needs more sleep than I—to awaken. The first thing which struck me was the inscription on a church: 'A virgin erected it, 10,000 martyrs hallowed it.' I confess that the simplicity of this anonymous inscription pleases me more than the ostentatious display of the names of private individuals on the façades of other churches. The church is dedicated to St Gregory—who, like all other Saints, must be invoked disinterestedly! . . . After Solfanelli's mass at St Gregory's we climbed up to the Cathedral, which has a façade decorated with a mosaic dating from 1207. A holy image, 'santa icone', of the Virgin, painted by St Luke, is revered there. About 100 paces from the Cathedral stands the Palazzo Campello. . . .

At 2 o'clock on Friday, in a calèche drawn by 2 excellent horses and driven by an ever-so-slightly odd coachman, we took the mountain road to Cascia. Arriving there at the time of the Ave Maria, we stopped at an hotel where accommodation was problematic—and at once went up to the home of the confessor of the nuns of the sanctuary of St Rita, diminutive of Margherita, the very Revd Father Pelacci. Salua had obtained a charming letter of introduction from Father Crettoni, an Augustinian, for me to give him. Pelacci gave us a very friendly welcome, was so kind as to procure horses and mules for our excursion to the *Madonna della Stella* the next day, and invited us to dinner on our return. St Rita's sanctuary, in which many miracles take place, is greatly venerated hereabouts. The body of the Saint, who was a 15th-century pauper, is preserved uncorrupted and gives off an aromatic odour. On Saturday morning, at 5.30, we set off on our pilgrimage to the *Madonna della Stella*, horses and mules carrying us there in 3 hours. A beautiful site, mountains, rocks, a stream, a chapel hewn into the rock, and a gravestone for Solfanelli's grandfather, Fra Venanzio, who died there at the age of 82, after spending 17 years as a hermit in this lonely spot. Solfanelli said mass—the present hermit participated in an *overcoat*, seeing that the Italian government prohibits the ancient dress. The others taking

---

[3] The letter was begun on the 7th and finished on the 8th.

part were Fortunato, the mule drivers, I myself, 2 dogs, and a little lamb, the hermit's companion. We had a hasty meal, with the provisions we had brought with us, and left again. The rain caught up with us once more *en route,* but did not prevent us from arriving before 1 o'clock for Father Pelacci's lunch, served in the nuns' refectory. After the pudding we exchanged a few words with the Mother Superior through the grille, visited the Blessed Rita[4] again, and before 9 o'clock were back in Spoleto. On the way I read about fifty pages of Rio's *L'Art chrétien,* on Cimabue, Giotto, *et al.*

At 10 o'clock on Sunday morning we prayed at the Porziuncola. St Francis's dear little chapel is situated in the middle of the new church of Santa Maria degli Angeli, erected under Gregory XVI between 1836 and 1840—an earthquake having destroyed almost the whole of the old church of Santa Maria degli Angeli, with the exception of the Porziuncola and of 2 other smaller chapels. Solfanelli said mass in the one in which St Francis died. We went to see the thornbush stained with the blood of St Francis and transformed into roses— and the chapel in which he laid on the altar 12 white and 12 red roses, in the presence of Jesus Christ and the Virgin Mary, while obtaining the *gran perdono* of the Porziuncola of the 1st of August.

The miracle of the roses was painted in fresco by Overbeck on the façade of the Porziuncola chapel in 1829. . . . So the memory of the artist remains gloriously associated with that of the miracle. With this letter I enclose some blood-stained thorns from St Francis's garden.

From Santa Maria degli Angeli to Assisi there is a climb of three-quarters of an hour. We lodged after a fashion at the Lion Hotel, beside the Bishop's Palace but rather far from St Francis's church. Prof. Cristofani is the author of a history of Assisi and of a short, commendable essay on St Francis and the works of art in his church. He and Father Ruggieri explained to us in detail the memorable things and the marvels of this great monument of Catholicism. Some of the frescoes in the upper church are still fairly well preserved—in particular the oldest by Cimabue. Likewise Giotto's sublime paintings of the 3 Vows—Poverty, Chastity, Obedience—and the triumph of St Francis, above the papal altar in the lower church. . . .

In the lower church Pietro Cavallini, a Roman, painted an admirable fresco of the Crucifixion—and just beside it a no less admirable one of the Madonna with 2 or 3 other figures, equally well preserved. St Stanislas, Bishop of Cracow, was canonized in St Francis's church in Assisi. I knelt down on the altar stone where his canonization took place. I also looked with delight upon the 2 figures of St Elisabeth of Hungary and St Clare, painted by Memmo, at the entrance

---

[4] Rita was not canonized until 1900.

to St Martin's Chapel. On Monday morning Solfanelli said mass at the altar in the underground church, before the body of St Francis. The massive and heavy sarcophagus from the time of Pius VII is no more in keeping with the relics of this sacred place than is a mass by Capponi. . . .

When you see Father Salua, please give him my best thanks for the letter of introduction to Father Pelacci, who gave us a very warm welcome. Tell him, too, that we visited his sister, the Mother Superior of St Catherine's Convent in Fabriano, Madre Giuseppina, a hearty woman of great merit. I recall a delightful remark of hers: 'Noi non siamo tagliati per la malinconia [We are not cut out for melancholy].'

We reached Fabriano at 5 o'clock on Monday. . . . After having seen all the interesting and curious things here, we leave this evening, Wednesday, for Loreto, where I hope to find a few words from Rome.

598. To Princess Carolyne. Grotta Mare, 8.00 p.m., Saturday, 11 July.
So here I am, at the end of my peregrination. At Loreto yesterday evening I found your note and telegram—and on arriving here, an hour ago, your brief letters of 6 to 7 July. My missive from Fabriano must have got to you in the morning of the day before yesterday. Maestro Pandolfi and Solfanelli's father insisted so much on keeping us for one more day, that I had to give in. We didn't leave Fabriano until yesterday morning; by about 5.00 we were at Loreto's *casa santa*. I shan't tell you much about it—my piety being by no means verbose!

As far as art is concerned, there is nothing remarkable in Loreto, I believe, apart from Sansovino's sculptures—which go right round the outside of the sanctuary, placed like the Porziuncola in the middle of the arm of the cross of the church. Santa Maria degli Angeli seemed to me to be more spacious than Loreto's Church of Our Lady. Sibyls abound, and are perfect company for the major and minor prophets, including Moses and Balaam. A hymn for the prophets and sibyls would be a splendid one to compose: I would undertake it rather in the manner of Gerbet's hymn to the obelisks of Rome: *Introduction de l'esquisse de Rome chrétienne.* Unfortunately I am too ignorant of sculpture to appreciate these statues at their worth. The plan of the ensemble of the tabernacle, which protects and ornaments the *casa santa*, is by Bramante. A rather singular *ex-voto* can be seen suspended in the interior, to the right of the altar: a cannon ball which nearly killed Pope Julius II at some battle which I no longer remember, and which he ordered to be kept there. . . .

As you know, Mgr. Vecchiotti's brother was *maestro di cappella* at Loreto. An *Ave maris stella* of his own composition enjoys quite a big reputation in Rome, where from time to time it is performed at St Peter's. It is an attractive bar-carolle in the style of Rossini—less full-bodied, however, than similar things by that master. I expressed the desire to look through some of Maestro Vecchiotti's scores, and, at 11.00 this morning, after the service of tierce, the choristers assembled in the choir for a special session, and performed, expressly for me, the *Ave maris stella* and various other works. To thank them for this most exceptional kindness, I invited the present choirmaster, plus the organist and the baritone, Steffani, to dinner. Vecchiotti died in '63—but Loreto still resounds with his glory. I also invited the Abbé La Trêche—French chaplain in Loreto for the last 22 years. . . . After many conversational digressions, he and I ended by talking about the Pcss Wittgenstein. I had a strong suspicion that his visit to the Babuino had not left him feeling too flattered. He told me that in a quarter of an hour you had examined him on Buddha and Napoleon, the mysteries of theology and the budget figures. This strange way of treating him like a schoolboy, while retaining exclusively for yourself the ultimate ruling on every question, greatly offended him! Despite the trenchant authority of the personage, I pleaded the Pcss's cause. In this I succeeded so well that my antagonist even ended up being amused about it—a little at his own expense!

This 8-day excursion has not increased my limited taste for travel. I certainly intend not to budge again for a long time—and, when I leave Grotta Mare, to return to Rome in a straight line. I am perfectly comfortable here at Count Fessili's. His residence is a *mezzo termine* between a palazzo and a house, conveniently laid out, very clean and well maintained. One of my bedroom windows looks out on to the sea, which is about 100 yards away—the other on to a hill, half wooded, flanked by a few houses and old turrets. I shall write to you about it at greater length next time. Wishing you much patience when correcting the proofs of the *Petits Entretiens*! 'In patientia vestra possidebitis animas vestras.'[5]

599. To Princess Carolyne. Grotta Mare, 19 July. This is my *orario*. I get up at about 6.00. As soon as I am dressed I go to church, just a hundred paces away. Between 7.00 and 8.00 Fortunato brings me coffee in my room, or rather my salon—for I have a separate bedroom as well as 2 salons and a gallery at my disposal. Solfanelli is obliged to stay in bed until 9.30. I see him only then, and we at once go to the chapel, for mass. At about 11.00 we read part of the breviary, either in the garden—rather restricted in size and not very luxurious, but containing a good many orange trees, fig trees, and vines—or in the

---

[5] 'In your patience possess ye your souls', Luke, 21: 19.

gallery. At 1 o'clock, lunch, on the floor below my rooms. There are about 12 of us at table. Every imaginable attention is shown me, being expressed in the form of cutlets, beefsteaks, beetroot, figs, and so forth. After lunch, siesta. At 5.00 Solfanelli and I continue our breviary, and do some reading in Italian or Latin. Then we take a walk on the beach; sometimes we say vespers and compline in a boat resting quietly on the sandy shore. At 9.00 Fortunato brings me my supper, which I prefer to eat alone. It suits me best to retire to bed before 11.00, except for reading a few more pages before going to sleep.

The rest of the time I read or write—but no music yet. I shall see about that next week perhaps. The sole and great event of the establishment is the arrival of the post at noon. Don't fear for one moment that boredom is taking hold of me over here, however. Given that I am not in Rome, there is nowhere I would rather be (or could better employ my time) than at Grotta Mare. Solfanelli assures me I am bothering no one. It is equally certain that no one is bothering me in any way whatever.

The post is arriving.

600. To Baron Augusz. Grotta Mare, 22 July. I am truly reproaching myself, very dear friend, for being so extremely late with you. . . . Your letter of the end of June reached me a few days before my departure from Rome. Between 3 and 12 July,[6] in the company of the Abbé Solfanelli, one of my best friends, I made a pilgrimage to Assisi and Loreto. In addition to its thrilling character of mysterious piety, the old double and triple church of St Francis still retains great artistic interest through the wonders of its paintings by Cimabue, and above all those by Giotto and his school. Many of them have become unrecognizable, to such a degree do the passing years deal barbarously even with paintings! Others, however, such as the three vows of poverty, chastity, and obedience (by Giotto), for example, haven't ceased to shine with their virginal beauty, remaining, so to speak, the imperishable *holy stigmata* of the Genius of Christian painting. It would be desirable for them to be put within everyone's reach in a permanent and convenient way by publishing them in the 'Arundel Society' of London's beautiful collection of chromolithographs, which I recommend to you. The price is modest, from 7 to 25 or 30 shillings a folio, which can each be acquired separately; and the reproduction of the drawings and colours of masterpieces by Masaccio, Lippi, Francia, Fra Angelico, *et al.* is very conscientiously done and satisfying for eyes and soul alike. . . .

---

[6] Liszt was often careless with dates. A letter to the Princess makes it clear that he reached Grotta Mare on the 11th.

For the last dozen days I have been here beside the Adriatic, at Grotta Mare (a small town with a population of about 3,000, famous as the birthplace of Sixtus V), at Count Fessili's, uncle of my friend Solfanelli. The latter has complete responsibility for this stay—an extremely pleasant one, for that matter—which did not come into my plans for the summer. I had firmly decided not to budge from Rome before Christmas, and consequently deprived myself of hearing *Die Meistersinger* in Munich, of attending the music festival at Altenburg, and even of taking advantage of the invitation to the festival in Debrecen. Last winter Solfanelli was severely tried and made extremely melancholy by a long illness, and rightly or wrongly I felt that I couldn't refuse to keep him company during his convalescence. We say our breviary together, and as we are not content to mumble it, we take 2 or 3 hours a day over it; in addition he makes me carry on with my feeble studies in Latin and theology, to which I am growing more and more devoted. That, too, takes a couple of hours, and the rest of the time passes only too quickly!

For the inauguration of your church, on St Michael's Day, I should very much like to send you my Szekszárd Mass. It is for me at once a debt of honour and of friendship, one which I shall discharge with joy. But grant me a little time, because it is impossible for me to write it at present. Do you know what I should like?—to compose it on some auspicious occasion at your place, in Szekszárd, under the immediate inspiration of my dear little prophetesses. . . . We'll talk about it again next year; in the mean time, be persuaded, very dear friend, that I am deeply moved by the honour you do me in putting up my medallion in the chancel of your church. Such a place for it is much more in agreement with my wishes than many a distinction; and if it depended only on me, I would also choose my place in the nearby cemetery. . . .

About the end of August I shall return straight to Rome, where I shall stay until January, at which time, as I have promised the Grand Duke, I shall go to Weimar.

The letter Reményi wrote to me from Hamburg this spring made a painful, I could almost say an annoying, impression on me. I was counting on his trip to Germany to have the effect of *solidifying* his reputation once and for all. Instead of that he falls ill. It is a bad trick that Dame Nature has played on him, and I fear that he may have played an equally bad if not worse one on himself by getting angry, like a spoilt child, at the criticisms of certain more or less notable newspapers which are at liberty to go about their work without artistes—who pursue more exalted goals—fretting about the articles they print. With a modicum of good sense one can even grow fat on a diet of bad criticisms. *Laissons dire, et sachons faire.* Finally, true public opinion doesn't consist in what this or that person said yesterday and repeats today, but in what one *would be* morally *obliged* to say. That is the secular translation of this beautiful utterance of St Francis of Assisi: 'Quantum homo est in oculis Dei, tantum est et non plus.'[7] I have put off replying to Reményi and will shortly send you a few lines which I ask you to be so good as to hand to him.

With a thousand cordial and affectionate greetings *en famille*, I am

Yours,   F. Liszt

601. To Princess Carolyne. [Grotta Mare] Saturday, 1 August. Gille has sent me a packet of articles on the Altenburg music festival. The main modern works on the programme were Berlioz's *Requiem* and *Symphonie fantastique*, my Psalm 13 with chorus and orchestra—and the famous *Künstlerchor*, performed and put to death at Karlsruhe in your presence.[8] My things seem to have obtained a certain success at Altenburg—and you will know its extent from the 3 short items I am sending you. *Vielleicht interessirt es Sie auch, so Geringfügiges zu wissen* [Perhaps it interests you, too, to know such trifles]! Berlioz won't need to complain about the share he has had in this *Musikfest*! If he hadn't put a spoke in our wheels, his own chariot would be moving better! The fact is that, outside the new musical Germany, of which Wagner is and must necessarily remain dictator, Berlioz can count only a very few supporters. They are still lying in hiding, and dare not put the shortest work of his on a programme, unless it be by way of homage to our school! It's a different matter for Schumann. He has had his following among musicians, and his regular representatives in the press, for the last dozen years.

What to say to Mme [Marie] Keller about her musical studies? Let her be careful not to imitate Psyche by lighting her lamp to know and understand the celestial harmonies singing in her soul! Moreover, the adventure ended in a secure marriage for Psyche, and she gained from it by being admitted to the ranks of the goddesses[9]—a position which Mme Keller occupies already! And so she will succeed in everything—even in knowing harmony better than Beethoven!

I regret that I was so whirled about during my last stay in Paris that I could not become better acquainted with M. Delsarte. He is a distinct personality in the group of celebrities. He has high aims in art and a noble character—if I am not mistaken, we shall find ourselves in agreement on the essential points. Art is not a religion apart—but the explicit embodiment of the true religion, the Catholic, Apostolic, and Roman one!

---

[7] 'What a man is in the sight of God, that he is and nothing more' (St Bonaventura, *Life of St Francis*, ch. 6).
[8] In 1853.   [9] As told by Apuleius in *The Golden Ass*.

I am astonished that, after so many years of experience, you still do not know that when I happen to ask for some information about art or industrial objects, it is never for myself. I frankly never desire anything, for the very simple reason that I have possessions well beyond my needs—and have no taste for collections, accumulations, curiosities, varieties of this and that! I make an exception only for books, which I confess I sometimes buy for the pleasure of possessing them—without succeeding in reading them, as I intend. Alas! I have very little time left in which to instruct myself. By going out only rarely, and keeping my relations with others to what is strictly necessary, I manage with great difficulty to read one volume a week. Treat me quickly to your *Prudences de serpent, et simplicités de colombe,*[10] which I am waiting for so that I can sample it in the moored boat—which is not even moored, but simply set down on the sandy shore—like a real professional and lifelong   *Contentone*

602. To Princess Carolyne. [Grotta Mare] Tuesday, 18 August. I don't know what you will think of my annotations.[11] If you find them utterly stupid, I shan't mind at all—and will only beg you to forgive the presumptuousness of my literary and other errors. Alas! my elementary education was more than neglected, and unfortunately I have never since been able to make good this cardinal deficiency whose consequences are so distressing to me. Want of study and sufficient knowledge reduces me, intellectually, to the sad condition of a shamefaced pauper! And I feel it all the more as my bit of celebrity brings me into frequent contact with the 'rich'! Some imagination and a certain integrity of character enabled me to get by when I was young—but I should now like to do better and learn more. This need is so imperative that my only thought is to satisfy it; and I am accordingly resolved to withdraw from the world and to live in the country, so that I may read, educate myself, and work peacefully and consistently until my dying day. Believe me, nothing better and more reasonable is left for me to seek in this world! I shall soon speak to you in more detail of my little plan, which you will help me to realize.

I shall be leaving Grotta Mare on Saturday or Sunday—and am saving up for my return a pile of laudatory things about your *Colombes-Serpents* that I prefer to say to you in person. Assuming that my annotations don't strike you as too absurd, I shall ask a favour of you—that of allowing me to communicate my reflections to you in the margins of the other volumes of your *petits Entretiens.* I didn't dare suggest doing so with your *Bouddhisme et Christianisme*

---

[10] The Princess's *Simplicité des colombes, prudence des serpents,* proofs of which reached Liszt ten days later.
[11] On the *Simplicité des colombes.*

—but you will give me real pleasure by putting up with my poodle's notes. Daniel Stern used to claim in days gone by that, from somewhere or other, ideas came to me that were not too stupid—my ambition would be to continue to justify her remark, by serving as your proof corrector.   F.L.

603. To Princess Carolyne. [Grotta Mare] Saturday morning, 29 August.
I thank God and you for these 2 months of tranquillity and simple contentment. The chief object of my journey was to acquaint myself with the breviary —Solfanelli has rendered me excellent service in that, and I am beginning to read the offices quite tolerably. Such an occupation is enough to live well and die well! Moreover, I can only give much praise to my Grotta Mare hosts, who, incidentally, would ask nothing better than to keep me longer. I have promised them a visit next year, perhaps when returning from Germany or Hungary.

This evening I shall be in Fano, where I shall spend tomorrow. The night train will bring me back to Rome on Monday morning, between 8 and 9 o'clock, I believe. Don't send a carriage for me. I am determined not to continue the expense of a horse, it being too disproportionate to my income—and procures me only a show of ostentation, which I prefer to do without. My acquaintances all live more or less in the same district. . . .

**604. To the Grand Duke Carl Alexander in Weimar.
Rome, 8 September**

Monseigneur,
The telegraph alone is to blame. For a wonder, it has done me two bad turns this last month. On the occasion of the *Musikfest*, Mgr. of Altenburg was so kind as to send me a very friendly telegram—which was a fortnight late in reaching me; and to date I have not received yours of 28 August. Fortunately, its content has been conveyed to me by your letter, Monseigneur, and I cannot tell you how touched I am by this token of Your Royal Highnesses', linked with the date of 28 August, which has long marked the happiest memories of my work in Weimar: in '49, the centenary of the birth of Goethe; in '50, the première of *Lohengrin*; later, the Carl August celebrations; and, last year, the Wartburg jubilee.

May I henceforth serve Your Royal Highnesses still better, and may they deign to count on the true feelings of gratitude and devotion with which I respond to their 'call' to return to Weimar. Yes, I shall be there early next January.

Forgive, Monseigneur, my long epistolary silence. I spent a sorry and sterile winter, exposed to the most commonplace curiosity (of very distinguished people, moreover). A superb American piano that the manufacturer, Mr Chickering, brought here himself at Christmas, served as a pretext for the mounting tide of visits. During the carnival, as during Lent, it was fashionable, especially with visitors to Rome, not *to hear*, but *to have heard*, the American piano played by Liszt, so that this famous instrument became a real nuisance for me—or, if you prefer a nobler comparison, drawn from my proximity to the Colosseum, a *Meta sudans*;[12] the difference, entirely to my disadvantage, being that the sound-waves did not refresh me in the least.

But I forget these past vexations, and shy away from the temptation to 'flee into a desert to avoid the approach of humans', firmly intending to make better use of my time next winter, near Your Royal Highness, of whom I have the honour to remain the very humble and faithful servant, F. Liszt

605. To Princess Carolyne [Rome, 14 September]. The 14th of September, feast of the Exaltation of the Cross, is one of the days in which I give most thought to my inner life. My Weimar testament was written on 14 Sept. [1860] —this morning, I took communion. For some time I have not been approaching the Lord's Table without being vividly carried back to the day of my first communion in my village—it seems to me that I have remained wholly a child before God, so thoroughly obliterated is the accumulation of bad impressions which are extraneous to me and contrary to my true character! Like the Emperor Heraclius, I divest myself of the weighty tinsel of my costume, to replace it with the Cross![13] Do not laugh at my comparison as too whimsically ambitious—I know that I am only a poor play-actor, and believe with Shakespeare that in general 'Man is a poor player'. But since Père Hyacinthe does not disapprove of Mme Mériman for professing her royal blood—I fancy he would also be indulgent to my Heraclius!

I shall come at about 9.00 this evening, after the service at the *Frati*. May your prayer rise towards God, like incense!

[12] Until it was finally removed—'barbaramente demolita', as an Italian writer has put it—in the 1930s, the *Meta sudans*, which stood close to the Colosseum and the Arch of Constantine, was Rome's only surviving example of a monumental fountain; literally, 'sweating goal', it owed its name to its conical shape, reminiscent of the goals in the circus, and to the water which, gushing from the top like a stream of sweat, ran down the cone to be collected in a circular basin.

[13] Referring to the legend—famously depicted in Piero della Francesca's frescoes of the *History of the True Cross* in the church of San Francesco at Arezzo—in which the Emperor Heraclius, having retrieved the Cross from, and slain, Khosroes at Nineveh, walked barefoot into Jerusalem carrying the Cross on his shoulders. This event, in 629, is commemorated in the Roman Catholic feast, alluded to by Liszt, of the Exaltation of the Cross.

606. To an unidentified person[14] [Rome, September]

Dear enthusiast,

I should protest sternly against your hyperbolic flattery. But you write it with such charming ardour, and such a tone of youthful sincerity, that I am much more tempted to listen to than scold you. Besides, enough people undertake to bring me *back to my senses*, sometimes in a way that is rather uncharitable. My numerous faults have been demonstrated to me so much that it would be impossible for me to be unaware of them; even if I had not already noticed them for myself. Doubtless, therefore, I need to be modest; but if people require me to be so to the point of pedantry, I shall demur, and since you are determined to think far too well of me, I very much wish you not to be entirely wrong.

The leaf you picked for me at the grave of Chopin is a charming memento of that beautiful, melancholy genius. His music remains an incomparable ideal of grace, tenderness, dreamy harmony, exquisite emotion, proud and noble passion! Therein can be found the very soul of Poland, with all its enchantments, its exaltation and its heartbreaks!

When you have decided what you are going to do with your life, write and let me know. In my opinion, Munich is now the place where your musical talent will develop to most advantage.

Asking you to be so good as to give my affectionate compliments to your mother and sister, I am   Yours most sincerely,   F. Liszt

607. To Agnes Street-Klindworth. Villa d'Este [October or November].
'Non licet omnibus adire Corinthum',[15] and, to boot, I totally lack any taste for travel. I have now been living in Rome for seven years without going to see Naples, which I know only from descriptions, pictures, photographs. Barring some necessary reason, why drag myself hither and thither? Now, since the death of my poor dear mother, there is nothing to take me back to Paris, where I have nothing further to do. This is not to say that I by any means underrate the great and wonderful things that can there be seen, heard, and admired: quite the contrary, I confess to a *chauvinistic* passion for Paris—above all the *Imperial* Paris of the present day—and, had fate not decided otherwise, would rather live there than anywhere else. Moreover, most of my Parisian friends being fonder of

---

[14] Of the female gender.

[15] 'It is not given to everyone to go to Corinth'—Latin translation of a Greek proverb expressing the fact that the pleasures of Corinth were so costly that not everyone could afford to go and stay there; used in connection with anything else that has to be given up for want of money and means.

travel than I am, we can very well run into one another beyond the boulevards —which you, I hope, will soon prove to me.

To escape having to practise, in excess, the small obligations of *la civilité puérile et honnête*,[16] I have withdrawn to the Villa d'Este for a few weeks. Tivoli has a population of seven thousand, they say, but I see very few of them, save in the Franciscan Church. This kind of *segregated* existence suits me best and I shall continue it, no matter where, for the rest of my days. At the end of December I shall go straight to Weimar (via the Brenner); three months will be enough for me to attend to my Germanic duties, after which I shall return here in April.

Let me ask you to be so kind as to tell me if Madame Kreutzer has received my letter addressed to Villa d'Avray. Although my long absence from Paris has rather weakened my relations with Léon and his wife, I have always held them in high regard and continue to be very fond of them, as I would have been able to show more effectively had we remained in closer proximity. . . . I congratulate you sincerely on all your successes, especially on your installation at the Batthyány Palace. It establishes the importance of [your father's] position, and I applaud it with a little selfishness, flattering myself that when you travel to Vienna this winter you, plus M. George and his Stradivarius, will spend some time in Weimar. Your visit will be an intellectual treat for me, and more.

Yours, F.L.

608. To Princess Carolyne. [Villa d'Este] Tuesday, 17 November. Things could not be better for me here. My rooms are very nice—there are carpets, 2 fireplaces, and all the comfort I could need, plus the view of the Roman Campagna with the dome of St Peter's and its *bambinello*, the dome of the Madonna del Rosario, on the horizon. I see them continually from the terrace, from my turret window, and even, without having to move, from my desk. For such a view, one would give all the royal and imperial palaces in the world! My *padrone* [Cardinal Hohenlohe] is most charmingly kind to me, and I am extremely grateful to him for adapting himself so nobly to my rather uncourtly character, defective as it is in so many ways.

Tomorrow, Wednesday, 18 November, feast of the dedications of the basilicas of St Peter and of St Paul, the Most Eminent will be going to Rome to take part in vespers. I suppose you will see him, and that he will offer you his congratulations on your volume *De la prière*,[17] which he is reading with great interest. I haven't dared ask him to lend it to me, for fear of being indiscreet

---

[16] 'Puerile and honest civility'—an expression used ironically by the French to indicate politeness.
[17] *De la prière, par une femme du monde.*

—but I hope I don't deserve the continual humiliation of hearing it praised by others, without knowing it! The *Agence Havas*, in reporting the theft of 200,000 francs from the home of the Princess Wittgenstein, bestows upon you the title of most distinguished woman of letters.

Times passes very quickly here, and I should like to prolong my stay at the Villa d'Este until 1 December. During the Cardinal's absence I shall certainly fare less sumptuously—however, the bill of fare displayed on the sign-board of the *Pace*, the most renowned restaurant in Tivoli, suffices for all my gastronomic desires.   *In sempiterno,*   F.L.

609. To Princess Carolyne. [Villa d'Este] Sunday, 22 November. . . .
Since the departure of my Patron I have neither made nor received visits. Among other advantages, a retired life offers one that I prize greatly—that of not saying silly things, and of not hearing any! Reading and writing lead us to them, it is true—but in a less bothersome way!

Two great potentates have disappeared almost at the same moment: Rossini and Rothschild, escorted by M. Havin, editor of *Le Siècle*![18] During their lives the pagan and the Jew teased one another. Rothschild was amused by Rossini, and the latter took advantage of it better to dine and enrich himself. But M. Havin weighed both of them on the free scale of public opinion. *Ipso facto*, Havin lorded it more imperturbably in the columns of his paper—than Rothschild from the height of his millions, and Rossini at the pinnacle of his successes! Don't be scandalized by my nonsense. My mood today is not turned to the funeral.
                                      Your very lowly servant,   F.L.

610. To Prof. Dr S. Lebert in Stuttgart. Villa d'Este, 2 December G

Dear friend,

The annotations to Schubert's Sonatas etc. required more time than I had expected. I have been working diligently at them for some weeks—and they are now finished *ad unguem*.

Our pianists are scarcely aware of what a glorious treasure they have in the piano compositions of Schubert. Most pianists play them over *en passant*, notice here and there repetitions, longueurs, examples of seeming carelessness ... and then put them aside. Of course, Schubert himself is somewhat to blame for the fact that his superb piano works are insufficiently cultivated. He was too

[18] Havin had died on 12 Nov., Rossini on the 13th, James Rothschild on the 15th. *Le Siècle* was a cheap, mainly working-class newspaper with a huge circulation.

immoderately productive, wrote incessantly, mingling what was trivial with what was important, what was great with what was mediocre, paying no heed to criticism and allowing his wings free flight. Singing his angelic melodies, he lived in music like a bird in the air.

O tender, ever-welling genius! O beloved hero of the heaven of my youth! From your soul's depths and heights pour forth melody, freshness, power, grace, reverie, passion, soothings, tears, and flames—and such is the enchantment of your world of emotions that we almost forget the greatness of your craftsmanship!——

Let us limit our edition of Schubert's piano compositions to: 2 Sonatas, the G major Fantasy (a Virgilian poem!), the magnificent *Wanderer*-dithyramb (C major Fantasy), 2 books of Impromptus, *Moments musicals* and the complete Waltzes (among them gems of the most exquisite quality). All this will be sent off to you at once; also the Weber Polonaises.

In the Sonatas you will find some variants which I find rather *appropriate*. Several passages, and the whole of the conclusion of the C major Fantasy, I have rewritten in the modern piano style, and flatter myself that Schubert would not be displeased with it.

Schubert's works for piano duet (*Holle's edition*) please send to Weimar, as I have no time left in Rome for *revising*. Add a copy of the *Aufforderung zum Tanz* [Invitation to the Dance], which people everywhere so rush through. You forgot to send this piece of salon-fireworks with the other music, and I didn't think of it either, precisely because many years ago, and on untold occasions, I had to play this *Aufforderung* over and over again—without the slightest *Anforderung* [request] on my part—and it became a dreadful torment to me. Nevertheless, such a showpiece must not be left out of Cotta's Weber edition.

Your visit to Weimar, dear friend, will be very welcome and agreeable to me. We shall then most conveniently be able to discuss, try out, and find out quite a lot.

With sincere thanks and friendliest good wishes, I remain

Yours,   F. Liszt

P.S. Of the French translation of your Method I have received not a word.

611. To Edvard Grieg in Christiania. Rome, 29 December

Sir,

I am glad to be able to tell you of the sincere pleasure it has given me to read your Sonata (Op. 8).[19] It bears testimony to a vigorous, reflective, and inventive creative talent of excellent quality—which to achieve the heights has only

---

[19] For piano and violin in F.

to take its natural course. I am pleased to think that in your own country you are meeting with the success and encouragement you deserve. These will not be wanting elsewhere either; and if you come to Germany this winter I cordially invite you to stop for a while in Weimar, so that we may get to know one another.[20]

I am, Sir, yours most sincerely,   F. Liszt

---

[20] Liszt and Grieg eventually met in Rome, Feb. 1870. See Biographical Sketches.

1869

5 January. Longfellow, Healy, and their families visit Liszt at Santa Francesca Romana.

12 January. Liszt arrives in Weimar, where a home has been prepared for him on the upper floor of the Hofgärtnerei (Court Gardener's House). Here, from this time forward, he will spend several weeks or months every year[1] until the end of his life.

20 January. He plays at a Court concert.

4 April. He is present at the first performance in Vienna of his *Legend of St Elisabeth*, conducted by Herbeck. Its success is so great that it is repeated on the 11th.

17–19 April. He visits Regensburg.

26 April. At the Vigadó concert hall in Pest, Liszt conducts a successful performance of his Hungarian Coronation Mass, and the Dante Symphony is conducted by Erkel.

30 April. Liszt conducts a further performance of the Mass; Erkel conducts *Hungaria* and the first performance in Hungary of Liszt's Psalm 137.

3 May. Liszt attends a recital given by his pupil Georg Leitert, who plays Beethoven's *Hammerklavier* Sonata and Liszt's Sonata in B minor, the Hungarian premières of these works.

5/6 May. *En route* to Rome, Liszt breaks his journey at Sagrado, where he is the guest of Princess Therese Hohenlohe.

6 June. His grandson Siegfried Wagner is born.

August. Liszt travels to Munich to attend the première of Wagner's *Das Rheingold*,[2] but the performance is delayed until 22 September, by which time he has returned to Rome.

WORKS. Mass (2nd version) for male chorus and organ, known as the Szekszárd Mass (S8/2). Psalm 116 (S15*a*), for male chorus and piano.[3] *Inno a Maria Vergine* (S39), for mixed chorus, harp and organ/piano duet/harmonium. *O salutaris hostia I* (S40), for female chorus and organ.

Two new oratorios were planned this year: *The Legend of St Stanislas* (S688) and *St Stephen, King of Hungary*. The first was never completed, the second barely begun.

612. To Princess Carolyne in Rome. Hotel Marienbad, Munich, Monday, 11 January. . . . Mme Laussot and Boisselot were at the station in Florence—and as the train stops there for a good hour, we had a leisurely meal with the *maestro* [*maestra*] *di cappella* of the Società Cherubini.[4] I was reckoning

---

[1] Apart from 1874, a year in which Liszt did not travel to Germany.

[2] The performance was mounted against the wishes of the composer, who did not attend it.

[3] Added to the Hungarian Coronation Mass as Gradual. See Letter 625 to Augusz.

[4] Mme Laussot was founder and conductor of this choral society.

on getting as far as Verona that same evening—but the train from Padua had already left when we got there. We were compelled to sleep at Padua on Friday —and the next day to waste a few hours in Verona, where I sought out my excellent Father Pietro, formerly *vice curato* at Monte Mario. We left Verona at 2.00 p.m. on Saturday—and got to Munich at 5.00 on Sunday morning. I immediately went to mass at St Boniface's—and then, on returning to the Marienbad, sent a note asking Hans to come round. At 2.00 lunched at Hans's place with his mother and his 2 daughters, Lulu and Bony,[5] who are really delightful. Spent the evening with Cornelius and Hans. Cornelius was very touched by your remembrance of him, and his wife is delighted with the beautiful parure in Roman mosaic that you sent her.

Tomorrow, Tuesday, I leave here at 6.00 a.m.—and will reach Weimar before midnight. As I telegraphed to you, the weather is very mild—and I have never had a more comfortable journey. My books keep me excellent company. . . .

613. To Princess Carolyne. Hofgärtnerei, Weimar, 1.00 p.m., Sunday, 17 January. For 3 days I have been trying to find half an hour to write to you conscientiously—impossible to extricate myself from visitors and urgent tasks! It is only from tomorrow that I shall manage to keep my mornings free. Frau von Schorn wrote to you on Thursday to say that it would be reasonable for me to accept the residence that Their Highnesses have prepared for me at the Hofgärtnerei. It is Preller's former studio—not the one close to the Catholic church, but the one in the same street, the Marienstrasse, at the start of the Belvedere Allee. Nothing has been neglected to make my dwelling-place agreeable and even elegant. It consists of 4 rooms: a 4-window salon, divided into two by red and green Algerian curtains, which can be drawn when desired; dining-room, bedroom and Fortunato's room. There are fine carpets everywhere, 4 Berlin stoves, double windows, curtains and portières all of a rich material, matching furniture, 3 bronze clocks, several 3-branch candlesticks in bronze, half a dozen or more carcel lamps, 2 gilt-framed mirrors, silver plate, glass and chinaware for six. I am told that the Grand Duchess and the Princesses took particular care over the choice of carpets, curtains, etc. The fact is, my new abode is of a 'Wagnerian' luxury—to which they have hardly been accustomed in this good town of Weimar. My near neighbours are the Helldorfs, Zedlitz, and Preller— who live in their attractive houses along the Belvedere Allee. When coming to see me on the morning after I took up residence here, Preller was amazed at the

---

[5] Nicknames of Daniela and Blandine respectively.

changes made to his old studio, of which he could no longer recognize even the staircase, now very dainty and fitted with a carpet.

Weimar diary: I reached the Erbprinz Hotel at about midnight, Tuesday, 12 January. From Munich to Weimar I was alone the whole time in a first-class [railway] compartment. . . . The next day, Wednesday, to mass at 8 o'clock. The priest was wearing the chasuble which you embroidered. My home is very near the church. Between 9 and 11 Preller and a few other people called. . . . About noon, visited Beust. He proposed that we should go to see the flat in the Hofgärtnerei—and took me there. At the door we found a superb grand piano, sent to me from Berlin by Bechstein.[6] Pauline[7] undertakes to do the housework—and Fortunato will easily find 2 or 3 dragomans of goodwill. . . .

On Thursday the 14th, after mass, Milde and a score of other people called. Letters and parcels arrived for me. I found it impossible to go out until 6.00, when I went to Herr von Loën's very roomy box. There, on a red velvet sofa, placed so that one can have a perfect view of the stage without being seen from the hall, I listened to the first act of Weber's *Oberon*. You know that the interior of the Theatre has been renovated; the former regular audience can hardly find their bearings any more than did Preller in his old studio—there are very attractive boxes, columns, velvet. In sum, one can be very satisfied with the embellishments and improvements which have signalled the advent in the Intendancy of Herr von Loën. The Grand Duke has reserved for himself a small stage-box, opposite the Intendant's, where he sent for me after the first act of *Oberon*. I stayed there tête-à-tête with him for the whole of the second act, and in the third I returned to Loën's box, which I shall make use of by preference and exclusively. It offers me the advantage of avoiding contact with the public. As I shall not take a seat in the front row, I shan't be seen. Besides, I shall not overdo the theatre. It will be enough for me to go there once or twice a week, when Schiller, Goethe, Shakespeare, and Hebbel are performed; or great operas. The small game of the repertory is no concern of mine. . . .

I reply to your question about the *Nibelungen*. Wagner has resumed work and is finishing *Der junge Siegfried*. Herr Richter will be able to copy the score, and perhaps even prepare the *Clavierauszug* [piano score]—but talk of a performance at the Crystal Palace is a simple canard. Two or three more years will certainly be needed before there is any question of performing Wagner's *Nibelungen*. When that point is reached, I think the theatre he is asking for will be built for him. . . .

---

[6] 'Accept a seven-octave chromatic scale of thanks for your kindness,' wrote Liszt to Bechstein.
[7] Pauline Apel, formerly a servant girl at the Altenburg, now became Liszt's housekeeper in his new home.

614. To Princess Carolyne. Tuesday evening, 26 January. During the course of the week Monseigneur paid me a couple of visits. I presented to him a Polish sculptor, M. Godebski, son-in-law of the cellist Servais.[8] It was during my last visit to Paris that I made the acquaintance of M. Godebski, who since then has made a large monument for Lima, Peru, as well as the full-length statue of Servais, with cello, which will be erected in Hal, Servais's native town, plus a bust of Rossini, finished shortly before the maestro's death.

My relations with Count Tarnowski are becoming very friendly. He will probably accompany me back to Rome. Should there be a suitable opportunity, I shall send you his 3 volumes of Polish poems, published in Leipzig. Further, Tarnowski has brought out his own Polish translation of Berlioz's famous *Traité d'instrumentation*—and of Brendel's outline *History of Music*. Last Sunday he sat beside me in the Catholic church, on the same bench from which so many prayers in Polish have been poured into the heart of God!—My new friend is sad, reserved, gentle, not very chatty—I hope that, personally, he will not fail to please you!

The 2 events of this week of some small note are the Court concert on 20 January for Pcss Marie's birthday, and the concert in the theatre yesterday evening, Monday. Reményi was to have arrived for the 20th, but my telegram reached him too late, and the consequent gap in the programme made the Grand Duchess and the Princesses extremely vexed. I tried to remedy the situation—and, after the last piece, unexpectedly seated myself at the piano—which was very graciously received! With the exception of 3 or 4 persons, everybody had heard me 50 times in that salon. It seemed to me that on this occasion it was better to perform once again with good grace—to entertain the third generation! My birthday bouquet was Rossini's *La charité*,[9] in which in days gone by I had accompanied the Grand Duchess. Yesterday, in the theatre, the orchestra gave a very spirited rendering of *Ce qu'on entend sur la montagne*. . . .

615. To Princess Carolyne. 4 February, evening. . . . Just imagine how Monseigneur classes the 4 great statesmen of modern times! At their head, and far above the others, Antonelli—then Napoleon III, Cavour, and Bismarck. The number being limited to 4, Beust[10] is excluded. Monseigneur grants him only a rare talent for drawing up dispatches, *pro memoria*, etc., much wit—but not

---

[8] For members of the Servais family, and Godebski, see under Franz Servais in Biographical Sketches.

[9] 'You cannot imagine the enthusiasm,' wrote Henriette von Schorn to Princess Carolyne; 'everyone who told me about it struggled to hold back tears: "He played like an angel and looked like a saint." '

[10] Not Count F. H. von Beust, Grand Marshal at the Weimar Court, but Count F. F. von Beust, the Austrian statesman.

enough intelligence to lay claim to the role of statesman. Unfortunately I am too great a blockhead to raise myself to the heights of intelligence—where reside those who watch over the destiny of nations. M. Guizot and Mme d'Agoult paralysed for ever my modest ability to appreciate men of responsibility! Between Cavour and Napoleon, Monseigneur hesitates to whom to give preference—but both the one and the other have to come before Bismarck.

On my return to Rome I shall try to set Longfellow's *Excelsior* to music for you. I have finally finished revising the 310 pages of the score of the *Elisabeth*. Before the end of the month I shall also have done with the proofs of the Requiem, which will soon be brought out by Repos in Paris. . . .

For the Grand Duchess's birthday [8 April], 2 operettas will be performed, both of them pretty and even distinguished: Lassen's *Le Captif*, an episode from Cervantes, successfully performed in Brussels—and Mme Viardot's *Le dernier des Sorciers*, the text of which is probably by Turgenev,[11] a close friend of Mme Viardot. She will be coming here next week to discuss with Lassen the orchestration of her *Sorcier*—of which she has as yet written only the vocal and piano score. Bronsart and Raff spent a couple of days in Weimar. Rubinstein will arrive the day after tomorrow, and Tausig during the course of the month. . . .

616. To Princess Carolyne. Friday, 12 February. Monday, 8 February,[12] I spent with God and His well-loved servant—whose memory is imprinted here on everything I look at. At 8 o'clock I took communion at that same altar where after long years you made me find the God of my childhood again. . . .

On Monday there was also Rubinstein's rehearsal and concert. His talent is complete, and of astonishing vigour and opulence. They appreciated him here better this time than formerly. The day after his concert he played admirably at the Grand Duchess's, in the little round salon; and on Wednesday evening at the home of Countess Styrum, a Dutchwoman, the Grand Duchess's Grand Mistress. He is planning a *steeplechase* of concerts throughout Europe, pending the American battue! His idea is to earn 2 or 300,000 francs with his piano-playing, so that in a couple of years he can live and compose independently. In Petersburg they are no longer given to excessive enthusiasm for him: his artistic requirements and brusque and moody behaviour have, it seems, displeased the Grand Duchess Helena. That doesn't surprise me at all—I admire, rather, the fact that for 9 years he has retained the position of Principal of the new

---

[11] Turgenev did indeed write the text of *Le Dernier Sorcier*, and also those of Pauline Viardot's other operettas, *Trop de Femmes* and *L'Ogre*.
[12] Princess Carolyne's birthday.

Conservatoire and of the concerts. I'll speak to you about him at greater length in person—for with Rubinstein it is the individual and the personage that interest me, *was er ist und was er vorstellt* [what he is and what he stands for]. He is tormented by an ideal that is not only inadequate but even a little incoherent! His great project now is to set the Bible to music, in the form of dramatic oratorios for which would be needed—as with Wagner's *Nibelungen*—a separate theatre, a Prince or a company of shareholders who would see to the costs, and an impresario—whose choice would present no difficulty, for Rubinstein would himself be this impresario. Wagner's theatre will be built—but Rubinstein's will be postponed to the Greek calends! . . .

Mme Viardot arrived last night, and this evening will sing at a grand orchestral concert, at Their Highnesses'. Tausig will be here on Monday. . . .

617. To János Ranolder, Bishop of Veszprém.
Weimar, 18 February

Monseigneur,

Your Lordship has been so kind as to favour me with a universally celebrated patriotic gift. Here in Thuringia, people say that Klingsor, the Magyar magician, was the first to make the 'Somlauer' known, at the time of the famous Wartburg contest; and historians state that at the Court of the Landgrave Ludwig, husband of Saint Elisabeth, the crusaders delighted in the Bishop of Veszprém's marvellous drink. On this point the whole world has remained orthodox; so I have ventured to share the small supply that I owe to Your Lordship's generosity, with the Landgrave Ludwig's successor, Monseigneur the Grand Duke of Saxe-Weimar, to whom we are indebted for the splendid restoration work at the Wartburg Castle. No less than at the time of the Crusades, the 'Somlauer'— very much improved again these last years through your good offices—will be highly appreciated here.

In the hope that I may soon be able to thank Your Lordship personally for His kind remembrance of me, I have the honour to be, Monseigneur, with feelings of the deepest respect,

Your very humble and devoted servant   F. Liszt

618. To Princess Carolyne. 16 March. To write to you so little and so poorly grieves me bitterly! Oh, how I envy Count Tarnowski, who tomorrow leaves for Rome! He brings you various little things from Frau von Schorn— and will give you news of me at length. Yesterday I received your new volume

—2 copies—which on my travels will keep me good and beautiful company. Here, I can scarcely manage to sneak a quarter of an hour's reading a day—and when I get into bed, my poor brain is no longer capable of attention. Monseigneur saw the volume on my table, but I took care not to offer it to him. . . .

Wagner is publishing as a booklet his old article on Judaism, *Das Judenthum in der Musik*. Far from confessing his guilt, he is making it worse by a Preface and an Epilogue addressed to Mme Kalergis. This dedication contrasts singularly with the one made recently, also to Mme Kalergis, by a Jewish professor, M. Caro—of his very striking little work entitled *Lessing et Swift*.

My days are spent in writing insignificant letters; in reading music manuscripts brought and sent to me from all quarters; in chatting with Monseigneur, who comes to see me twice a week; and explaining to 3 or 4 artistes, who have taken up their abode here for this purpose, how one sets about playing the piano. The names of my new temporary pupils are: Fräulein Mehlig from Stuttgart; Fräulein Steinacker; Herr Leitert from Dresden; and little Joseffy, son of a Rabbi in Pest. All have already given concerts in various capitals—and Joseffy is on the way to becoming a second Tausig. . . .

619. To Princess Carolyne. Meiningen, Tuesday, 23 March. Nothing new to tell you about my last week in Weimar. On Saturday morning Monseigneur left for Stuttgart, where he is to attend the confirmation of a daughter of Pce Hermann. The Grand Duchess again did me the honour of inviting me to dinner, after Monseigneur's departure. That same day, Stern of Dresden brought me the first part of our Beethoven Cantata.

The day before yesterday, Sunday, dined in Gotha with the Duke of Coburg. The previous day he had played the part of Tellheim in Lessing's *Minna von Barnhelm*, in his little Schloss theatre. The other parts were played by amateurs —with the exception of E. Devrient, the Duke of Gotha's *Hofrath* [Privy Councillor]. Mgr. of Weimar was not invited. The Duke told us at dinner that it was exactly 102 years since this same play was performed in this same little Court theatre. Then, it was his great-grandfather, also a Duke Ernst II, and Eckhoff, who played the principal parts.

At 10 yesterday morning, arrived here. The Duke [of Saxe-Meiningen] had me met at the station by his Court Marshal, Baron Stein. My accommodation at the Schloss is quite magnificent. Monseigneur of Meiningen will go to Ischia at the end of April to fetch his wife—and in May will spend a few days in Rome. Yesterday, a grand soirée at Bodenstedt's in which the Duke very kindly took part. Bodenstedt's prologue, with the programme of this evening's Bach concert, I am enclosing for you. . . .

Leitert, whom I have entitled my *Sgambati tedesco* [German Sgambati], insisted so much, and even wept, that I eventually yielded and am taking him with
me. This excellent young man of 16 has all the makings of a remarkable artiste.
He came here with me and will accompany me to Vienna and Rome.

Eduard gives me good news of Vienna—I shall see him the day after tomorrow, Thursday morning. . . .

620. To Princess Carolyne. At Eduard's,[13] **Vienna, midday, Tuesday,
20 April.** Leaving Vienna on Friday evening, St Fructuosus' Day, I spent 2
and a half days in Regensburg—from where I got back at 9 this morning. . . .
Although this trip to Regensburg increases my expenses by several hundred francs,
I do not regret it. It will bear, I hope, some good fruit in the field of Catholic
music. In this respect, Regensburg has more importance than various great capitals. I stayed with the publisher Pustet, greatly famed for his publications of
missals, antiphonals, etc. He is an excellent man, very sensible, simple, and discerning. His 2 brothers are associated with his publishing business, which has
capital estimated at several million. I made friends with the whole family, and
also with Herr Witt, a very distinguished ecclesiastic and founder of the new
Society of St Cecilia, which is unlikely to dilly-dally and moon about like the
congregation of St Cecilia's in Rome! Herr Witt also conducts, in a quite remarkable way, the little choir at St Emmeran's.

On Saturday evening, Bülow's concert. . . . On Sunday, Palestrina Mass at St
Emmeran's. Afterwards, dinner at the Bishop's, where there were about fifteen
guests. Three Fathers of the Company of Jesus were present; one of them, the
Revd Father Löffler, is one of the most celebrated preachers. During Sunday evening I made a visit to the Tour und Taxis, whom I had met the previous day at
the concert. The Bishop had been so delicately tactful as not to have a piano
brought into his apartment—and I took good care not to open the Taxis'. On
this topic, one of my Viennese responses has been reported in the *Fremdenblatt*:
'Show me to the door, Madame, but do not show me to the piano!'

Yesterday, Monday, I made a brief inspection of the astonishing music library
owned by Canon Proske, whom Cardinal Reisach knew—acquired after his death
by the Bishop of Regensburg. Next, dinner and supper at Pustet's—and, at 10
in the evening, climbed into the train to return here. . . .

[13] Eduard von Liszt's home was in the Schottenhof, where from this time forward Liszt stayed as a matter of course
during his visits to Vienna.

621. To Princess Carolyne. Pest, Friday, 30 April. . . . I was expecting
to be back in Rome on the eve of Ascension Day, and to participate in the Holy
Father's blessing, on the Thursday, at St John Lateran. That is no longer possible, for on Sunday I have to attend the performance of a mass by Mozart, the
one entitled Coronation Mass. The Church Music Society, of which I am a member, is preparing this performance in Buda expressly for me. On Monday a recital
is being given here by Leitert, to whom my absence would do a definite wrong.
So I shall leave on Tuesday morning, and before noon the next day will reach
Duino, from where Pcss [Therese] Hohenlohe has just telegraphed me. I shall
spend Ascension Day there with her; on Saturday I shall be in Florence, and
on Sunday in Rome.

From Augusz's letters and the newspapers you know that my little run of success is continuing. The first concert, last Monday, was a complete success—and
this evening's will not fail either. On Sunday I had the honour of dining at Court,
in a small gathering—and afterwards of producing for the Queen my little talents of a superannuated old pianist. Their Majesties left the next morning for
Gödöllő[14]—and so at the concert the royal box was empty. Pce Constantin, whom
I caught a glimpse of again at Andrássy's soirée on Sunday, returned to Vienna
on Monday evening. Mgr Haynald wanted to take me to his archiepiscopal residence at Kalocsa; Mgr the Primate[15] likewise invited me to Esztergom—and the
newspapers report that I am spending the summer in Szekszárd with my friend
Augusz! . . .

I have renewed acquaintance with Count György Apponyi, head of the
Catholic party in Hungary. His son[16] is a paragon of the education given by the
Jesuit Fathers, and seems very happily gifted in all respects. He came to Vienna
expressly to hear the *Elisabeth*, and, to offer his congratulations, paid me the first
visit—which gave me the opportunity to set foot inside the Apponyis' house
once again. As for my relations with society, I keep very much to myself—it
being my most decided intention no longer to depend on the salons, where I
expect to gain nothing. My path lies elsewhere—in Him who is the Truth and
the Life! You taught me it—and I bless you for it, and pray for you with all
my soul!

[14] A castle and estate about eighteen miles from Budapest which had been given to Franz Joseph and Elisabeth by
the Hungarian nation some months before their coronation as King and Queen of Hungary.
[15] See under Simor in Biographical Sketches.
[16] The later distinguished statesman and orator Count Albert Apponyi, whose *Memoirs* contain much of interest
about both Liszt and Wagner.

622. To Princess Carolyne. Sagrado, 6 May, morning. Here I am, already almost in Rome! Sagrado is a country seat in the style of Krzyżanowitz, but less manorial, unpretentious with pretty copses and a most extensive view. On my arrival, yesterday morning, the Princess gave me the kindest welcome. Before dinner, we went with her 2 sons to Duino—which you know from better descriptions than mine.[17] It is a trip of rather less than 2 hours in the carriage. What especially charmed me was that you were spoken of with total affection! Perhaps you will come here one day. . . . Tomorrow evening I shall be in Florence, where I shall spend Saturday. On Sunday, if you permit, I shall go from the station to mass at Sta Francesca—and will then come to the Babuino. . . .

I shall tell you about 2 works I am planning, for which I claim your co-operation: a *St Stanislas of Poland*—and a *St Stephen, King of Hungary*. I hope they will be composed in 18 months—as well as the Beethoven Cantata, the text for which Stern will be sending to Rome for me. This last work will not be a small-scale one. My passion for composing is keener than ever. I need only remain quietly in my room—and leave three quarters and a half of visitors at the door. Help me in this, I entreat you—no greater kindness can be done me! See you on Sunday!

About the end of the third week of August, Liszt again left Rome, his destination being Munich and—as he thought—the première of *Das Rheingold*.

623. To Princess Carolyne. [Munich] Tuesday evening, 24 August. Arrived with no hitches *en route* at 5.15 this morning. Since the train stopped for more than 3 hours in Florence, I put it to good use by going to the Cathedral of Sta Maria dei Fiori, with Brunelleschi's dome, and to Sta Maria Novella. . . .

My first visit here, after St Boniface's, was to Frau von Bülow.[18] Hans is in Berlin, to begin divorce proceedings. I can't do anything to help with that, and probably won't be seeing Hans this time. . . .

The Augsburg *Gazette* announces that the King—after getting back from his trip from Landshut to Berg—will spend his birthday with his mother at Hohenschwangau. So he will not be attending the performance of *Jessonda*[19] being given for his birthday tomorrow. Neither shall I, of course. But His Majesty is expected on Thursday or Friday—and doubtless He will attend the dress rehearsal of *Rheingold* on Friday. Notwithstanding many difficulties, delays, and

---

[17] Since Liszt's day Duino has become famous in literature, for it was here that, in 1912, Rainer Maria Rilke began his inspired *Duineser Elegien* (Duino Elegies).

[18] Franziska, mother of Hans, whose wife Cosima was now living in Switzerland with Wagner.

[19] Opera by Spohr, first performed at Kassel, July 1823.

criticisms, the performance of *Rheingold* is still fixed for next Sunday, the 29th. A mass of people will come from all parts. Among those already arrived, I can mention some friends of Emile: the daughter and son-in-law[20] of Théophile Gautier; the husband is a poet, and the wife—very beautiful, I am told—writes in prose. In addition, the Mathews, who are friends of Mme Laussot, Walter Bache—my pupil in days gone by, a colleague of Sgambati in Rome and now well established in London—and Mme Mouchanoff[21] with her husband. . . .

Henselt, Rubinstein, Saint-Saëns, and Pasdeloup are said to be arriving before the end of the week. The unveiling of the statue of Goethe will take place on Saturday, 28 August, the anniversary of Goethe's birth. . . .

624. To Princess Carolyne. [Munich] Tuesday, 31 August. Great disappointment! *Rheingold* was not performed on Sunday, and will probably not be performed for several months. The *Musikdirector* [Hans] Richter—to whom Wagner entrusted exclusive direction of the work—believed himself obliged to declare shortly after the dress rehearsal that, with such wretched scenery and so ridiculous a *mise-en-scène*, it was necessary to abandon the idea of performing *Rheingold*, and that he, Richter, absolutely refused to conduct it. Among other things there is a wooden rainbow, which greatly amused the French newspaper correspondents! Richter's resoluteness has been warmly approved by Wagner and his representative here, Mme Mendès—a charming and remarkably gifted woman. But Baron Perfall, the theatre Intendant, did not appreciate in all its haughtiness the artistic self-sacrifice of his *Musikdirector*—who by orders from above has been temporarily suspended from his duties. Lassen and other conductors present here have been invited to conduct *Rheingold*, for it seems that the King desires its performance. All have declined, fearing to offend Wagner.[22] A telegram from Tribschen in the evening of the day before yesterday accused the Intendancy and its adherents of *Schlechtigkeit, Niederträchtigkeit und Unfähigkeit* [badness, baseness, and incompetence]. Even so, the King has authorized Perfall to suspend Richter for insubordination—and how this whole mess will turn out can't really be foreseen. What Germans call the public's *Stimmung* [mood] is unfavourable to Wagner. . . . The dress rehearsal of *Rheingold*—although fairly satisfactory in a musical respect—made a sorry impression on the majority of those present, about 500 people. His Majesty had come back from Berg expressly to applaud the work of his glorious friend. According to what has been reported

---

[20] Judith and Catulle Mendès.   [21] The former Mme Kalergis.
[22] When the première finally took place, on 22 Sept., the conductor was Franz Wüllner.

to me, the King expressed his satisfaction with the performance as a whole
—including the *mise-en-scène*. No one in town talks of anything but *Rheingold*
—but not to praise it, nor its composer. As for me, I in no way enter into questions of detail, and maintain quite simply that *Der Ring des Nibelungen* is the
sublimest artistic endeavour of our epoch.

On 25 August Wagner sent the King for his birthday the finished score of
Der junge Siegfried. A child born at Tribschen in June bears the name of Siegfried.
Mme Mendès and Mme Mouchanoff correspond with Cosima. . . . Hans is still
in Berlin—and seems determined to settle in Florence shortly. All the children
are at Tribschen.

I see people from morning to night. Between 2.00 and 4.00 there is a 'reception' at my place. Yesterday, Monday, a full house: Mme Mouchanoff, her daughter Countess Coudenhove, Frau von Schleinitz, Mme Mendès, Mlle Holmès,*
Frau von Eichthal, Fredro—whose nickname is *perdreau rôti d'amour*!—Baron
Loën, Lassen, Saint-Saëns, and a score of others. In the course of the week I
have received Pauline Viardot, Turgenev, Serov, Herbeck, Chorley, Riedel, Gille,
Kahnt, Müller. . . .

I shall leave again at the end of the week, not at all regretting having come.
The ceremony inaugurating the statue of Goethe, on 28 August, went off very
properly—without attracting public attention. . . .

625. To Baron Augusz. Rome, 19 September

Very dear Friend. . . .

Among the great caravans of pilgrims—German, French, English, Italian, American—who came all agog to Munich to hear *Rheingold*, the *cara patria* [Hungary]
had only one representative: our friend Pál Rosty. He will relate to you the vicissitudes and excitements of the non-performance of Wagner's drama, which, taken
as a whole, is in my opinion the supreme work of this poet-musician of so lofty
a genius. To approach it in intelligence the public will need several years, seeing that in general, as Chamfort remarked, 'The public can raise itself only to
low ideas.' Rosty will also bring to my *prophetesses*[23] a nice copy, made in their
honour, of the Offertory and Benedictus from the Coronation Mass. In order
to make this work as little defective as possible, I again carefully revised and
corrected it before handing over the *definitive* score to Herbeck in Munich,
asking him to have the additions and alterations added to his Imperial Chapel
copy. They include, among others, an introduction and a few further bars for

---

[23] Augusz's daughters.

the Offertory, and Psalm 116,[24] 'Laudate Dominum omnes gentes', as Gradual. Next year I shall publish this Mass, the chief merit of which—its performance at the coronation—is due above all to you.

But let's talk about our Szekszárd festival. Between 1 July and 31 August [next year] I am entirely at your disposal. So fix the date which will best suit you. . . . On the day of the solemn Dedication of your church I should like my Mass for male voices, with simple organ accompaniment (*without orchestra*), to be performed by the Dalárda [philharmonic society]. A choir of about fifty well-chosen singers will broadly suffice; needless expense will thus be avoided and you will have to spend only a very modest sum on the musical part of the festival. The score and the vocal parts of my mass I shall send you in good time, and I undertake to conduct the final rehearsals. Further, Szekszárd will, for a few weeks, musically speaking, outdo the most prosperous capitals, and your home will become a kind of Athenaeum in which we shall have discussions and concerts of *transcendent* music with Reményi, Plotényi, Fräulein Sophie Menter,* and other celebrities of the same standing.

If Kaulbach were to decide to come at that time, it would give me extreme pleasure, even if we had to resume our discussions about his *Auto-da-fé*. However remarkable the vigour of the drawing and the pathos of what it depicts, I have urged him not to paint it, for a large part of its effect springs from an error, perpetrated by anti-Catholic historians, which should be rectified, not propagated still further. Without doubt, religious fanaticism played a terrible role in the horrors of the Spanish Inquisition, but other major causes—politics, wholly secular interests, the national character, the barbarity of the monks and of the legislation of the period, the fury of inveterate human malignity, ever quick, when God's mercy no longer restrains it, to turn to crime—certainly gave it powerful assistance. So to lay the entire blame on the Dominicans alone is unjust; and the misdeed of a perpetual calumny does not become a *super-eminent* artist like Kaulbach. Instead of portraying in a false philosophical light Torquemada or Pedro d'Arbues and this or that murderous monk, let him work at true glory and give us before very long his marvellous picture, *Nero*, in which he has so magnificently depicted that abominable scoundrel, emperor, play-actor and perpetrator of every dastardly deed, debauchery, and heathen ferocity, who, like an evil meteor, vanished before the true light of the crucified St Peter and the decapitated St Paul! . . .

Thank you for your letter, for the notelet with Anna's translation, and for so many, many other things that I couldn't finish listing them.

Ex toto corde, your   F. Liszt

---

[24] Vulg.; Ps. 117 in the AV ('O Praise the Lord, all ye nations') and BCP.

626. To Baron Augusz. Villa d'Este, 9 November. Éljen Szekszárd! dearest friend. Your home will be an oasis for me, and with you and your family I shall there enjoy the most agreeable comfort. Let's not determine the length of my stay but just agree that I shall stay as long as possible. . . .

As you know, in honour of the Beethoven Centenary I *must* this winter write a cantata, which will be performed at the music festival (end of May) in Weimar. To work on it at my ease, and to escape diversions, visits, and tiresome intrusions in Rome this season, I have withdrawn here, to Cardinal Hohenlohe's residence at the Villa d'Este. His Eminence has very graciously placed at my disposal some charming accommodation which I shall take advantage of on my own (for the Cardinal spends winter in Rome), but always in the very agreeable company of books and music, until my departure for Weimar in April.

Since last month I have been 58 years of age, and am beginning to feel old and tired, very dear Friend. My vocation does not incline me to make myself a hermit, and it is only through poetic intuition that I sometimes exclaim: 'O beata solitudo, o sola beatitudo!' But I feel a pressing need to live rather quietly from now on, and no longer to waste too much time with anybody and everybody. Consequently, during the remaining days that God leaves me in this world, I wish to isolate myself from common pleasures, worries, successes, and disappointments, so that I can concentrate the best of my powers on two works: our *Sz Tűz és Víz*[25]—and *St Stanislas* (a Polish oratorio in whose text I am passionately interested).

That will be my 'Nunc dimittis'!

See you, therefore, before as well as after St Michael's Day [29 September]. My grateful thanks to Mme Augusz, and a thousand affectionate respects to the prophetesses.   Yours,   F. Liszt

627. To Princess Carolyne. Rome, 27 November. Overbeck's death[26] makes me think of my own. I expressly desire, request, and enjoin that my obsequies take place without any pomp whatsoever, as simply and economically as possible. I protest against such a burial as Rossini's, and even against any summoning of friends and acquaintances, as at Overbeck's funeral. Let there be no ostentation, no music, no procession, no unnecessary lighting, no obligatory eulogizing, nor speeches of any kind at all. Let my body be buried not in a

---

[25] Referring to the planned—but never realized—oratorio *St Stephen, King of Hungary*, for which Liszt had asked Kornél Ábrányi (translator into Hungarian of the text of *St Elisabeth*) to render into verse Mór Jókai's prose work about St Stephen, *Szent Tűz és Szent Víz* (Holy Fire and Holy Water).

[26] On 12 Nov.

church, but in some cemetery—and above all may care be taken to see that it is not removed from that grave to any other. I desire for my remains no other resting-place than the cemetery made available to them at the place where I die, nor any religious ceremony other than a low mass—not a requiem sung at the parish church. The inscription on my tombstone could be: *Et habitabunt recti cum vulto tuo.* Ps. 139.[27] If I die in Rome, my wish is for my friend Don Antonio Solfanelli to officiate at this low mass. Lacking him, then perhaps some other priest can be found who may retain an affectionate memory of me. My last blessing belongs to you, as do those of each day of my life!

628. To Princess Carolyne. [Villa d'Este] Thursday morning, 2 December. The *Perfection chrétienne*[28] has reached me at the right moment. I shall immerse myself in it totally. One's time could not be better employed than with such reading, and the tranquil life I am leading here disposes me perfectly to it. Besides, don't imagine that I suffer in the least from the cold or the humidity. My room warms up marvellously, and, if I dare mention this detail, the jugs Fortunato has sent me maintain the most agreeable nocturnal temperature in the bedroom. When you see the Cardinal, tell him again that the Villa d'Este is a veritable El Dorado for me, and that I find in it in abundance everything I could desire. . . .

Monsignor Bishop Tota had the kindness to come and see me, and to get me to enjoy his very benign musical inspirations—amongst others a *Viva Maria* which Capocci has made famous in Rome by adding to it harmonies at once simple and learned. To Monsignor I also owe this charming definition: 'La musica è l'anticamera del Cielo [Music is the antechamber of Heaven].'

Devotissimo servo.   F.L.

629. To Franz Servais. Villa d'Este, 20 December. Your kind letter has given me most sincere pleasure, dear Monsieur Franz. I trust that you are in good health again, and immersing yourself to your heart's content in Bach—an admirable chalybeate bath! I shall keep you company, because for a Christmas present I have given myself the Peters small 8vo edition of the two Passions, Masses, and Cantatas of Bach, who could be called the St Thomas Aquinas of music.[29]

---

[27] Vulg. Ps. 140 in the AV and BCP ('The just shall continue in thy sight').

[28] Carolyne's book *Sur la perfection chrétienne et la vie intérieure.*

[29] A felicitous analogy and parallelism of the kind that Liszt was fond of and good at: Bach's B minor Mass was 'the Mont Blanc of church music', the middle movement of the *Moonlight* Sonata 'a flower between two abysses', the

Kahnt, who has sent me these scores, tells me how keen he is to bring Cornelius to Leipzig as editor of the *Neue Zeitschrift*, founded, as you know, by Schumann and valiantly carried on by Brendel. It is the only newspaper which for about thirty years has steadfastly, knowledgeably, and influentially upheld the works and men representing musical progress. . . .

I shan't do any travelling this winter, and will not be leaving my retreat at the Villa d'Este except to spend a few days in Rome. Several people have very kindly invited me to Paris; for the reasons of expediency that you know, I have declined. Henceforth it is not for me to put *myself* forward, but simply to continue to compose in full tranquillity and freedom of mind. This compels me to isolate myself; to avoid the salons, the half-opened pianos and the thousand pieces of drudgery inflicted on one by the big cities where I very easily feel out of place.

Hearty thanks for your propaganda on behalf of the *Missa choralis*; if you would write me a couple of words after the performance, I should be much obliged. Please also tell M. Brassin that I am very grateful to him for not being afraid to compromise his success as a virtuoso by choosing my Concerto.[30] Up to the present time, the best-known French pianists—with the exception of Saint-Saëns—have not ventured to play anything of mine other than *transcriptions*, my own compositions being necessarily considered absurd and insupportable. People know well enough what to think of them because of what is said about them by others, without needing to hear them for themselves.

In the Concerto, how did the orchestra and piano go together? Had care been taken to have sufficient rehearsals? Several passages are tricky; the modulations are abrupt, and the variety in the movements is somewhat disconcerting for the conductor. In addition, the treacherous *triangle* (proh pudor!), if it persists in coming in strongly with its mocking little motif, marked *pianissimo*, gives rise to scandal and uproar....

Notwithstanding all this pointless wrangling, for in such a matter all sensible people ought to be of the same opinion, I take it that M. Godebski's bust of Chopin will soon be placed in the foyer of the Warsaw theatre. Chopin well deserves this distinction, which need not prevent people giving thought to a larger monument in Lemberg, and raising an adequate sum for that purpose.

In Weimar we shall talk of Hal and of the pleasure it will give me to pay you a visit there. . . .   F. Liszt

---

Ninth Symphony 'the Great Pyramid', Beethoven himself 'a Janus, one of whose two faces is turned towards the past and the other towards the future', and Liszt's pupil Eugen d'Albert (a *great* pianist, or such a sobriquet would have been meaningless), 'Albertus Magnus'. Anyone might think of calling the organ 'the King of instruments'—but, seeing that it is associated less with castles and courts than with churches and chancels, Liszt's description is far more fitting and imaginative: 'the Pope of instruments'.

[30] Liszt's Piano Concerto No. 1 in E flat, which Louis Brassin had played at a concert in Brussels on 21 Nov.

1870

26–9 May. Liszt is the moving spirit of the Allgemeine Deutsche Musikverein festival held at Weimar in honour of Beethoven. On the programme of the final concert are the Second Beethoven Cantata (its première), the *Emperor* Piano Concerto (with Tausig), and the Ninth Symphony, conducted by Liszt.

14–26 July. Liszt attends performances, in Munich, of *Das Rheingold* and *Die Walküre*, sits to Lenbach for his portrait, and renews acquaintance with Smetana.

23 July. He sees the Passion Play in Oberammergau.

31 July to mid-November. Liszt stays in Szekszárd, leaving only for a brief visit to Pest and for excursions to Kalocsa and Nádasd.

25 August. At the Protestant church in Lucerne, Liszt's daughter Cosima marries Richard Wagner.

16 November. Liszt arrives in Pest, where he spends the next five months.[1]

14–16 December. A music festival is held in Pest to commemorate the centenary of the birth of Beethoven. At the Vigadó on the 16th Liszt conducts the Ninth Symphony, the Violin Concerto (with Reményi), and the first performance in Hungary of his own Second Beethoven Cantata.

WORKS. *Zur Säkularfeier Beethovens* (Second Beethoven Cantata) (A. Stern and F. Gregorovius) (S68, 1869–70), for soloists, double chorus, and orchestra. PIANO: *Mosonyi gyászmenete—Mosonyis Grabgeleit*[2] (S194). ORGAN: Prelude and Fugue on the name BACH (rev. version).

630. To Augusta Holmès in Paris. Villa d'Este, 12 January. To your sad and moving lines I respond with a prayer. Please regard me as a friend who is devoted to you with the sincerest respect. Of your extraordinary talents I have the highest opinion, and would wish to make clear to you other than by commonplace words the feeling of affection which you inspire in me. Can I be of use to you in any way? Always candidly and without ceremony regard the little I can do as being at your disposal. If your activities prevent your coming to

---

[1] This long sojourn in Hungary marks the beginning of the last phase of Liszt's life, the *vie trifurquée*, as he called it, in which his time was roughly divided between Pest, Weimar, and Rome. Pest was always the priority, as he explained in a letter of 7 May 1873 to Augusz: 'From birth to death, and despite my lamentable ignorance of the Hungarian language, I remain heart and soul a Magyar, and therefore earnestly wish to foster the development and practice of Hungarian music.'

[2] An elegy or funeral dirge for Mihály Mosonyi, who died on 31 Oct. that year.

Weimar in May, I shall regret it greatly. I am not likely to be going to Paris next year—and at my age one can no longer count on the following years.

When you find a moment, send a word about your work and plans to your most affectionate servant   F. Liszt

631. To Princess Carolyne. [Villa d'Este] 28 January. Yesterday morning, when leaving church, I was assailed by a good temptation. I wanted to go and wish you happiness on one of your feast-days—St John Chrysostom's Day. I know not what hare's prudence—that of the serpents is beyond my reach—held me back! And so we shall celebrate your Golden-Mouthed patron saint on the same day as his disciple and rival, 8 February. He often had a bone to pick with the great ones of this world, and at the secret council of Chalcedonia didn't stand on ceremony with the bishops. But the poor and the widows wept at his banishment—and by his genius and his learning he acquired immense glory. It has been said that St Paul, the preacher of truth, dictated to him in spirit several passages of his writings and sermons. I no longer know where I found mention of this detail of Chrysostom's biography—that he practised hospitality magnificently by never inviting anyone to dinner!

Having to do without your conversation yesterday, I compensated myself by reading a few chapters of your *Perfection chrétienne*—which could be defined as the ladder from the good to the better, and from the better to the perfect. . . .

Tarnowski spent the day before yesterday with me. He has gone to Subiaco, whence he returns today. Tomorrow evening he will bring you the *Revue de Toulouse*, containing 3 articles on the symphonic poems, by M. Gozlan, who looks like becoming—my Greppo.[3]

Umilissimo servo.   F.L.

632. To Baron Augusz. Villa d'Este, 8 March

Very dear Friend,

The precept *Age quod agis*[4] has, however, its bad side. Thus, because I have spent these last 2 months entirely absorbed in my Beethoven Cantata—which is to be performed on 28 May at the music festival in Weimar—I haven't found a moment to write to you. But this score, containing about a thousand bars,

---

[3] Weaver from Lyons, remembered as an invincibly faithful supporter of Proudhon.
[4] 'Do what you are doing' (without letting yourself be distracted).

has finally been finished, on Ash Wednesday [2 March]. Supposing that it's a flop, at least it will be a painfully deserved one. Be that as it may, I should very much like to invite you to come and hear it, and would insist still more were I not afraid of inconveniencing you, and above all were I still living in the Altenburg, where I could have allowed myself the pleasure of offering you an apartment suitable for Mme d'Augusz and the prophetesses. . . .

Sincere and affectionate greetings to the whole family,

Cordially yours,   F. Liszt

P.S. Mingled with the excellent qualities and rare talent of our charming Sophie Menter is, I regret to say, a certain capriciousness. Your home, in particular, was indeed not the place for her to appear anything other than the very *good-natured person* she basically is. I shall venture to give her a very gentle little lesson on this subject when I have the pleasure of seeing her again.

Do you remember Leitert? He has just left for Vienna, and his *taste for concerts* (on which Sophie nicely lampooned him) will perhaps soon take him to Pest. I recommend him to you only to *a certain extent*. He is without doubt an outstanding pianist, whom one can applaud at once; on the other hand there have come to my notice several little things concerning him which are less favourable, and which I don't want to know about in any detail. I mention this *in confidence*, knowing how kind you are, and how superlatively obliging to people I recommend to you.

633. To Princess Carolyne. Weimar, Wednesday morning, 20 April.

The best of my days from Maundy Thursday to Easter Day was spent in church. Our excellent priest hasn't grown quicker with the years. His mass lasts more than half an hour—and the services in Holy Week took several hours every day. This slowness, which I far prefer to the opposite fault, I put up with extremely well. It allows one better to absorb the texts, both their spirit and their letter. On Easter Day, after the sermon, the priest, at the moment of beginning mass and already wearing the priestly vestments, informed the congregation from the altar of the gift made by the Pcss Wittgenstein. At this name my heart leapt— and I had difficulty holding back my tears. Your beautiful carpet was laid out at the foot of the altar, where I see it every morning. Tell me when and how you sent it, if you worked on it yourself, what its origin is, and everything about it. I took communion last Thursday. On 3 May, Invention of the Holy Cross, and at Whitsun, I shall take communion again.

The Grand Duchess made her devotions on Thursday, and has remained in retreat the whole week. I have not seen her since Palm Sunday. The Grand Duke has twice favoured me with a visit. Yesterday morning he went to Meiningen to attend a performance of a new drama, a very daring one, entitled *Sixtus the Fifth*. On this subject have you read Montalembert's letter, written, I believe, on the eve of his death, to Baron Hübner, the latest historian of Sixtus V?

Eduard's promotion gives me very great pleasure. He is now drawing very close to a minister's portfolio. He would need only a little more flexibility and less merit! . . .   F.L.

634. To Baron Augusz. Weimar, 21 April

Very dear friend,

Leaving Rome in the evening of 2 April, and arriving here on the 6th, I didn't receive until Easter the two letters you had sent to Rome. Thank you with a full heart for everything that, for thirty years, you have said, done, asked, and *remained* for me. Be certain that I shall contrive to stay with you as long as possible; before leaving Weimar (around 10 July) I shall write and let you know my itinerary, of which Szekszárd remains the luminous point.

I hardly dare offer you again *your* hospitality in Weimar; out of discretion, therefore, I shall have to restrict myself to sending you the programme of the music festival, which is obliging me to write numerous letters and to read a quantity of others, not counting the manuscripts to look through and the visitors to receive. To keep myself going, physically and morally, in this task, I request of your ready friendship a signal service: send me, I beg you, at the earliest twenty or so bottles of your Szekszárd nectar (at a *florin* a bottle) similar to the kind you sent to Rome for me, with the Baron Augusz *label* and the scientific commendation of Baron Liebig. This wine absolutely must take part in the Beethoven Festival celebrations, which will be no more than a *Vorfeier* [curtain raiser] to our Szekszárd festival...

I am being interrupted—and will shortly write to you at greater length.

Yours,   F. Liszt

635. To Princess Carolyne. Monday, 25 April, feast of St Mark.

It is 5 years to the day since I entered holy orders. I bless God for it every day, while asking Him to shower His blessings upon you—you, to whom above all I owe the fact of being able to walk on the broad and luminous path of His commandments. 'Et meditabar in mandatis tuis, quae dilexi!'[5] Be so kind as to tell

---

[5] Ps. 118: 47, Vulg.; Ps. 119 in the AV and BCP ('And my delight shall be in thy commandments: which I have loved').

Cardinal Hohenlohe how deeply grateful I am to him for having thus brought me closer to the altar of the living God, from which my soul remains for ever inseparable.

I consider myself morally obliged to extend my stay here by a fortnight more than I had planned—seeing that from 15 June to 6 July the Weimar theatre will be giving *Mustervorstellungen* of operas by Wagner: *Tannhäuser, Lohengrin, Fliegender Holländer, Meistersinger*—and even *Tristan und Isolde*. For this last work the Grand Duke has just asked the King of Bavaria for the indispensable assistance of the 3 solo singers now able to play the principal parts. I should find it almost unseemly to leave the Hofgärtnerei before the end of these performances—which have been moved back a little because of the music festival, still fixed for 26 May. My Cantata will be performed at the closing concert, a Sunday, in the octave of the Ascension, 29 May. From 10 July to 25 August my plans are still uncertain—but I doubt that my path will bring me back to Rome at that time, as I would wish. I shall probably go with a number of other people to the Passion Play at Ammergau, and shortly thereafter to Szekszárd— whence at the beginning of October I shall return straight to Rome. It goes without saying that if you deem it advisable for me to return to Rome at an earlier date, I shall arrange matters accordingly.

Nothing new this week, except for the *Lisztsoirée* in Berlin—to which I was invited and of which I am sending you the programme. Notwithstanding the numerous outpourings of condemnation that for 15 years the newspapers, the professors, and many other influential persons have been bestowing upon my works, it seems that they are resisting and that their small effect on the public is *crescendo*. I don't know how the programme of the Berlin *Lisztsoirée* was received —but even if hisses were mingled with the applause, it is probable that there will be further such attempts! For my own part, I have only to let matters go forward—without bothering myself with anything other than writing the notes remaining in my head.

This evening I shall be dining with Monseigneur, and on Thursday with the Viardots and Turgenev, who are rather disposed to divide their time between Baden and Weimar—by spending the summer season in Baden and the winter here. Mme Viardot is giving lessons to the Grand Duchess's 2 daughters, and is also preparing several external pupils for the stage. She will shortly be singing the role of Fidès in *Le Prophète*—and [Gluck's] *Orfeo*, for a second time, at the theatre. I am spending my time pretty well in making her sojourn here more comfortable—finding that she is at once an illustrious adornment and an agreeable advantage for both Court and town. Besides, she and I get along sufficiently well for me not to aspire to being better understood by her! . . .

Wholly at your feet.   F.L.

636. To Princess Carolyne. Sunday morning, 15 May. I enclose the announcement of the Wagner performances. The King of Bavaria has written to the Grand Duke to express his regret at being unable to make Herr and Frau Vogl available, since they are indispensable for the Munich performance of *Die Walküre*, now in preparation. And so, impossible to do *Tristan* here. Between the music festival and the Wagner operas there is a strong possibility of the *Elisabeth* being done, either in the church or the theatre. I am putting no weight behind it, and last year was positively opposed to such a proposal.

The Vienna committee have invited me to conduct the *Missa solennis* at the Beethoven Festival in October. To conduct *Fidelio* they have invited Franz Lachner —and for the Ninth Symphony, Wagner. I have declined, pleading my *ganz passive Stellung in der musikalischen Welt* [wholly passive position in the musical world]—and I take it that Wagner will not accept either. . . .   F.L.

637. To Princess Carolyne. [Weimar] Tuesday, 21 June. . . . The day before yesterday, Sunday, Monseigneur very graciously invited himself to my so-called matinée. Its chief adornment, Mme von Mouchanoff, did the honours. Further, she appeared as *maestra*—accompanying at the piano several of Elsa's scenes sung by Frau Sternberg, who has sung this part in Brussels,[6] and delighting the too numerous audience with some of Chopin's mazurkas. Adelheid Schorn, Frau von Helldorf, Mme Mendès, and half a dozen German, French, and English journalists attended this brilliant private concert. In the Court chapel next Saturday several works of mine will be performed, shown on the programme I shall send you. The Grand Duchess was so kind as to make to Mme Mouchanoff a remark which flatters me: 'Liszt has the gift of doubling people's faculties while he is talking with them.' . . .

Yours with heart and soul.   F.L.

638. To Princess Carolyne. 1 July. I took communion yesterday, Thursday, 30 June. After mass, our worthy priest came to my place to take coffee— and I wanted to write to you without delay. But I was reckoning without my visitors, too numerous and relentless, alas! After 9 in the morning, at my home, the hail of letters and the rain of visits are incessant. You will not disapprove of me, I hope, for having asked Monseigneur to leave me out of it during the stay at the Belvedere of the Tsar of Russia. His Majesty and the Grand Duke Vladimir

---

[6] At the first (22 Mar. 1870), and subsequent performances, of *Lohengrin* in French.

arrived on Sunday at 11.00 p.m., and departed yesterday, Thursday, at 10.00 p.m. An entertainment and *tableaux vivants*, inspired by paintings of the Weimar School in the Belvedere orangery, were performed by the theatre artistes: on Monday, Halévy's *Eclair*, accompanied at the piano by Lassen; on Tuesday, the *tableaux*; on Wednesday, the 'august visitors' went to the last of the Wagner performances, *Die Meistersinger*. At the Belvedere soirées, from which I was excused, the few guests noticed the Tsar's little taste for expansive conversations. Monseigneur went to Eisenach, on Sunday, to meet his all-powerful cousin—and took him back there last night. Today, at 5 o'clock, I shall have the honour of dinner at the Belvedere with Fredro and Mme von Mouchanoff. . . .

I enclose the programme of the concert in the Schloss chapel, last Monday. Their Highnesses couldn't be present because of their most august guest. Nevertheless, the performance was very good and well received. . . .   F.L.

639. To Princess Carolyne. Vienna, Thursday, 28 July.[7] I shall at last be able to rid myself of the heavy burden of my several months of idleness! Having got here this morning, I shall leave again, for Szekszárd, the day after tomorrow—in order to avoid the Friday[8]—and shall be there on Sunday evening. By boat takes several hours longer than by rail—but I far prefer travelling by water. . . .

Summary of my stay in Munich—2 performances of *Rheingold* and of *Walküre*, 13, 17, 20, and 22 July. The King attended the 2 last. On the audiences in general, the *Walküre* made a greater and more favourable impression than *Rheingold*. The duet at the end of the First Act, between Siegmund and Sieglinde, was applauded very warmly; also the appearance of Brünnhilde to Siegmund, and the *Walkürenritt* [Ride of the Valkyries]. As for me, I profoundly admire the whole—without dwelling too much on the beauties of detail which limit the enthusiasm of the public. The great works should be embraced in their entirety, body and soul, form and idea, spirit and life. It's not a matter of wrangling with Wagner about longueurs—better to grow to his height!

Apart from these 2 works, I have heard no music in the theatre or at concerts in Munich—the people I have associated with being limited to the small number whose names I have mentioned. Cornelius will soon be sending you the first part of his translation of *St Stanislas*. Lenbach has done—so people say—a superb portrait of me, medium size, not standing, which he will exhibit

---

[7] La Mara has 'Thursday, 27 July'—but Thursday was the 28th.
[8] For superstitious reasons, Liszt did not like travelling on Fridays.

in Vienna and elsewhere. In addition to his portraits of the Imperial family in Petersburg, Lenbach has innumerable orders—for since last year's exhibition in Munich, to be painted by him is all the rage. Kaulbach is working on his *Nero*, but political preoccupations are raising his temperature. He would now be more disposed to seize a gun than to wield a palette! I went to him again on Monday, to take my leave of him—and despite our religious and political disagreements we parted company on friendly terms.

On Saturday, 23 July, we went on an excursion—I should prefer to say a pilgrimage—to Oberammergau, with Mme Mouchanoff, Their Excellencies M. and Mme Titoff, Mme Abazza, and Franz Servais. The last-named is accompanying me to Szekszárd; I shall be telling you about him shortly. What can I tell you about the Passion Play? As far as scenic representation is concerned, it is without doubt most remarkable, interesting, curious, and even edifying. Several of the *tableaux vivants*, such as those showing the miracle of the manna and of the Crucifixion, offer an ensemble of more than 100 people well costumed and perfectly motionless. The processions through the streets of Jerusalem, open to the 2 sides of the theatre, are astonishing. The chorus, 18 strong and stationed on a second row of boards in front of the theatre, appears and disappears at various moments in the divine tragedy, and invites the spectators to participate more intimately in the mystery of our redemption. The gestures of the principal actors are of a natural nobility, at once striking and charming; their attitudes and their language command a kind of respect for the sincerity and conviction with which they play their parts. So the great eulogies pronounced by Eduard Devrient and others on these performances are well deserved. However, it must be observed, although with regret, that the paintings used for the scenery would be better suited to the interior of a tavern, and that much inner composure is needed to put up with the dull, artless verse, adapted by a Benedictine monk, Ottmar Weiss, about 1830. Further, the music composed by the schoolmaster Rochus Dedler, who died in 1822, I found absolutely unbearable. His style is familiar to, and contains most of the drawbacks of, that of Weigl's *Schweizer-familie*. I advise musicians who visit Oberammergau to stuff a good deal of cotton wool in their ears. In the conception of the play, what I find especially satisfying is the division of each of the long scenes into 2 parts. Firstly, the 'figure' taken from the Old Testament, portrayed by a *tableau vivant* without narrative —and then its fulfilment by the Gospel. The tree of the Garden of Eden—and the Cross; Isaac, Joseph, Tobias—and Jesus. The manna, the vine—and the communion. The reciprocal action of the Old and New Testaments—very familiar to all those who have given ever so little of their time to the Holy Scriptures— is what gives the Oberammergau Passion Play its mystical character, which, for me, is paramount. . . .

640. To Princess Carolyne. Szekszárd, Wednesday, 3 August. . . . One feels almost ashamed of talking about oneself just now.[9] Yet I must tell you that I could not feel better here—and that I hope to put my time to fairly good use by writing a few pages of music. Augusz remains, as ever, the staunch and excellent friend that you know. The ways of the house are very peaceful—and my spacious, comfortable, handsomely furnished accommodation is very much to my liking. At 6.00 a.m. I go to mass. Afterwards, until 1.00 p.m., it is agreed that I be left alone; at 2.00 we dine, and at 8.00 tea is served. Franz Servais is occupying a room in the house, which is by far the most manorial in the town. Later, Reményi, Mosonyi, and Sophie Menter will come. For a fortnight and more, revision of the Hungarian Coronation Mass, and of other proofs and copies to be put in order, will prevent my beginning a new work. On 18 August, I shall go to the Pest *Sängerfest* [Festival of Song], which will last until the 22nd— the next day I shall return here, where reigns the most perfect tranquillity. The new church, built under the direction of Augusz, with a fund of 85,000 florins bequeathed by a lady who died in Szekszárd, is dedicated to the Holy Angels. The high altar is under the invocation of St Michael, and the 2 side altars under those of Gabriel and Raphael. I felt a deep joy on learning of the special patronage of the Angels in this church—for since I read your book *L'Amitié des Anges* my devotion for them has formed an essential part of my spiritual life. . . .

May the good angels keep you!   F.L.

641. To Princess Carolyne. Szekszárd, 11 August. From Szekszárd I shall have as little news to give you as from Tivoli. The Auguszes live a very retired life, and I spend three-quarters of my time as suits me, alone in my room. *Prima sera*, the two girls, Anna and Ilona, and I play a few piano duets together, with no other audience than Papa and Mama—and sometimes Franz Servais. He is a very gifted young man, whose blond locks and facial features remind me of my poor Daniel. Mme Servais, his mother, whom I have not the advantage of knowing personally, entrusted him to my care, to preserve him from the extravagances of the new musical school. I told him that it was a little like the story of Gribouille[10] who, for fear of being dampened by the rain, throws himself into the water! However, I shall try to prepare him well enough to win the composition prize at the Brussels Conservatoire next year. . . . His brother,[11] already decorated with a Cross of Portugal, is quitting his position as cello soloist in Weimar—and will probably have a brilliant virtuoso career in Petersburg and

---

[9] At the height of the Franco-Prussian War.
[10] Name denoting a simpleton. Cf. George Sand's *Histoire du véritable Gribouille*.   [11] Joseph Servais.

elsewhere. He is one of the 3 or 4 best cellists I know, and his father's fame will shine favourably on his own talent. His uncle, M. Damcke, is one of the composition teachers most in demand in Paris. Berlioz associated with him a good deal, although he belongs more to the old musical regime than the new. So he has not been able to instil much of his knowledge into Franz Servais, who, on my advice, spent 6 months in Munich, where he studied with Cornelius and Bülow, tristanizing at the top of his voice. . . . To exhaust the subject of the Servais family, I'll add that his brother-in-law, the sculptor Godebski, has various orders in Petersburg, has to do a small statue of Chopin in Warsaw, and has almost finished the one he is doing of his father-in-law. It will be unveiled next year in Hal, a quarter of an hour from Brussels, where Mme Servais is living in a de luxe property acquired by her late husband, to whom this statue is being erected at the town's expense. Up to now, with the exception of Paganini, no similar honour has been done to an instrumentalist. . . .

I shall pray to the Archangel Gabriel to be your Nuncio, and Raphael to cure me of my spiritual blindnesses.[12]   Your very humbly obedient   F.L.

642. To Princess Carolyne. Szekszárd, 28 September. . . . To my regret, I have not yet been able to begin *St Stanislas*. I feel little in the mood for work—the greater part of my days is spent reading newspapers, books, and music. After our visit to Kalocsa, we went *ossequiare* [to pay our respects to] our diocesan Bishop, Mgr. Kovács, at Nádasd, $3\frac{1}{2}$ hours away from Szekszárd. There, it was decided that the solemn ceremony of the dedication of the church, announced for 25 Sept., would be postponed until next year—which suits me in every respect.

Here, on the 25th, a concert to benefit the poor was given by Fräulein Menter, and that same evening there was a ball, likewise for charity. . . . I went to just the first, and heard the music of the ball, which went on until five in the morning, only from my bed. One of the ablest men in the Hungarian Government, M. Horvát, Minister of Justice, was visiting Mgr. Kovács in Nádasd on the same day as ourselves. By way of a toast, His Excellency did me the signal honour of reciting in its entirety, and from memory, the beautiful poem addressed to me in 1840 by Vörösmarty—a poem to which I believe I have responded to some extent with *Hungaria*, *Funérailles*, and other works. This surprising apropos of the minister was at once a *tour de force* of memory and an ultra-flattering incident for me.

---

[12] The name Raphael means, of course, 'God heals' or 'God's healer'.

At this very moment I have received today's telegram with these words: 'Detailed news from Magne.' And so I continue to wait patiently. A bizarre Hungarian proverb says: 'Patience is the Franciscans' ball.' I shall endeavour to learn its dances well! . . . My mental and physical health is perfect—so much so, that I feel this absolute liberty, indicated by Pascal: to know how to sit quietly on a chair. Even the chair is almost too much—if it broke, one would be able to avoid falling and to remain standing!

643. To Princess Carolyne. Szekszárd, Thursday, 13 October. Augusz's letter with the article from the Pest newspaper, a government mouthpiece, has informed you of the situation looming on my horizon. I have in no way desired it, and shall undertake it only after deliberation—as someone who would far prefer to remain ignored in some quiet corner. Although I am told that the press is coming out unanimously in favour of my settling in Hungary, and that in the Chamber and at the Ministry the question of funds to be obtained for the establishment of a new national Conservatoire under my direction or presidency will shortly be resolved, I am by no means persuaded of the matter, and am totally on my guard. Nevertheless, you will understand that it would not be proper for me now to quit a country where I am shown such honourable goodwill—and which is my own. Even if these preliminaries lead to no result, I must take them into consideration and put a good face on it. So I have decided to remain here until 15 November. After that I shall go to Pest to prepare the Beethoven Festival, the direction of which will be offered to me and which I shall accept. I shall also start rehearsals for the first part of my *Christus* oratorio —which will probably be performed *coi fiocchi*[13] during Christmas week. . . .

My present task is the revision and improvement of the 6 Hungarian Rhapsodies for orchestra. I imagine that after having slept in my cupboard for 10 years they will appear without disadvantage in the steps of the Rákóczy, which Schuberth will be publishing. Besides, they are almost indispensable to my expected position in Pest. For 22 Oct. a banquet, concert, and ball are being arranged! . . .   F.L.

---

[13] Literally, 'with tassels', meaning a first-rate performance.

2 January. Following a 'musical and aesthetic lecture' given by the Beethoven scholar Ludwig Nohl, Liszt and Reményi play the Kreutzer Sonata. The soirée is a 'very brilliant' success.

22 April. Leaving Pest, and travelling via Vienna (where he spends a week with Eduard von Liszt and his family) and Prague (where he sees his friends Smetana and Ambros), Liszt returns to Weimar, which he reaches on 3 May.

13 June. Liszt receives from the King-Emperor Franz Joseph the title of Royal Hungarian Councillor and an annuity of 4,000 gulden.

17 July. His great pupil Carl Tausig dies at the age of 29.

Mid-September to mid-November. Liszt spends two months in Rome.

22 October. Liszt's sixtieth birthday. Among his dinner guests at Santa Francesca Romana are Princess Carolyne, her daughter Princess Marie Hohenlohe, and Hans von Bülow.

25 November. At his new residence in Pest, Liszt's life is threatened by Olga Janina.

New Year's Eve. He is present at the performance in Vienna of the Christmas Oratorio from *Christus,* conducted by Anton Rubinstein. The organist is Anton Bruckner.

WORKS. *Ave verum corpus* (S44), for mixed chorus and organ (ad lib); *A lelkesedés dala— Das Lied der Begeisterung* (S91), for male chorus. The song *Die Fischerstochter* (Coronini) (S325). PIANO: Fantasia and Fugue on the theme B-A-C-H (S529); transcription (S448) of 'Am stillen Herd' from *Die Meistersinger* (Wagner); arrangement (S376), for solo voice, male chorus, and orchestra, of the song *Die Allmacht* (Schubert).

644. To Princess Carolyne in Rome. [Pest] **4 January.** The best part of my New Year is your telegram. I received it early on Sunday [New Year's Day], and it shines in my heart like the morning star! These last 3 days I have been giving my attention to a musical and aesthetic lecture on Beethoven which Nohl gave on Monday in the salon put at my disposal by Schwendtner. I enclose the invitation card for this soirée, which went off very brilliantly and was attended by several Excellencies. Besides the applause of a select audience, Nohl had 500 florins net profit. He left again yesterday, for Vienna, where he will give a few lectures of the same kind. Magne will probably attend them, for Nohl had the honour of being recommended to her by one of her brothers-in-law, Hohenlohe-Waldenburg—and yesterday I, too, wrote her a couple of words about him. The thesis he maintains is encountering numerous and important opponents in the official world of the press and the professors. It is that music did not end with Beethoven—that Wagner, and even your very humble servant, are not total spoil-trades. About this latter defendant I retain a few doubts—while wishing, however, that they may be more modest than just!

Orczy came to see me again, and I hope that we shall finish by getting along in harmony—unless he is carried away by his absolutist temperament and his propensity for irascibility.

Tomorrow I am invited to the home of one of the best known and most likeable men in the country, Mgr. Ipolyi, head of the seminary and renowned archaeologist. . . . F.L.

645. To Fortunato Salvagni. Pest, 22 January

My dear Fortunato,

My return to Rome is much delayed, and I now have to take up residence in Pest. Knowing that it would not suit you to live far away from your excellent wife, I propose that you remain with me no longer, and, with regret, give you your full liberty. For nine years you have been a loyal, honest, intelligent, and faithful servant. I thank you for it and shall always remember you most affectionately. Henceforth I have only one piece of advice to give you; it contains everything, and your good character will follow it willingly. Apply yourself ceaselessly to *living a Christian life*, as I try to do for my part. Man's real happiness and high dignity are found only in the observance of the precepts of our holy religion, whose rewards and promises are the only desirable and certain ones. Let us remain firmly attached to it until our last breath, my dear Fortunato, and count on the sincerely affectionate feelings of your old *padrone*, who knows no profitable satisfaction in this world other than that of humbly serving our Lord Jesus Christ! F. Liszt

646. To Princess Carolyne. Friday, 24 February. . . . You know that Grillparzer was nobly fêted in Vienna on his 80th birthday. The Emperor wrote to him and sent him the Grand Ribbon of Franz Joseph. Other sovereigns honoured him with admiring telegrams, shining out among them that of the Empress Augusta. Grillparzer responded to it by extolling Weimar, *das wahre Vaterland eines jeden gebildeten Deutschen* [the true fatherland of every educated German]. I enclose this beautiful phrase for you, printed in its entirety—with a letter from the Empress Augusta to the town of Weimar.

These last 4 days I have orchestrated Schubert's song *Die Allmacht*—the text of which is by Pyrker, the former Patriarch of Venice. An ecclesiastic of my acquaintance is to sing this *Lied*—to which I have added a male chorus—at a concert to be given shortly by the Buda Choral Society. . . .

647. To Princess Carolyne. St Casimir's Day, 4 March. The constancy of your admiration for the Emp. Napoleon [III] gives me extreme pleasure. I share it but, unlike you, without linking to it hope of the imminent reign of his son. Mme Mouchanoff told me in Munich that Napoleon occupied a far higher place in her esteem than all the rest of the French—and that for the full deployment of his genius it would have been desirable for him to govern a nation other than the impertinent people of Gaul! I found the idea singular—Napoleon, Emperor of Austria or Tsar of Russia! For 6 weeks, the opinion I have been very humbly expressing to my friends is that, in the present state of things political, the republican form of government seems to me the only possible one in France. Neither Henri V nor the Orléans would now manage to ascend a throne—still less remain on it! As for the Napoleons, their chances, although still alive, recede with the territorial cessions stipulated by the peace treaty. The name of Napoleon signified victory and the expansion of France—not defeat and surrender of provinces!

What a dreadful and heart-rending thought: that 18 centuries of Christianity, and a few more centuries of philosophy and of intellectual and moral culture, have not delivered Europe from the scourge of war! How much longer are we going to go on cutting one another's throats? When will the precepts of religion and the dreams of humanity succeed in achieving something positive? The Decalogue commands us not to kill; Christian and other philosophers constantly preach goodness, gentleness, and charity. Nevertheless, men kill one another ceaselessly, in fury and out of necessity! Suicides, duels, and battles stain the world with blood—even mankind's justice demands of the executioner the highest penalty! Oh! may God take pity on future generations, and may duels, wars, and the death penalty be abolished for ever! Statesmen ridicule these pastoral reveries, we know—but they have so often been mistaken in their fallacious wisdom that it is not utterly unreasonable to have aspirations that run counter to their pronouncements! Forgive me these humanitarian musings, which I shall abandon only with difficulty, while seeking to impose them on no one else at all.

The high opinion you have of Arnim's diplomatic capacity surprises me a little. It is a very rare wood, that from which the Bismarcks are made! For this wood to attain its full growth, an appropriate soil of events and circumstances is necessary. A Bismarck or a Napoleon is not conceived in an abstract manner, coming into existence by himself, like the great names of science and art—Newton, Kepler, Beethoven. These latter discover and give much more than they borrow, while the political personages are condemned to manipulate men—and succeed in becoming figures only if the zeros take it into their heads to be placed after them! . . .   B.B.

648. To Baron Augusz in Pest. Schottenhof, Vienna, 8.00 a.m., 23 April

Very dear friend,

I don't know how it came about that we hardly saw one another at the station yesterday evening.[1] I regret it all the more as I am reproaching myself for showing some slight irritability, certainly not towards you, nor towards anything you said *whatsoever*, but only towards this proposed accommodation, which would not suit me. Well, to avoid unnecessary discussion, I was bent on telling you my thoughts on the topic plainly and clearly. Forgive me, very dear Friend, if I did so too brusquely; my nerves have been set somewhat on edge by various extremely *inharmonious* matters, of which sundry visits yesterday were a painful reminder.... Once again, forgive me, and do please be aware that nothing you say to me will ever be understood other than in the sense of the noble, unwavering, and exemplary friendship you have shown me for some thirty years, for which remains *deeply* grateful to you your most cordially devoted   F. Liszt

649. To Princess Carolyne. Schottenhof, at Eduard's, Sunday, 23 April.

Coming into this house this morning, I half felt as though I were in your home. The better part of the furniture was given by you—your portrait adorns the drawing-room—and it is thanks to the constant and generous support you have given my cousin that his life has become easier and more agreeable. I have several times expressed my gratitude to you on this subject, and renew to you today, from the bottom of my heart, my thanks for the real kindnesses you bestow upon my very dear and very honourable cousin. His elder son shows great promise; he is studying hard—and making it clear that he is capable of doing honour to the name he bears. You would, I believe, like his sister Marie. Her features show nobility and a certain sweet and serious charm, totally devoid of affectation.

[1] Augusz had been among those seeing Liszt off from the station in Pest.

My last week in Pest became rather wearisome. Apart from the daily tedia, it was necessary to attend to the 2 soirées with dramatic performances and concert at the Karácsonyi Palace in Buda. If the audience could have been larger, at least its satisfaction was complete and demonstrative. . . .   B.B.

650. To Princess Carolyne. Prague, 2 May. I sent you a telegram from Vienna yesterday to say that I had received no letter from Rome since 22 April, the day of my departure from Pest. Although I profess permanent satisfaction and tranquillity, I admit that I couldn't understand this unusual silence. . . .

The last time I spent a week in Vienna, it was only a convenient stopping-place. After having spent the entire winter in Pest, I thought it absurd not to make a few visits in Vienna. Magne invited me to dinner, and to a very brilliant soirée—on Tuesday and Wednesday. Eduard was invited to both dinner and soirée. I played the *Glanes de Woronince*,[2] a Nocturne by Chopin, at the request of Prince Constantin, and a part of the 'Backhändl!'[3] for Princess Metternich, at whose home I dined on Sunday with Beust. The previous day there was a reception *chez* Pcss Schwarzenberg, where I was overwhelmed with kindly attentions —without music! The same day, I ran into Mme d'Eskeles again, at dinner in the home of her daughter, Frau von Gablenz.

In addition, I am more or less agreed with Herbeck that the first part of *Christus*, the Christmas Oratorio, will be performed in Vienna next winter between Christmas and Epiphany. . . . Tomorrow evening I hope to find news of you in Weimar. . . .   B.B.

651. To Princess Carolyne. Weimar, Sunday, 7 May, feast of St Stanislas. I join you in celebrating St Stanislas. Our priest, Hohmann, has been ill for 7 months—and his assistant is today saying mass at Jena. The church not being open, I prayed in my room—and am writing to you. . . .

Reaching Weimar at 5.00 p.m. on Wednesday, I was on Friday received by Their Highnesses with the most perfect grace—and a little more! It seems I had been reported as guilty of anti-German feeling.[4] I had it out straightaway with the Grand Duchess and Monseigneur, without hiding from them that the fall of Ollivier's government was a personal sorrow for me. I stood firm by my grateful admiration for the Emp. Napoleon—despite his terrible final blunder,

---

[2] Evidently as a compliment to his hostess, to whom they were dedicated.   [3] The *Soirées de Vienne*.
[4] During the recent war.

the culmination of everything that had gone on before—alas!—and made still worse by France's faults! As for M. Thiers, this is my opinion. His prodigious talents as a writer, orator, and political personage have to be admired—no one else is in so vibrant and unceasing communication with the greater number of the French. Unfortunately, it is not to their advantage that turn and turn about he has practised government and opposition, often mixing the two together. Without prejudging anything of his present influence on France—the necessity of putting one's trust in him will be, it seems to me, a great punishment. An old friend of Bismarck's told me in Vienna that the latter had recently commented to him: 'A pity Napoleon has fallen. He is mild, intelligent, and supremely capable of reigning. His only error consists in not having understood that instead of declaring war on Germany he should have pointed his cannons at the Parisian rabble and brought about another 2 December.'[5] . . .

In heart and mind, wholly at your feet.   F.L.

652. To Princess Carolyne. Weimar, Wednesday, 10 May. Thank you for the dear little picture of my Patron Saint—and for every line of your dearest last letter of 1 to 4 May, written despite rheumatism in your arm. You know that Mme Janina* has been in Rome for more than a fortnight, staying with her friend Mme Szemere. Your thoughts on her are extremely just—and I grieve to see a woman so gifted in intelligence, talent, and artistic feeling *à la tausend Teufel!* persist with a kind of fury on a path which will inevitably lead to her material and moral ruin. Unhappily, Gregorovius's sorry opinion of her still strikes me as very moderate. For years she has been nourishing her mind exclusively on the most depraved theories and sophisms. Her familiar litanies are the blasphemies, imprecations, and extravagances of Proudhon and the new atheist, agamist,[6] and anarchist school. Mme Sand she finds timid and squeamish. As regards poetry, she is mad about Baudelaire's *Fleurs du mal.* Last year, I was hoping that the stubbornness with which she was pursuing her musical studies, and her rare artistic talent, not devoid of reverie and charm, would gradually cause her to return to a path which, if not perfect, is at least more reasonable. It was an illusion—and you are not mistaken when you say *dass sie sich sehr zu ihrem Nachtheil ausgebildet hat* [that she has developed very much to her disadvantage]. What will become of her? The loss of her fortune and several attempts at suicide are not happy precedents for her future. Please, out of Christian charity, keep what I have just said to yourself. . . .

---

[5] Referring to the *coup d'état* of 2 Dec. 1851.   [6] One who opposes the institution of matrimony.

With Schuberth, who came to see me, I agreed that the first part of *Christus* would appear before the end of Sept., with a German translation by Cornelius. . . .   F.L.

653. To Princess Carolyne. Weimar, 23 May. Although meteorology isn't my strong point, and although I don't care about either rain or fine weather, with the exception of certain concert days—because of members of the audience without carriages—I shall tell you that it well and truly snowed here on 18 May, Ascension Day, for more than an hour. This little atmospheric phenomenon had been thoroughly prepared for by the days of incessant rain we have had since my arrival. . . .

My forecast of the results of Wagner's very brilliant stay in Berlin seems not to be wrong. He was acclaimed and fêted there with enthusiasm, and his concert attended by the Emperor and Empress. His *Kaisermarsch* was encored, and his conducting of Beethoven's C minor Symphony received and praised rapturously. Lastly, Pce Bismarck called on him and gave him several invitations. You know that Wagner addressed him a letter in verse, after Sedan. But here's the rub—neither the Emperor nor the Empress asked for or received him, notwithstanding his concert to benefit the *Wilhelmstiftung*. Herr von Hülsen[7] loudly declared that he could very well do without the pleasure of making the personal acquaintance of Herr Wagner—following which the latter considered he need not bother even to send his card to Hülsen. I have these details from a good source.

Frau von Schleinitz spent Friday afternoon and evening here with me, and returned to Berlin in the night, without seeing any Weimarians other than myself. The object of her visit was to tell me about the present great plan of Wagner's friends and to ask me to contribute to it. It's about providing a sum of 2 to 300,000 thalers with a view to mounting a performance of the *Ring* at Bayreuth, in Bavaria, next year. When the matter is a little riper, if indeed it does ripen, I'll tell you in what measure I shall be able to contribute to it.   B.B.

654. To Baron Augusz. Weimar, 17 July

Honoured and very dear friend,

To follow your excellent counsels, and to take ample advantage of your cordial friendship, is at once a very sound rule for me and my good fortune. Between us there is a logic of the heart, of intelligence, and of positive facts which has

---

[7] Intendant of the Berlin Court Theatre.

never proved faulty—from the evening of our torchlight march through Pest, to the time of my first stay with you at Szekszárd in 1846; from the Gran Mass to that for the coronation, and thence to the recent decree signed 'Andrássy', to which I very much hope to do some honour by sincerely and unwaveringly applying myself to giving noble service to Hungarian art, to our king, and to our country.

I gratefully accept the new service you are doing me by arranging an abode for me in the Palatingasse, opposite the Hotel Frohner, near the church of St Leopold. Several of our friends live in the vicinity, and I shall there be still nearer your home in Buda than I was at the Stadtpfarrei. The name of Széchenyi attached to the nearby promenade will remind me that I have something better to do than promenade.

A remarkable thinker, St Simon, ordered his valet to awaken him every morning with these words: 'Arise, M. le Comte, and remember that you have great things to do.' I shall not give a like instruction to Miska,[8] considering myself much too unimportant an individual for that; however, the least important are not forbidden to dream of great things, and even modestly to aim at them, according to the measure of their abilities.

It will now, very dear friend, be necessary to complete your new *hospitality* in Pest, and to ask Baroness Augusz to help you with it. I shall need some furniture—in particular a *desk* (to write my music on): a wide and commodious one with several drawers, like the one in my room at Szekszárd. My furniture as a whole must be very simple, *without any luxury at all*, for the sole luxury I can allow myself is that of my own person. . . .

I am extremely busy with the proofs of *Christus*, and very much bothered by numerous visits and letters. Forgive me for not writing to you at greater length today. But before I finish I shall let you into a little secret. The decree which *plants me* in Hungary is dated 13 June. It is the feast of St Antony of Padua, a Franciscan—and patron saint of lost objects, which his intercession causes to be found. Many of my acquaintances in Italy and elsewhere have invoked him fervently and effectively. For my own part, I admit, I have up to now had scruples about having recourse to his intercession for any objects whatsoever. But for this pious discretion of mine he is recompensing me nobly, and I bless him with an abundant heart for the *find* that my friends in Hungary—you at their head—are preparing for me.

Your F. Liszt

The day after tomorrow I go to Wilhelmsthal to spend a few days with Their Royal Highnesses. Until the end of the month my address remains Weimar.

---

[8] Miska Sipka, a Hungarian, was Liszt's manservant at this time and until his death four years later.

655. To Anton Rubinstein. Wilhelmsthal, 21 July

Honoured friend. . . .

Thank you for having thought of the *Christus* oratorio.[9] It is not a light work; may it not seem too heavy to the public! My intention was to bring out, in the first place, only its opening section, Christmas Oratorio, around Christmas this year. The score is now being engraved at Leipzig, and I shall send it to you in September. From November onwards I shall be taking up residence in Pest, and shortly before that I shall come and have a musical chat with you in Vienna—where I greatly desire not to inconvenience my friends in any way at all.

M. de Voltaire, of equivocal memory, used to put his friends in three categories: those who loved him, those who felt indifference for him, and those who detested him. Lacking his wit, one can share his experience.

You characterize the *good musician* very justly and wittily.[10] Indeed, he is only the lining of the material needed—which is supplied by the masters. However, we must appreciate and even extol this lining, provided it be of good quality.

Please remember me affectionately to Madame Rubinstein, and count on my old and unchanging feelings of sincere admiration and devoted friendship.

F. Liszt

656. To Princess Carolyne. Wilhelmsthal, Sunday, 23 July. Tausig's

loss I feel very deeply. He was a person of vigour, intelligence, and consequence, who had the exceptional capacity, the temperament, the talent, and the patient industry of a great artist. In addition, he had much practical ability, was very well read, and thoroughly suited to occupying an outstanding position in the world of music. He had been suffering for some 6 or 8 months, and an affair of the heart had still further aggravated his physical troubles. All last winter he had refused the numerous engagements offered him, and made absolutely no concert appearances. One fine morning he left for Naples, and immediately came back again. He no longer wished to continue his very flourishing piano school in Berlin, dismissed his assistant professors, and devoted himself passionately to philosophical studies—the systems of Kant, Schopenhauer, and Darwin had become familiar to him. On the other hand, he was working out and perfecting with admirable care a number of musical works: piano studies, a concerto,

---

[9] For performance in Vienna, where Rubinstein was to conduct a season's concerts for the Vienna Gesellschaft der Musikfreunde (Music Lovers' Society).

[10] In his letter to Liszt of 18 July, after news of Tausig's death, Rubinstein had written: 'I am all the more distressed since, with my brother and Bülow, he was the last great Virtuoso pianist—and the art of instrumental music can only lose by the disappearance of Virtuosity—it is not through "*good musicians*" that the art advances!!'

and unpublished transcriptions of several of the Beethoven quartets and Bach chorales. In June, he told me that he no longer knew what was to become of him, and that he felt inwardly broken. After a fortnight's illness, he was carried off last Monday by typhoid fever, at the Leipzig hospital, where patients are looked after with the utmost care. Countess Krockow never left him, and Mme Mouchanoff came from Baden to help during his final moments. Had the funeral taken place in Leipzig, I should have attended it. But his Berlin friends—and he had some very close ones—took his body to the Berlin cemetery, where they will adorn his grave with a little flower-bed.

I came here yesterday evening, and shall probably stay for some days in complete tranquillity. B.B.

657. To the Grand Duke Carl Alexander. Weimar, 13 August

Monseigneur,

Sincere thanks for your kindnesses! I am extremely grateful to you for having been so good as to mention the Allgemeine Deutsche Musikverein to HM the Empress. Under your protection it has been in active existence for 12 years; its reputation is increasing and its progress becoming more certain. Thanks to your recommendation, Her Majesty already showed some interest in it at the time of the Karlsruhe festival in 1864. I venture to hope that She will be a favourable auspice for it in Berlin.[11] . . .

Monseigneur asks my advice about Herr Müller of Königswinter's plan for a literary academy in Weimar. This project I find vague and lacking in vitality. Will Germany take upon herself the expense of support and money? I greatly doubt it. Most people will find it difficult to understand that an academy is being set up in Weimar by means of a national subscription. For such an institution to function honourably and usefully, three things are needed: men, means, and clearly defined goals.

The *men*, I can hardly see in Weimar, where we certainly have some literati of excellent standing, such as Herr Schöll, Herr Genast, *et al.*—but none of the outstanding names which have a dominating influence on the national mind. Is Herr Müller of Königswinter regarded as being among those in the very front rank? Will the latter be sought elsewhere? How to establish them in Weimar? What salary to allot them, and what premises as a meeting place? Your Royal Highness was thinking of the restoration of the Duchess Amalia's palace. Would it be adequate?

---

[11] In the event, the next ADM festival took place in Kassel.

As for the *means* and the *clearly defined goals*, they seem little clearer. The Académie française, which can be cited as an example, had its Dictionary to compile and publish; and it continues to reward deeds and works of exceptional merit by the Prix Montyon[12] and others. In Germany, the illustrious Grimm undertook the task of providing a Dictionary, and the Montyons have not yet appeared on the horizon of the academy in question.

Nevertheless, the idea of vigorously maintaining Weimar's intellectual tradition, identified with that of Your glorious House, remains a beautiful, great, and noble one, worthy of being followed up most keenly and respectfully. I congratulate Your Royal Highness on applying himself to it so firmly. If You are determined to proceed with this plan, You may perhaps recall the former project of the *Fondation Goethe*, combined with the revival of the Order of the Palm. I consider it far preferable to the proposals submitted to You since then, and believe that the protectorate which You exercise over the most notable associations in relation to Germany's intellectual and artistic development—the Schiller-Goethe Foundation, artists' and musicians' societies, etc.—will gain greatly in scope and lustre if You carry into effect one or two particulars of this same project.

I have the honour to be, Monseigneur, with sentiments of the most respectful gratitude, Your Royal Highness's very faithful and devoted servant   F. Liszt

658. To Princess Carolyne. Sunday evening, 13 August. I have been rather unwell for a few days. Don't worry about it, for it's only a nervous complaint—which has no other consequence than preventing me from writing. If I have a good night the trouble will be completely gone by tomorrow—and I shall reply without delay to your letter of the 6th. . . .

Between 3 and 6 Sept. the Society of St Cecilia will be holding its third general assembly in either Eichstätt or Regensburg. You know that I am seriously interested in this society, and believe that the men running it—Witt, Haberl—are the most capable of achieving something worth while in the field of church music. Their character as men of the Church, the intelligence and steadfast zeal they show, are reliable guarantees that the Society of St Cecilia will develop very considerably. So I have decided to attend this meeting, to which they have done me the honour of inviting me—and will there try to do some service to Catholic art. Eichstätt brings me nearer to Rome, which I hope finally to reach around 10 or 12 September.

May the good angels keep you sweet company!   F.L.

---

[12] The 18th-cent. philanthropist Baron de Montyon had founded several prizes for acts of virtue and works of moral value, to be awarded every year.

659. To Gaetano Belloni in Paris [September]

My dear Belloni,

No one appreciates more than I the noble sentiments by which you have always conducted your life. Among the honourable men I have known, you are one of the most honourable. Your probity, your lack of self-interest, your devoted zeal, are well known and deserve to be praised all the more seeing that, with such perseverance and for so many years, you have been practising them in a business and social environment which often leads to the vices which are their very opposite.

Accept with Christian resignation your share in the injuries and sorrows inflicted upon you by the immense disasters which have befallen France, and regain confidence in your occupation. God always comes to the help of those who are upright and hard-working.

I enclose the small sum you ask of me. I should like to multiply it tenfold, but, as you know, I am far from being rich. Excuse my poverty and count on the unchanging feelings of great esteem and affection of your very devoted friend

F. Liszt

660. To Baron Augusz. Santa Francesca Romana, Rome, 20 September. I shall have to give up for this year, dear excellent friend—not without appreciable regret—any idea of taking advantage of your cordial hospitality in Szekszárd. Having arrived in Rome in the evening of 9 September, I shall stay here until about the end of October. . . .

It pains me to speak to you of a person[13] of whom you remind me. My correspondence with her remains more than interrupted; but I shall never cast a stone at her, deeply though she offended me with her bad habits and behaviour in Pest last winter. Until I received your letter, I was *totally* unaware of the business of B.'s bill of exchange; if he writes to me, I shall not reply, for, having *no* hand in this equivocal predicament, I really can't start interfering in it. In other respects I am fully determined, and don't want to incur the reproach of having taken tolerance to extremes. When it goes beyond a certain limit, tolerance becomes connivance. Since 23 April (day of my arrival in Vienna) I have not seen the person in question, and shall not be seeing her again, anywhere. . . .

The newspapers report that Sophie Menter has broken off her American engagement. I paid her a call in Munich, but found only her mother, who is vociferously bewailing the marriage plan. In her opinion, it is a *degradation* for

---

[13] Probably Olga Janina.

the Menter family to be united with an Israelite. I tried to get her to understand that the sons of Abraham (according to the flesh) were nowadays among
the leaders in business and art, and that Sophie would always be able to manage very comfortably. 'Yes, perhaps,' she replied ... '*if* only he weren't a Jew!' To
such logic I had no further objection to make.

I have seen almost no one from local society, and, exceptionally, have spent
a couple of days in bed, thanks to Miska's unintended rashness in leaving my
windows open during the night, something considered very dangerous in Rome.
For the rest, Miska carries out his duties extremely well, and asks me to send
you his respects.

Yesterday I went to Count Kálnoky's (at the Austrian Embassy) and to
Cardinal Antonelli's. Both of them assured me that the Holy Father was in excellent health. . . .

I shall be very happy to see you and your family again in Pest and Buda at
the beginning of November, and ever remain your very grateful and devoted

F. Liszt

P.S. Mme la Pcsse. W. will shortly be publishing a new work. I gave her long
descriptions of my stay in Szekszárd and the charms of your home.

Give me some news of my friends in Pest, to whom I have not written since
my departure.

661. To Baron Augusz. Rome, 23 October

Honoured friend,

Your telegram of 22 October was *the first* I received, between 7 and 8 in the
morning, just as I got back from mass. It was a splendid beginning to this beautiful day, in which I had the joy of embracing Bülow, whom I had not seen for
two years. His health has improved and he plans to do a great concert tour this
coming winter, beginning in January with Vienna and Pest. In the spring he
will go to London, and in the autumn to New York.

As was the case in a previous year, Pcss Witt. and her daughter did me the
honour of inviting themselves to dinner at Santa Francesca Romana on the 22nd.
Among the guests they had asked for were Count Kálnoky (Austrian Minister
to the Holy See), Baron Des Michels (the present French chargé d'affaires), Mgr.
Ferrari (Archbishop of Lepanto), Pce Teano,[14] the Revd Father Theiner, Sgambati,
et al. After dinner, *Mazeppa* was performed on 2 pianos by self and Sgambati,

---

[14] The Duke of Sermoneta's son, Don Onorato.

and *Orpheus* by self and Bülow—who further amazed us with his playing of two solos.

During the course of the day several telegrams from Pest, from Countess Széchényi, Albert Apponyi, Reményi, Ábrányi, Rosty, *et al.*, gave me very great pleasure. . . .   Very cordially yours,   F. Liszt

662. To Princess Carolyne. Lamporecchio, Tuesday, 14 November.

Arrived here yesterday at noon, and was given an extremely kind welcome by the master and mistress[15] of the house. The weather being bad, I have not stirred from my room—from which, as I am told, one can see half Tuscany. Lamporecchio is a princely residence, and very well maintained. It does not lack visitors and letters. Joseph, the Princess's son, recently returned from his voyage to Peru, which he undertook alone—like Hübner, who travels without even a servant. Pcss Fanny told me again that the irritation felt against Germany by her family, friends, and acquaintances in France was so extreme—that she was being severely reproached for not breaking off all relations with Arnim. As you know, Lamporecchio was built by Bernini, for Clement IX. The chapel is separate, facing the palace and just a few yards away . . .   F.L.

663. To Princess Carolyne. [Pest] 29 November. . . .

Last Saturday I was caught up in a terrible dissonance, and was unable to resolve it until the evening before last. The Countess Janina—the title her Austrian passport now bears—spent those 3 days here. Spare me a recital of her violence and fury, and do me the kindness of not speaking about her to anyone at all. My guardian angel looked after me in this danger. After a further attempt at poisoning herself in my room, Mme Janina left for Paris, where she will probably remain. But, once again, I urge you not to talk about it—even to me—for as best I can I wish to forget this crisis, which, thanks to my good angel, turned into neither a catastrophe nor a public scandal. My friends the Auguszes and Mihalovich, knowing beforehand my resolve—as I wrote to them last summer—not to allow Mme Janina a prolonged stay in Pest, behaved with the utmost loyalty . . .   F.L.

---

[15] Prince and Princess Rospigliosi.

1872

16 February. At a soirée in the home of Count Imre Széchényi, Liszt and Reményi give the first performance of the *Epithalam.*

18 March. Liszt plays in a charity concert at the Vigadó before an élite audience which includes the King-Emperor, the young Crown Prince Rudolf, and other members of the Imperial family.

19 March. At the church of St Matthias in Buda, he conducts the Ofen Music Society in works by Hassler, Palestrina, and Bernabei.

Early April. Via Vienna, where he stays at the Schottenhof with his cousin Eduard, Liszt travels from Pest to Weimar.

26–30 June. He attends the music festival in Kassel.

2–6 September. Cosima and Richard Wagner stay in Weimar, where the reunion with Liszt effectively ends their estrangement from him.

8–14 October. Liszt is Cardinal Hohenlohe's guest at Schillingsfürst.

15–21 October. He stays with the Wagners in Bayreuth.

Late October. Via Regensburg and Vienna, Liszt goes from Bayreuth to Horpács, near Sopron, where he stays with Count Imre Széchényi and from where, on 4 November, he makes an excursion to Raiding. On 11 November he returns to Pest.

WORKS. PIANO: *Sunt lacrymae rerum* (S163/5, later included in the *Années de pèlerinage, troisième année*); Impromptu in F sharp (S191); transcriptions of Ballad from *Der fliegende Holländer* (S441), *Ich weil in tiefer Einsamkeit* (Lassen) (S495), *Frühlingsnacht* (Schumann) (S568, c.1872), *Bevezetés és magyar induló—Einleitung und ungarischer Marsch* (I. Széchényi) (S573). VIOLIN AND PIANO: *Epithalam zu E. Reményis Vermählungsfeier* (S129). SONGS: *La perla* (Princess Therese Hohenlohe) (S326); *J'ai perdu ma force et ma vie* (de Musset) (S327); *Wartburg-Lieder* (J. V. Scheffel) (S345), for solo voices, mixed chorus, and piano/orchestra.

664. To Princess Carolyne in Rome. [Vienna] 1 January, morning.

Happy and fruitful New Year, my good angel! Pray for me—so that I may better appreciate 'living in the present century in temperance, justice and piety'. . . .

My Christmas Oratorio produced a good impression on the majority of performers and audience. My friends in both Vienna and Pest tell me that it is a beautiful work—which will gain from being heard more often. Rubinstein conducted with great care. The *Stabat mater speciosa*, which was almost massacred at Ara Coeli, caused a little difficulty at the rehearsals here too, so far as maintaining the intonation was concerned. However, they liked it, and the performance itself was almost entirely satisfactory. Zellner told me he would be very happy to have written a single piece of this quality—and would thereafter believe himself a real composer. Tomorrow and the day after we shall read with what ears the critics listened to the Christmas Oratorio. Eduard will send you the main articles. For me, the great point henceforth will be to regain a few months of uninterrupted work every year. I hope to succeed in this in '72. . . .

I see fairly often a very charming young woman, the daughter of Madame Minghetti—Countess Dönhoff, whose husband is First Secretary at the Prussian Embassy.

I told Magne that you were very moved by her idea of having the portrait of the son she lost painted by Makart—and of intending it for the doctor who looked after him. . . . B.B.

665. To Princess Carolyne. [Vienna] Saturday, 6 January, Feast of the Epiphany. By the articles that Eduard has sent you, my little success of last Sunday is much contradicted and even invalidated. Hanslick, Bernsdorf, and their cronies dominate the musical press—with the approval of the professors of aesthetics, superannuated composers, salon blabberers, and others, including many of my friends. They indicate that as a person I am most amiable, very nearly respectable, whom one would be delighted to appreciate more. But unfortunately nature has not bestowed upon me the gifts necessary for a high-ranking musician—and as it is no longer possible to class me among the happy mediocrities, I must resign myself to finding 'no room at the inns' of the newspapers possessed by my antagonists. So be it! I shall remain in better company with the shepherds who heard the voice of the Angel—announcing peace to men of goodwill! During their journey the Three Kings will admit me into their retinue. . . . We shall thus proceed by the light of the Star of Bethlehem, and shall ascend the stations of Golgotha while blessing the God of Truth and Mercy!

Magne very graciously observed to me that in the symphonic poems, totally disapproved of only a short time ago, people are already recognizing a few little qualities! Unlike Pyrrhus, I perhaps need a few more failures, not to be lost as far as the public is concerned.[1]

We dined *à trois*, at the Augarten, the day before yesterday. Yesterday evening Bülow and I went into Pce Constantin's box, in the third act of *Lohengrin*.

---

[1] Pyrrhus I, King of Epirus 307 to 272 BC, defeated the Romans at Asculum in 279, but at so great a cost that he is said to have exclaimed 'One more such victory and we are undone.'

Another kindness I greatly appreciated—the Nuncio received me, with marked goodwill. At my visit the day before yesterday, I had twice almost taken my leave—but His Most Reverend Excellency kept me back, showed me some furniture, a plant, some little fish. He took me to the chapel, where in '60 I attended mass held by Mgr. Hohenlohe, who has just written me an extremely gracious letter. Assuming that the Nuncio was unaware of the reason for my present sojourn in Vienna, I mentioned in passing that on Sunday my Christmas Oratorio had been performed. He replied: 'Several of my priests went to it, and told me about it with emotion—you know that Romans have a feeling for music,' etc. I remarked that my reputation as a musician had been much contested, if not destroyed, by the important newspapers—and he interrupted me again with these words: 'Affaire des Juifs!'

Nevertheless, the great Jewish financiers also show me much amiability. Yesterday I dined in their company—and shall be doing so again tomorrow and the day after. On Monday, after Bülow's concert, I shall leave with him—and on Tuesday morning we shall be in Pest. . . .

Devotissimo servo.   F.L.

666. To Princess Carolyne. Pest, 10 January, morning.

Few things to add to my last letter from Vienna. . . . I need hardly say that I attended the Philharmonic Concert at which Bülow gave a magnificent performance of the Beethoven Concerto—and the next day, Bülow's first *Beethovensoirée*. The programme contained 4 Beethoven sonatas, plus 3 or 4 other works. Bülow's success is very considerable. He gives his concerts alone, as, in days gone by, I used to—and succeeds in holding the audience's attention, even in passionately arousing them, with more than 2 consecutive hours of piano pieces. . . . Be it said in passing, I did not touch a piano in Vienna this time, except at Rubinstein's and at Dr Standhartner's. Even in these 2 houses I abstained from solo performances—preferring by far to serve as 'partner' to Rubinstein.   B.B.

667. To Princess Carolyne. Pest, Sunday morning, 21 January, on my return from Pozsony.

. . . The day before yesterday, Friday, I spent almost the entire day in Pozsony with Bülow. His concert was at 11.30 a.m.; he played admirably a dozen pieces by Mozart, Mendelssohn, Beethoven, Schumann, Chopin, and, to finish, several of my things. As in Vienna and Pest, great success and a full house. It is no longer the *dritte Gesellschaft* [third society]—as his mother used to say—which fills Bülow's concerts, but the very first, which flocks there with the others. It seems that in Berlin and Leipzig all the tickets are already taken in advance. The Viennese and Hungarian newspapers are showing themselves, it can be said, to be unanimous in their praise of his immense talent, and they accord only to Rubinstein the honour of sharing with him the palm of virtuosity. If Tausig were still alive, there would be 3 great pianists towering above all the others, putting them at a greater or lesser distance, and many of them even very much in the shade. By his 3 *Beethoven soirées*—the programmes of which consisted exclusively of works by the master—Bülow very intelligently avoided entering into too provocative a rivalry with Rubinstein. The latter can from now on make no better decision than that of applauding with conviction such a colleague. He will, I hope, do it with good grace—notwithstanding his rather autocratic artistic temperament. On this point he resembles Berlioz. Two of his best lady friends and admirers, Mmes Schleinitz and Dönhoff, told me in confidence that he was reproaching them bitterly for their enthusiasm for Wagner, 'after he himself had declined to understand him' early enough, in Weimar. He even indicated that they showed me too partial an affection. Without always being of his opinion, I very sincerely esteem and admire Rubinstein. He is a noble, ardent, richly gifted, prodigiously hard-working personality—and far superior to the greater part of celebrated and distinguished artistes that one encounters. . . .

B.B.

668. To Cardinal Hohenlohe at Schillingsfürst. Pest, 22 January

Eminence,

The multiplicity of minor miseries caused by my very small portion of celebrity deprived me of the honour of thanking Your Highness earlier for his most gracious letter. However, I have not delayed in carrying out the commission relating to the indispensable addition to your furniture at Schillingsfürst; it will reach you shortly and will, I hope, meet with your approval. It is Herr Bösendorfer* (piano manufacturer to the Vienna Court) whom I have instructed to supply a *suitable* instrument to Your Eminence. For, in my opinion, his pianos are the most complete, the most sonorous and agreeable to play, among all those produced by factories in, and beyond, the Austrian Empire. Prince Constantin Hohenlohe values them likewise; and the most renowned pianists, Bülow, Rubinstein, *et al.*, prefer them for public performance. The piano destined for Your Eminence will, in its fittings and finish, be of the very finest; may He permit me to offer it to Him as a token of my gratitude for the exceptional musical hours which His kindness has promoted at the Vatican and the Villa d'Este.

If your stay at Schillingsfürst is prolonged, I shall certainly take advantage of it to come there this summer and pay my very humble court to the most eminent 'voluntary prisoner', on whom, be it quietly said, the public is already very loudly bestowing more immense honours. Today I venture to lay at His feet—in response to a very flattering allusion—*two* photographs, and beg Your Eminence to believe me ever

His very grateful and faithful servant,   F. Liszt

Monseigneur Haynald is most appreciative of Your Eminence's remembrance of him and will send Him his archaeological work (on Kalocsa Cathedral) as soon as it is published.

669. To Princess Carolyne. [Pest] 3 February, after dinner. In obedience to your wishes, I shall add a few details to the exact account, written the next day, of the horrible incident [2] with Mme Janina. In October she telegraphed me from New York: 'Leaving this week, to pay you for your letter.' The letter to which she refers was couched in the most moderate terms, but intimating that, with people I knew fairly well, I could hardly dispense with a certain degree of veracity. I understood at once what she meant by 'paying' me. In mid-November 2 letters—from Schuberth in New York and Hébert in Paris—warned me to be on my guard against the delirium of a provoked woman's vengeance. Apparently Mme Janina had openly informed her friends and acquaintances of her intention of coming to Pest, to kill first me and then herself. Indeed, she entered my room carrying a revolver and several bottles of poison—items she had already twice shown me last winter. I said calmly to her: 'What you intend doing is wicked, Madame. I advise you to give up such an idea—but am unable to prevent you.' After two hours, Augusz and Mihalovich found her with me; Mme Augusz came later. She told them very categorically that nothing was left her in this world other than to assassinate me and then to kill herself. I was absolutely against fetching the police, which would in any case have been quite pointless— for Mme Janina is perfectly capable of firing a revolver before being tied up. Enough, and too much, on this subject! The next day but one she left for Paris. For 7 weeks I have had an arrangement with Mihalovich (who saw a good deal of her in Weimar, Szekszárd, and Pest) whereby I shall send to him, sealed up, any and every letter she may write to me, without reading a single line. Mihalovich informed her of this. Once again, I beg you not to talk about Mme Janina with anybody. Don't write about her to Augusz—your silence will do me honour!

---

[2] See Letter 663 of 29 Nov. 1871.

670. To Princess Carolyne. [Pest] **Ash Wednesday [14 February].** I can't understand how I failed to send you a telegram last Thursday, 8 February —and am reproaching myself bitterly for this oversight. Certainly, my thoughts and my heart are constantly turned towards you, and all but overwhelmed with remembrance of you—but that even increases my faults of negligence. It would almost be better to love you less, and on certain days in the year to make myself a little more lovable! Having sincerely repented and made my confession, let me thank you for the gentleness of your reproach. . . .

You accuse me of going to extremes—and of jumping from Proudhon to Saint Ignatius. As a matter of fact, most of the intermediary expedients have for me only a transitory value; in theory, I incline little to the clever manœuvres which conceal the goal. From time immemorial, the reconciling of liberty and authority has been the great social problem which the legislators, the philosophers, the dreamers, and the lunatics have sought to solve. The ancient Greeks held forth brilliantly on liberty—while the vast majority of the population was formed of slaves. St Ignatius, too, was convinced he ought to grant his disciples the greatest amount of liberty compatible with their salvation—and in America, classic ground of our modern liberties, slavery has been abolished only recently. People have conceived of the idea of freedom of property. All right; but isn't it a bit like Montaigne's 2-handled jug, which everyone pulls from his own side without caring about the jug itself, in the process often broken? For matters political, we arrive, if not at a perfect accord between authority and liberty, at least at a compromise sufficient for them to get along together—but in religion the problem is bristling with difficulties, and seems rather like squaring the circle. Since the divine element necessarily holds sway, it goes beyond outer submission to impose absolute faith, commonly called the faith of the charcoal burner—whose legend contains more wisdom than many big books. It relates that the devil disguised as a hermit entered a charcoal burner's hut one day and, to tempt him, asked 'What do you believe?'—'I believe what the Holy Church believes.'—'And what does the Holy Church believe?'—'It believes what I believe.'. . . .   B.B.

Writing to Liszt from Basel on 17 January, Friedrich Nietzsche had told the composer that he was arranging for a copy of his *The Birth of Tragedy* to be sent to him; and, asking him to be favourably disposed towards the book, had remarked: 'When I look around me for the few people who have grasped with true instinct the phenomenon I have described, which I call Dionysian, it is to you above all that my eyes turn again and again: you in particular must be familiar with the most recondite mysteries of that phenomenon to such a degree that I consider you one of its most remarkable exemplifications, and have observed you time and again with the greatest theoretical interest.'

671. To Friedrich Nietzsche in Basel. Pest, 29 February ^G

Dear Sir,

Unceasing commitments prevented me from writing to you at an earlier date to express my most sincere thanks. Your enthralling book *The Birth of Tragedy* I have meanwhile read twice. In its pages there glows and blazes a powerful spirit which stirred me profoundly. I have, it is true, to admit that I lack adequate preparation and knowledge for a complete appraisal of your work: with Hellenism, and the idolatry which goes hand in hand with it by the men of learning, I have remained somewhat unfamiliar; as the highest spiritual achievement of the Athenians I would extol their erection of the altar 'Deo ignoto'—on which the whole of Olympus was shattered so soon as Paul brought tidings of the *unknown God.*[3] And my eyes do not wander around Parnassus and Helicon; rather does my soul turn unceasingly to Tabor and Golgotha.

Forgive me, therefore, dear Sir, if the admiration I am able to express is rather deficient, but not for that reason meagre or faint-hearted. Your exegeses of the 'Apollonian and Dionysian', of myth and tragedy, truly form what is 'earnest and impressive', doing so with astonishing lucidity and in glorious language. Nor have I found anywhere so beautiful a definition of Art—'the completion and fulfilment of existence leading to a continuation of life'; and expressions like 'A people—as, for that matter, a human being—is worth only as much as its ability to impress upon its experiences the seal of eternity' bring forth an echo from the very depths of one's soul.

God grant that the World's *Whim* and *Woe* be vanquished more and more by *Will.*

With most cordial good wishes I am, dear Sir, yours sincerely,   F. Liszt

672. To Baron Augusz. Weimar, 17 April

Most honoured, dear friend,

I enclose the instructions relating to the Chickering piano, the Erard-Alexandre piano-harmonium, and the toy glass harmonica which is at Bösendorfer's. The Chickering is destined for Szekszárd where, rather like the little pug in the lion's cage (as could formerly be seen in the Jardin des Plantes in Paris), the harmonica will be able to keep it company. As for the piano-harmonium, it will replace, in my study in Pest, the upright Viennese piano, which I would ask you to have returned at once to its rightful owner, whose name is not known to me.

---

[3] Acts 17: 23.

Yesterday I sent off to you a copy of my article on Franz, and you will shortly receive the programmes of the Erfurt and Leipzig concerts which I shall be attending. At Erfurt the *Elisabeth* will be performed, and in Leipzig Berlioz's *Requiem*—a gigantic work composed 35 years ago, but which in Germany has been heard in its entirety on only one occasion, at one of our music festivals in Altenburg, 4 years ago. . . .

The Grand Duchess's birthday was celebrated in a stately way last Monday (8 April). Her sister-in-law, the Empress Augusta, cut a most majestic and gracious figure at the Court dinner (for more than 200 persons), and at the performance of Gluck's *Armide*. She retains her fondness for Weimar, her *restricted* native country, where, in the lifetime of her mother, the Grand Duchess Maria Pavlovna, she used to spend a few weeks every year. Our Hereditary Grand Duke is in Italy with his bride-to-be, daughter of Prince Peter of Oldenburg. . . .

Please give my most affectionate respects to Mme d'Augusz, and a thousand fond regards to Anna, Ilona, and Clara. I wish the two boys the best possible rewards for their work and their merits, while remaining, dear Friend, ever your very sincerely grateful and devoted   F. Liszt

673. To Princess Carolyne. Sunday morning, 21 April. In the whole of this week I have received no letter from Rome. Here, my life is even and regular, without romantic incident. I have twice been invited to the Schloss for dinner—the day before yesterday to a soirée at Herr von Zedlitz's, to which Their Highnesses came too—and yesterday to a talk on metre and rhyme in poetry *chez* Mme la Grande Duchesse, who perfectly possesses the metre and rhyme of her demeanour and her situation. As in previous years, it is agreed that there will be music at my place between 11 and 1 on Sundays. Today the Grand Duke will probably come. . . .

So far as things musical are concerned, I have to tell you of 2 performances I shall attend—on 2 May, the *Elisabeth* at Erfurt, and on the 8th, Berlioz's *Requiem* in Leipzig, for the benefit of our new Beethoven Foundation. The 9th music festival[4] will probably be held in Kassel, between 26 and 30 June, if, as I hope, Monseigneur's influence causes us to obtain from Berlin the bounties which have enabled previous meetings of the same association—thriving despite a certain poverty—to be promoted at Karlsruhe, Meiningen, Altenburg, and Weimar. Between ourselves, this Allgemeine Deutsche Musikverein is the principal reason for my continuing sojourn in Germany. . . . It is something to which I devote

---

[4] Of the Allgemeine Deutsche Musikverein.

time and perseverance, convinced that I am thereby doing good. At Kassel the *Elisabeth* will also be performed, as will various symphonic works by Raff, Rubinstein, Mihalovich, *et al.* On the other hand the advent of the *Nibelungen* in Bayreuth is being asserted resoundingly, multifarious denials and difficulties notwithstanding. On 22 May, Wagner's birthday, the first stone of the new Bayreuth theatre will be laid. On this occasion Wagner will conduct Beethoven's Ninth Symphony, 'Freude, schöner Götterfunken', rendered by an immense number of performers in both orchestra and choruses, which Germany's main cities—Berlin, Vienna, Leipzig, and Weimar—are providing. . . . Many of my best acquaintances in Vienna, Berlin, and Leipzig will likewise be going there enthusiastically —and almost object to my not following their example. But on this subject my mind is made up: I shall not be going to Bayreuth just now. Not far from there, Cardinal Hohenlohe has again very graciously invited me to visit him at Schillingsfürst. . . .

                                                                                    B.B.

674. To Princess Carolyne. Thursday, 9 May, Feast of the Ascension of Our Lord. How could I 'put off' turning my thoughts inward and praying, on learning of the death of Caroline d'Artigaux! She was one of the purest earthly manifestations of God's blessing. Her long sufferings, endured with so much Christian meekness and resignation, ripened her for Heaven. There, she is at last entering into the joy of the Lord—the world's did not touch her at all, and the Infinite alone was worthy of her celestial soul! May God be blessed for having recalled her from earthly exile—and by her intercession may she obtain for us the grace of joining her!

The day before yesterday, 7 May—feast of St Stanislas!—our curate celebrated a Requiem Mass for a deceased lady, one whom I did not know—and who was also called Caroline. At this name, my heart nearly failed me! Another coincidence! Yesterday in Leipzig I heard Berlioz's *Requiem*—a prodigious work, sublime even—but in several places with a different feeling from that which the text of the Requiem inspires in me. The tones which move me most in this gigantic work are found above all in the Offertory, the Sanctus and the Agnus Dei.

Adelheid Schorn came to Leipzig with me yesterday morning—and I brought her back last night. She tells me that she wrote to inform you that the *Elisabeth* made an extremely good impression at Erfurt, last Thursday. The next day, Adelheid and the Helldorfs did me the kindness of accompanying me to Jena, where *Athaliah*, one of Handel's least known oratorios, was very appropriately performed. At my matinée on Sunday, Monseigneur favoured us with his presence. Have I already told you of the sudden death of Princess Hendryk of the

Netherlands, daughter of Duke Bernhard of Weimar? She was barely 43 years
of age. . . . B.B.

At Bayreuth on 22 May the foundation stone of Richard Wagner's Festspielhaus was
laid. Longing for Liszt's presence at this event, Wagner sent him on the 18th an invitation which ended 'Blessings and love whatever you decide!'

Feeling that the time had not yet come for a *rapprochement*, Liszt abided by his decision not to attend the ceremony. However, his gracious and conciliatory reply to the
invitation helped pave the way for the meeting and reconciliation that took place some
months later.

675. To Richard Wagner in Bayreuth. Weimar, 20 May ^G

Sublime, dear friend,

Profoundly moved by your letter, I am unable to thank you in words. But it
is my ardent hope that all shadows and considerations which bind me at a distance will disappear—and that we shall soon see one another again. Then it will
become clear to you, too, how inseparable my soul remains from *both of you*
—living again in your 'second higher life', in which you can achieve what you
could not have achieved alone. Therein I see Heaven's amnesty! God's blessing
be with both of you, as all my love! F.L.

I am more than reluctant to send these lines by post. They will be handed to
you on 22 May by a woman who has known my thoughts and feelings for several years.

It was the Baroness von Meyendorff to whom the postscript referred. 'The letter very
nice', thought Cosima, 'but the woman, unfortunately, very unpleasant. Her manner is
cold and disapproving.' (The two later became quite good friends.)

676. To Princess Carolyne. Weimar, 29 May. On their way back from
the very successful ceremony of 22 May at Bayreuth, Frau von Schleinitz and
Frau Dönhoff did me the kindness of spending a day in Weimar. And here
they ran into Rubinstein, more anti-Bayreuth than ever after the exaggerated
failure of his opera *Feramors*—based on Thomas Moore's *Lalla Rookh*—in Vienna
at the end of April. He attributes this failure to the Wagnerian clique in general,

and in particular to the *Wagnerverein* [Wagner Society] agent who—Rubinstein believes—posted hired booers at the performance of *Feramors*, just like Dingelstedt at the *Barber of Bagdad*. Naturally Rubinstein abstained from going to Bayreuth. Moreover, he had to direct the Düsseldorf *Musikfest*—a respectable and respected occasion, traditionally held at Whitsun. This year's fell 2 days before the solemn ceremony of the laying of the foundation stone of the *Nibelung* theatre in Bayreuth. So now, in Düsseldorf, Rubinstein was conducting his sacred drama *The Tower of Babel* and giving magnificent performances of Beethoven's Concerto in G major, the March from the *Ruins of Athens*, and *Erlkönig*—while in Bavaria was being erected the temple of the twilight gods, *Götterdämmerung*! As a recreation for him, I made the friendly suggestion, and not without some insistence, that he take part in the Kassel *Musikfest*, for which the Emp. of Germany has graciously granted us a subsidy of 1,000 thalers and the use of the theatre. But Rubinstein gave me an obstinate refusal—while protesting his keen and profound friendship for me. In this connection, I recalled that the role of certain friends, highly esteemed by me, consisted in showing themselves ready to render me every imaginable service except the one I had taken it into my head to ask them! 'Habitavi cum habitantibus Cedar.'[5] May the good angels keep you sweet company!

B.B.

677. To Princess Carolyne. 21 June. I have twice been to Ettersburg this last week.

My old bruises have prevented me from speaking to you in detail about the Bayreuth question. Here is a copy of Wagner's letter and of my reply. One always falls in the direction in which one is leaning—God will forgive me for coming down on the side of mercy, while beseeching his and wholly committing myself to it! As regards people, I'm not worried about the interpretation of this page of what you call my 'biography'. The only chapter I had longed to add to it is lacking—and about the remainder I am concerned only in so far as it is reasonable to be! For some months I have from time to time been writing to Cosima. Those of her letters that Bülow and Mme Mouchanoff showed me persuaded me that it was better not to sever all connection with her. When Grosse and about thirty other members of our orchestra departed for Bayreuth, I asked him to give Cosima a copy of *Christus*, which had just been published. She has already thanked me for it.

May the good angels keep you—and guide me to you in September.   B.B.

---

[5] Ps. 119: 5, Vulg.; Ps. 120: 5, BCP and AV: '[Woe is me, that] I dwell in the tents of Kedar!'

678. To Princess Carolyne. Sunday morning, 7 July. I have been feeling an urgent need to write to you ever since my return from Kassel on Monday evening. But your slight delay in replying to the letters I sent you was worrying me—and keeping me in a kind of hesitation. In this connection, allow me to say that you do me wrong in presuming that any occupation or preoccupation whatsoever can prevent me from listening to you with love and respect. Rest assured that in not a single hour of my life do I feel separated either from you or from prayer! Unfortunately my time is dreadfully cut up and sectioned off—letters, manuscripts, and visits rain down upon me from all sides, and I find it more and more difficult to write. If you were here to help me, my labours would be lightened considerably! In addition to my interminable correspondence, I have more than half a dozen pupils here, pianists and composers—Danes, Russians, Americans, Berliners, *et al.* I should reproach myself were I to neglect them totally; consequently, I have to give them at least 6 hours a week. Add to that my work—too limited, alas, for want of time—with various publishers, and you will see that I hardly have leisure for idling. . . . I beg you on my knees to believe firmly that any serious disagreement between us is impossible—and that I endeavour with all my might to become entirely according to the wishes of your heart.   B.B.

679. To Princess Carolyne. Monday, 8 July, continuing from yesterday. My stupid negligence in omitting to send you the photograph of the castle of Wilhelmshöhe[6] I shall put right at the earliest. The building with its façade of tall, thick columns impresses by its size; the grounds are extensive and in noble taste. An air of princely sumptuousness reigns in the rooms, and the fountains, almost as celebrated as those of Versailles, perhaps surpass them in variety of effect because of the structures over which they shoot up and spread out. I took little interest, for my own part, except in the custodian's fairly trivial account of Napoleon III's sojourn here. For want of a chapel, the Emperor had an altar placed in one of the salons and attended mass every morning. The Empress spent a day or two at Wilhelmshöhe; before her arrival she took care to send her husband a splendid collection of parlour games, so that he could keep himself amused whether alone or in company. . . .

May I venture to ask you to have 500 Roman cigars, *forti*, Virginia leaf, sent to my address? They are my sole favourite cigars, and almost indispensable, for it is in their regard that I practise the only jealousy known to me, never offering them to anyone. When, by chance, some ill-advised person asks if he can

---

[6] Castle near Kassel where Napoleon III had been confined after Sedan.

try one, I reply scornfully: 'You are not up to this ideal at a *baiocco* [farthing] apiece!'   B.B.

680. To Princess Carolyne. Weimar, 30 July. Several passages in your last 2 letters need pondering over. I shall try to turn them to good account, despite the difference in our points of view. . . . To your question, whether I go to mass every day, my answer is yes—but as our excellent Hohmann is still unwell, and his curate has been away for about ten days, the church has been closed this last week. I shall go there tomorrow, feast of St Ignatius Loyola. . . . I am morally compelled to give many gifts and alms. My little Weimar household with Pauline and Miska is very costly; I often grumble, but without managing to reduce my expenses. I refrained, for reasons of economy, from going to Leipzig to hear a church concert which interested me—and shall restrict myself to a little trip to Sondershausen, on Sunday, 11 August. The journey takes less than four hours. The Prince and his daughter were kind to me at Kassel—the Sondershausen orchestra continues to take part in all the music festivals that come within my scope, and frequently performs my works. On Sunday's programme appear the Faust Symphony and 2 orchestral pieces from the *Elisabeth*.

I approve with heart and soul the ceaseless continuity of what you call your satires. Won't you communicate some few fragments of them to me—or do you regard me as too inept? Unfortunately I have scarcely any time left to read—however, the amount I give to sleep I shall gladly reduce in order to absorb your thoughts more thoroughly. Do believe and be aware that the physical distance between us does not remove me from you in spirit. It weighs on me a lot, it is true—and sometimes I think of ways of ridding myself of it. When we see one another again, allow me to tell you everything I have on my mind. It will be a general confession, impossible to make in writing—after which I shall serenely await death!

Thank you for everything—and more than everything!   B.B.

681. To Princess Carolyne. Weimar, 'Capoue bourgeoise',[7] Sunday, 8 September. Last Sunday I received a letter from Wagner asking if a visit from him would be an annoyance for me now. Such a question had in no way sprung from any suggestion of mine. Since my response to his invitation to the

---

[7] It is not altogether clear why Liszt—presumably quoting the Princess herself—should designate Weimar a 'bourgeois Capua'. But since the expression *les délices de Capoue* (referring to a winter of luxury and idle living spent in that town by the soldiers of Hannibal) has become proverbial to signify a waste of precious time that could be employed more advantageously, perhaps Carolyne had again been chiding Liszt for not putting his own hours and days to better use.

ceremony in Bayreuth, on 22 May, I had not written a word either to Wagner or to my daughter. In such circumstances I could not refuse him; it would have been contrary to my character—which I do not separate from my conscience! And so I replied that he would always find in my home something worthier of him than a *friendly reception*. The next evening, Monday, Cosima and Wagner arrived here[8]—coming straight from Bayreuth, whither they returned the day before yesterday, Friday. I shall go and join them there for 2 or 3 days—probably for the feast of my daughter's patron saint, Cosmas, this coming 27 September, *en route* to Szekszárd. Bayreuth will take me only 3 or 4 hours out of my way. Before going there I shall enquire if Cardinal Hohenlohe is at Schillingsfürst —and if it suits him to receive me on the feast [29 September] of St Michael, patron saint of his family. If his reply is in the affirmative, I shall spend a couple of days there with him.

On the subject of my daughter, I especially remember your admirable solicitude for my 3 children—and bless you for everything you did for them during the long years of your set-backs and sorrows. Cosima is indeed my formidable daughter, as I called her in days gone by, an extraordinary woman of great merit, far above commonplace judgements, and altogether worthy of the feelings of admiration she inspires in those who know her—beginning with her first husband, Bülow! The enthusiasm with which she has dedicated herself to Wagner is absolute, like Senta's for the Flying Dutchman—and she will be the saving of him, for he listens to and follows her clear-sightedly. The very detailed sketch of *Siegfried's Tod*, last part of the *Ring des Nibelungen*, is finished. It is more than what a cartoon for a painting in fresco would be—because in this draft Wagner has indicated the orchestral combinations. He has now only to write the score at his ease in less than a year, without having to expend new invention upon it. . . .   B.B.

682. To Wilhelm von Lenz in St Petersburg. Weimar, 20 September

Honoured friend,

I owe you thanks in the 24 major and minor keys for your remembrance of me and the glowing style with which you proclaim it to the world. Your booklet[9] incurs one cardinal reproach: that of making me out to be too grand and

---

[8] And stayed at the Russischer Hof Hotel, where Liszt visited them that same evening. 'Wagner met me with a speech which lasted for about twenty minutes,' he told Alexander Siloti many years later. 'There was no one to hear it but his wife and myself. It was a speech I shall never forget. I was so touched by it that I forgot all except the good side in him.'

[9] *Die grossen Pianoforte-Virtuosen unserer Zeit* (Berlin, 1872), with chapters on Liszt, Chopin, Tausig, Henselt.

too fine. I confess, without any false modesty, that I am far from deserving such praise; but since it has pleased you to bestow it upon me, I can but bow in silence—and shake your hand.

No one possesses less than I the talent of communicating in writing; and the necessity of receiving more than a hundred letters a month (not counting notes and numerous deliveries of manuscript or printed works which I am obliged to read) likewise makes correspondence more than difficult for me. . . . Besides, most of the things which are readily said are of no importance to *me*, at least, and for those which I should like to say our everyday language does not suffice. . . .

What wit, sallies, and flashing sparks in your *Quartet* of Pianist-Virtuosi!— Let us not forget the etymology of the word 'Virtuoso', how it comes from the 'Cicerone' in Rome—and let's return to Chopin, the enchanting aristocrat of the most refined magic. Pascal's epigraph, 'one need not live on it; merely use it like perfume', is appropriate only to a certain extent. Let us breathe in the perfume and leave to the druggists the bother of making use of it. You exaggerate too, it seems to me, the influence on Chopin of the Parisian salons. His soul was not in the least affected by them, and his work as an artist remains transparent, marvellous, ethereal, and of an incomparable genius—far removed from the errors of a school and the twitterings of a salon. There is in him something of the angel and of the fairy; still more, the heroic string, which has nowhere vibrated with such grandeur, such fresh passion and energy as in his *Polonaises*, which you brilliantly designate 'Pindaric Hymns of Victory'.

No need to tell you that I entirely share your admiration and liking for Tausig and Henselt. . . .

Allow me to be especially grateful to you for a most understanding remark in your booklet (page 4)—'es war *thematisch*'—and accept, dear Lenz, the expression of my old and most cordial devotion.   F. Liszt

Are you in contact with musical *young* Russia and its very notable leaders: Messrs Balakirev, Cui, and Rimsky-Korsakov? I have recently read several of their works; they deserve attention, praise, and to be made known.

683. To Marie von Mouchanoff [Weimar, September]. You know that Cosima has always been a good part of my inner light. She gave me great joy by coming to Weimar with Wagner on 2 September—and I shall soon see them again in Bayreuth.

The monument of Germanic art, *Der Ring des Nibelungen*, is all but completed by the composition of *Götterdämmerung*, which Wagner showed me. All that remains for him to do is to write down the full orchestration; a great deal of work without doubt, but something he will easily be able to do in less than a year, seeing that the main orchestral combinations are settled and already noted in the sketched piano score.

However gigantic be the totality of this *œuvre* of the *Nibelungen*, it is its harmonious proportions and sustained sublimity that I admire above all. Down the centuries, in the realm of the fine arts in general, human genius has seldom manifested itself in analogous fashion. By the autocracy and vitality of its inspiration, Michelangelo's Sistine Chapel would perhaps be the closest term of comparison. . . .

Yours in full admiration and respectful affection.   F. Liszt

684. To Princess Carolyne. Schillingsfürst, Wednesday, 9 October.

Leaving Weimar on Saturday, I stopped for almost 2 days in Eisenach at the invitation of Their Royal Highnesses, with whom I spent the evenings of Saturday and Sunday at the Wartburg. Frau von Werthern, wife of the German minister in Munich, was there, and told us about some of the whimsicalities of the King of Bavaria. He has already created a lake in the winter garden of the Munich palace—His Majesty goes boating on it, catching colds from this exercise. To warm himself, he has just given orders, it is said, for a Vesuvius with eruptions ad lib to be erected in the middle of some picturesque site or other. That seems to me to be a charitable invention of some salon wit, and I mention it to you only with great reservations, for, as far as the King of Bavaria is concerned, I by no means side with the sneerers—quite the contrary. His poetic fancies—or peculiarities, if you like—are very innocent peccadilloes in a young man like him. If people aren't a little more tolerant and don't make so much of them, spite and other bad ingredients are chiefly responsible. To sit alongside the mockers is not to my taste—mockery is like pepper: it should be used only in moderation!

The day before yesterday, Monday, I spent the night at Ansbach. The Cardinal had asked the proprietor of the Stern Hotel to hand me at the station a few lines bidding me welcome to Schillingsfürst. To get here from Ansbach takes 3 hours by carriage. Having arrived yesterday at about midday, I plan to stay until Sunday. The Schloss is more spacious and looks larger than I had expected. It stands on rising ground, and the view extends over several leagues of countryside. . . . The Cardinal occupies the ground floor, and has given me accommodation near him. The library also serves him as a dining-room—mental and material nourishment all together! On the second floor are the guest rooms; on the first, those reserved for Pce Chlodwig and his wife. The latter has little liking for Schillingsfürst, and prefers to spend the summer in her villa at Aussee in Styria. His Eminence is in perfect health and spirits. . . .

Towards the end of the week I shall probably accompany him to Schloss Langenburg, a 4-hour journey from Schillingsfürst. Its châtelaine has just died —Princess Feodora, who, as sister of the Queen of England,[10] lived for a long time in that country. Her daughter, Feodora, Duchess of Meiningen, died so sadly last winter. Queen Victoria and the Empress Augusta wrote beautiful letters of condolence to Langenburg.   B.B.

685. To Princess Carolyne. Golden Cross Hotel, Regensburg, Tuesday morning, 22 October. Regensburg being on my route from Bayreuth to Vienna, I stopped here yesterday, to spend today, 61st anniversary of my birth, in tranquillity. I had intended to take communion this morning—but not seeing a single confessional in the cathedral, and not wanting to cause any bother in the sacristy, I confined myself to hearing mass, and to praying for you with all my soul. The day after tomorrow, I shall go to the Franciscan Church in Vienna to confess and to take communion. My devotion to St Francis leads me so far as always to prefer a friar of his Order to confess to. . . .

I stayed in Bayreuth from Tuesday until yesterday morning, Monday. Wagner is living temporarily in a rented house and having one built which will be his own property, the money to pay for it having been provided by the King of Bavaria. The town looks noble and pleasant—2 royal palaces—2 statues: King Maximilian and Jean Paul. Many fine houses dating from the beginning of the last century—a beautiful garden, the Schlossgarten—and the theatre, rococo style, very sumptuous, about which Frederick the Great reproached his sister[11] sharply for her extravagance. The sole Pce of the blood who now has a residence in Bayreuth is the Duke of Würtemberg, widower of Pcss Marie d'Orléans, Scheffer's pupil. He is said to be almost a misanthrope—he is cultivating a very beautiful park around his Villa Fantaisie, and has remarried morganatically.

The foundations of the new *Nibelung* theatre are beginning to rise—and Wagner societies are multiplying in Germany. The very extraordinariness of this

---

[10] Princess Feodora of Hohenlohe-Langenburg was the half-sister of Queen Victoria (same mother, different father). In the voluminous correspondence of the two, Liszt had been mentioned on at least one occasion—in Nov. 1864, when Feodora told the Queen of an enjoyable drive 'to the Monte Mario . . . where at present Liszt lives, retired from the world'.

[11] The celebrated Margravine Wilhelmine.

undertaking will probably make it succeed—despite criticism and censure, gossip and difficulties! Wagner leads a very retired life. Exceptionally, however, on Thursday evening he decided to invite about a dozen people[12]—among them the Regierungspräsident, the Dean, the Principal of the Gymnasium, the Burgomaster, and the *Nibelungen* banker, Herr Feustel. The last-named is a very important personage, recently appointed Minister of Finance in Munich, and wholly devoted to the work of the *Nibelungen*. The other days and evenings we remained completely alone, just the three of us. The 5 children dine separately—they are perfectly brought up and singularly charming. Cosima surpasses herself! Let others judge and condemn her—for me she remains a soul worthy of the *gran perdono* of St Francis and admirably my daughter!

Here, I have seen Witt and Pustet again; Haberl, now Kapellmeister at the Cathedral, is away. The Golden Cross Hotel is famed for its association with Charles V, who stayed here in 1544—the following year the hotel proprietress, Barbara Blomberg, gave birth here to Don John of Austria. The room in which I am writing to you bears his name and has several pictures and relevant autographs.   B.B.

686. To Princess Carolyne. Horpács, at Ct Imre Széchényi's, 29 October. The sketch of Wagner's *Parsifal*[13] that he read to me recently is stamped with the purest Christian mysticism. To admire the last scene of the second part of *Faust* and to excommunicate *Parsifal*, which, as it seems to me, is at least equally elevated in its mystical inspiration, would be a strange contradiction. I even admit that several of our poets, deemed religious and Catholic, make on me the impression of remaining well on this side of Wagner's religious feeling.

I rejoice at your new chapter on the beatitudes of Eternity, among them Art, added to the volume *De la matière*. Allow me, however, sometimes to feel nostalgia for the period of our close collaboration in Brendel's modest newspaper: our articles on Franz, Schumann, Berlioz, Chopin, Meyerbeer, our disputes over literary requirements, etc., etc. Destiny has not allowed us to continue this useful and honourably militant joint task. Your soaring has carried you away to sublimer regions—and I have remained alone in the rocky valley of ordinary, everyday Art. Your help therein, your aid, whose loss I feel, I often seek in my

---

[12] For Friday, according to Cosima's diary. 'In the evening my father plays for the people and captivates them all. Richard proposes a toast: "Noble spirit and good Christian, long live Franz Liszt!"'

[13] The première of this last of Wagner's music dramas took place in Bayreuth on 26 July 1882.

thoughts—while resigning myself and admiring you from the bottom of my heart. May God bless your chosen path!   B.B.

I was forgetting to tell you about Horpács, a very pleasant château,[14] in no particular architectural style, at the end of a village. Széchényi compares his property here to a ham—the château being situated at the end of the bone. There is a very well kept chapel, in which Count Széchényi's chaplain says mass every day at 8.30. Raiding is only a short distance away—perhaps I shall make an excursion there.

687. To Eduard von Liszt in Vienna. Horpács, 6 November ^G

Dearest Eduard,

My stay here has been prolonged a little, and I shall not be getting to Pest until next Sunday.

Széchényi's residence here is most decidedly pleasant and pleasing, and totally peaceful. In the private chapel the chaplain (an educated and estimable priest) celebrates mass daily. To our table conversation an old family doctor, Dr M., contributes a good deal. Among other delightful things he said, 'No one has yet understood what cholera is, apart from myself who have at last fathomed its *nature*. And its nature consists solely ... in *cholera* itself!'

The day before yesterday Széchényi, Mihalovich, and I went in under two hours to Raiding. A Herr Wittgenstein (probably an Israelite), who lives in Vienna, is now the leaseholder of this Esterházy property, which he sublets. To the house where I was born no marked alterations have been made since my last visit 24 years ago. The villagers recognized me immediately, came to the inn to pay their respects and, when we left, rang the church bell. . . .

All affectionate greetings to you and yours—from your devotedly attached

F. Liszt

I shall be seeing Augusz in Pest-Ofen.

Give Bösendorfer my friendly greetings and at the same time my praise for the excellent piano here which I have played a little.

If Zumbusch comes to Vienna, commission at once, as we arranged, a bust of me in marble and a pedestal for Bösendorfer.

---

[14] Years later an occasional guest at Horpács was the cellist Heinrich Grünfeld: 'There, which was counted an outstanding distinction, my accommodation was the Liszt room—that in which the celebrated Abbé had always stayed during his visits to Horpács. It was still crammed with all possible Liszt mementoes, and also contained a piano on which he used to play' (*In Dur und Moll*, Leipzig and Zurich, 1923, 157).

688. To Princess Carolyne. Horpács, Saturday, 9 November. Today I wish to write you a pile of contestations—affectionate ones! I contest your right to forbid me to admire you in telegrams, in letters, and in any way I please! Admiration is one of the soul's noblest feelings, and the most lacking in selfishness, of which a few particles often mingle even with self-sacrifice. We admire the heroes, the saints, the geniuses, the wonders of nature and art—and so on to God in His works. Why not allow me to admire you very sincerely with all my heart and with complete conviction? . . . B.B.

689. To Princess Carolyne. Pest, 11 November. To make a good start to my life here, I am writing to you and returning thanks for a score of things I am coming upon in this apartment: the carpet with the talisman, the volumes of yours, the large Roman portrait of you, etc.

We left Horpács with Mihalovich at about 5 o'clock yesterday and arrived here this morning. At 10.00, I went to my parish church, St Leopold's, to hear mass and to pray to God to grant me the joy of making you a little more satisfied with me. Today is the feast of St Martin [of Tours], a saint who belongs to Hungary by his birth—and to France by his episcopate. The oldest abbey, I believe, and the most celebrated in Hungary is the Benedictine Abbey on Martinsberg—which some day I propose to visit. In the office for today can be found this beautiful invocation to St Martin: 'O ineffable man whom work did not crush and whom Death was not to conquer—who neither feared to die nor refused to live! His eyes and his hands were ever lifted to Heaven, and his unwearying spirit did not cease to pray.' To cut our cloaks in two, to share them, as did St Martin, with the poor, is hardly one of our customs. People more readily cut a piece from someone else's cloak, to patch up their own! However, I am far from believing that charity is dying out in this world, where so many good works and beautiful things continue to be achieved. In opposition to incessant political and social lamentations, I maintain *stoutly* that we are better than people say, often even wholly good. . . . B.B.

690. To Princess Carolyne. Pest, feast of St Elisabeth, 19 November. . . . I hope that 'les bons Bessons' will together be able to attend the performance of Wagner's *Nibelungen*—a colossal and sublime work which, as you say, will do honour to its century. In fact, the German Emperor, the Grand Duchess Helena, Mme Meyendorff and your daughter have subscribed generously to the

Patronatsscheine;[15] likewise the Sultan, for 3,000 thalers! But, so far, the German Empress, Their Royal Highnesses of Weimar, Queen Olga of Würtemberg, and many of their august cousins, male and female, are refraining from so doing, not without some ill will towards the project itself. I shall send you the critical and psychological article by Hanslick that you have heard mentioned—which demonstrates, on the strength of a paper by a Munich psychiatrist, that Wagner has been attacked by a very well-known monomania: pride in oneself. Would this not be a desirable counterweight to another monomania still more prevalent and widely accepted—pride in one's stupidity?!

I shall take note of your hygienic recommendations. Moreover, I repeat to you that here, and even in Buda, the cholera is very mild, and people of good sense are not in the least afraid of it.

With all my heart,   B.B.

691. To Princess Carolyne. 27 December. It grieves me to write to you so little. Today, however, my conscience is not too bad, for I have written several pages of music this week. Now, you know that to express myself through letters is not easy for me—I attempt it only in certain hours, of which I always need several to stitch together forty lines or so. The fault lies in my very neglected early education—and in the long years of my anti-literary habits. I write to you as I pray and work: conscientiously, slowly, and with humility. Kindly take account of this frailty of my nature, which worsens with age. Perhaps I am more to be pitied than condemned! Besides, nobody is less acquainted with leisure than I— my days and years are wasted in not finding the hours I would seek! The happiest of my hours is now that in which I kneel near a few poor old women in my parish church, St Leopold's, or in the Franciscan Church, during morning mass. Lighting my *cerino*, I share it with my neighbours with a royal joy—while blessing the gentle yoke and light burden of Our Lord Jesus Christ.

The evening of Christmas Eve I spent *en famille* at the Auguszes'. No other guest but myself. . . .

The little packet of proofs, supplement to your work on *La Matière*, has not reached me. 'Art in Eternal Life' is a topic I have not dared catch a glimpse of until now. Nevertheless, what you reveal of it I shall endeavour to understand with the heart! . . .

Frau von Dönhoff will shortly be going to Rome to visit her mother. When you see her, ask her to play you an Etude by Tausig in *A flat*, dedicated to Mme Mouchanoff, which she makes a thing of marvellous poetry.

---

[15] Literally 'patronage certificates', whereby subscribers contributed to the cost of building Wagner's Festspielhaus.

Did you read in the *Revue des Deux Mondes* of 15 December the *conte fantastique* by Mme Sand, *Les Ailes de courage*?[16] It is more than charming, beginning with the dedication to her grandchildren—whom she calls on to interrupt her when they do not understand, reserving the right to explain herself in spoken words, which are always clearer than written ones! B.B.

---

[16] The correct title: La Mara has, erroneously, *Les Ailes du courage*.

12 January. Liszt plays, and works of his are performed by others, at a soirée in the Hotel Hungária.

March. He takes part in several other concerts in Budapest.[1]

2 April. He arrives in Vienna, where he stays at the Schottenhof with Eduard von Liszt.

Easter Day, 13 April. He attends a performance of the Gran Mass in Pozsony Cathedral.

29 May. In Weimar's town church Liszt conducts the first complete performance of *Christus.* Among those present are his daughter and son-in-law, Cosima and Richard.

Spring. Vincent d'Indy is introduced to Liszt and spends several months in Weimar.

23–6 June. Liszt is the Grand Duke's guest at Dornburg.

6 July. He attends a performance of the *Missa choralis* in Leipzig.

26 July–5 August. He stays in Bayreuth with the Wagners.

7 September. At a court concert given as part of the celebrations for the wedding of the Hereditary Grand Duke, Liszt plays his arrangement for piano and orchestra of Weber's Polonaise in E and his own Fantasia on Hungarian Folk Themes.

4 October. Liszt arrives in Rome where, on the 13th, he has a private audience with the Pope.

30 October. He returns to Budapest and a new residence in the Fish Market (Hal tér 4).

8–10 November. Celebrations are held to commemorate the fifty years which have passed since the Vienna concert (April 1823) at which Liszt's public career was consecrated by Beethoven. The chief event is a performance of *Christus,* conducted at the Vigadó on the 9th by Hans Richter.

WORKS. ORCHESTRA: Arrangement (S353) of Egressy and Erkel's *Szózat, Hymnus* (Vörösmarty and Kölcsey), 2 patriotic songs. PIANO: No. 3 of *Fünf kleine Klavierstücke*; *Fünf ungarische Volkslieder* (S245); transcription (S486, based on S353) of Egressy and Erkel's *Szózat und ungarischer Hymnus.*

692. To Princess Carolyne in Rome. Pest, 10 January.

Napoleon III is dead![2] Magnanimous heart, all-embracing intelligence, experienced wisdom, gentle and noble character—and ill-starred fate! He was an impeded, trammelled Caesar—but one that was quickened by a breath of the divine Caesar, ideal personification of the terrestrial Empire! In '61, in a rather long conversation we

---

[1] In January Buda and Pest were united to form the new name of the capital.

[2] He had died at Chislehurst, in Kent, where he was buried. His remains were later removed to St Michael's Benedictine Abbey, Farnborough.

had together, Napoleon remarked: 'I sometimes feel as though I were more than 100 years old.'—'Sire, you *are* the century,' I replied.

Indeed, I honestly believed then, and still do, that Napoleon's government was the one best suited to the needs and progress of our time. He set noble examples and accomplished or attempted great deeds: amnesties which were more complete than in any other reign; the rebuilding of Paris, Marseilles, Lyons, Brest, etc.; the wars in the Crimea and Italy; the protection of the Catholic Church in Rome and in all other countries; the great Paris Exhibition and the impetus given to more specialized exhibitions in the provinces; the active attention paid to the lot and interests of the rural and working classes; gifts and grants to scholars, writers, and artists—all these things are historical facts in which Napoleon not merely participated but often initiated and carried out, difficulties notwithstanding. They are not wiped out by the final disaster that befell him, terrible though it was! When the day of justice comes, France will bring back his coffin and give it a place of glory beside that of Napoleon I in the church of the Invalides! Until then, the Prince Imperial's accession to the throne seems most unlikely. The memory of Sedan weighs more heavily than that of Waterloo! It would need a miracle—and the young Napoleon is not like the Comte de Chambord, who himself remains outside his kingdom 'l'enfant du Miracle'.[3] One of the little sovereigns ousted peacefully remarked with *humour*: 'It seems we are no longer wanted. Henceforth, without too much inconvenience, we need only do without the peoples who so gladly do without us.' Without playing the courtier one can say that throughout his life the Emperor practised those all but synonymous sovereign virtues: goodness, kindness, liberality, generosity, magnificence, munificence! Among the fine character traits of Napoleon III that have often been remarked was his steadfast, scrupulous, and ingenious gratitude towards those who had done him some service. In all sincerity and humility, I endeavour to imitate him on this last point—and I begin with Napoleon himself, by blessing his memory and praying for him to the merciful God who allows nations to recover from their wounds.   F.L.

693. To Princess Carolyne. Pest, 6 March. Yesterday evening I received your latest letter, and at once reply to your question about my will. I am expressing in it my desire to be clothed, in my coffin, in the habit of the tertiary order of St Francis. It is my last homage to the great Saint who carried out his apostolate as a 'madman' of the Cross—and finished by obtaining from the Pope

---

[3] Referring to the fact that the Comte de Chambord, the Legitimist claimant to the throne of France, had been born after the murder of his father, the Duc de Berry.

the *gran perdono*, solemnized by the Church. Those who may be with me at the moment of my death I shall enjoin to cover my sorry remains in this vestment of St Francis. I shall also ask that I may be spared the honours of an ostentatious funeral. If possible, let me be taken to my last resting-place in the obscurity of evening—2 or 3 hired men will suffice to carry me. I should not like to trouble others to follow me to the cemetery—where I shall no longer be able to serve them!

694. To Cardinal Hohenlohe at Schillingsfürst. Vienna, 15 April

Eminence,

With all gratitude for the remembrance Your Highness deigned to express to me so affectionately on 2 April, I today make bold to join with my very humble thanks a few musical items, as directed in your letter.

With Beethoven, the choice is embarrassing—one runs a great risk of erring in preferring this or that work of his to others; *prudence* (a cardinal virtue) dictates that we embrace the whole; so I am sending Your Eminence the Complete Works of Beethoven for piano solo in the best edition yet published: that of Cotta—prince of publishers in Germany, as Didot is in France. In view of Bülow's notes and commentaries, which form a course of practical aesthetics, superlatively instructive and interesting, this edition far surpasses all its predecessors.

To the five Beethoven volumes I am adding two books of Beethoven's and Schubert's *Geistliche Lieder*, plus an *Ave Maria* written at the Villa d'Este, one which is sung in several churches in Germany.

When I have the honour of returning to Schillingsfürst, I shall bring other little works of mine, to which I shall ask you to grant the hospitality of your library.

My excellent friend Augusz is elated at your commendation of his Szekszárd wine, of which he yesterday dispatched to you a second supply, of superior quality.

This evening I return to Weimar, where I shall stay until the end of July.

Deign to accept the homage of sincere gratitude with which I have the honour ever to remain Your Eminence's affectionate servant, F. Liszt

695. To Princess Carolyne. Weimar, 17 May. Let us speak about the

title of your latest work.[4] To me, I admit, it seems almost rash; but since I have no competence in such a subject, I rely on your wisdom, which will not have neglected to seek similar enlightenment from trustworthy sources. It is under-

---

[4] Carolyne's *Causes intérieures*. (See Biographical Sketches.)

standable that the quest for the '*inner causes of the exterior weakness of the Church*' does not nowadays seem advisable to many personages highly placed in the Holy Father's confidence. They think, rightly, that regulating and determining the affairs of the Church belongs exclusively to them. Since you have in addition the misfortune to be a woman—it will be necessary, should the occasion arise, to submit to the role of silence assigned to your sex by Saint Paul.[5] The compliments of the salon and verbose civilities notwithstanding, the ecclesiastical authorities observe the same maxims. St Catherine of Siena spoke out, as before and after her a few other learned and holy women have done. You follow their example with admirable ardour and devotion. I hope that they will duly be recognized and that the Vatican clouds will disappear. But were it unfortunately to turn out otherwise, you can only submit and obey humbly, because this is the first duty of Catholics, one which can be neither altered nor evaded!

Have you noticed that this year, 25 May, feast of St Gregory VII, will be celebrated solemnly in France? The Holy Father has sent a special prayer for this purpose to the Bishop of Montauban, if I am not mistaken. . . .   B.B.

696. To Franz Servais in Hal. Weimar, 5 June

Dear Monsieur Franz,

My best wishes accompany you 'into the cage'.[6] You do well to enter it, and if the flight of your genius is momentarily rather impeded by the bars of counterpoint and fugue, it will soar all the more splendidly afterwards. I hope you will emerge from your cage crowned in glory. In case of mishap, don't grieve bitterly; cleverer and more valuable people than you and I, dear Franz, have had to exercise patience and go on doing so. When he said 'genius is patience',[7] M. de Buffon was wrong only in that he made an incomplete definition, taking the part for the whole; but that part is absolutely necessary in the practice of art, as in that of earthly life.

Be so good as to remember me very affectionately to your mother; give your brother a handshake from me—and always be assured of my feelings of fond affection.   F. Liszt

---

[5] I Cor. 14: 34–5: 'Let your women keep silence in the churches: for it is not permitted unto them to speak. . . . And if they will learn any thing, let them ask their husbands at home: for it is a shame for women to speak in the church.'

[6] On Liszt's advice, Servais was about to enter the competition (held in July) of the Brussels Prix de Rome—which he won—and writing to Liszt had perhaps jocularly described the *loge*, or separate room in which each of the candidates had to remain while preparing his work, as a 'cage'.

[7] Referring to the definition, attributed to Buffon, 'Le génie n'est qu'une grande aptitude à la patience' (Genius is nothing but a great aptitude for patience).

697. To Princess Carolyne. Weimar, Sunday, 29 June. From Monday to Thursday I stayed at Dornburg. Monseigneur's birthday, on Tuesday, was spent *en famille*. There were only the Court staff strictly necessary, 7 or 8 people— plus a deputation from Jena and Dornburg, and I myself. In the evening, Mme Milde and 3 of the theatre artistes sang Goethe's little rococo opera *Erwin und Elmire*. The dining-room had been prepared for this purpose. No stage, nor any décor other than plants and roses, but the four actors were in costume, and Lassen accompanied them at the piano. The rooms graciously allotted to me were those used by Goethe, who lived in them again in 1828 for a couple of months, and left in them a few words pencilled on the window sill. I humbly allowed myself to write to Magne on the old desk bearing this inscription: *Goethe's Secretär.* . . .

God bless   B.B.

698. To Princess Carolyne. Bayreuth, 1 August. Cosima has invited me to a little party for the men working on the *Nibelungen* theatre. It was to have been held last Saturday; but as Feustel the banker, principal personage of the administration of the whole undertaking, has had to go away on urgent business, the party has been postponed until tomorrow, Saturday. I shall attend it, and think it good to show in this subsidiary way the interest I am taking in the complete production—as per the majority of its author's altogether exceptional intentions—of the most extraordinary, and in my opinion most sublime, work of art of the century. Wagner has heroically finished composing it—all that remains for him to do is to orchestrate the 4th part, *Götterdämmerung*. The construction of the theatre is going forward—more than 200 workmen are toiling on it. Nearly half the sum necessary for the advent of the *Bühnen-Festspiel* has been collected—about 130,000 thalers; the estimated cost is 300,000. To determine subsequent measures, Wagner will shortly be summoning here the patrons of his work. I am sending you the report containing the theatre plans, recently published by Wagner. Simultaneously with his theatre, Wagner is erecting his admirably situated house,[8] adjoining the Hofgarten. He will be living in it by next spring—the King of Bavaria has given him 20 or 25,000 thalers to build it. Cosima and Wagner even wish to remain there, united in the grave—which has already been dug and consecrated at the entrance to the garden.

I hope to find a letter from you at Schillingsfürst—plus a few proof sheets.

B.B.

---

[8] Named Wahnfried ('Freedom from Illusion').

Yesterday we drove to the Hermitage, a charming park and Schloss half an hour from Bayreuth. M. de Voltaire appeared there as an actor, in his tragedy *Oedipus*, before the Margravine and her brother, Frederick the Great. Last Sunday, the Archbishop of Bamberg administered communion in the Catholic church here. I attended his mass, on Monday.

699. To Princess Carolyne. Schillingsfürst, 7 August. . . . Yesterday the Cardinal was so extremely gracious as to come as far as Ansbach station to meet me—$3\frac{1}{2}$ hours by road from Schillingsfürst. After an excellent lunch at the Star Hotel in Ansbach, and a stroll in the Schlossgarten, where King Ludwig I had a little memorial placed in memory of the murder of Caspar Hauser, we arrived here at about five o'clock. . . .

Yesterday evening I read the first fifty or so pages of your *Causes intérieures*, about which the Cardinal addressed a sensitive and sympathetic eulogy to me. With my admiration is mingled a little amazement—and even, dare I say it, fear. The work's very title, a striking and well-found one moreover, gives me some disquiet. Perhaps, by that, I am liable to the reproof that Our Lord Jesus administered to a disciple: 'O thou of little faith, wherefore didst thou doubt?'[9] I shall read, line by line, the 1,277 pages of your 2 volumes, and will then speak to you about them, very humbly, at full length. Hohenlohe has already told you that I take his approval to be from the general point of view. Permit me to observe that, in my opinion, the distribution of your book should be done only with much prudence on your part—consequently it is advisable for you to limit yourself to a small number of dispatches and letters to this end. Although your name does not appear on the title-page, people know the work is by you. . . .

The day before yesterday, Tuesday, Cosima, Wagner, and the 5 children accompanied me as far as Bamberg, from where they went on a short trip into Franconian Switzerland.

May the good angels continue to be your collaborators!   B.B.

700. To Princess Carolyne. Schillingsfürst, 8 August. I am advancing with a kind of terror in the reading of your *Causes intérieures*, but with trust in the guide! To your question as to whether Wagner is already working on *Parsifal*, I reply that he had earlier done only the draft of this poem. Before he has finished

---

[9] Matt. 14: 31.

the orchestration of *Götterdämmerung* and proceeded to the performance of the *Nibelungen* in Bayreuth, it would be rather unreasonable for him to busy himself with another work. M. Auber and other illustrious composers could easily produce works by the dozen—this is not the case with Wagner, be it said to his glory. Respond in the same manner to the inquisitive idlers, usually ill-willed, who question you on this topic.

Hohenlohe will be writing to you shortly.   B.B.

701. To Princess Carolyne. [Weimar] Sunday, 31 August. I shall be in Rome in a month. It is much too late for me, but because of the *Festspiel* at the Wartburg, on 21 Sept., I can't set out until 25 or 26 September. . . .

How very distressing for you those thefts must have been! After the large-scale lootings of which you have been a victim, one could have hoped you would be spared little domestic pilferings of that sort. . . .

I have written to Hohenlohe about your volumes, which he had given me as a present. They singularly provoke reflection, and above all controversy! In view of my slowness as a reader, it will take me a few weeks to finish these 2 volumes. To tell the truth, I would prefer not to send them back to Hohenlohe—for, as is my silly habit, I have marked several passages in pencil, and to remove all traces of them would be a bit of a job. . . . As for an indiscretion or even a negligence on my part in such a matter—I can affirm in good conscience that such things are quite out of the question. Among my numerous faults, I could not be reproached with that of causing trouble unnecessarily for anyone other than myself—and all my imprudences I reserve exclusively for my own use! And so do not fear either a display of your books in my sitting-room, or any chit-chat or nonsense about them! Further, I shall submit to your order not to bring them to Rome—while not in the least understanding what would be irrational in that. What is beautiful about obedience is to practise it out of faith —without understanding the reasons!

To give you complete information on the royal marriage,[10] I enclose the official newspaper for you. As soon as the programmes for next Sunday and Monday appear, the concert at the Schloss and the gala performance, you will receive them. . . . Monseigneur came to see me yesterday to talk about the arrangements relating to the festivities. The Empress Augusta is expected, and people say the Emperor will come too.   B.B.

---

[10] At Friedrichshaufen on 26 Aug. the Hereditary Grand Duke Carl August had married his cousin Princess Pauline of Saxe-Weimar, daughter of Prince Hermann (a son of the late Duke Bernhard).

702. To Princess Carolyne. Vienna, Sunday, 26 October. Instead of 48 hours, as the timetable indicated, the journey here from Rome took me 56. My second-class ticket did not allow me to take the fast train at Nabresina, and my sense of economy objected to paying the balance for a first-class ticket. So I arrived at 6 this morning, safe and sound—with no other incident *en route* than a meeting with a Franciscan lay brother at Mestre. The poor fellow had already been waiting at the station for several hours and seemed dejected. I chatted with him for a while about Assisi and Padre Marcellino, whom he knew, and invited him to supper. He declined, saying that as it was a Friday he was obliged to a fast and a *magro stretto*. Probably his purse was reduced to a *magro strettissimo*—but I tried to inspire confidence in him. Without further discussion I took him by the arm and into the restaurant, where he was served sardines, wine, an apple, and coffee. This little meal of which I was merely a witness, having already supped an hour earlier, gave me enormous pleasure. Even the proprietor's rather excessive bill—4 francs instead of 2—did not trouble him, and I was more than happy to settle it. Throughout the journey I was almost always alone in the compartment, my company being a few books and Miska, very silent with me. About a hundred pages of the *Causes intérieures*, Nietzsche's essay on Strauss,[11] and Dumas's preface to *Faust*, made these 2 days short and very interesting for me. . . . B.B.

703. To Princess Carolyne. [Budapest] Tuesday evening, 11 November. Everything went off very well—our festival[12] was a total success, from A to Z. . . .

I enclose 3 or 4 newspaper articles, one of which criticizes *Christus* in a way that strikes me as three-quarters laudatory—for the main reproach is that this work is Catholic. My response to that is that I composed my oratorio about Christ as I was taught about Him by my village priest and by the Church of the faithful, the Roman, Catholic, and Apostolic one—but that I would neither have known how, nor wished, to compose a work about the Christ of David Strauss.

You know already that the GD Constantine* telegraphed me to inform me of my nomination as an honorary member of the Imperial Academy of Music in Petersburg, of which he is President. The telegram from Their Highnesses of Weimar reads: 'In loyal remembrance and gratitude, and most cordial participation, we all send the fêted Master our good wishes for today's festival. Sophie,

---

[11] *David Strauss, der Bekenner und der Schriftsteller*, published that year.   [12] Celebrating Liszt's jubilee.

Carl Alexander.' The hereditaries also telegraphed me—as did the Grand Duchess of Strelitz, née Princess of Cambridge,[13] whom I had the honour of seeing in London from time to time before her marriage. The telegram in verse, signed Cosima and Richard Wagner, was read out at the banquet by Monseigneur Haynald; it was much applauded, and I shall send it to you in printed form. I received about a hundred congratulatory telegrams,[14] and almost as many letters.

On Sunday, 23 November, the day after St Cecilia's Day, the Gran Mass will be performed in Pozsony Cathedral for the second time. I have promised to go there for it and to spend a couple of days in Pozsony. In my reply to Monseigneur Haynald's toast, after which the medal was presented to me *coram populo*, I almost fulfilled your wish that I should say that I am the author of *Christus*, by saying more or less this: 'I thank God for having granted me a pious childhood. The same religious feelings inspire my compositions from the Gran Mass to the work you heard yesterday. It was thus that in complete sincerity and simplicity I was able to enter the Vatican, as you know,' etc. On some opportune occasion I shall come back to this essential point in my life. . . .   B.B.

704. To Princess Carolyne. Pest, 19 November. The Church today celebrates St Elisabeth, who is also your patron saint. This morning I besought her glorious prayers for the two of us—in order that we may scorn the false goods of this world, and ever rejoice in celestial consolations!

Your latest telegram follows your old habit of inventing merits for me! May I make this task less and less difficult for you! The sole quality I recognize as good in myself comes entirely naturally to me—a great need of truth. Hence my constant practice of sincerity, which has gained me the reputation of being a man of trustworthy character. Many a time have I said and written things similar to those you liked in my response to Monseigneur Haynald's toast. I had begun to make a draft of my little speech—but when the moment arrived, I spoke from an abundance of heart, without bothering about either the effect or the phraseology. It seems, however, that I made a good impression—and even several newspapers which usually praise only my talent as a pianist vouch that I displayed neither vanity nor ridiculousness. I do not know who is the author

---

[13] Augusta, elder daughter of the late Duke of Cambridge, had married the now reigning Grand Duke of Mecklenburg-Strelitz in 1843.

[14] Including one from St Petersburg signed by, *inter alios*, Balakirev, Borodin, Cui, Mussorgsky, and Rimsky-Korsakov: 'A group of Russians, devoted to art, believing in its everlasting progress and aspiring to participate in this progress, warmly greet you on the day of your jubilee. As a composer and performer of genius who has broadened the boundaries of art, as a great leader in the struggle against the old and routine, as an indefatigable artist before whose immense and lasting achievements we bow.'

of the *Dresdener Journal* article enclosed with this letter—it draws attention to the words about my entry into the Vatican. A French newspaper, *Le Danube*—whose correspondent is equally unknown to me—finds that I am totally unaccustomed to giving speeches, but states that everyone was deeply moved. . . .

Now, allow me to address a request to you—it will accord, I hope, with your own wish. On 9 November, when receiving the golden laurel wreath, offered to me in the name of Hungary, I at once declared that I considered it given to me only on trust, and that I intended it to take its place in the National Museum in Budapest, as a symbol of the country's noble generosity towards those who are devoted to it. To this wreath I wish to add 4 or 5 objects kept in your furniture-repository in Weimar. These are: the splendid gold conducting baton you gave me—I shall take care to have a label attached, with your name and the date of the gift; the piano given to Beethoven by the London firm of Broadwood, bearing the signatures of Ries, Cramer, and Moscheles, with the name of Beethoven inscribed above the keyboard; the solid-silver music rack which, at the Altenburg, was placed on Beethoven's piano—this rack, begun at Vienna in '46 or '47 by means of a subscription, was not finished until several years later; the little golden goblet given to me at Pozsony in 1840 by Countesses Batthyány, Károlyi, Széchenyi, Esterházy, *et al.*, whose names are inscribed on the goblet; and my Pest sabre. You have told me several times that in your opinion these objects should be given to the Museum. That was very much my intention too—I was only waiting for a suitable opportunity, and a more favourable one than the present could not be hoped for. So I should not like to delay further—and if possible hand over my gifts to M. de Pulszky, Director of the Museum, before the end of the year '73.   B.B.

On Sunday I paid a formal visit to the Prince Primate in Esztergom. He received me with great kindness and affability; on Monday evening he and I returned alone in the carriage, which gained me the advantage of a very instructive conversation of 3 to 4 hours.

705. To Princess Carolyne. Pest, 27 November. A letter from Magne, received the day before yesterday, tells me that after Gotha she spent 4 days in Weimar, wept in the garden of the Altenburg, visited the Hofgärtnerei—and that in the absence of their parents the hereditaries invited her to a soirée. The day before yesterday, too, Pce Constantin very kindly came to see me, and we chatted for a good quarter of an hour. Tomorrow morning, I shall go to His Majesty's audience, to congratulate him on the 25th anniversary of his reign. Since settling here in '71 I have not had the honour of speaking to the Emperor, and not seen him except at my concert last year, which he very exceptionally favoured with his presence. For the evening of the day after tomorrow Pce Constantin has had me invited to the Court reception, in the Palace of Buda. The Vienna concert for the benefit of the *K. Franz Joseph-Stiftung* [Emperor Franz Joseph Foundation] will take place in a fortnight. Yesterday a deputation from Vienna, announced the previous day by a telegram from the burgomaster, came to ask me if I would put my modest pianistic talent to use by taking part in this concert. I replied as I did to the first overture made to me about it by Albert Apponyi, before my visit to the Archbishop of Esztergom—that for me it was a matter of duty and honour. Indeed, short of suffering paralysis of the hands, I cannot get out of setting them in motion on such an occasion. It would be a strange way of recognizing the kindness shown to me by His Majesty, in honouring me with an honorary stipendium of 4,000 florins a year—to refuse to play a couple of pieces in Vienna, on behalf of the *Franz Joseph-Stiftung*! . . .   B.B.

I am delighted at the good result of your portrait by Hébert—its success is unquestionable, seeing that both you and he are satisfied with it, for neither of you is someone who is contented easily!

706. To Princess Carolyne. Pest, 2 December. At the Court reception on Saturday, in Buda, there were about a thousand men—the fair sex was represented exclusively by the Empress and her ladies-in-waiting. It was noticed that she deigned to speak to me most graciously. After the reception, Pce Constantin invited me to supper in his Chief Comptroller's rooms in the palace. About a dozen people gathered there: Count Andrássy, his 2 brothers, Pce Paul Esterházy, Pce Lobkowitz, *et al.*, and just one lady, the young Countess Festetics, a spinster, lady in waiting to the Empress. The piano did not stand idle, and I played several pieces with pleasure—beginning with the *Szózat* dedicated to Count Andrássy, about which he has written me a very kind note of thanks. . . .

                                                                              B.B.

I have just this moment received your letter of 24 to 27 November. The idea of the dialogue poem[15] by Longfellow, of which the Strasbourg bell-tower is the chief character, I find uncommonly appealing. For my 1874 New Year's gift make me a present of this poem, with a preliminary French or German translation—for I can scarcely understand the vile prose in English. It is quite impossible for

---

[15] *The Golden Legend*, the Prologue ('The Spire of Strasbourg Cathedral') to which inspired Liszt's *Die Glocken des Strassburger Münsters* (The Bells of Strasbourg Cathedral), composed the following year.

me to write any music before next year. All my time is taken up in dealing with letters, and in irremediable civilities—which my trip to Vienna will hardly reduce! As for the brevity of such a composition, I am by no means convinced of it. You speak of it with much greater ease than I shall have in writing it—trifle though you may think it!

707. To the Grand Duke Carl Alexander in Weimar. Budapest, 21 December

Monseigneur,

Goethe observes that to value oneself at less than one is worth is a great fault. Would I have committed it in thinking that Your Royal Highness would hardly notice the lack of a letter from me?

I have just written to HRH the Grand Duchess, to ask her to pardon the delay of my thanks in gratitude for Your Royal Highnesses' very gracious telegram on the occasion of my jubilee celebrations in Pest. Weimar was nobly represented there by the Intendant of your Theatre and his Kapellmeister, Baron Loën and Herr Lassen. At the very impressive ceremony of the presentation of a document from the town of Pest, and of addresses and wreaths, the speech pronounced by Baron Loën met with a most sympathetic reception, as did his toast at the next day's banquet.

Jena was also represented with great distinction by a poem in excellent Latin (praised by the experts here), and my sole regret is that these festivities of so exceptional and lofty a character could not be attended by my steadfast friend Gille. . . .

You will soon be receiving the two *Ave Maria* (for harp) the dedication of which you have been pleased to accept: the first, composed by Arcadelt in the sixteenth century; the second, by your humble servant—both of them excellently transcribed by M. Dubez, *kaiserlich königlicher Hofharfenspieler* [Imperial and Royal Court Harpist], formerly in St Petersburg and for some years a resident of Pest, where he is one of the five or six virtuosi greatly applauded at the theatre and in concerts. Your Royal Highness decorated him *of old* with the Weimar medal and ribbon, which he wears in his buttonhole. Permit me to remain invariably

Your faithful servant   F. Liszt

1874

8 January. Liszt arrives in Vienna where, at a charity concert on the 11th, he plays two works with orchestra: his Hungarian Fantasia and transcription of the Wanderer Fantasy.

15 January–17 February. He is the guest of Count Imre Széchényi at Horpács, and on 12 February plays at a charity concert in Sopron.

18 February–17 May. He remains in Budapest, with occasional visits to other towns.

16 March. At a soirée organized by the Hungarian Society of Authors and Artists, Liszt accompanies the singer Róza Laborfalvi in the first performance of his *A holt költő szerelme* (The Dead Poet's Love), a melodrama for voice and piano.[1]

19 April. Liszt plays, and his *Beatitudes* are performed, at a charity concert in Pozsony in which Sophie Menter also takes part.

21 May. He arrives in Rome, and soon takes up residence at the Villa d'Este, his headquarters until the following February.

WORKS. *Die heilige Cäcilia* (St Cecilia) (S5), a legend for mezzo-soprano, chorus, and orchestra. *Die Glocken des Strassburger Münsters* (Longfellow) (S6), for mezzo-soprano, baritone, chorus, and orchestra. *Elegie* (S130), for cello, piano, harp, and harmonium (plus versions for cello and piano/violin and piano). SONGS: *Ihr Glocken von Marling* (E. Kuh) (S328); *Und sprich* (Biegeleben) (S329). The melodrama *A holt költő szerelme* (S349). PIANO: transcription (S479) of Bülow's song *Tanto gentile e tanto onesta.*

708. To Princess Carolyne in Rome. Pest, New Year's Day. As usual, I spent the evening of New Year's Eve with the Augusz family, in Buda. When I returned home about half an hour after midnight, the telegraph messenger pushed under my door the telegram from 'Gregorio'—which expresses the supreme wish of my heart: that we once again live together! I pray to God to grant it.

In your last letter you again speak of my *Christbaum.*[2] I hope to publish it by next Christmas—and also the other little work of which I have for long been thinking: *Via crucis.* I shall need only 6 weeks of outer tranquillity to finish writing both of them. They will be no means be works of learning, or of display, but simple echoes of the emotions of my youth—these remain indelible through all the trials of the years!

---

[1] Roza's husband, the great novelist Mór Jókai, had written this poem about Petőfi especially for Liszt to set to music.
[2] A suite of piano pieces, eventually entitled *Weihnachtsbaum.*

I have omitted to tell you about a literary and musical soirée given last Monday, 29 December, by my friend Ábrányi. He read an excellent Hungarian dissertation on the right of nationality in music—and naturally claims this right for Hungarian music, the development of which has corresponded with other progress achieved in this country. At the end of the session I played 3 Hungarian pieces: *Puszta-Leben* by Mosonyi, whom you met in Weimar in days gone by; a Nocturne in Hungarian style by Ábrányi; and my transcription of a theme from Mosonyi's opera [*Szép Ilonka*]. The audience was very numerous, very well made up, and in the mood to applaud. Next Monday, 5 January, in the Vigadó's small hall, the Liszt Society will sing the jubilee cantata composed for me by Gobbi. My Psalm *Super flumina* will be on the same programme—and Mr Pinner, a young American pianist newly arrived here, will make a contribution —successfully, I hope. . . . Their Majesties are residing in Buda at present, until mid-January. The Emperor's journey to Petersburg has been postponed until much later—the Empress will go to Munich in about a fortnight, for her daughter's confinement. Happy New Year, dearest Gregorio! B.B.

709. To Princess Carolyne. At Count Imre Széchényi's, Horpács near Sopron, Friday, 16 January. Got here yesterday, at 5.30, after a journey of 6 hours. The *Neue freie Presse* articles on Sunday's rehearsal and concert I dispatched to you immediately. Eduard will send you some other articles, in particular the one written by Ambros for the official *Wiener Zeitung*, which I haven't had time to obtain—and will add to it those appearing today about Bösendorfer's soirée on Wednesday, at which I played 3 or 4 little pieces. . . .

At the Augarten on Wednesday morning I saw Magne and her husband again. The latter came to the Bösendorfer soirée, and was most amiable. The previous day I had been in his box at the performance of Schumann's *Genoveva*. My visit to Vienna offers no other incident than my little success as a pianist, which people say was a very complete one. The best echo of it you will find in the article by Ambros. If he avoids mentioning my Church compositions, the *Elisabeth* and *Christus*, he nevertheless ventures to say that the *symphonische Dichtungen* [symphonic poems] should not be totally rejected—and praises unreservedly my talents as orchestrator and transcriber, as also the Hungarian Rhapsodies. I thanked Ambros very sincerely for his eulogies, and am persuaded that he would willingly go further—did circumstances not constrain him to show prudence. It is one of the cardinal virtues which, in certain cases, must hold sway over the others, and even impose silence on them!

In the evening of the day before yesterday, when returning home, I found the third part of your *Causes intérieures*, which it was necessary to take out of bond. What a volume—1,149 pages! It formulates an entirely new constitution for the Church. When you were 15, I believe, you had written a constitution for Poland—may your recent work bear fruit more speedily! In the mean time, I say each day the *Veni Creator*[3] for the 'bisogni interni della Chiesa [internal needs of the Church]'—and this evening will begin reading Chapters III and IV, on the principle of election and the principle of nomination.

Although people are finding in general that I look well—and even going so far as to praise my persistent youthfulness—I feel extreme mental fatigue, and hope that I shall here be granted a fortnight's rest. . . . B.B.

710. To Princess Carolyne. Horpács, Friday, 23 January.[4] Perhaps it would be wise of me to keep silent about several points in which I venture not to be of your opinion—but the art of exchanging letters without saying anything to one another has not yet been invented! It is repugnant to me to tell you lies, or to write to you in the rather meaningless way that I do often enough to other people—and so all that remains to me is to vex you more often than I would wish. . . . There is no point in my saying to you once again that several of your ideas strike me as unsound. . . . Despite all my efforts, I have not so far succeeded in seeing in contemporary events an essentially Christian, and specifically Catholic, movement! Nevertheless, in reading the 3rd volume of your *Causes intérieures* I admire from the bottom of my heart your great militant spirit, while following it timidly and not without some terror. . . . B.B.

711. To Princess Carolyne. Horpács, 9 February. On completing my reading of your superb and sublime letter of the 2nd to the 5th, I come to you with a full heart. However feeble and stuttering my words, I cannot refrain from telling you at once of my rapturous gratitude. You protest against the word gratitude, in such a way as to make me feel twice as much! Once more, the 18 pages of your letter are superb and sublime. I bow down in thought before the loftiness of your sentiments and of your intelligence. This time, I have to contradict you only on the too great and glorious share you give to my weak

---

[3] *Veni, Creator Spiritus*, a hymn to the Holy Ghost which is sung at Whitsun vespers and on certain solemn occasions. Its authorship is usually attributed to the 9th-cent. abbot and bishop Rhabanus Maurus.
[4] Dated 22 Jan. in La Mara's edition—but Friday was the 23rd.

genius—whose works you glorify, while exaggerating their worth! Yes, dear holy Carolyne, I am a sincere believer and man of religion, and shall remain so to my very last breath. Believe me, accordingly, when I say that I pursue neither decorations, nor performances of my works, nor eulogies, distinctions, and newspaper articles, anywhere at all. My sole ambition as a musician has been, and will be, to hurl my spear into the undefined void of the future. . . . So long as this spear be of good quality and fall not back to earth, the rest is of no importance to me whatsoever! . . . I kiss your hands.   F.L.

712. To Princess Carolyne. Pest, Ash Wednesday, 18 February. I am delighted that my last letter, written with flowing heart and pen, gave you pleasure. Your pages from 6 to 12 February reached me at Horpács, late on the eve of my departure. The description of Schack's conversation and readings couldn't be more amusing. On some suitable occasion, ask his *alter ego*, Gregorovius, about the tragic story I've heard. Schack* is said to have been very much in love with a beautiful young woman, who suddenly died, a few hours before the wedding. It is to this that people attribute the rather singular—in the best sense of the word—direction his mind has taken. The idea of using an excerpt from my Dante Symphony as incidental music to his *Pisans*[5] is certainly an ingenious one. However, I ask you to give no further thought to it, for the outcome would be agreeable neither to the author of the *Pisans* nor to me—because of the present musical situation in general, and that of compositions adapted for tragedies in particular. It needed all the great weight of the name of Beethoven for people—after long years—to get into the habit of using his *Egmont* music in performances of the tragedy. The great success of the Overture at concerts came long before admiration for the complete *Egmont* music in the theatre. Meyerbeer wrote the most remarkable of his overtures and several excellent pieces for his brother's tragedy, *Struensee*.[6] Since that play is hardly ever performed, the music is almost unknown. Mendelssohn carried off the apple with his *Midsummer Night's Dream*—but here again, as with *Egmont*, it was the success of the Overture at concerts that assured its belated performance in the theatre. These considerations would not prevent me from writing an overture, entr'actes etc. for any tragedy whatever—if something came along that excited my very sluggish imagination. . . .

---

[5] Adolf von Schack's five-act tragedy *Die Pisaner* (1872), concerning the Pisan historical characters—above all Ugolino and Archbishop Ruggieri—immortalized by Dante (*Inferno*, xxxii. 124–39 and xxxiii. 1–90).

[6] Michael Beer's drama about the ill-fated Danish statesman, first performed, long after Beer's death, in Berlin, Sept. 1846.

Mme Dönhoff, whom Imre Széchényi had earlier invited to spend a few days at Horpács, came to the Sopron concert with Lenbach and Herr von Wartenegg. *La graziosissima contessa ed i suoi due cavalieri serventi* [The most gracious countess and her two gallants] visited Horpács on Saturday, and returned to Vienna on Sunday evening. I arrived in Pest at 6.00 this morning, in the company of Albert Apponyi and Mihalovich. . . .   B.B.

713. To Princess Carolyne. Thursday morning [Budapest, 19 February]. Apponyi dragged me off yesterday evening to *King Lear*, performed by an Italian company whose principal actor is Rossi. He has recently been very much praised in Vienna, and his success here is complete. Knowing nothing of the dramatic art, I refrain from expressing an opinion—and simply gave myself up to the poignant emotions of Shakespeare's drama, remembering above all the passionate emphasis with which you used to recite 'Blow, blow!'[7] . . .

714. To Princess Carolyne. Pest, 5 March.[8] Yesterday evening's concert has made me 3 days late with you. I needed to spend several hours practising scales and brushing up old pieces. The success of the concert was total. Rarely, in Pest, has there been so brilliant and so numerous a gathering. Monseigneur Haynald was in the front row—his health has improved. I undertook to remember you affectionately to him, for we run into one another fairly often—either at concerts or in the 2 or 3 houses that I cultivate as an old friend: those of Augusz, Karácsonyi, and even Leó Festetics. Otherwise, I visit hardly anyone, unless for some trifle or other. My intimacy with Apponyi is increasing, and the same with Mihalovich. They come and see me daily, and since our sojourn together with the Széchényis at Horpács, we call ourselves—the Three Horpácsists! Apponyi is the pearl of the young members of the aristocracy here—very serious, not boring, full of information, talent, and personal charm. . . .

Last week I sent you Nohl's latest volume, *Beethoven, Liszt und Wagner*. I am not urging you to read it. Magne very graciously accepted the dedication. A woman of learning and merit, Fräulein Ramann, a disciple of Brendel, consequently *aufgeklärt* and a rationalist, has just published an essay of more than 100 pages on my oratorio *Christus*. You are not obliged to read it—for your siege is done, and

---

[7] *As You Like It*, II. vii. 174. Liszt was probably thinking of 'Blow, winds, and crack your cheeks!' (*King Lear*, III. ii. 1).

[8] Dated 8 Mar. by La Mara, but the charity concert of the previous evening to which Liszt refers took place on the 4th. Full details of Liszt's activities in Budapest, and elsewhere in Hungary, in the last seventeen years of his life can be found in Dezső Legány's *Ferenc Liszt and His Country 1869–1873* and *Ferenc Liszt and His Country 1874–1886*.

perfect! Fräulein Ramann runs a thriving piano school in Nuremberg, where I am invited to give a concert for the Germanic Museum, the glorious foundation of our good-hearted acquaintance Aufsess, so bizarrely killed as the result of mistaken identity![9] What an irony of fate, that in Strasbourg the *Freiherr von und zu Aufsess* should be considered a suspicious Frenchman! . . .   B.B.

715. To the Grand Duke Carl Alexander in Weimar. Pest, 20 April

Monseigneur,

I have just spent two days in Pozsony, and on my return, this morning, I found your very gracious letter telling me of my promotion in the Order of the Falcon.

In bowing with gratitude before this further token of your goodwill, I remember that this decoration was the *first* I received. His Royal Highness the Grand Duke, your father, awarded it to me in 1841, and was also so kind as to promote me, some ten years later.

I have never considered decorations as items of dress (as several very decorated personages affect to call them), but very much as marks of honour corresponding to the degree in which services, talents, and merits are recognized, notified, and awarded from above. Now, for a long time, Monseigneur, I have interpreted the motto of your order, *Vigilando ascendimus*, in the Christian sense that 'every perfect gift is from above'—*Omne donum perfectum de sursum est*—and that one must draw near it by the assiduous practice of one's duties, by reflection, and by work.

Frederick the Great used to say: 'One should make a pleasure of one's duty.' This pleasure is not frivolous; it involves strictness, and sometimes resignation and sorrow. No matter; Frederick's remark strikes home and suits the valiant: Your Royal Highness will permit to abide by it His very grateful and faithful servant,

F. Liszt

716. To Cardinal Hohenlohe. Pest, 27 April

Eminence,

The day before yesterday, feast of St Mark and ninth anniversary of my admission into Your Eminence's residence, I particularly remembered all your kindnesses to me. The one which you are so good as to grant me by sheltering me

---

[9] Seventy-one years of age and unwell, Aufsess was staying in an hotel in Strasbourg when, because of a misunderstanding, he was violently assaulted, and as a result died not long afterwards.

yet again in your rooms (with the monogrammed doors) of the Villa d'Este, is for me *una grande consolazione*. I hope to find there once more a few months of peace and tranquil work, without *incommodo* for anyone, even Mgr. the Bishop of Tivoli, whose obsequious *lapsus linguae*, 'l'incommodo era mio [the inconvenience was mine]', deserves a place in an anthology of anecdotes.

On about 15 May I shall be leaving for Rome, and plan to take up my quarters at the Villa d'Este before the end of that month. . . .

Be so kind as to believe me unwaveringly Your Eminence's

very grateful and faithful servant,   F. Liszt

717. To Princess Carolyne. Monday morning, 27 April. . . . Annoyingly, some visits that I could not put off, and the dispatch of 2 or 3 urgent letters, have prevented my writing to you these last 2 days. In the evenings, after about 8.00 or 9.00, I am no longer fit for anything, unless it be to do some rather mixed reading. Most recently I have read the 3 short volumes of Victor Hugo's *Quatre-vingt-treize* and half of the *Lettres d'une inconnue à Mérimée*;[10] and the day before yesterday I let myself be tempted by *La Tentation de Saint Antoine*. It is a most extraordinary work, stupefyingly vivid and erudite. They say that Flaubert, of whose works I had not hitherto read a line, spent 25 years in elaborating and perfecting it.

No one more than I has felt the accuracy of this aphorism of Chamfort's: 'Celebrity is the punishment of talent and the chastisement of merit.' And so it was with good reason that my daughter wrote to me: 'I have long understood that the only service to render you is to leave you alone.' Among other things I am invited: to Cincinnati, to direct a music festival next month, and for this purpose to stipulate any sum I like; to Düsseldorf, to attend the performance of *Elisabeth* on 5 May; to Brunswick, so that I don't miss the next music festival, at which several of my works will be performed; to Vienna, Prague, Dresden, etc., etc., for various charity concerts to be graced by my strumming. I have, of course, declined everywhere. Forgive me this wearisome enumeration, and let's talk of something else! . . .

Very tired in body, but *valentissimo* in morale.   B.B.

---

[10] Evidently a *lapsus calami* for Mérimée's *Lettres à une inconnue*, a selection of which had been published—and read by Liszt—in the *Revue des Deux Mondes* of 1 Dec. 1873. Early in 1874 the complete letters had come out, and it is to these that he refers. The 'unknown woman' of the title was Jenny Dacquin.

718. To Princess Carolyne. Pest, Sunday, 3 May. Because I went out 1 or 2 days too early, the cold I had in Vienna and Pozsony took hold of me again—its only inconvenience is that it is rather boring. Since Thursday I have remained in my room, and shan't leave it until the day after tomorrow. . . .

Give me news of your new apartment. In Rome, I shall ask you to introduce me to Herr von Keudell,[11] whom I know only by his great reputation, in which music, too, has an accessory part. We have 2 points of admiration in common: Schubert and Robert Franz—in favour of whom Herr von Keudell made the very generous gift of 1,000 thalers. You tell me that he has transcribed for piano, with typical perfection, Schubert's Quartet in D minor, and that he plays it so that the 4 instruments can be heard with the tone peculiar to stringed instruments. I should be grateful if you would prevail upon Herr von Keudell to let me hear this beautiful work—and if you would assure him of the genuine interest I shall take in it, as well as of my sincere eagerness to appreciate his widely recognized talents and merits as a musician. Needless to add that if it were his intention to dedicate the Quartet to me,[12] I should be most honoured.

719. To Princess Carolyne. Villa d'Este, 5.00 p.m., Monday, 8 June.
A few newspapers and St Priest's book kept me pleasant company during the 4-hour journey from Rome. Having arrived at the olive grove, I made my way to the Villa on foot, in a beautiful sunset—tranquilly thinking back on many things. For many years the belief that the end of my life will be a good, sweet one has been familiar to me. It does not grow weaker, and I am far from treating it as illusory. May I only finish my journey while fighting the good fight and serving the faith! For the moment, it suits me extremely well to stay here at the Villa d'Este. Everything pleases me here: landscape, atmosphere, trees, bells, rooms, memories—and there is nothing in any of them to bother or disturb me! This morning I enjoyed arranging my books and music on the shelves; soon I shall reread *St Stanislas* and set it to music. Before mass at the Franciscan church adjoining the Villa, I entered the sacristy (where I was at once cordially recognized) to consult the little book showing the feast-days. St Philip Neri's has been transferred this year from 26 May, Whit Tuesday, to today, 8 June. So I began by invoking the patron saint of Rome, of the Oratory and of oratorios! He did not disdain music, and took a pious interest in musicians; so I find it a good augury that here, where I propose to follow more profoundly his intentions relating to the oratorio, the first music I heard was on his feast-day.

May the good angels assist you in your work, and give you strength! B.B.

---

[11] German Ambassador in Rome and a gifted amateur musician. [12] He did.

720. To Baron Augusz. Villa d'Este, 13 June, feast of St Antony of Padua.

My most cordial congratulations on your name-day, very dear Friend. This morning Padre Luigi, an old Franciscan of my acquaintance, said mass expressly for you at St Antony's altar in the Franciscan church adjoining the Villa d'Este, and, as I often do, I prayed for you, Tony, and your dear family. For 18 years, since the Gran Mass, August 1856, you have remained not only one of my best friends, but one of my benefactors too, considering the notable part you have played in various circumstances, all to my advantage. The independence of ingratitude being totally unknown to me, I feel happy to remain deeply and devotedly grateful to you. I have been residing here since Sunday evening [7 June]. The previous day, the Holy Father deigned to admit me to a small audience in the Vatican, and to give me his blessing. He seemed completely recovered from a slight indisposition which lasted only two days. He and Cardinal Antonelli have not left the Vatican since Rome became capital of Italy [1871]. . . .

My peaceful retreat at the Villa d'Este will probably be prolonged until the moment of my return to Pest in mid-January. No visitors have come to disturb me this week; with the exception of the *custode*, Signor Ercole (whose great-grandfather and his descendants have carried out the duties of custodian of the Villa), and of 2 old servants of Cardinal Hohenlohe, no one other than myself is in residence here at present. So I am living very much to my liking, quite alone, reading and writing. My sitting-room contains the Bösendorfer piano I had in Pest; it will serve me more in the summer than in the winter. I very much reckon on giving my fingers some exercise, but not my legs, and up to now I have not even gone down into the beautiful garden. My morning walk to the Franciscan church, and a few strolls around the long flat roof (beside my room), where a magnificent panorama of the Roman Campagna can be enjoyed, with the Dome of St Peter's and the thin line of the sea on the extreme horizon, are amply sufficient for my ultra-moderate need of locomotion. Bülow arrives here the day after tomorrow. His two astonishingly striking and *mordant* articles, published in the *Allgemeine Zeitung* (28 and 31 May), about the first performance of Glinka's opera (Russian) and Verdi's 'Requiem-festival' in Milan, have incensed a number of Italian journalists. Their hail of printed bullets will not trouble Bülow very much; he will bear it as cheerfully as the earlier ones in Munich and Berlin, where a verb has been invented in his honour: 'Die Critik wurde gebülowt!'

Affectionately yours, F. Liszt

721. To Princess Carolyne. Villa d'Este, Sunday, 14 June. I have never expected or desired any position or title whatsoever in Rome. If the Holy Father had put me in charge of the Papal Choir, I would have accepted with veneration for his kindnesses and out of obedience—and with the idea, perhaps erroneous, of rendering some service to religious art, but with no illusion about the fatigues and difficulties of such a task. Not to have them imposes no cross on me; on the contrary, it lightens the one I bear. Accordingly, I have no renunciation to practise in this matter, and, my inner freedom long being fully assured, I am dispensed from the bother of seeking what I already possess! Foot stamping and recriminating in sterile regrets are things absolutely contrary to my character. I know them only by hearsay—and no one in the world could reasonably reproach me with them, nor detect them in my words and doings. Once again, I have no reason at all to complain of anyone in Rome—but rather am well content with the graciousness and goodwill that several people have there shown, and continue to show, to me. Besides, I am not unaware of this judicious maxim: 'To pity oneself is ridiculous, to make oneself pitied is contemptible!'

Doubtless one can lie to oneself, just as one can lie to others—but were I to do such a thing, it would be as unknown to me as against my will! I call as witnesses numerous persons of my acquaintance who can attest that I apply myself constantly, scrupulously, and at times painfully, to telling the truth—to the point of eschewing even the little fibs that are the convention in good society. So I never decline an invitation on the ground of indisposition, unless I really am indisposed; and even at the risk of appearing gauche and ill-mannered I should have scruples about offering a false excuse. From your nephew Eugène Wittgenstein, who is himself a witty artist in little fibs, this pedantry has earned me the ironic title: the Friend of Truth. And so, as always, I am telling you the truth—were I in the confessional I could not do otherwise! . . . In 14 years, my entire activity has been restricted in Germany to 4 or 5 concerts given by the Allgemeine Deutsche Musikverein, which I more or less founded and do myself the honour of supporting—the Gran Mass in Paris and Amsterdam, not conducted by me; the *Elisabeth* in Pest and at the Wartburg; *Christus*, fragmentarily in Rome and Vienna, in its entirety in Weimar; plus ten or a dozen piano recitals, for the benefit of charitable organizations in Rome, Pest, Vienna, Sopron, and Pozsony. It is generally known that I have refused 50 other invitations. Without aspiring to soar like the eagle or the bird of paradise, I am keeping quiet here below, while hoping in the beyond! Allow me therefore to protest humbly, sorrowfully at your wrong judgement! From the depths of my heart I remain your loving and devoted   F. Liszt

722. To Princess Carolyne. Villa d'Este, Friday, 19 June. . . . Nothing could be simpler than my life here. It suits me perfectly—but I wouldn't know what to say about it, in view of its absolute tranquillity. As usual, in the morning I go to mass—then I read or write until lunchtime. This is served to me at 1 o'clock under the arcade of the flat roof, from where I enjoy the grandiose panorama of the Roman Campagna, with the dome of St Peter's on the extreme horizon. After lunch, a siesta for an hour or more—then I again read, write, and play the piano, until a cold supper at 9.00. Since my arrival no visitors other than Bülow—and, the next day, his 3 acolyte pianists, Sgambati, Buonamici, and Pinner, who took him back to Rome on Tuesday evening.

Ever your F.L.

723. To Hans von Bülow. Villa d'Este, 26 July

Dear unique one,

You overwhelm me. After the *Buch der Bücher—Geist und Welt* etc. which you discovered in Rome and asked Pinner to bring to me, you now favour me with Ida and Otto v. Düringsfeld's excellent *Proverbes des langues germaines et romanes*. These two books will henceforth have a permanent place on my table, being indispensable to my inner well-being. Like Sancho Panza, I have always had a taste for proverbs, adages, maxims, aphorisms, mottoes; thanks to you, I shall be better instructed in the wisdom of nations—reserving the right to derive only an intellectual and philosophical profit therefrom. But Pythagoras himself protested against the title of *sage*, and would allow only that of philosopher, which has also become very ambiguous. In this connection, I remember that Raff used at one time to dream of the *Pansophos*:[13] residence, Wiesbaden. . . .

D.S. has talked a lot about Dante and published a volume of dialogues about him.[14] Better than she, have you been inspired by the sublime poet in the sonnet *Tanto gentile e tanto onesta pare*:[15] a ravishing jewel of music, dedication of which is bound to make the Contessa Giulia Masetti very proud. For my part, I couldn't resist the temptation to transcribe it for piano, which I did yesterday. I shall send this sheet of paper to London for you, by our friend Bache, who has promised to visit me here in September.[16]

Affectionately yours,   F. Liszt

---

[13] Used by Homer to describe the extreme cleverness of Odysseus, this word might here be translated 'All-Wise One'. Raff lived in Wiesbaden 1856–77.

[14] For Daniel Stern's *Dante et Goethe* (of which a German translation by Bülow's daughter Daniela was published in 1911), see under d'Agoult in Biographical Sketches.

[15] One of the best-known sonnets in the *Vita Nuova*.

[16] Walter Bache saw Liszt in Rome and Tivoli in late August and early September, as he wrote enthusiastically to his sister Maggie: 'He is the *same as ever*, although he was last winter completely broken down by the fearful work and

724. To Princess Carolyne. Villa d'Este, 26 August. I expected a few words from you, and am uneasy at having received none. Are you perhaps unwell —or have I committed some new misdeed? If you do not send me a line, I shall not dare to come to Rome on Saturday as I was planning. The day before is the anniversary of the death of my father. On his death-bed, at Boulogne-sur-Mer, he told me that I had a kind heart and did not lack intelligence—but that he feared my life would be troubled, and I dominated, by women. Such a prediction was remarkable, for at that time, aged 16, I knew nothing about women, and naïvely asked my confessor to explain God's 6th and 9th commandments to me, fearing that I had perhaps broken them unwittingly. Later, my *amours* began only too sadly—and I resign myself to seeing them finish in the same manner! Even so, I shall never abjure Love, for all its profanations and false pretences! . . .

Antonio tells me he has received good news from the Cardinal. At the moment water is being brought back to the dried-up fountain in the courtyard of the Villa d'Este. My time passes rapidly, and I am very content with my retreat— so much so that I should like to prolong it for the rest of my life! B.B.

725. To Baron Augusz. Villa d'Este, 18 December. We know that life is only an apprenticeship for death. Nevertheless, the lessons given us by the death of our friends is an overwhelming one. This year I have lost three: Mme Mouchanoff, Cornelius, and Rosty. I rather envy than pity them. Mme Janicsáry wrote to tell me that until his very last moments Rosty was asking for the Benedictus from *our* Gran Mass, and that she and her daughter had it performed for him while he was dying! . . .

See you *chez vous* on 10 February. Very affectionately yours, F. Liszt

bothers of Pest: his teeth are going a little, and this sometimes slightly affects his pronunciation; but this is the only difference I notice. He played a great deal to me—several hours every day—as *magnificently as ever*; as Bülow said, all the pianists are "dumme Jungen" as compared with him!' (Constance Bache, *Brother Musicians*, 237).

11 February. Liszt arrives in Budapest.

3 March. His *Prometheus* choruses are performed at the Vigadó by the choir of the Liszt Society, the piano accompaniment being provided by Liszt and his former pupil Antal Siposs.

10 March. A Liszt–Wagner concert, attended by the Wagners, is held at the Vigadó. On the programme are Liszt's *Die Glocken des Strassburger Münsters* (its première), Beethoven's *Emperor* Piano Concerto, played by Liszt and conducted by Richter, and excerpts from Wagner's *Ring des Nibelungen*. Present at the rehearsal (9 March) of the Concerto is Count Albert Apponyi, who later recalls 'the perfection of the impression, or rather the impression of perfection, which one received from Liszt'.

15 March. At a charity concert in the small hall of the Vigadó, Liszt plays Weber's Sonata in A flat, Chopin's Polonaise in C minor, the Second Hungarian Rhapsody, and *Les Patineurs*.

30 March. Agoston Trefort, the Minister of Education, presents Liszt with his appointment as President of the new Hungarian National Academy of Music, to be opened later in the year.

April. After a week in Vienna and several days in Munich, Liszt returns to Weimar, which is his base until September.

23 April–1 May. Staying in Hanover with the Bronsarts, he attends a performance of *St Elisabeth* on the 24th, and the following day plays the Variations on *Weinen, Klagen, Sorgen, Zagen* at a concert to raise money for the Bach monument in Eisenach.

1–12 May. He is the guest at the Palace of Loo, near Apeldoorn, of King Willem III of Holland, who decorates Liszt and presents him with 'a magnificent writing-set in Egyptian alabaster and onyx'.

17 June. At the Tempelherrenhaus in Weimar, Liszt takes part in a concert in memory of Marie Mouchanoff.

29 July–17 August. Liszt stays in Bayreuth with the Wagners and attends rehearsals of Wagner's *Ring*.

3 September. He attends the ceremony, in Weimar, at which the equestrian statue of the Grand Duke Carl August is unveiled.

12 September. He plays at a private concert of his works mounted in Leipzig by the piano manufacturer Julius Blüthner.

19 September. Liszt arrives in Rome.

WORKS. Two festive songs, *Der Herr bewahrt die Seelen seiner Heiligen* (S48) and *Carl August weilt mit uns* (S92), both composed for the unveiling of the statue of Carl August. Hungarian Storm March (based on the *Seconde marche hongroise* for piano), for orchestra (S119) and for piano (S524). *Der blinde Sänger* (A. Tolstoy) (S 350), a recitation for voice and piano.

726. To Princess Carolyne in Rome. [Budapest] Sunday morning, 14 February. Having left Rome at 9.00 a.m. on Tuesday, I got to Buda at 8.30 on Thursday evening. Those 60 hours of travel provided only one very agreeable incident—the dinner that Mme Laussot and Hillebrand[1] had had prepared at Florence station on Tuesday evening. The spiritual nourishment of a friendly chat with my hosts was not wanting either—although the meal was abundant and distinguished enough, in a culinary respect, to do without anecdotes! During the night journey, Zarembski, whom I greatly appreciate, repeatedly insisted on wanting to cover me with his elegant rug, very like the one I had seen in your home. Not to upset him, I finally accepted—and the mystery was only revealed yesterday, here, when he brought me this same rug. The fact is, it did me very good service. . . .

You already know that like the theft committed in the Babuino, my dwelling-place in the Fish Market has served as scene of a similar exploit. The cupboards were forced, the silverware, linen, a gold ring, and several silver ones taken! The chief culprit is the servant of the owner of the house, M. Friedrich, a fencing-master. Miska is guilty only of excessive innocence—for the thief, now imprisoned, was frequently his table companion and obliging assistant, when Miska would favour him with confidential information about our possessions! My new *cameriere* is partly Montenegrin, speaks fluent German, Italian, and Hungarian, possesses favourable testimonials, shows himself eager to give me good service—and is called Spiridion Knezevics! You will understand that this baptismal name charmed me. *Vedremo*! . . . B.B.

727. To Princess Carolyne. Hanover, 25 April. The day before yesterday, on my arrival here, Bronsart handed me your letter of the 15th. No one fraternizes more than I do with Polish blood, the Slav ideal, Slav symbolism, Slav sentiment, and Slav hopes! But to infuse them in an oratorio, one should not proceed with brush and broom strokes, however great one's enthusiasm! That is why I have asked you to help me, and to deal with the literary structure of *St Stanislas*. Up to now, Poland has had only one great musician, Chopin, who remains immortally admirable, marvellous, sublime in grace and genius. But he

---

[1] Four years later Jessie Laussot and the historian Karl Hillebrand married.

composed only for the piano, and restricted himself to medium-scale forms, Ballades, Nocturnes, Scherzos, Polonaises—while enormously amplifying and rarefying the lyricism and enchantments of the patriotic muse. Moniuszko produced Polish operas and praiseworthy compositions inspired by poems of Mickiewicz. Perhaps the inspiration of his very noble, dreamy, and even moving afflatus was not enough! In 1875 one must write otherwise in honour of Poland. I am thinking about it, and believe I know more or less how—it is only a question of making the text of *St Stanislas* suit my way of doing so, in order to demonstrate that I am not a cretin! Will you accept this denial? . . .   B.B.

728. To Carl Gille in Jena. Weimar, 24 May

Very dear friend,

You asked me for the origin of the proverbial expression 'retourner à ses moutons'. It goes back to a dramatic farce of the fifteenth century, in which there is a judge who urges a litigant dealer not to digress and to return to his sheep. That, at least, is what I am told by an instructive and amusing booklet entitled 'petite Encyclopédie des proverbes français'.—

Alas! *Tristan und Isolde* will not be reappearing in our theatre for a long time. In their reply the Vogls have said that they won't obtain leave of absence in late June—the date that Loën had proposed to them for the performance. Consequently, it will be postponed until the next theatrical season, October or later. I shall then be at the Villa d'Este, whither I plan to return immediately after the Carl August celebrations here, on 3 September.

The *fourfold* division of my little life between Pest, Weimar, Rome, and the rest is very tiring and troublesome. And yet I have no reason to complain—rather to rejoice at my friends' kindness; and first of all at your devoted, long-standing, and loyal trustworthiness.[2]   F. Liszt

729. To Princess Carolyne. Weimar, Wednesday, 23 June. The great
sensation and emotion of the past week was *Tristan*. A good third of the very large audience consisted of visitors from elsewhere—the 2 performances were hugely applauded. One felt overwhelmed, ravished, and enraptured all at the same time—in several places one could only weep! After so poignant a work I do not know what will be left for our opera composers to do. Their task seems to me rather superfluous, and the best advice to give them would be to study

---

[2] This last paragraph of the letter was written in German.

Wagner's scores before resuming composition of their own—and patiently to attend performances of the *Nibelungen* in Bayreuth. M. Edouard Schuré, Wagner's French champion *par excellence*, has just published 2 volumes in 8ᵛᵒ entitled *Le Drame musical.* As yet I have done no more than skim through the second, which treats exclusively of the work and ideas of Wagner and sets them out in fine French style, absolutely apologistic.

You ask me for news of the commemorative matinée for Mme Mouchanoff. It went off very well. The Grand Duke took care to see that floral decorations adorned the salon in the Tempelherrenhaus. It was where in days gone by could be seen the colossal statue of Goethe devised by Bettina von Arnim. In the middle of this grove was placed Mme Mouchanoff's portrait, admirably painted by Lenbach. It is owned by Countess Coudenhove, who kindly consented to have it sent here from Vienna, to illustrate the commemoration of her mother. About 150 people were invited—Their Royal Highnesses and the Queen of Würtemberg were very graciously conspicuous. Frau von Schleinitz (accompanied by Herr von Redwitz, worthy and brilliant son of his father) and Cosima had arrived the previous day, and departed the day after the second performance of *Tristan.* The same evening, last Thursday, I saw Queen Olga again at a small private concert in the Belvedere. Her Majesty still shines with the charm of majestic perfections!

Tomorrow, the Grand Duke will spend his 57th birthday *en famille* at Ettersburg. The day after tomorrow, the Tsar of Russia is expected at the Belvedere. For several reasons, my humble self will probably have to go to Leipzig next Sunday.

May the good angels work with you on your *Causes*!   B.B.

730. To Princess Carolyne. Wilhelmsthal, 25 July. Before leaving Weimar I received a letter from Cardinal Hohenlohe, who wrote from Ragaz on the 18th. Several reasons prevent me making my very humble visit to him there. Firstly, watering-places are an aversion of mine. For more than 20 years I have been carefully avoiding them—to the point that I even spent a week in Karlsruhe without going to Baden, whither Mme Viardot and other friends were inviting me. Unless I had to take a cure, I should not know what to do in such places, except be bored to death and stupidly spend more money than elsewhere. Against Ragaz I now have a more determining reason: I should there be more of an embarrassment than a gratification for the Cardinal. He is too much in the public eye, and I not enough out of it, for the newspapers not to involve themselves in their own way; and as much as possible I try to spare him avoidable

vexations. The Empress Eugénie is staying in the same hotel as the Cardinal—
as are an Egyptian prince and a Berlin Geheimrath [Privy Councillor]. There will
certainly be a piano *chez le portier*! I shall be invited to display my little talents.
If I refuse, it will be attributed to pride—and if I consent, to foolishness! . . .

My little programme is therefore as follows. The day after tomorrow,
Liebenstein. I there owe the Duke of Meiningen a brief visit, and shall see the
Stahrs, with whom in Weimar I recently resumed our longstanding good relations. On Sunday, Nuremberg, because of my new biographer, Fräulein Lina
Ramann—an old friend and disciple of Brendel, an earnest, noble and dedicated woman.[3] If it is not granted to me to be good for anything—I try at least
not to be bad in anything.   B.B.

731. To Princess Carolyne. Bayreuth, Sunday, 15 August. After a very
successful run of 6 weeks, the preparatory rehearsals of the *Ring des Nibelungen*
finished last Thursday. On Friday, Wagner gave a splendid party in his home,
Wahnfried, for his entire staff of artistes, about 150 people: house and garden
brilliantly illuminated, military music and fireworks, abundant refreshments,
both solid and liquid. The whole thing served as a frame for the marvellous
speech Wagner gave. His principal theme was that in the 19th century it was
music's mission to regenerate and bring to life all the arts. 'Let us await events,'
said Pius IX! That of the performance of the *Nibelungen*, next year, towers grandly
above everything that other European theatres are doing or are able to do! I
enclose the small photographs of Wagner's house and theatre in Bayreuth—the
large size can hardly be sent by post.

Thanks with all my heart for the sweet things in your last 2 letters. I admire
how in Rome you have so good a memory of the tents pitched on the path to
the Ideal, of which we used to chat at Woronince! 'Orare et laborare'—without
respite! I shall tell you in person and at greater length of the course being taken
by all that concerns art in Germany—about which we were not mistaken at the
Altenburg. . . .   B.B.

732. To Baron Augusz. Bayreuth [16 August]. . . . The newspapers are
keeping you informed about preparations for the great event which will be
taking place here in August 1876. Bayreuth is becoming a new Mecca; but
more prodigious than the Kaaba is, to my mind, the tetralogy of the *Ring des*

---

[3] In the event, Liszt visited Liebenstein in mid-Aug. (18/19) and Nuremberg in mid-Sept. (16/17).

Nibelungen. In it, Wagner's sublime genius at its apogee has created, in poetry and music, the transcendental *drama* of our time. Those who have ears to hear, let them hear! . . .

733. To Marie Espérance von Schwartz in Chalépa, Crete [Villa d'Este, Autumn]

Dear and most excellent one,

What an excess of sufferings, sorrows, and torments! A broken leg, a fractured arm, a new dislocation, two assaults, and, as crowning tribulation, the too pathetic 'singer' Anita G.! I couldn't say anything to you about all that, other than that I profoundly admire your admirable and gentle resignation in enduring it, in practising the cardinal virtues, fortitude and temperance, to a heroic degree. So you are continuing to busy yourself with bricks and mortar, wine-harvests, zoophilia, charitable works of every kind, even with the hospice in Jena, into the establishment of which I again ask you not to put too much urgency. First of all, peacefully tend your 'financial wounds', translate the 'animal welfare sermon' and persevere victoriously in four languages in the most praiseworthy war against the 'atrocities' committed against animals in almost every country. They are—alas!—only a sad corollary of the countless atrocities and abominations committed by the human, so inhuman, race!—

But from where do you derive two strange ideas: (1) that I am not interested in animal welfare; (2—still worse) that it would ever be possible for me to 'disown' my friends? Without reproaching you, I protest vigorously against such false and unjust suppositions—about which we will not speak further. . . .

Replying to your question about my travels next year, I can inform you that, unless I suffer a broken leg or some equivalent accident, I shall remain here until mid-February. From 20 February until Easter in Budapest. Then in Weimar, where I hope to see you again, and shall ask you to accept me as a companion on the pilgrimage to your Jena hospice.

For mid-August is announced the marvel of the performances of the tetralogy, *Der Ring des Nibelungen*, 'im Vertrauen auf den deutschen Geist entworfen und zum Ruhme seines erhabenen Wohlthäters, des Königs Ludwig II. von Bayern, vollendet von Richard Wagner [planned with trust in the German spirit, and completed to the glory of his sublime benefactor, King Ludwig II of Bavaria, by Richard Wagner]'. Musically civilized Europe and America will then have to repair to Bayreuth. Please allow to invite you thither your most affectionate and grateful

F. Liszt

734. To Countess Alexei Tolstoy[4]

Madame la Comtesse,

It is only to share in your grief that I make bold to write to you. A celebrated poet, who was far from equalling your husband in nobility of soul and lofty intelligence, said: 'The only good thing remaining to me in the world is to have sometimes wept.'[5]

I feel this benefit when thinking of my noble friend Alexei Tolstoy; his memory is stamped with immortality.

Your cordially affectionate and respectful   F. Liszt

735. To Daniel Ollivier [Villa d'Este, late October]

Dear Daniel,

I thank you for your good wishes, and in assuring me that you are continuing to work hard you have given me much pleasure. To learn and to merit are the principal rules of life. With Latin you will also be studying history, 'witness of the ages', as it was called by Cicero, the familiar friend of your illustrious father, to whom I ask you to repeat my unchanged feelings of constant devotion. Remember me kindly to M. Démosthène and Madame Ollivier,[6] and be ever grateful to Providence for the happiness with which it is filling the days of your youth.

Your affectionate grandfather,   F. Liszt

736. To the Grand Duke Carl Alexander in Weimar.
Villa d'Este, 8 November

Monseigneur,

I should have forestalled your very gracious letter, received this morning. My delay is only in the *writing* and in no way invalidates the deeply grateful and devoted sentiments which ever bind me to Your Royal Highness, to His family, and to the glorious tradition of the house of Weimar.

---

[4] A note written in Rome or the Villa d'Este probably in mid- or late Oct.: Tolstoy had died in Krasnyi Rog on the 10th.

[5] The closing lines of Alfred de Musset's poem *Tristesse* (dated Bury, 14 June 1840), which Liszt set (1872) for voice and piano under the title of its opening line, 'J'ai perdu ma force et ma vie'.

[6] The father and the second wife (Marie-Thérèse) of Emile Ollivier.

Deign to accept my good wishes and felicitations for the marriage of your daughter,[7] and lay the very humble homage of my old fidelity at the feet of HRH the Grand Duchess and of the Princess Marie.

My sojourn at the Villa d'Este signifies retreat and the tranquil continuance of long musical toil, about which I labour under no delusion, regarding it as simply an obligatory task.

The newspapers announce my return to Pest now for the opening of the new Academy of Music, of which His Majesty, the King of Hungary, has been pleased to appoint me President. Without failing in my duty I can put off carrying it out for a while, and shall remain here until mid-February.

In Rome, the qualities, advantages, and virtues of Madame the Duchess of Sermoneta[8] receive great praise. Like Raphael, the Duke has his three manners— in marriage—and he is as successful in the third as in the first and second. His prodigious intellect and knowledge have never hampered his practical common sense.

The day before yesterday I had the honour of spending several hours with HRH Princess Friedrich Carl of Prussia and her two daughters, *chez* the new Ambassador, Baron Keudell. Notwithstanding his superiority in politics and diplomacy, Herr von Keudell takes a serious interest in music and cultivates it with rare distinction, so that it is always very agreeable to me to go to the piano, *chez lui.*

Your brother-in-law, HM the King of the Netherlands, graciously reinvites me to his Palace of Loo for next 15 May; not to accept would seem to me to be ingratitude.

A cordially eager welcome to Herr Ernst Koppel, author of the tragedy *Savonarola.* In returning his letter to you, I add the one addressed to Your Royal Highness by the composer of the oratorio *Luther,* Herr Meinardus, whom I take the liberty of again recommending to your goodwill. Were it to seem strange for a little Abbé like me to be meddling in matters concerning Savonarola and Luther, that would trouble my good conscience not in the least.

In the *Revue des Deux Mondes* of 15 October, M. Blaze de Bury has published an article pompously entitled *La Musique et ses destinées.* Happily, the latter do not depend on the decrees of M. Blaze de Bury, who from the height of his self-conceit despicably parodies one of the noble and beautiful remarks of Mme Mouchanoff, and in passing designates me as 'the most imperturbable

---

[7] Princess Marie had become engaged to Prince Heinrich VII von Reuss-Schleiz-Köstritz, whom she married on 6 Feb. 1876.

[8] Don Michelangelo's third wife was—like his second—an Englishwoman: Harriet Ellis, daughter of Lord Howard de Walden.

play-actor of this illustrious band'.[9] Imperturbable, yes; play-actor, no—and again no; but most loyally Your Royal Highness's

very faithful servant   F. Liszt

737. To Princess Carolyne. Villa d'Este, Wednesday evening and Thursday morning, 17/18 November. . . . After so many *pourparlers*, I shall need a few more months to get used to the fact that the Budapest Music Academy exists. Were it not for my antipathy to the writing down of bad jokes, I should have added, to vary the image of the millstone around the neck, that this academy had been for me, thus far, only an appalling collection of swords of Damocles, in the form of pianos and bothersome compositions, suspended above my head! Fortunately another Greek, Euripides, has given us this good advice: 'There is no point in getting angry with things, since that has no effect on them.' We'll meet in Rome on Sunday evening. Like mahogany and violins, I hope in ageing to improve a little.

B.B.

738. To Cardinal Hohenlohe. Villa d'Este, 24 December

Eminence,

Your gracious letter was a shining point for me in Rome, where I spent this last fortnight.

His Holiness, at whose feet I bowed with heart and soul, deigned to recognize me and say *Mio caro maestro* Liszt!

Various Vatican personages then asked me for news about Your Eminence's health; I gave them complete reassurance.

At the Palazzo Caffarelli, my good relations of former days are continuing as well as could be with Baron Keudell, whose most excellent *contegno* is greatly appreciated in Rome.

To celebrate the *buone feste* tranquilly, I have returned under your roof at the Villa d'Este. Ercole, Antonio, Saverio, Pietro, *et al.* look favourably upon me and regard me as one of their own—sincerely devoted to the service of Your Eminence.

A parish priest's servant is said to have had, like Raphael, her three manners. The first year, she said: 'M. le curé's hens'; the second year: 'our hens'; and the

---

[9] Liszt is not mentioned by name in this article, much of which is devoted to attacking Wagner. The sentence directed at him runs: '"Elles s'aiment en moi!" disait le plus imperturbable histrion de cette bande illustre en parlant des bons rapports ou vivaient entre elles ses vieilles maîtresses délaissées.'

third year: 'my hens'. In the same way I shall say that under my window I see with interest curtains being put in the *appartamento nobile*.[10] Myself, as a loyal acolyte, I put wholly at your feet.   F. Liszt

Tonight I shall attend the Christmas service in the cathedral here, and shall not leave *my* turret until about the end of January, to spend a few further days in Rome, and thence return straight to Budapest.

I caught scarcely a glimpse of Monseigneur Lichnowsky *chez* Count Bobrinsky, who has taken possession of the Villa Malta[11] and, by means of more than a million, rebuilt it from top to bottom, so that it has become a very princely dwelling-place, comfortable and in good taste. Lichnowsky arrived in Rome very ill; he has got thinner, but advantageously, for the embonpoint of prelates is not a state of grace: rather, their physical weight seems to hamper their moral importance.

739. To Princess Carolyne. [Villa d'Este] 30 December. Lina Ramann
has come to Weimar 2 or 3 times and is pursuing our late friend Brendel's idea concerning me. Hence the essay on *Christus*,[12] and the thankless task of a biography of F. Liszt—for which these last two years she has laboriously amassed a quantity of material: letters, articles, pamphlets, volumes, plus the numerous lowly works and transcriptions in my catalogue. More than 200 pages of this biography are already written. Please be so kind as to write and let me know if you authorize Lina Ramann to come to Rome at the end of January. I shall accompany her in a friendly way to St Peter's and the Colosseum—if only you are prepared to instruct her about the rest, which interests her more.

                                                      Infinitely,   B.B.

---

[10] The first-floor apartments. The Villa d'Este has four floors, from ground floor (*pianterreno*) to third, the rooms used by Liszt being on the second.

[11] Built on the site of the *horti Lucullani*, this Roman house has down the centuries been associated with a host of the famous and infamous. Among them: Messalina, Nero, Theodoric, Belisarius, Queen Casimira of Poland, and Goethe. In 1801 Wilhelm von Humboldt and his family settled here; and from 1827 it was, in the words of Gregorovius, 'for forty years the Sans Souci of the most art-loving of all German sovereigns, Ludwig I of Bavaria'. Early in the present century it became the home of Princess von Bülow (the former Maria Dönhoff) and her husband Prince Bernhard von Bülow, the German Chancellor.

[12] *Franz Liszts Oratorium Christus* (1874).

9 February. Liszt leaves Rome to return to Budapest, which he reaches on the 15th.

27 February. He receives an ovation after the first Budapest performance of *Hunnenschlacht*.

5 March. The Comtesse d'Agoult dies in Paris.

20 March. Liszt plays at a concert in the Vigadó to benefit flood victims.

26 March. His pupils at the new Academy of Music give their first concert.

6 April. He returns to Weimar.

Late April/early May. Works of his are performed—and he plays—at a music festival in Düsseldorf, where he renews acquaintance with Ferdinand Hiller and Clara Schumann.

15–25 May. Liszt is again the guest of King Willem III at Loo.

1 August–2 September. He stays in Bayreuth with the Wagners and attends all three performances of the *Ring*.

23 September–5 October. He stays in Hanover, where Hans von Bülow is seriously ill and being looked after by the Bronsarts.

21–31 October. Liszt is the guest of Baron Augusz in Szekszárd.

2 November. He returns to Budapest, where he remains until March.

WORKS. PIANO: *Weihnachtsbaum* (Christmas Tree) (S186, 1874–6), a suite of twelve pieces, first sketched in 1866; No. 4 of the *Fünf kleine Klavierstücke*; transcription (S555) of the *Danse macabre* of Saint-Saëns. PIANO DUET: *Festpolonaise* (S634b).[1]

740. To Princess Carolyne in Rome. Villa d'Este, 1 January. Flowers and fruit this morning told me again of your wishes, which I shall try to fulfil. Thank you, too, for the charming watch—it exhorts me to make good use of my time, in a way that will please you, and to make progress in the practice of the Christian virtues. . . .

What you tell me of the pedantically thorough Polish biography of Chopin,[2] and of the favourable return it caused you to make to our *Chopin*, pleases me enormously. Like you, I think that only a few words will need to be changed or added in Härtel's new edition, and I shall insist on only one particular, while sincerely acknowledging my error of times past. In 1849 I did not yet understand the intimate beauty of the last works of Chopin, the *Polonaise-fantaisie*

[1] Composed for the marriage of Princess Marie of Saxe-Weimar.

[2] Probably that by Karasowski, at this time available in Polish only.

and the *Barcarolle*—and had some reservations regarding their morbid tone. Now, I admire them totally—despite the pedantry of a few cloth-eared critics who fail to appreciate them. Without claiming that the last works of Chopin equal those of Beethoven's 3rd period, which for a long time were attributed to deafness and mental aberration, I affirm and shall maintain that they are not only very remarkable, but also very melodious, nobly inspired, and artistically proportioned, in all respects on a level with the enchanting genius of Chopin. No one else should be compared with him—he shines alone and unique in the artistic heavens. His emotions, grace, grief, power, and transports are unique to himself. He is a divine aristocrat, a feminine archangel with prismatic wings! Forgive me for expressing my thoughts in so bizarre a manner.

Talking of bizarre comparisons, in an article on the excavations in the Colosseum the correspondent of the *Moniteur universel* singularly flatters the poor Abbé Liszt. As a rule, the picturesque things written at my expense offer me very little on which to congratulate myself. All the more reason for thanking the correspondent for having observed the Abbé Liszt, with his tall figure, made still taller by the long cassock, devoutly making the stations of the Cross at the Colosseum—and for telling the public that 'in the immense arena this great shadow lengthened, in the setting sun, like the ghost of a Caesar!' Far below and outside the role of a Caesar who has come down in the world—to appear as the ghost of a Caesar seems to me most glorious!

Mme Minghetti[3] is 1,000 times right to find that I waste my time in salons —and so I shall give up this unfortunate habit. . . .

At this very moment the Tivoli orchestra is coming to greet me with an aubade in the *cortile* [courtyard] of the Villa d'Este.

With heart and soul,   B.B.

741. To Princess Carolyne. Villa d'Este, 6 January. I shall be very happy to reread with you the whole of our *Chopin*, and thank you with all my heart for such a good suggestion. In 2 or 3 evenings, and without any discussion about literary requirements, we shall finish the reading of this splendid former task of B.B. These last few days I have done a little work on my *Weihnachtsbaum*, which I shall finish soon. . . .

Allow me a single, very simple, remark about Fräulein Ramann's visit to Rome. This excellent person is, to be sure, not coming to enjoy herself. The entertainments of the Corso, of the *confetti e moccoletti* [sugar-almonds and small tapers], are

---

[3] Donna Laura Minghetti, mother of Maria Dönhoff.

no concern of hers—even the Colosseum and St Peter's hardly interest her. She is wholly absorbed in her task; if you will be so very kind as to help her with it, she will be profoundly grateful to you, and will comply with all your wishes. Do please, however, excuse her for being in rather a hurry to finish a book on which she has been working for 2 or 3 years, and which she would like to see published before the end of this year. Her duties at the school in Nuremberg are not a pretext to amuse herself elsewhere!

With heart and soul,   B.B.

742. To Princess Carolyne. Lamporecchio, 11 February.[4] I was unable to write any more in Florence—and am continuing at Lamporecchio, 4.00 p.m. Pce Rospigliosi at once handed me a telegram from Gregorio[5]—which he apologized for having opened inadvertently. The name Gregorio seemed to arouse his curiosity, but I did not consider it opportune to explain its meaning to him immediately upon arrival. In the *mezza oretta di conversazione* [short half-hour of conversation] I have just had with my host and hostess, the Princess reminded me that Arnim's father and grandfather committed suicide. Mme Fanny seems in good health—she hasn't perceptibly changed or lost weight. I shall see her again in the salon at 6.00; dinner is at 7.30. Tomorrow morning I shall be leaving for Venice.

At 6.30 yesterday evening, at Mme Laussot's, we had a delightful dinner chatting with Hillebrand and his near homonym Hildebrand, the greatly renowned sculptor, as well as Füssli, a painter likewise celebrated. Later I did a little strumming on the piano.[6] Mme Laussot will be sending you the American articles on Bülow; I have read them. You will find in them an ingenious observation: 'Bülow's talent stands out by reason of the same superior quality which is now making Germany stand out in Europe—discipline.'

The Duchess Colonna is living in the same house as Mme Laussot. I didn't find a moment to pay renewed respects to Marcello.[7] Her mother, Mme d'Affry, is with her, and also the Comte de Circourt,* whose memory of books, of facts, and of contemporaries more or less illustrious, makes him enormously erudite. I met him between 1830 and 40 at Lamartine's, with whom he was then very

---

[4] Continuation of a letter begun in Florence that morning.   [5] That is, from Princess Carolyne herself.

[6] Writing on 11 Feb. to Conrad Fiedler, Hildebrand remarked: 'La Laussot is lively and cheerful, and was yesterday so lucky as to have Liszt at her place . . . and he played. First a piece by Chopin . . . then something Viennese, Straussian, full of life and grace and just the thing to captivate the women. . . . Liszt, incidentally, has a wonderful head' (*Adolf von Hildebrands Briefwechsel mit Conrad Fiedler*, ed. G. Jachmann, Dresden, 1927, 57).

[7] The widowed Duchess Colonna di Castiglione devoted herself to sculpture, exhibiting her works—among which is said to be a statuette of Liszt—under the name of Marcello.

close. If he comes to Rome, I urge you to make his acquaintance—*man kann ihn angenehmst auspressen!*[8] Von Arnim told me that Circourt was at present functioning as a 'peace-maker in perpetuity' between Mme d'Affry and her daughter Mme Colonna.

The day after tomorrow, in Venice, I shall give you news of Lamporecchio. On Tuesday I hope to find a letter from you in Budapest.

With heart and soul, B.B.

743. To Princess Carolyne. Budapest, 17 February. Almost nothing to tell you about Venice, where I saw only the Széchényis and, in their home, half a dozen people of their acquaintance who are of no interest to you. After writing to you on Sunday morning I went to mass, in the sovereignly royal church of St Mark. This evangelist is my second patron saint—for it was on his feast-day, 25 April, that I received the minor orders at the Vatican. Until my last hour I shall say with a full heart: *Dominus pars hereditatis meae, et calicis mei.*[9]

You are quoting to Mgr. Strossmayer a verse of Goethe's which is by Schiller! In his prologue for the reopening of the Weimar theatre, Oct. 1798, Schiller said:

Wer den Besten seiner Zeit genug gethan,
Der hat gelebt für alle Zeiten.[10]

744. To Princess Carolyne. Tuesday, 29 February. The Danube dealt terribly severely last week with Komárom, Esztergom, New Pest, Old Ofen, the districts in the lower part of the town of Buda, Kalocsa, etc. Thousands of people find themselves with no other shelter than that of charity—their houses having been flooded. Pest was seriously threatened, from Thursday to Saturday —we were expecting a disaster similar to that of 1838. Numerous boats were positioned in various localities, and the Department of Public Safety was ready to act. Happily we got off with a fright; it will only be necessary to scrape together enough money to be able to provide temporarily for the essential needs of the flood victims. The Primate and Mgr. Haynald are giving the most generous example—the poor Franciscans and Capuchin friars are offering their

---

[8] One wonders if they met. The woman Humboldt had called 'the many-minded Princess' might well have met her match, and more, in the man Lamartine had described as 'a living chart of human knowledge'.

[9] The words (Ps. 16; Vulg. 15) Liszt had uttered when receiving the tonsure.

[10] 'He who has done enough to satisfy the best of his time, | has lived for all time.'

monastery as a refuge for hundreds of unfortunate people. By order of HM the King, Pce Hohenlohe has had the riding-school in the Hofburg outbuildings in Buda converted into shelter-rooms; in addition, the King and Queen have sent 30,000 fl. I, too, shall have to contribute to the relief of some of the victims—by making my old fingers available at a concert to be given shortly under the patronage of the President of the Council of Ministers, Tisza. This decision pains me a little, because I had made up my mind not to appear in Budapest again, in public, as a pianist—still less elsewhere! I was wanting, henceforth, to restrict my activity here to holding a class at the new Music Academy, of which His Majesty deigned to appoint me president. Having accepted this honour, my task is to carry out my duties thoroughly. I hope in a couple of years to have furnished proofs of my loyalty and ability. In addition I can tell you that yesterday,[11] after the performance of *Hunnenschlacht* at the Philharmonic concert, the audience's applause was so prolonged that I made bows of thanks from my seat in the dress circle of the Hungarian Theatre.   B.B.

745. To Princess Carolyne. Budapest, 14 March. I had taken care to write my letter to the Min. Trefort in elegant French.[12] The German newspapers translate it clumsily by adding to it a commonplace that I loathe: *bis zum Grabe* [until death]! That might almost have angered me, if over many years I had not grown indifferent to such clumsinesses.

The newspapers tell me of the death of Daniel Stern. Barring hypocrisy, I could not weep for her more after her death than while she was alive. La Rochefoucauld well said that hypocrisy is a homage rendered to virtue—but it is still permitted to prefer true homage to false. Mme d'Agoult possessed to a high degree a taste, and even a passion, for the false—except at certain moments of ecstasy, of which she could afterwards not bear to be reminded! At my age, moreover, condolences are no less embarrassing than congratulations. *Il mondo va da sè*—one exists in it, keeps oneself busy, frets, worries, deludes oneself, thinks better of it, and dies as one can! The most desirable sacrament to receive, it seems to me, is that of extreme unction! Very faithfully,   B.B.

You ask me why I shall be in Vienna on 2 April? Reply: I was here on the same date last year and the previous years. During the sad variabilities of my life, I am happy to retain some fixed point of affection. My cousin Eduard being

---

[11] Actually two days earlier, on Sunday the 27th.
[12] The letter of 1 Mar. in which Liszt had offered to play at a concert—given on 20 Mar.—in aid of the flood victims.

content with me, I most gladly celebrate with him on 2 April the feast of my patron saint, Francis of Paola, founder of the Order of Minims.

746. To Emile Ollivier in Saint Tropez. Budapest, 27 March

Dear Ollivier,

Thank you for having copied out for me Ronchaud's lines on the death of Madame d'Agoult. To make phrases does not become me: the memory I retain of Mme d'A. is a sorrowful secret; I confide it to God while asking Him to grant peace and light to the soul of the mother of my three dear children.

Nothing more appropriate than the legacy to Daniel Ollivier of Daniel Stern's literary property. . . .

In her *Esquisses morales*, Daniel Stern wrote: 'Forgiveness is merely a form of contempt.'[13] That is pretentious and false. The truth, with the sublime sweetness of forgiving, is revealed to us by the Gospel. And so let us pray 'Our Father which art in Heaven, forgive us our trespasses, as we forgive them that trespass against us.'

Please give to Madame Thérèse Ollivier the very affectionate regards of your

F. Liszt

747. To Princess Carolyne. Weimar, 8 April, morning. When I reached the Schottenhof at 6.30 on 2 April, Eduard at once handed me your letter and your magnificent bouquet. I should like to know how to thank you in words; but failing to succeed therein, and better still, I beg you to forgive me my errors and shortcomings! . . .

Nothing particularly interesting to tell you about my 4 days in Vienna. Eduard remains, as ever, most grateful and devoted to you. On 2 April we invited to dinner at the Schottenhof Herr and Frau Bösendorfer, of whom I am very fond, Camille Saint-Saëns, Gobbi from Pest, and Oncken. The last-named is exhibiting rather a large picture depicting some of the cypresses at the Villa d'Este. Magne spoke highly to me of this painting, which I went to see. Saint-Saëns obtained a very genuine success in Vienna as a pianist, and also for his compositions. His *Danse macabre*, a symphonic poem, is becoming popular. Next season his *Delilah*, a 4-act opera, is being performed in Vienna, and before that

[13] Her actual words were: 'Very often, forgiveness is only politeness, a kind of euphemism for contempt.'

in Weimar. For many years I have had a very high opinion of his talent, which is well known and appreciated. To define him for you in a word, I shall say that he is the French Rubinstein—so at once a distinguished virtuoso and a very productive composer, widely gifted, someone who can claim to excel in every genre: symphony, oratorio, chamber and salon music, and opera. Further, he is an admirable organist. Personally, I am on still more intimate terms with Saint-Saëns than with Rubinstein. He was so kind as to add distinction to the concert which the Conservatoire pupils put on for me on the spur of the moment last Monday, by conducting his *Danse macabre* and playing my Fantasy on themes from Beethoven's *Ruins of Athens*. . . .

You know that, by order, the first Berlin performance of *Tristan und Isolde* has been given for the benefit of the great work of Bayreuth. The Emperor and Empress were present from beginning to end, as was our Grand Duchess. The proceeds came to 5,000 thalers. For 2 months I have received no letters from Cosima—we understand one another without phrases! She, Wagner, and the whole of Wahnfried sent me a telegram on 2 April.

I shall repeat with all my heart, and also my lips, the beautiful Polish prayer for all those I have caused to sin or have been unable to keep from sinning. As for my reply to your letter 'to be read on the train'—it could be written only in sobs! May the good angels protect you!   B.B.

748. To Princess Carolyne. Palace of Loo, 20 May. During this fortnight Loo is not exactly a place of retreat and quiet meditation. His Majesty's extreme amiability towards his guests restricts their leisure hours. One would be ill advised not to feel flattered by it—and for my part I am truly moved by the kindnesses shown to me by His Majesty. There are about a dozen artistic celebrities here, painters and musicians. Gérôme, Cabanel, members of the Institut de France—Bouguereau, likewise well on the way to reaching the Institut—ten Kate, Rochussen, Heemskerk. As regards musicians, Vieuxtemps, Hartog, a young and mature Belgian composer, Batta, a cellist who has maintained his reputation for 40 years and finally taken up residence at Versailles—and Gevaërt, director of the Brussels Conservatoire, author of a noted book on the music of the ancient Greeks, and composer of several operas performed in Paris, where his *Quentin Durward* enjoyed a fitting success. In Gevaërt, exceptional erudition is combined with much wit. Ambroise Thomas, director of the Paris Conservatoire, and Saint-Saëns are expected. The King shows no inclination towards German art—consequently, neither painters nor musicians from Germany appear among the guests at the Palace of Loo. The fair sex is likewise now excluded from it—save on the stage, on which shine each evening the young lady artistes —recipients of grants from His Majesty—in magnificent costumes, artistically dressed and made up. I told you the meaning of the 'auditions' which keenly interest the King. Here enclosed is the programme for the first evening—the 14 following ones differ from and resemble each other. Gérôme, Cabanel, and Gevaërt talk very wittily; *bons mots*, jests and anecdotes fly around incessantly, from morning till night, with the King sometimes adding his sovereign note! It would need a very subtle historiographer to relate the ephemerides of Loo.

I pray to the good angels to continue their collaboration in your work of the *Causes*—and to protect minimally your most minimal and very unworthy servant, F.L.

749. To Princess Carolyne. Weimar, 26 May, morning. Before leaving Loo yesterday morning I wanted to write to you. But it was the Feast of the Ascension—to miss mass would have been a sin and a bad example. However, the little Catholic church, almost as modest as Weimar's, is at Apeldoorn, a good quarter of an hour from the château. On returning, I had time only to see to an autograph and pay a few essential visits. The King's gracious kindnesses to me continue *quasi crescendo*. He prepared for and assigned me the finest apartment in the château; in the salon was a piano with my photograph, that of the Pest Jubilee. His Majesty intends to have a Liszt Medal struck—as a pendant to the magnificent Malibran Medal. The gold model—value of the metal, 800 Dutch florins—would next year be the reward of honour for the most deserving female pianist among those receiving a grant from His Majesty. Further, His Majesty has invited me to attend, in Sept., a musical festival in Amsterdam, which He will be patronizing with his presence. Flattering though the invitation be, I doubt that I shall be able to take advantage of it. . . .

Today the Church celebrates one of the patrons of Rome: St Philip Neri. The breviary tells us that divine love swelled his heart so much that it could no longer be contained within its natural limits—and, by one of God's miracles, two of the Saint's ribs had to break and rise up to expand his chest.

I hope that the good angels have carried out their duties well by speedily curing the pain in your right hand. When you are so good as to speak to me again of your *Causes*—I shall be very grateful.

Constanter et fideliter. B.B.

The painter Siemiradzki, upon whom you bestow the title of rival of Chopin, is he in Rome at present?

750. To Princess Carolyne. Weimar, 2 June. Got back yesterday evening from Altenburg, where your latest letter reached me. . . .

Only with sadness do I obey your injunction to speak to you no more of the *Causes*. If I knew ever so little of theology and of politics, I would jib—but my ignorance condemns me to resignation. Allow me to remind you once again of the motto taken by my noble compatriot István Széchenyi, who achieved great and useful things in Hungary: 'Reine Seele, reine Absicht—ob erfolgreich oder nicht [Pure soul, pure intention—whether successful or not].' . . .

Lina Ramann is making her Whitsun pilgrimage to Rome—not *ad limina apostolorum*, but *ad limina*—of your authority and goodwill! She deserves a friendly welcome. Her religious propensities are consonant with the doctrine of her late friend Brendel and of Fräulein von Meysenbug.   F.L.

751. To Princess Carolyne. Weimar, Monday morning [12 June]. Magne and her husband spent 3 days here, from Wednesday, 7 June, until Saturday. . . . They stayed in the Russischer Hof Hotel, lunched at Court every day and returned there every evening. On Wednesday evening I was with them again at the Grand Duchess's, where there were only about a dozen people: the young Wedels, bride and groom, just returned from their honeymoon in Italy, Herr Rohlfs, the celebrated explorer of Africa, and the half-dozen persons-in-waiting. We chatted simply, seated around a tea-table. The next day, Pce Constantin had invited me to lunch at the Russischer Hof, but he and Magne had to go to a luncheon at Court, and for the evening had accepted an invitation from Monseigneur; on Friday, to lunch with the same—to which I was no more invited than to the previous day's. A concert for the Hohenlohes was announced for Friday evening. The programme was already printed—when, at 6 o'clock, Count Beust wrote to tell me that, in view of the alarming state of the Hereditary Grand Duchess's pregnancy, the reigning Grand Duchess was asking for the concert to be held at my place, the Hofgärtnerei. So I hastened first of all to the Hohenlohes, then to Lassen, Milde, Beust—and at 9.30 p.m. the music did its best in honour of the Hohenlohes, in this very room. Monseigneur had intended to come; he was prevented from doing so by preparations for the confinement of his daughter-in-law, who was safely delivered a few hours later, at 5 o'clock on Saturday morning. . . .

You ask me my impressions of the performance of the two parts of *Faust*. Were I intendant of any theatre whatsoever, it would for me be a duty to propagate the *mise-en-scène* of Goethe's sublime dramatic epic—despite all the confusion therein, and from which a way out will never be found, whatever they say. The commentaries on the *Apocalypse* seem to me to be clearer than those on *Faust*! Goethe himself in his last moments asked for *mehr Licht*!

Sempiternally yours,   B.B.

752. To Baron Augusz. Weimar, 30 June

Dear and honoured friend,

My best memories and feelings bind me to your home in Szekszárd. I should like to be there once again, heartily to chatter and make music *en famille*. Perhaps I shall find it possible next summer.

Until 25 July I am remaining here. Weimar, and the little Grand Duchy, are celebrating the birth of a son to the Hereditary Grand Duke. The christening will take place next Sunday, 9 July. In 1842 I attended the marriage of the grandfather, and in 1872 [1873] the wedding of his son, on which occasion was given the 'festival play', *The Bride's Welcome to the Wartburg*, with poetry by Scheffel and music by me. As I remarked to the Grand Duke at that time, I am one of his court's old pieces of furniture, rather useless but fully prepared to serve.

The whole of the month of August—Bayreuth. When this great and unique artistic event of the performance of the *Ring des Nibelungen* has been accomplished, its full significance will be understood, and, gradually, newspaper and theatre 'culture' will gain from what will have been seen and heard in Bayreuth. Be so good as to send me before the 1st of August about fifty bottles of your Szekszárd wine (with the 'Báró Augusz' label) to serve as refreshment after the emotions of the theatre. . . .

From Bayreuth I'll write to let you know what I shall be doing in September and October. I shall probably return to Rome; but certainly (barring serious illness, or death) will be in Budapest on 15 November, to spend the whole winter applying myself to my duties at the Academy of Music, fulfilling the benevolent intentions of HE Trefort, and with the co-operation of my friends Ábrányi, Erkel, and Volkmann.

In 1877 this Academy will have, I hope, full stability and standing.

Affectionately yours, and cordial good wishes to the whole Augusz family.

F. Liszt

753. To Princess Carolyne. Bayreuth, 10 August. Here, the great marvel of Germanic art is being achieved. No more doubt and no more obstacles; Wagner's immense genius has surmounted everything—his work, *Der Ring des Nibelungen*, shines on the world. The blind do not prevent the light—nor the deaf, music! . . .

The King of Bavaria was so gracious as to attend, from 6 to 9 August, the last 4 dress rehearsals, which were complete performances, with scenery and costumes. His Majesty had given orders that he was not to be fêted. However, the streets were hung with flags, and on Sunday evening the town was brilliantly illuminated. Wagner alone was constantly in the King's box, which, by order, had not been lighted. My daughter was summoned to this box, where the 5 children offered the King a bouquet. His Majesty stayed in his villa, the Hermitage, where he went on the night of Saturday to Sunday—without going through Bayreuth. It was only at Wagner's request that on Sunday, after *Rheingold*, the King consented to drive through the illuminated town in a closed carriage. To find fault with King Ludwig is very easy, and to the taste of the salons. For myself, I take no part in it—and sincerely admire the strange individuality of the sovereign who can thus pay tribute to the genius of Wagner.

The Emp. of Germany arrives the day after tomorrow, Saturday; his cousin of Bavaria prefers at that moment to be conspicuous by his absence. He left solitarily, as he had come, during the night of Wednesday to Thursday, after the rehearsal of *Götterdämmerung*. He will probably return for the 3rd and last series of performances, from the 27th to the 30th. The Hermitage villa will be occupied from Saturday evening to Tuesday morning by the Emperor, and his daughter and son-in-law, the Grand Duke and Duchess of Baden. They are the only guests that King Ludwig *verköstigt* [is boarding], putting at their disposal kitchen, carriages, etc.

The Emp. of Brazil,[14] the Grand Dukes of Mecklenburg-Schwerin and of Weimar, *et al.*, also arrive the day after tomorrow, a little before the Emp. of Germany. HM of Brazil will be housed in the Schloss owned by the Duke of Würtemberg, widower of Pcss Marie of Orléans, the very affectionate pupil of Ary Scheffer. Monseigneur [of Weimar] and his Mecklenburg cousin will enjoy the King's hospitality by staying in the palace, which has been newly furnished expressly for them; but they will have to defray the cost of their dinners and carriages. The Emp. of Germany will attend only 2 of the dramas of Wagner's tetralogy, *Rheingold* and *Walküre*, and on Tuesday morning will be proceeding to the manœuvres in Silesia. . . .

---

[14] See under Pedro II in Biographical Sketches.

A number of essays, and even a few volumes, are being published on Wagner. Principal champions of the good cause are: Nietzsche, a professor at Basel; Porges; E. v. Hagen; our friend Richard Pohl; Glasenapp, author of a 2-vol. biography of Wagner; and Nohl, biographer of Beethoven. Also Wolzogen, son of the Intendant of the Schwerin theatre. . . .

On Thursday evenings Wagner is at home to Ladies and Gentlemen—today there will be at least 80 of us. Every day there are half a dozen guests at dinner —the dining-room cannot seat more than 12. At Wilhelmsthal recently I said to Monseigneur: 'Bayreuth is now the *Musenhof* [Court of the Muses]; the absent will be in the wrong, and the hesitant will be accused of stupidity!'

Neither absent nor stupid—very humbly,   B.B.

754. To Princess Carolyne. Bayreuth, 19 August. The newspapers abound in articles and telegrams about Bayreuth. I restrict myself to sending you the little local *Moniteur*, which contains sufficient information. The Emp. of Germany attended performances of *Rheingold* and *Walküre* on Sunday and Monday, the 13th and 14th. His Majesty expressed his satisfaction to Wagner most graciously, complimenting him on the extraordinary success of the ensemble of the *National-Kunstwerk* [national work of art]—now the official title of the *Ring des Nibelungen*. After the Second Act, His Majesty deigned to talk to me too, and to assure me of his continuing goodwill. At 10 o'clock on Sunday evening, after *Rheingold*, the Emp. of Brazil sent for me. His conversation is agreeably intelligent—he rather wanted to hear me on the piano. I improvised after my own fashion, in a very dimly lit salon at the palace, during this tête-à-tête with His Majesty. Then, at about 11.00, I served him as chamberlain by accompanying him to Wagner's residence, where the Emp. spent a good quarter of an hour. This imperial incident caused a sensation here, and will be related by the newspapers. The Emp. of Brazil had come to Bayreuth almost on the spur of the moment, and stayed for one day only, leaving again on Monday morning.

The King of Bavaria will return in a week's time, for the 3rd series of performances. His personal and exclusive opinions, certainly very exalted ones, he reveals most emphatically—keeping apart from other sovereigns, whom he prefers not to meet. That seems strange—nevertheless, the friend of truth pays profound homage to King Ludwig II, to whom Wagner, Bayreuth, and the whole of this prodigious event of German art are indebted to the highest degree. Without him, Wagner would be reduced to experiencing only the depressing difficulties of a great genius. . . .

755. To Princess Carolyne. Bayreuth, 28 August. Forgive me for not complying with your request to send you as many newspapers as possible. They hardly enter Wagner's abode—and it would be bad taste on my part to ask for articles while I am living in this house. The German, Hungarian, English, and American press sent, at a cost, numerous correspondents here—as such, Wagner does not admit them into his home. It is only as personal exceptions that some of the most devoted of them can be seen at Wahnfried in the evenings, where *ricevimenti* [receptions] for 50 to 100 people are frequent. French newspapers are represented in Bayreuth by no more than half a dozen ardent admirers—at their head Mme Judith Mendès, daughter of Théophile Gautier. She is on the *Journal officiel*, the former *Moniteur*, but will scarcely find enough space in it to express more than a few small fragments of her enthusiasm. . . .

The 2nd series of performances, from 20 to 24 August, went off perfectly. The Grand Duchess of Baden, daughter of the Emp. of Germany, the Grand Duke and Duchess of Mecklenburg-Schwerin, and the Duke of Meiningen, attended them, in the Princes' box. When one thinks of the efforts and perseverance that were needed to obtain the result we see and hear—one can only bow before the supremacy of genius!

The King of Bavaria returned for the 3rd series, during the night of Saturday to Sunday. His Majesty forbade any ovation, and is keen to show that he does not condescend to popularity—while maintaining his royal support and esteem for Wagner's work. That is noble—if a little embarrassing for the local authorities! Despite the King's reserve, the town is bedecked with flags, and on Sunday evening was illuminated. Wagner alone is admitted to conversations with the King, in the theatre and at the Hermitage.

> Es soll der Sänger mit dem König gehen,
> Denn Beide wohnen auf der Menschheit Höhen.[15]

I do not know how to thank you for having finished the *Chopin*. We shall soon reread it together while remembering our beautiful days of struggle and of hope! On Saturday evening I shall be in Weimar, where I shall spend a fortnight. Afterwards, I shall go to see Bülow, who is extremely unwell. . . . He is now taking the cure at Godesberg, near Bonn.

Constanter et fideliter,   B.B.

---

[15] 'The singer should walk with the king, | For both dwell on mankind's heights' (Schiller, *Die Jungfrau von Orleans*, I. ii).

756. To Princess Carolyne. Weimar, 6 September. In all humility, I believe I do not deserve the letter I received from you today. With the most sorrowful sincerity I maintain what I told you in Rome: you are gravely mistaken about your daughter, about mine, and about me. God knows that to alleviate your sufferings was for many years my sole task! I have had little success, it seems! For my part, I wish to remember only the hours in which we have wept and prayed together, as one! After your letter of today I am giving up any thought of returning to Rome.   F.L.

757. To Princess Carolyne. Weimar, 16 September. Your latest letter is full of kindness and indulgence. I thank you for it with all my heart, which is still bleeding from recent wounds. Allow me to cure myself alone, without further discussion of my faults and wrongdoings! . . .

758. To Princess Carolyne. Hanover, 26 September. Bülow left Godesberg about ten days ago. At the pressing invitation of our friend Bronsart he came here, where I joined him last Saturday. He is convalescing well enough for us to hope for his complete recovery—after a few months of rest and care. When someone told you that Bülow had taken refuge in a lunatic asylum with a very high reputation, near Bonn, where Robert Schumann ended his days, they were mistaken. No trace of insanity with Bülow—but great exhaustion as a result of excessive work and of labours beyond measure. He disregarded a slight stroke which took him unawares in London last year. The doctors then advised him to take care of himself—whereupon he left as rapidly as possible for America, and there, in a period of 6 or 8 months, played more than a thousand pieces of music at 140 public concerts! On returning to London, he finally followed the doctors' orders, by betaking himself to Godesberg, near Bonn—there to undergo a *Stahlbadkur* [chalybeate bath cure] under the direction of the celebrated Dr Finkelburg. . . .

Your letter of 18 to 21 Sept., sent to Weimar, reached me here yesterday. My response would be very simple, if I could bring myself to return to Rome in October. Don't ask me to—to heal within, I need several months elsewhere—and before that I haven't the courage to present myself in your home. As I wrote, I shall be spending 3 or 4 days in Nuremberg and Regensburg, and returning to Hungary on about 10 Oct. There, I shall try not to test my true friends too severely, and to conduct myself so as to merit their approbation! Judge me not too harshly—but grant some charitable indulgence to your old   B.B.

759. To Princess Carolyne. Hanover, 28 September. To the enclosed letter—which I ask you to be so good as to give to Cardinal Hohenlohe—allow me to add a postscript for you, regarding the extreme dislike of Rome that you very wrongly attribute to me. True, I have never felt for Italy, its lemon trees and oranges, the *Sehnsucht* [longing] of Goethe's Mignon. Nevertheless, when I set the song *Kennst du das Land?* to music in Berlin in February 1842, after 50 other musicians, I identified myself as well as I could with the reveries of a young girl. Several of Goethe's friends, in particular Chancellor Müller, told me that I had succeeded pretty well—even that the emphasis on *dahin! dahin!* would not have displeased the great poet! Be that as it may, I no longer have to sing *dahin* for any of the regions of here below—but only for Purgatory, which by God's grace I hope to reach soon! . . .   B.B.

760. To Camille Saint-Saëns in Paris. Hanover, 2 October

Very dear friend,

In sending to you today the transcription of your *Danse macabre*, I ask you to excuse my lack of skill in reducing to the piano keyboard the marvellous colours of the orchestra.[16] No one is obliged to do what is impossible. To play the orchestra on the piano has as yet been given to no one. Nevertheless, the *Ideal* must always be aimed at, however unyielding and inadequate the form. Life and art, it seems to me, are good for that alone.

In sincere admiration and friendship,

Your very devoted   F. Liszt

761. To Princess Carolyne. Szekszárd, 26 October. The functions of the good fairies are not opposed to those of the good angels—they both have their hours in poetry as in real life. I should regret it if you abandoned 'Minette's' gracious wand entirely, to hold only the angels' censer! The peasants' party in the forest of Woronince in 1847—the golden conducting baton, garlanded with precious stones—the Midas, the symbolic inkstand—the *Chopin*, the *Bohémiens*, and 100 other things luminously fixed in my memory, belong to the reign of the good fairy! Your admirable letter of 22 October makes me hope that we shall celebrate our thirtieth anniversary together in Rome, in '77—Amen!

---

[16] In his reply of 6 Oct. Saint-Saëns remarked: 'You have produced a real masterpiece, and I never tire of admiring your "lack of skill".'

Augusz has already written to tell you that I feel very content in his home. His house is peaceful, comfortable, and even luxuriously maintained. This is the fourth time I have come here: to begin with, during the summer of '46, then in '65, after the performance of *Elisabeth* in Pest, and in August '70, at the time of the war. That last stay made me decide to settle in Pest, which I wasn't thinking of at all—but *vox populi* having expressed itself energetically, I accept the honour and the responsibility. For me, the main point can be summarized thus: having been born in Hungary, I should do something for it, little though it may be, through my musical talent. Without making a show of patriotism by mere words, I am keen to practise its duties—and so I hope that in 2 years the new Academy of Music in Pest will be on a sound footing.

Next Tuesday, Augusz and I are going to Kalocsa. We shall spend the 1st and 2nd of November at Mgr. Haynald's; the next evening, I shall be back in Pest, where I shall remain for the whole winter. My classes will take me at least fifteen hours every week; and my very onerous correspondence, which is my purgatory in this world, even longer. However, I shall try to save a few mornings to write a little music. It is the only work which rests me and keeps me in a state of equilibrium. . . .

Beethoven's Op. 106 is not a quartet but the great Sonata in B flat major for *Hammerklavier*. I can't tell you exactly why in 1821 Beethoven put this word into the title. It had been used on earlier occasions, but has fallen into disuse— just like that of *clavecin*. For years, pianoforte, or simply piano, has been used exclusively. If I am not mistaken, the *Hammerklavier* was the transition between the harpsichord (preceded by the spinet) and the Pianoforte that we know only too well. A talented composer, Theodor Kirchner, committed the pleonasm of calling one of his works *24 Klavierstücke für Pianoforte*. As for the marvellous Beethoven Sonata Op. 106, it consists of 4 movements: Allegro, Scherzo, Adagio, Prelude and Fugue, which take up 70 printed pages, if not more, and last almost an hour. I played it at the age of 10, doubtless very badly, but with passion—without anyone having taught it to me. My father wasn't equal to it, and Czerny was afraid to put me on such a diet. In those days, Hummel and Moscheles dominated the entire repertoire of pianists in Vienna and elsewhere. Several Beethoven sonatas were well known, and indeed profoundly admired, in particular the *Pathétique, Moonlight,* and *Appassionata*—but it was not the custom to play them in public. It wasn't until after the death of Beethoven that his works spread everywhere. The immense success of his symphonies at the Paris Conservatoire, from 1829 onwards, contributed greatly to making popular in Europe not only the symphonies but also the sonatas, quartets, etc. of this sublime and solitary genius, so full of human anguish and celestial ecstasy.

At the 2 side altars of the local church appear the archangels Gabriel and Raphael, the one announcing to Mary the salvation that humanity will receive from her; the other healing Tobias. The day before yesterday, feast of Raphael, I prayed to him to heal me too. The day after tomorrow, feast of the apostles St Simon and St Jude, I shall continue my constant prayer to the Holy Angels to assist you in your work—to console you in your sadnesses—and to fill your soul with divine blessings!   B.B.

762. To Princess Carolyne. Budapest, Saturday evening, 18 November. In your letters a tone of bitter desolation can often be heard! Can I not sweeten it by pruning away the doleful reasons which cause it! On 26 Oct. you wrote: 'Shall I die on straw?' If by any remote chance such an enormity came to pass—be assured that I would by lying on the floor beside your straw! My whole life long I shall avoid making to you anything resembling a remonstrance. However, I fail to understand how you can feel yourself to be surrounded by the emptiness of indifference; to be isolated, dying, alone with Jesus Christ on the Cross! Are you, then, forgetting your daughter, who loves you deeply? Are you taking no account of your very numerous friends and admirers, Cardinals and Bishops, Princes and Princesses, personalities and celebrities, scholars and artists, aristocrats and bourgeois, priests and nuns, men and women of society? Truly, it is a strange sort of isolation—that of associating with hundreds of people, of receiving and writing several thousand letters and notes a year! I make no mention of myself!

Sunday morning. Let us return to the subject of your domestic service! Serving well is not something that occurs frequently, in any echelon of society. You have several times reprimanded me for my indulgence towards servants. I am sticking to it, however, seeing the anomaly of conditions here below. Moderate your Christmas generosities. Pius IX, at Castel Gandolfo, while several prelates were playing billiards, quoted before dinner Horace's proverbial maxim: 'Ne quid nimis.'[17] It well applies to friendship—not between lovers, where too much is never enough! The good La Fontaine charmingly said:

'Rien de trop est un point
Dont on parle sans cesse, et qu'on n'observe point.'

The painting by Siemiradzki that you praised to me, depicting Nero's living torches, has created a sensation in Vienna, and will shortly be exhibited here. Siemiradzki had earlier painted a *Mary Magdalene*, to which little attention was

---

[17] An expression borrowed from the Greek *mēden agan*—'nothing to excess'.

paid at that time. Great artists have stages to go through and even failures to experience! . . . B.B.

763. To Ede Reményi in Paris. [Budapest] 6 December

Dear friend,

I cannot be annoyed with you for forgetting that I no longer travel. As it is, the journey from Budapest to Weimar and back is extremely tiring for me; yet I feel obliged to submit to it, having in both places unceasing duties to fulfil.

I wholeheartedly applaud from afar the glorious successes of composers and virtuosi in Paris, London, Petersburg, New York, etc., etc., but without in the least claiming to rank myself with them; consequently, I beg people to be so kind as to leave me *out* of concert programmes.

My long and very grateful memories of the *Erard firm* go back to the time of my arrival in Paris in 1823. Only too often did I play the piano in the salons of the rue du Mail, where I was in time to hear the masters of the fine old school, Hummel, Cramer, Moscheles, *et al.*, and later Thalberg and Döhler. They are dead, and I don't know why I outlive them....

As for the pianistic inauguration of the new Salle Erard, the honour devolves on younger and better artistes than I, named Bülow, Rubinstein, Saint-Saëns.

Rossini used to take pleasure in signing a good many of his photographs, 'Pianist of the third class'. For my part, I aspire only to the title of superannuated ex-pianist (without being classed or declassed in any way whatsoever).

Be so kind as to give Madame Erard my enclosed reply.

Yours, F. Liszt

764. To Princess Carolyne. Budapest, 27 December. Your telegram to

Augusz makes me think that you got wind of my little accident, which I did not wish to mention to you. This time it was not in the figurative sense that I came down on the side on which I was leaning. I quite simply fell my full length when getting out of the carriage, at the entrance to the Hotel Hungária, where I was making a call on the Revd Father Raymond, Pcss Raymondine Auersperg's Dutch Dominican priest. My fall was not a heavy one—no bruise worth the bother of a plaster! After a few days spent in my room, I am restored to good condition, apart from a little discomfort in my right arm, which will have gone by tomorrow. Besides, I had 2 other accidents during the course of the year: a bruise on the right thumb at Weimar in June, and in Szekszárd a rather deep razor cut to my left index finger, entirely my own fault. Stupidly, I raised my hand too high when enjoining something or other on Spiridion while he was shaving me—and in this way I learnt to hold in greater regard the excellence of his razor. Let's talk no more of such trifles! Several of my friends have broken their arms and legs. If such a thing happened to me, it wouldn't bother me too much—I should even prefer this kind of distraction to my usual pleasures, for it would obtain me more rest! . . .   B.B.

5 March. Liszt conducts his *Legend of St Elisabeth* at the Vigadó.

11–22 March. He stays in Vienna where, on the 16th, at a concert in aid of the city's Beethoven monument, he plays Beethoven's *Emperor* Concerto and Choral Fantasia. In the audience is the 11-year-old Ferruccio Busoni,* who plays to Liszt at the Schottenhof.

24 March–3 April. Liszt is the Wagners' guest in Bayreuth.

4 April. He arrives in Weimar, his headquarters for the next four months.

15–30 May. He stays in Hanover and participates in the festival of the Allgemeine Deutsche Musikverein.

1 July. Alexander Borodin visits Liszt in Weimar, and is frequently in his company during the next three weeks.

6/7 July. Liszt spends two days in Berlin, and at Potsdam on the 7th is the guest of the Crown Prince and Princess.

12–15 August. He again stays in Bayreuth with the Wagners.

19 August. He arrives in Rome, remaining here, and in Tivoli, until 17 November.

21 November. Liszt returns to Budapest.

WORKS. PIANO: *Sancta Dorothea* (S187); *Petőfi szellemének—Dem Andenken Petőfis* (S195); *Zweite Elegie* (S197); *Années de pèlerinage, troisième année* (S163): 1. *Angelus! Prière aux anges gardiens* 2. *Aux cyprès de la Villa d'Este: Thrénodie I* 3. *Aux cyprès de la Villa d'Este: Thrénodie II* 4. *Les Jeux d'eaux à la Villa d'Este* 5. *Sunt lacrymae rerum: en mode hongrois* (1872) 6. *Marche funèbre: en mémoire de Maximilien I, Empereur de Mexique* (1867) 7. *Sursum corda.*
Zweite Elegie (S131, an arrangement of S197), for violin/cello and piano. *Resignazione* (S263), for organ. The song *Sei still* (Nordheim, pen-name of H. von Schorn) (S330).

765. To Princess Carolyne in Rome. Budapest, 10 January. Let's argue no more about devotional practices! You have often recommended to me the narrow way of the Gospel; to make it easier for me you have also often tried to lighten the heavy crosses imposed upon me by my faults. Have I aggravated these still further by the least ingratitude towards you? I think not. The 30 years of our close relationship are full of the respect, admiration, and keen gratitude I have shown to you. As for the good crosses—I have always regarded them as a propitious means of penitence and salvation. In that, I associate myself with the sentiment of the penitent thief, who recognized that he had deserved his punishment, and put his trust in the promise given him by Our Lord Jesus Christ! Kindly, therefore, disapprove no more of my sincere devotion to the penitent thief!

You mention Napoleon III's allusion to the *Via Crucis*, during his journey from Sedan to Cassel. It was a Christian inspiration—my great admiration for the Emperor forbids me to make any criticism. However, all mortals being sinners, no one can compare himself to Jesus Christ, who alone is holy—as we say in the Gloria of the mass. Besides, I find it impossible to raise myself to your mystical viewpoint of Napoleon's voluntary sacrifice in his last campaign. Neither his uncle at Waterloo, nor he at Sedan, reckoned on such a frightful disaster—to enthrone their heirs more securely! They were defeated, without sacrificing themselves to any idea other than their national sovereignty. Otherwise, Tamerlane and Attila would, in comparison, be little saints! Let us leave to statesmen the task of providing for the well-being of nations! They are attending to it now in Constantinople—it's no concern of that foolish breed, poets and musicians!

What is most depressing for me in my old days is to find our opinions at variance. It was not thus from '47 to '62! Apart from a few disputes about literary requirements, and my follies, we were in total agreement on all essential matters. Rome and your transcendencies of mind have changed all that—but even now I acknowledge only the differences of opinion, not any disagreement of the heart—to which I shall *never* subscribe. . . .   F.L.

766. To Princess Carolyne. Budapest, 14 January. You see in your present satisfactions one of the forced smiles of fate—an ingenious remark which reminds me that before your marriage you said to Mme Patersi, 'I *will* force you to love me.' Wouldn't there, however, be a way of loving and helping one another in this world, in a Christian way and, so far as the fundamental miseries of our existence allow, even happily—without wearying St Jude in Rome with our lamentations, and above all without forcing anything? You will regard this simple question as a bucolic stupidity—so be it! You have a passion for the Great—and you reproach Hegel and Cardinal Antonelli with having not been great enough! I listen to what you say—and fail to understand! Baptism gave me for a patron saint, Francis of Paola, of obscure origins and founder of the Order of Minims. He fasted, mortified the flesh, did not write down his sermons, and concerned himself very little with literature. Your patron, St Charles Borromeo, scion of an illustrious family, early became a cardinal and so took part in the government of the Church. He even took an interest in music, and supported the reform of the Sistine Chapel which was allowed at that time, as desired by Palestrina. While fasting and mortifying the flesh, like St Francis of Paola, and taking 'Humilitas' as his motto—he remained Archbishop of Milan and *Porporato*.[1] Our differences of opinion are best explained by our respective patron saints. You soar on high, and I flounder about below. I attach myself to the Minim—and you are in harmony with the Great One, who must rule and govern! . . .

In very humble devotion to the Patron Saint of the Minims and to the penitent thief, your   F.L.

767. To Hans von Bülow. Budapest, 20 January. Rarely have I so choked with emotion as when reading your letter. It is heart-rending—and of a sublime goodness of heart. If tears were written down, my reply would be long; but to weep is not manly—I forbid myself to do so, and don't want to despair. That would be showing ingratitude towards the providence which has given me a friend such as you.

My misery is not less than yours, for all that it may seem set in a fairly ornate framework and sustained by my plebeian health. To bring together our two 'great miseries' is my great wish. United, they would without question be transformed into a treasure more enviable than the Rothschild millions. Your portrait of the '*Ideale*' (1863) with the inscription *nec vincere desistam* is before me.[2]

Let us be victorious: the blows of fate serve to spur us on; obstacles become means.

See you again soon, very dear and unique one. At the beginning of April I shall be back in Weimar. Tell me then where you can be found by

your faithful, saddened   F. Liszt

768. To Princess Carolyne. Budapest, 19 February. You speak admirably of God's great alchemy, which transforms evil into good. It is one of the attributes of His Providence, which we worship submissively! . . .

Do you know the photograph of a painting by Laszinski of Cracow, depicting the death of Chopin and entitled *Ostatnie chwile Chopina* [The last moments of Chopin]? It has been sent to me anonymously, and if you have not yet seen it I shall pass it on to you. I suppose the principal figure is Pcss Marcelina

---

[1] 'One clothed in purple', hence a cardinal.

[2] A photograph of Bülow holding the score of *Die Ideale*, with the inscription, in his own hand, 'Sub hoc signo vici et nunquam vincere desistam' (Under this sign I conquered, and shall never cease to conquer).

Czartoryska; behind her, one lady is kneeling, another standing, and a third hiding her face in tears. I don't know why the Abbé Jelowicki has been forgotten in this picture. Would the *beau monde* be turning rationalist to the point of taking fright at a cassock by a death-bed? The gentleman in plain clothes who seems to be sounding Chopin's chest makes no very picturesque effect—but, yet worse, in the corner of the room another gentleman is playing the piano. Poor Chopin, still having to hear the piano during his last moments, and to receive compliments which he could no longer decline with thanks!

At Dresden a new biography of Chopin is now being brought out in 2 vols., written in German by M. Moritz [Maurycy] Karasowski, 'nach authentischen Quellen, theils Mittheilungen der noch lebenden Schwester Chopin's, theils einiger seiner intimsten Freunde [according to authentic sources, partly communications from Chopin's surviving sister, partly from some of his closest friends]'.[3] In this biography 43 letters of Chopin's will be published, plus 2 unpublished letters by George Sand. . . .

Jules Janin's library—which contains treasures of the rarest erudition, in autographs and annotations, even in precious bindings—is being sold at auction. Mme Janin's offer of it as a gift, on condition that these treasures be kept in a room reserved for them alone and adorned with the name of Janin, the Académie Française did not accept.

Forgive me for resembling M. Duteil, saying to Mme Sand: 'Genius, inspiration, and superb phrases, George has and to spare—but logic, that's my business!' Mine own principal business would be to serve you

  constanter et fideliter, as   Bon Besson

769. To Princess Carolyne. Budapest, 7 March. I am greatly distressed to find you accusing me of ingratitude. If I thought I deserved this reproach, nothing would be left to me but to die at the very earliest. Having to bear the shame of ingratitude seems to me to be a fate worse than the forced labours of galley slaves! You also take me to task for not writing about what I am doing. Alas! I am hardly interested in my existence any more, and do not find that its details make an agreeable communication! During these last 4 months my time has been spent in reading about a thousand letters and notes—and in replying somehow or other to the most urgent. My best hours are those of my professorship at the new Academy of Music. Four times a week, between 4.00 and 6.00 p.m., I teach about fifteen artistes of both sexes—several of whom are already

---

[3] *Friedrich Chopin: sein Leben, seine Werke und Briefe* (Dresden, 1877).

distinguished talents—to play the piano and to understand music. In addition, I have attended about twenty concerts and ten opera performances: Goldmark's *The Queen of Sheba*, Erkel's *Bánk bán* and *Hunyady*, *Die Zauberflöte*, and *Geist des Wojwoden*. This last is a light opera by a composer from Warsaw, Grossmann, who has attempted a fusion of Polish and Hungarian music. I have also twice heard Verdi's *Requiem*, an important and serious work. Its great success, upheld by the insurance company of successes, is no less legitimate than that of Rossini's *Stabat Mater*. I remember that a priest in the outskirts of Paris once remarked to me: 'This year, death hasn't given!' But Verdi's *Requiem* will give good receipts at the theatres—for on certain days in the year one has to celebrate the memory of an illustrious dead person, in the country to which he belonged. Mozart's *Requiem* has become hackneyed, Cherubini's is too starchy, and Berlioz's too difficult. So—*Viva Verdi!* He has the double merit of composing conscientiously and profitably! . . .

I have by no means forgotten that you had written to me about a painting depicting the death of Chopin. But biographies, photographs, and posthumous narratives in honour of Chopin are multiplying to such a point that I was not sure if the mediocrely inspired picture was identical with the one you had told me about. If I could paint, how differently would I have depicted Chopin's last moments! This Herr Gutmann, seated on the bed as though coming back from a hunting expedition, and the other gentleman at the piano, are *seccature* [irritations]—and even Pcss Marcelina, in the attitude in which she is shown, strikes me as bourgeoisely bothersome.

Next Monday or Tuesday I shall be in Vienna. The concert for the Beethoven monument is on 16 March. Afterwards I shall stop for a day in Nuremberg, to chat with Lina Ramann, and will spend Holy Week at my daughter's in Bayreuth. . . . Augusz will tell you about the *Elisabeth*, performed the day before yesterday, and also about a charity concert to take place on Saturday. I shall participate by accompanying on a second piano Mme Sophie Popper-Menter,[4] who is, in my opinion, the best woman pianist in Europe. . . .

Very humbly, and without ingratitude, your F.L.

770. To Princess Carolyne. Weimar, Thursday, 5 April. To get here from Bayreuth, one passes through Meiningen—where, at the kind invitation of Duke Georg, I stopped for 24 hours, from the day before yesterday to yesterday. On Tuesday, at 5.00, I dined there *à quatre* with Pce Edward of

---

[4] Sophie Menter had in June 1872 married the cellist David Popper. 'Sophie, don't do it—you are not right for one another,' Liszt had warned her. To no avail, and after only a few years the couple separated.

Saxe-Weimar, whom I hadn't seen since Maria Pavlovna's funeral. He has acquired the best manner of London's high society, being both a native and a resident of that city. He has the rank of an English Major General, commanding officer of a Guards division; and he married morganatically Lady Augusta Gordon-Lennox, daughter of the Duke of Richmond. In the Schloss that evening we had a charming orchestral concert, which I made a little longer with 2 piano pieces, and then a seated supper for more than 50 people. You perhaps remember that Duke Georg's 3rd wife, now Baroness von Heldburg, was once a great friend of Cosima's in Berlin. Their relations were interrupted for a dozen years, but have resumed in Vienna and Bayreuth on their former close footing. Recently, Wagner and Cosima spent 3 days at the Meiningen Schloss—the Duke was then so amiably attentive as to have 3 performances given by his theatrical company, which now enjoys exceptional fame following its successes in Berlin, Vienna, and other German citites. The plays chosen were: Grillparzer's *Esther*, [Molière's] *Le Malade imaginaire* and [Shakespeare's] *Julius Caesar*.

The betrothal of the Duke's son to the daughter of the German Crown Prince took place in Berlin, last Sunday. The bride-to-be is not yet 17, and the marriage will be next year. People speak very well of the Hereditary Pce of Saxe-Meiningen, of whom I caught only a glimpse. He is a passionate enthusiast of the Greek tragic poets, and has composed music for the *Persae* of Aeschylus—a little too Greek, according to his father! . . .   B.B.

771. To Princess Carolyne. Weimar, 25 April.

Twelve years ago, on 25 April, feast of St Mark, I entered the Vatican as Mgr. Hohenlohe's acolyte. The sentiments which led me to it have not ceased—they date from the years of my childhood, and from my first communion in a little village church. . . .

Don't command me the practice *in extenso* of the customary civilities by letter or telegram! Correspondence has become my purgatory here on earth! Sometimes, after having foolishly spent the day pen in hand, I feel an absolute need to get my breath back a little, to sleep—and to dream of my old companion, music. . . .

26 April. I take up again the rosary of my replies to your questions. The Wagners go to London next Sunday. Have I spoken to you of Wagner's *Parsifal*? In the salons there is already much wagging of tongues about it; in Vienna, Pcss Metternich all but insisted that I play her its sublime melodies—not yet written! The fact is, Wagner has not yet finished the poem, the First Act of which he read to me on 2 April. On his return from London, he will get down to composing the music. Other venues for making money had been suggested to him, but he preferred 'perfidious Albion',[5] which will show herself, I hope, loyal and obliging in this instance. *The Times*, formerly very hostile to the works of Wagner, has become their apologist. That reassures the English public and the German public at one and the same time!

From Bayreuth to Nuremberg is but a short step. In my humble opinion, the best thing would be for Lina Ramann to limit her labours to a musical commentary on my works, the complete catalogue of which has just been published by Härtel. It would be sufficient for her to touch on the biographical side—very much outside her *deutsche Sittlichkeit* [German morality]—lightly in passing. If you have no objection, I ask you to advise her to restrict her work to a single volume of about 400 pages, which will deal with me as a musical individual, the pianist and composer such as I am. In this way she will certainly obtain the serious success she desires. Were it not immediate, it would increase in a few years! Forgive me this apparent fatuity—which conforms more with truth than would false modesty.

I am not of your opinion about the publication of Karasowski's *Chopin*. It will hardly serve, wholly mediocre as it is, to bring our *Chopin* into relief—for the public prefers things at its own level and according to its habits. . . .

After the *Faust* performances we have had here 4 successive evenings of Shakespeare's histories, *Richard II*, *Henry IV*, and *V.* Dingelstedt mounted in Weimar—about fifteen years before Vienna—the complete cycle of the 7 historical plays from *Richard II* and the *Henrys* to *Richard III*. It is the most brilliant feather in Dingelstedt's dramatic cap at Weimar and in Vienna. Magne has no doubt written to you about the success of these performances in Vienna. Those in Weimar interested me keenly—I followed them while reading the printed text. But what would interest me much more, would be to know the 5 full folios on the *Causes*! You are wrong to deprive me of them. If my ignorance justifies your excluding me from your literary and philosophical works, I resign myself to this humiliation only with deep sorrow! In earlier and better days, in Weimar and even in Rome, you were more generous towards me and did not entrench yourself so much in a kind of Tabor, inaccessible to simpletons of my sort!

F.L.

772. To Princess Carolyne. Hanover, 25 May.

Hanover's *Musikfest*, which ended yesterday, was a total success both artistically and financially. Thanks to the tact and vigilant steadiness of our excellent friend Bronsart, everything went off as desired—barring an unpleasant accident to one of the conductors,

---

[5] The expression *la perfide Angleterre* was coined by Bossuet; by the time of the Revolution it had become *la perfide Albion*.

indisposed [drunk] to the point of being unable to conduct the *Elisabeth* to the end. I am sending you the detailed programme, to which was added my Concerto in A, 'Let us inhale eternity!', brilliantly played by Pinner, and the Legend of St Cecilia, composed at the Villa d'Este. . . .

The orchestral works most warmly received by the public were Berlioz's *Symphonie fantastique*, which I conducted on this occasion; Bülow's ballad *Sängers Fluch*, a noble and beautiful work, quite equal to Uhland's ballad; the Andante and Finale from the Second Symphony of Tchaikovsky, whom I esteem—and, finally, the Dante Symphony. . . .

I flatter myself that I understand the *finesse* of your remark about the multiplicity of the arts in music. It has been well said that it is the only art which continues in Paradise!

I shall speak to you again about the performance of our friend Cornelius's *Barber of Bagdad*, admirable music with a very witty libretto, but lacking so far as theatrical requirements are concerned. Yesterday evening's success was more apparent than real. In my opinion, this charming musical work would have a chance of lasting in the theatre only if it were reduced to a single act—because nothing takes place on stage. However beautiful the music it is hearing, an opera audience cannot do without being entertained by what is happening on stage. Be that as it may, Bronsart acted nobly in having the *Barber of Bagdad* performed again, at the Hanover *Musikfest*. The scandal of the Weimar performance is thus fittingly made good. Cornelius's widow had come from Munich to attend yesterday evening's performance. . . .

Next Thursday I shall be in Weimar! May the good angels sing you the most beautiful celestial music!   B.B.

773. To Princess Carolyne. Weimar, Friday, 15 June. . . . Without complaining, I often suffer from living—health of the body remains to me, that of the soul is lacking. *Tristis est anima mea!* However, to my numerous real and alleged faults will never be added that of ingratitude, the very worst of all! From the bottom of my heart I bless you for persevering for 30 years in actively wishing for me the Good, the Beautiful, and the True. In this, you are heroic and sublime—and I feel unworthy to unlace your shoes! . . .

774. To Princess Carolyne. Dornburg, 25 June. Yesterday morning, when I got here from Weimar, Count Wedel spoke of your very kind present, a copy of the Titian—and Count Beust told me that he had just received a gracious letter from you, accompanied by your photograph. To the thanks sent to you by Wedel and his father-in-law Beust I can only add my profound regret about your remoteness from Weimar—your undue remoteness, it seems to me. But I have to get used to the fact that my words, whether spoken or written, no longer count for much! I am wrong to write that—but one quiet evening in the Babuino you will grant me permission to explain myself at greater length.

Because of mourning for the Queen of the Netherlands, Monseigneur's 59th birthday was celebrated here very quietly. At table, and in the evening, Their Royal Highnesses were surrounded by about ten high-ranking Court personnel at most. . . .

Have you read 2 singularly remarkable pages by Renan in the *Revue des Deux Mondes* on the late Queen?[6] She is described therein as the last of the great Princesses—a title that several of her close relatives by no means allow her! A close bond between Queen Sophia and Renan was formed by the great and virtuous Spinoza. From what the connoisseurs say, Daniel Stern's unfinished history of the Netherlands is her best work. The same authoress's *Mémoires* interest me only as literature. She was so amiable as to read me fifty or so pages from them in the spring of '66, and, still seeking a title at that time, asked my advice. *Dichtung und Wahrheit* belongs to Goethe, *Mémoires d'outre-tombe* to Chateaubriand, and *Confessions* have continued from St Augustine to Rousseau and as far as Alfred de Musset's *Confession d'un enfant du siècle*. What remains? . . . F.L.

775. To Princess Carolyne. Weimar, 14 July. For a number of years Frau von Schleinitz has been unwaveringly kind and affectionate to me. She is the devoted friend of my daughter, and made a notable contribution to the success of the great artistic event in Bayreuth. She will probably be back here with Cosima, in about ten days. Last week I paid her a friendly visit in Berlin—she and her husband insisted on my staying with them, at the Ministry of the King's Household, where I saw Mme Ada Pinelli again, who has written to you. Herr von Schlözer—minister in America, whom you remember from Rome—was at the soirée, and also at the dinner given the next day by the English Ambassador in Berlin, Lord Russell,[7] very well known and appreciated in Rome.

---

[6] The issue of 15 June. Queen Sophia, who had given Liszt so friendly a welcome in 1866, was regarded as one of the best-educated women in Europe. She and King Willem had long been separated, but it had been their practice once every year, in a vault-like apartment in Amsterdam, to have a formal meeting lasting a few minutes. Her own residence was at the Huis ten Bosch near The Hague. It was open to visitors, and every day at noon the Queen would send for the visitors' book to see who had called since noon the previous day. It was not by Sophia but by his second wife, Emma, that King Willem fathered the late Queen Wilhelmina.

[7] Odo Russell, later Baron Ampthill, was a brother of the 9th Duke of Bedford and a second cousin of the late Bertrand Russell.

At Potsdam on Saturday, before Russell's dinner, Their Highnesses the Crown Prince and Princess[8] deigned to give me a most gracious welcome. I stayed with them for about 2 hours, a few piano pieces being played without effort. The Crown Prince has a lofty, correct, and kindly simplicity, very becoming for great sovereigns; nor will his wife let him down. She was also so good as to show me an album containing the autographs of Pius IX, Cardinal Antonelli, and others. I shall speak to you again of this interview, very flattering for me. The Prince and his wife openly admire Wagner, which at once put me at ease in their presence. I remember that, at the Villa d'Este, Queen Olga of Würtemberg told me that no sensible person thought anything of the *Ring des Nibelungen*, an absurd work and impossible to perform according to the most learned professors of aesthetics. I permitted myself to observe very humbly to Her Majesty that infallibility was not the attribute of professors! The Bayreuth performances are a *fait accompli*—the condemned work exists and nobly makes its way to the honour of art; the name of Wagner is at once most glorious and very popular, above all the scowlings, stupidities, and insults of the critics! . . .

                                                                          F.L.

776. To Princess Carolyne. Villa d'Este, Friday, 31 August. Comte Gobineau's style is much better than his handwriting, difficult to decipher. I haven't managed to read several words, nor the name of the learned Milanese professor, author of the *Fonti Ariostee*,[9] which includes the knightly romances of the Middle Ages, above all those of the Round Table. This work would interest Wagner, and I shall send it to him, as soon as I can give the author's exact name to Löscher the bookseller. In Rome I shall ask you to give me instruction in Gobineau's hieroglyphics. In the mean time, his criticism of Renan's book strikes me as plausible.

Hohenlohe still shows me the most perfect and affectionate kindness. Just now he spoke to me about an excursion to Subiaco with the Revd Father Ceroni, a Rosminian of good intelligence and pleasant company—and at present a fellow resident of the Villa d'Este. At two o'clock he and I lunched with the Cardinal —there has so far been no other guest. . . . The piano arrived yesterday morning, and in the evening I made music tête-à-tête with Hohenlohe—who plays

---

[8] The subsequent Friedrich III, German emperor for three months in 1888, and his wife Victoria ('Vicky'), eldest child of Queen Victoria and Prince Albert. To her mother, the Crown Princess had written (7 July): 'Liszt is coming over here this afternoon to play to us, and I own I look forward to it greatly; it is so long since I have heard him.'

[9] Pio Rajna's *Le Fonti dell' 'Orlando furioso'* (Florence, 1876).

very agreeably, on both the harmonium and the piano, the *Ave maris stella* I composed at the Vatican.

As Grétry said to Napoleon[10]—still   B.B.

777. To Princess Carolyne. Villa d'Este, 3 September. Yesterday evening, when your letter arrived, Hohenlohe was in my room. Many thanks for having looked into the matter of the *Fonti Ariostee*, which on some suitable occasion I shall send to Cosima, for Wagner doesn't read Italian. I shall add to it Mgr. Gerbet's admirable work, *Du dogme générateur de la piété catholique*, which also contains the same author's splendid treatise on confession. Wagner wishes to learn about the Catholic conception of the dogma of the Eucharist, with a view to his present transcendental work *Parsifal*—in which, at the end of the First Act, the Knights of the Holy Grail take communion. He is calling his *Parsifal* a *Bühnenweihespiel* [sacred stage drama]—and I have told him that Gerbet's short volume would help him, better than large works—were they written by St Thomas Aquinas himself—to initiate himself into the sublimest of the mysteries of divine love.

You observe, judiciously, that I have knocked about the world only too much—please Heaven, may my travels cease! The trip to Subiaco has been postponed indefinitely—there will be no more mention of it.

Faithfully,   B.B.

778. To Princess Carolyne. Villa d'Este, Sunday evening, 23 September. These 3 days I have spent entirely under the cypresses![11] It was an obsession, impossible to think of anything else, even church. Their old trunks were haunting me, and I heard their branches singing and weeping, bearing the burden of their unchanging foliage! At last they are brought to bed on music paper; and after having greatly corrected, scratched out, copied, and recopied them, I resign myself to touching them no more. They differ from the cypresses of Michelangelo by an almost loving melody.

May the good angels make the most beautiful inner music for you—the music we shall hear fully, in its boundlessness, there above!   F.L.

Spiridion has just brought me your letter. Thank you for the information about Michelangelo's cypresses, and the small photograph showing them. . . .

[10] When Napoleon I asked Grétry his name twice in succession, the composer replied 'Still Grétry!'
[11] Referring to the composition of *Aux cyprès de la Villa d'Este*.

If he took a little trouble, Hohenlohe could play the *Cyprès*—for they are quite easy to play, technically speaking. Zaluski will play them fluently *a prima vista*.

779. To Princess Carolyne. Budapest, 26 November. My journey from Lamporecchio to Pest was completed in 36 hours, from Tuesday morning to Wednesday evening, without incident or interruption. Pce Rospigliosi made me the agreeable reproach of having paid him too short a visit, which according to him was like a doctor's visit! I replied that I absolutely had to be in Pest on St Cecilia's Day, 22 Nov., because of a musical discussion I was obliged to attend.

Let me give you some details of my domestic arrangements, much too luxurious in my opinion. Without my knowledge, Augusz arranged for me a complete Ministry of the Interior—consisting of 3 or 4 persons, not counting the inviolable Spiridion. They are: Mme Schwäger, a widow, a most respectable person and distinguished 'officier de bouche'—as cooks are called; Mme Fanny, the official charged with opening the door, receiving letters, visiting-cards and packets, in the absence of Spiridion, who is often out on errands, doing shopping, collecting or dispatching parcels; plus an assistant to polish the floors and undertake the essential task of cleaning them; and finally, Monsieur the porter and Madame his wife, or Mademoiselle his sister or relative, to whom falls the department of things more or less *ad libitum*. I at once remarked to Augusz that for my simple style of living a cook was a burdensome and very costly superfluity. As in previous years, here, in Weimar and at the Villa d'Este, a second-class restaurant would suit me perfectly well. It would even make good the few rare buffet *extras* on those occasions when celebrated artistes are passing through and do me the pleasure of readily coming to my place and being comfortable there. Nevertheless, the Ministry set up by Augusz before my arrival will last for a few months—despite the increase in expenses that it imposes on me and which I could have done without; I don't want to become a miser, but I do need to remain relatively thrifty. To gainsay my close friends is always extremely painful to me—and I shall in particular avoid distressing Augusz and his wife, whom I could hardly thank enough for their kind concern in my regard. So we shall have a very peaceful life in the Fish Market this winter—reserving the right to change the ministerial arrangements next year.

I have hardly left my room this week. The day after my arrival I took Hohenlohe's letter to Mgr. Haynald, who paid a very pleasant call on me a few hours later. Albert Apponyi, who possesses a great talent for oratory and is well on the way towards fulfilling his promise as leader of the intelligent Conservative party, continues to show me devotion and friendship. Likewise Ödön Mihalovich, and Géza Zichy,* president of the Music Conservatoire, a perfect gentleman with an attractive touch of Hungarian chivalry, writer, poet, musician, and remarkable pianist even, although he has only a left hand at his disposal, a hunting accident having deprived him of his right arm. . . .

Wholly at your feet,   F.L.

780. To Princess Fanny Rospigliosi at Lamporecchio. Budapest, 7 December

Madame la Princesse,

Under the continuing impression of your gracious welcome and your exquisite kindness, my journey from Pistoia to Pest passed without trouble. Here, people were surprised to find me looking tolerably well, for it seems that several newspapers had reported that I was ill. They will excuse me for not coming over to their opinion in that, and for contenting myself with some heavy colds, to which I pay no attention.

Ruysbroeck, 'the admirable',[12] deserves to be appreciated by you, Princess. His mysticism does not go on all fours; it has wings and shafts of celestial light. At a musical tangent, I sometimes 'half-hear' the harmonies of the mystical region in which Beethoven and other lofty geniuses soar during their great moments of inspiration. 'Who loves, understands.'

The work of which we spoke at Lamporecchio will reach you shortly. It is the most complete in this category that I know; M. l'abbé and your sisters of the tertiary order of St Dominic will take an interest in reading it. In addition to its chief merit, a full and faithful statement of the dogma, ethics, and creed of our holy religion, it offers an attraction that I permit myself to call a literary, historical, and even anecdotal one of noble *recreation*. The numerous notes added to the end of each chapter provide singularly edifying quotations from Voltaire, Jean-Jacques, Victor Hugo, Emile de Girardin, Macaulay, *et al.*, *et al.*

I venture to ask you to count on my most affectionate devotion, and to remember kindly to Prince Rospigliosi

Your most respectfully grateful servant   F. Liszt

Until the beginning of April I shall stay here; then in Weimar, and in the autumn (probably) in Rome. There, you were so kind as not to treat me *as a tourist*. It was exceptional at that time, and all but risky. And so I remain very humbly grateful to you.

---

[12] Whom Liszt had been reading in the translation by Hello.

781. To Princess Carolyne. Budapest, 14 December. I am sending direct to Sgambati the papers relating to the polemic that has begun about the number of pupils in the piano classes at the Liceo Reale di Santa Cecilia [in Rome]. Those opposed to them claim that there are too many pianists—I should very gladly be of their opinion, minus the silliness or malevolence. At all conservatoires the number of piano students far exceeds in total that of all other instrumentalists—not to mention unofficial piano schools, which in Vienna and Berlin count their pupils in hundreds. Those of Kullak and Horak, for example, provide at least a thousand pianists, and even little Weimar's *Orchesterschule* is swarming with them. The reason is very simple: the piano is the microcosm of music, as I am writing to Sgambati. Singers of both sexes, flautists and bassoonists, even cornettists and kettledrummers, have to learn the piano if they want to find their bearings intelligently in their own field. And so at the Vienna Conservatorium they have introduced a rule that a piano course of 2 or 3 years is obligatory for all pupils, whatever the instrument of which they are making a special study. This rule will be followed profitably by all conservatoires, if they do indeed wish to be of use to the honourable practice of the art.

Wholly at your feet,   F.L.

1878

4 January. At his home in Budapest, Liszt gives a soirée for Léo Delibes, a performance of whose *Coppélia* he had attended on the 3rd.

1–7 April. Liszt stays in Vienna with his cousin Eduard.

8–17 April. He is the guest in Bayreuth of the Wagners.

17 April. He arrives in Weimar, his headquarters until mid-August.

9–18 June. Liszt represents Hungary at the Paris Exhibition.

22–6 June. He attends the music festival in Erfurt.

20–31 August. He again stays in Bayreuth.

3 September. Liszt arrives in Rome, staying here, and in Tivoli, until the following January.

9 September. His friend Baron Augusz dies.

1 November. Liszt has an audience with Pope Leo XIII.

WORKS. *Septem sacramenta. Responsoria cum organo vel harmonio concinente* (S52), for solo voices, mixed chorus, and organ/harmonium. SONGS: *Gebet* (Bodenstedt, after Lermontov) (S331, *c.*1878); *Einst* (Bodenstedt) (S332, *c.*1878); *An Edlitam*[1] (Bodenstedt) (S333, *c.*1878); *Der Glückliche* (Wilbrandt) (S334, *c.*1878).

782. To Baron Augusz. Budapest, 2.00 p.m., Saturday, 19 January

Honoured friend,

No one could admire more than I the great heart and lofty intelligence of Mme la Pcsse W. For thirty years I have been saying to anyone who will, or will not, listen that Pcss. W. is a *sublime* woman, to whom I am singularly indebted and most respectfully grateful. Nevertheless, this does not compel me to run my little household in Budapest, Weimar, or elsewhere according to her ideas, which are extremely charitable, no doubt, but rather impractical. You have just told me that I make 'scenes'! Not at all: I desire the peace of men of goodwill, and am not aware that a single word of mine has ever seemed hurtful to a true friend such as yourself.

Your old and faithful   F. Liszt

---

[1] The name of Bodenstedt's wife, Matilde, spelt backwards—the poem being his tribute to her on the occasion of their silver wedding anniversary.

783. To Princess Fanny Rospigliosi at Lamporecchio. Budapest, 28 January

Madame la Princesse,

It is quite inexcusable of me not to have written until today to tell you of my lasting gratitude. Nothing could be more delightful than the pen surmounted by the *puttino*, copied from Michelangelo. I have shown this admirable jewel to the Director of the Pest Museum, M. de Pulszky; he envies me, and still more enviable than the gift are the grace and kindness of the giver.

Must I reply to the question about my health? As a rule I ask my best friends to give no thought to it. In times past, when I was twenty years of age, M. Buttini, a celebrated doctor in Geneva (and grandfather of Mme la Comtesse de Gasparin, authoress of excellent books more respected than read), made to me the relevant remark: 'Remember, young man, that health is the basis of all progress.' This last word I found singularly enticing at that time; I already had a notion of progress, but not that of taking care of myself. Since then, my practice of both these things has remained too faulty: to enjoy good health seems to me almost a puerile accessory in this world, where faith and virtue are the only salutary necessities.

I thank you for the good reception given at Spicchio to the new edition of the *Catéchisme de persévérance*.

Mgr. the Archbishop Haynald, whom I see frequently here, asks me to convey to you his affectionate regards, and I remain very faithfully, Madame la Princesse, your truly grateful servant,   F. Liszt

784. To Princess Carolyne in Rome, for 8 February 1878. On the day of your birth I very humbly repeat to you all the blessings and eulogies of my heart! You are ruled by a holy passion for the Good and the Beautiful—consumed by an evangelical hunger and thirst for justice—St Teresa [of Ávila] and St Catherine of Siena are your sisters! My fault, my very great fault, lies not in any failure to understand your sublime virtues, but in my unworthiness in following them! Nevertheless, please believe that my errors are quite involuntary and do not spring from obstinacy. Will you eventually grant them some mercy? Will you find that contrary to justice? Perhaps not. In any case, I shall persist in revering you as my good guardian angel! For 30 years you have been unceasingly good to me, and desire to go on being so—it would really be too despicable of me not to recognize this with the loving gratitude which alone is admissible. Our God remains, everlastingly, Truth and Mercy! This is already revealed in the Old Testament—how much more in the New! And so let every knee, in Heaven, on Earth and in Hades, bow before the Name of our Redeemer, Jesus!

According to the most ancient and widespread tradition, the good thief was called Dimas.[2] From now on, allow me to sign this name on telegrams replying to those from Gregorio. Neither Gregorovius nor Alexandre Dumas will take offence! Wholly at, and even under, your feet. F.L.

785. To Princess Carolyne. Budapest, 10 February. Pius IX was a Saint![3]
Never has anyone inspired, as he has done, so many countless panegyrics in all 5 parts of the globe. During his lifetime he was all but suffocated by universal praise—it will continue and even increase, if that is possible, after his death. The whole Catholic world is united in the cult—an almost adoring one—of the Pope who proclaimed the dogma of the Immaculate Conception of the Virgin Mary, and that of the dogmatic infallibility of the Supreme Pontiff, Vicar of Jesus Christ and legitimate successor of St Peter. The schismatics, the heretics, and even the majority of unbelievers have long made something of a show of devoted respect and praise for the person of Pius IX, not excepting those who contributed to 'relieving' him of his temporal royalty. To obey our Holy Mother Church we pray for Pius IX, but I am of the opinion that we should already beseech the late Pope to intercede with Jesus and Mary for us.

Wholly at your feet, F.L.

786. To Mme Katalin Engeszer. 8 March ᴳ

Dear Madam,

I repeat the request I made to you yesterday: *not* to have the Gran Mass performed here this year. In Budapest from now on I am to be regarded as neither pianist nor composer. I have declared that I no longer wish to play the piano in public, and want my compositions to remain unperformed.

I have told my friend Ábrányi to ask Kapellmeister Sándor Erkel to strike the Dante Symphony off the programme of the next Philharmonic concert. It is to be hoped that this instruction will be followed; if not, the performance will calmly be avoided by Yours sincerely, F. Liszt

---

[2] The spelling now commonly used is Dismas.
[3] The Pope had died on 7 Feb.; his successor, elected on 20 Feb., was Leo XIII.

787. To Princess Fanny Rospigliosi. Bayreuth, 11 April

Madame la Princesse,

The 'lilies and jasmines' of Spicchio give me constant delight. Thank you for so graciously remembering the feast of my patron, St Francis of Paola—patron of the *Minims*. Next week, as soon as I arrive in Weimar, I shall have the very agreeable pleasure of sending you my poor church melodies, which you have so kindly ventured to recommend to the Director of Fine Arts in Florence, Professor Maglioni.

Many things have long been said and printed about the *Reform* of church music. In 1839, the most illustrious Spontini, Count of Sant' Andrea, presented an excellent memorandum on this subject to Gregory XVI; twenty-five years later, Pius IX was so good as to tell me of his interest in this reform, advocated by its ardent French, Belgian, and German champions. It was a question of belling the cat; no one succeeded.

In my humble opinion, the best results obtained thus far are due to the *German* St Cecilia Association, whose chief town is Regensburg: (1) a rich and well-catalogued music library; (2) new and correct editions of the old masters continually brought out by Pustet (publisher to the Holy See); and, lastly, exceptionally fine church performances, thanks to the sustained efforts of the Abbé Witt, the Abbé Haberl, and other zealous continuators of the edifying and difficult task undertaken by Canon Proske about fifty years ago.

If the good examples set by Regensburg were followed, religious art and Catholic worship would gain in all countries.

You ask me my impression of O. d'Haussonville's articles on Mme Sand. They pleased me first and foremost by the omission of certain biographical details, which seems to me to be well bred; further, I appreciate the ingenious turn and elevated sense of the praise bestowed upon one of the most admirable of French geniuses. In d'Haussonville's pages, perfect homogeneity of thought is matched by distinction of style.

This week I am fortifying myself here in the home of my sublime friend R. Wagner, hard at work on the score of his marvellous poem *Parsifal*. Back in Weimar next Monday, there to remain until the end of July, will be

Your very humble and grateful servant,

F. Liszt

788. To Princess Carolyne. Bayreuth, Wednesday morning, 17 April.

I was hoping for a few lines from you here. I shall probably find them this evening, on arriving in Weimar. I had intended to leave Bayreuth last Saturday or Monday—but was detained. Much more than Pce Rospigliosi, who amiably reproached me with making to Lamporecchio only the visits of a hurried doctor, Wagner complains of the brevity of my visits to his home. His old idea that we should live in the same town has remained with him—fate has decreed otherwise.

Do you know the *Bayreuther Blätter*? It appears monthly, as mouthpiece of the *Bayreuther Patronatverein*. Wagner has published in it two remarkable articles, entitled 'Was ist Deutsch?' and 'Modern'. His adversaries, and even his lukewarm admirers and parasites, are encountering therein many a stumbling block. The war waged by pens and tittle-tattlers against one of the most sublime geniuses to have appeared in this world—where mediocrity must reign—will continue. Happily, he has already finished an act and a half of his *Parsifal*, in a very detailed sketch. The sublimity of this work borders on the impossible—not for its material performance, but for the inner understanding of it needed by the public, which, as Chamfort said, doesn't normally rise to other than low ideas. The big and overwhelming matter of the 120,000 Mark deficit created by the *Nibelungen* performances at Bayreuth in 1876 has finally been smoothed away, thanks to the royal generosity of King Ludwig II of Bavaria. How that came about, I'll tell you in person. Meanwhile, *Rheingold* and *Die Walküre* are shortly to be performed in Leipzig—*Siegfried* and *Götterdämmerung* will follow, as in Vienna, Munich, Hamburg, Schwerin, and Brunswick. HE Herr von Hülsen has forbidden performances of Wagner's tetralogy in Berlin and at the theatres, of which he is in charge, of Hanover and Wiesbaden—so our friend Bronsart is reduced to exercising patience.   F.L.

789. To Princess Carolyne. Paris, Wednesday, 12 June. Thus far, I have had nothing to do. Tomorrow, first session of the international jury of Class 13, at the Palais Bourbon. I shall begin by saying that I have come only to depart—seeing that the jury is so late in meeting. Yesterday there was a grand reception, with the entertainment of a ballet by Lully, *chez* the Minister of Education, Religion, and the Fine Arts, M. Bardoux. The President of the Republic[4] was there. I talked briefly only with Ambroise Thomas, Director of the Conservatoire; Robert Fleury, former Director of the French Academy in Rome; M. Garnier, architect of the Opéra; M. Guillaume, Director of Fine Arts; and three or four people involved with art. Pce Chlodwig Hohenlohe greeted me very affably in the procession, as did his wife. Their son Philipp, attaché at the German Embassy, had come to see me in the morning—and on Friday I shall dine at the German Emb.

[4] Marshal Mac-Mahon, President of the Republic 1873–9.

The telegram I sent you the day before yesterday told you that Mme Erard was giving me royal hospitality in her house, rue du Mail, 13. I had written to ask Belloni to hire a one-horse carriage for me—Mme Erard protested very effectively by putting a coupé at my disposal. I made use of it straightaway on the day of my arrival, Sunday, by going to La Muette to thank her. We dined there with the Olliviers and M. Daniel, already taller than his father. Before the Bardoux reception I dined at Passy with the Olliviers. This evening I shall call on d'Hennessy, and tomorrow on Mme de Blocqueville.

May the good angels keep you sweet company!   F.L.

All the Paris details I'll tell you of in Rome at the end of August.

790. To Princess Carolyne. Weimar, Thursday morning, 20 June. Got back here yesterday evening. I hope I neither uttered nor committed any stupidities in Paris this time, during the 10 days I spent there. My duties in Class 13 of the Exhibition were easy to carry out. At the very first session I was honoured by being unanimously elected Honorary President. The actual presidency fell by right to Gevaërt, Director of the Brussels Conservatoire—and the vice-presidency to Hanslick, Imperial aulic councillor, with whom on this occasion I was on very affable terms. . . . Mme Ollivier has written to you, and Mme de Blocqueville will give you news of the soirée at her home on Monday. In her study I admired your portrait, and, as the affectionate servant of Mme la Marquise of *La Villa des Jasmins*,[5] did not wait to be begged to play a Beethoven sonata. Between 5.00 and 6.00 on Friday my 10 old fingers were active again at Princess Chimay's, as desired by Mme la Maréchale de Mac-Mahon and the Comtesse de Flandres—the Princess had invited only about fifteen other people. Afterwards I dined at Princess Hohenlohe's, in the German Embassy, and accompanied the coffee with my little piano piece. Prince Chlodwig was in Berlin, but the Duke of Ratibor replaced him at table opposite the Princess—and his son Philipp sang very agreeably 2 *Lieder* by Schumann and Rubinstein. The same evening, from 10.00 to 11.00, I heard an act and a half of Gounod's *Faust* at the Opéra, in the box belonging to M. Maurice Richard, Minister of Fine Arts in 1870 and still a good friend of Ollivier's. On Tuesday I went to Pce Napoleon's; he said some nice things to me about you. And entirely in keeping with them, during the soirée at Victor Hugo's a few hours later, was the praise given by Renan to the author of the *Causes intérieures*. Hébert, painter of your

5 Mme de Blocqueville's novel *Les Soirées de la Villa des Jasmins*.

portrait, came to dinner at Mme Erard's at La Muette on Sunday—naturally we spoke of Rome and of Your 'Altesse Altitude'.

I have already told you that I am very grateful to Mme Erard for her princely hospitality. As well as the apartment of hers that I occupied, she generously provided me with kitchen service and a carriage. . . . People are talking of my return to Paris—I am giving no thought at all to such a thing, because it is becoming equally disadvantageous for me to appear there, whether as an old pianist or a young composer!

'Voilà pour le moment,' as my friend Belloni, of whom I am still very fond, used to say. He never lost trust in me—following, in that, the sentiments of my beloved mother! . . .   Wholly at your feet,   F.L.

On Trinity Sunday, at 10.30, I attended high mass in Notre Dame, with the Revd Father Mohr, a Jesuit and a person of rare intelligence and a noble heart. We had got to know one another well in Regensburg and Eichstätt—in Paris we became still closer. He has published excellent works of musical liturgy, the best I know of this kind.

791. To Princess Carolyne. Weimar, 5 July.

I talk constantly with you in heart and mind—you remain the supreme corollary of all my thoughts and aspirations! But it is becoming difficult for me to write to you as often as I should like.

I have already told you of my visit to Pce Napoleon. He had sent word by Ollivier that he would like to see me again, and I hastened to call upon him. To my regret I was unable to accept his dinner invitation because of prior engagements. If he returns to Rome while I am there, I shall make bold to thank him for the kind lines he has written to you about me.

Since Ollivier no longer sees Emile de Girardin, I abstained from contact with him. Quite another matter, however, as far as Victor Hugo is concerned. I have set several of his poems to music, *Ce qu'on entend sur la montagne*, etc., and I retain for him all my youthful admiration, plus something more, despite differences of opinion only too easy to understand. Informed by a friend of his that Hugo would be glad to see me again, I renewed to him in person the constant homage of my cult for genius—homage to which he responded most amiably, just as thirty or so years ago. I shall tell you about the evening I spent at Hugo's, an occasion on which Renan, Lacretelle, and General Wimpffen were present.

Adelheid and Lina Ramann have written to you about Erfurt—the *Musikfest* went off very well. A signal success for Bülow and Bronsart; the 2 friends returned to Weimar with me. Bülow yesterday went to the Duke of Meiningen's at

Liebenstein—he will spend August in Baden-Baden, and resume his Hofkapell-meister duties in Hanover at the end of September. Bülow now enjoys better health than Bronsart; he is mentally very lively and vigorous, superabundant in witty remarks and sallies, with a luxurious accompaniment of puns.

Here, we are all awaiting Monseigneur's jubilee celebrations.[6] Tomorrow the King of the Netherlands will be coming—and other august visitors are announced. Soon, news of these wonders will be sent to you by your sincere sclavichon,

F.L.

When you see Sgambati, tell him that his Quintet was greatly applauded at Erfurt.

792. To Princess Carolyne. Weimar, 26 July. Heavens, what an everlasting litany of sorrows and tribulations for poor humans in this vale of tears! Augusz has just suffered the untimely loss of his elder son, Saint-Saëns his younger, shortly after the death of his other child, who fell from a 3rd floor. Last week, my friend Moritz blew out his brains in Paris, and the wife of my Dutch friend Heckmann, who was well on the way to earning millions, writes to tell me that they haven't enough money left to buy bread! And you, dear sublime and incomparable one, have now been robbed in Rome for the 4th time—not counting earlier and greater thefts to which, moreover, you submitted heroically! Truly, you have painfully acquired the right to hold humanity in contempt—alas, my faults are too like everyone else's to allow me to ask for exception! My great refuge is my devotion to the penitent thief, St Dismas—I ask his intercession, and trust in the everlasting mercy of our Redeemer, Jesus Christ!

Wholly at your feet,   F.L.

At Ettersburg yesterday we celebrated the 26th birthday of the Hereditary Grand Duchess. . . . I am invited to Liebenstein by the Duke of Meiningen and Prince Hermann of Weimar, who has a charming *palazzo* there—inherited from his father, Duke Bernhard, a great lover of the pleasant countryside and agreeable environs of Liebenstein. I shall spend 2 days there, and will then continue my journey to Rome, via Bayreuth and Nuremberg. With regard to the last-named town, I can't make any further comments to Lina Ramann—and only wish her to find satisfaction in her work, which she will put right or spoil as she finds fit! From the moment she began it, I told her that I attached no importance to my biography. I have lived only too much, and not well enough, in my opinion! What's the good of sifting the details of the past? Had she listened to me, her volume would have been limited to a musical and aesthetic analysis of my works—

---

[6] It being twenty-five years since Carl Alexander's accession.

very defective, doubtless, but numerous enough to provide material for 100 or so pages of criticism, favourable or otherwise. By her noteworthy study of my *Christus*, Lina Ramann had made a good start on this path, which I advised her to follow, if indeed she wished to continue to occupy herself with me. Once again, experience has shown me that, with very few exceptions, good advice has been of little use. *Chacun avise à sa guise* [Everyone looks at things in his own way]!

793. To Baron Augusz. Bayreuth, 28 August ^G

Dear, good friend,

So you have been ill for six weeks!... And you still show me your unwearying and most attentively kind friendship. May God reward you!

After what you have told me I can no longer doubt that a new building for the Music Academy will materialize. It is essential that we have an appropriate organ in the large hall; please see that the competent authority leaves it entirely to me to choose and order this instrument. I shall make a point of attending to the matter as soon as I am back in Budapest. Perhaps the organ builder in Pécs would suit, which I should like, because our compatriots should always be given preference, in so far as their work is distinguished ... but if not, we shall have to look elsewhere.

I left Weimar on 17 August. The birthday [18 August] of our King I celebrated *chez* my Grand Duke at the Wartburg, kneeling before an old picture of St Elisabeth.

In the evening I visited the Duke of Meiningen in Liebenstein, and from there came here on Tuesday. Wagner and my daughter thank you most heartily for remembering them, and they appreciate your steadfast friendship for me. The marvel that is *Parsifal* is making powerful progress: the whole work will probably be completed by next summer, and performances will take place in 1880. Meanwhile, Wagner's tetralogy, *Der Ring des Nibelungen*, is appearing in all its splendour at theatres in Vienna, Leipzig, Dresden, Schwerin, Hamburg, etc.

To Rome, the day after tomorrow,[7] goes your old, loyal and grateful friend

F. Liszt

The foregoing, his last letter to Augusz, who died on 9 September, Liszt made a point of writing in German, the language Augusz knew best after Hungarian. To Imre Augusz he wrote a note in French thanking him for the lines 'which deeply grieve the old and faithful friend of your father'.

---

[7] In the event, Liszt left for Rome on the 31st.

794. To Princess Carolyne. Villa d'Este, 22 September. You have probably already had news of the musical *merenda* [snack] in the great throne room
of the Villa d'Este—provided last Thursday, after 5 o'clock, by the pupils of the
Greek College. There were 25 to 30 singers, and also a Roman violinist who
treated us to a *Cantabile* and to a rather tzigane-like *Allegro*—which I appropriated by continuing it at the piano. The party mood became general, and the
most eminent *Padrone di casa*[8] was himself so good as to go to the piano and
favour us with Weber's last inspiration. When the music was over we spotted
Pce and Pcss Massimo and their 2 sons on the garden terrace.[9] Hohenlohe sent
to invite them up, and we chatted for several minutes. On Friday I paid my
visit to the Massimos. Their house in Tivoli is modest to look at—the staircase
reminded me of yours at the Babuino, but the latter gains in the comparison!
. . . One of the sons plays the cornet very nicely—I told him that Tsar Nicholas
used to cultivate this instrument, on which Maestro Pezzini, conductor of the
concerto comunale tiburtino,[10] excels. I invited the Massimos to come and hear
him tomorrow.

As regards old Roman acquaintances, I have seen Countess Isabel Cholmeley[11]
here. She owns a pleasant, nicely situated little house with a view over the Temple
of Sibyl and the cascades of Neptune's grotto. Several of her works of sculpture,
among them my bust, adorn one of the salons. Mme Cholmeley's second husband is an adviser to the Prefecture in Venice. . . .

I have resumed work on a few pages of music for the *Via crucis*—they will
be finished shortly. Happily, the post has brought me only a dozen rather unimportant letters this week. I make an exception for one from Count Géza Zichy,
who makes a friendly offer to replace Augusz in official business of mine in
Budapest. Zichy is doubly my colleague: as pianist-composer—and as the new
President of the Music Conservatoire, founded 30 years before the Royal Academy of Music over which I preside. See you on 5 October!   Sclavichon

795. To J. N. Dunkl in Budapest. Rome, 25 November. [G]

Dear Sir, and former friend,

It was impossible for me to respond to your letter in a way that you would
find agreeable. Hence the delay; but, to remain clear and distinct, I must repeat
in writing what I have already told you in person.

---

[8] Cardinal Hohenlohe, of course.

[9] In a letter to Carolyne a week earlier, Liszt had remarked that he 'remembered Pcss Massimo very respectfully.
The gift of her pearl necklace, 100,000 fr., to benefit the poor of Arsoli, is a beautiful evangelical trait.'

[10] The adjective for Tivoli, anciently called Tibur.

[11] An Englishwoman who had sculpted a bust of Liszt for the South Kensington International Exhibition of 1862.

My connection with the Rózsavölgyi firm[12] is broken off. Whether for a shorter or longer period remains to be seen, and does not depend on my goodwill.

Even at the World Exhibition in Paris the Rózsavölgyi house particularly distinguished itself by ... exhibiting none of the works of Franz Liszt which belong to it.

Such people, who fear that they will compromise themselves with my honourable name, and merely trot out sophistries to suit themselves, I shall henceforth disregard.

With my customary sentiments—without the slightest quarrel or rancour—and friendliest regards to you personally,   F. Liszt

796. To Princess Carolyne. [Villa d'Este] Sunday, 22 December.[13]
Hardening one's heart against salutary exhortations and advice is one of the sins against the Holy Ghost—I shall try never to fall into it! You advise me Penitence—the practice of it is not unknown to me, first and foremost in the sacrament of the Church, infinitely sweeter than the unsought penitences inflicted elsewhere! But he who talks of penitence talks at the same time of full and complete reconciliation! Otherwise, the dissonance, to put it in the language of music, would not be resolved. . . .

Your Roman habits have given you a measure of absolutism which brooks no argument. The most discreet and respectful observations you regard as slights, and even as outrages! You no longer take any account of the logical honour of my life. It is by no means the salons which cause the divergence in our points of view, but your daughter, and to some extent mine too! When I am dead you will realize that my soul was and remained always deeply devoted to yours!

I shall probably not return to Rome until 2 January '79. Reply to these lines then, *viva voce, con un parlare vero ed amabile.*

797. To Princess Carolyne. [Villa d'Este] 25 December, morning. When having my supper yesterday evening, I found your very dear and consoling letter, surrounded by an admirable assortment of flowers. It made me almost ashamed of the lines I sent you the day before—forgive me for them, and for anything else which might seem like a diminution in my deep devotion to you! . . . At the midnight mass this morning I prayed for you with all my heart—and asked God to make me worthy of your supernatural sentiments!

---

[12] Distinguished Budapest publishing-house of which Dunkl was a partner.
[13] La Mara has the date 23 Dec.—but Sunday was the 22nd.

My confessor here, Father Alessandro, priest of the parish of St Francis, is very kind and affectionate to me. In this he concords—their differing nationalities notwithstanding—with my confessors in Weimar and Budapest, the parish priests Hohmann and Schwendtner. The last-named continues to give me his friendship. Father Alessandro took part in my supper yesterday evening, admired your flowers and also Visconti's beautiful saucer. I don't know if I shall dare carry it away, for I was very distressed when the previous one got broken—but in any case I shall take pleasure in making use of it at the Villa d'Este.

Your very humble and perpetual   Sclavichon

12 January. Liszt is summoned to the Vatican for a private audience with Leo XIII.

17 January. He arrives back in Budapest.

8 February. Eduard von Liszt dies in Vienna.

10–15 March. Liszt visits Kolozsvár, where on the 14th he and Zichy play for the benefit of victims of the floods in Szeged.

26 March. He takes part in a concert at the Vigadó, Budapest, for the benefit of the flood victims.

2–10 April. In Vienna, Liszt on the 4th plays at a soirée in the Bösendorfer-Saal, on the 7th participates in another concert on behalf of the flood victims, in the morning of the 8th hears parts of his *Septem Sacramenta* performed in the Hofburg Chapel, and in the evening conducts his Gran Mass at the Musikverein.

12–18 April. He stays in Hanover.

21 April. He attends a performance of *Christus* in Frankfurt, and the next day returns to Weimar.

3–9 June. Liszt attends the music festival in Wiesbaden.

21–31 August. He stays in Bayreuth with the Wagners.

4 September. He arrives in Rome.

9–12 October. Liszt stays in Albano, having been elected an honorary canon of the Cathedral.

30 December. He takes part in a charity concert at the Villa d'Este.

WORKS. *Via crucis, les 14 stations de la croix* (S53, 1878–9[1]), for solo voices, chorus, and organ/piano; *O Roma nobilis* (S54), for mixed voices and organ/solo voice and organ; *Ossa arida* (S55), for male voices and organ, 4 hands/piano, 4 hands. PIANO: Sarabande and Chaconne from Handel's *Almira* (S181); *Fünf kleine Klavierstücke* (S192, 1865–79); transcriptions of the Polonaise from Tchaikovsky's *Eugene Onegin* (S429) and Dargomyzhsky's *Tarentelle* (S483). ORGAN: *Missa pro organo* (S264); *Gebet* (S265). The song *Go not, happy day* (S335).[2]

798. To Princess Carolyne in Rome. Budapest, Sunday morning, 19 January. I asked Mme Laussot to write to you about my day in Florence. Enclosed is the note from Talleyrand, whom you will shortly be seeing again in Rome. His wife seemed very agreeable, and he the same as in Weimar. His house

---

[1] First sketched in 1866.   [2] Composed for a *Tennyson Album* published in London (n.d.).

in the Lungarno he has arranged very elegantly, and quite often invites the *beau monde* there for music and dancing. Pcss Rospigliosi having delayed her return by 2 or 3 days, I could not wait for her—but chatted for a good quarter of an hour with her husband, and handed him the images of the Holy Countenance, from Cardinal Hohenlohe. On this topic, Rospigliosi reminded me that the Pope in his family, Clement IX, I believe, was also archpriest at Santa Maria Maggiore.[3]

On Monday evening, at Mme Laussot's, I met Pcss Salm and Pcss Corsini again, the latter being the daughter of one of my former patronesses, the Marchesa Martellini. At the age of 80 the last-named is astonishingly well preserved; I have always remained very grateful to her for her kindnesses in times past. In 1838, my too long hair and irregular behaviour notwithstanding, she had the more than daring idea of getting the Grand Duke of Tuscany to bestow a decoration upon me. A critical observation (to which Mme Martellini made a lively retort) uttered by another Grand Duke, the heir to the throne of Russia who was passing through Florence, about the eccentricity of my person, deprived me of the Cross of St Joseph. My unfavourable antecedents at the Russian Court go back, as you see, a long way! Two years after Florence, the Tsaritsa's very first remark to me at Ems was: 'You will never come to Russia.' When I replied that it was my intention to make the journey quite soon, she added: 'That's just talk—you won't do it!'

At Hillebrand's I skimmed through the January issue of the *Deutsche Rundschau*—it contains a long article by Max Müller on Buddhism. Perhaps it will interest you; Herr von Keudell will have a copy. . . .

A charming and instructive read is provided by the little volume *Cahiers de Sainte-Beuve*. A few lines concern me; they are more well- than ill-wishing, although they refer to me as affected—an epithet bestowed upon me at the time of my début in the Paris salons. The truth is that at that time I was totally ignorant of the world, and didn't concern myself about it—unconstrainedly going adrift in a sea of passions, utterly unselfconsciously! Much later I realized that, to serve others, one had to some small extent to attend to oneself!

In Gorizia on Wednesday evening I spent several hours at Mme Augusz's. Count Carl Coronini came—I spoke to him about his *Fischerstochter*, and promised him the next dispatch of the printed score. I was strongly urged to stay for one more day—but was in a hurry to get here, and consequently missed the opportunity to present myself to the Comte de Chambord, now visiting Gorizia. Not since the years 1824–6, when I strummed the piano at Mme de la Bouillerie's,

---

[3] Giulio Rospigliosi, a native of Pistoia, was elected Pope on 20 June 1667, taking the name of Clement IX. He died on 9 Dec. 1669 and was buried in Santa Maria Maggiore.

mother of the bishop, before the Royal children, the Duc de Bordeaux and Mademoiselle his sister, have I seen the man who is the legitimate King, and steadfastly worthy of being so.

In Budapest my friends gave me a cordial welcome. Even Trefort, the Minister so overwhelmed by a triple family grief—the sudden death of his young son-in-law, Count Batthyány, the insanity of his daughter, and the death of his son in Bosnia—said to me yesterday: 'You know that we value you.' Mgr. Haynald will be returning from Kalocsa at the end of this week.

May the good angels keep you sweet company! Anna Augusz told me that she was reading your beautiful work *De l'amitié des Anges* to her father a few days before his death.   Wholly at your feet,   F.L.

The first performance of the *Roi de Lahore* was announced for yesterday evening—it has been postponed because the *prima donna* is indisposed.[4] The composer, M. Massenet, recently named a member of the Institut de France, is here and will be coming to my place this evening. He and the friend accompanying him claim that I am wrong not to accept the concert invitations addressed to me from Paris—where, it seems, my works are warmly appreciated!?

799. To Aladár Juhász [Budapest, 10 February] ᴳ

Dear Aladár,

I enclose Bülow's beautiful and remarkable ballad based on Uhland's *Sängers Fluch*. To play this poetic piece as a duet with you will give me great pleasure.

As you are coming to the Academy this afternoon, please bring with you the volume of my Marches.

With renewed thanks for your masterly performance of the Circassian March and that of the Three Holy Kings at Countess Livia Zichy's the day before yesterday, I remain, dear Aladár, ever your most sincerely devoted   F. Liszt

800. To Princess Carolyne. Kolozsvár, Transylvania, Thursday, 13 March. I am being greatly fêted here. On Monday, the day of my arrival, my

old and close friend Count Sándor Teleki published a brilliant article on me. For the vocal and instrumental serenade, more than 1,000 people gathered in front of Countess Teleki's home, where I am staying. This morning, the newspaper

---

[4] Referring to the first Budapest performance of Massenet's opera, the première of which took place at the Paris Opéra, Apr. 1877.

contains a few verses in my honour, signed by Veszeli, the parish priest at the cathedral. The day after tomorrow, Saturday, I return to Budapest with Count Géza Zichy, whom I accompanied here.

The whole of Hungary is in a state of agitation because of the frightful disaster at Szeged—one of the largest towns in the country—which has been all but destroyed by flooding. I shall not be able to avoid playing the piano publicly in Budapest once again, for the benefit of the Szeged victims, despite my extreme weariness with this exercise. To object to such an obol would be shameful!

On 2 April I plan to be in Vienna. My cousin[5] is so good as to insist that I stay in her home—I am accepting. The performance of the Gran Mass remains fixed for 8 April, Tuesday of Holy Week. In 4 or 5 days I shall write to you at length from Pest. In great haste—but ever invariably wholly at your feet, and with all my heart,   F.L.

801. To Princess Carolyne. Hanover, 17 April. I was hoping to receive a letter from you here, but it hasn't arrived. Tomorrow evening I shall be in Frankfurt am Main, where a performance of *Christus* is announced for next Monday. . . .

The Ninth Symphony, Berlioz's *Cellini* and my *Prometheus* choruses were admirably interpreted here this week, under the direction of Bülow. As a conductor he is absolutely outstanding, and can be compared only with Wagner, who has given up conducting other than in connection with Bayreuth. In my opinion, Berlioz, for all his prodigious knowledge and understanding of the orchestra, never equalled Bülow on the conductor's podium. The latter conducts even his baton—whereas Berlioz used to follow it anxiously! About mid-June Bülow returns to England, where he continues to astound his audiences, and arouse their passion, by his model performances, all in the same evening, of Beethoven's 5 last Sonatas.

From the depths of my heart, wholly at your feet.   F.L.

802. To Princess Carolyne. Weimar, 26 May. On Friday evening we heard Beethoven's sublime *Missa Solemnis*. An hour later, to entertain Pce von Waldeck, father of her new sister-in-law,[6] the Grand Duchess had a performance given, at the Schloss, of a *proverbe* of Musset's, *Il faut qu'une porte soit ouverte*

---

[5] Henriette von Liszt, widow of Eduard.

[6] In January the Grand Duchess's brother, King Willem III of Holland, had married Emma von Waldeck.

ou fermée, and of another little play, in which people say I slept—without snoring, I hope!

The day before yesterday, Saturday, and on Sunday, *Rheingold* and *Walküre*, 2 works which always keep me wide awake, and several parts of which move me to the very core of my being! You ask me my impression of Cassandra's scene. I believe that in composing *Les Troyens* Berlioz pursued a false ideal. Nowadays people are Persian, Hindu, or Scandinavian rather than ancient Greek, in music at least. No more than Beethoven did Berlioz have anything to do in this archaic gallery—excellent for professors of philology and aesthetics. Painters and sculptors can with impunity continue to find material in Homer and Virgil—musicians come a cropper in it, especially in the theatre, if they are not content with a few choruses accompanying the spoken tragedy, like Mendelssohn in *Antigone* and Gounod in Ponsard's *Ulysse*.

Another reply: M. Héritte married Mlle Louise Viardot, daughter of the most illustrious Pauline Viardot-Garcia—who has always had an excellent home life with her husband, Louis Viardot, by whom she has at least 4 children. The contrary is the case with Mme Héritte, legally separated, they say, from her husband—but retaining his name, which she joins to her father's. She composes, with all the bravura of genius, the great musical works I have mentioned to you: *Le Feu du Ciel, Caïn, Le Dieu et la Bayadère*. I have up to now met no female composer possessing a talent so vigorously frenzied! Mme Héritte-Viardot has liver trouble and left this morning for Carlsbad, from where she will be going to Sweden—and further!

Wholly at your feet,   F.L.

803. To Ferenc Erkel in Budapest. Weimar, 14 July [G]

Dear Herr Director and highly esteemed friend,

Many thanks for letting me know about the favourable course of this year's final examinations. To be sure, it surprises me to find among the pupils who have been awarded prizes a couple of names of which I did not expect such a distinction—but I have complete confidence in the discerning fairness of the judges and well understand that to strictness a little indulgence is sometimes to be admixed. . . .

The persistent poor health of Aladár Juhász grieves me. Why I suggested that he join the teaching staff of the Music Academy is known to you. In my opinion we need above all a young *virtuoso* pianist who is capable of playing difficult things to the pupils correctly. Juhász is most eminently suitable for this; but if his poor health definitely prevents him from joining, I want to find someone else of similar *virtuoso* calibre. And so the plan you suggest, although it offers some advantage and would be agreeable to me personally, I cannot adopt unconditionally.

What about Gobbi's misgivings? I should very much like to recommend three new assistant teachers to be engaged for piano and music theory: Juhász or a substitute **+ + +**: Heinrich Gobbi, and Gyula Erkel.

In sincere admiration and loyal friendship remains

Your ever devoted   F. Liszt

Until the end of this month I shall be remaining here.

804. To Princess Carolyne. Weimar, 18 July. Hohenlohe's kindnesses touch me deeply, and I admit that his telegram and his letter of yesterday caused me great, but very agreeable, surprise.[7] I replied at once by telegram and letter. . . . No one knows better than you my utter lack of ambition in regard to an ecclesiastical career. When I took the minor orders at the Vatican in 1865, in my 54th year, the idea of any outer advancement could not have been further from my thoughts. In simplicity and uprightness of heart I was merely following the old Catholic leaning of my youth. Had it not been thwarted in its first ardour by my dear mother and by my confessor, the Abbé Bardin, it might well have led me to the seminary in 1830, and later to the priesthood. My mother had no other support than myself, her only child; and the Abbé Bardin, something of a music-lover, took perhaps too much notice of my bit of precocious celebrity when advising me to serve God and the Church as an artist, without aspiring unrestrainedly towards the sublime virtues of the ministry. Thus randomly does one ratiocinate about the Ideal! I know of none as lofty as that of the priest practising, teaching, and meditating on the 3 theological virtues: Faith, Hope, and Charity—to the point of the voluntary sacrifice of his life, crowned by martyrdom, when God gives it! Would I have been worthy of such a calling? Divine grace alone could accomplish it! The fact remains that my mother's loving tenderness, and the Abbé Bardin's prudence, left me at grips with temptations that I have been able to overcome no more than inadequately! Poetry and music, not forgetting a few particles of innate rebellion, have subjugated me for too long! *Miserere mei, Domine!*   F. Liszt

My bad cold, with attendant sore throat, persisted for several days—and threatened to bother me for even longer! For once in a while I sent for Dr Brehme, who got rid of it. Yesterday I had several agreeable visits—not from the doctor. This evening I am expecting Henselt, a valetudinarian, and shall play him the

---

[7] Through Cardinal Hohenlohe, Liszt had been elected an honorary canon of Albano.

second melody of his Concerto, which in days gone by you adorned with the title 'affirmation of love'. . . .

805. To Princess Carolyne. Weimar, 30 July. You ask me to tell you about Henselt. The Petersburg atmosphere has so far been favourable to musicians only in the sense of lucre—*va bene*! After having taught the piano to the Russian grand duchesses, Henselt has become inspector of the piano classes of the Imperial Institutes for young noblewomen. As such, he is a Commander of the Order of Vladimir, with the corresponding title of Excellency—little Excellency, according to those Russians invested with the great one! Further, he is the owner of a pleasant house in Silesia, at Warmbrunn, where his wife resides throughout the year and where, for 3 or 4 months every summer, he goes for a rest after his autumn and winter fatigues in Petersburg. This holiday also helps to cure his rheumatism. His great talent as an artiste has almost gone astray in the subtleties and minutiae of teaching. He would gladly ask: 'How many grains of salt should be put on an egg?' The highly valued editions of Weber's piano works which he is bringing out are, in my opinion, a little overloaded. Besides this, he is adding a second piano accompaniment to Cramer's old Studies, probably for the use of a few thousand young noblewomen with places at the Imperial Institutes of Petersburg, Moscow, Odessa, and Kiev. He is correcting, equally painstakingly, the musical works of Pce Peter of Oldenburg, who has been favouring him with his patronage for a number of years, and doesn't fail to let him know it!

Personally, I have feelings only of real esteem and friendship for Henselt. He has composed his beautiful Concerto and his 24 remarkable Studies, of which more than half a dozen count among the most distinguished and successful productions of the new post-Chopin piano era, from 1833 to 1848. In Weimar he and I hardly mentioned music, contenting ourselves with strolling in the park and playing a few rubbers of whist.

I have already told you about a group of new and spirited Russian composers: Rimsky-Korsakov, Balakirev, Alexander Borodin, César Cui, and Anatol Lyadov. I like their works, which deserve serious consideration. Fashionable society in Petersburg as yet scarcely knows the names of these gentlemen. Mme Mouchanoff herself thought that I rated them too highly, and would admit only Tchaikovsky, several of whose works have been printed and performed in Germany. However, it remains my belief that the 5 musicians I have just named are ploughing a more fruitful furrow than the belated imitators of Mendelssohn and Schumann. Neither Henselt nor Rubinstein is of this opinion—from which contradiction will take nothing from its accuracy, when complete demonstration follows! . . .   F.L.

806. To August Manns in London [July] ^G

Dear Sir,

Replying with best thanks to your friendly letter, I have to inform you, with regard to my orchestration of Schubert's *Divertissement à la hongroise*, that only the second movement—Hungarian March—has so far been published (score and parts), together with three other Schubert Marches, by Fürstner of Berlin. I haven't yet found time to orchestrate the first and third movements of the *Divertissement*; but the publishing-house of J. Schuberth, Leipzig, has brought out my arrangement for orchestra, male chorus, and organ of Franz Schubert's glorious song *Die Allmacht*. This requires a powerful lyric tenor. The tempo should be *maestoso*, moderate and leisurely. I heard in Vienna a worthy performance of this version of *Die Allmacht*.

I have published orchestral arrangements of four other songs by Schubert: *Erlkönig*, *Gretchen*, *Die junge Nonne*, and *Mignon*. *Vide* the stout volume 'Verzeichnis von F. Liszt's Werken, Bearbeitungen, etc. [Catalogue of F. Liszt's Works, Arrangements, etc.]', the second edition of which was brought out last year by Breitkopf & Härtel of Leipzig.

If, dear Sir, you perform my symphonic poem *Die Ideale*, I would ask you, to facilitate the musical understanding of those listeners of goodwill, to add Schiller's poem of the same name to the programme, and perhaps affix the letters A, B, C, D etc. to the verses, in the sequence in which they appear in the score. Any further commentary would, it seems to me, be superfluous.

Most cordially yours,   F. Liszt

807. To Princess Carolyne. Villa d'Este, 8.00 p.m., Sunday, 14 September. Hohenlohe wrote to you today—he is returning to Rome on Thursday, for the consistory on Friday. My own intention is to surprise you on Saturday evening.

At the Villa d'Este, the dinner hour has changed. We sit down to table at about 6.00, and up till now I am the only guest—apart from a day when the *Canonico* Menghini came. Conversational topics are not lacking, and I admit that I singularly enjoy Hohenlohe's wit. My musical vein seems exhausted—all this week I have neither played nor written a note.

Some years ago I subscribed 100 francs for the statue of Thalberg in Naples. I don't know if it has already been finished and placed in position;[8] nor do I know the name of the sculptor. Apart from his marriage and its consequences, Thalberg was one of the most fortunate of artists—a passion for the ideal troubled him not at all; successes were enough.

Wholly at your feet,   D.

808. To Nikolai Rimsky-Korsakov in St Petersburg
[Rome, October]

Most honoured colleague,

Your letter of 22 September reached me only the day before yesterday. Please, therefore, excuse the delay in my reply and my sincere thanks. If, in one of your concerts, you are so kind as to conduct my *Triomphe funèbre du Tasse*, it will be for me a new proof of your goodwill, which I greatly value. The score of this work and a transcription for piano solo were brought out last year by Breitkopf & Härtel, in Leipzig. At the time of the performance, I should like the related commentary, taken from Tasso's biography, and which I have quoted at the head of the Härtel edition, to be printed in the programmes, to inform the public that this is not something frivolous.

'A bon entendeur salut [A word to the wise is enough].' And so reciprocal greetings; for we understand one another, and your works are very much to my liking.

I have had the pleasure of making the personal acquaintance of two of your collaborators in the *marvellous* jewel, the Variations and Paraphrases on a favourite theme, MM Cui and Borodin.[9] I beg you to remember me to them and to accept, dear colleague, the expression of the feelings of admiring esteem borne for the new *musical Russia* by

your devoted and affectionate   F. Liszt

---

[8] Six months later (Mar. 1880), Adolf von Schack was in Naples: 'At the end of the Villa Reale, towards Mergellina, I was surprised to see a marble statue with features, gazing in my direction, which I recognized at once. It was the piano virtuoso Thalberg, whom some years ago I visited in his villa at Posillipo. Even then he seemed to be ailing, and now, too soon for his many admirers, he has been carried off, while Liszt, a year or two his senior, is still vigorously active and, as I found in Rome recently, has lost nothing of the fire and passion of his playing. That Thalberg could win laurels in the same field as this King of the Piano, is no slight testimony to his mastery. His playing had not the spell-binding daemonic power of Liszt's, but was distinguished by the utmost delicacy and finish, as well as by great bravura' (*Ein halbes Jahrhundert*, iii. 345–6).

[9] Elsewhere writing of these 'chopsticks' variations as 'a work of serious value in the form of a jest', Liszt composed a variation of his own (as a prelude to Borodin's Polka), which he gave to Cui in July 1880 for the second edition of the *'marvellous'* work.

809. To Princess Carolyne. Rome, 3 November. We are extremely sad, are we not, very dear and adorable superhuman? But it is written: 'They that sow in tears shall reap in joy'![10] May the Father of mercy and of all consolation grant us here below His peace, which passeth all understanding! Let us not examine the faults of others, and let us hope, from the sole true, good, just and supreme Judge, for the loving forgiveness of our own!   Dismas.

810. To Count Géza Zichy. Rome, 22 December [G] [(F)]

Very dear friend!

That's really welcome news! You are back on your feet again—and I don't mean metaphorically speaking, for you have no need of such a recovery—but on the real feet of flesh and bone with which one walks. Beware of expressing to the illustrious Billroth[11] your plain opinion of the boundless enthusiasm shown to the genius of Brahms! He might turn nasty and have unkind thoughts about your healed foot.

I am glad that you have finished your poetic tale *The Witch of Leányvár*, and look forward to making her agreeable acquaintance at the earliest. Poetry and music try, as best they can, to remedy the irremediable sufferings of our earthly lives. Consolation and strength, however, are given only by the Cross of Jesus Christ! . . .

I am sorry that our friend Mihalovich is not gaining more ground. It is certainly not due to lack of talent and intelligence, but to lack of good fortune. That Ábrányi has married again, quite amazes me. This fact confirms the problem of divorce, whose greatest panegyrist, Alexandre Dumas, has with his latest works set the crown on his head. The skirmishes of the Pest Montagues and Capulets, Messrs D. and P., will not, if they continue their wrangling, hold the public interest for long. Neither of them realizes that their shop tills cannot play Romeo and Juliet. My most ardent wish is for the musical life and business of Budapest to be correct and complete (or so to become). This is the object of my endeavours; give me vigorous support, very dear friend. A certain unseemly routine, which is the custom in not a few countries, would be of no use in Hungary; on the contrary, we should lose thereby only the nobility of our origin. Let us then, putting it simply, be very seemly, even if sometimes clumsy, and always unwaveringly chivalrous, as befits the Magyars.

Au revoir in Budapest! Your ever cordially devoted   F. Liszt

[10] Ps. 126: 5.

[11] Zichy's injury had eventually been healed by the Austrian surgeon Theodor Billroth, a close friend of Johannes Brahms.

1880

January. Leaving Rome on the 11th, Liszt arrives four days later in Budapest, where he resumes his teaching activities and, as in previous years, plays a major part in the city's musical life.

16 January. He is present at a concert given by Pablo Sarasate.

23 January. He has a reunion, and reconciliation, with Joseph Joachim and attends the violinist's concert that evening (and a second concert on the 30th).

13 February. *Mazeppa* is performed at a Philharmonic Society concert in the Vigadó. On the same occasion Xaver Scharwenka performs his Piano Concerto in B flat minor (dedicated to Liszt) and several pieces for piano solo, among them Liszt's *Le Rossignol.*[1]

12 March. Liszt attends a benefit concert given by Géza Zichy, who, joined by Aladár Juhász, ends the programme with a three-hand version of the March of the Three Holy Kings from *Christus.*

14 March. A concert is given by Liszt's pupils at the Music Academy.

21 March. Liszt arrives in Vienna, where several works of his are performed during his ten-day sojourn in the city. He also plays at a soirée (24 March) given in his honour by the Wagner Society.

3 April. He arrives at the Hofgärtnerei in Weimar, his residence for the next four and a half months.

18–23 May. He visits Baden-Baden for the music festival (19–22 May).

29 August. Liszt arrives in Rome, soon returning to Tivoli.

16 September. He joins the Wagner family at their rented palazzo near Siena, returning to Rome, via Orvieto, on the 25th.

WORKS. *Romance oubliée,* for piano and viola/violin/cello (S132) and for piano solo (S527). *Angelus* (S378/2), for string quartet. PIANO: *In festo transfigurationis Domini nostri Jesu Christi* (S188); *Wiegenlied—Chant du berceau* (S198); Prelude (S207*a*) to Borodin's 'Chopsticks' Polka; transcription (S490) of 'Liebesszene und Fortunas Kugel' from *Die sieben Todsünden* (Goldschmidt); arrangements (S554) of two songs by A. Rubinstein: 1. *O! wenn es doch immer so bliebe.* 2. *Der Asra.* SONGS: *Verlassen* (G. Michell) (S336); *Des Tages laute Stimmen schweigen* (F. von Saar) (S337); *Und wir dachten der Toten* (Freiligrath) (S338, *c.*1880). *O Meer im Abendstrahl* (Meissner) (S344, *c.*1880), for soprano, alto, and piano/harmonium.

---

[1] Two months earlier Liszt had agreed to be godfather to Scharwenka's daughter, accordingly named Franziska.

811. To Princess Carolyne in Rome. Budapest, Saturday, 17 January.
I informed you by telegram yesterday that for this winter I have been lodged
in the Hotel Hungária—seeing that my superb flat in the building of the new
Royal Hungarian Academy of Music, of which I have the honour to be President, has not yet completely dried.[2] . . .

In Florence, a letter from Cosima told me that in Posillipo Wagner has caught
a second erysipelas. Fräulein von Meysenbug will give you the most authentic
news of my daughter and her husband.

Here, I have seen only 5 or 6 people close to me: Géza Zichy, Ábrányi—
Secretary of my Academy—Mihalovich, the Vöröses. Cardinal Haynald and Albert
Apponyi are in Vienna, in the delegation presided over by His Eminence. They
will not be returning to Budapest for another ten days or so. Yesterday I went
to Sarasate's concert—for several years the favourite violinist, and even the darling, of all audiences. He is a draw everywhere—this now being the supreme
sign of the glory of virtuosi! Joachim, whom I still esteem as the master *par
excellence* among contemporary violinists, will be playing here next week. I shall
applaud him with pleasure. My favourite woman pianist, Sophie Menter, will
be staying at the Hotel Hungária for several more weeks. Her husband is a cellist of talent and reputation—but hardly sees eye to eye with his wife, who is
by nature generous and independent. The relationships of artistes are even more
likely to go awry than others! . . .   F.L.

812. To Princess Carolyne. Budapest, 4 February. Just as you foresaw, my personal relations with Joachim have become pretty good once again,
after an interruption of 20 years. Since I esteem his talent as a great musician
very highly and sincerely, it is easy for me to say things to him which do not
displease him. I also find that the public are wrong to appreciate only his virtuoso side, and not sufficiently that of the composer. He does not have to reciprocate—for I can easily understand that my works are not to everyone's taste!
In this connection, my spirit of compromise passes the usual limits! On Friday
morning I accompanied Joachim to the rehearsal of his concert, and in the evening gladly applauded the same pieces: Concertos by Viotti and Brahms, Bach's
Chaconne, and above all a work of his own, *Variations sérieuses* with orchestra,
which I like greatly. The next day we dined quietly *à quatre* in my room, the
other two being his travelling companion, the pianist Bonawitz, and Géza Zichy.[3]

---

[2] In *Liszt and His Country 1874–1886*, Dezső Legány remarks: 'In fact, they were playing for time so that a young
architect, Sándor Fellner—just back from Paris—could decorate his apartment in a synthesis of French and Hungarian
styles intended to suit Liszt's personality and taste.'

[3] It was Zichy, as he relates in his memoirs, who had been instrumental in bringing Liszt and Joachim together.

The last-named told me afterwards that Joachim had confided to him that he felt at fault in my regard. That gives me a tacit satisfaction! . . .

813. To Princess Carolyne. Budapest, Saturday, 14 February. Although I think I haven't committed any great sins since I last took communion in Tivoli, I was keen to confess and take communion here. But my confessor is still unwell and can't be disturbed at any time, and, my days being taken up by a mass of things and ennuis of one sort and another, I failed to go and see him at the stated time. And so last Sunday I restricted myself to communing spiritually with you, with all my heart. . . . My evening was spent *chez* the 'English ladies', where about fifteen young ladies from 9 to 16 played piano pieces before an audience of at least 100 people. . . .

If my *Hunnenschlacht* has been listened to with some goodwill in Rome, that gives me sincere pleasure. Thank Sgambati again on my behalf. Yesterday evening the Philharmonic orchestra gave a very good performance of my *Mazeppa*, in the Vigadó's large hall. The audience applauded so much that I made 3 or 4 bows in acknowledgement. I shall soon have some definite news about the Liszt Concert being planned in Vienna. To tell the truth, I would prefer it not to take place—the weariness of age, and some inner sadness or other, fruit of a too long experience, are making it increasingly distressing for me to show myself in public. And so I have refused several recent and flattering invitations. My bit of celebrity weighs on me singularly—it is a tyrannical blind alley from which there is no escape! I should like to do nothing more but work, and pray in my corner—unattainable, it seems!

Why do you never speak to me of your own work, in which, unfortunately for me, I am prevented by my ignorance from participating other than by the most respectful admiration!

814. To Princess Carolyne. Budapest, 16 March. I am continuing my duties in Budapest, and will soon be attending to those of Weimar. It seems that a success is being prepared for me—perhaps even in Vienna, where I shall spend about ten days. . . .

Miss Anne Hampton Brewster has favoured me with a magnificent column in the *Boston Weekly Advertiser*.[4] Please give her my sincere thanks—and also to Mr Greenough for the photograph of the medallion of my sorry person. From what my friends say, the sculptor has well caught and brought out its character

---

[4] An American newspaper.

of meditative resignation. Several of my friendly local acquaintances, to whom I have shown this portrait, find that it has turned out admirably. If Mr Greenough, without putting himself out too much, could send another 2 copies of the photograph to me in Weimar, I should be greatly obliged to him. The one which belonged to me was carried off yesterday by a witty lady—who assured me that it was her definite intention not to return it to me. To gainsay her on this point would have been clumsy and stupid—and yet I should be glad to have it replaced. . . .

815. To Princess Carolyne. Schottenhof, Vienna, Wednesday morning, 24 March. I saw Magne yesterday morning. Notwithstanding the many nights she has been kept up, and all the worry she has had this last week, plus the continual fatigue, she looks quite well—rather better than last year. She seems reassured about her son's rather slow recovery and is devoting all her energy to looking after him. Consequently, she is still not going out in the evenings, and receiving only a small number of people. Pce Constantin came to my concert yesterday evening, but we didn't run into one another. I shall go back to the Augarten tomorrow evening, after dinner.

I enclose the programme of the concert—the impression received by the audience was most satisfying. The performance of *Die Ideale* and *Die Glocken des Strassburger Münsters*, excellent; slightly less so, but still acceptable, that of the Mass for Male Voices, which at the rehearsal worried several of my friends. The large audience was very kind and applauded me warmly. Dame Criticism took care to add her rather muddy water to my wine—I am inured to her procedures, and not complaining! My cousin [Henriette] will send you the main newspaper articles.

This evening the Wagner Society is giving a non-paying soirée musicale at the Bösendorfer-Saal in my honour. Tomorrow my *Missa Choralis*, written on Monte Mario, will be performed in the small Kirche am Hof. . . . On Easter Monday, in the Hofburg Chapel, Hellmesberger will again conduct the Coronation Mass. It has found a home in Vienna—having the advantage of being short and easy to perform. . . .

816. To Princess Carolyne. Vienna, Thursday morning, 1 April. . . . The newspaper critics here are jibbing at my public success, which they had neither foreseen nor desired. They deign to mention it this time, however, while ascribing it to my *liebenswürdige Personlichkeit* [likeable personality]! Let us leave our adversaries to grouse, growl, and grimace as they find fit—and ourselves quietly follow the motto 'Do what must be done, come what may'. *Excelsior!* . . .

817. To Bedřich Smetana in Prague [Weimar, 5 May] ^G

Dear friend,

Despite the hard test of your physical suffering, you have the great spiritual satisfaction of having achieved important things in art and for the honour of Bohemia. The name of Bedřich Smetana remains lastingly established in his native country. Your works guarantee this quite unmistakeably. One has only to read the symphonic cycle [*Má*] *Vlast* and the glorious, dazzlingly heroic Prelude to *Libuše*, performances of which in other towns than Prague are justified and desirable.

Much spiteful opposition restricts my 'influence' on concert managements everywhere; nevertheless, to those conductors who are well disposed towards me I shall not fail to make particular recommendation of the works of Smetana.

But first of all, dear friend, will you prevail upon the publisher Herr Urbánek to send the *parts* of the quartet *Aus meinem Leben* to me here in Weimar? My local quartet friends (the orchestra leader Kömpel, Grützmacher, *et al.*) will play this work gladly and beautifully.

Yours most sincerely,   F. Liszt

818. To Maurice Sand, Baron Dudevant [May]

Honoured friend,

Your affectionate remembrance is dear to me. I thank you for it most cordially and should be glad to make available to you the few letters written to me by your mother. With her, kindness of heart went hand in hand with genius of undying glory.

Unhappily, those letters were *stolen* from me by some autograph hunter or other—a rapacious tribe who flourish and function with no scruples whatever.

Please excuse me therefore for the wrongs of others and count on my affectionate feelings as of old.

F. Liszt

819. To Commendatore Prof. Giuseppe Ferrazzi in Bassano [Weimar, May]

Dear Commendatore,

The three symphonic works relating to Dante and Tasso, which I venture to offer you, are being sent to you by the publishers, Breitkopf & Härtel of Leipzig. In the prefaces to these 3 symphonic works you will find the idea which guided me.

As for my 3 Petrarch Sonnets, *Benedetto sia il giorno* (47), *Io vidi in terra* (123), and *Pace non trovo* (104), piano transcriptions of them were brought out long ago by Schott (Mainz); but I hesitate to publish the second original version (much modified and refined) for voice, for to express the feeling that I tried to breathe into the musical notation of these Sonnets would call for some poetic singer, enamoured of an ideal of love .... *rarae aves in terris.*[5]

Sincerely,   F. Liszt

820. To Marie Lipsius in Leipzig. Weimar, 10 June ^G

Dear friend,

Thank you so much for your persevering help. *Carmen* has just arrived, and I wonder if you would be so kind as to seek out and send me another of Mérimée's short stories, entitled *Les âmes du Purgatoire*. This relates the exploits of Don Juan de Marana, immortalized by Mozart and Lord Byron. Grabbe, too, paid this good-for-nothing poetic attention and associated him with Faust,[6] which might perhaps have amazed His Excellency von Goethe.

See you again soon in Leipzig or Weimar! Unceasing thanks from

Yours sincerely,   F. Liszt

Tomorrow I shall be writing to let the Härtels know that the edition of my writings[7] could not begin better than with your opportune German translation of the *Chopin*.

821. To Princess Carolyne. Saturday evening, 3 July. During this past fortnight Bülow has exercised a kind of terrorism here on about 20 pianists of both sexes. In a full session at my place he told them categorically that, with the exception of 3 or 4, they were unworthy to receive lessons from me, and

---

[5] 'Rare birds on earth'—the well-known phrase, made plural, of Juvenal (*Satires*, VI. 165).

[6] Grabbe's four-act tragedy *Don Juan und Faust* was first performed at Detmold in 1829, with music by Lortzing, who also played Don Juan.

[7] *Gesammelte Schriften*, ed. L. Ramann (6 vols., Leipzig, 1880–3).

too badly trained to profit from them. Almost all have already played in public concerts in Berlin, Hamburg, Frankfurt, Naples, and London, and aspire to
the celebrity of a Rubinstein or a Frau Schumann! Judge of their discomfiture
at being thus harangued by Bülow! Moreover, his sarcastic vein did not stop at
the non-sacred college of pianists—one of my friends, Baron Loën, Intendant
of the Weimar Theatre, was a particular sufferer. His name was travestied into
that of Baron Münchhausen, prototype of German liars! The fact is, my greatly
cherished Bülow breaks with the compromises and tergiversations of *la civilité
puérile et honnête*. His prodigious wit, and the haughtiness of his character of
admirable and indelible *noblesse*, make his relationships in general ever more complicated. Not with me, to be sure, but with most people, perpetual aggression
is becoming his method of sociability! . . .

The Infanta of Spain, Isabel, widow of Count Girgenti and elder sister of the
King of Spain, told me yesterday evening at the Belvedere concert that she was
passionately fond of music of whatever origin, Spanish, Italian, German, or French.
In her lively and charmingly gracious way she said that among modern composers Meyerbeer and Mendelssohn were her favourites. I observed respectfully
that musical eclecticism was in sovereign taste, and even convenient in the restrained
boldness it always showed—and yet 'not all things are alike!' . . .   F.L.

I still owe replies to several fair ladies who deign to write to me. At public sales
my autograph letters are now being sold, it is said, at up to 10 francs apiece.
Vanity without any benefit for me!

822. To the Grand Duke Carl Alexander. Weimar, 13 July

Monseigneur,

At the time of the centenary of the birth of Goethe, in 1849, I had the honour of presenting You with a project, printed shortly afterwards by Brockhaus
of Leipzig, relating to the *Fondation-Goethe*.

At Frankfurt in 1859, in the house in which Goethe was born, the *Freie deutsche
Hochstift* was set up; and recently the first volume of the *Goethe-Jahrbuch*, published by Professor Geiger, came out in Berlin.

To pretend not to know these obvious facts, or to take them only superficially into account, would be a great mistake, when it is a matter of royally
perpetuating the memory of Goethe. Granted, therefore, that Your Royal Highness is keen to carry out His idea of the *Fondation-Goethe*, I have to advise Him
to consult and work with the Frankfurt *Hochstift* and Geiger's *Jahrbuch* in Berlin. For this purpose, Baron von Beaulieu-Marconnay and Messrs Walther and
Wolfgang von Goethe are Your nearest advisers and fellow-workers.

The famous maxim *Divide et impera* always finds useful applications in politics, but *not* in matters concerning the fine arts and their protection. In this latter case, assimilation and agreement are needed. Being mistakenly prudent merely makes matters go completely awry.

Your old and faithful servant,   F. Liszt

823. To Count Géza Zichy. Weimar, 3 August

Very dear friend,

In transcriptions there is no need for too much invention: maintaining a certain conjugal fidelity towards the original is what is most suitable. The numerous variants I have attempted to find in your Bach *Chaconne*,[8] and which I enclose for you, have been done in this sense. Perhaps my 50 years' practice of the art of transcription (which I all but invented) has taught me to keep to the right proportion between too much and too little in this field. Had you remained in Weimar for a few more days, I should have explained my thoughts on this topic more clearly.

Very cordially yours,   F. Liszt

Send me the new copy of your Bach *Chaconne*; I shall add to it some fingering and pedal indications as seem to me to suit the transcription done by Géza Zichy. . . .

824. To Alexander Borodin in St Petersburg. Rome, 3 September

Dear Sir and Friend,

I am very late in telling You what You must know better than I: that the orchestration of Your very remarkable Symphony [No. 1 in E flat] has been done by a master hand, and is perfectly suited to the work. It gave me real and genuine pleasure to hear it at the rehearsals and concert of the Baden-Baden music festival, where You were applauded by the best connoisseurs and a large audience.

Herr Weissheimer conducted Your Symphony with intelligence and spirit. Do not disdain the two or three discreet cuts he ventured: they seem to me to be advantageous, and I advise You to retain them in the published score.

Sincere and affectionate regards,   F. Liszt

[8] Preparing a transcription for left hand alone of Bach's *Chaconne*, Zichy had sought Liszt's advice.

825. To Princess Carolyne. Torre Fiorentina, Siena, Friday morning, 17 September.

Awaiting me at the station yesterday, at 4 o'clock, were Cosima, Wagner, and the children—who were celebrating the return of their Grandpapa. Wagner's princely residence is a 20-minute carriage ride from Siena. It is overlooked by an ancient tower, and adorned by a stage which lacks architecture but is set out almost naturally like a terrace, surrounded by a bed of unwithered flowers. Some pastorals will certainly have been acted there in times past. Pius VII stayed at the Torre Fiorentina—I shall ask in which year. Now Wagner is renting it for 800 lire a month, which is not excessive. At the magnificent Villa d'Angri, in Posillipo, he paid a third as much again—and is continuing to pay the rent for another 2 months, without profiting from it. His health has improved, and I think he will stay here until his return to Bayreuth, in November, without taking the cure at Gräfenburg, as some doctor had advised him. Yesterday we were 11 at dinner—the 5 children, 2 governesses, we 3, and Zhukovsky.* The last-named is greatly devoted to the Wagners, and a perfect gentleman. His drawings for *Parsifal* are striking—and his portrait of Cosima admirable, I am told. Zhukovsky is continuing his *Parsifal* work down here.

This morning Cosima and I are going into Siena—first of all to the Franciscan Church, for today is the feast of the stigmata[9] of the *glorioso poverello di Dio*, St Francis—and then to the Cathedral.

Your perpetual sclavi, F.L.

826. To Princess Carolyne. Torre Fiorentina, Thursday morning, 23 September.

I shall be on my way again the day after tomorrow, Saturday, in the afternoon, reaching Rome early on Sunday morning. As usual, do not send me a carriage, but be so good as to inform the Hôtel Alibert of my return.

Here, little sociability—no visits. We are always the same persons—5 children, 2 governesses, one English and the other Italian, and Paul Zhukovsky. Wagner is in good health and excellent spirits. In about ten days he plans to settle in Venice for a month or two, before returning to Bayreuth.

Cosima committed a slight numerical error. It was Pius VI, not VII, who stayed for a while at the Torre Fiorentina. In my room is the framed document of the 'Indulti perpetui concessi dal Papa Pio VI' to the chapel adjoining the house, dedicated to the guardian angels. It was there that on Tuesday, and also yesterday and this morning, a Capuchin father said mass, attended by the children and myself. I have made the acquaintance of the father, who has the title

---

[9] The scars, corresponding to the five wounds of the crucified Christ, which appeared on St Francis's body in Aug. 1224 and which he bore until his death two years later.

of *Presidente*—for about fifteen years he has been attached to Siena's large hospital, and is actively employed with the construction of a small church and convent, 20 minutes away from here. Yesterday, Blandine, Siegfried, Zhukovsky, and I accompanied him there in the carriage. Zhukovsky has promised to paint a picture for the main altar: St Francis receiving the stigmata. Cosima tells me that Zhukovsky has painted a beautiful *Pietà*; it is in Bayreuth, where he intends to spend next winter.

Siegfried is showing extraordinary aptitude for architecture, and is drawing vaults, frontispieces, and towers. He has one of the liveliest and most charming children's natures I have encountered; and his sisters could not be better brought up or more gifted. All the younger members of the family show me very marked affection, and regret my early departure.

Through Giehrl's father I have received from Munich fairly reassuring news about Bülow's health. He is in Meiningen, where he is busy with his new duties as Intendant of the orchestra—without being deprived of either of his 2 hands, as the newspapers were saying. I have written 4 or 5 pages of music. *A bientôt —et toujours!*

827. To Princess Carolyne. Villa d'Este, Wednesday morning, 29 September.

I had as a travelling companion yesterday the *Sindaco* [Mayor] of Tivoli. He told me that Hohenlohe had gone the day before yesterday to Albano, where His Eminence will administer the sacrament of confirmation to his diocesans. I shall write to him this very day, feast of St Michael, the Hohenlohes' patron saint. The Gospel for today reveals to us that to enter the Kingdom of Heaven we must become like unto little children. . . .

For reading on the journey I continued a commendable biography of Palestrina, published in German by an ecclesiastic, Wilhelm Bäumker, whom I shall thank for having sent it to me. It is only 75 pages long and gives authentic information about the life—a rather distressing and troubled one—and works of the *Musicae Princeps*, the title inscribed on the tablet on his coffin. He lies in St Peter's, below the altar of SS Simon and Jude. Palestrina lived through the reigns of 8 or 9 Popes, among them Pius V and Sixtus V. One of his masses displeased Sixtus V, but the Pope changed his mind shortly afterwards and honoured the composer with eulogies and an increase in salary. He had already been appointed 'Maestro compositore della cappella papale' by Pius IV. This dignity has been bestowed on only one occasion since—on Anerio, at the end of the 16th century. Palestrina's patrons were Cardinals Borromeo, Vitellozzi, Ippolito d'Este (to whom he dedicated 2 vols. of motets), Aldobrandini, and

Duke Ferdinand of Tuscany. St Philip Neri was his confessor and friend. His principal artistic tribulation lay in having insufficient money to have all his works printed, and on his death-bed he earnestly enjoined his son Iginio to right this misfortune.

My Tiburtine *Sindaco* lent me on the train the latest issue of *Libertà, Mercoledì, 29 Settembre*. I urge you to read in it an extract from Alexandre Dumas's latest volume, entitled, I believe, *La femme qui tue.* . . .

828. To Princess Carolyne. Villa d'Este, 29 October. Showing discretion is no merit of mine, being simply something required by my very nature. I flatter myself that to pleasant conversations between friends and acquaintances I can bring other things than confidences or gossip! This kind is cultivated so luxuriously, moreover, that my dislike of the commonplace would alone be enough to make me desist from it!

I am jotting down a few observations on Lina Ramann's volume;[10] consequently I am reading it slowly, and not without sadness, despite my sincere gratitude for the too favourable sentiments of my biographer in my regard. No one will believe me if I say that I am becoming more and more impersonal! Yet it is the simple truth—to the point that to hear myself spoken of, even to be praised, often pains me. May God temper the wind to the shorn lamb!

This week I have written a few pages of music, pretty good ones perhaps, and have received no visits. The too numerous letters do not cease—but offer me no other interest than the onus of having to reply to them.

See you on Wednesday evening. Our music is arranged for 4 o'clock on Thursday, at Sgambati's. Your Sclavissimo

829. To Princess Carolyne. Villa d'Este, 10 November. In an article in the latest issue of the *Gazette de Hongrie* it is stated, correctly enough, that I did not carry off Mme d'Agoult inside a grand piano—as was said wittily in Paris at that time! The end of the article is accurate when it says that not a word escaped Comte d'Agoult, of honoured memory, in his own defence—nor a word against the Comtesse. 'It's all right, I shall bear it,' he contented himself with saying. It is also true that he said of me: 'Liszt is a man of honour.' I applied the same epithet to Mme d'Agoult's brother, Comte de Flavigny. I carried his

---

[10] Part One of Lina Ramann's *Franz Liszt als Künstler und Mensch* had been published earlier that month. Part Two, dealing with his life and work from 1839/40 to his death in 1886, eventually appeared in two volumes (1887 and 1894).

sister arm in arm with him from one room to the next at the time of her serious illness in '40. My conscience often pains me—but not always according to what other people like to say! That is why I have become absolutely impersonal!

In my letter to la Ramann I am asking her to rectify in the 2nd edition the very erroneous passage about my insistence on marrying Mme d'Agoult—in advising her, to that end, to convert to Protestantism. Whoever knows me, even minimally, will never attribute such a thing to me! . . .

Your perpetual Sclavissimo

1881

20 January. Liszt returns to Budapest, where he takes up residence in the Music Academy's new building.

14 and 18 February. He is present at recitals given by Hans von Bülow in the Vigadó.

9 March. Liszt's Second Mephisto Waltz is performed, and encored, at a Philharmonic Society concert in the Vigadó.

3 April. In Pozsony, Liszt takes part in a concert to raise money for a monument to Hummel.

7 April. He visits Raiding, where a plaque is unveiled on the house of his birth.

9 April. He plays at a charity concert in Vienna.

Easter Saturday, 16 April. Liszt arrives in Weimar.

25 April. He attends a performance of *Christus* in Berlin.

26 and 29 May. He is present at concerts of his music in Antwerp and Brussels.

30 May. He spends the day at the Servais home in Hal, near Brussels.

9–12 June. Liszt attends the Allgemeine Deutsche Musikverein festival in Magdeburg, where he and Alexander Borodin renew their acquaintance.

2 July. Liszt has a bad fall on the Hofgärtnerei stairs.

22 September–10 October. He stays in Bayreuth with the Wagners.

16 October. He arrives in Rome.

Christmas Day. Early in the morning a group of singers, organized by Nadine Helbig, give Liszt a surprise performance of his *Weihnachtslied* for tenor, female voices, and organ/harmonium.[1]

WORKS. *Cantico del sol di San Francesco d'Assisi* (rev. version, 1880–1), for baritone solo, male chorus, orchestra, and organ; Psalm 129 (S16), for baritone solo, male chorus, and organ. ORCHESTRA: Second Mephisto Waltz (S111, 1880–1); transcription (S364) of Zarembski's *Danses galiciennes. A magyarok Istene—Ungarns Gott* (Petőfi) (S339), for voice and piano with male chorus ad lib. *Ave Maria IV* (S341), for voice and organ/harmonium/piano. PIANO: *Toccata* (S197a, 1879–81); *Nuages gris* (S199); *Carousel de Mme Pelet-Narbonne* (S214a, 1875–81); *Valse oubliée* No. 1 (S215/1); *Puszta-Wehmut—A Puszta keserve* (S246, c.1881); transcriptions of the *Cantico del sol di San Francesco* (S499), Schumann's *Provenzalisches Lied* (S570), and the Second Mephisto Waltz (S515). PIANO DUET: transcription (S600) of the Second Mephisto Waltz. ORGAN: Prelude (S665) to the *Cantico del sol di San Francesco.*

---

[1] S49, adapted—exact date unknown—from the second piece (*O heilige Nacht*) of the *Weihnachtsbaum* for piano solo.

830. To César Cui in St Petersburg [Villa d'Este, early January]

Honoured friend,

I am overwhelmed with letters from all quarters. Yours[2] makes an exception; forgive me for not having thanked you for it sooner. . . .

I am waiting for your booklet *Music in Russia.* You know of my real appreciation of the present remarkable musical development in your country; in the course of time it will be more and more recognized elsewhere too. Without repeating M. de Voltaire's famous line, 'It is from the North that light comes to us nowadays,' I maintain that Russia possesses at the present time composers worthy of great consideration. You are one of them, and I remain your very devoted and affectionate   F. Liszt

831. To Princess Carolyne in Rome. [Rome] Friday morning [14 January]. The dinner at the Palazzo Caffarelli yesterday was for a very small number. Ten people: Frau von Keudell, Countess Arnim and her daughter, Frau Helbig, Cardinal Hohenlohe and his acolyte *poor me*,[3] Arnim, and the 2 military attachés at the Embassy, one of them being Franz Ratibor, your daughter's nephew. Keudell was absent from the dinner, coming only for the coffee, without taking any—he is suffering a loss of voice, which prevents him receiving people. We had a little private music. Hohenlohe deigned to play a chorale, *Wie schön leuchtet der Morgenstern*—and Rossini's *Carità*, from your very humble servant's manuscript. Keudell offered an attractive piano piece by Rossini, and Frau Helbig the *Aveu* and *Promenade* from Schumann's *Carnaval.* As for me, I contributed a Nocturne and accompanied Frau Helbig in a charming Fantasy by Schubert.

At 10 o'clock I was at Countess Malatesta's—always very agreeably crotchety! For midday today a lunch at the Bobrinskys' has been arranged. . . .

I shall be knocking on your door about 3 o'clock, and asking you to invite for this evening your old   Sclavissimo

832. To Princess Carolyne. Budapest, Thursday evening, 20 January. I arrived this morning. Not wanting to trouble people, I had abstained from letting anyone know the date and time of my arrival. However, Géza Zichy and Ábrányi were waiting at the station, and they took me to my spacious apartment, decorated in perfect taste. You know from the newspapers that ten

---

[2] Of 26 Nov. 1880.   [3] These two words written by Liszt in English.

or twelve ladies have been so kind as to decorate the armchairs and sofas with their embroidery. They are magnificent, worthy of a royal palace—Balzac would have taken pleasure in describing them with their monograms, crowns, and emblems. Various friends of mine have provided the carpets, which harmonize with the curtains and with the symphonic ensemble of the kindnesses paid to my dwelling-place! Everything is surpassed by the most precious and very dear tapestry-talisman that you embroidered in Weimar—it is still attached to the wall beside my bed, on which is spread, during the day, the beautiful efflorescent cover given by Cardinal Hohenlohe. . . . I am living in the Royal Academy's new building, in the Radialstrasse,[4] opposite the new *Künstlerhaus*, where exhibitions of painting and sculpture are held, and very close to the new and grand National Theatre, which will be finished next year.

In Florence, on Sunday, I paid only one visit—to Pcss Rospigliosi, who was confined to bed and could not see me. The day and evening passed very pleasantly with the Hillebrands, Sophie Menter, and Mme Minghetti and her daughter, Countess Dönhoff. . . .

833. To Princess Carolyne. Budapest, 26 February. The only excuse I can present for my long silence is rather a poor one—it is that for this last fortnight all my hours have been spent in scribbling on music paper. The setting of a poem by Petőfi, entitled *The God of the Magyars*,[5] tempted me. Its musical motif, which I found tolerable, almost good, and suitable, had come to me unexpectedly. I found it necessary to add about thirty bars, to adapt these to the Hungarian and German text, to arrange them for one hand at the piano, in honour of my friend Géza Zichy, and for 2 hands for the general run of pianists—and, finally, to correct the copies and prepare them for printing, which will follow shortly. The totality of this task took me much longer than I had expected. Further, since my Second Mephisto Waltz, written at the Villa d'Este in December, has to be performed here by full orchestra at the Philharmonic concert on 9 March, I have had to busy myself a little with some corrections connected with it—a rather tiring kind of work, after which I feel dazed.

Last week, Bülow's 2 recitals caused quite a stir. The public went to them in crowds—rarely, for a number of years, has the Vigadó's small hall, which holds from 6 to 700 people, been so packed; many people were unable to obtain tickets. It was the same at Bülow's last 2 concerts in Vienna, which were extremely successful in every respect. In short, Bülow is no longer only the marvellous and almost fabulous artiste we know—but he is becoming the fashion, and this time

---

[4] Now the Andrássy-út.   [5] *A magyarok Istene.*

fashion is quite right! In Vienna his first programme consisted of the 5 last Beethoven Sonatas—the second, of about fifteen pieces of mine, not a transcription among them, even a Rhapsody. He took care to explain this exclusion—not to my disadvantage—to several people little disposed to listen to my original works.

In Budapest he proceeded the other way about, by beginning with the Liszt soirée[6] and ending with the Beethoven. I had told my friends and acquaintances beforehand that Bülow was making no visits, and was refraining from dining in town—because of his migraines, his nerves, and above all his manifold and relentless work. . . .

May the good angels keep you agreeable company—and sing for you their loveliest melodies!

834. To Princess Carolyne. Budapest, Saturday morning, 2 April.

Tomorrow morning I shall leave Pest in the company of one of my best friends, Count Géza Zichy. In the evening a concert is being given to raise money for the statue of Hummel that is to be erected in his native city of Pozsony. There, Zichy will play several pieces in masterly fashion with his very dexterous left hand—I shall accompany him in the Rákóczy March, as I did in Kolozsvár and Vienna. To settle the programme of Pcss Marcelina Czartoryska's concert, I shall spend a few hours in Vienna the next day, Monday, when Magne has very kindly invited me to dinner at the Augarten. On Tuesday, Zichy and I shall be in Sopron, and on Wednesday in Raiding.[7] Your idea, in '48, of acquiring the humble house in which I was born, in the village of Raiding, has, as you know, recently been revived. I am still opposed to it, but haven't been able to prevent people putting it into effect. To make me illustrious before my death seems to me most inopportune! On Thursday I return to Vienna, where I shall stay until Wednesday of Holy Week.

Hanslick quotes Lina Ramann at some length in connection with the *Lac de Wallenstadt*. If, as is likely, I see Hanslick in Vienna—no grimace from me! He, not I, has to play the part of a man of consequence. So we'll remain on a footing of reciprocal good manners—he is free to do otherwise!

---

[6] The pieces Bülow played were: the B minor Sonata; *Au Lac de Wallenstadt*, *Au bord d'une source*, *Pastorale*, and *Les cloches de Genève*; *St François de Paule marchant sur les flots*; *Paysage* and *Feux follets*; *Waldesrauschen* and *Gnomenreigen*; Ballade No. 2, Polonaise No. 2, Mazurka, *Valse impromptu*, Scherzo and March. *Au bord d'une source* and *Gnomenreigen* were encored. 'No one could have surpassed him in performing [these works], wrote a critic, except for Liszt himself; though, for all its excellence, Bülow's playing lacked the personal freedom, genuine spontaneity, and fire of the inspiration of the moment, which made Liszt's playing so stirring' (Dezső Legány, *Liszt and His Country 1874–1886*, 154).

[7] In the event, Raiding was visited on the Thursday (7 Apr.).

On this feast of St Francis of Paola, patron of the humble minims, I kneel—
and beg you to ask Our Redeemer, Jesus Christ, to grant me the heavenly grace
of humility!

Your old minimal servant, F.L.

835. To Princess Carolyne. [Vienna] Tuesday morning, 12 April.

Through the *Pressburger Zeitung* and the *Extrablatt* of the *Oedenburger Bote*
that I sent you, you know the details of the concerts and festivities in those 2
towns, and also of the day we spent in Raiding. Above the entrance to the house
in which I was born, an inscription engraved in stone now shows the date of
22 Oct. 1811. A thousand or so of the villagers from Raiding and thereabouts
applauded the unveiling of this stone—at their head the parish priest and local
authorities. The *Vizegespan* [Deputy Chief] of the county of Sopron conducted
the day's ceremonies perfectly. The *Obergespan* [Senior District Chief] of the
county of Sopron, Pce Paul Esterházy, gave me generous hospitality, last Tuesday and Wednesday, in his residence! My charming and excellent friend, Géza
Zichy, and my cousin, Franz Liszt, were lodged opposite Esterházy's house in
the Benedictine monastery, where I was given a most cordial welcome. The Benedictines are men of ability, distinguished teachers of exemplary bearing—they
have 300 pupils.

Between Pozsony and Sopron, on Monday, 4 April, I spent a few hours in
Vienna, so that I could discuss the Ruthène concert with Magne. The title was
dropped from the programme just in time, and the proceeds will be divided
between the Red Cross and the foundation of a school in Lemberg. Although
the salon in the Education Minister's residence could hold only 240 people, the
cream of the Viennese aristocracy turned up—takings amounted to 3,500 fl. As
I said yesterday, Magne proved in this matter *ebenso gütig als verständig* [as kind
as she was sensible]. Without her, everything was going amiss—and I would
very discreetly have withdrawn from the affair. Marcelina Czartoryska gave
an admirable performance of the Chopin *Larghetto*,[8] as also of a Nocturne and
several Mazurkas by the same adorable artist. In the delicacy of his craftsmanship he is not a whit inferior to Cellini—and has, in addition, the entrancing
dreaminess that the greatest masters don't attain!

---

[8] Of the Piano Concerto in F minor, in which she was accompanied by Liszt at a second piano. He also played
Beethoven's Piano Trio in D, Op. 70 No. 1, with Hellmesberger and Sulzer; the *Romance oubliée* with Hellmesberger;
accompanied Caroline Gomperz-Bettelheim in the songs *Des Tages laute Stimmen schweigen* and *Es war ein König in
Thule*; and brought the programme to an end with some of the *Chants polonais*. His encore was one of the *Mélodies
hongroises*.

In Raiding I thought of the visit we made there in '48—and of the party we gave for the peasants in the Woronince woods in '47, on 22 October![9] On Thursday morning, the day after tomorrow, I shall be in Nuremberg—and on Saturday evening in Weimar.

Your old and very faithful sclavissimo,   F.L.

836. To Celeste Bösendorfer in Vienna. Weimar, Easter Day, 17 April.

Not to see you in Vienna this time, Madame, grieved me. It cast as it were a melancholy shadow over my stay, which otherwise passed so pleasantly.

The roses without thorns of your gracious remembrance accompany me, and my cordial and respectful devotion remains constant.   F. Liszt

Please give to Bösendorfer once again my most cordial regards.

837. To Princess Carolyne. Weimar, 14 May.

My cousin Franz—who is becoming prominent and already doing honour to our name—has written to tell you of the very pleasant day [7 May] I spent in Giessen with him and his charming wife. Here, the next day, I found your letter of Easter Week, from 17 to 28 April. The day before yesterday the one from 1 to 8 May arrived. I shall not cease to lay at your feet my very humble, most heartfelt gratitude! These last 30 years, from Woronince to Weimar and to Rome, you have divined my every thought, have helped me, succoured me, counselled, and protected me. Let us pray—*sursum corda*!

To take up the thread of my little successes, Freiburg [im Breisgau] and Baden-Baden must be mentioned. Between the two, the G.D. of Baden did me the honour of inviting me to dinner in Karlsruhe. . . . During the evening, Pcss Hohenlohe-Langenburg, née Margravine of Baden, spoke to me of her cousin the Cardinal—with whom I had spent a couple of pleasant days at Langenburg. Naturally the Villa d'Este, Albano, and Santa Maria Maggiore played a part in the conversation—just as they did last Friday in Baden-Baden, at a little dinner *chez* the Empress, where I ran into the Cardinal's sister again, Pcss Therese Hohenlohe and her husband, the illustrious family's genealogist. Tell the Cardinal of the loyal and very grateful devotion of mine that he knows. The Empress deigned to speak to me of him, in words suited only to persons who are 'gratissime'. She was also so good as to attend the second half of the Baden concert, on Friday, and remarked to me after the *Beatitudes*: 'That's truly admirable!'

---

[9] In celebration of Liszt's thirty-sixth birthday.

I have already told you that the Emperor was very gracious to me, in his manly way, in Berlin, when I had my audience with the Empress. To the extremely brilliant Schleinitz soirée came the cream of Berlin. I strummed on the piano and exchanged a few friendly words with the Duke of Ratibor.

I could catch only a glimpse of the Lubomirski at the Wagner Society concert in Vienna. When one belongs to the public, one no longer belongs to anyone! I suffer to a great degree from what was said so well by Chamfort: 'Celebrity is the punishment of talent and the chastisement of merit'!

On Sunday, 22 May, I shall be going to Antwerp—where my hosts are the Lynens. Your sclavissimo, F.L.

838. To Princess Carolyne. Antwerp, 27 May. Rarely have I encountered such lively and general goodwill as here in Antwerp. It takes my work more seriously and is not limited to my *liebenswürdige Persönlichkeit*, esteemed in several countries—nor to my celebrity as a pianist, which I have not yet had occasion to display here. The Gran Mass was performed and heard with enthusiasm yesterday—I dare use this word, which is the appropriate one! In Paris, in '66, this same work failed—it was brilliantly revived in Vienna last year, and even more brilliantly here in Antwerp, before an audience of at least 3,000. I am sending you the programme of the Liszt Festival of Antwerp, and will shortly write some details.

In Brussels tomorrow, for another big Liszt concert,[10] will be your most humble old Sclavissimo

839. To Princess Carolyne. Brussels, Monday, 30 May. The Brussels concert succeeded no less brilliantly than that of Antwerp. A packed hall, admirable orchestra, altogether first-class—and warm applause from the audience after each item on the programme. It is, I believe, the first time that posters in large letters on the street corners have declared 'Hommage à Liszt!' Franz Servais and Jules Zarembski brought the undertaking—which seemed to me to be slightly risky—to a very good end. The former conducted everything in masterly fashion. Zarembski and his wife, whom you know under the name of Wenzel, set the *Concerto pathétique* off to advantage as never before. Already at the Antwerp

---

[10] Details of both concerts, including quotations from the press, can be found in Malou Haine's *Franz Servais et Franz Liszt*.

Liszt Festival Zarembski's admirable talent obtained an enormous success for my *Totentanz*. This work, about fifty pages in length and taking 20 minutes to perform, was formerly a complete failure. Nikolai Rubinstein* released it from its captivity, playing it in Moscow and Warsaw with great *éclat*. Now it is gaining a chance of circulating, and is obtaining the approbation of some good judges, and of the public.

HM the Queen attended yesterday's concert, was so kind as to applaud and to speak to me most graciously. She observed to me that I was from her own country, Hungary, which her late father, the Archduke Joseph, Palatine of Hungary, governed wisely. His statue in Budapest perpetuates the memory of his reign, intelligent and blessed!

Between the 2 parts of the concert, Gevaërt, Director of the Brussels Conservatoire, presented me in public with the medal struck for 29 May, as a memento of the Brussels concert, in honour of F. Liszt. I shall show you the 3 models—gold, silver, and bronze.

Sclavissimo, F.L.

840. To Count Géza Zichy. Weimar, 10 July

Very dear friend,

My sincere condolences at the death of your brother. However prepared one may be for the sorrows of fate, there is always an element of surprise, which overwhelms one.

To suffer, and to go on suffering, remains the human motto. Blessed are those who attach their sufferings to the divine Cross of Our Lord Jesus Christ!

Yours, F. Liszt

841. To Princess Carolyne. Weimar, 18 July. I'm now more or less rid of the consequences of my silly fall.[11] A sore to which I had paid no attention has, however, forced me to stay in bed since yesterday, and will keep me there until tomorrow. Then I shall be back on my feet, for none of the limbs of my old body is broken, or even seriously affected—and all my ailments are mere bagatelles.

Having spent a fortnight here with her father, Daniela set out with him again on Saturday, 9 July, for Nuremberg. There, Cosima was to see Bülow again on

---

[11] On the Hofgärtnerei staircase, on 2 July.

Sunday—Daniela promised to write me a summary of this meeting, the first mention of which was made to me by her father while he was here. Naturally I strongly urged him to it—and await good results. From Nuremberg she and her mother will return to Bayreuth, where I shall join them before the end of August. . . . Bülow's health is now tolerable—but his mood does not turn to conciliation, nor to indulgence! He suffers from an excess of brain and wit, and from unceasing study, labour, travel, and fatigues. His horror of the Jews has not diminished—at any and every opportunity he heaps abuse upon them, witty abuse moreover, and his signature appears below the anti-Semitic petition.[12] If one is drawn up against the Freemasons he will sign that too—for his hatred of their methods and dealings is on a par with his hatred of the Israelites. Despite this, his successes as an artiste, and a strange kind of personal popularity, are increasing. His concerts draw crowds, and report makes known the wonders he achieves with the Meiningen orchestra—which, in his capacity as Intendant of HH the Duke, he presides over, directs, trains, instructs, and takes travelling. He can no longer tolerate being rigged out with the title of Kapellmeister. . . .

You know the good joke he has had printed and nailed to his door: 'Mornings not available; afternoons not at home.' How I should like to be able to regulate my life thus! . . .

A visit which was more than agreeable to me was Zarembski's. His latest compositions, *Danses galiciennes*, Mazurkas for piano duet, and his splendid Polonaise for piano solo, are truly of the highest quality, approaching without plagiarism Chopin's marvellous set of jewels. Zarembski is going to see his parents in Żitomir, and in September will be returning to his excellent position as professor at the Brussels Conservatoire.

Your old and faithful   Sclavissimo

842. To Emile Ollivier at Passy. [Weimar] 26 July

A great sorrow has befallen you and Madame Ollivier.[13] She, as mother, has the prerogative of grief. What consoles comes from God and re-ascends to Him! Here below, let us know how to suffer and persevere in work and resigned prayer.

Your   F. Liszt

---

[12] A petition, organized by Bernhard Förster and others, which, besides demanding the suspension of Jewish immigration, the barring of Jews from the Stock Exchange and the restriction of their activities in the press and in finance, also asked for a census to be taken of their numbers. (When, at Naumburg in 1885, Förster married Elisabeth Nietzsche, the date specially chosen for the ceremony was 22 May, birthday of an even better-known anti-Semite—Richard Wagner.)

[13] Their 10-year-old son Jocelyn had died.

843. To Princess Carolyne. Weimar, 4 August. I have enjoyed yet another *coda* to my silly fall. When I paid no heed to a wretched sore which was not hurting me, it began to swell and to bother me for several days. At last I am rid of it, I hope. Dr Brehme, a capable man, is satisfied with my condition, and I too am satisfied with it, with a relative satisfaction. You know my aversion to advice and condolences about my health. These last few weeks I have been overwhelmed with both—I am touched by them, but very tired. Fifty or more letters and telegrams are on my table. How to cope with the replies! I should find it more expedient to quit this earthly existence! All the same, I shall never be guilty of ingratitude. And so I shall remain as I am, with all the defects of my nature—which, I venture to say, is not an ungrateful one.

Even by the time of Woronince, my ideal horizon was rather wide—the pavilions of the ideal included. Since then—thanks to you—it has widened still further, in Weimar, Rome and Pest. My devotions to St Francis of Assisi, God's great madman, and to St Dismas, the penitent thief, remain most sincere! I shall shortly be publishing my *Cantico del sol di San Francesco*. To simplify them, and adorn them religiously, I have just done some more work on 'Messer il frate sol, suor luna, suor acqua, frate vento et frate fuoco'. How happy the world would be if we were living in it as in a monastery, in loving communion with St Francis—under the sweet and gentle yoke of Our Lord Jesus Christ! . . .

12 August. These lines, written on the 4th, were not posted. Piles of music needing prompt dispatch, have taken all my mornings; and then about twenty pupils, numerous visits, many letters and other things to send off cut short my days. Reisenauer, Pohlig, and Mlle Timanova, among others, have a future. In the evening I feel very tired—all the more since I must confess my lack of aptitude for living like this! . . .

844. To Princess Carolyne. Weimar, 6 September. Well, to continue to be truthful, I have to say that my recovery is not complete. There has been no relapse, nor pain—but it is dragging on, and an unpleasant sensation has remained in my right side. Furthermore, for about a year I have been suffering violent nausea when getting up each morning—not the rest of the day. I know the cause: an irregular diet, too many and too strong cigars, too much brandy, but not to the point that people say. I never drink it without a good portion of water, and I abstain from other drinks and strong wines. . . . My trouble is a simple contusion, without serious injury to any organ whatever. I must be patient for a while, take a dozen hot baths and perspire afterwards. To this end, I have been sent a bath tub from the Schloss. . . .

Spiridion left me[14] in mid-August. He was very well acquainted with my service. These last 3 weeks Pauline—an excellent and estimable woman who has remained devoted to me for 24 years—has been doing just about everything for me. Her husband gives her a little help when I have people to dinner—a Court servant willingly places himself at my disposal. That suffices perfectly, except for a few errands, which I entrust to this or that pupil.

This last fortnight I have been working enthusiastically at my *Cantico di S. Francesco*. Such as it now finally is, improved, expanded, ornamented, harmonized, and finished in full score, I consider it one of my best works. I shall have it performed again at some *Musikfest* next year—despite the antipathy of the critics, and of the public influenced by them, to religious works outside the conventional forms. I am going to write the arrangement for piano and organ of the new definitive version of the *Cantico di San Francesco*—and at Bayreuth shall finish scoring the symphonic poem *From the Cradle to the Coffin*[15] . . . Just imagine, Monseigneur, to whom I played my Second Mephisto Waltz, sketched at the Villa d'Este and finished here, finds it a masterpiece, filled with spirit, originality and youthful vigour! I am dedicating it to my friend Saint-Saëns. . . .

For ever, beyond the coffin, your faithful sclavissimo, D.

845. To the Grand Duke Carl Alexander in Weimar. Bayreuth, 9 October

Monseigneur,

Despite my extreme dislike of the epistolary style, so admirably cultivated since Mme de Sévigné and M. de Voltaire by so many others, in all languages, I am keeping my promise by writing to Your Royal Highness from Bayreuth.

The score of *Parsifal* is being completed. Its performance at the Wagner theatre in Bayreuth will be the great event in German art at the end of July 1882. You will be attending it in very lofty, sovereign company. Other echelons of society will be added to by thousands of spectators, the curious, the enthusiastic, the demented, the critical, the time-serving, the contradictory, the moderate, the immoderate, etc., etc. Happily, the works of Wagner are nowadays *de mode absolue*.

The beautiful Mme Judith Gautier has just had published in *Voltaire* (a Paris newspaper) some delightful articles on the recent Wagner performances in

---

[14] To get married.

[15] To the Princess's suggestion that the title be *From the Cradle to the Grave*, Liszt replied: 'I am adopting it with thanks; indeed, the coffin remains only a piece of furniture, whereas the grave becomes a metaphor.'

Munich. She has translated the libretto of *Parsifal* into French, brought out a superb Chinese play, spent three days here, and spoken of your kindness at the Wartburg, which she hopes will be renewed next year in Bayreuth, at the time of *Parsifal.*

I have not failed to convey your gracious compliments to my very dear granddaughter, Daniela von Bülow. She asks me to thank you respectfully, and this evening will be accompanying me when I leave for Rome. There she will remain until January with

Your very humbly grateful old servant   F. Liszt

846. To Princess Carolyne. [Rome] Friday [November or December].
I beg you not to take in bad part my absence today. The revision and extra ornamentation of my *Cantico di San Francesco* have been keeping me busy for several weeks. This canticle was composed and sung at Rome in '62—recently in Freiburg and Jena. After 2 or 3 previous versions, I shall this evening hand over the final one for printing. Painting has given the world several masterpieces depicting St Francis of Assisi, 'il gran matto di Dio'. The illustrious Gladstone invited me, when I am next in London, to see the one he owns—by Murillo or some other famous Spanish painter. In Antwerp last May I saw once again the superb painting of St Francis by Rubens. Why should music not add its note to the glorification of the Saint whom the Church has canonized and Dante exalted? I have tried to fill this gap—without flattering myself that I have succeeded as I should wish!   Sclavissimo

847. To Camille Saint-Saëns in Paris. Rome, 6 December

Dear and honoured friend,

You are not one of those who are easily forgotten, and your splendid reputation has been gained most valiantly. I have felt sincere admiration and gratitude for you for many years, and they are confirmed and increased by the proofs you give of constant and active fellow-feeling. . . .

Before Christmas, Fürstner the publisher will send you from me 3 copies (the score, plus arrangements for piano solo and duet) of my Second Mephisto Waltz, dedicated to Camille Saint-Saëns. My cordial thanks for the friendly reception you have already given it. No one feels more than I the disparity in my works between good intentions and what is actually achieved. Yet I go on composing—not without fatigue—from inner necessity and long habit. We are not forbidden to aim high: whether one has attained one's end remains the question. . . .

You hint in the most friendly way that I should return to Paris. Travelling becomes wearisome at my age, and I very much fear I should be found *out of place* in such capitals as Paris and London whither no immediate obligation summons me. This fear does not make me ungrateful to the public; nor, in particular, to my Parisian friends, to whom I acknowledge myself to be so greatly indebted. I should not, therefore, like wholly to give up the idea of seeing them again, although the woeful performance of the Gran Mass in '66 and the ensuing verbiage made a painful impression on me. That can easily be explained on both sides. Even so, to expose myself in future to similar misunderstandings would be too much. Without false modesty or foolish vanity, I cannot allow myself to be classed among those celebrated pianists who have gone astray in composing failures.

On this topic, let me ask you something. If I were to return to Paris, would you be prepared, dear friend, to *repeat the offence* of conducting a few works of mine at some orchestral concert or other? I dare not ask you to, but were a favourable opportunity to come along, I should be very proud to be present. Meanwhile, please be so good as to remember me to Vicomte Delaborde, and to give your colleague of the Institut, Massenet, my sincere thanks for his telegram. He will forgive me for not having replied at once. How to cope with his correspondence duties is an insoluble problem for your very grateful and devoted friend   F. Liszt

1882

28 January. Liszt leaves Rome and, stopping *en route* in Florence, Venice and Vienna, on 4 February reaches Budapest, where he resumes his duties at the Academy of Music.

25 March. He conducts his Hungarian Coronation Mass at the Inner City Church.

5–10 April. He is Cardinal Haynald's guest in Kalocsa, and on Easter Day, 9 April, plays at a concert in the archiepiscopal palace.

19 April. He returns to Weimar, his headquarters until the autumn.

3 May. In Brussels, Liszt attends the first performance in French of his *Legend of St Elisabeth.*

26 June. He conducts *Die Glocken des Strassburger Münsters* at a concert of sacred music in Jena.

Early July. Liszt attends concerts of his music in Freiburg am Breisgau and Baden-Baden.

8–13 July. He visits Zurich for the Allgemeine Deutsche Musikverein festival (9–11 July). Among his friends here is Saint-Saëns, who introduces to him the young Gabriel Fauré.[1]

15 July–5 August. Liszt stays in Bayreuth with the Wagners and attends rehearsals and performances of *Parsifal.*

24–30 August. He is again in Bayreuth, for the marriage of his granddaughter Blandine to Count Biagio Gravina.

22 October. Liszt's seventy-first birthday, the first for many years that he has spent in Weimar. Twice during the day works of his (including the *Pater noster* from *Christus*) are performed beneath his windows, and a banquet in his honour is given at the Erbprinz Hotel. The next day an all-Liszt concert is mounted at the Court Theatre.

19 November. Having journeyed via Nuremberg, Zurich, and Milan, Liszt arrives in Venice where, until January, he is the guest of the Wagners at the Palazzo Vendramin.

WORKS. The symphonic poem *Von der Wiege bis zum Grabe—Du berceau jusqu'à la tombe* (From the Cradle to the Grave) (S107, 1881–2). PIANO: *La Lugubre Gondola I* (S200/1); *Csárdás macabre* (S224, 1881–2); Hungarian Rhapsody No. 16 (S244/16); *Réminiscences de Simone Boccanegra* (Verdi) (S438); arrangement of 'Feierlicher Marsch zum heiligen Gral' from *Parsifal* (Wagner) (S450).

---

[1] Of this meeting, Fauré's son, Philippe Fauré-Frémiet, later wrote (*Gabriel Fauré*, Paris, 1929, 37): 'When he found himself in front of the marvellous old man, Fauré turned pale and began to tremble.' Nevertheless, Liszt gave the French composer his photograph, inscribed: 'F. Liszt à Gabriel Fauré: haute estime et affectueux dévouement.'

848. To Princess Carolyne in Rome. Venice, Tuesday, 31 January.
The telegram I sent you yesterday told you that I shall reach Vienna tomorrow, Wednesday, at 10.00 p.m. Imre Augusz is writing to you about my stay in Florence, from Saturday evening to Monday morning. The Pallavicini, husband and wife, were charming to me. I dined at their place [Palazzo Giarno] on both Saturday and Sunday, and there met an illustrious scholar with an outstanding knowledge of Sanscrit—Count Gubernatis. He was so kind as to write and recite some very beautiful Italian verses in my honour, containing an elevated thought.[2] If Augusz has not already sent you this short poem, I shall pass the autograph on to you.

Count Resse kindly offered me hospitality at his Palazzo Guadagni, Santo Spirito. I couldn't take advantage of it other than to use Resse's carriage, to go and see my former patroness in Florence, the Marchesa Martellini, aged 84—then I called on Pce Rospigliosi, who was out, and on Ctss Resse. I had no time to go and see Baron, now Count, Talleyrand—for at 6.00 I was to be back at the Pallavicinis'. . . .

At the station in Venice I found one of my excellent friends of former years, Count Francesco Alberti. He is several years older than me, and, expressly to see me again, had done the journey from Lake Como, where he lives. . . .

Before he leaves Vienna on Saturday, a further note will be sent to you by your very humble   Sclavissimo

849. To Princess Carolyne. Schottenhof [Vienna] Thursday morning, 2 February. I have never travelled in winter in such mild weather as yesterday's. Sunshine from morning to evening—cloaks and travelling rugs became almost unnecessary. The journey from Venice to Vienna takes 18 hours—we got here punctually at 10.00 in the evening. At the station Brichta, Standhartner, Bösendorfer, and Bülow were waiting for me; the last-named took me alone in his cab to the Schottenhof. There I found a few lines of welcome from Magne, and at 1 o'clock I shall be taking her your letter and the other items. This evening a concert by Bülow, whose programme consists exclusively of piano works by Brahms. . . .

6.00 p.m. Magne looks in rather better health than last winter, and seems to have put on a little weight, which does her no harm. Our conversation was brief, because of General Neipperg's visit. Tomorrow I shall be dining at the Augarten, and there will be ample talk of Rome. At Countess Dönhoff's . . . Bülow

---

[2] For Gubernatis and the verses, see Biographical Sketches.

had a long chat with Magne, and admitted candidly—that he was not at all fond of Pce Constantin Hohenlohe. The last-named will not be the least bit distressed by this privation and will everywhere, at Court and in town, easily find compensation for it! Apart from practising Christian charity, no need to like many people! A worldly mentality necessarily leads us to disparagement of others and to exaggeration of our own selfish vanities.

I am very pleased with the attentive and intelligent service given me by Achille.[3] On Saturday evening I shall be in Budapest. . . .

Vostrissimo Sclavissimo

850. To Princess Carolyne. Budapest, 9 February. I spent a very quiet day yesterday, feast of St John of Matha, one of the patrons of the Trinitarians. In memory of your birthday I went, exceptionally, to hear mass in the Inner City Church, which to my regret is no longer my parish church. The new district containing the Radialstrasse in which I live, belongs to the parish of St Teresa. . . .

Here, a short pamphlet entitled *Franz Liszt über die Juden* [Franz Liszt on the Jews] is stealthily going the rounds. It is not on sale, and I am told that the Jewish aristocracy is pretending to be unaware of it.[4] The author signs with the pseudonym of Sagittarius—his name is Max Schütz, an Israelite connected, as music critic, with the most influential German newspaper in Budapest, one which is even read elsewhere: the *Pester Lloyd.* As you know, there was something of an uproar about certain passages in our book on the gypsies. The pamphlet I am sending you in a separate packet reproduces the animadversions, censures, and curses heaped upon me by a part of the race of Israel. The simplest and wisest thing to do, it seems to me, is to keep silent. However, there would be certain clear and conclusive things to say—in opposition to the charges made

---

[3] Achille Colonello had succeeded Spiridion Knezevics as Liszt's manservant.

[4] In 1881 the Princess had had Liszt's book (for most of the writing and shaping of which she had been responsible) on the Hungarian gypsies and their music reissued, and, quite unnecessarily, had added to this new edition much material of an anti-Semitic (and, indeed, anti-Hungarian) nature—material which reflected her own views but which was quite alien to those of Liszt. Although guiltless, he now had to endure much hostility in Hungary, for out of loyalty to the Princess he could not reveal the real writer of the offensive opinions believed to have come from his pen. In *Liszt and His Country 1874–1886,* Dezső Legány writes: 'The fact that neither Carolyne's provocations under Liszt's name nor Max Schütz's distortions led to any noteworthy reactions can be credited to the level-headedness of the Israelite community in Budapest.' Legány also quotes the sensible and perceptive response of the newspaper *Fővárosi Lapok* (25 Nov. 1881): 'We should be surprised if we discovered that Liszt did in fact write these justifiably resented pages. But we have our doubts. Anyone who has ever read even a single page of Liszt's luxuriant, restless, splendid, warm writings, would not recognize the dry, stiff, and cold style of the additions as coming from his pen. He has not lived and acted for 70 years in a way that makes us easily believe in such a complete change from his human attitudes in his 71st year. . . . We would not be at all surprised if someone should come forward to affirm that somebody from the land of anti-Semitism has smuggled these pages into this book by the good old Liszt.' For the letter that Liszt eventually sent on this topic to the *Gazette de Hongrie,* see Letter 876 below.

against me of treachery, hypocrisy, frivolity, and Jesuitry. Tell me frankly if I should make any response. If I do, I shall of course entirely avoid making personal remarks about anyone. An eye for an eye, a tooth for a tooth—is a precept which runs counter to the Gospel. We belong heart and soul to Christ! I shall await your reply to help me make up my mind whether to remain silent or to protest about the hate-filled and perfidious designs very wrongly ascribed to me. They are wholly foreign to my character and to my spiritual practices!

851. To the Grand Duke Carl Alexander in Weimar.
Budapest, 28 February

Monseigneur,

In the little volume of *Lettres intimes* from Berlioz to his friend Ferrand, recently published, I read this: 'It is impossible to be more princely, or more of a charming Maecenas, than the Grand Duke of Saxe-Weimar.' Such a eulogy gives me so great a pleasure that I willingly forget the exclamation made by the same Berlioz about my Gran Mass: 'What a negation of art!' That he may be right about you, Monseigneur, and wrong about my work, remains my wish.

Your very agreeable lines of reproach reached me the day after the departure of my excellent friend Count Géza Zichy. He is now doing a tour of charity concerts in a few German towns—Munich, Nuremberg, Wiesbaden, Erfurt— to which lady patronesses of charitable institutions have invited him quite pressingly. Erfurt being very near Weimar, it is my opinion that, subject to your approval, Zichy should come to Weimar to present himself to you. I didn't mention this to him here, but today communicated to him by letter your virtual invitation, while regretting that I am not at the Hofgärtnerei to welcome him.

G. Zichy is one of the better kind of aristocrats: great talent as a poet (in Hungarian) and, from inclination, transiently, a celebrated left-handed pianist, the most dexterous imaginable. Your Royal Highness will enjoy making his personal acquaintance.

For about a fortnight we have been *en fête* here for Munkácsy*—banquets, receptions, concerts, academic and musical sessions (Munkácsy has just been named an honorary citizen of Budapest), and even a very brilliant fancy-dress ball at the Künstlerhaus. All these enthusiastic and patriotic ovations are genuine. No effort will be spared to provide the sum of 200,000 francs needed to purchase the picture, the grandiose masterpiece *Christ before Pilate*, and the government has just asked Munkácsy (to whom the necessary leisure is granted) for two new paintings, for the Budapest Academy and the Buda Cathedral.

Very humbly, your faithful old servant   F. Liszt

852. To Princess Carolyne. Budapest, Sunday, 5 March. I am a few days late in writing to you. It is the fault of a short Hungarian Rhapsody, written to fête Munkácsy. These 12 pages took me almost the whole week, because it was necessary to revise the copy before handing it over to be printed, and to make an arrangement for 4 hands. Before the end of the month it will be brought out by my friend Táborszky, a Budapest publisher—Sgambati will play it to you. I have made the acquaintance of Munkácsy and his wife, and am on friendly terms with them. In Vienna, and especially here, his latest picture, a most imposing one, done with great *maestria*, has had more than a success—it's all the rage. Nothing else is being spoken of: prelates, ecclesiastics, artists, laymen, strollers and saunterers, aristocrats, bourgeois, writers, poets, feuilletonists, politicians, society ladies, those of the *demi-monde*, Catholics, Protestants, heathens and Jews— they one and all admire the *Christ before Pilate* as a sublime masterpiece which equals the most glorious paintings of past centuries and surpasses those of contemporary art. If you do not already possess a photograph of this work, in which colour plays a great part, I shall be glad to send you the best that has appeared thus far. As you know, Munkácsy was originally a joiner—and to begin with his artistic calling caused him to go hungry—happily this transitional period was only of short duration. Since his painting *Last Hour of a Condemned Man*, his successes, with his *Milton* and now with his *Christ before Pilate*, have grown ever more brilliant. His next work, he thinks, will be a Crucifixion.

Personally, Munkácsy is distinguished by a genuine simplicity, akin to superiority. The very brilliantly exceptional ovations being given to him everywhere here he receives with modesty, without either silliness or poor taste. At the age of 38 he already has grey hair—and his face occasionally reflects some inner sadness. It is tempered by a sweetness of higher origin. . . .

My little *train de vie* in Budapest remains the same as in previous years. Despite the machinations of a few Israelites and their associates, the public displays open goodwill towards me, knowing that the name of Liszt signifies honour and loyalty. People have some reason for envying me for being thus coddled *in patria*.

Wholly at your feet, your old   Sclavissimo

853. To Cardinal Hohenlohe [Kalocsa, Good Friday, 7 April]

Eminence,

Numerous small local obligations in Budapest as well as some urgent work prevented me from thanking Your Eminence at once for his very gracious letter. . . .

Last Sunday, Cardinal Haynald said to me: 'You are very tired here; I am returning to Kalocsa tomorrow: come and spend Holy Week and Easter resting *chez moi.*' I accepted and arrived here on Wednesday. For the services they have kindly given me a stall in the choir; and so my title of honorary canon of Albano, which I owe solely to Your Eminence's kindness, is being honoured in Hungary.

Yesterday, at the Archbishop's Palace, there was a moving ceremony. After the washing of the feet, the twelve poor men representing the apostles, dressed in a kind of Hungarian overcoat of coarse white material, sat at table. Judas, as the thirteenth, stood in a corner, but was served equally with the others by the Cardinal, several prelates and ecclesiastics, half a dozen hussars and your very humble servant. The distinctive particular of this meal is that none of the guests touches any of the five or six dishes served to them; jugs of wine and victuals are immediately handed over intact to members of the guests' families who are waiting in the corridor. At the end of this symbolic meal the Cardinal addresses an edifying discourse to the twelve poor, enjoining them not to follow the example of Judas, *mercator pessimus*—and gives them thirty florins as a present. The clothing, with shirts and boots, comes likewise from archiepiscopal munificence.

In accordance with an ancient Kalocsa custom, the Archbishop yesterday gave another big dinner to about 60 people. A prelate of great distinction took pleasure in regaling us with rather a bizarre parallel: Bismarck proceeds like an animal tamer, going into the wild beasts' cages, whip in hand, laying about lions, tigers, bears, and hyenas with might and main until the whole pack lies timidly before him.

The musical matters I have to occupy myself with in Budapest are progressing rather slowly but uninterruptedly. In the autumn a suitable organ (costing 5,000 florins) will be placed in the hall adjoining my flat in the Royal Academy of Music. At an early date a class for the teaching of church singing will be instituted.[5]

854. To Princess Carolyne. Kalocsa, Easter Day [9 April]. Having, these last 3 days, attended morning and evening services in the Cathedral, where on Thursday morning and yesterday evening the Cardinal Archbishop officiated, I took communion this morning in a separate chapel which adjoins the Jesuit church. This was so crowded that, to attend mass, about 200 people had to stay outside in the square. My cousin Hennig—his mother was a sister of my father— for several years very praiseworthily performed the duties of rector of the large

---

[5] The only source for this letter is the copy made by Liszt himself, who did not trouble to record the valediction.

Jesuit college here; he continues to teach philosophy there, and in a serious way to direct the church singing. Nothing exceptional about his musical talent, but it suffices for the task that he accomplishes with edifying zeal. He has composed several masses, motets, and a *Stabat mater* for 2 and 4 voices. None of his works is printed; their style is simple, but the counterpoint well done, and tones of a noble piety can occasionally be heard. At the time of the performance of my Mass in Esztergom, he was curate at one of the parish churches in that town— a few years later he entered the Company of Jesus. We became good friends in Esztergom, and he has remained affectionate towards me—although we see one another very rarely, for he hardly ever leaves Kalocsa. Knowing from hearsay that he plays the organ quite well, I made him a present of your Mass, which he appreciates.

In the chapel, at 6.00 this morning, there was neither music nor participants— save Achille, who took communion at the same time as I. Hennig heard my confession yesterday evening, and today after mass took me to the present rector.

Cardinal Haynald constantly shows me the most gracious kindnesses and attentions. Yesterday we had a long tête-à-tête about Ollivier and Cardinal Antonelli. Despite the lack of cordiality in Haynald's initial relations with Antonelli, he retains a keen admiration for him. He praised almost to excess—as I thought, without saying so—the prodigious tenacity and flexibility of Antonelli's diplomatic genius. On the other hand, far fewer eulogies were heaped on Pio Nono! You would have enjoyed hearing opinions rather similar to your own. . . .

Tomorrow evening I return by boat to Budapest, which will take 12 hours— and on Thursday or Friday I shall be in Vienna. . . .

Your perpetual Sclavissimo,   F.L.

855. To Princess Carolyne. Antwerp, 6 May. The reception given me in Brussels this year was no less cordial than last year's. The performance of *St Elisabeth* was fairly tolerable—a large orchestra, choruses almost adequate, but conducted by someone not very well acquainted with this kind of music. Fortunately, the singer undertaking Elisabeth, Mlle Kufferath, had got into the part very well, and brought it off marvellously. She entirely deserved the very warm applause given to her by the extremely large audience, more than 2,000 people. . . . Between the 2 parts, the President of the Brussels Music Society presented me in my box with the diploma of honorary president of this society. It is illustrated by a very beautiful original drawing of St Elisabeth.

My most excellent friend Saint-Saëns had come from Paris expressly to attend this performance, and he had a seat in my box with Mme Gevaërt and the Zarembskis. In the interval Massenet and Planté came to offer their congratulations. . . .

In Brussels I was the guest of M. Tardieu, editor-in-chief of the *Indépendance Belge*. Its owner, M. Bérardi, gave a big dinner in my honour. Afterwards, several Hungarian pieces and also a Strauss waltz were well played by a dozen costumed gypsies who were passing through Brussels. Later, Zarembski and Planté went to the piano and played my *Tasso* and the Concerto in A, delighting the audience. Showing scrupulous tact, the mistress of the house, Mme Bérardi, did not ask me to go to the piano—and I did not deem it fitting to do so. This resulted in no cooling of the atmosphere!

On Tuesday, for the closing of the theatre, the season's 55th performance of Massenet's *Hérodiade*[6] was given—this time, under the direction of the composer. A shower, hail, and tempest of flowers, bouquets, and wreaths such as I had not hitherto seen. However, to enable the work to make its way elsewhere, some perceptible modifications to the libretto will be necessary. St John the Baptist in love with Salome is altogether too shocking a misinterpretation! I mentioned this *sub rosa* to Massenet, who had already decided to transform his false John the Baptist into some conventional theatrical personage for the forthcoming performances of *Hérodiade* in London and Petersburg. In my humble opinion, biblical subjects are almost impossible to make suitable for the theatre—with the exception perhaps of *Samson*, in which the love duet with Delilah is a stroke of luck for the composer, if not for Samson! Saint-Saëns has made admirable use of it, and his opera, first performed in Weimar, has just obtained a complete success in Hamburg. . . .

Your old Sclavissimo

856. To Edmond Hippeau in Paris. Weimar, 15 May

Dear Sir,

Please excuse the time it has taken me to express my sincere thanks for your kind lines. Of all the many things I lack, that of time for correspondence is the greatest.

You ask me to acquaint you with the letters written to me by Berlioz; unfortunately I no longer possess any, having given them all to various autograph collectors.[7]

---

[6] Four-act opera first performed at the Théâtre de la Monnaie, Paris, Dec. 1881.

[7] La Mara: 'When the Altenburg was vacated, a number of letters from Berlioz, as well as other letters and objects belonging to Liszt, had fallen among, and been sealed up with, Princess Wittgenstein's possessions, accordingly remaining inaccessible until after the Princess's death.'

Berlioz used to call album collectors 'albominable people'. I make an exception to the point of sometimes serving their *albominability*, while excluding my personal autographs, of no value.

From 1829 [1830] until '64 my relations with Berlioz could not have been simpler. Total admiration on my part; cordiality on his. That is how it was in Paris, Prague, and Weimar, where I consider it an honour to have mounted and conducted his *Benvenuto Cellini*, an admirable and magnificent work, most vividly coloured and rhythmic, brimming over with piquant melodies, whose *glorious* rehabilitation in Paris, through a Cellini-tenor of the kind that is rarely encountered, I very much desire.

After '64, without any foolish estrangement, the then burning Wagner question, nowadays very much cooled down, caused a loss of warmth between Berlioz and me. He did not think that Wagner was, as it were, the destiny of musical drama in Germany, going beyond Beethoven and Weber.

Sincerely,   F. Liszt

P.S. Please be so kind as to include me among subscribers to *Renaissance musicale*, and to send this excellent magazine to my Weimar address until the end of June, and then to Bayreuth (Bavaria), where I shall probably have the pleasure of seeing you at performances of *Parsifal*. At least thirty thousand people from *all countries* will attend them.

857. To Théodore Michaëlis in Paris. Weimar, 15 May

Sir,

The success of your grand publication of classical masterpieces of French opera is assured by the powerful patronage of the French Musical Institute, of the Ministry of Fine Arts, etc., etc. Your artistic collaborators of great merit, entrusted with the intelligently scaled-down editions for piano of these scores, will certainly make this publication worthy of esteem and of an extensive circulation.

To my regret, my modest income deprives me of the pleasure of adding my name to your list of subscribers. When I still happen to buy music, I admit that my choice falls on modern works. Nevertheless, two operas in your collection would be of particular interest to me: the *Tarare* and *Danaïdes* of Salieri, who, in Vienna in 1822 and '23, was so graciously kind as to teach me, not the art of composing—which can hardly be taught—but to know the different clefs and procedures used in the scores of his day. I remain deeply grateful to him.

I shall not fail to submit your prospectus to His Royal Highness the Grand Duke of Saxe-Weimar, accompanied by a well-deserved recommendation.

Yours,   F. Liszt

858. To Princess Carolyne. Weimar, Sunday, 21 May. Here, nothing out of the ordinary. Last week, at Court, there was a lecture by the very celebrated Haeckel, professor at Jena—who has refused the most brilliant offers from other universities, finding more time for work at Jena than elsewhere. A laboratory is now being built for him there, as was formerly done in Munich for Liebig. He told us some very interesting things about his recent trip to the island of Ceylon, illustrated by about a dozen water-colours done in his own splendid manner. In those parts, it seems, one can dine marvellously on roast bats and lizards—I forget the rest of the bill of fare, all in keeping. Someone of my acquaintance asked Haeckel if he had encountered in Ceylon the race much sought after, but not yet found, called Alali—forming the link between monkey and man. The illustrious scholar replied evasively, reserving the right to clear things up satisfactorily for the public later. . . .

About Bülow's marriage I know nothing positive, but have written to give him my heartfelt good wishes. He will do well to remarry, if only to rid himself of domestic bothers. Fräulein Schanzer is said to live up to her good reputation, both as an actress and a *personne comme il faut.*

Have you read the short poem by the Queen of Romania?[8] It is called *Jehovah,* and eloquently depicts the torments of Ahasuerus in perpetual quest of the true God—*Gott ist das ewige Werden* [God is eternal Becoming]! This formula was previously stated by Hegel, whom at Woronince in 1847 you declared 'not great'— and thus fairly snookered yourself! Nevertheless, the Queen of Romania's poem contains elements of pathos which seem to me to be worthy of Byron and of Victor Hugo. Nothing less! Should you not yet possess a copy of this little volume, published at Leipzig in a *de luxe* edition of the most elegantly erudite kind, I shall send you one. . . .

Very humbly, your old and faithful   Sclavissimo

859. To Princess Carolyne. Weimar, 25 May. My confidence in Bülow's new marriage is strengthened by the enclosed letter, which will inform you about his bride-to-be, whom I have heard spoken highly of by several people.

On Monday, at the soirée in the Amalia Palace, Otto Devrient gave us an interesting talk on Duke Ernst of Gotha, nicknamed the Pious. The audience consisted of about twenty people at most. The Amalia Palace is very attractively restored inside, in the simple and *piacevole* [pleasing] style of the time. . . . We had supper on the Duchess Amalia's own plates and dishes—her clavichord, her harp, her guitar, and a few pictures of the same origin adorn the modest suite

---

[8] Consort of King Carol I, the German-born Queen Elisabeth wrote under the pen-name of Carmen Sylva.

of rooms, which have no ostentation other than the revered memory of the Duchess herself. Your drawing-room at the Babuino is a little larger and more comfortable than hers. 'Comfort' has been practised for only a few years in Germany. Quite another matter the luxury of courts, Vienna and Dresden in particular—which was not the fashion formerly in Weimar. Nevertheless, the atmosphere of intelligence diffused by Carl August with Goethe, Schiller, Herder, Wieland, *et al.*, is not fading—despite many an influence to the contrary.

Adelheid will tell you about the Court concert, on Tuesday, mounted in honour of the Japanese embassy charged with delivering the grand decoration of the Mikado to the Grand Duke. . . .

Your old   Sclavissimo

860. To Princess Carolyne. Zurich, Monday morning, 10 July. Between the Freiburg concert and the Zurich *Musikfest* there was yet another Liszt Concert in Baden-Baden, put on unexpectedly on 5 July by our friend Pohl and the town authorities. Baden being only three hours away, I went there to please my old friend Pohl, who was most appreciative of your kind remembrance of him. . . .

The Grand Duke of Baden very graciously telegraphed me from Mainau. At Freiburg, your former architectural studies were constantly in my mind. At that time I could successfully follow them as far as the cathedral spire—now, your theological and political heights remain inaccessible to me! Unfortunately I am only a poor celebrated pianist of long ago—and, as a composer, one of the most opposed, even by his deceased friends, such as Berlioz! Yesterday, Saint-Saëns told me that at a performance of one of my symphonic poems, Berlioz went further than Schumann in showing disapproval. The last-named contented himself with shoving back his chair—Berlioz quietly left the Salle Erard, seeing that Liszt's music was the antithesis of music! In that, he had on his side the community of critics and the reigning tribe of loungers. All the same, my profound admiration for the genius of Berlioz remains intact! *Qui peu endure, peu dure!*

Your faithful   Sclavissimo

861. To Princess Carolyne. Bayreuth, 2 August. I am too late to tell you about *Parsifal*. All the newspapers, plus thousands of letters and telegrams, have been filled with it for 10 days—not counting the numerous earlier reports, favourable or otherwise. My viewpoint remains fixed: absolute admiration, excessive, if you like! *Parsifal* is more than a masterpiece—it is a revelation in music drama! It has been said, justly, that after the song of songs of earthly love, *Tristan und Isolde*, Wagner has in *Parsifal* gloriously depicted the supreme song of divine love, as allowed by the restricted possibilities of the theatre. It is the miracle work of the century! Calderón's *Autos Sacramentales* serve it as precedents; the Oberammergau performances of the Passion of our divine Redeemer Jesus Christ lead towards it—in a popular manner, in the good company of princes and newspapers.

Angelini, whom you recommended to me, will tell you that I gave him a good welcome—he has already communicated to *Libertà* and other Italian newspapers the delight given him by *Parsifal*. A comment I wrote[9] to Baron Hans von Wolzogen is being quoted: 'The pendulum of this sacred work swings from the sublime to the most sublime!'

The representative of the great and ancient house of Schott being here, as editor of the *Nibelungen* and of *Parsifal*, I have renewed my good relations with his firm—the only one which, for musical publications, has for more than half a century kept pace with Breitkopf & Härtel. The 3rd vol. of my *Années de pèlerinage* falls by right to Schott, publishers of the 2 previous vols. For this latest one I need a good photograph of the group of cypresses at the Villa d'Este.

Thank you with all my heart for your gift to Blandine[10]—she will be expressing her gratitude to you.   Umilissimo Sclavissimo,   F.L.

862. To Princess Carolyne. Weimar, Tuesday, 5 September.

I didn't see the Castellani bracelet that you were so kind as to give to my granddaughter Blandine—no doubt your choice was in the most exquisite taste.

Two German *savants* have assured me that the cypresses of Santa Maria degli Angeli have no connection with Michelangelo. To avoid superfluous contradictions, I have withdrawn from my Second Threnody the name of that great and most venerable sublime genius—a worthy second to his patron saint, the Archangel Michael. It will be published simply as No. 2 of the *Cyprès de la Villa d'Este*. Besides, I shall not be worthy of untying the shoe-laces of that supreme and austere artist, almost the martyr of his glory! In the history of art he has but one fellow—Beethoven. Like Goethe and Victor Hugo, Wagner now belongs to the Olympians. The cycle of his works from *Tannhäuser* to the *Nibelungen* and *Parsifal* can only be called prodigious.

---

[9] In a note of 27 July.   [10] For her wedding to Count Gravina. Liszt's present was 2,000 Marks.

In Bayreuth, at the last performance of *Parsifal*, I saw Monseigneur. He was in august company, as the late Maltitz used to say—that of the Duke and Duchess of Edinburgh,[11] the Grand Duke and Grand Duchess Vladimir, *et al.*, all full of enthusiasm, as was the German Crown Prince at the previous performance. Wagner naturally saw none of Their Highnesses, save the Grand Duke of Weimar, who at my invitation paid him a visit. What he needs is not further enthusiastic bravos—but the financial means to ensure that his Bayreuth theatre can continue to mount annual performances. Patrons will find themselves under the marvellous aegis of King Ludwig II of Bavaria—without whom Wagner would be reduced to inadequate expedients. The King did not come to Bayreuth—but has the intention, it is said, to have *Parsifal* performed in Munich for himself alone.   Umilissimo Sclavissimo

863. To Princess Carolyne. Weimar, 10 September. My last letter had grown so long that I omitted the postscript: why am I in Weimar? Is that an error, a fault or a folly? Perhaps all three at once! Nevertheless, for more than thirty years now I have been, as it were, adhering to the house of Weimar. Musically, by works, teaching, publication, I make use of it myself as a base of operations in Germany—where more than elsewhere instrumental, choral, and serious music has taken root through Bach, Haydn, Mozart, Beethoven. Mendelssohn and Schumann have continued along this path. Italy invented opera and caused it to make brilliant progress, aided by numerous talents, composers and singers —and one great genius, Rossini, who for more than half a century dominated the theatres and salons of Europe. In his last years he poked friendly fun at the discovery of infinite melody! Nevertheless, Wagner, with the *Nibelungen* and *Parsifal*, is making it prevail. To understand one another well, too many explanations should be avoided! I have reached the point of keeping silent a good deal.

864. To Princess Carolyne. Weimar, 25 September. I attach no value to my opinions, other than in music—and even in that I generally take care not to express them. On other subjects—which I have not had the means of studying in depth—I find it more convenient, and more agreeable, to remain silent, as one uninformed. In my youth I often spoke without rhyme or reason. Nowadays I profit more from listening and reading than from speaking—and

---

[11] Alfred, second son of Victoria and Albert, and Marie, only daughter of Tsar Alexander II.

take more pleasure in turning my tongue over a few times than in using it for conversation. I submit to it when the topic concerns matters of no importance, by which it is sometimes necessary to embellish one's dealings with friends and acquaintances.

My musical writings are slowly making progress. I am correcting the final proofs of the 3rd vol. of my *Années de pèlerinage, Villa d'Este, Cyprès*—and scoring the symphonic poem based on [Mihály] Zichy's drawing *Du berceau jusqu'à la tombe.*

At Bayreuth, Baron Zhukovsky had begun a large portrait of me—at Monseigneur's invitation he is now finishing it here, in a studio at the *Kunstschule* [Art School] that Monseigneur has placed at his disposal. The portrait is destined to adorn the music salon of a big piano manufacturer[12] in Toronto, Canada. . . .

With heart and soul,   Sclavissimo

865. To Princess Carolyne. Weimar, Tuesday, 10 October.

What an immense labour these 22 volumes of the *Causes*—how much learning, inspiration, and ardent zeal for God's house they contain! With what skill and vigour you so magisterially set out and develop the theses and hypotheses of the politics, administration, organization, hierarchy, disciplines, and reforms of the Church. Truly, you are proceeding from St Augustine, St Bernard, St Thomas, St Teresa, St Catherine of Siena—and a little, too, from Joseph de Maistre, since, if you will allow me, you share his militant and prophetic understanding. Between the two of you there is just this difference: he was crudely called the prophet of the past—you appear as prophet of the future of the Church and of human societies, to be restored to their place under the beneficent protectorate of Catholicism. That would be the beginning of the reign of God on earth, besought of our Heavenly Father every day in the simple and sublime prayer taught us by our divine Saviour, Jesus Christ. Napoleon I recommended it to Larévellière-Lépeaux in these words: 'You desire the sublime, Monsieur—then say the *Pater noster!*' . . .

The day before yesterday I finished scoring the symphonic poem *Du berceau à la tombe*—and delivered up to Kahnt, for printing, St Francis's *Cantico del sol.* In addition, he is undertaking 2 or 3 short compositions for single voice, with piano or organ accompaniment—and also the Psalm *De profundis*,[13] composed in Rome, Nov. '81. . . .

F.L.

---

[12] Mason and Risch.   [13] 'Out of the depths', Liszt's Psalm 129 (Vulg.; Ps. 130 in the AV).

866. To Princess Carolyne. Weimar, Sunday, 29 October. I was writing the first words of my profound thanks for your adorable lines in response
to my condolences on the death of Audisio[14]—when I received your letter, no
less adorable, for my birthday on the 22nd. Adelheid tells me that she is to ask
me on your behalf if I have any recollection of the celebrations of 22 October
at Woronince in 1847, in the woods—and above all in your great heart! I reply
with these words of the *Thrénodies*: 'Memor ero et tabescet in me anima mea
[I shall remember and my soul will pine within me].'

   You honour me and remain right in thinking that I know what you wish for,
and what you are aiming at—but I hope you are singularly mistaken in fancy-
ing that I can be opposed to what you do, or that I am against your writings,
whatever they may be. As a matter of fact, I understand nothing of politics,
or of theology—consequently, three-quarters of your work remains beyond my
reach. As for aesthetics, I admit likewise that I have not as yet found the thread
of Ariadne which will lead me out of the maze of the numerous systems of philosophers ancient and modern. Let us hope that I shall at last grasp the true thread
in your lucid theory of Emotions and Sensations! Until then, I see myself sentenced to a sceptical mortification.

   I am returning your pages on the gradual abolition of war—that terrible, perpetual, crowning outrage of *lèse-humanité*! Why did you put these beautiful and
just thoughts as footnotes? They deserve to be printed in type of the usual size.
Joseph de Maistre believed, astonishingly, that war was of divine institution! Herr
von Moltke, in a memorable historic letter that you refer to, declares himself
in favour of the temporary necessity of permanent armies. He does so simply,
with the lofty intelligence and conciliatory dignity of a great man—but he does
not make a parade of it, being aware of his genius for patience, and for great
generalship.   Sclavissimo

Audisio's pen and ink-well are precious relics. Your letter to Cantù will add
lustre to his memory.

867. To Princess Carolyne. Weimar, 3 November. Ladislas Mickiewicz
has brought out this year a new translation of his father's poetical masterpieces,
containing *Konrad Wallenrod*, *Dziady*—some fragments of which have been set
to music by Moniuszko—and the book of the *Polish Nation* and the *Polish Pilgrims*.
At the beginning of the '30s, Montalembert, Lamennais, George Sand, Quinet,
and Michelet admired him to the point of enthusiasm. The *Paroles d'un croyant*

---

[14] The ecclesiastical writer Canon Audisio had been on very friendly terms with the Princess.

are drawn from the same source. I have reread this volume with fervour, fright, terror, and compunction. It is Poland panting on the Cross! The prayer and litany which close the book of the *Pilgrims* made me sob.

Thank you for the photograph of Duprez's *St Francis at Assisi*; I was going to ask you for it. Quite possibly the statue is a beautiful and admirable work. As far as I am concerned, however, the chief characteristic of the *gran poverello di Dio* is not brought out. Duprez has made of it a companion piece to Houdon's most admirable statue of St Bruno, in Santa Maria degli Angeli. 'It would speak, were this not against the Rule of the Order,' runs a well-known witticism. Well, St Francis spoke and even sang—his Rule does not impose silence, nor total confinement within the cloister. He has in common with St Bruno only saintliness. In my opinion, he must be portrayed on his knees, arms outstretched, lovingly asking for the divine stigmata—which Our Lord Jesus Christ granted him. In the antechamber of my flat in the Villa d'Este there is a photograph of St Francis of Assisi, given to me last year by Cardinal de Falloux. It is framed in wood—kindly send it to me. It will perhaps serve as a vignette to my *Cantico*. . . .

Monseigneur returns here from Biarritz and Paris on Tuesday; the Grand Duchess a few days later. I shall wait for them—in view of the long time I have lingered in Weimar, my departure, just before their return, would be ill-mannered. About 15 Nov. I shall be in Venice.   Very humbly,   Sclavissimo.

For the feast of St Charles, tomorrow, I lay at your feet 35 years of admiration, respect, and loving gratitude.

868. To Malwine Tardieu in Brussels. Weimar, 6 November

Chère bienveillante,

I am still detained here, partly because of a stupid indisposition; nothing serious, but lasting a disagreeably long time. I make a rule of never bothering about my health, and I beg my friends never to take an interest in it either.

Thank you for sending the 3rd volume of the *Correspondance de George Sand*. The long 20-page letter to Mazzini, dated 23 May '52, seems to me to be a masterpiece of judgement and foresight. In 1852 few politicians had settled on a viewpoint lofty enough to permit them an overall view of the fluctuations of socialism and an understanding of its necessary value. Mazzini himself was mistaken about it, as he was, too, about the importance of achieving universal suffrage. Forgive me for wandering off like this into political matters which I don't understand at all and which are no concern of mine. I shall, however, quote a remark which surreptitiously went the rounds at Petersburg in 1842. A beautiful lady of my acquaintance told me that Tsar Nicholas had said to her of me: 'I like neither his hair nor his political opinions.' I asked the same lady to convey my response in these terms: 'His Majesty has every right in the world to criticize me as he pleases. Nevertheless, I venture to beg him not to take me for an imbecile. Now, it would certainly be imbecility on my part to flaunt political opinions. The Tsar will know them when he deigns to put 300,000 soldiers at my disposal.'

Coming back to George Sand's letters, those addressed in '52 to Prince Jérôme Bonaparte and Louis Napoléon, about *reprieving* several democrats, are in exquisite taste: in them can be seen the genius of a great heart. . . .

Has the *Indépendance belge* mentioned a highly interesting and superb volume: *Correspondance et œuvres musicales de Constantin Huygens* (17th century),[15] edited by Jonckbloet and Land, professors at the University of Leyden, and published in Leyden, magnificently, by Brill? It is a work which deserves to be paid attention.

To the kindly lines published in the *Indépendance* about the concert of 23 October with the Liszt programme, I add the observation that the real title of my 'transcription' of the Rákóczy March should be 'symphonic paraphrase'. It has more than double the pages of Berlioz's very well-known one, and was written *before* his. From delicacy of feeling towards my illustrious friend, I delayed its publication until after his death; for he had dedicated to me his orchestral version of the Rákóczy, for which, furthermore, one of my earlier transcriptions had served him—chiefly for the harmonization which differs, as is only too well known, from the rudimentary chords generally used in performances of this same march by gypsies and other small bands. . . .

In about ten days I shall rejoin the Wagners, and shall spend more than a month with them at the Palazzo Vendramin, Venice.

Cordial regards to your husband, from your

Very grateful and affectionate   F. Liszt

869. To Princess Carolyne. Zurich, Friday morning, 17 November.[16]
Here I am *en route* and with half the journey done! On Sunday evening I shall be in Venice, where I expect to stay until New Year's Day—then returning straight to Budapest.

---

[15] Constantijn Huygens was not merely the father of the great physicist and astronomer Christiaan Huygens, but an outstanding, multi-talented figure—endowed with great physical beauty and strength—in his own right: athlete, gymnast, painter, engraver, linguist, lutenist, composer, diplomat, and, in the words of Edmund Gosse, 'the most brilliant figure in Dutch literary history'.

[16] La Mara has the date 16 Nov.—but Friday was the 17th.

On the eve of my departure from Weimar, and also the previous day, Their Royal Highnesses invited me to a private dinner. The first evening, in the Hereditaries' rooms, the Grand Duchess did not put in an appearance—only her husband, her 2 daughters Marie and Elsi, and her son-in-law, Prince Reuss, were there. After dinner the Grand Duchess received me alone, in her room fitted with white cupboards, containing books and engravings. She told me she was fairly well recovered from her serious illness, a diphtheria—however, enough traces of it remain to prevent her from taking any other nourishment than oysters and mashed meat. The next day, in her own quarters—in the little round salon with the statue of the fallen angel—she graciously took a place at table, for the first time since her return from Heinrichsau, as Monseigneur told me, but without tasting a morsel. For the rest, the conversation turned animatedly on the usual subjects—further, there was only one foot muff, which she was most kindly insistent that I should accept, assuring me that she possessed an outstanding collection of such things. Before the pudding, she told a servant to take my muff to the Hofgärtnerei straightaway.

I am very proud that my impression of the *St Francis of Assisi* is identical to yours. The engraving of my *Cantico*—score, arrangement for piano—will not be finished until the end of December. Your chapter on war please address to me, soon, at *Venezia, Palazzo Vendramin*, which used to belong to Mme la Duchesse de Berry. . . .

Mme Meyendorff's 3rd son, Clement, born in Rome, is showing a remarkable talent for painting. In between his college studies, brought to a successful conclusion in Weimar, he drew, almost secretly, a large sketch of the *Bells of Strasbourg*, after hearing my work based on Longfellow's Legend. He is now studying at the painting academy in Rome, whither his mother has taken him—so that he may progress by seeing the great Vatican masterpieces. . . .

Your faithful   Sclavissimo

870. To Adelheid von Schorn in Weimar. Palazzo Vendramin, Venezia la bella, Monday, 20 November

Dear friend,

I wouldn't want you to learn from others of my safe arrival here. Wagner and the whole family are, thank Heaven, in perfect health.

Your brother will write from Nuremberg to tell you that the method of whist all but invented, and certainly perfected, by you, is also being propagated under your name at L. Ramann's in the Dürerplatz. Getting rid of all the aces first, is really glorious.

Apart from one incident that more severe people than I would call a statutory swindle by the Milan customs-house, and which I got out of by paying a fine of 70 francs for bringing 50 cigars (!) in with me, my entire journey passed very well.

In Zurich I was given the same friendly reception by several members of the committee—Herr Roemer, the President of the town, at their head—as at the *Musikfest* last July. The proprietor of the Hôtel Bellevue, Herr Pohl (no relation of his namesake in Baden), insisted on my accepting gratis some charming accommodation, plus dinner, supper, etc. and some excellent wines. Such munificence would have made the late Hemleb of the *Erbprinz* break into a hot sweat, and his associates won't be imitating Herr Pohl's gracious courtesy. So I beg you to recommend the very comfortable, first-rate Hôtel Bellevue to any friends and acquaintances of yours who may pass through Zurich. Without promising them that they will be lodged *gratis*, I can assure them that they will find a beautiful view over the lake, well-kept rooms, an excellent *cuisine* and attentive service. The Duke of Altenburg and other princes have stayed there and signed their names in the visitors' book.

Your friend Ada Pinelli is still here, staying with Princess Hatzfeldt at the Palazzo Malipieri; I shall call and see her tomorrow. For the rest, I shall practise moderation in the matter of visits. Wagner pays very few, and as best I can I shall imitate him on this point. My most illustrious friend has given me magnificent accommodation in a spacious apartment in the superb Palazzo Vendramin, which formerly belonged to Madame la Duchesse de Berry. Her son, the Duc della Grazia, is now the owner and, for a year, Wagner the tenant. The splendid furniture bears the impress of the old princely regime, and has been perfectly preserved. The main, inhabited part of the Palazzo Vendramin is likewise in excellent repair, so that Wagner incurred no particular expense, even for stoves and other necessary items, often neglected.

Ever since my very first visit in 1837 [1838], I have been in love with Venice: this feeling will not diminish this time, quite the contrary.

Cordially and sincerely,   F. Liszt

Try to find out something about Bülow, and let me know. Not seeing him again in Meiningen was heart-breaking.

871. To the Grand Duke Carl Alexander. Palazzo Vendramin, Venice, 24 November

Monseigneur,

Coming through the magnificent St Gotthard tunnel, I shared the ultra-French feeling of the idler who cried out in the Place Vendôme: 'Oh, when one looks at the column, how proud one is to be French!' Yes, one is proud to belong to the human race when the enormous intellectual and material achievements of our century are considered. Each of us should contribute to them as much and as well as he can. Above all, Terence's famous line, *Homo sum: humani nihil a me alienum puto*,[17] must be practised as loftily as it was by Your ancestors, and by Goethe, Humboldt, and their colleagues, including my most illustrious friend R. Wagner. I am his guest at the Palazzo Vendramin, where I shall stay, enjoying princely accommodation, until the New Year. He neither makes nor receives visits, and goes out solely to take the air. For thinkers and labourers alike that is a good example, and I regret that I can follow it only rarely. The pincers of daily life hold me in a kind of worldly grip, one which often runs counter to the Ideal I dream of and sometimes strive to express in music.

Your gracious lines reached me a moment ago, and I hasten to thank you for them. Sincerely sharing in the happy news of the full recovery in health of HRH the Grand Duchess, I venture to ask you to lay at the feet of Her Royal Highness the most humble homage of my unwavering gratitude. Perhaps you will add, too, my thanks for the comfortable foot muff which She so kindly deigned to bestow upon me, and which, on my journey, rendered me excellent service. Even here, it is continuing its cosy function under my desk.

Writing to Géza Zichy, I told him that Princess Elisabeth was granting his studies for the left hand the favour of studying them. I listen and applaud at a distance.

D'Albert will everywhere do honour to the title of *Hofpianist* [Court Pianist] which Your Royal Highness has conferred upon him. He is a prodigious virtuoso who will outlast many a pianistic celebrity, and he has the *durable* quality which is needed. . . .

Your old and faithful servant F. Liszt

I stopped in Milan only from the evening to the morning; long enough, however, to gaze in profound awe at the harmonious splendour of the Cathedral. Its stones and stained-glass windows unceasingly sing the *Gloria in excelsis*.

I also admire the square laid out before the Cathedral, with the superb Galleria Vittorio Emanuele. When the ensemble of adjoining buildings is finished—and

---

[17] 'I am a man: I count nothing human indifferent to me', *Heauton Timorumenos* (The Self-tormentor), I. i. 25.

that won't take long—this square will count among the most glorious in modern Europe. The Seven Wonders of the ancient world have long been crumbling, delivered up to the investigations of the archaeology which is officiating at their too ostentatious obsequies. We need new wonders; evidence of them is not lacking for those who did not receive their eyes not to see, and their ears not to hear.

872. To Princess Carolyne. [Venice] 28 December. *St Stanislas* has so entirely absorbed me these last 3 days, that I formed an extreme aversion to corresponding by letter. So I have written only lines of music, much scratched and crossed out—no others! In Venice, the musical event of the month is the *in camera* performance of a symphony by Wagner, which remained in manuscript and has been rediscovered in Dresden. It is the young Hercules subduing the serpents—and taking an Olympian pleasure in this labour. Wagner conducted the orchestra himself, and after 5 rehearsals it went very well. The evening was in honour of Cosima, to celebrate her birthday on Christmas Eve. After the fashion of the King of Bavaria, no guests! There was only family, 7 of us, plus the faithful Zhukovsky from Bayreuth, the President of the *Liceo*, Count Contini, and Humperdinck, the orchestra's assistant conductor—in the attractive foyer at La Fenice, festivally illuminated. Two other persons were admitted at the last moment only on my recommendation. . . .

Hohenlohe sent me direct the photograph of the statuette of St Francis given me at the Villa d'Este by Cardinal de Falloux. It will hardly serve as the title picture of my *Cantico del sol*—neither the gesture nor the accessories, the crown of thorns and the skull, suit the *Cantico*, brought to an end by the great Pardon! From Assisi I received an invitation to take part in the celebrations there, in October, of the *gran poverello di Dio*, by a Sonatina for piano! The invitation reached me only here, 6 weeks after the date—giving me a twofold reason for being unable to accept. If you can without too much inconvenience obtain the picture of St Francis that you tell me about, with arms held out towards the stigmata—I beg you to send it to me. My *Cantico* is being engraved, but will not be out until mid-March. . . .

Umilissimo Sclavissimo

873. To Princess Carolyne. Venezia, Dec. What a charming remark, worthy of Balzac, about Pcss Massimo: 'Having lacked beauty in her youth, she now appears to possess it, in as much as her features are harmonizing as she grows older.'

Wagner and Cosima were the warmest friends and admirers of Gobineau[18] —they have told me a score of times that there was a crying injustice in the lack of appreciation and success met by his works. The public were unaware of them, and the connoisseurs kept silent. Apart from a minor prize of 15,000 francs from the Académie française for his volume *La Renaissance*, he was treated as a diplomat who, to make his way, had no need of literature and the sciences. In the Dec. issue of the *Bayreuther Blätter* you will find a remarkable article on Gobineau.

I ought to write a little letter of congratulations to Ollivier.[19] But you know what a sad feeling is inspired in me by children—their future is exposed to so many contrary chances! Human life is so full of bitterness and disappointments, that I can no longer rejoice very much at the coming into the world of a little creature subject to all our frailties, follies, and misfortunes. On the other hand, I do not grieve excessively at the deaths of those I have known. I even find their fate enviable—for they no longer have to bear the heavy yoke of life and of the responsibility it implies. The sole positive and very keen feeling I retain is that of compassion—with the intense vibrations of human sorrows. Sometimes, for brief moments, I feel those of the sick in the hospitals, of the wounded in war, and even those of people condemned to torture or to death. It is something analogous to the stigmata of St Francis—without the ecstasy, which is for the Saints alone! This strange hypertrophy of the feeling of compassion came to me at the age of 16—when I wanted to let myself slowly die of hunger in the cemetery of Montmartre. It opened my heart to the sublime consolations of Christianity! . . .

---

[18] Who had died in Turin on 13 Oct.
[19] The Olliviers' daughter, Geneviève-Carolyne (after Ollivier's mother and the Princess, her godmother), had been born on 2 Nov.

1883

13 January. Liszt leaves Venice to return to Budapest.

27 January. He attends a performance of Erkel's opera *Bánk bán.*

13 February. Richard Wagner dies in Venice.

16 February. Liszt attends his pupils' concert in the Music Academy.

17–19 February. He visits his cousin Marie in Székesfehérvár.

18 March. He conducts *The Legend of St Elisabeth* in Pozsony.

27 March. He attends a performance of Boito's *Mefistofele* at the Budapest Opera House.

Early April. En route from Budapest to Weimar, Liszt spends several days in Vienna where, on the 6th, his admirer Hugo Wolf is introduced to him. He reaches Weimar on the 7th.

1 May. He attends a performance of *St Elisabeth* in Marburg, where he is the guest of his cousin Franz von Liszt.

2–7 May. He visits Leipzig for the festival (3–6 May) of the Allgemeine Deutsche Musikverein.

22 May. A Wagner memorial concert is mounted in the Weimar Theatre. After several works have been conducted by Müller-Hartung, Liszt brings the occasion to an end by conducting the Prelude and *Karfreitagszauber* (Good Friday music) from *Parsifal.*

3 August and late September. Liszt visits Leipzig for performances of Berlioz's *Benvenuto Cellini.*

21 October. On the eve of Liszt's seventy-second birthday, the Weimar Court Theatre presents a stage performance of *St Elisabeth.*

19 November. Liszt attends a concert of his works in Leipzig.

1–3 and 15/16 December. Liszt visits Meiningen to hear the Meiningen orchestra under its conductor Hans von Bülow.

WORKS. *Zur Trauung* (*Ave Maria III*) (S60), an arrangement for organ/harmonium, unison female voices ad lib, of *Sposalizio* (S161/1). *Nun danket alle Gott* (S61), for organ (voices, brass, drums ad lib). *Magyar király-dal—Ungarisches Königslied* (S93), for various combinations of voices, accompanied or unaccompanied. *Am Grabe Richard Wagners* (S135), for string quartet, harp ad lib. Arrangement (S368) for voice and orchestra of two songs by Korbay: 1. *Le matin* (Bizet) 2. *Gebet* (Geibel). PIANO: *R.W.—Venezia* (S201); *Am Grabe Richard Wagners* (S202);[1] *Schlaflos, Frage und Antwort* (S203); *Valses oubliées* Nos. 2, 3, 4 (S215/2, 3, 4); Third Mephisto Waltz (S216); Mephisto Polka (S217); *Bülow-Marsch* (S230); transcription of *Symphonisches Zwischenspiel zu Calderón's Schauspiel 'über allen Zauber Liebe'* (Lassen) (S497, *c.*1882–3).

---

[1] Composed on 22 May, 70th anniversary of Wagner's birth.

874. To Princess Carolyne in Rome. Budapest, Sunday, 14 January.
Your nice letter reached me yesterday morning in Venice. The train left at 2.15, and brought me straight here in less than 22 hours. Mild temperature, the compartment windows not frozen—a peaceful journey, with no company other than Achille, with whom I am always very content. To the telegram I sent you immediately, I add my constant and unchanging thanks for your kindnesses to me. They are nothing short of prodigious! . . .

Please be so good as to thank Sgambati for his intention of making known my *Lugubre gondola*. I doubt that it will obtain any success at concerts—in view of its sad, sombre character, scarcely mitigated by a few dreaming shadows. The public demand other things—and if they were wrong, that would not worry them! Nevertheless, I shall have the *Lugubre gondola* published. It will appear after Easter, and I shall send it to Sgambati without delay.

For the title-page of the St Francis *Cantico*, the picture by Alonso Cano will do. You asked Magne to send it to me, and I have received it. Beautiful though it may be, it does not express my own idea of the Saint. I believe I have already told you that I did not imagine the *gran poverello di Dio* as a St Antony the Hermit or a St Bruno, for his saintliness frequents a different tonality from theirs. If I could paint, I would represent him not with clasped hands but with arms outstretched in an ecstasy of love, imploring the *gran perdono di Dio* for the sinful world, and the stigmata for himself!

From Venice you will receive Wagner's letter on his youthful Olympian symphony. Mme Dönhoff is in Rome for the winter, and will tell anyone interested that the rumour of her marriage with Lenbach is just as false as many another salon heresy.

875. To Princess Carolyne. Budapest, Sunday, 4 February. The
Vereshchagin photographs you ask for are going to be put in the post. They are: the man eater—the pyramid of human skulls—erected during the Russo-Turkish War, to which I am adding another large photo, Skobeleff haranguing his soldiers, and a small one, showing 3 small paintings of great effect. The inscription on them is taken from a Russian dispatch: 'All calm in Shipka.' It reminds one of General Paskevich's unfortunate remark, after the taking of Warsaw: 'Order reigns in Warsaw.'! In the same packet you will find Vereshchagin's portrait and the catalogue of his exhibition in Budapest—in which no place could be found for the painting showing the Pce of Wales's entry into India, because of its great size. One of Vereshchagin's chief merits consists in his new and superior way of dealing with atmosphere, lights, and skies, to which in India and Russia he devoted

long and hazardous studies. Photography cannot render the strange effects of his colouring of skies and clouds—and also gives no more than an incomplete idea of the astonishing effects of perspective. It is said that on the day of the battle of Pleven—liberated on the birthday of Tsar Alexander II—a table bearing wines and victuals was made ready on the hillock where the Tsar and his staff officer found themselves. The painter had at first depicted Alexander II holding a glass, drinking to the health of the army; but when a high personage observed that this realism ran the risk of offensive comments, Vereshchagin painted out the table and wines. The Tsar is simply seated, with some old Marshal or other beside him—as you will see in the small photograph joined to the catalogue.

At long last, the 3rd volume of my *Années de pèlerinage*, and my 3 *Sonnets de Petrarque* for voice, have been brought out by Schott, Mainz. You will receive them at the same time as the Vereshchagin photographs. The vignette of the *Hymne aux Anges*[2] has been done after Zhukovsky's painting, which adorns the large salon at Wahnfried. My 3 granddaughters, Daniela, Blandine, and Eva, appear in it as angels with wings and musical instruments. In the painting, Siegfried, Cosima, and Zhukovsky himself also appear—it was better to restrict the vignette to the 3 girls. The 2nd illustration in the *Cyprès de la Villa d'Este* reproduces the photograph that you were so kind as to send me. Bock of Berlin has not yet published my last symphonic poem, *Du berceau à la tombe*. As soon as it comes out, I shall send it to you in 3 editions, the full score and arrangements for piano. Another day I'll tell you about my other musical peccadilloes now in the press. Among this number I do not count the *Cantico di San Francesco*, the engraving of which is not yet finished—I believe Kahnt will be publishing it around Easter, or shortly afterwards.

The large portrait that Zhukovsky painted of me continues to obtain numerous and serious votes. And now, a young sculptor with a great deal of talent, by the name of Stróbl, is undertaking a bust of me, after having last winter modelled a large seated statue of my person, which is to be executed in marble and placed as a pendant to the statue of the most celebrated composer of Hungarian operas, F. Erkel. He is the composer of *Hunyady*, *Bánk bán*, etc., which have had hundreds of performances here, without ever passing the Hungarian frontier. The 2 statues will be placed at the entrance to the new grand theatre, in the Radialstrasse. HM the King has ordered the opening of this theatre, now being completed, for October or November next year, '84. . . .

Your umilissimo Sclavissimo,   F.L.

---

[2] The *Angelus! Prière aux anges gardiens*, first of the *Années de pèlerinage, troisième année*.

876. To the Editor[3] of the Gazette de Hongrie.
Budapest, 6 February

Sir,

It is not without regret that I send you these lines; but since something of a fuss has been made here about my alleged hostility to the Israelites, I have to rectify this false and unfounded rumour.

In the world of music it is a matter of common knowledge that a number of illustrious Israelites, Meyerbeer first and foremost, have given me their friendship and esteem; just as, in the literary world, Heine and others have done.

I find it unnecessary to enumerate the many proofs that I have given, for fifty years, of my active loyalty towards Israelites of talent and ability; I further refrain from speaking of my voluntary contributions to Jewish charitable institutions in various countries.

The motto of my patron saint, Francis of Paola, is 'Caritas!' To this motto I shall remain faithful my whole life long!

If, by a few mutilated quotations from my book on the Hungarian gypsies, it has been sought to pick a quarrel with me—what in French is called *une querelle d'Allemand*—I can in all good conscience affirm that I feel guilty of no other misdeed than that of having feebly reproduced the argument of the kingdom of Jerusalem put forward by Disraeli (Lord Beaconsfield), Georges Elliot [*sic*] (Mrs Lewes),[4] and Crémieux, three Israelites of high degree.

I am, Sir,

Yours etc., F. Liszt

877. To Lina Ramann in Nuremberg. Budapest, 9 February. [G] . . .

My winter existence in Budapest this time is very much like that of previous years: every day at least 4 hours of letter-writing; visits—business and other—then await; proofs to attend to; in the afternoons, three times a week, several hours of piano lessons with a dozen pupils, some of whom acquit themselves in masterly fashion; in the evenings, sometimes concerts to attend and, for recreation, a game of whist.

Here, I can hardly get down to my *real* work. It was easier for me in Venice. There, I wrote various things, among them a *third* elegy, dedicated to Lina Ramann. Don't be frightened by the title, 'die Trauer Gondel' ('la gondola lugubre'). As you know, I bear in my heart a deep sorrow; now and then it has to break out in music. . . .

---

[3] Amadé Saissy.

[4] Although with her novel *Daniel Deronda* she did great service to the cause of Jewish nationalism, George Eliot was not herself Jewish; nor did she ever marry G. H. Lewes.

878. To Princess Carolyne. Budapest, 10 February. I usually have the honour of sitting near Cardinal Haynald at public concerts. Yesterday evening[5] I conveyed to him your admiring respects, which he will reciprocate when the opportunity offers. . . .

Local circumstances, difficult to appreciate elsewhere, have made me decide to have published in the *Gazette de Hongrie* my letter relating to the criticism of the Israelites which is wrongly attributed to me. To publish this letter last winter seemed to me to be timorous—and the foolish courage of fear is not known to me!—I incline rather in the other direction! I now think I shall not be committing a shameful retraction. Kindly let me know your opinion, without any reserve whatsoever. You quote to me Sainte-Beuve's just remark in 1833 [1834] on Lamennais, after the fulgurating publication of *Paroles d'un croyant*: 'He has changed his public, but will not gain by the change.' For my humble part as an artist, I try to serve the public nobly—without anxiety about gain or loss—whether by pleasing, or by confronting, it.

879. To Adelheid von Schorn in Weimar. Budapest, 14 February. If you were here, dear friend, you would perhaps find a way of bringing a little order into the hundreds of letters that rain down upon me from all sides. The bothers and burdens of the amiability with which I am credited are becoming unbearable; and I have a good mind, one of these days, to cry from the house-tops that I beg the public to consider me one of the most disagreeable, crotchety, and disobliging of men.

Until our cordial meeting at Weimar in early April. Ever your very affectionate and grateful   F. Liszt

880. To Princess Carolyne. Székesfehérvár, 19 February, morning. As I telegraphed you the day before yesterday, I shall remain in Budapest until Easter. In that first moment[6] I wrote to ask Cosima if it suited her for me to join her in Venice and accompany her back to Bayreuth. Through Daniela she replied in the negative. Actually, Cosima finds herself in a tumultuous confusion of condolences, respects, and admiration. At Bayreuth there will be a hubbub of very legitimate enthusiasm and glorification. Wagner's funeral will have all the *éclat* of Victor Emmanuel's or Gambetta's. From afar I associate myself

---

[5] At a concert in the Vigadó to benefit victims of floods in Gyor.   [6] Of the news of Wagner's death.

with it in thought, while keeping my old distance from festive or funerary ceremonies. Barring absolute necessity, my personal preference is to stay away from
them. You know my sad feeling about life: dying seems to me to be simpler
than living! Death, even when preceded by the long and frightening pains
of 'dying'—according to Montaigne's striking remark—is our deliverance from
an involuntary yoke, a consequence of the original sin. Job is my patron saint
of the Old Testament—and the penitent thief, St Dismas, that of the New. In
6 weeks I shall, unhurriedly and at my leisure, see Cosima again in Bayreuth.[7]

The kind approval you give to my Semitic letter has pleasantly surprised me.
In writing it, I feared that in view of local circumstances I might go astray. When
you approve of what I do, I am sure of staying on the right path.

As my cousin Frau von Saar is in the 8th month of her interesting condition, I came here yesterday to see her. I think highly and fondly of her as a
woman of distinction who does honour to her name of Liszt—following in that
the example of her father and of her brother Franz. Her husband, Heinrich von
Saar, is a Major in a regiment of uhlans, an instructor in military tactics and
strategy. . . .

Back in Budapest at midday will be your umilissimo Sclavissimo,   F. Liszt

881. To Antal Siposs. Budapest, 27 February. [G] Your letter of yesterday
brings into the consistently friendly relations we have had for many years a discordant note which I find most disagreeable.

A candid comment, the musical appropriateness of which is quite evident,
you regard as an insult. In the face of such an error on your part, I need no
apology.

Herr Hlavach's crude *dérangement* of the softly murmuring F minor Etude of
Chopin ranks among the very worst *distortions*. Just as does the previous day's
clumsy, unauthorized performance, on 2 pianos, of the same work. They were
vying to see which could make it worse.

Precisely because I have frequently taken the opportunity conscientiously
to praise the Siposs school and talented pupils, I unfortunately had this time
conscientiously to put a curb on the production of Hlavach's objectionable programme. No sensible musician will blame me for that.

---

[7] In the event, this did not happen. Thus Adelheid von Schorn, writing of Liszt's visit to Leipzig in early May: 'He
had earlier told me that he would be going on from there to Bayreuth. I went to Leipzig for one day only, to hear
Liszt's *Prometheus*, and found him in a dreadfully excited state: he had received a letter from Wahnfried asking him to
postpone his visit as Frau Wagner could see *no one*. That his daughter was shutting herself away from *everyone*, Liszt
knew, but that *he* was to be no exception, hurt him bitterly.'

As far as Kücken's *Polonaise* is concerned, I repeat that such vapid charlatanism does not deserve to be admitted on to decent concert programmes, but ought to be expelled to that place where the great Molière dispatched the 'sonnet d'Oronte', with the celebrated line:

'Franchement, il est bon à mettre au cabinet.'[8] . . .

In the expectation that reflection and justness will recommend to you the simple retraction of your tetchy letter, I remain, with my customary loyal and invariable sentiments,   Yours,   F. Liszt

882. To the Grand Duke Carl Alexander in Weimar. Budapest, 4 March. Today, Monseigneur, prepare for a long letter. First of all, I ask you to lay the very humble homage of my steadfast gratitude at the feet of Her Majesty the Empress, your sister, who for a good many years has been so very graciously kind to me. I am deeply grateful for it and venture to say that between Her and myself there is an indissoluble bond that I call my exalted *feeling for Weimar*, and for the traditional and perpetual glory of your illustrious House.

As for the modest part which falls to music, I allow myself to claim Your Royal Highness's attention in honour of the memory of Berlioz. Of the great French composers, it is he who has the most links with Weimar. His *Benvenuto Cellini*, with its wonderful verve and originality, has several times been performed in your theatre, despite the failure that unjust prejudices and a violent cabal caused it to suffer in Paris and, some fifteen years later, in London. In accepting the dedication of *Cellini*, Your august mother redressed the wrongs committed by other theatres.

Berlioz's second opera (lighter and *di mezzo carattere*), *Béatrice et Bénédict*, has remained in the repertoire of the Weimar theatre, and I know that it is appreciated by one of the most discerning connoisseurs in Europe: the reigning Grand Duchess.

Had there been no cessation of my own activities in your theatre—and those activities were, I confess, a little too energetic so far as the average temperature in the town was concerned—I would certainly have mounted a *complete* performance of *Les Troyens*, a most remarkable and superb work which in the composer's lifetime obtained no more than a *succès d'estime* in Paris. You know some excerpts from it, Monseigneur, and you also remember that Berlioz had the honour of conducting his admirable symphonies at your Court concerts.

---

[8] The words in *Le Misanthrope* with which Alceste gives Oronte his opinion of the latter's sonnet. An equivalent remark today, in colloquial English, might be: 'Frankly, I'd put it down the loo.'

I am sending to Baron von Loën the letter addressed to me by the committee for the Berlioz statue. Chairman: Vicomte Delaborde, permanent secretary of the Académie des Beaux Arts. Members: A. Thomas, Saint-Saëns, Massenet, *et al.*, of the Institut de France.

In my opinion, it is not advisable literally to accept the invitation of the Paris committee by setting up subcommittees in Weimar and Budapest. In Germany and Hungary we have to provide for so many national monuments and—alas!— for so many flood victims that our purses are generally empty.

Here, I have asked some kind friends—Cardinal Haynald, Géza Zichy, Albert Apponyi, and others—to give me their contributions towards the Berlioz monument. From Weimar, should Your Royal Highnesses be pleased to make a donation, Baron von Loën would be the qualified intermediary.

Your very humble and faithful old servant, F. Liszt

883. To Malwine Tardieu in Brussels. Budapest, 6 March

Dear, kind friend,

Silence best suits deep mourning. I shall be silent on Wagner, prototype of an initiatory genius.

Cordial thanks for your telegram of yesterday.[9] No one rejoices more than I in Saint-Saëns's successes. He deserves them, beyond any doubt; but Dame Fortune, a great sovereign of dubious morals, often shows no eagerness to side with merit. To make her listen to reason, one must keep on tweaking her ear tenaciously (as Saint-Saëns has done).

Be so kind as to send me the issue of the *Indépendance* with the article on *Henry VIII*. I shall ask M. Saissy, editor of the *Gazette de Hongrie* and Professor of French literature at the University of Budapest, to reproduce this article in his *Gazette*. Saissy is a friend of mine; consequently, he will publish what is favourable to *Henry VIII*.

Saint-Saëns has sent me the score of his *splendid* work *La Lyre et la Harpe*. Alas! Anything not pertaining to the *theatre* and not belonging to the repertoire of the old classical masters, Handel, Bach, Palestrina *et al.*, still doesn't enjoy the attentive and paying—the decisive criterion—regard of the public. Proof of this was provided in his lifetime by Berlioz.

Please give my friendly regards to your husband, and accept my devoted and grateful affection. F. Liszt

---

[9] On the successful première, at the Paris Opéra on 5 Mar., of Saint-Saëns' four-act opera *Henry VIII*.

884. To Princess Carolyne. Budapest, 6 March. French being the language most familiar to you, I sent you yesterday the Paris *La Renaissance musicale.* You will find in it the flowery language of the newspapers on Wagner, and an unpublished letter from him to M. Monod, pastor and professor in Paris. Other letters and notes from Wagner are being sought avidly and published with *éclat.* I have been asked for letters he sent to me—my response was to say that I shall not hand over a single one. The Wagnerian cult is assuming colossal dimensions, very just ones in my opinion. In his honour, 7 statues are already planned —it's Homeric!

These last few days I have done nothing but write letters relating to the Berlioz monument. . . . After my personal contribution last year of 300 fr., I am adding 350 fr., due to the kindness of Counts Géza Zichy, Albert Apponyi, *et al.,* as well as that of Cardinal Haynald, who appreciates the Berlioz masterpieces only with great reservation. Long ago, Cardinal Haynald said to me: 'Dear Liszt, I am fond of *you*—but understand nothing of your works.'—'Tanto meglio, Eminenza [So much the better, Eminence]', I replied. A witty remark by Count Gyula Andrássy, my very kind patron: 'I understand nothing of music, but I understand Liszt.' . . .   F.L.

885. To Princess Carolyne. Pozsony, Palm Sunday, 18 March. Thank you for reminding me of my old wish, to be buried without any fuss whatsoever, or any funeral service other than a low mass—consequently, without music. More than fifteen years ago, I had asked in Budapest that on my deathbed my body should be clothed in the habit of the tertiary order of St Francis of Assisi. At that time I also had that habit cut to my measurements, at the Franciscan Monastery in Budapest. If it is lost, to have a new one tailored in the same fashion—no matter where I die—will not be difficult. . . . The sublime *poverello di Dio*, St Francis, the ardent lover of poverty, as Dante so admirably glorified him[10]—also remains the almost extravagant and intoxicated apostle of the divine madness of the Cross, of the *gran Perdono.* Before coming to Rome, in '61, I sent you the will I drew up in Weimar. I beg you to carry it out with your usual charity, and to favour my daughter Cosima in connection with those possessions of mine which, according to your instructions, have remained locked up in Weimar. Some, which I have already mentioned to you, must go to the Budapest Museum: Beethoven's piano, the accompanying music-rack, of which you provided two-thirds of the cost, and the famous Hungarian sabre, presented

10 *Paradiso,* XI.

to me in 1840 at the end of a concert in the Pest National Theatre. For the other objects, I rely on your kindness to distribute them as you see fit, which will certainly be in perfect agreement with my own wishes. I add only that my watch from the Geneva Conservatoire, in 1837 [1836], is to go to my former secretary and disinterested friend Gaetano Belloni. He was at Woronince—it was his Austerlitz!

If you wish graciously to participate in the subscription, a rather meagre one, for the statue of Berlioz—that will be splendid. 100 francs from you will suffice. In the few lines accompanying whatever you send, I urge you to recall that it was to you that Berlioz dedicated *Les Troyens*. . . .

Sclavissimo,   F.L.

886. To Princess Carolyne. Weimar, 26 April. I am reproaching myself greatly for not having written to you sooner. What prevented me more than anything else was a foolish obligation I had incurred by promising one of my godsons, Francis Korbay, born in Pest and well settled in New York, to orchestrate 2 of his *Lieder*, which he intends to sing soon in London. This task would, I thought, take me no more than 4 or 5 mornings. How wrong I was! More than double that time was needed for me to make them presentable. To keep my promise as best I could, I was struggling and sweating. Probably Korbay will be dissatisfied, for to lead to a possible success my work had to run very much counter to his. When I write on music paper, there is no possibility of writing letters the same day, in view of visits and local obligations. In the evenings I am overcome by fatigue, and no longer feel capable of anything other than playing whist—an amusement which will not ruin me as my partners consent to play for nothing. The knaves, queens, and kings of cards are acquaintances more inoffensive than the humans corresponding to the same titles! Without any misanthropy whatsoever, my age allows me some lassitude!

The day after I got here, Monseigneur came first thing in the morning to give me a cordial welcome—it was his wife's birthday, 8 April. She received about thirty people at midday, myself among them, as also at the dinner, the following Monday, for 7 or 8 persons. . . . Yesterday, dinner for an even more limited number. At a small Court concert Mme Jaëll, an artiste of distinction, performed pianistic prodigies. She is outstanding, and far above the reputation she has gained. Otto Roquette has just published a volume entitled *Friedrich Preller, ein Lebensbild*. Several pages concern you.

Thank you for your subscription of 100 francs for the *scuola gregoriana* in Rome, at the Anima. When I return to Rome I shall add another 100 lire to the 300 I gave when this *scuola* was founded. It is very much to be recommended, but its prosperous progress could be hindered by the prevailing influence of the autochthonous *maestri*.

Next Monday I shall be at my cousin's home in Marburg. I enclose the announcement of the performance of the *Elisabeth* on the occasion of the 600th anniversary of the consecration of the church of St Elisabeth at Marburg. On Wednesday, 2 May, I shall arrive in Leipzig for the music festival, which will last until 6 May. As soon as the complete programme appears, you will receive it.   Umilissimo, devotissimo Sclavissimo

887. To Théodore Michaëlis in Paris. 25 June[11]

Dear Monsieur Michaëlis,

Receiving about fifty letters every week, I find myself necessarily condemned, so far as the replies are concerned, to the practice of frequent *ritardandi*, and even of *fermate*. Kindly disposed people grant me indulgence, and the others don't preoccupy me at all.

This autumn I shall send you the short voice and piano score of *Le Devin du village*,[12] suitable for your collection of masterpieces of French opera. I shall add a transcription of some songs from Jean-Jacques Rousseau's *Consolations des misères de ma vie*; and I thank you for having sent me the original edition of this work.

As regards subscribing to Jean-Jacques's monument, the fact that I am an Abbé makes it quite out of the question, notwithstanding all my admiration for the great genius of the writer and his dazzling influence on the political destiny of France.   Yours etc.

888. To Princess Carolyne. Weimar, 26 July. Once again the reason, or rather the unreason, for the delay in my letters lies in my tiresome habit of writing music. To correct myself of it in my old days is no longer possible! Fontenelle used to say of his brother, the abbé: 'In the mornings he says mass; in the evenings he knows not what he says.' I resemble the Abbé Fontenelle, with this variant that, in the evenings, worn out by the fatigues of the day—I no longer know what to say, and limit myself to corresponding mentally!

---

[11] Written either in Weimar or at Dornburg.
[12] 'The Village Soothsayer', a one-act opera by Rousseau; its first performance was at Fontainebleau on 18 Oct. 1752.

The numerous celebrations of the 400th anniversary of the birth of Luther have again brought a Catholic work into the limelight, one which, having gone through several previous editions, was very prominent already. It is the one by Jansen, a professor at some college in Frankfurt am Main. These 2 or 3 vols. contain a history of the Reformation—done from the Catholic viewpoint—as well as documents which, if not unknown, are at least very skilfully drawn up in battle array. The author has added a volume addressed to his critics, written in a tone at once moderate, firm and steadfast—which, according to what is said by competent judges, does not put his adversaries at their ease. I have not read the work—but if you would like to make its acquaintance, I shall send it to you.

A new Parisian music magazine, *La Renaissance musicale*, is publishing a series of articles, entitled *Berlioz intime*,[13] which will form a volume. Our glorious and too embittered friend is not gaining from the posthumous publication of his letters. His forename, Hector, brought him no luck—the Achilles, Wagner, having arrived on the scene to dominate contemporary music drama.

Wilhelmsthal, 31 July. For three days I have as usual been the guest of Their Royal Highnesses. On 3 August I shall be in Leipzig for the performance of Berlioz's *Benvenuto Cellini*—about which will shortly be writing to you your

Umilissimo Sclavissimo

889. To Princess Carolyne. Weimar, 29 September. I went back to Leipzig to hear *Cellini* again, a work I don't weary of admiring. Even the defects—that narrow criticism might reproach Berlioz with—have their brilliant aspect, and a youthful verve that is quite astonishing. The King [Albert] of Saxony attended this performance—being in Leipzig on some business or other. His Majesty was so gracious as to send for me during an interval, to the salon adjoining the royal box—and to talk to me, with great goodwill, for 10 minutes. To his observation that this kind of music needed to be heard several times to be appreciated, I responded plainly with: 'It is worth the trouble and the pleasure!' . . .

I owe Keudell a letter of thanks for the dedication of his excellent transcription of the Schubert quartet—but, for me, writing letters is becoming not so much tedious as torturous! The kind of celebrity I possess leads to cretinism—and so I told a friend that I was thinking of settling in the Valais canton, classic ground of cretins!

---

[13] By Edmond Hippeau.

In our Weimar church we pray every day, after mass, for the salvation of the sovereign Pontiff—of his Catholic flock, and for the conversion of sinners!

Umilissimo Sclavissimo,   F.L.

Despite the many interruptions, I continue to blacken music paper, and do nothing but cross out and erase. Most of the things I could write don't seem to me to be worth the trouble!

890. To the Emperor Dom Pedro II of Brazil [Autumn]

Sire,

Your Majesty is so good as to honour me with his kind remembrance, on the occasion of the first performance of *Lohengrin* in Rio de Janeiro. Wagner dedicated this admirable work to me, and its première was mounted in Weimar under my direction, in 1850. From that time onwards I understood what Wagner's sublime genius was to create in *Tristan*, the *Nibelungen* tetralogy, and *Parsifal*.

I shall not fail to convey to Mme Wagner, the Countess Schleinitz, and His Eminence Cardinal Hohenlohe, Your Majesty's gracious good wishes.

Your Majesty's very humble servant,   F. Liszt

891. To Princess Alexander Bibesco at Epurény Castle, Romania [Autumn]

Madame la Princesse,

My very humble thanks for remembering me so graciously and kindly. I retain a lively memory of your fine talent: its charm penetrates and embellishes the very compositions that you interpret. Similarly, I recognize it again in the ravishing inspiration of Carmen Sylva in connection with one of my little works.[14] It at one and the same time abashes me and fills me with pride. Infinitely better than my poor musical notes has the royal poet known how to express the *Waldesrauschen* and the mysterious murmurings of the forest.

Be so good, Madame la Princesse, as to put at the feet of Her Majesty the Queen the profound and grateful respects of your most affectionately devoted servant,   F. Liszt

---

[14] Referring to the poem Queen Elisabeth had been inspired to write after hearing Liszt's *Waldesrauschen*.

892. To Princess Carolyne. Meiningen, Sunday morning, 2 December.

Getting here at 6.00 p.m. yesterday, and having accommodation in the Schloss, I met the Cardinal [Hohenlohe] and his sister Mme Lauchert. At 7.00 we were at the rehearsal of this evening's Beethoven concert, conducted by Bülow. The Meiningen orchestra performs prodigies—nowhere else does one find such an understanding of the different works, such precision in the rendition, with the subtlest and most appropriate rhythmic and dynamic nuances. A circumstance very favourable to concerts in Meiningen was the Duke's abolition of the opera, about twenty years ago. Having no duties at the opera, the orchestra are left with time for a good number of partial and full rehearsals without getting tired. Bülow is almost prodigal of rehearsals in the way that, had he had the means, Berlioz would have been. The result is admirable, and in certain respects unrivalled—the Paris Conservatoire and other celebrated concert institutions not excepted. Thanks to its present conductor, Meiningen's little phalanx is in advance of the biggest battalions. People say that Rubinstein and a few others have expressed themselves disapprovingly about several of Bülow's unusual *tempi* and expressive nuances—in my opinion, their criticism is misplaced.

4 o'clock. On Sundays, Hohenlohe says mass in the new church, which has turned out fairly well, with 5 or 6 stained glass windows and a good organ—I went there with him. For weekdays he has a chapel in his apartment at the Schloss. At 11.00, a further assembling of the orchestra, for the performance of the March *Vom Fels zum Meer*, Berlioz's *King Lear* overture, my *Ideale*, the Prelude to the *Meistersinger*, and Brahms's Variations on a Theme of Haydn. . . . Here's something astonishing! Beethoven's most difficult work for quartet—the last great Fugue Op. 133, which because of its complexities never appears on programmes —is performed by the Meiningen orchestra with a perfect ensemble of all the stringed instruments, more than thirty players. This is, up to now, a unique achievement, before which every musician must raise his hat. On a previous occasion in Meiningen I also heard Bach's celebrated *Chaconne*, given a virtuoso performance by a dozen violins in unison.

893. To Princess Carolyne. Weimar, 5 December.

I returned here, with Bülow, on Monday. Yesterday there was his concert to benefit the *Orchesterschule*; the audience were amazed by his outstanding gifts as conductor and pianist. This time, it was works by Raff which filled the entire programme—among them all, the *Waldsymphonie* is one of the most successful, and seems to me to have a chance of lasting. . . . The decrees of Dame Criticism are not absolute. She had utterly condemned my *Totentanz*: for about fifteen years this piece, after the thundering fiasco it made at its first 2 performances, was consigned to the mortuary of oblivion. And then Nikolai Rubinstein took it up and, through his admirable talent, restored it to life in Moscow, Warsaw, and Petersburg. In these 3 cities, the young Conservatoire pupils play it with passion—and in Germany, too, it is beginning to be rife, under the brilliant fingers of Fräulein Remmert and of several pianists on their way to becoming famous. Recently in Leipzig, *proh pudor*,[15] a young and remarkably talented Russian pianist, assisted by Weimar's *Orchesterschule*, risked a Liszt Concert—and after the *Totentanz* he was much applanded by the audience. The delinquent's name is Siloti. Before studying with me he was regarded as the most distinguished of Nikolai Rubinstein's pupils. He possesses everything necessary to succeed as a celebrated pianist—plus the very favourable negative advantage of not being a composer. I went to Leipzig for Siloti's *Liszt-Conzert*. Programme: Goethe March and Crusaders' March (*Elisabeth*), *Lieder*, and 4 or 5 piano pieces. All went well, performance and audience—I was given my revenge for my failures of days gone by!

If Bülow conducts the Meiningen concert of Sunday, 16 December, I shall attend it. The Duke and his wife, Baroness von Heldburg, are always very gracious to me.

894. To Princess Carolyne. Meiningen, 16 December. I have written a few words to Magne[16]—to see those about them die, remains the sad fate of the living! The ancients thought that to die young was a signal favour of the gods! As Christians, we say with the voice heard by St John: 'Blessed are the dead which die in the Lord!' I hope that it will soon be the case with me— until the last moment I shall bless your great and holy soul, superabundant in sublimities!

Without leaving the thought of death, I shall mention that my daughter Cosima is doing her utmost not to survive Wagner. From what I am told—for I neither receive nor request direct news—she spends hours every day at Wagner's tomb, despite all pleas to the contrary. A decisive vocation!

Umilissimo Sclavissimo,   F.L.

The Cardinal is no longer in Meiningen, but will perhaps return here at Christmas—his sojourn in Germany having to be prolonged a little with the authorization of HH Pope Leo XIII. The GD Constantine Constantinovich of

---

[15] 'Oh, for shame!' In the past, Leipzig had generally been hostile to Liszt's music.
[16] Whose 14-year-old son Wolfgang had just died.

Russia is passing through with his fiancée, Pcss of Altenburg, niece of the Duke of Meiningen—the wedding will take place in the spring, at Petersburg. The young man talked to me very sensibly about music—I asked him to renew to his father my warmest thanks for the triple telegram he sent me in Budapest at the time of my 50th anniversary as an artiste, in Nov. '73. That telegram made a sensation, as was to be expected.

895. To Princess Carolyne. Weimar, 28 December. Thank you for the telegram, signed with a dearly remembered pseudonym.[17] For today, I have only some rather distressing news about my household to send you. Achille's illness is getting worse. As well as catarrh of the stomach he now has a swollen liver—further, acute pains in both sides. Their scientific name escapes me, but they prevent Achille not only from sleeping comfortably, but even from lying at full length in bed without difficulty. He usually reclines on a chair like Napoleon I, and without suspecting the profundity of Pascal's remark: 'All mankind's misfortunes come from not knowing how to sit quietly in a chair.' In saying that, Pascal was rather forgetful of the fact that the chair required a joiner and an owner, and these latter some sort of shelter—hence labours, bothers, trade, disputes, and social complications without end! In this way the sublimest thoughts of the greatest minds break down when confronted by the implacable necessity of things here below! May the will of Our Father, who is in Heaven, be done—to correspond to and co-operate with it, as our frailty allows, is our task! Let us fill it with the *Charitas* which unites us to Him and to humanity! It will probably be necessary to put Achille, despite his aversion to the idea, in the Weimar or Jena *Krankenhaus* [hospital]. If he has recovered by 12 January he will accompany me to Budapest—if not, I shall take the necessary steps. I envy Hübner on one single point—he went around the world without a servant! . . .

Same old story—for the second time this year a hundred francs or so have been taken from my drawer. It is what Sue elegantly called 'borrowing without prior notice'! He and others formerly suspected of this behaviour Comte Horace de Viel-Castel—who figured as something of a wit and extreme mischiefmaker in Parisian society as far back as the 1830s. He held on under the Empire, through the protection of Princess Mathilde and the limitless indulgence of Napoleon.

Sundry persons are, contrary to my wishes, busying themselves with my health —which I pride myself that I can look after adequately. I'll tell you the honest

---

[17] Probably 'Gregorio'.

truth on this topic. No real malady, no organ attacked—but, more often than in previous years, nervous troubles which interrupt or spoil my work and sometimes oblige me to go to bed *prima sera*.

Happy New Year of '84, with a good reunion in Rome! *Semper ubique* umilissimo Sclavissimo,   F.L.

1884

4 February. Liszt arrives in Budapest.

24–6 February. He visits Pozsony where, on the 25th, he conducts the Hungarian Coronation Mass in the Cathedral.

2/3 March. He is the guest in Esztergom of Cardinal Simor.

17 March. He attends a concert given by Vladimir de Pachmann.

5 April. Liszt takes part in a private concert at the English Ladies' Institute. 'As he did so often in his old age, he ended the concert with *La Charité* transcribed from Rossini, with its brilliant octave progressions.'[1]

6 April. At a choral concert given by the Academy of Music, *Nun danket alle Gott* is performed, for the first time in Hungary.

9–14 April. Liszt spends Easter in Kalocsa with Cardinal Haynald.

25 April. He arrives in Weimar.

23–6 May. At the festival of the Allgemeine Deutsche Musikverein, held in Weimar, Liszt conducts an orchestra for the last time.

23–6 June. Liszt is the Grand Duke's guest at Dornburg.

12 July–8 August. He stays in Bayreuth to attend performances of *Parsifal.*

Late August/early September. Liszt goes to Munich, and is then the guest of Sophie Menter at Schloss Itter, her home in the Tyrol.

28 September. Visiting Eisenach for the unveiling of a statue of J. S. Bach, to the cost of which he had contributed 3,000 thalers, Liszt also attends a performance of the B minor Mass, and on the 29th a Bach concert.

1 October. Liszt attends a concert of his music given at the Leipzig Gewandhaus by his pupils Friedheim and Siloti.

30 October. He arrives in Budapest.

1–17 November. He is the guest of Count Zichy at Tetétlen. Here, on the 10th, he, Zichy and one of the latter's daughters (with her piano teacher) give a concert for the local countryfolk. 'After the concert the great master excelled himself in kindness, waiting upon his unsophisticated guests, offering them food and filling their glasses with wine. . . . After Liszt had captivated everyone, despite his inability to speak Hungarian fluently, a snow-white old man went up to him at the end of the meal and, glass in hand, said: "What you are *called*, the Count has told us; what you can *do*, you have shown us; but what you *are*, we have seen for ourselves—and for that, may the great God of the Hungarians bless you!" '[2]

---

[1] Legány, *Liszt and His Country 1874–1886*, 240.
[2] Graf G. Zichy, *Aus meinem Leben* (3 vols., Stuttgart, 1911–20), iii. 61.

22/4 November. Liszt attends concerts given by Bülow and his Meiningen orchestra in the Vigadó. At the second concert Johannes Brahms plays his Piano Concerto in B flat major.

5 December. The 16-year-old Archduchess Maria Valeria (daughter of the Emperor Franz Joseph) and other royal personages visit Liszt, who receives them graciously and delights them with his playing.

8 December. Liszt leaves Budapest to travel, via Florence, to Rome.

WORKS. *Mariengarten (Quasi cedrus)* (S62, *c.*1884), for solo voices and organ. *Qui seminant in lacrimis* (S63), for mixed voices and organ. PIANO: *Csárdás* (S225/1); Hungarian Rhapsody No. 17 (S244/17). *Introitus* (S268/1), for organ. *Le Crucifix* (Hugo) (S342), for alto and piano/harmonium.

896. To Princess Carolyne in Rome. Nuremberg, 2 February. Having

left Weimar the day before yesterday, I here received news of the death of Achille.[3] He spent almost the whole of January in the *Krankenhaus*, and I regarded him as lost from the very beginning of his illness, which became more and more complicated and finished with an incurable dropsy. In my last conversation with him, I urged him to exercise patience and to trust in Our Lord Jesus Christ— while assuring him that he would return to my service and join me again in Budapest. He answered me most affectingly: 'Per Vostra Eccellenza vengo a piedi [For Your Excellency I'll come on foot].' Achille was the best *cameriere* I have ever had—upright, quiet, home-loving, well-schooled, and not easily put out. His failings were certainly far fewer than those of his master, and his qualities very praiseworthy. He performed his duties as a Catholic unpretentiously, went to mass, to confession, and took communion at Easter. At Kalocsa we took communion together in the chapel of the Jesuit College, at the mass performed by my very respectable cousin Father Hennig. My old friend Gille will take care to have Achille's coffin accompanied to the Weimar cemetery by the Catholic priest. A cross with an inscription will be placed over his grave. An intelligent and alert young man[4] is provisionally serving me as an aide—as they say in America—on my journey to Budapest. He will continue with his good offices for 6 weeks—I should gladly keep him longer, but he is engaged in someone

---

[3] The telegram giving notice of his manservant's death was handed to Liszt by Lina Ramann whom he was visiting in Nuremberg: 'I gave him the telegram; he was very shaken, it trembled in his hand and a tear fell upon it.' (L. Ramann, *Lisztiana*: *Erinnerungen an Franz Liszt in Tagebuchblättern, Briefen und Dokumenten aus den Jahren 1873–1886/7*, Mainz, 1983, 221.)

[4] Carl Lehmann, a servant of Baroness von Meyendorff.

else's service, from which I cannot in good conscience entice him away. Spiridion has offered to return to his old duties—but I have other ideas! Achille's successor will be found in Budapest.[5]

897. To Princess Carolyne. Hotel Paluguay, Pozsony, 25 February, morning. The letter of yours that went astray has turned up, and I thank you from the bottom of my heart for the one I received recently. I got here yesterday, for the jubilee commemorating the 50 years that Mgr. Heidler has been in the priesthood. He has long been *Stadtpfarrer* [parish priest] in Pozsony, a mitred abbé with the title of bishop without diocese. He is also President of the *Kirchenmusikverein* [Church Music Society], and has always shown me great kindness. . . . For his jubilee, the Cardinal Primate of Esztergom and numerous bishops are sending him congratulatory telegrams; yesterday, the Emperor sent him the cross of Commander of the Iron Crown. At 10.00 today he will officiate in the Cathedral, and I shall conduct my Coronation Mass—already known here through 2 very tolerable performances, I am told. . . . Tomorrow morning I return to Budapest—and next Sunday I shall probably pay a very humble visit to the Cardinal Primate, in Esztergom. HE Simor has, through Lippert his architect, directed the work of restoration being carried out on Pozsony Cathedral. . . .

I do not know who mentioned a supposed estrangement between Cardinal Haynald and me. Not the shadow of one! I often meet Haynald, either at concerts, where I am usually his neighbour, or in the homes of persons of our acquaintance—and he everywhere shows me much kindness. I shall take good care not to abuse it—consequently, our relations will remain uniformly very flattering for me and without any inconvenience for him. In general I escape tangles and entanglements by my pacific and respectful straightforwardness towards my superiors, and by strict observance of the consideration due to my equals and inferiors. When I happen to have a difference of opinion with either, my practice is to avoid angry clashes—unless they prove absolutely necessary. Even then, I now try to keep them within reasonable limits! . . .

Umilissimo Sclavissimo, D.

My eyes are weakening perceptibly. A celebrated oculist whom I consulted assures me that I have no cataract to fear—but he advises me to read little, and to write still less.

---

[5] The last of Liszt's manservants, a Hungarian named Mihály Kreiner, entered his service on 1 Mar.

898. To the Grand Duke Carl Alexander in Weimar.
Esztergom, 3 March

Monseigneur,

When you come to Hungary, do not fail to visit Esztergom. Here you will find architecture worthy of renown: the propylaea of the Basilica—8 very lofty, imposing, and massive columns. In my opinion they are worth far more than the Basilica itself, which turned out rather mediocre, excessive consultation resulting in a muddle. Right beside the Basilica stands the ancient chapel of the King of Hungary, St Stephen. Cardinal Prince-Primate Simor's architect, named Lippert, has restored it in a wholly worthy manner. In certain countries artists are half-dead in their lifetime: if they deserve glory, it comes to them posthumously. Paris, London, and Brussels take the lead—with very few exceptions.

Lippert has also built the Cardinal Prince-Primate's new palace, admirably situated on the right bank of the Danube, here very imposing. The palace is excellently planned, and has a library of more than 30,000 volumes plus a gallery containing several hundred paintings, engravings, and drawings, some of which would fill Herr Ruland[6] with understandable envy.

As in previous years, my winter in Budapest is going by tranquilly. I hope to be of some use in a musical respect. The task of those who do not seek their reward in this world is to serve others.

After Holy Week, back to Weimar will come Your Royal Highness's old and faithful servant   F. Liszt

899. To Princess Carolyne. Budapest, 12 March. Last Wednesday my
Hunnenschlacht was given quite a decent performance at a Philharmonic Society concert.[7] I enclose the insolent lines that appeared in the *Pesther Lloyd,* a newspaper of importance—so that ministers are obliged to come to an understanding with the editor-in-chief, M. Falk, an Israelite. Now, Israelites currently form the unquestioned majority of concert audiences, here and elsewhere. Nothing surprising in that—they rule the 2 greatest powers in the world, the Stock Exchange and the Press. Without them, the sovereigns would have no idea how to make either war or peace. With but a few exceptions, the greatest lords are obliged to enter into a compact with these potentates, whom, unlike some of my close friends, I have never censured. Quite the contrary: in the days of my youth, as

---

[6] Director of the Weimar Museum.

[7] At this concert, of 5 Mar., Vladimir de Pachmann played Chopin's Piano Concerto in F minor and Liszt's *Au bord d'une source.*

now in my old age, I showed myself to be friendly towards, and glad to help, numerous Israelites—not those privileged by wealth—and shall continue in the same way, without any pretention whatsoever. The professed anti-Semite, Bülow, has just pronounced a bellicose tirade against the Theatre Royal in Berlin, which he calls 'the Hülsen circus'. The incident caused a rumpus—one which may, I fear, be unfavourable to Bülow's career. . . . He has added to it a flash of wit à la Voltaire: his letter of recantation, in which he begs the circus directors, Renz, Salamonsky, and Schumann, not to feel offended by the designation of the Hülsen circus!

900. To Princess Carolyne. Weimar, Sunday, 27 April. When I arrived here, on Friday evening, Adelheid [von Schorn] was waiting for me at the Hofgärtnerei. She has already written you a good report about my good health. Next month, I shall need to go to Leipzig several times, and even once to Dresden—where for more than 25 years I have stopped for only one day, in honour of Countess Dönhoff. In Leipzig I shall see *Helianthus*, a highly ambitious opera, the text and music of which are by my friend Goldschmidt, whom Bülow openly ill-treats. Nor do other critics spare him, but perhaps he has it in him to last—that's the question!

Riedel is keen to give a second performance of my oratorio *Christus* in Leipzig, on 18 May. I have in vain tried to dissuade him—after they have been written, corrected, and published, my poor works preoccupy me not in the least. I generally even advise against their performance.

Umilissimo Sclavissimo,   D.

901. To Princess Carolyne. Weimar, 29 May. Our music festival went off very well. Despite the programme being extended so much, the works were performed satisfyingly—several even excellently. Those which made a particular impression were: Berlioz's *Te Deum*, Draeseke's Symphony, the *Salve Polonia*, and, to my surprise—the Gran Mass. At the instigation of Countess Schleinitz and Mme von Meyendorff—who got Monseigneur and his daughter Elsi to participate in their innocent little plot—the *Salve Polonia* was repeated at the next day's concert. Mme Viardot, her daughter Mme Héritte, and above all my most excellent and illustrious friend Saint-Saëns, responded to it with emotion. I feel rather tired—just enough to begin to be sociable again at the performances of *Parsifal* at Bayreuth in July and August. The very valiant Arnauld used to say: 'Haven't we eternity to rest?'

In a note from Bayreuth in July to his friend and pupil Lina Schmalhausen, Liszt wrote, *inter alia*, referring to an occurrence in June: 'Last month a small sum of money was once again stolen from my home, the Hofgärtnerei. I'll tell you in person about this incident, which occasioned a great outburst of anger ... (not from me).'

Publishing the note in his biography[8] of the composer, Julius Kapp remarked: 'The theft brought Liszt yet another bitter disappointment. Similar thefts had already been committed from time to time, and a number of people had been wrongly suspected. Then, one day, Liszt's servant succeeded in catching the thief as, using a duplicate key, he took money from Liszt's desk. The culprit turned out to be—one of Liszt's oldest friends! Arriving at that very moment, Liszt took in the situation at a glance and, although deeply shocked, retained his composure so far as to protect his friend from the servant, saying scoldingly: "But Miska, what are you thinking of! Let go of Herr X at once; I gave him the key myself just now, to fetch something for me." Before everyone else, too, he maintained his outer association with this gentleman—but to him, who in his immeasurable goodness simply could not conceive of such a thing, the incident had given bitter pain.'

One has no wish to cast a stone at Liszt's old friend Carl Gille if he was not the miscreant—or even if he was—but two notes that Liszt wrote to him in the month in question make it plain that, for whatever reason, Gille was very reluctant to face Liszt at this time.

902. To Carl Gille. Weimar, 11 June. ^G I hope you will soon return to your senses, dear friend. Then we'll mention not a word of the wretched gossip ... and will continue to associate serenely and tranquilly.

Your affectionate, grateful and devoted old   F. Liszt

Baroness Meyendorff had invited you for this evening. Don't hesitate to give me your hand—and here.

903. To Carl Gille. Weimar, 14 June ^G

Dear friend,

About the *alleged* 'heavy blow' you have suffered, I neither can nor wish to know anything. Its consequences are by no means to be feared: I'll bet 100 to 1 —with the certainty of my old experience—gossip and tittle-tattle never count

⁸ *Franz Liszt*, 525.

with me. Whoever doesn't feel at ease in my home can avoid it. To see *you* at a third place, after this unpleasant incident, strikes me as quite inappropriate. And so come, dear friend, just as you have done for so many years, calmly and with clearest conscience to your ever-loyal

F. Liszt

904. To Princess Carolyne. Dornburg, Thursday morning, 26 June.

At Dornburg the day before yesterday there was, as is customary for Monseigneur's birthday, a stage performance. Pailleron's *Etincelle* I found quite charming. Yesterday, and on Monday evening, whist was arranged, to some extent for my sake. The players were the Hereditary Grand Duke, his sister Elisabeth, Beust, Wedel, Loën, and your very humble servant. Monseigneur knows absolutely nothing of cards, and my mood for conversation grows ever less. Is this the weakness of age?

At 10.00 this morning I shall be in Jena—for a church concert at which my Gran Mass will be performed.

Sclavissimo, D.

Herr Sauer whom you recommended, and who is here nicknamed 'the Spaniard from Hamburg', is studying very diligently.[9] Three or four of my disciples now in Weimar are in some respects more advanced than he: Friedheim and Siloti, for example, both from Russia; van de Sandt, a young Dutchman of 20; and Reisenauer, who is unfortunately too subject to physical *embonpoint*, without which his reputation as an artiste would already be bigger! Virtuosi appearing before the public ought to show a certain slenderness—it's the professors who can be plump!

Weimar. Friday, 27 June. Yesterday's church concert, in Jena, was attended by Monseigneur, his family, and their attendants—come from, and returning to, Dornburg. Just for a joke, I shall say that the Gran Mass is like the Russian soldiers of whom Frederick the Great remarked: 'When they have been killed, they still remain standing.'—'Perseverando' is my old motto. . . .

---

[9] In his reminiscences of Liszt, the pianist Emil von Sauer remarked *inter alia*: 'Liszt possessed a genius of prodigious diversity. To understand him well, it is necessary to take into account the vast knowledge of this man. . . . If destiny had not opened the Elysian fields of music to him, he would have excelled—I am convinced of it—in like manner in any other vocation. He could just as well have been proclaimed a great cardinal, diplomat, savant, poet, man of letters, lawyer, doctor, etc.... except a banker or merchant. His absolute mastery springs from this universality. . . . With his exquisite and unequalled gifts were associated the qualities of a being both fascinating and of the first rank. Grand seigneur from head to toe, a fervent Catholic, stern towards himself, indulgent towards others, with integrity of character, a perfect model from all points of view, I found in him but one fault: an overabundance of goodness and clemency, of whose abuse he did not take cognizance. It is a sad fact that a great many so-called pupils took advantage of his good nature, wasting his valuable time and expending his patience' (*Emil Sauer: Disciple of Liszt*, trans. Gilles Hamelin, Musical Scope Publishers, New York, 1975).

905. To Princess Carolyne. Bayreuth, Thursday, 24 July. Monday and yesterday, the first 2 performances of the revival of *Parsifal* in Bayreuth. Complete success with a large German and international audience, filled with enthusiasm for this wonderful masterpiece. It will continue in the same way for the whole fortnight. Wagner must be glorified—we had a presentiment of it in Weimar, as early as '49. The following years confirmed our feelings—and today, the theatre is everywhere dominated by Wagner. His true glory is never to have deviated from his great calling—which he followed through many an obstacle. To him belongs the immortality of a great earthly renown! . . .

My daughter remains engulfed in her mourning. I have not seen her again.[10] Her children, whom I see every day, are prospering.

Umilissimo Sclavissimo, D.

906. To Princess Carolyne. Weimar, Sunday morning, 10 August. On getting back, yesterday evening, I found your sweet letter. Here are the continuation and end of my brief reports on Bayreuth.

No doubt about the success of the 10 performances of *Parsifal,* concluded the day before yesterday. Large, admiring, and enthusiastic audiences—the majority of whom had come from other countries. The ensemble of these astonishing performances—to which the talents of the singers, the orchestra, and even the stage-designer and scene-shifter, give a unique character—cannot be praised too highly. It must also be said that no work has ever been rehearsed and learnt in every last detail with so great a care as *Parsifal.* The relentless energy and practical knowledge which for several months in '82 Wagner brought to the rehearsals and *mise-en-scène* were truly prodigious. The result, since then, has been completely secure and unshakeable—the work has passed into its interpreters' flesh and blood!

Daniel Ollivier has presumably acquainted you with his impressions. Personally, he made a very good one—his 4 female cousins took a great liking to him, and I am happy to tell you that his *contegno* [demeanour] was that of a young man of tact and good breeding. As regards people you know from Rome, I saw Frau Helbig and her mother, Countess Voss, and Comtesse La Tour. . . . As an out-and-out Wagnerian, Joseph Rubinstein was in Bayreuth as a matter of course. He will extend his stay there, and again plans to spend the winter in Rome, to give Wagnerian concerts with Countess Dönhoff in the salons rented by Lenbach at the Palazzo Borghese. To conclude, Countess Schleinitz, her husband and her

---

[10] Liszt was not staying at Wahnfried, but at a house in the Siegfriedstrasse.

mother, Pcss Hatzfeldt, presided very amiably at the *Bühnenweihfestspiel,* as in previous years. Among august visitors, after the Queen [Olga] of Greece can be mentioned [her father] the GD Constantine of Russia, who preserved his incognito, several young Dukes of Dessau and Mecklenburg, the reigning Duke of Meiningen and, after him, his son and the Pcss his wife, daughter of the Crown Pce of Germany. I have wrongly kept to the end the Duchesse d'Alençon, formerly engaged to the King of Bavaria, and her sister-in-law, née Coburg-Kohary. These 2 princesses wished to hear me play the piano, and to this end came to my lodging, where I obliged with good grace. Finally, Bülow attended, incognito, the penultimate performance.

Blandine's marriage with Gravina seems very happy. At the beginning of July they spent a week in Meiningen, sharing Bülow's residence. They will be going back to Palermo in the autumn, with their baby, Manfred—who isn't walking yet, but charms his parents and the public by his good looks and calm good humour. . . .   D.

Cosima I caught a glimpse of for barely a minute, in the darkness at the end of one of the *Parsifal* rehearsals. Her mother in days gone by took as a motto: 'In alta solitudine.' Cosima's altitude is her widowhood!

907. To Princess Carolyne. Thursday, 11 September. At Schloss Itter I quietly thought back on our travels [1858] in the Tyrol with Magne, who was still rather unwell at that time. Even the *vetturino*, the *zither*, and the Tyrolean songs, more vulgar than artless—seemed admirable, as you were there! Oh! that good and lovely time when the common run of people said we were unhappy!

Friday morning until Sunday evening I spent visiting Their Royal Highnesses. Pcss Hendryk of the Netherlands, a young widow, was staying at the Wartburg with her suite of ladies-in-waiting and chamberlains; there was no room left for me. That suited me, for I am by no means a lover of tiny spiral staircases, nor of romantic, uncomfortable nooks and crannies. I was given good accommodation in Eisenach, at the Schloss, where my next-door neighbour was Herr Voss—not our former dancing-master at the Altenburg, but the dramatist and writer with a growing reputation. He told me he had had the honour of seeing you in Rome now and then.[11] His opinions are those which predominate nowadays, even among princes and princesses of the blood—free-thought is very much the fashion in literature and the salons. It is the great temptation to which one must not succumb! As you know, Voss has a house in Berchtesgaden and

---

[11] See Richard Voss, *Aus einem phantastischen Leben* (Stuttgart, 1920), 95–7.

stayed for several months in Frascati. His plan to write a volume on the Roman Campagna will soon be taking him back to those parts. The accommodation he would now prefer to any other is an apartment at the Villa d'Este—and he is of course fully prepared to pay for renting it. I am giving him a note of introduction to Cardinal Hohenlohe. Be so kind as to tell His Eminence that it would be more agreeable to me to recommend to him for the Villa d'Este a good Catholic, such as my friend Dimmler, than a free-thinker. Nevertheless, I hope Voss will find a good welcome and shelter there, for he has an agreeable and attractive personality.

After the unveiling of the statue of Bach in Eisenach, on 28 Sept., your umilissimo Sclavissimo will write and tell you what is to become of him in October.

D.

Adelheid has had to perform the sad duty of transferring her brother from Nuremberg to a lunatic asylum in Würzburg. I have just composed for chorus and organ what was formerly called a motet, on this verse from Ps. 125 [126]: 'Qui seminant in lacrimis, in exultatione metent [They that sow in tears shall reap in joy].'

908. To Mily Balakirev in St Petersburg. Weimar, 21 October

Dear and honoured colleague,

My admiring appreciation of your works is well known. When my young disciples wish to give me pleasure, it is your compositions, and those of your valiant friends, that they play to me. I cordially salute in this intrepid Russian musical phalanx the *maîtres* endowed with so exceptional a vital energy. They suffer not in the least from an anaemia of ideas—a malady extremely prevalent in various countries; more and more will their merits be recognized and their names renowned. I accept with gratitude the honour of the dedication of your symphonic poem *Tamara*, which I hope to hear next summer with full orchestra. When the piano-duet edition comes out, you will greatly oblige me by sending me a copy. Between mid-January and Easter I shall be in Budapest.

Accept, dear colleague, the expression of my feelings of high esteem and cordial devotion.

F. Liszt

909. To Comtesse Louise de Mercy-Argenteau. 24 October. Certainly, very dear and kind friend, you are 100 times right to appreciate and relish present-day musical Russia. Rimsky-Korsakov, Cui, Borodin, and Balakirev are *maîtres* of outstanding originality and worth. Their works compensate me for

the tedium caused me by others more widely known and praised, of which it would be difficult for me to say what Léonard once wrote to you from Amsterdam after a *Lied* by Schumann: 'What soul, also what a success!' Rarely does success hasten to escort *soul*. In Russia the new composers, despite their remarkable talent and ability, have as yet had only a limited success. High society at Court is waiting for them to succeed elsewhere before applauding them in Petersburg. In this connection, I recall a striking remark made to me in '43 by the late Grand Duke Michael: 'When I have to put my officers under arrest, I send them to performances of operas by Glinka.' Customs grow gentler—and MM Rimsky, Cui, Borodin have themselves the rank of colonel.

For a number of years now, the annual concerts of the Allgemeine Deutsche Musikverein have, at my suggestion, performed a work by the Russian composers. Little by little a public will be formed. Next year our festival will take place in June, at Karlsruhe. Saint-Saëns will be coming; why not you, too, dear friend? You would also hear something Russian there. . . .

Putting aside politeness and ceremony, I can tell you with the utmost sincerity that your instincts did not lead you astray on the day when this music so deeply delighted you. Continue your work, therefore, in the firm conviction that you are doing what is right.

Above all I beg you not to think that I am exaggerating. When you knock, I shall not merely bid you to enter, I shall come forward to meet you. To return to Paris, there to put myself forward as a young composer, or to follow the trade of an old pianist in the salons, doesn't tempt me in the least. I have other things to do elsewhere. Faithful regards, F. Liszt

910. To Princess Carolyne. Budapest, Tuesday morning, 18 November. In an 8-hour journey, with 2 or 3 stops, Géza Zichy and I got back here from Tetétlen yesterday evening. He sets out again this morning, and will be giving ten or so charity concerts in Augsburg, Stuttgart, and the Rhenish towns. As for me, I shall wait here for Bülow's 2 concerts, of 22 and 24 Nov., and shortly afterwards will finally come and see you. At Tetétlen I hardly moved from my room—and from the almost adjacent house in which Zichy lives with his wife and 4 children—other than to go to chapel. It is extremely simple and small, but well maintained—better by far than our poor church in Weimar, where the only precious thing is your beautiful carpet!

At Tetétlen, as on other manorial estates in Hungary, the chief diversion is hunting, in the noisiest of forms. The remainder of the days and evenings is divided among sundry games: *croquet* and its near cousins in exercise, according to fashion, billiards and cards. I accompanied Countess Zichy in the carriage to a hunt one morning, dispensed with the *croquet* etc., and restricted myself to the very enjoyable game of whist. The stake did not exceed 1 or 2 fl.—but the conversation was all the more agreeable. . . .   D.

911. To Victor Hugo in Paris. Rome, 15 December

Glorieux immortel,[12]

In the years of my youth you honoured me with your kindnesses, and during my last visit to Paris with your gracious remembrance. These precedents make me hope that you will indulge the request I venture to address to you today: to accept the dedication of the French edition of the biography of Garibaldi, prepared according to authentic documents communicated by the General to the authoress, Frau E. von Schwartz. Before and after Caprera[13] she nobly assigned a considerable part of her fortune to the cause of Italian unity. A most eulogistic article on Frau von Schwartz, by St René Taillandier, was published long ago in the *Revue des Deux Mondes*.

There is nothing I need say to you of myself, except that for 50 years I have been reading your works with the keenest and most profound admiration. This has prompted me to set to music two of your wonderful poems: *Ce qu'on entend sur la montagne* and *Mazeppa*; as also several of your love songs, and recently your adorable *Crucifix*: 'Vous qui pleurez, venez à ce Dieu, car il pleure.'

Of the universal Majesty of Your Genius the very humble and faithful servant,   F. Liszt

---

[12] Members of the Académie française are popularly known as *Les immortels*.

[13] The island (now an Italian national monument) off the north-east coast of Sardinia which Garibaldi acquired in 1854; from which he escaped when, in 1867, he was arrested by the Italian government; and where he died (1882) and is buried.

1885

25 January. Liszt leaves Rome, and four days later arrives in Budapest.

7 February. He attends a concert given by his pupils.

22 February. He plays several pieces at a musical soirée given by the university lecturer József Árkövy.

9–10 March. Liszt visits Esztergom as the guest of Cardinal Simor.

16 March. Pupils of the National Conservatoire perform a number of works by Liszt at a concert in the Vigadó.

28 March. Liszt gives his annual private concert—admission by invitation only—at the English Ladies' Institute.

2–6 April. He spends Easter with Cardinal Haynald at Kalocsa, on the 4th taking part in a concert at the archiepiscopal palace.

13 April. He attends a concert given by Anton Rubinstein in Pozsony to raise money for a statue of Hummel.

19 April. Liszt arrives in Weimar.

27 May–1 June. He visits Karlsruhe for the festival of the Allgemeine Deutsche Musikverein.

3–15 June. He is present at concerts of his music in Strasbourg, Antwerp and Aachen; in Hal, on the 11th, a soirée musicale is given in his honour by Franz Servais and others.

18 July. He visits Robert Franz in Halle.

15 October. Liszt leaves Weimar and, via Kassel, Munich, Schloss Itter, and Innsbruck (where on the 22nd he celebrates his 74th and last birthday), returns to Rome, which he reaches on the 25th.

WORKS. *Pax vobiscum!* (S64), for male voices and organ. *Qui Mariam absolvisti* (S65), for baritone, unison mixed voices and organ/harmonium. *Salve regina* (S66), for mixed voices. PIANO: *La Lugubre Gondola II* (S200/2); *Historische ungarische Bildnisse—Magyar történelmi arcképek* (S205);[1] *En rêve, nocturne* (S207); *Unstern: sinistre, disastro* (S208, c.1885); *Bagatelle ohne Tonart—Bagatelle sans tonalité* (S216a); *Csárdás obstiné* (S225/2); Hungarian Rhapsodies Nos. 18 and 19 (S244/18/19); *Abschied* (S251); transcription (S482) of Cui's *Tarentelle*.

---

[1] Musical portraits of six eminent deceased Hungarian contemporaries: István Széchenyi, Ferenc Deák, László Teleki, József Eötvös, Mihály Vörösmarty, and Sándor Petőfi, plus the funeral music for Mihály Mosonyi. The sixth and seventh items are identical, respectively, with S195 (1877) and S194 (1870).

912. To an unidentified person. Rome, 16 January

Dear friend,

Without the shadow of a reproach, I am not of the opinion that you should withdraw from the world. To be sure, it hasn't only delights to offer: roses do not lack thorns and sometimes even thistles mingle with them. All the same, one must know how honourably to endure and adapt oneself. In your capacity as a singer of excellence, solitude doesn't suit you at all. Music is necessarily sociable, immediate, humanitarian. Come down, therefore, from your *Montagne Pistoiesi*, and, if it isn't inconvenient, come and see me again, not far away, at the Universe Hotel in Florence. I shall be spending two days there at the end of next week, and will telegraph you beforehand.   Cordial good wishes,   F. Liszt

Thank you for your chivalrous defence; the newspaper containing the diatribe will probably not have printed your reply.

We come nowhere near that sort of thing, and in perfect tranquillity let us say with the Psalmist: *Ab auditione mala non timebit.*[2]

913. To Princess Carolyne in Rome. Florence, Tuesday, 27 January, feast of one of your patron saints, John Chrysostom.

Got here yesterday morning, without incident other than a long conversation on the train with my very agreeable travelling companion, Count Gubernatis, editor of the *Revue internationale*, and a few hours of good sleep. Yesterday I had breakfast and lunch with Mme Hillebrand, almost tête-à-tête, for apart from the 2 ladies who live with her, no one else was present. I have for many years cherished the sincerest feelings of esteem and friendship for Mme Hillebrand—who possesses a noble character and an extremely well-stocked mind. During the evening, in response to an invitation she had issued before my arrival, the day of which was not known to her, several interesting people called to see her. Firstly, the young but already celebrated sculptor Hildebrand—the recent exhibition of his works in Berlin obtained a real success and numerous admirers. He is now working on a monument for the tomb of Hillebrand, his quasi homonym, of whom he had already made a superb bust, bought by the Crown Princess. Other guests yesterday evening: Mr Mackenzie, a Scottish composer—his opera *Colomba*, based on a short story by Mérimée, and a cantata of his have been greatly applauded in London; Ximenes, formerly Spain's ambassador to Pius IX; and a new English literary

---

[2] Ps. 112 (Vulg. 111), 7: 'He [the righteous man] shall not be afraid of evil tidings.'

celebrity, Miss Zimmern. She is of German origin but writes in English—and has attracted attention with a volume on Schopenhauer and some magazine articles.

Between 4.00 and 6.00 I paid a call on Pcss Rospigliosi, wholly given up to putting her new and very princely *villino* in order, and appreciably better in health. She invited me to have lunch with her today, but on the train I had already promised Gubernatis—consequently, I shall not be able to return to the Princess's until this evening. I also made the acquaintance of one of your illustrious Hebrew correspondents: Consolo—translator of Job and more than eighty years of age. . . . Tomorrow morning I shall be in Budapest.

914. To Princess Carolyne. Budapest, 2 February. On Friday evening, at the home of Mlles Wohl, I saw Cardinal Haynald, who amiably reproached me with having told you that he lacked the time to read your books. He was amazed at their prodigious theological, political, administrative, universal learning—especially at the unparalleled knowledge you have acquired and demonstrated of the whole network of matters pertaining to the Catholic Church. Your analysis of the distinctive character of the huge ecclesiastical staff, from the little abbés, monks, and nuns, up to the bishops and cardinals, he finds strikingly accurate. It is Haynald's opinion that, in this regard, no ecclesiastical or secular writer equals your astonishing expertise—very occasionally they have just about managed to come close to it. If, according to the proverb, Gros-Jean taught his grandmother to suck eggs—you will do the same, more deliberately, magisterially, and victoriously, to the most outstanding minds among the College of Cardinals—and all the more to the lay authors, their fellow workers, supporters, and even those who dissent from them. Your prediction to Haynald, that the 25 vols. of the *Causes* will be read attentively by his successor, reminded me of the remark made by an Englishman to an 18th-century Pope: 'I am enchanted with Rome. I have conscientiously seen everything here, more than once—the only thing remaining is a conclave.'

Haynald told me, too, of a 15- or 20-page letter you once wrote him. The résumé he tried to make of it came to this: 'The Princess considers me a great donkey!' I replied by saying that, to my shame, I had had to draw the same conclusion from several of the letters you have addressed to your very humble servant.

Yesterday evening your latest letter reached me. So many things! My name saint, Francis of Paola, is the patron of the humble and of the minims—I belong to them with all my heart.   Your Sclavissimo

915. To Princess Carolyne. Budapest, Easter Tuesday [7 April]. From Maundy Thursday until Easter Monday I was in Kalocsa with Cardinal Haynald. When I got back yesterday evening, I found your 2 very dear letters. As regards my portrait, it was on Hébert's recommendation that I posed for M. Layraud, *premier prix de Rome*, who announced himself as a Berlioz of painting. I am grateful to Pce Radziwill for having acquired this portrait. Pcss Marcelina Czartoryska, née Radziwill, will take great care not to hang a large-size effigy of Liszt in her music salon—at most she would allow in a photograph!

Cardinal Haynald is always very busy and overburdened. There is nothing that people don't ask him, sometimes impudently. His Eminence's portrait, painted by Munkácsy, is very beautiful, but makes him look a little older, people say.

Next Tuesday I shall be in Vienna, at the Schottenhof.

Your umilissimo Sclavissimo

916. To Princess Carolyne. Weimar, 24 May. As well as trouble with my eyes and with music paper, I have had other *impicci* [bothers] these last weeks: numerous letters relating to the Karlsruhe *Musikfest*, and various musical obligations. I have barely managed to reply to half—my usual helper, Gille, having been detained in Jena by performances of *Luther*, and having, thus far, found no one here to replace him. A trip to Sondershausen, in honour of Reisenauer's concert, took me 2 days—and I am now feeling extremely tired. I suffer quite often from bad nerves, to the point that I have to lie down.

Tomorrow I go to Mannheim, where I shall see Isolde and Eva, who will spend a day or two in Karlsruhe with me. The 1st concert, with Wagner's *Kaisermarsch*, Berlioz's Requiem and my *Prometheus choruses*, will take place next Thursday. Invitations to *Lisztconzerte* have come to me from Strasbourg and Freiburg im Breisgau—I have declined, but will return to Antwerp on 4 June. My Mass for male voices will be performed there by an impressive choir—also some of my symphonic works.

Today I can only tell you of my great embarrassment for my transgression in being so epistolarily negligent!

Umilissimo Sclavissimo

My relations with Their Royal Highnesses are always most affectionate. I have dined at the Schloss 2 or 3 times, and was the only person present who was not a member of the family. . . . Adelheid has shown me your commentary on *Parsifal*, which you link with Buddhism. The difference between religion and religiosity you explain in masterly fashion. Have you seen Mgr. Fraknói, a non-honorary but very well paid canon of the rich chapter of Grosswardein? He has returned to Rome to continue his research in the Vatican archives on the historical relations between the Popes and the Hungarian bishops. . . .

917. To Princess Carolyne. Weimar, 16 July. The bad accident suffered by Princess Elisabeth, who fell from her horse, has this last fortnight been the sad topic of conversation in Weimar. She has suffered dreadfully—and despite some respite, danger still threatens.

It was only in the imagination of certain newspapers that my trip to Holland was made! After the Karlsruhe *Musikfest*, and the round of very successful Liszt concerts in Strasbourg, Antwerp, and Aachen, I returned here in mid-June to keep body and soul together at the Hofgärtnerei until September. Then, *vedremo*! People know that I go back to Rome only to see one most eminent person there—yourself! What has become of your plan to leave Rome temporarily this summer?

I am sending your lines to Daniela. She has written nothing to me about the date of her marriage—and I am only advising her to keep the engagement as short as possible. Her father had intended to come and see me here the day before yesterday—gastric trouble is keeping him in Meiningen.

A new sensational book being much talked of in Germany is *The Conventional Lies*! The author, [Max] Nordau, had already attracted attention with his previous volumes—*From the Kremlin to the Alhambra*[3] and *Paradoxes*. The ultimate import of his works comes back to the ancient wisdom of King Solomon, very much the fashion nowadays: 'Everything of this world is only a lie, vanity of vanities!' This notwithstanding, we shall keep trust and unshakeable hope in the divine love of our crucified Redeemer, Jesus Christ!

Umilissimo Sclavissimo,   F.L.

918. To Princess Carolyne. Weimar, 30 July. The latest bulletins on Pcss Elsi confirm that she is making slow progress. I enclose yesterday's bulletin, with a few quite fair lines of praise taken from the Leipzig illustrated *Gazette*.

You are swimming in Buddhism—and I for my part am immersing myself musically in Magyarism through 6 or 7 historical portraits: István Széchenyi, Deák, László Teleki, Eötvös, Vörösmarty, Petőfi, and the funeral procession of my friend Mosonyi—the whole thing ending with a fanfare apotheosis.

---

[3] *Die konventionellen Lügen der Kulturmenschheit* (Leipzig, 1884) and *Vom Kreml zur Alhambra. Kulturstudien* (2 vols., Leipzig, 1880).

My *Via crucis* and *Septem Sacramenta*, plus the *Rosario*, will not be published by Pustet of Regensburg, the Catholic publisher I wanted. He has declined politely, very much to my chagrin—finding that the compass of these works exceeded that of his numerous usual publications. Another and worse reason lies at the root of it—my works in this field do not sell, which will not prevent me from doing justice to those of Witt, Haberl, *et al.*, and from contributing as well as I can to promoting the German Society of St Cecilia. In certain cases my rule remains: 'As you will do, I shall not do.'

In August, Liszt's one-armed friend Count Géza Zichy, pianist and poet, was involved in a duel, a consequence of the insult he deemed had been done him at a Hungarian spa earlier in the year (before a company which included Ferdinand de Lesseps and Jules Massenet) by a 'turbulent young man' named Pulszky. 'The duel was fought in Budapest with sabres, but without a serious outcome,' recalled Zichy. 'In the afternoon of the same day I visited my adversary, who was being tended by his very lovely wife. It was a remarkable scene when the lady grasped my hand and said: "Oh, how happy I am that this divinely gifted hand has remained uninjured!"'

919. To Count Géza Zichy in Budapest. Weimar, 23 August

Very dear friend,

The Budapest *Tageblatt* of 22 August tells me of your encounter with Charles [Károly] Pulszky. *Convinced* of your irreproachable chivalry, I am certainly not asking you for any explanation of the reasons behind this affair, and only beg you to dictate to one of your secretaries the reply to this question: was it Pulszky's seconds, or yours, who proposed that the duel be with *sabres*—and not *pistols*?

In view of my devoted friendship for you, very many questions about this matter are being put to me, for which reason I am keen to be well informed. The report in the Budapest *Tageblatt* is written in a most friendly tone. . . .

Very cordially yours,   F. Liszt

920. To Count Géza Zichy. Weimar, 31 August ᴳ ⁽ᶠ⁾

Very dear friend!

I knew indeed, right from the start, that you would proceed in a noble manner on all occasions, and the detailed report of your duel published in the Budapest *Tageblatt* has confirmed me in my conviction. It is a conviction about you that I shall stick to in any and every conceivable circumstance. Lesseps' letter also gives you a very rich measure of satisfaction. The distinction of Lesseps' person and his place in history turn this incident very much to your advantage. I have written a few words of thanks to Massenet, who remembered me at the Franco-Hungarian banquet. I enclose a note about your *Künstlerfahrt* that I am sending to the publisher, Herr Simrock. I believe he possesses enough taste to publish your work, which is indeed its own recommendation. Enlighten him with a few lines.

Affectionately yours,   F. Liszt

Please be so good as to express to Countess Géza Zichy my unchanging admiration and devotion.

921. To Princess Carolyne. Weimar, 21 September. Every year a mass is celebrated with the 'Memento vivorum Carolinae' in our poor old chapel in Weimar. This time, I chose the feast of the stigmata of St Francis of Assisi, the sublime poet of the *Cantico del sol* and ardent apostle of the *gran perdono*. In his *Paradiso*, Dante seraphically glorified the divine madman St Francis!

A pamphlet[4] on my Psalms, which will be a continuation of the one on the oratorio *Christus*, has been read to me in manuscript these last few days. It seems to me to be distinguished in its understanding of my musical wishes. The authoress will pay you the humble homage of her dedication, which I ask you to accept.

Walter Bache's recent visit here has induced me to undertake a trip to London next April, unless something unforeseen clashes with it. In mid-Oct., after Monseigneur's return, I shall leave Weimar to go to Rome.

Your umilissimo Sclavissimo

922. To Sophie Menter in St Petersburg. Rome, 30 December [G]

Kind diplomatist and very dear friend,

Together with my most humble thanks for his gracious invitation, I am writing to tell the Grand Duke Constantine[5] of my very well-founded misgivings about my age and failing eyesight—and above all of my *unfitness* for playing the piano and conducting an orchestra. This deters me from making any claims to a fee; yet you know, dear friend, that my small income is insufficient to pay for accommodation and a carriage in Petersburg.

[4] Lina Ramann's *Franz Liszt als Psalmensänger* (Leipzig, 1886).
[5] In a letter to Liszt of 4/16 Dec., Constantine had expressed the hope that the composer would be present at the 'music festival planned for this winter'.

From 1 to 12 April I am detained in London. If it is *not then too late*, to Petersburg will come

       Your ever faithful and most devoted   F. Liszt

In mid-January I return to Budapest. . . . From the Grand Duke Constantine's next letter I await the decision whether my journey to Petersburg is approved for *mid-April*, or not.

1886

8 January. Liszt dines at the Villa Medici, where Claude Debussy* makes his acquaintance.

16 January. A farewell concert is given in Liszt's honour by the German Society of Artists; many works of his are performed and, to the audience's delight, he brings the proceedings to an end by a spontaneous performance of the Thirteenth Hungarian Rhapsody.

20 January. Liszt leaves Rome and, via Florence, Venice and Gorizia, returns to Budapest, which he reaches on the 30th.

10 March. The Academy of Music gives a farewell concert in his honour.

11 March. At 11.00 p.m., after attending a farewell recital given for him by his pupil István Thomán,[1] Liszt takes the train from Budapest for the last time, travelling initially to Vienna. Here, on the 14th, he plays at the home of Adalbert von Goldschmidt before a company which includes his fervent admirer Hugo Wolf.

16–18 March. He attends a concert of his works in Liège (17 March) and stays, at nearby Argenteau, with the Comtesse Mercy-Argenteau.

20 March. He arrives in Paris. Waiting to greet him are, among others, the Munkácsys, Pauline Viardot-Garcia, and the conductors Colonne and Lamoureux. The next day he receives a standing ovation after a performance of *Les Préludes*.

22 March. At the end of a grand soirée musicale given in his honour by Mme Munkácsy, in which works of his are performed by Saint-Saëns, Louis Diémer and others, Liszt plays two pieces to the assembled company.

25 March. Colonne conducts the Gran Mass at Saint-Eustache—so successfully that it has to be repeated a week later.

26 March. Liszt has a long audience with the President of the Republic, Jules Grévy. In the evening, with Emile and Daniel Ollivier, he sees the last act of Massenet's *Le Cid* at the Opéra.[2]

3 April. Leaving Paris, Liszt travels to England where, for the next fortnight, he is the guest, at Westwood House, Sydenham (a south London suburb), of Henry Littleton, head of the Novello firm.

5 April. He attends the 'full grand rehearsal' of *The Legend of St Elisabeth* at St James's Hall in central London.

6 April. He visits the Royal Academy of Music (Tenterden Street, Hanover Square), to endow a Liszt scholarship, and plays to the assembled students. In the evening he is

---

[1] Who was later a professor of piano at the Academy of Music, where Bartók and Dohnányi were among his pupils.
[2] Seated in another box was Giuseppe Verdi. 'In spite of this close proximity,' writes Dezső Legány, 'the two great contemporaries did not meet.'

given a memorable ovation after the performance of *St Elisabeth* at St James's Hall, where he meets, among other royal personages, the Prince and Princess of Wales.

7 April. Liszt travels to Windsor Castle, at the invitation of Queen Victoria, to whom he plays several pieces.

8 April. After dinner at the Langham Hotel, Portland Place, Liszt and his party proceed to the Grosvenor Gallery, Bond Street, for a reception and musical soirée mounted by Walter Bache. After a short programme of his music, Liszt delights the very distinguished company by playing two pieces.

9 April. Liszt is present at a concert of his works in St James's Hall. On the programme are, *inter alia,* the March of the Three Holy Kings, the symphonic poem *Orpheus,* the Piano Concerto in E flat, played by Emil Bach, and the ballad *Die Vätergruft* (orchestrated by Liszt for this occasion), sung by Georg Henschel.

10 April. At a concert in the Crystal Palace, Liszt's pupil Bernhard Stavenhagen plays the Piano Concerto in E flat and some solo pieces, and August Manns conducts performances of various orchestral works, including *Les Préludes* and *Mazeppa.*

11 April. Liszt attends mass at the Brompton Oratory, South Kensington. Later he visits, and plays to, the Duchess of Cambridge in St James's Palace before going to Marlborough House for dinner with the Prince of Wales.

14 April. At the Lyceum Theatre, Wellington Street, he sees Henry Irving play Mephistopheles in a stage version of *Faust,* and then joins Irving, Ellen Terry, Bram Stoker and others for supper.

15 and 16 April. He attends recitals given by his pupils Lamond and Stavenhagen.

18 April. Liszt again attends mass at Brompton Oratory, and later visits Baron Orczy at his home in Wimpole Street. In the evening he plays to the dinner guests—among them Henry Irving and Ellen Terry—at Westwood House.

20–7 April. Liszt spends Easter in Antwerp with his friends the Lynens.

28 April–15 May. He stays with the Munkácsys in Paris, where on 8 May *St Elisabeth* is performed at the Trocadéro.

17 May. He returns to Weimar.

2–6 June. He visits Sondershausen for the music festival.

1 July. Leaving Weimar for the last time, Liszt goes to Bayreuth where, on the 3rd, his granddaughter Daniela marries Henry Thode.

5–20 July. He stays with the Munkácsys at Colpach in Luxembourg, and on the 19th plays several pieces at a concert given in his honour by the Luxembourg Music Society.

21 July. In very poor health, and tormented by a dreadful cough, Liszt returns to Bayreuth for the festival performances.

23 and 25 July. Despite his deteriorating condition he attends performances of *Parsifal* and *Tristan.*

31 July. Shortly before midnight, at his lodgings in Bayreuth, Liszt dies.

WORKS. The song *Ne brani menya, moy drug* (Chide me not, my friend) (Alexei Tolstoy) (S340*a*). Arrangement (S371) for voice and orchestra of *Die Vätergruft.*

923. To the Grand Duke Constantine of Russia
[Rome, early January]

Monseigneur,

Your Imperial Highness honoured me with his gracious kindness at the time of the fiftieth anniversary of my career as an artiste, in Budapest. He is so good as to continue it by inviting me to return to St Petersburg. On this subject I have serious scruples: my health and my sight are failing; more evident still is my inability to function effectively, either as the pianist of former times or as conductor of an orchestra.

I therefore greatly fear my uselessness, and to cut a sorry figure in Russia would badly repay the kindness of Your Imperial Highness, whom I beg to judge of my difficulties.

Until 12 April I shall be detained in London. Thereafter it will perhaps be too late to renew personally to Your Imperial Highness my most humble respects and sincere gratitude.[3]

924. To Princess Carolyne in Rome. At Princess Hatzfeldt's, Palazzo Malipieri, Venice, Tuesday, 26 January. Mme Hillebrand wrote to you yesterday about my short stay in Florence—or, rather, at a good half-hour from Florence, in Count Pio Resse's superb villa at Maiano. In town I heard mass at Santa Croce—then visited the studio of the very celebrated sculptor Hildebrand, about whom I have already spoken to you. One of his latest works is a fine bust, *Pensieroso*, of the Grand Duke, done in Weimar.

Pcss Rospigliosi is still suffering greatly, and told me she was barely able to walk. But the graces of her mind bloom unimpaired. She again most graciously invited me to stay in her princely *villino* in Florence. To Pcss Hatzfeldt I quoted yesterday the remark made by Leo XIII to one of his painters, the Irishman Thadeus [*sic*]: 'Popes have no age.'[4] Without infallibility—very beautiful and above all very intelligent women aspire to the same prerogative! . . .

This evening I shall be at my cousin's [Marie von Saar] in Gorizia—and on Sunday in Budapest.   F.L.

---

[3] Source of the letter is Liszt's own draft, on which he did not trouble to record any valediction or signature.

[4] H. Jones Thaddeus reproduced this papal apophthegm, of which he had evidently told Liszt, in his *Recollections of a Court Painter*. About the composer himself he remarked: 'Liszt spoke most beautiful French, possessing the true Parisian accent, so rare amongst foreigners. Even in his old age women adored him, and followed him about as if he were a magnet attracting them. He told me that there is no exaggeration in the story of how in Russia after one of his concerts the ladies present, exuberantly enthusiastic, stormed the stage, battling to embrace him and obtain a memento of the occasion, and that he was in a fainting condition when, eventually, he was rescued . . . from the midst of this surging, hysterical mob of women, minus much of his clothing, which had literally been cut off his back for souvenirs.'

925. To Princess Carolyne. Budapest, 11 February. The reply from Paris that I was expecting here has not arrived. On the other hand I am accepting an invitation from Liège for a Liszt Concert in mid-March. On 1 April I shall be in London where, after the performance of *Elisabeth*, on the 6th, 2 Liszt Concerts with full orchestra are already announced for the 9th and 10th. My trip to Petersburg is still expected but rather doubtful—for the GD Constantine, who has so graciously invited me, has to be away at the end of April. No point in wearying you in advance with my comings and goings!

Here, everything remains the same. I enclose Cardinal Haynald's card—it will prove to you that there has been no estrangement between His Eminence and your umilissimo   Sclavissimo

Although they don't hurt me, my eyes continue to get weaker, so that reading and writing are becoming very difficult.

926. To Walter Bache in London. Budapest, 11 February ᴳ

Very dear friend,

They seem determined in London to push me to the piano.

I cannot agree to this in public, because my 75-year-old fingers are no longer suited to it, and Bülow, Saint-Saëns, Rubinstein, and you, dear Bache, play my compositions much better than my dilapidated self.

Perhaps it would be opportune if friend Hueffer[5] would be so kind as to let the public know, by a short announcement, that Liszt ventures to appear only as a grateful visitor, and neither in London nor anywhere else as a person with an interest in his fingers.   Friendliest regards,   F. Liszt

927. To Princess Carolyne. Budapest, 10 March. Thank you for writing to me in large letters. My sight is becoming lamentably weak, and I should not like to ask anyone to read what you write to me. As I have already told you, the day after tomorrow, Friday morning, I shall be in Vienna, where I shall remain until Monday. On 15 March I arrive in Liège, and on the 20th, Paris. I greatly hesitate to 'attempt' a 2nd performance of the Gran Mass at St Eustache. M. Aubry assures me that the vocal rehearsals are going well and spiritedly. The poster indicates 6 choirmasters from Paris churches, and the total number of performers will be 400, under the direction of Colonne—in short, a success is

[5] Music critic of *The Times* (and, later, translator of the Liszt–Wagner correspondence).

expected. Moreover, in Paris I am rather like a character in [Racine's] *Athalie* who fears 'everything' and 'has no other fear'![6]

I always appreciated the rather odd qualities of mind of Eugène Wittgenstein.[7] My personal relations with him were affectionate on my side. He called me 'the friend of truth'—and I could only desire him to adore Him who remains the Way, the Truth and the Life!   Umilissimo Sclavissimo

928. To Sophie Menter in St Petersburg. Argenteau (Liège), 18 March [G]

Dear, honoured diplomat,

A week before 19 April (Russian style) I shall arrive in Petersburg. Do please make *as little ceremony as possible* for my humble self. The 2 programmes seem appropriate; my small part in them I'll tell you of only when I get to Petersburg. On 19 April, therefore, *Elisabeth*; on the 23rd, a concert. Tell the committee to send me their *invitation* to both performances to 'Novello & Co., Music Publishers, 1 Berners Street, London.' From 1 to 12 April I am Novello's guest. How do matters stand with regard to my lodgings in Petersburg, for which my meagre income will not suffice? From you, dear friend, I shall expect to hear something definite in London. However honourable for me the invitation to Warsaw would be, I could not accept it just now. I have to be back in Weimar before the end of May, because of the music festival in Sondershausen. Yours most affectionately,   F. Liszt

929. To Princess Carolyne. Argenteau, near Liège, Friday, 19 March.

I had written from Pest to tell Magne that my visit to Vienna would be very brief this time. On my arrival at the Schottenhof, I found a note from Magne inviting me to dinner *en famille* that very evening, Friday. Pce Constantin was in the best of humours. You are better informed than I about measles at the Augarten, and Pce Constantin's short anodyne course of treatment. Physically, intellectually and morally Magne is getting along admirably!

The day before yesterday, the Liszt Concert in Liège was a brilliant success. Tomorrow evening I shall be in Paris. My accommodation is still to be decided.

---

[6] Liszt is misquoting from the line (Act One, Scene One) 'Je crains Dieu, cher Abner, et n'ai point d'autre crainte' (I fear God, dear Abner, and have no other fear). See Letter 266 to Stahr.

[7] Who had died on 18 Feb.

930. To Princess Carolyne. Hôtel de Calais, rue des Capucines, Paris, 23 March. Belloni telegraphed you yesterday—*Les Préludes* received with cheers at Colonne's concert. It will be repeated next Sunday, with *Orpheus* and a Hungarian Rhapsody. The newspapers are very favourable this time—not as in '66, of awful memory! 'Qui veut durer, doit endurer!'

Munkácsy is painting a large-scale portrait of me. His house here is of a magnificence that many princes couldn't match. Rubens was only a discreet precursor!

A telegram from Petersburg tells me that the Russian Court will be in the Crimea at the end of April—consequently, my journey to Petersburg is postponed.

Sclavissimo

931. To Princess Carolyne. Paris, 2 April, morning. Ollivier and the Marquise de Blocqueville have written to tell you that the favourable reception given to myself and my works goes beyond my expectations. I have only to humble myself on this day of the feast of St Francis of Paola, my patron and that of the Minims! At midday, 2nd performance of the Gran Mass—rehabilitated henceforth, despite the contrary opinion of Berlioz in '66, and of his scribe d'Ortigue, a good Catholic and friend of my youth!

Tomorrow evening I shall be in London, where I shall write to you *subito* [immediately].

Your umilissimo Sclavissimo

932. To Princess Carolyne. Westwood House, Sydenham, Tuesday morning, 6 April. Left Paris on Saturday, 3 April, at 11.00 a.m., and arrived here before 8.00 p.m. Walter Bache was waiting for me at Dover; Mackenzie and Littleton, my host, had come as far as Calais. Mackenzie, a distinguished composer of great fame here, will this evening conduct the *Elisabeth*. The final rehearsal yesterday was attended by more than 1,500 people. I am overwhelmed with attentions and testimonies of goodwill—it's more than a success! I'll send you some newspapers, and next Sunday a report will be written for you by your umilissimo

Sclavissimo

933. To Princess Carolyne. Westwood House, Sydenham, Thursday, 8 April. Report: Magnificent performance of *Elisabeth* the day before yesterday in St James's Hall. During the interval the Pce of Wales came to the artistes' room and took me back into the hall to present me to his wife and to his sister-in-law, the Duchess of Edinburgh. Yesterday, at 3 o'clock, I was at Windsor, by command of the Queen. She was most gracious this time and conversed in good German; I played her 3 or 4 short piano pieces, including a Nocturne [Op. 9/1] by Chopin.[8] The audience consisted of three ladies-in-waiting and a Prince of Battenberg—plus Mr Cusins, conductor of the Queen's orchestra, who number about thirty. Next Sunday, at 8.30, I am invited to dinner with the Pce of Wales. I had expected to be leaving two days later, but a second performance of *Elisabeth* is announced for Saturday, 17 April, at the Crystal Palace—and I have promised to attend it. The singers and players, under the excellent direction of Mackenzie, will be the same as at St James's Hall. Mme Albani identified herself admirably with the part of Elisabeth, and earned warm applause from the audience.

9 April. Every day I receive at least 25 letters and notes. A sculptor greatly renowned in England, and very well regarded at court, Mr Boehm, is doing a bust of me. I am expecting the photograph based on my portrait by Munkácsy, greatly admired in Paris, and shall send it to you. There is much talk about the performance of *Elisabeth* in Paris, in the vast hall of the Trocadéro.

934. To Princess Carolyne. Westwood House, Sydenham, Monday, 12 April.

Continuation of London report: Tuesday, 6 April, in the afternoon, shortly before the performance of *Elisabeth*, a session at the Royal Academy of Music. Following a proposal by Walter Bache, a prize for young musicians—to be called 'Liszt Scholarship'—was founded. The awarding of the scholarship, for which £1,000 has already been set aside, falls to me.[9] At the time of my Jubilee in Budapest the city authorities placed a similar sum at my disposal, and every year I distribute the interest to young musicians.

Thursday, the 8th: A grand soirée at Grosvenor Gallery, with several works of mine, and a supplement from my ten fingers.

[8] Liszt and the Queen met in the Red Drawing-Room. As well as an improvisation he also played the Miracle of the Roses from *St Elisabeth* (at the Queen's request), and a Hungarian Rhapsody. To her daughter the Crown Princess of Prussia, Victoria wrote that same day: 'We have just heard Liszt, who is such a fine old man. He came down here and played four pieces beautifully. What an exquisite touch. . . .' The *Court Journal* recorded that the Queen, while complimenting Liszt on his artistry, 'had also much to speak with him about the past'. 'He is a courtier,' it continued, 'and speaks as well as he plays.'

[9] Liszt played to the RAM students one of the *Chants polonais* and *Cantique d'amour*. 'We had most of us felt some reserve beforehand,' recalled Orsmond Anderton, 'but no sooner did he appear than the whole gathering rose in a sort of frenzy of enthusiasm. Such was his peculiar hypnotic influence. He was persuaded to play . . . [and] no piano has ever sounded the same to me, before or since.' Another student remembered the event almost 80 years later. Thus the *South Wales Argus*, Sept. 1965: 'Mrs. Rose Cullimore, Newport's oldest inhabitant, celebrated her 104th birthday in St. Woolos Hospital on Monday. . . . She received her musical training under the guidance of Sir Walter MacFarren at the Royal Academy of Music. . . . One of her more outstanding memories is of Liszt. "He was a funny-looking old man with long white hair and a sweet smile," she said today, "and his playing was wonderful."'

Friday, 9 April: Liszt Concert with full orchestra, given by Emil Bach—not Walter Bache. Entirely successful. Then, at 10.30, the smoking concert, with an orchestra made up of *dilettanti*—such distinguished ones that to my knowledge there is not a comparable amateur orchestra in Europe. The Pce of Wales was so kind as to make me sit next to him.

Saturday, 10 April: Another Liszt Concert, very well conducted by Manns, at the Crystal Palace—complete success!

Sunday, 11 April: Mass of Palestrina's at the [Brompton] 'Oratory', the main Catholic church in London.[10]   Sclavissimo

935. To Princess Carolyne. Westwood House, Sydenham, Friday, 16 April.

Continuation of report: The Duchess of Cambridge had asked for me for about 7 o'clock. In '40 she showed me great kindness. She is now over 80, but still mentally alert and most gracious. Since her ear was causing her some pain, I played her 2 short pieces, with the soft pedal, on an upright piano. At 8.00, dinner with the Prince of Wales at Marlborough House.[11] About twenty guests, among whom shone out the very celebrated beauty of Lady Herbert's daughter. The 2 ambassadors present, Stael and Corti, were not unknown to me. Corti reminded me of an evening at Ettersburg, after the Congress of Berlin. As *chasse-café*, my little piano pieces were received most favourably.

During the week: sessions with England's eminent sculptor, Boehm, a native of Vienna who has been a naturalized Englishman for more than 20 years. The bust he is doing of me will make a pendant to Munkácsy's portrait of me, in Paris admired as a masterpiece. HE Cardinal Manning received me kindly. That will make clear to you that here, no more than in Hungary or elsewhere, am I in bad odour with the Catholic authorities. I'll pass over the invitations to dinner and *lunch*, of which I have been able to accept barely half. Wednesday: performance of *Faust*;[12] in the interval, after a Hungarian March of mine had been played, the audience began to applaud so warmly that I bowed a few times from my box. Afterwards, England's great actor, Irving, treated us to a magnificent supper, at which I met and established friendly relations with the most illustrious Max Müller, gloriously established at Oxford.[13]

---

[10] Westminster Cathedral was not built for more than another decade.

[11] The mansion off Pall Mall built (1709–11) by Wren for the first Duke and Duchess of Marlborough (John and Sarah Churchill) had been the official residence of the Prince of Wales since 1850.

[12] W. G. Wills's spectacular stage version, with Henry Irving (as Mephistopheles) and Ellen Terry.

[13] In a brief note dated Antwerp, 25 Apr., Liszt told Max Müller that he hoped 'next year to accept your kind invitation to Oxford'.

6.00 p.m., 17 April. I'll again pass over 2 successful concerts I attended, and mention merely that today the 2nd performance of *Elisabeth*, at the Crystal Palace, was given an ovation. . . .

936. To Princess Carolyne. Boulevard Léopold, Antwerp, 21 April.

As in previous visits, I am staying at the home of M. Lynen—who, in accordance with the precept of our illustrious friend Visconti, is putting his fortune to noble use! I shall be staying here until Easter Tuesday, and carrying out my duties as an abbé in the church services of Holy Week. I have asked my friend Walter Bache to write you a kind of postscript to my London report. Bache is a *perfect gentleman* and an excellent artiste. For years he has made financial sacrifices to secure performances of my works in London. I have several times tried to dissuade him, but he has replied imperturbably: 'C'est mon affaire!'

Between 27 April and 10 May I shall be residing in the princely and most artistic home of my illustrious compatriot and friend, Munkácsy. The performance of *Elisabeth* at the Trocadéro is announced for 8 May. Before that, two concerts with a Liszt programme.

937. To Princess Carolyne. At M. de Munkácsy's, 53, Avenue de Villiers, Paris, 5 May.

Last Sunday my Hungarian Coronation Mass was to have been performed at the church of St François de Sales, my present parish church. But the performance was prevented by a serious oversight on the part of Schuberth, the Leipzig publisher, who was late sending the parts. But there has been something much better than that. In his sermon the parish priest very tactfully told his parishioners of the omission of my music already announced by several newspapers—and went so far as to enjoin them to attend the performance of *Elisabeth*, on 8 May, at the Trocadéro, while speaking very highly of the composer.

That same Sunday I left my name at Pce Napoleon's, and at Pcss Mathilde's —and also left my card with M. Popelin. The Pce very kindly visited me on Monday. We talked of you—and I have just received from His Imp. Highness a gracious note inviting me to dinner next Sunday.

938. To Princess Carolyne. Paris, Sunday morning, 9 May.

Yesterday, between 2.00 and 5.00, the *Elisabeth* in the immense hall of the Trocadéro, which holds at least 7,000 people. The hall was pretty well filled by *tout Paris*. Very large halls are disadvantageous to my works—the details, which I flatter myself

I attend to to the last iota, are lost. Nevertheless, the general impression of the audience yesterday was favourable. After the miracle of the roses, Gounod remarked to me: 'There are aureoles therein—it is haloed with a mystic dust.' And after the final chorus: 'The stones with which it is built are holy ones.' Mme Ollivier will tell you about it, and Belloni will send you some newspapers, which confirm an evident success.

This evening, dinner at Pce Napoleon's—on Wednesday, at Pcss Mathilde's.

Umilissimo Sclavissimo

939. To Princess Carolyne. Weimar, 21 May. Having left Paris on Saturday evening, I arrived here quietly in the evening of Monday, 17 May, with no company on the train other than my Mihály. The next day, Cosima came to see me—I had not seen her since Venice, a few weeks before Wagner's death. On 3 July I shall attend the wedding in Bayreuth of my granddaughter Daniela to Herr Thode—a paragon of talents and qualities, I hear from all sides. Before the marriage he will be coming here, to make my personal acquaintance. Between 5 and 18 July I shall probably be at the Château de Colpach, Luxembourg, home of my excellent friends the Munkácsys. Thank you for having written to Mme Munkácsy, a kind-hearted woman who professes an admiring devotion for me, with nothing untoward mingled therein.

The cycle of performances of *Parsifal* and *Tristan* in Bayreuth begins on 20 July and ends on 23 August. Although I had written to Daniela to say that I would not be going to Bayreuth this year, her mother's visit changed my mind —consequently, I shall become a Bayreuthian again from late July until 23 August, without staying at Wahnfried, as in Wagner's lifetime.

Parisian details: An indisposition, now passed, deprived me of the pleasure of accepting an invitation from Pcss Mathilde. After the Gran Mass at St Eustache, a well-known preacher said to me: 'Of all the musical works I know, it is the most theological.' This opinion is gaining credence, despite many hesitations.

940. To Princess Carolyne. Weimar, 22 May. P.S. to my letter of yesterday: Mme Erard's flat, rue du Mail, which I occupied for about ten days in '78, at the time of the Exhibition, is now inhabited by some of her next of kin. Consequently, I took accommodation at the Hôtel de Calais—but when I asked to pay my bill, I was told that Mme Erard had paid it—including the cost of the carriage I had used from morning till night. At Sydenham, Littleton's splendid hospitality put a carriage at my disposal. Here, I am making up in simplicity for all these luxuries when travelling! Nevertheless, I do not allow my few guests, such as Gille, Riedel, and others who come from here and there to see me, to dry up from thirst: the only drink rarely served at my table is champagne. My former Pauline Apel of the Altenburg has married the brother of her deceased husband. She is proving remarkably resistant to the attacks of age, looking almost the same as she did in '50, and continuing to do the housework for me very nimbly.[14]

I was pleased to see Frau von Helldorf again yesterday.   Sclavissimo

941. To Cécile Munkácsy [Weimar, 27 May] G (F)

My dear, good friend!

Munkácsy's *Goldwasser*[15] has just arrived, and I hasten to send you my thanks for it.

I am intending this elixir for my most personal use, even though I have several times—very wrongly—been forbidden its consumption.

My eyesight is deteriorating from day to day. I shall be consulting the celebrated Gräfe in Halle. Perhaps he will be able to help me somehow or other. If not, I must resign myself to the thought of going totally blind.[16]

942. To Princess Carolyne. Weimar, Whit Monday, 14 June. Of the

success of the Sondershausen concerts you have been sent word by Adelheid [von Schorn], who attended this *Musikfest*. I don't want to ask her to tell you about my physical condition, and am writing direct to you about it, holding nothing back. For a dozen days my weakening sight has reached the point that I have had to dictate all my letters, and shall continue to do so this week too. Further, some kind of trouble with my legs is bothering me once again—without causing me any pain at all, it reveals itself by a slight swelling. The result of my consultation at Halle [1 June] of 2 eminent doctors, Volkmann and Gräfe, is by no means pleasant. To put my legs right, Volkmann has prescribed me a cure

---

[14] Pauline continued to look after the Hofgärtnerei—or Liszt Museum, as it became—until shortly before her death, at the age of 88, forty years later. She, too, remembered Liszt with deep affection. Writing to Carl Lachmund during a visit to Weimar in 1922, another former pupil remarked: 'Pauline was weeping when talking of Liszt; she is very well preserved and talked like a young person' (Lachmund, *Living With Liszt*, 361).

[15] A cognac which Liszt had particularly enjoyed in Paris.

[16] The source for this letter provides no valediction or signature.

at Marienbad, or another place that he will tell me about later—after that, Gräfe thinks I shall probably have to undergo an operation, nowadays very anodyne, he assures me. You know my dislike of water cures, of which I have only once made use, in Aachen, 30 years ago. Having my left eye operated on is almost more attractive to me!

How my time is being spent: On Wednesday, 23 June, I shall be at Dornburg, for the Grand Duke's birthday on the 24th; on 3 July in Bayreuth, for Daniela's wedding. Until 30 June I shall remain in Weimar. I beg you not to worry—and I promise to behave very sensibly. Two of my pianist disciples of the male sex read to me for several hours a day.

Umilissimo Sclavissimo,
to whom the doctors promise a long life, provided he take care of himself!

943. To Count Géza Zichy. Jena, 25 June ᴳ

Dear friend!

As I have not got to the stage of being able to read and write, on receipt of your Sonata I at once asked an excellent pianist, Herr Göllerich, to play it to me. It sounds good and when nicely played will make an effect. Without being a hunter of reminiscences—a very silly hunt—I was nevertheless struck by the similarity between the triplets in your first movement and the triplets in my *Tasso, Lamento e Trionfo*, and still more those in Rubinstein's *O! wenn es doch immer so bliebe*, a conservative song but no longer an unknown one. This kinship can't be helped, and you can therefore calmly admit to being a cousin. . . .

Your most affectionately devoted   F. Liszt[17]

944. To Princess Carolyne. Bayreuth, Friday, 2 July. Last Tuesday, Herr Thode came to Weimar to see me. He made an excellent impression on me—without being a good-looking lad, he has a pleasant appearance, and strikes me as the stuff of which men of ability are made. His manners are distinguished, without any kind of ridiculous pedantry or presumptuousness. He offered to

---

[17] Publishing this letter in his memoirs, Zichy remarked that, like two earlier letters in June, it had been dictated (in German) and 'signed only with a trembling hand'. 'A few weeks later this great and noble man was dead. I received the sad news in a small, remote village in the Hungarian mountains, so late that I had no time to get to the funeral in Bayreuth. Franz Liszt is the most beautiful memory of my life. In loyal love and gratitude I remember my great friend, whose friendship constitutes the greatest pride and the greatest joy of my existence.'

accompany me here—but I had promised to dine at the Belvedere on Wednesday, and did not wish to detain him here a further day. I have had read to me part of his very remarkable volume on St Francis of Assisi and his influence on the fine arts during the period of the Renaissance.[18]

Daniela's marriage contract will be signed at Wahnfried tomorrow evening: on Sunday the religious ceremony will take place in the Protestant church. Thode's father and mother arrived here today. The bride and groom will leave Bayreuth on Sunday evening, returning here in a fortnight. After the *Festspiele* they will be going to Bonn, where Thode is qualified to lecture at the university on the history of art. At Colpach, G.D. of Luxembourg, will be arriving in the evening of 5 July your umilissimo   Sclavissimo

Daniela yesterday wore the elegant brooch with the inscription Roma-Amor that you gave her. For my part, I shall give her no present at the moment, for this year will be costly for me—and the weakening of my eyes prevents me from supplying the transcriptions which pay!

945. To Sophie Menter. Bayreuth, 3 July ^G

Very dear friend,

Tomorrow, after the church wedding of my granddaughter Daniela von Bülow to Herr Professor Henry Thode (art historian), I shall be setting out to the home of my excellent friends the Munkácsys, *Château of Colpach, Grand Duchy of Luxembourg*.

On 20 July I shall be back here again for the first 7 or 8 performances of the *Festspiel*; then I unfortunately have to undergo what is, for me, the very disagreeable cure at Kissingen, and in September an eye operation with Gräfe in Halle awaits me. This past month I have been quite unable to read, and barely able to write a couple of lines with difficulty. Two secretaries kindly help me by reading to me and writing letters at my dictation.

How nice it would be, dear friend, if I could visit you at your fairy-tale castle of Itter! But I see no immediate opportunity of doing so.

Perhaps you will come to Bayreuth, where from 20 July to 7 August will be staying   Your affectionately devoted   F. Liszt

---

[18] Years later Thode's acquaintance was made by the dancer Isadora Duncan, who devoted some interesting pages to him and his mother-in-law, and published his photograph, in her *My Life* (London, 1928) (in which she also remarked, in passing, that she had been initiated into the 'full spiritual meaning' of the 'inspired and holy music of Liszt').

946. To Princess Carolyne. Colpach, G.D. of Luxembourg, Tuesday, 6 July. In Bayreuth, on Saturday evening, all went well. After the marriage contract had been signed, there was a big *ricevimento* at Wahnfried for more than 80 people. The Burgomaster, who is on very friendly terms with the Wagner family, gave a most appropriate address. The gathering was made up of notable townspeople and of the artistes engaged here, singers and instrumentalists already busy with the *Parsifal* rehearsals. Refreshments were provided by a good buffet, adequately supplied with cold dishes; Isolde, Eva, and Siegfried were so good as to attend to the serving. About forty guests were seated—myself beside Princess Hatzfeldt. At Berlin in mid-June her daughter, the former Countess von Schleinitz, took as her second husband Count Wolkenstein, Austrian Ambassador in Petersburg. Wagnerism will therefore be brilliantly represented [in that city] by its two most ardent and stubborn propagandists: Countess von Wolkenstein and Baroness von Bülow, the former Countess Dönhoff. The latter is now the wife of an important diplomatic personage, one who is, likewise, well on the way to becoming German Ambassador.[19]

The day before yesterday, Sunday, the nuptial blessing took place at the Protestant church, quite packed with people. The pastor took as his text, persuasively, St Paul's *First Epistle to the Corinthians*, 13, on Love, *Charitas*. At midday a luncheon for 30 people in the restaurant beside Wagner's theatre. I was placed between Daniela and Princess Hatzfeldt. The young couple went that very evening to Nuremberg, and today will arrive in Geneva, to visit Bülow.

Yesterday evening at Colpach I once again came into contact with Cardinal Haynald—always most kindly disposed towards me. Tomorrow he will have an audience with the King in Brussels, and thence will return to Hungary—to give his blessing at the marriage of Count Emmanuel Andrássy's daughter to Karácsonyi's son.

Shortly, news of Colpach will be sent to you by your umilissimo Sclavissimo.

The foregoing innocuous lines were the last ever penned by Liszt to his Princess—and thus was brought to an end the long series of letters addressed by the great composer-pianist to that most devoted friend, companion, and counsellor over a period of nearly forty years.

Letters were sent after this date, however, to several other correspondents; to the Baroness von Meyendorff no fewer than three (6, 12, and 17 July), in the last of which Liszt wrote: 'To my physical condition, already so pleasant, has now been added these five days a most violent cough which plagues me day and night. To comfort me, the

---

[19] Attached to the German Embassy in Petersburg at this time, Bernhard von Bülow, later Count and then Prince, was indeed eventually appointed an Ambassador (to Rome), but rose yet higher, being from 1900 to 1909 Chancellor of the German Empire.

doctor says that this type of cough is very tenacious. So far, neither cough medicine nor infusions, nor mustard plasters, nor foot-baths have rid me of it.'

On Monday, 19 July, at a concert given in the city of Luxembourg in his honour, Liszt appeared at the piano for the last time. 'With the first of his *Liebesträume*,' writes La Mara, 'the *Chant polonais* from the *Glanes de Woronince*, and the sixth of his *Soirées de Vienne*, Liszt's magic playing fell silent for ever.'

The next day he left Luxembourg by train, spending the night in Frankfurt and reaching Bayreuth in the afternoon of Wednesday the 21st. 'When he arrived at his rented accommodation in the home[20] of Herr Fröhlig, a forestry commissioner, he was in a feverish condition,' recalled his pupil August Göllerich. 'I made sure that he went to bed at once. Towards evening he broke out in a mild sweat, but about 8.00 Siegfried and Eva Wagner appeared, to fetch him for a soirée at Wahnfried. . . .'

On Thursday, Liszt was too unwell to go to morning mass, as he wished, and was obliged to spend the whole day in his room. In the early morning of Friday, as Göllerich was reading to him from the breviary, they were joined by another pupil, Lina Schmalhausen. Liszt's daughter arrived before long, however, and the two young people had perforce to withdraw. From this day forward Cosima came every morning at 5.00 and stayed with her father until 8.00. Later in the day, for the next few days, it was mainly the two pupils who kept Liszt company. The reading to him of some passages from the *Divina Commedia* during this time gave him 'one last joy', remembered Göllerich. 'This book has accompanied me on all my travels,' he exclaimed; 'it counts among the profoundest achievements of the human mind.' In the evening of the 23rd he attended the performance of *Parsifal* at the Festspielhaus, seated in the Wagner family's box 'more asleep than awake'.

On Saturday the 24th, Adelheid von Schorn and Zhukovsky found Liszt seated on the sofa playing whist; among his companions were Sophie Menter, Lassen, Siloti, and Lessmann. 'He was coughing, nodding off for a moment or two and then resuming play, scarcely aware of who was there and hardly able to hold himself upright,' recalled Adelheid. 'Deeply distressed, we went away, for there was nothing we could do. . . .'

On Sunday the 25th, having given his promise to his daughter, and despite his deteriorating condition, Liszt insisted on attending the performance of *Tristan*. Permitting him to do so, the local doctor, Landgraf, ordered him to rest thereafter, to have no visitors, and to keep conversation to a minimum. In the theatre, to stifle his constant coughing and gasping, he was obliged to hold a handkerchief pressed against his mouth.

From the following day he was confined to bed. Lina Schmalhausen again spent several hours with him, reading to and trying to divert him. Holding her hand seemed to be of comfort, but, too weak for conversation, he constantly dozed off.

On Tuesday, summoned by a telegram from Cosima, Dr Fleischer from Erlangen comfirmed pneumonia. After his departure, Cosima gave strict instructions to Liszt's servant Mihály to admit thenceforth no one but family.

---

[20] The residence, in the Siegfriedstrasse, in which he had stayed in 1884. The street is now called the Lisztstrasse, and the house contains a Liszt museum.

On Wednesday the 28th, Liszt's pupil August Stradal arrived. He, too, was barred from the sickroom but, after pleading with Mihály, was allowed to stand at the threshold and gaze upon his slumbering master. 'His dreams must have been pleasant ones,' he wrote later to Lina Ramann, 'for he was smiling and the expression on his features was a happy, ecstatic one.'

From Thursday onwards, as Liszt was now almost constantly delirious or unconscious, Cosima began to sleep in the adjoining room, the better to keep watch. In the early hours of Saturday the 31st, the pain caused to Liszt by his heart spasms, and by his difficulties in breathing, caused him to utter shrieks loud enough to ring round the house and neighbourhood; as he did so, he sprang out of bed, his hand pressed against his heart. When, at Cosima's summons, Dr Landgraf arrived, the composer lay diagonally across the bed, ice-cold and still. Revived to some extent by a prolonged massage, he did not regain consciousness.

The remainder of the day was spent by Cosima at her father's bedside. Towards evening his breathing grew more laboured, and at about 9 o'clock his heartbeat became irregular. Injections were administered by one of the doctors present—but about half an hour before midnight Liszt's heart stopped beating.

The funeral, which took place on Tuesday, 3 August, was described by Constance Bache in the September issue of the *Monthly Musical Record*. 'Many, very many,' she wrote, 'who would have wished to show the last honours to the memory of the great Master, were precluded from doing so by the impossibility of arriving in time, and many actually came only just in time to join the funeral *cortège* as it emerged from Wagner's house into the road. The streets were hung with black flags, and the lighted lamps were veiled in crape. Both sides of the road were lined with spectators, as the long procession wended its slow way to the sound of the distant bell.

'The religious service over, the mayor of Bayreuth spoke a few words over the lowered coffin, and alluded in touching language to the great loss they, we, all the world, has sustained. One or two other speeches followed, including a few broken words from an old and beloved friend of the Master's, Herr Hofrat Gille, from Jena, but his words were almost incoherent from the sobs that broke from him, and everyone must have deeply sympathized with the grief of the poor old man, who had just lost his old and dear friend—and *such* a friend!'

Among those who sent wreaths and floral tributes were Liszt's friends Carl Alexander and Sophie of the royal house of Saxe-Weimar, the Crown Prince of Germany, whose large laurel wreath was placed on top of the coffin as it was borne to the cemetery, and Queen Victoria.[21] 'There were wreaths from Robert Franz; Sophie Menter; Frau Materna; a faithful and loving disciple of the Master's in London;[22] and many others . . . and even for many days afterwards floral homage continued to be paid to the Great Dead.'

---

[21] To her daughter the Crown Princess of Germany she wrote in a letter of 12 Aug.: 'I also forgot in each letter saying how grieved we were at old Liszt's death. Such a distinguished man and so sad that he should be taken after all his successes. But I fear his visit here and all the parties he was asked to killed him.'

[22] Constance's brother, Walter Bache.

'I have had to take to my bed, for, although so foreseen, the blow came unexpectedly,' wrote Princess Carolyne to Adelheid von Schorn. Remaining in Rome and devoting her energies to her *magnum opus*, the *Causes intérieures*, she completed the 24th and final volume early the following year, on Ash Wednesday, 23 February.

The last days of the Princess have been described by Adelheid von Schorn as told her by Princess Marie Hohenlohe, who journeyed to Rome at the beginning of March 1887 in response to disquieting news she was receiving. 'She spent a week at her mother's bedside. No one was expecting such a quick end, least of all the patient herself—with her work completed there was no reason for her to remain in Rome any longer, and she was making travel plans for the summer. Feeling tired, towards evening she sent every-one out so that she could sleep. Cardinal Hohenlohe had in the mean time called to see his sister-in-law; as they were conferring in the salon, wondering if it would be advis-able to bring the Princess's confessor to her the next day, the maid keeping watch at the door of the sickroom came to say that everything was "so deathly quiet". Death had indeed come to the Princess and "taken her gently by the hand". Her head was inclined slightly to one side, her expression infinitely peaceful.'

Some lines the Princess had written shortly after Liszt's death provide not only a sur-passingly apt epitaph for him who had been 'the sun of her life', but, in their conclud-ing words, also offer an insight that has lost little of its truth even today, after the passing of more than a hundred years:

In higher, heavenly spheres he will be happier than here, where, for all the homage, he was so profoundly misunderstood.

BIOGRAPHICAL SKETCHES

Agoult, Comtesse Marie Catherine Sophie d' (Frankfurt am Main, 31 Dec. 1805–Paris, 5 Mar. 1876), née de Flavigny, was the daughter of a French vicomte who had served in the army of emigrant princes; her mother was a member of the German banking family of Bethmann. In 1827 she married Comte Charles d'Agoult (1790–1875)—an ex-army officer whom she respected but did not love—and for about a decade from 1833 was the mistress of Liszt, to whom she bore three children.

When, six years her junior, Liszt made Marie's acquaintance *chez* the Marquise Le Vayer, there was an immediate mutual attraction. He was soon invited to her home, and their friendship developed—with ups and downs—until, in the spring of 1835, Marie's pregnancy compelled their flight into Switzerland. That, as the years passed, the relationship became ever more turbulent, was the result partly of their long periods of separation, partly of Liszt's behaviour with other women, partly of a jealous, intolerant streak in Marie herself. Two years after the end of their liaison, and perhaps prompted by Balzac's *Béatrix* and George Sand's *Horace*, in both of which she had herself been the target, she published (under her pen-name of Daniel Stern) a *roman à clef*, entitled *Nélida*, in which she sought to settle scores with her former lover. The eponymous heroine is meant to be a portrait of Marie herself (Nélida is an anagram of Daniel), and Guermann Régnier, a painter of plebeian origin who becomes her unworthy lover, to represent Liszt, denigration of whom is the real object of the book, many of the incidents of which are taken from Franz and Marie's life together in the 1830s. Eventually commissioned by the Grand Duke of W*** to paint a huge fresco, Guermann finds that his abilities are far inferior to his aspirations. Dying not long afterwards, he has a death-bed reconciliation with the nobly forgiving Nélida, whom he had earlier abandoned. Even apart from the inaccuracy of such a portrayal of Liszt (whose Weimar years showed him to be more than equal to great artistic challenges), *Nélida* is at best a mediocre novel, for Marie's turn of mind was analytical and exegetical rather than creative. Years later she herself dismissed it as an 'early literary sin that I gladly forget'.

Pride, an ingrained intolerance, and an inability to give and take spoiled several of her closest relationships. That with George Sand foundered because of criticisms of the novelist made by Marie in letters to their common friend Mme Marliani. Offending both of them, she had no contact with either her daughter Blandine or her son Daniel during the last two or three years of their lives; her relations with her mother turned sour before the latter's death; and she was long on uneasy terms with her brother, Maurice de Flavigny, for several reasons but, above all, because of her loathing of his wife. There was in fact a strain of mental instability in the Bethmann family. Her half-sister drowned herself in the Main, and in her early married life Marie had to be restrained from throwing herself into the Seine. (Her nephew Léon Ehrmann actually did so but was fished out.) Nearly forty years later, in April 1869, she had to be put into a strait-jacket and given treatment in a clinic, on the journey to which she was tormented by the notion that she was going to be dissected alive.

Of her physical attractions, a description was penned by Comtesse Dash: 'She was not exactly pretty, but her elegance, her distinction, her blond hair, her eyes and her charm made a beauty of her.' However, she was chaste by temperament, and, with the possible exception of the Swiss *littérateur* Charles Didier, it is likely that her husband and Liszt were the only men with whom she ever had intimate relations. This was not for want of opportunity: among her many admirers were Sainte-Beuve, Emile de Girardin, Henry Lytton Bulwer and—most faithful of all—Louis de Ronchaud. Gratified by their attentions, she seems nevertheless to have kept them at arm's length. When a declaration of love was made to her for the last time she was 56 years old.

The possessor of a fine intellect—Angelo de Gubernatis even wrote of her 'sovereign intelligence'—she collaborated with Liszt on his essays in the *Gazette musicale* and elsewhere, and later presided over a successful salon, which was at first literary and artistic but later of a more political tone, her sympathies being strongly pro-republican. Deeply interested in education—in her *Esquisses morales* she quoted approvingly Hegel's 'I know everything, more or less, and believe that everyone could and should know everything' —she herself acquired enormous erudition, much of which can be found in her writings. Among her books—published, like *Nélida*, under the name of Daniel Stern—are *Essai sur la liberté* (1847); *Esquisses morales* (1848); *Histoire de la Révolution de 1848* (1851–3); *Florence et Turin* (1862), discussions of art, history, and politics, the fruit perhaps of her friendship with Manin and acquaintance with Mazzini and Cavour; and *Histoire du commencement de la République aux Pays-Bas* (only the first part was completed, published in instalments between 1855 and 1870, and as a volume in 1872). Her *Dante et Goethe*, dedicated to Cosima and consisting of five long dialogues, came out in instalments in 1864 and two years later in book form; autobiographical allusions make it clear that the principal speaker, named Diotima (after the instructress of Socrates), represents Marie herself. Packed with learning, but written simply and unpretentiously, it forms an appealing introduction to the two great poets and their respective masterpieces, and seems to have been read with interest by the composer of the Dante and Faust symphonies.

In addition to short stories, articles, and reviews, Marie also wrote three plays, *Jeanne d'Arc* (1856), performed to great acclaim in her presence at Turin in 1860; *Trois journées de Marie Stuart* (1856); and *Jacques Cœur* (1858). Daniel Stern's *Mes Souvenirs 1806– 1833* came out a year after her death; *Mémoires 1833–1854*, edited by her grandson Daniel Ollivier, appeared under her real name in 1927. This latter work contains her diary account of the 'years of pilgrimage' with Liszt; and some months after her last meeting with him, in 1866, she wrote in the margin of the manuscript some final words on the relationship which had represented both the highest point and the tragedy of her life: 'What has *he* done with these twenty-eight years? And what have *I* done with them? He is the Abbé Liszt and I am Daniel Stern! And, between us, how much despair, how many deaths, tears, sobs, and griefs!'

Ambros, August Wilhelm (Mauth [now Vysoké Mýtó] 1816–Vienna 1876), Austrian music historian, university lecturer, critic, and composer, a nephew of the musicologist Raphael Kiesewetter. Most important of his writings is his monumental *Geschichte der*

Musik, for which he carried out extensive research in various German and Italian cities but died before completion of the fourth volume, which had to be prepared from his notes. (A fifth volume was added some years later.) Liszt liked and admired this learned and witty man, whom he saw regularly during his visits to Prague and who, as Ambros remarked in his essay 'The Abbé Liszt in Rome' (*Bunte Blätter*, 1872), in his turn visited him at the Vatican and Santa Francesca Romana. When, in 1880, a monument was to be erected over Ambros's grave in Grinzing, it was Liszt who made the largest single contribution towards costs.

Anderson, Miss Janet (b. Berwick-upon-Tweed 1816). This Scottish governess of the young Marie Wittgenstein travelled with the latter and her mother from Woronince to Weimar in 1848, and there dwelt with them—and Liszt—for the next dozen years, remaining at the Altenburg even after Marie's marriage and Carolyne's departure to Rome. When in August 1861, at the age of 45, she returned to Britain (to live with her brother in Somerset), Marie's husband, Prince Constantin Hohenlohe, awarded her an annual pension of 300 silver roubles.

Arnim, Bettina (Elisabeth) von (Frankfurt am Main 1785–Berlin 1859), née Brentano, German woman of letters and the wife, from 1811, of the poet and novelist Ludwig Achim von Arnim (1781–1831). By the time she and Liszt first encountered one another, during the weeks of his Berlin triumphs of early 1842, she had been on friendly terms with a number of great men, including Beethoven and Goethe. She and the fêted pianist at first enchanted one another. Years later the friendship turned sour, to a large extent, apparently, because of Liszt's disinclination to share Bettina's obsessive worship of Goethe, of whose genius he was fully aware and appreciative, but to whom, as a man, he preferred Schiller; and it was probably with some relief that, at their last meeting (1854), he heard her words of farewell: 'I shall see you no more! I shall see you no more today, no more tomorrow, no more ever!' Her main contributions to literature were *Goethes Briefwechsel mit einem Kinde* (1835), a correspondence freely adapted, with cuts, alterations, and inventions, from letters she had exchanged with the poet, and the originals of which she destroyed; and *Die Günderode* (1840), based in a similarly imaginative—or eccentric—way on the letters of a friend who had taken her own life when thwarted in love.

Of Bettina's seven children, best known to Liszt were the three daughters: Maxe (1818–94), who in 1853 married Eduard, Count von Oriola; Armgart (1821–80), the wife, from 1860, of Albert, Count von Flemming; and Gisela (1827–89), whose husband, from 1859, was the essayist and short-story-writer Hermann Grimm, son of the philologist and folklorist Wilhelm Grimm.

There was a connection between Bettina and Marie d'Agoult, for the former's brother, Clemens Brentano (1778–1842), had in 1807 been lured into matrimony by Marie's half-sister Auguste Bussmann (1791–1832)—a union into which the poet entered in 'the utmost anguish' and from which, filled with horror and loathing, he several times tried to escape, until released by a formal separation in 1810. Auguste later married a rich Strasbourg merchant, J. A. Ehrmann, bore him children and, in April 1832, drowned herself in the Main.

Augusz, Baron Antal (1807–78), Hungarian magnate who, making Liszt's acquaintance early in the latter's virtuoso years, soon became, and remained, the closest of all his friends in his native country. A talented amateur pianist and singer, and the dedicatee of the Eighth Hungarian Rhapsody, Augusz was Liszt's host at his home (which now houses a Liszt museum) in Szekszárd, southern Hungary, on four occasions: in October 1846 and September 1865, for more than three months in 1870, and again in 1876. 'We were *one* in heart,' wrote Liszt when, in September 1878, news reached him of the death of this generous and loyal friend and compatriot.

Bache, Walter (Birmingham 1842–London 1888), English pianist, conductor, and teacher who from 1862 to 1865 studied with Liszt in Rome and in later years regularly attended the masterclasses in Weimar. In a series of annual orchestral concerts beginning in 1871, he introduced his mentor's music to audiences in London. At the sixth concert (24 February 1876) he conducted *The Legend of St Elisabeth*; at the tenth (11 March 1880), with August Manns, the first performance in England of the Faust Symphony. At the last of his orchestral concerts (8 February 1886) he played three concertos: Beethoven's in C minor, Liszt's in A, and Chopin's in E minor. A year later (21 February 1887) he gave the first performance in England of the Dante Sonata. It was he who induced Liszt to come to England in April 1886; he, too, was largely responsible for setting up the Liszt Scholarship at the Royal Academy of Music, where he was a professor of piano.

Bache was always deeply distressed by the ingratitude shown to his revered master by so many. 'Liszt is the most ill-used genius the world ever saw,' he wrote in 1877 to Jessie Laussot. 'All are ungrateful to him. No Wagner, Bülow, Joachim or Klindworth would be here but for Liszt. . . . I lose courage with my abominable fellow-creatures!' When Liszt's correspondence with Wagner was published, the same friend was asked: 'Is there *one* of us (even your dear self) who does not feel guilty of having sometimes judged the great Departed unjustly, even impertinently, according to our small views, and not in harmony with his much greater ones? I allude to many small matters which we put down to weakness, old age, etc., which now appear to me as parts of his enormous and unflinching plan of *self-abnegation*, in which he had reached a height that is almost incomprehensible to us.'

Of Bache's six brothers and sisters, two are of special interest: Edward, a very promising composer and pianist who died young, and Constance, author of *Brother Musicians: Reminiscences of Edward and Walter Bache* and translator of, *inter alia*, the first two volumes of Liszt's letters in the series edited by La Mara.

In *Brother Musicians*, Constance mentions a photograph showing Sophie Menter, Liszt, and Bache standing together in front of Sophie's 'fairy-tale' home of Schloss Itter—an interesting contribution to the Liszt iconography which, unfortunately, is reproduced nowhere in the literature.

Bacheracht, Therese von (Stuttgart 1804–Java 1852), née von Struwe, German novelist. It was in Hamburg, where she was wife of the Russian Consul General, that she made Liszt's acquaintance; and in October 1848, accompanied by her friend Fanny Lewald, she visited him and Princess Carolyne at the Altenburg. After leaving her husband she devoted herself to the writer Karl Gutzkow—secretary of the Schiller Foundation in Weimar from 1861 to 1864—and later married her cousin Baron Heinrich von Lützow, with whom in 1849 she emigrated to Java.

Balakirev, Mily Alexeyevich (Nizhny-Novgorod 1837–St Petersburg 1910), Russian composer and pianist, guiding spirit of the group of composers—himself, Borodin, Cui, Mussorgsky, and Rimsky-Korsakov—known as 'the Five' or *moguchaya kuchka* (mighty handful). It is to be regretted that Liszt never met this extraordinary musician with whom he had in common not only the gift of leadership and the desire to help others, but even a similar warmth and generosity of temperament: 'Liszt is a real Balakirev, a great-hearted man indeed,' wrote Borodin. Although not a phenomenal virtuoso of the calibre of a Tausig or a Rubinstein, Balakirev was none the less a master pianist, and had Liszt, in the last year of his life, made the planned trip to St Petersburg, he might well have enjoyed hearing his music interpreted by so individual an admirer. 'Liszt occupied the throne at our gatherings,' recalled A. A. Olenin of the Tuesday soirees at Balakirev's; 'and how Mily Alexeyevich played him!'

It was to Liszt that Balakirev, who kept a portrait of the Hungarian master above his desk, dedicated his symphonic poem *Tamara*. An earlier work, the famous and formidable *Islamey*, he had dedicated to Nikolai Rubinstein, but afterwards declared that it had been 'made known in the musical world thanks to Liszt'. Long after the latter's death he wrote: 'I cannot imagine that after Liszt it is possible for the art of the piano to be taken any further—unless this instrument be *considerably improved*, enabling some future genius, on the scale of a Liszt, to advance 'pianistic instrumentation' still more. Of such geniuses, however, only one a century is born!'

Balakirev's pupil Sergei Lyapunov (Yaroslavl 1859–Paris 1924) composed some fine *Etudes d'exécution transcendante* which complete the key sequence begun by Liszt in his own. The twelfth and last of the set is entitled *Elegiya pamyati Frantsa Lista* (Elegy in memory of Franz Liszt).

Beaulieu-Marconnay, Baron Carl Olivier von (Minden 1811–Dresden 1889), Court Marshal in Weimar from 1848, Intendant of the Court Theatre 1850–2 and 1854–7, and author of, among other things, *Anna Amalia, Carl August und der Minister von Fritsch* (Weimar, 1874).

Beethoven, Ludwig van (Bonn 1770–Vienna 1827), German composer whom Liszt revered all his life, whose symphonies he transcribed for piano, and his renditions of whose greatest works for that instrument have been called the sublimest achievements in the history of piano-playing. It was thanks to Liszt, above all, that in 1845 it was possible to erect a monument to the dead colossus in his native city.

Throughout his life Liszt told friends and acquaintances that Beethoven had come to his Vienna concert of 13 April 1823 and there embraced and kissed him. This assertion has been challenged on the ground that remarks in the Beethoven conversation books seem to indicate that the composer—by this time almost completely deaf—did not attend the event in question. Such an argument must, however, be regarded as not proven.

The remarks certainly support a scenario in which Beethoven was not present—but they all equally well support one in which he was. Even if those books contained a comment which might at first glance seem to make the matter conclusive, such as someone writing, 'I'm sorry you did not go to little Liszt's concert the other day,' it would actually do no such thing. (Beethoven might, for example, have replied, 'Oh, but you're mistaken, my friend: on the spur of the moment I *did* suddenly decide to go, and from what I could judge with eyesight alone rather enjoyed it.') Since, without Beethoven's spoken utterances, the conversation books prove nothing, they have to be set aside, and we are left with Liszt's own words. And just as, generally speaking, we tend to believe what any fundamentally honourable person tells us about the events of his or her life, when there is no evidence to show that he or she is not speaking the truth, surely we should do the same courtesy to Liszt.

Belgiojoso, Princess Cristina (Milan 1808–Milan 1871), née Trivulzio, Italian patriot, social reformer, writer, and translator into French of Vico's *Scienza Nova*. An epileptic, she was at the age of 16 so unfortunate as to marry Prince Emilio Belgiojoso, who soon infected his bride with syphilis, a disease which, in the words of her biographer, 'was to lead her on a *via crucis* for the next forty years'. It was to flee this husband, and the agents of Metternich, to whom her political opinions were unpalatable, that she settled in Paris, where she soon became one of the most brilliant of the salon hostesses and the admired friend of, amongst others, Balzac, Heine, and de Musset. The father of her only child, a daughter born in 1838, was the historian Mignet.

'Slim, *distinguée*, pale, eyes as big as saucers, very slender hands, grand and gracious manners, extremely intelligent, *de l'esprit comme un démon*', runs a description of Cristina as she was at about the time that Liszt made her acquaintance in the early 1830s—a pen portrait which makes it easy to understand his long devotion to her. It was at a charity matinée in her Paris home that his historic keyboard contest with Thalberg took place; and it was to her that he dedicated the *Hexameron* and *Réminiscences des Puritains*.

Belloni, Gaetano (*c.*1810–87). Known to Liszt as early as the mid-1830s, Belloni was interviewed by Mme d'Agoult in August 1840 when her lover was seeking a secretary and concert manager. 'I have seen Belloni,' she wrote on 22 August, 'and am more than content with him. He accepted gladly, without any ifs or buts. He doesn't want to make any special arrangement, putting himself entirely in your hands. He hopes to accompany you on all your travels, and seems to have a perfect understanding of what he will have to do. Mlle Delarue answers for his integrity.' Beginning his duties in February 1841, Belloni remained with Liszt until the musician's career as a professional pianist came to an end in late 1847.

Berlioz, Hector (La Côte-Saint-André, Isère, 1803–Paris 1869), French composer whose first meeting with Liszt was on 4 December 1830, eve of the première of the *Symphonie fantastique*. 'Liszt came to see me,' he recalled. 'We felt an immediate affinity. . . . He came to the concert and was conspicuous for the warmth of his applause and his generally enthusiastic behaviour.' After the concert, 'Liszt literally dragged me off to have dinner at his house and overwhelmed me with the vigour of his enthusiasm.' This was the beginning of a long and close friendship. Liszt championed the works of Berlioz, transcribed several of them for piano, mounted a number of Berlioz Weeks at Weimar in the 1850s, and, in 1855, brought out a long and appreciative essay, *Berlioz and his Harold Symphony*. On the other hand, although a great admirer of his friend's pianistic genius, Berlioz showed little interest in or understanding of him as a composer; and, when the Gran Mass was performed in Paris in 1866, even denounced it as 'the negation of art'. (Some years earlier he had, it is true, described as 'a great work' the Faust Symphony dedicated to him.) By this time, however, the friendship had already begun to founder, for the reason outlined in Liszt's letter of 15 May 1882 to Edmond Hippeau (Letter 856). Nevertheless, Liszt remained an admirer of Berlioz, towards the cost of a statue of whom he contributed 300 francs himself and sought donations from others. (See Letter 882 of 4 March 1883 to the Grand Duke Carl Alexander.)

Berlioz's two wives, neither of whom brought him much happiness, were the Irish actress Harriet Smithson (Ennis, Co. Clare, 1800–Paris 1854), by whom he had a son, and the Franco-Spanish singer Marie Recio (1814–62), née Martin, who had been his mistress for many years when he married her some months after the death of Harriet.

Bibesco, Princess Hélène, née Costaki-Epureano, the wife of Prince Alexander Bibesco. A talented pianist and pupil of Anton Rubinstein, this Romanian aristocrat was also a friend of Camille Saint-Saëns, who dedicated to her his *Valse nonchalante*, Op. 110.

Blessington, Marguerite, Countess of (Knockbrit, nr. Clonmel, 1789–Paris 1849), née Power, Irish authoress who at Genoa in 1823 was daily in the company of Byron, the literary outcome of which was her *Conversations of Lord Byron with the Countess of Blessington* (London, 1834), a book eagerly sought by Liszt and Mme d'Agoult even before its publication. In 1836, some years after the death of Lord Blessington, she moved into Gore House, a mansion in Kensington which stood on the site now filled by the Royal Albert Hall. Her friend Count Alfred d'Orsay (Paris 1801–Paris 1852), a dandy and charmer universally recognized as *arbiter elegantiarium*, officially occupied the villa next door, and between them this glamorous couple 'wielded a sort of supremacy over a considerable circle of the artistic and fashionable world of London'. Liszt, during his sojourns in the city in 1840 and 1841, seems to have enjoyed their society, and he might have done so even more had he known Lady Blessington, by now in her early fifties, at the time, some years earlier, when she had been described by another connoisseur of female beauty as 'one of the most lovely and fascinating women I have ever seen'.

Boisselot, Dominique François Xavier (1811–93), head of the family piano-manufacturing firm in Marseilles after the death of his brother Louis (1809–50), until the latter's son Franz (named after Liszt, his godfather) attained his majority. Louis accompanied Liszt during his visit to Spain in 1844–5.

Boissier, Valérie (Geneva 1813–Rivage, nr. Geneva, 1894), Swiss authoress whose many writings were mostly published under her married name of the Comtesse Agénor de

Gasparin. The daughter of Caroline and Auguste Boissier, a well-to-do patrician couple resident in Geneva, she was accompanied by her mother to her lessons with Liszt in Paris in late 1831 and early 1832; and it is Caroline Boissier whom posterity has to thank for valuable descriptions of the young musician as he was at this time. 'There are very bright lights in his head,' she wrote on one occasion, 'as well as strong and new ideas. If he hasn't genius, and a genius which will become creative, then I know nothing about it, and the prodigious impression made on me both by his music and his conversation would be inexplicable without this certainty.'

Borodin, Alexander Porfiryevich (St Petersburg 1833–St Petersburg 1887), Russian composer (a chemist by profession) and member of the St Petersburg group whose works Liszt much admired. Meetings between the two at Weimar in 1877 and Magdeburg in 1881 were described by Borodin in fascinating detail in letters to his wife and to Cui; and in gratitude for Liszt's kindness, and for recommending his First Symphony for performance at Baden-Baden in 1880, he later dedicated to him the 'orchestral picture' *V srednei Azii* (In Central Asia).

It had been Borodin's wife Ekaterina (1832–87), née Protopopova, a gifted pianist and admirer of Chopin, Liszt, and Schumann, who had converted him to their music at a time when his tastes lay elsewhere.

Bösendorfer, Celeste (d. Vienna 1882), née von Possbach, sometime actress and 'femme d'élite' of whom Liszt was evidently very fond. Ludwig Speidel, in his brief memoir written shortly after her death, remarked that, to those persons whom she wished particularly well, Frau Bösendorfer used to present a copy of the *Meditations* of Marcus Aurelius—an idiosyncrasy which, if he knew of it, might in itself have been enough to endear her to Liszt.

Her husband **Ludwig Bösendorfer** (Vienna 1835–Vienna 1919) was head of the famous Viennese piano-manufacturing firm after his father's death in 1859, a leading figure in the musical life of Vienna, and a devoted admirer of Liszt. In 1872 he turned the Liechtenstein riding-school in the Herrengasse into a concert hall, the Bösendorfer-Saal, inaugurated that same year by a recital of Hans von Bülow's and on several occasions the venue of appearances by Liszt. The last concert to be given in this much-loved building before its demolition, forty years later, was described movingly by Stefan Zweig in his *The World of Yesterday*: 'When the last bar of Beethoven, played more beautifully than ever by the Rosé Quartet, had died away, no one left his seat. We called and applauded, several women sobbed with emotion, no one wished to believe that this was a farewell. . . . A half hour, a full hour, we remained as if by our presence we could save the old hallowed place.'

Brendel, Karl Franz (Stolberg 1811–Leipzig 1868), German writer on music who, as editor—from 1845 until his death—of the *Neue Zeitschrift für Musik*, was able to do great service to the cause of the new music represented by Liszt and Wagner. After Liszt's move to Rome in 1861, Brendel's letters also helped him keep in touch with musical developments in Germany.

Brockhaus, Heinrich (Amsterdam 1804–Leipzig 1874), German publisher whose services to science and literature were rewarded in 1858 by an honorary doctorate from the University of Jena, and in 1872 by the freedom of the city of Leipzig.

Bull, Ole (Bergen 1810–Lysøen, nr. Bergen, 1880). Although he made a number of visits to Paris in the 1830s, this legendary violinist and Norwegian national hero seems not to have met Liszt until the spring of 1840, in London. 'We have played together and are mutually inspired with admiration and sympathy for each other,' wrote Bull to his wife on 15 May; a few weeks later they performed the Kreutzer Sonata at a Philharmonic Society concert. Their paths crossed again on several later occasions—in Vienna, Rome and, in 1878, in Budapest. A ceaseless traveller, Bull played all over Europe and made many trips across the Atlantic; at Giza on his sixty-sixth birthday he even climbed to the top of the Great Pyramid and, gazing out over the Valley of the Nile, there played his most enduring piece, *Et saeterbesøg*. His life, it has been said, is 'a fairy story to enthral every Norwegian child'.

Bülow, Hans Guido von (Dresden 1830–Cairo 1894), German pianist and conductor who as a boy made the acquaintance of both Liszt and Wagner, at the age of 19 met and admired Liszt anew ('He is a quite perfect man. . . . His playing, and his whole personality, have completely enchanted and inspired me'), and in 1850, after hearing Liszt conduct *Lohengrin*, decided to abandon his legal studies and pursue a career in music. Between 1851 and 1853 he was Liszt's pupil in Weimar. In August 1857, while a teacher at the Stern Conservatorium in Berlin, he married Liszt's younger daughter; in 1864 he was appointed conductor of the Royal Opera in Munich. After Cosima had left him to live with and devote herself to Wagner, he spent two years in Italy before resuming the itinerant life of a public performer. From 1880 to 1885 he was conductor of the Meiningen Court Orchestra, which he transformed into one of the finest in Europe. The second wife of this witty, eccentric, irascible depressive was the actress Marie Schanzer (1857–1941), who later wrote his biography and published his letters. In early 1894, seeking to alleviate an 'incurable malady', he travelled to Egypt, but, within a week of his arrival, died in hospital. Six weeks later his remains were cremated in Hamburg.

Bülow was the dedicatee of, *inter alia*, Liszt's Fantasia on Hungarian Folk Themes, *Totentanz*, and transcriptions (when published complete) of the Beethoven symphonies. As well as the first performance of the Fantasia (Pest, 1853) and the *Totentanz* (The Hague, 1865), he also gave that of the B minor Sonata, at a Berlin concert of 22 January 1857 which inaugurated the first Bechstein grand piano. It was he who conducted the première of Wagner's *Tristan und Isolde* (Munich, 1865) and of *Die Meistersinger* (Munich, 1868) and gave the first performance (Boston, USA, 1875) of Tchaikovsky's Piano Concerto in B flat minor, which the composer dedicated to him. In his later years he was also closely associated with the music of Brahms.

Bulyovszky, Lilla (Kolozsvár 1833–Graz 1909), née Szilágyi, Hungarian actress and authoress who seems to have become enamoured of Liszt during his visit to Hungary in the summer of 1856. One of their subsequent meetings was at Breslau in May 1859; twenty years thereafter, in a letter (28 October 1879) in which she expressed among other things her lifelong gratitude, she wrote of 'the tiny little prayer book which it was my good fortune to receive from your celebrated hand, in the Hotel Zedlitz, at the time of my first guest appearance in Breslau. My God, what memories. . . .'

Busoni, Ferruccio Dante Michelangiolo Benvenuto (Empoli 1866–Berlin 1924), German-Italian pianist and composer, one of the greatest names in the history of piano-playing. It is a matter for regret that it was not the adult Busoni, rather than the 11-year-old, who encountered Liszt, of whose works he was to become so outstanding an exponent. When, in December 1899, he played the *Réminiscences de Norma* to Liszt's pupil William Dayas, the latter—reported Busoni to his wife—'with eyes nearly starting out of his head' sprang up and said, 'What a pity the "Old Man" did not hear it! He would have given you his sword and died in peace.' One can only wonder how such a performance might have compared with Liszt's of the same work, such as he gave at Olmütz in 1846, described as 'so breathtaking that it was frequently interrupted by storms of applause'. Like Liszt, or because of him, Busoni was drawn to Weimar, where, in the summer of 1900 (and again in 1901), he gave masterclasses in the Tempelherrenhaus. (It was at this time that the aged Grand Duke made to him the historic observation: 'Liszt *was* what a Prince *ought to be*!') 'In those Weimar days,' recalled his pupil Vladimir Cernikoff, 'I remember also a concert at which he played with orchestra the two E flat Concertos of Beethoven and Liszt. In *his* hands they were *both* Emperors, not only the so-called Beethoven one. In later years I gratefully recollect his memorable series of Liszt recitals in Berlin, which were a revelation, even to the jaded and supercilious Berlin critics.'

'We are all descended from Liszt radically, without excepting Wagner, and we owe to him the lesser things we can do. César Franck, Richard Strauss, Debussy, the penultimate Russians, are all branches of his tree,' wrote Busoni. 'It can compromise no pianist if he shows himself to be of the same opinion as Liszt, otherwise it must follow that he excels Liszt as a musician and pianist. Such a pianist is, up to now, not known to me. I am myself respectfully conscious of the distance which separates me from his greatness.'

Caetani, Don Michelangelo, Duke of Sermoneta (Rome 1804–Rome 1882), thrice-married Roman politician, man of letters and authority on Dante, whose masterpiece he described as 'unquestionably the greatest work of art ever produced by human genius'. (As a Caetani he was, of course, a collateral descendant of the man who was for Dante the great enemy, Pope Boniface VIII.) As well as writing valuable commentaries on certain cantos of the *Commedia*, he also sought to reconstruct the Dantesque topography, publishing his conclusions under the title *La materia della Divina Commedia di Dante Alighieri dichiarate in sei tavole* (1865). Liszt was but one of the many outstanding men with whom Don Michelangelo associated during his long life; as the Prince of Teano—he succeeded to the dukedom in 1850—he had been on friendly terms with, among others, Balzac, who dedicated to him the novels *La Cousine Bette* and *Le Cousin Pons*, and Sir Walter Scott. During his last years, after the failure of an operation for cataract, he had to endure blindness.

Also well known to Liszt were Don Michelangelo's two children (by his first wife, née the Countess Calista Rzewuska): Don Onorato (1842–1917), Duke of Sermoneta from 1882, sometime Mayor of Rome, Minister of Foreign Affairs and Senator, and Donna Ersilia (1840–1925), a passionate student of Roman history and antiquities— she has been called 'the most learned of Italian women'—who in 1859 married Count Giacomo Colombo Lovatelli (d.1879). Of Don Onorato's five children by his English-born wife Donna Ada, the eldest, Leone, Duke of Sermoneta from 1917, was self-taught in oriental languages, became a world authority on Islam, and emigrated to Canada; the second, Roffredo Michelangelo Francesco, was musically gifted—he became a composer— and one of Liszt's many godchildren. Leone's daughter, Sveva Caetani, became a painter whose major work, an extraordinary series of fifty-six watercolours, was inspired by the lifelong passion of her great-grandfather, the *Divina Commedia* of Dante.

Carus, Carl Gustav (Leipzig 1789–Dresden 1869), German physiologist, psychologist, and landscape painter whose memoirs record several meetings with Liszt. Having made his acquaintance during his virtuoso years, in September 1853 he ran into him, as well as Princesses Carolyne and Marie, at a musical soirée hosted by Baron Lüttichau in Pillnitz. Enjoying their company—'among the crowd of guests, these three delighted me above all'—he arranged to meet them again in Dresden the following day. 'The elder Princess . . . accompanied me to the gallery, where she everywhere expressed herself in a lively, imaginative manner. All three then came to my home and inspected my collection of skulls, where many things likewise attracted their attention, giving me a good opportunity quietly to note many interesting psychological traits in these people.'

Visiting Weimar in August 1858, Carus was invited to the Altenburg, where he heard several performances by his host and others, and enjoyed above all a 'great Fantasy' played by Liszt himself: 'What can't such a huge grand piano do under those hands!'

Cessiat, Valentine de (1820–94). This capable niece and—in later life—adopted daughter of Alphonse de Lamartine has been thus described, as she was at about the time that Liszt made her acquaintance: 'a thin young girl with a remarkably large nose and mouth' who was less physically attractive than her sisters and a 'confirmed dyspeptic'. On the other hand, 'though not strictly beautiful, if her features were examined separately, her clear pale skin, her melodious voice and her stately carriage conveyed an impression of beauty and won much general admiration' (Ragg, *The Lamartine Ladies*). Liszt was evidently one of the admirers, and Valentine is the only woman to whom he is known to have proposed marriage. (In the case of Princess Wittgenstein, the initiative may well have been hers.)

That his offer was rejected was no secret. Years later his daughter Blandine wrote to him, after meeting Valentine: 'She tries to please, but she lacks charm. She's a horsy type: not very intelligent and possessing the merest smattering of knowledge—and certainly not worth the tip of your little finger nail.' Remaining a spinster, and more than once suffering the distress of being jilted, Valentine was to devote much of her life to looking after her adored uncle and, after his death, to collecting, sorting and editing his correspondence. That she became his wife, as was rumoured, is improbable.

Charnacé, Claire Christine de (1830–1912), younger of the two daughters of Charles and Marie d'Agoult. At the age of 19 she married Comte Guy de Charnacé (1825–1909), from whom she was legally separated six years later. Both became writers, and Claire was also a painter of talent.

Chopin, Fryderyk Franciszek (Żelazowa Wola, nr. Warsaw, 1810–Paris 1849). For several years after his arrival in Paris, in 1831, this great composer-pianist was a close friend and comrade of Liszt. Later, however, certain matters, such as the quarrel between their mistresses, caused something of a chill to descend upon the relationship. Chopin was also offended when his apartment was used by Liszt for a tryst with Marie Pleyel—causing him to complain angrily, or so we are told, that the pair had even got together 'under my mother's portrait!' None of these things affected Liszt's fundamental regard for Chopin, his memoir of whom has often been criticized, but, as was remarked by George Sand—and a better judge could hardly be found— nevertheless contains 'very good things and very beautiful pages'. Nor could anyone who knows certain of the letters Liszt wrote in later years (for instance, Letters 727 and 740 of 25 April 1875 and 1 January 1876 to the Princess Wittgenstein), doubt for one moment his deep and lasting admiration and affection for the Polish genius and his incomparable creations.

Circourt, Comte Adolphe de (Bouxières, nr. Nancy, 1801–Celle-Saint-Cloud 1879), French polymath and polyglot. Not a genius in the sense of being the possessor of extraordinary creative power, this likeable and profoundly religious man—who constantly quoted Septimius Severus's 'Laboremus' (Let us work) and applied to himself the words 'Io che d'altro che d'imparar non ho voglia'[1]—might perhaps be considered a near-genius for the scarcely paralleled range of his erudition. Like Bacon, he seems to have 'taken all knowledge to be his province'; and, as a latter-day Pico, to have been eminently capable of defending nine hundred theses *de omni re scibili*. Liszt made his acquaintance at Lamartine's; and it was Lamartine who penned a memorable description of this man who lived to learn: 'He had devoted himself to studies which would have absorbed the lives of several men, but which in his own were mere diversions. Languages, races, geography, history, philosophy, travels, constitutions, religions of peoples from the infancy of the world to our own day, from Tibet to the Alps, he had incorporated everything into himself, reflected on everything, retained everything: one could question him on the totality of facts and ideas which make up the world without his having need, to reply, of other books than his memory. Breadth, width, and vast depths of learning, neither the bottom nor the limits of which could ever be reached, a living chart of human knowledge. . . .'

'With Circourt,' added his biographer Huber-Saladin, 'one could enter into the most curious and secret details concerning the most illustrious personages, and the most unknown. On his special predilections he was inexhaustible. Dante's *Divina Commedia* he knew by heart, from first line to last. . . .'

---

[1] 'I who have no wish other than to learn.' This seems to be a paraphrase of Petrarch's 'Io ch'altro diletto che 'nparar non provo' (*Trionfo d'Amore*, i. 21).

His much-admired wife (Moscow 1808–Paris 1863), née Anastasia de Klustine, an 'incomparable Russian' who at her home in the rue des Saussaies presided over one of the most notable of Parisian salons, was in the audience at the Hôtel de Ville on 9 April 1835 when Liszt fainted at the keyboard. In later years she was a valued friend and supporter of Cavour, the book of whose letters to her—*Count Cavour and Madame de Circourt: Some Unpublished Correspondence*, ed. Count Nigra (London, 1894)—is prefaced by her portrait.

Cohen, Hermann (Hamburg 1821–Spandau, Berlin, 1871). Coming to Paris from Germany in the summer of 1834, this talented young pianist had one lesson from Chopin, one from Zimmermann (teacher of, amongst others, Alkan, Franck, Gounod, and Bizet), and then attached himself to Liszt, whom he soon idolized. ('The ascendancy Liszt achieved over others amounted almost to fascination,' he recalled.) In Geneva in 1835, at Liszt's recommendation, Puzzi—as he was nicknamed—was (despite his youth) appointed a professor of piano at the Conservatoire. In that same city, however, he became addicted to gambling; and the next dozen years were largely swallowed up by this and associated pursuits. In 1847, writes his biographer, Hermann was 'like another Saul, struck by Divine Grace'. Renouncing Judaism, he asked for baptism (his godmother was the Duchesse de Rauzan), devoted himself to a life of penitence and sacrifice, and in October 1849 became a Discalced Carmelite with the name of Brother Augustin-Marie-du-Très-Saint-Sacrement. 'God alone knows how far he advanced towards perfection,' remembered a fellow Christian. 'Those who lived in intimacy with him would, I think, have had some trouble to point out a defect.' In late 1870 Hermann journeyed to Berlin in order to minister to French prisoners of war at Spandau. There, in January 1871, he died of smallpox (or typhoid fever) and was buried in the church of St Hedwig.

His relations with Liszt had gone badly wrong by 1840, and the letter from Liszt to Mme d'Agoult of 7 December 1841 even attributes to Hermann the theft of large sums of money. It should be said, however, that when, years later, he was leading an exemplary life, Hermann wrote of 1841 as the year in which 'a plot, prepared with the most diabolical cunning', had been the cause of his estrangement from Liszt. Be that as it may, when they met in Rome in 1862 there was much affection on both sides. Twenty years on again, writing to Hermann's biographer, Liszt referred to the deceased as 'my pupil who was later my revered friend'.

Now, in the 1990s, Hermann is a candidate for beatification and eventual canonization, much stress being laid on his conversion in London of several condemned Spanish criminals to whom he administered Holy Communion and, during the night before their public execution, the Holy Viaticum. Thus far, the movement to enrol him in the canon of saints has not succeeded; should it eventually do so, Liszt—whose childhood reading was the *Lives of the Saints*, some of whose finest music was inspired by saintly legends, and whose letters in later life abound with references to saints and saints' days —will also have been the friend and mentor of a saint.

Constantine Nikolaevich (St Petersburg 1827–St Petersburg 1892), Russian Grand Duke of whom it was remarked that his 'intellectual power and encyclopaedic knowledge would have made him a remarkable man in any sphere of life'. The second, and ablest, of the four sons of Tsar Nicholas I—and a cousin of Liszt's friend and patron Carl Alexander of Saxe-Weimar—he was a zealous supporter of the reforms carried out by his brother Tsar Alexander II; indeed, he incurred the odium of many in Court circles by his remark that the Russian nobility were 'not worth even spitting upon'. A music-lover and amateur cellist, he was the dedicatee of the piano score of Smetana's *The Bartered Bride*. Liszt he seems to have held in very high regard, nominating him an honorary member of the Imperial Academy of Music in St Petersburg at the time of his jubilee celebrations in 1873, and inviting him to that city in early 1886—a formidable journey which in the event the 74-year-old composer was spared from undertaking.

Cornelius, Peter (Mainz 1824–Mainz 1874). Making Liszt's acquaintance at Weimar in 1852, this versatile German composer—a nephew of the homonymous painter—soon became a valued and very well-liked member of the Altenburg circle, and an enthusiastic supporter, with an able pen, not only of the Hungarian master but also of Berlioz and Wagner. Already a composer of choral works, chamber music, and sonatas, he had studied acting, was a gifted linguist and translator, and had written good poetry and several opera libretti as well as some excellent articles on music. The fiasco, for extramusical reasons, of the première of his sparkling comic opera *The Barber of Bagdad* did not deter him from further ventures in this field. *The Cid* was performed successfully at Weimar in 1865; a third opera, *Gunlöd* (a subject taken from the *Edda*), remained unfinished.

'I can't tell you how sad I feel,' wrote Princess Wittgenstein to Adelheid von Schorn on learning of Cornelius's untimely death. 'I knew so much about him, and he about me! He always wanted to write my biography! . . . Let us thankfully and joyously remember his great qualities, his splendid talent, his noble soul, and his understanding heart!'

Cui, César Antonovich (Vilna 1835–Petrograd 1918), Russian military engineer, propagandist for Russian national music, and member of the group of composers known as the *moguchaya kuchka*. The arrangement made by Liszt—whom he visited at Weimar in the summer of 1876 and again in 1880—of his *Tarentelle* was the very last of the Hungarian master's many transcriptions for piano of works originally written for orchestra.

Czerny, Carl (Vienna 1791–Vienna 1857), Austrian pianist, composer—above all of technical exercises for the piano—and pedagogue of whom it has been said that he could have answered most impressively two questions so often asked of musicians, 'With whom did you study?' and 'Have you any interesting pupils?' To the first, his reply would have been 'Beethoven'; to the second, 'Yes, Liszt among others'. The former, to whom Czerny was taken as a boy, remained a lifelong friend and mentor. Of the latter, whom he taught from the spring of 1822 until the autumn of 1823, he afterwards wrote: 'It was plain that Nature herself had here formed a pianist.' 'The result of little Liszt's unfailing cheerfulness and good spirits, together with the extraordinary development of his talent, was that my parents loved him like a son, and I like a brother; and I not only taught him entirely gratis but also provided him with all the works he needed from the music literature as it then existed.' Although the pupil occasionally chafed at the master's pedagogical methods, he remained keenly aware of what he owed him—a debt which in after years he acknowledged publicly, as it were, with the dedication to Czerny of the *Grandes Etudes* and their later versions, the *Etudes d'exécution transcendante*. (See, also, Letter 346 to Pruckner.)

Debussy, Achille-Claude (Saint-Germain-en-Laye 1862–Paris 1918), French composer. As a young Prix de Rome winner living at the Villa Medici, Debussy thrice came into contact with Liszt, according to François Lesure (from details provided by the diary of Gabrielle Hébert, wife of Ernest Hébert, director of the Villa Medici) in his *Claude Debussy*: on 8 January 1886, when Liszt dined at the Héberts' and Debussy and Vidal played the Faust Symphony on two pianos; on the 9th, when Hébert, Debussy, and Vidal visited Liszt (this presumably being the occasion, recorded by Vidal in his memoirs, when he and Debussy played Chabrier's *Valses romantiques*); and on the 13th, when Liszt was again a guest at the Villa. On this last occasion he played three pieces to the assembled boarders, among them *Au bord d'une source* and his transcription of Schubert's *Ave Maria*. Long afterwards, Debussy recalled Liszt's use of the pedal, in a manner which, as it were, made the piano *breathe*. 'I have heard only two fine pianists,' he remarked, 'my old piano teacher and Liszt.'

Deguerry (or **Du Guerry**), **Abbé Gaspard** (Lyons 1796–Paris 1871), French priest and popular preacher who became *curé* at the Madeleine and in 1868 was entrusted with the religious education of the Prince Imperial. It was he who, in February 1869, administered the last rites to the dying Lamartine. Arrested (10 April 1871) as a hostage by order of the Commune, he was first held at the Mazas prison and then, together with Darboy and Bonjean, shot (24 May) in the courtyard of the prison of La Roquette.

Dingelstedt, Franz (von) (Halsdorf, Hessen, 1814–Vienna 1881), German poet, novelist and dramatist who was appointed Royal Librarian at Stuttgart in 1843, Intendant (general manager) of the Munich Court Theatre in 1851, and six years later to the equivalent post in Weimar. In 1867 he became director of the Vienna Opera and, in 1870, of that city's Burgtheater, where he remained until his death.

As a *littérateur* and man of the theatre, Dingelstedt possessed very considerable talent. Among his memorable productions in Weimar were a 'masterpiece' of a *Winter's Tale* in 1859, the two parts of Hebbel's *Nibelungen* in 1861, and an outstanding cycle of Shakespeare's histories in the tercentenary year of 1864; he was also a notable translator of Shakespeare and a founder of the German Shakespeare Society. By common consent, however, the man was by no means as admirable as some of his achievements. Having obtained the Intendancy in Weimar (after being dismissed from the Munich Theatre) with the help of Liszt, he quickly set to work to undermine him, the culmination of his efforts being the débâcle at the première of *The Barber of Bagdad* and Liszt's resignation. Later, he also caused the loss to the Weimar Theatre of the universally admired Rosa von Milde. 'A more delightful companion there could hardly be—so long as it suited him,' remembered Adelheid von Schorn; 'his mind and his mood could change from one moment to the next.' The same source records that the Grand Duchess Sophie summed up Dingelstedt, simply and succinctly, as 'un caractère abominable'.

Draeseke, Felix (Coburg 1835–Dresden 1913), German composer who attended Liszt's Leipzig Gewandhaus concert of 26 February 1857, there met the composer—who seemed a 'supernatural personality'—and became one of his most enthusiastic adherents. In the summer of 1858 he was Liszt's guest at the Altenburg, a memorable experience which, at the time of his seventieth birthday nearly half a century later, he recalled in an article, 'My First Long Stay at Franz Liszt's in Weimar' (*Neue Zeitschrift für Musik*, 4 Oct. 1905), penning therein also his impressions of such fellow guests as Alexander Serov and Wilhelm von Kaulbach. Liszt admired Draeseke's opera *König Sigurd*, but his hopes of mounting a performance of the work were dashed when, in December 1858, he found it necessary to resign from his Kapellmeister duties following the reception accorded to an outstanding work by another of his protégés.

Dunkl, Nepomuk János (Johann Nepomuk) (Vienna 1832–Budapest 1910), Hungarian pianist, and a partner in the Rózsavölgyi music publishing-house, who as a boy was a pupil of Liszt, as he recalled in his *Aus den Erinnerungen eines Musikers* (Vienna, 1876).

Eckstein, Ferdinand, Baron d' (Copenhagen 1790–Paris 1861), French man of letters of Danish origin, described thus by Lamartine in his *Cours de Littérature*: 'Philosopher, poet, publicist, Orientalist, a Brahmin of the West, misunderstood by his contemporaries, living in one century but actually present in another.'

Engeszer, Katalin, née Marsch, Hungarian singer who seems to have been active in promoting Liszt's works in Budapest, and who sang the title role in the performance of *The Legend of St Elisabeth* conducted by Liszt at the Vigadó on 5 Mar. 1877.

Erard, Pierre (Paris 1796–Passy 1855), head of the French piano-manufacturing firm from 1831. When the 12-year-old Liszt and his parents arrived in Paris in December 1823, they took accommodation at the Hôtel d'Angleterre which, standing in the rue du Mail, was very near the home of the Erard family, among whom were at this time the founder of the firm, Sébastien Erard (1752–1831), his brother Jean-Baptiste (1749–1826), and the latter's son Pierre. In a short time the two families were on such good terms that the young pianist came to regard the Erards as his 'adoptive family'. For years it was Erard instruments—with their new double-escapement action—that he played whenever possible. He was always on particularly friendly terms with Pierre, who in 1824 accompanied Adam and Franz to London, where the firm had a branch for nearly a century.

The Erards also owned the splendid Château de la Muette. Once a royal residence, this mansion, standing at the Passy Gate opening into the Bois de Boulogne, was surrounded by 'the largest and most beautiful private grounds in Paris'. Originally named La Meute (as the place where Louis XV reared dogs for hunting in the Bois), it had been acquired by the wealthy Sébastien Erard, renamed, and filled with the many artistic treasures he had accumulated. Even in later life, long after the death of Pierre, Liszt was occasionally the guest here of his friend's widow, the charitable Mme Camille Erard (1813–89), who attracted to La Muette under the Second Empire an intellectual élite among which—as was to be expected—music was especially well represented. Every year, the Erard firm presented a grand piano to the winner of the first prize at the Conservatoire, Pleyel giving one to the runner-up.

Erkel, Ferenc (Gyula 1810–Budapest 1893), Hungarian composer, pianist, and teacher. Remembered above all for his two greatest operas, *Hunyady László* (1844) and *Bánk bán* (1861), he was also the composer of the Hungarian national anthem. When, in 1875, Budapest's Royal Academy of Music was opened, Liszt was its President, Erkel its Director.

Ernst II (Coburg 1818–Reinhardsbrunn 1893), Duke of Saxe-Coburg-Gotha from 29 January 1844. Liszt, who arranged for piano solo the 'Halloh! Jagdchor und Steyrer' from the Duke's opera *Tony*, conducted the première of his *Santa Chiara*, and attended those of *Zaire* and *Diana von Solange*, evidently thought rather well of this keen music-lover and amateur composer. Someone who, towards the end of the Duke's life, took a more jaundiced view of him was his great-niece Marie, the subsequent Queen of Romania, who in her memoirs devoted several delightful pages to the 'dissolute old reprobate' and his wife, daughter of a Grand Duke of Baden: 'She was a mild lady, perfectly virtuous, perfectly colourless and resembling her sister-in-law, Queen Victoria, only by her unlimited and (in her case) inexplicable adoration of her lord and master. He treated her with abominable, insulting indifference, and was known all over Germany for his never-ending and often none too dignified amorous adventures. . . .'

Evans, Mary Ann or **Marian** (Arbury Farm, nr. Nuneaton, 1819–Chelsea 1880), English novelist known, after the publication in early 1857 of the first of her *Scenes of Clerical Life*, under the pen-name of George Eliot. Deeply impressed by the playing and personality of Liszt, whom she met when she accompanied G. H. Lewes to Weimar in 1854, she wrote of him at length in her diary, in her letters, and in an article ('Liszt, Wagner, and Weimar') published the following year in *Fraser's Magazine* ('Take him all in all, he is a glorious creature—one of those men whom the ancients would have imagined the son of a god or goddess, from their superiority to the common clay of humanity'). Liszt and the Princess seem likewise to have thought well of the interesting couple from England whose relationship—and the fact that they were never able to marry—had not a few points in common with their own: the lively, versatile, partly French-educated Lewes, and the sympathetic, deep-feeling, enormously intellectual Miss Evans. They might, however, have felt some astonishment had they known that when, twenty-six years later, this outwardly unremarkable Englishwoman came to die, it was proposed that she be buried in Westminster Abbey on the ground that her achievements were 'without parallel in the previous history of womankind' (John Tyndall to Dean Stanley, Christmas Day, 1880). Her remains actually lie, near Lewes's, in Highgate Cemetery.

Ferrazzi, Giuseppe Iacopo (Cartigliano 1813–Bassano 1887), Italian priest and patriot, and the author or compiler of, *inter alia*, a *Bibliografia Petrarchesca*, a *Bibliografia Ariostesca*, a *Torquato Tasso* and, above all, a very useful and well-received *Manuale Dantesco*, which appeared in five volumes, 1865–77.

Franck, César Auguste (Liège 1822–Paris 1890), Belgian composer, organist, pianist, and teacher, one of the numerous outstanding nineteenth-century musicians who was given a helping hand by Liszt. Their first meeting was probably in April 1837, at a concert in which Liszt made a guest appearance and the 14-year-old Franck played a Fantasy by Hummel. Liszt later showed particular interest in the younger composer's three Piano Trios, Op. 1, which he played at Weimar, and in gratitude for his support and encouragement Franck dedicated to him the Piano Trio, Op. 2.

Gille, Carl (Weimar 1813–Ilmenau 1899), legal adviser in Jena who was for many years a close friend of Liszt and, after the composer's death, first Curator of Weimar's Liszt Museum. After concerts in Jena, Liszt and his entourage of pupils—and on one occasion Alexander Borodin—often repaired to Gille's home for refreshments, as described in a letter (1873) by Amy Fay, an American pupil: 'At seven we were all invited to tea at the house of a friend of Liszt's. He was a very tall man, and he had a very tall and hospitable daughter, nearly as big as himself, who received us very cordially. The tea was all laid on tables in the garden, and the sausages were cooking over a fire.' (The daughter was Gille's foster daughter, Anna Spiering.)

Gregorovius, Ferdinand (Neidenburg, East Prussia, 1821–Munich 1891). To do research for his *magnum opus*, *Geschichte der Stadt Rom im Mittelalter*, a multi-volume history of Rome from AD 400 until the death of Pope Clement VII in 1534, this distinguished German historian lived in the city for more than twenty years; here, from the early 1860s, he was frequently in the company of Liszt and the Princess Wittgenstein, both of whom are mentioned *passim* in his *Roman Journals*. Several of his graphic descriptions of Liszt —'a striking, uncanny figure ... tall, thin, and with long grey hair', 'a truly sovereign personality', 'a piano-centaur', 'Mephistopheles disguised as an abbé'—rank among the best known of the composer by his contemporaries.

Among his other works are *History of the Emperor Hadrian and His Time*, *Corsica*, *Lucrezia Borgia*, *The Tombs of the Popes*, and *History of the City of Athens in the Middle Ages*.

Grieg, Edvard Hagerup (Bergen 1843–Bergen 1907), Norwegian composer who, at a time early in his career when the outlook was bleak, received out of the blue a friendly letter from Liszt which provided impressive support to his application—consequently successful—for a travel grant. (See Letter 611 in the present volume.) In Rome he was given a warm welcome and much encouragement by the older musician, who played at sight part of Grieg's Violin and Piano Sonata in G ('He was literally all over the whole piano at once, without a note being missed. And how, then, did he play? With majesty, beauty, genius beyond compare . . .') and the whole of the Piano Concerto. 'In him,' wrote Grieg, 'I have learned to know not only the most talented of all pianists, but what is more—a phenomenon of spirit and greatness, with no limits in the domain of art.'

Gubernatis, Count Angelo de (Turin 1840–Rome 1913), Italian orientalist and man of letters who taught Sanscrit and comparative philology in Florence 1863–90, and Italian literature, as well as Sanscrit, in Rome 1890–1908. It was at Florence in January 1882 that he made Liszt's acquaintance, as he recalled in his *Fibra: Pagine di Ricordi*:

Liszt's old friend, Princess Wittgenstein, had urged him to spend just one night in an hotel, and to continue his journey in the morning without seeing anyone; and she begged Baron Imre Augusz, who was devoted to Liszt, to look after him. Count Géza Kuun, the Marchese Czáky Pallavicino—married to a Contessa Orsini, a dear and intelligent Sienese lady—and I were told by Augusz that Liszt would be passing through Florence, and between us we hatched a plot to abduct him at the station. The Marchesa was absolutely insistent on having him in her palazzo, and without more ado she ordered an elegant banquet in his honour. At the station, Baron Augusz, Count Kuun, and I met him with the Marchese's carriage. Liszt thought we were taking him to the hotel; instead, we entered an illuminated palazzo which, to welcome him, had been made festive and adorned with flowers; smiling most pleasantly, the gracious Marchesa walked towards him. At first astonished, Liszt then showed his delight. The elegant and sumptuous meal ended, by way of a toast, with an improvisation of mine. Having heard from Liszt, while we were awaiting the meal, how gratified he was to have received in his early youth a kiss on the brow from Beethoven, the Jupiter of music, and since Liszt was now giving himself wholly to sacred music, I took this for my theme:

> A te stampava un dì Giove sul fronte,
>   Di Beethoven col bacio, l'armonia;
>   E un fiume uscì da la sacrata fonte,
>   Un fiume di vibrata poesia;
>
> Corse plaghe diverse e mille genti,
>   Nel vario e ratto suo vibrar, commosse;
>   Cercando il porto, alfin, fra preci ardenti,
>   Sull'ali de la fede, a Dio si mosse.

Gubernatis also wrote admiringly of the Comtesse d'Agoult, excerpts from whose letters were published as an appendix to his book *Etincelles*.

Hagn, Charlotte von (Munich 1809–Munich 1891), made her début in 1826 and, beautiful, intelligent, gifted, and graceful, was soon one of the most admired of German actresses. Much of her career—she retired from the stage in 1846 after her marriage (short-lived) to Alexander von Oven—was spent in Berlin, where she met Liszt at the time of his unparalleled triumphs in that city. Mutually attracted, they remained on good terms after Liszt's departure; her feelings, in particular, seem never to have waned, and in a letter of May 1849 in which she thanked him for helping her protégée Fräulein Fastlinger (the first Ortrud in *Lohengrin*), she wrote: 'Years have passed since I found and lost you, but I must admit that because of you I have been spoilt for all other men; for none, *not a single one*, can bear the least comparison. You are and remain *unique*.'

Haynald, Lajos (Szécsény 1816–Kalocsa 1891), Hungarian prelate who, when Liszt made his acquaintance in 1856, was Bishop of Transylvania; but in 1862, having fallen foul of the Austrian Government about matters pertaining to that diocese, he resigned his see and went into a six-year exile, much of it spent in Rome. Returning to Hungary after the establishment of the Dual Monarchy, he was soon afterwards made Archbishop of Kalocsa—where Liszt was on several occasions his guest—and in 1879 a Cardinal. Distinguished not only as a churchman, he also possessed eminent gifts as writer, states-man, diplomat, orator, and *savant*. Very charitable, and an outstanding botanist, he founded the Haynald Fund for promoting scholarship, art, and science, and to the Hungarian National Museum presented a valuable library with a herbarium collected over forty years and accounted one of the richest in Europe. Not surprisingly, Liszt, whom he much admired, much admired him.

Henselt, Adolf von (Schwabach, Bavaria, 1814–Warmbrunn, Silesia, 1889), German pianist, composer, and teacher whose acquaintance Liszt made in St Petersburg in 1842. Apparently terrified of performing in public, Henselt made few appearances, but by the cognoscenti was nevertheless very highly regarded. Clara Schumann said that so glori-ous and 'fragrant' a touch as his she had never heard, nor would ever herself achieve. 'Liszt, Chopin, and Henselt are continents; Tausig, Rubinstein, and Bülow are coun-tries,' observed Wilhelm von Lenz. And Rubinstein himself opined that, to know what genuine piano-playing meant, 'one must have heard Chopin, Liszt, Thalberg, and Henselt'. A sympathetic pen-portrait of this interesting figure was drawn by his pupil Bettina Walker in her *My Musical Experiences* (London, 1890).

Hiller, Ferdinand (Frankfurt am Main 1811–Cologne 1885), German composer, pianist, conductor, and critic, a friend of Liszt in Paris in the late 1820s and early 1830s, but in after years, as a musical conservative, deeply hostile to his music (and that of Wagner), as he made clear at the time of the Lower Rhine Music Festival in 1857. His book *Künstlerleben* (Cologne, 1880) contains an 'Open Letter to Franz Liszt' which is super-ficially friendly in tone and includes some reminiscences of their acquaintance in Paris and Milan more than forty years earlier.

Hippeau, Edmond Gabriel (1849–1921), French writer and music critic, author of *Berlioz intime* (Paris, 1883) and *Berlioz et son temps* (Paris, 1890).

Hohenlohe-Schillingsfürst, Cardinal Prince Gustav Adolf von (Rothenburg ob der Tauber 1823–Rome 1896), played an important part in Liszt's life from the early 1860s onwards, firstly by working behind the scenes to prevent his marriage to Princess Wittgenstein. Once that matter was out of the way, however, he proved himself a good friend to the composer. It was he who, in 1865, when still Papal Grand Almoner, gave him the tonsure and provided him with accommodation in the Vatican. From the mid-1860s he also generously made available to him an apartment at the Villa d'Este—thus securing him a refuge from the bustle of Rome, and the solitude, in entrancing sur-roundings, so necessary for his work.

Several of Cardinal Hohenlohe's relatives and acquaintances wrote of his hatred of the Jesuits and his conviction that they would eventually murder him, probably by poison. According to Lady Helena Gleichen, he was even 'obliged to keep a taster, as in medieval times, who tasted all his food before he touched it'. Richard Voss, in his memoirs, stated categorically that the Cardinal did, indeed, suffer an unnatural death, 'brought about, at the instigation of his enemies, by one of those official servants of his upon whom he had lavished so many kindnesses'. (*The Times* in its obituary gave the cause of death as 'apoplexy'.) However that may be, the description of this engaging prelate by his niece Princess Marie von Thurn und Taxis makes it easy to understand Liszt's affection for him: 'He was a typical *grand-seigneur*—actually more *grand-seigneur* than priest. As he was very slender, he looked taller than he was; he had fair hair, very blue eyes, regular features and his whole appearance was very youthful. . . . He was excellent company, very amusing, dangerously sarcastic, a spendthrift, and always in debt; nevertheless he had the best horses of the entire College of Cardinals, and his servants wore magnificent (and entirely correct) liveries—pure white trimmed with red and silver galloons and embroidered with the leopard, the Hohenlohe crest.'

Also well known to Liszt were Gustav's three brothers: **Prince Victor** (1818–93), Duke of Ratibor, soldier, politician, and philanthropist; **Prince Chlodwig** (1819–1901), who in 1874 was appointed German Ambassador in Paris, in 1885 Governor of Alsace Lorraine, and between 1894 and 1900 was Chancellor of Germany and Prime Minister of Prussia; and **Prince Constantin** (1828–96). The last-named, an official at the Austrian court, in October 1859 married Princess Marie von Sayn-Wittgenstein.

Hohenzollern-Hechingen, Prince Friedrich Wilhelm Constantin von (1801–69), a keen music-lover who was on several occasions Liszt's host at Löwenberg in Silesia. Among his guests at other times were Berlioz and Wagner; and in his memoirs the French composer penned a splendid description of a concert at Löwenberg, where the orchestra was directed for a number of years by Max Seifriz (1827–85), regarded by Liszt as 'one of the most intelligent and experienced conductors in Germany'. The Prince's first wife was a Princess of Leuchtenburg (1808–47); in 1850 he entered into a morganatic alliance with the 18-year-old Countess von Rothenburg, a marriage which thirteen years later ended in divorce.

Holmès, Augusta (Paris 1847–Paris 1903), French composer of Irish parentage, but possibly the daughter of Alfred de Vigny, who showed great interest in her upbringing. In 1875 she became a pupil of César Franck, on whom her beauty and personality had a pronounced effect, as they did on many others. 'We were all in love with her,' said Saint-Saëns, whose offer of marriage she declined (but not the overtures of Judith Gautier's husband, Catulle Mendès, father of her three daughters). Among her works are operas (to her own libretti), symphonies, symphonic poems, and choral works. She was also a pianist and singer. Her reception by Wagner at Tribschen in 1869 was witnessed by Marie Mouchanoff: 'Wagner was very cool to begin with; he found her manner of singing Isolde *frightful*, but gave sincere praise to her compositions. Little Holmès was pale and trembling, nothing left of her aplomb, nor of her make-up and toiletries. A modest black dress and curtsies down to the very floor.'

Hugo, Victor-Marie (Besançon 1802–Paris 1885), French poet, novelist, and dramatist, the outstanding figure of the Romantic movement in France. It was in May 1829, at the time when the young Liszt was studying French literature (and much else) with the utmost enthusiasm, that he was introduced to 'the great Victor'; thereafter he saw him frequently and eagerly devoured his works as they made their appearance. Several of them inspired creations of his own—half a dozen songs, the official title (*Après une lecture de Dante*) of the Dante Sonata, two symphonic poems, and the late *Le Crucifix*.

Following the *coup d'état* of 2 December 1851, and until 1870, Hugo lived in exile on the Channel Islands. He and Liszt met again—for the last time—in 1878. For his birthday in 1854, however, Liszt had received a telegram from Reményi, visiting Jersey, and been delighted to read a message added to it by the great writer: 'The exile of Jersey shakes hands with the Orpheus of Weimar.'

Humboldt, Baron Alexander von (Berlin 1769–Berlin 1859), German naturalist, geographer, traveller, and all-round man of science, younger brother of the philologist Wilhelm von Humboldt. Between 1799 and 1804, accompanied by the French botanist Aimé Bonpland, he undertook a scientific expedition to South America in which he climbed Mount Chimborazo, almost to the top—a feat, taking him to the highest altitude ever reached by a human being up to that time, which brought him great celebrity; he was later said to be the most famous man in Europe after Napoleon. In 1829, at the invitation of Tsar Nicholas, he carried out scientific studies in the Urals (where thanks to him, and while he was present, the first diamond deposit in Russia was discovered), before pushing on through the Siberian steppes as far as the border with China. By the time he arrived back in Berlin (a city to which he far preferred Paris—just as he preferred French to German—and lived in only at the express wish of the King) he had travelled a distance equal to nearly half the circumference of the globe.

One of his numerous eminent acquaintances was Goethe, who in conversation with Eckermann spoke admiringly of Humboldt's many-sidedness and of the generosity with which he shared the inexhaustible wealth of his intellectual treasures. 'What a man he is! Long as I have known him, he ever surprises me anew. One may say he has not his equal in knowledge and living wisdom.'

Among the literary achievements of this outstanding man, and great humanitarian, are *Aspects of Nature*, his most popular book, and the monumental *Cosmos*, a vast and comprehensive survey of natural phenomena. 'His canvas was the universe, and he used his pencil with a master hand,' observed his obituarist in *The Times*. 'His merits are of such transcendent quality that praise is out of place.'

Hummel, Johann Nepomuk (Pressburg [Pozsony] 1778–Weimar 1837), Austrian pianist, composer, teacher, and conductor who studied with, among others, Mozart, Haydn, and Salieri, and was later on friendly terms with Beethoven. Among his own pupils were Henselt and Hiller—but cupidity lost him the chance of one of far greater distinction, as Liszt recalled in the postscript to Letter 510.

That the two pianists did, however, encounter one another is made clear in Adam Liszt's letter of 14 August 1825 to Czerny (from Paris): 'We gave our concert at the theatre . . . and a second at Erard's. . . . But Hummel did not attend; probably so as not to have to see for himself that someone can have a larger audience than he. But that did not bother me, and at his next soirée I placed my boy at his side to turn the pages for him.' Said Hummel, when he heard the playing of his young colleague, 'the fellow's an iron-eater!'

From 1819 he was one of Liszt's predecessors in Weimar where, like Liszt in his last years, he lived in the Marienstrasse. His widow Elisabeth, née Röckel, long survived him, dying in that same town in 1883 at the age of 90.

Janina, Olga (b. 1845). At Rome in the spring of 1869 this eccentric young Pole became a pupil of the 57-year-old Liszt and was soon infatuated with him. 'With her wide mouth, turned-up nose, close-cropped hair, she made an impression of no great beauty,' remembered the sculptor Josef von Kopf. 'But that soon faded away when she spoke, or when she sat at the piano and gave a virtuoso performance of her sonatas. . . . She was terribly jealous of the Master; and for her rivals, of whom there were dozens, she felt a violent hatred.' By Gregorovius she was summed up as 'a little witty, foolish person, mad about Liszt'.

Her real name was Olga Zielinska. In 1863 she had married Karol Janina Piasecki; adopting his middle name, she then gave herself out to be the Countess Janina.

The 'Cossack Countess', as she has been called, also spent time with Liszt at the Villa d'Este, in Tivoli, and in due course followed him to Weimar, Pest, and even Szekszárd. When, however, her unseemly behaviour caused him to sever relations, she sought revenge, first by threatening him with a revolver and then by writing a book—*Souvenirs d'une Cosaque*, published (1874) under the pseudonym 'Robert Franz'—which told the world, truthfully or otherwise, that a certain 'X' (only too easily identifiable as the Abbé Liszt) had been her lover. There followed from the same pen other books of a similar nature.

It was thought by Liszt that after the scene in Pest in which she threatened his life, Olga then fled to Paris. Following the publication of Malou Haine's *Franz Servais et Franz Liszt*, we now know that it was with the Servais family in Hal that she found refuge, until eventually being sent about her business by Servais's mother. When she left she was accompanied by Servais, who thought very highly of the pianistic talent of this 'great artiste'—which, he wrote, was 'not of those that can be acquired in this world'.

When, years later, Olga had fallen on hard times and was trying to earn a living by teaching, Liszt sought to assist her anonymously. 'She was not wicked,' he remarked, 'just exalted.'

Joachim, Joseph (Kitsee [now Köpcsény], nr. Pozsony, 1831–Berlin 1907), Austro-Hungarian violinist greatly helped by Liszt, at whose recommendation he was in 1850 appointed leader of the Weimar orchestra and, two years later, to a more lucrative position in Hanover. 'I shall see his departure with *great regret*,' Liszt remarked, 'but I have his interests too much at heart to prevent him advancing his career.' In 1857, however, in response to a friendly invitation he had sent to Joachim to attend the music festival in Weimar, he received from the violinist—who had probably been offended by Wagner's anti-Semitic tract *Judaism in Music* and certainly come under the baneful influence of Clara Schumann and her clique—a letter which not only referred slightingly to Liszt's works but virtually severed all relations. From that time forward the 'grateful pupil', as he had styled himself, seems to have regarded his benefactor and would-be friend as an enemy. 'We must oust the name of Liszt,' became his watchword. In 1860, with Johannes Brahms and two others, he went so far as to put his name to an absurd 'manifesto', published in a Berlin newspaper, which protested against the music, theories, and tendencies of the New German School; i.e. those of Liszt, Wagner, and their disciples. From 1868 he was director of Berlin's Hochschule für Musik, where one of his diktats was to ban the study of works by Liszt. After a further dozen years, apparently impelled by regret and shame, he sought a reconciliation, being then very warmly and generously received by the composer whose creations he had for a quarter of a century opposed so unrelentingly.

Cosima Wagner in her diary described Joachim as a 'thoroughly bad person'—an opinion which, though he was incontestably less admirable as a man than as a player, seems a trifle harsh and perhaps owes something to her second husband's loathing of the violinist as well as to the anti-Semitic views Cosima shared with both her husbands. A juster assessment is probably that of Adelheid von Schorn: 'Joachim was regarded by Liszt's and Wagner's supporters as a two-faced apostate. I knew him well later and found him, not two-faced, merely weak and feeble.'

Juhász, Aladár (1856–1922), Hungarian pianist and writer on music of whom Géza Zichy penned a graphic description: 'A small, frail little man, the type of a Socrates, Aladár Juhász is one of the most remarkable artistic figures I have ever known. Highly gifted and erudite, philosopher, musician, and pianist in one person, he totally lacked any kind of ambition or vanity, practised his art only for his own enjoyment, and never undertook concert tours or gave himself airs. The fact that he was for many years my children's teacher gave me an opportunity to get to know and admire not only his knowledge but also his noble, chivalrous turn of mind. . . . His studies and interests were varied: for a while he immersed himself in Brahmanism, then in Christian theology, studied philosophy, the Zend-Avesta, then medicine, and finally devoted himself passionately to chess. . . . How often did I find him lying under the piano solving chess problems! He is much too gifted an individual, and all these fruits could not come to full ripeness. Pathologically he is a miracle. A more wretched body, possessing such tremendous strength in its hands, I have never seen. Having begun to spit blood when still in his early youth, he eventually became so weak and frail that the doctors gave him up for lost. This was repeated several times—but he recovered nevertheless, and still lives today' (*Aus meinem Leben*, 3 vols., Stuttgart, 1911–20, ii 77–9).

Kalergis, Marie, see **Mouchanoff**.

Kaulbach, Wilhelm (von, 1866) (Arolsen 1805–Munich 1874), German painter. A pupil of Cornelius in Düsseldorf, he lived from 1826 in Munich, where in 1837 he became Court Painter to King Ludwig I and in 1839 Director of the Academy. Liszt made his acquaintance here in 1843 and they became good friends. Felix Draeseke, a fellow guest of Kaulbach's at the Altenburg in 1858, found the painter quite unmusical, and felt that he 'probably had not the least understanding of Liszt the composer, whereas Liszt, who had a fine understanding of the sister arts in general, and of painting in particular, will have valued Kaulbach at his true worth'. In conversation, he added, the painter was 'witty, charming, and fascinating'.

The painter of numerous portraits, among them two of Liszt (as well as a drawing and a caricature), Kaulbach also specialized in murals depicting scenes from history and mythology, and it was one of these that inspired the symphonic poem *Hunnenschlacht.*

Ketten, Henrik (Baja 1848–Paris 1883), Hungarian pianist and composer. 'This lad, scarcely seven years of age, completely stupefied me with his outstanding musical gifts,' wrote Bülow to Liszt in March 1855. 'He can transpose into different keys even the pieces he is seeing for the first time. An astonishing dexterity of fingers *born* for piano-playing, and a fabulously acute sense of hearing, make this little fellow truly interest-ing. He can decipher the most unusual chords without mistaking a single note, even when they follow one another rapidly. . . . I played him the opening bars of *Prometheus* and was amazed by the accuracy of his responses. . . .' Assessing the boy's ability in Weimar soon afterwards, Liszt promised Ketten *père* that he would try to obtain a grant for the young prodigy from the King of Prussia; he also advised him to put his son in Bülow's hands. To Bülow himself he wrote (10 June 1855): 'There is every reason to suppose that if you take an interest in him he will soon safely cross the straits of medio-crity in which so many others remain stranded more or less their whole lives long.'

Studying in Paris with Marmontel and Halévy, Ketten became a well-regarded pianist and composer of popular salon pieces, and died at the age of 35.

La Mara, see **Lipsius**.

Lamennais, Félicité Robert de (Saint-Malo 1782–Paris 1854), French thinker, Chris-tian democrat and religious writer, ordained in 1816, who first attracted attention with his *Essai sur l'indifférence en matière de religion* (1817–23), a work intended to arouse his contemporaries from their state of spiritual apathy. In September 1830 he brought out the first issue of *L'Avenir*, a journal which carried the epigraph 'God and Liberty' and advocated reforms of both a religious and a political nature. When it was condemned in the encyclical *Mirari vos*—promulgated as Lamennais, Lacordaire, and Montalembert were returning to France in August 1832 after a fruitless interview with Pope Gregory XVI—Lamennais submitted and the journal was withdrawn. Two years later, however, he finally rebelled against Rome in *Paroles d'un croyant*, a book—revealing an apoca-lyptic imagination and penned by a writer of genius—which created an almost unex-ampled sensation. It, too, was swiftly condemned by an encyclical, *Singulari nos* (25 June 1834).

Shortly before publication of *Paroles d'un croyant*, the 22-year-old Liszt was introduced to the charismatic rebel. 'I have made the acquaintance of Liszt, whom I liked greatly, a young man full of soul,' wrote Lamennais to Montalembert on 18 April 1834. To another, later correspondent he described Liszt as 'one of the finest and noblest souls I have met on this earth, where they are not excessively common'. Nor was he any less enthusiastic about his new friend's talent, remarking that Liszt was 'the greatest pianist he had ever heard or who had ever existed'. It was to Lamennais (in 1835 a courageous supporter of certain rebellious Lyonnais workmen who were brought to trial) that Liszt dedicated *Lyon* (opening piece of the *Album d'un voyageur*) as well as the unfinished *De profundis*.

Among the young disciples of 'Monsieur Féli' who at various times were members of his small Christian community at La Chênaie, prominent are the names of Lacordaire, Gerbet, Montalembert, and Maurice de Guérin. The last-named, a visitor in 1832, wrote to his father, and to his equally famed sister Eugénie, descriptions of his host, the house and grounds not unlike those sent by Liszt two years later to Marie d'Agoult.

In 1840 Lamennais was tried for a breach of the laws against the press and sentenced to a year's imprisonment. Among the achievements of later years was a translation of Dante. He died unreconciled with the Church and, at his own wish, his remains were interred (at Père Lachaise) in the common burial ground reserved for paupers.

Lassen, Eduard (Copenhagen 1830–Weimar 1904), composer of Danish origin brought up in Brussels and in 1851 winner of the Belgian Prix de Rome. Visiting Weimar, he was so enchanted by Liszt and his circle that he settled in the town, where in 1857 two performances were mounted of his opera *Landgraf Ludwigs Brautfahrt*. He later succeeded Liszt as Court Kapellmeister.

Adelheid von Schorn enjoyed a close friendship with Lassen and after his death came into possession of his letters to his parents, from which she quotes extensively in her *Das nachklassische Weimar*. 'Not only did he do excellent work for the theatre,' she remarks, 'he was also very popular in society, playing and conducting, composing and helping, as often as he was asked. . . . He had hardly a single enemy, but on the contrary a circle of friends who received each of his compositions with joy. His operas obtained little success, but there are wonderful things among his songs, which today—and quite unjustly—are almost forgotten. Liszt liked and esteemed him, but sometimes gave a superior smile if, in their praise of Lassen's works, the latter's admirers got a little too carried away. . . .'

Laussot, Jessie (1827–1905), née Taylor, English-born musician who, accompanied by her mother, in September 1854 presented herself at the Altenburg in Weimar, receiving 'ineffaceable impressions' at one of Liszt's Sunday musical matinées and becoming thereafter one of his most valued friends and supporters. Much of her life was spent in Florence, where she founded and directed a choral society named—after a distinguished musical son of that city—the Società Cherubini. In her youth she had been a good friend of Hans von Bülow, and it was with her that he found refuge when, in psychological turmoil after his wife had abandoned him, he left his native Germany for a time. After the death in 1879 of her mentally disturbed husband, Eugène Laussot, from whom she had long been separated, Mme Laussot married her friend Karl Hillebrand (Giessen 1829–Florence 1884), German cultural historian and author of, *inter alia*, the seven-volume *Zeiten, Völker und Menschen*, a work read and enjoyed by Liszt.

Lebert, Sigmund (Ludwigsburg 1822–Stuttgart 1884), né Levy, German pianist and teacher, a founder of the Stuttgart Conservatorium and, with Ludwig Stark, editor of the 'Grosse Klavierschule' for which Liszt wrote the concert studies *Waldesrauschen* and *Gnomenreigen*.

Lehmann, Heinrich (or **Henri**) (Kiel 1814–Paris 1882), German historical and portrait painter whom Liszt and Marie d'Agoult knew well in Paris (whither he came in
1831 to study with Ingres) and later saw much of in Rome, and whom they nicknamed
'Clear placid', or simply 'Clear'—from Byron's apostrophe, in *Childe Harold*, to Lake
Geneva: 'Clear, placid Léman!' Of his two portraits of Liszt, it was that done at Lucca
in 1839 which, when exhibited at the Paris *Salon* of 1840, helped earn Lehmann a Gold
Medal. His much admired Marie d'Agoult he painted or drew at least five times.

His brother **Rudolf** (Ottensen, nr. Hamburg, 1819–Bushey, Herts, 1905), likewise
a painter, made Liszt's acquaintance on Heligoland in September 1849, as he did, too,
that of the Princess Wittgenstein, whom in his memoirs he recalled as being 'irresistibly
hypnotized by Liszt's marvellous personality, which had in it a rare mixture of strength
and sweetness, of genius and worldly wisdom'. Settling in London in 1850, Rudolf later
took British nationality.

Lenz, Wilhelm von (Riga 1809–St Petersburg 1883), Russian writer on music who in
his *Die grossen Pianoforte-Virtuosen unserer Zeit* (Berlin, 1872) penned valuable character sketches and reminiscences of Liszt, Chopin, Tausig, and Henselt. His other most
notable book is *Beethoven et ses trois styles* (2 vols., St Petersburg, 1852), in which he
proposed the division of Beethoven's works into three styles.

Lichnowsky, Prince Felix von (Grätz 1814–Frankfurt am Main 1848), a grandson of
Prince Carl von Lichnowsky, the friend and patron of Mozart and Beethoven, made
Liszt's acquaintance early in 1841 and was soon his closest male friend as well as, from
time to time, his host and travelling companion. Felix's early death occurred after he
had gone to Frankfurt as a delegate at the National Assembly. Out riding, he was ambushed
by revolutionary elements, pursued, cornered, and virtually hacked to death, the *coup
de grâce* being provided by a bullet. It was him to whom Liszt also referred when, in
his memoir of Chopin, he wrote of the composer as 'one of the two dearest friends we
have ever known on earth'.

Lipsius, Marie (Leipzig 1837–Schmölen, nr. Wurzen, 1927), German musicologist, known
by her pseudonym of La Mara, one of Liszt's most devoted admirers. Her many publications include eleven volumes of his letters and another three of letters addressed to
him by distinguished contemporaries, her labours on which she described in the memoirs *Durch Musik und Leben*. She also translated his book on Chopin for inclusion in
the German collected edition of his writings. Her unique contribution to Liszt studies
was acknowledged by Jessie Laussot when, seventeen years after his death, she paid Marie
Lipsius a merited tribute: 'Merely being aware that he lived, does one good. And yet
that noble and wonderful man is still far from being recognized, as man and artist, as
he deserves to be. And so I am grateful to all who help to do him fitting justice. Among
them, you are in the forefront.'

Liszt, Adam (Edelsthal [Nemesvölgy], nr. Pozsony, 16 Dec. 1776–Boulogne-sur-Mer,
28 Aug. 1827) and **Anna** (Krems, Lower Austria, 9 May 1788–Paris, 6 Feb. 1866), née
Lager, the parents of Franz Liszt. Employed by Prince Nicholas Esterházy as *ovium rationista*

(superintendent of sheep), Adam, an educated man and friend of Haydn and Hummel, was also a keen amateur musician, whose talent was summed up—from information supplied by his son—in the biographical study of Franz Liszt written by Joseph d'Ortigue: 'Without being a pianist of the first order, Adam Liszt possessed rather a remarkable talent as a performer. A consummate musician, he could play nearly all instruments. Had his family possessed a greater fortune, and had fourteen or fifteen brothers and sisters not laid claim to the greater part of the sacrifices necessary to open up a brilliant career for him, and to obtain him opportunities for development, he could have become a distinguished artiste.' The same source tells us that Adam derived consolation from the exceptional nature of his son's talent, his firm belief in which impelled him to move the whole family from Raiding to Vienna. By so doing, he laid the foundations of the phenomenal career that was to come—as Franz gratefully acknowledged in the letter to his mother of 12 September 1862. It may be concluded that it was from his father that Franz inherited his courage, determination, strength of purpose, superior intelligence, mystical tendencies, and—in even greater measure—his musicality.

Adam was himself the second child of the thrice-married Georg Adam Liszt (György Ádám List), a village schoolmaster (among other occupations) who altogether fathered twenty-five children.

Anna was at one time employed as a chambermaid in Vienna, but then went to stay with a brother in Mattersdorf; and it was here that she met Adam. After his death she settled in Paris, a city of which she became very fond and which remained her home for the rest of her life. As devoted a grandmother as she was a mother, she was entrusted by Liszt in the 1840s with the care of his children, all of whom returned in full the love and affection she lavished upon them.

A contemporary report tells us that when Anna Liszt died, in her seventy-eighth year, her coffin was followed by an 'endless line of carriages of the old hereditary nobility and of the aristocrats of finance, of senators and deputies, of poets and writers, of journalists, artists and actors'. That this once semi-literate chambermaid had been acquainted with so many personages of distinction may be ascribed to the celebrity of her son; that they liked her, respected her, and sought her company, was a tribute to her own warm-heartedness, sincerity, and uprightness of character.

Liszt, Blandine (Geneva, 18 Dec. 1835–Saint-Tropez, 11 Sept. 1862), **Cosima** (Como, 24 Dec. 1837–Bayreuth, 1 Apr. 1930), and **Daniel** (Rome, 9 May 1839–Berlin, 13 Dec. 1859), the children of Liszt and Marie d'Agoult. Exemplary though it was in so many ways, Liszt's life is not wholly above reproach. Blame can be attached to him for his failure to have regular personal contact with his children during their formative years, after his break with their mother. By entrusting them to his own mother, he ensured that they would be lovingly cared for, and he took pains to see that they received an excellent education. But by allowing more than seven years (1846–53) to go by without a meeting with them—and since they were at that time forbidden to see Mme d'Agoult— he inadvertently condemned them to the existence of orphans. Happily, his relations with them from the mid-1850s onwards, particularly after the marriages of the two girls, were warm and affectionate. News of the death of Blandine came to him as a shattering blow. And had this charming and adoring daughter been granted a normal lifespan, the later years of Liszt's own life would surely have been far happier.

Also at one time a loving daughter, Cosima changed perceptibly after she had abandoned her first husband, Hans von Bülow, and thrown in her lot with Wagner, whose arrogance she soon matched, and whose Pan-Aryan, Francophobe, and anti-Semitic obsessions—if she did not share them already—she readily espoused. Although her diaries reveal that she was pleased to see her father from time to time after the renewal of relations in September 1872, they also record many foolish remarks about him and his music, not all of them utterances of Wagner. After the disappearance from the scene of this second husband, however, she reached heights of absurdity that can only be called monumental.

A letter of 12 August 1884 from Marie-Thérèse Ollivier to Princess Wittgenstein about young Daniel Ollivier's visit to that year's Bayreuth performances, also attended by Liszt, is amusingly revealing about the (unintentional) comedy enacted there by Wagner's widow, who, a year and a half after his death, was still refusing to see or associate with anyone other than her children. 'Daniel returned from Germany yesterday. . . . He didn't set eyes on his aunt, apart from a day when he caught a chance glimpse of her skeletal figure in the garden. She and Liszt, it seems, had a similar encounter in the corridors of the theatre. Her response to the words he addressed her was merely—a spectral silence. "Non è finita la commedia." . . . Either from fatigue or boredom, and to the great indignation of the holy family, Liszt slept a lot during the apotheoses. That can be called a witty way of getting out of an awkward situation. . . .' (Anne Troisier de Diaz, *Emile Ollivier et Carolyne de Sayn-Wittgenstein: Correspondance 1858–1887*, 310–11).

'What would poor Blandine have said, had she known that her son would spend a week at the door of the sister she so loved, and that that sister would not open her arms to receive him?' wondered Emile Ollivier, giving vent to his own indignation at the 'perpetual comedy'.

After another two years, realizing that the presence of her father would add lustre both to the wedding of her daughter Daniela and to that year's festival performances, and after having—for no known reason, unless it was a bitter and belated revenge for her childhood—excluded him from her life for more than three years, Cosima granted him once again the status of *persona grata*. When, during the festival, his life drew to its close, she seems to have attended to the nursing requirements dutifully but in a manner devoid of warmth and affection. She herself, the grim old matriarch of 'the royal family of Bayreuth', lived on for another forty-four years.

The most gifted and, with Blandine, most likeable of Liszt's three children was Daniel. At school, after a slow start, he strove to live up to his father's expectations, and succeeded with distinction, carrying off a number of prizes, including, in 1855, first prize in a national competition in Latin; a year later, when graduating from the prestigious Lycée Bonaparte, he was awarded the *Prix d'honneur* in rhetoric.

As a teenager he got to know his admired father very well, spending several long and happy holidays with him in Weimar. In mid-1857 he repaired to Vienna where, that autumn, he began law studies. The circumstances of the death, two years later, of this exceptionally promising young man are described in detail in Letter 427 of 15/16 December 1859.

Liszt, Eduard (**von**, 1867) (Margarethen am Moos 31 Jan. 1817–Vienna 8 Feb. 1879), youngest child of Georg Adam Liszt by his third and last wife, and therefore a half-brother of Adam Liszt. Being actually more than five years older than this step-uncle, Franz Liszt used generally to refer to Eduard, of whom he was very fond, as 'cousin' or 'uncle-cousin'. A gifted musical amateur, Eduard spent most of his life in Vienna, where he enjoyed a distinguished career as lawyer and jurist, becoming Royal and Imperial Public Prosecutor. From the 1850s onwards he was his nephew's legal and financial adviser; and for the last seventeen years of his life, when visiting Vienna, Franz stayed at Eduard's home in the Schottenhof, continuing to do so even after Eduard's death.

By his first wife, Karoline (1827–54), née Pickhart, who died of cholera, Eduard fathered: Franz Maria (1851–1919), who became a distinguished jurist, Karoline (1852–3), and Marie (1853–1919). In later years Liszt was particularly fond of the last-named, who on his sixty-sixth birthday (22 Oct. 1877) married Heinrich von Saar (1836–84).

To Eduard's second wife, Henriette (1825–1920), née Wolf, were born Henriette (1860–4), Hedwig (1866–1941), who in the last years of her stepcousin's life took part in his masterclasses in Weimar, and Eduard (1867–1961), who became a lawyer and contributed to the Liszt literature the useful *Franz Liszt: Abstammung, Familie, Begebenheiten*.

Manns, August (**Sir**) (Stolzenberg, nr. Stettin, 1825–London 1907), German-British conductor of the Crystal Palace concerts, Sydenham, 1855–1901. Knighted in 1903.

Massart, Lambert-Joseph (Liège 1811–Paris 1892), Belgian violinist who in the 1830s and 1840s was a close friend of Liszt, and his intermediary with Mme d'Agoult after the break between the two in 1844.

Menter, Sophie (Munich 1846–Munich 1918). 'My only legitimate piano daughter', was how Liszt described this great German pianist, whose ideal he had been from her childhood onwards. Whether she was ever his pupil, in the usual sense, is a question on which La Mara commented: 'When they first got to know one another she was already a finished artiste, but it was he who was responsible for her final and highest development; and to none of those who sat at the feet of the Great One did so much of the magic of his playing pass as to Sophie Menter, in whom has been recognized "the centrepiece of what has been bequeathed to us by Liszt the pianist".'

It was to Sophie that Liszt dedicated his transcription of the Saint-Saëns *Danse macabre*. Her own *Ungarische Zigeunerweisen* (Hungarian Gypsy Melodies) for piano and orchestra have been thought by one or two scholars to be the work of Liszt in his last years. There is, however, no real evidence (internal or external) for his authorship of this glittering, shallow piece, which is so unlike—and so inferior to—the great, forward-looking works he was creating at this time; and it is extremely probable that his part (if any) in its composition was limited to correcting Sophie's efforts and to helping her combine her themes into a coherent whole. The orchestration was done by Tchaikovsky, and when, at Odessa in February 1893, Sophie gave the first performance of the work, it was he who conducted.

Mercy-Argenteau, Comtesse Louise de (Paris 1837–St Petersburg 1890), née de Riquet, Comtesse de Caraman, daughter of Prince Alphonse de Chimay, and the wife, from 11 April 1860, of Comte Eugène de Mercy-Argenteau (1838–88). A loyal friend and confidante of Napoleon III, whom she twice visited during his captivity at Wilhelmshöhe, Louise was a passionate music-lover and an excellent pianist. Recalling her girlhood, she remarked in her reminiscences, 'I played Chopin and Liszt with more pleasure than other composers, and continue to do so'. In 1882 she discovered contemporary Russian music and was quite enchanted by the works of 'the Five', and of Cui in particular. She learnt Russian, made several trips to St Petersburg, wrote *César Cui. Esquisse critique* (Paris, 1888), invited Borodin and Cui (and, later, the entire Cui family) to the Château d'Argenteau (near Visé, north-east of Liège), organized concerts of their music and a performance of Cui's opera *Kavkazskiy plennik* (A Prisoner in the Caucasus), and in general promoted the Russians in Belgium and France much as Liszt had done in Germany. His letters to her make plain his admiration and affection for this beautiful and gifted woman, whose acquaintance he seems to have made, through his daughter Blandine, during his visit to Paris in 1861. In the spring of 1886 he, too, was a guest at Argenteau.

After Louise's death at the age of 53, her remains were brought back to Argenteau and buried in the family vault. The portrait painted of her by Ilya Repin in the last weeks of her life, showing her features ravaged by cancer, today hangs in Moscow's Tretyakov Gallery. Her younger sister, Susanne, married Marcel, son of Chopin's friend and pupil Princess Czartoryska, another musical noblewoman known to Liszt and mentioned in his letters.

Metternich, Prince Richard von (Vienna 1829–Vienna 1895), Austrian diplomat, eldest son of Prince Clement Metternich and his second wife, was appointed envoy to the Saxon Court at Dresden in 1856 and, three years later, Ambassador in Paris. His wife, **Pauline** (Vienna 1836–Vienna 1921), whose parents were Count Moritz Sándor and Leontine, a daughter of Metternich by his first wife, was therefore also his stepniece. As a couple they were much in evidence at the court of Napoleon III, particularly—when it was a matter of devising new amusements—the witty and vivacious Princess, whose description of herself, 'le singe à la mode' (the fashionable monkey), became the appellation by which she was known. She was also extremely popular in her native city, where a verse composed in her honour ran:

> Es giebt nur a Kaiserstadt,
> Es giebt nur a Wien;
> Es giebt nur a Fürstin,
> Es ist die Metternich Paulin!

'I always had a great liking for Franz Liszt, not only as an artist, but as a man,' she wrote. 'Personally he was more sympathetic to me than Wagner. Liszt was indeed vain —what great artist is not?—but he was so infinitely kind-hearted, so magnanimous, so loyal in his friendships, that one readily overlooked his little vanities, when one came into closer contact with him and got to know him thoroughly.'

Meyendorff, Baroness Olga von (1838–1926), née Gorchakova. When Liszt made her acquaintance in the 1860s, this erudite Russian lady was the wife of Baron Felix von Meyendorff, First Secretary at the Russian Embassy in Rome. Later appointed Ambassador to the Court of Weimar, the Baron was in 1870 transferred to Karlsruhe— but died suddenly in 1871. His widow seems then to have written the composer some kind of declaration. 'Will I be worthy of the sentiment, enigmatic but overflowing with conviction and loyalty, which you have vowed to me?' he replied. Returning to Weimar with her four young sons, and finding a residence near Liszt's, the Baroness was able to provide him with stimulating companionship as well as the domestic comforts less readily available in his existence at the Hofgärtnerei. His letters to her show that their relationship—far more intense on her side than on his—was founded above all on shared literary and intellectual interests. A competent pianist, she was the dedicatee of the Impromptu in F sharp, *Fünf kleine Klavierstücke*, and transcription of Lassen's *Ich weil' in tiefer Einsamkeit*.

Michaëlis, Théodore, music publisher in Paris.

Mickiewicz, Adam (nr. Nowogródek, Lithuania, 1798–Constantinople 1855), Polish poet and patriot, author of, *inter alia*, *Konrad Wallenrod*, *Dziady* (Forefathers' Eve) and— his masterpiece—*Pan Tadeusz* (Messire Tadeusz), a narrative poem which has been called 'the greatest of the nineteenth century'. His *Books of the Polish Pilgrims* was, in French translation, greatly admired by Lamennais, whose *Paroles d'un croyant* it influenced.

Paris, which was to be the base of his activities in the second half of his life, he reached in the early 1830s (having earlier become a close friend of Pushkin in Russia, whither he had been deported in 1824, and visited Goethe in Weimar). Here, and else-where, his passionate and engaging personality as much as his poetic gifts, intelligence, and learning—he was for a time Professor of Latin literature at the University of Lausanne, and then Professor of Slavic literature at the Collège de France—gained him many friends and sympathizers. One such was Margaret Fuller, who, in a letter of early 1847, reported the poet's appraisal of the two great contemporary composer-pianists: 'Chopin talks with spirit[2] and gives us the Ariel view of the universe. Liszt is the eloquent *tribune* to the world of men, a little vulgar and showy certainly, but I like the tribune best.'

Another admirer was Mme d'Agoult, who, some years after his death, evoked his mem-ory in a startling—because of a name that is conspicuously absent—list of the 'choir of the invisible dead who accompany me: my father, my mother, Léon, Louise, Blandine above all!—Then the geniuses: Manin, Cavour, Lamennais, Mickiewicz!' (Diary, 31 July, 1863.)

When Princess Wittgenstein visited Paris in September 1855, Liszt suggested that she contact her famous compatriot. In that very month, however, Mickiewicz travelled to Turkey to help organize a Polish detachment to serve in the Crimea—and there, on

---

[2] One takes it that, here, 'with spirit' does not mean 'spiritedly' but 'with the spirit world'.

26 November, he died of cholera. His remains, having long lain in Montmorency, were in 1890 interred in the Wawel Cathedral, Cracow, the Westminster Abbey of Poland.

Milde, Feodor von (Petronell, nr. Vienna, 1821–Weimar 1899). This gifted baritone spent most of his career in Weimar, where he sang the role of Telramund at the première of *Lohengrin* in 1850. The part of Elsa was sung on the same occasion by the soprano Rosa Agthe (Weimar 1827–Weimar 1906), who a year later became Milde's wife. 'Whoever saw Feodor and Rosa von Milde in their starring roles, received an impression rarely to be approached,' wrote Adelheid von Schorn. 'In addition to their magnificent voices, there was their wonderful artistry, their inspired acting, and not least their striking good looks. As human beings, too, the Mildes could not have been more highly regarded by the people of Weimar.'

Montez, Lola (Limerick 1818–New York 1861), née Marie Dolores Eliza Rosanne Gilbert, strikingly beautiful thrice-married Irish adventuress and 'Spanish' dancer whose encounter—how close, is a matter of conjecture—with Liszt at Dresden in February 1844 seems to have been regarded by the Comtesse d'Agoult as the final straw in her own relationship with the composer. A year and a half later Lola also turned up at the Beethoven Festival in Bonn, behaving, in Liszt's company, in a manner that he may have been none too pleased about. In Munich, where she danced in 1846, she became the mistress of the infatuated King Ludwig I, who, creating her Countess of Landsfeld, allowed her considerable power and influence—until, in 1848, king and courtesan alike were swept away by revolution. If, in her account of a conversation she had with Liszt later that same year, Fanny Lewald reported accurately his outburst of enthusiasm *vis-à-vis* the turbulent dancer, he had evidently long forgotten and forgiven her less endearing qualities: ' "She is the most perfect, most enchanting creature I have ever known!" he cried with enthusiasm. . . . "Ever new, ever plastic! Creative at every moment! She is truly a poetess. The genius of charm and love! All other women pale beside her! One can understand everything that King Ludwig has done and sacrificed for her! Everything!" '

Mosonyi, Mihály (Boldogasszonyfalva [now Frauenkirchen, Austria] 1814–Pest 1870), né Michael Brand, Hungarian composer who became a friend and admirer of Liszt after taking part, as a double-bass player, in the first performance of the Gran Mass. Nine years later he played the same instrument at the première of *The Legend of St Elisabeth*. Liszt composed a Fantasy on Mosonyi's opera *Szép Ilonka* ('La belle Hélène') and, in his memory, the piano piece *Mosonyi gyászmenete* (Mosonyi's Funeral Procession), which he later included in the *Hungarian Historical Portraits*.

Mouchanoff-Kalergis, Countess Marie von (Warsaw 1823–Warsaw 1874), née Nesselrode, music-loving Polish aristocrat and beauty known for her political activities, her brilliant salon in Baden-Baden, and her championship of the music of Liszt and Wagner, to both of whom can be found many interesting references in her *Briefe an ihre Tochter*. At the age of 16 she entered into a marriage, which lasted only a few months, with a Greek diplomat named Kalergis. Years later (Sept. 1863) she became the wife of Count Serge Mouchanoff. Her pianistic talent was appreciated by both Chopin (who gave her lessons a year or two before his death and described her playing as 'truly admirable') and Liszt, who made her acquaintance in Warsaw in 1843, later dedicated to her his *Petite valse favorite* and transcription of 'Salve Maria de Jérusalem' from *I Lombardi*, and called her the 'good fairy' in his life. Wagner, whom she gave generous financial assistance, dedicated to her his notorious *Judaism in Music*. 'We are losing one of the noblest, most intelligent and universally cultured women on the face of the earth,' remarked Hans von Bülow at the time of her early death. (See also under **Tausig**.)

Munkácsy, Mihály von (Munkács 1844–Endenich, nr. Bonn, 1900), né Lieb, Hungarian painter who took his surname from the place of his birth. In his letter of 5 March 1882 to Princess Carolyne in which he reported having made the acquaintance of this fêted compatriot, Liszt remarked that Munkácsy's face 'occasionally reflects some inner sadness'—a perception containing within it a tinge of the prophetic, for towards the end of his life the painter's mind clouded over, and his death took place in the same asylum in which more than forty years earlier Robert Schumann had died. His wife **Cécile** (1845–1915), née Papier, was a native of Luxembourg and, according to Rudolf Lehmann, 'a very loquacious, masterful lady'.

Nietzsche, Friedrich (Röcken, nr. Lützen, 1844–Weimar 1900), German philosopher who in early 1872 sent Liszt a copy of his newly published first major work, *Die Geburt der Tragödie aus dem Geiste der Musik*, eliciting the friendly and appreciative reply reproduced in the present volume (Letter 671). Much more closely associated with Wagner —as friend and foe—than with Liszt, Nietzsche did nevertheless have personal contact with the latter on at least one occasion, according to La Mara: 'On 26 February [1869] we welcomed Liszt to Leipzig . . . and at his side in the Thomaskirche heard Riedel's performance of Handel's *Israel in Egypt*. Later we fêted him at a festive supper in the Hôtel de Pologne, at which Friedrich Nietzsche, a pale young man, joined us at table and was introduced to him as a promising philologist and keen music-lover.'

Nourrit, Adolphe (Montpellier 1802–Naples 1839), French tenor of outstanding gifts who had many parts written for him by such contemporaries as Rossini, Meyerbeer, Auber, and Halévy, but who withdrew from the Paris Opéra when his role of Arnold in *William Tell* was given to Duprez. After touring the French provinces he went to Italy, achieving considerable success there—but he had begun to reveal symptoms of mental illness, and in Naples one morning he threw himself to his death. A post-mortem examination showed serious degeneration of the heart and intestines, and an enlarged heart. At his memorial service in Marseilles the organ was played by Chopin. The four known letters from Liszt to Nourrit are reproduced in the present volume—and if any of the ill-fated tenor's friends had cause to reproach themselves with failing to write to him affectionately and encouragingly, Liszt was certainly not one of them.

Ollivier, Emile (Marseilles 1825–Saint-Gervais-les-Bains 1913), French lawyer and politician. Having, early in 1870, been charged by Napoleon III with forming a constitutional ministry, Ollivier was Prime Minister at the outbreak of the Franco-Prussian War some months later, a conflict into which he led his country 'with a light heart'

—words which, despite his immediate explanation, have haunted his reputation and his memory. Long before these fatal events he had married Blandine Liszt, whose father he met for the first time at Weimar in January 1858 and came to admire greatly. It was to be with Liszt and Princess Wittgenstein that the grief-stricken Ollivier visited Rome after Blandine's death.[3] Her grandmother, the aged Anna Liszt, who was very fond of him, he continued to house and look after until her own death a few years later. In 1869 he married the much younger Marie-Thérèse Gravier (1850–1934).

Emile and Blandine's son **Daniel** (1862–1941) became a lawyer and, in later life, the editor of several volumes of his grandfather's correspondence.

Ortigue, Joseph Louis d' (Cavaillon 1802–Paris 1866), French musicologist, writer and critic who settled in Paris in 1829 and was soon on friendly terms with Liszt, his biographical study of whom was published in the *Gazette musicale* of 14 June 1835.

Oven, see **Hagn**.

Pasqué, Ernst (1821–92), opera producer at Weimar in the 1850s.

Pedro II (Rio de Janeiro 1825–Paris 1891), Emperor of Brazil from April 1831 until a military revolt in November 1889 compelled his abdication, after which he went into exile in Europe, already known to him from visits in earlier years. Liszt played to him at Bayreuth in August 1876, again in Vienna in March 1877, and renewed acquaintance with him and the Empress a month later when the Imperial couple visited Weimar *incogniti*. Dom Pedro was a model constitutional sovereign, a gifted linguist, and a generous patron of science and letters.

Pictet, Major Adolphe (Geneva 1799–Geneva 1875), Swiss artillery officer and philologist, nicknamed 'l'Universel', who accompanied Liszt, Marie d'Agoult, and George Sand on their excursion from Chamonix to Fribourg in early September 1836, an experience which inspired his *Une Course à Chamounix. Conte Fantastique.* 'Let me add a few words about our friend Franz,' he had written to Marie some months earlier. 'From the very first moment, which is extremely rare with me, I felt extremely attracted to him. That mixture of warmth, heart, and reflection, of youth and maturity, of artistic fire and philosophical calm, of genius and *naïveté*, singularly impressed and delighted me. That moment when I met him I shall count as one of the happiest of my life.'

Planté, Francis (Orthez, Basses-Pyrénées, 1839–Mont-de-Marsan 1934). 'The Abbé Liszt expects you at rue de la Chaussée d'Antin; you can display your admirable talent beside

---

[3] Anthony B. North Peat's *Gossip From Paris During the Second Empire* (London, 1903) contains this curious passage (p. 296): 'M. Emile Ollivier first married a daughter of the great pianist Liszt. The lady died and was buried in the enclosed cemetery of St. Tropez. You enter by a great gate, closed during the night to the public, but there is likewise a side door, of which M. Ollivier was given the key, in order that he might indulge his grief by moonlight, if it so pleased him. During the elections the Mayor and M. Ollivier . . . came to open warfare, and on the hustings M. le Maire got the worst of it. Now access by this side door to the cemetery was a privilege his worship alone could grant. Feeling himself aggrieved, he had a padlock put on the door. M. Ollivier stormed and wrote letters, and reported the affair in such high quarters that M. le Maire had nothing for it but to have the padlock taken off, and humbly restore to the deputy of the Opposition his right to mourn over his wife's grave.'

his without fear,' wrote Mme Olympe Rossini on 9 May 1866 to this outstanding French pianist. In a letter (Rome, 5 July 1867) after learning of a private performance Planté and Saint-Saëns had given of *Tasso* and *Héroïde funèbre*, Liszt remarked: 'Your brilliant hands I shake most cordially; they have given charm to works which, rightly or wrongly, people have been very eager to suspect, even to disparage, as being devoid of both charm and sense. Thank you for having understood me better, dear Monsieur Planté. . . .'

In 1855, asked to contribute to the album of the Marquise de Blocqueville, Henri Herz jotted down a 'musical' portrait of his hostess. To this piece Planté added years later a *Lento religioso* intended to depict the more elevated side of the lady's character. When the album was shown to Liszt he in his turn was inspired to contribute 'a page of the most serene beauty': *La Marquise de Blocqueville, portrait en musique*. The three pieces were published in *Le Figaro*, 14 April 1886.

Pleyel, Marie, known as Camille (Paris 1811–St Josses-ten-Noode, nr. Brussels, 1875), née Moke. Daughter of a Belgian father and a German mother, this talented French pianist—by all accounts one of the finest of her time—is perhaps best remembered for the part she played in the life of Berlioz, who recalled their engagement, her jilting of him, and his plan to murder her, in some of the most notable pages of his *Memoirs*. She has been called a nymphomaniac, and her marriage to the much older pianist, music publisher, and piano manufacturer Camille Pleyel (Strasbourg 1788–Paris 1855) lasted only until the time when he could endure her infidelities no longer; they were legally separated in 1835. The father of her daughter, born in 1836, was the Hamburg merchant George Parish. Chopin, a friend of her husband, dedicated to her in 1833 his three Nocturnes, Op. 9. Liszt, with whom she seems to have had a brief *affaire*, dedicated to her his paraphrase of the Tarantella from the *Muette de Portici*, and also the *Réminiscences de Norma*, publication of which, with a letter addressing her as 'dear and ravishing colleague', did nothing to heal the widening rift between him and Mme d'Agoult. Between 1848 and 1872 she taught at the Brussels Conservatoire; dying near that city she was buried, like Malibran, in the cemetery at Laeken.

Prokesch von Osten, Count (1871) **Anton** (Graz 1795–Vienna 1876), Austrian diplomat, officer, writer, numismatist, and Orientalist who, after representing his country in Athens and Berlin, was for many years Ambassador in Constantinople. 'During my visit there in the spring of 1870, I spent the most delightful hours at Prokesch's,' recalled Adolf von Schack. 'It was admirable to see the keen interest with which he devoted himself to German literature even amidst the many duties imposed upon him by his ambassadorship. In the evenings he used to read out to his family circle, and with a truly youthful fervour, poems which had made an especially strong impression upon him. . . . I took my departure with the melancholy feeling that I was leaving a man who, in the variety of his intellectual culture and his keen sympathy for higher endeavours, surpassed almost everyone I had known' (*Ein halbes Jahrhundert*, ii. 101–2).

Pruckner, Dionys (Munich 1834–Heidelberg 1896), German pianist who studied with Liszt in the early 1850s and was in 1859 appointed a professor at the Stuttgart

Conservatorium. Nicknamed Dionysius by Liszt, he was the dedicatee of the concert studies *Waldesrauschen* and *Gnomenreigen.*

Raff, Joseph Joachim (Lachen, Lake Zurich, 1822–Frankfurt am Main 1882), Swiss composer and teacher. Making himself known to Liszt at Basel in 1845, he was given much help in finding suitable employment, first in Cologne, then in Stuttgart and Hamburg, where he worked for the music publisher Schuberth. In early 1850 he joined his benefactor in Weimar, assisting him as music copyist, adviser on orchestration (in which, at that time, Liszt had had little practice), and general musical factotum. At the Weimar Court Theatre a year later Liszt helped prepare the première of the younger composer's opera *King Alfred.* In 1856 Raff moved on to Wiesbaden, where he gave piano lessons and composed prolifically. While living here he married Doris Genast (1826–1912), daughter of the Weimar stage manager Eduard Genast and elder sister of the singer Emilie Merian-Genast. From 1877 until his death he was director of the Hoch Conservatorium in Frankfurt. 'Raff was one of those people who are not amiable with everybody, but doubly so with those they like,' remembered Adelheid von Schorn. 'I found the strange man quite fascinating, and enjoyed talking to him, for he was extremely clever—and always very kind to me.'

Ramann, Lina (Mainstockheim, nr. Kitzingen, 1833–Munich 1912), German musicologist, teacher, composer, and writer of the nineteenth century's most notable Liszt biography, in the preparation of which she was helped by both Liszt and Princess Carolyne. Her valuable *Lisztiana* was not published until 1983, more than seventy years after her death. Among her other contributions is the *Liszt-Pädagogium.*

Ranolder, János (Pécs 1806–Veszprém 1875), Hungarian ecclesiastical writer who was Bishop of Veszprém from 1849 and also a distinguished vine-dresser.

Reinecke, Carl (Altona 1824–Leipzig 1910), German pianist, composer, teacher, and, for many years, conductor of the Leipzig Gewandhaus concerts. Unsympathetic, by temperament and environment, to Liszt the composer, he greatly admired Liszt the pianist, writing: 'He played in a way that no other pianist has ever played, before or since. His marvellous, unsurpassed bravura and virtuosity were always blended with poetic feeling and the keenest musical intelligence. Boldness, passion, grace, elegance, humour, simplicity of expression—all were there when appropriate, compelling a boundless admiration.'

Rellstab, Ludwig (Berlin 1799–Berlin 1860), German writer who has been called 'the first great music critic'. In a series of articles in the *Vossische Zeitung* he discussed in detail and at length Liszt's Berlin concerts of late 1841 and early 1842, concluding in the very first that 'that charm which passes to the physical state from a higher, psychic one Thalberg possesses in such small measure, or Liszt so much *more*, that in comparison with the former's we could call the latter's an inspired art'. Having been a scathing critic of the works of Chopin, Rellstab later changed his tune and, planning to wait upon that composer in Paris, asked Liszt for some lines of introduction. (See Liszt's tactful letter to Chopin of 26 February 1843.)

Poems of Rellstab's inspired three of Liszt's songs and several by Schubert, including the first seven of *Schwanengesang*. It was he, too, who bestowed upon Beethoven's Piano Sonata in C sharp minor the nickname *Moonlight*.

Reményi, Ede (Miskolc 1828–San Francisco 1898). Exiled from his native land throughout the 1850s following his part in the War of Independence, this Hungarian violinist, who in 1854 became solo violinist to Queen Victoria, was the possessor of an original talent much appreciated by Liszt, who invited him and Johannes Brahms to the Altenburg when the two young musicians were touring together in 1853. Reményi, it seems, had the habit of unconsciously colouring with Hungarian characteristics all the music he played, a habit which, according to Liszt's pupil William Mason, 'gave rise to a story about his treatment of the concluding strain of the first theme in the slow movement of the "Kreutzer Sonata", namely that, forgetting himself, he added to Beethoven's music [a] peculiar Hungarian termination . . . as a final ornament. Whether this story is true or not, it was widely circulated and caused a great deal of merriment all over Germany.'

Repos, E., a music publisher in Paris.

Rimsky-Korsakov, Nikolai Andreyevich (Tikhvin, nr. Novgorod, 1844–Lyubensk, nr. St Petersburg, 1908), Russian composer (initially a naval officer), Inspector of Music Bands of the Navy Department, and the teacher of, amongst others, Glazunov, Lyadov, Arensky, Grechaninov, Ippolitov-Ivanov, and Stravinsky. Unlike Borodin and Cui he never met Liszt, who thought very highly of his music and lost no opportunity to acquaint himself with it, as was noted by Vincent d'Indy when, in 1873, he witnessed Liszt and the Weimar Court Orchestra trying out Rimsky's *Sadko* and other Russian works. 'How delightful it was,' he recalled, 'to see the old master listening eagerly to those pieces whose conception and style of writing were then so new. . . .'

Rospigliosi, Princess Françoise ('Fanny') (1825–99), née de Nompère de Champagny, daughter of the Duc de Cadore. Noted for her humanitarian activities, Princess Fanny, and her husband Prince Clemente (1823–97), were on friendly terms with Liszt soon after his arrival in Rome in 1861. Frequently a visitor to the Palazzo Rospigliosi at 43 via Quirinale (where, in the Casino, can be seen Guido Reni's famous *Aurora and the Hours*), Liszt also on several occasions broke his journeys between Rome and Budapest at the monumental Rospigliosi villa—built by Bernini for Pope Clement IX (Giulio Rospigliosi)—at Spicchio, Lamporecchio, nr. Pistoia.

Rubini, Giovanni Battista (Romano, nr. Bergamo, 1794–Romano 1854), renowned Italian tenor who toured with Liszt in late 1842 and early 1843. Noted for his exceptionally high range, he was associated above all with operas by Bellini and Donizetti.

Rubinstein, Anton Grigorevich (Vykhvatinetz, Podolia, 1829–Peterhof 1894), Russian pianist, composer, and conductor. When, in the early 1840s, young Anton was taken on an extensive tour of Europe and, in Paris, first heard Liszt, he was so overcome that he had a severe nervous seizure. 'Liszt took the boy in his arms,' writes Rubinstein's biographer, 'put him to bed and stayed several hours by his side until he was quiet and slept.' Although not generally regarded as one of the pianistic mentors of the gifted boy, Liszt did years later remark to La Mara: 'Rubinstein went through my school too, first in Paris, later in Vienna,' from which it may be inferred that some tuition was given. Of the many comparisons that have been made between the two, as pianists, of special interest is that of Saint-Saëns, an admirer of both and himself a notable virtuoso:

With his irresistible charm and superhuman playing Rubinstein could stand up fearlessly to the memory of Liszt. He was very different from him, of course, and if Liszt was an eagle then Rubinstein was a lion. Those who heard him play can never forget the sight of that great sheathed claw of his stroking the keyboard with its powerful caress! Neither one nor the other was ever, at any moment, 'the pianist'. Even when they played the smallest things very simply they remained great, without deliberation and through the grandeur of complete integrity. They were living incarnations of their art and worked miracles, imposing a sort of holy terror beyond the limit of ordinary admiration. (James Harding, *Saint-Saëns and His Circle*, 103–4)

Rubinstein had no great understanding of Liszt the composer. Nevertheless, on New Year's Eve 1871, as director of the Vienna Philharmonic Concerts, he conducted the Christmas Oratorio from *Christus*; and at his celebrated Historical Concerts of the 1880s, which covered the whole range of keyboard music from Byrd to Tchaikovsky, played several of Liszt's original piano works as well as Rhapsodies and transcriptions. He was the dedicatee of the *Weinen, Klagen, Sorgen, Zagen* variations, and his wife Vera that of the arrangement of Anton's song *O! wenn es doch immer so bliebe*.

Rubinstein, Nikolai Grigorevich (Moscow 1835–Paris 1881). Anton's brother and likewise a pianist of outstanding gifts, to whom Liszt dedicated the Fantasy on themes from Beethoven's 'Ruins of Athens', Nikolai was the founder and first Principal of the Moscow Conservatoire, and the teacher of Sergei Taneyev, Alexander Siloti, and Emil Sauer. It was his early and much lamented death that inspired the composition of Tchaikovsky's Piano Trio in A minor, dedicated 'to the memory of a great artist'.

Saint-Cricq, Caroline de (1812–72), a pupil, and the first love, of the young Liszt. His feelings for her were reciprocated, but, after the death (30 June 1828) of Caroline's mother, who had looked favourably upon the attachment of the two young people, her father, the Comte de Saint-Cricq (a minister of Charles X), terminated the lessons and made it plain that the two were to meet no more. Caroline thus lost in quick succession both her mother and the man she loved. The shock and distress of so sudden and brutal an end to the relationship seem to have caused Liszt, for his part, some kind of breakdown, and for nearly a year thereafter he made no public appearances. At her father's behest, Caroline married Bertrand d'Artigaux, a landowner in Pau; it was here, in 1844, that she and Liszt next encountered one another. Marie Wittgenstein, who met Caroline in Paris in the 1850s, noted that 'her manner was not characterized by charm, but rather by the stiffness of restrained passion and deeply-felt misfortune'. The destiny Caroline endured with her loveless marriage, the cares of nursing an incurably sick daughter, and unrealized hopes of further meetings with the man she thought of as 'the single shining star' of her life, was indeed a melancholy one. In his will, written in 1860, Liszt bequeathed her one of his talismans set in a ring; and, when she died, twelve years later, wrote of her with emotion as 'one of the purest earthly manifestations of God's blessing'.

Saint-Saëns, Camille (Paris 1835–Algiers 1921), French composer, pianist and, for twenty years (1857–77), organist at the Madeleine. Before knowing Liszt he was already a keen admirer of the symphonic poems; when the two did eventually meet they became good friends. Liszt warmly championed the music of the younger composer, most notably the opera *Samson and Delilah* which, thanks to his support, was premièred at Weimar in December 1877. (Contrary to what has been stated so often, Liszt was not himself present, being in Budapest at that time.) In gratitude, and without informing Liszt beforehand—'otherwise,' remarked Liszt, 'I would have begged him not to risk such an undertaking'—Saint-Saëns mounted (Mar. 1878) a concert of his benefactor's music at which he conducted, *inter alia*, the Dante Symphony and parts of *Christus*.

Of the occasion when he first heard Liszt the pianist, Saint-Saëns recalled: 'I already considered him to be a genius and had formed in advance an almost impossible conception of his playing. Judge of my astonishment when I realized that he far exceeded even this expectation. The dreams of my youthful fancy were but prose beside the Dionysiac poetry evoked by his supernatural fingers. . . .' Liszt, for his part, was 'filled with wonder' on hearing his *St François d'Assise: la prédication aux oiseaux* performed on the organ by the versatile musician he hailed as the 'extraordinary king of organists'.

Saissy, Amadé (Cannes 1844–Paris 1901), French *littérateur* and translator who lived for some years in Budapest, where he edited the *Gazette de Hongrie*, led the 'Cercle français' of which Liszt was a member, and became Professor of French literature at the University.

Salvagni, Fortunato, Roman manservant of Liszt's *c*.1862–71, whose German wife was Princess Carolyne's housekeeper at the Via Babuino. When Adelheid von Schorn visited Rome in 1874 she found him, by then a widower, the proprietor of a *trattoria* built into the walls of the Baths of Diocletian. His successors as Liszt's manservants were the Hungarian **Miska Sipka**, 1871–5, the Montenegrin **Spiridion Knezevics**, 1875–81, the Italian **Achille Colonello**, 1882–4, and the Hungarian **Mihály Kreiner**, 1884–6.

Sand, George (Paris 1804–Nohant 1876), pen-name of the French novelist Baroness Dudevant, née Armandine-Lucile-Aurore Dupin, who was on very friendly terms with Liszt for several years, although, unlike de Musset, Chopin, and others, he was never her lover. She (and her children) joined him and Marie d'Agoult in Switzerland in the summer of 1836, later that year shared their apartment in Paris (this being the time when Chopin was introduced to her by Liszt), and in 1837 was twice their hostess at Nohant, her home near La Châtre in Berry. The letters Liszt wrote to her in the mid-1840s—after her quarrel and his break with Marie—in an attempt to renew their friendship, did not wholly achieve that object. A decade later, Mme Sand responded in friendly fashion to his request to her to give Princess Carolyne a cordial reception. Nevertheless, he and she seem not to have met again after the early 1840s.

Liszt's letters make plain his admiration of George Sand's early novels, above all *Lélia* (1833), as well as of the famous *Lettres d'un voyageur* (1834–6). Of these last, the one addressed to 'mon cher Franz' and published in the *Revue des Deux Mondes* of 1 September 1835 was that to which Marian Evans (George Eliot) referred when, writing from Weimar to a friend two decades later, she remarked: 'When I read George Sand's letter to Franz Liszt in her *Lettres d'un voyageur*, I little thought that I should ever be seated tête-à-tête with him for an hour, as I was yesterday, and telling him my ideas and feelings.'

The *Rondeau fantastique sur un thème espagnol* ('El contrabandista'), which Liszt dedicated to Mme Sand, was the inspiration for her story 'Le Contrebandier'.

In the 1830s Liszt also saw much of Maurice and Solange Dudevant, Mme Sand's children by her husband Casimir, Baron Dudevant, from whom in the mid-1830s she obtained a legal separation. As **Maurice Sand** (Paris 1823–Nohant 1889), the elder child became known both as a writer and as an illustrator of his own and his mother's books, the best of the former being, apparently, *Masques et bouffons*, a study of the Commedia dell'Arte.

Solange (1828–99) married the sculptor Auguste Clésinger. Writing to La Mara in 1892, she recalled the Liszt she had known at Nohant more than fifty years earlier: 'He was very kind. Because of my hatred of my lessons and my wild behaviour, I was an extremely naughty and recalcitrant child. Forever being punished for some misdeed or other, I would refuse to say that I was sorry. Well! Out of sympathy for me when I was confined to my room without dinner, M. Liszt used to come and beg me to ask my mother's forgiveness. His friendly request was the only thing that made me give in.'

Saxe-Weimar, royal family of. Although they are mentioned from time to time in his letters, two of the most notable rulers of the Duchy had already passed from the scene when Liszt first set foot in Weimar. **Anna Amalia** (Wolfenbüttel 1739–Weimar 1807), daughter of Duke Carl of Brunswick, came to the town in 1756 as the bride of Duke Constantin. In 1758, left a widow with two infant sons, she took control of affairs of state, remaining as regent until the elder boy, Carl August, attained his majority at the age of 18. A competent, humane, and responsible ruler with intellectual interests and a gift for friendship, it was she who, by appointing C. M. Wieland tutor to the two princes, brought to Weimar the first of the literary luminaries whose presence was to shed so great a lustre on court and town. The tribute that Wieland later paid the Duchess was a striking one: 'The longer I live the more I am convinced that, *telle qu'elle est*, she is one of the most delightful and splendid mixtures of human, womanly, and royal qualities that have been on this earth of ours.'

Known as the Wittumspalais, and described in Letter 859, the residence into which Anna Amalia moved after her withdrawal from the affairs of government still stands in Weimar and now houses a Wieland Museum.

During the reign of **Carl August** (Weimar 1757–Graditz, nr. Torgau, 1828) Herder and Schiller settled in Weimar, as did, above all, his great friend Goethe, whose enlightened counsel was of benefit to both ruler and Duchy. (At the Congress of Vienna in 1815 the Duchy was elevated to the status of Grand Duchy, giving Carl August the right to call himself Royal Highness.) 'Napoleon, Frederick the Great, Peter the Great and Carl August have a family resemblance, in so far that no one could oppose them,' remarked Goethe to Eckermann. 'Everything that I undertook under his direction succeeded. . . . If the daemonic spirit deserted him, as it often did for a time, and only the human remained, his perceptions were certainly less clear and, strange to say, everything went wrong.' For Carl August's liaison with Caroline Jagemann, see Letter 217.

The elder son of Carl August and his wife, Princess Luise of Hesse-Darmstadt, was the amiable, unintellectual **Carl Friedrich** (Weimar 1783–Weimar 1853), who in 1804 married the Imperial Grand Duchess **Maria Pavlovna** (St Petersburg 1786–Weimar 1859), a sister of the reigning Tsar Alexander and of Tsar Nicholas. About the Romanov background of this kindly, charitable, art- and music-loving patroness of Liszt's some rather awed words were penned by the great dramatist Friedrich Hebbel, who dined with Maria Pavlovna in 1858, more than fifty years after her entry into Weimar in the lifetime of Anna Amalia: 'I could not leave off thinking: this is the daughter of Tsar Paul who was murdered while, in the adjoining room, the piano was being played loudly to prevent her, a young girl, from hearing the dying gasps of her father as he was being strangled; this is the sister of the mighty Nicholas who came to so sudden an end, like a slater; this is that same Maria Pavlovna to whom, half a century ago, Schiller addressed his *Huldigung der Künste*. . . . I felt as though I were dreaming of Shakespeare!' Long after her death, Liszt himself wrote of 'the late Grand Duchess Maria Pavlovna, whose name I shall never mention without blessings and gratitude'.

The second of Carl Friedrich and Maria Pavlovna's three children was **Augusta** (1811–90), Princess of Prussia when Liszt made her acquaintance, later the German Empress. Her brother **Carl Alexander** (Weimar 1818–Weimar 1901), who succeeded his father on 8 July 1853, proved a cultivated and enlightened ruler as well as a loyal friend to Liszt. However, for all his burning desire to bring back to Weimar the glory it enjoyed during his grandfather's reign, he let slip the greatest opportunity, despite Liszt's earnest entreaty. (See Letter 366.) With Liszt and Wagner living and working together in the town, Weimar might well have known a second 'golden age' to rival the earlier one. Even so, what Liszt achieved, as it were single-handedly, during the decade of his Kapellmeistership, has caused those years to be remembered as Weimar's 'silver age'.

Carl Alexander's consort, the Grand Duchess **Sophie** (The Hague 1824–Weimar 1897), a daughter of King Willem II of the Netherlands, was also his cousin, her mother, Anna Pavlovna, being another daughter of Tsar Paul. It was to Sophie, whose calm dignity and ceaseless humanitarian work were much admired, that the last Goethe, Walther, bequeathed the Goethe estate and papers; to her initiative was owed the institution of Weimar's Goethe and Schiller Archive. She was the dedicatee of Liszt's Second Beethoven Cantata and song *Was Liebe sei*. 'Weimar has possessed an Anna Amalia, a Duchess Luise, and a Maria Pavlovna,' observed Adelheid von Schorn. 'Different though they were, each was great in her way—and the Grand Duchess Sophie perhaps the greatest in intellect, character and selflessness.'

Carl Alexander and Sophie's son **Carl August** (Weimar 1844–Pegli 1894)—the little boy mentioned in Letter 308—predeceased his father; Carl Alexander was therefore succeeded by his grandson Wilhelm Ernst (1876–1923), an enthusiast of Prussian militarism who, abdicating on 9 November 1918, was the last of the rulers of the Grand Duchy of Saxe-Weimar-Eisenach.

In his letters Liszt also refers from time to time to Prince **Edward of Saxe-Weimar** (1823–1902), son of the Grand Duke Carl August's younger son, Duke Bernhard (1792–1862), and Princess Ida of Saxe-Meiningen (1794–1852), sister of Queen Adelaide of England. Making a career in the British army and rising to the rank of field-marshal, Prince Edward died at a house in Portland Place, London, and was buried, with military honours, in Chichester Cathedral.

Sayn-Wittgenstein, Princess Carolyne von (Monasterżyska, Ukraine, 8 Feb. [NS] 1819–Rome, 9 Mar. 1887), daughter of a rich Polish landowner, Peter Ivanovsky, and his wife Pauline (née Podovska), and the dominating figure in Liszt's life from the late 1840s until his death. At the age of 17 she married—with the utmost reluctance and only when compelled to do so by her father—Prince Nicholas von Sayn-Wittgenstein, an officer in the Russian cavalry. Early the following year their daughter Marie was born; in 1840 the mismatched couple agreed to lead separate lives; and in 1844, on her father's death, she inherited an immense fortune. In Kiev three years later she encountered Liszt, and the effect upon her of his playing, personality, and conversation was overwhelming. 'To see him, hear him and fall in love with him were one and the same for the Princess,' wrote their later acquaintance La Mara. 'The ardent, art-thirsting soul of the lonely woman succumbed to the magic which held in thrall the whole of educated Europe.' By mid-1848 he and she—both devout Catholics—had settled in Weimar and the long struggle had begun to obtain the annulment of Carolyne's marriage. (In 1855 Prince Nicholas, a Protestant, obtained his own divorce and soon took a second wife.)

By January 1861, after a dozen years of intermittent crises and traumas, all obstacles had been surmounted and the couple were at last free to marry. Instead of doing so quickly and quietly, however, they delayed; and when, nine months later, on the eve of the day (Liszt's fiftieth birthday) finally appointed for the wedding, word came from the Vatican that the ceremony was to be postponed (new objections having been lodged by those who had a material interest in preventing the marriage), the Princess seems finally to have conceded defeat. According to her friend Adelheid von Schorn, an additional factor, outweighing all else, was her perception—accurate or otherwise—that during the year and a half of their separation Liszt had grown indifferent to the idea of marriage and was now prepared to take her to the altar only as a matter of honour. When, two and a half years later, Prince Nicholas died, and nothing could any longer have prevented their union, the subject seems not to have arisen.

Comprehensive details of Liszt and Carolyne's efforts to become man and wife, of the difficulties they had to contend with and of the forces ranged against them, are provided by Alan Walker and Gabriele Erasmi in their richly-documented *Liszt, Carolyne and the Vatican: The Story of a Thwarted Marriage*.

In compensation for her plain features, dumpy figure, yellowish complexion and—by her early thirties—blackish teeth (remarked on by George Eliot among others), Carolyne possessed an acute intellect and great eloquence; and during the long, lonely years before the fateful meeting with Liszt she acquired enormous erudition, as was acknowledged by such contemporaries as Alexander von Humboldt ('the many-minded Princess'), Hans von Bülow ('I doubt if there ever was a woman of such astonishing knowledge and such quick and penetrating intelligence'), Adolf von Schack ('a phenomenon who has at the present time no equal'), and Gerhard Rohlfs ('one of the most brilliant women I have ever met'). It was surely these qualities of the mind that captivated the highly intelligent and cultured Liszt, ever eager to expand his own intellectual horizons. During their life together in Weimar, as well as providing him with stimulating companionship and conversation, Carolyne also collaborated in his literary writings; and after their marriage plans were abandoned it was to books and articles of her own—mainly on religious and ecclesiastical topics—that she devoted her energies. At her home in Rome's Via Babuino where, as the years passed, her life became ever more eccentric, were indited: *Bouddhisme et Christianisme*; *De la prière, par une femme du monde*; *Entretiens pratiques à l'usage des femmes du monde* (3 vols: *Religion et monde, L'Amitié des anges, La Chapelle Sixtine*); *La Matière dans la dogmatique chrétienne*; *L'Eglise attaquée par la médisance*; *Petits entretiens pratiques à l'usage des femmes du grand monde pour la durée d'une retraite spirituelle* (8 vols.); *Simplicité des colombes, prudence des serpents. Quelques réflexions suggérées par les femmes et les temps actuels*; *Souffrance et Prudence*; *Sur la perfection chrétienne et la vie intérieure*; and, her *magnum opus*, *Causes intérieures de la faiblesse extérieure de l'église en 1870*, in 24 volumes, some of which were quickly placed on the Vatican's *Index librorum prohibitorum*.

These works having remained largely unread, the quarter-century taken to produce them could easily be considered a pitiful waste of time. It is, therefore, heartening to learn that Henri Lasserre, editor of *Le Monde catholique*, made a point of revising one of the volumes of the *Petits entretiens*, to bring it to a wider public; and that, because it had 'helped and guided them on their path', he and his family made a pilgrimage to the Princess's grave (in the German cemetery at the Vatican) and there, in gratitude, knelt to offer their thanks. (See also under **Schack**.)

Sayn-Wittgenstein, Princess Marie von (Woronince, Ukraine, 1837–Schloss Friedstein, Styria, 1920). When, visiting Woronince in early 1847, Liszt first met this only child of his interesting new acquaintance Princess Carolyne, she had just celebrated her tenth birthday. Later that year, during his second and much longer sojourn there, he composed and dedicated to her the lovely *Glanes de Woronince*. From 1848 until her marriage in 1859 to Prince Constantin von Hohenlohe, Marie lived at the Altenburg in Weimar, where, as she grew up, she was constantly in the company of Liszt, who seems to have regarded her as the stepdaughter she almost became. It was to her that he gave the attention craved by his own children in faraway Paris; and during his absences from Weimar he would write to her very charmingly and affectionately.

After the composer's death, the Grand Duke Carl Alexander decreed that the rooms he had occupied at the Hofgärtnerei should be preserved as a Liszt Museum; and when, on her mother's death seven months later, Princess Marie inherited Liszt's possessions, she at once presented them to the new museum, thereby providing the nucleus of the collection of Lisztian memorabilia to be seen there today.

Schack, Adolf Friedrich, Count von (1876) (Schwerin[4] 1815–Rome 1894), wealthy German writer and art patron among whose works are poems, epics, tragedies, translations from Spanish, Portuguese, and the Persian of Firdusi, *History of Dramatic Literature and Art in Spain, Poetry and Art of the Arabs in Spain and Sicily*, and *History of the Normans in Sicily*. His memoirs, *Ein halbes Jahrhundert* (Half a Century), record his many travels around Europe and the Near East (among them a journey to Athens with Prince and Princess Chlodwig Hohenlohe), as well as his impressions of numerous distinguished contemporaries, beginning with Otto Nicolai, a guest at Brüsewitz in Schack's childhood ('It was not so much his musical talent which impressed us children as the dexterity with which he performed all manner of conjuring tricks'). Among other musicians of his acquaintance were Berlioz, whose 'great admiration for Weber particularly delighted me'; Mendelssohn, who asked Schack to prepare an opera libretto for him but died before its completion; and Wagner, for a time his next-door neighbour in Munich and a frequent visitor to the Schack picture gallery in that city.

'Since my youth,' wrote Schack, 'I have striven to struggle up out of the dust, to take possession of everything great and beautiful that past and present can offer, to follow in the steps of the great and noble beings who have gone before, and to learn as much as possible with the mental powers I possess.' Given this outlook, his creative gifts and his vast cultural and historical knowledge, it is not surprising that Schack should have been held in high esteem by idealists such as Liszt—whose acquaintance he made at Weimar in 1850—and Princess Wittgenstein, to both of whom his memoirs pay tribute. Expressing his admiration of Liszt the musician and humanitarian, he also singled out for special praise the 'extraordinary beauty' of the Schubert *Lieder* transcriptions. Of the Princess, to whose 'intellectual court'—Liszt's expression—in Rome Schack repaired on each of his visits to that city, he wrote: 'Only posterity will recognize the full extent of her genius when a wider readership is gained for her many writings, which are distinguished as much for their breathtaking eloquence as for their astounding wealth of knowledge. . . . The basis of these works, it is true, is Catholicism, but they are filled with such lofty views that they offer rich intellectual nourishment even to the most thoroughgoing freethinker. . . . The Princess's noble heart and high-minded outlook have caused me to regard her friendship as a treasure beyond price, and there have been several occasions in my life when, at moments of depression, I would have succumbed, had *she* not somehow helped and sustained me' (*Ein halbes Jahrhundert*, i. 389).

Scheffer, Ary (Dordrecht 1795–Argenteuil 1858), French painter who as a young man became drawing-master to the children of Louis-Philippe, remaining thereafter on particularly close and affectionate terms with Princess Marie of Orléans. In 1830 he

---

[4] Reference books give Schack's birthplace as Brüsewitz. In his memoirs, however, he writes: 'I was born at Schwerin in Mecklenburg . . . but spent my childhood on our nearby estate of Brüsewitz.'

fathered an illegitimate daughter, his beloved Cornélie, who, as Mme Marjolin, is mentioned in Liszt's Letter 308 of 17 July 1854. His well-known portrait of the composer, dating from 1837, hangs in the Liszt Museum, Weimar.

Schober, Franz von (Torup, nr. Malmö, Sweden 1796–Dresden 1882), Austrian poet whose acquaintance Liszt seems to have made in the late 1830s, probably in Vienna. Cultured and worldly-wise, Schober had in earlier years been a close friend of Franz Schubert, who set many of his poems to music, among them the well-known *An die Musik*. From about the mid-1840s he was a *Legationsrat* (secretary of legation) in Weimar. In 1856 he entered into a short-lived marriage and settled in Dresden; but his friendship with Liszt had already waned by this time, partly because of the poet's increasing conventionality, partly because of the musician's justified criticisms of the libretto Schober had provided, long before, for Schubert's opera *Alfonso und Estrella*, the première of which Liszt conducted in 1854 as an 'act of piety to the composer'. In old age Schober conceded that the libretto had indeed been 'such a miserable, still-born, bungling piece of work that even so great a genius as Schubert was not able to bring it to life'.

Schoelcher, Victor (Paris 1804–Houilles 1893), French republican politician—sometimes styled 'the French Wilberforce'—who early in life espoused various humanitarian causes, especially that of emancipation of the negroes; later, as Under-Secretary for the Marine, he presided over a commission which led to abolition of slavery in the French colonies. He also had a hand in the abolition of flogging in the Navy. Expelled from France after the *coup d'état* of 1851, he settled in London, where he wrote a life of Handel, published simultaneously in French and English. ('Readers at the British Museum were struck by this tall, ungainly, and extremely plain but intellectual-looking foreigner,' was the rather ambiguous comment of his obituarist in *The Times*.) Returning to France in 1870, he was a colonel in the National Guard during the siege of Paris, and in 1874 became a life Senator.

Schorn, Henriette von (Nordheim 1807–Weimar 1869), née von Stein, lady-in-waiting to the Grand Duchess Maria Pavlovna and Princess Wittgenstein's closest woman friend during her Weimar years. Her daughter **Adelheid** (Weimar 1841–Weimar 1916) came to know both Liszt and the Princess very well, corresponded with them, paid several visits to Rome to see the Princess, and often acted as Liszt's amanuensis during his final years at the Hofgärtnerei. Her two volumes on the history of Weimar under the Grand Dukes Carl Friedrich and Carl Alexander are a mine of information on the events and personalities of those two reigns; the more personal *Zwei Menschenalter* provides a similar wealth of detail about her own and her family's relations with Liszt and the Princess. Her mother's collected stories she published under the title *Geschichten aus Franken*. Marie and Otto von Schorn were the two children of the first marriage of her father Dr Ludwig von Schorn.

Schumann, Robert Alexander (Zwickau 1810–Endenich, nr. Bonn, 1856). When, having enjoyed a cordial correspondence, this German composer and Liszt first met, in 1840, they got on tolerably well. Schumann had already dedicated to Liszt his Fantasy in C, and on hearing his playing was overwhelmed. Later, however, friendly feelings turned into antagonism on the part of both Schumann and his wife. Liszt was, admittedly, rather tactless when he visited them at Dresden in 1848, but in the following years could hardly have been a better friend—writing Schumann warmly encouraging letters, giving performances in Weimar of his *Scenes from Faust* and *Manfred*, offering him hospitality in the event that he visited Weimar, and travelling to Leipzig to give support at the première of *Genoveva*, of which he later mounted a production of his own. ('During all these years the Schumanns accepted everything and gave Liszt nothing,' has been aptly observed by Alan Walker.) In his letter to Eduard Liszt of 29 March 1854 Liszt did, it is true, describe Schumann as 'a kind of Arius'—i.e. heretic—'in the little Church we are trying to build', a comment which, in view of Schumann's evident opposition to the music of the 'New German School', was by no means unfair or inappropriate. That, on the other hand, after the tirelessly generous help and loyal support he had received from Liszt, Schumann could refer to him in a letter (Oct. 1853 to Joachim) as the 'Judas Iscariot' of Weimar—perhaps the most monstrously unjust gibe to which even Liszt has ever been subjected—brings one to the conclusion that poor Schumann was already afflicted by the mental deterioration which led not long afterwards to his attempted suicide, incarceration in an asylum, and tragic end.

The pianist **Clara Schumann** (Leipzig 1819–Frankfurt am Main 1896), née Wieck, Robert's wife from 1840, came, by the early 1850s, to dislike Liszt intensely, possibly because of a certain flamboyance in his behaviour which was alien to her, probably because of his superiority on their instrument, and certainly because of her total inability and failure to understand and appreciate his works, the sheer inanity and obtuseness of her comments on which are hard to believe (the epoch-making Sonata in B minor, dedicated to Robert, was 'merely a blind noise', the great *Harmonies poétiques et religieuses* 'dreadful stuff'). It has also been suggested—by one of her own biographers—that while Clara deplored, and was 'disgusted' by, the attentions Liszt paid to, and was paid by, various members of her sex, she may unconsciously have resented the fact that he never showed a similar interest in her. The hostility she felt did not, however, prevent her from writing to Liszt ('most revered friend') twice in October 1854 to entreat him to secure her a concert engagement in Weimar. Responding to her appeal by mounting a concert of her husband's works in which she appeared as soloist in the Piano Concerto, and by arranging for her to play at the Dowager Grand Duchess's, the chivalrous Liszt went even further in championing Clara at this difficult period of her life (earlier in the year Robert had been admitted to an asylum) by writing a very sympathetic and supportive article about her for the *Neue Zeitschrift für Musik*, the magazine founded by her husband.

This remarkably mean-spirited woman's way of showing her gratitude, not long afterwards, was to refuse to appear at the Mozart centenary concerts in Vienna (Jan. 1856) because of Liszt's participation. Having in every conceivable way shown himself a true, loyal, and generous friend, Liszt seems after this to have given up; thereafter, they encountered one another very little. (Düsseldorf in 1876 and Frankfurt in 1879 are the only occasions that come to mind.) Conceding his genius and supremacy as a pianist, Frau Schumann—whom Liszt wittily, and most aptly, called 'die Musikpäpstin' (the Popess of music)—remained unwaveringly hostile to his creations, after his death remarking that they would soon disappear 'now that he has gone'. Doubtless she would have desired the same fate for the equally despised works of Berlioz and Wagner. (The former's *Roméo et Juliette* was 'infernal, devilish music'; the latter's *Tristan und Isolde* 'the most repulsive thing I ever saw or heard'.) More than a century later, however, it is her own music—derivative of her husband's and lacking precisely that greatness and originality which is the lifeblood of his and theirs—that has disappeared, consigned by time and posterity to the very brink of oblivion.

Schwartz, Marie Espérance von (Southgate, Herts, 1821–Ermatingen, Switzerland, 1899), philanthropist, anti-vivisectionist, and supporter of Garibaldi who wrote under the pseudonym of Elpis Melena, the Graecized form of her name. Much of her life was spent on Crete, where she founded hospitals, asylums, schools, and a hospice for sick animals, and valiantly sought to raise educational standards. The admiration Liszt felt for this exceptionally charitable woman was expressed in a letter to her of 22 March 1883: 'Your life seems to me to be one vast *symphony* of generosity, munificence, alms, charities, gifts, and attentions as delicate as they are costly. Beginning with Garibaldi and his people, and continuing indefinitely with those poor German fellows, ill in Rome, and buried there at your expense; then the fighting Cretans, the invalids in your hospital at Jena, the societies for the protection of animals, etc., etc. I admire you and bow before your unending acts of kindness and goodness—all the more because you perform them unobtrusively, as it were in the shade, without any beating of drums or fanfares on trumpets.'

Servais, François-Mathieu (Franz) (St Petersburg 1846–Asnières, nr. Paris, 1901), Belgian composer and conductor—son of **Adrien-François Servais** (Hal 1807–Hal 1866), the 'Paganini of the cello', and his Russian-born wife **Sophie**, née Feygin (St Petersburg 1820–Ixelles 1893)—who became a disciple and protégé of Liszt after going to him, in Weimar, in 1869. Thereafter spending time with his mentor in Italy and Hungary, as well as in Germany, Servais also played a major part in most of the visits made to Belgium in the 1880s by Liszt, in whose honour a soirée musicale was mounted in June 1885 at the Servais villa in Hal, near Brussels.

As early as 1870 Servais was able to write about Liszt, 'What he is doing for me is wonderful, and I truly look upon him as a second father'. Some sixty years later, pointing to the facial similarity between the older and younger musician, and the identical forenames, the music critic Ernest Newman argued that Liszt was, in fact, Servais's real father—by, according to Newman, the Princess Wittgenstein. In her *Franz Servais et Franz Liszt*, however, Malou Haine has recently published a facsimile of the relevant baptismal certificate, making it clear beyond peradventure that Servais was born in March 1846, the son of Adrien-François and Sophie, nearly a year before Liszt and his Princess so much as set eyes upon one another.

Another to be added to the rollcall of spurious Lisztian offspring is found in *Irish and Other Memories* (London, 1922) by the Duke de Stacpoole, who in 1876 took rooms beneath Princess Wittgenstein's in the Via Babuino: 'The famous composer and pianist frequently visited her at her flat, where I often met him and heard him play. Sometimes his masterly touch would collect a crowd in the street. Years later, whilst at Simbirsk in Eastern Russia, I chanced to meet the organist of the Cathedral, and was struck by his extraordinary likeness to Liszt. I learned that he was a son of the great man, and was himself very talented. Seldom have I heard anyone play the organ as he did.'

Before embarking on an outstanding solo career, Servais's brother **Joseph** (Hal 1850–Hal 1885) was for a time a cellist in the Weimar orchestra. Their brother-in-law, the Franco-Polish sculptor **Cyprien Godebski** (Méry-sur-Cher 1835–Paris 1909), was also known to Liszt; a photograph of his model of a planned—but never realized—Liszt monument is one of the many illustrations in Haine, *Franz Servais et Franz Liszt*.

Sgambati, Giovanni (Rome 1841–Rome 1914), became a pupil of Liszt in Rome in 1862; thereafter they enjoyed a cordial friendship. 'The Italian's admiration for the great Hungarian was profound; for his part, Liszt at once discerned Sgambati's merits, both as pianist and composer,' Mary Tibaldi Chiesa has written (*Nuova Antologia*, July 1936). 'Putting all his experience at the younger man's disposal, and revealing to him the beauties of the classics, he realized that he had found someone who would be a valuable collaborator in making German instrumental music known in Italy, and also in helping with, and continuing, the task of reforming music in Rome.'

It was Sgambati who conducted the première of a large part of *Christus*, as well as the first performances in Rome of the *Eroica* and Dante symphonies. He was also an admirer of Wagner, whose acquaintance he made during that composer's visit to Rome in 1876.

Shestakova, Lyudmila Ivanovna (Novospasskoye [now Glinka], Smolensk district, 1816–St Petersburg 1906), sister of Mikhail Glinka who, after his death, and with the help above all of Balakirev, toiled devotedly to bring about publication of his complete works: a task which was almost finished at the time of her own death. Liszt made the acquaintance of Glinka and his music when visiting St Petersburg in 1842; and in a letter to Mme Shestakova of 14 June 1879 he hailed him, fittingly, as 'the patriarch-prophet of music in Russia'.

Simonffy, Kálmán von (Tápiószele 1831–Budapest 1888), Hungarian song composer who idolized Liszt until, in 1859, he learnt that the book *Des Bohémiens et de leur musique en Hongrie* credited the gypsies, rather than the Hungarians themselves, with creation of the nation's music, when he at once took up a position against him.

Simor, Cardinal János (Székesfehérvár 1813–Esztergom 1891). The salient points of the career, and something of the character, of this high-ranking Hungarian prelate and occasional host of Liszt's, are brought out in his obituary in *The Times* (24 Jan. 1891): 'He was the son of a mechanic . . . and there was not much in his education, his character, or his manner to prepare him for the high position he was to fill. He was a man of short stature, rather rough, outspoken, and little inclined to yield in any argument. By force of talent, however, he made his way to an ecclesiastical professoriate, was appointed Court Chaplain in 1850, and in 1857 became Bishop of Raab [Győr]. In 1862 he became Archbishop of Gran [Esztergom], and, officiating as Primate, he five years later crowned the Emperor and Empress of Austria as King and Queen of Hungary. He received the Cardinal's hat in 1873. . . . Cardinal Simor lived in great simplicity. One of his peculiarities was an aversion to railways, and he travelled on them as little as possible. His journeys between Gran and Budapest were always made in a carriage and four, and, when business took him to Vienna, he preferred the Danube route. He was a great lover of books, and collected a magnificent library in his new palace at Gran. . . .'

Siposs, Antal (Ipolyság 1839–Révfülöp 1923), Hungarian composer, pianist (pupil of Liszt 1858–61) and teacher who, in 1875, opened a music school in Budapest largely with the aim of preparing gifted youngsters for higher studies with Liszt.

Smetana, Bedřich (Litomyšl 1824–Prague 1884), Bohemian composer whom Liszt captivated and inspired with his Prague concerts of 1840 and gave much help and encouragement to in 1848 and thereafter (especially in the matter of finding a publisher for the *Six morceaux caractéristiques* for piano, which Smetana dedicated to him). He visited him in 1856, gave him hospitality at Weimar in 1857 (when Smetana attended the first performance of the Faust Symphony) and 1859, and was with him again at Pest in 1865, catching sight of him at a public rehearsal of *St Elisabeth* and jumping down from the stage to kiss and embrace him, and in Prague in 1871. On this last occasion Smetana—a pianist of genius—played to him excerpts from *Dalibor* and conducted for him the overture to *The Bartered Bride*. Among other works appreciated by Liszt were the opera *Libuše*, the great cycle of symphonic poems forming *Má Vlast*, the G minor Trio and the String Quartet No. 1, *Aus meinem Leben*.

Unlike so many whom Liszt helped, Smetana remained lastingly grateful, as he showed in some heartfelt words penned in a letter of May 1880: 'I have *him to thank* for everything I have achieved; it was he above all who gave me self-confidence and showed me the path I had to take. Since then he has been my *master*, my *example* and for all of us surely an *unattained ideal*. My reverence, my admiration, and my gratitude know no bounds.'

When, in 1884, Liszt received news of Smetana's distressing end, he was profoundly moved and remarked: 'He was indeed a genius!'

Spohr, Rosalie (Brunswick 1829–Berlin 1919), German harpist (daughter of the piano manufacturer Wilhelm Spohr and niece of the composer Louis Spohr) who as a 15-year-old attended Liszt's two Brunswick concerts of March 1844 and received 'the greatest musical impressions of her young life'. Entering upon a musical career she became 'the Liszt of the harp' and, according to Hans von Bülow, 'the most ideal representative of her beautiful instrument'. She played to Liszt for the first time at Weimar in February 1851, finding him, as she wrote to her uncle, 'more interested in the harp than any pianist I have known'. Although, on her marriage to Count Xaver von Sauerma-

Zülzendorf in 1855, she retired from the concert platform, she remained on friendly terms with Liszt until the end of his life. Two short letters to Countess Sauerma were among the last he wrote.

Stahr, Adolf (Prenzlau 1805–Wiesbaden 1876), German writer who made Liszt's acquaintance on Heligoland in 1849. The two were introduced by the novelist and travel-writer **Fanny Lewald** (Königsberg 1811–Dresden 1889), who in 1855 became Stahr's second wife. Anna (1835–1909) and Helene Stahr (1838–1914), the offspring of his first marriage, were given much help and encouragement by Liszt. Becoming piano teachers, in their Weimar home they gave musical matinées at which his pupils were invited to play. Second to none in their admiration of the great composer-pianist, they wrote after his death to Henriette von Liszt: 'Never again will the light come into our lives—for, with him, down into the history of art has gone the sun of the universe.'

Street-Klindworth, Agnes (Bremen 1825–Paris 1906). Ostensibly for piano studies with Liszt—actually for intelligence-gathering purposes on behalf of her father Georg Klindworth, Metternich's master spy—this attractive young woman, briefly married to an Englishman, first came to Weimar in the autumn of 1853. In December, accompanied by her mother, she journeyed to Hamburg, where the first of her four children was born (21 Jan. 1854). Bringing the infant George with her, she returned to Weimar in the autumn of that year; and it seems to have been about this time that she and Liszt became lovers. In April 1855 she moved to Brussels. Missing Agnes badly, Liszt not only wrote to her frequently (her letters to him, to prevent the consequences of their falling into Princess Carolyne's hands, were sent to safe addresses elsewhere in Weimar), but also contrived trysts with her in other towns and cities. He was the father of none of Agnes's four children (one, possibly two, of whom died in infancy), and as time went by their love-affair was transformed into a good, honest friendship. Although, later on, there were occasional periods in which no correspondence was maintained, they never quite lost contact, and the last of Liszt's letters to this former mistress was penned just three weeks before his death.

For a detailed study of the relationship, and some sage comments on Liszt's love for two women (Agnes and Carolyne) simultaneously, see Alan Walker's 'Agnes Street-Klindworth: A Spy in the Court of Weimar?' The edition of Liszt's letters to Agnes published by La Mara in 1894 was heavily expurgated. A complete edition is now being prepared by Pauline Pocknell.

Streicher, Johann Baptist (Vienna 1796–Vienna 1871), Austrian piano manufacturer. His wife Friederike, née Müller, was a pupil of Chopin and the dedicatee of his *Allegro de Concert*, Op. 46.

Tardieu, Malwine (d. Brussels 1896), née Wetzlar. Wife of Charles Tardieu, editor-in-chief of the *Indépendance Belge*, this lady kept Liszt informed, in his last years, of musical events and publications in the Belgian capital. She was his hostess when he visited Brussels in the spring of 1882.

Tausig, Carl (Warsaw 1841–Leipzig 1871), Polish pianist and composer who was brought to Liszt at the age of 13 and, with such a mentor and his own innate talent, developed into one of the most remarkable virtuosi of the century. In 1864 he entered into a short-lived marriage with the pianist Szerafina Vrabély, with whom he settled in Berlin. Here, in 1865, he opened a School of Advanced Piano-Playing which was attended some years later by the American pianist Amy Fay, whose graphic descriptions of Tausig's classes—he was a reluctant and tyrannical teacher—and playing can be read in her *Music Study in Germany*.

Liszt's reaction to the tragically early death, from typhoid fever, of his great pupil was described by Emilie Merian-Genast in a letter (10 Aug. 1871) to Eduard Lassen which also casts a little light on Tausig's compatriot Marie Mouchanoff, who was at his bedside during his final moments: 'Liszt was deeply shaken by Tausig's death, and the first few days were made very difficult by uncertainty over whether or not the body was to be taken to Berlin. In the end it was, which spared Liszt the melancholy duty of attending the funeral. Mme Mouchanoff came to Weimar for two days, but was so badly affected by the sad events that I can't help feeling concerned about her. . . . She is a quite wonderful woman and means all the more to me because she has an aversion to superficial relationships—an aversion that she acts on with enormous determination, in this way saving herself much time-wasting and allowing her to get what is best and most important from the people with whom she does associate. She told me wonderful things about Tausig. In the evening, as she, Liszt and I were sitting together really quietly and solemnly, he suddenly opened the piano and played—your song *Das Leben draussen*. I wish you could have shared the impression it made on us, and I think it is bound to give you pleasure to know that this was the only music he could endure that evening' (Schorn, *Das nachklassische Weimar*, ii. 295–6).

Thalberg, Sigismond (Paquis, nr. Geneva, 1812–Posillipo 1871), Austrian pianist and composer who specialized in florid display pieces for his instrument in which a melody played in the middle of the keyboard by the thumbs, and sustained by the pedal, was surrounded by rippling passagework above and below, with an effect of three hands. 'He created a great sensation in Paris and became the idol of the public, principally, perhaps, because it was felt that he could be imitated, even successfully, which with Chopin and Liszt was out of the question,' recalled Charles Hallé. When Liszt returned to Paris from Geneva in late 1836 there was much rivalry between the two—and still more, per-haps, between their respective admirers—until the day when they appeared together at the Princess Belgiojoso's, the outcome, according to Jules Janin, being 'two victors and no vanquished'. The severity of Liszt's criticism of Thalberg's music antagonized the Austrian pianist's supporters, but its justness has been amply confirmed by the verdict of posterity, which has consigned to oblivion almost everything that 'Old Arpeggio', as he was nicknamed, ever wrote. The type of showpiece of his own composition on which his programmes of the 1830s were built, he was still offering to audiences in the 1860s, at a time when Liszt had behind him the great achievements of his Altenburg years—including, amongst so much else, the Faust and Dante symphonies, the Gran Mass and B minor Sonata—and had started work on *Christus*.

Theiner, Augustin (Breslau 1804–Civitavecchia 1874), Catholic historian. Becoming a priest, he entered the Congregazione dell'Oratorio and in 1855 was appointed Prefect of the Vatican Archives. At the time of the First Vatican Council (1869–70) he was dismissed from office for making documents available to opponents (above all to Cardinal Hohenlohe) of the dogma of papal infallibility. When, some years later, Father Theiner lay dying, his servant and landlady telegraphed to obtain absolution for him. It came, and with it the Pope's special benediction.

Tolstoy, Count Alexei Constantinovich (St Petersburg 1817–Krasnyi Rog, Chernigov district, 1875), Russian poet, novelist, and dramatist who spent much of the last ten years of his life in Rome, where he was on very friendly terms with Liszt. His wife, the recipient of Liszt's letter of condolence, was described by Gregorovius as being 'thoroughly versed in literature and eager for knowledge'. 'Although looking like a Mongolian, she attracts all who come near her. Her intellect is not original, but she has a beautiful mind, and her face is always lighted up from within.'

Viardot, Pauline (Paris 1821–Paris 1910), née Garcia, French mezzo-soprano of Spanish origin. Younger sister of Maria Malibran and Manuel Garcia *fils*, and herself exceptionally gifted, both vocally and dramatically, she achieved enormous success in such parts as Fidès in Meyerbeer's *Le Prophète* and the title role in Gluck's *Orfeo*. Her husband from 1840 was the writer Louis Viardot (1800–83). Not blessed (or cursed) with beautiful features, she could nevertheless count numerous admirers, among them Turgenev, who fell in love with her in St Petersburg in 1843 and remained devoted until his death. Maurice Sand was also long infatuated. 'What made her so captivating, more perhaps than her talent as a singer, was her personality, assuredly one of the most remarkable I have ever encountered,' recalled Camille Saint-Saëns, who dedicated to Pauline his opera *Samson and Delilah*. An outstanding pianist (as a girl, a pupil of Liszt, for whom she suffered the pains of unrequited love) and talented composer, she wrote, *inter alia*, several charming operettas; and her arrangements of some of his Mazurkas were admired by Chopin. Although not drawn to the music of Liszt and Wagner, she was always an enthusiast of Liszt's pianistic prowess. 'After him I shall not for a long time be able to listen to anyone else playing the piano,' she wrote after hearing him at Weimar in 1858. 'He is still *the colossus*.'

Wagner, Wilhelm Richard (Leipzig 1813–Venice 1883), German composer whose friendship with Liszt, one of the most famous in the history of music, began inauspiciously when the little-known Kapellmeister and the ultra-celebrated pianist first encountered one another. Liszt had no way of knowing of the musical and dramatic gifts concealed in the rather awkward German; and the latter, likewise, could hardly discern, at that time, that there was so much more to the fêted Hungarian than dazzling pianism. Later, after Liszt had attended a performance of *Rienzi*, and come to know and admire *Tannhäuser*, their friendship—for long kept up largely by correspondence—developed rapidly. When, in 1849, Wagner paid a fraught and fleeting visit to Weimar after his part in the ill-fated Dresden uprising, Liszt gave the fugitive both shelter and financial assistance. A year later he conducted the première of *Lohengrin*; in the summer of

1853, and again in 1856, he visited the exile in Zurich; and throughout the 1850s he responded to Wagner's stream of requests and entreaties with unfaltering encouragement and, when possible, material support.

When, in the early 1860s, Wagner was at last allowed back into Germany without fear of prosecution, he was evidently greatly disappointed to find that Liszt was about to settle in Italy. Since, in his single-minded way, Wagner generally discarded people when they were no longer of use to him, his correspondence with Liszt more or less petered out soon after the latter's departure for Rome.

The severest test the friendship had to face came at the end of the 1860s, when Liszt's daughter, Cosima, abandoned her husband Hans von Bülow and, taking their children with her, joined Wagner—to whom she had already borne two daughters and whose son she was carrying—on a permanent basis, marrying him in 1870. Feeling morally obliged to stand by the wronged Hans, for all the latter's inadequacies as a husband, Liszt sorrowfully broke off relations with Cosima and Richard, thus bringing about an estrangement of several years' duration. A reconciliation took place in 1872; and four years later, at the first Bayreuth Festival, Wagner, though not given to bearing a burden of gratitude, paid fitting tribute to the man who had been his staunchest ally in earlier, more traumatic years: 'I have one person to thank, without whom not a single note of my music would have been known; a dear friend who, when I was outlawed from Germany, was the first to recognize me and, with matchless devotion and self-denial, to draw me into the light. To this dear friend the highest honour is due. It is my sublime friend and master, Franz Liszt!'

Liszt's letters and relevant essays make plain his boundless admiration of the Wagnerian music dramas, in defence of which he even crossed swords with the Princess Wittgenstein. The admiration was not unreciprocated. Wagner acknowledged the influence on his harmony and orchestration of the works of Liszt (above all the symphonic poems, of which he made a close study), appropriated certain Lisztian themes for his own use, wrote to him with the utmost enthusiasm of the Sonata in B minor ('beyond all conception beautiful, great, lovely, deep and noble, sublime even as thyself'), and expressed profound appreciation of the Faust and Dante symphonies. (This latter work was dedicated to him with words quoted from Dante's tribute [*Inferno*, i. 85] to Virgil: 'Tu se' lo mio maestro e 'l mio autore'; and one can only wonder if, when penning them and thus equating Wagner with Virgil and himself with Dante, it crossed Liszt's mind that, while Virgil is a very great poet, Dante is an even greater.)

As the years passed, however, and Wagner became ever more scornful about and dismissive of the music of great contemporaries, no exception was made for the introspective and experimental late works of Liszt, of which he had not the least understanding. Cosima's diary records several occasions during the two composers' last reunion, in Venice, in which Wagner—when Liszt was not present—would speak scathingly of his old friend's creations and behaviour alike. (This last was generally nothing more than that Liszt had chosen to spend the evening out with friends rather than *chez* Wagner.) There may also have been occasional displays of Wagnerian petulance and ill humour when Liszt *was* present. To read the diary is in any case to be reminded both of Liszt's admirable tolerance in old age and of his difficult circumstances in those years. Finally to wash his hands of the boorish nonsense and egomania of his son-in-law—who could, in his heavy Teutonic way, be good-humoured and affectionate when nothing was 'vexing' or 'annoying' him (occurrences that were all too frequent), and who even urged Liszt to make his home with the family permanently—would also have meant the severing of relations with his only surviving child and her children. Following Wagner's sudden death a month after the end of the visit, however, the lonely and unsuspecting Liszt, who wished only to be in harmony with those nearest to him and who was by nature conciliatory and forgiving, then found that he had further—and far more contemptible—nonsense to put up with. (See under **Cosima Liszt**.)

Wieck, Clara, see **Schumann**.

Wolff, Pierre-Etienne (b. 1810), Swiss pianist and teacher who was one of Liszt's earliest pupils. They renewed acquaintance when Liszt visited Geneva in 1831, when Wolff stayed in Paris in 1834, and again when Liszt and Marie d'Agoult settled in Geneva while awaiting the birth of their first child. Of the certificate (incorrect in certain details regarding the mother) recording this event, Wolff, a professor at the newly opened Geneva Conservatoire, was one of the three witnesses, the others being Liszt himself and James Fazy.

Zhukovsky (Joukovsky), Paul von (Frankfurt am Main 1845–Weimar 1912), German painter, son of Vasily Andreyevich Zhukovsky the distinguished Russian poet and translator who was a friend of Pushkin and tutor to the Tsarevich (the later Alexander II). The painter, in 1882, of a portrait of Liszt for the Canadian piano manufacturers Mason and Risch, Paul was also a close associate of the Wagner family; it was he who on 20 February 1883 sent Liszt a detailed account of the circumstances of the death of Wagner. His later years were spent in Weimar, where he was a close friend of Adelheid von Schorn.

Zichy, Count Géza (Sztára 1849–Budapest 1924), Hungarian pianist, composer, and poet who at the age of 14 lost his right arm in a hunting accident but became, nevertheless, a celebrated—and most 'dexterous'—left-handed virtuoso. From 1875 to 1918 he was Director of the National Conservatoire in Budapest, and between 1891 and 1894 Intendant of the Royal Hungarian Opera. His devotion to Liszt, from whom he received much help and encouragement, is made clear in his memoirs, in which he also recalled their first meeting, in March 1873, after a concert in which Zichy's ballad *Klára Zach* had been performed: 'Franz Liszt came and spoke very kindly to me, inviting me to visit him. . . . So friendly an invitation I could not resist. Liszt seated himself at the piano and played my ballad; and, oh, gracious Heavens, *how* he played it! Passages which struck him as too monotonous he changed on the spot; the main themes he transposed and broadened, enriching them with a wealth of passagework; and he did not leave off saying again and again: "I know! I know! *This* is how you imagined it, but not how it came out! . . ." As I left the great man I felt dizzy, and a new world opened before my eyes.'

Zichy's wife, Melanie, was the daughter of Liszt's friend Count Guido Karácsonyi.

SOURCES

ABBREVIATIONS

BDL   R. Bory, 'Diverses lettres inédites de Liszt', *Schweizerisches Jahrbuch für Musik-wissenschaft*, iii (Aarau, 1928)

BLB   La Mara (ed.), *Briefwechsel zwischen Franz Liszt und Hans von Bülow* (Leipzig, 1898)

BLC   La Mara (ed.), *Briefwechsel zwischen Franz Liszt und Carl Alexander, Grossherzog von Sachsen* (Leipzig, 1909)

B*RS*   R. Bory, *Une retraite romantique en Suisse* (Lausanne, 1930)

C*FL*   W. von Csapó (ed.), *Franz Liszt's Briefe an Baron Anton Augusz 1846–1878* (Budapest, 1911)

CLA   D. Ollivier (ed.), *Correspondance de Liszt et de la Comtesse d'Agoult* (2 vols., Paris, 1933–4)

CLM   D. Ollivier (ed.), *Correspondance de Liszt et de sa fille Madame Emile Ollivier 1842–1862* (Paris, 1936)

CM*B*   G. Colli and M. Montinari (eds.), *Briefe an Friedrich Nietzsche* (Berlin, 1977)

D*BZ*   S. A. Dianin, *Borodin: Zhizneopisanie materiali i dokumenti* (Moscow, 1960)

FLB   La Mara (ed.), *Franz Liszt's Briefe* (8 vols., Leipzig, 1893–1905)

GCL   M. Gravina (ed.), 'Une Correspondance inédite de Liszt', *La Revue hebdomadaire*, Mar. 1927

IAN   W. Ilges, 'Aus dem Nachlasse Munkácsys', *Deutsche Revue*, 26/3 (Sept. 1901)

K*GS*   W. Karénine, *George Sand: Sa vie et ses Œuvres* (4 vols., Paris, 1899–1926)

K*WL*   E. Kloss (ed.), *Briefwechsel zwischen Wagner und Liszt* (2 vols., 3rd rev. edn., Leipzig, 1910)

LBM   La Mara (ed.), *Franz Liszt's Briefe an seine Mutter* (Leipzig, 1918)

LDM   La Mara, *Durch Musik und Leben im Dienste des Ideals* (2 vols., Leipzig, 1917)

LLU   D. Legány (ed.), *Franz Liszt: Unbekannte Presse und Briefe aus Wien 1822–1886* (Budapest, 1984)

M*PC*   A. Malvezzi, *La Principessa Cristina di Belgiojoso*, ii (Milan, 1936)

M*RM*   T. Marix-Spire, *Les Romantiques et la musique: Le cas George Sand 1804–1838* (Paris, 1954)

N*FC*   F. Niecks, *Friedrich Chopin als Mensch und als Musiker*, i (Leipzig, 1890)

O*AM*   D. Ollivier (ed.), *Autour de Mme d'Agoult et de Liszt (Alfred de Vigny, Emile Ollivier, Princesse de Belgiojoso): Lettres publiées avec introduction et notes* (Paris, 1941)

P*LB*   M. Prahács (ed.), *Franz Liszt: Briefe aus ungarischen Sammlungen, 1835–1886* (Budapest, 1966)

Q*AN*   L. Quicherat, *Adolphe Nourrit: Sa vie, son talent, son caractère*, iii (Paris, 1867)

R*LE*   L. Ramann, *Lisztiana: Erinnerungen an Franz Liszt in Tagebuchblättern, Briefen und Dokumenten aus den Jahren 1873–1886/7* (Mainz, 1983)

RLS L. Rabes (ed.), *Liszt Saeculum*, 35 (Älvsjö, 1985)
RMI *Rivista musicale italiana*, 39 (Turin, 1932)
SLG A. Stern (ed.), *Franz Liszts Briefe an Carl Gille* (Leipzig, 1903)
SZM A. von Schorn, *Zwei Menschenalter: Erinnerungen und Briefe* (Berlin, 1901)
VFL J. Vier, *Franz Liszt—L'Artiste, le clerc: Documents inédits* (Paris, 1950)
WLG C. Wagner, *Franz Liszt: Ein Gedenkblatt von seiner Tochter* (2nd edn., Munich, 1911)
ZAL Graf G. Zichy, *Aus meinem Leben* (3 vols., Stuttgart, 1911–20)

1. *FLB* i. 6–8.
2. *LBM* 12–13.
3. *LBM* 13–14.
4. *LBM* 14–15.
5. *CLA* i. 19–20.
6. *CLA* i. 22–3.
7. *CLA* i. 25–6.
8. *CLA* i. 26–8.
9. *CLA* i. 31–2.
10. N*FC* 262–3.
11. *CLA* i. 35–6.
12. *CLA* i. 36–7.
13. *CLA* i. 37–8.
14. *CLA* i. 39–40.
15. *CLA* i. 42–3.
16. *CLA* i. 47–8.
17. *CLA* i. 49.
18. *CLA* i. 59–60.
19. *CLA* i. 68–9.
20. *CLA* i. 72–4.
21. *CLA* i. 77–9.
22. *LBM* 10–11.
23. *LBM* 18.
24. *CLA* i. 81–4.
25. *CLA* i. 87.
26. *CLA* i. 89–90.
27. BDL 15–17.
28. *CLA* i. 102–3.
29. *CLA* i. 105–6.
30. *CLA* i. 109.
31. *CLA* i. 109–11.
32. *LBM* 15–16.
33. *CLA* i. 117–21.
34. *CLA* i. 122–4.

35. *LBM* 16–17.
36. M*RM* 610–11.
37. *LBM* 19–22.
38. M*RM* 612–15.
39. *LBM* 25–7.
40. *LBM* 27–8.
41. *LBM* 28–31.
42. K*GS* ii. 254–6.
43. B*RS* 99–102.
44. M*RM* 616–18.
45. *CLA* i. 139–41.
46. *CLA* i. 141–2.
47. *CLA* i. 142–5.
48. *CLA* i. 145–7.
49. *CLA* i. 153–5.
50. *CLA* i. 158–60.
51. *CLA* i. 163–4.
52. *CLA* i. 164–7.
53. V*FL* 27.
54. *CLA* i. 169–71.
55. *CLA* i. 180–2.
56. *CLA* i. 186–90.
57. *CLA* i. 190–1.
58. *CLA* i. 193–5.
59. M*PC* 235–6.
60. M*RM* 618–19.
61. *CLA* i. 209–10.
62. *CLA* i. 210–11.
63. B*RS* 131–3.
64. V*FL* 39–43.
65. Q*AN* 376–7.
66. *CLA* i. 213–15.
67. *CLA* i. 215–18.
68. M*PC* 237–40.

69. *CLA* i. 218–19.
70. *CLA* i. 220–1.
71. *CLA* i. 221–2.
72. *CLA* i. 222–3.
73. *FLB* i. 18–20.
74. *CLA* i. 226–9.
75. *CLA* i. 230–1.
76. Q*AN* 377–8.
77. *LBM* 48–9.
78. B*RS* 144–6.
79. Q*AN* 381–3.
80. *LBM* 49–50.
81. V*FL* 48–53.
82. Q*AN* 383–5.
83. B*RS* 154–8.
84. *FLB* i. 24–6.
85. *FLB* i. 26–8.
86. M*PC* 271–2.
87. *CLA* i. 264–8.
88. *CLA* i. 280–3.
89. *CLA* i. 285–8.
90. *CLA* i. 292–6.
91. *CLA* i. 310–13.
92. *CLA* i. 330–7.
93. *CLA* i. 340–4.
94. *CLA* i. 344–8.
95. *CLA* i. 349–53.
96. *CLA* i. 355–7.
97. *CLA* i. 372–3.
98. *CLA* i. 390–2.
99. *CLA* i. 405–8.
100. *CLA* i. 414–15.
101. *CLA* i. 416–17.
102. *CLA* i. 421–2.

103. *CLA* i. 427–8.
104. *CLA* i. 428–30.
105. *CLA* i. 433–4.
106. *CLA* i. 440–1.
107. *CLA* i. 441–3.
108. *CLA* i. 443–4.
109. *CLA* i. 446–7.
110. *CLA* i. 450–1.
111. *CLA* ii. 11–12.
112. *FLB* i. 37–8.
113. *CLA* ii. 14–15.
114. *CLA* ii. 16–19.
115. *CLA* ii. 22–3.
116. *CLA* ii. 25–6.
117. *CLA* ii. 26–7.
118. *CLA* ii. 34–5.
119. M*PC* 300–2.
120. *CLA* ii. 40–2.
121. *CLA* ii. 53–5.
122. *CLA* ii. 59–61.
123. M*RM* 621–2.
124. *CLA* ii. 74–6.
125. *CLA* ii. 135–6.
126. *CLA* ii. 147.
127. *CLA* ii. 148–9.
128. *CLA* ii. 149–50.
129. *CLA* ii. 151–2.
130. *CLA* ii. 159–61.
131. *CLA* ii. 161–3.
132. *CLA* ii. 163–5.
133. *CLA* ii. 165–6.
134. *CLA* ii. 166–8.
135. *CLA* ii. 168–9.
136. *CLA* ii. 173.
137. *CLA* ii. 174.
138. M*PC* 332–4.
139. *CLA* ii. 177–80.
140. *CLA* ii. 181–4.
141. *CLA* ii. 188–90.
142. *CLA* ii. 191–2.
143. *CLA* ii. 194–5.
144. *CLA* ii. 197–202.
145. *CLA* ii. 261–5.

146. *CLA* ii. 204–5.
147. *CLA* ii. 210–13.
148. *CLA* ii. 220.
149. *CLA* ii. 223–5.
150. *CLA* ii. 226–9.
151. *CLA* ii. 229–30.
152. *CLA* ii. 230–1.
153. *CLA* ii. 238–41.
154. *CLA* ii. 242.
155. *CLA* ii. 247.
156. *CLA* ii. 249–51.
157. *CLA* ii. 253–4.
158. *FLB* viii. 31.
159. *CLA* ii. 272–3.
160. *CLA* ii. 274–5.
161. *CLA* ii. 277–9.
162. *CLA* ii. 279–81.
163. *CLA* ii. 283.
164. *CLA* ii. 287–8.
165. *CLA* ii. 291–2.
166. *CLA* ii. 293–5.
167. *CLA* ii. 303–5.
168. *CLA* ii. 320–3.
169. *CLA* ii. 325–7.
170. *CLA* ii. 329–31.
171. *CLA* ii. 331–2.
172. *CLA* ii. 334–5.
173. *CLA* ii. 338.
174. *CLA* ii. 339.
175. *CLA* ii. 340.
176. *CLA* ii. 340.
177. *CLA* ii. 341.
178. *CLA* ii. 342.
179. *LBM* 55–6.
180. *LBM* 57–8.
181. M*RM* 568–9.
182. *LBM* 60–2.
183. O*AM* 185–8.
184. *CLM* 25–6.
185. V*FL* 66–9.
186. V*FL* 77–8.
187. *LBM* 62–3.
188. *CLA* ii. 343–4.

189. *FLB* viii. 40–2.
190. *FLB* viii. 42–4.
191. *LBM* 65.
192. *RMI* 259–60.
193. *RMI* 261–2.
194. *CLA* ii. 345.
195. *CLA* ii. 349–54.
196. O*AM* 193–5.
197. *CLA* ii. 354–8.
198. *BLC* 7–12.
199. *CLA* ii. 365–9.
200. *LBM* 72–5.
201. C*FL* 41–3.
202. *CLA* ii. 369–73.
203. *LBM* 75–7.
204. *CLA* ii. 374–7.
205. *FLB* iv. 2–5.
206. *CLA* ii. 377–80.
207. *FLB* iv. 6.
208. *FLB* iv. 7–8.
209. *CLA* ii. 380–3.
210. *BLC* 15–19.
211. *CLA* ii. 384–9.
212. *FLB* viii. 50–1.
213. *LBM* 79–81.
214. *BLC* 19–21.
215. *CLA* ii. 390–2.
216. *FLB* iv. 15–16.
217. *FLB* iv. 22–6.
218. *FLB* iv. 27–8.
219. *FLB* iv. 29–30.
220. *FLB* viii. 58.
221. *FLB* iv. 31–2.
222. *FLB* i. 71–2.
223. K*WL* i. 11–12.
224. *LBM* 100–1.
225. *BLC* 22–4.
226. *FLB* i. 76–8.
227. *FLB* i. 78–9.
228. *BLC* 26.
229. *CLM* 37–9.
230. *BLC* 30.
231. V*FL* 97–100.

232. *FLB* viii. 61–2.
233. *FLB* viii. 65–7.
234. *FLB* viii. 70–1.
235. *KWL* i. 69–70.
236. *LBM* 87–8.
237. *CLM* 48–51.
238. *LBM* 88–90.
239. *CLM* 54–7.
240. *LBM* 91–2.
241. *CLM* 62–5.
242. *FLB* iv. 40–1.
243. *FLB* iv. 42–3.
244. *FLB* iv. 49–51.
245. *FLB* iv. 51–4.
246. *FLB* iv. 56–7.
247. *FLB* iv. 64.
248. *FLB* iv. 65–7.
249. *FLB* iv. 70–2.
250. *FLB* iv. 72–3.
251. *LBM* 93–5.
252. *KWL* i. 107–9.
253. *FLB* i. 95–8/*LLU* 133.
254. *CLM* 68–70.
255. *FLB* iv. 88–9.
256. *FLB* iv. 96–8.
257. *FLB* iv. 104–5.
258. *FLB* iv. 105–6.
259. *FLB* iv. 106–9.
260. *FLB* iv. 109–10.
261. *FLB* iv. 111.
262. *FLB* iv. 112.
263. *FLB* iv. 113–15.
264. *FLB* iv. 117–19.
265. *FLB* iv. 121–2.
266. *FLB* viii. 86–8.
267. *LBM* 99–100.
268. *KWL* i. 144–6.
269. *KWL* i. 147–9.
270. *KWL* i. 160–1.
271. *FLB* i. 109–10.
272. *FLB* i. 110–11.
273. *FLB* iv. 126–8.

274. *FLB* iv. 129–30.
275. *FLB* iv. 130–1.
276. *FLB* iv. 38–9.
277. *LLU* 139.
278. *WLG* 74–6.
279. *KWL* i. 173–5.
280. *FLB* i. 113.
281. *FLB* viii. 98–9.
282. *FLB* i. 114.
283. *FLB* i. 120–5.
284. *KWL* i. 192–7.
285. *KWL* i. 202–4.
286. *FLB* viii. 100–2.
287. *FLB* i. 133–4.
288. *FLB* iv. 137–8.
289. *FLB* iv. 139–41.
290. *FLB* iv. 142–6.
291. *FLB* iv. 146–7.
292. *FLB* iv. 148–50.
293. *FLB* iv. 152–3.
294. *FLB* iv. 155–7.
295. *FLB* iv. 158–61.
296. *FLB* iv. 164–5.
297. *FLB* iv. 179.
298. *FLB* iv. 181–2.
299. *FLB* iv. 184–5.
300. *LLU* 145–7.
301. *WLG* 76–8.
302. *LBM* 102–3.
303. *CLM* 100–1.
304. *FLB* iv. 190–1.
305. *FLB* iv. 193–4.
306. *FLB* iv. 194–7.
307. *FLB* iv. 198–9.
308. *FLB* iv. 203–4.
309. *FLB* iv. 205–7.
310. *FLB* iv. 208–9.
311. P*LB* 79–80.
312. *CLM* 106.
313. *FLB* viii. 116–18.
314. *FLB* i. 191–2.
315. *FLB* i. 198–9.
316. *FLB* iv. 212–13.

317. *FLB* iv. 213–14.
318. *FLB* iv. 217–19.
319. *FLB* iii. 20–3.
320. *KWL* ii. 71–3.
321. *FLB* iii. 23–5.
322. *FLB* iii. 25–8.
323. *FLB* iii. 30–1.
324. *FLB* iv. 222–3.
325. *FLB* iv. 230–2.
326. *FLB* iv. 232–3.
327. *FLB* iv. 234–7.
328. *FLB* iv. 237–9.
329. *FLB* iv. 239.
330. *FLB* iv. 240.
331. *FLB* iv. 243–4.
332. *LBM* 103–5.
333. *FLB* iv. 248–51.
334. *FLB* iv. 252–3.
335. *FLB* iv. 253–4.
336. *FLB* iv. 257–8.
337. *FLB* iv. 259–60.
338. *FLB* iii. 45.
339. *FLB* iv. 278–80.
340. *FLB* iv. 288–90.
341. *FLB* iv. 297–8.
342. *FLB* iii. 57–9.
343. *FLB* iii. 59–62.
344. *FLB* iii. 63.
345. *BLB* 171–5.
346. *FLB* i. 218–20.
347. *KWL* ii. 110–12.
348. *LBM* 107–9.
349. *FLB* iii. 73–4.
350. *KWL* ii. 127–9.
351. *KWL* ii. 133–4.
352. *FLB* iv. 312–14.
353. *FLB* iv. 315–17.
354. *FLB* iii. 77–80.
355. *FLB* iv. 317–18.
356. *FLB* iv. 322–4.
357. *FLB* iv. 325–6.
358. *FLB* iv. 328.
359. *FLB* iv. 328–30.

360. *FLB* iv. 331–3.
361. *FLB* iv. 333–5.
362. *FLB* iv. 335–6.
363. *FLB* iv. 338.
364. P*LB* 92–3.
365. P*LB* 93–4.
366. *BLC* 51–2.
367. C*FL* 75–81.
368. *CLM* 182–3.
369. C*FL* 81–4.
370. *FLB* iv. 349–50.
371. K*WL* ii. 154–6.
372. *LBM* 111–13.
373. *FLB* iv. 360–2.
374. *FLB* iv. 363–4.
375. *FLB* iv. 364–6.
376. *FLB* iv. 366–8.
377. *FLB* iv. 370–2.
378. *FLB* iv. 372–3.
379. K*WL* ii. 176–8.
380. *FLB* iv. 377–8.
381. *FLB* iv. 379–82.
382. *FLB* iv. 384–5.
383. *LBM* 116–18.
384. *FLB* iv. 391–2.
385. *FLB* iv. 392–4.
386. *FLB* iv. 396–8.
387. *FLB* iii. 94–5.
388. *CLM* 189–90.
389. *FLB* i. 286.
390. *CLM* 193–4.
391. K*WL* ii. 179–80.
392. *CLM* 200–2.
393. *FLB* i. 295–6.
394. K*WL* ii. 197–8.
395. *FLB* iv. 403–5.
396. *FLB* iv. 406–8.
397. *FLB* iv. 408–9.
398. *FLB* iv. 410.
399. *FLB* iv. 412–14.
400. *FLB* iii. 105–8.
401. *FLB* iv. 422–4.
402. *FLB* iv. 428.

403. *FLB* iv. 429–36.
404. *FLB* iv. 432–4.
405. *FLB* iv. 440–1.
406. *CLM* 209–12.
407. *LBM* 118–20.
408. *FLB* viii. 141–2.
409. K*WL* ii. 220–4.
410. *CLM* 220–2.
411. *FLB* iii. 113–15.
412. K*WL* ii. 245.
413. *FLB* iv. 444–5.
414. *FLB* iv. 447–8.
415. *FLB* iii. 115–16.
416. *FLB* iv. 459–61.
417. *FLB* iv. 461.
418. *FLB* iv. 470–1.
419. *FLB* iv. 476–7.
420. *FLB* iv. 480–2.
421. *FLB* iii. 120–2.
422. P*LB* 105.
423. *FLB* iv. 492–3.
424. *FLB* iv. 494–5.
425. *FLB* iv. 497–9.
426. *BLC* 83–4.
427. *FLB* iv. 500–7.
428. *CLM* 232–3.
429. C*FL* 93–6.
430. *BLC* 87–93.
431. *FLB* v. 7–10.
432. *FLB* iii. 122–3.
433. K*WL* ii. 283–5.
434. *FLB* v. 13.
435. *FLB* v. 14–15.
436. *FLB* v. 15–17.
437. *FLB* iii. 124.
438. *FLB* v. 17–19.
439. *FLB* v. 23–4.
440. *CLM* 248–9.
441. *FLB* v. 25–6.
442. *FLB* v. 26–8.
443. *FLB* v. 28–9.
444. *FLB* v. 34–6.
445. *FLB* v. 38–40.

446. *FLB* v. 40–1.
447. *FLB* v. 42–3.
448. *FLB* v. 43–6.
449. *FLB* v. 47–9.
450. *FLB* iii. 129–32.
451. *FLB* v. 63–6.
452. *LBM* 131–2.
453. *FLB* v. 67–8.
454. *BLC* 99–101.
455. *FLB* v. 73–4.
456. *FLB* v. 79–80.
457. *FLB* v. 85–6.
458. *FLB* iii. 135–8.
459. *FLB* v. 94–5.
460. *FLB* iii. 138–40.
461. *FLB* v. 113–18.
462. *FLB* v. 119–22.
463. *FLB* iii. 143–5.
464. *FLB* v. 126–8.
465. *FLB* v. 131–3.
466. *FLB* v. 135–8.
467. *FLB* v. 138–41.
468. *FLB* v. 141–4.
469. *FLB* iii. 145–6.
470. *CLM* 266–70.
471. *FLB* v. 148–51.
472. *FLB* v. 159–61.
473. *FLB* v. 168–75.
474. *FLB* iii. 150–2.
475. *FLB* v. 177–9.
476. *FLB* v. 179–81.
477. *FLB* v. 182–4.
478. *FLB* v. 185–8.
479. *FLB* v. 190–4.
480. *FLB* v. 194–9.
481. *FLB* v. 199–201.
482. *FLB* v. 202–3.
483. *FLB* v. 205–6.
484. *FLB* v. 209–12.
485. *FLB* v. 215–19.
486. *BLC* 103–5.
487. *FLB* v. 224–6.
488. *FLB* v. 228–31.

489. *FLB* v. 232–4.
490. *FLB* v. 234–6.
491. *FLB* v. 238.
492. *CLM* 296–8.
493. *BLC* 106–9.
494. *FLB* viii. 153–5.
495. P*LB* 111–12.
496. *FLB* vi. 1.
497. *FLB* vi. 2.
498. *FLB* vi. 2–3.
499. *FLB* vi. 5–6.
500. *CLM* 305–6.
501. *CLM* 307–10.
502. *FLB* vi. 11.
503. *CLM* 314–16.
504. *FLB* vi. 9.
505. *FLB* vi. 10.
506. *CLM* 319–21.
507. *CLM* 321–3.
508. *FLB* ii. 16–21.
509. *FLB* vi. 8.
510. V*FL* 110–12.
511. V*FL* 112–14.
512. *FLB* vi. 12–13.
513. *BLC* 114–18.
514. *CFL* 97–9.
515. *LBM* 144–7.
516. *FLB* vi. 14.
517. *FLB* vi. 14–15.
518. V*FL* 118–19.
519. V*FL* 120–2.
520. *FLB* ii. 39–41.
521. *FLB* ii. 41.
522. *FLB* ii. 46.
523. *LBM* 147–9.
524. *FLB* iii. 161–2.
525. *FLB* ii. 50–3.
526. *FLB* iii. 163–4.
527. *FLB* ii. 57–8.
528. *FLB* ii. 58–61.
529. *FLB* iii. 167–70.
530. *FLB* viii. 169–70.
531. *FLB* vi. 22.

532. *FLB* vi. 25.
533. *FLB* vi. 26–7.
534. *FLB* vi. 27–31.
535. *FLB* vi. 31–4.
536. *FLB* vi. 34–6.
537. *FLB* vi. 36–41.
538. *FLB* vi. 46–9.
539. *FLB* vi. 49–51.
540. *FLB* vi. 51–2.
541. *FLB* vi. 53–5.
542. *FLB* vi. 55–8.
543. *FLB* vi. 59–61.
544. V*FL* 135–6.
545. *FLB* iii. 177–9.
546. *FLB* vi. 67–9.
547. *FLB* vi. 69–70.
548. *FLB* vi. 70–5.
549. *FLB* vi. 75–6.
550. *BLC* 130–1.
551. *FLB* vi. 77.
552. *FLB* ii. 80–2.
553. *FLB* iii. 181–3.
554. P*LB* 121–2.
555. *FLB* vi. 79.
556. *FLB* vi. 82–4.
557. *FLB* vi. 84–6.
558. *FLB* vi. 86–7.
559. *FLB* vi. 89–91.
560. *CFL* 102–4.
561. *CFL* 105–7.
562. *LBM* 151–2.
563. *CFL* 107–8.
564. *FLB* viii. 173.
565. *FLB* vi. 95–7.
566. *FLB* vi. 97–100.
567. *FLB* vi. 100–2.
568. *FLB* vi. 105–7.
569. *FLB* vi. 107–9.
570. *FLB* vi. 110–11.
571. *FLB* vi. 111–12.
572. *FLB* vi. 113–15.
573. *FLB* vi. 116–17.
574. *FLB* vi. 117–18.

575. *CFL* 115–18.
576. *FLB* vi. 119–20.
577. *FLB* vi. 120–1.
578. *FLB* vi. 125–6.
579. *FLB* viii. 183–4.
580. *CFL* 120–2.
581. *FLB* iii. 188–90.
582. *BLC* 136–7.
583. *FLB* iii. 190–2.
584. *FLB* vi. 130–2.
585. *FLB* vi. 133–7.
586. *FLB* vi. 137–40.
587. *FLB* vi. 142–3.
588. *FLB* vi. 148.
589. *FLB* vi. 149–50.
590. *FLB* vi. 153–5.
591. *FLB* vi. 155–7.
592. *FLB* vi. 157–9.
593. *FLB* vi. 159–60.
594. *FLB* vi. 160–2.
595. *FLB* iii. 200–1.
596. *FLB* ii. 122–3.
597. *FLB* vi. 165–70.
598. *FLB* vi. 170–3.
599. *FLB* vi. 174–5.
600. *CFL* 146–9.
601. *FLB* vi. 177–9.
602. *FLB* vi. 183–4.
603. *FLB* vi. 186.
604. *FLB* viii. 201–2.
605. *FLB* vi. 186–7.
606. *FLB* viii. 199–200.
607. *FLB* iii. 203–4.
608. *FLB* vi. 189–90.
609. *FLB* vi. 191–2.
610. *FLB* ii. 132–3.
611. *FLB* ii. 135–6.
612. *FLB* vi. 194–5.
613. *FLB* vi. 195–9.
614. *FLB* vi. 199–200.
615. *FLB* vi. 202–4.
616. *FLB* vi. 205–6.
617. P*LB* 135.

618. *FLB* vi. 211–13.
619. *FLB* vi. 213–14.
620. *FLB* vi. 217–18.
621. *FLB* vi. 219–20.
622. *FLB* vi. 220–1.
623. *FLB* vi. 223–4.
624. *FLB* vi. 224–6.
625. C*FL* 154–7.
626. C*FL* 157–9.
627. *FLB* vi. 228–9.
628. *FLB* vi. 229–30.
629. *FLB* ii. 152–4.
630. *FLB* viii. 212–13.
631. *FLB* vi. 232–3.
632. C*FL* 161–4.
633. *FLB* vi. 238–9.
634. C*FL* 164–5.
635. *FLB* vi. 239–41.
636. *FLB* vi. 243–4.
637. *FLB* vi. 248.
638. *FLB* vi. 249.
639. *FLB* vi. 254–6.
640. *FLB* vi. 257–8.
641. *FLB* vi. 258–60.
642. *FLB* vi. 265–7.
643. *FLB* vi. 268–9.
644. *FLB* vi. 282–3.
645. *FLB* viii. 222.
646. *FLB* vi. 288–9.
647. *FLB* vi. 289–91.
648. C*FL* 167–8.
649. *FLB* vi. 295–6.
650. *FLB* vi. 296–7.
651. *FLB* vi. 297–9.
652. *FLB* vi. 299–300.
653. *FLB* vi. 300–1.
654. C*FL* 171–3.
655. *FLB* viii. 226.
656. *FLB* vi. 306–7.
657. *BLC* 149–50.
658. *FLB* vi. 308.
659. *FLB* viii. 232.
660. C*FL* 175–8.

661. C*FL* 178–80.
662. *FLB* vi. 312.
663. *FLB* vi. 316–17.
664. *FLB* vi. 320–2.
665. *FLB* vi. 322–3.
666. *FLB* vi. 324.
667. *FLB* vi. 327–8.
668. *FLB* viii. 239–40.
669. *FLB* vi. 330.
670. *FLB* vi. 331–2.
671. CM*B* 557–8.
672. C*FL* 183–4.
673. *FLB* vi. 341–2.
674. *FLB* vi. 345–6.
675. K*WL* ii. 308.
676. *FLB* vi. 346–7.
677. *FLB* vi. 349.
678. *FLB* vi. 351–2.
679. *FLB* vi. 352–4.
680. *FLB* vi. 355–6.
681. *FLB* vi. 359–60.
682. *FLB* ii. 174–6.
683. *FLB* viii. 252–3.
684. *FLB* vi. 362–3.
685. *FLB* vi. 365–7.
686. *FLB* vi. 368.
687. *FLB* ii. 177–8.
688. *FLB* vi. 369–70.
689. *FLB* vi. 370–1.
690. *FLB* vi. 372–3.
691. *FLB* vi. 374–5.
692. *FLB* vii. 2–3.
693. *FLB* vii. 10.
694. *FLB* viii. 264–5.
695. *FLB* vii. 19–20.
696. *FLB* ii. 187.
697. *FLB* vii. 22–4.
698. *FLB* vii. 26–7.
699. *FLB* vii. 27–9.
700. *FLB* vii. 29.
701. *FLB* vii. 33–4.
702. *FLB* vii. 38.
703. *FLB* vii. 41–3.

704. *FLB* vii. 43–5.
705. *FLB* vii. 46.
706. *FLB* vii. 47.
707. *BLC* 156–7.
708. *FLB* vii. 48–50.
709. *FLB* vii. 52–3.
710. *FLB* vii. 53.
711. *FLB* vii. 57–8.
712. *FLB* vii. 59–60.
713. *FLB* vii. 58.
714. *FLB* vii. 61–3.
715. *BLC* 160–1.
716. *FLB* viii. 273–4.
717. *FLB* vii. 68–70.
718. *FLB* vii. 70–1.
719. *FLB* vii. 72–3.
720. C*FL* 199–201.
721. *FLB* vii. 73–4.
722. *FLB* vii. 75.
723. *BLB* 389–90.
724. *FLB* vii. 81–2.
725. C*FL* 203.
726. *FLB* vii. 86–7.
727. *FLB* vii. 100.
728. *SLG* 60.
729. *FLB* vii. 106–7.
730. *FLB* vii. 109–10.
731. *FLB* vii. 111–12.
732. C*FL* 209–10.
733. *FLB* viii. 297–8.
734. *FLB* viii. 300.
735. *FLB* viii. 300–1.
736. *BLC* 170–1.
737. *FLB* vii. 118.
738. *FLB* viii. 303–4.
739. *FLB* vii. 121–2.
740. *FLB* vii. 122–3.
741. *FLB* vii. 124–5.
742. *FLB* vii. 127–8.
743. *FLB* vii. 128–9.
744. *FLB* vii. 129–30.
745. *FLB* vii. 131.
746. *FLB* viii. 309.

747. *FLB* vii. 132–4.
748. *FLB* vii. 138–9.
749. *FLB* vii. 139–40.
750. *FLB* vii. 140–1.
751. *FLB* vii. 141–3.
752. C*FL* 221–2.
753. *FLB* vii. 150–2.
754. *FLB* vii. 152–3.
755. *FLB* vii. 154–5.
756. *FLB* vii. 155.
757. *FLB* vii. 155.
758. *FLB* vii. 156–7.
759. *FLB* vii. 157–8.
760. *FLB* ii. 243.
761. *FLB* vii. 162–4.
762. *FLB* vii. 165–6.
763. *FLB* viii. 322–3.
764. *FLB* vii. 168–70.
765. *FLB* vii. 170–1.
766. *FLB* vii. 172–3.
767. *BLB* 398.
768. *FLB* vii. 175–6.
769. *FLB* vii. 177–8.
770. *FLB* vii. 184–5.
771. *FLB* vii. 188–91.
772. *FLB* vii. 191–2.
773. *FLB* vii. 193.
774. *FLB* vii. 195–6.
775. *FLB* vii. 196–7.
776. *FLB* vii. 201.
777. *FLB* vii. 201–2.
778. *FLB* vii. 202–3.
779. *FLB* vii. 205–6.
780. GCL 464–5.
781. *FLB* vii. 208.
782. C*FL* 225.
783. GCL 465.
784. *FLB* vii. 208–9.
785. *FLB* vii. 209–10.
786. P*LB* 195.
787. GCL 465–6.
788. *FLB* vii. 214–15.
789. *FLB* vii. 222.

790. *FLB* vii. 223–4.
791. *FLB* vii. 224–6.
792. *FLB* vii. 227–9.
793. C*FL* 227–8.
794. *FLB* vii. 232–3.
795. P*LB* 207.
796. *FLB* vii. 237.
797. *FLB* vii. 237–8.
798. *FLB* vii. 238–40.
799. P*LB* 210–11.
800. *FLB* vii. 244.
801. *FLB* vii. 248–9.
802. *FLB* vii. 253–4.
803. P*LB* 216–17.
804. *FLB* vii. 258–9.
805. *FLB* vii. 259–61.
806. *FLB* viii. 351–2.
807. *FLB* vii. 264.
808. *FLB* viii. 358.
809. *FLB* vii. 266.
810. Z*AL* ii. 79–81.
811. *FLB* vii. 272–3.
812. *FLB* vii. 273–4.
813. *FLB* vii. 275–6.
814. *FLB* vii. 277–8.
815. *FLB* vii. 278–9.
816. *FLB* vii. 280–1.
817. *FLB* viii. 366.
818. *FLB* viii. 368.
819. *FLB* viii. 368.
820. *LDM* i. 338.
821. *FLB* vii. 292–3.
822. *BLC* 183–4.
823. P*LB* 231.
824. D*BZ* 243.
825. *FLB* vii. 297–8.
826. *FLB* vii. 298–9.
827. *FLB* vii. 299–301.
828. *FLB* vii. 302.
829. *FLB* vii. 303.
830. *FLB* viii. 379.
831. *FLB* vii. 306–7.
832. *FLB* vii. 308.

833. *FLB* vii. 310–11.
834. *FLB* vii. 312–13.
835. *FLB* vii. 313–15.
836. *FLB* ii. 306.
837. *FLB* vii. 316–18.
838. *FLB* vii. 318–19.
839. *FLB* vii. 319–20.
840. P*LB* 243.
841. *FLB* vii. 322–4.
842. *FLB* viii. 387.
843. *FLB* vii. 324–5.
844. *FLB* vii. 325–8.
845. *BLC* 186–7.
846. *FLB* vii. 330–1.
847. *FLB* ii. 316–17.
848. *FLB* vii. 331–2.
849. *FLB* vii. 332–3.
850. *FLB* vii. 333–5.
851. *BLC* 187–8.
852. *FLB* vii. 335–6.
853. *FLB* viii. 392–3.
854. *FLB* vii. 338–9.
855. *FLB* vii. 341–3.
856. *FLB* viii. 396–7.
857. *RLS* 81–4.
858. *FLB* vii. 344–5.
859. *FLB* vii. 346.
860. *FLB* vii. 349.
861. *FLB* vii. 351.
862. *FLB* vii. 355–6.
863. *FLB* vii. 356.
864. *FLB* vii. 356–7.
865. *FLB* vii. 357–8.
866. *FLB* vii. 359.
867. *FLB* vii. 360–1.
868. *FLB* ii. 335–7.
869. *FLB* vii. 361–3.
870. *SZM* 433–5.
871. *BLC* 192–4.
872. *FLB* vii. 366–8.
873. *FLB* vii. 368–9.
874. *FLB* vii. 370–1.
875. *FLB* vii. 372–4.

876. *FLB* ii. 345–6.
877. R*LE* 201.
878. *FLB* vii. 374–5.
879. *SZM* 439.
880. *FLB* vii. 375.
881. P*LB* 257.
882. *BLC* 200–1.
883. *FLB* ii. 349–50.
884. *FLB* vii. 376–7.
885. *FLB* vii. 377–8.
886. *FLB* vii. 379–80.
887. *FLB* viii. 406–7.
888. *FLB* vii. 384–5.
889. *FLB* vii. 387–8.
890. *FLB* viii. 410.
891. *FLB* viii. 410–11.
892. *FLB* vii. 391–3.
893. *FLB* vii. 393–4.
894. *FLB* vii. 395.
895. *FLB* vii. 396–7.
896. *FLB* vii. 397–8.
897. *FLB* vii. 399–400.
898. *BLC* 205–6.
899. *FLB* vii. 402.

900. *FLB* vii. 404–5.
901. *FLB* vii. 406–7.
902. S*LG* 76.
903. S*LG* 77.
904. *FLB* vii. 407–8.
905. *FLB* vii. 408.
906. *FLB* vii. 409–10.
907. *FLB* vii. 411–12.
908. *FLB* ii. 370–1.
909. *FLB* ii. 371.
910. *FLB* vii. 417.
911. *FLB* viii. 414.
912. *RMI* 465.
913. *FLB* vii. 418–19.
914. *FLB* vii. 419–20.
915. *FLB* vii. 421.
916. *FLB* vii. 422–3.
917. *FLB* vii. 425–6.
918. *FLB* vii. 427.
919. P*LB* 283–4.
920. Z*AL* iii. 68.
921. *FLB* vii. 429.
922. *FLB* ii. 387–8.
923. *FLB* viii. 418.

924. *FLB* vii. 430–1.
925. *FLB* vii. 431.
926. *FLB* ii. 389.
927. *FLB* vii. 432–3.
928. *FLB* ii. 390.
929. *FLB* vii. 433.
930. *FLB* vii. 433–4.
931. *FLB* vii. 434.
932. *FLB* vii. 434.
933. *FLB* vii. 435.
934. *FLB* vii. 436.
935. *FLB* vii. 436–7.
936. *FLB* vii. 438.
937. *FLB* vii. 439.
938. *FLB* vii. 439–40.
939. *FLB* vii. 440–1.
940. *FLB* vii. 441.
941. IAN 331.
942. *FLB* vii. 441–2.
943. Z*AL* iii. 92.
944. *FLB* vii. 442–3.
945. *FLB* ii. 393–4.
946. *FLB* vii. 443–4.

SELECTIVE LIST OF OTHER
WORKS CONSULTED

AGOULT, COMTESSE D', *Mémoires 1833–1854*, ed. D. Ollivier (Paris, 1927).

ATTWATER, D. and JOHN, C. R., *The Penguin Dictionary of Saints* (London, 1995).

BACHE, C., *Brother Musicians: Reminiscences of Edward and Walter Bache* (London, 1901).

BARTOS, F., *Bedřich Smetana: Letters and Reminiscences*, trans. D. Rusbridge (Prague, 1955).

BELLAIGUE, C., 'Un Evêque Musicien', *Revue des Deux Mondes*, 15 Sept. 1922.

BELLAS, J., 'François Liszt et le "département des livres"', *Studia musicologica*, 28 (Budapest, 1986).

BERLIOZ, H., *Memoirs*, trans. D. Cairns (London, 1970).

BOTTING, D., *Humboldt and the Cosmos* (London, 1973).

BOWEN, C. D., *'Free Artist'—The Story of Anton and Nicholas Rubinstein* (New York, 1939).

BROMBERT, B. A., *Cristina: Portraits of a Princess* (London, 1978).

BURGER, E., *Franz Liszt: Eine Lebenschronik in Bildern und Dokumenten* (Munich, 1986).

BUSONI, F., *Letters to His Wife*, trans. R. Ley (London, 1938).

CARAMAN-CHIMAY, T. DE, *Violets for the Emperor: The Life of Louisa de Mercy-Argenteau 1837–1890* (London, 1972).

CARUS, C. G., *Lebenserinnerungen und Denkwürdigkeiten*, ii (Weimar, 1966).

CERNIKOFF, V., *Humour and Harmony* (London, 1936).

DALMONTE, R., *Franz Liszt: La Vita, L'Opera, I Testi Musicati* (Milan, 1983).

DANDELOT, A., *Francis Planté: Une belle vie d'artiste* (Paris, 1920).

DAVIES, L., *César Franck and His Circle* (London, 1970).

DENT, E. J., *Ferruccio Busoni* (London, 1933).

DUPÊCHEZ, C. F., *Marie d'Agoult* (Paris, 1989).

ECKHARDT, M., 'Schubert's and Liszt's Friend and Poet: Franz von Schober', *Liszt Saeculum*, 56 (Stockholm, 1996).

—— 'Une femme simple, mère d'un génie européen: Anna Liszt. Quelques aspects d'une correspondance', *Revue Musicale*, 405–7 (Paris, 1987).

FAY, A., *Music Study in Germany* (London, 1886).

FITZLYON, A., *The Price of Genius: A Life of Pauline Viardot* (London, 1964).

GARDEN, E., *Balakirev: A Critical Study of his Life and Music* (London, 1967).

GERARD, F., *A Grand Duchess: The Life of Anna Amalia Duchess of Saxe-Weimar-Eisenach and the Classical Circle of Weimar* (2 vols., London, 1902).

GLADSTONE, W. E., *The Gladstone Diaries*, vi, ed. H. C. G. Matthew (Oxford, 1978).

GÖLLERICH, A., *Franz Liszt* (Berlin, 1908).

GREGOROVIUS, F., *Roman Journals 1852–1874* (London, 1911).

GUBERNATIS, A. DE (ed.), *Carteggio Dantesco del Duca di Sermoneta* (Milan, 1883).

—— *Fibra: Pagine di Ricordi* (Rome, 1900).

HAIGHT, G. S., *George Eliot: A Biography* (Oxford, 1968).

HAINE, M., *Franz Servais et Franz Liszt: Une amitié filiale* (Liège, 1996).

HARDING, J., *Saint-Saëns and His Circle* (London, 1965).

HUBER-SALADIN, Le Colonel, *Le Comte de Circourt: Son temps, ses écrits. Madame de Circourt: Son salon, ses correspondances* (Paris, 1881).

HUGO, H. E. (ed.), *The Letters of Franz Liszt to Marie zu Sayn-Wittgenstein* (New York, 1953).

KAPP, J., *Franz Liszt* (Berlin and Leipzig, 1909).

KEELING, G., 'Liszt and the Legion of Honour', *The Liszt Society Journal,* 10 (London, 1985).

LACHMUND, C. V., *Living with Liszt: From the Diary of Carl Lachmund, an American Pupil of Liszt,* ed. A. Walker (New York, 1995).

LA MARA (ed.), *Briefe hervorragender Zeitgenossen an Franz Liszt* (3 vols., Leipzig, 1895–1904).

—— *Liszt und die Frauen* (Leipzig, 1911).

LEGÁNY, D., *Ferenc Liszt and His Country 1869–1873,* trans. G. Gulyás (Budapest, 1983).

—— *Ferenc Liszt and His Country 1874–1886,* trans. E. Smith-Csicsery-Rónay (Budapest, 1992).

LESURE, F., *Claude Debussy* (Paris, 1994).

LISZT, E. RITTER VON, *Franz Liszt: Abstammung, Familie, Begebenheiten* (Vienna and Leipzig, 1937).

LISZT, F., *An Artist's Journey: Lettres d'un bachelier ès musique 1835–1841,* trans. and annotated by C. Suttoni (Chicago, 1989).

—— *Des Bohémiens et de leur musique en Hongrie* (Leipzig, 1881).

—— *Frederick Chopin,* trans. J. Broadhouse (London, 1879).

—— *Gesammelte Schriften,* ed. L. Ramann (6 vols., Leipzig, 1880–3).

—— *Lettres à Cosima et à Daniela,* ed. K. Hamburger (Liège, 1996).

MARIE, Queen of Roumania, *The Story of My Life,* i (London, 1934).

MASON, W., *Memories of a Musical Life* (New York, 1901).

MOUCHANOFF-KALERGIS, M. VON, *Briefe an ihre Tochter,* ed. La Mara (Leipzig, 1911).

ORTIGUE, J. D', 'Franz Liszt: Etude biographique', *Gazette musicale,* 14 June 1835.

POCKNELL, P., 'Franz Liszt and the Caetanis', *Liszt Saeculum,* 46 (Stockholm, 1991).

—— (ed.), 'Franz Liszt: Fifteen Autograph Letters (1841–1883)', *Journal of the American Liszt Society,* 39 (Nashville, 1996).

RAABE, P., *Franz Liszt: Leben und Schaffen* (2 vols., 2nd rev. edn., Tutzing, 1968).

RAGG, L. M., *The Lamartine Ladies* (London, 1954).

RAMANN, L., *Franz Liszt als Künstler und Mensch* (3 vols., Leipzig, 1880–94).

SAFFLE, M., *Liszt in Germany 1840–1845* (New York, 1994).

SCHACK, A. F. Graf von, *Ein halbes Jahrhundert: Erinnerungen und Aufzeichnungen* (3 vols., Stuttgart and Leipzig, 1888).

SCHLÖZER, K. VON, *Römische Briefe 1864–1869* (Berlin, 1924).

SCHORN, A. VON, *Das nachklassische Weimar,* ii (Weimar, 1912).

SEARLE, H., *The Music of Liszt* (New York, 1966).

SEARLE, H., and WINKLHOFER, S., 'Liszt', *The New Grove: Early Romantic Masters I* (London, 1985).

STERN, D., *Dante et Goethe: Dialogues* (Paris, 1866).

—— *Esquisses morales: Pensées, réflexions et maximes* (Paris, 1856).

—— *Nélida* (Brussels, 1846).

SUTTONI, C., 'Liszt and Louise de Mercy-Argenteau', *Journal of the American Liszt Society*, 34 (Nashville, 1993).

—— 'Liszt Correspondence in Print: An Expanded, Annotated Bibliography', *Journal of the American Liszt Society*, 25 (Blacksburg, Va., 1989).

—— 'Liszt the Writer', *Liszt and the Arts* (Columbia University, NY, 1996).

SYLVAIN, Abbé C., *Life of the Reverend Father Hermann*, trans. Mrs. F. Raymond-Barker (London, 1882).

THADDEUS, H. J., *Recollections of a Court Painter* (London, 1912).

THURN UND TAXIS, PRINCESS MARIE VON, *Memoirs of a Princess* (London, 1959).

TROISIER DE DIAZ, A. (ed.), *Emile Ollivier et Carolyne de Sayn-Wittgenstein: Correspondance 1858–1887* (Paris, 1984).

VICTORIA, Queen of Great Britain : Victoria, Empress of Germany, *Beloved and Darling Child: Last Letters between Queen Victoria and her Eldest Daughter 1886–1901*, ed. A. Ramm and R. Fulford (Sutton, 1990).

WAGNER, C., *Diaries*, trans. G. Skelton (2 vols., London, 1978–80).

WAGNER, R., *My Life* (2 vols., London, 1911).

WALKER, A., *Franz Liszt: The Virtuoso Years: 1811–1847* (New York, 1983).

—— *Franz Liszt: The Weimar Years: 1848–1861* (London, 1989).

—— 'Liszt and Agnes Street-Klindworth: A Spy in the Court of Weimar?', *Studia musicologica*, 28 (Budapest, 1986).

—— and ERASMI, G., *Liszt, Carolyne and the Vatican: The Story of a Thwarted Marriage* (New York, 1991).

WATERS, E. N. (ed.), *The Letters of Franz Liszt to Olga von Meyendorff 1871–1886*, trans. W. R. Tyler (Dumbarton Oaks, DC, 1979).

WILLIAMS, A. (ed.), ' "Fantastic Cavalcade": Liszt's British Tours of 1840 and 1841 from the Diaries of John Orlando Parry', *Liszt Society Journal*, 6 (London, 1981) and 7 (London, 1982).

—— *Portrait of Liszt: By Himself and His Contemporaries* (Oxford, 1990).

ZWEIG, S., *The World of Yesterday* (London, 1943).

INDEX OF LISZT'S WORKS

GENERAL INDEX

Italic type implies that information is provided in the Biographical Sketches